Lecture Notes in Computer Science 9844

Commenced Publication in 1973
Founding and Former Series Editors:
Gerhard Goos, Juris Hartmanis, and Jan van Leeuwen

Editorial Board

Yogesh K. Dwivedi · Matti Mäntymäki
M.N. Ravishankar · Marijn Janssen
Marc Clement · Emma L. Slade
Nripendra P. Rana · Salah Al-Sharhan
Antonis C. Simintiras (Eds.)

Social Media: The Good, the Bad, and the Ugly

15th IFIP WG 6.11 Conference on
e-Business, e-Services, and e-Society, I3E 2016
Swansea, UK, September 13–15, 2016
Proceedings

 Springer

Editors
Yogesh K. Dwivedi
Swansea University
Swansea
UK

Matti Mäntymäki
University of Turku
Turku
Finland

M.N. Ravishankar
Loughborough University
Loughborough
UK

Marijn Janssen
Delft University of Technology
Delft
The Netherlands

Marc Clement
Swansea University
Swansea
UK

Emma L. Slade
Swansea University
Swansea
UK

Nripendra P. Rana
Swansea University
Swansea
UK

Salah Al-Sharhan
Gulf University for Science and Technology
Hawally
Kuwait

Antonis C. Simintiras
Gulf University for Science and Technology
Hawally
Kuwait

ISSN 0302-9743   ISSN 1611-3349 (electronic)
Lecture Notes in Computer Science
ISBN 978-3-319-45233-3   ISBN 978-3-319-45234-0 (eBook)
DOI 10.1007/978-3-319-45234-0

Library of Congress Control Number: 2016948250

LNCS Sublibrary: SL1 – Theoretical Computer Science and General Issues

Printed on acid-free paper

This Springer imprint is published by Springer Nature
The registered company is Springer International Publishing AG Switzerland

Preface

This book presents the proceedings of the 15th International Federation of Information Processing (IFIP) Conference on e-Business, e-Services, and e-Society (I3E) which was held in Swansea, UK, during September 13–15, 2016. The annual I3E conference is a core part of Working Group 6.11, which aims to organize and promote the exchange of information and cooperation related to all aspects of e-business, e-services, and e-society (the three *E*s). The I3E conference series is truly interdisciplinary and welcomes contributions from both academicians and practitioners alike.

The central theme of the 2016 conference was "Social Media: The Good, the Bad, and the Ugly!" although, in line with the inclusive nature of the I3E series, all papers related to e-Business, e-Services, and e-Society were welcome. The ubiquity of social media has had a profound effect on the way we communicate and is of significant importance to the three *E*s. Despite this, research regarding social media is still evolving and in-depth reviews of existing literature reveal a multiplicity of gaps for future research to address (e.g., Abed et al. 2015; Dwivedi et al. 2015; Plume et al. 2016). Therefore, the aim of the conference was to bring together a community for the advancement of knowledge regarding the adoption, use, impact, and potential of social media across e-business, e-services, and e-society.

Social media tools have helped break down geographical barriers that once restricted communication and have led to an explosion of e-participation, virtual presence, and diverse online communities (Pan et al. 2014). The widespread adoption and use of mobile phones and hand-held wireless devices (Shareef et al. 2016) is acting as a catalyst for the further growth, adoption, and use of social media platforms and related applications particularly in the context of developing countries. Professional benefits of social media include sharing of information, publicity, and giving and receiving support and advice. Consumers have become increasingly empowered to exert an influence on brands (Labrecque et al. 2013) and businesses are able to acquire rapid feedback and garner insight into individual preferences that can be used for service and product development (Rathore et al. 2016). Social media tools also enable citizens to share advice and information with their local community, and are becoming increasingly important for civic engagement and political campaigns (Kapoor and Dwivedi 2015).

The radical transformation of the world that has been enabled by social media presents a fascinating environment for academics from all backgrounds. Social media applications provide a source of valuable big data – the focus of the 14th I3E conference (Janssen et al. 2015). Automated techniques and systems are emerging that can analyze and manage the big data generated. Analytics help businesses to ensure their social media activities are adding value and helping to accomplish business goals, although some organizations are failing to measure return on investment (McCann and Barlow 2015). Analysis of data derived from social media is also being increasingly used to predict political election results (Burnap et al. 2016).

With seemingly endless benefits it is perhaps easy to overlook the disadvantages of social media, which are an increasingly important consideration as social media platforms continue to proliferate. Social media has facilitated a loss of ownership and control of content as private, public, and institutional domains increasingly overlap. Users are becoming more aware of how their behavior on social media affects others' impressions of them (Marder et al. 2016). Other drawbacks include time pressure, plagiarism, misrepresentation, addiction, and negative psychological consequences. The benefits of citizens' social media reporting can quickly be outweighed by rumor mongering (Oh et al. 2013). Research has also highlighted more sinister use of social media to facilitate terrorist attacks (Oh et al. 2011), but even the use of social media for overarching benefits to society, such as detecting and managing crises, presents ethical issues and privacy concerns (Johansson et al. 2012).

The Call for Papers solicited submissions in two main categories: full research papers and short research-in-progress papers. Each submission was reviewed by at least two knowledgeable academics in the field, in a double-blind process. The 2016 conference received submissions from more than 25 countries across the world, including Australia, Canada, China, Germany, India, Japan, Mauritius, Saudi Arabia, South Africa, Sweden, and the USA to name a few. The best papers were selected for inclusion in a special issue of *Information Systems Frontiers* or the opportunity to enhance the manuscript for fast-track review and publication in the *Journal of Enterprise Information Management*, *Transforming Government: People, Process and Policy*, or *International Journal of Electronic Government Research*. The final set of 64 full and short papers submitted to I3E 2016 and appearing in these proceedings were clustered into eight groups, each of which are outlined below.

The papers appearing in Part I address social media strategy and digital business. Based on a literature review, Ogbuji and Papazafeiropoulou suggest a social media strategy framework that organizations can use for business value. Spil, Effing, and Both develop a 3E framework for creating social media strategies based on case studies from the airline industry. The exploratory study by Kwayu, Lal, and Abubakre reveals how social media is reforming strategy within the telecom industry by exerting influence on organizational processes. Moghrabi and Al-Mohammed analyze the effect of social media on the business environment and present recommendations regarding the integration of social media into business operations. Singh, Kumar, Gupta, and Madaan develop a conceptual model of the effect of social media on the competitiveness of electronics manufacturing. Alkhowaiter explores the use of Instagram as a selling platform by Saudi female entrepreneurs and presents some of their success stories. Salichos, Polemi, Douligeris, and Qusa et al.'s paper is the final paper in this cluster and presents an ICT tool, namely, Daedalus, as a best practice example for enabling cross-border collaboration and exchange of information regarding the supply and demand of labor in the Mediterranean basin.

Part II contains papers relating to digital marketing and customer relationship management. Alalwan, Rana, Algharabat, and Tarhini's paper is the first in this part and provides an overview of the main themes and trends of existing social media research in the marketing context. Qi and Mitra's research highlights the need for higher education institutions to create an integrated presence on different social media platforms to truly create a buzz about the institution when marketing postgraduate courses. Bühler, Cwierz, and Bick consider the interplay between social media and traditional offline advertising channels on cause-related marketing campaigns. Using interviews with campaign creators, Elden, Cakir, and Bakir explore the effect of new communication technologies on corporate social responsibility campaigns. Colicev and O'Connor present preliminary findings relating to how the social media efforts of brands influence consumer mind-set metrics that underlie the purchasing decision. Jalonen and Jussila develop a conceptual model of the relationships between an organization's social media behavior, negative consumer emotions, and brand disloyalty. Using a netnography approach, Peeroo, Samy, and Jones uncover the ways customers react to corporate messages on social media and how value can be created and destroyed. Baur, Henne, and Bick conduct an exploratory study to ascertain opportunities, pitfalls, and success factors organizations report when using social customer relationship management to leverage customer experience. By contrast, Rathore, Shioramwar, and Ilavarasan undertake a quantitative study to explore how social media affects customer relationship management, comparing B2B and B2C relationships. As the final paper in this group, Zhang, Kotkov, Veijalainen, and Semenov apply situational crisis communication theory to explore interaction of airlines with customers on Facebook and how this affects brand image and reputation.

Incorporating a core theme of previous I3E conferences, Part III comprises manuscripts relating to adoption and diffusion. Abdullah and Chan employ focus groups to explore the use of social media among teenagers in Brunei Darussalam. Adopting a different method, Alryalat, Rana, Sarma, and Alzubi use surveys to examine adoption of Facebook by young adults in a rural state of India. Wamba and Akter investigate the role of perceived connectivity on intention to use social media. Abed extends the Technology Acceptance Model to examine the antecedents of continued usage intention of Facebook users in Saudi Arabia and implications for social commerce. Namankani, Moxham, and Tickle develop a conceptual framework for achieving social media adoption in small to medium enterprises. Eginli, Ozdem, and Aktuglu utilize content analysis to discover how GSM operators in Turkey are using Twitter. Marriott and Williams's paper develops a theoretical model to explain antecedents of consumer acceptance of mobile shopping. Baabdullah, Nasseef, and Alalwan adopt a quantitative method to examine factors affecting adoption of mobile government in Saudi Arabia. Gao, Zhang, and Peng undertake an empirical study of factors affecting adoption of smart wearable devices in China. Through case studies of two Indian banks, Sahu and Singh investigate the critical success factors for successful adoption and implementation of green information systems. Finally, Praditya, Sulastri, Bharosa, and Janssen propose a conceptual model to analyze the adoption and implementation of eXtensible Business Reporting Language standard.

Part IV continues the core theme of the conference to draw together manuscripts related to information sharing on social media. Plume and Slade review the theoretical concepts used to explain sharing on social media to date and propose future developments. Bahia and Simintiras consider how value from social media information is created from a combination of sharing, persuasion, and timing. Alajmi and Farhan empirically test a model to examine the influence of source, message, and recipient characteristics on information exchange via Twitter. Ismagilova, Slade, and Williams provide a review of the literature related to effectiveness of electronic word-of-mouth (eWOM) and an overview of the determinants of eWOM persuasiveness. Kapoor and Gunta utilize a case example to consider the impact of anonymity on eWOM behavior on social media. Mikalef, Pappas, and Giannakos's paper concludes this cluster with an empirical examination of how utilitarian and hedonic features on social media platforms affect purchase and eWOM behavior.

Complementing the previous two clusters, Part V contains papers related to impression, trust and risk management. Thordsen, Murawski, and Bick undertake a structured literature review to devise a research model of the factors affecting self-disclosure in social networks. Gonibeed and Ravishankar conduct interviews with Indian IT professionals to explore how individuals manage their image when interacting with professional contacts online. Aggarwal, Rai, Jaiswal, and Sorensen investigate how the norm of reciprocity affects trustworthiness in social media. Kaur, Arif, and Akre conduct a literature review to explore the positive and negative effects of social media interactions on trust among virtual team members. Abdelghani, Zayani, Amous, and Sédes consider concepts and properties of social Internet of Things, and the models that have been proposed for trust management in these environments. Dordevic, Safieddine, Masri, and Pourghomi seek to identify the variables that influence the process, speed, and success pace of fighting misinformation online. Tackling privacy risks and misuse, Hashimoto, Ichino, Kuboyama, Echizen, and Yoshiura present a method that uses machine learning to link social network accounts to resumes. Kumar, Dasari, Nath, and Sinha's paper concludes this part with a discussion of techniques to control and mitigate targeted socioeconomic attacks that can result from social media.

Significant opportunities and challenges are presented by the large volumes of data resulting from social media. The papers in Part VI address data acquisition, management, and analytics. Mian, Mäntymäki, Riekki, and Oinas-Kukkonen extend the concept of the Internet of Things to develop a conceptual framework of the Social Sensor Web along with five dimensions that can guide the design of future health and wellness technologies. Based on a case study of a large telecom company, Wahyudi and Janssen derive process patterns for dealing with big data comprising various qualities. Setiya, Ubacht, Cunningham, and Oruç seek to uncover the kind of business intelligence on opinion formation that can be derived from user-generated content on Twitter. Bosangit, McCabe, and Hibbert use discourse analysis of blogs to demonstrate how qualitative analysis of language can provide rich insights into consumption experiences. Lakhiwal and Kar utilize more than 40,000 tweets about a major economic event in India to explore social media personality dimensions. Amirkhanyan and Meinel collect and analyze social geotagged data and propose filters to provide situational awareness. Using semistructured interviews, Marbouti and Maurer seek to provide insight into the challenges that practitioners face when trying to extract emergency-related information from social media. Saumya, Singh, and Kumar investigate the role of social media users in predicting stock price movements in India. Brous, Janssen, and Herder's paper completes this section with an exploration of the impact of data governance on asset management decision-making.

Part VII draws together all papers related to e-government and civic engagement. Pal and Gonawela's paper starts with an examination of growing social media use for political communication in low- and middle-income countries. The literature review undertaken by Sivarajah, Weerakkody, and Irani seeks to examine the opportunities and challenges that Web 2.0 technologies offer to public authorities. Bolívar adopts a quantitative method to explore the perceptions of local government policy makers about the governance model for management of Web 2.0 applications used for the delivery of public services. Mitra, Gupta, and Bhattacharya seek to derive insight from mobile governance initiatives by urban and local bodies in India. Kumar, Singh, and Gupta propose a framework for smart governance through social media. Raghavan, Wani, and Abraham empirically investigate the role of personality traits and technology perspectives in affecting use of social media for civic engagement. The final paper in this group by Hossain, Chan, and Dwivedi undertakes a quantitative study to identify the factors that influence intention to share political content on social media and the moderating effect of collective opinion.

The final section of these proceedings, Part VIII, presents manuscripts focused on e-society and online communities. Gao and Zhang propose a framework of four overarching dimensions of business model concepts to explore the sharing economy in China. Jenkins, Lin, and Jeske empirically examine the influences and benefits of role models on social media. Hattingh and Matthee explore the ways in which Facebook is used in the quest for finding missing persons in South Africa. Sircar and Rowley use a case study analysis of Hillsong megachurch to understand how social media can be used for the growth of engagement in large scattered communities. Tripathi explores the effects of Indian higher education institutions' unofficial presence on social media. Al-Hamad, Kollar, Asim, and Mishra, propose a mathematical integrated connected-ness model to monitor effectiveness of teaching and learning strategies, assuming identical importance of the six learning domains. The final paper contained within the 15th IFIP I3E proceedings is by Majekodunmi and Harris who explore the factors affecting adoption of social media banking.

In addition to the aforementioned papers, we were delighted to welcome Prof. H. Raghav Rao, Prof. Viswanath Venkatesh, and Prof. Ben Light as our keynote speakers. Professor H. Raghav Rao is AT&T Distinguished Chair in Infrastructure Assurance and Security at the University of Texas San Antonio College of Business. His interests are in the areas of management information systems, decision support systems, e-business, emergency response management systems, and information assurance. He was ranked no. 3 in publication productivity internationally in a 2011 Communications of the Association for Information Systems study. Professor Rao's keynote, authored in collaboration with Onook Oh from the University of Colorado Denver, Priya Gupta from Amrita School of Business, Bangalore, and Manish Agrawal from the University of South Florida, was entitled "ICT Mediated Rumor Beliefs and Resulting User Behaviors During a Community Crisis." In this work, authors attempted to explore an extreme case of the ICT-mediated rumor incident – the August 2012 hate rumor(s) targeted toward a specific ethnic community in the technological hub of Bangalore in India – which led to the mass exodus of a targeted group of citizens. A survey of the targeted citizens suggests that kin ties and communication media characteristics influ-enced rumor belief, which, in turn, prompted extreme behavioral responses such as mass exodus. Confirming the relevance of rumor belief as a trigger of extreme collective behaviors, the authors found that people who believed the received rumors as true information took both informational (rumor-spreading) and behavioral (safety-seeking) actions. People who believed the hate rumors as true messages tended to take more extreme actions (e.g., rush to leave their own community) rather than mild or moderate actions (e.g., check safety of their acquaintances or stay at home without going outside).

Professor Viswanath Venkatesh is Distinguished Professor and Billingsley Chair in Information Systems at the Walton College of Business, University of Arkansas. His research focuses on understanding the diffusion of technologies in organizations and society. He is recognized as one of the most influential scholars in business and economics, with about 55,000 cites in Google Scholar and about 13,000 cites in the Web of Science. Professor Venkatesh's keynote was entitled "Pursuing the United Nations' Millennium Developmental Goals: Lessons Learned from a Project in Villages in India." The pursuit of the Millennium Development Goals (MDGs) of the United Nations is of economic and social significance to the poorest citizens of less developed countries. Information and communication technologies are seen to have the potential to help achieve these goals. Yet, the presence of a digital divide, which is the gulf between the information and communication technology (ICT) *haves* and *have-nots,* exists across a variety of demographic, ethnic, and geographic dimensions. Overcoming the digital divide by successfully deploying ICTs in developing countries can have major socioeconomic implications for those countries. ICTs can be a cornerstone for the development of these countries by providing a better quality of life through greater access to education, health care, and government. ICT success, typically defined in terms of adoption and use, is rare, with up to 85 % failing to some degree in developing countries. To this end, Professor Venkatesh discussed a large-scale longitudinal (10+ years) research project being conducted in India among more than 3,000 farming families across 10 villages. Against the backdrop of this project, potential research opportunities were discussed.

Ben Light is Professor of Digital Society at University of Salford, UK. His research concerns people's everyday experiences of digital media with a focus on (non)consumption, digital methods, gender and sexuality. His book, Disconnecting with Social Networking Sites was published in 2014. Professor Light's keynote was entitled "The Internet of Us: Increasing Convergence Amongst Digital and Physical Actors". The notion that the online and offline are separate elements of life where social media is concerned has been significantly undermined due to various sociotechnical theorizations and practical developments. In recent years, there has been much discussion of algorithmic culture, the politics of platforms, the quantified self, geolocation, bots and the Internet of Things for instance. In his talk Prof Light explored what this increasing convergence of the physical and the digital means for many of us where social media is integral to our lives, particularly where previously somewhat such separate sociotechnical arrangements are brought into being together. Ultimately, he argued that we are seeing a shift not only to an Internet of Things, but also towards an Internet of Us and this has significant implications for how we approach the study of social media.

The success of the 15th IFIP I3E Conference was a result of the enormous efforts of numerous people and organizations. Firstly, this conference was only made possible by the continued support of WG 6.11 for this conference series and for selecting Swansea to host I3E 2016, and for this we are extremely grateful. We are privileged to have received so many good-quality submissions from authors across the globe and the biggest thank you must go to them for choosing I3E 2016 as the outlet for their current research. We are indebted to the Program Committee, who generously gave up their time to provide constructive reviews and facilitate the improvement of the manuscripts submitted. We would like to thank the School of Management and Swansea University for hosting the conference as well as the EMaRC and i-Lab research centers and Gulf University of Science and Technology, Kuwait, for supporting the conference. Finally, we extend our sincere gratitude to everyone involved in organizing the conference, to our esteemed keynote speakers, and to Springer LNCS as the publisher of these proceedings, which we hope will be of use for the continued development of research related to the three *E*s and social media in particular.

July 2016

Yogesh K. Dwivedi
Matti Mäntymäki
M.N. Ravishankar
Marijn Janssen
Marc Clement
Emma L. Slade
Nripendra P. Rana
Salah Al-Sharhan
Antonis C. Simintiras

References

Abed, S, Dwivedi, YK, and Williams, MD (2015) SMEs' adoption of e-commerce using social media in a Saudi Arabian context: a systematic literature review, *International Journal of Business Information Systems*, 19(2), 159–179.

Burnap, P, Gibson, R, Sloan, L, Southern, R, and Williams, M (2016) 140 characters to victory? Using Twitter to predict the UK 2015 General Election, *Electoral Studies*, 41, 230–233.

Dwivedi, YK, Kapoor, KK, and Chen, H (2015) Social media marketing and advertising, *The Marketing Review*, 15(3), pp. 289–309.

Janssen, M, Mantymaki, M, Hidders, J, Klievink, B, Lamersdorf, W, van Loenen, B, and Zuiderwijk, A. (2015) Open and big data management and innovation, *Proceedings of the 14ᵗʰ IFIP WG 6.11 Conference on e-Business, e-Services, and e-Society, I3E*, Delft, October 13–15, Lecture Notes in Computer Science, Springer.

Johansson, F, Brynielsson, J, and Quijano, M (2012) Estimating citizen alertness in crises using social media monitoring and analysis, *Proceedings of the 2012 European Intelligence and Security Informatics Conference*, Odense, 22-24 August, 189–196.

Kapoor, KK and Dwivedi YK (2015) Metamorphosis of Indian electoral campaigns: Modi's social media experiment, *International Journal of Indian Culture & Business Management*, 11(4), 496–516.

Labrecque, LI, Esche, JVD, Mathwick, C, Novak, TP, and Hofacker, CF (2013) Consumer power: Evolution in the digital age, *Journal of Interactive Marketing*, 27 (4), 257–269.

Marder, B, Slade, EL, Houghton, D, and Archer-Brown, C (2016) I like them but won't 'Like' them: An examination of impression management associated with visible political party affiliation on Facebook, *Computers in Human Behavior*, 61, 280–287.

McCann, M and Barlow, A (2015) Use and measurement of social media for SMEs, *Journal of Small Business and Enterprise Development*, 22(2), 273–287.

Oh, O, Agarwal, M and Rao, H (2013) Community intelligence and social media services: A rumour theoretic analysis of tweets during social crises, *MIS Quarterly*, 37(2), 407–426.

Oh, O, Agarwal, M and Rao, H (2011) Information control and terrorism: Tracking the Mumbai terrorist attack through Twitter, *Information Systems Frontiers*, 13(1), 33–43.

Pan, Z, Lu, Y, and Gupta, S (2014) How heterogeneous community engage new-comers? The effect of community diversity on newcomers' perception of inclusion, *Computers in Human Behavior*, 39, 100–111.

Plume, CJ, Dwivedi, YK, and Slade, SL (2016) *Social Media in the Marketing Context: A State of the Art Analysis and Future Directions*, Chandos Publishing Ltd, Oxford, UK

Rathore, AK, Ilavarasan, PV, and Dwivedi YK (2016) Social media content and product co-creation: an emerging paradigm, *Journal of Enterprise Information Management,* 29(1), 7–18.

Shareef, M A, Dwivedi, YK, and Kumar, V (2016) Mobile Marketing Channel: Online Consumer Behavior. Springer.

July 2016

Organization

Conference Chairs

Yogesh K. Dwivedi	Swansea University, UK
MP Gupta	Indian Institute of Technology Delhi (IITD), India
Marc Clement	Swansea University, UK
Michael D. Williams	Swansea University, UK
Antonis Simintiras	Gulf University for Science and Technology (GUST), and Swansea University, UK
Nick Rich	Swansea University, UK

Program Chairs

Yogesh K. Dwivedi	Swansea University, UK
Matti Mäntymäki	University of Turku, Finland
M.N. Ravishankar	Loughborough University, UK
Marijn Janssen	Delft University of Technology, The Netherlands
Marc Clement	Swansea University, UK
Emma L. Slade	Swansea University, UK
Nripendra P. Rana	Swansea University, UK
Salah Al-Sharhan	Gulf University for Science and Technology (GUST), Kuwait
Antonis Simintiras	Gulf University for Science and Technology (GUST), and Swansea University, UK

Organization Chairs

Michael D. Williams	Swansea University, UK
Nick Rich	Swansea University, UK
Nripendra P. Rana	Swansea University, UK
Emma L. Slade	Swansea University, UK
Vigneswara Ilavarasan	IIT Delhi, India
Arpan Kumar Kar	IIT Delhi, India
G.P. Sahu	MNNIT Allahabad, India
Mahmood Shah	University of Central Lancashire, UK

Conference Administrator

Helen Snaith	School of Management, Swansea University, UK

I3E 2016 Keynote Speakers

H. Raghav Rao   The University of Texas San Antonio, USA
Viswanath Venkatesh   The University of Arkansas, USA
Ben Light   Salford University, UK

I3E 2016 Program Committee

Dolphy M. Abraham   Alliance University, India
Shweta Aggarwal   Management Development Institute (MDI), India
Swati Agrawal   Indraprastha Institute of Technology, Delhi, India
Jamal Ahmad Al Nsour   Al-Balqa' Applied University, Jordan
Ali Abdallah Alalwan   Al-Balqa' Applied University, Jordan
Fatmah M.H. Alatawi   University of Tabuk, Saudi Arabia
Adel Alferaih   Independent Researcher, Saudi Arabia
Raed Algharabat   University of Jordan, Jordan
Wassan Alkhowaiter   Qassim University, Saudi Arabia
Mohammad Alryalat   Al-Balqa' Applied University, Jordan
Jafar A. Alzubi   Al-Balqa' Applied University, Jordan
Aggeliki Androutsopoulou   University of the Aegean, Greece
Chris Archer-Brown   University of Bath, UK
Mohammed Arif   University of Salford, UK
Md. Mahfuz Ashraf   University of Dhaka, Bangladesh
Hernan Astudillo   Universidad Tecnica Federico Santa María, Chile
Lazaro M. Baccallao-Pino   University of Zaragoza, Spain
Piyush Bansal   International Institute of Information Technology,
                               Hyderabad, India
Ana Margarida Barreto   Universidade Nova de Lisboa, Portugal
Aaron Baur   ESCP Europe Business School Berlin, Germany
Khalid Benali   LORIA – Université de Lorraine, France
Justin Beneke   University of Winchester, UK
Djamal Benslimane   Lyon 1 University, France
Paul Beynon-Davies   Cardiff University, UK
Markus Bick   ESCP Europe, Berlin, Germany
Thomas Bortolotti   Swansea University, UK
Carmela Bosangit   Coventry University, UK
Stefania Boscari   Swansea University, UK
Laurence Brooks   Brunel University London, UK
David Brown   Lancaster University, UK
Margo Buchanan-Oliver   University of Auckland, New Zealand
Julian Bühler   ESCP, Germany
Lemuria Carter   Virginia Commonwealth University, USA
Wojciech Cellary   Poznan University of Economics, Poland
Antonio Cerone   IMT Institute for Advanced Studies Lucca, Italy
Hing Kai Chan   University of Nottingham Ningbo, China
Yannis Charalabidis   University of the Aegean, Greece

François Charoy	LORIA – Université de Lorraine, France
Hsin Chen	Independent Researcher, Taiwan
Christy M.K. Cheung	Hong Kong Baptist University, SAR China
Thom Cochrane	Auckland University of Technology, New Zealand
Ioanna Constantiou	Copenhagen Business School, Denmark
Joep Crompvoets	KU Leuven – Public Governance Institute, Belgium
Gisele da Silva Craveiro	Universidade de São Paulo, Brazil
Gareth Davies	Swansea University, UK
Rahul De	Indian Institute of Management Bangalore, India
Peter De Bruyn	University of Antwerp, Belgium
Daniele Doneddu	Swansea University, UK
Christos Douligeris	University of Piraeus, Greece
Cathal Doyle	University College Cork, Republic of Ireland
Rameshwar Dubey	Symbiosis International University, India
Andreas Eckhardt	German Graduate School of Management and Law, Germany
Amany Elbanna	Royal Holloway, University of London, UK
Jocelyn Finniear	Swansea University, UK
Americo Nobre G.F. Amorim	John Hopkins University, Brazil
Mohit Gambhir	Founder-Director, PiVerse Inc., India
Mila Gasco	ESADE, Spain
Denis Gillet	EPFL, Switzerland
Dion Goh	Nanyang Technological University, Singapore
Yiwei Gong	Wuhan University, China
Anuradha Goswami	Symbiosis International University, Symbiosis Centre for Information Technology, India
Marie Griffiths	University of Salford, UK
M.P. Gupta	Indian Institute of Technology New Delhi, India
Ankit Gupta	Birla Institute of Technology, India
Anabel Gutierrez	Regent's University London, UK
Nick Hajli	Newcastle University London, UK
Margeret Hall	Karlsruhe Institute of Technology, Germany
Wu He	Old Dominion University, USA
Mohammad Hossain	RMIT University, Australia
David Houghton	University of Birmingham, UK
Vigneswara Ilavarasan	Indian Institute of Technology New Delhi, India
Sarah Jack	Lancaster University, UK
Marijn Janssen	Delft University of Technology, The Netherlands
Jonna Järveläinen	Turku School of Economics, Finland
Ambikesh Jayal	Cardiff Metropolitan University, UK
Anand Jeyaraj	Wright State University, USA
Jason Jung	Chung-Ang University, South Korea
Sajal Kabiraj	Dongbei University of Finance and Economics, China
Sara Kadry	The Irish Centre for Cloud Computing and Commerce (IC4), Dublin City University, Republic of Ireland

Sowmya Kamath S.	National Institute of Technology Karnataka, India
Atsushi Kanai	HOSEI University, Japan
Atreyi Kankanhalli	National University of Singapore, Singapore
Kawaljeet Kapoor	Brunel University London, UK
Arpan Kar	Indian Institute of Technology New Delhi, India
Hannu Kärkkäinen	Tampere University of Technology, Finland
Farhan Khan	National University of Sciences and Technology, Pakistan
Khalil-Ur-Rahmen Khoumbati	University of Sindh, Pakistan
Anjala Krishen	University of Nevada, USA
S. Krishna	India Institute of Management Bangalore, India
Adrian Kuah	James Cook University, Singapore
Maneesh Kumar	Cardiff Business School, Cardiff University, UK
Prabhat Kumar	National Institute of Technology Patna, India
Ewelina Lacka	University of Strathclyde, UK
Banita Lal	Nottingham Trent University, UK
Winfried Lamersdorf	University of Hamburg, Germany
Sven Laumer	University of Bamberg, Germany
Heejin Lee	Yonsei University, South Korea
Hongxiu Li	Turku School of Economics, Finland
Ben Light	Queensland University of Technology, Australia
Merlyna Lim	Carleton University, Canada
Yong Liu	Aalto University, Finland
Euripidis Loukis	University of the Aegean, Greece
Ben Lowe	University of Kent, UK
José Machado	University of Minho, Portugal
Christian Maier	University of Bamberg, Germany
Matti Mäntymäki	Turku School of Economics, Finland
Ben Marder	University of Edinburgh, UK
Ricardo Matheus	Delft University of Technology, The Netherlands
Ulf Melin	Linköping University, Sweden
Jani Merikivi	Aalto University, Finland
Sian Miller	Independent Researcher, UK
Nishikant Mishra	University of East Anglia, UK
Rakesh Mishra	University of Huddersfield, UK
Amit Mitra	University of the West of England, UK
José María Moreno-Jiménez	Universidad de Zaragoza, Spain
Claire Moxham	University of Liverpool, UK
Arunabha Mukhopadhyay	Indian Institute of Management Lucknow, India
Jari Multisilta	University Consortium of Pori/Tampere University of Technology, Finland
Rajendran Murthy	Rochester Institute of Technology, USA
Robin Nunkoo	University of Mauritius, Mauritius
Onook Oh	University of Colorado Denver, USA

Ilkka Ojansivu   University of Oulu, Finland
Adegboyega Ojo   National University of Ireland Galway,
                                  Republic of Ireland
Natasha Papazafeiropoulou   Brunel University London, UK
Anthony Patterson   University of Liverpool, UK
Sanjay Pawar   Symbiosis Institute of Management Studies (SIMS),
                                  India
Olivier Perrin   Loria, France
Luiz Pereira Pinheiro Jr.   Getulio Vargas Foundation, Brazil
Nineta Polemi   University of Piraeus, Greece
Usman Qamar   National University of Sciences and Technology
                                  (NUST), Pakistan
Vishnupriya Raghavan   Manipal Global Education Services, India
Nripendra Rana   Swansea University, UK
M.N. Ravishankar   Loughborough University, UK
Nick Rich   Swansea University, UK
Sian Roderick   Swansea University, UK
G.P. Sahu   Motilal Nehru National Institute of Technology
                                  (MNNIT), India
Florence Sedes   IRIT, Paul Sabatier University, France
C.S. Kanimozhi Selvi   Kongu Engineering College Perundurai, India
Mahmud A. Shareef   North South University, Bangladesh
Santosh Shrivastava   Newcastle University, UK
Ben Silverstone   Arden University, UK
Antonis Simintiras   Gust University of Science Technology, Kuwait,
                                  and Swansea University, UK
Jyoti Prakash Singh   National Institute of Technology Patna, India
Mohini Singh   RMIT University, Australia
Nitish Singh   St. Louis University, USA
Sanjay Singh   Abu Dhabi University, UAE
Uthayasankar (Sankar)   Brunel University London, UK
  Sivarajah
Emma Slade   Swansea University, UK
Ainin Binti Sulaiman   University of Malaya, Malaysia
Zhaohao Sun   University of Ballarat, Australia
Reima Suomi   University of Turku, Finland
Ashish Sureka   ABB Corporate Research Center, India
Juliana Sutanto   Lancaster University, UK
Sarmah Tapati   Symbiosis Institute of International Business, India
Ali Tarhini   Brunel University London, UK
Alok Tiwari   King Abdulaziz University, Kingdom of Saudi Arabia
Fujio Toriumi   The University of Tokyo, Japan
Rakhi Tripathi   FORE School of Management, India
Panayiota Tsatsou   University of Leicester, UK
Heidi Tscherning   Deakin University, Australia

Contents

Adoption and Diffusion

Information Sharing on Social Media

Impression, Trust, and Risk Management

Data Acquisition, Management and Analytics

e-Government and Civic Engagement

e-Society and Online Communities

Social Media Strategy
and Digital Business

Social Media Strategies for Companies: A Comprehensive Framework

Bibian Ogbuji[✉] and Anastasia Papazafeiropoulou[✉]

Brunel University London, London, UK
{bibian.ogbuji,anastasia.papazafeiropoulou}@brunel.ac.uk

Abstract. Companies when strategizing are looking for innovative ways to have a competitive advantage over their competitors. One way in which they compete is by the adoption of social media. Social media has evolved over the years and as a result, new concepts and applications are developed which promises to provide business value to a company. However, despite the usefulness of social media, many businesses fail to reap its full benefits. The current literature shows evidence of lack of strategically designed process for companies to successfully implement social media. The purpose of this study is to suggest a framework which provides the necessary alignment between social media goals with business objectives. From the literature review, a social media strategy framework was derived to offer an effective step by step approach to the development and implementation of social media goals aligned with a company's business objectives. The contribution to this study is the development of a social media strategy framework that can be used by organisations for business value.

Keywords: Social media · Social media strategy · Social networks · Social media · Platforms

1 Introduction

Social media are online platforms that aid global collaboration and sharing amongst users. With the rapid growth and availability of network bandwidth and technology, social media has a significant increase in user count. This has also led to the increase in user-generated content [18]. Hence, it enables users to connect with one another and share information. These platforms are extensively adopted by users of all age group, educational, cultural and economic background [29].

The inarguable growth of social media has allowed profound changes in the environment. Social media is altering the business while introducing development, new learning skills and communication management processes [25]. Social media has changed the traditional marketing methods which is a one-way flow of information (for example, television and radio) while encouraging a two-way communication flow. The use of social media allows easy sharing of information to a wider audience while increasing brand awareness and promoting company's products and services. As a result of this exposure, companies strive to maintain a positive image, have an active online

© IFIP International Federation for Information Processing 2016
Published by Springer International Publishing Switzerland 2016. All Rights Reserved
Y.K. Dwivedi et al. (Eds.): I3E 2016, LNCS 9844, pp. 3–14, 2016.
DOI: 10.1007/978-3-319-45234-0_1

presence to communicate with their customers and also satisfy customers' needs. Companies are following the trend of having a presence on social media by creating multiple social media accounts without clear objectives or a strategic approach for its business use. Previous research has shown the implementation of social media is to be done carefully by designing a framework or method to provide the necessary integration between social media and the business goals. Resources such as time, skills, human resource and technology are needed when adopting social media. Therefore, the need to measure return on investment (ROI) arises [25]. Nonetheless, it is a challenge to measure the efficiency and return on investment on a social media approach that has not been strategically designed.

However, so many companies have adopted the use of social media practice in their business. The gap in the literature shows limited availability of social media strategy framework for the implementation of social media for business use. Despite the advantages, some companies are yet to identify clearly what their social media presence entails [18]. Recent research has shown that companies do not have a strategy in the selection of a suitable social media platform for their business [29]. In the absence of a strategic process, a company cannot gain the full benefit that social media provides [15]. Hence, this study aims to address the gap of a lack of a comprehensive social media strategy.

The next section presents the use of social media by companies which leads to the lack of social media strategies in business. Second, we elaborate on existing social media strategies. Third, we discuss the selection process of suitable social media platforms by companies. Fourth, we present a proposed framework. Finally, the conclusion of this study.

2   Use of Social Media by Companies

For many businesses, it is important to engage in social media to benefit from the opportunities it provides. According to Harris and Rae [13], companies have recognised the opportunities that lie in the adoption of social media. For example, it helps build trust and commitment with key stakeholders, employees, and customers.

The different social media platforms such as Facebook, Twitter, LinkedIn, and YouTube are used to enable online interaction share and collect information about products and services. These platforms can serve as a place where different ideas can be collected from a vast range of population concerning the development of a business or its products.

Previous research has shown that social media adoption has created a high positive impact on businesses that incorporates this technology as an innovative process in comparison to firms that are yet to do so [30]. According to Li & Li [24], social media creates a cordial relationship between a company and its customers thereby, influencing various aspects of consumer behaviour which includes purchase behaviour, awareness, information acquisition, post-purchase communication and opinions [28]. According to Jiang et al. [16] from a business perspective, social media can be used in various ways to improve operations and enhance business profile. The process can be done by improved communication, maintaining a good relationship with existing customers and attracting new customers, intensify word of mouth effect, advertising company's products and services, improving brand awareness and increasing traffic to websites. Businesses are increasingly attempting to adopt and implement social media as an integral part of work life and to enhance competitive advantage [7].

According to Weisgerber & Butler [34], social media has enabled organisations to gain exposure to the needs, opinions, and desires of a wider audience and also provide an opportunity for connecting with a highly targeted population that could be potential customers to the organisation. From the organisations' perspective, social media creates a better communication process between customers, stakeholders and the organisation itself which leads to the start of an innovative process in the organisation [23].

2.1 Lack of Social Media Strategy

In the early 2000 s, during the inception of social media which brought the launch of platforms like Fotolog, Myspace, hi5, Friendster and del.icio.us, companies have established a presence on these platforms to explore the benefits of social media for business. The early adopters were intrigued by the number of users subscribed to these platforms and its increasing usage among its customer base. Previous research has shown that most companies randomly establish a presence on social media while others avoid these platforms altogether because of unknown business risk and lack of understanding of the social media environment [21]. Establishing a presence on several social media platforms without a strategically defined approach does pose some risks to companies. Nevertheless, during the adoption process of social media, companies use up time, human resource, efforts, technology and skills, these parameters need to be put into consideration so the return on investment can be measured accurately. Strategic content planning, resources or undefined job responsibility can lead to the inconstancy of content flow. Therefore, companies will not be able to keep customer's interest for long [26].

In the excitement of creating a presence on social media platform (for example, Facebook page) to enable customers to join (like), or for the display of adverts especially videos which have the tendency to go viral. The video can expose a company in either a positive or negative way; a positive exposure can generate more revenue while a negative exposure can affect the business and the company's reputation [5]. The nature of social media makes it difficult to govern as it is user generated and difficult to control [9]. However, after a careful study of social media mechanisms companies can foresee social media risks and provide quick response to them. Lardi and Fuchs [21] states that the adoption of social media brings an advantage to a company's value when properly incorporated into the company's context. Recent research shows companies are beginning to understand the need to adopt a social media strategy, clearly defining the objectives of the use of having a social media presence for their business, identifying the target audience and the selection of suitable social media platform(s) for specific business needs [21].

A strategic business change impacts all the aspects of the company; people, culture, process, technology and also the implementation of social media strategy. Applying social media as a business strategy and not just a platform for marketing allows companies to find an appropriate use for social media with a maximum business value [26].

3   Existing Social Media Strategy Framework

Companies are challenged as they face an environment where the adoption rate of social media has massively increased by customers and employees. However, companies face tremendous pressure to create a presence on various platforms as expected by customers [22]. For this reason, they are struggling to implement social media strategically in their business for it is not enough to just create a presence but to use it systematically and enjoy its benefits. However, many companies find implementing a successful social media strategy difficult [4, 18]. There is a few social media strategy that concentrates on different aspects of social media.

Effing and Spil [12] framework provides significant key elements and areas of concern for the development of a social media strategy. The seven elements are as follows; (i) Target audience: companies should define what target group they intend to address using social media. (ii) Channel choice: it is important to select the appropriate choice of channel for different target groups. (iii) Goals: to gain business value, social media should be aligned with business goals. (iv) Resources: adequate resources should be allocated to the success of social media strategy. (v) Policies: should be structured to manage the use of social media in the company. (vi) Monitoring: businesses should listen to what is been said about the company\products and services. (vii) Content activities: a clear content post and timeframe are defined to allow regular contribution on the platforms. These elements are derived from the literature review as the components required for a comprehensive social media strategy.

Secondly, Kietzmann et al. [18] framework which is called "The Honeycomb of social media" consist of seven functional building blocks of social media they are: (i) Presence: refers to the availability of users on the platform. (ii) Relationship: is how users relate to one another, (iii) Reputation: is the degree to which users know each other, (iv) Groups: is when users form communities. (v) Identity: this relates to the level of which users reveal themselves, (vi) Conversation: refers to how users communicate with one another, (vii) Sharing: is the exchange of information among users. Hence, these functional building blocks describe the extent in which users engage with social media.

While Kiralova and Pavliceka [19] social media strategy is concerned with using social media as a useful tool for marketing. The paper discussed the competitive advantage gained by the alignment of business strategies with social media in the tourism sector. While Oliveira and Figueira [26] social media strategy concentrated on using social media to develop a functional communication strategy.

The above frameworks do not possess the significant factors needed in a comprehensive social media strategy as they do not contain the necessary requirements for evaluating readiness, development and the implementation of social media in companies.

The Lardi and Fuchs [21] social media strategy framework forms the core of this study (Fig. 1). This framework gives a detailed step by step process on the implementation of social media strategy while considering the goals and objectives of the business.

Phase 1 – Development Strategy. This stage is important as it allows a replete assessment of the company's competence regarding readiness, abilities, objectives and capabilities to adopt social media into their business [16]. This stage also puts into

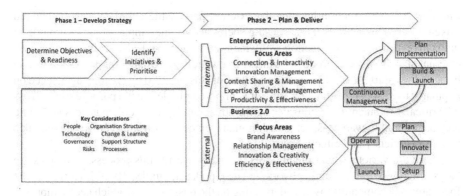

Fig. 1. Social media strategy framework [21]

consideration the organisational structure, people, process carried out, governance, changes social media brings to the business process, technology to be adopted and risk involved.

Phase 2 – Plan & Deliver. Phase 2 has two parts: Enterprise collaboration (Internal) and Business 2.0 (External).

Enterprise Collaboration: This section focuses on the use of social media within the company. The enterprise collaboration gives power to the employees by slowly getting rigid of the traditional corporate structure in a company. The implementation of enterprise 2.0 creates an opportunity for businesses to tap into the creativity of their employees to enhance productivity and daily work activities [14].

In regards to the focus areas (see Fig. 1) connection and interactivity in the enterprise collaboration is a process of exchange of information. The interactive innovation of social media offers two-way communication, which aids in the easy flow of information between employees to achieve effectiveness and productivity [35]. The continual interaction of employees in enterprise collaboration encourages brainstorming and enhances the chances of the birth of new ideas or innovation.

Enterprise collaboration process is carried out in three stages; (i) Plan implementation: at this stage, companies substantiate the functional requirements, develop a business case that fits the business and employees requirements. Furthermore, they identify a particular business area where social technology can be defined and implemented. Important factors like training for employees, development of unique skills and adoption process are considered critically. (ii) Build and launch: the actual building and launching of the social media platform are done at this point. For example, if the company does not want to use existing third-party applications like Facebook etc. they would develop a platform within the corporation to suit their needs (iii) Continuous management: Monitoring and analysing the adopted or developed platform to measure the quality, usefulness. Ongoing analysis of the platform is required for maintenance and future development [21].

Business 2.0: This section handles the external part of the company; customers and stakeholders. This area focuses on using social networking applications in promoting innovative teamwork, interaction with their customers and also collaborating with external stakeholders to produce business innovation [6]. Many companies are at risk because they start the implementation process of Business 2.0 by creating a presence on popularly used social media platforms. It is important to define the purpose of Business 2.0 critically in business by considering the advantage(s) to specific business areas like increasing brand awareness, relationship management, innovation, creativity and also increase efficiency and effectiveness.

There are various social media tools company use for this process. Examples are blogs, microblogging, social networking sites, podcast, etc. [8, 10, 33]. However, the focus area of a company may vary depending on the business area which needs improvement. There are processes outlined for the implementation of Business 2.0 such as; (i) Plan: at the planning stage, a clear identification of the target audience or target group(s) and the social media platforms they use are determined. For example, if a company provides services for different target groups, different messages will be sent to these various groups. Hence, sending a clearly defined message relevant for each target groups is an effective communication strategy to reaching out to customers. Furthermore, the most efficient way to benefit from Business 2.0 initiatives is by the selection of suitable social media platforms [19]. (ii) Innovate: this is where the creative ideas emanate. According to Berman and Hagan [2], innovation is changing the basis of competition, rather than competing heads on with other competitors; companies create new ideas to exploit a growing market need in order have an edge over its competitors and also to gain market advantage. (iii) Setup: before the implementation of Business 2.0 a few adjustments are required to accommodate social media activities in the company. Setup stage is the modification of company's policies and development of social media policies to allow the business handle the necessary change the implementation process brings [12]. Furthermore, social media tools and accounts are setups. The content messages for the target groups and time frame for posting are determined at this point [21]. (iv) Launch: The launch stage is the final stage after the above steps are completed. The launch takes place after the platform(s) are developed and ready for the reveal. The platform(s) can are revealed same day or separate days. The launch approach varies amongst companies. (v) Operate: After the platform(s) have been initiated, the effect of how social media activities are influencing and creating traffic to the corporate websites is monitored [12].

The social media strategy framework is structured in an easy to follow steps. However, it does not include a systemic approach for companies to identify the suitable social media platform to employ for their business.

4   Selection of Social Media Platform

Social media platforms have a vast advantage for social activities hence it is not just a means of sharing information on day-to-day operations; it is a valuable and cost-effective way for businesses to reach their customers. Regardless, it is not appropriate for companies to create an account on all the social media platforms available. Determining the right social media platform(s) for a company is not to be overlooked [11].

Recent studies have shown that companies do not take strategic procedures in selecting suitable social media platform(s) to meet their business values [26]. This has been identified as a gap in the literature. The study for the process of selecting social media platform has little attention in this research area. However, Tavana et al. [31] derived a network structure of factors to consider in the selection process of a suitable social media platform for business. This structure consist of six elements; content, impression score, cost, look & feel and audience fit. These elements describe the different important factors to consider during the selection process.

The social media platform evaluation in Fig. 2 shows the elements and the inter-connection between them. A brief description of the items is discussed below.

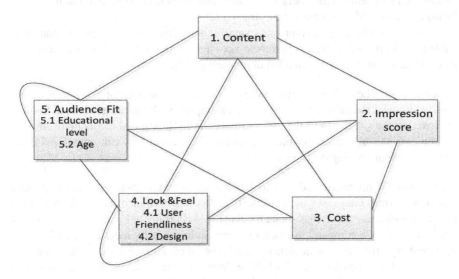

Fig. 2. Social media platform evaluation [31]

Content: With the increased growth of social media in the community, the tools and strategies companies use to communicate with customers have changed appreciably. This significant change allows consumers to generate content online with the intent on sharing and educating one another about products, services, experiences and brands [3]. According to Tavana et al. [31] the content of a social media platform is used to measure the amount of pertinent information on that platform. Hence, content is significant because it can keep customers interested or customers can lose interest then switch to a different platform. Barnes [1] states that it is important to create a schedule for content updates to ensure frequent participation in the platform(s). Kaplan and Haenlein [17] indicates that social media is about sharing and interacting with the audience, so it is important to ensure an active presence whereby posting new updates and also engaging in discussions with customers and target audience.

Impression Score: According to Kiralova and Pavliceka [19] research on tourism destination, social media is used as a promotional or marketing tool which has a high number of visitors using social media applications. Therefore in other to monitor these visits impression score is employed. "Impression score is a subjective score used to capture the behaviour of visitors in a site" [31].

Cost: Initially, social media began as a medium for entertainment, then after it became the most common tool for marketing because of the vast advantage it brings to the business area. To create a presence on most social media platforms, this can be done free of charge or at low cost. As a result of it cost- effective nature, it is considered to be the preferred marketing tool in the business environment. Hence, companies have employed social media as an excellent approach and a marketing strategy to reach their customers and potential customers. Companies benefit from cost reduction on marketing by using social media as a marketing strategy [20].

Therefore, multinational companies, small and medium-sized enterprises, non-profitable organisations and even government agencies all implore social media because of it cost effective nature and high level of efficiency [17].

Look and Feel: The look and feel of a site are stated to mean the design and user friendliness of a social media site. Furthermore, it can represent the need for minimal training expense and the simplicity of the tool Tavana et al. [31]. A social media platform with an intuitive and user-friendly interface ensures that customers can engage with the systems without training or difficulty [21].

Audience fit: Companies are advised to define what target groups to address using social media platforms. They have to prioritise their customers to identify the degree of the population who use and access social media [12]. According to Edwards [11], the most effectual way for a company to reach its target audience is by identifying its business goals and objectives and the audience suitable for the business. For example, age group, educational level, gender, etc. all of these determines an audience fit. Therefore, if a company is interested in the young audience, a good example of social media platform to concentrate on would be snap chat and Instagram.

Having seen Figs. 1 and 2, this study has merged both structures to form a comprehensive social media strategy framework.

5 Proposed Framework

A gap from the literature suggests that there is a lack of focus on the capability and readiness for companies to adopt social media. The literature states a limitation in research on social media strategy frameworks for business use and the evaluation of social media platform. The merging of social media strategy frameworks in Fig. 1 and the social media platform evaluation in Fig. 2 address their independent limitations. As discussed in the social media strategy framework in Fig. 1, the framework considered the readiness of an organisation to adopt social media and how it is used in specific business context. However, it lacks a systemic approach for selection of social media platform(s) that is suitable for its business which Fig. 2 addresses by merging both frameworks. While studying Figs. 1 and 2 independently, it was considered that the frameworks were incomplete because they do not contain the necessary factors needed for the implementing of social media strategy in an organisation. The existing frameworks as discussed in Sect. 3 have some limitations which the comprehensive social media strategy in Fig. 3 addresses. For example "The Honeycomb Framework" [18] is designed to help understand social media and its functionalities, so this does not necessarily focus on social media readiness or how it can be implemented successfully in a company [27].

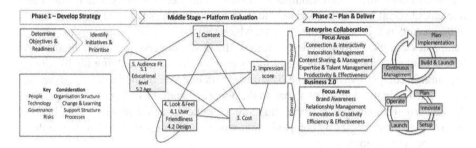

Fig. 3. A comprehensive social media strategy framework

The social media strategy framework (see Fig. 1) gives a detailed illustration on how social media can be implemented by a company effectively. While considering the company's readiness, transparency to employees and customers, the merging between social media and existing business activities and the importance of defining the target audience for social media use [32]. Nonetheless, the social media strategy framework (Fig. 1) lacks a profound process to select a suitable platform for both the Enterprise Collaboration (internal) and Business 2.0 (external) which the framework in Fig. 2 addresses.

The Platform evaluation process (see Fig. 2) shows the key factors necessary for consideration in the evaluation process for selecting a suitable social media platform. The literature shows there is a lack of a framework to determine the right social media platform for businesses. Although Edwards [11] suggested ways in selecting the right social media platforms by having a good knowledge of user statistics such as daily active users, monthly active users and overall users of each platform. More so, gave an explanation of how these platforms can be used, however, this is not an efficient way to determine the precise social media platform for it is based on number counts. Different platforms are developed for a different purpose with distinct functionality and separate target audience [32]. For example, LinkedIn is known to be a platform for work professionals.

From Figs. 1 and 2 forms the comprehensive framework for social media strategy implementation and platform evaluation process. This framework provides the necessary need for adoption and improvement of an existing social media practice and the useful method for the selection of social media platform. The framework was merged and is presented in Fig. 3. We suggest this framework as a comprehensive way for the adoption and implementation of social media in companies.

6 Conclusion

The continual development of information technology brings both opportunities and challenges in the world. Managers are faced with the technologically progressive environment. Hence, social media networks have become a necessary tool for business. Social media creates a platform for companies through which they can improve their business and customer experience. Social media provide several opportunities but also come with some risks. Companies need to evaluate which social media platform is appropriate for its business. It is important for businesses to select the best few platforms that suit its company's need. Companies need a social media strategy to help adopt and implement social media appropriately to their business. The suggested framework aids in this regard as it presents a mechanism, which various companies such as, the service companies can use to identify what areas of the business need improvement and how best to exploit social media for the business purpose. Thus, intensifying the likelihood of gaining a competitive advantage. The framework is also contributing to the advancing of knowledge in the domain of social media adoption from the company's perspective. As the current literature is not providing any theoretical frameworks in the application of social media strategies by companies our work is offering a practical well as a theoretical tool in this domain.

References

1. Barnes, I.: Twitter in special libraries: a distributed social media strategy. Public Serv. Q. **10**(1), 62–65 (2014). http://www.tandfonline.com/doi/full/10.1080/15228959.2014.875789
2. Berman, S.J., Hagan, J.: How technology-driven business strategy can spur innovation and growth. Strategy Leadersh. **34**(2), 28–34 (2006)
3. Blackshaw, P., Nazzaro, M.: Consumer-generated media (cgm) 101: word-of-mouth in the age of the web-fortified consumer. Nielsen BuzzMetrics, New York (2006)
4. Bottles, K., Sherlock, T.: Who should manage your social media strategy. Physician Executive **37**(2), 68–72 (2011)
5. Brodie, R.J., Ilic, A., Juric, B., Hollebeek, L.: Consumer engagement in a virtual brand community: An exploratory analysis. J. Bus. Res. **66**(1), 105–114 (2013)
6. Burrus, D.: Social networks in the workplace: the risk and opportunity of business 2.0. Strategy Leadersh. **38**(4), 50–53 (2010)
7. Carmichael, D., Cleave, D.: How effective is social media advertising? a study of facebook social advertisements. In: 2012 International Conference for Internet Technology and Secured Transactions, pp. 226–229 (2012)
8. Chiang, H.S.: Continuous usage of social networking sites: the effect of innovation and gratification attributes. Online Inf. Rev. **37**(6), 851–871 (2013)
9. Dijkmans, C., Kerkhof, P., Beukeboom, C.J.: A stage to engage: social media use and corporate reputation. Tourism Manage. **47**, 58–67 (2015)
10. Dioko, L., Harrill, R., María Munar, A.: Tourist-created content: rethinking destination branding. Int. J. Cult. Tourism Hospitality Res. **5**(3), 291–305 (2011)
11. Edwards, V.: Determining the right social media networks for your business. J. Digital Soc. Media Mark. **3**(3), 217–228 (2015)
12. Effing, R., Spil, T.A.M.: The social strategy cone: towards a framework for evaluating social media strategies. Int. J. Inf. Manage. **36**(1), 1–8 (2016)

13. Harris, L., Rae, A.: Social networks: the future of marketing for small business. J. Bus. Strategy **30**(5), 24–31 (2009). http://www.emealdinsight.com/doi/pdf/10.1108/02756660910987581
14. Husin, B., Heikal, M., Swatman, P.M.C., bin Husin, M.H., Swatman, P.M.C.: Removing the barriers to enterprise 2.0. In: 2010 IEEE International Symposium on Technology and Society (ISTAS), pp. 275–283 (2010). http://ieeeplore.ieee.org/xpls/abs_all.jsp?arnumber=5514627
15. Jansen, B.J., Zhang, M., Sobel, K., Chowdury, A.: Twitter power: tweets as electronic word of mouth. J. Am. Soc. Inf. Sci. Technol. **60**(11), 2169–2188 (2009)
16. Jiang, H., Luo, Y., Kulemeka, O.: Leading in the digital age: a study of how social media are transforming the work of communication professionals. Telematics Inform. **33**(2), 493–499 (2016). http://www.sciencedirect.com/science/article/pii/S0736585315001264
17. Kaplan, A.A.M., Haenlein, M.: Users of the world, unite! the challenges and opportunities of social media. Bus. Horiz. **53**(1), 59–68 (2010). http://www.sciencedirect.com/science/article/pii/S0007681309001232
18. Kietzmann, J.J.H., Hermkens, K., McCarthy, I.P.I., Silvestre, B.S.B.: Social media? get serious! understanding the functional building blocks of social media. Bus. Horiz. **54**(3), 241–251 (2011). http://www.sciencedirect.com/science/article/pii/S0007681311000061
19. Kiralova, A., Pavliceka, A.: Development of social media strategies in tourism destination. Procedia – Soc. Behav. Sci. **175**, 358–366 (2015). http://www.sciencedirect.com/science/article/pii/S1877042815012719
20. Kirti, A.K., Karahan, F.: To be or not to be in social media arena as the most cost-efficient marketing strategy after the global recession. Procedia - Social and Behavioral Sciences **24**, 260–268 (2011). http://www.sciencedirect.com/science/article/pii/S1877042811016119
21. Lardi, K., Fuchs, R.: Social media strategy. vdf Hochschulverlag AG, Zurich (2013)
22. Larson, K., Watson, R.: The value of social media: toward measuring social media strategies (2011)
23. Lehmkuhl, T., Baumol, U., Jung, R.: Towards a maturity model for the adoption of social media as a means of organizational innovation. In: 2013 46th Hawaii International Conference on System Sciences (HICSS), pp. 3067–3076. IEEE (2013)
24. Li, S., Li, J.: Linking social media with open innovation: an intelligent model. In: Proceedings of the 7th International Conference on Intelligent Computation Technology and Automation (ICICTA) (2014). http://ieeexplore.ieee.org/xpls/abs_all.jsp?arnumber=7003550
25. Schroeder, M.H.: Social media in business strategy: the learning and development implications. Dev. Learn. Organ. Int. J. **28**(6), 12–15 (2014)
26. Oliveira, L., Figueira, Á.: Benchmarking analysis of social media strategies in the higher education sector. Procedia Comput. Sci. **64**, 779–786 (2015)
27. Omosigho, O.E., Abeysinghe, G.: Evaluating readiness of organizations to adopt social media for competitive advantage. In: 2012 International Conference on Information Society (i-Society), pp. 16–21. IEEE (2012)
28. Paniagua, J., Sapena, J.: Business performance and social media: Love or hate? Bus. Horiz. **57**(6), 719–728 (2014). http://www.sciencedirect.com/science/article/pii/S0007681314000974
29. Persaud, A., Spence, M., Rahman, M.: Social media implementation in small service firms. Int. J. E-Bus. Dev. (2012)
30. Smith, F., Taglino, F.: Semantics-based social media for collaborative open innovation. In: 2014 International Conference on Collaboration Technologies and Systems (CTS), pp. 345–352 (2014). http://ieeexplore.ieee.org/xpls/abs_all.jsp?arnumber=6867587

31. Tavana, M., Momeni, E., Rezaeiniya, N., Mirhedayatian, S.M., Rezaeiniya, H.: A novel hybrid social media platform selection model using fuzzy ANP and COPRASG. Expert Syst. Appl. **40**(14), 5694–5702 (2013)
32. Value, B.: Quarterly executive (2010)
33. Viégas, F.B.: Bloggers' expectations of privacy and accountability: an initial survey. J. Comput.-Mediated Commun. **10**(3) (2005)
34. Weisgerber, C., Butler, S.H.: Social media as a professional development tool: using blogs, microblogs, and social bookmarks to create personal learning networks. Cutting-edge Technol. High. Educ. **3**, 339–363 (2011)
35. Zolkepli, I.A., Kamarulzaman, Y.: Social media adoption: the role of media needs and innovation characteristics. Comput. Hum. Behav. **43**, 189–209 (2015)

Enable, Engage and Evaluate: Introducing the 3E Social Media Strategy Canvas Based on the European Airline Industry

Ton A.M. Spil[1,2,3(✉)], Robin Effing[1,2,3], and Menno P. Both[1,2,3]

[1] University of Twente, P.O. Box 217, 7500 AE Enschede, The Netherlands
{a.a.m.spil,r.effing}@utwente.nl
[2] Saxion University of Applied Sciences,
P.O. Box 70.000, 7500 KB Enschede, The Netherlands
[3] Both Social, Enschede, The Netherlands
menno@bothsocial.nl

Abstract. The strategic use of social media has increased in importance. However, there is a lack of theory to design and evaluate social media strategies. In a competitive environment, airlines need to excel on service, customer satisfaction and marketing. Social media could support those areas of business. This paper comprises the results of both a systematic literature review and case studies at European airlines. The literature study was based on 85 academic articles, regarding the prevalent approaches to social media strategies. The case studies were conducted within three North-western-European airlines in Germany, France and the Netherlands. As a result, a new conceptual framework and tool for creating social media strategies is created. Engagement, Evaluation and Enabling are its main concepts. The new theoretical framework is more complete and was derived from existing literature and case studies. The 3E Social Media Strategy Canvas can serve both as a decision-making tool and as a theoretical framework for comparison.

Keywords: Social media strategies · Facebook · Business model canvas · Policy · Engagement

1 Introduction

In recent years, social media channels such as Facebook, YouTube, Twitter and Instagram have increased in importance within the airline industry [1–3]. Since this is an information intensive sector, social media is predominantly used at airlines as a communication channel for providing customers with relevant information [4,6]. One study found that airlines social media use is found to be heavily advertising focused [1]. Social media could also be important as a tool for customer service. The risks of not effectively addressing customers by social media are apparent. For example, United Airlines reputation was affected because one of their customers made a viral YouTube video [7]. The reason was that United

© IFIP International Federation for Information Processing 2016
Published by Springer International Publishing Switzerland 2016. All Rights Reserved
Y.K. Dwivedi et al. (Eds.): I3E 2016, LNCS 9844, pp. 15–30, 2016.
DOI: 10.1007/978-3-319-45234-0_2

Airlines refused to compensate a musician whose 3,500 dollar guitar was broken. This example stresses the importance of managing business reputation on social media. Because social media could be useful to contribute to marketing, customer-satisfaction and service goals more knowledge is required regarding effective social media strategies. However, there is a lack of theory to underpin the design of social media strategies within companies [8]. In a highly competitive field such as the travel and hospitality sector it is of major importance to adapt to the needs of clients including their expectations regarding social media presence.

The main aim of this paper is to systematically combine important aspects of social media strategy into a practical tool for designing such strategies. As a result, the 3E Social Media Strategy Canvas is introduced in this article as a tool for organizations to design and revisit their social media campaigns. Therefore the main research question of this research is: How to design a social media strategy canvas as a tool to meet business and customer requirements? This research paper is designed to meet the dual objectives of engaged scholarship, thus producing relevant insights for both theory and practice [9]. A canvas tool could help to design, compare and revisit new and existing social media strategies in practice. Osterwalder and Pigneur [10] have showed with their Business Model Generation Canvas that practical tools can be developed from a theoretical background. The concepts of a social media canvas tool should be based on both theoretical and empirical insights. We derive key elements of a social media strategy from a literature review and construct a framework entitled the 3E Social Media Strategy Canvas. Furthermore, to support the design of a new canvas tool, interviews were conducted with three airlines in North-western-Europe.

The remainder of this article is structured as follows. First, the research method is shown and second, the theoretical background for key elements of social media strategy is presented. Third, the results of the qualitative interviews are presented in order to validate the key elements of social media strategy. Fourth, the key elements are used to design a framework for designing social media strategies in a discussion section. Finally the conclusions are drawn.

2 Research Method

The method consists of the following parts. First, there is a literature review that aims to find key elements of social media strategies. According to Webster and Watson [11]: "relevant literature is an essential feature of any academic project". In order to have a systematic approach regarding the identification of key elements and concepts of social media strategy we follow the method of a systematic literature review [12]. The literature review was based on desk research using electronic scientific literature databases to which access is provided by academic library services including ISI Web of Science, Scopus, EBSCO INSPEC and EBSCO Business Source Elite. This multi-disciplinary set included the top journals of the field of information systems [13]. In order to include recent literature the articles had to be published between 2005 and 2016 at the time of selection. 85 papers were selected of which 9 delivered key elements for this study (Table 1). Selection criteria were empirical evidence and being part of a series of elements. The case studies included three airline carriers in Europe.

The second part of the method is based on qualitative case studies [14]. Three case studies were conducted at airlines in Western-Europe. The selection criteria for the included cases were based on industry type, and European origin. The interviews do not strive to provide us with a complete evaluation of the industry nor a reliable view on the state of the field. The sample was relevant to the universe of the grounding of theory [15]. While a larger selection of cases would have contributed to presenting more generalizable claims, generalization of the entire population would still be problematic [16,17]. Because of the limited amount of people working on social media strategies and since the homogeneous nature of this group only a few interviews per airline were conducted with social media managers and on-line sales and marketing assistants and with social media experts, totaling 9 interviews. The qualitative open interviews were held to test to what extent the key elements of social media strategy from literature were recognized and used in practice. The list of key elements of social media strategies (Table 1) was used as a guideline for the topics of the framework of the interviews. Furthermore, the interviews were semi-structured. For its qualitative cause we were also open for new, unexpected elements, concepts and motivations that could be present in practice but were not yet found in literature. Next to the interviews, the actual airlines social media activities were observed and analyzed to obtain objective comparative data.

The third part of the method was the design of a canvas tool that was based on thorough analysis of both results from literature and practice. Based on systematic comparison of the results the social media canvas tool was designed. The design of the canvas is partly a creative task. Other designs are possible but we have created multiple designs and tested them in practice with actual users. The canvas tool design is an initial version based on three iterations of the design. We used the hypothesis-driven experimentalism for market exploration testing to derive the canvas tool [70].

3   Theoretical Background

Table 1 presents the key elements of social media strategies as found in literature. After analysis we have defined three overarching concepts that comprise the elements: Enable, Engage and Evaluate. These categories were assigned by sorting processes. Based on these three concepts we will highlight relevant findings from literature in the following sections.

3.1   Enable

We have recognized various key elements of social media strategy and combined them into three concepts. The first concept of 'Enable' is about preparing and setting up social media activities and campaigns. Policies intend to provide

Table 1. Key elements of social media strategy in literature

Category enable	Category engage	Category evaluate	References
Resources	Target audience	Monitoring	[50]
	SM choice		
	Goals		
	Goals	Monitoring	[42]
	Activity plan		
	Target audience	Monitoring	[4]
	SM choice		
Policies resources	Target audience	Monitoring	[22]
	Goals		
	Activity plan		
Policies employees/consultants	Sharing content	Evaluation	[20]
	Relationships		
	Users		
	Platforms		
	Goals		
Development	Relationships		[38]
	Conversations		
	Users		
Policies	Content	Monitoring	[18]
	Target audience		
	SM choice		
	Goals		
	Activity plan		
Partners staff investment	Messages		[34]
	Magnet		
	Paths		
	Customers		
Guidelines employees technology investments	Engagement	Learn listen	[19]
	SM types		
	Customers		

guidelines for employees usage of social media [26, 27] by directing them in what they can and cannot do at the organizational level [24]. However, the companies should be careful not to overly constrain their employees and limit their personal freedom of expression [28]. Social media policies often address ethical issues [28]. This does not differ from the responsibilities a companies has beyond social media, which is why these policies tend to rely on the common rules and regulations valid for the entire organization [24].

Partners is a topic of social media strategy that includes both internal and external social media resources. Internal partners are employees that are responsible for social media [18–20]; external partners are professional consultants that support organizations with social media use [20]. It is important that an organization clearly defines responsibilities [20]. All social media members should have both IT and communication skills and should be able to develop relationships with customers [19,20]. Several authors agree that in order to successfully deploy social media, the companies need to provide specific training and education for the employees allocated to this task [19,29–35]. Furthermore, it is important to define specific tasks properly among the staff, so that each employee plays a certain role in maintaining the social media sites [20,23].

Social media investments include all financial costs with regard to the social media use of an organization [18,20,22,36]. Resources include the financial part, namely the budget for implementing such a strategy with all related technological expenses such as Facebook Ads and tool subscriptions, as well as the allocation of the dedicated time and staff [35–37]. In the present paper resources contain expertise or training that is needed, quality control of messages [18] and necessary technology [19].

3.2 Engage

The second concept 'Engage' comprises of all those aspects and key elements of social media strategy about reaching out, getting attention of certain target audiences and interacting with them. Schaffer [41] recently mentioned eleven essential elements of social media strategies and ten of these elements can be placed within engagement.

For a successful social media presence, it is moreover essential to define your target audience in your social media strategy [22,25,50,51,61,62]. In order to design the social media presence in a way that different types of customers are addressed, it is important to reconsider different group characteristics [18,20,38]. Gaining a significant reach and attracting enough attention among the selected target audience is the foundation for creating value with social media [3,63]. Social media is primarily used for approaching customers, but a reason to be present might also be to interact with suppliers or vendors of the firm [64]. Another option for a target audience is to reach out and try to address the key opinion leaders on social media platforms [36,63].

Goals build the basis for a social media strategy. Therefore, companies that deploy social media strategies also need to determine their ideal objectives [23,39,50,51]. These goals need to be measurable [42] so that the strategy can be evaluated and constantly adapted if necessary. The determination of these goals needs to be completed before entering in the social media business to guarantee a successful implementation [52]. To define the goals for utilizing social media corporately, an alignment between these objectives and the overall business goal is required [20,21,53]. There should be specific attention for engagement and interaction goals [46,48,57]. Integrating social media into the consumption and purchase experience for customers rather than utilizing the sites as pure marketing channels is found to be advantageous for the companies [59].

Various authors point out that the content published on social media is one of the core elements of a strategy [22,30,37,45,46]. Othman et al. [42] propose that companies should develop an individual content strategy for the social media presence. Primarily, the content has to be relevant [25,47]. The social media content should fit the company culture and should be of significant quality [3, 47,48]. Organizations need to design a recognizable social media presence that contains interesting information or objects (e.g. videos, pictures, sounds) in order to enhance customer engagement [20,34]. Organizations can start discussions, develop games, or present campaigns where customers can get involved in [38]. Furthermore it is important that organizations see the relation with their social media users as a friendship based on trust. Aggressive advertising and other disturbing activities may lead to a lower engagement of users [19,38].

Social media channels differ in appropriateness and effectiveness for disparate or complementary communication goals [34,60]. There are differences in the extent to which users can see that other users exist, where they are, and if they are available. Social media channels differ also in the amount to which they share such information with their users. Furthermore the popularity of social media channels differs between countries [19]. Organizations need to understand these connections [20] in order to reach the highest amount of customers [18]. First an overview of the existing platforms is provided. Facebook, Twitter and YouTube are regularly named the most popular social media channels [5,6,37,62], with Facebook being the worlds dominating platform by the number of users [3].

An action plan for a social media strategy can imply the creation of a schedule for corporate posts [39,48,49]. This schedule might include information about the organizations social media activity concerning the specific time of the day, the frequency and the subject of the post. The regularity of the postings is important for finding a right balance [57]. In order to foster engagement, posting questions on the platforms is likely to create awareness and a sense of membership among users [3,57]. The questions tend to support the interaction on the social networking site. However, it is found that companies still do not use the full potential of the platforms [57]. There are also social media publishing tools available for the development of an activity plan [45].

3.3   Evaluate

The third concept 'Evaluate' comprises of various ways of using data, statistics and insights to learn, adapt and measure whether the companys activities on social media are delivering desired effects. The literature largely agrees on the importance of monitoring the social media activities for a successful social media strategy [3,20,43,44,46,47,52,55,65,66]. The outcome of monitoring social media platforms, namely the vast quantities of data, is considered equally as beneficial as a thorough marketing research [30]. Several authors agree that listening to their audience is an essential part of operating social media strategically [19,25,26,30,39,40,42–44]. With listening to the customers voice, the organizations are more likely to gain insights into their preferences and needs [25,43]. Companies that fail to carefully monitor their social media channels lose a significant amount of valuable insights from the market. Therefore, clearly monitoring the buzz is important for companies operating social media platforms for it can lead to a better understanding of the consumer behavior and feelings of the mood in the market [44]. The outcome of the monitoring process can moreover aid in the creation of customized offerings for the users [66]. With sufficient information about the potential customer, a company is able to adapt their advertisements to the individual needs and therewith increase the likeliness of attracting the followers attention. Measuring the success of a social media strategy can more specifically occur through monitoring the amount of likes, posts or retweets on companies social media sites [4]. These structured metrics can provide a company with a decent overview of the value of their activities. The process of monitoring can be done with the aid of available monitoring tools [26,43]. Evaluation of return is the final important aspect of social media as indicated in literature. Organizations have two possibilities to measure the success of social media use, namely key performance indicators and financial returns [18]. Performance indicators could include simple metrics such as likes, shares, retweets or followers [18,20], whereas financial returns focus on pure monetary gains. To measure return, there could be measurable indicators such as increase in website traffic, customer satisfaction, and so on. Evaluating the results of social media use helps to estimate to what extent social media goals are reached and to adjust the social media strategy in case of weaknesses [18].

4 Results

This section will show the interview results within the three theoretical concepts given above. First, it was essential to investigate whether the airlines were familiar with the elements of a social media strategy and to what extent they were integrated into their social media operations. Therefore, the interview framework was constructed in such a way that all elements of a social media strategy supported by the literature research were present (see Table 1).

Thereby, it became apparent how the airlines included these elements in their approaches. The interviews were analysed according the theory of Miles and Huberman [67]. In the case the participant provided a positive answer to a question, they are classified as aware of that element, if not they are classified as unaware (i.e. + for aware, − for unaware). When the answers were more reflective they were classified as aware but not yet implemented (+/−). Table 2 summarizes the airlines comprehension of the elements of a social media strategy defined in the literature review and after that all concepts are described for all three airlines.

Table 2. Comprehensions of social media strategies in the studied cases

Elements	Airline 1	Airline 2	Airline 3
Enable	+/−	+/−	+/−
Engage	+	+/−	+
Evaluate	+	−	+

4.1   Airline 1

Enable. Airline 1 identifies social media as an instrument for customer retention and therefore tries to respond to all customer questions and also react to online given feedback. The goal of Airline 1 is to expand their social media operations in such a way that the networks will eventually serve as service channels for the customers. Airline 1 controls the usage of social networking sites with several rules summarized in their social media policy. This policy consists of the manner in which the employees are advised to approach their followers, the principles they have to consider before publishing content on the sites and the actions they are supposed to take in case uncontrollable online behavior occurs. The usage policies of Airline 1 essentially consist of guidelines for the employees behavior on their social networking sites. An intern is also taking part in the social media activities and decision-making next to the responsible employee.

Engage. Consumer engagement is key at Airline 1. It developed their strategy from being purely advertising focused to a more interactive strategy. There are monthly meetings that discuss the overall plans and content for the upcoming weeks. Additionally, the spontaneous social media actions appear to be scheduled as well, such as events, press news/releases, job vacancies and offerings. A clear goal of airline 1 is: "For the future we plan on increasing our social media activities regarding CRM in order to guarantee the customers and optimal 24/7 support service". The airline plans on significantly increasing their response rate and, thereby, improving the engagement of their followers. They focus on users of age 18–35, thus mainly the young adults. Airline 1 indicates that social media has a high significance for their organization. The interviewee indicated: "We fill [our Facebook] page on a daily basis with interesting content regarding the topics flying and traveling and we act as a direct contact person in case of questions and problems to our fans. Through our social media channels we build a relationship with our fans and respectively potential customers and generate direct feedback this way." The airline takes their differing purposes into account when deciding about the content that is to be published. This particularity shows the separate attention that the content of their strategic social media operation receives. Airline 1 is also very explicit about the content they post on their social networking sites: "[...] there is content that is regularly posted, e.g. content about price campaigns and events [...] and [additionally] special content is created in order to encourage fans to interact and play a part in our conversations [...] such as games, competitions or [we] ask our fans questions."

Evaluate. In monthly meetings Airline 1 discusses the topics and major activities that will be posted to the social media platforms of the airline. Regarding the frequency of their posts, the interviewee provided the information in another part of the interview and mentioned that they fill the sites on a daily basis. Airline 1 puts the focus on the interaction with the customers. Airline 1 is moreover aware of the importance of monitoring the online activities. They monitor the effectiveness of their social media presence with the aid of the Facebook statistics and an additional monitoring tool. Airline 1 utilizes social media for their Customer Relationship Management (CRM) next to the advertising focused usage.

4.2   Airline 2

Enable. Since Airline 2 only established their online presence a year ago, they have yet to reach their desired capabilities in this division. Airline 2 aims to expand its social media team in the near future. The outcome of the question concerning the allocation of required resources shows that Airline 2 do not have a separate department or employees that work on social media full time. The social media operations are done by both the online marketing department and the website management department. Furthermore, the employees responsible for this division have responsibilities beyond social media and can, thus, not completely engage their time and efforts into the social media operations. Therefore, in total, one person is responsible for the social media operations at Airline 2.

Engage. Airline 2 targets on a B2C and B2B audience. Hence, Airline 2 does not only wish to appeal to potential customers of their flight tickets, but also to other industry members, such as suppliers. So far, there is no strategic planning involved in the one-year old social media presence. At the time of research Airline 2 is very active on social media. Compared to Airline 1 they have almost double amount of comments and surpasses their numbers of shares by more than 15 times, even though they did not mention any strategic concepts or purposes for their social media. The post with the highest number of likes included a hint about an ending competition, in which users were able to win two flight tickets. The second highest amount of likes received a post including a question towards the online community, asking them about their guesses regarding a following football match. Airline 2 is the 'smaller' airline in number of followers and likes on social media, but it catches more attention with their posts than Airline 1.

Evaluate. At this point there was no clear evaluation at Airline 2. It appears to skip the "Plan" stage and directly move to the "Do" stage, with defining their targets, choosing a social media platform and allocating resources, and, hence, does not consider following up and adapting their operations with evaluation.

4.3   Airline 3

Enable. Airline 3 won various prizes for their use of social media. Their social media cases are used by other companies to get inspired. The main pillars of the social media strategy of Airline 3 are service, reputation, engagement and commerce. Service is key because that is the reason that people follow us. Airline 3 has formed specific social media teams. For example, they have 4 editors within the communication department who are responsible for the engagement goals. The e-commerce department is responsible for both service and commerce purposes of social media. On top of that they have specific agents for webcare to answer questions of clients. Furthermore, Airline 3 frequently hires agencies to help them with creating visual content for specific campaigns. As these examples make clear, Airline 3 has assigned significant resources for social media tasks. Airline 3 says that they do not target for one target audience but let this depend on their specific social media campaigns.

Engage. Airline 3 has shown advanced ways of engaging with their customers such as interactive content and attractive campaigns. They have even linked social media relationships to their internal customer relationship systems (such as Salesforce) to track the individual customer experiences. Because of service purposes it matters whether: a customer that has lost its suitcase six times making it a different discussion than when it is the first time an issue with his lost suitcase. Furthermore Airline 3 is taking social media monitoring serious for continuous improvement of the organization: we really try to retrieve a top 10 of complaints and improve processes in our organization.

Evaluate. Airline 3 is stating that they are capable of getting quite a positive return on their investments: We are easily capable to earn back our investments Because of the highly advanced targeting and social advertising capabilities of social media they can target on specific niche markets. As a result they have been successfully selling seats in planes that they were not capable of selling before: "you see conversion rates increase as high as 900 percent". As Table 2 makes clear, Airline 3 showed attention to most key concepts from the social media strategy. Furthermore, they have been in the opportunity to assign significant resources (both staff and budget) to execute their social media plans.

5   Analysis

Based on careful analysis of the results and the structured literature study the following design is proposed for a Social Media Canvas as a new business tool to design social media strategies in Fig. 1. Following Osterwalder and Peigneur [10] we split content and engagement on the one hand and channel choice on the other hand. The canvas integrates the key elements of social media strategy from the findings of this research. It can help companies such as airline carriers to revisit and design their social media strategies during brainstorm meetings and

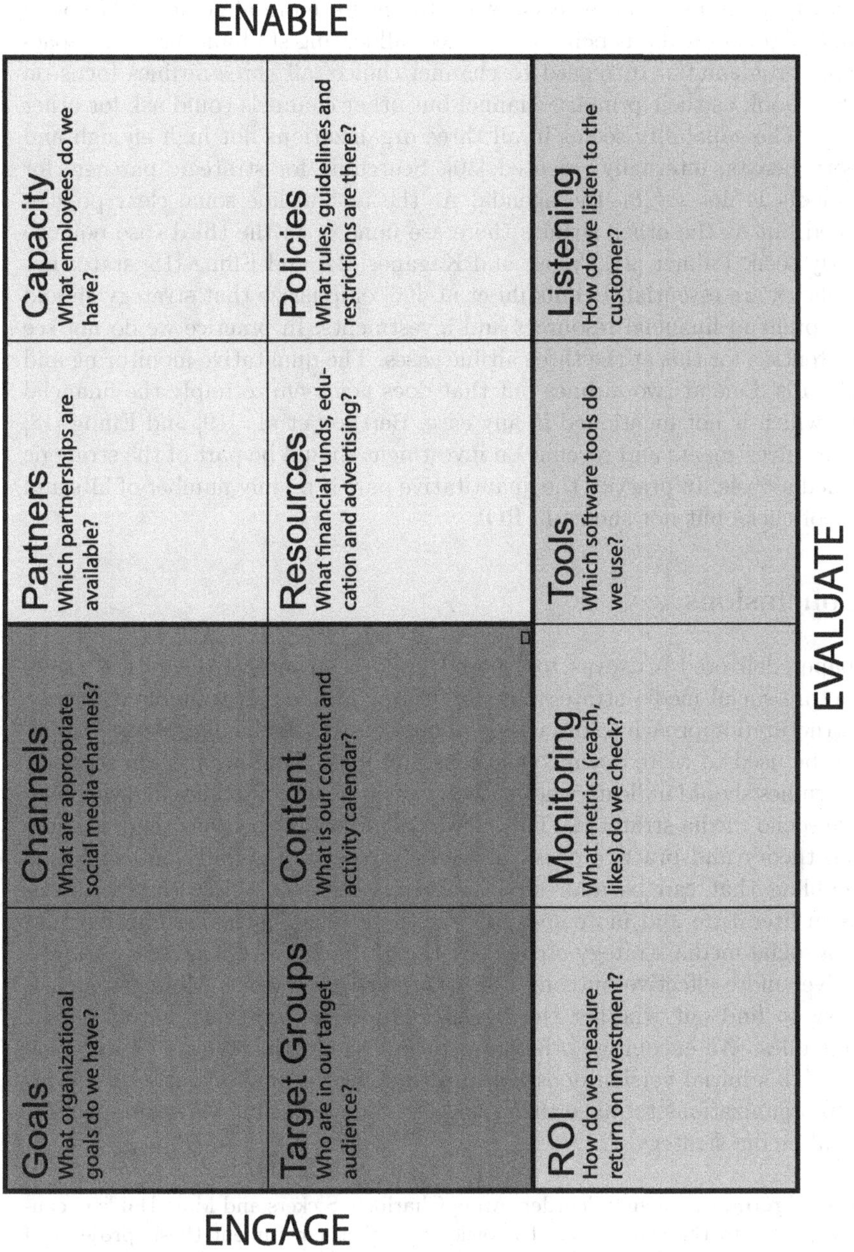

ENABLE

Capacity What employees do we have?	Partners Which partnerships are available?	Channels What are appropriate social media channels?	Goals What organizational goals do we have?
Policies What rules, guidelines and restrictions are there?	Resources What financial funds, education and advertising?	Content What is our content and activity calendar?	Target Groups Who are in our target audience?
Listening How do we listen to the customer?	Tools Which software tools do we use?	Monitoring What metrics (reach, likes) do we check?	ROI How do we measure return on investment?

ENGAGE

EVALUATE

Fig. 1. 3E social media strategy canvas

decision-making processes. As the case results show, alignment between business goals and social media goals can be improved. As mentioned in theory the social media seem very agile and difficult to plan [48]. Therefore, we design the goals and activity planning close to each other to ensure more alignment. Although the value of social media is being recognized, allocating staff and partner capacity seems problematic. In regard to channel choice, all three airlines focus on using Facebook as their primary channel but other channels could ask for other activities. The capability seems in all three organizations not high enough and as theory boasts, internally oriented [30]. Searching for strategic partners for social media is not yet on the agenda. At the first airline some clear policies are issued but at the other airlines there are none or in the third case none to be clearly seen. Palmer [21], Vaast and Kaganer [24] and Effing [18] state that clear policies are essential. Lehmkuhl et al. [66] emphasize that strategy should also comprehend financial resources and investments. In practice we do not see much attention for this at the three airline cases. The qualitative monitoring and evaluation is done at two airlines but that does not seem to imply the financial revenue which is not mentioned in any case. Berthon et al., [19] and Effing [18] show that investments and revenue on investment should be part of the strategic social media cycle. In practice the quantitative part is mainly number of hits and number of clicks but not shown in ROI.

6   Conclusions

This paper delivered a canvas tool based upon a structural theoretical study to structure social media strategy in the future. The tool is valuable to have a more structured approach to discussion about these social media strategy topics and can be used to write down conclusions and ideas from brainstorm sessions. Future studies should indicate whether this canvas helps companies in developing effective social media strategies. This canvas is important because there is a gap between theory and practice of social media strategy, especially on evaluation and enabling that can be addressed now. It is more complete than previous models in literature and more specific. Yet there remains the assumption that having a social media strategy created by the 3E Social Media Strategy Canvas will deliver more effective outcomes or return on investment. More research is necessary to find out whether the strategic approach will have better results for companies. We encourage other researchers to use this canvas in empirical research. This initial version does not aim to deliver a final layout. Our canvas can help organizations to make their own decisions regarding various aspects of the social media strategy.

Acknowledgements. Jenny Schrder, Anna Charlotte Sickers and Mart Hakkert contributed greatly to the generation of knowledge with their student thesis projects of both the University of Twente and Saxion University of Applied Sciences. We hereby express our great gratitude to them for being part of the broader research program.

References

1. Hvass, K.A., Munar, A.M.: The takeoff of social media in tourism. J. Vacation Mark. **18**(2), 93–103 (2012)
2. Xiang, Z., Gretzel, U.: Role of social media in online travel information search. Tourism Manag. **31**, 179–188 (2010)
3. Hsu, Y.L.: Facebook as international eMarketing strategy of Taiwan hotels. Int. J. Hospitality Manag. **31**, 972–980 (2012)
4. Hays, S., Page, S.J., Buhalis, D.: Social media as a destination marketing tool: its use by national tourism organisations. Curr. Issues Tourism **163**, 211–239 (2013)
5. DiStaso, M.W., McCorkindale, T.: A benchmark analysis of the strategic use of social media for fortunes most admired U.S. companies on Facebook, Twitter and YouTube. Public Relat. J. **71**, 1–33 (2013)
6. Escobar-Rodriguez, T., Carvajal-Trujillo, E.: An evaluation of Spanish hotel websites: informational vs. relational strategies. Int. J. Hospitality Manag. **33**, 228–239 (2013)
7. Aula, P.: Social media, reputation risk and ambient publicity management. Strategy Leadersh. **386**, 43–49 (2010)
8. Pham, P.H.M., Gammoh, B.S.: Characteristics of social-media marketing strategy, customer-based brand equity outcomes: a conceptual model. Int. J. Internet Mark. Advertising **9**(4), 321–337 (2015)
9. Wagner, D., et al.: Toward a conceptualization of online community health. In: International Conference of Information Systems, Auckland (2014)
10. Osterwalder, A., Pigneur, Y.: Business Model Generation: A Handbook for Visionaries, Game Changers, and Challengers. Wiley, Hoboken (2010)
11. Webster, J., Watson, R.: Analyzing the past to prepare for the future: writing a literature review. MIS Q. **262**, 13–23 (2002)
12. Wolfswinkel, J.F., Furtmueller, E., Wilderom, C.P.M.: Using grounded theory as a method for rigorously reviewing literature. Eur. J. Inf. Syst. **22**(1), 45–55 (2011)
13. Schwartz, R.B., Russo, M.C.: How to quickly find articles in the top IS journals. Commun. ACM **47**(2), 98–101 (2004)
14. Yin, R.K.: Case Study Research: Design and Methods. Sage, Thousand Oaks (1994)
15. Calder, B.J., et al.: The concept of external validity. J. Consum. Res. **9**, 240–244 (1982)
16. Lee, A.S., Baskerville, R.L.: Generalizing generalizability in information systems research. Inf. Syst. Res. **14**(3), 221–243 (2003)
17. Shadish, W.R., Cook, T.D., Campbell, D.T.: Experimental and Quasi-Experimental Designs for Generalized Causal Inference. Wadsworth Cengage Learning, Belmont (2002)
18. Effing, R.: Social media strategy design. In: 2nd Scientific Conference Information Science in an Age of Change, Insitute of Information and Book Studies, University of Warsaw, Warsaw (2013)
19. Berthon, P.R., et al.: Marketing meets Web 2.0, social media, and creative consumers: implications for international marketing strategy. Bus. Horiz. **553**, 261–271 (2012)
20. Kietzmann, J.H., et al.: Social media? get serious! understanding the functional building blocks of social media. Bus. Horiz. **54**, 241–251 (2011)
21. Palmer, L.A.: Social media infrastructure: supporting communication practices from behind the scenes. In: SIGDOC 13 Proceedings of the 31st ACM International Conference on Design of Communication, pp. 191–192 (2013)

22. See-Pui Ng, C., Chung Wang, W.Y.: Best practices in managing social media for business. In: Thirty Fourth International Conference on Information Systems 2013, Milan, pp. 1–11 (2013)
23. Meijer, A., Thaens, M.: Social media strategies: understanding the differences between North American police departments. Gov. Inf. Q. **30**, 343–350 (2013)
24. Vaast, E., Kaganer, E.: Social media affordances and governance in the workplace: an examination of organizational policies. J. Comput. Mediated Commun. **19**, 78–101 (2013)
25. Thackeray, R., Neiger, B.L., Keller, H.: Integrating social media and social marketing: a four-step process. Health Promot. Pract. **132**, 165–168 (2012)
26. Constantinides, E., Lorenzo-Romero, C., Gomez Boria, M.A.: Social media: a new frontier for retailers? Eur. Retail Res. **22**, 1–28 (2008)
27. Weber, R.: Constrained agency in corporate social media policy. J. Tech. Writ. Commun. **433**, 289–315 (2013)
28. Gotterbarn, D.: Corporate social media use policy: meeting business and ethical responsibilities. IFIP AICT **386**, 387–398 (2012)
29. Carim, L., Warwick, C.: Use of social media for corporate communications by research-funding organisations in the UK. Pub. Relat. Rev. **39**, 521–525 (2013)
30. Malthouse, E.C., et al.: Managing customer relationships in the social media era: introducing the social CRM house. J. Interact. Mark. **27**, 270–280 (2013)
31. Munar, A.M.: Social media strategies and destination management. Scand. J. Hospitality Tourism **12**(2), 101–120 (2012)
32. Hotopp, D., Willecke, L.: Twitter als werkzeug des online-marketings: richtlinien fur erfolgreiches twittern. Informationswissenschaft Hildesheim **61**, 419–422 (2010)
33. Picazo-Vela, S., Gutierrez-Martinez, I., Luna-Reyes, L.F.: Understanding risks, benefits, and strategic alternatives of social media applications in the public sector. Gov. Inf. Q. **29**, 504–511 (2012)
34. Gallaugher, J., Ransbotham, S.: Social media and customer dialog management at starbucks. MIS Q. Executive **9**(4), 197–212 (2010)
35. Linke, A., Zerfass, A.: Social media governance: regulatory frameworks for successful online communications. J. Commun. Manag. **173**, 270–286 (2013)
36. Chandy, R.: Making your social media strategy work. Lond. Bus. Sch. Issue **1**, 77 (2014)
37. Parent, M., Plangger, K., Bal, A.: The new WTP: willingness to participate. Bus. Horiz. **54**, 219–229 (2011)
38. Kaplan, A.M.: If you love something, let it go mobile: mobile marketing and mobile social media 4 x 4. Bus. Horiz. **55**(2), 129–139 (2012)
39. Barnes, I.: Twitter in special libraries: a distributed social media strategy. Public Serv. Q. **101**, 62–65 (2014)
40. Mortleman, J.: Social media strategies. Comput. Fraud Secur. **2011**, 8–11 (2011)
41. Schaffer, N.: Eleven essential components of a social media strategy. Graph. Arts Mon. **18**(4), 28–30 (2015)
42. Othman, I.H., Bidin, A., Hussain, H.: Facebook marketing strategy for small business in Malaysia. In: 2013 International Conference on Informatics and Creative Multimedia, pp. 236–241 (2013)
43. Jansen, B.J., et al.: Twitter power: tweets as electronic word of mouth. J. Am. Soc. Inf. Sci. Technol. **6011**, 2169–2188 (2009)
44. Woodcock, N., Green, A., Starkey, M.: Social CRM as a business strategy. Database Mark. Customer Strategy Manag. **181**, 50–64 (2011)
45. Goldner, S.: A guide to social media what tools are worth paying for? EContent, 6–7 (2013)

46. Heath, D., Singh, R., Ganesh, J.: Organizational engagement in social media to motivate strategic directed action: a revelatory case. In: Proceedings of the Nineteenth Americas Conference on Information Systems, pp. 1–10 (2013)

47. Salo, J., Lankinen, M., Mantymaki, M.: The use of social media for artist marketing: music industry perspectives and consumer motivations. Int. J. Media Manag. **151**, 23–41 (2013)

48. Midyette, J.D., Youngkin, A., Snow-Croft, S.: Social media and communications: developing a policy to guide the flow of information. Med. Ref. Serv. Q. **331**, 39–50 (2014)

49. Mergel, I., Bretschneider, S.I.: A three-stage adoption process for social media use in Government. Public Adm. Rev. **733**, 390–400 (2013)

50. Rodriguez-Donaire, S.: Changing business model dynamics by means of social media. In: Proceedings of the 2012 IEEE ICMIT, pp. 370–377 (2012)

51. Bottles, K., Sherlock, T.: Who should manage your social media strategy? Phys. Executive **372**, 68–72 (2011)

52. Andzulis, J.M., et al.: A review of social media and implications for the sales process. J. Pers. Selling Sales Manag. **323**, 305–316 (2012)

53. Arvidsson, V., Holmstrom, J.: Social media strategy: understanding social media, IT strategy, and organizational responsiveness in times of crisis. Cutter IT J. **2612**, 18–23 (2013)

54. Palmieri, M.: Learning to like social media. Paperboard Packag. 21–24 (2012)

55. Drula, G.: Strategy of social media in the media companies. In: MindTrek10 Proceedings of the 14th International Academic MindTrek Conference, pp. 215–223 (2010)

56. Larson, K., Watson, R.T.: The value of social media: toward measuring social media strategies. In: Thirty Second International Conference on Information Systems, Shanghai, pp. 1–18 (2011)

57. Shen, B., Bissell, K.: Social media, social me: a content analysis of beauty companies use of Facebook in marketing and branding. J. Promot. Manag. **19**(5), 629–651 (2013)

58. Mills, A.J.: Virality in social media: the SPIN framwork. J. Public Aff. **122**, 162–169 (2012)

59. Oestreicher-Singer, G., Zalmanson, L.: Content or community? a digital business strategy for content providers in the social age. MIS Q. **372**, 591–616 (2013)

60. Kaplan, A.M., Haenlein, M.: Users of the world, unite! the challenges and opportunities of social media. Bus. Horiz. **53**, 59–68 (2010)

61. Dutta, S.: Whats your personal social media strategy? Harvard Bus. Rev. **88**(11), 127–130 (2010)

62. Hanna, R., Rohm, A., Crittenden, V.L.: Were all connected: the power of the social media ecosystem. Bus. Horiz. **54**, 265–273 (2011)

63. Leeflang, P.S.H., Verhoef, P.C., Dahlstrom, P., Freundt, T.: Challenges and solutions for marketing in a digital era. Eur. Manag. J. **32**, 1–12 (2014)

64. Ferrell, L., Ferrell, O.C.: Redirecting direct selling: high-touch embraces high-tech. Bus. Horiz. **55**, 273–281 (2012)

65. He, W., Zha, S., Li, L.: Social media competitive analysis and text mining: a case study in the pizza industry. Int. J. Inf. Manag. **33**, 464–472 (2013)

66. Lehmkuhl, T., Baumol, U., Jung, R.: Towards a maturity model for the adoption of social media as a means of organizational innovation. In: 46th Hawaii International Conference on System Sciences, pp. 3067–3076 (2013)

67. Miles, M.B., Huberman, A.M.: Qualitative Data Analysis: An Expanded Sourcebook. Sage, Thousand Oaks (1994)

68. Effing, R., Spil, T.A.M.: The social strategy cone; towards a framework for evaluating social media strategies. Int. J. Inf. Manag. **36**(1), 1–8 (2016)
69. Lau, E.K.W.: Understanding a company's social media strategies and customer engagement. In: Uden, L., Heričko, M., Ting, I.-H. (eds.) KMO 2015. LNBIP, vol. 224, pp. 438–450. Springer, Heidelberg (2015)
70. Apgar, D.: The false promise of big data: can data mining replace hypothesis-driven learning in the identification of predictive performance metrics? Syst. Res. Behav. Sci. **32**(1), 28–49 (2015)

Strategy Reformation? Materialization of Social Media in Telecom Industry

Shirumisha Kwayu$^{(\boxtimes)}$, Banita Lal, and Mumin Abubakre

Nottingham Trent University, Nottingham, UK
Shirumisha.kwayu2014@my.ntu.ac.uk,
{Banita.lal,Mumin.Abubakre}@ntu.ac.uk

Abstract. The pervasive use of social media is influencing change within organization. This paper uses sociomaterial lens with agential view to understand how social media is reforming strategy in Telecom organization through exploring changes brought by social media to organization, evaluating the changes with selection of strategic theories as well as providing insight on adoption of social media by telecom organizations. Following an interpretivist philosophy with exploratory purpose the study uses case study methodology employing secondary data and observation to explain how social media practices are shaping strategy at Vodacom. Social media is reforming strategy within telecom industry by exerting influence on organizational process for instance product development and marketing strategy.

Keywords: Social media · Strategy · Sociomateriality

1 Introduction

There are significant changes within organizations as result of widespread use of social media application such as Facebook, Twitter, WhatsApp, Instagram, Snapchat, You-Tube and Viber. For instance, social media has influenced marketing strategy of organizations (Gallaugher and Ransbotham 2010; Culnan et al. 2010), where the wide use of these social media applications has had implications on how organizations and customers interact with one another (Culnan et al. 2010). (Dabner 2012) defines social media as Internet and mobile-based applications that integrate technology, telecommunication and social interaction to facilitate creation and dissemination of words, videos images and audio. According to Mangold and Faulds (2009, p. 358), "the 21st century is witnessing an explosion of Internet-based messages transmitted through these media". Despite the fact that it is becoming a major factor for consideration for both businesses and consumers, the impact of social media for organizations is not yet clearly identified. Thus, it is difficult to determine the extent to which the transformation-taking place in organizations results from social media (Treem and Leonardi 2012). For the purpose of this study, focus of this paper is on the telecommunications sector in Tanzania with the following objectives:

Y.K. Dwivedi et al. (Eds.): I3E 2016, LNCS 9844, pp. 31–41, 2016.
DOI: 10.1007/978-3-319-45234-0_3

- To Investigate what changes social media brings into an organization
- To evaluate the selection of a theory that will provide a specific research angle to study social media within the Tanzanian telecommunications sector
- To understand social media adoption in Tanzania

2 Literature Review

2.1 Sociomateriality

Sociomateriality, which is a new way of investigating and theorizing information system (IS) phenomena within organization and society at large, is appealing to Information System (IS) scholars. It has stirred an interesting and enriched discussion on how it could be used to study IS phenomena and its implication on studies undertaking this perspective. Significantly sociomateriality has extended and challenged the prevailing knowledge among IS scholars and practitioners on the ontological relationship between technological and social (Kautz and Jensen 2013). (Orlikowski 2007) defines socio-materiality as a recursive intertwining of human and technology in practice. (Orlikowski 2007) further argues that for years IS scholars have been struggling to figure out the recursive intertwining of human and technology in practice: as means of moving from the usual framing of social and material as a separate factors even when they interact. (Orlikowski 2007) then proposes to view organization practices as sociomaterial - an approach that views an inherent inseparability between technical and social. Thus, given the high level of human involvement and dependency of technology within social media, the sociomateriality approach appears to be a suitable angle from which to investigate this phenomenon.

Using the sociomaterial perspective, this paper uses the agential realism as theoretical foundation. Agential realism views actors and objects as self-contained entities that influence each other to composite and shifting assemblages (Barad 2003). Thus, with agential realism actor (social) and objects (material) are relational and ontological. Hence sociomaterial view fits in agential realism belief that social and material are inherently inseparable. Holding to this view, reality is not given but performed through relations in practice. Further, this paper has decided to adopt sociomaterial perspective as (Scott and Orlikowski 2014) argue that it's a more sensible approach for studying technology such as social media to understand a reality that is dynamic, multiple and entangled. Sociomaterial perspective is going to enrich the analysis in this by examining the relationship between social media practice (usage) and what happens in strategy within organization.

Currently, there are two studies on social media that have used sociomaterial lens footed on agential realism, both studies are done by same scholars (Scott and Orlikowski 2012, 2014) and are on the travel sector. The first study explored the materialization of social media in the travel sector and the other one performing anonymity through social media. Starting with the latter, they explored entanglement in practice by comparing the production of anonymity between the institutionalized accreditation scheme offered by the AA and an online social media website hosted by TripAdvisor. The use of sociomateriality aided the focus from perceiving technology as a distinct object influencing human being to examining how actions and relations are materially constituted in practice. (Scott and Orlikowski 2014) perceive social media as interesting area to study sociomateriality in practice as they are characterized with active engagement and online contribution producing novel form of knowledge that provides deep entanglement of meaning and materiality. Sociomateriality centers the empirical interest on how and when specific characteristics and consequences of practice are produced through particular material enactment. In simple terms, material enactments is an emphasis on practices that draw focus on how everyday activities constitute reality, which supports the analysis of emergence, dynamism and multiplicity of organization context. The study of Orlikowski using sociomateriality was able to challenge the literature that viewed anonymity as single attribute of some agent or system to find that anonymity is multiple dynamic and sociomaterial as its not fixed or binary in state (Scott and Orlikowski 2014).

The former study of (Scott and Orlikowski 2012) explored the moral and strategic implication of social media using sociomaterial perspective to examine online rating and ranking mechanism by analyzing how their performance reconfigures relations of accountability. Their study focused on the use of social media in particular TripAdvisor. The relationship between online rating and ranking mechanism with social media is the boost provided by social media. The power charging of online rating and ranking perform a redistribution of accountability. The study was done with a case of Village Inn hotel, which is located in remote part of England. TripAdvisor transformed the business in fundamental ways for instance; sales increased nine fold, it instituted a weekly practice of reflecting customer reviews. It also changed the marketing practice from traditional ways like magazines to online and social platform like TripAdvisor.

This brief review highlights power of sociomateriality as a theoretical foundation of exploring the complexity of social media and its implication in organization. It also shows the importance of focusing on practice rather than on distinct technology in understanding the impact of technology which can be multiple, dynamic and complex to organization. Further, despite the theoretical power of sociomateriality that footed on agential realism there is inadequate of social media literature conducted by this theory, as it is evident from the two studies explained above. Thus the use of this method will contribute to our understanding of the use of social media in organization as well as adding knowledge of sociomaterial perspective in IS.

3 Methodology

This paper follows an interpretivist philosophy, which believes there are many interpretation of reality and these interpretations are part of the scientific knowledge (Hammersley 1993). Following the interpretivist philosophy the paper is exploratory, as (Saunders et al. 2009) suggest it provides a valuable means of finding out what's happening, to seek new insights, to ask questions and to assess phenomena in new light. The paper intends to give insight on the possible effects of social media on strategy formation within organization.

The paper adopts a case study method as it intends to provide in depth knowledge on a real life phenomenon (Yin 2013). It uses Vodacom Tanzania as a case organization. Vodacom is a leading Telecom company in Tanzania. It owns 35 % of subscription market share as of September 2015 (TCRA 2015). Vodacom is a representative sample of Tanzanian telecom organization. The rationale for choosing case method is its ability to explain a decision(s), why they were taken and the way they were implemented. Furthermore, this paper makes use of secondary data and observation of social media practices to explain the reformation of strategy that (Mutch 2008) explains as concerned with external face of organization and how it translates into imperative for internal activities. Thus the paper intends to explain the external face of telecom organization in Tanzania using the case of Vodacom by linking it with social media practices.

4 Analysis

The prolific use of social media in the world is also experienced in Tanzania (Pfeiffer et al. 2014). Most of social media users in Tanzania use them for communication purposes. The access to social media in Tanzania is through mobile phones. Thus use of social media in Tanzania has direct effects on telecom industry. These effects are in two ways: (1) Social media substitutes the generic service provided by telecommunication industry by enabling text and verbal communication; (2) Telecommunication companies are using social media to advance their business process for instance they provide Internet to majority of social media user in Tanzania, and in addition they use social media platform for marketing and maintaining customer relations. These two factors make the relationship between social media use and telecommunication organizations an interesting area to explore especially in the context of Tanzania. Without telecommunication companies in Tanzania, majority of social media users cannot access the Internet with the current state of infrastructure. Profoundly, the telecom companies continue to support the use of social media although it substitutes their generic service. The relationship between social media and telecom companies that seems to influence the development of each other creates the rationale to explore and understand how social media impacts the telecom industry in Tanzania and how telecom industry perceives strategy on social media.

Internet user in Tanzania have increased tremendously in the recent years, they have increased from 5 million in 2010 to above 11 million in 2014 (TCRA 2015). The increase in Internet usage attributed by the increase of mobile service that has increased from 20 million in 2010 to 34 million in 2014 whereas there has been a decline in fixed phone service from 174,511 to 142,950 (TCRA 2015). It is arguable that the increase use of Internet service is associated with the use of social media because most of social media users in Tanzania access them through their mobile. The increasing use of social media has exerted pressure on the telecom industry. Strategic literature suggests that changes in external environment have great influence on internal (operational) process of organization (Ben-Menahem et al. 2013). The data above not only shows a shift in technological environment but also on social practice, which portrays a change in business environment for telecom organization. For instance using (Henderson and Venkatraman 1989) strategic alignment model, which aligns between external and internal environment of organization, motivates us to understand how the adoption of social media by the public in Tanzania is reshaping strategy within organization in this case Telecom Company. The analysis below examines how strategy is reformed with the influence of social media by exploring products of telecom industry and how they market their products.

4.1   Product/Service Strategy

(Belasen and Rufer 2013) argues that new products is the lifeblood for firms that hope to remain competitive in high-technology industries such as telecommunication because they are faced with fast shrinking product life cycles thus developing new products that match with market needs is their secret for survival. (Belasen and Rufer 2013) research highlights the sensitivity of telecom organization to changes that occur in the market. This means that the product strategy of telecom industry reacts to changes that occur within the business environment. Thus it is highly expected the emergency of social media to influence the product strategy of the telecom organization.

Exploring the product offered by Vodacom, a significant influence of social media can be noted. First, they have reformed their packages to attract social media user. For instance, on their prepaid offer they have Facebook SMS, a service that allows individual to receive their Facebook notification on their phone (Vodacom 2016). Another example from Vodacom that shows that social media has enormous influence on their product strategy is on their Value Added Services where several of the services are social media for instance SIMU.tv is YouTube channel that is dedicated to provide video clips and live broadcasts from several TV channels in the country. Furthermore the influence of social media in reforming product strategy of Vodacom cannot be overstated as some of their product such as Rafiki Chat are in-company initiated social media application that intend to lure their customers with taste of social media offered by external organization such as Facebook, Alphabet (Google+) Inc. There are other several products that can show the influence of social media on Vodacom new products.

In addition, there is an indirect influence of social media on Vodacom's products. There is no social media without Internet. Internet has become a dear product of Vodacom. For instance on their *Cheka Bombastik* bundles they sell minutes and text but they also include internet (Data) that is significant product in the bundle the Table 1 below is the *Cheka Bombastic* package:

Table 1. Cheka Bombastik

All network bundles					
Duration	Price in Tsh.	Minutes	SMS	Data (MB)	Validity
Daily	499	6	40	2	Midnight
	649	10	100	6	24 h
	999	19	200	16	24 h
Weekly	1,999	22	200	60	7 Days
	4,999	70	500	120	7 Days
	9,999	180	1,000	120	7 Days
Monthly	9,999	125	1,000	500	30 Days
	14,999	200	1,500	500	30 Days
	19,999	330	2,000	500	30 Days
	29,999	550	3,000	500	30 Days
	49,999	1,000	10,000	500	30 Days

Source: Vodacom Tanzania 2016

Social media is a significant driver for mobile Internet consumption among other uses. In Tanzania with 11 million individual Internet users (TCRA 2015), 2.7 million use Facebook (Internet World Stats 2016). This is a significant amount as it accounts for a quarter of Internet usage. Thus social media usage has indirect influence on product strategy of Vodacom. For instance, on the monthly bundle the 500 MB of data service does not increase with price, this cap forces user to buy extra data service when already consumed the allowance thus the data services are included in the bundle to sustain the minutes and SMS service. If the cap on data service is not imposed it means that people will have more power to substitute the generic product of telecom that is SMS and the Minutes. Moreover competitors of Vodacom such as Tigo have exclusive data bundles that allow free WhatsApp within the *Minikabang* or *Tigo Xtreme bundles* (Tigo 2016). The repacking of bundles is evidence of how use of social media is indirectly influencing product strategy within telecom industry.

There is probability that social media has influenced Vodacom to diversify some of their product services. This is difficult to measure. Since diversification is moving away from associated service, the methodology we are using cannot validate this claim but it raises a question whether there is any correlation between the diversification of Vodacom services or it is just an assumption. Vodacom has diversified to financial services such as *M-Pesa*, which helps to transfer, receive and borrow money, it has also moved to entertainment industry with music streaming services like *Mkito Plus*. This diversification could potentially be linked with social media usage. Consciously or unconsciously Vodacom may have diversified to escape or create resilience of the negative effects of social media to the company. The service such as *M-Pesa*, *M-Pawa* (Saving service) and *M-Kopa* (borrowing service) helps to retain customers, thus if the competition exerted by social media in different dynamics challenges Vodacom, Vodacom could resist the effects social media. For instance, if other telecom companies decide to reduce the price of Internet and influence a lot of customer to move, the M-Pawa service could still retain the customers. This scenario could be possible considering Tanzania is a low income country with only US Dollar 920 Gross National Income (GNI) per capita (World Bank 2016) hence having customers who are extremely sensitive to price change. Thus the diversification to other products can be a strategy of Vodacom to reduce the negative power of social media user to influence the performance of organization.

Exploring the products development at Vodacom with sociomaterial lens assists us in understanding how strategy is reformed in Tanzania telecom industry. Sociomaterial is interested with daily practice (Cecez-Kecmanovic et al. 2014), looking at the daily use of social media by Tanzania public influences the product development in telecom industry, likewise telecom industry influences the use of social media. A user buys a bundle in order to access social media, the user can only use the bundle and finish the allowance or the allowance expires with time, the bundle controls the extent of using social media but also give the organization opportunity to manipulate social media usage for instance allowing a free WhatsApp while limiting other social media application. Likewise, the use of social media by the public goes beyond as telecom companies are learning and developing products such as Facebook SMS and Simu TV.

Thus it is this relation in practice that influences reality which in this case is telecoms strategy of developing and delivering this products to social media user in Tanzania. Therefore, this paper argues that the existence of social media related products offered by telecom organizations provide evidence of how social media has influenced strategy. The reality of these products is not given but exists as a result of social media usage. This is in line with the Agential philosophy that reality is not given but enacted through practice (Scott and Orlikowski 2013).

4.2 Marketing Strategy

Literature (Gallaugher and Ransbotham 2010; Culnan et al. 2010) indicates how social media has influenced marketing strategy of organizations. Many organization use social media for marketing related purposes. Social media use in Tanzania has influenced Vodacom's marketing strategy to a significant level. A brief overview of Facebook pages statistics in Tanzania highlights the influence of social media on Vodacom marketing strategy.

Table 2. Facebook statistic page

No	Page name	Total fans	Ratings	Descriptions	Comments
1	JamiiForums	1,318,938	10	Social media forum	Vodacom advertises on their forum
2	Tigo Tanzania	1,085,577	8	Telecommunication company	Vodacom's competitor
3	Diamond Platnumz	1,071,953	8	Artist/Musician	He's Vodacom's Brand ambassador
4	Bongo Movies	924,685	N/A	Tanzania movie industry	
5	Airtel Tanzania	858,537	7	Telecommunication company	Vodacom's competitor
6	East African television (EATV)	803,486	10	TV station	
7	Vodacom Tanzania	735,128	8	Telecommunication company	
8	Fastjet	703,051	0	Airline company	
9	Midcom East Africa	499,235	7	Telecommunication company	Vodacom's competitor
10	Lady Jaydee	499,230	0	Artist/Musician	

Source: Social Baker 2016

The above Table 2 shows the top ten Facebook pages in Tanzania with highest fans. The telecom industry dominates the list. This shows how social media has become a competition arena for telecom organizations. Furthermore, visiting the Facebook pages of this telecom industry, the companies use them to promote their service, to engage customers and also to respond to some of the queries of customers. The domination of the list by Telecom industry is by itself an explanation why social media is adopted by telecom organization in Tanzania. (Braojos-Gomez et al. 2015) using a social competitor theory found that firms adopted and developed their social media competence once their competitors have done so. Thus the competition exhibited in the table above is an additional evidence to explain adoption and validate the social competitor theory. Also domination of telecom industry reveals that social media practice is key strategy within the telecom industry.

In addition, the table above signifies how marketing decision of telecom organization are influenced by social media usage. JamiiForums is a social platform and Vodacom advertises on the platform, in the list JamiiForums appears to attract a lot of social media users and thus attracting Vodacom to capitalize on their popularity to influence their user. Likewise, Vodacom hired Diamond Platnumz as their brand ambassador. The selection of Diamond Platnumz as their brand ambassador may have been influenced among other factors by the number of social media fans he has on his page. Thus, this shows that social media usage continues to influence the marketing strategy of Vodacom.

The selection of Diamond and JamiiForums is a strategic practice of Vodacom to influence social media user. (Kumar and Mirchandani 2012) suggests that identifying influential individual who can spread organization message is important for gaining success in social media. Organization can use data to identify influential individual. In the above case we see Vodacom practice of identifying individual using the Facebook statistics. While presenting Diamond to the press conference as a Vodacom brand ambassador, Ian Ferrao, Vodacom's Managing director acknowledged the power of social media in influencing people, stating, *'just as an example we going to think power of the internet and the power of social media and how that is creating use of this lads, diamond and Vodacom are both committed to one another we going to work together on this journey'* (Vodacom Press 2016).

The above table can be demonstrated on the diagram below where we see an intra action of activities that enact (reforms) strategy at telecom organizations in Tanzania. The bigger wheel represents the 2.7 million Facebook users in Tanzania, the other wheel represents Telecom organizations and the last wheel represents the influencer. Each of the wheels has its own practice but the practice of one group influences another group. Thus the relationship of these actors they reform strategy. For instance, a social media user can directly contact the organization and likewise the organizations can directly contact an individual user. However, there is a group of people that the organization cannot contact directly but can do so through influencers such as Diamond who can influence on behalf of the organization. It is through this relationship that the telecom organization is strategically advancing its marketing objectives (Fig. 1).

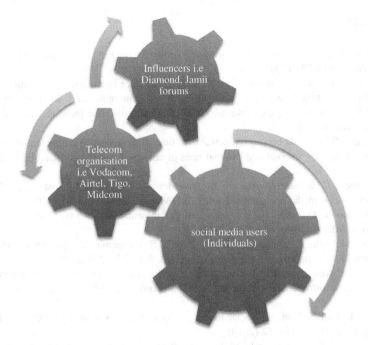

Fig. 1. Facebook intra-action

5 Conclusion

Adopting a sociomaterial lens in this paper has demonstrated the changes social media brought in telecom organization. With a framework of strategic theories the paper explained strategic practices which are influenced by social media as well as providing insight on the adoption and use of social media by telecom organization. First, sociomaterial lens by providing focus on practice enables to correlate public usage of social media and organizational practices with each influencing the other. For instance, the public follows the influencer (for example Diamond) and the organization (Vodacom) uses influencer to reach the public. In other word the public is influencing the choice and the organization is responding rational (strategic) to the public. Second, with aid of theories like strategic alignment the paper was able to explain how changes in external environment are influencing internal (operational) practices of organization. For instance how the pervasive use of social media is influencing product development in telecom industry such as free WhatsApp, Facebook SMS and *Cheka Bombastick*. Lastly, with aid of social competitor theory, the study could interpret the intensity and dominance of telecom industry in the Facebook statistics page. Sociomaterial with agential perspective demonstrates how reality is performed through practice (Kautz and Jensen 2013). This lens provides a basis of explaining how strategy in Tanzania telecom organization is reformed through social media practices and how telecom organization conceive their strategy with social media in mind, the evidence of this can be obtained in product development and marketing processes of Vodacom.

References

Barad, K.: Posthumanist performativity: toward an understanding of how matter comes to matter. Signs **28**(3), 801–831 (2003)

Belasen, A., Rufer, R.: Innovation communication and inter-functional collaboration: a view from the competing values framework for corporate communication. In: Pfeffermann, N., Minshall, T., Mortara, L. (eds.) Strategy and Communication for Innovation, pp. 227–240. Springer, Berlin (2013)

Ben-Menahem, S.M., et al.: Strategic renewal over time: the enabling role of potential absorptive capacity in aligning internal and external rates of change. Long Range Plan. **46**(3), 216–235 (2013)

Braojos-Gomez, J., Benitez-Amado, J., Llorens-Montes, F.J.: How do small firms learn to develop a social media competence? Int. J. Inf. Manage. **35**(4), 443–458 (2015)

Cecez-Kecmanovic, D., et al.: The sociomateriality of information systems: current status, future directions. MIS Q. **38**(3), 809–830 (2014)

Culnan, M., Mchugh, P., Zubillaga, J.: How large U.S. companies can use Twitter and other social media to gain business value. MIS Q. Exec. **9**(4), 243–259 (2010)

Dabner, N.: 'Breaking ground' in the use of social media: a case study of a university earthquake response to inform educational design with Facebook. Internet High. Educ. **15**(1), 69–78 (2012)

Gallaugher, J., Ransbotham, S.: Social media and customer dialog management at Starbucks. MIS Q. Exec. **9**(4), 197–212 (2010)

Hammersley, M.: Social Research: Philosophy. Politics and Practice. Sage, Thousand Oaks (1993)

Henderson, J.C., Venkatraman, N.: Strategic alignment: a process model for integrating information technology and business stategies (1989)

Kautz, K., Jensen, T.B.: Sociomateriality at the royal court of IS: a jester's monologue. Inf. Organ. **23**(1), 15–27 (2013)

Kumar, V., Mirchandani, R.: Increasing the ROI of social media marketing. MIT Sloan Manag. Rev. **54**(1), 55 (2012)

Mutch, A.: Managing Information and Knowledge in Organizations: A Literacy Approach. Routledge, Abingdon-on-Thames (2008)

Orlikowski, W.J.: Sociomaterial practices: exploring technology at work. Organ. Stud. **28**(9), 1435–1448 (2007)

Pfeiffer, C., et al.: The use of social media among adolescents in Dar es Salaam and Mtwara, Tanzania. Reprod. Health Matters **22**(43), 178–186 (2014)

Saunders, M., Lewis, P., Thornhill, A.: Research methods for business students (2009)

Scott, S.V., Orlikowski, W.J.: Entanglements in practice: performing anonymity through social media (2004)

Scott, S.V., Orlikowski, W.J.: Sociomateriality - taking the wrong turning? A response to Mutch. Inf. Organ. **23**(2), 77–80 (2013)

Scott, S.V., Orlikowski, W.J.: Reconfiguring relations of accountability: materialization of social media in the travel sector. Acc. Organ. Soc. **37**(1), 26–40 (2012)

Treem, J.W., Leonardi, P.M.: Social media use in organizations: exploring the affordances of visibility, editability, persistence, and association. Commun. Yearb. **36**, 143–189 (2012)

Yin, R.K.: Case Study Research: Design and Methods. Sage Publications, Thousand Oaks (2013)

Internet World Stats (2016). http://www.internetworldstats.com/stats1.htm. Accessed 17 Feb 2016

Social Bakers (2016). http://www.socialbakers.com/statistics/facebook/pages/total/tanzania/. Accessed 17 Feb 2016

TCRA. Tanzania Communication regulatory Authority (2015). http://www.tcra.go.tz/images/documents/telecommunication/telcomStatsSept15.pdf. Accessed 17 Feb 2016

Tigo (2016). http://www.tigo.co.tz/sw/personal/voice-sms/hot-offers. Accessed 17 Feb 2016

Vodacom (2016). https://www.vodacom.co.tz. Accessed 17 Feb 2016

Vodacom Press (2016). https://www.youtube.com/watch?v=j6fLJ453CGI (minute 3:40- 4). Accessed 12 June 2016

World Bank (2016). http://data.worldbank.org/country/tanzania. Accessed 12 June 2016

Social Media or Social Business Networks?

Issam A.R. Moghrabi[✉] and Abdullah R. Al-Mohammed

Gulf University for Science and Technology, Mishref, Kuwait
{moughrabi.i,GUST1303102011}@gust.edu.kw

Abstract. Social media has incurred changes that can be seen in developing new customer centric strategies, objectives, and goals, to realigning operations to meet the constantly changing and highly sensitive demands of customers, among others. The increase in value of social media channels is more than just a luxury gateway; rather those channels have become quintessential venues of communication between the customer and the organization. The purpose of this paper is to analyze the effect of social media on the business environment with particular emphasis on how it impacts both the customer and the organization. This will be accomplished through focusing on several facets such as social media and globalization, social media vs. traditional media, bridging the gap between the customer and the organization, and how social media empowers the customer. The paper presents some recommendations and precautions pertinent to the utilization of social nets into the core business processes.

Keywords: Social media · Viral marketing · Business networks · Online reputation systems

1 Introduction

Social media platforms have become a forum where users can share content and interact with one another. Though the involvement of the word "social" indicates the big role played by the people in sharing their social life on those digital platforms, such platforms are largely becoming business networks or media [1]. They are shaping new business models and moving the market into new prospects. Social media have also shaped the existence of online communities that share common interests and tendencies [1, 2].

In the previous decade, organizations have been working by cutting edge levels of data and correspondence. Technology innovations define new methods for communication and socializing. Technology is primarily adopted as a means to decrease the communication barriers. Innovative technology has become an enabler of a new era of communication with a huge impact on business, thus creating new means of interactions and introduced us to a new socializing median called social media [3, 6].

Social media has seized a considerable share of everyday life activities, especially due to the multitude of purposes of social media activities. Therefore, it only makes sense that companies and businesses would decide to take advantage of the benefits offered by social media, and integrate social media within their organizations in order to help them achieve their strategic goals and objectives. Social media had the power to

Published by Springer International Publishing Switzerland 2016. All Rights Reserved
Y.K. Dwivedi et al. (Eds.): I3E 2016, LNCS 9844, pp. 42–52, 2016.
DOI: 10.1007/978-3-319-45234-0_4

transform organization's business model from operations, marketing, and not ending with sales. Whether they were small businesses or big operating companies, many businesses nowadays cannot operate without the aid of social networking accounts. In fact social media now is dramatically affecting traditional business-to-customer models as well as business-to-business models [4]. Moreover, since the year 2010, social networking has been regarded the internet buzzword, utilized as a cultural facilitator as well as a business tool. Social networks are different from the traditional online marketing-channels because they have the ability to gather, parse, and sort valuable demographic data, on daily basis. Social networking includes a variety of services, evolutions and communications that happen in the cyberspace [3, 14]. Social networking has attracted a lot of attention due to its ability to bring together huge customer bases to organizations of all sizes, including the small ones that target niche markets. Social networks have undeniably transformed businesses. The changes in business induced through the incorporation of social media can be seen in developing new customer centric strategies, objectives, and goals, to realigning operations to meet the constantly changing and highly sensitive demands of customers, to the establishment of social media dedicated units and budgets, to bridging the gap between the organization and the customer, to developing an IT infrastructure to meet the demands of such social media units. In addition, it has the potential to empower clients and end users [3, 12]. Further, it has the ability to make customer-metrics more granular. Social networks bring several functionalities. Through business analytics/intelligence, one is able to obtain demographic data, location data, friends and relationships data, real time trends and content, and user-interaction data. The new social media seems to have become the new telephone and/or the new email [1, 9].

The paper is organized as follows: Sect. 2 addresses the main aim of the paper; Sect. 3 brings some insight into the issues being addressed here and sheds light on the repercussions of utilizing social media into businesses to create a transformation in the concept of doing business at a price that could be costly to organizations both financially and morally. Section 4 mainly embodies recommendations and precautions related to the adoption of the use of social networks to become the business networks or the social business. Finally, in Sect. 5, the conclusions are presented.

2   Research Question

The motivation behind this paper is to explore, investigate, and break down the impact of online networking on the business environment with specific accentuation on how it sways both the client and the association, both positively and negatively. This is done through concentrating on online networking and globalization, online networking versus conventional media, overcoming any issues between the client and the business, how online networking enables the client, which is accomplished at lower expenses and higher scope than customary media. Also, in this paper, we will raise the issue of whether businesses can make due in today's rapidly changing business environment without online networking, and we will be presenting our recommendations on how organizations can best utilize long range social networking to enhance their brand image and achieve higher customer loyalty. The article will also be giving guidelines of what entrepreneurs should look at when constructing social marketing strategies [4, 13].

The main hypothesis here is that social networks have caused a migration in the business culture and have themselves emerged as business networks. Thus, guidelines need be established as to the adoption of such networks to become an integral part of the business processes.

3   Some Insight

We start this section by exploring the impact of social media on the business environment from (a) business perspective, and from (b) customer perspective.

From a business perspective, integrating social media inside of a business and aligning it with an organization's strategies and goals has turned out to be less of an alternative, and even more a need in today's aggressive and dynamic business environment. The reason is that organizations must recognize the demands of the global competitive business environment and respond promptly in addition to ensuring that they predict trends in that environment – be proactive [4]. By embracing online social networking, and building up a culture of client centricity supported by the use of the social networking channels, organizations can develop a competitive advantage. This can be achieved by reengineering the organizations primary business functions such as marketing, advertising, public relations, and customer experience management to be driven by and be highly dependent on social media platforms [4, 5].

Social media has forced companies to change their infrastructure, influence their strategies, and transform their objectives to include a social media specific target – such as obtaining 1 M followers online, create a dedicated social media team, a dedicated budget, and minimize the volume of poor comments which may reflect negatively on the organization's image [4, 6].

Furthermore, not only has social media affected business and consumers, but it has also, on a larger scale, affected the economy as a whole by creating new jobs and new job titles, such as social media officers. Moreover, it also created new types of organizations such as social media agencies and consultancy [4].

Looking at Twitter platform, it has given people an opportunity to link with those who are like minded. For instance, business people meet, share ideas and they learn from each other. Using business intelligence and social-media analytics [9], engaging-content strategy can be formed to monitor interactions that take place within it and detect trends to improve decision making. There are also web tools in various social sites to help users knowledge-base their usage of the social net to maximize output for a certain purpose [2, 7]. Though useful for a period of time, most of the sites provide publishing platforms. For instance, in Facebook, there are plugins that allow users to post something on Twitter. Analytics, coupled with broadcasting have enabled sites such as ping.fm to add analysis tools, hence differentiating themselves. These work together with seismic, to produce the best results. There are also other web analytics tools used by e-commerce sites that do not properly analyze users' opinions and sentiments. However, these have been improved by enhancing their capabilities to connect to social-media analytics that collect user information that relates to products and various brands. They also collect trends, including competitors' insights [7].

There are several social media sites whose success is not determined much by their technology parameters, but rather by their users base. LinkedIn, Twitter, Facebook and YouTube, are among such social sites that have the most contributing and engaged audiences. Years back, people would take much pride if they had many follows in Facebook and Twitter. Things have changed today, and instead, marketers have targeted certain categories of followers whereby they post content that is of interest to those and this helps to keep the followers engaged [8, 9]. Users have also learned the art of attracting friends intelligently. Since people can access large amounts of data, they are no longer very much interested in public image. On the contrary, they want in-depth material. Regarding content, people consistently seek out for comprehensive material, since they are empowered [1, 7]. Business intelligence helps to engage and to nurture consumers, as this is what they expect, as well. They want to be part of the product/ brand, and not to simply purchase. Big data is obtained from the social networks, configured and then delivered through various programming interfaces. There are also available tools that help to format data from one form to another [10, 11].

Tagged based advertising is the expansion of the Facebook pages. This methodology will be useful for the organization to advertise their item, image. Tagged based advertising permits the association to tag the input of the item to their client [12]. Once the tag has been done then this tag will then be obvious to the Friend List of the client in the News Feed. The advantage of the tag based promoting is: when an organization takes input about any item from the shopper and with his/her authorization, the criticism is tagged on the purchaser profile. This tag will now be visible in the News Feed of the Friend List of the shopper, which helps in the powerful showcasing; trust of the item will be expanded in the buyer's circle by purchaser's impact. This is the roundabout promoting that the association would be doing with minimal effort when contrasted with the other advertising media. The significant advantage of this advertising is the trust of the item which is critical in today's aggressive business sector. A sample from Kuwait would be Social Media Consulting Agency Ghaliah Tech which was established in 2011, with the reason for serving businesses or individuals trying to connect and promote their brand/image across online networking platforms. The agency offers services such as brand creation, online networking accounts administration, web promoting, web improvement, among others. Such organizations would not have existed without the emergence of online networking, and this is only one sample of the many organizations and jobs that were made possible by the social technology.

Viral marketing is well known as a word of mouth way of passing messages or information. As a marketing strategy, the study has focused on showing how communication among friends in social media such as Facebook, Twitter, YouTube, and Instagram among others, has been utilized heavily to market products as it facilitates the spread of "word of mouth" direct and indirect marketing. Branding in practice and philosophy is facing significant challenges due to the rise of digital and social media platforms that ease and allow electronic "Word of mouth". Many scholars [3, 8, 9, 11] emphasize the opportunities and benefits that online social networking could offer to companies. In recent times, critical research has stressed that even strong brands are open to these new environments because of the greater transparency, consumer empowerment, and online activism. IBM managers, for instance, reportedly believe that the social media communications of employees to be an enterprise-level threat, and have worked to teach employees as to corporate policy in this regard. Social media are playing important roles in political campaigning and shaping competition in which reputational factors could make the difference between success and failure.

From a customer perspective, social media has facilitated for the shift of power from the business to the consumer. This has become possible due to several different variables. Firstly, increased competition has led to increased options for consumers who have become more educated, more aware, due to the higher and better access to knowledge and feedbacks that are available on social media platforms. This has led not only for competitors to offer better products and services to consumers, but also, it has also led to product reengineering through involving the consumer in the product development process through customization, and customer interactions on social platforms. One such example of involving the customer in the product development process is the Lay's marketing campaign on social media platforms where consumers are asked to vote for their favorite potato chips flavor using hash tags on social media platforms, where the most voted for chips flavoring will be developed, and sold in the Middle East and North Africa markets.

Another example of the shift in power from businesses to consumers is while in the past negative customer experiences and complaints would sit idly in complain boxes at the business headquarters, or are not taken seriously or even ignored by the business, nowadays, the higher transparency and wider reach of social media networks means that negative experiences are not hidden from other customers. Furthermore, bad news travels faster today across social platforms to reach larger audiences. One specific example is the "United Broke my Guitar" incident where a Canadian musician's guitar at Chicago O'Hare airport was destroyed by United cargo staff, leading the musician to complain to the customer care unit and ask to be reimbursed in full, and when the musician tried to resolve the issue peacefully, but United Airlines failed to reimburse him in full. He decided to utilize the power of social media to get his voice heard, by creating a song which went viral thanks to the power of social media, reaching millions of viewers around the world, and leading United to lose 10 % of their share value, which is equivalent to $180 M USD [15]. This example shows that consumers, no matter who they are, or how small they are, can have their voices heard loud, owing that to the power of social media.

Due to the fact that customers can access information regarding most of the products and businesses they have taken interest on, they have become more informed and hence more selective and aware. It is essential not to ignore the fact that customers will communicate to others when it comes to social media. Social media marketing has caused increased customer awareness and product knowledge among customers and has hence enhanced the decision making process for the consumer. In the past, marketers held the power to influence product awareness and thus influencing product sales. The marketers based it on the purchase funnel. This divided product purchase into three stages. The first stage involved product awareness, followed by a mental note to purchase the product, and finally, purchasing of the product. This has greatly changed due to the impact of the social media. This change involves the effect of comments from other users regarding the subject in question. People will tend to use the product that has been proposed to them by others. Social media marketing has taken the role of creating consumer awareness from the marketer and entrusted that role to the consumer himself. The modern day consumer has the ability to research on a commodity instead of relying on the information provided by the marketer.

We now discuss how social media has promoted the creation of a new level of global understanding among cultures. Due to the advancements in telecommunication technologies, people have become more interconnected than ever before. Social media has contributed significantly to that by "bridging the gap" that existed not only among cultures, but between people and businesses as well. To elaborate, social media has added a human element to organizations [12, 16]. More people nowadays perceive a business as an individual due to the interaction taking place between the business and the individual on a daily basis, regardless of whether a business transaction occurs or not – something which would have been unthinkable a decade ago. Furthermore, social media has bridged the gap by being available to both customers and businesses anywhere, any time – something again which would have been unthinkable a decade ago.

In addition, social media has bridged the gap through creating a unified language for everyone to use regardless of their race, nationality, origin or background. Such language includes symbols of affection such as likes, and thumbs ups, and symbols of dissatisfaction such as dislikes, and thumbs downs, along with symbols of approval and common interests such as hash tags and/or retweets as signs of agreement. The bottom line is that social media has bridged the distance, time, and culture gaps which have led to a flatter, more engaged, better connected and interacted world, not only among individuals themselves, but also between individuals and organizations alike [17].

From a Customer Relationship Management (CRM), social media has created a new medium for customers to express their feelings, frustrations, experiences, ask questions, and simply send and receive feedback to the organization. Moreover, social media engagement by organization can lead to the better development of the organization's Customer Relationship Management system, as it allows the organization to build up on its existing CRM software. This can be done through enhancing the customer database via low cost techniques thus allowing the business to access customer social media patterns, activities and interests, who they follow, what they post about. This allows the business to understand what can be created to satisfy current customers, and possibly attract new ones, along with allowing the organization to view what their competitors are offering to their customers, and what can be offered to pull away those customers from the competition [4, 9].

In fact, taking a close look at the revenue figures of the top social networking companies gives a clear indication of the scale and volume of how popular those are to businesses embracing the services, tools and facilities of the social networks. Even further, it is evident that those social networks have themselves practically and tangibly become businesses that boost profits competing with that of the largest business enterprises in the world. Table 1 is plainly one evidence of many found in the literature as to the size of such social businesses [21].

Table 1. Comparing both the revenue and revenue per employee in 2012 ([21])

Company	2012 Reported revenues	Employees	Revenue per employee
Facebook	$5,089,000,000	4,619	$1,101,753
Zynga	$1,281,267,000	2,916	$439,391
Twitter	$350,000,000	900	$388,888
Automattic (WordPress)	$45,000,000	150	$300,000
LinkedIn	$972,309,000	3,458	$281,176
Groupon	$2,330,000,000	10,000	$233,000
LivingSocial	$536,000,000	4,500	$119,111
Yelp	$137,600,000	1,214	$113,344
Tumblr	$13,000,000	151	$86,092
Foursquare	$2,000,000	100	$20,000

4   Prospects and Recommendations-the Good, the Bad and the Ugly

After discussing the different effects social media has made on the business environment, we will answer the question raised earlier in this paper, and that is whether companies can survive without social media, followed by a recommendation on how companies can best utilize social media to enhance their image, generate higher profits and achieve higher customer satisfaction and hence loyalty.

All the above stresses the fact that social networks have promoted the emergence of social business networks which brings to the front the main question businesses are often confronted with and that is "To Social Media or not to Social Media". From a personal perspective, the benefits of utilizing social media by organizations greatly outweigh any negatives of social media usage. This again is due to several reasons already presented in this paper such as wider and faster reach, better cost savings, and higher customer satisfaction, among others. However, this only applies to industry specific organizations such as organizations that are highly customer centric such as the services industry. So yes, organizations with high customer focus must utilize social media in order to survive. That being, organizations with very low, to non-existent customer focus such as B2B organizations do not essentially require the utilization of social media to survive.

As a consequence of the induced electronic "word of mouth", there is a growing emphasis on reputation management and reputation risk assessments in brand management. It is noted in [17, 18] that there is a shift in power in the relationship between marketers and online consumer networks whereby transparency impact has grown, suggesting more consumer criticism and selectivity towards brands. Latest contributions suggest that there is an urgent need for a rapprochement between branding and reputation management perspectives in the utilization of social media, as noted in [5, 11]. Moreover, there is a growing interest in the role of corporate reputation, reputation fostering, and reputation management in organizations. Social media have received an increasing attention in the branding and marketing literature. There is a lack of practical studies and theoretical elaborations exploring the company's reputation management maneuvers under the influence of social media. Reputation management is an issue that is gaining growing importance and hence companies must invest resources to work on the development of effective electronic systems to handle that issue while integrating such systems with social networks. This is not optional any more in today's business markets.

We now move into presenting the main recommendations pertaining to the integration of social media into the business operations of any organization. These go as follows:

- Social media is not to be employed as a replacement to traditional media but should rather be used as a supplement to it. Though large is the reach of social media, it does not reach all customer segments, as some segments are still loyal to traditional media, so it is recommended to utilize them concurrently. This especially applies to the older generations.
- Despite the current emphasis placed on social media platforms by some organizations, it should be emphasized that this does not take away the importance of traditional face-to-face interaction [19], as that is equally important. As such, a balance must be formulated between the organizations "intangible" social media persona, and the organizations "tangible" real life persona.
- Social media is often used to mislead customers through unrealistic advertisements, false promises, buying followers, while it should be the case that the quality of, rather than the quantity, of the customers is what needs to be quantified.
- It must be stressed that social media is a cost saving tool, and organizations should not make it a costly platform through excessive and exaggerated pricing for online promotions and campaigns.
- Organizations should avoid taking advantage of the free nature of social media and abuse it by excessive overloaded postings.
- Social nets have reshaped the concept of *online reputation systems*. Many organizations are trying to develop social media policies in order to protect their reputation as social media problems emerge. Insurance coverage designed to provide resources in instances of reputational damage (including online mishaps) have been formulated [1].
- Social networks have proven to be a useful tool in investment and entrepreneurship. This has created a considerable impact on entrepreneurships worldwide in relation to social media as an effective marketing tool. These effects can be seen in relation to its effect on cost, organization, objectives and marketing strategies. Strategies have evolved to include business networks-related goals and rules.
- Social marketing is seen to be the future of marketing. This can be determined from the rate at which it is being embraced in the corporate world and the importance accorded to it [20]. Its popularity is rising fast such that there are social media marketing companies on the rise. However, it is imperative to note that the success of any social media marketing project is based on proper planning and evaluation of the target market. This can be done by following the steps outlined below:
  (a) Carefully analyse the effects of social media marketing on the business in order to determine whether the business is capable of absorbing any problems or burden related to the integration of social networks as a marketing tool.
  (b) Analyse the social networks with the aim of finding the most suitable one for the desired target customer segment.

(c) Ensure that educated, specialized, and experienced personnel are assigned for handling the use of the media.

(d) Choose the best way to manage your social media channel or channels in case you opt for different social media platforms.

(e) Set up a strategy by which you will be operating after setting up the social media channel. This will also include business rules associated with the use of such channels.

(f) Find the optimal manner to interact with the target group. Finding the best content through which you can keep your target group keeping up with the social media channel developed.

(g) Establish a means through which a business can profit from the social media channel. This means developing the ability to distinguish between socializing and marketing. The latter should be the main target.

(h) Carefully allocate time for managing the social media channel.

- Due to the diversity of users of the social networks who come from different education levels, backgrounds, ages, interests and experiences, the use of such media is mostly time consuming and distracting. Dedicated staff, with time management skills, must be appointed to handle the influx of postings and to manage the platform.

We now briefly shed some light on the ugly ingredients and repercussions of social networking.

- "Piracy", "Cybercrimes", "Cyberbullying", "Cyber-stalking", "Child safety", "potential for misuse", "unauthorized access", lack of physical interaction, and the psychological and behavioral consequences of social overload are global challenges that communities are facing today. It is very hard to take something back once it is posted, even if it gets deleted [9]. The response has to be both careful and expeditious. Otherwise it is quite useless to respond at all postings and could be damaging.

- Burden of the marketing shift induced by the new trends pose new challenges of carefully formulating customer relationships that focus on inviting customer involvement. Companies have to develop stories that promote the culture of the product instead of simply outlining its particular benefits.

- Customer empowerment is one of the burdens placed on the businesses. Disappointments travel quickly to the friends' circles and eventually to wider circles of networkers.

- Accidental postings of improper statements will create a long lasting effect and cannot be retracted.

- Starting wrong without proper adequate research and preparation will likely be fatal and backtracking might be very costly.

- "Social Media is Creating Bad Customers", a post published by Jeff Wilson, Partner/ Chief Customer Experience Designer at Sensei Marketing, that is sparking discussion among digital marketers. In the post, Wilson argues that social media equips the average person with four "factors empowering bad behavior, particularly against companies:" (1) No Guilt (2) The Mob (3) Relative Anonymity and (4) No Accountability. "If anything, social media has increased the importance of building positive customer experiences online and off". This view is correct especially if the social media is the only or main source the public derives feedback from. The questions he suggests businesses ought to consider are important: "What are the risks?" and "What is the compelling reason for you to use social media?" If it is because competitors are using it, this is not good enough reason.

5   Conclusion

Social media has, today, become a parcel of the business ecosystem, rather than a separate isolated entity. Businesses need to integrate social networking with their business processes. Social networking can fundamentally help change the business. Social media offer interaction over the web as it offers content that is user-generated. Through the social media, a modern cultural infrastructure is formulated, which is more responsive to customer behaviors. This interaction has become very interlinked with organizational processes, leading to Enterprise Social Marketing (EPM). Social media and EPM allow for authenticity, increased granularity, improved responsiveness, value creation, proper targeting, analytics, and flexibility.

Social media has transformed the business world, from bridging the gap with the customers, to higher marketing cost savings, to better damage control, to higher customer satisfaction, to greater lead generation, among many others. Moreover, social media although available to all organizations, can create a competitive advantage for the organizations that know how to best utilize it, and this competitive advantage is the fine line between success and failure in today's highly competitive global business environment.

To understand the full impact of social networks, they need to be addressed from the perspectives of both the business and the customer. This paper has done so and presented some highlights and guidelines that users often disregard or undermine. Such media is a tool for maintaining a good customer relationship though the effect could be detrimental, if misused. It also can be a useful platform for globalizing a business or a brand name. Quite a large number of businesses have recognized the fact that social or, more appropriately, business networks have also developed to be a reputation management tool that can promote the reputation of the organization or otherwise, if mismanaged.

Given the fact that this paper has shown how social networks have actually transformed into business social networks, embracing the integration of such networks into the core business processes has become more than a luxury if a business needs to be constantly connected to its customers as well as suppliers, and to the public at large. The adoption however needs to be done carefully and for this a list of recommendations has been presented, taking into account some precautions.

References

1. Kaplan, M., Haenlein, M.: Users of the world, unite! The challenges and opportunities of Social Media. Bus. Horiz. **53**(1), 59 (2010)
2. Livingstone, S.: Taking risky opportunities in youthful content creation: teenagers' use of social networking sites for intimacy, privacy and self-expression. J. New Media Soc. **10**(3), 393–411 (2008)
3. Mohammad, Y.A.: Integration of social media in businesses. Int. J. Bus. Soc. Sci. **5**(8) (2014)
4. Rodriguez, M., Ajjan, H., Peterson, R.M.: CRM/Social media technology: Impact on customer orientation process and organizational sales performance. J. Mark. Dev. Competitiveness **8**(1), 85–97 (2014)
5. Logofatu, M.C.: The social media impact on small and medium sized businesses. Young Econ. J./Rev. Tinerilor Econ. **9**(18), 214–218 (2012)
6. Pfeiffer, M., Zinnbauer, M.: Can old media enhance new media? How traditional advertising pays off for an online social network. J. Adv. Res. **50**(1), 42–49 (2010)
7. Laroche, M., Habibi, M., Richard, M.: To be or not to be in social media: how brand loyalty is affected by social media? Int. J. Inf. Manag. **33**(1), 76–82 (2013)
8. Andzulis, J., Panagopoulos, N., Rapp, A.: A review of social media and implications for the sales process. J. Pers. Sell. Sales Manag. **32**(3), 305–316 (2012)
9. Chau, M., Xu, J.: Business intelligence in blogs: understanding consumer interactions and communities. MIS Q. **36**(4), 1189–1216 (2012)
10. Goi, C.: The impacts of social media on the local commercial banks in Malaysia. J. Internet Bank. Commer. **19**(1), 1–10 (2014)
11. Harrysson, M., Metayer, E., Sarrazin, H.: How 'social intelligence' can guide decisions. Mckinsey Q. **4**, 81–89 (2012)
12. Oh, O., Agrawal, M., Rao, H.: Community intelligence and social media services: a rumor theoretic analysis of tweets during social crises. MIS Q. **37**(2), 407–426 (2013)
13. Rohan, M.: Social media and its implications for viral marketing. Asia Pac. Public Relat. J. **11**(1), 1–3 (2011)
14. Recine, M., Prichard, J., Chaudhury, A.: Social media and evolving marketing communication using IT. Commun. Assoc. Inf. Syst. **33**, 115–128 (2013)
15. Singh, N.: Social media and corporate agility. Glob. J. Flex. Syst. Manag. **14**(4), 255–260 (2013)
16. Bronstein, J., Aharony, N.: Personal and political elements of the use of social networking sites. Inf. Res. **20**(1) (2015)
17. Boyd, D.M., Ellison, N.B.: Social network sites: definition, history, and scholarship. J. Comput. Mediated Commun. **13**(1), 210 (2007)
18. Cabot, J.E.: The information age; Manuel Castells; the rise of the network society. Res. Policy **32**(1141), 57–68 (2003)
19. Chauhan, S.: Factors affecting use of mobile social networking. Vilakshan, XIMB J. Manag. **11**(1), 41 (2014)
20. Men, L.R., Tsai, W.H.: Toward and integrated model of public engagement on corporate social networking sites: antecedents, the process, and relational outcomes. Int. J. Strateg. Commun. **7**(2), 257–273 (2013)
21. http://www.web-strategist.com/blog/2013/03/18/social-networks-by-revenue-and-employees-facebook-stands-above-all/

The Social Media Cone: Towards Achieving the Manufacturing Competitiveness Goals

Manoj Kumar Singh[✉], Harish Kumar, M.P. Gupta, and J. Madaan

Department of Management Studies, Indian Institute of Technology,
Delhi 110016, New Delhi, India
manojksiet@gmail.com, harishkr08@gmail.com,
{mpgupta, jmadaan}@dms.iitd.ac.in

Abstract. The competitiveness among the different organizations in any industry might be raised due to changes in the technology, emergence of new competitive forces, devising and adopting newer business models, developing innovative products with differentiating pricing methods. The social media strategy is adopted by organization to harness the potential and get advantage in terms of the profit. Social media has provided both the opportunities and challenges for the organizations particularly to the high end manufacturing. The study undertakes the literature survey and the expert opinion on the factors which influences the electronics manufacturing industry. The findings suggest the key factors and a model in which the social media plays the important role to enhance the performance of electronics manufacturing sector.

Keywords: Social media · Electronics manufacturing sector · Competitiveness · Performance of industry

1 Introduction

The growth of the electronics manufacturing industry (EMI) could impact the socio-economic condition of any country. The EMI ranks high among the various segments that can contribute significantly to GDP of any nation. The core philosophy of manufacturing sector has shifted from Plan-Do-Check Act (PDCA) to operational expenditure based model now. Most of the demand for electronics hardware in India is met by the imports. The government had announced National Policy for Electronics in 2012, with an objective to achieve a turnover of about $400 billion by 2020. The government has taken various initiatives such as 100 % FDI through automatic route, capital subsidy of 25 % under Modified Special Incentive Package Scheme (20 % for Special Economic Zones) for ten years from the date of approval of the project, 2–5 % benefits for export under Focused Product Scheme (FPS), 75–100 % skill development assistance for sector on total cost of the project, preference to domestic manufacturing in government procurements, availability of land for Electronics Manufacturing Clusters, and setting up semiconductors wafers fabrication manufacturing facilities etc. for boosting this sector.

The perception of competitiveness varies from firm, industrial and national level [10]. At firm level it is the ability to persuade customers, ability to improve

Y.K. Dwivedi et al. (Eds.): I3E 2016, LNCS 9844, pp. 53–58, 2016.
DOI: 10.1007/978-3-319-45234-0_5

continuously their process capabilities. Whereas at the industrial level competitiveness could be understood by comparing the performance of industry with that of other nations. India lags behind in hardware manufacturing because of various reasons, such as high power cost, lack of fund, high transaction cost, poor supply chain, etc. The cutting edge technology in the industry is the need of the hour [4] to sustain. The next generation technology including social media, big data analytics and cloud may play a significant role for the growth of such industries [1, 7, 11]. The consumers have adopted the social media platform on a massive scale over which they can suggest the changes in the products, innovative solutions, and priorities for the development [6]. The market could be sensed from the interactive discussions with customers over social media [3, 11].

2   Literature Review

Indian IT hardware and electronics industry is still in a nascent stage of development. However the country has well performed in the software industry and highly competitive in the global market. The electronics industry has the potential of creating enormous employment opportunities including skilled and semiskilled manpower. The competitiveness of electronics sector has shown its influence on the spread of education and health care through ICT (e-learning) and tele-health services to both rural and urban areas as well as implementation of e-Governance [5]. The social media is the platform for sharing the information online. The research shows that organizations that are using social media in B2B environment, they are getting the advantages of online feedbacks regarding their products and services. This would help the organizations to improve their products and policies which simultaneously enhance the company's trust and brand value.

Today, most of the organizations are using community discussion, employees' forums, blogs, Facebook, linked in groups and Twitter for the discussions, policy design and decision making [8]. The customers based industries must explore social media for online marketing and customer complaints. Social media must be integrated with overall manufacturing strategy so that customers will get the desired products [2]. Some of the key observations regarding India from the literature are (i) 66 % of the current demand is met by imports for electronics products; (ii) High value added manufacturing is likely to be restricted to less than 7 % in 2015 depicts opportunity loss of $200 billion between 2011 and 2015 in the absence of intervention; (iii) Raise in domestic manufacturing to 50 % till 2015 to create employment for nearly twenty lacs people; and (iv) Therefore, it is very critical to recognize the EMI as a priority sector and provide favorable conditions for its growth in the country.

3   Challenges in Using Social Media

Despite of vast potential benefit of using social media technology in EMI, there are considerable challenges that need to be addressed, some of these identified through the literature are-

(1) Level of accountable and control by both consumer and manufacturing organisation.
(2) Clashes between social media platform and organisation due to hierarchy in organisational structure.
(3) Governance issue with changing in social media platform for the manufacturing organisation.
(4) Fear of employees working on social media platform may be distracted by social media and hence be less productive at work.
(5) Concern of for loss of commercially sensitive information when using social media platforms.
(6) Because of pear pressure on manufacturing organisational, they adopt the latest platform of social media.

4 Research Methodology

The various factors affecting the EMI are identified from the extensive literature survey. The identified 48 factors have been listed in appendix-1 in the study. The study utilizes the expert opinion to identify those factors which are influenced by customers through social media and showing significant impact on manufacturing sector. The experts were mainly chosen from the government, industry and academic fields. The brief details of the experts are listed in Appendex-2 along with their experiences. The personal details are not discussed in order to maintain the confidentiality of the experts. The total eleven experts were chosen, five from industry, three from government organizations and three from the academic field. The experts were asked to give their response in yes or no in front of each factor. In first phase, the factors were mailed to the experts and responses were recorded. In second phase, a separate version was recorded from each expert in order to avoid the biasness in opinion on the factors. For few factors the consensus were not achieved. Then the decision was made on the basis of majority.

5 Findings and Discussions

Indian EMI is facing infrastructure and supply chain issues, which are hampering the competitiveness [9]. The major ones are related to the high cost of power, finance, logistics, high transaction costs and high raw material costs due to cascading taxes and inverted duties on dual use inputs. The in-house production raises the cost of goods by 8–12 % depending on the value addition.

Based on the expert opinions, the study finds seven key factors which are influenced by customers and have significant role in manufacturing process. These factors are product quality, product design, customer needs, service quality, product cost and government regulations. The customers may suggest to the manufacturing unit regarding the product requirement, its quality, product looks, and how much they are willing to pay for the product. The big organizations having integration with social media platform are analyzing various discussion happening over social media among the consumers to mine the relevant information regarding their own products, services and product competitors available in the market. Such analysis prompts the organizations to make their strategies to attract the customers with high quality and low cost products or services. This makes the market players to be competitive and compete each other by providing the sustainable products or services to their customers.

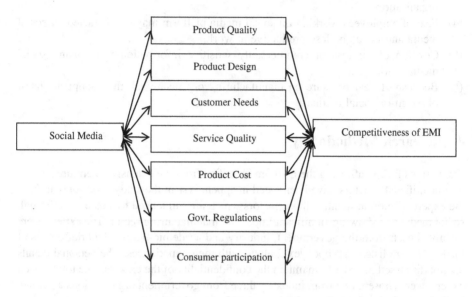

Fig. 1. Research Model for impact of social media on electronics manufacturing sector

A conceptual model has been designed to show the social media effect on competitiveness of manufacturing sector (Fig. 1).

6   Conclusions and Further Research

The next generation technologies are impacting the industries and have the immense potential for influencing growth. Therefore, the manufacturing industries also need to identify the technology options to craft the strategy to influence their sustainable growth. The designed model explains how the social media plays the key role to improve the performance of electronics manufacturing sector while placing the customers' opinions and feedbacks in center of the production.

The factors identified by the literature survey and the expert opinion are open tofurther discussion and future research. We would support the research framework may be used in future studies for clear understanding the importance of social media strategies in view of manufacturing sector. The proposed research framework could be further refined and validated by incorporating case based research.

Appendix-1. List of Factors Affecting Manufacturing Sector Identified from the Literature

1. Size of domestics market for EMI	2. Growth rate of industry
3. Government policies for facilitation the EMI	4. Need for common tax structure
5. Availability strong legal and regulatory framework	6. Incubation for entrepreneurship
7. Low cost of capital (interest on capital)	8. Availability of resources at low cost
9. Numbers of new firms registered	10. Investment in infrastructure building
11. Low cycle time of registration of the firm (online facility and ease of registration)	12. Substantial R&D Expenditure on EMI by government and private org.
13. Availability of transportation infrastructure	14. High exchange rate risk of currency
15. Proposition for joint research collaboration for EMI	16. Expenditure on science and technology education for building technological capability
17. Availability of Supplier network	18. Marketing excellence
19. FDI investment in host country for industry	20. Ease of Doing Business
21. Good macro-economic condition of the country	22. Ease of regulations for the sector
23. Human resource development	24. Export of electronics goods
25. Global export share	26. Share of industry in % of GDP
27. No. of patents registered by the industry	28. Quality products by the industry
29. Low cost products by the industry	30. Need for product differentiation
31. Integration of industry with research institutions/universities	32. Complicated and time taking decision making in government approvals process
33. Efficient operational capabilities	34. Inter-state trade restrictions
35. Unavailability of skilled manpower required for industry	36. Low level of R&D and Innovations investments by EMI
37. Unavailability of raw material and components at competitive cost	38. Focus on research and innovations of electronics products and manufacturing
39. Service quality of the products	40. Mergers and acquisitions
41. Usage of renewable energy source by the manufacturers	42. Customer focus (The willingness and ability to bring the customer to the focus of organizational)
43. Effective cost leadership to deliver the quality product at low cost	44. Customer feedback for the product
45. Internationalization of Industry	46. Competitiveness performance of Industry
47. Customer participation and engagements	48. Product design and new product innovations

Appendix-2. Personal Details of the Experts Selected for the Study

S. No	Designation	Experience
Industrial background		
1	Sr. Manager production from the electronics manufacturing industries	22 yrs
2	Manager marketing of electronics manufacturing	17 yrs
3	Industrial consultant	5 yrs
4	Manager, Production of electronics manufacturing	9 yrs
5	Manager, Production and Industrial of electronics manufacturing	6 yrs
Government organisations		
6	Scientist from the government organization	11 yrs
7	Undersecretary from the government organization	7 yrs
8	Sr. Scientist from the government organization	11 yrs
Academicians		
9	Professor, from reputed institution	8 yrs
10	Professor, from reputed institution	18 yrs
11	Professor, from reputed institution	12 yrs

References

1. Bottles, K., Sherlock, T.: Who should manage your social media strategy? Phys. Executive **37**(2), 68–72 (2011)
2. Dutta, S.: What's your personal strategy. Harvard Bus. Rev. **88**(11), 127–130 (2010)
3. Gallaugher, J., Ransbotham, S.: Social media and customer dialog management at starbucks. Manag. Inf. Syst. Q. Executive **9**(4), 197–212 (2010)
4. Gupta, M., Jana, D.: E-government evaluation: a framework and case study. Gov. Inf. Q. **20**(4), 365–387 (2003)
5. Gupta, M.P., Kumar, P., Bhattacharya, J.: Government Online: Opportunities and Challenges. Tata McGraw-Hill, New Delhi (2004)
6. Hoffman, D., Fodor, M.: Can you measure the ROI of your social media marketing? MIT Sloan Manag. Rev. **52105**, 40–50 (2010)
7. Hvass, K.A., Munar, A.M.: The takeoff of social media in tourism. J. Vacation Mark. **18**(2), 93–103 (2012)
8. Khan, M.U.: A comparison of the electronics industry of India and Korea. Technovation **18**(2), 111–123 (1998)
9. Liu, X., Grant, D.B., McKinnon, A.C., Feng, Y.: An empirical examination of the contribution of capabilities to the competitiveness of logistics service providers: a perspective from China. Int. J. Phys. Distrib. Logistics Manag. **40**(10), 847–866 (2010)
10. Ng, C., Wang, C.: Best practices in managing social media for business. In: Thirty Fourth International Conference on Information Systems, Milan, pp. 1–11 (2013)
11. Thakur, B., Gupta, R., Singh, R.: Changing face of India's industrial policies : a look. Int. J. Sci. Res. Publ. **2**(12), 1–7 (2012)

The Power of Instagram in Building Small Businesses

Wassan Alkhowaiter[(✉)]

A-Qassim University, Buraydah, Saudi Arabia
wkhoietr@qu.edu.sa

Abstract. Instagram is a relatively new channel of communication that allows its users to share photos and videos. Since its launch in October 2010, there has been a rapid growth in the number of its users worldwide. In Saudi Arabia women, entrepreneurs in particular have discovered new ways to exploit Instagram accounts to start and manage small online businesses. The use of this application allows them to target and reach interested users and customers, especially given the limited involvement of Saudi women in the labor force. Although social media channels such as Instagram offer a significant opportunity to address the high female unemployment rate in Saudi Arabia (SA) by creating new jobs, no research has yet identified the factors affecting the success of Instagram-based small businesses. Therefore, the current research explores the uses of Instagram as a selling platform by Saudi women entrepreneurs and presents some of their success stories.

Keywords: Social media · Instagram · Saudi women entrepreneurs · Small business

1 Introduction

Instagram is a social networking service and mobile application that enables its users to share their life moments through photos and videos, publicly or privately [4]. It was launched in October 2010 and since then the number of active users has increased from 100 million in 2011 to more than 400 million in 2016 [9]. The extraordinary success of Instagram corroborates the recent Pew report, which states that photos and videos have become the key social currencies online [8].

Social media channels such as Instagram now play a dominant role not only as entertainment and interaction tools but also in business [13]. According to AlGhamdi and Reilly [1], 83 % of marketers place a high value on social applications because of their important role in reaching and retaining customers, and most importantly in creating new business opportunities.

Social media have made it very easy for entrepreneurs to reach potential customers and tell them about their products. They also provide a solid platform for them to advertise, promote and deliver their ideas and products. Many studies have explored the effectiveness of social media as business marketing tools e.g. [6, 7, 12]. Their main

© IFIP International Federation for Information Processing 2016
Published by Springer International Publishing Switzerland 2016. All Rights Reserved
Y.K. Dwivedi et al. (Eds.): I3E 2016, LNCS 9844, pp. 59–64, 2016.
DOI: 10.1007/978-3-319-45234-0_6

finding is that social media platforms represent a unique interaction channel for businesses to advertise their products, maintain relationship with customers, and most importantly identify public needs.

Like people in other countries around the world, Saudi citizens now use many different social media channels. Saudi Arabia is ranked 7th in the world for social media users [2]. In fact, the various social applications provide important platforms for interaction between individuals in Saudi society.

With this increased use of social channels, Saudi entrepreneurs and especially women have begun to recognize the important role of social media in growing business, by generating content and ideally promoting their products. Use of these media also helps them to target and reach as many customers as possible around the country.

Instagram is one of the social media platforms that female entrepreneurs exploit to start up small companies in the emerging economy of Saudi Arabia. It is ranked the fourth most popular social network application in the country, with 15 % of the Saudi population considered active users [11]. These users have posted around 80 million photos on Instagram, with more than 5.3 billion likes per day [2].

With the popularity of Instagram, Saudi women have started using their accounts to create online stores, mainly to sell their own products, often handmade. Such online stores provide many advantages for these women, especially given the restrictions to Saudi women entering the labor market, due to the cultural characteristics of Saudi society [1]. The use of an Instagram account as the only presence for a small business allows the owner to remain physically close to her family so as to maintain the integrity of the household. Another benefit for these women is the low or negligible cost of starting a business in this way, as creating and maintaining an Instagram-based small business is less expensive than running a professional website [1, 5]. Kahlid Al-Khudair, founder and chief executive officer of an organization dedicated to female employment, is reported as saying in interview that "social media has provided a venue for women who undergo some social restrictions or prefer not to work or deal with men". He adding, "Starting a business on Instagram is very easy and the only obstacle they may face is the marketing aspect" [3].

For the last three years, Saudi media have reported and discussed success stories of Instagram-based businesses. Meanwhile, Saudi business analysts have strongly urged the government to adopt and improve this new business model, in the belief that supporting such businesses could help the government to create new job opportunities, thus contributing to a reduction in the high unemployment rate among women, which in turn would alleviate the current economic problems being experienced in Saudi Arabia.

Despite the success of these businesses, at this point it seems that few if any studies have examined the factors that could be contributing to the success of using such platforms to run businesses. Therefore, this paper can be seen as a first step toward identifying the factors that enable some Instagram-based business to use Instagram. The following sections will present some of the success stories of these businesses, as well as discussing their reasons for using such a platform. The paper concludes by stating the contribution and limitations of the research and suggesting some future research directions.

2   The Power of Instagram to Sell Products

Among the different social media platforms, e.g. Facebook, Twitter and YouTube, Instagram was found to be the most effective tool for reaching customers and marketing a business [5]. Instagram was basically designed for mobile phones, and since smart-phones help to connect people to social media on the move, it makes it easier for a business to reach its customers wherever they are, which explains why more than 50 % of businesses use Instagram to market their products and services [5].

[13] Studied the use of Instagram as a marketing tool by Emirati business women. They found seven main factors making Instagram a powerful marketing tool. The two main reasons for women entrepreneurs to use Instagram are that it is a user-friendly application and that it allows them to reach more people. Other reasons given are that Instagram is free to use, that its use in not restricted by regulations, that users are engaged through comments and likes, and finally, that the process of sharing pictures makes an Instagram account into an interesting type of online catalog.

In another recent study, [1] found that women and especially Saudi entrepreneurs used Instagram to sell their products because it can provide them access to the market while helping to maintain their privacy, confidentiality, and safety. It also enables women to remain physically close to their families while running their businesses, thus allowing them to maintain the integrity of their households. Finally, there is no issue of start-up costs, as the application is free of charge.

3   Success Stories of Instagram-Based Businesses in Saudi Arabia

As mentioned before, there is a lack of studies of Instagram as a selling platform; instead, most of the studies of Instagram in business have considered its use as a marketing tool. Therefore, this section presents some of the most successful stories of Saudi women entrepreneurs who have started and run online stores through Instagram.

The first is a 26-year-old female who runs one of most successful Instagram-based businesses. Her profile on Instagram, @Lace, presents her brilliant work in wedding planning and hosting grand events locally. Reports of her work in the press include magazines such as *Arab News*, *Sayidaty* and *Jeddah Destination*, which have featured the owner of @Lace as one of the first females to have used Instagram as a platform for selling. She has stated in interview that the application allows her customers to know her personally as well as to know what she is doing, while using the features of Instagram such as posting photos and videos allows her to share her work in progress as well as the finished product. This helps her followers to interact with her and feel that they are part of her work and projects. Users of Instagram started tagging their friends, which helped her to increase the numbers of followers and gained her more events in neighboring countries such as Kuwait and the United Arab Emirates.

A twenty-year-old college student who used Instagram to spread her fashion designs said that one of the main ways of gaining many followers is her way of using videos and photos to present her work, using herself as a model for her products. This way of working has built trust in her work among customers. Presenting her work by using Instagram features has also allowed her to collaborate with national brands and celebrities. Her amazing personality and hard work have led the well-known fashion magazine *Hia* to list her account among the five most important accounts to follow.

One of the most inspiring stories concerning the commercial use of Instagram is that of a girl who started her profile by posting photos and videos of her daily life. After she exceeded the one million followers mark, she started to think of using her fan base as customers and exploit the platform by marketing cosmetic products, notebooks and other products, using her name as a logo. Today she has more than four million followers and earns more than 10.000 SR monthly. [3] Cites her as saying "Instagram made it easier for her to get to know people and to make her a young business woman". The comment bar that Instagram provides allows her to take decisions and go on with her business after receiving positive feedback from her followers. Such comments and feedback help her to shape her business and products to fulfill her followers' needs. In an interview with the MBC channel, she said, "I never thought I would become a business woman or my brand would exist if there was no Instagram" [3].

Another online store on Instagram, called @SaudiCorner, sells traditional fashionable women's clothes designed and made by Saudi sisters who started their business on Instagram. They post videos of their designs and write details of the products such as availability and prices in the comment section. Having gained many followers and reaching their goal of becoming well known in the Saudi market, they decided to start shipping not only locally but also worldwide. They state that Instagram is a helpful tool that has enabled them as Saudi young women to work from home and avoid unwanted restrictions.

Another profile, named @Ido, is based in Jeddah and run by a Saudi female who designs and produces personalized wedding and engagement-related products, such as cards, hangers, boxes, and props. She ships her products not only to Jeddah but to destinations throughout Saudi Arabia. The account on Instagram gave her the opportunity to make a business out of her craft skills and to earn a monthly income. She says that running such a business online makes it easier to avoid losing money and to make a good profit [3].

A final story is from my personal experience of using Instagram to purchase a product. I came across an account selling homemade cakes. An unemployed lady in her twenties runs the online shop, designing and baking cakes for special occasions. She bakes and decorates her cakes in a very creative way that has allowed her to compete with major commercial bakeries in her region. Starting an online shop through Instagram has helped her to avoid the high expense of owning a physical store and paying employees. She said that Instagram gave her the opportunity to present her work to local customers by tagging and spreading her account to the point where customers have to order in advance and pay a deposit before she will take the order. She has told me that running her own online store is particularly convenient, as she can work at any time without leaving the house.

3.1 Advantages of Using Instagram

From the inspiring stories reported in the previous section, the two main reasons for Saudi women to use Instagram as a business platform are that the application is free of charge and that it does not consume much time or effort. Another important factor mentioned by the owners of @SaudiCorner and @Lace is the power of the application to reach not only local customers but also a global market. One of the main practical reasons for such business women to use Instagram is the ability it gives them to run their businesses from home, which helps these women to balance their personal and business lives.

Three of the six owners of Instagram-based businesses also believe that the application has helped them to interact with their followers, all of whom they consider to be potential customers. Interacting with them through the comment and tagging features has helped them to identify customers' needs and try to fulfill them.

All these reasons could contribute to the use of Instagram as a selling platform, which in return will help to create more job opportunities for young Saudi women. For Middle Eastern women today, owning a business is as important as education for financial security.

4 Conclusion

This paper has discussed some of the factors that attract Saudi women to use Instagram as a selling tool. The lack of charges and ease of use were the most frequently cited reasons for using such a platform. Reaching more customers and interacting with them also drives business women to own online stores and run them through Instagram. It can be concluded that Instagram is a great tool not only to market products but also to sell them.

4.1 Research Contributions

To my knowledge, there have been few if any studies that have examined the role of social media in building small businesses. Therefore, this research represents the first step in providing insight into the current situation of these businesses and the reasons behind their success. Understanding the current situation by looking over a success stories will contribute to providing an insight on the reasons that contributed to the success of these business therefore building a theoretical framework to identify the factors affecting the use of social media in business and therefore the success of these businesses. Such a framework will serve as a guideline for female entrepreneurs, offering a valuable new way to start a business through social media in general and Instagram in particular, even if their resources are limited. Saudi market analysts have urged the Saudi government to take advantage of Social media-based business to address unemployment, especially among women. The findings of this research will therefore serve as a reference for the Saudi government to understand the current situation of Instagram-based business and the factors affecting its use.

4.2   Limitations and Future Research Directions

The main limitation of this paper is the lack of empirical data that would help to determine the main reasons for running a successful online store through Instagram. To address this limitation, a recommendation for the future direction of ongoing research is to conduct an in-depth analysis of both qualitative and quantitative data to determine the enabling factors and barriers affecting the use of Instagram-based businesses. Therefore, in the near future I intend to collect such data in order to build a theoretical model for the exploration of the factors affecting the conducting of Instagram-based businesses in Saudi Arabia.

References

1. AlGhamdi, E., Reilly, D.: Social media based business in Saudi Arabia. In: Dalhousie Computer Science In-House Conference, pp. 1–3 (2013)
2. Arab News. Saudi Arabia social media (2015). http://www.arabnews.com/saudi-arabia/news/835236. Accessed 10 June 2016
3. BloombergBusiness.com. Saudi business women tap Instagram to bypass men, attract clients (2015). http://www.bloomberg.com/news/articles/2015-08-17/saudi-businesswomen-tap-instagram-to-skirt-men-attract-clients. Accessed 2 March 2016
4. Instagram. Instagram statistics (2016). http://instagram.com/press/. Accessed 20 Feb 2016
5. Miles, J.: Instagram Power: Build Your Brand and Reach More Customers with the Power of Pictures. McGraw-Hill, New York (2013)
6. Odhiambo, C.A.: Social media as a tool of marketing and creating brand awareness. Master thesis. University of Applied Science, USA (2012)
7. Paquette, H.: Social Media as a Marketing Tool: A Literature Review. Major Papers by Master of Science Students. Paper 2 (2013)
8. Rainie, L., Brenner, J., Purcell, K.: Photos and videos as social currency online. Pew Internet & American Life Project (2012)
9. Social Media in Business.com. Why most companies fail at social media (2013). http://socialmediainbusiness.com/why-most-companies-fail-atsocial-media. Accessed 10 March 2016
10. Statista. Instagram monthly active users (2016). http://www.statista.com/statistics/253577/number-of-monthly-active-instagram-users/. Accessed on 2 March 2016
11. Statista. Social media daily users by country (2016). http://www.statista.com/statistics/270229/usage-duration-of-social-networks-by-country/. Accessed 2 March 2016
12. Stelzner, M.: 2014 Social Media Marketing Industry Report: How Marketers Are Using Social Media to Grow Their Businesses. Social Media Examiner (2014). http://www.socialmediaexaminer.com/report2014/. Accessed 10 March 2016
13. Wally, E., Koshy, S.: The use of Instagram as a marketing tool by Emirati female entrepreneurs: an exploratory study. In: 29th International Business Research Conference. World Business Institute Australia, Australia, pp. 1–19 (2014)

Daedalus: An ICT Tool for Employment within the Mediterranean Basin Region

P. Salichos[1(✉)], D. Polemi[1], C. Douligeris[1], H. Qusa[2],
Y. Elhallaq[2], and G. Koukoulas[3]

[1] Department of Informatics, University of Piraeus, Piraeus, Greece
petros.salichos.0@gmail.com, {dpolemi,cdoulig}@unipi.gr
[2] University College of Applied Sciences, Gaza, Palestine
hqusa@ucas.edu.ps, y.elhallaq@gmail.com
[3] Unisystems S.A., Athens, Greece
koukoulasg@unisystems.gr

Abstract. The latest web technologies can be instrumental in allowing the dissemination of job opportunities to under-represented groups and in making these groups aware of the job market needs and requirements This paper presents the design, architecture and functionalities of DAEDALUS, an ICT tool that provides collaborative employment services to young people from the Mediterranean basin countries involving regional entrepreneurs, ICT companies, and employment associations. Special attention is paid to the presentation of the services offered by Daedalus that assist regional administrators to monitor the current and forecast the future national and regional matching of market demands and supply needs in order to enhance the regional labor market. Challenges and shortcoming of this effort as well as future evaluation directions are highlighted.

Keywords: Employment · Mobility · Cross-border · Interoperability · Collaboration · Architectural design

1   Introduction

The modern European digitalized society is in the threshold of globalization where the free migration movement is one of the most essential fundamental civil rights of European citizens. The European Commission (E.C) sets as one of its most important objectives the facilitation of legal immigrants to the access of equal employment opportunities. The role of the Information and Communication Technologies (ICT) has become essential in the labor mobility and in the fight against unemployment in the European Union (EU), since ICT significantly supports the efforts of legal immigrants to seek employment in EU regions and of EU citizens to expand their search for employment outside the EU. The continuously changing face of the cyberspace is transforming the shape of the societal structure affecting all types of activities, including the employment seeking and the integration of legal immigrants.

© IFIP International Federation for Information Processing 2016
Published by Springer International Publishing Switzerland 2016. All Rights Reserved
Y.K. Dwivedi et al. (Eds.): I3E 2016, LNCS 9844, pp. 65–75, 2016.
DOI: 10.1007/978-3-319-45234-0_7

Digitalization, however, triggers the phenomenon of social exclusion since it may lead to the low participation of disadvantaged groups such as migrants and disabled people [1]. The European society must confront this phenomenon efficiently and effectively. The E.C., acting towards the direction of bridging this digital gap, aims to create a Single European Information Space [2] in order to enhance social cohesion and support ICT initiatives that can boost employability. Moreover, since the EU labor market is also affected by the increased global connectivity, the global trends of de-localization and re-localization of services and the international monetary relations, it is in need of an innovation-based growth strategy for Europe regarding employment and inclusiveness.

Driven by this motivation, this paper presents Daedalus as a best practice example for enabling cross-border collaboration and exchange of information about career and employment opportunities in the Mediterranean basin that takes into advantage innovative ICT technologies such as the Web 2.0 [3], social networking [4], and the semantics web [5]. Daedalus engages all the relevant stakeholders (regional employers, youngsters, youth organisations, academic institutions and migration offices) having as its main objectives the posting of job vacancies seeking qualified young people that are available in the Mediterranean and EU markets, the identification of partnerships and of potential investment opportunities and the development of cross-border business plans using advanced ICT tools.

More specifically, the Daedalus integrated services consist of interactive web interfaces, interactive maps, online forms, dynamic questionnaires, Web 2.0 technologies and applications, web conferencing tools and instant messaging all of which improve the readiness of the young people to enter regional markets and create a liaison with the policy, business and scientific community in the Mediterranean area, trying to remove the digital gap from a social, technological and business perspective.

The remainder of this paper is structured as follows: Sect. 2 presents a literature review in the research fields of e-employment and e-migration at the EU level, Sect. 3 presents the Daedalus notion and architecture, Sect. 3 reveals pending issues and Sect. 4 provides conclusions and future research directions.

2   Literature Review

Bridging the digital gap, enhancing free movement and integrating migrants using ICT tools has been in the center of research in EU, since the global changes in the information and communication technologies [6] may allow migration to contribute to the European prosperity and growth [7]. Since the Riga declaration, the goal of reaching high levels of electronic inclusion of these groups has led to several efforts to use ICT towards this direction [8]. Since employability lies in the center of European ICT initiatives because deprivation of work is one of the most important factors leading to social exclusion [9], ICT tools that work towards this direction are of paramount importance.

The various information and communication technologies and the use of the Internet can provide useful and powerful tools in today's society [10] and they can affect the way that modern human resource planning and improvement are achieved [11]. There are several Internet innovations addressing job seekers and employers [12] that have affected the way the Labor Market operates in various ways, such as in searching for a job, in searching for an employee, in the delivery of labor services and in the way that local labor markets shape their demand [13]. Research on this field is underlying the fact that online job searches can shorten the time needed in order to find a job and they provide better outcomes in the labor market [13–15]. Kuhn [16] has emphasized the benefits for an employer in the online search process referring to the lower search costs, the larger number of applicants for a job, the exact matching of the set prerequisites and the shorter time needed for a recruitment.

"The importance of the Internet for job procurement is increasing primarily because the three quarters of the people in the employment age are online" [17]. However, a success in the procedure of finding a job electronically is closely related with the high level of service quality that is required [18]. This kind of high quality is expected from both the employers and the employees to fulfil their reliability [19] reliability, validity, trust, responsiveness, portal aesthetics, privacy and ease-of-use goals [18]. Additionally, the quality and quantity of the job postings together with the customization of a job search are considered very important factors for successful results [20].

The need to adopt automated procedures and to integrate the available technological tools that can approach in a more holistic way the issue of employability and free movement have introduced many software tools at the EU level that provide advising and employment e-services, information and statistical data for work, study abroad and generally cross-border commuting, opportunities, search services, job vacancies, the legislation framework and legal proceedings [21–24].

One of the major problems that arise within the framework of employability, is the fact that the available skills are neither monitored nor benefiting integration efforts and the enhancement of the European market competitiveness, creating negative consequences in businesses, society and economy [25]. Employers and employees may face numerous obstacles in the process of seeking employment, building partnerships, identifying synergies and specifying effective business plans at a transnational level. The need to match the existing market needs with skills availability, especially during an economic recession, is urging. The establishment of collaboration frameworks that could enable all the relevant stakeholders in the field of employment to interact and cooperate may come forward as the most fruitful approach of the technology-driven public sector reform, capable to shape a new vision where information sharing, transparency, openness and collaboration constitute the main opportunities of significant added value. Social inequalities in employment dictate the course of action towards the development of new policy and business intelligence frameworks and mechanisms [26].

Daedalus is an effective open source system that reduces the gap between the supply and the demand in the labor market by offering collaborative cloud services, guiding young residents that seek employment in the labor markets of the Mediterranean Sea Basin and stakeholders to post employment vacancies, seek qualified competitive employees and explore investment opportunities in a collaborative way.

3   Description of Daedalus

Daedalus addresses the following objectives:

- Meets the needs of young residents seeking employment in the labor markets of the Mediterranean Sea Basin by searching targeted categorized job vacancies in their own language;
- Enhances young residents' career and business opportunities by advising them in improving their business portfolio (curriculum vitae–CV-, cover letter and job interviews templates);
- Matches the qualifications and skills of job seeking individuals with existing needs in neighboring countries;
- Enables young people, entrepreneurs, ICT companies, regional and local employment associations to collaborate and build synergies (Fig. 1).

Fig. 1. Daedalus' Home Page (http://daedalusportal.eu/home)

3.1   Daedalus Users

Daedalus addresses three different type of users, the opportunity seekers, the opportunity providers and the advisor:

The Opportunity Seeker: EU and non-EU citizens seeking employment online, trying to match their qualifications with the existing needs of the labor market. Giovanilli [27] stated that "making the young protagonists of their own choices by providing them with practical tools for a careful self-analysis and that of the world around them, to develop the capacity for self-direction and participation in social life with a greater attention to their project of life.; Developing skills for citizenship, which allow individuals to be active citizens in economic and social context in which they live; Increase their "employability", increasing awareness of their skills, strengths and potential of their own, buying strategies and methods to integrate successfully into the world of work".

The Opportunity Provider: Entrepreneurs, institutions, nongovernmental organizations (NGOs), universities, colleges and the private sector in general that can provide the opportunities for the job-seekers and capitalize on the advantages of a dynamic portal such as broader data analytics, plan management tools, web-based plan comparison and a series of functionalities that facilitate the procedures of finding an employee. An employer hires employees either in full-time jobs or in part-time ones, like as exempt employees who receive a salary for completing a whole job or hourly workers who are paid an hourly wage. The employers need to be aware and compliant with all the governmental and legislative restrictions of the country that their organization is registered.

The Advisor: A person, an institution, NGOs, universities or colleges that give advice and help the job seeker in writing a professional CV and career profile; a person who enriches the knowledge of the opportunity seeker through writing awareness articles in the employment field. The advisor needs to be aware and inform the job seekers for the realistic conditions and restrictions (legal, governmental, societal, insurance policy) for the country that he/she seeks employment. Such a supporting service in the form of articles, discussion groups and entrepreneurial advice can advance the quality of a job-providing oriented portal [28]. Information regarding the labor conditions and the type of contracts as training options may become truly helpful to people seeking for a job [29].

3.2 Daedalus Services

The services offered by Daedalus (see Fig. 2) are classified into the following categories:

- *Public Library services:* Since Daedalus is a cross-border network that involves non-EU citizens seeking jobs in EU and vice-versa, it has integrated in its basic functional requirements a public library with all the external links leading to all the institutions of the national stakeholders that support the procedures of issuing an employment visa, recognition of skills and degrees and the legislation framework that is needed for the transition to another country. The governmental restrictions applied in the employment related issues is often a discouraging factor into working abroad and the provision, the sequencing of information, and the placement and the identification of those hyperlinks are of major importance. The clarification of citizenship/visa status for employment is one of Daedalus most important assets, facilitating the opportunity seekers wishing to migrate.

- *Profile Services*: The users can build their own CVs. The system stores all the information concerning their educational background, training, work experience and their career aiming to create an attractive image for entrepreneurs that will be able to access one's background easier and choose employees more efficiently. Moreover, the organizations and the companies can create their own profiles, present the type and the scope of their vacancies and attract efficient employees.

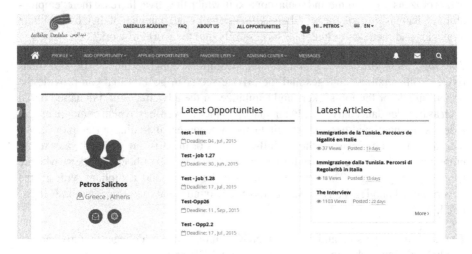

Fig. 2. Daedalus Dashboard

- *Search services* that may provide access to a pool of CVs and to opportunity listings:
  - *for an opportunity provider:* Registered users and visitors may search for a job, an internship, a seminar or a scholarship. The sequence actions of this process starts when the user enters the search keyword. The system will search about this keyword in many fields, such as in the job title, the job description and the skills.
  - *for an opportunity seeker:* Employers may filter opportunity seeker profiles based on category, qualifications, preferred salary and location. Employers can see the latest job seekers via an RSS feed link based on specific search criteria.
  - *for employment and migration documents:* Related documents (legislation, employment migration requirements/procedures/documents, guidelines) may also be found in the structured repository.
- *Application and Testing services:* An opportunity seeker has the capability to apply for a vacancy found within the system. Daedalus gives the employer an option to perform a skill test for specific candidates. The opportunity seeker will take the test upon an employer invitation to test his experience level. The employer can create a skills exam for job seekers to test their experience level. The exam may contain true or false, multiple-choice and open questions. The exam time can be time-limited. After filtering the applicants' CVs, the employer can specify a short list for interviews, and set the date and time for each applicant. The Daedalus communication tools are necessary for the necessary interaction for finding a job.

- *Advising Services:* Daedalus provides a series of helpful articles in the employment field supported by the Advisors, and an asynchronous community in an effort to create an educational interactive space with vital information related, among others, with the procedure of finding a job, creating a CV, creating a cover letter and preparing for an interview to develop a robust career advisory portal.

Daedalus follows a distributed architecture which we will describe in the next section.

3.3 The Architectural Principles of Daedalus

The architectural principles adopted by Daedalus [30] are divided into three categories. The data, the application and the technological principles. These principles ensure on one hand that the strategic objectives of the system will not be compromised and on the other hand that the use of the web portal will be maintained.

The Data Principles, such as security and privacy are integrated into all the architectural layers to preserve confidential information from unauthorized access and disclosure in order to enhance the users' trust upon Daedalus. Data are monitored by mechanisms and categorized based on sensitivity considerations. The validity of input data is also one of Daedalus major considerations and it can be ensured by different

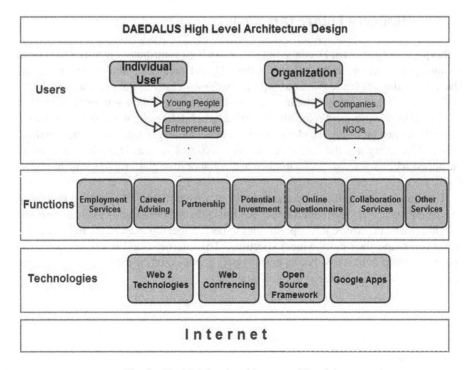

Fig. 3. The high level architecture of Daedalus

types of data validation such as by Field Level Validation, Form Level Validation, Data Saving Validation and Search Criteria Validation.

The *Application Principles* ensure an improved efficiency and a user-friendly environment, system availability and its supporting applications and infrastructures, system performance (highest level of functionality, provision of sufficient capacity to allow the supported system to perform as required), system reliability and system manageability (administering, monitoring and managing the IT resources).

The *Technological Principles* address the Open Standards Policy, the implementation of practicable open source software and the Operating System Independence. the independence of the applications from the infrastructure allows applications to be developed, upgraded and operated in the most cost-effective and timely manner (Fig. 3).

Daedalus seeks to employ open-source technologies in creating solutions for its stakeholders. The adopted standards are open standards wherever practicable.

An open source approach is fundamentally more compatible with an agile approach as innovative changes can be integrated more easily.

The technologies used for the development of Daedalus system are: Grails[1] as a back-end framework for JAVA, Laravel[2] for PHP, AngularJS[3] as a JavaScript framework, Twitter Bootstrap as a front-end framework, jQuery library as a DOM selector, Respond.js and html5shiv.js, Google charts and GotoMeeting API/Skype API which are the only commercial choices that the Daedalus technological partners have integrated in the development of the tool.

4 Conclusions – Future Directions

In this paper we presented Daedalus, an ICT tool which contributes towards the problem of unemployment of young people in the EU and non- EU Mediterranean region. Daedalus addresses the regularized migration, the matching of the demand and supply in the pan-European market, the integration of migrants and the labor mobility.

The delocalization and relocalization of services define a new European course of action that must be taken in order to face the new challenges that rise in the threshold of the 21st century and the digitalized society. Systems such as Daedalus combine all the necessary characteristics of a modern and collaborative platform towards this direction.

Immigration, integration and unemployment are among the EU growing problems. The recent events in the Mediterranean Sea Basin dictate the urgency to create realistic solutions that can provide job opportunities to people seeking work in the EU and Europeans to expand their employment spectrum. The internet could be the most fruitful space that can provide cross border employment services setting the ground for the new age of migration (e-migration) in the digital era.

---

[1] https://grails.org/.

[2] https://laravel.com/.

[3] https://angularjs.org/.

Concerning the recommendations for further improvement, it is necessary for Daedalus to expand its use to Open Data and Interconnectivity. The legal mining of useful data, such as opportunity postings and internships from universities as well as from other portals will boost and enhance Daedalus' utility and strengthen its current status in the job-seeking market. Interconnecting with other portals, either of governmental institutions, such as of ministries providing the necessary information when it comes to moving abroad (visa information etc.) or of European websites and Observatories that are operating in the same field, may be the most important strategic step for Daedalus, in order to be established as an innovative, competitive and modern portal in the market. Moreover, a continuous evaluation of the way users perceive, use, comment and navigate through Daedalus is under way, in order to have an up-to-date, user-friendly and effective platform.

The Daedalus project has already done its first basic steps towards the creation of a fully operational platform which combines a data pool of opportunities addressed to job seekers in the Mediterranean Sea Basin (e-opportunities services) together with the provision of all the necessary procedures and documents that a user should be aware of, in his efforts to work abroad. Technologically wise, the platform complies with the modern trends on the net and provides a friendly interface to the user together with some innovative services in the e-opportunities field. The most important future directions include the vision that the Daedalus system and the associated services can contribute towards the utilization and feasibility of national and European policies and Directives, especially the Employment, Immigration and Labour policies as a paradigm for regularized migration in the digital era and set a prototype for the future migration flows in the 21st century, the e-migration paradigm.

Acknowledgments. This publication has been produced with the financial assistance of the European Union under the ENPI CBC Mediterranean Sea Basin Programme. The contents of this document are the sole responsibility of Unisystems S.A/Partners and can under no circumstances be regarded as reflecting the position of the European Union or of the Programme's management structures. This work has also been partially supported by the University of Piraeus Research Center.

References

1. European Commission, Directorate-General for Employment, Social Affairs and Equal Opportunities, Unit G4: 'Media4Diversity, Taking the Pulse of Diversity in the Media, A Study on Media and Diversity in EU Member States and 3 EEA countries'. European Commission (2009)
2. European Commission: i2010—A European Information Society for growth and employment{SEC(2005) 717}(COM [2005] 229). European Commission, Brussels (2005)
3. Juffinger, A., Weichselbraun, N.T., Wohlgenannt, A., Granitzer, G., Kern, M., Scharl, R.: Distributed Web2.0 crawling for ontology evolution. In: The Proceedings of the 2nd International Conference on Digital Information Management, ICDIM 2007, 28–31 October 2007, vol. 2, pp. 615–620 (2007). ISBN: 978–1-4244-1475-8
4. Peers, S.: Key legislative developments on migration in the european union. Eur. J. Migr. Law **4**, 339–367 (2002)

5. van Harmelen, F.: The semantic web: what, why, how, and when. In: IEEE Distributed Systems Online 1541–4922 © 2004, vol. 5(3). IEEE Computer Society, March 2004

6. Borkert, M., Cingolani, P., Premazzi, V.: The state of the art of research in the EU on the uptake and use of ICT by immigrants and ethnic minorities (IEM). JRC Scientific and Technical Reports, EUR EN (2009)

7. European Commission: A common immigration policy for europe: principles, actions and tools, COM (2008), 359 final. European Commission, Brussels (2008a)

8. Kluzer, S., Haché, A., Codagnone, C.: Overview of digital support initiatives for/by immigrants and ethnic minorities in the EU27. *JRC* Scientific and Technical Reports, EUR 23566 EN (2008)

9. Bradshaw, J., Kemp, P., Baldwin, S., Rowe, A.: The Drivers of Social Exclusion. A review of the literature (Office of the Deputy Prime Minister, London) (2004)

10. Yang, Z., Jun, M., Peterson, R.T.: Measuring customer perceived online service quality. scale development and managerial implications. Int. J. Oper. Prod. Manage. **24**(11), 1149–1174 (2004)

11. Mansourvar, M., Yasin, N.B.M.: Development of a job web portal to improve education quality. Int. J. Comput. Theory Eng. **6**(1), 43–46 (2014)

12. Nakamura, A.O., Shaw, K.L., Freeman, R.B., Nakamura, E., Pyman, A.: Jobsonline. In: Autor, D.H. (ed.) Studies of Labor Market Intermediation, pp. 27–65. University of Chicago Press, Chicago (2009)

13. Autor, D.H.: Wiring the labor market. J. Econ. Perspect. **15**(1), 25–40 (2001)

14. Bagues, M., Labini, M.S.: Do online labor market intermediaries matter? the impact of Alma Laurea on the university-to-work transition. Working Paper No. 13621, National Bureau for Economic Research, Washington, DC (2007)

15. Stevenson, B.: The impact of the internet on worker flow. Working paper, The Wharton School, University of Pennsylvania, Philadelphia, PA (2006)

16. Kuhn, P., Skuterud, M.: Internet job search and unemployment durations. Am. Econ. Rev. **94**(1), 218–232 (2004)

17. Dorn, N., Naz, T.: Integration of Job Portals by Meta-search. Vienna University of Technology, Wien (2007)

18. Zeitman, V., Parasuraman, A.A., Malhotra, A.: Service quality delivery through web sites: a critical review of extant knowledge. J. Acad. Mark. Sci. **30**(4), 362–375 (2002)

19. Stemmer, P.M., Montgomery, Jr., B., Moore, J.P.: Career guidance services at michigan university: linking careers and education through virtual tools – a lifespan career development model [online]. (http://files.eric.ed.gov/fulltext/ED478219.pdf). Accessed 12 December 2015

20. Liljander, V., Riel, A., Pura, M.: Customer satisfaction with e-services: the case of an online recruitment portal [online] (2002). (http://citeseerx.ist.psu.edu/viewdoc/download?doi= 10.1.1.199.2974&rep=rep1&type=pdf). Accessed 12 December 2015

21. Eures. (http://ec.europa.eu/eures/)

22. EURAXESS Jobs Portal. (http://ec.europa.eu/euraxess/)

23. Eurodesk. (http://www.eurodesk.eu)

24. European Youth Portal. (http://europa.eu/youth/en)

25. Fleischmann, F., Dronkers, J.: The effects of social and labour market policies of EU-countries on the socio-economic integration of first and second generation immigrants from different countries of origin. EUI-RSCAS Working paper 2007/19 (European Forum Series) (2007)

26. Kate, M., Niessen, J.: Guide to Locating Migration Policies in the European Commission. EPIM and MPG (2008)

27. Giovanilli, P.: Moriento.it. In: Good practices in the use of ICT in providing guidance and counselling, pp. 39–41 [online] (2012). (http://www.eunec.eu/sites/www.eunec.eu/files/mebers/attachments/good_practices_in_the_use_of_ict_in_providing_guidance_and_counselling.pdf). Accessed 12 December 2015
28. Liljander, V., Riel, A., Pura, M.: Customer satisfaction with e-services: the case of an online recruitment portal [online] (2002). (http://citeseerx.ist.psu.edu/viewdoc/download?doi=10.1.1.199.2974&rep=rep1&type=pdf). Accessed 12 December 2015
29. Donato, E., Botto, C.: E Portfolio: improve the situation in the labour market by reconstructing the career path'. In: Good Practices in the use of ICT in providing guidance (2012)
30. Daedalus Deliverable, II-B/4.1/0903: Daedalus Design Document, September 2014

Digital Marketing and Customer Relationship Management

A Systematic Review of Extant Literature in Social Media in the Marketing Perspective

Ali Abdallah Alalwan[1], Nripendra P. Rana[2(✉)], Raed Algharabat[3], and Ali Tarhini[4]

[1] Amman College of Banking and Financial Sciences,
Al-Balqa' Applied University, Amman, Jordan
alwan.a.a.ali@gmail.com

[2] School of Management, Swansea University Bay Campus, Swansea, SA1 8EN, UK
n.p.rana@swansea.ac.uk

[3] The School of Business Department of Marketing, The University of Jordan, Amman, Jordan
r.gharabat@ju.edu.jo

[4] Department of Information Systems, Sultan Qaboos University, Muscat, Oman
Ali.Tarhini@hotmail.co.uk

Abstract. Social media applications have been extensively used and adopted by individuals and organisations in most aspects of daily life. Likewise, researchers have spent much effort in examining and exploring the effectiveness and efficiency of engaging such applications over the marketing context. This study, therefore, realizes the necessity of conducting a review of prior literature of social media over the marketing context especially in the light of the fact that only a small number of studies have been reviewed and conducted in this area. Accordingly, the aim of this study is to systematically review the current literature of social media in the marketing context. By reviewing approximately 71 articles, this study provides an overview of the main themes and trends covered by the relevant literature such as the role of social media on advertising, the electronic word of mouth, customers' relationship management, and firms' brands and performance.

Keywords: Social media · Marketing · Systematic review · CRM · Advertising

1 Introduction

Social media platforms have become an integral part of our daily life. The most human interactions have been moving to take their place over virtual platforms (i.e. Facebook, Instagram, LinkedIn and Twitter) and people are more likely to formulate a positive attitude and perception towards such technologies [12, 57, 67, 75].

By the same token, social media innovative applications (hardware and software) have been available for firms and customers worldwide and can be utilised to effectively interact with customers, create and share a sufficient content, and enhance interoperability [6, 27, 35, 48]. According to [6], there are three main aspects that could differentiate social media in comparison with traditional computer-mediated communications and are summarised by [6] as follows: (a) by using social media platforms, customers

© IFIP International Federation for Information Processing 2016
Published by Springer International Publishing Switzerland 2016. All Rights Reserved
Y.K. Dwivedi et al. (Eds.): I3E 2016, LNCS 9844, pp. 79–89, 2016.
DOI: 10.1007/978-3-319-45234-0_8

have more points (i.e. PC desktop, mobile phone, personal digital assistance, iPad) to access the targeted websites; (b) more interactivity can be attained using social media to communicate with customers, and accordingly customers are more to be value creator rather than just receiver; (c) the third aspect is related to the fact that by using social media, customers have more power to influence and to attain the best offers. Accordingly, social media has been largely realised as an effective mechanism that contributes to the firms' marketing aims and strategy; especially in the aspects related to customers' involvement, customer relationship management and communication [25, 63].

Therefore, social media-related issues represent worth directions to be considered and examined as highly recommended by academics over the relevant area [8, 14, 33, 61]. This could be attributed to the need to understand the feasibility of using social media over the marketing context. Such thought has been assured by [33] who highly supported the importance of examining the role of social media over different contexts to expand the existing knowledge toward such important issues of social media. As well as, in their recent review study, [25] argued that even though social media-related issues have been the focus of attention for many researchers worldwide, there is still a necessity to formulate a rigorous theoretical framework clarifying the main aspects that could hinder or contribute to such technology from either the customers' perspective or the firms' perspective.

In fact, social media-related issues have recently been the focus of attention of researchers worldwide and many studies have been conducted in this regard over different sectors, countries and from different perspectives as well [see 6, 12, 25, 48]. The marketing area has received the largest part of these studies; researchers have examined the role of social media as mentioned by [12]. It is also worth noting that different aspects and factors have been examined over the prior literature regarding social media marketing as well as different research approaches that have been applied to test such issues. Accordingly, the current study realised a necessity of conducting a systematic review of the relevant literature of social media over the marketing context to synthesise and organise the main areas covered by these studies and how these studies examined such issues.

2 Literature of Social Media Over the Marketing Context

In line with the main aim of this study, it has been restricted to studies that have examined the role of social media over the marketing area. Accordingly, other studies that have considered the role of social media over different areas (i.e. education, social, politics, and management) have been excluded. In addition, this study was also restricted to articles published in impact factor journals written in the English language.

Indeed, over the period extending from September 2015 to January 2016, this study has started looking at the main database research engine (i.e. Sciencedirect, Emeraldinsight, EBSCO, and Google scholar) to collect the related articles. Researchers have used a number of terms to reach the relevant articles such as marketing along with social media, marketing and Web 0.2, customers along with social media, social media marketing, and social media and branding. The researchers also used specific names of the most well-known social media applications: Facebook, Twitter, YouTube, Google+ along with marketing, customers, and brands terms to reach the targeted articles. Such approach to reach the most relevant articles has been adopted by [22, 25, 74] in their review studies.

In total, 71 articles were collected. These articles were found to be in different interests and themes and therefore they were segmented in subgroups as presented in the six subsections as follows:

2.1 Social Media and Advertising

Businesses worldwide seem to be more interested in conducting their promotional and advertising campaigns through social media vehicles [70]. This is due to the ability of social media sites enhancing the interactive communication between firms and their customers. In this regard, [42] asserted the importance of considering social media as an integral hybrid component for a promotional mix. [21] demonstrated that Facebook advertising could have different aims to influence the customers' perception, awareness, knowledge, preferences, their willingness to purchase or even their actual buying behaviour. Accordingly, a good number of marketing researchers have paid attention to examine the related issues of advertising over the social media platforms [i.e. 14, 19, 42, 48, 54, 66]. Indeed, the extent to how much advertisement activities were able to reach their aims in the term of effectiveness and efficiency has been evaluated based on the customers' attitudes toward such activities [i.e. 21]. By the same token, [12] argued that so as to attain a desirable level of customer attitudes, social media advertising activities should comprise of hedonic parts to provide customers a more entertaining experience.

2.2 Social Media and Electronic Word of Mouth

Social media applications have empowered customers to share their own experiences with a large number of people than the old traditional ways. This makes the scope and impact of electronic word of mouth more crucial. Therefore, there are many studies that have focused on the electronic word of mouth (e-WOM) [i.e. 16, 18, 32, 44, 55, 68]. This could be attributed to the nature of social media as a more interactive way to share any kind of content about firms and their brands to a large number of people who use these platforms [32, 55]. For instance, [18] examined the impact of a number of factors (i.e. source, network, relationship, and message/content) on the customers' reaction and response towards word of mouth distributed by way of social media platforms. The main findings of such a study indicated that the traditional word of mouth still has more influence on customer response than those that come from the social media platforms [18].

2.3 Social Media and Customer Relationship Management

As stated by [10, 25, 69], having a strong customer relationship largely depends on the ability of firms to emotionally and cognitively involve their customers with its brand.

Recently, most companies are looking to take advantage of social media applications (i.e. Facebook, Twitter) so as to leverage customer experience as well as customer relationship management [18]. Indeed, communication, relationship development and promotion are fostered through the posting and sharing of content with consumers [e.g. 30, 62] as well as through exchange and interaction facilitated through social media [23, 43, 56]. [23, 30, 43, 62] acknowledged that levers comprised in social media platforms that enable customers and firms to commonly post, share, and interact play a highly positive role in enhancing the level of communication, customer relationship management and the efficiency of promotional activities. Over the prior literature, many marketing scholars have tested how using social media could impact the customer relationship management (CRM) [i.e. 1, 5, 7, 25, 26, 32, 41, 53, 56, 69, 73].

2.4 Social Media and Brand

Several researchers [e.g. 27, Kapla35] have supported the effective role of social media in enhancing the brand's image due to its ability to tailor the messages sent according to the personal preferences of the users. Indeed, firms are able to engage their customers with their brands with a higher degree of customisation and interactivity as stated by [25]. Theoretically, many recent marketing studies that have tested brand issues over the social media platforms [i.e. 7, 11, 15, 19, 24, 27, 28, 32, 37, 38, 45, 46, 60]. For instance, in their conference paper, [24] indicated that the customers' willingness to follow brands on social media is derived by five factors: brand affiliation, investigation, opportunity seeking, conversation, and entertainment. A qualitative study conducted by [59] who interviewed fourteen ladies in Ireland indicated that social media platforms such as Facebook and Twitter have an important role in shaping the female's perception and awareness of their needs toward online fashion brands.

2.5 Social Media and Customer Behavior and Perception

Indeed, as a part of their daily life, customers nowadays depend largely on the social media over the whole stages of his or her purchasing process: collecting information, conducting actual purchasing, adoption, and even in forming their attitudes and future behaviour (loyalty, commitment, retention) [41]. Therefore, social media plays an important role either in the term of helping customers to attain information required or by enabling them to create their own content and share it with others [20]. For instance, more than 20 % of customers, according to [54], have a strong thought that social media is a considerable source of information when they are in the process of finalising their purchasing decision. This makes social media platforms one of the most important factors predicting customer behaviour and decision-making [50].

The important role of social media has been largely discussed by different researchers over the relevant area of marketing and social media [i.e. 20, 50, 54, 59, 72, 73]. For example, a recent study undertaken in the hotel context in the USA by [40] reported that customer experience with social media has an influence on consumer attitudes towards both Twitter and Facebook. Moreover, the dimensions pertaining to the high degree of interactivity and personalisation have contributed to both customers' experience as well as the information resources needed by customers in their purchasing decisions as stated by [13, 21, 31, 50, 72] indicated that customers' intention to purchase is significantly predicted by the role of involvement. [72] noticed that customers' involvement was largely enhanced by using social media. Three factors - enjoyment, internalisation and identification - were found by [34] to be key predictors contributing to travellers' behaviour to share their experiences on the social media platforms.

2.6 Adoption of Social Media

The related issues of adoption and usage of social media have derived an interest by marketing researchers [i.e. 9, 13, 14, 17, 28, 36, 47, 49, 65, 74]. Indeed, there are number of factors that have been tested to predict the adoption behaviour of social media platforms. For example, both perceived benefits and perceived risk have been proven to have a strong influence on the individuals' intention to use social media as reported by [47, 49]. Customers' behaviour, intention and interactions with social media are largely influenced by website integrity, credibility and subjectivity as founded by [74]. [28] also attempted to explain the key drivers justifying why customers are willing to adopt social media applications. In this regard, three kinds of different users' behaviours related to social media adoption were identified by [28]; they are the general use of social media platforms; joining brands' page on social media; and opt on ads on the social media. To do so, [28] formulated their conceptual model based on the decomposed theory of planned behaviour. Their results strongly supported the role of attitudes, relative advantage, complexity, compatibility, and self-efficacy in shaping the adoption of social media platforms. Based on both the Technology Acceptance Model and the Resource Based Theory, [65] were able to prove the significant influence of perceived ease of use, image, and perceived barriers on the perceived usefulness pertaining to the social media.

3   Methods Adopted in Examining the Role of Social Media in the Marketing Context

A closer look at the main methods implemented by researchers in examining the related issues of social media over marketing context leads the researchers to observe many approaches adopted in this area. A quantitative approach using a questionnaire survey has been commonly used by different studies [i.e. 14, 15, 23, 24, 29, 32, 43, 72]. It is also worth mentioning that most of these quantitative approaches have tested their empirical data using the Structural Equation Modelling (SEM) [i.e. 14, 24, 28, 32, 34]. The qualitative approach has been largely used by researchers to explore the associated area of social media marketing (i.e. [1]). Importantly, content analyses of material posted over social media platforms were noticed to be extensively used by most qualitative studies [56]. Another group of qualitative studies [i.e. 7, 59] were found to be using the interview approach to collect the required data. The mixed method has been noticed in a number of studies [28, 53, 54]. Case studies have been considered as a suitable research approach to explore the related issues of social media by a number of marketing researchers [i.e. 36, 43]. [22, 25, 27, 74] have used a systematic review approach of most papers and studies conducted over the related area of social media and marketing. Other parts of social media studies were found in the form of a theoretical framework and conceptual model papers [i.e. 8, 51, 52, 58, 61, 68, 73].

4 Discussion

By reviewing the main papers that have examined the role of social media over the marketing context, it was concluded that social media-related issues represent an emerging trend capturing more interest by practitioners and researchers. This was proved by the large number of papers that have been published between 2010 and 2016 in addition to the fact that most of these papers have been published after 2014 [i.e. 25, 39, 57, 64, 74, 75]. Such recent interest conveys a sign about the importance of examining the related issues of social media over the marketing context.

It is also worth considering that the reviewed studies have addressed different practices for social media in the marketing context and from different perspectives. For instance, a number of studies concentrated on the effective use of social media for promotion and advertising activities [i.e. 14, 19]. However, most of these studies [i.e. 42, 48, 66] recommended examining such issues of advertising by considering other factors and using different research methods as well. Further, there is still a need to see how the effectiveness of such advertising activities could be different from one platform to another (i.e. Facebook vs YouTube). In this regard, [25] did not consider the different kinds of Facebook advertising and accordingly recommended examining if different forms of Facebook advertising could reflect a variation in the customers' attitudes.

Researchers were also able to notice that considerable attention of the reviewed studies was on how firms can successfully use social media applications either in terms of e-WOM [i.e. 16, 18] or in terms of enhancing CRM [i.e. 56, 69, 73]. This means that using social media for the related issues of e-WOM and CRM is critical and requires further understanding and research as recommended by [1, 5, 7, 44]. It is also important to consider how such mechanisms (personalization, interactivity, and digital community) could be accelerated using social media applications, and accordingly, contributing to both CRM and e-WOM [see 18, 25, 74].

A number of studies were found to be interested on the impacting role of social media on customers' perception and behaviour towards firms, their brands, and products [i.e. 15, 19, 20, 24, 27, 28]. Indeed, it was observed that such a role has been addressed differently; while some studies capture the customers' point of view regarding how social media has been an important source of information to them [i.e. 20, 54], other studies have looked at how customers' attitudes and purchasing behaviour could be predicted by social media [i.e. 40]. In this regard, as discussed by [1, 3] in their paper examining the adoption of mobile banking, social media tools could also be used by banks to accelerate the adoption of such emerging technologies. Therefore, another important research trend could be in testing the effective use of social media in teaching customers and enhancing their intention and adoption toward such technologies as assured by [2, 4].

The last important theme pertained to examining the factors predicting adoption of social media platforms [i.e. 36, 47]. Several factors have been examined to predict the customers' adoption towards such technologies such as: perceived benefits and perceived risk [47, 49]; website integrity, credibility and subjectivity [i.e. 74]. Further, quite a few of these studies have formulated their model according to well-established theories such as the Technology Acceptance Model and the Resource Based Theory [65]; and the theory of planned behaviour [28]. However, there is still a need to systematically select the related factors that could influence the adoption of social media by users. Furthermore, the theoretical foundation proposed should clearly explain the related issues of adoption of social media from the customers' perspective. In this regard, the new model by [71] could be used as this model has accurately proposed to predict the adoption of system applications from the customers' perspective as proved by [3] in their study to examine the adoption of Internet banking.

5 Conclusion

This study was conducted with the intention to systematically review the prior literature of social media over the marketing context. Indeed, such a review was important to be conducted to see how practitioners and researchers addressed the implications of social media for marketing issues. This study began by providing an introduction about social media and its importance from the marketing perspective. It also provided further discussion regarding the concept of social media and social media marketing. In section three, literature of social media over the marketing context, it was mentioned that such literature could be categorised into six main themes: social media and advertising; social media and e-WOM; social media and CRM; social media and brand issues; social media and customers' perception and behaviour; social media from the firms' perspective; and adoption of social media. In this study, it also looked at the main research methods and approaches adopted by studies reviewed (i.e. quantitative approach; qualitative approach; mix method questionnaire survey; content analyses; review studies). In the discussion section, it provided further explorations for the main six themes as well as what main directions were required for further examination.

5.1 Limitations and Future Research Directions

As any other reviewing studies, the current study is restricted by a number of limitations. For instance, all social media articles reviewed in the current study were over marketing context. Therefore, other kinds of social media studies over different contexts are very important to be considered as well. This study also conducted a systematic review of these studies. As mentioned in Sect. 4, there are a good number of papers that have conducted a quantitative approach. Accordingly, future studies could easily employ a meta-analysis method to discover the most frequently and influential factors over the related studies of social media marketing. It also indicated that social media-related issues are emerging trends and there is need for further examinations and exploration, and accordingly, there is still a need to conduct more studies over different cultures and context by using different approaches.

References

1. Abreza, G., O'Reilly, N., Reid, I.: Relationship marketing and social media in sport. Int. J. Sport Commun. **6**(2), 120–142 (2013)
2. Alalwan, A.A., Dwivedi, Y., Rana, N.P., Williams, M.D.: Consumer adoption of mobile banking in Jordan: examining the role of usefulness, ease of use, perceived risk and self-efficacy. J. Enterp. Inf. Manage. **29**(1), 118–139 (2016)
3. Alalwan, A.A., Dwivedi, Y.K., Williams, M.D.: Customers' intention and adoption of telebanking in Jordan. Inf. Syst. Manage. **33**(2), 154–178 (2016)
4. Alalwan, A.A., Dwivedi, Y.K., Rana, N.P., Lal, B., Williams, M.D.: Consumer adoption of Internet banking in Jordan: examining the role of hedonic motivation, habit, self-efficacy and trust. J. Financ. Serv. Mark. **20**(2), 145–157 (2015)
5. Ballings, M., Van den Poel, D.: CRM in social media: predicting increases in Facebook usage frequency. Eur. J. Oper. Res. **244**(1), 248–260 (2015)
6. Berthon, P.R., Pitt, L.F., Plangger, K., Shapiro, D.: Marketing meets Web 2.0, social media, and creative consumers: implications for international marketing strategy. Bus. Horiz. **55**(3), 261–271 (2012)
7. Bianchi, C., Andrews, L.: Investigating marketing managers' perspectives on social media in Chile. J. Bus. Res. **68**(12), 2552–2559 (2015)
8. Billings, A.: Power in the reverberation why Twitter matters, but not the way most believe. Commun. Sport **2**(2), 107–112 (2014)
9. Bolton, R.N., Parasuraman, A., Hoefnagels, A., Migchels, N., Kabadayi, S., Gruber, T., Solnet, D.: Understanding generation Y and their use of social media: a review and research agenda. J. Serv. Manage. **24**(3), 245–267 (2013)
10. Brodie, R.J., Ilic, A., Juric, B., Hollebeek, L.: Consumer engagement in a virtual brand community: an exploratory analysis. J. Bus. Res. **66**(1), 105–114 (2013)
11. Bruhn, M., Schoenmueller, V., Schäfer, D.B.: Are social media replacing traditional media in terms of brand equity creation? Manage. Res. Rev. **35**(9), 770–790 (2012)
12. Carrillat, A.F., Astous, A., Grégoire, E.M.: Leveraging social media to enhance recruitment effectiveness: a Facebook experiment. Internet Res. **24**(4), 86–123 (2014)
13. Chandra, B., Goswami, S., Chouhan, V.: Investigating attitude towards online advertising on social media-an empirical study. Manage. Insight **8**(1), 1–14 (2013)
14. Chang, Y.T., Yu, H., Lu, H.P.: Persuasive messages, popularity cohesion, and message diffusion in social media marketing. J. Bus. Res. **68**(4), 777–782 (2015)
15. Christou, E.: Branding social media in the travel industry. Procedia-Soc. Behav. Sci. **175**, 607–614 (2015)
16. Chu, S.C., Kim, Y.: Determinants of consumer engagement in electronic word-of-mouth (eWOM) in social networking sites. Int. J. Advert. **30**(1), 47–75 (2011)
17. Clavio, G., Kian, T.M.: Uses and gratifications of a retired female athlete's Twitter followers. Int. J. Sport Commun. **3**(4), 485–500 (2010)
18. Coulter, K.S., Roggeveen, A.: "Like it or not" - consumer responses to word-of-mouth communication in on-line social networks. Manage. Res. Rev. **35**(9), 878–899 (2012)
19. De Vries, L., Gensler, S., Leeflang, P.S.: Popularity of brand posts on brand fan pages: an investigation of the effects of social media marketing. J. Interact. Mark. **26**(2), 83–91 (2012)

20. Drews, W., Schemer, C.: eTourism for all? online travel planning of disabled people. In: Gretzel, U., Law, R. (eds.) Information and Communication Technologies in Tourism, pp. 507–518. Springer, Heidelberg (2010)
21. Duffett, R.G.: Facebook advertising's influence on intention-to-purchase and purchase amongst millennials. Internet Res. **25**(4), 498–526 (2015)
22. Dwivedi, Y.K., Kapoor, K.K., Chen, H.: Social media marketing and advertising. Mark. Rev. **15**(3), 289–309 (2015)
23. Eagleman, A.N.: Acceptance, motivations, and usage of social media as a marketing communications tool amongst employees of sport national governing bodies. Sport Manage. Rev. **16**(4), 488–497 (2013)
24. Enginkaya, E., Yilmaz, H.: What drives consumers to interact with brands through social media? a motivation scale development study. Procedia Soc. Behav. Sci. **148**, 219–226 (2014)
25. Filo, K., Lock, D., Karg, A.: Sport and social media research: a review. Sport Manage. Rev. **18**(2), 166–181 (2015)
26. Gamboa, A.M., Gonçalves, H.M.: Customer loyalty through social networks: lessons from Zara on Facebook. Bus. Horiz. **57**(6), 709–717 (2014)
27. Gensler, S., Völckner, F., Liu-Thompkins, Y., Wiertz, C.: Managing brands in the social media environment. J. Interact. Mark. **27**(4), 242–256 (2013)
28. Gironda, J.T., Korgaonkar, P.K.: Understanding consumers' social networking site usage. J. Mark. Manage. **30**(5–6), 571–605 (2014)
29. Gummerus, J., Liljander, V., Weman, E., Pihlström, M.: Customer engagement in a Facebook brand community. Manage. Res. Rev. **35**(9), 857–877 (2012)
30. Hambrick, M.E.: Six degrees of information: Using social network analysis to explore the spread of information within sport social networks. Int. J. Sport Commun. **5**(1), 16–34 (2012)
31. He, W., Zha, S.: Insights into the adoption of social media mashups. Internet Res. **24**(2), 160–180 (2014)
32. Hudson, S., Huang, L., Roth, M.S., Madden, T.J.: The influence of social media interactions on consumer-brand relationships: a three-country study of brand perceptions and marketing behaviors. Int. J. Res. Mark. **33**, 27–41 (2016)
33. Hutchins, B.: Twitter follow the money and look beyond sports. Commun. Sport **2**, 122–126 (2014)
34. Kang, M., Schuett, M.A.: Determinants of sharing travel experiences in social media. J. Travel Tourism Mark. **30**(1/2), 93–107 (2013)
35. Kaplan, A.M., Haenlein, M.: Users of the world, unite! the challenges and opportunities of social media. Bus. Horiz. **53**(1), 59–68 (2010)
36. Killian, G., McManus, K.A.: marketing communications approach for the digital era: managerial guidelines for social media integration. Bus. Horiz. **58**(5), 539–549 (2015)
37. Kim, A.J., Ko, E.: Do social media marketing activities enhance customer equity? an empirical study of luxury fashion brand. J. Bus. Res. **65**(10), 1480–1486 (2012)
38. Kim, S., Koh, Y., Cha, J., Lee, S.: Effects of social media on firm value for US restaurant companies. Int. J. Hosp. Manage. **49**, 40–46 (2015)
39. Leeflang, P.S., Verhoef, P.C., Dahlström, P., Freundt, T.: Challenges and solutions for marketing in a digital era. Eur. Manage. J. **32**(1), 1–12 (2014)
40. Leung, X.Y., Bai, B., Stahura, K.A.: The marketing effectiveness of social media in the hotel industry a comparison of Facebook and Twitter. J. Hosp. Tourism Res. **39**(2), 147–169 (2015)
41. Malthouse, E.C., Haenlein, M., Skiera, B., Wege, E., Zhang, M.: Managing customer relationships in the social media era: introducing the social CRM house. J. Interact. Mark. **27**(4), 270–280 (2013)

42. Mangold, W.G., Faulds, D.J.: Social media: the new hybrid element of the promotion mix. Bus. Horiz. **52**(4), 357–365 (2009)
43. McCarthy, J., Rowley, J., Ashworth, J.C., Pioch, E.: Managing brand presence through social media: the case of UK football clubs. Internet Res. **24**(2), 181–204 (2014)
44. Munar, A.M., Jacobsen, J.K.S.: Trust and involvement in tourism social media and web-based travel information sources. Scand. J. Hosp. Tourism **13**(1), 1–19 (2013)
45. Naylor, R.W., Lamberton, C.P., West, P.M.: Beyond the "like" button: The impact of mere virtual presence on brand evaluations and purchase intentions in social media settings. J. Mark. **76**(6), 105–120 (2012)
46. Nguyen, B., Yu, X., Melewar, T.C., Chen, J.: Brand innovation and social media: Knowledge acquisition from social media, market orientation, and the moderating role of social media strategic capability. Ind. Mark. Manage. **51**, 11–25 (2015)
47. Nusair, K.K., Bilgihan, A., Okumus, F., Cobanoglu, C.: Generation Y travelers' commitment to online social network websites. Tourism Manage. **35**, 13–22 (2013)
48. Okazaki, S., Taylor, C.R.: Social media and international advertising: theoretical challenges and future directions. Int. Mark. Rev. **30**(1), 56–71 (2013)
49. Parra-López, E., Bulchand-Gidumal, J., Gutiérrez-Taño, D., Díaz-Armas, R.: Intentions to use social media in organizing and taking vacation trips. Comput. Hum. Behav. **27**(2), 640–654 (2011)
50. Patino, A., Pitta, D.A., Quinones, R.: Social media's emerging importance in market research. J. Consum. Mark. **29**(3), 233–237 (2012)
51. Pedersen, P.M.: A commentary on social media research from the perspective of a sport communication journal editor. Commun. Sport **2**, 138–142 (2014)
52. Pegoraro, A.: Twitter as disruptive innovation in sport communication. Commun. Sport **2**, 132–137 (2014)
53. Pereira, H.G., de Salgueiro, M.F., Mateus, I.: Say yes to Facebook and get your customers involved! relationships in a world of social networks. Bus. Horiz. **57**(6), 695–702 (2014)
54. Powers, T., Advincula, D., Austin, M.S., Graiko, S., Snyder, J.: Digital and social media in the purchase decision process. J. Advert. Res. **52**(4), 479–489 (2012)
55. Priyanka, S.: A study of online advertising on consumer behaviour. Int. J. Eng. Manage. Sci. **3**(4), 461–465 (2013)
56. Pronschinske, M., Groza, M.D., Walker, M.: Attracting Facebook 'fans': the importance of authenticity and engagement as a social networking strategy for professional sport teams. Sport Mark. Q. **21**(4), 221–231 (2012)
57. Rathore, A.K., Ilavarasan, P.V., Dwivedi, Y.: Social media content and product co-creation: an emerging paradigm. J. Enterp. Inf. Manage. **29**(1), 7–18 (2016)
58. Rowe, D.: Following the followers sport researchers' labour lost in the twittersphere? Commun. Sport **2**, 117–121 (2014)
59. Ruane, L., Wallace, E.: Generation Y females online: insights from brand narratives. Qual. Mark. Res. Int. J. **16**(3), 315–335 (2013)
60. Saboo, A. R., Kumar, V., Ramani, G.: Evaluating the impact of social media activities on human brand sales. Int. J. Res. Mark. (2015) (In press)
61. Sanderson, J.: What do we do with Twitter? Sage J. (2014). Communication & Sport
62. Sanderson, J., Hambrick, M.E.: Covering the scandal in 140 characters: a case study of Twitter's role in coverage of the Penn State saga. Int. J. Sport Commun. **5**(3), 384–402 (2012)
63. Saxena, A., Khanna, U.: Advertising on social network sites: a structural equation modelling approach. Vis. J. Bus. Perspect. **17**(1), 17–25 (2013)
64. Shilbury, D., Westerbeek, H., Quick, S., Funk, D., Karg, A.: Strategic Sport Marketing, 4th edn. Allen & Unwin, Sydney (2014)

65. Siamagka, N.T., Christodoulides, G., Michaelidou, N., Valvi, A.: Determinants of social media adoption by B2B organizations. Ind. Mark. Manage. **51**, 89–99 (2015)

66. Steyn, P., Ewing, M.T., Van Heerden, G., Pitt, L.F., Windisch, L.: From whence it came: Understanding source effects in consumer-generated advertising. Int. J. Advert. **30**(1), 133–160 (2011)

67. Taylor, D.G., Lewin, J.E., Strutton, D.: Friends, fans, and followers: do ads work on social networks? how gender and age shape receptivity. J. Advert. Res. **51**(1), 258–276 (2011)

68. Tham, A., Croy, G., Mair, J.: Social media in destination choice: distinctive electronic word-of-mouth dimensions. J. Travel Tourism Mark. **30**(1–2), 144–155 (2013)

69. Trainor, K.J., Andzulis, J.M., Rapp, A., Agnihotri, R.: Social media technology usage and customer relationship performance: a capabilities-based examination of social CRM. J. Bus. Res. **67**(6), 1201–1208 (2014)

70. Tuten, T.L., Solomon, M.R.: Social Media Marketing, 2nd edn. Sage, Thousand Oaks (2015)

71. Venkatesh, V., Thong, J.Y., Xu, X.: Consumer acceptance and use of information technology: extending the unified theory of acceptance and use of technology. MIS Q. **36**(1), 157–178 (2012)

72. Wang, X., Yu, C., Wei, Y.: Social media peer communication and impacts on purchase intentions: a consumer socialization framework. J. Interact. Mark. **26**(4), 198–208 (2012)

73. Williams, J., Chinn, S.: Meeting relationship–marketing goals through social media: a conceptual model for sport marketers. Int. J. Sport Commun. **3**(4), 422–437 (2010)

74. Zeng, B., Gerritsen, R.: What do we know about social media in tourism? Rev. Tourism Manage. Perspect. **10**, 27–36 (2014)

75. Zhu, Y.Q., Chen, H.G.: Social media and human need satisfaction: implications for social media marketing. Bus. Horiz. **58**(3), 335–345 (2015)

Conversations in Search of Audiences: Prospects and Challenges of Marketing UK's Postgraduate Higher Education Using Social Media

Baomin Qi[1] and Amit Mitra[2(✉)]

[1] Bolton Business School, University of Bolton, Bolton, UK
[2] Bristol Business School, University of the West of England, Bristol, UK
Amit.Mitra@uwe.ac.uk

Abstract. It is no surprise that there are serious disparities between the rhetoric of education and the realities of education. Marketing of university curricula is a challenge that is increasingly becoming a difficult proposition as advances in social media (SM) are enabling prospective students to form opinions and inform their decisions like never before. Whilst the Universities and Colleges Admissions Service (UCAS) plays a central role in matching undergraduate students to courses in universities yet the same does not apply to postgraduate admissions which are sought after by a large number of applicants from overseas as well. This paper looks at some of the areas where SM has been successfully used. The papers then goes onto develop taxonomy of popular SM tools that are being widely used. Using this taxonomy it explores barriers and promoters that exist in the interface between universities and their audiences.

Keywords: Social media · Higher education · Postgraduate · Online conversation · Online marketing

1 Introduction

About a couple of decades ago nobody expected to measure popularity by the number of Facebook friends one had. Whilst people find less time to meet each other in the real world they seem to be drawn towards spending more time in the virtual community of social media. Visiting shops on the high street, talking to sales staff about features of products seem to have been replaced by reviews and experiential accounts of fellow social media punters. Ubiquitous online access through different interfaces has brought about a world where consumption of goods is prefaced by surveys and recommendations of friends and family. Reliability of views of friends and family seems to have assumed a special significance where sellers increasingly use viral marketing to inform the world of products and services. Lack of time to speak to high street salesmen seems to have been replaced by an abundance of views within social media platforms. The advent of such a resource that potentially enriches prospects of product sales has influenced many customer-facing businesses to consider ways of reaching out to potential markets through a dynamic personalisation of products and offerings.

Y.K. Dwivedi et al. (Eds.): I3E 2016, LNCS 9844, pp. 90–104, 2016.
DOI: 10.1007/978-3-319-45234-0_9

At a time when being social may mean being active online, it is obvious that for Higher Education Institutions (HEIs) to cultivate audiences may require consistent engagement with participants on social media platforms. As more people are registering on social media sites, we are gradually moving towards a mature social media usage environment. Whilst in the late 1990s use of social media platforms like Facebook was taken to be a must have, the advent of recent protest movements, its use for anti-state activities, as well as becoming infamous for being a ploy for time wasting, has relegated possession of a Facebook account to a 'could have' status. For instance, one does get to hear tales of employers declining jobs to prospective candidates if they are known to be active Facebookers. However, with the progress of technology, ubiquity of the online world has meant that an ever increasing number of people are now accessing social media platforms through a variety of interfaces like smartphones and tablets. In a context where opinions and reviews are central to generating stickiness and market share, HEIs would be an exception if they were to overlook opportunities to market their offerings through social media platforms. Just like creating a website with goods and services does not mean that eCommerce traffic can be successfully generated by it, similarly engagement and mediation are imperative to successfully develop audiences that could then be converted into market share for HEIs.

In a fiercely competitive recruitment market, uniqueness of offerings can be a key differentiator that enables a university to not be beaten on price. Given the ability of social media platforms to enable a two-way communication, it is feasible that fulfilment maybe more easily attainable in comparison to platforms devoid of SM links. It is often argued that marketing communications will be a differentiating feature that an institution can offer its potential students and the diverse promotion and marketing could be a key driving factor to the sustainable success of the HE sector [40]. The recent phenomena of social media (SM) technologies provides a potential solution to ensure the two-way communication with prospective students, who, especially in an increasingly competitive market place, want and indeed expect to feel valued. As [15] points out an overwhelming student preference seem to be to make up their own minds through bespoke searches of online offerings. They actively seek out institutions that understand their needs and can facilitate them in achieving their aspirations [3]. Thus, HEI's should be looking at new ways of communicating with students and try to build better relationships with them. With a proliferation of search tools and recommendation engines, audiences are wary of actually losing their ability to customise products. By facilitating a personal comment sharing platform it is likely that some of informal communication will add to a better management of expectations.

Many universities have already broached the concept of using SM to communicate with potential students. It is clear that more recently evolved universities require innovative mechanisms to attract and sustain audiences. According to [1], "Edge Hill University was one of the first HEIs in the UK to exploit social networking services such as Facebook." They used this platform to raise their profile among the targeted student base in order to create a 'buzz' about their institution and also to engage in two-way communication with new, existing and past students. However, the social media arena is deemed by many HEIs as frivolous, and the significance of SM is yet to be widely realised. Though, recent statistics reveals that social networking and blog sites are now more popular than e-mail as a means of social communication, indeed they eclipsed email in global reach at 68.4 % vs 64.8 % in February 2009. [24] also identified that 40 % of respondents of a study undertaken by Oracle believe that social networking is now easier to utilise than software currently adopted in the workplace. The following table is an attempt to classify some well-known SM tools that are used by audiences to gauge market opinion at the same time be able to consolidate public opinion through viral discussions (Table 1).

Table 1. Taxonomy of social networking tools

Activity	Tools	Influence/uptake
Viral informal platform	Facebook, Bebo, MySpace	Early adoption by vast numbers, successful in quick mobilisation of public opinion.
Professional networking	LinkedIn, Ning, Ecademy,	Popular professional networking tools that seems to have motivated people across a multiple range of professions to set up links. To some degree it may be said that new expectations have been created by the advent of these networking platforms.
Blogging	Wikipedia, blogger.com, wordpress.com, Typepad, Jux, Blogetery, LiveJournal, Blogsome, freeblogit, blog dive, vabalu.com	Situational commenting has led to the creation of repositories that lead people to express their views within readily accessible platforms.
Microblogging	Twitter, Tumblr, Posterous Spaces, Thoughts.com, Typepad Micro	Instant communication within the world at large within a defined character set that can enable commenting on dynamic activities.
Content management systems	Weebly, Moonfruit, Squarespaces	Website development tools that can be used to launch a business. Not much use as SM tools.
Video sharing	YouTube	Widely used to provide snapshots of work/profile. Especially beneficial when performing arts types of courses are being considered.
Audio sharing	iTunes, Podcast.net	Audio feature compositions on specific topics can be listened to by audiences.
Live-casting	BlogTalkRadio, Live 365	Live transmission of real time debates and conversations, Tends to work best when issues are topical and directed.
Virtual worlds, Avatars	Second Life	So far have been used to facilitate game playing environments

The term 'social web' and Web 2.0 are often used interchangeably. These terms incorporate social networking sites (e.g. Bebo, Facebook, LinkedIn, MySpace, Ning, etc.), Blogging sites (e.g. Blogger.com, Wikipedia and Wordpress) as well as micro-blogging sites (e.g. Twitter). Such an umbrella may also include Video (e.g. YouTube), Audio (e.g. iTunes and Podcast.net) and live-casting (e.g. BlogTalkRadio and Live 365), and the virtual worlds (e.g. Second Life). This clearly outlines the complexity surrounding the term social media, however the one commonality between all of the above areas is that they all focus on building online communities within which people interact and influence each other. For the marketer the adoption of social media marketing tools will require a paradigm-shift, as [39] illustrates "...the marketer's role changes from broadcaster pushing out messages and materials to an aggregator who brings together content and enables collaboration with communities." Although there are numerous articles written regarding the power of social media marketing, yet the literature is embryonic with regard to the public sector in general and the Higher Education sector in particular. Besides, as [6] has identified marketers in the public and private sectors to have considerably differing viewpoints on the relevance and importance of social media.

2 Opportunities for Social Media Adoption

[33] well known work entitled 'Screw blackboard... do it on Facebook' demonstrates some of the lack of reverence that the student community has towards structured engagement. Also given that many prospective students based overseas are going to only have access to Facebook it is likely that many interesting discussions could be had using it. The continued development and growing integration of social media technologies into many activities presents numerous hitherto non-existent opportunities for institutions to engage with the virtual community [30]. They allow prospective students to "...self-evaluate, self-segment, self-support, self-organise, self-advertise, self-police, and self-program..." [34:11]. If HEIs do not adapt their teaching, learning and research practices in order to engage with students and potential students on the social media, they could easily be usurped by their competitors. The following sections will explore available opportunities that institutions may use to develop competitive advantage.

2.1 Experience Sharing with Current Students

[38] concurs that social media enables powerful feelings to be shared immediately with friends, colleagues, acquaintances and the general public. By setting up social networking sites and encouraging current students to write blogs about their experiences in universities, provides prospective students with an authentic student-to-student communication platform on 'real' life as a student and what to expect [1]. It is therefore possible to enable students to feel part of the university community even before formally starting university life. Add to the social media's ability to build 24/7 virtual communities that share experiences, it is also feasible and particularly useful for an overseas student to access recommendations and feedback left by current and graduating students about an institution without leaving their home country.

From the literature review, what is also evident is that social media is here to stay, and people are empowered from utilising the internet and specifically social media sites, that provide free access to user-generated information. Though when enabling these channels, institutions should monitor currently active conversations and respond and engage as appropriate [11]. This is a particularly delicate issue as negative student feedback can quickly go out of control and situations can be easily blown out of proportion. The authors have experience of seeing Facebook pages created by students on why they consider certain lecturers to be unpopular. Just like fan mail of popular lecturers can sometimes have little to do with the actual content of the lecture and may be more with how somebody is perceived similarly unflattering comments can sometimes make tutors demons where subject itself might not be riveting material.

[37] observes that the social media arena is rapidly expanding, with innovative applications developing on an almost daily basis; with some institutions using tools such as Twitter to collate student opinion on tangible facilities on campus. Indeed, [37:37] identifies that "…Twitter is continuing to grow in popularity and evolve as both a social network and marketing tool…" Furthermore, individual's usage of Twitter varies presenting new marketing opportunities. However, it would be prudent for institutions to have identified who they are communicating to, what they are trying to communicate and which medium they wish to communicate on prior to communicating on these platforms [17].

Although HEI's have the platform to promote their achievements, this is not always effective. It would be more meaningful for them to encourage students to promote their successes. This is primarily because the student is the most transparent tool to deliver an honest review of life from within the institution [20]. Besides, the social media tools enable real time sharing of reactions and responses from individuals within that community [38]. In a way this makes it tricky for institutions as a balance needs to be struck between positive long term views on student experiences and the individual here and now snapshots.

2.2 Word of Mouth Marketing and Brand Building

[32] argue that social networks are ultimately creating influence among students. By developing and cultivating these networks, HEIs are able to create an opportunity to nurture the trust that results in increased numbers. Indeed, [11] have highlighted that "… 26 % of marketers say that social networking and word of mouth activities are the most likely marketing activity to increase…" This is corroborated by [12] who believes that social networking and proximity marketing will be increasingly utilised in order to deliver targeted offers, generating word-of-mouth recommendations. [12] expects that increasing overlaps between social networking and proximity marketing in the near future that will enable further experimentation by marketers and brand managers.

Evidently, [21] identified that individuals are more inclined to believe information received from a word-of-mouth source. This is because such sources are the only ones that are from customers, by customers and for customers. In a social media context due to the personal nature of the environment participants feel encouraged to comment on personal experiences. Once collated these then may become significant vehicles to influence future participants. Thus there is no hidden agenda and so future students feel that the information contained therein is transparent. However, with this point in mind, HEIs need to be careful when trying to transfer word-of-mouth into the online social arena. Within such an arena the content being primarily controlled by the customer and therefore if the customer was dissatisfied in any way, implications of spreading unflattering messages may be serious.

A common feature of social networking is that individuals are drawn to those who have similar interests and/or behaviour to their own [23]. Thus, using social media to bring like-minded people together to discuss about their experiences on institutions could aid the building of brand awareness and raise the profile of the institution. Indeed, [13] highlighted that many HEIs have realised the potential benefits of e-recruiting after applicants converted to registered students through a continued electronic dialogue and consistent communication. Clearly such innovation can only consolidate the success of the HEIs. [35] also concurs and goes on to add that engaging in social media would involve customising the communication that will then engage the student, building trust and loyalty and thus embrace its potential as a tool to encourage a community ethos among students.

If an HEI leveraged its influence effectively across a mix of social media (i.e. micro-blogging, blogging and a presence on social network sites) they could wield considerably seductive marketing and branding system [22]. Such an approach will assume importance as traditional blanket marketing campaigns will get substituted by audience preferences of personalised conversation enabled through social media [29].

2.3 Market Research

[19] has identified that "...social networking enables institutions to discover not just the answers to their questions, but the answers to questions they'd never thought of asking - that's both customer service at its best and a marketers dream..." This issue was reiterated by in [7]) who noted that in order to identify which market segments would be most profitable, market research would be essential. Indeed, without market research it would be difficult to know what the appropriate marketing mix would be for the segment, whether the information content would appeal to them and which media would be most effective in reaching them, consequently resulting in generating user demand.

Admittedly, Social Media may be deemed to be a direct and cost-effective market research tool for educating HEI's on identifying their customer base [25]. For instance, by using a YouTube channel to upload promotional videos, HEIs would be able to reduce costs of newspaper, radio and TV coverage [5]. Furthermore, [11] have identified that "...as more businesses integrate social networking sites into their digital marketing media mix, companies are increasingly focusing on measurement techniques to better understand the return on investment from social media.." Given financial constraints that are to be placed on HEI's in the future, cost-savings across all areas of the institutions will be essential.

Indeed, as a market research tool social media and the analytical tools that can be adopted should enable HEI's to not only listen to what is currently being said about their programmes and services, but also to engage with these conversations. By gathering

Table 2. Key opportunities of SM applications for HEIs

Experience sharing	Direct marketing and building brand awareness	Market research
SM removes barriers and encourages conversations between prospective and current students	SM can be used to build brand awareness and raise the profile of the institution.	Social Media has to be the purest, direct and cost-effective market research tool for educating HEI's on their customer base
SM engages in two-way communication between institutions and prospective students	SM helps reach hundreds of millions of targetable consumers	By gathering data on the targeting and segmentation of their messages, HEIs will be able to tailor the communications to specific platforms and to identify which platforms they should have a profile on
SM enables powerful feelings to be shared immediately with friends, colleagues, acquaintances' and the general public	SM simplifies content management systems and increases the overall quality and effectiveness of marketing messages	Social media tools enable real time sharing of reactions and responses from individuals within that community
SM is ultimately creating influence among students, by developing and cultivating networks and if HEis can influence the flow of conversation they will have achieved a significant competitive advantage	SM enables HEIs to co-opt staff, existing and former students to provide a realistic image of the institution, its people and environment	Social networking and proximity marketing will increasingly overlap in the coming years which will enable more experimentation by marketers and brand managers
SM can enable potential students to join the institution with an understanding of the culture and expectations that they may encounter	SM is rapidly expanding, with more innovative applications developing on an almost daily basis	Tools such as Twitter could be used to collate student opinion on the tangible facilities on campus
	Perception that information gained via social networks is more trustworthy than information that is only available from the corporate hymn sheet	

data on the targeting and segmentation of their messages, they will be able to customise communications to specific platforms and to flexibly determine which platforms they should have a profile on. [9:7] has identified that "...social media is the word on the street, proof of bragging, culture and shortcuts..." Hence, the more profiles HEI's have the more they will be able to raise their brands and drive traffic to their main sites.

Having reviewed the available literature, Table 2 summarises, by embracing the social media technologies, the main opportunities that are presented to HEIs.

3 Challenges to Social Media Adoption

Much has been written about the wonders of social media adoption, however as [13] has identified there are a number of institutional barriers to adoption within this sector such as, lack of horizontal communication, functional specialism, and decentralisation, lack of planning and expertise, lack of budget, lack of integration with Content Management Systems (CMS), corporate culture and fear of change.

3.1 Internal Issues Impacting Adoption

The need for academic buy-in to new technologies is not a new phenomena, though as widely acknowledged that for many, too little time to learn new technologies is an issue. Moreover, [18] identified that within institutions "...35 % don't track any conversions, 32 % do with admissions info inquiries (47 % wish they did) and 29 % with online applications (44 % wish they did)..."

Understanding the role of innovative technologies with regard to skill development of staff is exceedingly important. How can an institution expect academic colleagues to participate and champion the use of new media, if they have not been given the opportunity to develop their skills in this area? Further for those who have used social media platforms for engagement are aware of impulsive potential of negative feedback generation and may be reluctant to integrate social media as a front line marketing tool in place of obtaining traditional avenues.

According to the [10] it will become the role of the marketing departments to become facilitators that aid the entire institution to realise that transparent, open communication and excellent customer service with their potential and existing market is essential to their continued survival. Besides, [8] believes that if marketing is to be utilised as an agent of change, then it must first demonstrate that it understands and empathises with the essence of Higher Education generally and second the individual characteristics and cultures of individual institutions. There is preponderance among HEIs to have marketing departments that are not sufficiently integrated with academic programs. Hence there may be a disconnect between agendas of academic programme directors and marketing groups.

As mentioned previously, [13] has identified a number of institutional barriers, not least that of culture. The cultural barriers- as with any innovation, is often a formidable challenge. For instance, regardless of the numerous successful social media platforms, many individuals remain sceptical of the value of investing time on these arenas and have voiced concerns regarding the perceived risks associated with adoption of such technologies [22]. Academics in HEIs are usually driven by individual goals and norms – carrying out their tasks. Use of social media platforms has an expectation of a group norm and collective endeavour. The latter might be alien and unattractive to existent traditional mind sets.

[23] reported that management often does not fully appreciate the role of social media within an institutions promotional arsenal. Indeed, "...the Higher Education sector is one that should be at the forefront of Twitter use and innovation, but which instead has been slow to adopt this technology..." [37:63]. HEIs that are deemed to be progressive tend to claim that they are enabling social media within their programs. However, they may not necessarily use it as a tool to attract and sustain audiences of prospective students. This is regardless of the fact that it magnifies the significant impact of customer-to-customer communication within the virtual marketplace and as yet they have not been able to articulate how to shape these communications in the future.

This is corroborated further by [20] who concur that adoption will be unsuccessful without the backing of the Managing Board within the HEI; who in turn would require a substantial business case to encourage investment. Although individuals may be convinced of the potential benefits, this alone is not enough. This is further exacerbated as "... marketing and academia are seen as diametric opposites in terms of both character and purpose..." [8:30], which again reiterates the importance of garnering support from the top of the institution down. There may also be HEIs that have its top management interested in implementing social media capacity but may not have a plan to implement as they themselves are not users of social media. Consequently academics may be daunted by the challenges to develop capacity in the absence of any official allocation of time for such activities.

It is apparent that many academics and other staff are not overtly predisposed to engaging with online communities. In keeping with the availability of new technology, it is a part of the expected norm for teaching staff to continually upgrade delivery of modules. Consequently, it is commonplace to find a much higher amount of technology enhanced interactivity between students and staff in comparison to delivery frameworks of the past. This sort of continued pursuit of technology enhancement tends to produce a kind of indifference among academics who perceive that as long as a one to one relationship works to facilitate module delivery, external effort to be part of a one to many relationships is probably an additional capacity feature that may or may not add to the student experience. This type of institutional inertia by staff is a significant barrier to adoption of social media, however the risk from doing nothing and being left behind is much higher than from doing something [1].

3.2 Absence of Policy and Legal Guidelines

[22] argue that HEI's are struggling with the legal ramifications of embracing this new push for interactivity, clearly there are a minority who embrace innovation and have taken steps to deal with the challenges with which they are now faced, but it should be remembered they are a minority.

Many staff within HEIs are reluctant to embrace the technology fully, for fear of opening themselves to law suits due to lack of a clear policy. However, this can be addressed by developing guidelines and policies for using the tools. Indeed [11], have identified that the UK Consumer Protection from Unfair Trading Regulations 2008, provide information on legal requirements for transparency whilst online and using social media; this could be incorporated into policies and guidelines that HEIs produce.

Furthermore, HEIs often find themselves in a dilemma regarding the need to develop institutional on-line social networking policies [14]. Given the speed at which this arena is evolving there is not always sufficient time for universities to develop succinct policies on its use [1]. As universities become more driven by the need to sustain quality standards, the need for honest feedback from students is assumes importance. Whilst formal feedback generation is useful in ensuring the right levels of delivery specification is adhered to yet informal feedback like that available on social media platforms may have genuine substance. Ironically it is lack of clear policy that is impacting on adoption the most.

Moreover, HEIs need to remember that customer-to-customer communication can work both ways and as a result social network sites can also pose a threat, especially if a dissatisfied customer chooses to spread their views [29]. For example, members who perceive themselves to being tricked and who may not have received expected levels of transparency may have become dissatisfied very quickly, an event that would not prove beneficial to the institution. Especially given that "...increasingly students will formulate their opinions of a potential university on the feedback they receive on such sites from current students..." [30:15]. Somehow the juxtaposition of current student opinion with that of prospective students makes it an ongoing long term challenge for HEIs. Clearly it is an issue of considerable challenge for HEIs when they have to demonstrate the seriousness with which they treat current student feedback, if they are to rely on transmission of positive stories by current to prospective student audiences.

3.3   Lack of Understanding of the Medium

It is evident that many HEI's have a presence in the social media arena; it is equally evident that such a presence remains underutilised. Furthermore, many feel that having a presence on these platforms is intrusive and does not realise the potential first hand conversation advantages can offer [16]. Indeed, some sceptics believe social media is no more than a digital mailing list. Again, overlooking the opportunities it offers to share and comment on topics, and what an effective marketing communications tool it can actually be if utilised effectively [38].

There is also a significant gap between the potential of the technologies available and the manner in which they are currently being utilised [35]. For example, some HEIs use social networking to deliver learning, whilst other academic colleagues use it to interact with groups of students that are brought together. However, this has led to allegations of bullying or intimidation by staff and student alike [1]. [30] believes that if an institution has a reputation for academic collaboration, it would seem inevitable that a small number of individuals will already be communicating using these technologies.

Table 3. Mapping of information/feedback on various stages of the recruitment process

Stage	Activity	Type of information	Prospective student perspective
1	Matching of expectations with availability	Courses on offer	Actual content needs to fit with student interests
2	Assessment of attainment at point of entry	Pre-requisites to enrol on the course	Background information may enable students to have a clear fit as well as enable comparison of notes on strengths and weaknesses
3	Finances	Fee levels/Costs	Best value/Convenient payment arrangements
4	Reputation	Feedback of past students	Reiteration of value derivation in pursuit of the course
5	Prospects	Job prospects and associated advantages	Job prospects in the market post completion of the course

The following Table 3 articulates the phases through which the marketing/recruitment activities may be mapped on the social media landscape.

It is clear from Table 3 above that social media can enable the recruitment process substantially as conversations around each of the stages may enable prospective students to appreciate the process of entry into a HEI through evaluation of what contributors on social media platforms may say. Both students within the UK as well as those without need specific information in the first instance and then assurances on that information to ensure that they are making meaningful choices that would have some kind of return on investment. Specific strengths of courses may enhance marketability through social media conversations. Further social media platforms like LinkedIn may be able to bring together opportunities in the job market as well as introductions of networks that may facilitate further addressing of aspirations of prospective students. More disturbingly, it has also been alleged that some HEI's have used their presence on these platforms to 'snoop' on how students are presenting themselves. Such activity can be potentially damaging and does little to develop a community of trust and transparency. Indeed, [31] has identified that for many the use of social media as a marketing tool in HE is controversial, added to this is of course ethical implications of how and what institutions are communicating with individuals. Moreover, some individuals see this method of communication as intrusive and if institutions get it wrong it can be an instant turn off [27].

The audiences using the social network arena are more educated and are no longer predisposed to accept every message a marketer wants to foist on them [12]. Rather, they will extract information that matches their needs and interests. According to [38:17] "…this can work two ways for marketers – some people will respond to direct engagement that cuts through the clutter. Others will instead ignore your noise alongside everyone else marketing a product or service…"

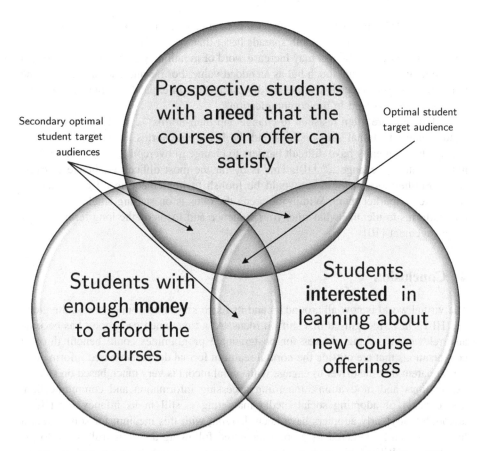

Fig. 1. Relationship between types of student expectations source: adapted from [2]

In order to gain competitive advantage from utilising social media technologies, HEIs need to implement proper market segmentation and positioning [4]. Figure 1 below presents this to enable visualisation of the intersections of student interests and how a specific target student audience can be located. However, this would prove difficult if staff do not understand the medium they are now delving into. Indeed, human nature dictates that we are often fearful of situations we don't understand and thus often allow others to venture out before us [32]. However, on this occasion, this type of strategy could prove extremely risky for the HEI and result in them being left behind.

It is equally apparent that many within this sector are still uncertain about the lifecycle of this phenomena as well as implications of engagement. This was corroborated by [28] who identified that HEIs are struggling with what information and content is suitable for incorporation in social media (such as Twitter), whilst also trying to come to terms with how these mediums work. Although no one could argue that tools such as Twitter are not powerful additions to the social media marketeers toolkit, this would only be the case if utilised with a specific focus and end goal in mind.

[19] (2011:29) posits that "...with each person having an average of 130 friends on Facebook, negative word of mouth spreads faster than ever..." Moreover, [26] believes that although social networks may increase word of mouth they should not be used as a substitute of the personal touch but as an added value. For instance, what would be the point of being on twitter if you are not investing time in expanding your audience by getting others involved in the communication?

Individuals are often resistant to change and their norms "...are influenced by the cultural and situational surroundings and the behaviour norms and attitudes of their peers, who frequently have difficult barriers to change to overcome, or who are simply not motivated to change..." [10]. This is by far the most difficult challenge to overcome. Furthermore, institutions would be foolish to implement an all out attack on social media market share. Within the arena the onus is on starting small, monitoring the platforms to identify what suits your audience and focus on the long-term strategy on engagement [10].

4   Conclusion

The virtual world is now all around us and its reach knows no bounds across the globe and HEI's have recognised this shift in focus. At a time when geography has become an irrelevance, making choices for postgraduate programmes could benefit through conversations that are outside the normal realm of formal document based information. It is apparent that the driver to engage with social media is very much based on student expectations and motivations, regarding accessing information and communication. The concept of adopting social media marketing is still in its infancy for HEI's, although many early adopters have been dallying with this medium for some time, it has only recently garnered its current increased following and thus truly risen to the attention of HEI's. This taxonomy presented in this paper has identified numerous applications that fall under the 'social media' umbrella, including social network sites such as Facebook as well as blogging sites such as Twitter. However, it would be prudent to highlight that these media are far more successful and beneficial when used in conjunction with each other and not exclusively. Therefore, for a HEI to truly raise its profile and create a buzz within these arenas, they need to have a multi-faceted action plan that meets their institutional goals. Also if they wish to raise their profile and create a 'buzz' about the institution, they shouldn't first establish which social media applications their customer base are currently using and the focus should primarily on fostering long-term relationships that will build trust and credibility.

It is clear that there is a crying need to address informal conversations that could support standard admission procedures within the postgraduate market. By being able to engage in narratives of student expectations and what the HEI is trying to deliver it is likely that a human face of the organisation would be identifiable by the student community. As graduating students can sometimes be the inspiration for newer students, validation of perceptions gained through other means could be developed through personalised conversations that a social media tool like Facebook enables.

It is also evident that for social media marketing to be successful and thus beneficial to the institution, compatibility with the content management systems within the HEI is essential. This therefore, raises issues in relation to the possible lack of suitable IT infrastructures to support the adoption of the social media applications.

Within the current financial climate, lack of funding to invest in what could be perceived as a 'flash in the pan' innovations are a major challenge for adoption of social media applications. In order for HEI's to truly benefit from adoption of social media marketing, they need to produce a strong business-case; that would encourage the strategic management level to invest in the infrastructure, with emphasis on the cost-effectiveness of integration in the long-term, to facilitate this adoption. However, a word of caution, it would be ill advised for HEI's to use these media without having a clear strategy of what they are aiming to achieve by doing so. Adoption will also require a complete paradigm-shift of the academic staff within the HEI, the marketers role will no longer be as a broadcaster pushing content and messages at a targeted audience but as an aggregator who endeavours to pull the audience to them by means of collaboration and building of relationships within communities.

References

1. Armstrong, J., Franklin, T.: A review of current and developing international practice in the use of social networking (Web 2.0) in higher education. Franklin Consulting (2009). http://franklin-consulting.co.uk/
2. Barker, M., Barker, D., Bormann, N., Neher, K.: Social Media Marketing: A Strategic Approach. South-Western, Mason (2013)
3. Barnes, C.: B2B is still person to person. The Marketer, January 2011
4. Bonnema, J., Van der Waldt, D.L.R.: Information and source preferences of a student market in higher education. Int. J. Educ. Manage. 22(4), 314–327 (2008)
5. Brabazon, T.:YouTube has merit, but enough already of cat videos. Times Higher Education (2009). http://www.timeshighereducation.co.uk/story.asp?storycode=409416
6. Brennan, R.: Should we worry about an "academic-practitioner divide" in marketing? Mark. Intell. Plan. 22(5), 492–500 (2004)
7. Caemmerer, B.: The planning and implementation of integrated marketing communications. Mark. Intell. Plan. 27(4), 524–538 (2009)
8. Callan, J.: Marketing's Role in Developing and Delivering Corporate Strategy: What Vice-Chancellors Really Think About Marketing. Callan Associates, London (2007)
9. Campbell, H.A.: When Religion Meets New Media. Routledge, London (2010)
10. CIM: Don't stop me now: marketing in central government. The Chartered Institute of Marketing (2009)
11. E-Consultancy. Online PR and Social Media Trends Briefing (2009). http://econsultancy.com/reports/online-pr-and-social-media-trends-briefing
12. Gray, R.: Location is where it's at. The Marketer, October 2011
13. Gurau, C.: Integrated online marketing communication: implementation and management. J. Commun. Manage. 12(2), 169–184 (2008)
14. Harris, K.: Using social networking sites as student engagement tools. Diverse Issues High. Educ. 25(18), 40 (2008). http://diverseeducation.com/#
15. Headworth, A.: Why twitter should be a key part of your institution's marketing strategy. In: UCAS Social Media Marketing Conference, London (2010)
16. Hayes, A., McGrath, S., Campbell, J.: Using apps as a marketing tool. In: UCAS Social Media Marketing Conference, London (2010)

17. Hearn, G., Foth, M., Gray, H.: Applications and implementations of new media in corporate communications: an action research approach. Corp. Commun. Int. J. **14**(1), 49–61 (2009)
18. HigherEdExperts: The State of Web and Social Media Analytics in Higher Education Report (2010). http://www.higheredexperts.com
19. Hilpern, K.: Does your marketing serve. The Marketer, March 2011, p. 29 (2011)
20. Jadu: An Investigation into the Challenges, Application and Benefits of Social Media in Higher Education Institutions. Jadu Research Report (2010). http://www.jadu.co.uk/downloads/file/18/research_into_the_challenges_usage_and_benefits_of_social_media_in_higher_education_institutions
21. Kotler, P.: Marketing Management, 11th edn. Pearson Education Inc., Upper Saddle River (2003)
22. Leader-Chivee, L., Hamilton, B.A., Cowan, E.: Networking the way to success: on-line social networks for workplace and competitive advantage. People Strat. **31**(4), 40–46 (2008)
23. Mangold, W.G., Faulds, D.J.: Social media: the new hybrid element of the promotion mix. Bus. Horiz. **52**, 357–365 (2009)
24. Manning, C.D.: Part-of-speech tagging from 97 % to 100 %: is it time for some linguistics? In: Gelbukh, A.F. (ed.) CICLing 2011, Part I. LNCS, vol. 6608, pp. 171–189. Springer, Heidelberg (2011)
25. Marken, G.A.: Social media .... the hunted can become the hunter. Public Relat. Q. **52**(4), 9–12 (2009)
26. Matthews, D.: Word of Mouth. The Marketer, November 2010, p. 30 (2010)
27. McGrath, S.: Using apps as a marketing tool – what do students want? In: Proceedings of UCAS Social Media Marketing Conference, London, pp. 21–25 (2010)
28. Other Side Notes: 10 ways universities can (and should) use twitter (2010). http://www.othersidenotes.com/10-ways-universities-can-and-should-use-twitter/
29. Palmer, A., Koenig-Lewis, N.: An experiential, social network-based approach to direct marketing. Direct Mark. Int. J. **3**(3), 162–176 (2009)
30. Precedent: Traditional universities' websites: Trends, Observations & Best Practice (2008). http://www.precedent.co.uk/precedent/.../the-higher-education-communication-specialists
31. Reuben, R.: The Use of Social Media in Higher Education for Marketing and Communications: A Guide for Professionals in Higher Education (2013). http://doteduguru.com/wp-content/uploads/2008/08/social-media-in-higher-education.pdf
32. Safko, L., Brake, D.K.: The Social Media Bible. Wiley, New York (2009)
33. Selwyn, N.: Social media in higher education. In: The Europa World of Learning, pp. 1–10 (2012). www.educationarena.com/pdf/sample/sample-essay-selwyn.pdf
34. Sheth, J.N., Sisodia, R.S.: A dangerous divergence: marketing and society. J. Public Policy Mark. **24**(1), 160–162 (2005)
35. Singh, T., Veron-Jackson, L., Cullinane, J.: Blogging: a new play in your marketing game plan. Bus. Horiz. **51**(4), 281–292 (2008)
36. Sugden, J.: Universities on Twitter: we'll be brief about this. TimesOnline (2009). http://www.timesonline.co.uk/tol/life_and_style/education/student/article6802305.ece
37. Thomases, H.: Twitter Marketing: An Hour a Day. Wiley Publishing Inc., Indianapolis (2010)
38. Treadway, C., Smith, M.: Facebook Marketing: An Hour a Day. Wiley Publishing Inc., Indianapolis (2010)
39. Weber, L.: Marketing to the Social Web. Wiley, Hoboken (2009)
40. Yeshin, T.: Integrated Marketing Communications, 2nd edn. Butterworth-Heinemann, Oxford (1998)

The Impact of Social Media on Cause-Related Marketing Campaigns

Julian Bühler$^{(\boxtimes)}$, Natalia Cwierz, and Markus Bick

ESCP Europe Business School Berlin, Berlin, Germany
{jbuehler,mbick}@escpeurope.eu,
natalia.cwierz@edu.escpeurope.eu

Abstract. Traditional offline media channels have always served as a reliable backbone for all kinds of marketing campaigns. But with the emergence of new digitally-driven ways of communication, other contenders arise. Very prominent and fostered by ongoing technological advantage are social media services. In this empirical study, we analyze the interplay between two traditional offline channels, print and point-of-sale (PoS) advertising, and two leading social media services, Facebook and YouTube. These channels were used by the brand Volvic during a recent cause-related marketing (CRM) campaign. It supports local supply of drinking water in Ethiopia, and serves as the basis for our investigations. We developed an online survey and asked 114 participants for their perception of four alternating campaign displays. Based on the communication model of Te'Eni, we then calculate an ordinal logistic regression and results reveal that Facebook and YouTube can add significant value to CRM campaigns.

Keywords: Social media · Facebook · YouTube · Caused-related marketing · Ordinal logistic regression · Organizational communication model · Media synchronicity theory

1 Introduction

The statue of liberty is well-known as an iconic, prestigious symbol representing core values and convictions of the United States of America. More than three decades ago, this symbol was in bad conditions and restauration was inevitable, but high costs delayed the necessary operations. The financial service company American Express realized that they could draw significant positive attention by supporting the process and took over the lead of a what later was established as their "Historic Preservation Initiatives" program [1]. After few prior company initiatives in predominantly local markets had been executed [2], this was the first move into a concept nowadays recognized as cause-related marketing (CRM) [3].

Marketing strategies in general have to be adapted constantly to keep pace with people's continuously enhancing usage behaviors. This includes new communication platforms that got established with technological progress, especially social media service. Despite various understandings of the term behind it, social media includes

© IFIP International Federation for Information Processing 2016
Published by Springer International Publishing Switzerland 2016. All Rights Reserved
Y.K. Dwivedi et al. (Eds.): I3E 2016, LNCS 9844, pp. 105–119, 2016.
DOI: 10.1007/978-3-319-45234-0_10

social networks like Facebook, microblogging services like Twitter, video services like YouTube, platforms for social collaboration, and other social services or software.

In this article we shift from a broader marketing research perspective on general cause-related activities towards a selective comparative analysis of traditional and social media-driven channels. Our goal is to differentiate between these channel types by identifying unique key characteristics and bring the strength of both sides together. We contribute to this by an extensive analysis of the Volvic CRM campaign which was launched to call attention to the need of people in Africa for drinking water. The campaign was executed through two social media channels, Facebook and YouTube, and two traditional channels, print advertising and point-of-sale advertising. Based on media theories by Te'Eni [4] and Dennis et al. [5], we calculate separate ordinal logistic regressions for all channels two answer the main research question: "Can social media channels – compared to traditional channels – have a different impact on the user perception of cause-related marketing campaigns?"

Our research agenda is composed of a CRM literature review and utilization of two media theories for the Volvic case in Sect. 2. We approach our research question with the help of an online questionnaire. Its setting is described as part of the research methodology in Sect. 3. Survey results in Sect. 4 lead to the discussion part, Sect. 5. We conclude this study in Sect. 6 with an overview of potential avenues for future research.

2 Theoretical Perspective on CRM and Social Media Integration

2.1 Evolution of CRM Research

The case of American Express in 1983 was constitutional for companies and the integration of CRM into many overall business strategies. But beside theses practical consequences, it also stimulated the academic research activities. In this section, we will provide a literature review of selected articles dealing with CRM and discuss how the role of media changed with the rise of social media in the last decade.

Researchers had begun studying CRM in the early to mid-80 s and the first explorative articles emerged from existing corporate involvement examinations [6]. Soon, a critical perspective on CRM was added mainly based on trade literature, and arguments against it were based on predictions that traditional donations made by companies would significantly decrease [2]. With the continuous emergence of CRM, research was in need of a more precise structure. Varadarajan and Menon consolidated different understandings of what CRM represents, including sales promotion, a forming of philanthropy, corporate sponsorship, charity, and funding [7]. To their understanding, CRM is a "marketing activity" that contains elements of these concepts. They provided a first formal definition:

> Cause-related marketing is the process of formulating and implementing marketing activities that are characterized by an offer from the firm to contribute a specified amount to a designated cause when customers engage in revenue-providing exchanges that satisfy organizational and individual objectives [7].

According to this definition, CRM is not limited to a certain industrial segment or branch. And indeed during the following years up to now, prominent companies of all sizes made intensive use of various CRM campaigns bearing in mind their resources. Prominent examples include Starbucks, the Coca Cola scholar program[1] that awarded sustainable scholarships to students [8], or a Procter & Gamble campaign called "Open Minds"[2] that supported children with special needs. CRM activities pervaded other areas like sports, e.g. a NIKE cooperation with Lance Armstrong's Livestrong foundation [9]. This example, however, also envisions potential risks which exist for companies, e.g. if bad headlines (here a doping incident) are associated with the campaign.

One of the main characteristics lies in the nature of CRM to produce benefit for many groups involved including nonprofit organizations that often receive the donations made by companies [3]. Because potential benefits are arguably obvious for donating companies and receiving organizations, a large CRM research stream evolved for a third group of entities, the customers. Roberts early reflected CRM from this perspective and identified a grown awareness of customers towards the companies' manufacturing processes [10]. For companies, CRM is also a direct reaction to demonstrate social responsibility for the environment in front of customers. Hence, they need to draw the excitement of customers and get them involved, as all "CRM campaigns should benefit from involvement" [11].

2.2 Conceptualization of Media Research Frameworks: Te'Eni and MST

Regardless in which way interaction and communication between companies, donationving organizations and consumers is perceived by the three respective entities, the various types of CRM all have a strong media integration in common. Media support through diverse channels has always been the key factor since the beginning of CRM campaigns, accompanied by additional actions [12].

Research on selection of appropriate media channels to initiate communication has a long tradition, starting with basic conceptualizations of information transfers between senders (or transmitters) and receivers by Shannon and Weaver [13]. A first framework for media selection that is still widely used today for theoretical foundations was the Media Richness Theory [14]. The differentiation ranged between lean media types like (bulk) e-mails and posters, and effective, rich types like face-to-face meetings or later, supported by technological progress, video conferences. These types, from a technical perspective, form the basis for Te'Eni's cognitive affective model category "medium" [4]. The communication process constituted in this model consists of a "goal", "strategies" to fulfill this goal which are selected by the sender and affected by the chosen "medium" and "message form". The combination of all four elements account for the overall level of "communication complexity" [15]. We will use this theoretical conceptualization of Te'Eni as the basis for the design of our empirical study and apply it to the case of Volvic in the next section.

---

[1] http://www.coca-colacompany.com/stories/education/.

[2] http://nichestudio.com.my/openminds/.

Beside Te'Eni's model, the Media Synchronicity Theory (MST) was first intro-duced in 1999 at the HICSS conference [16] and completely postulated by Dennis et al. [5] in 2008. The authors predominantly focus on two transmission features which they call "conveyance" and "convergence". Conveyance describes the processing of a message that is of high content quality, is spread out slowly from multiples sources, and requires low synchronicity between both ends of the communication (sender and receiver). Convergence, on the other hand, takes the obverse characteristics: lower content quality, fast, and with a high level of synchronicity. Fur our purposes, we choose MST as a supporting concept, as we mainly focus on media selection and interaction of various media channels in this study. This focus is not originally intended by the MST authors who aim at explaining media performance with their model. Media selection was only part of a later extension of MST [17].

2.3   CRM in the Social Media Era: The Case of Volvic

Our digital perception changed over the last decade, triggered by the technological progress. Unidirectional devices like televisions turned into media centers and are connected with mobile devices, predominantly smartphones and tablets. Ley et al. [18] identified specific roles we as users attribute to our devices, and new concepts evolved and culminated with the rise of social media services [19]. Popular services we are familiar with including Facebook, YouTube, Twitter, Instagram, LinkedIn and countless other variations are established on the digital market nowadays. Kaplan and Haenlein categorize the concept of social media and understand services in this field as "a group of Internet-based applications that build on the ideological and technological foundations of Web 2.0, and that allow the creation and exchange of User Generated Content" [20]. We follow this definition for the purpose of our study.

CRM is used by companies to actively communicate their social engagement, on the one hand to draw attention to the corresponding cause, and on the other hand to allure new potential customers. According to the theoretical concepts of Te'eni and MST, media as the transmitting unit plays a key role. Companies not only participate in social media services, but also have begun to capitalize from expanding their general marketing strategy to the social media environment. Ongoing research in this field reveal that CRM initiatives increase users' brand awareness and their willingness to share their appreciation with friends through invitations [21]. Furlow [22] gives a case-study based overview of three CRM campaigns on Facebook by Procter & Gamble (P&G), Target, and Walmart. Among them, one (P&G) describes the suc-cessful connection between an offline purchase of a product and online involvement in a bird rescue project via Facebook. This motivated us to deeper investigate the CRM campaign by Volvic which also made use of a combination of on- and offline channels.

Based on previous theoretical analyses, we decided to empirically investigate the CRM campaign "1L =10L for Africa" of Danone via its brand "Volvic" in this study[3]. The concept behind this campaign which started in 2005 is a pioneering idea of

---

[3] In cooperation with UNICEF, the campaign "1L =10L for Africa" was also named "Drink 1, Give 10" (http://drink1give10.com/).

combining bottled water purchases with social engagement: For each liter of bottle Volvic water sold, the company obligates to provide 10 L of drinking water for people in need from Ethiopia and other countries in Africa. The campaign was initially launched in Germany, and at later stages extended into other markets in industrialized countries, e.g. USA, UK, France or Japan. We used the CRM campaign of Volvic in this study as bottled water is an archaic, timeless product everyone is most likely confronted with. Water is also specifically eligible in the field of CRM and corporate social responsibility research, and other research projects successfully applied the combination of CRM and social media, e.g. Paek et al. [21]. The campaign itself was successful from an economic point of view as Danone could increase the brand awareness of Volvic and respective sales [23]. However, less is known about the different communication channels used in this campaign and their joint impact on the consumers. Hill and Moran [24] confront research findings from studies which analyzed on- and offline-driven social marketing campaigns. They reveal a contradiction between studies in terms of stronger behavioral influence caused by on- or offline

Table 1. Volvic's CRM campaign applied to Te'Eni's model of communication [4]

Attribute	Explanations	Volvic campaign
Goal	**Influence**: "Attempting to influence behavior and attitude [...]" **Instruction Action**: "Getting the receiver to act according to the sender's wishes."	Drawing compassion for people in need of drinkable water Forwarding of the campaign; Buying Volvic water
Strategies	**Contextualization**: "Provision of affective components (emotions, moods) in messages." **Attention focusing**: "Directing or manipulating the receiver's information processing."	 Pictures (print) Video (YouTube)
Medium	**Channel capacity**: The medium's potential to transmit a high variety of cues and languages.	Picture + Text (Facebook) Video (YouTube) Picture (Print) Positioner / Poster (PoS)
Message Form	**Size**: Number of semantic units. **Organization**: The extent to which the message is ordered to support mutual understanding.	Limited to area of campaign (offline); Unlimited (social media) Interaction through comments (YouTube, Facebook) No interaction (Offline)

campaigns. The Volvic case is suitable in this sense, as it was put into practice through four different channels: (1) The social network service Facebook, (2) the video platform YouTube, offline with (3) magazine and newspaper advertisement (print) as well as (4) in stores at the point-of-sale (PoS).

We contribute to CRM research in the way that we combine these four different communication channels without hierarchically preferring one over another. According to the conceptual model of Te'eni [4], we apply the Volvic campaign to the four pillars "goal", "strategies", "medium", and "message form" (Table 1).

It is necessary to analyze the whole Volvic campaign and, thus, to receive information on all four communication channels. In order to differentiate between the channels more adequately, we use the "conveyance" and "convergence" characteristics of MST. Both offline channels, print and PoS, can be characterized as rather conveyance ways to present a message. Multiple sources, i.e. advertisements in various magazines in newspapers, spread out the message of people in need of drinkable water slowly and passively, though intensively shaping "the understanding of the receiver" [15]. Depending on how Facebook and YouTube are used, both social media services can be classified as conveyance or convergence processes [25]. Volvic presented a video on YouTube showing children in Africa in front of already constructed fountains as a stimulus (element supporting conveyance), still allowing users comments below the video (element supporting convergence). On Facebook, users received, besides the picture also presented in the magazines and newspapers, additional news updates via the timeline by Volvic employees. A crosslink to the YouTube channel was also integrated, making Facebook a hybrid communication channel as well. Based on these classifications, we derived the following research model which we use as the basis for our empirical analysis (Fig. 1):

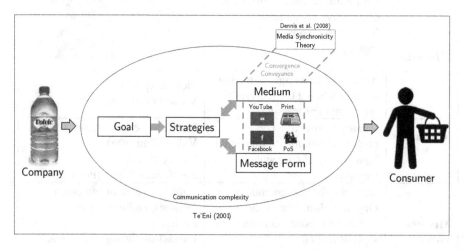

Fig. 1. Research model of the Volvic CRM campaign

3   Research Methodology: Online Questionnaire Design

Volvic's CRM campaign "1L =10L for Africa" was simultaneously launched online on Facebook and YouTube, offline through various print advertisings in magazines, newspapers, and at point of sale. In order to analyze how consumers react on this stimulus, we decided to develop a questionnaire that reflects the individual perception of participants through all four communication channels. In line with its business model, YouTube was exclusively used by Volvic as a platform to share the campaign video. Thus, an online survey suited best for our purposes because it was possible to directly integrate the video within the survey system. We used the free open-source software "Limesurvey"[4] to implement the survey.

Our questionnaire design followed a funnel approach design, narrowing down from general to specific, content-related questions [26]. It was split into several sections and started with initial questions on demographics ("age", "gender", "profession") including online behavior. In a second section we asked the respondents to assess their engagement in the society. Questions included participation in blood donations, waste separation, and ecology among others. It helped us to receive a general understanding of each participant's mindset before we focus on questions addressing the purchase behavior in terms of water, like frequency, brands, and Volvic in particular (e.g. "How often do you drink Volvic", "How often do you buy Volvic", "How well do you know Volvic as a brand").

We than addressed the core topic of our empirical investigation, Volvic's CRM campaign. For both the two offline channels as well as the two social media services, we combined the unique form of display used by Volvic with an identical set of homogeneous questions. Directly after presenting the campaign display, a "Timeline Screenshot" (Facebook), the integrated "campaign video" (YouTube), an original "advertising" from a magazine (print), and a visualization of a "positioner in a shop" (PoS), we asked participants to rate how emotionally provoked they are by the display. They then should state their "intention to purchase Volvic bottled water" and, depending on their answer, were ask to give reason for their decision. The full sequence of questions is visualized in Fig. 2.

Volvic did not concentrate on a specific target group with their campaign. The cause of affordable, drinkable water in Africa should be recognized by as many consumers as possible. However, the campaigns on the respective markets varied in terms of language and content. Hence, we focused on Germany as the campaign was first started in this market and it is an important one with the highest amount of still mineral water exports for Volvic. We followed this approach and neither limited the questionnaire access to a specific target group. The link to the survey was distributed through various on- and offline channels including short URL aliases to ease mobile access. Most of the questions were designed as single choice checkboxes and, especially in the CRM campaign (4) as 5-point Likert scales in preparation for the ordinal logistic regression analysis. Both descriptive results and results of our regression analysis are discussed in the next section.

---

[4] https://www.limesurvey.org.

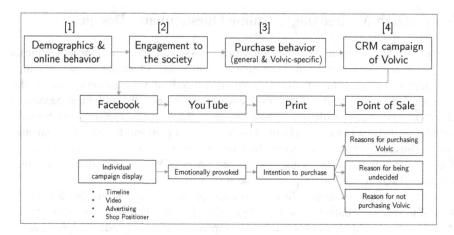

Fig. 2. Section and path of the Volvic CRM campaign questionnaire

4 Results

4.1 Initial Descriptive Outcomes

Our online survey was accessible to the public in a timeframe between 20 November and 12 December 2015 on Limesurvey after a phase of two weeks in which we pretested and optimized especially the section where the campaigns were displayed. We received n = 131 responses that were completely filled. An initial analysis of these answers revealed that according to the response time that was tracked at runtime, 17 participants finished the survey in less than five minutes. However, the YouTube display – a video of 2.48 min' length – suggests that it is impossible to answer all questions appropriately in under five minutes. As data reliability was not given for them, we excluded these participants and received a final sample size of n = 114.

To understand the demographic structure of our sample, we first analyzed the descriptive results of the first survey section. For this and all further calculations, the statistics software IBM SPSS Statistics 22 was used. A weak majority of participants are female (n = 68; 59.6 %) compared to slightly fewer males (n = 46; 40.4 %). On average our respondents are 26.84 (sd: 5.28) years old. From the initial data screening we could see that a minority of people were older than 35 years at the time of their responding. Thus, we decided to go deeper with our investigations and analyzed the age structure in a histogram. Compared to the normal distribution, we can see a potentially high kurtosis with a strong peak around mean. We calculated the values for measure of central tendency and divided the value for kurtosis (5.85) over its corresponding standard error (0.449). The excess value we received (13.01) indicates a heavy-tailed distribution [27]. The skewness of the sample is near normal distribution and only few older outliers influence the measurement. Overall, further calculations are not likely affected by the age distribution.

Results for online and social media behavior reveal a high penetration rate within our sample. Regular internet availability – a crucial barrier for CRM initiatives that are also

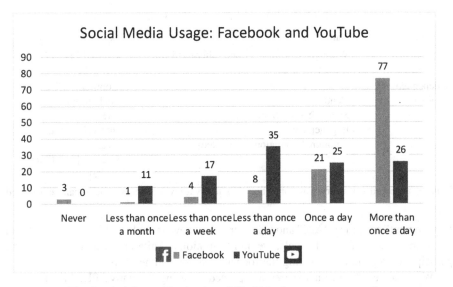

Fig. 3. Activity on Facebook and YouTube in our survey sample

run online – is no factor because nearly all participants (n = 112; 98.2 %) accessed the internet more than once a day, the two remaining participants on average once a day. Both social media services are frequently used in this sample, with Facebook (n = 96, 84.2 %) dominating over YouTube (n = 45; 48.3 %) regarding daily user visits (Fig. 3).

Concerning the social and environmental engagement, the overall commitment is on an average level. On a 5-point Likert scale, a majority of n = 47 (41.2 %) participants indicate moderate involvement (score of 3). Waste separation was the individual activity with the highest level of commitment: 74 respondents (64.9 %) separate their waste regularly. Section three of the questionnaire addresses the purchase behavior with regard to water in general, and Volvic in particular. A majority of 73.7 % (n = 84) buys water on a regular basis more than once in a month and n = 17 (14.9 %) of the participants claim to buy large amounts of water ahead (n = 17). They favor a huge variety of 28 different local, national, and international brands. Only the remaining 13 respondents exclusively drink tap water. Volvic is the first choice of 17.5 % (n = 10) participants, but it is in favor of as many as 36 % (n = 41) who state that they have a "positive" or "very positive" attitude towards the brand.

4.2 Ordinal Logistic Regression Analysis

For the final core Sect. 4 of our questionnaire, we calculated an ordinal logistic regression for all four communications channels, with Facebook and YouTube representing social media while print and PoS account for traditional channels. This regression type is dedicated to ordinal dependent variables which we use in all four scenarios [28]. "Willingness to buy Volvic" was measured on an ordinal scale with the answer options "Yes" and "No" as well as "Maybe" in between. As independent variables, we took into account one case-related and two basic demographic variables also used by Webb and Mohr [29] in their CRM study, "Social & Environmental

Table 2. Overview of regression variables

Variable type	Name	Scale
Dependent variable	Willingness to buy Volvic [alternated for each channel]	Ordinal [Yes | No | Maybe]
Independent variables	Age	Continuous [in Years]
	Gender	Dichotomous [male | female]
	Social & Environmental Engagement	Interval [1–5 Likert scale][a]
	Emotional Agitation [alternated]	Interval [1–5 Likert scale]

[a]Equidistance and symmetry was controlled thus interval level of measurement can be assumed

Engagement" as well as "Age" and "Gender". As a new variable to differentiate between social media and offline channels, we add "Emotional Agitation" which measures the participant's reaction after facing the four alternative channel displays (Table 2).

We followed the ordinal regression procedure using the native PLUM estimation offered by SPSS. For all four channels, the regression was calculated individually with the corresponding values for the alternating independent and the dependent variable. We calculated the two social media models first and started with Facebook. First, we looked at the model fit and the deviance goodness-of-fit test indicated that the model was a good fit to the observed data as the Chi-Square is not significant ($\chi 2$ $(188) = 183.877$, $p = .071$). However, the Pearson value was significant though and we refer to the likelihood-ratio instead to decide. Here, the complete model with all four independent variables revealed a better fit than the intercept model ($\chi 2$ $(4) = 25.784$, $p < 0.001$) indicating a suitable model fit. We proceeded to derive the regression equation for the Facebook case. In an ordinal regression with three categories ("No", "Maybe", "Yes"), two equations exist to describe the threshold between the categories. The regression then predicts with the help of probabilities in which category a person will be classified based on his or her characteristics (in terms of the independent variables) [30]. For Facebook, the following regression estimates result from the survey:

$$\ln\left(Buy\_Volvic_{Facebook \leq "No"}\right)$$
$$= -1.463$$
$$- (-.119 * male - 0.117 * age + 0.144 * engagement + 0.710 * emotion\_Facebook)$$

$$\ln\left(Buy\_Volvic_{Facebook \leq "Maybe"}\right)$$
$$= -0.054$$
$$- (-.119 * male - 0.117 * age + 0.144 * engagement + 0.710 * emotion\_Facebook)$$

Table 3 (a-d). Ordinal logic regression results

Facebook (FB)		Estimate	Std. Error	Wald	df	Sig.	Exp_B
Threshold	[FB_buy = 0]	-1.463	1.639	1.426	1	0.232	0.231
	[FB_buy = 1]	-0.054	1.594	0.002	1	0.965	0.948
Location	Age	-0.117	0.043	7.328	1	0.007	0.889
	Engagement	0.144	0.209	0.473	1	0.492	1.155
	Emotion	0.710	0.183	14.980	1	0.000	2.034
	[Gender = 0]	-0.119	0.386	0.095	1	0.758	0.888
	[Gender = 1]	0[a]			0		1.000

Link function: Logit. | a. This parameter is set to zero because it is redundant.

YouTube (YT)		Estimate	Std. Error	Wald	df	Sig.	Exp_B
Threshold	[YT_buy = 0]	-0.535	1.235	0.188	1	0.665	0.585
	[YT_buy = 1]	1.340	1.242	1.163	1	0.281	3.819
Location	Age	-0.090	0.040	5.118	1	0.024	0.914
	Engagement	-0.320	0.216	2.194	1	0.139	0.726
	Emotion	1.102	0.211	27.345	1	0.000	3.011
	[Gender = 0]	0.053	0.404	.0170	1	0.896	1.054
	[Gender = 1]	0[a]			0		1.000

Link function: Logit. | a. This parameter is set to zero because it is redundant.

Print		Estimate	Std. Error	Wald	df	Sig.	Exp_B
Threshold	[Print_buy = 0]	-0.545	1.257	0.188	1	0.665	0.580
	[Print_buy = 1]	1.341	1.267	1.120	1	0.290	3.821
Location	Age	-0.105	0.045	5.520	1	0.019	0.900
	Engagement	0.011	0.217	0.002	1	0.961	1.011
	Emotion	1.026	0.192	28.643	1	0.000	2.790
	[Gender = 0]	0.229	0.400	0.327	1	0.568	1.257
	[Gender = 1]	0[a]			0		1.000

Link function: Logit. | a. This parameter is set to zero because it is redundant.

Point of Sale (PoS)		Estimate	Std. Error	Wald	df	Sig.	Exp_B
Threshold	[PoS_buy = 0]	-2.164	1.350	2.569	1	0.109	0.115
	[PoS_buy = 1]	-0.330	1.340	0.061	1	0.805	0.719
Location	Age	-0.129	0.047	7.331	1	0.007	0.879
	Engagement	-0.152	0.228	0.446	1	0.504	0.859
	Emotion	1.076	0.190	32.142	1	0.000	2.932
	[Gender = 0]	-0.476	0.410	1.347	1	0.246	0.621
	[Gender = 1]	0[a]			0		1.000

Link function: Logit. | a. This parameter is set to zero because it is redundant.

The negative log odd value coefficients result from the fact that the ordinal scale of the dependent variable "Willingness to buy" was categorized from 0 = "No" to 2 = "Yes". For age, an increase of one year results in an increase in the odds of considering to buy a bottle of Volvic water after seeing the Facebook campaign. The odds ratio is 0.889 and significant (Wald $\chi2(1)$ = 7.328, p < 0.01). Emotional agitation after the display on Facebook has the highest coefficient in the equation and its impact (odd ratio: 2.034) is also highly significant (Wald $\chi2(1)$ = 14.980, p < 0.001). We applied this procedure three more times for the CRM campaigns on YouTube, the print campaign and PoS. All results are summarized in Tables 3 a–d:

5 Discussion

The empirical results and especially those of our ordinal logistic regression contribute to finding an answer to the main research question which was initially drawn in the introduction. According to our data, social media channels can have a different impact on the outcome and perception of a cause-related marketing campaign. Results further reveal that companies can consider online channels, and especially social media services, as appropriate and adequate.

If we compare both social media services which we analyzed in this study, we see from the coefficients that Facebook has a lower overall impact compared to YouTube. Emotional agitation is for both services the most influencing trigger in the equation towards user perception that drives the buying intention in the end. This is supported by the strong statistical significances. However, contrasting both services with each other reveal differences. Videos as presented by Volvic on YouTube can touch users deeper than a mixture of various stimuli like it was the case on Volvic's Facebook appearance. In fact, if we take all four channels into account, this Facebook display underperforms. Both point-of-sale and print advertising displays drew more attention to the participants, resulting in stronger coefficient values.

Concerning the other input variables, gender and social engagement differences also contribute to the success of a CRM campaign, but play a minor role. Gender difference did not occur as the Volvic cause addresses a problem everyone is involved in and which does not include any gender-specific topics in particular. Age is an important factor and significant for all channels on the 1 % (PoS and FB) or 5 % (Print and YouTube) confidence interval. Estimates range between −0.09 (YouTube) and −0.129 (PoS). These low difference can be explained by the high kurtosis in our sample that sets up a rather centroid distribution.

As described in the theoretical section and visualized in our research model, we mainly lean on Te'Eni's model of communication and its focus on message transfer with the help of adequate media. Volvic's campaign can be assessed as successful not only regarding the overall perception by customers. Additionally, it can be seen as a positive example of how the interplay can work out between various on- and offline channels, or – to use Te'Eni's vocabulary – types of "media". Volvic's CRM campaign capitalized from the individual opportunities offered by the channels, thus transferring the "message" in effective manners. They presented a campaign video and offered user comments on YouTube which according to MST fulfils both conveyance and convergence.

Our empirical results revealed that the impact of the Facebook campaign was rather low, but still existent. Most likely, that is also caused by the combination of conveyance and convergence and the fact that more users are active on Facebook.

In summary, our empirical findings reveal a strong impact of social media services on the perception of cause-related marketing campaigns. A key advantage is that most likely different target groups will be addressed. While PoS and print advertising in newspapers or magazines draw the attention of all user groups, social media can also address all these groups, but is specifically interesting for younger users [31]. Thus, a holistic coverage of all age groups can be established and CRM campaigns can capitalize from synergies of both sides. Instead of replacing traditional channels like print advertising or point-of-sale, companies should strive for a mélange of various channel types. By applying this "strategy", they can draw the attention of as many customers as possible through alternating displays and ultimately reach their pursued "goal" and the deepest impact.

6 Conclusion

In this study we contribute to the question if and in which way social media services like Facebook and YouTube can support a positive customer perception of cause-related marketing campaigns. Our empirical results reveal, based on ordinal logistic regression analyses, that social media services have a huge impact, but must not be seen isolated. These findings lead to more implications relevant for practitioners and raise new questions for further research projects.

Some practical insights for successful CRM campaigns can be derived from our findings. Companies should rely on social media services as many potential or active customers use these services and can be addressed easily. Key to achieving positive effects is an adequate display suitable for the respective service. For YouTube, a single video with an enabled comment function can be enough to gain these effects. Facebook, however, can primarily serve as a more general first place to go in the social media environment. With respect to their overall marketing strategy, companies benefit best from implementing social media services into it rather than replacing traditional services like print or PoS.

From an academic perspective, this study helps social media research to position itself more appropriately. It provides researchers with a way to convey established communication frameworks like Te'Eni's model or MST to researchers of other fields. In particular, we aimed at getting better connected with established marketing research streams without obliterating its technological uniqueness. Also, we strengthened social media research in term of empirical investigations of effects caused by services like Facebook or YouTube. However, our findings are limited by some assumptions we had to make in our research design and which can serve as links to further research. First, we concentrated on two dominant services, but social media is a fast moving topic. Thus, more services on the rise, e.g. Twitter or Instagram, should be addressed. Second, we have a decent sample, but it is focused on German-speaking participants. Research projects based on our setting could analyze CRM campaigns in other countries, and focus on intercultural differences regarding social media utilization.

References

1. American Express Company. http://about.americanexpress.com/csr/pip.aspx
2. Ross Iii, J.K., Patterson, L.T., Stutts, M.A.: Consumer perceptions of organizations that use cause-related marketing. J. Acad. Market. Sci. **20**, 93 (1992)
3. Berglind, M., Nakata, C.: Cause-related marketing: more buck than bang? Bus. Horiz. **48**, 443–453 (2005)
4. Te'Eni, D.: Review: a cognitive-affective model of organizational communication for designing IT. MIS Q. **25**, 251–312 (2001)
5. Dennis, A.R., Fuller, R.M., Valacich, J.S.: Media, tasks, and communication processes: a theory of media synchronicity. Bus. Horiz. **32**, 575–600 (2008)
6. Stroup, M.A., Neubert, R.L., Anderson, J.W.: Doing good, doing better: two views of social responsibility. Bus. Horiz. **30**, 22–25 (1987)
7. Varadarajan, P.R., Menon, A.: Cause-related marketing: a coalignment of marketing strategy and corporate philanthropy. J. Market. **52**, 58–74 (1988)
8. Slater, J.: Philanthropy for profit. Far Eastern Econ. Rev. **163**, 48 (2000)
9. McGlone, C., Martin, N.: Nike's corporate interest lives strong: a case of cause-related marketing and leveraging. Sport Market. Q. **15**, 184–188 (2006)
10. Roberts, J.A.: Will the real socially responsible consumer please step forward? Bus. Horiz. **39**, 79–83 (1996)
11. Grau, S.L., Folse, J.A.G.: Cause-related marketing (CRM). the influence of donation proximity and message-framing cues on the less-involved consumer. J. Advertising **36**, 19–33 (2007)
12. Smith, S.M., Alcorn, D.S.: Cause marketing: a new direction in the marketing of corporate responsibility. J. Serv. Market. **5**, 21 (1991)
13. Shannon, C.E., Weaver, W.: The Mathematical Theory of Communication. University of Illinois Press, Champaign (1949)
14. Daft, R.L., Lengel, R.H.: Organizational information requirements, media richness and structural design. Manag. Sci. **32**, 554–571 (1986)
15. George, J.F., Carlson, J.R., Valacich, J.S.: Media selection as a strategic component of communication. MIS Q. **37**, 1233–1251 (2013)
16. Dennis, A.R., Valacich, J.S.: Rethinking media richness: towards a theory of media synchronicity. In: Proceedings of the 32nd Annual Hawaii International Conference on Systems Sciences (HICSS), p. 1017 (1999)
17. Dennis, A.R., Fuller, R.M., Valacich, J.S.: Media synchronicity and media choice: choosing media for performance. In: Hartmann, T. (ed.) Media Choice: A Theoretical and Empirical Overview. Routledge, New York (2009)
18. Ley, B., Ogonowski, C., Hess, J., Reichling, T., Wan, L., Wulf, V.: Impacts of new technologies on media usage and social behaviour in domestic environments. Behav. Inf. Technol. **33**, 815–828 (2014)
19. Boyd, D.M., Ellison, N.B.: Social network sites: definition, history, and scholarship. J. Comput. Mediated Commun. **13**, 210–230 (2007)
20. Kaplan, A.M., Haenlein, M.: Users of the world, unite! The challenges and opportunities of Social Media. Bus. Horiz. **53**, 59–68 (2010)
21. Jeong, H.J., Paek, H.-J., Lee, M.: Corporate social responsibility effects on social network sites. J. Bus. Res. **66**, 1889–1895 (2013)
22. Furlow, N.E.: Find us on Facebook: how cause marketing has embraced social media. J. Market. Dev. Competitiveness **5**, 61–64 (2011)

23. Brei, V., Böhm, S.: '1L=10L for Africa': corporate social responsibility and the transformation of bottled water into a 'consumer activist' commodity. Discourse Soc. **25**, 3–31 (2014)
24. Hill, R.P., Moran, N.: Social marketing meets interactive media. Int. J. Advertising **30**, 815–838 (2011)
25. Bühler, J., Lauritzen, M., Bick, M.: Social Media communication in European airlines. In: Proceedings of the 20th Americas Conference on Information Systems, Savannah, GA (2014)
26. Hair, J.F., Black, W.C., Babin, B.J., Anderson, R.E.: Multivariate Data Analysis. Prentice Hall, Upper Saddle River (2010)
27. Miles, J., Shevlin, M.: Applying Regression & Correlation: A Guide for Students and Researchers. SAGE Publications, London, Thousand Oaks (2001)
28. Agresti, A.: Categorical Data Analysis. Wiley-Interscience, Hoboken (2013)
29. Webb, D.J., Mohr, L.A.: A typology of consumer responses to cause-related marketing: from skeptics to socially concerned. J. Public Policy Market. **17**, 226–238 (1998)
30. O'Connell, A.A.: Logistic Regression Models for Ordinal Response Variables. SAGE Publications, Thousand Oaks (2006)
31. van Bergh, J.D., Behrer, M.: How Cool Brands Stay Hot. Branding to Generation Y. Kogan Page, London, Philadelphia (2011)

Corporate Social Responsibility Campaigns in the Digital Age: The Case of Vodafone "Red Light Application/Between Us"

Muge Elden, Sinem Yeygel Cakir, and Ugur Bakir[✉]

Ege University, İzmir, Turkey
{muge.elden.pogun,sinem.yeygel,ugur.bakir}@ege.edu.tr

Abstract. The aim of this study is to reveal how new communication technologies affect corporate social responsibility campaigns by analyzing the new dimensions that corporate social responsibility campaigns acquired in the new digital era from the standpoint of the advertisers who have created these campaigns. Within the scope of this study, the social responsibility campaign undertaken by Vodafone has been investigated in its various characteristics and the study data has been obtained using the in-depth interview technique with the team of the advertisers who created the campaign. In the analysis of data obtained after interviews with the participants forming the team that created the Vodafone "Red Light Application/Between Us" social responsibility campaign it was seen that the data is grouped around three themes: These are; (1) society lifting, (2) effects of digital media and (3) "Between us" Campaign.

Keywords: Corporate social responsibility · Digital marketing · Society lifting · Vodafone · Red Light Application

1 Introduction

In terms of a corporation creating a positive image for its target groups, in addition to having quality goods and services, efficient distribution channels, successful pricing policies and a deep-rooted history, a significant factor is the demonstration of sensitivity towards social issues. In this respect, corporate activities, which are created to increase public awareness of social responsibility in contemporary marketing, have begun to gain more significance.

Moreover, these days it is no longer sufficient for a corporation's social responsibility activities to direct attention towards a single social problem, and raise public awareness about it. Target groups expect corporations to create behavioral change or to have an effect on the public as well, and the corporations that succeed in this are those that sign up for more resourceful social responsibility activities. These kinds of social responsibility campaigns, which create participation on the behavioral level beyond that of creating social awareness and create strong changes in attitudes, cause society to develop through the solving of social problems, raising societies to higher levels of awareness.

© IFIP International Federation for Information Processing 2016
Published by Springer International Publishing Switzerland 2016. All Rights Reserved
Y.K. Dwivedi et al. (Eds.): I3E 2016, LNCS 9844, pp. 120–127, 2016.
DOI: 10.1007/978-3-319-45234-0_11

In addition to this, along with current developments in information communication technologies, corporations are able to involve individuals more effectively in their social responsibility campaigns and their target groups become team friends and solution partners. Digital media that has a personalized communication structure makes it possible to reach a specific audience or a specific person as a target audience with a specific content (Zeff and Aronson 1999:11). At this point, information and communication technologies, specifically created for the target audience, can change the users' attitude and behaviors by using symbolic and perceptual contents for senses; and can operate a convincing communication process by directing the target audience (Canaday 2004).

In this respect, the Vodafone Red Light Application/Between Us social responsibility campaign on violence towards women, carried out by Vodafone in 2015, is a successful example of integrating informative communication technologies with corporate social responsibility campaigns.

2   Background

Corporate social responsibility campaigns are applications which involve a corporation focusing attention on a social problem in order to create a benefit at the point of strategically reaching its marketing goals and serve to create a mutual benefit for both the society and the brands (Pringle and Thompson 1999:3). When a changing market and contemporary consumer structures are taken into consideration, corporate social responsibility becomes of increasing concern and holds strategic implications for companies across industries (Hsu 2012:189). As the research conducted also shows, consumers are more willing to buy goods that are specifically created for social responsibility campaigns, or associated with these campaigns, changing their buying preferences in the favor of those corporations that are more sensitive in terms of their social responsibility (Assioras et al. 2010:211). With regard to this aspect, besides making a positive contribution by showing their sensitivity towards the social environments in which they are active, thereby attributing a positive quality to their corporate image, corporate social responsibility campaigns are activities that generate additional financial benefits for the corporations.

The most important fundamental factor influencing the success of a corporate social responsibility campaign is that the campaigns' objectives are integrated into society; in other words, individuals can be made an integral part of the campaigns. At this point, the Internet and social media attract attention, as effective tools for making individuals a part of a social responsibility campaign, triggering the masses in the axis of a common goal. The pressure- removing characteristic of information communication Technologies in terms of time and geographical borders, adds strength to corporate social responsibility campaigns in the sense that they are applicable for whatever reason, by anyone, at any place and time. So much so, that this flexibility brings along with it the opportunity for corporations to act together with their shareholders through global networks in corporate social responsibility campaigns (Hasnaoui and Freeman 2010:397).

Corporations transmit their corporate social responsibility principles, philosophies and detailed information about the corporate social responsibility they implement to their target groups, through official websites and are able to shape networks that consist of businesses, civil society organizations or shareholders (Wang 2009:63). In addition, new media environments, such as Facebook and Twitter, embody a strong effect in their own structure, which removes limitations of time and place in speed, direct interaction, and dialogue, creating participation. This characteristic allows groups, which geographically inhabit different places, to easily come together and share with each other and the network movements, activism, increase the new social movements (Schultz et al. 2013:685). In terms of a movement being initiated in this direction, Web 2.0 applications, which have a more dynamic and interactive structure and efficiency in terms creating social media in which context is produced by users themselves, have assumed a more significant role than Web 1.0 technologies, the websites of which have a static appearance (Bakker and Hellsten 2013:808).

In particular, the effective use of new media in corporate social responsibility campaigns has given provided a platform for the formation of a sustainable structure during the process of communication. During the corporate social responsibility campaigns carried out using social media channels, corporations carry the responsibility of spreading the themes, thoughts, and facts through the Networks in which they are also involved. Information communication technologies, in particular social media channels, present the opportunity for active participation in the creation and management of information (Hasnaoui and Freeman 2010:398). The magic, which is inherent in the Internet, offers advantages to corporations, in terms of spreading information in corporate social responsibility applications, adding understanding and acceleration, and presenting depth through multi channels, realizing problem management immediately on the receipt of feedback, and building a democratic structure in the communication process (Nwagbara and Reid 2013:410).

The structure of social media, which consists of groups that cluster around common points of interest, gives rise to applications that are carried out with common objectives and understandings; something that is regarded as normal in the corporate social responsibility campaigns realized through this channel (Hasnaoui and Freeman 2010:399). This paves the way for the birth of corporate social responsibility applications, which are continuously enriched contextually by the members of the network, where interactive communication within the scope of applications is achieved at the top level, and thus are added to the process by making the participation of the target group to the campaign possible, sustainable, and fast spreading, whereby numerous shareholders are able to come together from different geographical areas and with high synergy.

3   Campaign Overview

Violence towards women is a widely seen social problem in Turkey, which results in many women being the victims of serious physical injury and mental abuse every year, and in some cases causing their death. Vodaphone's social responsibility campaign on violence towards women is built on an application operating in smart phones, which used by women to call for help if they are being subjected to violence. The Vodafone Red Light Application, which allows women to easily notify the police or their significant others, makes it possible to call three people with a single button, to ask for help and send an emergency message by shaking the phone. So that men do not understand what the application does, it is only women to know, it is uploaded on phones to appear like a flashlight. In addition, the application has been presented to women where men had no access; women have been informed about the red light application in areas such as ladies' rooms, lingerie tags and waxing strips which change color when heated. In addition, Vodafone, which has advertised in newspapers and areas such as ladies' rooms, where only women can visit, has videos containing the secret message of the campaign to direct them to microsites. The scope of the campaign has resulted in hundreds of thousands of women downloading the application on their phones within a short period of time, sharing it on social media through coded messages which men cannot understand. Vodafone's Between Us campaign has received the Grand Prix award at the Cannes Lions International Creativity Festival, in the Media category, the Grand CLIO award, the Golden Award, in the Integrated Campaign award at the CLIO Awards, and the silver award in the Digital category.

4 Methodological Considerations

In this study, corporate social responsibility campaigns, which take on new shapes within the scope of developments in the information communication technologies of the digital age, are dealt with through the campaign creators' perspective. In this study, qualitative research is preferred and a sample case is analyzed, showing how advertisers approach social responsibility campaigns in the digital age, and the new application styles in these campaigns are dealt with through the Vodafone "Red Light Application/Between Us" application, which has recently received awards on the international platform, and the perspective of the team which created it.

The research data were obtained from participants who were identified by snowball sampling using in depth interview technique. Participants working within body of Team Red that was established as an "exclusive" agency to carry out the activities of marketing communications regarding Vodafone in tandem with Young & Rubicam (Y&R) took active part in the process of creating "Between Us" campaign.

Interviews with participants were conducted through internet. First of all, each participant was informed about the aim of the research, and then each participant answered research questions independently from one another. Since the interviews were conducted in Turkish, the research was analyzed in Turkish and translated into English after the whole analysis had been completed. Interpretative phenomenology analysis was used in the analysis of the research data. First of all, researchers read the transcriptions line by line, categorized similar data into the same groups, and developed main themes. Each theme included the opinions of the participants (Table 1).

Table 1. Interviewees

Participant	Workplace	Title
A	Y&R Team Red Istanbul	Strategic planner
B	Y&R Team Red Istanbul	Copywriter
C	Y&R Team Red Istanbul	Art director
D	Y&R Team Red Istanbul	Account executive

After the analysis of the data had been completed, member checking was carried out. Within the scope of member checking, research findings were emailed to the participants, and they were asked if the text reflected their views. After all of the participants gave their approval, the study took its final shape. The data obtained from the research were used in the study with the permission of Y&R Team Red Istanbul and Vodafone Turkey.

5   Findings

After the data obtained from the interviews carried out with the participants involved in the team having created the social responsibility campaign of Vodafone "Red Light Application/Between Us" had been examined, it was observed that the data was collected within the scope of three themes: (1) society lifting, (2) the effects of digital media, and (3) "Between us" Campaign.

5.1   Society Lifting

Advertising professionals interviewed agreed upon the fact that the communication activities that brands carry out due to their social sensitivities can contribute to the solution of social problems. According to them, when right strategies, or implementations are developed, and social responsibility campaigns are not regarded as "show business", socially favorable outcomes are generated. What Strategic Planner A said about this is:

"Today, the fact that governments are unable to completely solve the problems in their countries, the impacts that companies have on the world, and many other reasons attach significant responsibilities to brands and thus, to advertisements. Today, many brands are now trying to provide solutions to issues/problems/social problems stemming from governments or themselves through their communication efforts. The contribution of the brands can be at local level like reviving a local language on the brink of extinction, or at global level like collecting donations to raise awareness for ALS disease."

Advertising professionals state that social responsibility campaigns contribute to brands at more levels than image campaigns do. Although image campaigns are important in terms of establishing emotional ties with consumers by describing the brand philosophy and belief, the expectations of consumers are changing today. What Copywriter B said is:

"While image campaigns remain at one level, communication campaigns focusing on society lifting can leave more long-lasting marks on the lives of consumers. Because image campaigns describe what the company does and its range of products etc. Thus, this means establishing a bond with consumers to some extent. However, communication studies focusing on society lifting usually find solutions to the problem of consumers. I think Turkish consumer, the problem of whom has been addressed never forgets that brand."

5.2   The Effects of Digital Media

According to the Advertising professionals interviewed, digital media has a power of establishing bilateral and effective communication with less people when compared to traditional media. Therefore, corporate social responsibility campaigns find more opportunities to touch the lives of the society in our era by making use of the social media. Nevertheless, benefitting both from the traditional media and corporate social responsibility campaigns may yield effective results in developing counties, especially the ones such as Turkey. What Copywriter B said about this is:

"Since the use of digital media channels is cost-effective, it is beyond that the advantages they offer are great. You can create ten times greater effect by using ten times lower budget compared to the traditional media. Nevertheless, we should not forget the great power of traditional media. Let's not forget your possibility to reach out to the whole Turkey when one of your campaign films is broadcasted during prime time."

5.3   "Between Us" Campaign

The team having created the "Between Us" campaign stated that the aim of their communication and media strategies was to convey the message of "Feel safe with Red Light" to women by using the channels to which only women can be exposed without mentioning the name "Vodafone", and to use the contents that women are sharing on the Internet more day by day. In this regard, the advantages that traditional media offer have not been ignored although this campaign predominantly operates through digital channels. Moreover, all the professionals in the team told that the most important feature of the campaign was the confidence it created by seeking a solution to a social problem with the promise of "confidentiality". The team members told that the insight of the "Between Us" campaign was to "reach out to women target audience through the channels only women can understand, in which men are present".

According to Copywriter B, the general idea of the campaign stemmed from the aim to help women in the presence of violence. Because the previous campaigns run by different brands provided solutions either prior to or after violence. What was aimed with Red Light application is how to stop violence in the presence of violence. Therefore, an application that can be used by women when they are exposed to violence has been created, and was introduced to women through confidential ways, and it was ensured that they used this application when they were exposed to violence.

Art Director C told that the campaign succeeded due to the number of downloads, and making Vodafone innovative, reliable and recommended brand in the eyes of women. Copywriter B gave the following tangible information regarding the success of the campaign:

"A tangible criterion was how many times the application had been downloaded and activated. Application has been downloaded more than 280.000 times, and was activated more than 103.000 times In order to call for help. These results are very good for the work done. On the other hand, they are upsetting results as they show the extent of violence in Turkey. If only we could bring an end to violence, and the violence to women became something we never would come across."

6   General Discussion

Society lifting campaigns offering sustainable and effective solutions to social problems are highly likely to be more successful by differing from other advertisement campaigns. In this context, society lifting campaigns may contribute to the brand preference, consumption and profitability despite not in the short term. The brand health researches conducted regularly by Vodafone brand proved this. Providing bilateral communications with the target audience in corporate social responsibility campaigns, digital media makes campaigns more useful both for the brand and society. However, media planning studies should not be ignored since traditional media can easily access to a greater target audience, particularly in developing countries.

7   Limitations and Future Research

The basic limitations of this study are that the study approaches the subject only from advertisers' perspective, and the data obtained from depth interview technique is related only to the analyzed case. Regarding the limitations of the study, for future studies analyzing the similar cases, it would be useful to address the issue from both brands' and consumers' perspective.

References

Assiouras, I., Siomkos, G., Skourtis, G., Koniordos, M.: Consumer perceptions of corporate social responsibility in the Greek mobile telecommunication industry. Int. J. Manag. Cases 13(3), 210–216 (2010). Special Issue of CIRCLE International Conference

Bakker, F.G.A., Hellsten, I.: Capturing online presence: hyperlinks and semantic networks in activist group websites on corporate social responsibility. J. Bus. Ethics 118(4), 807–823 (2013)

Canaday, V.D.: Persuasive Technology and Emotional Agents. Technical report. Norfolk State University (2004)

Hasnaoui, A., Freeman, I.: Diffusion and implementation of corporate social responsibility (csr): the role of information and communication technologies (ict). Rev. Manag. et Avenir (RMA) 39, 386–406 (2010)

Hsu, K.: The advertising effects of corporate social responsibility on corporate reputation and brand equity: evidence from the life insurance industry in Taiwan. J. Bus. Ethics 109, 189–201 (2012). doi:10.1007/s10551-011-1118-0

Nwagbara, U., Reid, P.: Corporate social responsibility communication in the age of new media: towards the logic of sustainability communication. Rev. Int. Comp. Manag. 14(3), 400–414 (2013)

Pringle, H., Thompson, M.: Brand spirit: how cause related marketing builds brands. Wiley, Chichester (1999)

Schultz, F., Castello, I., Morsing, M.: The construction of corporate social responsibility in network society: a communication view. J. Bus. Ethics **115**(4), 681–692 (2013)

Wang, A.: Perceptions of corporate social responsibility practices on mobile phone companies. Int. J. Mob. Mark. **4**(1), 62–68 (2009)

Zeff, R., Aronson, B.: Advertising on the Internet, 2nd edn. Wiley, New York (1999)

The Impact of Brand Actions on Facebook on the Consumer Mind-Set

Anatoli Colicev[1] and Peter O'Connor[2(✉)]

[1] Graduate School of Business, Nazarbayev University, Astana, Kazakhstan
anatoli.colicev@essec.edu
[2] Essec Business School, Cergy Pontoise, France
oconnor@essec.edu

Abstract. Despite all the surrounding hype, it is still not clear exactly how social media affects consumer behavior. In an effort to contribute to the current debate on the effectiveness of social media marketing this study aims to theorize and empirically demonstrate how brand's social media efforts influence a wide array of consumer mind-set metrics that underlie the consumer purchase decision-making process. Specifically, we relate key dimensions of a brand's social media actions (intensity, valence and richness) to well established consumer mind-set metrics ranging from awareness through attitude to satisfaction. We hypothesize that brand actions' intensity (more brand posts) with neutral valence and richer content will have a strong impact on the consumer mind-set. Using a unique data set that captures both social media and consumer mind-set metrics for multiple brands, we propose empirically testing our model with panel vector auto regression.

Keywords: Social media · Mind-set metrics · Panel vector auto regression

1 Introduction

US companies now spend on average more than 13 % of their marketing budgets on social media (The CMO Survey 2016), with marketers increasingly supplementing traditional marketing efforts with social media activities (Srinivasan et al. 2015). Most Fortune 500 companies have invested in social media presences, including Twitter accounts (73 %), Facebook fan pages (66 %), and YouTube channels (62 %; Heggestuen and Danova 2013). In addition to simply being present, brands typically also engage in proactive activities on social media by creating, developing, and managing online content to help drive consumer conversations (Peters et al. 2013). Brands also try to gain social media exposure through voluntary brand mentions, comments and recommendations from users, all in an effort to ultimately help increase demand for their products. However, to be able to justify the necessary budgets, brands need to be able to demonstrate the impact of these efforts on consumers, something that is currently difficult to do (Hoffman and Fodor 2010).

© IFIP International Federation for Information Processing 2016
Published by Springer International Publishing Switzerland 2016. All Rights Reserved
Y.K. Dwivedi et al. (Eds.): I3E 2016, LNCS 9844, pp. 128–133, 2016.
DOI: 10.1007/978-3-319-45234-0_12

Brands typically conduct marketing campaigns to understand, inform, involve and satisfy consumers (Keller 2008). Thus the objective of marketing actions is to affect consumers' hearts and minds (Hanssens et al. 2014). To measure the effect of their efforts, brands collect survey metrics that purport to reflect the consumer mindset. These include measures such as awareness, attitude, purchase intent and satisfaction, which collectively are held to represent the essence of the consumer purchase decision-making process (Wiesel et al. 2011). The central premise of the "consumer mind-set" is well established and posits that customers move toward a purchase through a series of stages, including a cognitive-awareness (e.g., need recognition, information search and being aware of the brand), an affective (e.g., consumer attitudes, evaluation of alternatives and consideration set inclusion), and ultimately, a conative (e.g. purchase intent and actual customer) stage (Rogers 1995, 1962; Wiesel et al. 2011).

Whilst classical marketing mix elements have been shown to impact these metrics (Srinivasan et al. 2010) the effect of social media actions remains to a large extent under-explored. Given that the relative importance of traditional marketing mix elements is declining (Mangold and Faulds 2009) as consumers place more trust in social media channels (Srinivasan et al. 2015), understanding how brands' social media actions affect the consumer mindset has taken on increased urgency.

Several studies have already attempted to link social media activity to consumer mindset metrics. For example Rishika et al. (2013) find that customers' social media participation increases website visit frequency and profitability. Similarly, Goh et al. (2013) analyze how user- and brand-generated content on a brand's Facebook page impacts purchase behavior. Colicev et al. (2016) demonstrated that social media actions affect brand equity, with the relationship mediated by brand awareness and willingness of consumers to recommend the brand through word-of-mouth. Although these studies provide important insights into the impact of social media on consumers, most are based on a single brand and employ a limited set of social media data (e.g. Facebook posts (Goh et al. 2013), Facebook likes and unlikes (Srinivasan et al. 2015)). Furthermore, these studies do not examine the more extensive and complex relationship between brands' social media efforts and the consumer mind-set.

We aim to fill this research gap by extending current research on the effect of social media actions to the consumer mind-set. Overall, we argue that firm's social media actions may directly "feed the funnel" by bringing in prospective customers. To provide a granular approach to social media actions, this paper separate various dimensions of a brand's social media actions (i.e., valence, intensity and richness) and relate them to the consumer mind-set. The first dimension captures the intensity of the brand effort, represented by how often a brand posts on its Wall. To capture the second dimension, we analyse the polarity of efforts that represents the valence (positive, negative, and neutral) of brand's posts. Finally, richness refers to the various forms of content that a brand can post, flowing along a continuum from simple textual status updates to more information dense photos or videos. In theory, messages with richer content are more likely to be noticed and shared as they are more engaging and informative than simple text (Smith et al. 2012). Accordingly rich messages should in theory generate more consumer engagement and therefore play a more significant role in influencing consumers (Daft and Lengel 1986).

Our aim thus is to answer the question "Which social media metrics under control of managers positively impact consumers' engagement and ultimately their mind-set?", enriching our understanding of the value of brand social media activity and helping managers better justify their expenditure on social media marketing.

2 Data and Methods

To test our theory, we have assembled a novel, comprehensive, dataset that combines measures of the intensity, valence and richness of brand's social media efforts on Facebook with consumer engagement and consumer mind-set metrics. Data on social media activity was collected using a series of third-party automated tools, each of which had been previously validated by manually crosschecking its output against actual data from the selected brands' social media presences. Firstly, over a period of ten days we accessed each brand's Facebook page and manually collected our desired metrics (e.g., "fans" of a brand page, "likes", "shares", "comments" on brands' posts). We also counted each brand's daily Facebook posts over the same period. In the second step, we compared the collected data with the data vendor's records. Finding no discrepancies suggested that the data provider reliably collects and archives data from Facebook.

To capture the consumer mindset metrics we follow the marketing literature and rely on survey data (Aaker 1996; Lehmann et al. 2008; Steenkamp et al. 1997). To obtain high validity survey metrics requires active recruitment and interaction with a large diverse set of participants (Steenkamp et al. 1997). Therefore, we obtained our consumer mindset metrics from YouGov Group, which uses online consumer panels to monitor brand perceptions. YouGov monitors multiple brands in multiple industries by surveying 5,000 randomly selected consumers (from a panel of 5 million) on a daily basis For estimation of the model as depicted we combine the traditional VAR approach with the panel-data approach, thus allowing for unobserved individual (brand-level) heterogeneity. Panel Vector Auto Regression (PVAR) (Holtz-Eakin et al. 1988) is a relatively new econometric technique that is a variant of the vector autoregression for use with panel data. We will adopt the reduced form of PVAR models in which each dependent variable is endogenous and is a linear function of its own past values, the past values of all other dependent variables, a set of exogenous variables, and an error term. While the use of PVAR is fairly nascent, it has been recently employed in the marketing (see for e.g. Borah and Tellis 2015) and information systems fields (Dewan and Ramaprasad 2014).

We adopt the reduced form of PVAR in which each dependent variable is endogenous and is a linear function of its own past values, the past values of all other dependent variables, a set of exogenous variables, and an error term. Based on the unit root and cointegration tests, we specify the PVAR model in Eq. (1):

$$
\begin{bmatrix}
Satisfaction_{it} \\
PurchaseIntent_{it} \\
Consideration_{it} \\
Awareness_{it} \\
Earned(volume)_{it} \\
Earned(valence)_{it} \\
Owned(richness)_{it} \\
Owned(neutral\_valence)_{it} \\
Owned(positive\_valence)_{it}
\end{bmatrix}
= \sum_{n=1}^{p}
\begin{pmatrix}
\gamma_{1,1}^{n} & \cdots\cdots & \gamma_{1,9}^{n} \\
& \vdots & \\
\gamma_{9,1}^{n} & \cdots\cdots & \gamma_{9,9}^{n}
\end{pmatrix}
\begin{bmatrix}
Satisfaction_{it-n} \\
PurchaseIntent_{it-n} \\
Consideration_{it-n} \\
Awareness_{it-n} \\
Earned(volume)_{it-n} \\
Earned(valence)_{it-n} \\
Owned(richness)_{it-n} \\
Owned(neutral\_valence)_{it-n} \\
Owned(positive\_valence)_{it-n}
\end{bmatrix}
+
\begin{pmatrix}
\phi_{11} \cdot \phi_{1,2} \\
\vdots \\
\phi_{9,1} \cdot \phi_{9,2}
\end{pmatrix}
\begin{bmatrix} x_1 \\ x_2 \end{bmatrix}
+
\begin{bmatrix}
u_{1i} \\ u_{2i} \\ u_{3i} \\ u_{4i} \\ u_{5i} \\ u_{6i} \\ u_{7i} \\ u_{8i} \\ u_{9i}
\end{bmatrix}
+
\begin{bmatrix}
e_{1it} \\ e_{2it} \\ e_{3it} \\ e_{4it} \\ e_{5it} \\ e_{6it} \\ e_{7it} \\ e_{8it} \\ e_{9it}
\end{bmatrix}
$$

$$(1)$$

Where Satisfaction = Satisfaction mindset metric, Purchase Intent = Purchase Intent mindset metric, Consideration = Consideration mindset metric, Awareness = Awareness mindset metric, Earned (volume) = earned social media volume, Earned (valence) = earned social media valence, Owned (Richness) = owned social media richness, Owned (Neutral) = owned social media neutral valence, Owned (Positive) = owned social media positive valence. The off-diagonal terms of the matrix $\Gamma - \gamma_{kl}^{n}$ estimate the indirect effects among the endogenous variables and the diagonal terms estimate the direct effects. The exogenous vector contains the advertising awareness variable and a deterministic trend t to capture the impact of omitted, gradually changing, variables.

3 Implications

This study aims to contribute to the literature in several ways. The paper is currently at the conceptual stage with further developments expected in the coming months. We aim to provide a theoretical explanation as to why social media metrics should affect mind-set metrics as this link is currently underexplored in the current marketing literature. Examining this relationship should reveal new insights on the importance of social media for organizations. Our research answers the question on the return on investment (ROI) on social media marketing by establishing that social media positively affects consumer behavior.

Improving the way in which consumer reach their purchase (or repurchase) decision is a key goal in marketing, which can now be systematically related to drivers in social media metrics. For example, marketers could use social media activity both as an influencer and as a predictor of customer mind-set metrics. Alternatively, marketers could potentially use consumer engagement as a predictor of their consumers' mind-set, or could influence consumer engagement and mind-set by actively posting appropriate content in the appropriate format at the appropriate interval on their Facebook presence. In addition, by considering different dimensions of social media and consumer mindset our research underscores that not all social media are created equal and, therefore may not affect the consumer mindset in a similar fashion. Finally, marketers could estimate the feedback loops from the consumer mind-set to online consumer engagement metrics to identify how consumer mind-set can drive consumer engagement.

Our model will this potentially allow managers to estimate the immediate and long-term impact of their social media actions. On the one hand, the immediate impact is relevant as managers need to be able to monitor social media conversations so as to be able to estimate customer mind-set metrics almost in real time to allow for accurate predictions. In addition, being able to measure the long-term impact should also allow managers to better justify company investments in social media marketing and obtain their much needed funding.

4 Preliminary Findings

The Power of Consumer Voice: Earned Social Media. Our findings emphasize the importance of earned social media in shaping the consumer mindset. First, we find that the *valence* of earned social media has strong positive effects on all consumer mindset metrics. We find that "what" consumers say (*valence*) is more important than how often they say it (*volume*). In light of these findings, managers should acknowledge the power of earned social media and incorporate it into their extended marketing mix. Social media enables the wisdom of the crowd, in effect making levers under the direct control of the brand less manifest.

Volume and Valence of Owned Social Media. Social media managers have at their disposal several other tools that they can use to influence the consumer mindset. Our study suggests four managerial levers: namely the three dimensions of owned social media and advertising. Our findings indicate that the *volume* of brand posts can have a beneficial effect on *Awareness*. In other words, more frequent brand posts translate into more consumers discovering the brand. Interestingly, we find that the hallmarks of persuasive marketing messages in traditional settings - adopting a positive language (advertising-like tone) - can have a negative effect on social media. Brand posts with a positive *valence* have a negative effect on purchase intent. In contrast, we find that adopting a neutral *valence* positively affects the purchase intent. This is consistent with our previous argument that a neutral tone conveys more objectivity, which can be perceived by social media audiences as being more trustworthy and informational.

Richness of information. Another key finding relates to the *richness* of the posts that managers use to convey information to their consumer base. Rich posts are the strongest predictors of purchase intent and satisfaction. In other words, to positively impact consumer choices, managers should create richer content using photos, videos and /or music.

References

Aaker, D.: Measuring brand equity across products and markets. Calif. Manage. Rev. **38**, 102–120 (1996)

Borah, A., Tellis, G.J.: Halo (spillover) effects in social media: do product recalls of one brand hurt or help rival brands? J. Mark. Res. **53**(2), 143–160 (2015). Ahead of P

Colicev, A., O'Connor, P., Vinzi, V.E.: Is investing in social media really worth it? How brand actions and user actions influence brand value. Serv. Sci. **8**, 152–168 (2016)

Daft, R.L., Lengel, R.H.: Organizational information requirements, media richness and structural design. Manage. Sci. **32**, 554–571 (1986)

Dewan, S., Ramaprasad, J.: Social media, traditional media, and music sales. MIS Q. **2**, 101–121 (2014)

Goh, K., Heng, C., Lin, Z.: Social media brand community and consumer behavior: quantifying the relative impact of user-and marketer-generated content. Inf. Syst. Res. **24**, 88–107 (2013)

Hanssens, D.M., Pauwels, K.H., Srinivasan, S., Vanhuele, M., Gokhan, Y.: Consumer attitude metrics for guiding marketing mix decisions. Mark. Sci. **33**, 534–550 (2014)

Heggestuen, J., Danova, T.: Brand Presence: How To Choose Where To Be On Social Media [WWW Document]. Business Insider, Bangalore (2013)

Hoffman, D.L., Fodor, M.: Can you measure the ROI of your social media marketing? MIT Sloan Manag. Rev. **52**, 41–49 (2010)

Holtz-Eakin, D., Newey, W., Rosen, H.S.: Estimating vector autoregressions with panel data. Econometrica **56**, 1371–1395 (1988)

Keller, K.L.: Strategic Brand Management, 3rd edn. Prentice Hall, Englewood Cliffs (2008)

Lehmann, D.R., Keller, K.L., Farley, J.U.: The structure of survey-based brand metrics. J. Int. Mark. **16**, 29–56 (2008)

Mangold, W.G., Faulds, D.J.: Social media: the new hybrid element of the promotion mix. Bus. Horiz. **52**, 357–365 (2009)

Peters, K., Chen, Y., Kaplan, A.M., Ognibeni, B., Pauwels, K.H.: Social media metrics — a framework and guidelines for managing social media. J. Interact. Mark. **27**, 281–298 (2013)

Rishika, R., Kumar, A., Janakiraman, R., Bezawada, R.: The effect of customers' social media participation on customer visit frequency and profitability: an empirical investigation. Inf. Syst. Res. **24**, 108–127 (2013)

Rogers, E.: Diffusion of Innovations. The Free Press of Glencoe, New York (1995)

Rogers, E.: Diffusion of innovations, 1st edn. The Free Press of Glencoe, New York (1962)

Smith, A.N., Fischer, E., Yongjian, C.: How does brand-related user-generated content differ across youtube, facebook, and twitter? J. Interact. Mark. **26**, 102–113 (2012)

Srinivasan, S., Rutz, O.J., Pauwels, K.H.: Paths to and off purchase: quantifying the impact of traditional marketing and online consumer activity. J. Acad. Mark. Sci. **1**, 1–14 (2015)

Srinivasan, S., Vanhuele, M., Pauwels, K.H.: Mind-set metrics in market response models: an integrative approach. J. Mark. Res. **47**(4), 672–684 (2010)

Steenkamp, J.-B.J., van Trijp, H.C.M., Trijp, H.Van: Attribute elicitation in marketing research: a comparison of three procedures. Mark. Lett. **8**, 153–165 (1997)

The CMO Survey: CMO Survey Report: Highlights and Insights, Feburary 2016

Wiesel, T., Pauwels, K.H., Arts, J.: Practice prize paper–marketing's profit impact: quantifying online and off-line funnel progression. Mark. Sci. **30**, 604–611 (2011)

Developing a Conceptual Model for the Relationship Between Social Media Behavior, Negative Consumer Emotions and Brand Disloyalty

Harri Jalonen[1]([✉]) and Jari Jussila[2]

[1] Turku University of Applied Sciences, Turku, Finland
harri.jalonen@turkuamk.fi
[2] Tampere University of Technology, Tampere, Finland

Abstract. Companies have been facing the dark side of social media. Particularly, the odds of customer complaints and brand insults have increased tremendously. Social media has given a voice to disappointed consumers. They use the voice when they feel negative emotions, for example, due to product failures, service problems or unethical behavior. It seems reasonable to expect that the more ubiquitous social media becomes, the more it persuades people to share also their negative experiences. However, although social media raises new challenges for companies, it also gives them new opportunities. Social media enables companies to trace disappointed customers, evaluate their impressiveness and communicate with them. The conceptual paper aims to develop a model for the relationship between social media behavior, negative consumer emotions and brand disloyalty. The argument of this paper is that although social media gives consumers more power which is manifested in sharing negative emotions related to the company, the effect this has on brand disloyalty depends on the company's behavior.

Keywords: Social media · Negative emotions · Brand disloyalty

1 Introduction

A great deal of social media content is emotionally loaded. People express the highs and lows of their everyday life, establish new friendships and break up old ones, share holiday and party pictures, praise and complain about brands, idolize the achievements of their descendants and pets through different social media sites – behavior which is strongly affected by emotion. Emotions can be expressed through words, pictures, emoticons and videos.

Social media has transformed the ways companies and customers interact. Metaphorically, social media has punctured holes into companies' walls and made them transparent in an unforeseen way. Social media has intensified the development in which the competition is based more on brands' ability to inspire emotional experiences, than on technical details of products. Consequently, companies are nowadays obliged to encounter their customers and other stakeholders more openly. Many companies have

© IFIP International Federation for Information Processing 2016
Published by Springer International Publishing Switzerland 2016. All Rights Reserved
Y.K. Dwivedi et al. (Eds.): I3E 2016, LNCS 9844, pp. 134–145, 2016.
DOI: 10.1007/978-3-319-45234-0_13

witnessed that social media has given customers a powerful medium to voice their negative emotions related, for example, to product failures, service problems or unethical behavior.

For some companies, social media provides new opportunities, whereas many others just face problems. Presumably, the distinction lies in whether or not the company is able to trace disappointed customers, evaluate their impressiveness and communicate with them. Be it fair or not, social media forces companies to deal with emotionally rationalized criticism and complaints.

Many studies have touched upon negative consumer emotions shared in social media – particularly studies that have been based on electronic word-of-mouth (eWOM) approach. These studies have, for example, identified various motivations for sharing negative information in social media [1]. Studies have also found out the stronger impact of negative eWOM (NWOM) compared to positive eWOM [2]. Despite of existing research, at least four research gaps can be identified. Firstly, previous studies have not explored the social media behavior of people as an antecedent to sharing negative emotions raised by negative experiences. Secondly, the relationship between disclosing negative emotions in social media behavior and brand disloyalty have received scant attention in the literature to date. Due to the lack of research it is not known whether disclosing negative emotions can contaminate brands and make customers disloyal. Thirdly, there is lack of research related to the mobile use of social media. Of particular interest should be whether mobile social media will increase the odds that negative experiences are expressed and shared. Fourthly, although companies cannot manage the ways their brands are discussed in social media, they are not unarmed. Social media has enabled companies to interact directly with their customers. However, there is lack of research with a focus on companies' customer retention tactics and their consequence on brand loyalty in the case of negative eWOM. The paper presumes that the methods of creating loyal customers in the age of social media may have been oversimplified. In order to increase customer loyalty, it is suggested that it is useful to look at the hidden side – i.e. the relationship between negative consumer emotions and disloyalty.

This conceptual paper aims to introduce a theoretically sound model for the relationship between social media behavior, negative consumer emotions and brand disloyalty. The argument of this paper is that although social media gives consumers more power, which is manifested in sharing negative emotions related to the company, the effect this has on brand disloyalty depends on the company's behavior.

The rest of the paper is organized as follows. Section 2 shortly reviews the key literature and presents the theoretical foundation for the paper. Section 3 introduces the conceptual model. In Sect. 4 the paper concludes with short managerial implications, including limitations and venues for future research.

2 Literature Review and Theoretical Foundation

Emotion refers to an emotional state involving thoughts, physiological changes, and an outward expression or behavior. Emotions are expressed in facial reactions, gestures or postures and they are intuitively or intentionally directed toward a certain target. [3] Psychological literature typically classifies emotions into two axes that describe their valence and arousal. Valence indicates whether the affect related to an emotion is positive or negative, and arousal indicates the personal activity induced by that emotion [4].

The relationship between negative emotions and social media has been addressed from various perspectives. The following will give a short overview of studies which have focused or at least touched upon the question of how negative emotions manifest themselves in social media. Firstly, psychologically oriented studies have found out that negative emotions can be so popular in social media because people who suffer psychosocial problems appreciate the ability to stay connected with others without face-to-face communication. According to these studies disorganised, anxious and lonely people use social media sites as they provide a context for holding relationships at a psychological arm's distance and modulating negative emotions associated with these problems [5]. Secondly, consumer behaviour studies have identified several motivations for negative online word-of-mouth (WOM). These include sharing dissatisfaction in order to get a solution, disclosing unfavorable experiences to prevent others from enduring similar bad experiences, and ventilating feelings on a bad experience to give the company a chance to improve its practices [1]. Thirdly, sociologically inspired studies have focused on cultural and demographic differences in social media behaviour. These studies indicate that age and gender affect emotional behaviour in social media [6, 7]. Studies have also shown cultural differences in emotional behaviour in social media [8]. Fourthly, some studies have addressed social media sites which are dedicated to allowing people to vent. Rant-sites, as they are called, provide people a forum to rant, for example, about firms and their products and services. Rant-sites particularly attract people who feel anger [9].

As this paper focuses on emotions which have negative valence and positive arousal, the psychological approach falls out of the paper's scope. Recognizing the existence of socio-demographically oriented studies, this paper is not aiming to study age, gender or cultural factors that may influence on NWOM. Ranting sites are left out, in turn, because they represent, albeit interesting, extremely negative emotions and marginalised behaviour. The majority of social media users do not commit cyber trolling or bullying.

By concentrating on moderate ways of expressing disagreements in social media, this paper leans on consumer behavior studies [10]. These studies have shown that instead of rational decisions based on utilitarian product attributes and benefits, consumers' decisions are "biased" by emotions. Negative consumer emotions can result from various sources. A dysfunctional product, impolite customer service or insulting ads, to name a few, typically cause frustration, discontentment and other negative emotions. Negative consumer emotions pose a threat to companies for two main reasons. Firstly, negative emotions elicited from bad experiences may decrease customer loyalty, and secondly negative emotions can be spread through eWOM to a large audience. Negative consumer emotions do no good for the brand.

The importance of brand has been known for several decades. Studies have found out that consumers are willing to pay more for a brand because they perceive some unique value in the brand compared to a generic product [11]. Companies invest in building loyal customer relationships because of numerous benefits such as premium price [12], long lasting customer retention [13], lower price sensitivity by customers [14], higher profitability [15] and greater market share [16]. Oliver [17, p. 34] defines brand loyalty as "a deeply held commitment to rebuy or repatronize a preferred product/service consistently in the future, thereby causing repetitive same-brand or same brand-set purchasing, despite situational influences and marketing efforts having the potential to cause switching behavior". Oliver's definition includes two aspects of brand loyalty – behavioral and attitudinal [18]. Behavioral loyalty consists of repeated purchases of the brand, whereas attitudinal loyalty refers to emotional ties with the brand.

Intuitively thinking, it seems that brand disloyalty is just opposite to brand loyalty. However, it is worthwhile to notice that as satisfied customers are not necessarily loyal, dissatisfied customers are not always disloyal [19]. Although a company can effectively handle unpleasant issues in a way which reduces dissatisfaction, the result is not necessarily satisfaction. On the other hand, while the company can behave badly and cause negative affect, the customer may keep purchasing the brand. A bit paradoxically, satisfied customers can defect, while dissatisfied customers remain faithful. Apparently due to this paradox, Söderlund [20] has suggested that satisfaction and dissatisfaction may, in fact, be two orthogonal axes rather than a bipolar measurement.

The paper defines brand disloyalty *as a deeply held negative attitude and emotionally motivated rejection to buy a certain brand in the future, despite customer retention efforts by the company responsible for the brand.* Brand disloyalty can take various forms. Adapting Dick and Basu [21], Rowley and Dawes [19] have identified four different manifestations of brand disloyalty: disengaged, disturbed, disenchanted and disruptive. Disengaged customers have typically no intention to purchase, nor direct experience of the brand. Disturbed customers have purchased the brand, but whether they buy in the future is uncertain because of recent dissatisfied experience. Disenchanted customers have purchased previously but are not likely to buy in the future because of many negative experiences. Disruptive customers have so many negative experiences that they have no intention to purchase in the future. In addition, disruptors actively discourage their peers to consider the brand.

3   A Conceptual Model – A Nexus Between Social Media Behavior, Negative Consumer Emotions and Brand Disloyalty

Social media refers herein to a constellation of Internet-based applications that derive their value from the participation of users through directly creating original content, modifying existing material, contributing to a community dialogue and integrating various media together to create something unique [22]. Consumer-generated content (CGC) is obviously a double-edged sword that can cause both positive and negative outcomes. Sometimes CGC can help companies, for example, with identifying hidden customer needs and cultivating brand communities [23, 24], while in other occasions CGC insults companies and damages brands [24, 25]. Electronic WOM is a particular form of CGC. By definition, it means any positive or negative statement made by potential, actual, or former customers about a product or company, which is made available to a multitude of people and institutions via the Internet [2].

Social media has notably lowered the threshold of eWOM. Nowadays anyone can post her or his opinions about brands.

Studies indicate that negative eWOM may have very strong effects on companies' performance. Wangeheim [26], Chevalier and Mayzlin [27] and Park and Lee [28], among others, have identified that negative evaluations of products and services have a stronger effect than positive ones. Negative eWOM affects brand image negatively [29], consumers' preferences [30] and purchase decisions [31]. Consumers share negative experiences mainly for three reasons [1]. Firstly, sharing negative experiences can serve to lessen the frustration and reduce the anxiety associated with the event. Secondly, negative experiences are shared for warning and preventing others from enduring similar events. Thirdly, consumers can share their negative experiences in order to help companies improve their practices. All in all, eWOM is more often negative than positive [32]. Social media has empowered consumers to voice negative experiences and opinions about brands with reduced physical and psychological costs [33]. Therefore, the paper presumes that negative disclosures are particular forms of CGC. Furthermore, it is argued that how these negative social posts influence brand disloyalty depends on companies' own behavior. Figure 1 illustrates the factors which are discussed in more detail in the following sections.

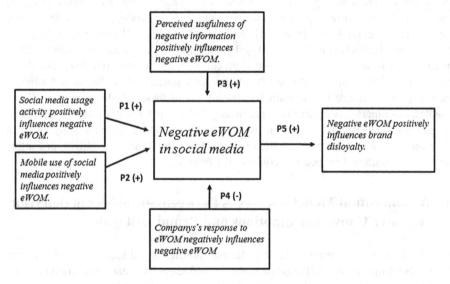

Fig. 1. A conceptual model of the relationship between social media behavior, negative consumer emotions and brand disloyalty

3.1 Social Media Usage Activity and Negative eWOM

The social media era has significant implications for the spread of negative eWOM. Negative opinions about brands are formed and spread by thousands or millions of people within hours via social media [34]. In recent years the adoption of social media has surged. As an indicator of this development, 73 % of Fortune 500 companies had a

Twitter account and 66 % a corporate Facebook page in the year 2012 [35]. In the year 2015, 78 % of Fortune 500 companies have a Twitter account and 74 % a corporate Facebook Page, and only 2 % companies do not use any social media [36]. The amount of time consumers spend online and on social networking has also kept increasing. Time spent online via PCs, laptops, mobiles and tablets has increased from 5.55 h in 2012 to 6.15 h in 2014, and the time spent on social networks has climbed from a daily average of 1.61 to 1.72 h in the same time period [37].

As more and more companies are adopting social media, and consumers are spending more time online and on social networks, the more rapid can also be the spread of negative eWOM. Thus, the paper formulates the following proposition.

P1: Social media usage activity positively influences negative eWOM.

3.2 Mobile Use of Social Media and Negative eWOM

Mobile phones and devices have become increasingly popular. For instance, 90 % of Americans own a mobile phone, and most people rely so heavily on their mobile phones that they wouldn't dare to leave home without them [38]. Nearly two-thirds (64 %) of mobile phones owned by Americans are smartphones [39] that make it possible to have all the social media applications (e.g. Facebook, Twitter, etc.) at the disposal of consumers all the time. Mobile social media has also introduced new characteristics for social media use, such as time-sensitivity and location-sensitivity [38]. The transfer of traditional social media applications to mobile devices has increased the immediacy of feedback [38, 40] and thus made the use of social media applications more time-sensitive. For example, traditionally you would have to log in to Twitter with your computer in order to determine whether you have received any new messages or if there are any discussions that mention you. Whereas, using a mobile device, you get an immediate notification whenever someone posts a message or mentions you in a post (e.g. on Twitter, Facebook, LinkedIn and other applications). Exchange of messages with relevance for one specific location at one specific point of time [38], with mobile applications such as Foursquare and Facebook Places, has introduced a new dimension of interacting with consumers and businesses. For instance, consumers receive discounts to shops or restaurants based on their location information. Location-based services revenues are forecasted to increase from €10.3 billion in 2014 at an annual growth rate of 22.5 % to €34.8 billion in 2020 according to a recent market report [41]. With such growth rates in location-based services it is likely that the mobile use of social media will impact the spread of negative eWOM as well. It has been noted that a mobile device is a 'telephone', the primary objective of which is message transmission, while a PC is a 'processor', with the primary objective of data transmission [42]. Presumably the differences between the objectives affect the behavior. Thus, the paper formulates the following proposition.

P2: Mobile use of social media positively influences negative eWOM.

3.3 Perceived Usefulness of Negative Information and Negative eWOM

Social media has enabled consumers an easy way to post their experiences of products and services. These experiences are based not only on facts (what has actually happened) but also on consumers' subjective opinions. Unsurprisingly, brands are forced to face fair and unfair negative eWOM. Social networking sites and online review sites, among others, have considerably increased the probability that peer information is taken in to consideration when consumers make judgements about brands. The importance of negative peer information and eWOM can be addressed from two complementary perspectives.

Firstly, information seeking theories suggest that people perceive negative information, in general, to be more persuasive than positive information [43, 44]. Based on the accessibility–diagnosticity model [45], Anderson and Salisbury [32] and Yang and Mai [46] have found out that negative information is more diagnostic and persuasive than positive. For example, information about a product that does not work as it should is more diagnostic than information about a product that does work as it should. In case of product failure, negative information is given more weight because it differs from the expectations. It can be said that negative framing is more effective than positive framing [47]. Ahluwalia [48] has described this "negativity affect" arguing that negative product attributes are believed to be more characteristic of a poor quality product, than positive attributes are for a high quality product [33].

Secondly, eWOM is considered a relatively credible and trustworthy source of information and therefore is more influential than advertising and other marketing information provided by the companies [49]. The credibility of negative eWOM is dependent on the perceived competence of the source providing the information and on the emotional relationship between the information provider and its receiver. If the information source is ranked as an expert (i.e. she/he possesses greater awareness and knowledge about a market and products within it or by virtue of his/her occupation, social training or experience), the knowledge he/she provides is more useful and persuasive than information provided by a non-expert [49–52]. In addition to competence, the emotional relationship between the information provider and its receiver influences the credibility of messages. Pan and Chiou [53], for example, have shown that negative online messages were perceived credible when the messages were posted by those perceived to have close social relationships.

The more diagnostic and credible the given information is, the more probable it is that information will be retrieved as an input to judgement about brand. Thus, the paper formulates the following proposition.

P3: Perceived usefulness of negative information positively influences negative eWOM.

3.4 Company's Behavior and Negative eWOM

Negative eWOM can damage a company's brand. However, it can be expected that the amount of damage depends on the company's behavior. Recent experiences clearly show that no response is not an option [e.g. 34, 54]. Instead, companies are encouraged to put an effort on handing negative eWOM. There is no shortage of studies which point out that competent complaint management is an effective means of reducing the impact of negative WOM (traditional and online) on brand and purchase intention [24, 55–59].

Two aspects seem of particular importance in attenuating negative eWOM. Firstly, because individual negative experiences easily escalate into online fire-storms [34] and digital groundswells [60], it is important to act timely. A timely response to online complaints offer two potential benefits as it not only resolves the issue with the complainant and prevents follow-up attacks from the consumers who exposed themselves to the original complaint, but can also decrease consumer disloyalty [24, 33, 61]. Secondly, the tone of response should be considered carefully. In the worst case, the company's response can engender a spiral of negative effect undermining its intended goals [24, 61]. In order to avoid the backfire, Kelleher [62] and van Noort and Willemsen [33], among others, have emphasized the conversational human voice approach. Kelleher [62] defines the conversational human voice as "an engaging and natural style of organizational communication as perceived by an organization's publics based on interactions between individuals in the organization and individuals in publics". Contrary to corporate voice, which is profit-driven and persuasive [63], human voice invites individuals to communicate in a non-persuasive manner [33]. The more quickly and the more emphatically the company responses to online complaints the more probable it is that the damage of eWOM can be limited. Thus, the paper formulates the following proposition.

P4: Company's response to negative eWOM negatively influences negative eWOM.

3.5 Negative eWOM and Brand Disloyalty

As described earlier, brand disloyalty is not just opposite to brand loyalty. This means that customers can be loyal to certain brands even if they are dissatisfied, whereas satisfied customers can defect. Instead of disloyalty, the latter behavior represents no loyalty [21]. Disloyalty differs from no loyalty in that it includes a negative attitude toward the brand [19]. Disloyalty is an emotionally motivated rejection to buy a certain brand in the future, despite customer retention efforts by the company responsible for the brand.

Brand disloyalty, as distinct from brand loyalty, in the social media context has received scant attention in previous research. However, based on the studies which examined the relationship between eWOM and brand loyalty, there are reasons to suspect that negative eWOM impacts brand disloyalty. Several studies have identified that negative eWOM has a significant power that affects brand loyalty and purchase decisions [64–68].

In spite of lack of studies on eWOM and disloyalty, one important remark can however be introduced. Because of the diagnosticity of negative information [45], it can be argued that a negative review on a brand is a valuable information source for consumers. Consumers can use negative eWOM for avoiding frustration, dissatisfaction and other negative emotions elicited by buying certain goods or services [68].

In other words, negative eWOM may increase emotional rejection toward a brand. Thus, the paper formulates the following proposition.

P5: Negative eWOM positively influence brand disloyalty.

4 Conclusions

Advancing the current understanding on the relationship between social media behavior and NWOM on brand disloyalty the conceptual model claims that social media usage and mobile use of social media are antecedents that increase the odds that negative events, such as bad customer experiences, are disclosed in social media. Similarly, the model argues that negative information about something, for example about product usability, is perceived as more useful than positive or neutral information about the same something. The value of negative information is based on its diagnosticity. It is worth noting that companies can influence the audibility of negative eWOM. Through quick and empathetic responses it may be possible to prevent the worst from happening. If, however, eWOM takes place, the result is brand disloyalty – a negative attitude and emotionally motivated rejection to buy a certain brand.

Obviously the conceptual model has its limitations. As antecedents of sharing negative emotions in social media and the relationship between sharing negative emotions in social media and brand disloyalty have received little attention in the literature, this paper has induced the need for empirical research. The authors will conduct a study to validate the proposed model. It will be carried out as follows: (i) a socio-demographically representative consumer population will be recruited, (ii) the data will be gathered through questionnaire survey with Likert-scale components, (iii) the structural equation modeling using partial least squares (SEM-PLS) estimation will be employed to test hypothesized relationships among constructs. This approach will be favored over single regression analyses because it allows testing the conceptual model as a whole [69]. It is expected that empirical research will contribute to the development of understanding of the antecedents and consequences of negative consumer emotions expressed in social media.

References

1. Verhagen, T., Nauta, A., Feldberg, F.: Negative online word-of-mouth: behavioral indicator or emotional release? Comput. Hum. Behav. **29**(4), 1430–1440 (2013)
2. Hennig-Thurau, T., Gwinner, K.P., Walsh, G., Gremler, D.D.: Electronic word-of-mouth via consumer-opinion platforms: what motivates consumers to articulate themselves on the Internet? J. Interact. Mark. **18**(1), 38–52 (2004)
3. Cacioppo, J.T., Gardner, W.L.: Emotion. Annu. Rev. Psychol. **50**, 191–214 (1999)
4. Russell, J.A.: A circumplex model of affect. J. Pers. Soc. Psychol. **39**(6), 1161–1178 (1980)
5. Nitzburg, G.C., Farber, B.A.: Putting up emotional (Facebook) walls? Attachment status and emerging adults' experiences of social networking sites. J. Clin. Psychol. **69**(11), 1183–1190 (2013)
6. Shen, A.X.L., Lee, M.K.O., Cheung, C.M.G., Chen, H.: Gender differences in intentional social action: we-intention to engage in social network-facilitated team collaboration. J. Inf. Technol. **25**(2), 152–169 (2010)

7. Przybylski, A.K., Murayama, K., DeHaan, C.R., Gladwell, V.: Motivational, emotional, and behavioral correlates of fear of missing out. Comput. Hum. Behav. **29**(4), 1841–1848 (2013)
8. Koh, N.S., Hu, N., Clemons, E.K.: Do online reviews reflect a product's true perceived quality? An investigation of online movie reviews across cultures. Electron. Commer. Res. Appl. **9**, 374–385 (2010)
9. Martin, R.C., Coyier, K.R., van Sistine, L.M., Schroeder, K.L.: Anger on the Internet: the perceived value of rant-sites. CyberPsychol. Behav. Soc. Netw. **16**(2), 119–122 (2013)
10. Laros, F.J.M., Steenkamp, J.-E.E.M.: Emotions in consumer behavior: a hierarchical approach. J. Bus. Res. **58**(10), 1437–1445 (2005)
11. Keller, K.: Conceptualizing, measuring and managing customer-based brand equity. J. Mark. **57**(1), 1–22 (1993)
12. Doyle, P.: Building successful brands: the strategic options. J. Consum. Mark. **7**(2), 5–20 (1990)
13. Reichheld, F., Sasser, W.: Zero defects: quality comes to services. Harvard Bus. Rev. **68**(5), 105–111 (1990)
14. Krishamurthi, L., Raj, S.P.: An empirical analysis of the relationship between brand loyalty and consumer price elasticity. Mark. Sci. **10**(2), 172–183 (1991)
15. Hallowell, R.: The relationship of customer satisfaction, customer loyalty and profitability: an empirical study. Int. J. Serv. Ind. Manag. **7**(4), 27–42 (1996)
16. Assael, H.: Consumer Behavior and Marketing Action. South-Western, Cincinnati (1998)
17. Oliver, R.L.: Whence consumer loyalty? J. Mark. **63**, 33–44 (1999)
18. Chaudhuri, A., Holbrook, M.B.: The chain of effects from brand trust and brand affect to brand performance: the role of brand loyalty. J. Mark. **65**(2), 81–93 (2001)
19. Rowley, J., Dawes, J.: Disloyalty: a closer look at non-loyals. J. Consum. Mark. **17**(6), 538–549 (2000)
20. Söderlund, M.: Customer satisfaction and its consequence on customer behaviour revisited. Int. J. Serv. Ind. Manag. **5**(8), 21–38 (1998)
21. Dick, A., Basu, K.: Customer loyalty: toward an integrated conceptual framework. J. Mark. Sci. **22**(2), 99–113 (1994)
22. Kaplan, A.M., Haenlein, M.: Users of the world, unite! The challenges and opportunities of social media. Bus. Horiz. **53**(1), 59–68 (2010)
23. Muñiz, A.M., Schau, H.J.: How to inspire value-laden collaborative consumer-generated content. Bus. Horiz. **54**(3), 209–217 (2011)
24. Noble, C.H., Noble, S.M., Adjei, M.T.: Let them talk! Managing primary and extended online brand communities for success. Bus. Horiz. **55**(5), 475–483 (2012)
25. Kucuk, S.U.: Negative double jeopardy: the role of anti-brand sites on the internet. Brand Manag. **15**(3), 209–222 (2008)
26. Wangenheim, F.V.: Postswitching negative word of mouth. J. Serv. Res. **8**(1), 67–78 (2005)
27. Chevalier, J., Mayzlin, D.: The effect of word of mouth on sales: online book reviews. J. Mark. Res. **63**(3), 345–354 (2006)
28. Park, C., Lee, T.M.: Information direction, website reputation and eWOM effect: a moderating role of product type. J. Bus. Res. **62**(1), 61–67 (2009)
29. Jansen, B.J., Zhang, M., Sobel, K., Chowdury, A.: Twitter power: tweets as electronic word of mouth. J. Am. Soc. Inform. Sci. Technol. **60**(11), 2169–2188 (2009)
30. Khare, A., Labrecque, I.I., Asare, A.K.: The assimilative and contrastive effects of word-of-mouth volume: an experimental examination of online consumer ratings. J. Retail. **87**(1), 111–126 (2011)
31. Fagerstrom, A., Ghinea, B.: On the motivating impact of price and online recommendations at the point of online purchase. Int. J. Inf. Manag. **31**(2), 103–110 (2011)

32. Anderson, E.W., Salisbury, L.C.: The formation of market-level expectations and its covariates. J. Consum. Res. **30**(1), 115–124 (2003)
33. Van Noort, G., Willemsen, L.M.: Online damage control: the effects of proactive versus reactive webcare interventions in consumer-generated and brand-generated platforms. J. Interact. Mark. **26**(3), 131–140 (2011)
34. Pfeffer, J., Zorbach, T., Carley, K.M.: Understanding online firestorms: negative word-of-mouth dynamics in social media networks. J. Mark. Commun. **20**(1–2), 117–128 (2014)
35. Barnes, N., Lescault, A., Andonian, J.: Social Media Surge by the 2012 Fortune 500: Increase Use of Blogs, Facebook, Twitter and More. Charlton College of Business Center for Marketing Research, Dartmouth (2012)
36. Barnes, N., Lescault, A., Holmes, G.: The 2015 Fortune 500 and Social Media: Instagram Gains, Blogs Lose. UMass, Darthmouth (2015)
37. Mander, J.: Daily Time Spent on Social Networks Rises to 1.72 hours. Global Web Index, London (2015)
38. Kaplan, A.M.: If you love something, let it go mobile: mobile marketing and mobile social media 4×4. Bus. Horiz. **55**(2), 129–139 (2012)
39. Smith, A.: U.S. Smartphone Use in 2015. Pew Research Center, Washington, DC (2015)
40. Jussila, J.: Social Media in Business-to-Business Companies' Innovation, vol. 1333. Tampere University of Technology Publication, Tampere (2015)
41. Research and Markets: Mobile Location-Based Services, 9th edn. (2015). http://www.researchandmarkets.com/reports/3396579/
42. Okazaki, S.: Social influence model and electronic word of mouth – PC versus mobile internet. Int. J. Advert. **28**(3), 439–472 (2009)
43. Fiske, S.T.: Attention and weight in person perception: the impact of negative and extreme behaviour. J. Pers. Soc. Psychol. **38**(6), 889–906 (1980)
44. Crowley, A.E., Hoyer, W.D.: An integrative framework for understanding two-sided persuasion. J. Consum. Res. **20**(4), 561–574 (1994)
45. Herr, P.M., Kardes, F.R., Kim, J.: Effects of word-of-mouth and product attribute information on persuasion: an accessibility diagnosticity perspective. J. Consum. Res. **17**(4), 454–462 (1991)
46. Yang, J., Mai, E.: Experiental goods with network externalities effects: an empirical study of online rating system. J. Bus. Res. **63**(9–10), 1050–1057 (2010)
47. Maheswaran, D., Meyers-Levy, J.: The influence of message framing and issue involvement. J. Mark. Res. **27**(3), 361–367 (1990)
48. Ahluwalia, R.: How prevalent is the negativity affect in consumer environments? J. Consum. Res. **29**(2), 270–279 (2002)
49. Brown, J., Broderick, A.J., Lee, N.: Word of mouth communication within online communities: conceptualizing the online social network. J. Interact. Mark. **21**(3), 1–17 (2007)
50. Gotlieb, J.B., Sarel, D.: Comparative advertising effectiveness: the role of involvement and source credibility. J. Advert. **20**(1), 38–45 (1991)
51. Schiffman, I.G., Kanuk, L.L.: Consumer Behavior, 9th edn. Prentice Hall, Upper Saddle River (1955)
52. Mitchell, A.A., Dacin, P.A.: The assessment of alternative measures of consumer expertise. J. Consum. Res. **23**(3), 219–239 (1996)
53. Pan, L.-Y., Chiou, J.-S.: How much can you trust online information? Cues from perceived trustworthiness of consumer-generated online information? J. Interact. Mark. **25**(2), 67–74 (2011)
54. Hemsley, J., Mason, R.M.: Knowledge and knowledge management in the social media age. J. Organ. Comput. Electron. Commer. **23**(1–2), 138–167 (2013)

55. Fornell, C., Wernefelt, B.: Defensive marketing strategy by customer complaint management: a theoretical analysis. J. Mark. Res. **24**(4), 337–346 (1987)
56. Tax, S.S., Brown, S.W., Chandrasherakan, M.: Customer evaluations of service complaint experiences: implication for relationship marketing. J. Mark. **62**(2), 60–76 (1998)
57. Blodgett, J.G., Anderson, J.: A Bayesian network model of the consumer complaint process. J. Serv. Res. **4**(2), 321–338 (2000)
58. Von der Heyde, F.D., dos Santos, P.: The antecedents of the consumer complaining behavior (CCB). Adv. Consum. Res. **35**, 584–592 (2008)
59. Sandes, F.S., Urdan, A.T.: Electronic word-of-mouth impacts on consumer behaviour: exploratory and experimental studies. J. Int. Consum. Mark. **25**(3), 181–197 (2013)
60. Li, C., Bernoff, J.: Groundswell – Winning in a World Transformed by Social Technologies. Harvard Business Review Publishing, Boston (2009)
61. Lee, Y.L., Song, S.: An empirical investigation of electronic word-of-mouth: informational motive and corporate response strategy. Comput. Hum. Behav. **26**(5), 1073–1080 (2010)
62. Kelleher, T.: Conversational voice, communicated commitment, and public relations outcomes in interactive online communication. J. Commun. **59**(1), 172–188 (2009)
63. Locke, C., Weinberger, D., Searls, D.: The Cluetrain Manifesto: The End of Business as Usual. Perseus Publishing, New York (2004)
64. Chiou, J.-S., Cheng, C.: Should a company have message boards on its web sites. J. Interact. Mark. **17**(3), 50–61 (2003)
65. Gruen, T.W., Osmonbekov, T., Czaplewski, A.J.: eWOM: the impact of customer-to-customer online know-how exchange on customer value and loyalty. J. Bus. Res. **59**(4), 449–456 (2006)
66. Jones, S.A., Aiken, D.K., Boush, D.M.: Integrating experience, advertising, and electronic word of mouth. J. Internet Commer. **8**(3–4), 246–267 (2009)
67. Khammans, M., Griffiths, G.H.: 'Arrivederci CIAO.com, Buongiorno Bing.com' – electronic word-of-mouth (eWOM), antecedents and consequences. Int. J. Inf. Manag. **31**(1), 82–87 (2011)
68. Bambaeur-Sachse, S., Mangold, S.: Brand equity dilution through negative online word-of-mouth communication. J. Retail. Consum. Serv. **18**(1), 38–45 (2011)
69. Henseler, J.: On the convergence of the partial least squares path modeling algorithm. Comput. Stat. **25**(1), 107–120 (2010)

Generating Customer Engagement and Customer Enragement on Facebook Pages of Tesco and Walmart

Swaleha Peeroo[1(✉)], Martin Samy[2], and Brian Jones[2]

[1] Université des Mascareignes, Pamplemousses, Beau Plan, Mauritius
speeroo@udm.ac.mu
[2] Leeds Beckett University, Leeds, UK
{M.A.Samy,B.T.Jones}@leedsbeckett.ac.uk

Abstract. Social media are compelling businesses to review their way of managing customer experiences. There is a dearth of research as to why customers interact with businesses on social media in the grocery sector. This paper aims to explore how customers react to corporate messages on Facebook pages of Tesco and Walmart. Netnography approach was adopted to gain an insight into the various ways customers engage with the grocery stores on its Facebook pages. Findings show that the social customer is both a curse and a blessing to Tesco and Walmart as they can create or destroy value for the business. This paper contributes to knowledge by uncovering the various ways customers react with the business and how value can be created and destroyed.

Keywords: Social media · Customer engagement · Relationship marketing · Customer empowerment · Grocery stores · Facebook

1 Introduction

The social media revolution has impacted the business world, pushing companies to adapt to a new social order [1]. Social media have empowered customers by giving them a voice to spread their opinions on products and services to a very wide audience and at an incredible speed [2]. The potential benefits of adopting social media platforms have appealed to businesses of all sizes across several industries [3]. Dreading to lose the social media battle, managers have hastily integrated social media within their business strategies [4]. However, many managers are still uncertain of the opportunities and threats relating to social networks owing to the lack of knowledge of their structure and operation [5].

Extant literature covers the field of social media as a marketing tool to build relationship with customers, however there is a dearth of research on the use of social media in the grocery sector, though practitioners in this field are increasingly incorporating social media in their marketing strategy [6]. Following the calls for research for understanding the expectations and motivations of customers to interact with businesses on social media [7, 8], this paper aims to uncover the reasons customers engage with grocery stores on social media and to show how customer interactions on social media can be

© IFIP International Federation for Information Processing 2016
Published by Springer International Publishing Switzerland 2016. All Rights Reserved
Y.K. Dwivedi et al. (Eds.): I3E 2016, LNCS 9844, pp. 146–156, 2016.
DOI: 10.1007/978-3-319-45234-0_14

both a blessing and a curse. In this article, we provide a brief literature of social media, and customer engagement. We outline the netnographic method and present a model based on the findings of the study focusing on the challenges and opportunities that these phenomena present to retailers of the grocery sector. We then conclude, present the limitations and suggest future research directions.

2   Literature Review

2.1   Social Media

Social media are a collection of Internet-based applications that build on the ideological and technological foundations of Web 2.0 [5] and mobile technology [9] and they allow the creation and exchange of user-generated content (UGC). Social media are bringing about a societal revolution, as they are an open platform enabling multi-way communication, they are fast and affordable [1]. Social media empower customers and virtual communities to send and broadcast information to a global audience cheaply and instantaneously on the net [1].

Individuals leverage social networks and blogs to create, recommend and share information hence outspreading the reach of marketing influence [10]. Consumers in the digital age use the Internet and social media platforms to find information about products and services, to engage with the businesses they purchase from, and to connect with other customers who may provide valuable insights [10].

Traditional management methods can no longer be used with consumers on social media as they expect firms to listen to them, engage and respond accordingly [9]. Social networking sites are increasingly being used by businesses to establish their marketing network, since social media platforms facilitate the establishment of communication and ongoing real time conversations [11].

Research has identified that large companies use their Facebook pages to (1) promote their products and services such as launching new products and announcing sales promotions; (2) promote sponsored events for e.g. donations or sponsoring sports activities; (3) carry out surveys to get feedback from their fans; (4) make informational announcements for e.g. new opening hours or new business locations; and (5) post fun messages usually in a question style linked to a recent or forthcoming event [12].

Customers connect to a Facebook brand page because (1) they consume the products and services of the company, (2) they hope to get discounts and promotions, (3) they want to show to others that they like a particular brand, (4) they want to get information about the brand before others do, and (5) they wish to have access to exclusive content [13]. Four benefits that customers gain from using social networks are: (1) social benefits by interacting with other members of the community, (2) informational benefits by accessing information about the products and services of the company, (3) hedonic benefits by enjoying and having fun on the social network for e.g. games, and finally (4) economic benefits by obtaining promotional deals. These benefits encourage community members to continue visiting and being active on social networking sites, therefore offering opportunities to firms to strengthen relationships with their customers [14]. Research has been carried out to understand motivations of customers for interacting with businesses in the apparel sector [8] where customers are highly involved in the purchase. These authors suggested that further research is required to understand motivations of customers to connect with retailers in various sectors. This paper therefore aims to fill this gap by analysing the motivations of customers to interact with grocery stores, which sell mostly low involvement products by analysing responses of customers to customer and company initiated messages.

When brands and consumers co-create brand stories, brand owners do not have full control of their brands [15] as consumer-generated brand contents can spread as quickly as those created by companies [16]. In this social media era, marketers find themselves at the mercy of customers who can post comments about their brands. As this new marketing paradigm evolves, there is genuine excitement about the potential of social media to add value for businesses, but also apprehension about the difficulty of seizing the full promise of this new medium [17].

Co-creation is one of the virtues of the new age marketing enabled by social media. However, for marketers who need to manage their brands, UGC and social media do not only provide opportunities but also threats [18]. Social media and UGC are a potential threat to the efforts of organisations to build, manage and protect their brands because such content is outside their immediate control [15, 18, 19]. Interestingly, technologies and tools of Web 2.0 seem to ease the co-creation of value by the company and the customer [20, 21].

The open-comment platform of Facebook and the anonymity offered by the Internet produce the ideal conditions for public outrage to be vented on corporate walls [22]. Furthermore, social media have empowered customers and the public by giving them a voice and weakened the position of companies by rendering them vulnerable to customer attacks, negative publicity and corporate reputation damage [23]. The voice of the customer in brand communities may be a threat to the organisation if it carries a negative content [24]. Social media users can generate huge waves of outrage within a short period of time when reacting to a questionable activity or statement of an organisation [25]. Such a phenomenon is qualified as an online firestorm, which is "the sudden discharge of large quantities of messages containing negative word of mouth and complaint behaviour against a person, company, or group in social media networks" [25].

Despite the threats posed by the democratisation of communication, marketers are increasingly using social media to connect and engage with their customers. Customer engagement is believed to be the key outcome of social media campaigns [26].

2.2 Customer Engagement

Social media channels such as mobiles and online videos provide new opportunities to engage customers [27]. By giving access to online content and communication through virtual tools, social media enable and facilitate consumer experiences, which may generate customer engagement with specific brands [28]. Though customer engagement has various interpretations, it is often viewed as a motivational concept, with varying intensity. It encompasses an object (i.e. a brand) and a subject (i.e. the customer) [29], and has either a positive or negative valence [30, 31].

Customer engagement encompasses the connection that users form with businesses, following their experiences with the products, services and activities of the business [32]. Hollebeek defines customer brand engagement as "the level of a customer's motivational, brand-related and context dependent state of mind characterized by specific levels of cognitive, emotional and behavioural activity in direct brand interactions" [32, p. 790]. In this definition of customer engagement, there are the three dimensions that have been extensively cited in the literature, namely the cognitive, emotional and behavioural perspectives [30, 33]. From a cognitive standpoint, engagement is a positive state of mind that is represented by high commitment, energy, and loyalty towards a firm [34], for e.g. the person's level of concentration or engrossment in the brand [32]. From a behavioural viewpoint, engagement refers to actions toward a firm that go beyond transactions [34], for e.g. participation, vigour and interaction with the focal brand [33]. From an emotional perspective, customer engagement may be characterised by feelings of an individual towards a brand [28], for e.g. a customer's level of brand-related inspiration and/or pride [32].

Unlike authors who have used multidimensional perspectives, van Doorn et al. focus only on the behavioural dimension of customer engagement [35]. According to these scholars, customer engagement consists of behaviours, which go beyond transactions [35]. Customers engage in several behaviours that boost their relationship with the brand. Behavioural manifestations do not only mean purchases, but also include other activities of the customer such as word of mouth, customer co-creation and complaining behaviour [36], recommendations, helping other customers, blogging, writing reviews and even engaging in legal actions [35]. By moving along the customer engagement cycle, value is generated both for the customer and the company. However, when organisations fail to engage customers, they have to face the potential threat of customer enragement [37], a situation where customers can easily become value destroyers instead of value creators for companies [38, 39]. This forces businesses to be increasingly reactive, or even proactive, to avoid negative brand image consequences which in turn may lead to increased value co-destruction.

3   Methodology

A netnographic study was undertaken to observe reactions of customers to company posts on Facebook pages of grocery stores. Netnography is a participant-observation method used for data collection to research the consumer behaviour of online communities and cultures present on the Internet [40]. The aim of this netnographic research was to analyse the reactions of customers of grocery stores to messages posted by the grocery stores on their official Facebook pages. The researchers have observed interactions on the official Facebook pages of Tesco and Walmart. For a rigorous and reliable research approach, the researchers have adhered to the five stages and recommended procedures: (1) making entrée, (2) data collection and analysis, (3) providing trustworthy interpretation, (4) research ethics, and finally (5) member checks. [40].

For the entrée, the researchers have chosen Tesco and Walmart, the leading grocery stores in the world according to the March 2013 Global Food Retail report. These two grocery stores have been selected as they have both implemented an international strategy and have stores in several countries. Additionally there are high traffic of postings and a large number of discrete posters on both Facebook pages.

For data collection, the researchers downloaded conversations occurring on the official Facebook pages of Tesco and Walmart during a one-month period during which saturation of data occurred [40]. The data were saved in word documents, the data added up to 8008 pages of texts using Arial font size 11. The data were analysed through the qualitative software, NVivo.

The third step of netnography is to provide trustworthy interpretation [40]. Research is reckoned to be reasonable and trustworthy when conventional procedures of netnography are followed while collecting and analysing data [40]. Triangulation of data was used to enhance credibility of the study. Triangulation is achieved through the use of a large number of customers who have posted comments [41]. Additionally site triangulation has been achieved through the participation of customers from two different grocery stores (Tesco and Walmart) in order to lessen the effect on the research of particular local factors belonging to one specific grocery store.

The ethical procedure recommended by Langer and Beckman has been adopted in this research [42]. Comments posted by customers of Tesco and Walmart on the official Facebook page are considered to be publicly available data as they are not password restricted. Therefore the researchers did not need to obtain permission before using these data. However, anonymity and privacy of the participants have been respected.

Finally, the fifth step is carrying out member checks [40]. Member check is a technique whereby part or all of the research findings are given to the participants of the research in order to seek their comments [41]. However, the researchers did not carry out member checks since this research is conducted entirely unobtrusively, and Langer and Beckman argue that in such conditions, it is unnecessary to present the findings back to members of the community who participated [42].

4   Findings and Discussions

When customers respond to company posts or initiate conversations on the Facebook pages of Tesco and Walmart, they provide insights into the reasons why they engage with businesses on social media. This study reveals that social media have empowered customers, have influenced the relationships customers have with the grocery stores and have generated customer engagement.

4.1   Empowered Customers Within the Grocery Sector

While interacting with Tesco and Walmart on their official Facebook page, customers perceive that they have been empowered since they can voice out their opinions to the virtual brand community and they can also add or destroy value for the business. Co-creation of products and modification of products are not areas in which customers can add value in the grocery sector, since grocery stores do not manufacture products but only source products from their suppliers to sell to final customers. However, this study reveals that customers of Tesco and Walmart add value to the relationship by suggesting products that they would like to have, by informing the grocery stores of their needs and wants, by recommending products to their peers, and by giving advice to other customers as illustrated by the following quote:

"Let's all go to tescos [sic] where allegra [sic] gets her best cloths [sic] their [sic] all half price she thinks that's nice"

Additionally, the researcher has observed that Facebook has given a voice to the customer, which extends far beyond the circle of relatives, friends and colleagues known to the customer. By giving a voice to the customer, Facebook has empowered customers since it is easier for customers to post complaints on the page, to criticise actions of the company, than to call the company or write a letter of complaint as illustrated below.

"I will never buy food at Walmart and risk my life. Walmart, please improve your quality…
………..dont [sic] go down to any level to lower your prices. Do not risk the lives of people to save a few cents"

4.2 Relationship Building Within the Grocery Sector

As the modern food retail industry is booming worldwide and competition in this sector is rife, grocery retailers aim to provide superior customer value to gain customer satisfaction. To improve the satisfaction levels of customers, retailers are increasingly using social media to enrich their shopping experience [43]. Tesco and Walmart have set up their official Facebook pages to communicate, interact and engage their customers to strengthen the relationship with them.

In this study, the researcher found that customers have commented on the relationship they have with grocery stores by posting comments in which they have expressed satisfaction and loyalty towards Tesco and Walmart. This study reveals that customers tend to post positive comments in which they inform the company and other customers about the product or service that they have bought and how satisfied they are with the purchase as illustrated in the following quote:

"Walmart the best store in the whole world, everything that I need is there, yeah [sic] because after looking in the other stores website comparing prices at end Walmart is the my favourite and I finished my day in Walmart."

Emotional bonding is a prerequisite to strong brand relationships [19]. Customers of Tesco and Walmart have demonstrated their emotional commitment to the firm by posting comments in which they express their affection and attachment to the firm for e.g. by using the word 'love'. These emotional bonds therefore provide a sustainable competitive advantage [44].

However, this study has also revealed numerous cases of dissatisfied customers who have either complained about a product or service or criticised an action of the organisation and who have vouched that they are terminating the relationship with the grocery stores as illustrated by the following quote:

"Why am I being plastered with ads from this miserable store? I hate wmart [sic]!!!!!

When retailers fail to meet expectations of customers, the relationship is broken and customers turn to competitors [45]. However, engaging with customers on Facebook, Tesco and Walmart can help build and maintain relationships with them.

4.3 Customer Engagement Within the Grocery Sector

Tesco and Walmart aim to engage customers on their official Facebook pages. This study reveals that the three most extensively cited dimensions of customer engagement occur on the Facebook page of Tesco and Walmart: cognitive, emotional and behavioural. Cognitive engagement occurs at Tesco and Walmart, whenever customers post comments in which they provide information and help to other customers, or when they give advice to other customers. Another form of cognitive engagement is when customers post comments about their loyalty towards the stores as illustrated below:

> "Love tescos [sic] have shopped there for the last 29yrs [sic] since I had my first son. £1 delivery slots will definitely make me shop on line!! [sic]"

Emotional engagement also occurs whenever customers post comments about their feelings and emotions. Four main emotions have been expressed on the Facebook pages of Tesco and Walmart: enthusiasm, humour, sarcasm and scepticism. Enthusiasm and humour bring positive value to the online community, while sarcasm and scepticism destroy value and even damage the image of the store. Emotional engagement influences the nature of the relationship between the customer and the business [30, 44].

Behavioural engagement occurs when customers request for more information, entertainment, additional incentives and when they participate by responding to posts of the stores. This study reveals that customers converse with other customers on Facebook, share advertisement, give advice to other customers, get or provide feedback to other customers, criticise other customers, help other customers, make themselves or someone else known to other customers and also provide support and encouragement to other customers.

When customers are engaged, the levels of utilitarian and hedonic value that they perceive to experience increase [33]. However, findings have revealed that engaged customers also post negative comments, which may harm the organisation. When this occurs, instead of engaging customers, retailers generate customer enragement [37]. This study reveals that customers destroy value when they post comments to complain, to criticise, to provide information about competitors, to warn customers against a product/service, and to boycott a store. When UGC contains negative brand information, it may damage a brand [46].

4.4 Influence of Social Media on the Grocery Sector

From the findings of this study, it can be concluded that the four main constructs of the study are interconnected: social media, relationship marketing, customer empowerment, and customer engagement. In the retail sector, more specifically the grocery sector, Facebook generates online customer engagement which influences the relationships customers have with Tesco and Walmart. Empowered customers use Facebook to convey their satisfaction or dissatisfaction to Tesco and Walmart as well as to the members of the community by posting comments. The interconnectedness of the constructs is depicted in Fig. 1.

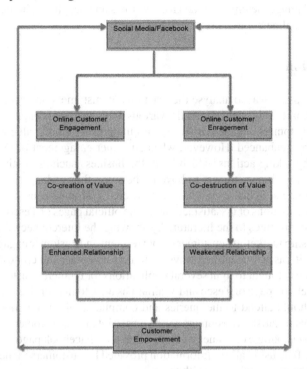

Fig. 1. Customer reactions to messages posted on Facebook pages of Tesco and Walmart. (Source: developed by the authors)

The model depicts the reactions of customers to messages posted on the Facebook pages of Tesco and Walmart. Tesco and Walmart use Facebook to engage their customers. This study shows that customers interact with the grocery stores by 'liking', 'sharing' and 'commenting' posts on the Facebook page. This study has revealed that online customer engagement can either create value or destroy value. Positive online customer engagement results in co-creation of value, which leads to a stronger relationship between the grocery stores and their customers. While negative online customer engagement also known as online customer enragement leads to co-destruction of value, which weakens the relationship between the parties.

In this social media era, whether the customer is satisfied or dissatisfied with the products and services of the grocery stores, the customer feels empowered as Facebook and social media offer a voice to the customer. When the customer has a positive customer experience, he/she wants to share this experience with the other members of the virtual community. Therefore, the happy and satisfied customer goes back to the Facebook page and posts a positive message, which may eventually positively influence the members of the online community. Conversely, when the customer experiences a negative outcome resulting in online customer enragement, he/she wants to share his/her experience with the other members of the virtual community. Hence, the disgruntled and angry customer posts a negative comment on the Facebook page. This customer backlash may damage the image of the grocery stores and negatively influence the other members of the online community.

5   Conclusion

The aim of this paper was to analyse the reactions of customers on Facebook pages of Tesco and Walmart. This paper shows the various ways customers engage with grocery stores. When customers engage positively with the grocery store, value is created and the relationship is enhanced. However, when customer enragement occurs, customers destroy value by taking actions, which harm the business such as posting complaints and criticisms or asking customers to boycott the store, thus endangering the relationships with customers. Social media have empowered customers who use Facebook to express their satisfactions or dissatisfactions on the official pages of Tesco and Walmart.

This paper contributes to the literature by showing the interconnectedness of social media, relationship marketing, customer empowerment and customer engagement in the grocery sector. It has also identified ways customers co-create and co-destroy value.

This paper has brought to light several implications for retailers. Customers perceive the official Facebook page of Tesco and Walmart as a customer service channel. Therefore retailers should attend to the queries and complaints of customers efficiently on Facebook, so that unsatisfied customers can be turned into loyal customers. Additionally, retailers should encourage customer co-creation on their Facebook page and should also harness CRM 2.0 by using all the information provided by customers in their comments to personalise the communication with them.

The limitation of the paper is related to the nature of the netnography method, which constrained the analysis to those customers who have commented on Facebook, therefore neglecting other sources such as offline customer feedback. Future research might offer a comparative analysis of the use of Facebook by grocery stores and might analyse the social media strategies adopted by these firms. Another avenue for future research could be to focus on one grocery store operating in several countries to identify differences and similarities between social media communication in different country contexts. This will provide the opportunity to look at how communication is customised to specific locations i.e. the influence of place and culture.

References

1. Arnaboldi, M., Coget, J.F.: Social media and business: we've been asking the wrong question. Organ. Dyn. **45**, 47–54 (2016). http://dx.doi.org/10.1016/j.orgdyn.2015.12.006
2. Constantinides, E., Romero, C., Boria, M.: Social media: a new frontier for retailers? Eur. Retail Res. **22**, 1–28 (2008)

3. Ureña, G.V., Murillo, D.H., Murillo, N.H., Garza, F.J.M.: Purposes of the communication between companies and their Facebook followers. Rev. Lat. de Comun. Soc. **70**, 110–121 (2015). doi:10.4185/RLCS-2015-1037en. http://www.revistalatinacs.org/070/paper/1037mx/07en.html
4. Schultz, D.E., Peltier, J.: Social media's slippery slope: challenges, opportunities and future research directions. J. Res. Interact. Mark. **7**(2), 86–99 (2013)
5. Kaplan, A., Haenlein, M.: Users of the world, unite! the challenges and opportunities of social media. Bus. Horiz. **53**, 59–68 (2010)
6. Tarnowski, J.: Social studies. Progress. Grocer **90**(7), 85–130 (2011)
7. Tsimonis, G., Dimitriadis, S.: Brand strategies in social media. Mark. Intell. Plan. **32**(3), 328–344 (2014)
8. Anderson, K., Knight, D., Pookulangara, S., Josiam, B.: Influence of hedonic and utilitarian motivations on retailer loyalty and purchase intention: a Facebook perspective. J. Retail. Consum. Serv. **21**, 773–779 (2014)
9. Kietzmann, J.H., Hermkens, K., Mccarthy, I.P., Silvestre, B.S.: Social media? get serious! understanding the functional building blocks of social media. Bus. Horiz. **54**, 241–251 (2011)
10. Hanna, R., Rohm, A., Crittenden, V.L.: We're all connected: the power of the social media ecosystem. Bus. Horiz. **54**, 265–273 (2011)
11. Coulter, K.S., Roggeveen, A.: "Like it or not": Consumer responses to word-of-mouth communication in on-line social networks. Manage. Res. Rev. **35**(9), 878–899 (2012)
12. Dekay, S.H.: How large companies react to negative Facebook comments. Corp. Commun. Int. J. **17**(3), 289–299 (2012)
13. Pereira, H.G., Salgueiro, M.F., Mateus, I.: Say yes to Facebook and get your customers involved! relationships in a world of social networks. Bus. Horiz. (2014). doi:10.1016/j.bushor.2014.07.001
14. Park, H., Kim, Y.K.: The role of social network websites in the consumer–brand relationship. J. Retail. Consum. Serv. **21**, 460–467 (2014)
15. Mangold, W.G., Faulds, D.J.: Social media: the new hybrid element of the promotion mix. Bus. Horiz. **52**, 357–365 (2009)
16. Yan, J.: Social media in branding: fulfilling a need. J. Brand Manage. **18**(9), 688–696 (2011)
17. Lipsman, A., Mudd, G., Rich, M., Bruich, S.: The power of "like" how brands reach (and influence) fans through social-media marketing. J. Advert. Res. **52**(1), 40–52 (2012)
18. Bergh, B.G.V., Lee, M., Quilliam, E., Hove, T.: The multidimensional nature and brand impact of user-generated ad parodies in social media. Int. J. Advert. **30**(1), 103–131 (2011)
19. Fournier, S., Avery, J.: The uninvited brand. Bus. Horiz. **54**, 193–207 (2011)
20. Harrison, T.M., Barthel, B.: Wielding new media in Web 2.0 exploring the history of engagement with the collaborative construction of media products. New Media Soc. **11**(1-2), 155–178 (2009)
21. Thackeray, R., Neiger, B.I., Hanson, C.L., McKenzie, J.F.: Enhancing promotional strategies within social marketing programs: use of Web 2.0 social media. Health Promot. Pract. **9**(4), 338–343 (2008)
22. Champoux, V., Durgee, J., McGlynn, L.: Corporate Facebook pages: when "fans" attack. J. Bus. Strat. **33**(2), 22–30 (2012)
23. Schulze Horn, I., Taros, T., Dirkes, S., Huer, L., Rose, M., Tietmeyer, R., Constantinides, E.: Business reputation and social media - a primer on threats and responses. IDM J. Direct Data Digital Mark. Practice **16**(3), 4 (2015). http://www.palgrave-journals.com/dddmp/index.html
24. Lee, H., Han, J., Suh, Y.: Gift or threat? an examination of voice of the customer: The case of MyStarbucksIdea.com. Electron. Commer. Res. Appl. (2014). doi:10.1016/j.elerap.2014.02.001

25. Pfeffer, J., Zorbach, T., Carley, K.M.: Understanding online firestorms: negative word-of-mouth dynamics in social media networks. J. Mark. Commun. **20**(1–2), 117–128 (2014). doi: 10.1080/13527266.2013.797778
26. Malhotra, A.: Defining purpose and meaning in social media. Vikalpa: J. Decis. Makers **37**(4), 102–105 (2012)
27. De Valck, K., van Bruggen, G., Wierenga, B.: Virtual communities: a marketing perspective. Decis. Support Syst. **47**, 185–203 (2009)
28. Vivek, S., Beatty, S., Morgan, R.: Customer engagement: exploring customer relationships beyond purchase. J. Mark. Theory Pract. **20**(2), 122–146 (2012)
29. Dessart, L., Veloutsou, C., Morgan-Thomas, A.: Consumer engagement in online brand communities: a social media perspective. J. Product Brand Manage. **24**(1), 1–33 (2015)
30. Brodie, R.J., Hollebeek, L.D., Juric, B., Ilic, A.: Customer engagement: conceptual domain, fundamental propositions, and implications for research. J. Serv. Res. **14**(3), 252–271 (2011a)
31. Hollebeek, L., Chen, T.: Exploring positively- versus negatively-valenced brand engagement: a conceptual model. J. Product Brand Manage. **23**(1), 62–74 (2014)
32. Hollebeek, L.: Demystifying customer brand engagement: exploring the loyalty nexus. J. Mark. Manage. **27**(7/8), 785–807 (2011)
33. Hollebeek, L.D.: The customer engagement/value interface: an exploratory investigation. Australas. Mark. J. **21**(1), 17–24 (2013)
34. Porter, C., Donthu, N., MacElroy, W., Wydra, D.: How to foster and sustain engagement in virtual communities. Calif. Manage. Rev. **53**(4), 80–110 (2011)
35. van Doorn, J., Lemon, K.N., Mittal, V., Nass, S., Pick, D., Pirner, P., Verhoef, P.C.: Customer engagement behavior: theoretical foundations and research directions. J. Serv. Res. **13**(3), 253–266 (2010)
36. Bijmolt, T.H.A., Leeflang, P.S.H., Block, F., Eisenbeiss, M., Hardie, B.G.S., Lemmens, A., Saffert, P.: Analytics for customer engagement. J. Serv. Res. **13**(3), 341–356 (2010)
37. Leeflang, P.S.H., Verhoef, P.C., Dahlström, P., Freundt, T.: Challenges and solutions for marketing in a digital era. Eur. Manage. J. **32**, 1–12 (2014)
38. Verhoef, P., Beckers, S., van Doorn, J.: Understand the perils of co-creation. Harv. Bus. Rev. **91**(9), 28–32 (2013)
39. Verhoef, P.C., Reinartz, W.J., Krafft, M.: Customer engagement as a new perspective in customer management. J. Serv. Res. **13**(3), 247–252 (2010)
40. Kozinets, R.V.: The field behind the screen: using netnography for marketing research in online communities. J. Mark. Res. **39**, 61–72 (2002)
41. Lincoln, Y.S., Guba, E.G.: Naturalistic Inquiry. Sage Publications, Beverly Hills (1985)
42. Langer, R., Beckman, S.C.: Sensitive research topics: netnography revisited. Qual. Market Res. Int. J. **8**(2), 189–203 (2005)
43. Pookulangara, S., Koesler, K.: Cultural influence on consumers' usage of social networks and its' impact on online purchase intentions. J. Retail. Consum. Serv. **18**, 348–354 (2011)
44. Harridge-March, S., Quinton, S.: Virtual snakes and ladders: social networks and the relationship marketing loyalty ladder. Mark. Rev. **9**(2), 171–181 (2009)
45. Zeithaml, V., Berry, L., Parasuraman, A.: The behavioral consequences of service quality. J. Mark. **60**(2), 31–46 (1996)
46. Cheong, H., Morrison, M.: Consumers' reliance on product information and recommendations found in UGC. J. Interact. Advert. **8**(2), 1–29 (2008)

Customer Service Experience Through Technology-Enabled Social CRM – An Exploratory Analysis in the Automotive Industry

Aaron W. Baur[1(✉)], Johannes S. Henne[2], and Markus Bick[1]

[1] ESCP Europe Business School Berlin, Berlin, Germany
{abaur,mbick}@escpeurope.eu
[2] City & Bits GmbH, Berlin, Germany
johannes.henne@gmx.de

Abstract. In recent years, social media and the Web 2.0 have rapidly gained an increasing popularity. Companies have recognized this development and anticipate higher customer satisfaction, customer loyalty and customer lifetime value through the use of social media for commercial purposes. Social customer relationship management (SCRM) professionalizes the use of social media and aims at value cocreation of companies and their customers. Through a combination of high tech and high touch, this new way of interaction with customers also offers plenty of opportunities to enhance customer service experience.

In this inductive, exploratory study, eighteen interviews were held with professionals from several vertical levels of the automotive industry (original equipment manufacturers, suppliers, market research agencies, and strategy consultancies). We aimed at exploring which opportunities, pitfalls and success factors organizations report when using technology-based Social CRM to leverage customer service experience. The findings are then discussed and practical recommendations given.

Keywords: Customer relationship management · CRM · Customer service experience · Social CRM · Value cocreation · Social media · Service economy

1 Introduction

A constantly growing number of activities of private and public organizations are engineered and managed as services, often times creating innovations for economic prosperity and social welfare. This development is mirrored in the Information Systems (IS) discipline. Examples include the use of services as the organizing logic for providing information systems, the use of services as an architectural paradigm (Service Oriented Architecture, SOA), and the development of Cloud/Internet-based services for information, processes, applications, and IT-infrastructures [1].

Along with a service-oriented economy in a highly competitive environment, there is an ever growing pressure to deliver customers a unique service experience to ensure customer satisfaction, retention and referrals. This necessity to deliver outstanding

© IFIP International Federation for Information Processing 2016
Published by Springer International Publishing Switzerland 2016. All Rights Reserved
Y.K. Dwivedi et al. (Eds.): I3E 2016, LNCS 9844, pp. 157–172, 2016.
DOI: 10.1007/978-3-319-45234-0_15

service can be supported through a mixture of technology and personal interaction, that is, by 'high tech and high touch' [2, 3]. Likewise, only few people can imagine their life without the daily involvement in social media services like Facebook, Twitter, or YouTube. Social media and Web 2.0 have advanced to an important part of economic, social, and technology concept of the Internet, which enables users to create content and build a network with other users [4]. The results from user participation, such as posts, friend lists, and profiles, are accessible by other parties of the community [5]. This development attracts attention of companies that aim to take advantage of the opportunities that come with them, such as improving reputation, influencing the purchase decision process of potential buyers, increasing marketing efficiency, supporting cost reductions, receiving post-purchase feedback, and innovating their products through cocreation [6–9].

Combining the developments of a predominantly service-based economy with the pervasiveness of social media customer interactions, the relatively new term social customer relationship management (SCRM) was born [10]. Social customer relationship management is a philosophy and business strategy that professionalizes the affiliation to customers using social media and aims at realizing mutual benefits. The relevance of the opportunities and challenges are underpinned by the reports of the renowned Marketing Science Institute (MSI), which biennially issues its 'Research Priorities'. The Research Priorities papers capture "the areas of most interest and importance to MSI member companies" [11]. The number one ranked priority, *Understanding Customers and the Customer Experience,* explicitly emphasize the importance of more research of the customer service experience.

In this paper, we apply a qualitative interview approach to answer the following research question:

> RQ: *Which opportunities, pitfalls and success factors do companies on several vertical levels of the automotive industry report when applying technology-based Social Customer Relationship Management to enhance Customer Service Experience?*

The intention is to build a better understanding of the interaction between Social CRM and the intended delivery of 'memorable events' [12] of commercial firms when operating in a business-to-consumer (B2C) or business-to-business (B2B) context.

In the remainder of this research paper, we first draw a picture of the interactions between a service economy, a necessary high level of customer service experience and social media/Social CRM. We then explain the research methodology, before we present and discuss the results. A conclusion, also explaining limitations and avenues of further research, close the paper.

2   The Interplay of Service, Customer Service Experience and Social Technology

For decades, marketing was primarily constructed around physical products. Traditional understandings following the historic goods-dominant logic identify value as something that could be manufactured or created within a business and then distributed to customers, thus, making value at the point of exchange the prime issue. With the advent of the 'service-economy' [13, 14], however, the services that go along with products and services as stand-alone offerings moved into the focus of most researchers. The service-dominant logic thinking diffused into ICT development. The Information Systems discipline contributes to the interdisciplinary research stream of Service Science since its first inception about 10 years ago.

However, even in the service-dominant logic, research in marketing focused on defining value from a company's perspective [15]. More recent approaches have been to explain the notion of value from the customers' point of view [16, 17]. As most services can only be delivered in conjunction with the customer, the ensuring and managing of the customer service experience became the center of thought.

Customer experience is the subjective, internal response customers have to any direct or indirect contact with a firm [18]. Customer service experience entails any aspect of a firm's offering, such as the quality of customer care, product and service features, usability, advertising, and packaging. As CEOs oftentimes focus on costs rather than on the customer value, literature is full of bad customer service experiences, such as mystifying phone carrier minutes to discourage comparison shopping and thus price war, hard-to-obtain rebates to stimulate a purchase, or offering electronic surrogates on company hotlines to slash staffing costs. These customer experiences provoke regrets and then the determination to do business elsewhere [19]. At the same time, the advent and success of the service paradigm challenges previously established separations between B2B and B2C relationships, corporate IS and consumer IS, or internal IS and external services.

The Paradigm Shift from Web 1.0 to Web 2.0. In parallel, profound changes in society, business and technology took place, revolutionizing (online) communication [20]. Central keywords in this context are Web 2.0 and Social Media [4]. Web 2.0 describes second generation web technologies [21] focused on the active, simultaneous and bi-directional involvement of professional and non-professional users [22]. Social Media are corresponding internet-based applications that enable participation in creating, communicating, and sharing content such as text messages, posts, images, or short clips [23]. The availability of easy-to-use forums, blogs, special interest groups, and other social media channels has opened up opportunities for ordinary people to engage easily with large governmental or corporate bodies by creating user-generated content (UGC). UGC was the main factor responsible for the massive growth of Web 2.0 and the unprecedented availability of information-rich content. Commercial companies have actively gathered and analyzed these customer reviews, ideas, and opinions since the early years of this century [24, 25]. This 'wisdom-of-the-crowd' [26], however, was not only received, but also actively triggered, shaped, and influenced [27]. Through value cocreation, companies have harnessed their own customers in reducing product flaws or developing completely new products and services [28]. More and more, manufacturers and users of products are entering a symbiosis, with the Web 2.0 being a "key piece of organizational infrastructure that links and engages employees, customers, and suppliers as never before" [29].

Customer relationship management (CRM, [30]) is another promising field of application of Web 2.0, based on this more intimate relationship. Web 2.0 can provide "the means to facilitate dialogue and bonding not simply with individual consumers, but with multiple participants. This in turn may allow these various participants to benefit from an internet dialogue which is based upon community" [31]. In other words, Web 2.0 enables consumer-centric management and offers novel opportunities for direct interaction and collaboration and thus an increased exchange. This 'Web 2.0 supported CRM' is termed Social CRM (SCRM), addresses the potential for advanced customer integration, and deals with the deployment of Web 2.0 principles and practices in CRM [32]. According to Greenberg [33], SCRM is "[...] a philosophy and a business strategy, supported by a technology platform, business rules, processes and social characteristics, designed to engage the customer in a collaborative conversation in order to provide mutually beneficial value in a trusted and transparent business environment."

The term social customer service consequently generally refers to customer service offered via social media platforms such as Facebook, Twitter, or YouTube [34]. Examples of user activities are joining groups, placing like- or dislike flags, adding others to the friend list, reading specific texts, watching videos, and changing profile information. With these activities, consumers receive a better customer service experience and benefit from participating companies through relationship advantages, first hand reviews, product updates, brand interaction and exchange, and influence on business processes [35]. Examples are discounts, special promotions, and the acceleration of the fulfilment of support requests. Business opportunities arise in the form of leads (i.e., potential customers), enriched customer profile information, and a better understanding of interests and markets [36]. Fliess et al. [8] state that "activities of customers can be considered as an economic resource". User activities in social media create value and stimulate companies' revenues [37].

Social customer service is more than establishing a channel for customers' requests and complaints, but rather a complete realignment of the online communication philosophy and strategy [38]. The objective is to provide companies and their customer service organizations with the tools needed to move customers from a satisfied and loyal experience to avid brand advocates [39]. It combines personal interaction between company staff and the customer with state-of-the-art technology, also referred to as 'high tech, high touch' [2, 3]. This technology-employee pair is especially suitable to create a high customer service experience [40].

3 Research Methodology

The review of literature in the abovementioned areas revealed that applications of Social CRM actually used in practice for the purpose of enhancing customer service experience are not well researched. We therefore chose an explorative, inductive, interview-based method, as this is deemed most suitable for discovering new ideas and arguments [41, 42]. Three constituting considerations led us to the choice of the automotive industry as our research subject: first, automobiles are very complex products [43]. They therefore – in theory – yield abundant motives and possibilities for customers to engage with the manufacturers or suppliers. Second, the high relative value people assign to automobiles being status symbols leads – in practice – to a massive amount of automobile-related online user-generated content [44] as a basis for

Table 1. Question blocks of interview guideline

Block Number	Area of Questions
1	Demographics & role of interviewee; general situation of the company
2	Overview CRM landscape and offline service channels
3	Social media channels
4	Relevance of social media services for CRM
5	Implementation of social media strategy
6	Customer focus and customer service experience excellence
7	Overall assessment

future increases customer service experience. And third, the automobile industry still plays a decisive role in many countries' economies, making the findings highly relevant for practical purposes.

After the target industry had been fixed, we developed an interview guideline comprising seven question blocks that adhered to common qualitative research standards [45]. The guideline was first pre-tested with six final year Master's students enrolled in management-related degrees (Table 1) [46].

Eighteen semi-structured practitioner interviews were then carried out on the practitioners' own premises (*field research,* [47]). The selection of the interview partners and the eleven companies which they work for, respectively, was based on a diligent, purposive, theory-driven sampling strategy, that is, relevance was more decisive than representativeness [48]. This ensured the inclusion of most aspects of the underlying theories in the evidence gathered from the informants [45, 49]. It also enabled comparisons as well as theoretical and literal replication [50]. The inclusion criteria were 'automotive company' or 'professional service firm working for the automotive industry', the interviews continued until a theoretic saturation had been reached [51]. The literature confirms that multiple cases enhance validity [49, 52], and the convergence of statements and observations increases confidence in the findings [49]. The interviews lasted between 51 and 96 min. More than one interviewee was questioned at most companies to avoid a respondent bias and so that a first triangulation of findings could be done (see the descriptions of companies and interview partners in Appendix A). The inclusion of managers from different hierarchical ranks, working for firms at several vertical levels of the industry (original equipment manufacturers (OEMs), suppliers and service providers), should ensure the formation of a holistic picture and mitigate the possibility of missing important insights [53, 54]. The interviews were transcribed [45] and coded following an open coding process [55]. Relevant passages were identified and categories were subsequently refined in an axial coding phase. The analysis was diligently carried out to fulfill the common requirements for qualitative research (e.g., [48, 56, 57]). The interpretation process was rule-driven and documented ("procedural validity"). Finally, consensus was derived through discussions with several of the interviewees [58].

4 Results and Recommendations

The analysis of the coded interview transcripts gives a solid picture of current practices of using Social CRM to enhance customer service experience. The research categories and codes used for analysis were not based on a certain framework or theory, but emerged completely out of the interview data. We then iteratively rearranged them until we got seven rather homogenous concepts. Besides *pros* and *pitfalls*, we derived *processes, plans, proactivity, personnel*, and *personality*.

In the following section, we summarize and discuss the findings (see Table 2 for sample evidence). As the topic is especially relevant for practitioners trying to leverage the technology for the benefit of their clients and their own bottom line results, we decided to deviate from standard procedures and present the findings in the form of practical recommendations.

First of all, personnel need to understand the overall meaning and significance of customer service experience for their clients and of Social CRM for their company. Both managers and employees should attend workshops and training sessions to obtain the necessary social media and customer centricity awareness. Only under these circumstances the use of Facebook, Twitter and other services will increase the service experience and add value to the company. Otherwise, the services will be ends in themselves and can even be a threat. All interviewees confirmed that Social CRM offered through social media has taken a center stage. Resources in form of capital and man power need to be allocated.

If the company has decided to offer Social CRM, it has to make sure to align it with the overall business model, corporate vision, mission, and strategy. This is the task of the top tier of managers, who then have to convey the new thinking to the whole organization.

Another responsibility of the top management is to ensure that all divisions are involved in equal measure. One key challenge is to reply to customers' request virtually in

Table 2. Sample qualitative evidence from interviews

Research Constructs	Codes	Findings	Exemplifying Quotes O = OEM I S = Supplier M = Market Research C = Strategy Consultancy
Pros	Competitive Advantage	competitive advantage through a relationship based on better understanding customers' needs	**C2:** "we really do believe we attain superior customer service experience through our Social CRM initiatives"
	Reach	potentially millions of contact points reachable with a mouse-click, penetration of smartphones/mobile devices important driver	**O1:** "we reach more customers with Social CRM than with all other communication channels combined" **O2:** "about every second a customer uses a Social Media channel"

(Continued)

Table 2. (*Continued*)

Benefits	Mone-tary Benefit	almost no variable costs, very effective communication channel (many customer replies possible in short amount of time) increase of customer equity	**S2:** "the application of successful social customer service has almost doubled the sales compared to other communication channels"
	Timeli-ness	fast, almost synchronous communication without the disadvantages of phone calls; great customer service experience higher frequency of interaction possible	**M1:** "we can get back to our client without any delays, and can give expert advice due to real-time access to user-related data"
	(e-) word-of-mouth	word-of-mouth for free, one Twitter follower can stipulate hundreds of other ones; loyalty and increased customer-lifetime value; improved image	**O2:** "many of our satisfied customers share their experience over the Web" **C2:** "we experience higher revenue of customers who also use Social Media channels"
	Data Access	customer interactions yield massive amount of data, which can be mined to create up-selling opportunities	**O3:** "our marketing campaigns are much more tailor-made and reach exactly the specified target group"
Pitfalls	Non-Use	massive competitive disadvantage, threat of 'unofficial' company representation (e.g., fake Twitter account)	**S1:** "today, non-use is a no-go. There is only one worse thing: doing Social CRM sloppily or infrequently"
	Speed	sheer speed of information dissemination threatening, moderated replies need to be posted within 24 hours	**O1:** "one of the biggest hurdles to responding to social media customer feedback is the challenge of operating in real time" **M2:** "our policy is to react within two hours in 95% of cases, which is hard, but doable"
	Negative com-ments	people even more likely to talk about negative experience; anonymity of internet lowers threshold	**O2:** "moderated, but open discussion helps" **S2:** "we capitalize in negative tweets by solving the issue promptly" **O3:** "the risk of shitstorms is always there"
	Data Privacy	public channels not suitable for the exchange of customer data; here, the switch to more secure, private channels is mandatory	**C1:** "we had to transfer certain traffic to other channels due to data privacy concerns"
Processes	Com-prehen-sion & realiza-tion of value-ad	all hierarchical levels need to be aware of the 'why' and the associated opportunities, risks and technical requirements	**S1:** "we realized that top-management needs to show deep commitment to customer service experience supported by Social CRM"

(*Continued*)

Table 2. (*Continued*)

	Integration of 'social' into strategy	Inclusion of social media in corporate vision, mission & strategy; right social media approach match business model simple, integrated solutions, not fragmented, burdensome ones	**S2:** "customer service experience and satisfaction are central parts of our corporate self-image, which is codified in our mission. Social CRM is a way to get there."
	Collaboration of all departments	free flow of information between departments crucial to enable short customer response times; one 'voice' to the outside world sales and marketing do not monopolize points of contact with customers	**M3:** "our social media, PR and marketing departments closely coordinate their actions with virtually any other function to gain maximum alignment and credibility"
	Technology as enabler	powerful technology as a necessary commodity, but not as the means to an end technology enables monitoring, closed-loop process required	**C3:** "a proprietary tool helps us to track all action on Facebook" **S2:** "we use the fastest hardware and online connection, this is out of question"
	Key Performance Indicators	easy to collect and quantify data information from data then needs to be acted on	**M1:** "gathering business-relevant data, like degree of customer satisfaction, is now constantly monitored"
Plans	Knowledge Management	guidelines and handbook need to codify Social CRM strategy, voice and tone of voice	**S1:** "in a large corporate like us, there have to be rules pertaining to how we express and present ourselves in social media channels; this has worked well in the past"
	Escalation- and crisis plans	Emergency rules as how to handle sensitive data, criteria for incoming messages, exemplary replies and information of relevant contact persons	**O1:** "speed is decisive, even if things go wrong. We therefore developed a set of explicit emergency do's and don'ts, available and known to all employees"
Proactivity	Anticipation of trends and customer demands	constant monitoring of trends and developments ensure a fast adaption of the company, e.g., through new products or services delivered to the customer	**O3:** "indeed, we today get more ideas and suggestions from outsiders via social media channels than what we actively generate with internal product development"

(*Continued*)

Table 2. (*Continued*)

Personnel	Reduction of support need of customers	best-of-class Social CRM not only reacts, but proactively creates content that helps customers getting the most out of the company's products or services, without support.	**O2:** "for us, this idea of proactively trying to avoid customer requests – in its best sense – and to deliver an extraordinary service experience was very innovative"
	Recruiting	job descriptions, recruiting ads and hiring policies have to completely match the actual job and skill requirements; outsourcing of Social CRM not advisable completely new philosophy for employees: more authority, more rewarding job position, enhanced team work, higher salary	**C2:** "our CEO is personally responsible for hiring new employees and takes specific care to employ friendly, honest and integer colleagues, especially in the outside-facing departments. We developed an additional code of behavior for new employees as well"
	Training and qualification	training is key, especially in topics such as adherence to communication policies, service level agreements, user post handling, or response times.; well-trained personnel boosts motivation and leads to competitive advantage	**S1:** "our full-time staff responsible for Facebook are very well qualified and constantly trained" **M2:** "the manual is permanently updated and communicated" **C1:** "the fast pace of change in the social media landscape necessitates perpetual training"
Personality	First Contact Resolution	speed and credibility of reply to customer inquiry decisive, no automated answers if possible, solution-oriented thinking	**S2:** "we specifically stress the importance of a satisfactory solution on the first attempt" **O2:** "we really strive for making our customers feel appreciated"
	Treatment of Customer	professional etiquette, even if customers are impolite or insulting always take the customer's view point	**O1:** "we would never use inexperienced interns or part-timers to handle our Social CRM inquiries – what better asset than our customers do we have?"

real-time and thus, every division needs a designated person being responsible for the process [59]. Regular office hours will not necessarily meet the actual user behavior in the social media environment and additional resources have to be allocated to guarantee quick response rates at all time.

As part of the Social CRM strategy, risk planning has to be considered in possible cases of extraordinary situations. Again, this is important for all divisions because the company has to appear as one coherent entity. Every member should document interactions with customers to simplify the review process afterwards.

All previous recommendations make great demands on employees and, therefore, every company should have appropriate recruiting and training procedures. Within the recruiting process, demands regarding social competence and service-oriented qualities as well as communication skills should be assured. Another option would be to out-source Social CRM to an external partner [60]. However, for the most part, the managers interviewed do not recommend this as customer relationship management, be it with traditional or with ne means and technologies, has been and will remain a crucial success factor for the entire company.

In terms of continuous process improvement, the company needs to offer constant, advanced training to be enable staff staying ahead of the fast moving evolution of social media services [61]. Software product updates and new internal policies have to be effectively communicated to every employee involved in the social customer service process.

Finally, the decision which social media service to adopt first to establish Social CRM is important. It is nearly impossible for companies to enter multiple services at the same time [39]. Thus, they should focus on the most dominant service in the desired national market. Facebook has a leadership role and was deemed to be a rea-sonable starting point for most of the companies. Customers' expectations, which are of high importance, should be weighed up with the firm's own resources and capabilities.

5 Conclusion

In this research paper, the authors analyzed how Social CRM can interact with and be beneficial to customer service experience. Our study took an inductive, explorative stance with qualitative interviews as the method of data collection and coding as the means of data analysis. We advanced the body of research in the Service Science field from an IS academic viewpoint by answering the following research question:

Which opportunities, pitfalls and success factors do companies on several vertical levels of the automotive industry report when applying technology-based Social Cus-tomer Relationship Management to enhance Customer Service Experience?

As customers have a greater number of choices than ever before, more complex choices, and more channels through which to pursue them, companies need to focus on delivering an excellent customer service experience [62]. Spreading important clues that address all five senses of the customer, that is, seeing, smelling, tasting, hearing or touching, can at least partially be supported through Social CRM methods [63, 64]. However, many companies just seem to follow a trending social media path everyone is using without adding significant elements to their overall business model [65]. They have not realized until now how to integrate social media service into their strategic concept in order to differentiate themselves and create unique selling propositions [66], as well as igniting value cocreation [28].

The rapidly developing and changing social media environment and the hitherto changing relationship between companies and its customers can be regarded as the rationale for conducting this study (cf. also [67]). As more and more power shifts from the companies to the customers, new concepts, technologies and recommendations have to be created and provided [68]. This explorative approach with first empirical elements helps to set the research agenda for upcoming studies.

In conclusion, we could identify opportunities, pitfalls and success factors of Social CRM when it comes to enhancing customer service experience. In the end we agree with March [36, 69] who states that "by choosing social media over other communications channels, millions of customers have given voice to their concerns in what has become an increasingly public arena."

However, some limitations occur in this study which we would like to address. As is common with qualitative research, the number of data points gathered is limited. Eighteen interviews from eleven firms are a good start, but it remains unclear whether talking to eighteen other managers would yield the same or similar results. Cultural differences were also not taken into consideration. In addition, the interviewees were all related to the automotive industry, which can be counted as very mature. Questions of external validity, that is, whether the results can be transferred to other, potentially more dynamic industries, remain unacknowledged.

Further research can address more companies of various sizes, industries and cultural backgrounds. Switching from a commercial context to the public or non-profit sector may be worthwhile. Looking at the issue from the other side, the customer's point of view, could also bring up new perspectives and triangulate the findings. The increasing ubiquity of a service society calls for more relevant and rigorous research that reaches across traditional geographical and disciplinary boundaries.

Appendix A: Description of Interview Partners and Companies[1]

Group	Company	Number of Interviews	Company Type	Interview Partner
Automotive OEM	O1	1	European premium OEM	Head of Communication Insights
Automotive OEM	O2	3	European mass OEM	Head of Strategy
Automotive OEM	O2	3	European mass OEM	Senior Manager Digital/ Brand Marketing
Automotive OEM	O2	3	European mass OEM	Team Lead Communication Strategy/ Branding & Marketing Management
Automotive OEM	O3	2	European premium OEM	Associate Brand Strategies, Market Research and Competitor
Automotive OEM	O3	2	European premium OEM	Associate Product Management, Small Vehicles
Automotive Supplier	S1	1	European supplier of steering systems, top 50 of global suppliers	Vice President Personnel and Services
Automotive Supplier	S2	2	European supplier of driveline and chassis technology, top 20 of global suppliers	Head of Market Development, Market Intelligence & Sales Coordination
Automotive Supplier	S2	2	European supplier of driveline and chassis technology, top 20 of global suppliers	Project Manager Car Powertrain Technology
Market Research Agency	M1	1	European branch of a global leader in (market) research, insight, consultancy	Director Automotive
Market Research Agency	M2	1	Leading agency for content marketing & social media strategy	Director Social Media Strategies
Market Research Agency	M3	1	Specialized agency for innovation, product development, idea generation & idea management	Team Lead Social Media Research
Strategy Consultancy	C1	4	Global strategy consultancy (top 10)	Partner, EMEA Head of Digital Business Practice
Strategy Consultancy	C1	4	Global strategy consultancy (top 10)	Partner, EMEA Head of Automotive Practice
Strategy Consultancy	C1	4	Global strategy consultancy (top 10)	Partner, EMEA & Global Head of Strategic IT Practice, Global Head of Digital Business Practice
Strategy Consultancy	C1	4	Global strategy consultancy (top 10)	Partner, Vice President Knowledge Services
Strategy Consultancy	C2	1	Global strategy consultancy (top 10)	Manager Technology Practice
Strategy Consultancy	C3	1	Global strategy consultancy (top 10)	Manager Digital Services
Sum	11	18		

---

[1] Industry rankings (e.g., 'top 50') are based on the fiscal year 2015.

References

1. Poeppelbuss, J., Tuunanen, T. and Wijnhoven, F.: CfP ECIS 2016: Service Innovation, Engineering, and Management (2016). http://www.ecis2016.eu/files/downloads/Tracks/T27. pdf
2. Wunderlich, N.V., Wangenheim, F.V., Bitner, M.J.: High tech and high touch: a framework for understanding user attitudes and behaviors related to smart interactive services. J. Serv. Res. **16**, 3–20 (2013)
3. Davis, M.M., Spohrer, J.C., Maglio, P.P.: Guest editorial: how technology is changing the design and delivery of services. Oper. Manag. Res. **4**, 1–5 (2011)
4. Musser, J., O'Reilly, T.: Web 2.0 Principles and Best Practices. O'Reilly Media, Sebastopol (2007)
5. Ang, L.: Is SCRM really a good social media strategy? J. Database Mark. Cust. Strategy Manag. **18**, 149–153 (2011)
6. Smith, T.: Conference notes – the social media revolution. Int. J. Mark. Res. **51**, 559 (2009)
7. Baird, C.H., Parasnis, G.: From social media to social customer relationship management. Strategy Leaders. **39**, 30–37 (2011)
8. Fliess, S., Nadzeika, A., Nesper, J.: Understanding patterns of customer engagement – how companies can gain a surplus from a social phenomenon. J. Mark. Dev. Compet. **6**, 81–93 (2012)
9. Jahn, B., Kunz, W.: How to transform consumers into fans of your brand. J. Serv. Manag. **23**, 344–361 (2012)
10. Lehmkuhl, T., Jung, R.: Value creation potential of web 2.0 for SME - insights and lessons learnt from a European producer of consumer electronics. Int. J. Coop. Inf. Syst. **22**, 1–22 (2013)
11. Keller, K.L.: MSI 2014–2016 Research Priorities. http://www.msi.org/uploads/files/MSI_RP14-16.pdf
12. Pine, B.I., Gilmore, J.H.: Welcome to the experience economy. Harv. Bus. Rev. **76**, 97–105 (1999)
13. Vargo, S.L., Lusch, R.F.: Evolving to a new dominant logic for marketing. J. Mark. **68**, 1–17 (2004)
14. Vargo, S.L., Lusch, R.F.: Service-dominant logic: continuing the evolution. J. Acad. Mark. Sci. **36**, 1–10 (2008)
15. Tynan, C., McKechnie, S., Hartley, S.: Interpreting value in the customer service experience using customer-dominant logic. J. Mark. Manag. **30**, 1058–1081 (2014)
16. Heinonen, K., Strandvik, T., Voima, P.: Customer dominant value formation in service. Eur. Bus. Rev. **25**, 104–123 (2013)
17. Heinonen, K., Strandvik, T., Mickelsson, K., Edvardsson, B., Sundström, E., Andersson, P.: A customer-dominant logic of service. J. Serv. Manag. **21**, 531–548 (2010)
18. Kuepper, T., Lehmkuhl, T., Wieneke, A., Jung, R.: Technology use of social media within customer relationship management: an organizational perspective. In: Proceedings of the 19th Pacific Asia Conference on Information Systems, pp. 1–17, Singapore (2015)
19. Meyer, C., Schwager, A.: Understanding customer experience. Harv. Bus. Rev. **85**, 116–126 (2007)
20. Georgi, S., Jung, R., Lehmkuhl, T.: Die große Veränderung – Social Media revolutioniert die Online-Kommunikation. Controlling **23**, 632–637 (2011)
21. DiNucci, D.: Fragmented future. Print **53**, 32–35 (1999)
22. Dellarocas, C.: The digitization of word of mouth: promise and challenges of online feedback mechanisms. Manag. Sci. **49**, 1407–1424 (2003)

23. Kaplan, A.M., Haenlein, M.: Users of the world, unite! the challenges and opportunities of social media. Bus. Horiz. **53**, 59–68 (2010)
24. Berry, A.J., Otley, D.: Case-based research in accounting. In: Humphrey, C., Lee, B. (eds.) The Real Life Guide To Accounting Research: A Behind-The-Scenes View of Using Qualitative Research Methods, pp. 231–256. Elsevier, Amsterdam (2004)
25. Bryman, A.: Social Research Methods. Oxford University Press, Oxford (2012)
26. Berthon, P.R., Pitt, L.F., Plangger, K., Shapiro, D.: Marketing meets Web 2.0, social media, and creative consumers: implications for international marketing strategy. Bus. Horiz. **55**, 261–271 (2012)
27. Janssen, M., Matheus, R., Zuiderwijk, A.: Big and open linked data (BOLD) to create smart cities and citizens: insights from smart energy and mobility cases. In: Tambouris, E., Janssen, M., Scholl, H.J., Wimmer, M.A., Tarabanis, K., Gascó, M., Klievink, B., Lindgren, I., Parycek, P. (eds.) EGOV 2015. LNCS, vol. 9248, pp. 79–90. Springer, Heidelberg (2015)
28. Akaka, M.A., Corsaro, D., Kelleher, C., Maglio, P.P., Seo, Y., Lusch, R.F., Vargo, S.L.: The role of symbols in value cocreation. Mark. Theor. **14**, 311–326 (2014)
29. Bughin, J., Chui, M., Manyika, J.: Ten IT-enabled business trends for the decade ahead. McKinsey Global Institute, pp. 1–13 (2013)
30. Payne, A., Frow, P.: A strategic framework for customer relationship management. J. Mark. **69**, 167–176 (2005)
31. Szmigin, I., Canning, L., Reppel, A.E.: Online community: enhancing the relationship marketing concept through customer bonding. Int. J. Serv. Ind. Manag. **16**, 480–496 (2005)
32. Askool, S., Nakata, K.: A conceptual model for acceptance of social CRM systems based on a scoping study. AI & Soc. **26**, 205–220 (2011)
33. Greenberg, P.: The impact of CRM 2.0 on customer insight. J. Bus. Ind. Mark. **25**, 410–419 (2010)
34. Ryals, L.: Making customer relationship management work: the measurement and profitable management of customer relationships. J. Mark. **69**, 252–261 (2005)
35. Gallaugher, J., Ransbotham, S.: Social media and customer dialog management at starbucks. MIS Q. Exec. **9**, 197–212 (2010)
36. March, J.: Five Ways To Socialize Your Customer Service Team. http://www.conversocial.com/blog/entry/five-ways-to-socialize-your-customer-service-team, http://www.conversocial.com/blog/entry/five-ways-to-socialize-your-customer-service-team
37. Yang, C.C., Tang, X., Dai, Q., Yang, H., Jiang, L.: Identifying implicit and explicit relationships through user activities in social media. Int. J. Electron. Commer. **18**, 73–96 (2013)
38. Brinsmead, A.: Create a successful social customer service strategy. CRM Mag. **17**, 11 (2013)
39. Malthouse, E.C., Haenlein, M., Skiera, B., Wege, E., Zhang, M.: Managing customer relationships in the social media era: introducing the social CRM house. J. Interact. Mark. **27**, 270–280 (2013)
40. Sashi, C.M.: Customer engagement, buyer-seller relationships, and social media. Manag. Decis. **50**, 253–272 (2012)
41. Sonnenberg, C., vom Brocke, J.: Evaluation Patterns for Design Science Research Artefacts. In: Helfert, M., Donnellan, B. (eds.) EDSS 2011. CCIS, vol. 286, pp. 71–83. Springer, Heidelberg (2012)
42. Sonnenberg, C., vom Brocke, J.: Evaluations in the science of the artificial – reconsidering the build-evaluate pattern in design science research. In: Peffers, K., Rothenberger, M., Kuechler, B. (eds.) DESRIST 2012. LNCS, vol. 7286, pp. 381–397. Springer, Heidelberg (2012)

43. Abrahams, A.S., Jiao, J., Fan, W., Wang, G., Zhang, A.: What's buzzing in the blizzard of buzz? Automotive component isolation in social media postings. Decis. Support Syst. **55**, 871–882 (2013)
44. Eastin, M.S., Daugherty, T., Burns, N.M.: Handbook of Research on Digital Media and Advertising. User Generated Content Consumption. Information Science Reference. IGI Global, Hershey (2011)
45. Kvale, S., Brinkmann, S.: InterViews. Learning the Craft of Qualitative Research Interviewing. Sage, Thousand Oaks (2015)
46. Moody, D.L., Shanks, G.G.: Improving the quality of data models: empirical validation of a quality management framework. Inf. Syst. **28**, 619–650 (2003)
47. Abraham, R., Aier, S., Winter, R.: Fail early, fail often: towards coherent feedback loops in design science research evaluation. In: Proceedings of the 35th International Conference on Information Systems. Auckland, New Zealand (2014)
48. Miles, M.B., Huberman, A.M.: Qualitative Data Analysis. Sage, Thousand Oaks (1994)
49. Eisenhardt, K.M.: Building theories from case study research. Acad. Manag. Rev. **14**, 532–550 (1989)
50. Yin, R.K.: Case Study Research. Design and Methods. Sage, Beverly Hills (2003)
51. Miles, M.B., Huberman, A.M., Saldaña, J.: Qualitative Data Analysis. A Methods Sourcebook. Sage, Thousand Oaks (2013)
52. Eisenhardt, K.M., Graebner, M.E.: Theory building from cases: opportunities and challenges. Acad. Manag. J. **50**, 25–32 (2007)
53. Creswell, J.W., Plano Clark, V.L.: Designing and Conducting Mixed Methods Research. Sage, Thousand Oaks (2007)
54. Ghauri, P.N., Grønhaug, K.: Research Methods in Business Studies. A Practical Guide. Financial Times Prentice Hall, Harlow (2005)
55. Corbin, J., Strauss, A.: Grounded theory research: procedures, canons, and evaluative criteria. Qual. Sociol. **13**, 3–21 (1990)
56. Flick, U.: Managing Quality in Qualitative Research. Sage, London (2008)
57. Hesse-Biber, S.N., Leavy, P.: The Practice of Qualitative Research. Sage, Thousand Oaks (2006)
58. Wrona, T.: The case study analysis as a scientific research method. ESCP-EAP European School of Management, Berlin, Germany (2005)
59. Kuepper, T., Jung, R., Lehmkuhl, T., Walter, S., Wieneke, A.: Performance measures for social CRM: a literature review. In: Proceedings of the 27th Bled eConference, Bled, Slovenia (2014)
60. Trainor, K.J., Andzulis, J., Rapp, A., Agnihotri, R.: Social media technology usage and customer relationship performance: a capabilities-based examination of social CRM. J. Bus. Res. **67**, 1201–1208 (2014)
61. Kuepper, T., Wieneke, A., Lehmkuhl, T., Jung, R.: Evaluating social CRM performance: an organizational perspective. In: Proceedings of the 19th Pacific Asia Conference on Information Systems, Singapore (2015)
62. Sheth, J.N., Parvatiyar, A., Shainesh, G.: Customer Relationship Management: Emerging Concepts, Tools, and Applications. Tata McGraw-Hill Pub Co., New Delhi (2001)
63. Berry, L.L., Carbone, L.P.: Build loyalty through experience management. Qual. Prog. **40**(9), 26–32 (2007)
64. Ding, D.X.: Clues, flow channels, and cognitive states: an exploratory study of customer experiences with e-brokerage services. Serv. Sci. **3**, 182–193 (2011)
65. Boulding, W., Staelin, R., Ehret, M., Johnston, W.J.: A customer relationship management roadmap: what is known, potential pitfalls, and where to go. J. Mark. **69**, 155–166 (2005)
66. Kotler, P., Keller, K.: Marketing Management. Prentice Hall, Upper Saddle River (2011)

67. Haenlein, M., Kaplan, A.M.: The impact of unprofitable customer abandonment on current customers' exit, voice, and loyalty intentions: an empirical analysis. J. Serv. Mark. **26**, 458–470 (2012)
68. Ordenes, F.V., Theodoulidis, B., Burton, J., Gruber, T., Zaki, M.: Analyzing customer experience feedback using text mining: a linguistics-based approach. J. Serv. Res. **17**, 278–295 (2014)
69. March, J.: 5 Reasons Why Your Business Needs Social Customer Service. http://www.ddw.us.com/5-reasons-why-your-business-needs-social-customer-service, http://www.ddw.us.com/5-reasons-why-your-business-needs-social-customer-service

Social Customer Relationship Management as Predictor of Customer Relationship Performance: An Empirical Study of B2B and B2C Companies

Ashish K. Rathore, Sakshi Shioramwar, and P. Vigneswara Ilavarasan[✉]

Indian Institute of Technology Delhi, New Delhi, India
ashishriitd@gmail.com, shiivva07@gmail.com, vignes@iitd.ac.in

Abstract. Using an empirical survey conducted among B2B and B2C companies in India, the paper examines the linkage between social media use, customer relationship management (CRM), social customer relationship management (SCRM) and the customer relationship performance (CRP). A framework was constructed using literature review and validated by the regression analysis. The findings show that the social media use and CRM capabilities interact positively to build SCRM capabilities which then have positive impacts on CRP. The linkages differ slightly for business to business (B2B) and business to consumers (B2C) companies. The paper also shares the challenges faced by the businesses in implementing the SCRM.

Keywords: Customer relationship management · Social media · Social Customer Relationship Management · Customer Relationship Performance · India

1   Context

Social media platforms are becoming an indispensable part of strategies in reaching out to the customers and to maintain the relationship with them. They act as touch points and serve as building blocks for personalized experiences in a socially networked ecosystem. There are social media uses without external customer interactions which are aimed at improving the internal collaboration of the businesses. The examples include internal social networking platforms, internal wikis, social media recruiting and image sharing boards. It is said that degree of social media use for internal collaboration might be an important influencing factor for successful external collaboration for the businesses [1]. The traditional customer relationship management (CRM) focuses on aggregating and analyzing customer data in order to automate workflows for business process optimization and address issues related to customers in order to deliver high quality service to the customers. The new practices focus on engaging customers on a real time basis through multiple social media platforms and social monitoring tools [2]. This integration of social media in CRM is called as social CRM (SCRM). The SCRM enables not only employee to customer interactions but also customer to customer interactions and help in forming communities.

© IFIP International Federation for Information Processing 2016
Published by Springer International Publishing Switzerland 2016. All Rights Reserved
Y.K. Dwivedi et al. (Eds.): I3E 2016, LNCS 9844, pp. 173–182, 2016.
DOI: 10.1007/978-3-319-45234-0_16

Efforts are being made by the practitioners to implement the social CRM in an optimum way resulting in higher profitability to the businesses. Many social media technologies and their applications are being labeled as SCRM, but there is still a dearth of guidelines for SCRM design and implementation [3]. As the social media technologies are also evolving, the extant literature on this emerging space seems to be inadequate. The paper attempts to fill this gap. The paper is broadly divided into two parts. First, we construct a framework for businesses that seek SCRM implementation in Indian context. Second, we validate this framework based on survey research to examine inter-relationship of elements within the framework.

1.1 Customer Relationship Management

Customer Relationship Management is a comprehensive strategy and process of acquiring, retaining, and partnering with selective customers to create superior value for the company and the customer. It involves the integration of marketing, sales, customer service, and the supply-chain functions of the organization to achieve greater efficiencies and effectiveness in delivering customer value [4]. As the new technologies are emerging, the way customers are interacting with the businesses is changing. There are different touch-points and platforms to facilitate customer relationship management. There is a need for understanding the factors that facilitate the effectiveness in an organization [5]. It is no secret that businesses are exploring more and new strategies for better customer relationship management to tackle the increasing competition in market place where customer retention, satisfaction and delivering value are imminent [6]. In a dynamic market environment, building and fostering relationships with customers and further fortifying in order to track of the demands and understand their innate needs are essential to retain the customers [7]. The businesses have never been able to interact with customers and engage them in such large numbers before and at so many touch-points and in real time basis.

1.2 Customer Relationship Performance

In organization, resources and capability determine the success of the business processes. The effectiveness in converting the resources into capabilities defines the business performance [8]. This performance can be determined with customer based measures like loyalty and satisfaction. The paper uses the customer relationship performance as 'the extent to which firms are successful at satisfying and retaining loyal customers' [8, p.5]. The customer based measures can also be included in parameters for examining performance measurement items like sales growth and profitability etc. [9]. The customer satisfaction has a significant effect on their repeat purchase behavior and buying more than their regular product purchases [10, 11]. Also, customer retention also lowers the level of customers' complaints. The customer satisfaction and retention enhance their relationship with the organization positively, subsequently resulting in improved performance in terms of low cost, more ROI, higher profitability, and high market share [12]. It is also observed in the literature that organization can achieve a competitive advantage by integrating recourses like CRM technology to social technology for customer-linking capabilities. Finally customer relationship based on social media technology can also add value to organization by accelerating the communication flow between market and businesses.

1.3 Social Media

Social media is seen as platform where customers can interact among themselves and is also defined as a set of applications enabling a way of communication among users and developing different communities [13]. It works on Web 2.0 technologies and is expected to have user generated content. The user generated content can be of all possible content formats – images, audio, video, and text etc. Further, seven functional blocks were delineated while differentiating the social media platforms: identity, conversations, groups, reputation, relationships, presence, and sharing [14]. Any social media platform shall perform one or more functions predominantly.

The challenges to utilize the social media at an optimum level are many as the platforms are dynamic and user based activities cannot be controlled. The platforms should not also be used on one-time exchange basis. A continuum should be followed in exchange which would then lead to co-creation of values. Businesses really need to focus on or try to adapt themselves to new and different approaches in order to get customer attention or engage them. They have to shift from goods dominant logic which is focused more on achieving sales target for withstanding the new empowered and well-informed customers and their activities in the platforms. Social media platforms can themselves be used to interact with the customers. They have expanded the realms of these interactions in such a vast space that there is an ever increasing amount of data available on the behavior of customers [8]. Social media based approaches have intensified the need for hyper agility of businesses. It is imperative that businesses need to know, track and understand the tone, content of remarks, talks, discussions, and actions of customers towards certain product, brand, or organization and then utilize this data to co-create value with customers in order to build and maintain customer relationship and achieve customer relationship performance and deliver high service quality [15].

1.4 Social Customer Relationship Management

Social Customer Relationship Management is often referred as the integration of customer-facing activities, including processes, systems, and technologies, with emergent social media applications to engage customers in collaborative conversations and enhance customer relationships [3]. The emerging ecosystem of SCRM involving different stakeholders is wide, diverse, complex and challenging. Nevertheless, such an eco-system can be leveraged to facilitate new ideas generation for innovation, new product or service development, market research, trends analysis, sentiment analysis, word-of-mouth marketing, and customer reviews.

It has been proved that social media use has a positive association with CRM capabilities [8]. The businesses with customer centric management systems may further facilitate employees of an organization to assimilate information from interactions and networks in social media platforms. The customer-centric management systems and social media use interact and positively affect the social CRM capabilities organizations [8]. The capabilities of an organization are determined by ability of organization to assimilate and integrate resources in a useful way in order to differentiate itself and deliver high customer relationship performance. The literature also reiterates that resources are needed to be integrated and used to achieve the business performance [16]. It is evident that social media technologies along with other organizational resources will contribute highly and positively towards achieving the business performance [17].

The extant research provides inadequate insights on development and implementation frameworks for SCRM in general and more specially in the Indian context. In the light of the above, we suggest that social media use and CRM practices in any business shall predict the SCRM which in turn predict the customer relationship performance (CRP).

2   Methodology

2.1   Sample

The data were collected by surveying managers who are at either mid-management level, senior level or at C-level from organizations spread across a wide spectrum of industries located in India. The respondents are working in the departments of marketing, sales, and media and communication. They were from both business to business (B2B) and business to consumers (B2C) segments. A total of 48 responses were collected from 31 organizations. 23 responses were collected by conducting telephonic interviews and rest was collected using an online questionnaire. All the questions were closed ended. In few cases the respondents gave long responses which are used by the authors in this paper, just to illuminate the findings, rather than treating the study as a mixed design. The respondents were assured of protection of identity while canvassing for the survey.

The data were collected using a questionnaire. The questionnaire consisted of 35 close-ended questions. It contained Likert type items to examine social media use, CRM and SCRM. The data were fed into SPSS v.20 for analysis. The regression analysis was performed to find the linkage between the elements in the empirical evaluation of our conceptual framework.

2.2   Measures

The questionnaire used various indexes developed by the earlier researchers and modified wherever required. For social media technology use, we used an index developed by [2]. We asked respondents to mark in a list of social media technologies which were used in their organization. It determines the usage of various social media technologies by each organization. The aggregate score of this analysis was further used as an observed measure.

We adapted a scale [18] developed to operationalize the Social CRM capabilities. This scale represents an organization-wide system for acquiring, disseminating, and responding to customer information referring to customer information generated from social media applications. Further, customer relationship performance was evaluated adapting a scale developed by [12] to examine whether organizations are successful in retaining and have satisfying customers. Following were the items for which yes or no responses were sought: once we get new customers, they tend to stay with our company; our loyal customers also promote our firm; our customers are satisfied with our company; and customer retention is very important to our firm.

3 Results

The sample firms were divided into two major categories – B2B and B2C. The most widely used social technologies in organizations are Facebook, YouTube, twitter, direct mail, social analytics, social collaboration, online conferencing and LinkedIn.

72 % of the respondents rated Facebook as an important platform. The Facebook is used for various purposes like interacting with customers, disseminating information about discounts, new products, deals, and increasing brand's visibility. For B2C companies, Facebook posts are used to address specific cosmetic product's users whose contact numbers were asked on Facebook and were called later in order to get the product review and help research department in the company. It also helped them understand customer sentiment for the product. While in B2B companies, Facebook is used majorly for branding purposes and recruitment. It is also seen as mainly a hygiene factor in many B2B companies. The reasons for the same can be attributed to clients' online behavior, customers reach, and business needs such as maintaining confidentiality of clients' information, high cost of each deal, as per the qualitative data.

Further, Twitter and LinkedIn are rated as important by 58 % of the respondents. The Twitter is used for promoting campaigns and competitions held by companies, sharing updates, interacting with online customer base and responding to queries, conducting research such as identifying trends, sentimental analysis, being part of groups and analyzing their behavior, providing experts' insights by sharing white papers on Twitter.

LinkedIn is mainly used for recruitment purposes. It is also used for ad spots, publishing articles such as white papers and to be part of relevant groups like specific cause related associations. It is also used for identifying specific groups and identifies the potential customers. Mails are sent to email id of CEOs on LinkedIn and campaigns were held to reach out to CEOs who were the present and potential customers. 56 % of the respondents rated online conferencing/webinar as important for their businesses. Webinar is mainly used in B2B companies to interact with clients and teams spanning across different geographical locations. In B2C companies, it is used for employee to employee interaction. 72 % of the respondents rated direct mails as important as well. The direct mails are mainly used to contact customers and provide assistance by responding to queries or requests. They are usually followed or preceded by phone calls at customer centre through the interactive voice response (IVR) systems. 66 % of the respondents rated YouTube as an important platform. YouTube is mainly used for passive promotion, i.e., ads are there but they are not core to customer acquisition or retention.

To understand interactive effects of CRM in an organization and its social technologies use on SCRM of the organization, multiple regressions analysis were undertaken. The results are presented in Tables 1 and 2. In analysis, SCRM and CRP (dependent variables in separate cases) were considered as a function of all independent variables. Based on their significance level, the models included only the significant factors with $p \leq 0.05$ in the regression equation and omitted all of the other insignificant factors. In addition, the value of R square measures the percentage of variance explained by the independent variables. Literature suggests that the value more than 0.60 are considered as good result.

Table 1. Social customer relationship management in B2B Companies

Independent variables	Dependent variable	Adjusted R^2	P
CRM	SCRM	0.0070	<0.757
Social media use		0.3470	<0.016
CRM and Social media use (Both)		0.3900	<0.039
CRM	CRP	0.4140	<0.007
SCRM		0.0005	<0.9327
CRM and SCRM (Both)		0.3250	<0.030

Table 2. Social customer relationship management in B2C Companies

Independent variables	Dependent variable	Adjusted R^2	p
CRM	SCRM	0.141	<0.167
Social media use		0.742	<3.65E−05
CRM and social media use (Both)		0.699	<0.0002
CRM	CRP	0.265	<0.049
SCRM		0.422	<0.008
CRM and SCRM (Both)		0.426	<0.014

The predictor, social media use explained a significant proportion of variance in SCRM scores. Although CRM as an individual predictor in the model does not have significant effect on SCRM, while social media use as an individual predictor has significant effect on SCRM. On the CRP, SCRM did not explain a significant proportion of variance unlike CRM. But the collective effects of CRM and SCRM on its CRP in B2B industry, explained a significant proportion of variance in CRP. In other words, in B2B companies, mere use of social media does not translate into SCRM automatically, but it should have good CRM practices. Also, CRP is predicted by combination of CRM and SCRM, not just SCRM. The research underlies that extant CRM practices are important for establishing the linkage between social media use and customer relationship performance.

For B2C companies, the results are slightly different. Social media use predicted the SCRM, not the CRM. The combined effect of CRM and social media use also predicted the SCRM with relatively higher amount of causality. CRP is predicted successfully by CRM and SCRM.

4   Discussion

The study suggests that there is a strong causal linkage between social media use and SCRM. SCRM focuses on a firm's capability to engage with internal and external customers with the help of social media. The association between the two is higher in B2C companies as compared to B2B companies. As discussed earlier, in different ways and strategies social media technologies have been used to engage with customers, create value for them and with them. The results reflect on how pervasive SCRM should be in customer engagement across organizations.

The possible explanation for differences between B2B and B2C businesses can come from the nature of customers. In B2B companies, the target segment is relatively smaller than the B2B segment and is reached out on a more person to person basis. While in B2C companies, the target segment is large and can be reached out via social media beside other media and person to person basis. There is a possibility that social media platform like Facebook or Twitter could be seen as hygiene factor in B2B companies.

There is also significant interactive effect of social media use and CRM towards SCRM in both B2B and B2C companies. But no positive association could be seen between SCRM and CRM in both B2B and B2C companies. It is possible that SCRM and CRM are seen as two separate entities and under different lights in Indian context. Either a company does CRM through social media or it doesn't. The level of SCRM implementation in a company doesn't have an effect on how it manages customer relationship through other media like IVR, call centre, customer care team. It is also important to note that parameters used to measure CRM and those used to measure SCRM and different and need not have high relation between the two. It is possible that because the processes that come under CRM and SCRM do not overlap and because companies who implement high CRM need not implement the same level of SCRM, there is no significant association found between CRM and SCRM. This linkage needs to be explored further in future studies.

Further the study also indicates positive interactive effects of SCRM and CRM towards achieving CRP but with different individual effects. In B2B companies, while SCRM doesn't seem to have significant impact, although positively influencing the CRP, interactive effects of SCRM and CRM are significant in effecting CRP. In B2C companies, while CRM doesn't seem to have significant impact, although positively determining the CRP, interactive effects of SCRM and CRM are significant in effecting the CRP. This may be due to less focus on SCRM as compared to CRM in B2B companies and less focus on CRM as compared to SCRM in B2C companies. It should be noted that CRM alone has significant effect on CRP in both B2B and B2C companies, while SCRM alone has a positive significant effect on CRP only in B2C companies.

In B2C companies, there is more focus on managing customer relationship via social media technologies whereas in B2B companies, social media is mainly used for brand awareness, recruitment purposes, research and not for engaging or communicating with clients. The clients are reached out at a personal level and social media is not sought for maintain relationship with clients. It is done as clients are usually executive level employees who also believe in person to person meetings and each product solution transaction cost is very high.

5 Challenges in Implementation of SCRM

The questionnaire had listed seven possible challenges faced by the businesses while implementing the SCRM. The data indicated three top challenges. 20 % of the managers believed that the organization size was one of the challenges in implementing SCRM in organization. Both too small and too large sizes of organizations were seen as challenges. Shortage of sufficient and skilled manpower to gain social media technologies capabilities was a challenge identified in organizations of small size. While complexities in integrating social media activities and derived capabilities, large number of stakeholders, lack of expertise and large consumer base due to increased scope and scale of organization were seen as challenges in organizations of large size.

Further discussion with a respondent who is a senior executive explained that how a larger size became a problem, as the structure is more complicated in large organizations, especially the sales team. Lack of common data sharing platform in an organization is seen as a problem. A consultancy's communication manager explained that how due to large size of the company, a SCRM implementation had become too centralized when it should be decentralized in an ideal situation. Currently marketing and communication unit alone handle the SCRM and operations person has to tell the marketing person to take a necessary action and then only it is acted upon resulting in longer time.

28 % of the managers reported that lack of clarity in measuring return on investment (RoI) for implementing SCRM was one of the challenges. Although sales target is achieved and online visibility is observed, measuring ROI of SCRM is still seen as a challenge in implementing SCRM. Possible reasons for the same may be lack of clear and well-defined key performance indicators when it comes to implementation of SCRM in an organization.

Further, 20 % of the responses reported that lack of expertise to implement SCRM was one of the challenges in implementing SCRM in organization. This was a challenge prevalent irrespective of size of organizations. Although, a marketing manager of an e-commerce company shared that one of the challenges faced while measuring success and implementing SCRM was that there was no 100 % overlap between people liking posts, pages etc. and real customers. This creates a problem in identifying true customers and understanding their behavior. Also everyone in the company believed in SCRM but not many really knew how to implement it as the required expertise was lacking in organization.

6 Implications

This study provides a preliminary framework for companies to implement SCRM. It provides a road-map so as to head-start with or to identify the right elements to achieve high CRP. It also throws light on interactions abilities of different factors within the framework. This study also suggests that investment in social media technology can provide businesses with substantial CRM benefits. The comparative analysis of SCRM implementation B2B and B2C industries highlights the differences in usage and approach. It shows why earlier models proposed for implementation of SCRM towards achieving CRP cannot be as it is applied to Indian industries. While there seems to be a high correlation between customer-centric processes and SCRM capabilities [8], this study doesn't support such high correlation between these components.

The study clearly indicates that SCRM alone will not result in performance, especially in the B2B domains. It needs to be aligned with the best of CRM processes. Although the sample is very broad and diverse which may help to capture insights from different industries like ones which are transactional in nature, technology oriented, e-commerce, retail etc. The research findings can be used as a stepping stone to understand SCRM related issues in Indian industries and in developing confidence in the preliminary framework designed for implementation of SCRM.

The paper reinforces the importance of customer centricity required in Indian businesses. The CRM measure is uniform across both B2B and B2C companies as it is an important factor for realizing the CRP in businesses. The CRM capabilities affect SCRM capabilities by interacting with social media use and also affect CRP by interacting with SCRM capabilities. The B2B companies came across as more inclined towards developing CRM capabilities, while B2C companies came across as more inclined towards developing SCRM capabilities. The linkages between CRM and SCRM capabilities in Indian organizations are weak unlike given in the extant research that are mostly done in the high income countries. The framework needs further validation in the context of low and middle income countries like India wherein the Internet penetration or information eco system is not in the advanced stages. The study also raises importance of unpacking the differences between B2B and B2C domains in the use of social media platforms for business use, especially in the customer interaction centric ones.

References

1. Defining Social Media: 2006–2010. http://www.briansolis.com/2010/01/defining-social-media-the-saga-continues/. Accessed 10 May 2015
2. Jayachandran, S., Sharma, S., Kaufman, P., Raman, P.: The role of relational information processes and technology use in customer relationship management. J. Market. **69**(4), 177–192 (2005)
3. Social CRM? Really? REALLY? http://www.mycustomer.com/selling/crm/paul-greenberg-social-crm-really-really. Accessed 10 May 2015
4. Parvatiyar, A., Jagdish, N.: Customer Relationship Management: emerging practice, process, and discipline. J. Econ. Soc. Res. **3**(2), 1–34 (2001)
5. Law, M., Lau, T., Wong, Y.: From Customer relationship management to customer-managed relationship: unraveling the paradox with a co-creative perspective. Market. Intell. Plan. **21**(1), 51–60 (2003)
6. Jensen, H.: Antecedents and consequences of consumer value assessments: implications for marketing strategy and future research. J. Retail. Consum. Serv. **8**(6), 299–310 (2001)
7. Sheth, J.N., Sisodia, R.S.: Marketing productivity: issues and analysis. J. Bus. Res. **55**(5), 349–362 (2002)
8. Trainor, K.J., Andzulis, J.M., Rapp, A., Agnihotri, R.: Social media technology usage and customer relationship performance: a capabilities-based examination of social CRM. J. Bus. Res. **67**(6), 1201–1208 (2014)

9. Ahearne, M., Jelinek, R., Rapp, A.: Moving beyond the direct effect of SFA adoption on salesperson performance: training and support as key moderating factors. Ind. Market. Manag. **34**(4), 379–388 (2005)
10. Hogan, J.E., Lehmann, D.R., Merino, M., Srivastava, R.K., Thomas, J.S., Verhoef, P.C.: Linking customer assets to financial performance. J. Serv. Res. **5**(1), 26–38 (2002)
11. Szymanski, D.M., Henard, D.H.: Customer satisfaction: a meta-analysis of the empirical evidence. J. Acad. Market. Sci. **29**(1), 16–35 (2001)
12. Rapp, A., Trainor, K.J., Agnihotri, R.: Performance implications of customer-linking capabilities: examining the complementary role of customer orientation and CRM technology. J. Bus. Res. **63**(11), 1229–1236 (2010)
13. Hoffman, D.L., Fodor, M.: Can you measure the ROI of your social media marketing? MIT Sloan Manag. Rev. **52**(1), 41–49 (2010)
14. Kietzmann, J.H., Hermkens, K., McCarthy, I.P., Silvestre, B.S.: Social media? Get serious! Understanding the functional building blocks of social media. Bus. Horiz. **54**(3), 241–251 (2011)
15. Woodcock, N., Green, A., Starkey, M.: Social CRM as a business strategy. J. Database Market. Customer Strategy Manag. **18**, 50–64 (2011)
16. Roberts, N., Grover, V.: Investigating firm's customer agility and firm performance: the importance of aligning sense-and-respond capabilities. J. Bus. Res. **65**(5), 579–585 (2012)
17. Melville, N., Kraemer, K., Gurbaxani, V.: Review: information technology and organizational performance: an integrative model of IT business value. MIS Q. **28**(2), 283–322 (2004)
18. Srinivasan, R., Moorman, C.: Strategic firm commitments and rewards for customer relationship management in online retailing. J. Market. **69**(4), 193–200 (2005)

Online Stakeholder Interaction of Some Airlines in the Light of Situational Crisis Communication Theory

Boyang Zhang$^{(\boxtimes)}$, Denis Kotkov, Jari Veijalainen,
and Alexander Semenov

Department of Computer Science and Information Systems,
University of Jyvaskyla, Jyvaskyla, Finland
{boyang.zhang,jari.veijalainen,
alexander.semenov}@jyu.fi, deigkotk@student.jyu.fi

Abstract. The purpose of this paper is to explore the participation of main actors in Facebook. The engagement shows different degrees of participation that directly affect the brand image and reputation. This research applies Situational Crisis Communication Theory (SCCT) to interaction in the social media. It provides possibilities for decision makers to monitor diverse messages online, understand stakeholder concerns and reply to them adequately, which is especially important in crisis situations. Seven airline organizations were selected for a comparative analysis concerning their online discussions. The verified Facebook and Twitter accounts of those airlines were investigated, the status updates of the airlines and comments issued by other users during 2009-2016 collected along the replies and comments issued by the airlines themselves. The main methods are sentiment analysis, categorization of the messages into four categories and counting.

Keywords: Situational Crisis Communication Theory · Stakeholder theory · Airlines · Sentiment analysis · Facebook · Twitter

1 Introduction

Nowadays all large organizations have established own verified accounts on all major social media platforms to gain attention for their brands and activities, because customers and other stakeholders are reachable through them. Organizations need to protect their reputational assets among stakeholders. They can publish new products or services, information about organizational changes and other news through their social media accounts. The globally accessible platforms such as Facebook, LinkedIn and Twitter have attracted hundreds of millions of users, making the communication through them vitally important to society and business.

This paper explores the Situational Crisis Communication Theory (SCCT) with the observed communication behaviors of some airlines in Facebook and Twitter. SCCT deals especially with crisis situations. Particularly in them, negative word-of-mouth disseminates virally in social media [9] which may lead to damages in organizational image and harm the reputation. The literature on social media shows that also scholars

© IFIP International Federation for Information Processing 2016
Published by Springer International Publishing Switzerland 2016. All Rights Reserved
Y.K. Dwivedi et al. (Eds.): I3E 2016, LNCS 9844, pp. 183–192, 2016.
DOI: 10.1007/978-3-319-45234-0_17

have begun to explore the multiple voices of stakeholders [1, 7, 12], including customers, Facebook account owners, crew, authorities and so on. Organizations have become more visible online attracting different voices and clearly being scrutinized by the public and governing organizations [10].

This paper reviews the interactions on the verified Facebook and Twitter accounts of seven airlines and investigates how these seven airlines performed in their customer interactions as exhibited by their Facebook and Twitter account behavior. The hypotheses are: organization in crisis communicates more/less with the stakeholders' activities; organization in crisis experiences more negative sentiment from stakeholders than before. The contribution of this paper is to test SCCT theory in online crisis situation, and questions whether the theory should be enhanced towards the social media activities of organizations.

2   Situational Crisis Communication Theory

Social media is important due to the billions of user profiles hosted by them and their potential to disseminate information to the general public and specific stakeholder groups [2]. Thus, organizations establish verified (official) accounts at major social media sites to post information online and engage stakeholders [7]. The immediate online sharing can enhance brand loyalty. However, negative publicity ("social media rage") can unexpectedly trigger organizational crises [13] and financial ramifications for the involved organizations which may even lead to bankruptcy.

It is noticeable that researchers increasingly scrutinize changes of public opinion towards organizations that experience crises [4, 8]. To illustrate methods of responses in crisis situations, organizations are beginning to seek ways to enhance brand protection and prevent losses in reputation. Because of the complexity of crises, multiple response strategies may be required. Coombs [5] developed the Situational Crisis Communication Theory (SCCT) referring mainly to blogs and web sites as the main discussion venues in Internet, in addition to traditional mass media and direct contacts. Since coining it, SCCT has been applied to several organizational crises, such as the Amazon crisis in 2009 [3], and to the love Parade crisis in Germany in 2010 [11]. Figure 1 [6] presents the major concepts and their relationships in SCCT. In the center there are the crisis responsibility and organizational reputation. These are related with the emotions towards the organization (arrow C), crisis history (the timeline of the current crisis and earlier crises, arrows B1–B2), and prior relationship reputation (how the organization was perceived earlier, arrows B3–B4). Crisis response strategies are employed to mitigate the harm to reputation of the organization among the stakeholders and calm negative emotions. They are related with crisis responsibility (arrow F1) and organizational reputation (arrow F2) and they affect the emotions (arrow F3) among the stakeholders and their behavioral intentions towards the organization (arrow E). The latter are also directly influenced by the perceived reputation (arrow D).

In most situations the theory encourages an active response strategy in interactions with the stakeholders, "dealing" with the crisis rather than "denying" the crisis. The theory suggests three crisis categories and different crisis response strategies based on the crisis category, including deny, diminish, rebuild, or perform reputation repair by

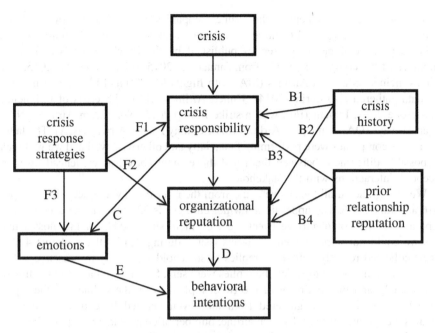

Fig. 1. SCCT central concepts and relationships (Coombs [6], Fig. 1)

apology [3]. According to Coombs [6] categories are victim cluster, accidental cluster and preventable cluster.

However, it may be more difficult to clarify the situation to the social media audiences and enhance organizational compliance in this environment [8]. Therefore, we will focus the analysis on online interaction in Facebook and Twitter, and scrutinize how actively certain Facebook and Twitter account owners engage with their stakeholders in the online environment in various crisis situations and in normal operation. The reason we select SCCT theory is because we plan to investigate whether airlines have followed advices suggested by SCCT theory. For those airlines that are not in an acute crisis, it is the question of preventive reputation maintenance, for others it is mainly active reputation maintenance and repair. Referring to Fig. 1, we will concentrate on the emotions of the stakeholders, their intentions and organizational reputation development among the stakeholders. Indirectly, we will report the activities airlines exert towards the stakeholders in social media and draw conclusions about the crisis response strategies based on them.

3 Methodology, Data and Findings

The data gathered relate to three airline organizations with a major or smaller crisis in 2010–2016, and data from four further airlines with no major crisis. The data was collected using Facebook graph API and Twitter REST API.

To assess the engagement of the airline companies, we analyzed their Facebook pages using the Graph API (https://developers.facebook.com/docs/graph-api). We collected posts, comments and replies published by the Facebook users and representatives of the companies mainly from January 1, 2015 to December 31, 2015. The airlines include: Malaysia Airlines (MA; with flights MH370 and MH17 lost in 2014 and data gathered also during 2014); United Airlines (UA) with crisis of turbulence amid probe 2015; Finnair (Fin) with a strike in Sep 2015; Norwegian Airlines (NA); Qatar Airways (QA); Singapore Airlines (SA); Cathay Pacific Airways (CA). The latter four airline companies were performing financially and otherwise well and we will seek for possible differences between them and those three above, as evidenced by their Facebook interactions with the stakeholders.

We also gathered all tweets we could from their verified Twitter accounts in April 2016 and June 2016. The upper limit Twitter enforces is 3200 tweets per account. For some airlines we could retrieve tweets sent by them since 2009, for the most active ones we could not retrieve even all tweets issued during 2015. Of the almost 40000 tweets collected roughly 25000 are replies to stakeholders, mostly to passengers. We also collected the tweets to which the replies were sent. So we could analyze the time it took to reply and the sentiment of the tweet replied to by the airline and the reply. Table 1 is based on data gathered from the seven verified Facebook accounts. It contains the number of posts by each airline, number of comments and replies from the stakeholders, and number of replies of the airlines to the comments. The identified stakeholder types were mainly airline customers who have relevant questions to the organization, and (the representatives of) the airline organizations in Facebook. The interactions happened mostly in form of answering to questioning, apology making to complaints, and greetings encountered by greetings.

Table 1. Owner performance based on the contrastive result of comments and replies versus account owner replies, Facebook accounts

Airlines	MA March 2014	MA 2015	UA 2015	Fin 2015	NA 2015	QA 2015	SA 2015	CA 2015
Statuses	25	92	54	81	75	114	57	87
Comments	3155	8900	14046	1704	2961	13726	562	851
Replies (customers)	539	4034	10502	289	649	2541	147	63
Replies (account owner)	1	1059	3649	81	106	340	103	12

Table 2 shows that most of airline organizations actively engage in the dialogue with relevant stakeholders in Facebook. In order to test the SCCT theory, we performed a content analysis and divided the replies into four different types: Acknowledgements or greetings in various situations (A); Answers to services or booking-related questions (B); Redirecting people to other client services or websites (C); and Apology making (D).

Table 2. Content analysis of the replies from the verified Facebook accounts of the airlines

Type	MA March 2014	MA 2015	UA 2015	Fin 2015	NA 2015	QA 2015	SA 2015	CA 2015
A	1	453	712	6	15	48	75	3
B	0	438	1394	45	74	68	16	8
C	1	52	831	25	18	279	13	0
D	0	293	790	14	23	54	4	1

The mapping of the messages into one category was performed based on the major information content conveyed, although in some cases the message could have been placed into several categories. For example on December 19, 2015 MA replied: "Hi Elizabeth, we're sorry for letting you down with our services. May we recommend that you drop us a formal feedback/complaint at customer@malaysiaairlines.com so that our Customer Care team could look into this issue better? Thank you." This was considered to belong to category D, but it could be also categorized into C.

Concerning the Malaysia Airline case, the March 2014 data from Facebook was collected immediately after the MH370 was lost. The collection started from 7th March 2014 and lasted to 26th April 2014. The bad performance of the MA in Facebook is evidenced by the fact that there was only one reply from the verified account owner of MA towards customers. The situation has improved in 2015, as evidenced by the hundreds of replies and apologies issued by MA mainly towards its customers.

The ownership changes of MA are also worth noticing, Khazanah National Berhad (sovereign wealth fund of the government of Malaysia) which is the majority shareholder of MA begins to compensate the minority shareholders and purchase remaining ownership to renationalize the organization in August 2014. MAS (Malaysia Airlines System) was ceased operations on 31st August 2015, MAB (Malaysia Airlines Berhad) was launched to rebrand with reduced working employees and routes adjusting on 1st September 2015. This could be the trigger event of the attitude changes on the performance of MA Facebook verified account.

The financial reports of MA in the web indicate that the company made more losses in 2014 than in 2015. The current estimates tell that the company will be profitable again by 2017. The other 6 companies in the sample were profitable in 2015.

United Airlines had a turbulent period 2015, but still the company was profitable in 2015 while exhibiting a strong Facebook engagement with customers. Finnair had labor force strike in May 2015. It shows active engagement towards its customers throughout the year.

We performed a sentiment analysis on the collected Facebook and Twitter data, recording positive/negative/neutral sentiment score of the whole comment (pos/neg/neu). The range of all scores is [0,1]. A comment might include several sentences. In this case the score of each sentence is calculated separately in a similar format. In Fig. 2 there is a graph for the entire comment set gathered from UA Facebook account in 2015. Most comments are mainly neutral and positive sentiment overwhelms during most days the negative sentiment. In Fig. 3 there is a similar analysis performed for the Finnair posts and comments. The peak of negative message at the end of Nov. 2015 requires

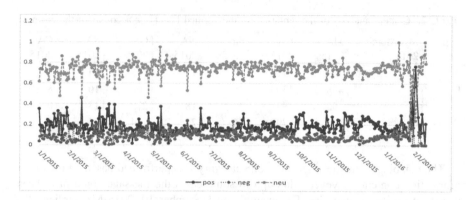

Fig. 2. Sentiment analysis on Facebook comments, 2015 full year average, United Airlines

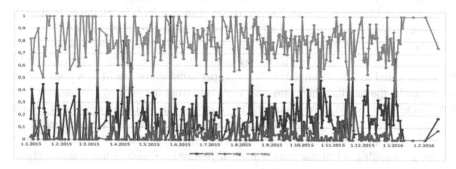

Fig. 3. Sentiment analysis on Facebook comments, 2015 full year average, Finnair

further study. Table 3 lists number of tweets sent by the seven airlines year by year, percentage of replies, average response time to show the comparison. In Fig. 4, there is the sentiment analysis on tweets that were replied to by Cathaypacific Airline.

Table 3 contains the overall analysis results of the Twitter data collection. In most columns there is a date, such as 11.10 under Finnair (Fin) on the row 2008. It denotes the date when the Twitter account collected here was established. For instance, the account with the screen_name @Finnair was established on October 11, 2009. If the date is missing from the table, it means that it was established in the year the first tweets were sent. This is the case for several Cathay Pacific subsidiary accounts. Most accounts were established in 2008–2010, although United has established it on April 2, 2011 and Singapore Airlines on February 2, 2011. The dates show when social media presence has become important for the airlines. All other accounts are verified, except @Fly_Norwegian. From the account description and contents of the tweets one can still infer that the latter account is controlled by the Norwegian.

The bottom row named 'Statuses' tells how many Twitter status updates the airline had issued on a verified account by June 13, 2016. It tells how active the airline has been at Twitter. United has tweeted almost 600,000 tweets in total and others mostly ten to thirty thousand times. Because Twitter only allows 3,200 tweets to be collected

Table 3. Number of tweets collected from the seven airlines, percentage of replies among the collected tweets, percentage of the retrieved replied-to tweets response times

Year	Airline MA	UA	Fin	Fhelp	Fsuomi	NA	QA	SA	CA	CA_ZA	CA_CA	CA_UK	CA_IN	CA_AU	CA_US
2008			11.10.			29.4.			22.10.						
2009	17.1.									14.10.	91	9	9	9	4.5.
2010					19.8.				2	16	237	67	67	45	3
2011		4.3.					17.2.		1	113	151	24	24	126	
2012				2.4.					3	269	292	114	114	390	
2013				422					9	130	795	132	132	556	129
2014				872					1	83	425	24	248	639	907
2015	464		2019	993	676		1372		2558	136	359	709	709	637	1866
2016	3884	6438	1780	2225	435	6451	2843	3221	1096	137	163	351	351	212	478
Collected	4348	6438	3799	3218	2405	6451	4215	3221	3670	884	2513	2780	1654	2614	3383
Replies, %	93%	99%	69%	95%	46%	94%	75%	95%	84%	8%	28%	51%	12%	49%	55%
Replied %	61%	93%	87%	1%	0%	92%	100%	91%	81%	46%	58%	68%	63%	74%	77%
Med. resp.	9h30'	0h16'	3h05'			1h10'	7h10'	0h22'	7h15'	15h	4h 10'	6h40'	6h 30'	5h40'	2h45'
Avg. resp	10h12'	1h20'	6h38'			2h47'	7h51'	1h21'	8h57'	12h21'	7h 42'	9h17'	8h 05'	7h49'	6h23'
Statuses	26700	598000	11100	9166	2405	26300	27500	27600	16300	887	2519	2786	1669	2614	5944

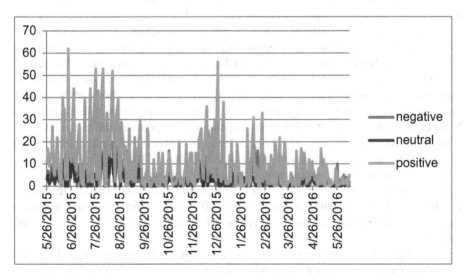

Fig. 4. Sentiment analysis on tweets that were replied to by Cathaypacific Airline

from an account, for most airlines we could only retrieve tweets from 2015–2016. Unfortunately, we cannot thus follow development over a longer period of time, except for some Cathay Pacific subsidiaries, for which the data starts from 2009. The row 'Collected' tells how many tweets we were able to collect from the corresponding Twitter account of the airline. They show a tendency to increasing volumes. The total number of collected tweets from the accounts is roughly 51,600.

We parsed the tweet contents into a database table and marked into the records which ones were replies to earlier tweets. In total, we parsed 67 attribute values from a tweet, if available. We paid attention especially to the replies, because they especially show the interaction with the stakeholders. The row 'Replies' in Table 3 indicates which percentage of the collected tweets are replies to some earlier tweets. This varies a lot between airlines and accounts. High percentage shows that the airline uses Twitter as a vehicle to interact with the stakeholders. Low percentage indicates that the airline uses the account more for informing the stakeholders. To analyze the replied_to tweets, we attempted to collect as many replied-to tweets as possible using the statuses_lookup function of the Twitter library. The row 'Replied' tells how many replied-to tweets we could collect for the replied tweets. For instance, United had almost all tweets replies (6,392 tweets out of 6,438) in the collected data set. We could collect 93 % of the tweets to which United replied, i.e. 5,944 earlier tweets sent by other stakeholders to whom United replied. These were either directly sent to the United account @united or @united was mentioned in the tweet text alone or among other screen_names. In the latter case Twitter forwards the tweet to those "mentioned" in the text.

The other data set containing the replied-to tweets contains roughly 30,000 tweets. Thus, we could retrieve about 57 % of the replied-to tweets in average. We did not analyze the reasons why we could not retrieve the missing 40 %. One can still see that the more recent the originally collected tweet is, the more probable it is that the replied-to tweet can be retrieved and vice verso, as the United account shows. The reasons for failing to retrieve the replied-to tweets is for further study, but obvious reason are that the user has protected his or her tweets, or the account is closed.

One aspect of the reputation of a company is related with the reaction time of the company to customer tweets or other messages, like emails, phone calls, or text messages. Because we collected the replied-to tweets, we could calculate the duration between the replied-to tweet and the subsequent reply. We consider this as the response time to the customer. There are striking differences between the average and median response times between the accounts. United and Singapore Airlines responded in tens of minutes, measured by the median response time, Norwegian responded in less than 2 h. The average response time was still over an hour in all cases. The rest responded roughly in half a day. The data contains over 1,700 instances where the response time is between 1 and 2 days. In about 3,400 (11 %) of the cases the response time exceeds one day.

Who were the stakeholders to whom or to which the airline responded? We investigated a tiny sample of replied-to tweets and the accounts. Most tweets seemed to deal with problems the airline passengers had (luggage lost, reservation number does not work, call center is not reachable), but there were also positive tweets telling how wonderful the business class of the airline was. The replies were often requests for the customer to send a direct message to the airline, apologies for the inconvenience experienced by the passengers, or advice to call the call center. Further contents analysis is required to better understand what the issues were handled in replies. A longer tweet history should also be collected in order to understand, for instance, how a crisis influences the contents and sentiment, as well as tweet frequency.

4 Conclusions

The number of Facebook messages during 2015 varies among the airlines, from less than 1,000 to circa 25,000 and does not seem to correlate in any clear way with the customer base size. It requires more analysis, whether number of messages in different categories is correlated with problems in services or other kind of crises. MA evidently decided to put resources into Facebook and Twitter account handling in spite of financial losses during 2015, after the catastrophic 2014, during which it did not reply to customers.

According to our findings, the hypothesis has been accepted that organization in crisis experiences more negative sentiment from stakeholders than before, for example in January 2015, Cathay Pacific had the crisis of scales back expansion plans, blames cockpit crew dispute, in Fig. 4, the amount of negative sentiments are more than positive ones.

As mentioned before, SCCT focuses on how to react to crisis, based on causes and responsibilities [11] for crises, and in most situation, applying SCCT centers on "dealing" with the crisis rather than "denying" the crisis. We noted that supportive replies to customers concerns formed most of the owner account replies. Apology making strategies were commonly used to comfort those expressing anger and negative comments. Therefore, this research provides empirical evidence on SCCT theory that Facebook account owners try to repair reputation after crisis through appropriate apology making strategies in which support the hypothesis that organization has communicated more with stakeholders' activities. Meanwhile, also redirecting strategies were visible that take away grounds for dissatisfaction and provide positive solutions, in the case of crisis situation, an organization's strong engagement helps reputation repair.

SCCT theory emphasizes that key responsible actors, in the case of the airlines this relates to managers taking responsibility, efficient and effective engagement of the online dialogue, providing organizations opportunities to monitor social media and other online world-of-mouth. SCCT theory provides a reality-based guidebook when encountering different crisis situations. Applying the perspective in this study shows that airline organizations are "dealing" with the crisis, taking responsibility which may exert a profound impact on their brand images, such as by apology making. When considering SCCT theory as a whole, there are several categories: deny, diminish, and rebuild [5]. In this research, rebuild category is selected to deal with the crisis and apology making strategies is one of the major process to reputation repairing, future research could illustrate more on various perspective.

In this study, several limitations exist in the analysis and data collection. Similarly, the financial performance of each airline could get attention, because degradation in profitability could be a cause or an effect of a crisis. In the data analysis, topic modeling and text mining techniques could be utilized to decompose the content of comments and replies. These steps will be performed in the future.

Acknowledgements. The authors were supported in part by the Academy of Finland, grant number 268078 (MineSocMed).

References

1. Botha, E., Mignon, R.: To share or not to share: the role of content and emotion in viral marketing. J. Public Aff. **13**(2), 160–171 (2013)
2. Chou, W.S., Yvonne, M.H., Hunt, E.B.B., Richard, P.M., Moser, P., Bradford, W.H.: Social media use in the United States: implications for health communication. J. Med. Internet Res. **11**, 4 (2009)
3. Coombs, W.T., Holladay, J.S.: Amazon.com's Orwellian nightmare: exploring apology in an online environment. J. Commun. Manag. **16**(3), 280–295 (2012)
4. Coombs, W.T., Hollday, J.S.: How publics react to crisis communication efforts. J. Commun. Manag. **18**(1), 40–57 (2014)
5. Coombs, W.T.: Crisis Management and Communications. Institute for Public Relations, 30 October 2007. http://www.instituteforpr.org/crisis-management-and-communications/
6. Coombs, W.T.: Protecting organization reputations during a crisis: the development and application of situational crisis communication theory. Corp. Reput. **10**(3), 1–14 (2007)
7. Elefant, C.: The 'Power' of social media: legal issues and best practices for utilities engaging social media. Energy Law J. **32**(1), 1 (2011)
8. Freberg, K.: Intention to comply with crisis messages communicated via social media. Public Relat. Rev. **38**(3), 416–421 (2012)
9. Edward, C.M., Haenlein, M., Skiera, B., Wege, E., Zhang, M.: Managing customer relationships in the social media era: introducing the social CRM house. J. Interact. Market. **27**(4), 270–280 (2013)
10. Seungahn, N., Saxton, G.D.: Modeling the adoption and use of social media by nonprofit organizations. New Media Soc. **15**(2), 294–313 (2013)
11. Schwarz, A.: How publics use social media to respond to blame games in crisis communication: the love parade tragedy in Duisburg 2010. Public Relat. Rev. **38**(3), 430–437 (2012)
12. Sinha, V., Subramanian, K.S., Bhattacharya, S., Chaudhary, K.: The contemporary framework on social media analytics as an emerging tool for behavior informatics, HR analytics and business process. Manag. J. Contemp. Manag. Issues **17**(2), 65–84 (2012)
13. Shari, R.V., Petrun, L.E., Roberts, H.A.: Issue management gone awry: when not to respond to an online reputation threat. Corp. Reput. Rev. **15**(4), 319–332 (2012)

Adoption and Diffusion

Social Media Use Among Teenagers in Brunei Darussalam

Annie Dayani Ahad Abdullah[1(✉)] and Calvin M.L. Chan[2]

[1] Universiti Brunei Darussalam, Jalan Tungku Link,
Gadong BE1410, Brunei Darussalam
annie.ahad@ubd.edu.bn
[2] SIM University, 461 Clementi Road, Singapore 599491, Singapore
calvinchanml@unisim.edu.sg

Abstract. This paper presents a study on the use of social media among teenagers in Brunei Darussalam. The aim is not merely to reveal the social media usage behavior of teenagers in Brunei Darussalam, but also to illustrate the benefits and challenges brought about by social media usage among youths in the social-cultural context of Brunei Darussalam and its national ideology of Malay Islam Monarchy. Four findings of social networking, romantic intimacy, social media addiction, and cyberbullying are presented and the corresponding social-cultural implications and interventions are discussed. It is hoped that such awareness of how social media usage among youth is perceived in a different social-cultural context will bring about greater mutual understanding in this increasingly divisive world.

Keywords: Social media · Teenagers · Youth · Brunei Darussalam

1 Introduction

Social media is widely used among all strata of societies, its use is most prevalent among teenagers [35]. Even as social media has brought about benefits to and enhancement of social relations [15], it has also brought about negative effects that detriment and degrade social relations [50]. While there is considerable study of social media use among teenagers [7, 14], these studies are mainly based in the United States of America, which is a primarily liberal and westernized country [6, 14, 18]. Considering that social media use among teenagers is a global phenomenon, it is necessary to study this phenomenon in countries that are less liberal and westernized in order to have a complete understanding of this contemporary phenomenon. This paper explores the use of social media among teenagers in Brunei Darussalam, which is a quaint and largely conservative, Islamic country.

The aim of this paper is not merely to reveal the social media usage behavior of teenagers in the social-cultural context of Brunei Darussalam, with its national ideology of Malay Islam Monarchy. It is also hoped that a greater awareness on how social media usage is perceived in different social and cultural context can help to bring about greater mutual understanding amidst dissimilarities in this increasingly divisive world.

© IFIP International Federation for Information Processing 2016
Published by Springer International Publishing Switzerland 2016. All Rights Reserved
Y.K. Dwivedi et al. (Eds.): I3E 2016, LNCS 9844, pp. 195–205, 2016.
DOI: 10.1007/978-3-319-45234-0_18

The paper is organized as such: the next section provides a brief review on social media. This is followed by a description of the social and cultural context of Brunei Darussalam and its national ideology of Malay Islamic Monarchy. The research methodology is then discussed before findings from this study is presented. The implications and proposed follow up to address the findings are then discussed before the paper is concluded.

2 Social Media

Social media can be defined, "as a group of online applications that allow for the creation and exchange of user-generated content" [20]. Social media can be classified by their social presence or media richness and self-presentation or self-disclosure, which, according to [22], can be further categorized into five groups: (1) collaborative projects (e.g. Wikipedia); (2) blogs or microblogs (e.g. Blogs, Twitter); (3) content communities (e.g. YouTube); (4) social networking sites (e.g. Facebook, Instagram) and (5) virtual gaming or social worlds (e.g. HumanSim). In 2015, active social media users exceeded 2 billion worldwide, with Facebook being the most widely adopted social media platform with about 1.366 billion active users across the world [23].

In most societies, teenagers are perceived to be more expressive, more open to changes and even deemed as trendsetters [6]. Compared to earlier generations, most teenagers are exposed to new technologies such as computers, mobile phones, and the Internet at a very young age [6, 7]. Thus, it is somewhat unsurprising that teenagers are among the most active social media users [14, 19].

Research showed that social media are commonly used for communication or social networking; to post comments and sending instant messages to friends or classmates [15, 28, 35, 38]. Additionally, the use of social media to enhance learning among students is also apparent [4]. In studies of social networking use among American teenagers, it was found that the students collaborated via social networks to discuss their homework or group projects [4]. Similarly, students' use of social media to access their learning contents during class session was also reported [32]. Indeed, for the purpose of the students' learning and conveniences, online videos are uploaded onto the social media platform for sharing purposes. Interestingly, social media is also widely used to strengthen social intimacies, particularly among young people who are involved in a romantic relationship [8, 17].

Nevertheless, as much as technologies (such as the social media) are celebrated for their benefits, they are also condemned for some detrimental effects. A number of studies revealed how high levels of social media use is positively connected to addiction-like behaviors [44, 48]. Other studies also illustrated that cyberbullying via social media is prevalent among young people. Previous research investigated the types of cyberbullying experienced by young people and these include name-calling, susceptibility to rumors, gossips and threats [13, 25, 36, 49].

3   Brunei Darussalam

Brunei Darussalam is located in South East Asia, on the island of Borneo. It has a land area of 5,765 km^2, with a population of about 420,000. The official languages are Malay, English and Chinese, and Islam is the national religion.

Brunei Darussalam was a British Protectorate from 1889 till it gained its full independence in 1984. The country is ruled by a king, the Sultan of Brunei. He is the head of state and also head of government. He is concurrently the Prime Minister, Defense Minister, Finance Minister, as well as the Foreign Affairs Minister. The Malay Islamic Monarchy is the country's distinctive ideology which guides social norms and government administration, "promoting Islam as the state religion and monarchical rule as the sole governing system" [45].

Apart from the Shari'a law (Islamic law), applicable only to Muslims in the case of divorce, inheritance or sexual crimes (immoral activities such as adultery known as *zina*, close proximity between sexes in secluded areas known as *khalwat*, or illicit sex resulting in unlawful pregnancy), Bruneian judicial system practices the Secular law, originating from English common law [45]. The sale of alcohol is prohibited by law and the sale of pork is limited to certain restaurants and markets. In comparison to other predominantly Muslim South-East Asian countries (e.g. Indonesia and Malaysia) and more liberal jurisdiction in the Middle East (e.g. Egypt, Dubai and Qatar), Brunei Darussalam is culturally and religiously more conservative.

Socio-cultural norms values and attitudes are heavily influenced by the Malay Islamic Monarchy ideology. Some of these norms, values and attitudes include respect for the elders, good manners, honesty, trustworthiness and obedience to religious practices and obligations. Families are close-knitted and it is not uncommon to find multi-generations living under one roof.

About 50 % of Brunei's population is below the age of 24. As education is fully funded by the government to Bruneian citizens in state schools and is made compulsory, the youth literacy rate is at a high of 99 %. Courses on Islam and the national ideology of Malay Islamic Monarchy is made mandatory by the Ministry of Education. Moreover, Muslim students are also required to attend religious schools, in addition to studying at the state schools.

The teenagers in Brunei are largely technology savvy as information technology is well integrated into the education system. Majority of the educational institutions are equipped with computer laboratories and Internet access.

According to the official 2013 Brunei Darussalam Household Information communication technology (ICT) Survey Report, the most frequently used social media platform in Brunei is Facebook, followed by Instagram [2]. The mobile penetration rate is at 114 %, among the highest in South-East Asia. Most Bruneian access the Internet through the mobile subscription lines. However, there is little or no research on social media use and their implications towards Bruneians.

4   Research Methodology

The phenomenological strategy of inquiry is adopted in this study. The rationale behind using the phenomenological approach in this study derived from the importance of describing the little known yet complex phenomenon of social media use among teenagers in Brunei.

The phenomenological approach seeks to understand human experience from the everyday lives of those who experience an event, phenomenon or object [11, 26]. The phenomenological approach is useful where the focus of a study is on the subjective views of people, describing specific and in-depth information from the actors or subjects [26]. As argued by [26], by using an interpretive phenomenological dimension, the study can contribute significantly to the "practical theory, which can be used to inform, support or challenge policy and action" [26, p. 1]. The phenomenological approach has close affinity with other qualitative research strategies such as ethnography, and case studies, and methodology such as grounded theory, hermeneutics and symbolic interactionism [5, 26, 34].

Qualitative methods are used to collect data as it enables holistic and descriptive data upon which new insights into the lived experiences of the participants can be generated [29, 30]. Indeed, qualitative methods can be used to understand social life and social change [33]. The qualitative method emphasizes an interpretive, naturalistic approach to research inquiry, involving a combination of different research methods such as in-depth interviews, personal observations and case studies to ensure research rigor and credibility of the research inquiry [12].

A total of 143 Bruneian teenagers between the ages of 13 and 19, involving both males and females, are recruited for this study. They are selected randomly throughout the four Districts of Brunei Darussalam, i.e. the Brunei-Muara, Belait, Tutong and Temburong districts. The teenagers are divided into 30 separate focus groups. Each focus group ranged from four to six participants. Each focus group discussion lasted for approximately 60 to 90 min.

The collected data are recorded and transcribed verbatim, segmented and coded. Open coding and axial coding techniques [41] are used to identify categories and later connected to discover broad themes respectively. Direct quotes from respondents that emphasized those themes were incorporated into the thematic data analysis [10, 46].

5   Findings

The findings reveal four social media related behaviors among teenagers in Brunei Darussalam.

5.1   Social Networking

Many teenagers shared that they used social media for its intended purpose of social networking with friends and relatives. Although some admitted to stalking their friends, others shared that they used social media to communicate with their teachers and follow up on school work. Some of the supporting evidence for this is shown in Table 1 below.

Table 1. Evidence of social networking.

Evidence of social networking	
Plain social networking	*To connect, ask my friends this and that...all through Facebook.*
	I tend to share or update status, like for example. "I'm bored. I'm bored."
Stalking	*I'm a stalker...I visit others' pages.*
	Same here, the most I do is check (on others) when I go on Facebook.
Follow-up on school work	*Sometimes we discuss about school work.*
	We ask friends whatever that we may have forgotten or anything about school.
	I ask about homework, plus we can easily contact our teachers.
	We ask about our homework, what to bring for the subject on the next day, ask about our studies...We also Facebook with our teachers. If we don't know their mobile phone number, we contact them through their Facebook instead.

5.2 Romantic Intimacy

Another social media usage behavior among teenagers in Brunei Darussalam is to attain some degree of romantic intimacy with their 'boyfriend' or 'girlfriend'. While most uses social media to connect and keep in touch with their 'boyfriend' or 'girlfriend' or to coordinate social outings, some post pictures of themselves in intimate or sexy posture. Supporting evidence for this is shown in Table 2.

Table 2. Evidence of romantic intimacy.

Evidence of romantic intimacy	
Connecting with 'boyfriend' or 'girlfriend'.	*My boyfriend and I would be joking, and talk about just anything.*
	My boyfriend, I use it often to contact him.
	What's good is that I can just call my girlfriend.
	I use it a lot to contact my boyfriend, so it's good in terms of keeping in touch, no matter where you are.
	To be in contact with our boyfriend, because we're in different school.
Post pictures of themselves in intimate or sexy posture	*Like on Facebook, you tend to see pictures of them kissing or hugging, and they are our school friends... in fact, guys like us will judge those girls who take pictures of them like that, it's like if they're like this, they're guaranteed to have bad personalities, they're cheap and guys will not be serious with them.*
	Yes, we know that girls now are pretty much daring, they would take sexy pictures of themselves, we have seen these pictures of our own friends, but we don't do it, it's disgusting.

5.3   Social Media Addiction

When asked about the unintended or negative implications of their social media activities, the teenagers admitted they are addicted to and easily distracted by their social connectivity. This, they said, made them to be less focused in their studies and spend less time on their school work, and even distract them from performing their prayers, which is an obligation as Muslims are expected to pray five times at specified time period each day. They also stayed up till late at night to engage in long online chats, affecting their sleep. Supporting evidence for this is shown in Table 3.

Table 3. Evidence of social media addiction.

Evidence of social media addiction	
Distracted from performing religious obligation	*Especially in terms of our studies and performing prayers... like if it's time to pray, we still play on the mobile phone, got shouted by dad. But yeah, still play with it and go to the room...*
	Religiously, I think kids are already far left behind... like me, at noon time I'm a good boy. By night time, I would be different. I would be (on) Facebook, going online and chat with my friends, sometimes, dirty chats like that... so I'm not confident to say that I'm holy; if I am, I won't be leaving or skipping my prayers.
Affect sleep	*Like me I would chat till morning, during school holidays that is, like if I want to stop, (I can't). I soon changed my mind (and continue chatting online).*
	I chat a lot, with my friends online, till the break of dawn. (We) talk about anything...
Distracted from school work	*I get scolded by my parents for being too busy with my social media activities, like during exam period, I hardly study.*
	I've always been scolded by my parents, because I'm always playing games and Facebooking, and my homework usually left undone.

5.4   Cyberbullying

Cyberbullying is also frequently mentioned by teenagers. According to them, the use of social media to send insulting messages and spread rumors or gossips, as well as name-calling, is widespread. Such cyberbullying often progress into the real world, resulting in discord among the teenagers in school. Supporting evidence for this is shown in Table 4.

Table 4. Evidence of cyberbullying.

Evidence of cyberbullying	
Cyberbullying	*There was one time, someone commented on my picture, saying my face looked like a pig, so we ended up fighting.*
	It's just bad because, sometimes things like bullying and spreading of rumors on Facebook and all can create family problems, break relationships, you insult each other, you say this, they say that.
	Because of saying things on the Facebook, like name-calling, like laughing at your dad's name which they think is funny, so you end up fighting in school.

6 Discussion

The findings of this study provide a glimpse into the use of social media among teenagers in Brunei Darussalam. The findings of this study also add to a growing body of literature [7, 24, 27, 46] on how teenagers use social media. It reveals that, apart from using social media for its intended purpose of social networking, teenagers in Brunei Darussalam are also using it to achieve a degree of romantic intimacy with their 'boyfriends' or 'girlfriends'. In addition, there are also signs of social media addiction and cyberbullying. While these findings are consistent with studies on the use of social media among teenagers in other countries [7, 9, 16, 47], its significance lies in the context of Brunei Darussalam, especially considering its conservative and Islamic culture as embodied by its national ideology of Malay Islamic Monarchy.

A key use of social media among teenagers in Brunei Darussalam is for social networking. This is unsurprising as this is a primary intent of social media [20]. What is perhaps intriguing is that these teenagers also uses social media to follow-up on their school work, and even to connect with their teachers. While this is a positive use of social media in itself, reports in other countries about such mentoring relationship morphing into illicit sexual relationship between teachers and students [1] can be a red flag for more care to be exercised. To prevent mentors from becoming predators, it will be prudent for schools or even the Ministry of Education to establish some guidelines or code of ethics on how teachers and students can engage one another on social media. The challenge is not so much in the establishment of such guidelines but on where the line should be drawn in such a way that facilitates the use of social media to encourage learning, but yet inhibit the development of illicit relationship. Further research is needed to not only understand the substance of such guidelines, but also how it can be effectively enforced.

Another finding from this study reveals that youths in Brunei Darussalam use social media as a platform to connect with their 'boyfriends' or 'girlfriends', or share pictures of their intimate behaviors. While the development of romantic relationship or even intimacy among teenagers may not be an issue in liberal western societies, such behaviors is a major concern in Brunei Darussalam as it does not conform to the values and beliefs of the Malay Islamic culture. These practices contravene the teachings of Islam, where, in Quran verse (17:32), 'the wrong doings of 'zina' or sexual involvement without marital relationships, are despicable and carries a huge sin and which is 'haram' or forbidden' [21].

While addiction to social media are also found in other countries [31, 42], most of these have only revealed how such addiction has led to being distracted from school work and affecting sleep quality [51]. This study shows that social media addiction has also distracted the teenagers from performing their religious obligation of praying five times every day.

Taking the findings on romantic intimacy and social media addiction together, the use of social media among youths in Brunei Darussalam has brought about behavior that are deemed to be unacceptable in Islamic beliefs. This indicates a tendency for teenagers to be less pious towards the teaching of their Islamic faith. However, instead of dismissing the use of social media altogether, not least because it has the potential to bring about positive outcomes such as enabling teenagers to follow up on the school work, a more enlightened approach is to engage the teenagers through social media such as dissemination of religious information and teachings. Indeed, similar approaches of active engagement and education have also been posited by other scholars [7]. Further research is needed to study how such engagement and education can be effectively implemented, especially in culturally and religiously conservative context such as the situation in Brunei Darussalam.

Cyberbullying is another finding revealed in this study. Cyberbullying via social media has become a convenient alternative to traditional forms of bullying among teenagers [43] and this form of bullying has been found to be widespread in some countries [37]. In extreme cases, cyberbullying is also known to induce depression and even suicidal thoughts among teenagers [39, 40]. Considering the pervasiveness of cyberbullying around the world, it will be advisable for schools and the Ministry of Education to proactively put in place cyberbullying awareness and prevention programs as well as train teachers to be effective counsellors of both cyberbullies and their victims [3]. More research is also needed to understand the effectiveness of such awareness and prevention programs.

7 Conclusion

This paper presents a study on the use of social media among youths in Brunei Darussalam, revealing the presences of social networking, romantic intimacy, social media addiction and cyberbullying behaviors. The unique implication of these behavior to the social-cultural context of Brunei Darussalam, especially in terms of its national ideology of Malay Islamic Monarchy, are discussed. Corresponding interventions approaches as well as future research directions are also proposed.

As with all research, there are limitation to this study which should be cautioned when understanding and using the findings. Even as the interpretive phenomenological methodology adopted in this study limits the transferability of findings to other context, the intent of this study is not about establishing findings that are transferable to other context. Instead, this paper aims to bring about an awareness of how social media usage among youth are perceived in a different social-cultural context and bring about awareness of different worldviews and greater mutual understanding in this increasingly divisive world. Readers are thus cautioned against simply extracting the findings in this paper and extrapolate onto other context. More importantly, this paper alludes that despite differing cultural norms and religious beliefs, similarities and general consensus about the good, the bad and the ugly of social media exist. Such a consensus can be harnessed to bring about greater cooperation and exchange of knowledge in making social media less bad and ugly on one hand, and more good and beautiful on the other.

References

1. Abbott, T.: More Teachers are Having Sex with Their Students. Here's How Schools Can Stop Them. Washington Post (2015). https://www.washingtonpost.com/posteverything/wp/2015/01/20/more-teachers-are-having-sex-with-their-students-heres-how-schools-can-stop-them/
2. AITI.: Brunei Darussalam Household ICT Survey Report 2013, Authority for Infocommunications Technology Industry (2013). http://www.aiti.gov.bn/downloadables/Downloadables%20Library/Brunei%20Darussalam%20Household%20ICT%20Survey%202013.pdf
3. Ang, R.P.: Cyberbullying: its prevention and intervention strategies. In: Deb, S. (ed.) Child Safety, Welfare and Well-being: Issues and Challenges. Springer, India (2015)
4. Boyd, D.: Taken Out of Context: American Teen Sociality in Networked Publics. University of California, Berkeley (2008). http://www.danah.org/papers/TakenOutOfContext.pdf
5. Babbie, E.: The Basics of Social Research. Thomson/Wadsworth, Belmont (2008)
6. Bolton, R.N., Parasuraman, A., Hoefnagels, A., Migchels, N., Kabadayi, S., Gruber, T., Loureiro, Y.K., Solnet, D.: Understanding generation Y and their use of social media: a review and research agenda. J. Serv. Manag. **24**(3), 245–267 (2013)
7. Boyd, D.: It's Complicated: The Social Lives of Networked Teens. Yale University Press, New Haven (2014)
8. Blais, J.J., Craig, W.M., Pepler, D., Connolly, J.: Adolescents online: the importance of Internet activity choices to salient relationships. J. Youth Adolesc. **37**(5), 522–536 (2008)
9. Campbell, M.A.: The Impact of the Mobile Phone on Young People's Social Life (2005). http://eprints.qut.edu.au/3492/
10. Chen, Y.F., Katz, J.E.: Extending family to school life: college students' use of the mobile phone. Int. J. Hum Comput Stud. **67**(2), 179–191 (2009)
11. Castro, A.D.: Introduction to Giorgi's Existential Phenomenological Research Method (2003). http://redalyc.uaemex.mx/pdf/213/21301104.pdf
12. Denzin, N.K., Lincoln, Y.S.: Collecting and Interpreting Qualitative Materials. Sage Publications, Thousand Oaks (1998)
13. DeHue, F., Bolman, C., Völlink, T.: Cyberbullying: youngsters' experiences and parental perception. CyberPsychol. Behav. **11**(2), 217–223 (2008)
14. Duffet, R.G.: Facebook advertising's influence on intention-to-purchase and purchase amongst millennials. Internet Res. **25**(4), 498–526 (2015)
15. Ellison, N.B., Steinfield, C., Lampe, C.: The benefits of Facebook "friends:" Social capital and college students' use of online social network sites. J. Comput. Mediated Commun. **12**(4), 1143–1168 (2007)
16. Engel, G., Green, T.: Are we dialing up disaster? TechTrends **55**(2), 39 (2011)
17. Fox, J., Warber, K.M.: Romantic relationship development in the age of Facebook: an exploratory study of emerging adults' perceptions, motives, and behaviors. Cyberpsychol. Behav. Soc. Network. **16**(1), 3–7 (2013)

18. Forbush, E., Foucault-Welles, B.: Social media use and adoption among Chinese students beginning to study in the United States. Int. J. Intercultural Relat. **50**(1), 1–12 (2016)
19. Goldenberg, B.: The rise of the digital client. Customer Relat. Manag. **11**(1), 12 (2007)
20. Hamm, M.P., Chisholm, A., Shulhan, J., Milne, A., Scott, S.D., Given, L.M., Hartling, L.: Social media use among patients and caregivers: a scoping review. BMJ Open **3**, 5 (2013)
21. Holy Quran. Selangor, Malaysia: Khazanah Rabbani (2010). Print
22. Kaplan, A.M., Haenlein, M.: Users of the world, unite! The challenges and opportunities of social media. Bus. Horiz. **53**(1), 59–68 (2010)
23. Kemp, S.: Digital, social & mobile worldwide in 2015. We are Social (2015)
24. Kumjonmenukul, P.: The behavior of young people when using mobile phones and its impact on Thai culture and lifestyle: a case study of Kalasin Municipality in Kalasin Province. Am. J. Sci. Res. **22**, 57–64 (2011)
25. Kokkinos, C.M., Antoniadou, N., Markos, A.: Cyber-bullying: an investigation of the psychological profile of university student participants. J. Appl. Dev. Psychol. **35**(3), 204–214 (2014)
26. Lester, S.: An Introduction To Phenomenological Research (1999). http://www.sld.demon.co.uk/resmethy.pdf
27. Leung, L., Wei, R.: More than just talk on the move: uses and gratifications of the cellular phone. J. Mass Commun. Q. **77**(2), 308–320 (2000)
28. Lenhart, A., Purcell, K., Smith, A., Zickuhr, K.: Social media & mobile Internet use among teens and young adults millennials. Pew Internet & American Life Project (2010)
29. Mariampolski, H.: Qualitative Market Research: A Comprehensive Guide. Sage Publications, Thousand Oaks (2001)
30. Marshall, C., Rossman, G.B.: Designing Qualitative Research. Sage Publications, Thousand Oaks (1999)
31. Muller, K.W., Dreier, M., Beutel, M.E., Duven, E., Giralt, S., Wolfling, K.: A hidden type of Internet addiction? Intense and addictive use of social networking sites in adolescents. Comput. Hum. Bahav. **55**(A), 172–177 (2016)
32. Moran, M., Seaman, J., Tinti-Kane, H.: Teaching, Learning, and Sharing: How Today's Higher Education Faculty Use Social Media. Pearson Learning Solution & Babson Survey Research Group, Boston, MA (2011)
33. Mackay, H., Maples, W., Reynolds, P.: Investigating Information Society. Routledge with The Open University, London (2001)
34. Rubin, H.J., Rubin, I.S.: Qualitative Interviewing: The Art of Hearing Data. Sage Publications, Thousand Oaks (2005)
35. O'Keefe, G.S., Clarke-Pearson, K.: The impacts of social media on children, adolescents, and families. Pediatrics **127**(4), 800–804 (2011)
36. Patchin, J.W., Hinduja, S.: Bullies move beyond the schoolyard a preliminary look at cyberbullying. Youth Violence Juv. Justice **4**(2), 148–169 (2006)
37. Patchin, J.W., Hinduja, S.: Cyberbullying among adolescents: implications for empirical research. J. Adolesc. Health **53**(4), 431–432 (2013)
38. Park, N., Kee, K.F., Valenzuela, S.: Being immersed in social networking environment: Facebook groups, uses and gratifications, and social outcomes. CyberPsychol. Behav. **12**(6), 729–733 (2009)
39. Reed, K.P., Cooper, R.L., Nugent, W.R., Russell, K.: Cyberbullying: a literature review of its relationship to adolescent depression and current intervention strategies. J. Hum. Behav. Soc. Environ. **26**(1), 37–45 (2016)
40. Shpiegel, Y., Klomek, A.B., Apter, A.: Bullying, cyberbullying, depression and suicide ideation among youth: comparing online to paper-and-pencil questionnaires. Int. J. Child Adolesc. Health **8**(2), 161–167 (2015)

41. Strauss, A., Corbin, J.: Basics of Qualitative Research – Techniques and Procedures for Developing Grounded Theory, 2nd edn. Sage Publications, London (1998)
42. Tang, J.-H., Chen, M.-C., Yang, C.-Y., Chung, T.-Y., Lee, Y.-A.: Personality traits, interpersonal relationships, online social support, and Facebook addiction. Telematics Inform. **33**(1), 102–108 (2016)
43. Tokunaga, R.S.: Following you home from school: a critical review and synthesis of research on cyberbullying victimization. Comput. Hum. Behav. **26**(3), 277–287 (2010)
44. Tsitsika, A., Janikian, M., Schoenmakers, T.M., Tzavela, E.C., Ólafsson, K., Wójcik, S., Macarie, G.F., Tzavara, C., Richardson, C.: Internet addictive behavior in adolescence: a cross-sectional study in seven countries. Cyberpsychol. Behav. Soc. Network. **17**(8), 528–535 (2014)
45. U.S Department of State.: Bureau of Democracy, Human Rights, and Labor (2008)
46. Walsh, S.P., White, K.M., Young, R.M.: Over-connected? A qualitative exploration of the relationship between Australian youth and their mobile phones. J. Adolesc. **31**(1), 77–92 (2008)
47. Weerakkody, N.D.: Mobile phones and children: an Australian perspective. Issues Inform. Sci. Inf. Technol. **5**, 459–475 (2008)
48. Wilson, K., Fornasier, S., White, K.M.: Psychological predictors of young adults' use of social networking sites. Cyberpsychol. Behav. Soc. Network. **13**(2), 173–177 (2010)
49. Whittaker, E., Kowalski, R.M.: Cyberbullying via social media. J. School Violence **14**(1), 11–29 (2015)
50. Wegge, D., Vandebosch, H., Eggermont, S., Walrave, M.: The strong, the weak, and the unbalanced the link between tie strength and cyberaggression on a social network site. Soc. Sci. Comput. Rev. **33**(3), 315–342 (2015)
51. Xanidis, N., Brignell, C.M.: The association between the use of social media sites, sleep quality and cognition function during the day. Comput. Hum. Behav. **55**(A), 121–126 (2016)

An Empirical Study of Facebook Adoption Among Young Adults in a Northeastern State of India: Validation of Extended Technology Acceptance Model (TAM)

Mohammad A.A. Alryalat[1], Nripendra P. Rana[2(✉)],
Hiren K.D. Sarma[3], and Jafar A. Alzubi[1]

[1] Al-Balqa Applied University, Salt, Jordan
{mohammad.alryalat,j.zubi}@bau.edu.jo
[2] School of Management, Swansea University Bay Campus,
Swansea SA1 8EN, UK
n.p.rana@swansea.ac.uk
[3] Department of Information Technology,
Sikkim Manipal Institute of Technology, Sikkim, India
hirenkdsarma@gmail.com

Abstract. The purpose of this paper is to explore the adoption of a social networking site called Facebook in context of a landlocked and one of the least populous states in India. The adoption of Facebook is examined by considering technology acceptance model (TAM) as a basic model along with additional constructs such as subjective norm and perceived trust in it. The data were collected from 202 young adults from couple of degree level colleges from one of the least populous and landlocked states called Sikkim in India. The empirical outcomes provided the positive significant connections between nine hypothesised relationships among seven constructs. The article also discusses the resulting theoretical contributions for Facebook adoption and discusses practical implications of Facebook adoption for Facebook providers and users.

Keywords: Facebook · Adoption · Usage · Young adults · India · TAM

1 Introduction

People's interest in social networking sites has considerably increased in recent years [1]. Social networking sites such as Facebook are virtual communities, which allow people to connect and interact with each other on a specific subject or to just hang out "together" online [2]. The prior research has shown that social network site usage is not randomly distributed among Internet users, and that user's demographic background and socio-economic status can play a significant role in the specific social network site adoption [3].

Social media sites, such as Facebook and Twitter, can expedite direct, one-to-many communication with a large audience at a little to no cost [4]. The research indicates that more than 500 million people spend about 700 billion minutes on Facebook every

© IFIP International Federation for Information Processing 2016
Published by Springer International Publishing Switzerland 2016. All Rights Reserved
Y.K. Dwivedi et al. (Eds.): I3E 2016, LNCS 9844, pp. 206–218, 2016.
DOI: 10.1007/978-3-319-45234-0_19

month and half of them log into their account in a given day with an average user has about 130 contacts [1]. As far as India is concerned, it is the second biggest market for Facebook after the US. Facebook has 125 million average users with the number of mobile users stands at 114 million. On a daily basis, 59 million users in India access Facebook and 53 million are accessing it through mobile phones [5].

The adoption of Facebook across the young adults constitutes a natural experiment providing insight into how technological innovations spread across to the young population [4] particularly in the relatively trailing states in India as such social media sites allow the young generations to get connected to the world and to get updated to what is happening in the world without putting in much effort to know them. The adoption of Facebook by young adults also allows us to understand the degree to which the people want and intend to get connected to all those they are acquainted with and are available online. It also gives the idea about the people's interest toward following certain other public figures, brands, organisations for which they are interested in and want to follow their updates by liking them.

Realising that such a large number of people use Facebook in India and only a few research studies (e.g., [6, 7]) have attempted to analyse the adoption of this social networking site in Indian context, it is timely and relevant to explore the adoption of Facebook among young adults in one of the least populous and landlocked states in India called Sikkim located in the Himalayan mountains.

2 Theory Development and Research Hypotheses

This section will provide overview of the proposed research model and the statements for hypotheses based on the relationships between seven constructs.

2.1 Overview of the Proposed Research Model

Our theoretical development will follow up and emerge from the TAM. The TAM carries on being the most extensively and commonly used dominant theoretical model for examining the individual's acceptance of information systems [8]. Adapted from the theory of reasoned action (TRA) [9] and firstly proposed by Davis [10], it presumes that acceptance of information system/information technology (IS/IT) at the individual level is established by two key variables; namely, *perceived ease of use* and *perceived usefulness*. The IS/IT community has also considered TAM as a prudent and powerful theory for more than two decades [11].

Perceived ease of use is defined as, the degree to which an individual believes that using a particular system would be free of effort [12]. Perceived usefulness is defined as, the degree to which an individual believes that using a particular system would enhance his or her job performance [12]. These two constructs are found to determine individual's attitude to adopt Facebook. *Attitude* can be defined as individual's positive or negative feelings about accomplishing the target behaviour [9]. Perceived usefulness and perceived ease of use influence the individual's attitudes toward using the technology (intention). According to TAM, intentions to use technology will determine whether a person will use the technology or not (behavior) [12].

TAM has been revised in various studies (e.g., [13]) to fit a specific context of technology being examined. One important and well-received revision of TAM has been the inclusion of *subjective norm* in predicting the usage behavior of a technology by its users [14]. *Subjective norm* is defined as an individual's perception that most people who are important to him think he should or should not perform the behavior in question [9]. Legris et al. [15] performed a qualitative meta-analysis and concluded that TAM was a useful model but had to include the human and social change process variable such as subjective norm.

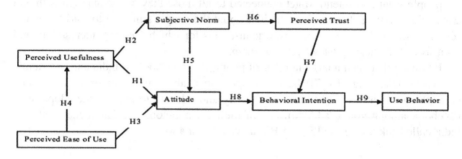

Fig. 1. Proposed research model (Source: Adapted from Davis, [12])

Inclusion of *subjective norm* in the proposed research model is also important as this model examines the adoption of a social network service such as Facebook for which the people's opinions who are close to the user are very important. Similarly, employing trust perceptions in the uncertain context of social media is also reasonable. Drawing upon these constructs, this paper theoretically develops and empirically validates a research model (see Fig. 1) that predicts young adults' acceptance of Facebook in a relatively straggling state like Sikkim in India.

Table 1. Hypotheses development

H#	Hypothesis statement	Source(s)
H1	Perceived Usefulness → Attitude	[16]
H2	Perceived Usefulness → Subjective Norm	[17]
H3	Perceived Ease of Use → Attitude	[13, 18]
H4	Perceived Ease of Use → Perceived Usefulness	[19]
H5	Subjective Norm → Attitude	[20]
H6	Subjective Norm → Perceived Trust	[21]
H7	Perceived Trust → Behavioral Intention	[22]
H8	Attitude → Behavioral Intention	[23, 24]
H9	Behavioral Intention → Use Behavior	[12, 25]

2.2   Hypotheses Development

Under the proposed research model, we have formulated nine hypotheses based on the relationships between seven constructs adopted. A brief summary of the various hypotheses is presented below in Table 1.

3   Research Methodology

The sample of this study consists of young adults including undergraduate and post-graduate students and young members of faculties within the age range of 19–39 years from couple of degree level colleges from one of the smallest states called Sikkim in India. We conducted the web-based questionnaire survey through the young students and faculties in these colleges during their computer lab sessions and provided them the Google document link to click and respond to the online questionnaire. The whole exercise was done through various lab sessions, which were conducted in a week of time in September 2015. The concerned faculties of the modules were also requested to take part in the survey although it was completely done in a voluntary manner.

A seven-point Likert scale of [1–7] was chosen as the key instrument in the questionnaire. All the questions were close-ended to make sure that the respondents do not face any difficulty while responding to the questions. After a week time, we were able to obtain 211 completed responses out of which nine responses were discarded because the respondents' age range was found to exceed 39 years mark. This scrutiny was done to avoid any influenced results being obtained due to biased responses. As result, we were left out with 202 usable responses, which made the basis for our empirical analysis for measuring users' behavioral intentions and use of Facebook.

4   Results

4.1   Respondents' Demographic Profile

As per the questionnaire results, the average respondents' age ranges from 19 to 25 with 72.3 % of the overall respondents lie in this age group, with males accounting for 76.7 % of the sample and 23.3 % were female. As far as the extent of use of Internet is concerned, largest 53 % of the respondents used Internet several times a day whereas 23.8 % used it even on hourly basis. In terms of the Facebook use, the highest 43.1 % of the overall respondents were found to use it several times a day whereas 6.4 % used it on hourly basis. When we asked them about the number of friends on Facebook, the largest 34.7 % indicated to have more than 500 friends in their friend list.

4.2   Descriptive Statistics and Measurement Model

The high overall mean values (see Table 2) for most of the constructs indicate that respondents react favorably to the all the measures directly or indirectly related to respondents' actual use of Facebook. The overall minimum mean for perceived trust as

Table 2. Descriptive statistics

Variable	Mean	S.D.
Perceived Ease of Use (PEU)	5.79	1.12
Perceived Usefulness (PU)	4.56	1.17
Attitude (AT)	5.20	1.18
Subjective Norm (SN)	4.73	1.29
Perceived Trust (PT)	4.39	1.43
Behavioral Intention (BI)	5.17	1.50
Use Behavior (UB)	5.05	1.14

Legend: S.D. = Standard Deviation

'4.40' on the Likert scale [1–7] indicates that although respondents have not shown remarkable trust on the use of Facebook, they have not distrusted its various features and applications either.

Convergent and discriminant validity of the scales were tested with confirmatory factor analysis. Convergent validity is examined using three ad hoc tests recommended by [26]. Table 3 lists the standardized factor loadings, composite reliabilities, and average variance extracted. Standardized factor loadings are indicative of the degree of association between scale items and a single latent variable [27]. The loadings are highly significant in all the cases. Composite reliabilities for all the variables were found well beyond the minimum limit of 0.70.

Table 3. Results of Confirmatory Factor Analysis (CFA)

Measure	FL	CR	AVE
Perceived Ease of Use (PEU)		0.857	0.784
PEU1	0.79		
PEU2	0.87		
PEU3	0.69		
PEU4	0.74		
Perceived Usefulness (PU)		0.775	0.589
PU1	0.54		
PU2	0.63		
PU3	0.73		
PU4	0.64		
PU5	0.65		
Attitude (AT)		0.856	0.603
AT1	0.73		
AT2	0.75		
AT3	0.78		

(*Continued*)

Table 3. (*Continued*)

Measure	FL	CR	AVE
Subjective Norm (SN)		0.739	0.580
SN1	0.73		
SN2	0.70		
SN3	0.66		
Perceived Trust (PT)		0.897	0.705
PT1	0.80		
PT2	0.81		
PT3	0.87		
Behavioral Intention (BI)		0.725	0.554
BI1	0.71		
BI2	0.72		
BI3	0.62		
Use Behavior (UB)		0.774	0.648
UB1	0.69		
UB2	0.72		
UB3	0.78		

Legend: AVE: Average Variance Extracted, CR: Composite Reliability, FL: Factor Loading

Average variance extracted (AVE) is a measure of the variation explained by the latent variable to random measurement error [28] and ranged from 0.554 to 0.784 for all constructs. Again, these estimates exceed the recommended lower limit of 0.50 [29]. All tests support the convergent validity of the scales. Discriminant validity was assessed with the test recommended by Anderson and Gerbing [26]. The squared correlation between a pair of latent variables (see Table 4) should be less than the AVE of each variable (Table 4). Each combination of latent variables was tested, and each pairing passed, providing indication of the discriminant validity of the scales.

Table 4. Squared pairwise correlations and alpha internal reliabilities

Var	PEU	PU	AT	SN	PT	BI	UB
PEU	0.885[b]						
PU	0.450[a]	0.767[b]					
AT	0.537[a]	0.641[a]	0.776[b]				
SN	0.312[a]	0.446[a]	0.547[a]	0.761[b]			
PT	0.335[a]	0.379[a]	0.441[a]	0.441[a]	0.839[b]		
BI	0.473[a]	0.558[a]	0.616[a]	0.517[a]	0.466[b]	0.744[b]	
UB	0.424[a]	0.596[a]	0.615[a]	0.467[a]	0.503[b]	0.655[b]	0.805[b]

Legend: [a]Square root of AVE shown on the main diagonal
[b]Significant at p < 0.01

4.3 Structural Model Testing

The overall model fit is acceptable, as can be seen from Table 5. As the Chi-square test of absolute model fit is absolute to sample size and non-normality, a better measure of fit is Chi-square over degrees of freedom [27]. The ratio of Chi-square over degrees of freedom (i.e., 1.495) is well within suggested 3 to 1 bracket [30, 31]. Typically, researchers also report a number of fit-statistics to examine the relative fit of the data to the model (see Table 5). We found the fit-indices and RMSEA (Root Mean Square Error of Approximation) well within the recommended level, which measures the discrepancy per degree of freedom [32].

Table 5. Model fit summary for the proposed research model

Fit index	Model	Recommendation
Chi-Square	354.40	N/A
Degree of Freedom (DF)	237	N/A
P	0.000	Non-Significant
Chi-Square/DF	1.495	<3.000 (see [30])
GFI (Goodness-of-Fit Index)	0.903	>0.90 (see [33])
AGFI (Adjusted GFI)	0.848	>0.80 (see [30])
CFI (Comparative Fit Index)	0.951	>0.90 (see [34])
TLI (Tucker-Lewis Index)	0.950	>0.95 (see [35])
RMSEA	0.050	<0.06 (see [35])

Having established the relative adequacy of the model's fit, it is appropriate to examine individual path coefficients corresponding to our hypotheses. This analysis is presented in Table 6. All nine hypotheses are supported.

All relationships except between PEOU and AT were found significant at the levels of p < 0.001 whereas that of between PEOU and AT was found significant at p < 0.01 level. The higher level of significance and strong path coefficients for majority of

Table 6. Path coefficients and hypotheses testing

H#	Hypothesis	PC	CR	Sig.
H1	Perceived Usefulness → Attitude	0.514	4.405	***
H2	Perceived Usefulness → Subjective Norm	0.633	5.972	***
H3	Perceived Ease of Use → Attitude	0.218	2.959	**
H4	Perceived Ease of Use → Perceived Usefulness	0.591	6.101	***
H5	Subjective Norm → Attitude	0.339	3.797	***
H6	Subjective Norm → Perceived Trust	0.587	6.430	***
H7	Perceived Trust → Behavioral Intention	0.226	3.649	***
H8	Attitude → Behavioral Intention	0.849	9.121	***
H9	Behavioral Intention → Use Behavior	0.866	9.178	***

Legend: CR: Critical Ratio, H#: Hypothesis Number, PC: Path Coefficient, Sig.: Significance relationships are also indicated by relatively higher critical ratios between different relationships. The variance explained by the validated research model on dependent variables including perceived usefulness, subjective norm, attitude, behavioral intentions and use behavior were found as 35 %, 40 %, 34 %, 84 % and 75 % respectively.

5 Discussion

Among all other social media portals, Facebook has become a universal phenomenon to support users' communication, interactions, entertainment and social bonding. Motivated by the global and unparalleled popularity, this research seeks to understand what leads to acceptance of such social media usage [13] by young adults from academic institutions located in a landlocked and one of the least populous states in India. Figure 2 presents the validated research model using the data collected through young adults on Facebook adoption from one of the remotest and least populace states in India.

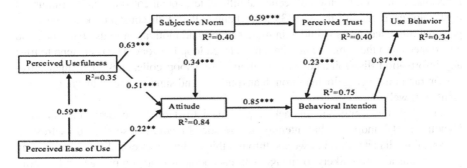

Fig. 2. Validated research model

Firstly, the strong and significant impact of perceived usefulness on user's attitude (i.e., Hypothesis H1) indicates that perceived usefulness or benefits derived from using Facebook influences users' positive beliefs, feelings and positive thoughts toward using it. One of such obvious benefits could be to use Facebook to interact with the friends, community and society. It is consistent with the findings of prior studies (e.g., [13, 36]) on social media adoption. The results also indicated the strongly positive and significant impact of perceived usefulness on subjective norm (i.e., Hypothesis H2). This indicates that the perceived usefulness or benefits offered by this social networking channel would allow the existing Facebook users to refer it to their friends, family and colleagues.

Secondly, perceived ease of use was found to significantly influence users' attitude (i.e., Hypothesis H3) and perceived usefulness (i.e., Hypothesis H4). The findings supporting these hypotheses indicate that designers and developers of social media websites, applications, and pages should focus more on how to create value for the social media users [13]. In other words, the developers and designers of Facebook should make sure that users can easily perform activities including photo and file uploading and downloading, profile editing, and using the menus efficiently [37]. Managing such features and Facebook content without much effort would influence users' attitude toward using this social media channel. Also, easy to access interface and features provided by designers would help users to better understand Facebook's usefulness and benefits, which eventually help them accept and use this social media channel.

Thirdly, subjective norm was found to exert significant impact on attitude (i.e., Hypothesis H5) and perceived trust (i.e., Hypothesis H6). The significant impact of subjective norm on attitude indicates that social network users are more likely to base their positive perceptions integrating their sense of image and opinions from their informal social network rather than following the fad blindly [20]. This relationship indicates that users' attitude toward using Facebook is socially influenced by their friends, colleagues, family or any significant others who already have their presence on this social media site [38]. Moreover, the support to use social media site such as Facebook from significant others also leads to significantly improved trust toward using this channel. Many early adopters of the social media sites such as Facebook stop using it because of the combination of technical difficulties, social collisions and a rupture of trust between users and the site [39]. We believe that with constant social and inter-personal influence, users would gain more support and motivation to use Facebook and get connected to their important others in a closed loop network. The users tend to trust any information disseminated through their closed loop colleagues more than information randomly being floated through anyone else and significance of this relationship justifies it well.

Fourthly, the significant impact of perceived trust on behavioral intention (i.e., Hypothesis H7) indicates that intention to use social media is also shaped by trust on the social media site. In other words, through this finding, it is established that trusting young adults are more likely to engage with Facebook. Reports on privacy and security concerns on social media sites such as Facebook have made everyday front-page news. In order to freely participate and engage, users need to trust this site [13]. From its moderate path-coefficient on intentions, it can be inferred that trust apparently plays a role in enhancing intentions (Shin, 2010). The findings support prior research on trust and emphasised the value of trust in the online environment [40, 41]. This is largely up to developers and designers to provide adequate security and privacy provisions in the site that allows the users to trust it and so improves their intentions to use it. Also, in the prior online environment research, trust has been found to be indispensable to virtual community members' intention to exchange information with other members [42–44].

Finally, the strong and significant impacts of attitude on behavioral intention (i.e., Hypothesis H8) and behavioral intention on use behavior (i.e., Hypothesis H9) indicate that users' positive believes lead to their intention to know more friends and use Facebook to interact with their friends and continue to use it in the future, which in turn results in its use for enjoyment and interacting with improved efficiency in sharing information and connecting with others. The facilitators of Facebook should keep very close eyes on this social media system to meet the users' expectations and constantly improves its interface keeping the users' requirements in mind. A number of studies (e.g., [13, 41]) on social network have supported these relationships.

5.1   Implications for Researchers and Practitioners

This research provides several implications for information systems (IS) researchers as well as Facebook service providers. Researchers have advocated extending and re-validating past theories and frameworks in a new context [13] [45]. Following that, this study represents the first widespread investigation of the user acceptance of a social media site such as Facebook using scales derived from existing literature and in a completely new context of young adults from one of the smallest, technologically lagging and landlocked states in India. The composite reliabilities of our constructs (such as PEU, PU, AT, SN, PT, BI and UB) reflect reliable instruments that can be adopted for future studies in the field of social media adoption.

The findings from factor analysis and the measurement model help in classifying the significant dimensions for the extended TAM model for social media adoption. We believe that this contribution is a substantial accumulation to the social media literature [13]. The study sheds light on developing a new theory by grounding additional variables (i.e., subjective norm and trust) in the TAM and applying it in the emerging context of Facebook adoption in context of India. The inclusion of additional variables found valid and significant in this study. This result ensures a consistent model of the drivers for social technology and established theory development. Hence, the proposed research model provides a significant contribution to emerging literature on social media adoption [41] in developing countries' context in general.

Similarly, this study can draw practical implications of this research for vendors, managers and Facebook service providers. To develop good practices of managing and developing social media related strategies, the research findings based on extended TAM model can be referenced by practitioners of social media as well [13]. The inclusion of trust in the model and its positive impact on behavioral intentions indicate that vendors should establish user's trust by ensuring that their services are conducted in accordance with users' expectations [41]. The Facebook providers also need to understand the ease of services provided to users so that they can easily explore the Facebook to seamlessly avail all its features and get in touch with their online friend community.

The results of this research are also important to academic community to get in touch with each other and by realising the actual benefits of using Facebook in real sense. For instance, its usefulness in terms of using the "Facebook Chat" and special feature of "News Feed" allow users to sense the presence of their friends in Facebook and accept it as a social media channel to use it on 24 × 7 basis [46]. Particularly, with widespread adoption of smartphones and the use of Facebook messenger in them have allowed users to come even closer to their friends for all recent updates and news.

5.2   Limitations and Future Research

First, the sample size considered for this research was only 202 young adults from degree colleges in one of the Northeastern states in India. The future study should consider even larger and diversified sample to analyse the adoption of Facebook in Indian context. Second, the study represents mostly the student users of Facebook.

Therefore, the care must be taken when extrapolating the findings to the other types of online social networks that target different groups of users such as professionals in LinkedIn or Twitter. Third, as the responding users of this research are young adults, it does not provide a comprehensive picture of the entire social media community. The future research can consider a sample of different groups of users across the various age groups.

6 Conclusion

This research proposed an extended TAM model for enhancing our understanding of a social media user's attitude and intentions to use Facebook. The findings indicate that usefulness, ease of use, friends and family influence, trust and positive attitude are some of the significant factors that positively influence young adults' intention and actual use of the social media sites like Facebook. Based on the TAM model, this research also validates the attitude-intention-behavior relationship in the context of the social media site Facebook. Moreover, adding additional constructs such as subjective norm and perceived trust makes the TAM model more meaningful for understanding the acceptance and use of social media.

References

1. Koc, M., Gulyagci, S.: Facebook addiction among Turkish college students: the role of psychological health, demographic, and usage characteristics. Cyber Psychol. Behav. Soc. Network. **16**(4), 279–284 (2013)
2. Murray, K.E., Waller, R.: Social networking goes abroad. Int. Educ. **16**(3), 56–59 (2007)
3. Hargittai, E., Litt, E.: The tweet smell of celebrity success: explaining variation in Twitter adoption among a diverse group of young adults. New Media Soc. **13**(5), 824–842 (2011)
4. Harris, J.K., Mueller, N.L., Snider, D.: Social media adoption in local health departments nationwide. Am. J. Public Health **103**(9), 1700–1707 (2013)
5. PTI: Facebook user base has now climbed to 125 million users in India. Press Trust of India (2015). http://tech.firstpost.com/news-analysis/facebook-user-base-has-now-climbed-to-125-million-users-in-india-272186.html
6. Ahmed, S., Diesner, J.: Information network analysis to understand the evolution of online social networking sites in the context of India, Pakistan, and Bangladesh. Growth 3(3/4), 1–6 (2012)
7. Kumar, N.: Facebook for self-empowerment? A study of Facebook adoption in urban India. New Media Soc. pp. 1–16 (2014). DOI:10.1177/1461444814543999
8. Lee, Y., Kozar, K.A., Larsen, K.R.: The technology acceptance model: past, present, and future. Commun. Assoc. Inf. Syst. **12**(1), 752–780 (2003)
9. Fishbein, M., Ajzen, I.: Belief, Attitude, Intention and Behavior: An Introduction to Theory and Research. Addison-Wesley, Reading (1975)
10. Davis, F.D.: A Technology Acceptance Model for Empirically Testing New End-user Information Systems: Theory and Results. Doctoral dissertation. Massachusetts: Sloan School of Management, Massachusetts Institute of Technology (1986)

11. Venkatesh, V., Davis, F.D.: A theoretical extension of the technology acceptance model: four longitudinal field studies. Manag. Sci. **45**(2), 186–204 (2000)
12. Davis, F.D.: Perceived usefulness, perceived ease of use, and user acceptance of information technology. MIS Q. **13**(3), 319–340 (1989)
13. Rauniar, R., Rawski, G., Yang, J., Jhonson, B.: Technology acceptance model (TAM) and social media usage: an empirical study on Facebook. J. Enterp. Inf. Manag. **27**(1), 6–30 (2014)
14. Schepers, J., Wetzels, M.: A meta-analysis of the technology acceptance model: investigating subjective norm and moderation effects. Inf. Manag. **44**(1), 90–103 (2007)
15. Legris, P., Ingham, J., Collerette, P.: Why do people use information technology? A critical review of the technology acceptance model. Inf. Manag. **40**(3), 191–204 (2003)
16. Porter, C.E., Donthu, N.: Using the technology acceptance model to explain how attitudes determine Internet usage: the role of perceived access barriers and demographics. J. Bus. Res. **59**(9), 999–1007 (2006)
17. Teo, T.: The impact of subjective norm and facilitating conditions on pre-service teachers' attitude toward computer use: a structural equation modeling of an extended technology acceptance model. J. Educ. Comput. Res. **40**(1), 89–109 (2009)
18. Molla, A., Licker, P.S.: e-Commerce systems success: an attempt to extend and respecify the DeLone and McLean model of IS success. J. Electron. Commer. Res. **2**(4), 131–141 (2001)
19. Huang, Y.M., Huang, Y.M., Huang, S.H., Lin, Y.T.: A ubiquitous English vocabulary learning system: evidence of active/passive attitudes vs. usefulness/ease-of-use. Comput. Educ. **58**(1), 273–282 (2012)
20. Lu, J., Yao, J.E., Yu, C.S.: Personal innovativeness, social influences and adoption of wireless Internet services via mobile technology. J. Strateg. Inf. Syst. **14**(3), 245–268 (2005)
21. Li, X., Hess, T.J., Valacich, J.S.: Using attitude and social influence to develop an extended trust model for information systems. ACM SIGMIS Database **37**(2–3), 108–124 (2006)
22. Papadopoulou, P.: Applying virtual reality for trust-building e-commerce environments. Virtual Reality **11**(2), 107–127 (2007)
23. Ajzen, I., Fishbein, M.: Understanding Attitudes and Predicting Social Behavior. Prentice-Hall, Englewood Cliffs (1980)
24. Taylor, S., Todd, P.A.: Decomposition and crossover effects in the theory of planned behaviour: a study of consumer adoption. Int. J. Res. Mark. **12**(2), 137–155 (1995)
25. Davis, F.D., Bagozzi, R.P., Warshaw, P.R.: User acceptance of computer technology: a comparison of two theoretical models. Manag. Sci. **35**(8), 982–1003 (1989)
26. Anderson, J.C., Gerbing, D.W.: Structural equation modeling in practice: a review and recommended two-step approach. Psychol. Bull. **103**(3), 411–423 (1988)
27. Belanger, F., Carter, L.: Trust and risk in e-government adoption. J. Strateg. Inf. Syst. **17**(2), 165–176 (2008)
28. Netemeyer, R.G., Johnston, M.W., Burton, S.: Analysis of role conflict and role ambiguity in a structural equations framework. J. Appl. Psychol. **75**(2), 148–157 (1990)
29. Fornell, C., Larcker, D.F.: Evaluating structural equation models with unobservable variables and measurement error. J. Mark. Res. **18**(1), 39–50 (1981)
30. Chin, W.W., Todd, P.A.: On the use, usefulness, and ease of use of structural equation modeling in MIS research: a note of caution. MIS Q. **19**(2), 237–246 (1995)
31. Gefen, D.: e-commerce: the role of familiarity and trust. Omega Int. J. Manag. Sci. **28**(6), 725–737 (2000)
32. Steiger, J.H., Lind, J.C.: Statistically-Based Tests for the Number of Common Factors. Annual Spring Meeting of the Psychometric Society, Iowa City (1980)
33. Hoyle, R.H.: The Structural Equation Modeling Approach: Basic Concepts and Fundamental Issues. Sage Publications, Thousand Oaks (1995)

34. Bentler, P., Bonett, D.: Significance tests and goodness of fit in the analysis of covariance structures. Psychol. Bull. **88**(3), 588–606 (1980)
35. Hu, L.T., Bentler, P.M.: Cutoff criteria for fit indexes in covariance structure analysis: conventional criteria versus new alternatives. Struct. Equat. Model. Multi. J. **6**(1), 1–55 (1999)
36. Mansumitrchai, S., Park, C.H., Chiu, C.L.: Factors underlying the adoption of social network: a study of Facebook users in South Korea. Int. J. Bus. Manag. **7**(24), 138–153 (2012)
37. Mazman, S.G., Usluel, Y.K.: Modeling educational usage of Facebook. Comput. Educ. **55** (2), 444–453 (2010)
38. Pedersen, P.E.: Adoption of mobile Internet services: an exploratory study of mobile commerce early adopters. J. Organ. Comput. Electron. Commer. **15**(3), 203–222 (2005)
39. Ellison, N.B.: Social network sites: definition, history, and scholarship. J. Comput. Mediated Commun. **13**(1), 210–230 (2007)
40. Hassanein, K., Head, M.: Manipulating social presence through the web interface and its impact on consumer attitude towards online shopping. Int. J. Hum Comput Stud. **64**(12), 1230–1242 (2007)
41. Shin, D.H.: The effects of trust, security and privacy in social networking: a security-based approach to understand the pattern of adoption. Interact. Comput. **22**(5), 428–438 (2010)
42. Chu, S.C., Kim, Y.: Determinants of consumer engagement in electronic word-of-mouth (eWOM) in social networking sites. Int. J. Advert. **30**(1), 47–75 (2011)
43. Jarvenpaa, S.L., Knoll, K., Leidner, D.E.: Is anybody out there? Antecedents of trust in global virtual teams. J. Manag. Inf. Syst. **14**(4), 29–64 (1998)
44. Ridings, C.M., Gefen, D., Arinze, B.: Some antecedents and effects of trust in virtual communities. J. Strateg. Inf. Syst. **11**(3/4), 271–295 (2002)
45. Berthon, P., Pitt, L., Ewing, M., Carr, C.: L: Potential research space in MIS: a framework for envisioning and evaluating research replication, extension, and generation. Inf. Syst. Res. **13**(4), 416–427 (2002)
46. Cheung, C.M., Chiu, P.Y., Lee, M.K.: Online social networks: why do students use facebook? Comput. Hum. Behav. **27**(4), 1337–1343 (2011)

Impact of Perceived Connectivity on Intention to Use Social Media: Modelling the Moderation Effects of Perceived Risk and Security

Samuel Fosso Wamba[1(✉)] and Shahriar Akter[2]

[1] Toulouse Business School, 20 Boulevard Lascrosses, 31068 Toulouse, France
fossowam@gmail.com
[2] Faculty of Business, University of Wollongong, Northfields Ave,
Wollongong, NSW 2522, Australia
sakter@uow.edu.au

Abstract. The main objective of this study is to assess the impact of perceived connectivity (PC) on the intention to use (IU) social media in organizations, as well as the moderating effects of perceived risk (PR) and perceived security (PS) on this relationship. Data were collected from 2,556 social media users across Australia, Canada, India, the UK, and the US to test our proposed research model. Our results found that PC has a significant positive effect on the IU social media in organizations, and non-significant moderating effects of PR and PS. The study concludes with the implications for practice and research.

Keywords: Social media · Adoption and use · Intention · Perceived connectivity · Perceived risk · Perceived security · Moderation

1 Introduction

Social media tools are currently emerging as the new means for value creation and realization for many organizations across all industries. Indeed, social media tools (e.g., Facebook, Twitter) have the capability of transforming the way firms conduct their businesses, by allowing for example, an improved way of identifying products with high market potential [1], a superior mechanism for engaging (e.g., attract and retain) with online consumers [2], a robust platform for marketing communication [3], and a better collaboration channel with all firm stakeholders [4, 5]. It is probably for these reasons that some scholars argue that social media are at the core of the "social commerce", which is considered as the new wave of electronic commerce, and defined as "a form of Internet-based social media that allows people to participate in the marketing, selling, comparing, and buying of products and services in online marketplaces and communities" (p. 215) [6].

The high operational and strategic potential of social media as enabler of organizational change for competitive advantage has been acknowledged by the professional literature as well as the emerging research on the topic. However, technological innovation history tells us that the path toward the wide acceptance of any given innovation by businesses can be quite long. Therefore, it is critical to look at the key

© IFIP International Federation for Information Processing 2016
Published by Springer International Publishing Switzerland 2016. All Rights Reserved
Y.K. Dwivedi et al. (Eds.): I3E 2016, LNCS 9844, pp. 219–227, 2016.
DOI: 10.1007/978-3-319-45234-0_20

determinants that may drive the adoption and use of social media by organizations. More specifically, this study examines the following research questions:

1. What is the impact of perceived connectivity on the intention to use social media in organizations?
2. What is the moderating effect of perceived risk and security on this relationship?

To address these research questions, the study explores the embryonic literature on social media, the diffusion of innovation theory, risk and security issues to develop a conceptual research model. More precisely, we argue that social media's perceived connectivity will have a positive impact on the intention to use social media. Then, perceived risk and perceived security will have moderating effects on the said relationship. The proposed model was tested using data from 2,556 social media users for their daily activities across various industries in Australia, Canada, India, the UK, and the US. The rest of the paper is structured as follows: first, we present the conceptual model and hypotheses; next, we discuss the research methodology; the following section presents the results; then we present the discussion, implications, limitations and future research perspectives; finally, we present the conclusion of the study.

2 Theoretical Development

From the emerging literature on social media, the diffusion of innovation theory, risk and security issues, a conceptual model based is presented in Fig. 1. In the model, we argue that Perceived connectivity (PC) of social media in organizations will have a positive impact on the intention to use (IU) social media. However, this relationship will be moderated by both perceived risk (PR) and perceived security (PS).

Perceived connectivity which is defined as the ability of a social media platform to bring together people who share common interests or goals [7] is considered as an important determinant of IT adoption and use [8, 9]. The importance of this construct is

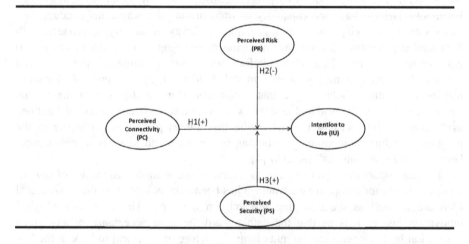

Fig. 1. Research model

even greater for interactive innovations since their adoption and effective use by a critical mass of users will impact positive network externalities on all users [10]. Evidence supporting this postulate exists in prior studies on the user acceptance of enterprise instant messaging [8], and the acceptance of electronic mail (e-mail) and instant messaging (IM) [9].

Perceived risk and perceived security play an important role in IT adoption and use. Perceived risk is defined as "the extent to which a functional or psychosocial risk a user feels he/she is taking when using a product", whereas perceived security is defined as "the subjective probability with which users believe their sensitive information (business or private) will not be viewed, stored, and manipulated during work sessions by unauthorized parties in a manner consistent with their confident expectations" (p. 165) [8].

Due to the emergence of Web 2.0 and social media in the last decade, there is an increasing trend in the creation and exchange of user generated contents. People express themselves in virtual communities for communication, networking or amusement through constant interaction in the form of information creation, redistribution and exchange [11]. Indeed, social network sites and many online platforms are used by individuals to share private information effortlessly and seamlessly in great detail and volume [11]. These massive amounts of data, referred to as big data, often used for personalized offers or targeting potential customers. However, Akter & Wamba [12] report that unexpected consequences can have on perceived risk and security when marketers target consumers in the big data environment. Because, it raises the question of safe handling of individual and organizational privacy and data security (e.g., names and addresses, social security numbers, credit card numbers, and financial information). Although consumers increasingly share personal information in e-commerce sites or in social networks, it is expected for firms not to breach consumers' privacy because consumers disclose information expecting it to be confidential under 'terms of use' [13]. Despite consumers' expectations for anonymous data to protect their security and risk, the ever growing big data environment and social commerce raise the question of perceived risk and security. Scholars have identified the current environment as informal and poorly structured [14, 15]. Moreover, prior studies on social media adoption and use by organizations have identified perceived risk [3] and perceived security as s factors that can slow down their adoption.

Thus, we propose the following hypotheses:

H1: *PC has a significant positive effect on the IU social media in organizations.*

H2: *PR negatively moderates the relationship between PC and IU social media in organizations.*

H3: *PS positively moderates the relationship between PC and IU social media in organizations.*

3   Methodology

This study is part of a larger study conducted by the Institute for Innovation in Business and Social Research (IIBSoR) of the University of Wollongong in Australia.

In this study, a web based-survey employed to collect data from 2,556 social media users within their workplaces in Australia, Canada, India, the UK, and the US in January 2013. The data collection process was handled by a leading international market research provider called *Survey Sampling International (SSI)*. All items used in the study were taken from prior studies and adapted to the context of social media adoption and use in organizations [8, 16]. They were measured using 7-point Likert scale with anchors ranging from Strongly Disagree (1) to Strongly Agree (7) (Appendix).

For the data analysis, a statistical Excel add-in tool called XLSTAT-PLS (version of 2013.6.04) was used using Partial Least Squares (PLS) based Path Modeling. In this study, the reliability and validity of the items were evaluated. For model assessment, all item loadings values that are higher than 0.70 are considered to be adequate. A composite reliability value that is higher than 0.70 is considered to be acceptable [17]. For average variance extracted (AVE), a value that is higher than 0.50 is considered as acceptable measure justifying the use of a construct [17].

For the moderating effects testing, we use the two stage approach proposed by [3] using XLSTAT as following [18]: (1) we ran the main effect model, (2) extract the latent variable scores, (3) use the extracted latent variable scores as indicators of the exogenous and endogenous variables, and (4) use the element wise product of the latent variable scores of the exogenous variable and the moderator variable as the indicator of the interaction term.

4 Results and Discussion

Table 1 presents the descriptive statistics of our manifest variables. PC is the latent variable with the items with the highest means. Indeed, all PC items have a mean greater than five (5) with items measure using a Likert scale ranging from 1 to 7. On the other hands, PS is the latent variable with the lowest items values (3.68 and 3.706).

Table 1. Descriptive statistics of measured manifest variables

Latent variable	Items	Minimum	Maximum	Mean	Std. deviation
PC	PC1	1	7	5.154	1.685
	PC2	1	7	5.047	1.755
	PC3	1	7	5.162	1.693
	PC4	1	7	5.565	1.557
IU	IU1	1	7	3.748	2.076
	IU2	1	7	4.597	2.011
	IU3	1	7	3.752	2.099
	IU4	1	7	4.598	1.989
PS	PS1	1	7	3.680	1.841
	PS2	1	7	3.706	1.790
PR	PR1	1	7	4.440	1.749
	PR2	1	7	4.228	1.808

Table 2. Factor loadings, Cronbach's Alpha, composite reliability and AVE

Latent variable	Items	Standardized loadings	Cronbach's alpha	D.G. rho (PCA)	AVE
PC	PC1	0.948	0.890	0.929	0.749
	PC2	0.919			
	PC3	0.942			
	PC4	0.606			
IU	IU1	0.842	0.902	0.932	0.776
	IU2	0.920			
	IU3	0.844			
	IU4	0.914			
PS	PS1	0.973	0.942	0.972	0.945
	PS2	0.971			
PR	PR1	0.994	0.809	0.913	0.780
	PR2	0.756			

Table 3. Correlations matrix (The bold values on the diagonal are the square root of the AVE)

	PC	PS	PR	IU
PC	**0.865**			
PS	0.271	**0.972**		
PR	-0.050	-0.189	**0.883**	
IU	0.506	0.626	-0.198	**0.881**

Table 2 displays all factor loadings, Cronbach's alpha values, composite reliability and average variance extracted (AVE) of the latent variables. From Table 2, we can see that all values meet the recommended acceptable threshold values—respectively, 0.6, 0.7, 0.7 and 0.5 [19] —and consequently justify the use of all our constructs in the model.

Table 3 represents the correlation matrix with the square root of the AVEs in the diagonals. From the table, we can see that all values exceed the inter-correlations of the construct with the other constructs in the model, and therefore confirming the discriminant validity [20–22]. In fact, the discriminant validity is confirmed when all the bold values on the diagonal representing the square root of the AVE are higher than the inter-correlations of all constructs in the model.

Table 4 presents a value of 0.644 for the absolute goodness of fit (GoF) and a value of 0.980 for the relative GoF, which are all above the threshold values. Indeed, an absolute GoF greater than 0.5 is considered satisfactory, and a relative GoF that is close to 0.90 is considered as a great fit of a model [23], and accordingly, we can conclude that the research model has an excellent fit.

Figure 2 presents the research results. From the figure, we see that the standardized path coefficient of the relationship between PC and IU social media in organizations is significant at a level of 0.001, and thus supporting our hypothesis (H1). However, all the standardized path coefficients related to the moderating effects of PR and PS are not

Table 4. Goodness of fit index

	Goodness of fit index
Absolute	0.644
Relative	0.980

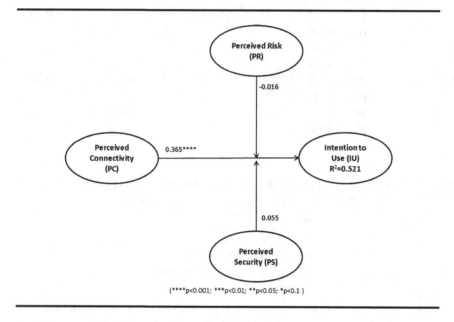

Fig. 2. Research results

significant, and therefore, we have to reject H2 and H3. In addition, the coefficient of determination, R^2 is 0.521 for the IU social media in organizations, thus suggesting a good fit of the data with our proposed model.

Consistent with prior studies [9, 18], this study found that PC of social media is a significant predictor of IU. This result confirms that users perceived positive network externalities of social media have a positive impact on their use of social media [9]. However, the study found no moderating effects of PR and PS on the relationship between PC and IU. A possible explanation of this result may be the fact that within organizations, several protection mechanisms related to the use of media have been implemented to create a safe usage environment.

5   Conclusion and Future Research Directions

The main objective of this paper was to assess the impact of perceived connectivity (PC) on the intention to use (IU) social media in organizations, as well as the moderating effects of perceived risk (PR) and security (PS) on this relationship. Our proposed model provides strong empirical evidence that perceived connectivity positively impact users' intention to use social media in organizations. However, the study found no moderating effects of both perceived risk and security.

Still, the big data driven social media environment raises enormous questions on risk and security as a result of mass scale surveillance, manipulation, and profiling. Undoubtedly, the current environment has challenged the autonomy of individuals by neglecting their consent and acknowledgment. Since social connectivity are increasingly used for security, marketing, health, business, and many other social aspects, the predictions and decisions that are made using social data should be scientific, error- free and objective.

The study presents some limitations: First, the data were collected using a cross-sectional design. Future studies should consider using a longitudinal study or case study to gain a deeper understanding related to social media adoption and use within organizations. Second, the study doesn't assess cultural differences within the sample. Future research could focus on analysing the impact of cultural factors on the adoption and use of social media within organizations. Third, this study doesn't consider a specific type of social media platform. In fact, prior studies suggest that adoption factors vary depending on the type of social media platform under study [24]. Therefore, future studies could focus on one specific type of social media platform.

Appendix: Adapted from [18]

	Strongly Disagree	Moderately Disagree	Slightly Disagree	Undecided	Slightly Agree	Moderately Agree	Strongly Agree
Perceived Connectivity							
Most of my colleagues use social media tools	1	2	3	4	5	6	7
Among the colleagues I communicate with regularly, many use social media tools	1	2	3	4	5	6	7
A large percentage of my colleagues use social media tools	1	2	3	4	5	6	7
From my observation, the number of social media tools users is large	1	2	3	4	5	6	7

(Continued)

(Continued)

	Strongly Disagree	Moderately Disagree	Slightly Disagree	Undecided	Slightly Agree	Moderately Agree	Strongly Agree
Intention to Use							
If I have to temporarily use a computer without social media tool(s), I intend to install it (them).	1	2	3	4	5	6	7
If I own a computer with social media tool(s), I intend to use it (them).	1	2	3	4	5	6	7
Given that I have a computer with social media tool(s), I predict that I will use it (them) at work.	1	2	3	4	5	6	7
I plan to use social media tools in the near future.	1	2	3	4	5	6	7
Perceived Risk							
I think using social media tools is risky.	1	2	3	4	5	6	7
Using social media tools will bring risk to my work	1	2	3	4	5	6	7
Perceived Security							
I think my information on social media tools is secure.	1	2	3	4	5	6	7
Using social media tools is secure	1	2	3	4	5	6	7

References

1. Liang, T.-P., Turban, E.: Introduction to the special issue social commerce: a research framework for social commerce. Int. J. Electron. Commer. **16**(2), 5–14 (2011)
2. IBM: Social Commerce Defined. IBM (2009)
3. Munnukka, J., Järvi, P.: Perceived risks and risk management of social media in an organizational context. Electron. Markets **24**(3), 219–229 (2014)
4. Culnan, M.J., McHugh, P.J., Zubillaga, J.I.: How large US companies can use Twitter and other social media to gain business value. MIS Q. Executive **9**(4), 243–259 (2010)

5. Burke, W.Q., Fields, D.A., Kafai, Y.B.: Entering the clubhouse: case studies of young programmers joining the online scratch communities. J. Organ. End User Comput. **22**, 21–35 (2010)
6. Stephen, A.T., Toubia, O.: Deriving value from social commerce networks. J. Market. Res. **47**(2), 215–228 (2010)
7. Benbasat, I.: A program of studies to improve the communication between customers and online stores. In: Galletta, D.F., Zhang, P. (eds.) Human-Computer Interaction and Management Information Systems: Application. Advances in Management Information Systems (2006)
8. Trinchera, L.: Unobserved heterogeneity in structural equation models: a new approach to latent class detection in PLS path modeling, p. 338. Universita degli Studi di Napoli Federico II, Napoli(2007)
9. Strader, T.J., Ramaswami, S.N., Houle, P.A.: Perceived network externalities and communication technology acceptance. Eur. J. Inf. Syst. **16**(1), 54–65 (2007)
10. Fosso Wamba, S., Chatfield, A.T.: A contingency model for creating value from RFID supply chain network projects in logistics and manufacturing environments. Eur. J. Inf. Syst. **18**(6), 615–636 (2009)
11. Gritzalis, D., et al.: History of information: the case of privacy and security in social media. In: Proceedings of the History of Information Conference (2014)
12. Akter, S., Wamba, S.F.: Big data analytics in e-commerce: a systematic review and agenda for future research. Electron. Markets **26**, 1–22 (2016)
13. Martin, K.E.: Ethical issues in the big data industry. MIS Q. Executive (2015, Forthcoming)
14. Pantelis, K., Aija, L.: Understanding the value of (big) data. In: 2013 IEEE International Conference on Big Data (2013)
15. George, G., Haas, M.R., Pentland, A.: Big data and management. Acad. Manag. J. **57**(2), 321–326 (2014)
16. Davis, F.D.: Perceived usefulness, perceived ease of use, and user acceptance of information technology. MIS Q. **13**(3), 319–340 (1989)
17. Leung, J., Cheung, W., Chu, S.-C.: Aligning RFID applications with supply chain strategies. Inf. Manag. **51**, 260–269 (2014)
18. Luo, X., Gurung, A., Shim, J.P.: Understanding the determinants of user acceptance of enterprise instant messaging: an empirical study. J. Organ. Comput. Electron. Commer. **20**(2), 155–181 (2010)
19. Guadagnoli, E., Velicer, W.: Relation of sample size to the stability of component patterns. Psychol. Bull. **103**, 265–275 (1988)
20. Chin, W.W.: The partial least squares approach for structural equation modeling (1998)
21. Chin, W.W.: How to write up and report PLS analyses. In: Handbook of Partial Least Squares, pp. 655–690 (2010)
22. Fornell, C., Larcker, D.F.: Evaluating structural equation models with unobservable variables and measurement error. J. Market. Res. **18**, 39–50 (1981)
23. Rahimnia, F., Hassanzadeh, J.F.: The impact of website content dimension and e-trust on e-marketing effectiveness: the case of Iranian commercial Saffron corporations. Inf. Manag. **50**(5), 240–247 (2013)
24. Fosso Wamba, S., Carter, L.: Twitter adoption and use by SMEs: an empirical study. In: The 46 Hawaii International Conferences on System Sciences (HICSS), Maui, Hawaii, US (2013)

An Empirical Examination of Factors Affecting Continuance Intention Towards Social Networking Sites

Salma S. Abed[(⊠)]

Department of Management Information Systems, College of Business (COB),
King Abdulaziz University, Rabigh, Saudi Arabia
sabid@kau.edu.sa

Abstract. This study examines the factors that affect consumer continuance intention to use social networking sites as a business tool. Using the Technology Acceptance Model (TAM) as the theoretical framework, the researcher tested the research model and related hypotheses using structural equation modelling. The results from a survey of 304 Facebook users in Saudi Arabia indicate that trust, perceived usefulness, and perceived enjoyment had significant positive effects on behavioural intention to continue to use social networking sites. Furthermore, perceived ease of use was found to have a significant positive effect on perceived usefulness, perceived enjoyment, and trust. Discussion of the findings and research contribution as well as limitations and future research directions are presented.

Keywords: Social networking sites · E-commerce · S-commerce · TAM · Consumers · Saudi Arabia

1 Introduction

Virtual communities and Social Networking Sites (SNS) allow people to connect with each other in general or on a particular subject online [26, 32]. Recently, the number of members of online social networks has increased explosively. For example, the social networking site "Facebook" registered 1.06 billion monthly active users, 618 million daily active users, and 680 million mobile active users in December 2012 [40]. Indeed, the popularity of SNS is highly demonstrable through the huge number of people using them, as it has quickly become a new phenomenon that has transformed online communication [29]. Consequently, Saudi Arabia has witnessed the biggest growth of diffusion of social media in the Arab world, which is the strongest empowering factor to e-commerce adoption within the Kingdom of Saudi Arabia (KSA) [35]. According to [8], around 87 % of social media users covered by the survey in the Arab world are subscribed to Facebook. In Saudi Arabia, the subscription rate is 80 % of total users of Facebook, 81 % of current Facebook subscribers in KSA access the channel on a daily basis, and 76 % of social media users in KSA visit Facebook through their smartphones and/or tablets. As a result, firms are starting to make wider use of SNS to build closer links with suppliers and customers [1, 24]. Therefore, many firms have been

Y.K. Dwivedi et al. (Eds.): I3E 2016, LNCS 9844, pp. 228–239, 2016.
DOI: 10.1007/978-3-319-45234-0_21

creating new ways to make profitable use of SNS applications [2]. Accordingly, the development of SNS has improved a new e-commerce model called social commerce (s-commerce). The term 's-commerce' is defined as a concept of Internet-based social media, which enables people to participate actively in the selling and marketing of different products and services in online marketplaces [28]. This dynamic process helps consumers obtain better information about different products and services provided by companies [22]. However, very limited empirical research has been conducted in this context [22, 28, 33, 34, 36–38], specifically in the Arab world and particularly in Saudi Arabia. Accordingly, this study aims to investigate factors affecting consumer continuance intention to use SNS as a business tool. The following sections of the paper include the relevant literature review and hypothesis development in the second section. These are followed by the methodology, data collection, as well as results and discussion outlined in the third, fourth, and fifth sections respectively. Finally, the research contribution, conclusion and limitations are delivered in sections six, seven, and eight.

2 Literature Review and Hypothesis Development

As Davis' technology acceptance model integrates findings from the information systems literature, the model's use became widespread in the diffusion of innovation literature. The previous studies have explained the importance of the Technology Acceptance Model (TAM). Many research studies have provided better empirical support for TAM in information technology research regardless of the country concerned i.e. [16, 22, 23, 39, 43]. Accordingly, TAM has been utilized in the Saudi Arabian context in various studies. [4] used TAM to examine biometric technology to determine user identity in e-commerce. [7] examined factors that influence the online banking adoption behaviour of 400 customers based on the TAM. [5] presented a conceptual framework that was extended from the advanced TAM to examine social media effects. [9] utilized TAM to examine consumers' online shopping intention and risk perceptions in both Saudi Arabia and the United States. [6] extended the TAM to examine the influence of user acceptance of m-government services. [3] investigated factors influencing customers' behavioural intention to adopt mobile services during their travel process using TAM and DOI. Finally, [8] investigated the adoption of self-service technologies by consumers in Saudi Arabia using the TAM model. In the s-commerce context, a number of studies have examined TAM in different geographical contexts; this includes the UK [21, 22], USA [38], and South Korea [34]. Accordingly, it is worthy to investigate s-commerce adoption utilizing TAM in the Saudi Arabian context.

In fact, TAM was developed for the explanation of the factors affecting computer acceptance in general rather than for a specific topic. As a result, a further modification of TAM is essential to explain consumer Behavioural Intentions (BI) to continue to use SNS. In this section, the researcher highlights the original constructs of TAM, specifically perceived usefulness (PU) and perceived ease of use (PEOU), followed by perceived enjoyment (PE) and trust (TR), which has been examined in s-commerce in other geographical contexts and found to be significant, PE [37, 38], TR [21, 22, 27, 33] and are worth further investigation in the Saudi Arabian context. The proposed hypothesis of this study are presented:

Perceived Usefulness (PU): Perceived usefulness is defined as the degree to which a user is aware of specific information technology innovation and how it will improve his/her work performance [13]. In fact, there is widespread research in the Information Systems (IS) context that provides evidence of the significant effect of PU on BI [43]. For the present research, the proposed relationship between PU and BI is based on studies that have found perceived usefulness to have a positive effect on behavioural intention to use s-commerce [22, 33, 37, 38]. Accordingly, the following hypothesis has been formulated:

H1: Perceived usefulness will have a significant positive effect on behavioural intention to continue to use social networking sites.

Perceived Ease of Use (PEOU): Perceived Ease Of Use refers to the degree to which the users' expectations about using information technology innovations would be free of effort [13]. Over the past decade, much research has provided evidence of the significant effect of PEOU on BI, either directly or indirectly through its effect on PU [13, 43]. Furthermore, other studies have found the PEOU to have a significant effect on Perceived Enjoyment (PE) as well as Trust (TR). In the context of SNS acceptance and adoption, [34] found that PEOU has a significant effect on BI. In contrast, [21] found the effect of PEOU on IB to be non-significant. Furthermore, few studies have found that PEOU has a significant positive effect on PU [21, 34, 39]. Additionally, other studies in the literature found that PEOU has a significant positive effect on PE [11, 12]. Finally, a number of studies have integrated trust to the TAM [19, 31, 34] and found the PEOU has a significant positive affect on Trust [30]. By extending the results of this study, the author proposes the following hypotheses for SNS intention of continuous usage:

H2: PEOU will have a significant positive effect on behavioural intention to continue to use social networking sites.

H3: PEOU will have a significant positive effect on perceived usefulness of social networking sites.

H4: PEOU will have a significant positive effect on perceived enjoyment of social networking sites.

H5: PEOU will have a significant positive effect on the Trust of social networking sites.

Perceived Enjoyment (PE): In this study, the researcher defines PE as the degree to which a person believes that using social networking sites for business purposes will be associated with enjoyment. If the user can enjoy the adoption of new technology, his attitude toward the adoption will be more positive than if that same technology was not enjoyable. Several studies on PE have indicated that PE significantly affects intention to use a technology [14, 39, 41, 42]. Previous studies of s-commerce have empirically added PE to the TAM [38]. Furthermore, limited studies in the context of s-commerce have found that PE has a significant positive effect on BI [36, 38]. In contrast, [37] found the relationship to be non-significant. Therefore, we hypothesize that:

H6: Perceived enjoyment will have a significant positive effect on behavioural intention to continue to use social networking sites.

Trust (TR): [19] defined trust as "an individual willingness to depend based on the beliefs in ability, benevolence, and integrity". According to [18, 19], trust is a key feature to enable e-commerce and is linked to uncertainty in most economic and social transactions. Furthermore, trust has a direct effect on online buying intention and on reducing uncertainty in e-commerce sites. Various studies on e-commerce adoption found trust to be a key aspect of e-commerce adoption [18, 27, 28, 30, 31]. This feature needs additional consideration in cyberspace, as customers and e-vendors are not face-to-face. However, the development of s-commerce and SNS can help improve customers' trust. Customers on SNS can support each other virtually with their ratings, reviews, and recommendations. In the context of s-commerce, some studies have found that trust has a significant positive effect on behavioural behavioural intention [21, 22, 27, 33]. Accordingly, the following hypothesis has been formulated:

H7: Trust will have a significant positive effect on behavioural intention to continue to use social networking sites.

3 Methodology

This study utilized scale items derived from the literature of technology adoption in order to measure the selected variables; i.e. Perceived Enjoyment and Trust, in addition to other variables adopted from the TAM. To do that, several items were used in order to measure the variables of the TAM which were adapted from [13]. Additionally, perceived enjoyment items have been adopted from [10]. Furthermore, Trust items were selected from [19, 25, 27, 34]. The degree of responses was estimated using the seven-point scale, ranging from 'strongly agree' to 'strongly disagree'. In regard to the language of the data collection tool, the questionnaire was translated into Arabic to overcome cultural and linguistic differences [9]. A pilot study was then conducted using 15 questionnaires that were distributed to Facebook users in Saudi Arabia who were asked to give their feedback in case they faced any difficulties in answering the questionnaire [20]. Accordingly, the questionnaire's items were rechecked in terms of clarity, language simplicity, and length.

When it came to the sampling, this study implemented a convenience sampling, as the researcher does not have a list of Facebook users. Moreover, convenience sampling is cost-effective [15, 17], and the results of a convenience sample can be generalised more appropriately since it allows for the presence of a variety of profiles and characters of potential users [17]. The survey questionnaires were distributed as online web links using the online survey software Qualtrics. The web link was sent to different Saudi Arabian e-commerce groups on Facebook as this was the most popular SNS to examine users' intentions rather than non-users. Due to space constraints, scale items cannot be provided in the paper but will be available upon request.

4   Data Collection

The demographic details show that 59.2 % of the respondents were female, while 40.8 % were male respondents. In regard to the respondents' age, the descriptive statistics demonstrate that the largest age population was within 21–29 years old with 62.5 %, followed by the age group of >=18–20 with 18.8 %. The rest of the respondents were divided among the age groups of 30–39 (11.8 %) and 40–49 (6.9 %), with no respondents aged 50 and above. In regards to educational level, the majority of the respondents hold a Bachelor's degree, representing 49.0 % of the total sample. The second largest group were high school graduates (34.5 %) followed by 10.2 % postgraduates and 5.9 % diploma holders. A very small percentage of respondents held less than high school qualification (0.3 %). Table 1 shows the demographic details of the respondents in the survey sample.

Table 1. Respondents' profile and characteristics

Variable	Group	Frequency	Percent
Gender	Male	124	40.8
	Female	180	59.2
	Total	**304**	**100.0**
Age	>=18–20	57	18.8
	21–29	190	62.5
	30–39	36	11.8
	40–49	21	6.9
	50 and above	0	0.0
	Total	**304**	**100.0**
Education	Less than High School	1	0.3
	High School	105	34.5
	Diploma	18	5.9
	Bachelor's degree	149	49.0
	Postgraduate	31	10.2
	Total	**304**	**100.0**

5   Results and Discussion

5.1   Validation of the Measurement Model

A confirmatory factor analysis was conducted to assess the validity of the measurement model using AMOS 22.0. To examine the overall model fit for the CFA and SEM, GOF indices were reported for this study; each of them describes the model fit from a different perspective. In the first run, most of the GOF indices fit the data well. The normed chi-square was (2.115), the GFI (.910), the AGFI (.877), NFI (.907), and RMSEA (.061):

Table 2. Summary of fit indices for the measurement model

	X^2	Df	X^2/df	GFI	AGFI	CFI	NFI	RMSEA
Criteria			3:1	≥ 0.9	≥ 0.8	≥ 0.95	≥ 0.9	< 0.07
1st run	264.341	125	2.115	.910	.877	.948	.907	.061
2ed run	204.553	120	1.705	.929	.899	.968	.928	.048

χ^2: chi-square, df: degrees of freedom, χ^2/df: normed chi-square, GFI: goodness-of-fit, AGFI: adjust goodness-of-fit, CFI: comparative fit index, NFI: normed fit index, RMSEA: root mean square error of approximation.

all in the acceptable benchmarks; yet, the CFI was slightly lower than the acceptable range (.948). To improve the model fit, the modification indices were checked in AMOS 22.0. Accordingly, PEOU2 and PEOU4 were correlated, and PEOU3 and PEOU4 were correlated as well. Additionally, TR1 and TR2, TR2 and TR3, and TR3 and TR4 were correlated. This indicated a good fit in the second run (X^2/df: 1.705; GFI: .929; AGFI: .899; CFI: .968; NFI: .928; RMSEA: .048). Table 2 shows the results.

5.2   Item Reliability, Internal Consistency, and Discriminant Validity

After the validation of the measurement model, to evaluate the reliability and validity of the research model, item reliability, internal consistency, and discriminant validity were examined [20]. Item reliability was measured using factor loadings. Item reliability is considered practically significant if each factor loading exceeds 0.5 [20]. The results of the item reliability show that all the examined items exceeded the threshold ranging from .640 (PEOU3) to .904 (PE2). This suggests that the survey tool was appropriate for evaluating each construct individually. The researcher used Cronbach's alpha for evaluating internal consistency. [20] suggested that Cronbach's alpha should exceed 0.7 for sufficient construct reliability. The results of the analysis show that Cronbach's alpha exceeds this threshold, ranging from .779 to .889. Table 3 shows the results for item reliability and internal consistency.

Lastly, discriminant validity was measured using the average variance extracted (AVE). For sufficient discriminant validity, the square root of each of the AVE's constructs should exceed its correlation with any other construct [20]. Table 4 reveals sufficient discriminant validity by indicating that the correlation of each construct does not exceed the square root of its AVE.

5.3   Structural Model Assessment

Structural Equation Modeling (SEM) was utilized for testing hypotheses using AMOS 22.0. This approach produces two vital pieces of information that are used to indicate how well the structural model can predict the hypothesized relationships. Namely, the standardized path coefficients estimate (β) assesses the strength of the causal relationship between two constructs, and the squared multiple correlations (R^2) measure the percentage of the predictive power of the dependant construct [20]. As shown in Table 5,

Table 3. Reliability test for investigated constructs (Cronbach's alpha)

Construct	Item	Mean	Std. Deviation	Factor Loading	Cronbach's alpha
Perceived Usefulness	PU1	5.56	1.368	.730	.779
	PU2	5.61	1.277	.766	
	PU3	5.34	1.419	.702	
Perceived Ease of Use	PEOU1	5.40	1.463	.683	.789
	PEOU2	5.26	1.370	.729	
	PEOU3	5.50	1.442	.640	
	PEOU4	5.36	1.509	.712	
Perceived Enjoyment	PE1	5.60	1.468	.810	.867
	PE2	5.65	1.395	.904	
	PE3	5.54	1.444	.785	
Trust	TR1	4.50	1.774	.643	.843
	TR2	4.59	1.581	.664	
	TR3	4.46	1.709	.800	
	TR4	4.43	1.628	.756	
	TR5	5.05	1.501	.671	
Behavioural Intention	BI1	5.29	1.432	.833	.889
	BI2	5.13	1.496	.836	
	BI3	5.15	1.530	.895	
Valid N (listwise) 304					

Table 4. Results for discriminant validity

	PU	PEOU	PE	TR	BI
PU	**0.812**				
PEOU	.431**	**0.798**			
PE	.446**	.527**	**0.910**		
TR	.381**	.286**	.332**	**0.830**	
BI	.510**	.469**	.550**	.513**	**0.925**

Square root of AVE is shown on the diagonal in **bold**.
** Correlation is significant at the 0.01 level (2-tailed).

Table 5. Summary of fit indices for the structural model

	X^2	Df	X^2/df	GFI	AGFI	CFI	NFI	RMSEA
Criteria			3:1	≥ 0.9	≥ 0.8	≥ 0.95	≥ 0.9	< 0.07
Model GOF	224.978	125	1.800	.923	.895	.963	.921	.051

χ^2: chi-square, df: degrees of freedom, χ^2/df: normed chi-square, GFI: goodness-of-fit, AGFI: adjust goodness-of-fit, CFI: comparative fit index, NFI: normed fit index, RMSEA: root mean square error of approximation.

The results of the structural model indicate a good fit for all indices (X^2: 224.978; df: 125; X^2/df: 1.800; GFI: .923; AGFI: .895; CFI: .963; NFI: .921; RMSEA: .051).

As the structural model indicated a good fit, the proposed hypotheses were examined using standardized path coefficients (β). As presented in Table 6, all the proposed hypotheses are supported except H2. First, PU had a significant positive effect on Behavioural Intention ($\beta = .28$, $p < 0.001$), providing support for H1 and confirming the effect of the PU of SNS on consumers' continuous intention to use the technology. Second, PE had a significant positive effect on behavioural intention. The path coefficient between PE and BI was .27 ($p < 0.001$), providing support for H3 and suggesting that consumers who enjoy using SNS for business purposes intend to continue to use the technology in the future. Third, Trust had significant positive effects on behavioural intention to continue to use SNS. The path coefficient between TR and BI was .34 ($p < 0.001$), providing support for H4 and suggesting that consumers who trust SNS for business purposes intend to continue to use the technology in the future. Furthermore, PEOU had significant positive effects on PU, PE, and TR. The standardized path coefficients between perceived ease of use and these three constructs were 0.62 ($p < 0.001$), 0.67 ($p < 0.001$), and 0.43 ($p < 0.001$), respectively. As a result, H5, H6, and H7 are supported. The hypothesis suggests that consumers who finds SNS easy to use for business purposes are more likely to perceive it as useful, enjoyable, and trustworthy. Finally, PEOU had no significant effect on BI ($\beta = .11$, $p = .237$), providing no support for H2. This finding suggests that consumers are already familiar with using SNS as a business tool. Accordingly, ease of use dose not predict behavioural intention to continue to use the technology.

PU, PE, and TR explained approximately 56 % of the variance in behavioural intention to continue to use SNS for business purposes. Furthermore, PEOU explained 45 % of the variance in PE, and 39 % of the variance in PU. Finally, PEOU explained 18 % of the variance in TR. Table 6 summarizes the results of the tested hypotheses.

Table 6. Summary of hypotheses test

H#	Hypothesis		β	S.E.	C.R.	P	Supported
	Dependent Variable	Independent Variable					
H1	PU	BI	.28	.090	3.643	***	YES
H2	PEOU	BI	.11	.110	1.182	.237	NO
H3	PEOU	PU	.62	.083	7.630	***	YES
H4	PEOU	PE	.67	.096	8.402	***	YES
H5	PEOU	TR	.43	.096	5.647	***	YES
H6	PE	BI	.27	.074	3.591	***	YES
H7	TR	BI	.34	.056	5.607	***	YES

6 Research Contribution

The results of this study provide both academic and practical implications. In fact, the current study makes a significant contribution for academics by proposing the TAM model for examining the adoption of s-commerce technologies, which is a novel modern technology. Furthermore, the study also expanded the applicability of TAM by focusing on a new cultural context (Saudi Arabia). Finally, this study is able to extend the theoretical horizon of the TAM by including other external factors from the technology adoption literature, including Perceived Enjoyment and Trust. In practice, the proposed model provides business owners, managers, and marketers in developing countries understanding of continuous intention to use s-commerce technologies. It provides a suitable approach to define which factors require further attention in order to obtain the highest benefits from the adoption of s-commerce technologies by ensuring that consumers continue to accept the modern way of interacting via social media platforms to conduct business. Based on the proposed model, business owners, managers, and marketers needs to pay closer attention to some issues, particularly the finding that the most significant predicted constructs of behavioural intention to continue to use SNS is Trust. This means that business owners, managers, and marketers need to pay closer attention to build online trust with consumers, by connecting with them and providing online privacy and security policy, as well as encouraging user ratings, reviews, and recommendations on SNS to develop user generated content, which will lead to consumer trust. Furthermore, perceived ease of use was found to be a strong predictor of perceived enjoyment as well as perceived usefulness. This means that business owners, managers, and marketers needs to ensure that the SNS they are using to connect with their consumers are easy to use, and as a result, consumers will enjoy using the SNS to conduct business, and find them useful in their daily lives.

7 Conclusion

This study aims to identify the important factors that influence customer behavioural intention to continue to use social networking sites. The TAM has been identified as a suitable theoretical foundation for proposing a conceptual model. The study has added two further significant factors, perceived enjoyment and trust, along with TAM constructs to formulate the model. In order to accomplish the study's objectives, a quantitative field survey was circulated to obtain data from a convenience sample of Saudi customers and a self-administered questionnaire used for data collection, before the respondents' profile and characteristics were presented. Next, the study results and discussion was offered, including validation of the measurement model, item reliability, internal consistency, and discriminant validity for the investigated variables. Finally, structural model assessment and hypothesis testing was conducted. The findings indicated that trust, perceived usefulness, and perceived enjoyment play a significant role in behavioural intention to continue to use social networking sites.

8 Limitations and Future Research Directions

This study is limited in that the researcher views the behavioural intention of consumers of SNS rather than the consumers actual use. Future research should be conducted on consumers' actual usage behaviour within the context of social networking sites. Additionally, this study could be further strengthened to better understand the relationships between variables. Future research could explore new additional constructs to better predict the intention and actual use of SNS. Furthermore, the population of the study limits this research. As the respondents resided in Saudi Arabia, the results might not be generalizable to other populations. Accordingly, future research needs to investigate other cultures. Finally, this study did not measure how frequently the respondent consumers made use of SNS. Therefore, future research should aim to determine how often consumers participate in SNS and to what extent it motivates their purchasing decisions.

References

1. Abed, S.S., Dwivedi, Y.K., Williams, M.D.: Consumers' perceptions of social commerce adoption in Saudi Arabia. In: Janssen, M., Mäntymäki, M., Hidders, J., Klievink, B., Lamersdorf, W., van Loenen, B., Zuiderwijk, A. (eds.) I3E 2015. LNCS, vol. 9373, pp. 133–143. Springer, Heidelberg (2015). doi:10.1007/978-3-319-25013-7_11
2. Abed, S.S., Dwivedi, Y.K., Williams, M.D.: Social commerce as a business tool in Saudi Arabia's SMEs. Int. J. Indian Cult. Bus. Manag. **13**(1), 1–19 (2016)
3. Al-Gethmi, M.A.: Mobile commerce innovation in the airline sector: an investigation of mobile services acceptance in Saudi Arabia. Doctoral dissertation, Ph.D. Thesis, Brunel University School of Engineering and Design (2014)
4. Al-Harby, F.M., Qahwaji, R., Kamala, M.: The feasibility of biometrics authentication in e-commerce: user acceptance. Paper Presented at the IADIS International Conference WWW/Internet, Freiburg, Germany (2008)
5. Al-Mowalad, A., Putit, L.: The extension of TAM: the effects of social media and perceived risk in online purchase. In: 2012 International Conference on Innovation Management and Technology Research (ICIMTR), pp. 188–192. IEEE, May 2012
6. Al-Rowili, T.F., Alotaibi, M.B., Al-Harbi, M.S.: Predicting citizens' acceptance of M-government services in Saudi Arabia: an empirical investigation. In: 2015 9th Annual IEEE International Systems Conference (SysCon), pp. 627–633. IEEE (2015)
7. Al-Somali, S.A., Gholami, R., Clegg, B.: An investigation into the acceptance of online banking in Saudi Arabia. Technovation **29**(2), 130–141 (2009)
8. Arab Social Media Report: Arab Social Media Influences Summit. TNS (2015). www.wpp.com/govtpractice/~/media/.../arabsocialmediareport-2015.pdf. Accessed 30 May 2016
9. Brislin, R.: Comparative research methodology: cross-cultural studies. Int. J. Psychol. **11**(3), 215–229 (1976)
10. Brown, S.A., Venkatesh, V.: Model of adoption of technology in households: a baseline model test and extension incorporating household life cycle. MIS Q. **29**, 399–426 (2005)
11. Bruner, G.C., Kumar, A.: Explaining consumer acceptance of handheld internet devices. J. Bus. Res. **58**(5), 553–558 (2005)

12. Cyr, D., Head, M., Ivanov, A.: Design aesthetics leading to M-loyalty in mobile commerce. Inf. Manag. **43**(8), 950–963 (2006)
13. Davis, F.D.: Perceived usefulness, perceived ease of use, and user acceptance of information technology. MIS Q. **13**, 319–340 (1989)
14. Dickinger, A., Arami, M., Meyer, D.: The role of perceived enjoyment and social norm in the adoption of technology with network externalities. Eur. J. Inf. Syst. **17**(1), 4–11 (2008)
15. Dwivedi, Y.K., Choudrie, J., Brinkman, W.P.: Development of a survey instrument to examine consumer adoption of broadband. Ind. Manag. Data Syst. **106**(5), 700–718 (2006)
16. Dwivedi, Y.K., Ramdani, B., Williams, M.D., Mitra, A., Williams, J., Niranjan, S.: Factors influencing user adoption of web 2.0 applications. Int. J. Indian Cult Bus. Manag. **7**(1), 53–71 (2013)
17. Franzosi, R.: From Words to Numbers: Narrative, Data and Social Science, vol. 22. Cambridge University Press, Cambridge (2004)
18. Gefen, D., Straub, D.W.: Consumer trust in B2C e-commerce and the importance of social presence: experiments in e-products and e-services. Omega **32**(6), 407–424 (2004)
19. Gefen, D., Karahanna, E., Straub, D.W.: Trust and TAM in online shopping: an integrated model. MIS Q. **27**(1), 51–90 (2003)
20. Hair, J.F., Black, W.C., Babin, B.J., Anderson, R.E.: Multivariate Data Analysis, 7th edn. Pearson, Upper Saddle River (2010)
21. Hajli, M.: An integrated model for e-commerce adoption at the customer level with the impact of social commerce. Int. J. Inf. Sci. Manag. (IJISM) **16**, 77–97 (2012). (Special Issue)
22. Hajli, M.N.: Social commerce for innovation. Int. J. Innov. Manag. **18**(4), 1–24 (2014)
23. Irani, Z., Dwivedi, Y.K., Williams, M.D.: Understanding consumer adoption of broadband: an extension of the technology acceptance model. J. Oper. Res. Soc. **60**(10), 1322–1334 (2009)
24. Jamal, A., Coughlan, J., Kamal, M.: Mining social network data for personalisation and privacy concerns: a case study of Facebook's Beacon. Int. J. Bus. Inf. Syst. **13**(2), 173–198 (2013)
25. Jarvenpaa, S.L., Tractinsky, N., Saarinen, L.: Consumer trust in an internet store: a cross-cultural validation. J. Comput. Mediated Commun. **5**(2) (1999)
26. Kang, J.Y.M., Johnson, K.K.: How does social commerce work for apparel shopping? Apparel social e-shopping with social network storefronts. J. Custom. Behav. **12**(1), 53–72 (2013)
27. Kim, S., Park, H.: Effects of various characteristics of social commerce on consumers' trust and trust performance. Int. J. Inf. Manag. **33**(2), 318–332 (2013)
28. Kim, D.J., Ferrin, D.L., Rao, H.R.: A trust-based consumer decision-making model in electronic commerce: the role of trust, perceived risk, and their antecedents. Decis. Support Syst. **44**(2), 544–564 (2008)
29. Kuitunen, K.: Social media in international brand communication of SMEs: a multiple case study of small Finnish design-intensive companies. Master's thesis, Turku School of Economics, University of Turku, Turku (2012)
30. Li, R., Kim, J., Park, J.: The effects of internet shoppers' trust on their purchasing intention in China. JISTEM – J. Inf. Syst. Technol. Manag. **4**(3), 269–286 (2007)
31. McCloskey, D.W.: The importance of ease of use, usefulness, and trust to online consumers: an examination of the technology acceptance model with older consumers. J. Organ. End User Comput. **18**(3), 47 (2006)
32. Murray, K.E., Waller, R.: Social networking goes abroad. Int. Educ. **16**(3), 56 (2007)
33. Ng, C.S.P.: Intention to purchase on social commerce websites across cultures: a cross-regional study. Inf. Manag. **50**(8), 609–620 (2013)

34. Noh, M., Lee, K., Kim, K., Garrison, G.: Effects of collectivism on actual S-commerce use and the moderating effect of price consciousness. J. Electron. Commer. Res. **14**(3), 244–260 (2013)
35. de Kerros Boudkov Orloff, A.: E-commerce in Saudi Arabia: driving the evolution adaptation and growth of E-commerce in the retail industry. Sacha Orloff Consulting Group (SOCG), 17 June 2012. http://www.scribd.com/doc/136654512/E-Commerce-in-SaudiArabia-Driving-the-Evolution-Adaptation-and-Growth-of-Ecommerce-in-the-Retail-Industry. Accessed 30 May 2016
36. Sharma, S., Crossler, R.E.: Disclosing too much? situational factors affecting information disclosure in social commerce environment. Electron. Commer. Res. Appl. **13**(5), 305–319 (2014)
37. Sharma, S., Crossler, R.E.: Intention to engage in social commerce: uses and gratifications approach. In: Proceedings of the 20th Americas Conference on Information Systems (AMCIS), pp. 1–12 (2014b)
38. Shen, J.: Social comparison, social presence, and enjoyment in the acceptance of social shopping websites. J. Electron. Commer. Res. **13**(3), 198–212 (2012)
39. Sun, H., Zhang, P.: Causal relationships between perceived enjoyment and perceived ease of use: an alternative approach. J. Assoc. Inf. Syst. **7**(9), 618–645 (2006)
40. Tam, D.: Facebook by the Numbers: 1.06 billion monthly active users. CNET News, 8301–1023 (2013)
41. Teh, P.L., Ahmed, P.K.: MOA and TRA in social commerce: an integrated model. In: 2011 IEEE International Conference on Industrial Engineering and Engineering Management (IEEM), pp. 1375–1379. IEEE (2011)
42. Teo, T., Noyes, J.: An assessment of the influence of perceived enjoyment and attitude on the intention to use technology among pre-service teachers: a structural equation modeling approach. Comput. Educ. **57**(2), 1645–1653 (2011)
43. Venkatesh, V., Morris, M.G.: Why don't men ever stop to ask for directions? Gender, social influence, and their role in technology acceptance and usage behavior. MIS Q. **24**, 115–139 (2000)

A Conceptual Review of Social Media Adoption in SMEs

Hanaa Namankani[1,2(✉)], Claire Moxham[1], and Matthew Tickle[1]

[1] University of Liverpool Management School, Chatham Building, Chatham Street,
Liverpool, L69 7ZH, UK
{hanaa,c.moxham,m.tickle}@liverpool.ac.uk
[2] Faculty of Computing and Information Technology, KING Abdul-Aziz University, Jeddah,
Kingdom of Saudi Arabia

Abstract. Small to Medium Enterprises (SMEs) are not well equipped to use Social Media (SM) and struggle to utilise its full potential in the context of adding value to the business. It is suggested that SMEs often need strategic guidance and support, particularly with regard to optimising SM. The question remains as to how effectively SM is embedded in the business operations of SMEs. This study examines how SM adoption can be realised by SMEs. It considers how SMEs can adapt their business strategies under changing circumstances by adopting SM in their daily practice. By integrating the current models of technology adoption (including the Technology-Organization-Environment (TOE) and Innovation-Decision-Process from Diffusion of Innovation (DOI) frameworks) a conceptual framework for achieving SM adoption is developed and presented. The results of this study provide a helpful synthesis of the extant literature and act as a useful springboard for further work in this important area.

Keywords: Social media · Small to medium sized enterprises · Technology adoption

1 Introduction

This study investigates how Social Media (SM) adoption can enable effective and improved business performance in Small to Medium sized Enterprises (SMEs). The study considers two practical dimensions identified as Technology-Organization-Environment (TOE) and Innovation-Decision-Process from Diffusion of Innovation (DOI) theories with the aim of exploring the role each theory plays in developing and supporting an environment whereby SMEs can create a sustainable business. A framework for achieving SM adoption is presented which highlights the interaction processes as well as the various stages of developing a SM adoption plan. Important criteria, models and factors were considered to evaluate the extant literature, and how SMEs may practically progress from one level to the next in order to keep growing their business. The main objective of this study is to reveal the extent to which SM adoption is applied in SMEs and how it may contribute to the success within SMEs. It is envisaged that the successful implementation of the SM adoption framework will allow SMEs to increase both their flexibility and internal capabilities.

© IFIP International Federation for Information Processing 2016
Published by Springer International Publishing Switzerland 2016. All Rights Reserved
Y.K. Dwivedi et al. (Eds.): I3E 2016, LNCS 9844, pp. 240–250, 2016.
DOI: 10.1007/978-3-319-45234-0_22

2   Small to Medium Enterprises (SMEs)

Although large firms are leading the market in most industries and dominating some industries' market shares, many studies have concluded that the global economy is enhanced by SMEs that are focused, small, innovative and flexible and are run by highly skilled resources, especially IT [1–3]. Additionally, SMEs provide a great opportunity of employment, wide production base and support for large organizations [4]. [3] define a SME as an independent business organization that is run by its owners or part owners and has a small market share, and where the number of employees is not larger than a specific predefined number that slightly differs across nations (mainly between 50 to 500 for medium sized enterprises, and less than 10 or 50 for small enterprises).

The European Commission (EC) Recommendation 96/280/EC [5] presents a slightly different view of SMEs, placing them in the micro, small, and medium-sized enterprises (SMEs) category. This is a set of enterprises that employ less than 250 employees and have an annual turnover estimated at 50 million euro, and/or an annual balance sheet total not exceeding 43 million euro, and are not more than 25 % owned by a non-SME. In addition, the European Commission [5] categorizes SMEs in terms of the number of employees: 0-9 employees is a micro enterprise; 10-99 employees is a small enterprise; and 100-250 employees is a medium enterprise. Nevertheless, no clear evidence or affirmative consensus on the SME definition itself is claimed, as variations occur between countries, industries and even agencies within one country.

Even though the size and market share of SMEs is relatively small, many researchers assert the important contribution they play in the national economy [6]. For instance, in most developed countries in Europe, around 85 % to 99 % of enterprises are considered SMEs if the definition focuses on the number of employee and market share [7]. As a result, the development and sustainability of SMEs has gained significant attention [8], and conducting research to improve this sector of the economy is vital.

3   Social Media (SM)

The nature of business and the associated economic environment has frequently changed over time. Mainly within this decade, such change is happening continually and rapidly, thus urging the need for updated studies and research to help organizations understand and effectively react to these changes and challenges [9]. One of the most important global changes is the use of SM to achieve the business goals and objectives of maintaining sustainable productivity and competitive advantage [10–12]. According to [13], the adoption of SM is very important to any economic system. Crucially, the utilization of SM is one of the latest examples of the vital role of technology in supporting and changing the business environment [10, 14]. SM is being considered as one of the effective mediums to reach target audiences of not just business organizations, but any governments, communities, or types of society (e.g. political or social) [15].

Figure 1 details the various features of a SM platform. Studies that examine or research SM phenomena in a business context and SM influence in business are becoming extremely important due to the rapid diffusion of SM globally [11, 16] as well as the continuing rise in penetration and access rate of social media [17, 18]. SM is a widely spread phenomenon, however the adoption of SM as part of businesses is still surprisingly slow [19]. Therefore researchers need to investigate the factors affecting SM adoption and develop an understanding of why SM is being slowly adopted by businesses. Appropriate frameworks and models that help organizations in different sectors to adopt and use SM effectively are therefore required. A clear understanding of how SMEs in particular can gain SM advantages and benefits and avoid and overcome SM disadvantages and barriers is important [17, 18]. This study therefore focuses on SM adoption in SMEs and perceives its use as a powerful source and significant factor in improving SMEs performance and productivity [10–12, 20–22].

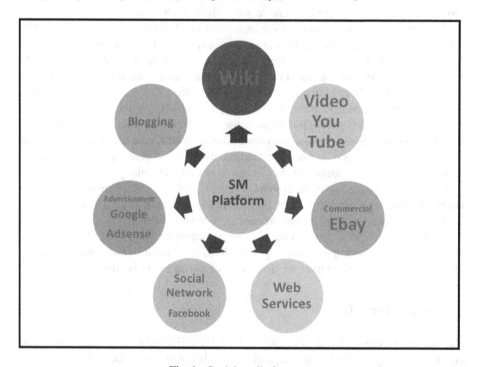

Fig. 1. Social media features

There are several research studies that have examined SM in the business context; however, these studies mainly focus on the effect of SM on organizations [10] or on the user, with little being known about SM from a company adoption perspective [23]. Also, many studies have looked at SM from a purely marketing perspective [24]. The focus of many studies is mainly concentrated on developed countries, where there is a prevalence of plenty of strong academic research centres and institutions [9]. Only a limited number of studies considered the SME perspective [25, 26] and the factors affecting the adoption decision stages, with little or no focus on the implementation and confirmation or after adoption stages [23].

Moreover, there are many unrevealed factors affecting SM adoption by SMEs that need to be discovered and explored, especially in fast growing developing countries [9].

Furthermore, most of the studies in this field preferred the use of quantitative data, mostly from surveys and questionnaires [23], which reflects the need for qualitative research for a deeper analysis and understanding. From the literature review it has been found that there are very few research studies that have been carried out to study SM adoption from the perspective of Saudi Arabian SMEs as a context of a developing country. Accordingly, the objective of this study is to explore and investigate the factors that affect the SM adoption decision process in SMEs in Saudi Arabia; and the extent to which these factors are critical to such adoption and why.

4 Small Medium Enterprises and Social Media

Although many research studies have investigated SM and its significance to business, there is still only a vague understanding as to how SMEs can utilize SM adoption effectively [27], particularly as SMEs may not have the budget nor the experience to copy international or large business approaches and strategies [19]. SMEs play a major role in the national and global economy, and it is undeniable that they represent the highest percentage of organizations in almost all developed countries [4].

Some SMEs tend to adopt a new technology, such as SM, for its perceived opportunities and to copy the market trend, yet do not have appropriate how-to-knowledge [28]. Such under-utilization of technology might lead to problems in terms of ineffective adoption and results. Therefore, it is important to explore the impact of a new technology on SMEs as well as how to effectively adopt it in order to avoid any problematic implementation and results [27]. Therefore, SMEs need to prepare for SM adoption by extensively planning operations including finance, marketing, human-resource-management and production [29].

[30, 31] posit that SMEs can strongly benefit from using SM as it requires minimal cost, simple participation and low technological skills. Whereas [31] suggest SM adoption can improve customer relations and business networks, [32] asserts that SMEs believe it is "a must" to adopt SM in business. [33] affirms that the "wait attitude" toward internet technologies adoption decision is no longer valid. As such these points support the argument that SM adoption is a necessary element for SMEs.

5 Current Models

Very few studies have looked at SM adoption from the perspective of SMEs [25, 26]. As previously mentioned, there is a shortage of studies examining the factors affecting the adoption decision stages, with no focus on the implementation and confirmation or after adoption stages [23]. To begin to address this shortfall, this study examines the adoption of SM by SMEs. It considers two key theoretical concepts; the Technology-Organization-Environment (TOE) and the Innovation-Decision-Process from Diffusion of Innovation (DOI). By integrating these dimensions, a conceptual framework for achieving SM adoption is developed and presented. Each of these theoretical concepts is now considered in turn.

5.1   Technology-Organization-Environment Framework (TOE) Theory

Developed by [34], the Technology–Organization–Environment (TOE) framework is described as the entire process of innovation. It extended from the development of innovations by engineers and entrepreneurs to the adoption and implementation of those innovations by users within the firm context. [35] suggests that the TOE framework represents one segment of the process on how the firm context influences the adoption and implementation of innovations. In this case this framework represents an organization-level theory that explains the three different elements of a firm's context influencing the adoption decisions and process which are; (i) the technological context, (ii) the organizational context, and (iii) the environmental context. All three contexts are posited to influence the technological adoption in its practical application.

The first context, "Technological" includes all of the technologies that are relevant to the firm which are both (i) technologies that are already in use at the firm, as well as (ii) those that are available in the marketplace but not currently in use. The second context, "The Organizational" refers to the characteristics and resources of the firm, including linking structures between employees, intra-firm communication processes, firm size, and the amount of slack resources. There are several ways in which this context affects adoption and implementation decisions. First, mechanisms that link internal sub-units of the organization or span internal boundaries promote innovation [36, 37]. The presence of informal linking agents such as product champions, boundary spanners, and gate-keepers is associated with adoption. Besides, cross-functional teams and employees that have formal or informal links to other departments or to other value chain partners are additional examples of such mechanisms. Finally the third context "The Environmental" includes the structure of the industry, the presence or absence of technology service providers, and the regulatory environment. Industry structure has been investigated in several ways [35]; for instance, intense competition stimulates the adoption of innovation [38, 39]. Also, dominant firms within the value chain can influence other

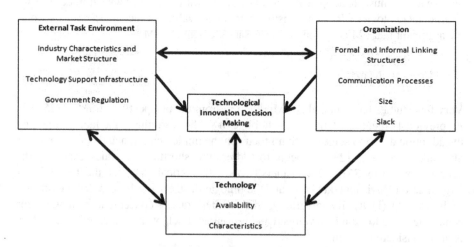

Fig. 2. The technology–organization–environment TOE model framework (Source: [34])

value chain partners to innovate [40]. The clear picture of the TOE model is depicted in Fig. 2 below.

5.2 Diffusion of Innovation (DOI) Theory

It is generally accepted that Roger's [41] Diffusion of Innovation (DOI) model is one of the most dominant and inclusive in the technology adoption field. This model is also empirically used and applied in multiple fields, including history, economics, technology and education. In this model, technology is defined as "a design for instrumental action that reduces the uncertainty in the cause-effect relationships involved in achieving a desired outcome" [41:13]. Hardware is defined as "the tool that embodies the technology in the form of a material or physical object" and software is described as "the information base for the tool" [41:259]. Rogers also states that the lower the observability of an innovation such as software, the lower the adoption rate. Again by definition, adoption means "the full use of an innovation as the best course of action available" and rejection is defined as "not to adopt an innovation" [41:177]. Diffusion is "the process in which an innovation is communicated through certain channels over time among the members of a social system" [41:5]. The key concept of DOI is identified as The Innovation-Decision Process, which is described as "an information-seeking and information-processing activity, where an individual/organization is motivated to reduce uncertainty about the advantages and disadvantages of an innovation" [41:172]. The innovation-decision process involves five continuous stages in the following order: (i) knowledge, (ii) persuasion, (iii) decision, (iv) implementation, and (v) confirmation.

Firstly "The Knowledge" stage is expressing "what the innovation is and how and why it works" [41:21]. Knowledge composes of three types, which are awareness-knowledge, how-to-knowledge, and principles-knowledge. Awareness-knowledge represents the knowledge of the innovation's existence, which can motivate individuals to learn more about the innovation and the other two types of knowledge. The how-to-knowledge contains information about the right and effective way of using the innovation concept. Finally, the principles-knowledge describes the basic popular knowledge of how and why an innovation works as well as how it can be used. Knowledge is crucial in avoiding a lack of continuity later in the process cycle. The second stage "The Persuasion" explains that "The formation of a favourable or unfavourable attitude toward an innovation does not always lead directly or indirectly to an adoption or rejection" [41:176]. The third stage "The Decision" is the critical function to adoption which reflects the "full use of an innovation as the best course of action available" or to reject which means "not to adopt an innovation" [41:177].

The fourth stage, "The Implementation" is the stage where "some degree of uncertainty is involved" [41:6]. Being uncertain regarding the result of the implementation of a new innovation might cause a problem at this stage. This can be handled by involving out-sourced technical experts or specialized change experts. This is one area that this study wishes to address by producing a best practice framework or model of how to adopt a technical innovation (enhancing knowledge at all of its levels); in particular SM adoption within SMEs. In the final stage, "The Confirmation", it is assumed that the adopter will need some form of support for their decision of whether to continue the adoption process or not. The decision to discontinue may be due to the adoption of another better (yet similar) innovation, or due to the innovation becoming less appealing and/or convincing due to its performance during the implementation stage. The DOI model is illustrated in Fig. 3 below.

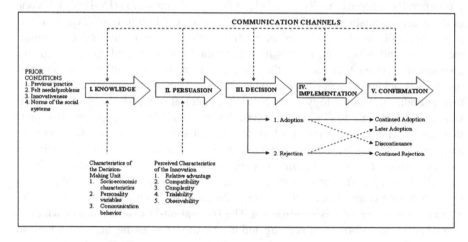

Fig. 3. The Diffusion of Innovation (DOI) model framework (Source: [41])

TOE and DOI are chosen as they remain among the most prominent and widely utilized theories of organizational innovation and technology adoption. In fact [35] believes that TOE is one of the more important future directions in empirical research as this model has been shown to be useful in the investigation of a wide range of innovations and contexts. It is anticipated that these two models, when integrated in the research specific context of SM adoption by SMEs, contributes to the creation of a new model.

6   The Gap

The extant literature has shown that the empirical study of SM adoption in SMEs is still lacking. There have been limited studies investigating the influencing factors (either internal or external) that affect the SM adoption decision process in SMEs. It is perceived that the integration of the two existing models of Technology-Organization-Environment (TOE) and Diffusion of Innovation (DOI) will permit robust exploration to address this current shortfall within SMEs. It is anticipated that the DOI will investigate the SMEs decision process and innovation attributes, while the TOE is used to examine the wider context of factors that affect the SM adoption process. The results are therefore expected to offer motivational factors that will benefit SMEs in running their businesses. Subsequently the influencing factors of who, why, and how SM can be effectively adopted can then be revealed further.

Existing models such as TOE [34] and DOI [41] have often been criticised as being too simplistic and offering no clear advice that can be used by SMEs as a form of guidance to motivate them. There are no clear indications of the influencing factors that SMEs need to be aware of or avoid, nor are there any suggested critical actions to conduct in order to apply SM adoption successfully. The impact of the successful SM application after the adoption is also not identified. The conundrum remains that the probability of SMEs succeeding in applying SM is not clearly presented; as a result, a gap is identified as exploring the influencing factors of why the SM adoption process is not fully applied within SMEs. The questions persist regarding "how, what and why" the implementation of the SM adoption process is not fully realized in the context of SMEs, when in reality SMEs should have benefited from it to help expedite their business expansion.

7   Conceptual Framework

Based on the current models for studying innovation and technology adoption, TOE and DOI were perceived as the most suitable as they provide the ability to look at the adoption process from different perspectives; the adoption decision process and the innovation attributes. The models consist of several theories, thus providing a flexible choice to use the most relevant theories that best serve the research objectives and aim. These models are considered the most appropriate to be used for this study for 2 reasons; firstly, the idea of SM is an innovation in itself, and secondly, this research is looking at the adoption process by SMEs. The DOI model was developed based on Rogers' five stages innovation-decision process model (knowledge, persuasion, decision, implementation, and confirmation). These stages are anticipated as critical in determining the SM adoption process throughout the implementation. The journey of SM adoption can be mapped in these processes. In addition to DOI, TOE contexts are identified as being appropriate to study the adoption of innovation by considering both organizational and environmental factors. These factors are essential for investigating technology adoption by organizations [42]. Organization and environment are used to assess the influencing factors persistent in the organization and surrounding environment. According to [43], "as long as new technologies are developed, and as long as novel contexts for adoption can be identified, the need to understand the adoption of innovation in organizations indicates that the TOE framework is capable of providing insights for researchers and practitioners." Thus, the TOE framework has been combined for a better understanding of the phenomena under investigation.

Figure 4 illustrates the proposed conceptual framework that was developed by integrating the conceptual theory of DOI [41] and TOE [34] to investigate the gap in order to carry out new findings. The DOI model is used to focus on the "five stages model" of innovation adoption decision process consisting of knowledge, persuasion, decision, implementation and confirmation which will look into the SM adoption process stages in SMEs. At this stage the processes will be examined to map the journey of SMEs involved in the SM adoption process. It is assumed that this staged process will contribute to finding answers to the research question of how SM is adopted in SMEs. On the other hand, the TOE framework is viewed from the perspective of the 3 main factors of technology, organization and environment. It is assumed that the contribution will result in the combination of internal and external influencing factors that affect the

SM adoption progress. Based on this conceptual framework, it is anticipated that the integration of DOI and TOE will begin to address the current gap around the factors that most influence the SM adoption process within SMEs. The result is therefore perceived to be either the effective functional SM adoption or otherwise the rejected slow progress / no changes.

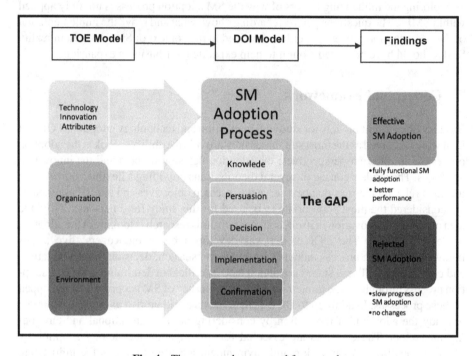

Fig. 4. The proposed conceptual framework

8   Conclusion

The findings from the literature revealed concepts and techniques that are believed to be of interest to SMEs as well as to academics and can be explored further. It is antici-pated that this study is able to produce some helpful guidance that will add value to SMEs in improving and sustaining their business. The significant contributions of this study are a new conceptual framework and a new paradigm for business within SMEs, both of which can be used to inform policy and practice. It is believed that this framework will be able to assist bodies supporting SMEs in mapping their current state and assessing their ability to potentially move to the next level of business development and sustain-ability. As such, the main intention of this study is to assist SMEs to sustain/improve their business performance by adopting SM.

References

1. McAuley, A.: International Marketing: Consuming Globally Thinking Locally. Wiley, New York (2001)
2. McAuley, A.: Looking back, going forward: reflecting on research into the SME internationalisation process. J. Res. Mark. Entrepreneurship **12**, 21–41 (2010)
3. Bahaddad, A., Al Ghamdi, R., Houghton, L.: To what extent would e-mail enable SMEs to adopt e-commerce? Int. J. Bus. Manage. **7**, 123–132 (2012)
4. Al-Mahdi, H.: Supporting SMEs by universities: an emprical study in Saudi Arabia towards building a conceptual model for best practices. BBS Doctoral Symposium, Brunel University (2009)
5. European Commission: European energy and transport: Trends to 2030 (2003)
6. Fathian, M., Akhavan, P., Hoorali, M.: E-readiness assessment of non-profit, ICT SMEs in a developing country: the case of Iran. Technovation **28**, 578–590 (2008)
7. Storey, D.J.: Understanding the small business sector. In: Entrepreneurship, University of Illinois at Urbana-Champaign's Academy for Entrepreneurial Leadership Historical Research Reference in Entrepreneurship (1994)
8. Ozmen, E., Oner, A., Khosrowshahi, F., Underwood, J.: SME buying behaviour: literature review and an application agenda. Mark. Rev. **13**, 207–227 (2013)
9. Poorangi, M.M., Khin, E.W., Nikoonejad, S., Kardevani, A.: E-commerce adoption in Malaysian small and medium enterprises practitioner firms: a revisit on Rogers' model. Anais Acad. Bras. Ciên. **85**, 1593–1604 (2013)
10. Jagongo, A., Kinyua, C.: The social media and entrepreneurship growth. Int. J. Humanit. Soc. Sci. **3**, 213–227 (2013)
11. Indrupati, J., Henari, T.: Entrepreneurial success, using online social networking: evaluation. Educ. Bus. Soc. Contemp. Middle Eastern Issues **5**, 47–62 (2012)
12. Barnes, N.G., Jacobsen, S.: Adoption of social media by fast growing companies: innovation amongst the Inc. 500. J. Mark. Dev. Compeitiveness **7**, 11–17 (2013)
13. Nasco, S.A., Toledo, E.G., Mykytyn, P.P.: Predicting electronic commerce adoption in Chilean SMEs. J. Bus. Res. **61**, 697–705 (2008)
14. Tapscott, D., Williams, A.: Wikinomics: How Mass Collaboration Changes Everything. Penguin, New York (2007)
15. Terblanche, N.S.: You cannot run or hide from social media - ask a politician. J. Public Aff. **11**, 156–167 (2011)
16. Kietzmann, J.H., Hermkens, K., McCarthy, I.P., Silvestre, B.S.: Social media? get serious! understanding the functional building blocks of social media. Bus. Horiz. **54**, 241–251 (2011)
17. Godes, D., Mayzlin, D.: Firm-created word-of-mouth communication: evidence from a field test. Mark. Sci. **28**, 721–739 (2009)
18. Godes, D., Mayzlin, D., Chen, Y., Das, S., Dellarocos, C., Pfeiffer, B., Verlegh, P.: The firm's management of social interactions. Mark. Lett. **16**, 415–428 (2005)
19. Abed, G.T. (ed.): The Palestinian Economy: Studies in Development Under Prolonged Occupation. Routledge, Oxon (2015)
20. Brown, S.L., Tilton, A., Woodside, D.M.: The case for on-line communities. The McKinsey Quarterly **39**(1) (2002)
21. Tickle, M., Michaeledes, R., Kehoe, D.: The Challenge Of Creating Virtual Communities. Information Resources Management Association, Vancouva (2007)
22. Koch, H., Leidner, D.E., Gonzalez, E.: Digitally enabled social networks: resolving IT-culture conflict. Inf. Syst. J. **23**, 501–523 (2013)

23. Kawaljeet, K., Dwivedi, Y.K., Williams, M.: Rogers' innovation adoption attributes: a systematic review and synthesis of existing research. Inf. Syst. Manage. **31**, 74–91 (2014)

24. Armstrong, G., Kotler, P.: Principles of Marketing. Pearson Prentice Hall, London (2011)

25. Lee, J.: Adoption of information technology in small business: testing drivers of adoption for entrepreneurs. Entrue J. Inf. Technol. **1**, 21–36 (2002)

26. Simpson, M., Docherty, A.J.: E-commerce adoption support and advice for UK SMEs. J. Small Bus. Enterp. Dev. **11**, 315–328 (2004)

27. Durkin, M., McGowan, P., McKeown, N.: Exploring social media adoption in small to medium-sized enterprises in Ireland. J. Small Bus. Enterprise Dev. **20**, 716–734 (2013)

28. Drury, G.: Social media: should marketers engage and how can it be done effectively? J. Direct Data Digit. Mark. Pract. **9**, 274–278 (2008)

29. Demirbas, D., Hussain, J.G., Matlay, H.: Owner-managers' perceptions of barriers to innovation: empirical evidence from Turkish SMEs. J. Small Bus. Enterp. Dev. **18**, 764–780 (2011)

30. Derham, R., Cragg, P., Morrish, S.: Creating value: an SME and social media. In: PACIS 2011 Proceedings (2011)

31. Constantinides, E., Lorenzo-Romero, C., Gómez, M.A.: Effects of web experience on consumer choice: a multicultural approach. Internet Res. **20**, 188–209 (2010)

32. Durkin, M.: Tweet me cruel: perspectives on battling digital marketing myopia. Mark. Rev. **13**, 51–63 (2013)

33. Drew, S.: Strategic uses of e-commerce by SMEs in the east of England. Eur. Manage. J. **21**, 79–88 (2003)

34. Tornatzky, L.G., Fleischer, M., Chakrabarti, A.K.: Processes of Technological Innovation. Lexington Books, Lexington (1990)

35. Baker, J.: The technoloy-organisation-environment framework. In: Dwivedi, Y.K., Wade, M., Schneberger, S. (eds.) Information Systems Theory: Explaining and Predicting our Digital Society, pp. 231–246. Springer, New York (2011)

36. Galbraith, J.R.: Designing Complex Organizations. Addison-Wesley, Reading (1973)

37. Tushman, M., Nadler, D.: Organizing for innovation. Calif. Manage. Rev. **28**, 74–92 (1986)

38. Mansfield, E.J.: The Economics of Technological Change. Longmans, London (1968)

39. Mansfield, E.J., Rapoport, J., Romeo, A., Wagner, S., Beardsley, G.: Social and private rates of return from industrial innovations. Q. J. Econ. **91**, 221–240 (1977)

40. Kamath, R.R., Liker, J.K.: A second look at Japanese product development. Harvard Bus. Rev. **72**, 154 (1994)

41. Rogers, E.: Diffusion of Innovations. Free Press, New York (2003)

42. Damanpour, F., Gopalakrishnan, S.: Theories of organisational structure and innovation adoption: the role of environmental change. J. Eng. Technol. Manage. **15**, 1–24 (1998)

43. Dwivedi, Y.K., Weerakkody, V., Janssen, M.: Moving towards maturity: challenges to successful e-government implementation and diffusion. ACM SIGMUS Database **42**, 11–22 (2012)

Social Media Usage of GSM Operators in Turkey: A Content Analysis of Twitter Use

Aysen Temel Eginli[✉], Ozen Okat Ozdem, and Isil Karpat Aktuglu

Communication Faculty, Ege University, Izmir, Turkey
{aysen.temel.eginli,ozen.okat,isil.karpat}@ege.edu.tr

Abstract. Social network sites with the increasing importance, take place in the centre of people's life. By the way companies have taken place in social networks for the aim of both to maintain their presence in the virtual environment and also create customer loyalty, improve brand image and customer satisfaction. Recently, Tweeter, has been preferred both companies and customers to transmit the message fast and clearly. Accordingly, this study aims to examine the current state of Turkey GSM Operators' Twitter usage, in the term of passing through 4.5G (IMT-Advanced) band speed. In addition to this, within the framework of this study focused on the Turkey GSM Operators usage of Twitter as a marketing tool and how do they use it and what do they tweet about in the term of passing through 4.5G band speed, the content analysis is used.

Keywords: Information communication technologies · Social networks · Uses and gratifications theory · Social influence network theory · Tweeter · Customer engagement

1 Introduction

Within the improvements in the information communication technologies, computer mediated communication has gain importance in people's lives. With social network sites, computer mediated communication has stepped into people's lives expeditiously. Individuals have felt the need to get in touch and communicate online with their families, friends and working environment. In this sense, having an account on social networks and being constantly available have become the most important aspects in daily life practices. Companies can reach their customers fast and inform them about their products and services via social networks, thus the users can retrieve information about services and products of the brands.

With the effect of social media in 21st century, changes have been observed in behaviors such as awareness in customer behaviors, purchasing behaviors, post-purchasing behaviors, ideas and attitudes. Social media has become the focal point in consumer to consumer sharing that's why it has become one of the promotional mix elements in terms of marketing efforts.

According to this situation, this study aims to reveal how GSM operators use Twitter, as one of the most technologic companies in Turkey, in terms of informing their

© IFIP International Federation for Information Processing 2016
Published by Springer International Publishing Switzerland 2016. All Rights Reserved
Y.K. Dwivedi et al. (Eds.): I3E 2016, LNCS 9844, pp. 251–260, 2016.
DOI: 10.1007/978-3-319-45234-0_23

customers about the new technology, 4.5G. In this sense, GSM operators made very huge advertising campaigns via conventional media. The campaign has been broadcast throughout the conventional media, and the main purpose of this research is to reveal how the campaign have been represented in social media, especially in Twitter. According to this, social network sites, twitter usage, uses and gratifications theory, and social influence network theory in social media are the bases of this study.

2 Literature Review

With the development of Web 2.0 technologies, social communication and therefore community have gained importance. Within this context, concepts of social network, online community and virtual reality have started to gain importance (Jansen et al. 2009: 2169). Transferring all web-based applications along with social networks into mobile medium both provides constant communication among people, and it also points the characteristic of promoting communication (Tong 2008).

Kaplan and Haenlein (2010: 60) defined social media 20 years ago as "Open Diary", which is the oldest form of social network sites. The term was stated as "weblog" when it was first used, later it is defined as "we blog". Social media is a virtual environment that came into existence in order to form social interactions among users with pulling out all the stops. Social media enables its users to speak by providing an opportunity to be in an environment where people want to share ideas at specific subjects without time or geographic restrictions (boyd et al. 2010). Social media helps consumers make decisions quickly with its user generated content feature (Huang et al. 2010). Baruah (2012: 8) points out the advantages of social network sites as follows, sharing of ideas, low cost/cost effective, less time consuming, bridges communication gap, important marketing tool, important customer interaction tool, important crisis communication tool.

With social media's coming to the fore, communication instruments that companies carry out in their communication strategies with their customers have undergone a change. In this sense, "Social media encompasses a wide range of online, word-of-mouth forums including blogs, company sponsored discussion boards and chat rooms, consumer-to-consumer e-mail, consumer product or service ratings websites and forums, Internet discussion boards and forums, moblogs (sites containing digital audio, images, movies, or photographs), and social networking websites (Mangold and Faulds 2009: 358)". In other words, "Social media as a medium of promotion contributes, through its immediacy, to a healthy and direct relation between brands and their public in an online environment (Baruah 2012: 1)".

Kaplan and Haenlein (2010) have categorized social media as blogs, social network sites (e.g. Facebook), virtual social worlds (e.g. Second Life), collaborative projects (e.g. Wikipedia), content communities (e.g. YouTube), and virtual game worlds (e.g. World of Warcraft). At this point, social network sites put forth the motives and satisfaction related to online media usage as a form of social media.

Boyd and Ellison (2007: 211) have defined social network sites as "social network sites as web-based services that allow individuals to (1) construct a public or semi-public profile within a bounded system, (2) articulate a list of other users with whom they share a connection, and (3) view and traverse their list of connections and those made by others within the system" and stated that the concept of social network sites refers to public discourse and clarifies the field where people get in touch with others and maintain this connection.

Ellison et al. (2007) have stated that social network sites offer people a place that they can exist and at the same time, they can create and manage their own social networks and communicate with other people in their online circle. Baruah (2012: 8) points out the advantages of social network sites as follows:

- **Sharing of ideas:** Social network sites provide their users the opportunity of sharing ideas, emotions, thoughts and interests.
- **Low Cost/Cost effective:** Using social network sites for personal or business purposes is not only quite cost effective because of its feature of enabling people to reach others simultaneously, but it is also very cost-efficient.
- **Less time consuming:** It helps users manage their time effectively in terms of reaching and sharing the information needed.
- **Bridges communication gap:** Social networks enable possibilities to share posts on mutual grounds and carry out activities between the people with the same interests by acting as a bridge.
- **Important marketing tool:** It is an important medium in order for the companies to reach out vast majorities of people on their products and services. It also provides convenience to their customers to get feedback on their suggestions and complaints.
- **Important customer interaction tool:** It creates a very important medium in order to create customer services and to have a one-on-one communication.
- **Important crisis communication tool:** It is the fastest tool to reach out and to inform the public on occasion of any given catastrophe or crisis about any corporate, company and/or country.

Twitter has been detected as the most popular social network site according to the number of users. "Twitter is a "social-networking and micro-blogging" service developed in San Francisco and lunched in October 2006" (Tong 2008). Twitter is a system, which was developed to increase text message usage in the beginning of microblogging service year, offers people to send messages by using "@user" syntax. In a sense, it is a new communication platform that has combined social network sites and blogs. "Twitter users follow others or are followed. Unlike on most online social networking sites, such as Facebook or MySpace, the relationship of following and being followed requires no reciprocation" (Kwak et al. 2010).

In addition to providing communication with other people by creating a profile, Twitter enables its user to send direct messages and allow them to follow other people. Besides, it is also possible to see personal messages and comments in chronological order, as on a blog. Unlike other social media tools, in order to choose a topic and enable its users to follow those topics easily, Twitter uses hashtags (#), which is the most important feature of it. Also, this feature makes it easy to know the trend topic and analyzing them. Moreover, retweet button, which is used to share someone else's tweets, provide convenience in communication. However, limiting the tweets with 140 characters is usually seen as a restriction regarding the subject that is desired to be shared.

Therefore, when people retweet the messages they tend to make some changes in the main messages (Boyd et al. 2010).

Why people use social networks and what do they get by using social media, can be explained with Social Influence Network Theory and Uses and Gratifications Theory. In 1950s and 1960s, usage of mass media tools and which gratifications are created by this usage were defined by analyzing social and psychological variables. Answers to the questions of why people listen to the radio and why do they watch TV were sought. Ruggerio (2000: 27) claimed that the U&G theory has provided "a cutting edge approach in the initial stages of each new communication medium: newspaper, radio, television, and now the Internet". Katz et al. (1973) explains that motivations and reasons why people choose to use media tools vary between users.

Uses and Gratifications Theory which explains why people use media tools also guides researchers to explain consumer behaviors and motivations. Explaining why people use social networks, what are the motivations of using them and the gained satisfaction from using social networks can also explain the desire for using the new technological tools. Ancu and Cozma (2009) have stated that social network sites offer "network" that enable its users to create self-presentation profiles and connect to other profiles. Uses and gratifications theory analyzed with computer mediated communication, it is seen that it becomes difficult to make a distinction between needs and motive. Besides, it has been stated that users choose a media tool based on personal preferences and motivations, and "user taste" may differ from person to person and the media tool (Karimi et al. 2014).

Social influence network theory suggests that people are affected by feelings and thoughts of other people in their networks and they tend to change their feelings and thoughts according to group decisions (Wallach 2014: 66). The theory was developed by mathematician and social psychologists in the 1950s. The theory explains how network of interpersonal effects have an impact on decision making process based upon formal theory of social power. In 1999, Friedkin and Johnsen have generalized the theory by stating that how effective a network is on sociological work in the formation process of an idea. The theory has 6 elements: Cognitive Weighted Averaging, Fixed Social Structure, Determinism, Continuance, Decomposability.

Social influence network theory shows how interpersonal effects follow a process during the data processing through network. The theory explains how a group of actors' opinions on a subject affect other people. Social networks can be divided into two groups. These groups are affiliation networks, and membership networks or hypernetworks. Also these groups can be defined as affiliation or involvement relation (Hui and Buchegger 2009). Social impacts enable other people to adopt actors' opinions and attitudes, especially in groups, and create a common understanding among the group members or make decisions as a group and even cause them to take part in collective activities together (Friedkin and Johnsen 1999).

Virtual brand organizations founded via social networks and social network websites, have changed consumer behavior of the customers and created new patterns of purchase (Ioanăs and Stoica 2014). Consumers who consume in the new pattern are exposed to social influence; however, this social influence operates through social networks. These people who use social networks for many purposes such as making friends, obtaining social support also share information and comments about products or services with other people, which makes their decision making process easy and enables them to obtain information about products and services (Kozinets et al. 2010).

"Social media marketing consists of the attempt to use social media to persuade consumers that one's company, products and/or services are worthwhile. Social media marketing is marketing using online communities, social networks, blog marketing and more" (Neti 2011: 3). Consumers have control in sending and receiving messages that are about companies and their products. Especially social networks enable customers to share and interactions with other people. In social networks, the relationship between customers are close and profitable (Waad Assaad 2011). Therefore, the aim of the companies today is to create consumer engagement in social media. At this point, consumer engagement has different components for each customer. The first step to create a consumer engagement is to observe, evaluate, analyze and measure the customers on the social media and take possible actions for the decision making process (Zailskaite-Jakste and Kuvykaite 2012: 195).

Kidd (2011) has stated that in order for companies to establish social media engagement and maintain their relationship with the customers, they need to create an environment that encourages the customers to share their personal histories and express their opinions. Zailskaite-Jakste and Kuvykate (2012) have developed "The conceptual model of consumer engagement in brand equity building in social media" model by using watching, sharing, commenting, producing, curation stages defined by Li and Owyang (2010) to create consumer engagement in social media.

3   Methodology

This study examined the current state of Turkey GSM Operators' Twitter use, in the term of passing through 4.5G (IMT-Advanced) band speed. The aim of this study is to reveal firstly, whether "Turkey 4.5G Auction" has an influence on Turkey GSM Operators' Twitter accounts and second - if it yes - to examine how Turkey GSM Operators use Twitter and what they tweet about.

According to the aim, this study is focusing on the following research questions: Do Turkey GSM Operators use Twitter as a marketing tool and if yes, how do they use it and what do they tweet about in the term of passing through 4.5G band speed?

1. Does the 4.5G Auction in Turkey have an influence on whether Twitter is used or not?
2. Does the 4.5G Auction in Turkey have an influence on the content of Tweets?
3. Does the GSM Operators use Twitter as a marketing tool?

According to the previous research (Thoring 2011) the only research method adequate to answer these questions is the content analysis; bearing in mind the analytic aim, a quantitative, standardized approach was chosen.

In Turkey, there are three GSM Operators called, Turkcell, Vodafone and Turk Telekom – Avea. These three operators are persistently competing. As indicated in the literature review, Turkey's GSM internet band speed is 3G. In 27th of August 2015 BTK (Turkey's Information Technologies and Communication Foundation) opened an auction for 4.5G Band Speed. Turkey's three GSM Operators has joined to the auction. The auction was for 20 different frequency package sales. For all packages Turkcell offered 1.63 billion euro, Turk Telekom – Avea offered 954 million euro and Vodafone offered 777 million euro. All three operators bought different megahertz (800, 900, 1800, 2100 and 2600) frequency band packages. This result means a very big enterprise and according to this result, it can be predicted that GSM operators will compete fiercely in marketing area. So, this study focuses on three GSM Operators' tweets after 4.5G auction.

4   Results

4.1   Participation

The analysis reveals that all GSM operators have at least two Twitter accounts. Turkcell has eight accounts: One of them is @Turkcell, which announces marketing campaigns and this is the main account of the company; @TurkcellHizmet, which is working as a customer relations; and different accounts for various purposes as @Tcellplatinum, @superonlineTR, @TurkcellMuzik, @TurkcellAkademi, @TurkcellTVPlus, @TurkcellNews.

Vodafone has seven accounts: One of them is @VodafoneTR, which announces marketing campaigns and this is the main account of the company; @VodafoneDestek, which is working as a customer relations; and different accounts for various purposes as @VodafoneArena, @VFreeZone, @VodafoneMedya, @VodafoneVakfi, @GeciyorMuyuz.

Turk Telekom and Avea are mergers. At the auction time its name was Avea but now the company called as Turk Telekom. In this study it is considered the last name of the company. As Turk Telekom the company has two original and several fake accounts, so that it has been considered only two original accounts: One of them is @Turk_Telekom which announces marketing campaigns and this is the main account of the company; the other one is @Galatasaray_TTA, which is about a specific sponsorship campaign.

In this study, only main accounts of company's are considered for the sample. These are, @Turkcell, @VodafoneTR and @Turk_Telekom.

@Turkcell had joined Twitter in 23rd of August 2007, @VodafoneTR had joined Twitter in 21st of December 2008 and @Turk_Telekom had joined Twitter in 3rd of November 2011. @Turkcell has 602,736 followers, @VodafoneTR has 606,124 followers, @Turk_Telekom has 307,427 followers in 11th of March 2016. Turk Telekom's follower number is half of the other company's because of its Twitter join date. As being the oldest communication company in Turkey 2011 is very late to join Twitter.

Turkcell has 4301, Vodafone has 35,626 and Turk Telekom has 2068 tweets at all times. Vodafone's huge number of tweets is because of duplication. In the term of analyze, Turkcell tweeted 0.71, Vodafone tweeted 1.14, Turk Telekom tweeted 0.45 tweet per day.

4.2   Interactivity

A users activity on Twitter can be examined by analyzing its Retweets and Replies. Turkcell has 21 retweets and 2 replies; Vodafone has 11 retweets and 85 replies; Turk Telekom has 5 retweets and 8 replies. In the period that tweets were analyzed, 15 % of all Turkcell tweets are retweets, 4.89 % of all Vodafone tweets are retweets, 5.56 % of all Turk Telekom tweets are retweets; 1.3 % of all Turkcell tweets are replies, 37.78 % of all Vodafone tweets are replies and 8.89 % of all Turk Telekom tweets are replies. Reply number reflects direct interaction. According to that statement Vodafone is the most interactive GSM operator account as 37.78 % reply rate.

In the sample Turkcell tweets accounted for 16.42 % of all tweets retweets and replies, Vodafone tweets accounted for 42.6 % of all tweets retweets and replies and Turk Telekom tweets accounted for 14.4 % of all tweets retweets and replies. This result indicates that the most interactive account in the sample is Vodafone, according to its replies and retweets.

4.3   Connectivity

Because of the limited length of Tweets, Twitter – more than other social networking sites and blogs – functions as a distributor which drives traffic to other sites (Thoring 2011). As seen on Fig. 1, Vodafone has the maximum hyperlink number. According to this result, Vodafone use Twitter mostly as an indicator.

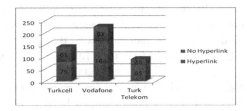

Fig. 1. Categorization by hyperlink

4.4   Channels of Tweeting

As seen on Fig. 2 Of all tweets in the sample most were sent directly on Twitter web page. Turk Telekom used also Android Phone, Tweet Deck, Twitter Ads as a Twitter channel. Turkcell used Twitter Ads and Echofon beside web channel. Vodafone used Twitter Ads, Twitter for iPhone, Periscope and a social responsibility project web page of Vodafone called "DuslerGercekOlsun".

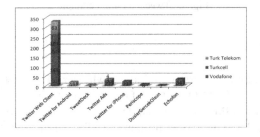

Fig. 2. Channels of tweeting

4.5 Content of Tweets

According to the Fig. 3 Vodafone used Twitter by various contents. The number of "Tweets About Miscellaneous Topics" indicates that result. Also Vodafone used Twitter as a social responsibility projects communication channel. Twitter usage as a marketing tool, nearly same for all GSM operators.

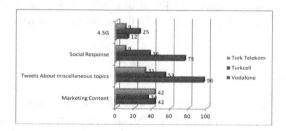

Fig. 3. Content of tweets

According to the research questions, the main aim of this study is analyzing tweets, which are about 4.5G and marketing content. As seen on Fig. 4 Turkcell used Twitter as 4.5G marketing area directly more than the others. By of all their tweets, Turkcell used direct/indirect 4.5G messages 17.85 %, Turk Telekom 10 % and Vodafone 5.3 %. According to the percentage of tweets, it can be said that Vodafone doesn't use Twitter as a 4.5G marketing tool. As the money that operators spend for 4.5G auction, this result is not surprising. The biggest 4.5G investment is made by Turkcell. As expected, Turkcell has to spend marketing efforts about 4.5G technology.

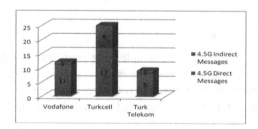

Fig. 4. Tweets by 4.5G content

5   Conclusion

The aims of this study were, firstly to find out whether "Turkey 4.5G Auction" has an influence on Turkey GSM Operators' Twitter accounts and second - if it yes - to examine how Turkey GSM Operators use Twitter and what they tweet about. As the results, it can be said that there is an influence on Twitter messages even if it is few. As a tweet subject, 4.5G is seen on Twitter messages. The owner of the biggest investment, Turkcell's number of tweets about 4.5G is more than the other GSM

Operators. Also other GSM operators are investor for 4.5G technology. As their amount of investment, their tweet numbers about 4.5G are parallel. GSM operators used 4.5G content, mostly directly. Also this situation indicates direct marketing messages.

According to the last question of research, it can be said that, as being a profit, GSM operators used Twitter as a marketing tool. Turk Telekom marketing tweets accounted for 46.66 % of all Turk Telekom tweets. Turkcell marketing tweets accounted for 24.28 % of all Turkcell tweets and Vodafone marketing tweets accounted for 18.66 % of all Vodafone tweets. As this result, nearly half of Turk Telekom's tweets are marketing content.

In Turkey GSM operators made very big campaigns on traditional media. In parallel with it was expected that GSM operators would use social media as traditional media, although the real life doesn't indicate the expected. As ratios, there is a social media usage via Twitter about 4.5G, but the numbers of all tweets are very few. 4.5G is becoming a technological item, to market it, social media, as a technological media, didn't considered properly as a marketing tool. May be this because of the internet usage 49 % and Twitter usage 6 % in Turkey.

References

Ancu, M., Cozma, R.: Myspace politics: uses and gratifications of befriending candidates. J. Broadcast. Electr. Media **53**(4), 567–583 (2009)

Baruah, T.D.: Effectiveness of social media as a tool of communication and its potential for technology enabled connections: a micro-level study. Int. J. Sci. Res. Publ. **2**(5), 1–10 (2012)

Boyd, D.M., Ellison, N.B.: Social network sites: definition, history, and scholarship. J. Comput.-Mediated Commun. **13**(1), 210–230 (2007)

Boyd, D., Golder, S., Lotan, G.: Tweet, tweet, retweet: conversational aspects of retweeting on Twitter. In: HICSS-43. IEEE: Kauai, 6 January 2010

Ellison, N., Steinfield, C., Lampe, C.: The benefits of Facebook "friends": social capital and college students' use of online social network sites. J. Comput.-Mediated Commun. **12**, 1143–1168 (2007)

Friedkin, N.E., Johnsen, E.C.: Social influence networks and opinion change. Adv. Group Process. **16**, 1–29 (1999)

Huang, Y., Basu, C., Hsu, M.: Exploring motivations of travel knowledge sharing on social networking sites: an empirical investigation of U.S. college students. J. Hospitality Market. Manag. **19**(7), 717–734 (2010)

Hui, P. Buchegger, S.: Groupthink and peer pressure: social influence in online social network groups, social network analysis and mining. In: International Conference ASONAM 2009, pp. 53–59 (2009)

Ioanăs, E., Stoica, I.: Social media and its impact on consumers behavior. Int. J. Econ. Pract. Theor. **4**(2), 295–303 (2014)

Jansen, B.J., Zhang, M., Sobel, K., Chowdury, A.: Twitter power: tweets as electronic word of mouth. J. Am. Soc. Inf. Sci. Technol. **60**(11), 2169–2188 (2009)

Kaplan, A., Haenlein, M.: Users of the world, unite: the challenges and opportunities of social media. Bus. Horiz. **53**(1), 59–68 (2010)

Karimi, L., Khodabandelou, R., Ehsani, M., Ahmad, M.: Applying the uses and Gratifications Theory to compare higher education students' motivation for using social networking sites: experiences from Iran, Malaysia, United Kingdom, and South Africa. Contemp. Educ. Technol. 5(1), 53–72 (2014)

Katz, E., Gurevitch, M., Hass, H.: On the use of mass media for important things. Am. Sociol. Rev. 38, 164–181 (1973)

Kidd, J.: Enacting engagement online: framing social media use for the museum' in information. Technol. People 24(1), 64–77 (2011)

Kozinets, R.V., Valck, K., Wojnicki, A.C., Wilner, S.J.S.: Networked narratives: understanding word-of-mouth marketing in online communities. J. Market. 74(2), 71–89 (2010)

Kwak, H., Lee, C., Park, H., Moon, S.: What is Twitter, a social network or a news media? In: International World Wide Web Conference Committee (IW3C2), Raleigh, North Carolina, USA (2010)

Li, C., Owyang, J.: Social marketing analytics (2010). http://www.web-strategist.com/blog/2010/01/21/socialgraphics-help-you-tounderstand-your-customers-slides-and-recording/

Mangold, W.G., Faulds, D.J.: Social media: the new hybrid element of the promotion mix. Bus. Horiz. 52, 357–365 (2009)

Neti, S.: Social media and its role in marketing. Int. J. Enterp. Comput. Bus. Syst. 1(2), 1–15 (2011)

Ruggiero, T.: Uses and gratification theory in the 21st century. Mass Commun. Soc. 3(1), 3–37 (2000)

Thoring, A.: Corporate tweeting: analysing the use of Twitter as a marketing tool by UK trade publishers. Publ. Res. Q. 27(2), 141–158 (2011)

Tong, C.: Analysis of some popular mobile social network systems. In: TKK T-110.5190 Seminar on Internetworking (2008)

Waad Assaad, J.M.G.: Social network in marketing (social media marketing) opportunities and risks. Int. J. Manag. Public Sect. Inf. Commun. Technol. (IJMPICT) 2(1), 13–22 (2011)

Wallach, K.: A content analysis of twitter use: factors that might increase music sales during an award show? Elon J. Undergrad. Res. Commun. 5(1), 1–2 (2014)

Zailskaite-Jakste, L., Kuvykaite, R.: Consumer engagement in social media by building the brand. In: Electronic International Interdisciplinary Conference, pp. 194–202 (2012)

Developing a Theoretical Model to Examine Consumer Acceptance Behavior of Mobile Shopping

Hannah R. Marriott[✉] and Michael D. Williams

School of Management, Swansea University, Swansea, UK
{632527,m.d.williams}@swansea.ac.uk

Abstract. Mobile activity is increasing in popularity with Smartphones and Tablets being used for a variety of daily online activities. However, the number of mobile users utilizing mobile devices for the purpose of shopping is relatively low and there has been limited theoretical research examining the acceptance behavior of consumers in the UK. This research aims to develop a theoretically grounded adoption model to examine UK consumers' mobile shopping acceptance behavior. Through consideration into findings from existing research, a theoretically grounded model is developed by extending UTAUT2 with perceived risk, trust, mobile affinity and innovativeness. This theoretical model can subsequently be empirically tested with data gathered from the UK.

Keywords: Acceptance · Consumer behavior · Mobile shopping (m-shopping) · Perceived risk · UK · UTAUT2

1 Introduction

Smartphones and Tablets ('mobile devices') are considered a new generation of operating system allowing for an array of computer-like functions whilst providing consumers with higher levels of convenience than previously experienced with computers [1, 2]. Mobile devices have become heavily integrated into the lives of modern day users and are used for a variety of daily activities, including conducting in mobile banking (m-banking), mobile learning (m-learning), mobile payments (m-payments) and mobile shopping (m-shopping). M-shopping comprises of the online searching, browsing, comparing and purchasing of goods and services through wireless mobile devices [3–5]. This research examines m-shopping at the consumer level, with primary consideration into business-to-consumer relationships.

Increased functionality in mobile devices has seen the growth of Internet sales, with mobile orders expected to increase at 21–29 % by the end of 2016 [6]. Although m-shopping activity is increasing, it remains the least preferable and least trusted means of online shopping worldwide [2]. Risk perceptions subsequently limit the number of consumers adopting m-shopping activities and practitioners have stressed the significance of developing effective marketing techniques and mobile systems to increase adoption willingness [7]. However, there is limited empirical research examining m-shopping acceptance behavior of UK consumers, restricting validity of findings to

Y.K. Dwivedi et al. (Eds.): I3E 2016, LNCS 9844, pp. 261–266, 2016.
DOI: 10.1007/978-3-319-45234-0_24

geographical contexts. Insight into UK consumers will further validate the significance of various theoretical acceptance factors and provide a more geographically holistic understanding into m-shopping acceptance behavior.

This paper provides an overview of theories and models used in mobile-related research, establishing those most commonly used and those most underutilized, for the purpose of identifying an appropriate research model for m-shopping acceptance behavior in the UK, that can be tested using empirical data. The conceptual model incorporates acceptance factors and barriers towards m-shopping in a contemporary light. The remainder of this paper is as follows. First, in reviewing acceptance literature surrounding m-commerce, m-banking, m-payment and m-shopping literature, the most commonly used Information Systems (IS) theoretical adoption models to date will be highlighted. Second, exploration into the most appropriate adoption model will be discussed, followed by its proposed extensions. The paper concludes with an overview of findings and discussion into areas for further empirical work.

2 Overview of Theories and Models in Mobile-Related Research

Technology acceptance research has utilized a variety of theoretical models to explain consumer behaviors across various areas in the digital environment. In the digital retail environment, comprising of electronic commerce (e-commerce) and mobile commerce (m-commerce), the most commonly adopted theoretical models have been the Theory of Reasoned Action (TRA) [8], Theory of Planned Behavior (TPB) [9], Technology Acceptance Model (TAM) [10], Unified Theory of Acceptance and Use of Technology (UTAUT) [11, 12] and the Diffusion of Innovation Theory (DOI) [13].

A review of the literature, conducted through keyword searches via *Google Scholar* and *EbscoHost*, revealed 26 quantitative studies relating to consumer m-shopping behavior between 2002 and 2016. Of these studies, one adopts TPB, six adopt TAM, with two utilizing UTAUT; 17 studies fail to adopt a defined theoretical research model but re-affirm some significant variables within existing models. Due to limitations in m-shopping literature, it is appropriate to consider literature surrounding other sub-categories of m-commerce to further develop an appropriate conceptual model. Therefore, research relating to m-commerce, m-services, m-Internet and m-payments will also be considered. The analysis of the subsequent 77 quantitative studies reveals TAM as the most commonly used IS adoption model, with 44.1 % of studies utilizing it. The number of studies not adopting a grounded theoretical model accounts for 29.8 % of these studies, leaving a small percent of studies adopting DOI, TPB, TRA and UTAUT.

As the most commonly used research model, TAM has been empirically extended to incorporate trust, innovativeness and affinity. Aldás-Manzano et al. [14] extended TAM to include personality variables of innovativeness and mobile affinity and found that the variance of m-shopping intention is 8 % higher when the two personality variables are added to TAM. Although not extended to TAM, Bigné et al. [15] provides support for the inclusion of mobile affinity as their study explained over 60 % variance on intention when included in their model.

TAM is also the most regularly utilized model when examining perceived risk ('risk') and trust. Zhang et al. [16] observes trust as having 85.7 % and risk as having 87.5 % significance on behavioral intention. Furthermore, Nassoura [17] considers trust to be a significant positive predictor of m-commerce adoption. UTAUT has increased in popularity in more recent years and has been used to further explain trust. UTAUT has been most regularly extended with trust within m-banking research; Foon and Fah [18] found trust to be a significant predictor of behavioral intention and that the extended model explains 56.5 % of variance. Furthermore, Chong [3] observed trust to have a significant positive relationship with behavioral intention towards m-commerce in China and accounts for 33.4 % of variance.

3 Selection of Theoretical Model

The TRA, being a development of the Information Integration Theory (IIT), collaboratively examines consumer beliefs and evaluations on their attitudes and normative beliefs to predict their behavioral intention and actual behavior [8, 19]. Although TRA has made fundamental advances in consumer behavior research, it has been criticized regarding its lack of consideration into behavioral control; TRA has subsequently been replaced by TPB, which examines the effects of attitude, subjective norms and perceived behavioral control on behavioral intention, and increased variance from 32.7 %, in TRA, to 44.05 %. Although the significance of incorporating perceived behavioral control is maintained in e-commerce literature, its application to intention-related research is limited [11, 20].

Due to limitations in TPB, TAM is considered the most widely adopted theoretical model in IS adoption research as it is considered a better predictor of overall intention than TRA and TPB [19, 21]. TAM incorporates perceived usefulness (PU) and perceived ease of use (PEOU) on behavioral intention. Due to its minimalistic nature, researchers have drawn attention to it as having reached saturation point. Following its establishment in 2003, UTAUT offered a more explanatory theoretical model through the incorporation of performance expectancy, derived from PU, effort expectancy, derived from PEOU, social influence and facilitating conditions, alongside the moderating effects of age, gender, experience and voluntariness of use [11].

Although UTAUT is a widely accepted IS adoption model, the high numbers of its citation are considered not to be truly representative of its actual utilization as a theoretical research model [22]. Furthermore, its application to m-shopping research has been minimal. Nevertheless, UTAUT was designed to explain and predict employee technology acceptance within organizations, rather than in a consumer context. In response to its limitations, Venkatesh et al. [12] proposed an extension of this model to accommodate the consumer context, giving rise to UTAUT2. UTAUT2 incorporates the original UTAUT constructs of performance expectancy, effort expectancy, social influence and facilitating conditions and includes hedonic motivation, price value and habit. Furthermore, due to the removal of the employment context, voluntariness of use is not included in UTAUT2 as it is presumed that consumers adopt technologies voluntarily, leaving gender, age and experience as moderators.

Since its establishment in 2012, UTAUT2 has been considered a substantial improvement in explaining consumer behavioral intention and has since been used in m-payments, m-internet and m-banking research. UTAUT2 has increased the explained variance of behavioral intention from 56 % to 74 % and of use behavior from 40 % to 52 % [12]. Despite significant developments of UTAUT2, it remains significantly underutilized in m-shopping research. Furthermore, although UTAUT2 was originally developed with consideration into American consumers, it has been recommended for its use to stretch across geographical contexts [12]. Consequently, applying UTAUT2 to an m-shopping acceptance context within the ambit of the UK provides both theoretical and practical contributions.

4 Proposed Extensions of UTAUT2

Across the mobile research environment, theorists have seldom applied theoretical models without also extending them. Venkatesh et al. [12] stressed the importance of further research extending UTAUT2 for the purpose of finding other key acceptance factors across different research contexts. It is therefore appropriate for both the application and extension of UTAUT2 to examine UK consumer m-shopping acceptance behavior. Through analysis into m-shopping and m-commerce literature, it can be proposed that UTAUT2 be extended to incorporate mobile affinity, personal innovativeness, multi-dimensional risk and multi-dimensional trust.

Mobile affinity is the personal closeness with a user's mobile devices and examination into its various situational contexts is significant in mobile related research [2, 23]. Although UTAUT2 is better suited to consumer related contexts, it does not directly relate to m-shopping situations. In incorporating mobile affinity into UTAUT2, UK m-shopping acceptance behavior can be further explained.

Innovativeness is the willingness of individuals to try something new in relation to their experience [13]. Although it is suggested that innovativeness is incorporated with hedonic motivation, within UTAUT2 [12], innovativeness relates more to an individual's predisposition to adopt technology rather than towards their perceived enjoyment of that technology. Innovativeness will subsequently be considered in this research as it has previously been considered one of the most significant predictors of behavioral intention [14].

Risk is a multidimensional construct, comprising of financial, psychological, physical, social, time and performance risks, providing feelings of anxiety and uncertainty, reducing the likelihood of consumers adopting technologies [24]. Although risk has been regularly implemented into existing models, it is seldom considered multi-dimensionally and has not been examined in relation to m-shopping acceptance. Due to the various types of risk, it is appropriate to examine risk as a multidimensional construct in this research as a negative determinant of behavioral intention.

Trust is the belief that one party will fulfil their obligations, which is also of a multidimensional nature. There are many origins of trust throughout the m-shopping process, including trust in the m-vendor, the m-shopping platform and the mobile device itself. Although trust is often considered a unitary concept, this research aims to extend UTAUT2 to incorporate various dimensions of trust and to examine its direct effect on behavioral intention and its effect on risk reduction.

5 Conclusion

Despite the increase of m-shopping acceptance literature across a variety of geographical contexts, examination into UK consumer's behavior towards m-shopping has remained in its infancy. This research has developed a theoretical consumer adoption model to examine and help predict consumer acceptance of m-shopping in the context of the UK. Due to the increasing utilization of UTAUT2 in consumer research, it has been applied to this research and extended to include perceived risk, trust, mobile affinity and innovativeness. To further validate these theoretical extensions to UTAUT2, this research requires empirical investigation. Furthermore, future research in this area can further examine UTAUT2 alongside other acceptance variables to further contribute to m-shopping knowledge.

References

1. Büllinger, F., Stamm, P.: Mobile Commerce via Smartphone & Co: Analyse und Prognose des zukünftigen Marktes aus Nutzerperspektive. Hg. v. Verbraucherzentrale Bundesverband eV. Wissenschaftliches Institut für Infrastruktur und Kommunikationsdienste GmbH. Büyüközkan, G. (2009) Determining the mobile commerce user requirements using an analytic approach. Computer Standards and Interfaces 31(1), 144–152 (2012)
2. Holmes, A., Byrne, A., Rowley, J.: Mobile shopping behaviour: insights into attitudes, shopping process involvement and location. Int. J. Retail Distrib. Manag. 42(1), 25–39 (2014)
3. Chong, A.Y.L.: Predicting m-commerce adoption determinants: a neural network approach. Expert Syst. Appl. 40(2), 523–530 (2013)
4. Groß, M.: Exploring the acceptance of technology for mobile shopping: an empirical investigation among Smartphone users. Int. Rev. Retail, Distrib. Consum. Res. 25(3), 215–235 (2014)
5. Yang, K., Kim, H.Y.: Mobile shopping motivation: an application of multiple discriminant analysis. Int. J. Retail Distrib. Manag. 40(10), 778–789 (2012)
6. Mulpuru, S., Johnsob, C., Wu, S., Roberge, D., Naparstek, L.: US Mobile Retail Forecast, 2012 to 2017. Forrester Research (2014). https://www.forrester.com/US+Mobile+Phone +And+Tablet+Commerce+Forecast+2013+To+2018/fulltext/-/E-res115514#AST971255
7. Hung, M.C., Yang, S.T., Hsieh, T.C.: An examination of the determinants of mobile shopping continuance. Int. J. Electron. Bus. Manag. 10(1), 29 (2012)
8. Fishbein, M., Ajzen, I.: Belief, Attitude, Intention and Behavior: An Introduction to Theory and Research. Addison-Wesley, Reading (1975)
9. Ajzen, I.: The theory of planned behavior. Organ. Behav. Hum. Decis. Process. 50(2), 179–211 (1991)
10. Davis, F.D.: Perceived usefulness, perceived ease of use, and user acceptance of information technology. MIS Q. 13(3), 319–340 (1989)

11. Venkatesh, V., Morris, M.G., Davis, G.B., Davis, F.D.: User acceptance of information technology: toward a unified view. MIS Q. **27**(3), 425–478 (2003)
12. Venkatesh, V., Thong, J.Y., Xu, X.: Consumer acceptance and use of information technology: extending the unified theory of acceptance and use of technology. MIS Q. **36**(1), 157–178 (2012)
13. Rogers, E.: Diffusion of Innovations, 4th edn. Free Press, New York (1995)
14. Aldás-Manzano, J., Ruiz-Mafe, C., Sanz-Blas, S.: Exploring individual personality factors as drivers of M-shopping acceptance. Ind. Manag. Data Syst. **109**(6), 739–757 (2009)
15. Bigné, E., Ruiz-Mafé, C., Sanz-Balz, S.: Key drivers of mobile commerce adoption. An exploratory study of Spanish mobile users. JTAER **2**(2), 48–60 (2007)
16. Zhang, L., Zhu, J., Liu, Q.: A meta-analysis of mobile commerce adoption and the moderating effect of culture. Comput. Hum. Behav. **28**(5), 1902–1911 (2012)
17. Nassuora, A.B.: Understanding factors affecting the adoption of m-commerce by consumers. J. Appl. Sci. **13**(6), 913 (2013)
18. Foon, Y.S., Fah, B.C.Y.: Internet banking adoption in Kuala Lumpur: an application of UTAUT model. Int. J. Bus. Manag. **6**(4), 161 (2011)
19. Wong, C.H., Lee, H.S., Lim, Y.H., Chua, B.H., Tan, G.W.H.: Predicting the consumers' intention to adopt mobile shopping: an emerging market perspective. Int. J. Netw. Mob. Technol. **3**(3), 24–39 (2012)
20. Grandón, E.E., Nasco, S.A., Mykytyn, P.P.: Comparing theories to explain e-commerce adoption. J. Bus. Res. **64**(3), 292–298 (2011)
21. Mathieson, K.: Predicting user intentions: comparing the technology acceptance model with the theory of planned behavior. Inf. Syst. Res. **2**(3), 173–191 (1991)
22. Williams, M.D., Rana, N.P., Dwivedi, Y.K., Lal, B.: Is UTAUT really used or just cited for the sake of it? A systematic review of citations of UTAUT's originating article. In: ECIS, June 2011
23. Matthews, T., Pierce, J., Tang, J.: No smart phone is an island: the impact of places, situations, and other devices on smart phone use. IBM RJ10452 (2009)
24. Jacoby, J., Kaplan, L.B.: The components of perceived risk. Adv. Consum. Res. **3**(3), 382–383 (1972)

Consumer Adoption of Mobile Government in the Kingdom of Saudi Arabia: The Role of Usefulness, Ease of Use, Perceived Risk and Innovativeness

Abdullah Baabdullah[1][✉], Omar Nasseef[1], and Ali Alalwan[2]

[1] Department of Management Information Systems,
Faculty of Economics and Administration, King Abdulaziz University,
Jeddah, Kingdom of Saudi Arabia
{baabdullah,onasseef}@kau.edu.sa
[2] Amman College of Banking and Finance, Al-Balqa' Applied University,
Amman, Jordan
alwan.a.a.ali@gmail.com

Abstract. Utilising Mobile Government (M-Gov) services would raise socio-economic benefits. Thus, it is essential to examine the factors that may increase the adoption of M-Gov services within the context of Saudi Arabia. This research aims to examine potential users' intentions towards different variables that may be significant for supporting higher behavioural intention to use the M-Gov services in Saudi Arabia. This study embraces the following variables: perceived risk, innovativeness, perceived usefulness, perceived ease of use and behavioural intention. Data was collected by means of a self-administered questionnaire on a convenience sample that consisted of 600 subjects with a response rate of 69.67 %. The findings were gathered and the statistical analysis suggested that the related variables are perceived as significant by participants and they have a strong behavioural intention to use the M-Gov services. Furthermore, the findings show that perceived ease of use significantly influences perceived usefulness.

Keywords: Saudi Arabia · M-Gov · TAM · Perceived risk · Innovativeness

1 Introduction

M-Gov deals with the group of services concerning the organised usage of the governmental services and utilisations that are mainly attainable via mobile phones [37]. The Saudi Government has aimed at increasing the adoption of M-Gov in order to offer citizens more accessibility to governmental services compared with traditional methods in terms of time and cost [7]. Nevertheless, the traditional channels for communicating and transacting with the government are still common in Saudi Arabia [3]. Saudi citizens have not adopted it quickly due to the risks associated with the adoption of M-Gov as well as the lack of Saudi infrastructure [2]. This study aims to explore the citizens' (potential users) perceptions on the significance of certain factors regarding the issue of M-Gov adoption in the domain of Saudi Arabia.

© IFIP International Federation for Information Processing 2016
Published by Springer International Publishing Switzerland 2016. All Rights Reserved
Y.K. Dwivedi et al. (Eds.): I3E 2016, LNCS 9844, pp. 267–279, 2016.
DOI: 10.1007/978-3-319-45234-0_25

2 Literature Review

Theoretically, within the field of IT/IS, researchers have integrated and formulated different theories and models in order to get in-depth knowledge and thoughtful understanding of the customers' behavioural intention towards M-Gov. Examples include the Theory of Reasoned Action (TRA) which was embraced by [8]. The Theory of Planned Behaviour (TPB) was applied by [32]. The Technology Acceptance Model (TAM) has also been implemented by [35], and it proposed to predict the customers' behavioural intention to use M-Gov. The Unified Theory of Acceptance and Use of Technology (UTAUT) [34] were implemented by [37]. The low level of M-Gov adoption in the context of Saudi Arabia was referred by [5]. [7] referred that the overt lack of consumers' awareness and the low levels of trust were considered as the main problems when it comes to the actual adoption of the M-Gov service on a larger scale. It is obvious that due to the newly established E-Gov services in Saudi Arabia, the issue of M-Gov has not, so far, been studied comprehensively. Consequently, this matter requires further research to investigate the shortage of M-Gov adoption.

3 Conceptual Model and Research Hypotheses

TAM has been recognised as the most adopted theory within IT/IS research [34]. In order to solve the matter of inaccuracy in prediction with behavioural intention, the TAM has been extended by a number of researchers [6]. For example, within the context of M-Gov, [3] extended the TAM model to include factors from the IDT model (relative advantage, compatibility, trialability). Likewise, [31] added elements from the IDT and UTAUT models to the TAM model. [8] developed their conceptual model relying on factors from TAM, TRA and UTAUT. As Fig. 1 shows, this study adopts PU and PEOU from TAM and extended it to include perceived risk (PR) and innovativeness (INN).

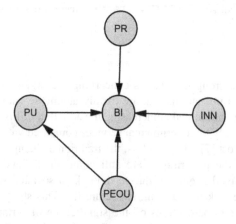

Fig. 1. The proposed research model. Adopted from [13]

Perceived Usefulness (PU) is defined as 'the degree to which a person believes that using a particular system would enhance his or her job performance' [14]. A considerable number of studies have affirmed the important role of PU over BI within the context of M-Gov (e.g. [22, 25]). Thus, the following hypothesis is: H1: PU positively influences Saudi customers' intention to use M-Gov. *Perceived Ease of Use (PEOU)* is described as 'the degree to which a person believes that using a particular system would be free of effort' [14]. Because of the unique trait of M-Gov which necessitates a specific amount of skill and knowledge, PEOU might have a significant role in influencing the customers' behavioural intention to adopt this service [30]. Furthermore, PEOU indirectly influences BI through facilitating the influence of PU on BI [38]. Accordingly, this paper concludes: H2: PEOU positively influences Saudi consumers' BI to adopt M-Gov. H3: PEOU positively influences PU of using M-Gov. [27] defines *Perceived Risk (PR)* as 'the consumer's subjective expectation of suffering a loss in pursuit of a desired outcome.' In M-Gov, the effect of PR on BI was significant [8, 31]. Similarly, it can be assumed that: H4: PR has a negative significant impact on consumers' BI to adopt M-Gov. [29] described *Innovativeness (INN)* as 'the level to which an individual is comparatively early in using novel thoughts than other members of a social system.' [3] referred that increased levels of innovativeness led to a higher positive influence on consumers' adoption of M-Gov services. The following hypothesis can be formulated for the M-Gov context: H5: Innovativeness has a significant and positive relationship with consumers' BI to adopt M-Gov.

4   Methodology

Since the researchers presupposed as having no list of Saudi M-Gov potential adopters and because the citizens are dispersed in different areas, this research employed convenience sampling (i.e. in Jeddah, Riyadh and Dammam). Twenty-two items of the selected constructs were derived from [1, 4, 13, 15, 23, 39]. The level of responses was measured by the seven-point Likert scale.

5   Results

5.1   Response Rate

Table 1 outlines the distributed sample along with the returned responses, incomplete and problematic responses, and finally valid responses.

Table 1. Response rate

	M-Gov	%
Sample	600	100
Returned responses	418	69.67
Incomplete and problematic responses	22	3.67
Valid responses	396	66

5.2   Data Screening

Data screening was able to check whether the data was clean, reliable, useable and valid with a normal distribution before conducting further multivariate statistical analysis such as Structural Equation Modelling (SEM) [12].

Treatment of Missing Data. The amount of missing data and their distribution pattern has been examined in the data set based on [11] role, and the amount of missing data per construct was less than 0.05 and in an acceptable level. In addition, the p value of missing completely at random (MCAR) was found to be non-significant in the data set ($p = 0.483$). This indicates that the missing data over the data set is in a random manner and its values also existed non-systematically. All the missing values have been filled by the variable mean value as recommended [33].

Outliers. Based on AMOS 22.0 outcomes, Mahalanobis-D squared distance (D^2) was used to screen multivariate outliers with a p value of 0.000 over the data set as shown below in Table 2. In fact, the small amount of outliers is not problematic in the large sample size [24]. In addition to this, removing outliers may negatively reflect the generalisability of the results. Accordingly, it was decided to keep these outliers, as they could not improve the multivariate statistical results [18].

Table 2. Multivariate outliers: Mahalanobis-D squared distance (D^2)

Observation number	Mahalanobis d-squared	p1	p2
61	86.862	.000	.000
341	70.379	.000	.000
20	70.017	.000	.000
225	63.930	.000	.000
29	63.617	.000	.000
325	60.903	.000	.000
158	60.758	.000	.000
111	52.108	.000	.000
233	50.717	.000	.000

Assessment of Normality. Assessment of normality is meant to ensure that the attained data is normally distributed in a symmetrical shape. Accordingly, the univariate normality of each variable was examined by the skewness-kurtosis approach [10]. According to [36], the cut-off point of skewness and kurtosis values should be 3 and 8 respectively. As seen in Table 3 that represents AMOS 22.0 outcomes, the skewness-kurtosis approach was used over the data set, and all statistical values of this approach were found to be in an acceptable range.

Table 3. Assessment of normality

Construct		M-Gov	
	Variable	Skewness	Kurtosis
Perceived Usefulness (PU)	PU 1	−1.320	.754
	PU 2	−1.044	.085
	PU 3	−1.025	.034
	PU 4	−1.087	.132
Perceived Ease of Use (PEOU)	PEOU 1	−.729	−.271
	PEOU 2	−.687	−.370
	PEOU 3	−.733	−.401
	PEOU 4	−.969	.312
Innovativeness (INN)	INN1	−1.133	1.138
	INN2	−1.287	1.680
	INN3	−.448	−.604
	INN4	−1.038	.584
	INN5	−.861	−.590
	INN6	−.671	−.686
Perceived Risk (PR)	PR1	.077	1.221
	PR2	.635	2.939
	PR3	.274	.486
	PR4	.072	.378
	PR5	−.037	−.388
Behavioural Intention (BI)	BI1	−1.415	1.043
	BI2	−1.531	1.420
	BI3	−1.327	.787

6 Respondents' Profile and Characteristics

Table 4 below shows the demographic characteristics of respondents (i.e. Gender, Age, Education, Occupation, and Monthly Income).

Table 4. Demographic characteristics of respondents

Demographic profile	Number of respondents (N = 307)	Percentage (%)
Gender		
Male	228	57.6
Female	168	42.4
Total	396	100
Age		
>=18–20	25	6.3
21–29	40	10.1
30–39	230	58.1

(Continued)

Table 4. (*Continued*)

Demographic profile	Number of respondents (N = 307)	Percentage (%)
40–49	64	16.2
50 and above	37	9.3
Total	396	100
Education		
Less than high school	7	1.8
High school	57	14.4
Diploma	82	20.7
Bachelor	170	42.9
Postgraduate	80	20.2
Total	396	100
Occupation		
Student	35	8.8
Government employee	253	63.9
Private sector employee	63	15.9
Self employed	45	11.4
Total	396	100
Monthly income (Saudi Riyals)		
1000–4000	30	7.6
4001–8000	64	16.2
8001–14000	212	53.5
14001–20000	44	11.1
More than 20000	46	11.6
Total	396	100

7   Structural Equation Modelling (SEM)

SEM is an approach that is made from two stages. The first stage is the reliability and validity of the constructs and then the fitness of the model are examined via CFA [10]. The second stage (i.e. structural model) examined the path coefficients between the endogenous variables (i.e. PU, PEOU, PR and INN) and the exogenous construct (i.e. BI) were checked. The relationship was also tested between PEOU and PU.

7.1   Measurement Model: Confirmatory Factor Analysis (CFA)

Model Fitness. For the purpose of testing the level of unidimensionality and the model's goodness of fit, a number of fit indices were used as seen below in Table 5 [21]. All the latent constructs were measured and their own indicators (22 items). The model is fitting the data according to the fit indices. According to [9], there is a need for a few respecifications and refinements. This process is meant to improve the model fitness by looking at standardised regression weights, modification indices and

Table 5. Measurement model

Fit indices	Cut-off point	Measurement model	Modified measurement model
CMIN/DF	≤ 3.00	1.900	1.488
GFI	≥ .90	.922	.955
AGFI	≥ .80	.901	.937
NFI	≥ .90	.935	.965
CFI	≥ .90	.968	.988
RMSEA	≤ 0.08	.048	.035

standardised covariance matrix. It was observed that PR1, 3 and INN1, 5 and 6 had an unacceptable higher value based on the modification indices, and thus all of them were removed. It was also found that the standardised residual values were within the acceptable range of ±2.58 as recommended by [17]. Finally, and as suggested by [10], the CFA was tested once more to ensure the goodness of fit of the modified measurement model to see if it was sufficiently enhanced. Accordingly, no extra modifications were conducted regarding the measurement model.

Construct Reliability. Internal consistency (Cronbach's alpha), CR and AVE were employed to check the reliability of each construct after unidimenstionality of the goodness of fit of the measurement model was tested [9]. Accordingly, and as Table 6 shows, adequate values of internal consistency, CR and AVE were realised.

Table 6. Constructs' reliability

Latent constructs	Cronbach's alpha (α)	Composite reliability (CR)	Average variance extracted (AVE)
PU	.910	.909	.715
PEOU	.874	.875	.637
PR	.780	.775	.535
INN	.758	.843	.649
BI	.947	.947	.860

Construct Validity. The CFA was used to examine the constructs' validity of the conceptual model; both convergent and discriminant. [19] indicated that all items should have standardised regression weights above the cut-off value of .50. As seen in Table 7, all values were above .50. A threshold that is less than .85 has to be attained for all of the inter-correlation measurement [19]. According to the correlations table, the measurements of all of the inter-correlations attained this condition. As it can be seen in Table 8, the inter-correlation values with other similar constructs were no more than the square root of AVE given for each latent constructs [16]. Therefore, the conceptual model's estimations achieved a reliable level when it comes to the validity of convergent and discriminant.

Common Method Bias. This study considered Harman's single factor in order to check the common method bias (CMB) in the data set, and the 17 scale items [20]. All items in

Table 7. Constructs' validity

Latent constructs	Items	Factor loading
PU	PU1	.915
	PU2	.818
	PU3	.810
	PU4	.835
PEOU	PEOU1	.803
	PEOU2	.759
	PEOU3	.814
	PEOU4	.813
PR	PR2	.661
	PR4	.774
	PR5	.755
INN	INN2	.860
	INN3	.599
	INN4	.921
BI	BI1	.931
	BI2	.945
	BI3	.901

Table 8. Discriminant validity

Latent constructs	PU	PEOU	PR	INN	BI
PU	**.846**				
PEOU	.710	**.798**			
PR	−.317	−.363	**.732**		
INN	.563	.515	−.449	**.805**	
BI	.618	.578	−.447	.578	**.927**

Table 9 were inspected by using an unrotated factor solution after loading the items into the EFA. According to [28], the first factor was able to account for less than the cut-off value of 50 % as shown in the statistical results (44.864 % of variance); otherwise, no factor was able to develop. Thus, the data set is perceived to be reliable, and there are no concerns about the CMB.

Structural Model. The conceptual model was validated and the causal paths between the dependent and independent factors were tested - See Fig. 2. The structural model was examined at the second stage of the SEM. The structural model adequately fits the data based on the fit indices (see Table 10). A variance of .50 in BI and of .53 in PU was explained. The standardised estimates of the structural model are detailed below in Table 11.

Table 9. Common method bias test

Total variance explained

Component	Initial Eigenvalues			Extraction sums of squared loadings		
	Total	% of Variance	Cumulative %	Total	% of Variance	Cumulative %
1	7.627	44.864	44.864	7.627	44.864	44.864
2	1.802	10.600	55.464			
3	1.298	7.637	63.101			
4	1.200	7.058	70.158			
5	1.096	6.446	76.604			
6	.649	3.816	80.420			
7	.538	3.163	83.583			
8	.466	2.740	86.323			
9	.441	2.594	88.917			
10	.359	2.111	91.028			
11	.314	1.849	92.877			
12	.308	1.810	94.687			
13	.240	1.412	96.099			
14	.211	1.242	97.340			
15	.180	1.060	98.400			
16	.164	.962	99.363			
17	.108	.637	100.000			

Extraction Method: Principal Component Analysis

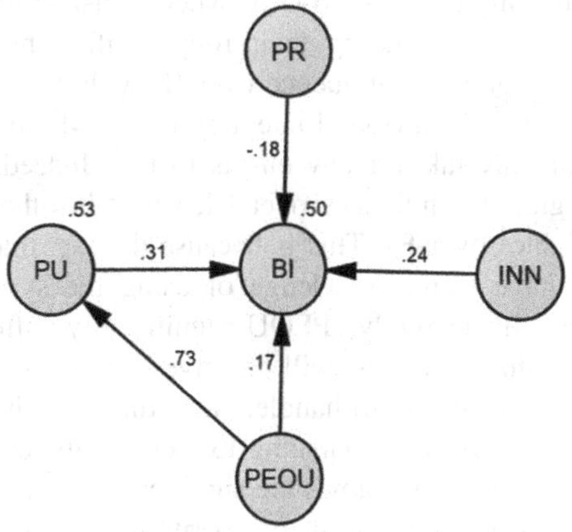

Fig. 2. Validation of the conceptual model

Table 10. Structural model

Fit indices	Cut-off point	Structural model
CMIN/DF	≤ 3.00	1.714
GFI	$\geq .90$	.948
AGFI	$\geq .80$	.928
NFI	$\geq .90$	.958
CFI	$\geq .90$	.982
RMSEA	≤ 0.08	.043

Table 11. Standardised estimates of the structural model

Path	Standardised estimate	Critical ratio	P-value	Significance
PU→BI	.308	4.500	***	Significant
PEOU→BI	.173	2.418	.016	Significant
PR→BI	−.184	−3.306	***	Significant
INN→BI	.243	4.334	***	Significant
PEOU→PU	.729	13.090	***	Significant

8   Discussion

The statistical findings affirmed the predictive power of the adopted conceptual model in interpreting suitable variances explained on the dependent factors (i.e. PU and BI) - see Fig. 2. In detail, the statistical findings strongly affirmed that PU is a main factor anticipating of BI with ($\gamma = .31$). This means that Saudi customers tend to have a stronger behavioural intention to use M-Gov when considering this technology as productive, useful and effective during their routine life. The empirical outcomes asserted that PEOU has significant influence over BI with 17 %. As such, the Saudi customers will have a higher behavioural intention to use M-Gov when they perceive the service is easy and only takes a few efforts to use. Indeed, it can be seen that although PEOU has significant influence over BI; yet, it has the least effect amongst other independent variables over BI. This is because the fact that conducting M-Gov requires customers to have some knowledge of using the system which might be difficult in some cases. Interestingly, PEOU significantly influences the PU with ($\gamma = .73$). This indicates that customers will perceive M-Gov as a useful service when considering that this service is easy to handle. Accordingly, it is considerably importance to assert the role of INN when pursuing to increase the customers' behavioural intention to use M-Gov. This study shows the significance of this path ($\gamma = .24$). This can be explained by the idea that economic prosperity in the Kingdom of Saudi Arabia allows the consumers to experience new technologies and novel products or services such as M-Gov. This study measured the negative importance effect of PR over BI in M-Gov ($\gamma = -.18$). Thus, this paper suggests that PR is recognised by Saudi customers as a significant aspect in shaping their behavioural intention to accept or discard the M-Gov in terms of social, financial, performance, and psychological risks [26].

8.1   Contribution

The achievement of this research is estimated to add to the context of M-Gov and to Saudi Arabia's initiatives in developing M-Gov applications as well as citizens' behavioural intention towards using this new promised service. Furthermore, this study theoretically adds to the literature by extending TAM to include two powerful factors to enhance the citizens' intention to shape an actual behaviour.

9   Conclusion

This study measured the influence of PU, PEOU, INN and PR on BI to use M-Gov within the Saudi Arabian context. The findings indicated that the aforementioned independent factors positively influenced BI; also, PEOU significantly influences PU.

9.1   Limitations and Future Research Directions

This study only examines M-Gov which, in turn, adversely reflects on the outcomes' generalisability to other types of mobile services. Future research should consider other contexts and technologies such as the Mobile Internet. As this study considers investigating behavioural intention instead of actual use of M-Gov in Saudi Arabia, future research should provide a complete view about the actual usage in addition to new effective factors to provide a more comprehensive model.

References

1. Agarwal, R., Prasad, J.: A conceptual and operational definition of personal innovativeness in the domain of information technology. Inf. Syst. Res. **9**(2), 204–215 (1998)
2. Ahmad, T., Ansari, A.A., Akhtar, A., Parveen, S.: Current review of ICT and m-government services in Saudi Arabia. Int. J. Comput. Eng. Appl. **7**(2) (2014)
3. Al-Busaidi, H.A.S.: A model of intention to use m-gov services. (Doctoral dissertation, Victoria University) (2012)
4. Aldás-Manzano, J., Ruiz-Mafé, C., Sanz-Blas, S.: Exploring individual personality factors as drivers of m-shopping acceptance. Ind. Manag. Data Syst. **109**(6), 739–757 (2009)
5. Al-Khalifa, H.S.: Development of m-gov websites: a functional design approach. In: Proceedings of the 13th International Conference on Information Integration and Web-based Applications and Services, pp. 455–458. ACM (2011)
6. Aloudat, A., Michael, K., Chen, X., Al-Debei, M.M.: Social acceptance of location-based m-gov services for emergency management. Telemat. Inform. **31**(1), 153–171 (2014)
7. Alsenaidy, A., Ahmad, T.: A review of current state m-gov in Saudi Arabia. Department of Biochemistry, King Saud University (2012)
8. Althunibat, A., Zain, N.A.M., Ashaari, N.S.: Modelling the factors that influence m-gov services acceptance. Afr. J. Bus. Manag. **5**(34), 13030–13043 (2011)
9. Anderson, J.C., Gerbing, D.W.: Structural equation modelling in practice: a review and recommended two-step approach. Psychol. Bull. **103**(3), 411–423 (1988)

10. Byrne, B.M.: Structural Equation Modeling with AMOS: Basic Concepts, Applications and Programming, 6th edn. Taylor and Francis Group, New York (2010)
11. Churchill, G.A.: Marketing Research Methodological Foundation, 6th edn. The Dryden Press, Orlando (1995)
12. Coakes, S.J.: SPSS: Analysis Without Anguish: Version 14.0 for Windows. Wiley, Milton (2006)
13. Davis, F.D.: Perceived usefulness, perceived ease of use, and user acceptance of information technology. MIS Q. **13**, 319–340 (1989)
14. Davis, F.D., Bagozzi, R.P., Warshaw, P.R.: User acceptance of computer technology: a comparison of two theoretical models. Manag. Sci. **35**(8), 982–1003 (1989)
15. Featherman, M.S., Pavlou, P.A.: Predicting e-services adoption: a perceived risk facets perspective. Int. J. Hum. Comput. Stud. **59**(4), 451–474 (2003)
16. Fornell, C., Larcker, D.F.: Evaluating structural equation models with unobservable variables and measurement error. J. Mark. Res. **18**(1), 39–50 (1981)
17. Hair Jr., J.F., Anderson, R.E., Tatham, R.L., Black, W.C.: Multivariate Data Analysis with Readings. Prentice-Hall, Englewood Cliffs (1995)
18. Hair Jr., J.F., Black, W., Babin, B., Anderson, R.E., Tatham, R.: Multivariate Data Analysis, 6th edn. Prentice Hall, New Jersey (2006)
19. Hair Jr., J.F., Black, W.C., Babin, B.J., Anderson, R.E.: Multivariate Data Analysis: A Global Perspective, 7th edn. Pearson Education International, London (2010)
20. Harman, H.H.: Modern Factor Analysis, 3rd edn. University of Chicago Press, Chicago (1976)
21. Hooper, D., Coughlan, J., Mullen, M.R.: Structural equation modelling: guidelines for determining model fit. Electron. J. Bus. Res. Methods **6**(1), 53–60 (2008)
22. Hung, S.Y., Chang, C.M., Kuo, S.R.: User acceptance of mobile e-government services: an empirical study. Gov. Inf. Q. **30**(1), 33–44 (2013)
23. Karaiskos, D.C., Kourouthanassis, P., Lantzouni, P., Giaglis, G.M., Georgiadis, C.K.: Understanding the adoption of mobile data services: differences among mobile portal and mobile internet users. In: 8th International Conference on Mobile Business, ICMB 2009, pp. 12–17. IEEE (2009)
24. Kline, R.B.: Principles and Practice of Structural Equation Modelling. The Guilford Press, New York (1998)
25. Lu, J., Liu, C., Yu, C.S., Wang, K.: Determinants of accepting wireless mobile data services in China. Inf. Manag. **45**(1), 52–64 (2008)
26. Nunnally, J.C.: Psychometric Theory. McGraw-Hill, New York (1978)
27. Pavlou, P.A.: Integrating trust in electronic commerce with the technology acceptance model: model development and validation. In: De Gross, J. (ed.) Proceedings of the Seventh Americas Conference in Information Systems, pp. 816–822. ACM, New York (2001)
28. Podsakoff, P.M., MacKenzie, S.B., Lee, J.Y., Podsakoff, N.P.: Common method biases in behavioral research: a critical review of the literature and recommended remedies. J. Appl. Psychol. **88**(5), 879 (2003)
29. Rogers, E.M., Medina, U.E., Rivera, M.A., Wiley, C.J.: Complex adaptive systems and the diffusion of innovations. Innov. J.: Public Sect. Innov. J. **10**(3), 1–26 (2005)
30. Shareef, M.A., Archer, N., Dwivedi, Y.K.: Examining adoption behavior of mobile government. J. Comput. Inf. Syst. **53**(2), 39–49 (2012)
31. Susanto, T.D., Goodwin, R.: Factors influencing citizen adoption of SMS-based e-government services. Electron. J. e-Gov. **8**(1), 55–71 (2010)
32. Susanto, T.D., Goodwin, R.: User acceptance of SMS-based e-government services: differences between adopters and non-adopters. Gov. Inf. Q. **30**, 486–497 (2013)

33. Tabachnick, B.G., Fidell, L.S.: Using Multivariate Statistics. Pearson Education, Boston (2007)
34. Venkatesh, V., Morris, M.G., Davis, G.B., Davis, F.D.: User acceptance of information technology: toward a unified view. MIS Q. **27**, 425–478 (2003)
35. Wang, C.: Antecedents and consequences of perceived value in mobile government continuance use: an empirical research in China. Comput. Hum. Behav. **34**, 140–147 (2014)
36. West, S.G., Finch, J.F., Curran, P.J.: Structural equation models with non-normal variables: problems and remedies. In: Hoyle, R.H. (ed.) Structural Equation Modelling: Concepts, Issues, and Applications, pp. 56–75. Sage, Thousand Oaks (1995)
37. Yfantis, V., Vassilopoulou, K., Pateli, A., Usoro, A.: The influential factors of m-government's adoption in the developing countries. In: Daniel, F., Papadopoulos, G.A., Thiran, P. (eds.) MobiWIS 2013. LNCS, vol. 8093, pp. 157–171. Springer, Heidelberg (2013)
38. Zarmpou, T., Saprikis, V., Markos, A., Vlachopoulou, M.: Modeling users' acceptance of mobile services. Electron. Commer. Res. **12**(2), 225–248 (2012)
39. Zhou, T.: Understanding users' initial trust in mobile banking: an elaboration likelihood perspective. Comput. Hum. Behav. **28**(4), 1518–1525 (2012)

Understanding the Adoption
of Smart Wearable Devices to Assist
Healthcare in China

Shang Gao[1(✉)], Xuemei Zhang[2], and Shunqin Peng[2]

[1] School of Business, Örebro University, Örebro, Sweden
shang.gao@oru.se
[2] School of Business Administration,
Zhongnan University of Economics and Law, Wuhan, China
xuemo123@foxmail.com, shunqinpeng@outlook.com

Abstract. With the development and advancement of information communication technology, smart wearable devices are playing a more and more important role in peoples' daily lives. This study aims to investigate the adoption of smart wearable devices to assist healthcare in China. Based on the previous technology diffusion theories (e.g., TAM, IDT), a research model with ten research hypotheses was proposed in this research. The research model was empirically tested with a sample of 180 users of smart wearable devices in China. The results indicated that seven of the ten research hypotheses were significantly supported. The most significant determinant for users' attitude towards smart wearable devices was trust. However, personal characteristics did not have a significant positive impact on both users' attitude and behavior intention to use smart wearable devices.

Keywords: Adoption · TAM · Trust · Smart wearable devices

1 Introduction

Building smart cities has been a popular topic in China recently. Smart cities can be explained as those cities that utilize information and communication technologies with the aim to increase the life quality of their inhabitants while providing sustainable development [4]. Consequently, the cities are able to become more intelligent in their management of resources.

With peoples' increasing demand for high quality of life, healthcare has been an essential issue in peoples' daily lives. For example, people who go to large hospitals usually need to wait for a long time to see a doctor and pay high medical costs. Having treatments in the medical community is an alternative for patients. It can save patients' waiting time. Furthermore, primary healthcare services have low operating costs and can save a lot of expenses for patients in taking treatments and buying drugs.

With the development and advancement of information communication technology, smart wearable devices (SWD) with variety of sensors are playing a more and more important role in peoples' daily lives. Smart wearable technologies can

© IFIP International Federation for Information Processing 2016
Published by Springer International Publishing Switzerland 2016. All Rights Reserved
Y.K. Dwivedi et al. (Eds.): I3E 2016, LNCS 9844, pp. 280–291, 2016.
DOI: 10.1007/978-3-319-45234-0_26

sometimes enable people to live in their own homes and monitor their own wellbeing rather than being hospitalized or institutionalized [28]. Smart wearable technologies can help patients manage their wellbeing by examining the relevant indexes. Taking the advantage of SWD, the medical community is able to make it more convenient for people to get medical treatments, optimize the allocation of resources and form a rational advanced medical system.

User preferences for the use of SWD in their daily lives need to be studied before actual use of these devices becomes a common practice. To our knowledge, there is a lack of literature that explores the perceptions of peoples' attitude towards SWD to assist healthcare in China. The objective of this paper is to study the adoption of SWD to assist healthcare in China. The major constructs from technology diffusion theories (e.g., TAM [7] and IDT [32]) are chosen to form a research model to examine the potential factors that affect users' adoption of SWD in China.

The remainder of this paper is organized as follows: the literature review is provided in Sect. 2. Section 3 proposes the research model and research hypotheses. This is followed by the illustration of the research method and the research findings in Sect. 4. The discussion of the findings is presented in Sect. 5. In Sect. 6, we conclude this research and point out future research directions.

2 Literature Review

2.1 Smart Wearable Devices

Wearable technology and wearable devices are phrases that describe electronics and computers that are integrated into clothing and other accessories that can be worn comfortably on the body [36]. While these devices carry out many of the same tasks as handheld technologies such as mobile phones and laptop computers, they can actually surpass them in performance due to sensory and scanning features such as biofeedback and tracking of physiological function. Examples of wearable devices include watches, glasses, contact lenses, e-textiles and smart fabrics, headbands, beanies and caps, jewelry such as rings, bracelets, and hearing aid-like devices that are designed to look like earrings [36]. The major providers of SWD in China include: Baidu, iGeak, SmartQ, BabyTree, Tenghai Shiyang, Qihoo360, Hoolai Games.

SWD have the potential to monitor and respond to both the patient and the patient's environment. For monitoring patients' wellbeing, an SWD may include a wide range of wearable or implantable devices, including sensors, actuators, smart fabrics, power supplies, wireless communication networks (WCNs), processing units, multimedia devices [6].

2.2 Technology Diffusion Theory

An important and long-standing research question in information systems research is how we can accurately explain user adoption of information systems [8]. Several models have been developed to test the users' attitude and intention to adopt new technologies or information systems. These models include the Technology

Acceptance Model (TAM) [7], Theory of Planned Behavior (TPB) [1], Innovation Diffusion Theory (IDT) [32], Unified Theory of Acceptance and Use of Technology (UTAUT) [29]. Among the different models that have been proposed, TAM, which is the extension of the Theory of Reasoned Action (TRA) [11], appears to be the most widely accepted model. TAM focus on the perceived usefulness (PU) and perceived ease of use (PEOU) of a system and has been tested in some domains of E-business and proved to be quite reliable to predict user acceptance of some new information technologies, such as electronic commerce [30], and online shopping [19].

However, TAM's limitations relative to extensibility and explanation power have been noted [5]. Many researchers have suggested that TAM needs to be extended with additional variables to provide a stronger model [12, 15, 24]. Some researchers have also indicated that the major constructs of TAM cannot fully reflect the specific influences of technological and usage-context factors that may alter users' acceptance [29]. Therefore, PU and PEOU may not fully explain people's intention to adopt mobile services. We believe that TAM has limitations when investigating users' adoption of mobile services, which is also confirmed by prior research work in [17, 37]. Moreover, although UTAUT unifies more factors and consolidates the functions of the technology acceptance model with the constructs of eight prominent models in IS adoption research, this increases the complexity, so that it is more complicated to test its applicability.

There are only few studies addressing the adoption of smart wearable devices. For example, Kim and Shin [22] developed an extended technology acceptance model to examine the adoption of smart watches in South Korea. The results indicated that affective quality and relative advantage of smart watches were found to be associated with perceived usefulness, while the sense of mobility and availability induced by smart watches led to a greater perceived ease of the technology's use. Furthermore, Gao et al. [18] examined the factors associated with consumers' intention to adopt wearable technology in healthcare.

To our knowledge, there is a lack of empirical studies which address the adoption of smart wearable devices to assist healthcare in China. This explorative study aims to begin to fill this knowledge gap. All the findings above motivate the development of a research model, which is described in next section.

3   Research Model and Hypotheses

3.1   Research Model

A research model that identifies important factors as significant antecedents of users' intention to use SWD was developed. The proposed acceptance model is an extension of TAM. In addition to the constructs from TAM, the model includes Trust, Perceived Risks, Personal Characteristics, Compatibility as other factors to study users' adoption of SWD. Table 1 summarizes the definition of the constructs in the research model (see Fig. 1).

Table 1. The definitions of the constructs

Construct	Definition	Reference
Perceived usefulness	The degree to which a person believes that using a particular system would enhance his or her task	[7]
Perceived ease of use	The extent to which a person believes that using a particular system would be free of effort	[7]
Compatibility	The extent to which a potential customer's value, self-demand, precious experiment are matching with a particular system	[32]
Attitude	The possibility of a user to accept a particular system	[7]
Behavior intention	The user's desire to accept a particular system	[7]
Personal characteristics	The extent to which user's gender, sex, age, education background and occupation that affect the acceptance to a particular system	[14]
Trust	The extent to which a person believes that using a particular system would be safe and high quality	[20]
Perceived risks	The risks to which a person believes that using a particular system	[10]

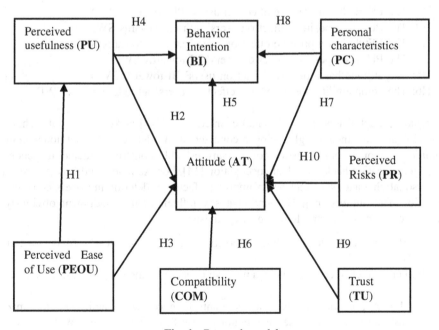

Fig. 1. Research model

3.2 Research Hypotheses

Previous studies have found the positive relationship between perceived ease of use and users' attitude in the IS context (e.g., [13]). In the original TAM model, Davis proposed that perceived ease of use (PEOU) affects perceived usefulness (PU). There are extensive empirical evidences that perceived ease of use positively influences perceived usefulness (e.g., [13, 25]). For example, Van der Heijden [33] found that this relationship holds true for website usage in an Internet environment. Furthermore, Perceived usefulness was found to have a strong effect on technology adoption (e.g., including adoption of WWW [21], and wireless internet [26]). The empirical findings in these studies demonstrated the importance of perceived usefulness on behavior intention (BI) to use the technologies. Rogers [32] indicated that innovation that are perceived by individuals as having greater relative advantage, compatibility, trialability, and observability, and less complexity will be adopted more rapidly than other innovation. To further understand users' attitude towards SWD, one factor from IDT was also included into our research model. Compatibility can be seen as users' belief in the consistency of using SWD with the way they live. Previous research also demonstrated that the importance of Compatibility to the adoption of new technologies (e.g., e-banking [23]). Furthermore, Gao et al. [16] also confirmed that compatibility was one of the important determinants to influence older adults adoption of smartphones in China. Therefore, the following hypotheses were proposed.

H1: The PEOU has a positive effect on users' PU towards SWD.
H2: The PU has a positive effect on users' attitude towards SWD.
H3: The PEOU has a positive effect on users' attitude towards SWD.
H4: The PU has a positive effect on users' BI towards SWD.
H5: The attitude has a positive effect on users' BI towards SWD.
H6: The compatibility has a positive effect on users' attitude towards SWD.

Personal Characteristics (PC). Personal characteristics [14] as key factors of technology diffusion are increasingly being recognized in academic and practitioner communities. Personal characteristics cover many possible constructs, including gender, sex, age, education background and occupation [14]. For example, gender as one aspect of personal characteristics can be an important factor in determining one's consumer behavior. The authors in [34] found that sex influences final judgment obviously. Therefore, we proposed the following hypothesis:

H7: Personal characteristics have a positive effect on the users' attitude towards SWD.
H8: Personal characteristics have a positive effect on to the users' BI towards SWD.

Trust (TU). A potential adopter usually wants to maximize benefits and minimize risks. Trust can help reduce the uncertainties a use faces when using SWD. Previous research has found that trust is one of the important factors to the adoption of online information services (e.g., [20]). In [20], the authors extended TAM with trust in the service provider to study user acceptance of online shopping. They found that trust-related issues have a considerable effect on user acceptance of online shopping.

In [13], the authors found that trust has a positively direct effect on the intention to use mobile information systems in Norway. To better explain the importance of trust to users' attitude towards SWD, we propose the following hypothesis:

H9: Trust has a positive effect on users' attitude towards SWD.

Perceived Risks (PR). Perceived risk is considered as felt uncertainty regarding possible negative consequences of using a product or service. Featherman and Pavlou [10] define perceived risk as the potential for loss in the pursuit of a desired outcome of using an e-service. People are often anxious about the diverse types of risks presented when engaging in activities or functions involved in a new technology. Liebermann and Paroush [25] proved that adoption rates of newly offered goods depend crucially on the marketer's ability to mitigate perceived risk involved with new goods offered. Thus, a user of SWD may be deterred from increasing usage due to perceived risk of the new technology. Previous research suggests that perceived risk is an important construct to affect users' attitude towards new technologies (e.g., [9]). For example, Donthu and Garcia [9] found that Internet shoppers are less risk averse than Internet non-shoppers are. Wu and Wang [37] found the positive influence of perceived risk on behavioral intention to use mobile commerce. The implicit uncertainties involved in using SWD have rendered risks as inevitable elements. Therefore, we proposed the following hypothesis:

H10: The perceived risks have a negative effect on users' attitude towards SWD.

4 An Empirical Study

In this empirical test, our research model was examined through the use of SWD in China.

4.1 Instrument Development

The validated instrument measures from previous research were used as the foundation to create the instrument for this study. Previous studies were reviewed to ensure that a comprehensive list of measures were included. In order to ensure that the instrument better fit this empirical study, some minor words changes were made to ensure easy interpretation and comprehension of the questions. All the items were adopted from prior studies ([7, 10, 14, 20, 32, 35]) and modified to fit the domain of using SWD. A questionnaire was developed first in English and then translated into Chinese. Back-translation was conducted by bilingual third parties to improve the translation accuracy. As a result, 26 measurement items[1] were included in the questionnaires. In addition, a seven-point Likert scale, with 1 being the negative end of the scale (strongly disagree) and 7 being the positive end of the scale (strongly agree), was used to examine participants' responses to all items in the survey.

---

[1] The measurement items are available at this link: http://tinyurl.com/jtclbxy.

4.2 Samples

The data for this study was collected through paper-based questionnaires from 20th Dec to 30th Dec 2015 in the residential area in the biggest city in the central China. People were asked to participate in the survey voluntarily. Firstly, we explained who we were, what they were supposed to do during our survey, and the purpose of the survey. The participants were also informed that the results would be reported only in aggregate and their anonymity would be assured. After participants experienced the SWD, they were asked to complete the questionnaires and submitted them to us. 180 completed questionnaires were collected, among which 145 of them were valid questionnaires (i.e., valid respondent rate 80.6 %). Among the participants, 67 of the participants were male, and 78 were female. In terms of age, 68 participants were 25 years old and under 25 years old, while 77 participants were over 25 years old.

4.3 Measurement Model

The quality of the measurement model is determined by (1). Content validity, (2). Construct reliability and (3). Discriminant validity [2]. To ensure the content validity of our constructs, a pre-test of the questionnaire with 3 researchers in the field of information systems was conducted in Oct 2015. And we found that the questionnaire was well understood by all the researchers.

To further test the reliability and validity of each construct in the research model, the Internal Consistency of Reliability (ICR) of each construct was tested with Cronbach's Alpha coefficient. As a result, the Cronbach's Alpha values range from 0.615 to 0.977. Robinson et al. [31] indicated that a reliability coefficient of 0.6 was marked as a lowest acceptable limit for Cronbach's Alpha for exploratory research. All the constructs in the research model were above 0.6. Consequently, the scales were deemed acceptable to continue.

Convergent validity was assessed through composite reliability (CR) and the average variance extracted (AVE). Bagozzi and Yi [3] proposed the following three measurement criteria: factor loadings for all items should exceed 0.5, the CR should exceed 0.7, and the AVE of each construct should exceed 0.5. As shown in Table 2, all constructs were in acceptable ranges.

The measurements of discriminant validity were presented in Table 3. According to the results, the variances extracted by the constructs were more than the squared correlations among variables. The fact revealed that constructs were empirically distinct. As good results for convergent validity and discriminant validity were achieved, the test result of the measurement model was good.

4.4 Structural Model and Hypotheses Testing

The structural model was tested using SmartPLS. Table 4 presents the path coefficients, which are standardized regression coefficients. Seven (H1, H2, H3, H4, H5, H6, H9) of the ten research hypotheses were significantly supported. According to the results, perceived ease of use, perceived usefulness, trust and compatibility were found to have

Table 2. Means, Factor loadings, Composite reliability, and AVE for each item

Construct	Item	Factor loading	Composite reliability	AVE	Cronbach's Alpha
Perceived usefulness	PU1	0.858	0.893	0.677	0.937
	PU2	0.836			
	PU3	0.800			
	PU4	0.795			
Perceived ease of use	PEOU1	0.814	0.867	0.684	0.977
	PEOU2	0.845			
	PEOU3	0.822			
Compatibility	COM1	0.844	0.879	0.708	0.810
	COM2	0.818			
	COM3	0.861			
Personal characteristics	PC1	0.591	0.839	0.656	0.836
	PC2	0.922			
	PC3	0.521			
	PC4	0.561			
Perceived risks	PR1	0.931	0.802	0.588	0.615
	PR2	0.808			
	PR3	0.595			
Trust	TU1	0.700	0.878	0.592	0.782
	TU2	0.804			
	TU3	0.689			
	TU4	0.838			
	TU5	0.804			
Attitude	PR1	0.940	0.935	0.878	0.861
	PR2	0.933			
Behavior intention	BI1	0.919	0.901	0.820	0.854
	BI2	0.892			

Table 3. Discriminant validity

Variables	AT	BI	COM	PC	PEOU	PR	PU	TU
AT	0.9							
BI	0.7	0.9						
COM	0.6	0.5	0.8					
PC	−0.1	−0.2	−0.1	0.5				
PEOU	0.5	0.5	0.7	−0.1	0.8			
PR	0.1	−0.0	0.1	0.1	0.2	0.8		
PU	0.5	0.5	0.7	−0.1	0.7	0.1	0.8	
TU	0.6	0.5	0.6	−0.0	0.6	−0.0	0.6	0.8

Note: Diagonals represent the average variance extracted, while the other matrix entries represent the squared correlations.

Table 4. Test of hypotheses based on path coefficient

Hypothesis	Path coefficient	Hypothesis result
H1: PEOU to PU	0.693[a]	Supported
H2: PU to AT	0.343[a]	Supported
H3: PEOU to AT	0.327[a]	Supported
H4: PU to BI	0.233[b]	Supported
H5: AT to BI	0.549[b]	Supported
H6: COM to AT	0.368[b]	Supported
H7: PC to AT	−0.093	Not Supported
H8: PC to BI	−0.109	Not Supported
H9: TU to AT	0.4[b]	Supported
H10: PR to AT	0.052	Not Supported

[a]$p < 0.05$; [b]$p < 0.01$; [c]$p < 0.001$.

a statistically significant effect on users' attitude towards SWD, while perceived risk and personal characteristics did not have significant impact on users' behavior of using SWD.

The R^2 (R square) denotes to coefficient of determination. It provides a measure of how well future outcomes are likely to be predicted by the model, the amount of variability of a given construct. In our analysis, the R^2 coefficient of determination is a statistical measure of how well the regression coefficients approximate the real data point. According to the result, the amount of variance in Behavior Intention was 0.466, which means the explained variance of Perceived Usefulness factor is 46.6 %. Similarly, the percentage of variance explained for attitude is 50.6 %. The percentage of variance explained for PU is 48 %.

5   Discussion

The findings of this empirical study provided some insights on the adoption of SWD to assist healthcare to both researchers and practitioners in China. On the one hand, from an academic perspective, this study contributed to the literature on the adoption of SWD by identifying and validating the potential factors affecting the adoption of SWD by identifying and validating the potential factors affecting the findings demonstrated the appropriateness of the research model and hypotheses for measuring the adoption of SWD. On the other hand, from a business perspective, the statistical results of the research model also provided some insights for practitioners to offer better SWD with a high user acceptance in China.

According to the results, we found that 7 research hypotheses were supported. PU (0.343), PEOU (0.327), compatibility (0.368), Trust (0.433) explain 50.6 % of the observed variance in users' attitudes toward SWD. Both PU and PEOU have significant positive impacts on users' attitude towards SWD. This is consistent with the findings from previous study (e.g., [22]).

This study also has some practical implications. The results of this empirical test also provided guidelines and suggestions to services providers. The influence of trust on users' attitudes towards SWD was the most significant which is followed by compatibility, PU and PEOU. Thus, when considering the customers' attitude towards SWD, the companies should pay more attention the trust construct. The devices should be able to provide precious measurements and send some essential health-related messages timely. Users also expected that the primary care units are able to provide services to patients by taking advantage of SWD. Furthermore, it is essential to make sure that it is easy to use SWD.

To better understand the findings of this study, an interview with a doctor from local primary care unit was carried out in February 2016. The interviewee indicated that the primary care in China was far away from what it is like in developed countries (e.g., Sweden and Canada). While they have a proper system to care about every citizen, we are in desperate need more investments on infrastructure construction. Primary care services (e.g., home care) were provided in theory. However, it hasn't been applied to the real setting in most residential areas. Most doctors and nurses have too many patients in their units. Therefore, they did not get time to visit patients' homes. The interviewee also indicated that collecting citizens' daily health data like heartbeats and heart rate do help doctors a lot when making a definite diagnosis in the long term. However, this requires nearly all citizens to use SWD in appropriate ways. In addition to this, a sound database must be constructed to collect and analyze all those information that come from the patients. Otherwise, the collected data will become a string of numbers, which is meaningless to the doctors. They are often too busy to find out the meanings behind the numbers. Lastly, he indicated that another essential precondition for the widespread of SWD to assist healthcare in China: the support from the government. Therefore, it is believed the government plays an important role in the success of the promotion of using SWD to assist healthcare in China.

However, we were also aware of some limitations. Firstly, we only tested the research model and research hypotheses with samples from one of the big cities in China. This sample might not be fully representative of the entire population in China. Secondly, all the data were collected using self-reported scales in the research. This may lead to some caution because common method variance may account for some of the results. This has been cited as one of the stronger criticisms of tests of theories with TAM and TAM-extended research [27]. However, our data analysis with convergent and discriminant validity does not support the presence of a strong common methods bias.

6   Conclusion and Future Research

This research was designed to explore users' adoption of SWD to assist healthcare in China. A research model with ten research hypotheses was proposed. The results indicated that seven of the ten research hypotheses were significantly supported. And the most significant determinant for users' attitude towards SWD was trust. However, personal characteristics did not have a significant positive impact on both users' attitude and behavior intention to use SWD.

Continuing with this stream of research, we plan to examine some additional constructs' influence on the adoption of SWD. Future research is also needed to empirically verify the research model with larger samples across China.

References

1. Ajzen, I.: The theory of planned behavior. Organ. Behav. Hum. Decis. Process. **50**(2), 179–211 (1991)
2. Bagozzi, R.P.: The role of measurement in theory construction and hypothesis testing: toward a holistic model. In: Ferrell, O.C., Brown, S.W., Lamb, C.W. (eds.) Conceptual and Theoretical Developments in Marketing, pp. 15–32 (1979)
3. Bagozzi, R.P., Yi, Y.: Specification, evaluation, and interpretation of structural equation models. J. Acad. Mark. Sci. **40**(1), 8–34 (2012)
4. Bakıcı, T., Almirall, E., Wareham, J.: A smart city initiative: the case of Barcelona. J. Knowl. Econ. **4**(2), 135–148 (2013)
5. Benbasat, I., Barki, H.: Quo vadis TAM. J. Assoc. Inf. Syst. **8**(4), 211–218 (2007)
6. Chan, M., Estève, D., Fourniols, J.-Y., et al.: Smart wearable systems: current status and future challenges. Artif. Intell. Med. **56**(3), 137–156 (2012)
7. Davis, F.D.: Perceived usefulness, perceived ease of use and user acceptance of information technology. MIS Q. **13**(3), 319–340 (1989)
8. DeLone, W.H., McLean, E.R.: Information systems success: the quest for the dependent variable. Inf. Syst. Res. **3**(1), 60–95 (1992)
9. Donthu, N., Garcia, A.: The internet shopper. J. Advertising Res. **39**(3), 52 (1999)
10. Featherman, M.S., Pavlou, P.A.: Predicting e-services adoption: a perceived risk facets perspective. Int. J. Hum. Comput. Stud. **59**(4), 451–474 (2003)
11. Fishbein, M., Ajzen, I.: Belief, Attitude, Intention and Behavior: An Introduction to Theory and Research. Addison-Wesley, Boston (1975)
12. Gao, S., Krogstie, J., Chen, Z., et al.: Lifestyles and mobile services adoption in China. Int. J. E-Bus. Res. (IJEBR) **10**(3), 36–53 (2014)
13. Gao, S., Krogstie, J., Siau, K.: Adoption of mobile information services: an empirical study. Mob. Inf. Syst. **10**(2), 147–171 (2014)
14. Gao, S., Krogstie, J., Siau, K.: Developing an instrument to measure the adoption of mobile services. Mob. Inf. Syst. **7**(1), 45–67 (2011)
15. Gao, S., Krogstie, J., Zang, Z.: The effect of flow experience and social norms on the adoption of mobile games in China. Int. J. Mob. Hum. Comput. Interact. (IJMHCI) **8**(1), 83–102 (2016)
16. Gao, S., Yang, Y., Krogstie, J.: The adoption of smartphones among older adults in China. In: Liu, K., Nakata, K., Li, W., Galarreta, D. (eds.) ICISO 2015. IFIP AICT, vol. 449, pp. 112–122. Springer, Heidelberg (2015)
17. Gao, S., Zang, Z.: An empirical examination of users' adoption of mobile advertising in China. Inf. Dev. **32**(2), 203–215 (2016)
18. Gao, Y., Li, H., Luo, Y.: An empirical study of wearable technology acceptance in healthcare. Ind. Manag. Data Syst. **115**(9), 1704–1723 (2015)
19. Gefen, D.: TAM or just plain habit: a look at experienced. online shoppers. J. End User Comput. **15**(3), 1–13 (2003)
20. Gefen, D., Karahanna, E., Straub, D.W.: Trust and TAM in online shopping: an integrated model. MIS Q. **27**(1), 51–90 (2003)

21. Johnson, R.A., Hignite, M.A.: Applying the technology acceptance model to the WWW. Acad. Inf. Manag. Sci. J. **3**(2), 130–142 (2000)
22. Kim, K.J., Shin, D.-H.: An acceptance model for smart watches: implications for the adoption of future wearable technology. Internet Res. **25**(4), 527–541 (2015)
23. Kolodinsky, J.M., Hogarth, J.M., Hilgert, M.A.: The adoption of electronic banking technologies by US consumers. Int. J. Bank Mark. **22**(4), 238–259 (2004)
24. Legris, P., Ingham, J., Collerette, P.: Why do people use information technology? A critical review of the technology acceptance model. Inf. Manag. **40**(3), 191–204 (2003)
25. Liebermann, Y., Paroush, J.: Economic aspects of diffusion models. J. Econ. Bus. **34**(1), 95–100 (1982)
26. Lu, J., Yu, C.-S., Liu, C., et al.: Technology acceptance model for wireless internet. Internet Res. **13**(3), 206–222 (2003)
27. Malhotra, N.K., Kim, S.S., Patil, A.: Common method variance in IS research: a comparison of alternative approaches and a reanalysis of past research. Manag. Sci. **52**(12), 1865–1883 (2006)
28. Menschner, P., Prinz, A., Koene, P., et al.: Reaching into patients' homes–participatory designed AAL services. Electron. Mark. **21**(1), 63–76 (2011)
29. Moon, J.-W., Kim, Y.-G.: Extending the TAM for a World-Wide-Web context. Inf. Manag. **38**(4), 217–230 (2001)
30. Pavlou, P.A.: Consumer acceptance of electronic commerce: integrating trust and risk with the technology acceptance model. Int. J. Electron. Commer. **7**(3), 101–134 (2003)
31. Robinson, J.P., Shaver, P.R., Wrightsman, L.S.: Criteria for Scale Selections and Evaluation. Academic Press, San Diego (1991)
32. Rogers, E.M.: The Diffusion of Innovations. Free Press, New York (1995)
33. Van der Heijden, H.: Factors influencing the usage of websites: the case of a generic portal in The Netherlands. Inf. Manag. **40**(6), 541–549 (2003)
34. Venkatesh, V., Morris, M.G., Ackerman, P.L.: A longitudinal field investigation of gender differences in individual technology adoption decision-making processes. Organ. Behav. Hum. Decis. Process. **83**(1), 33–60 (2000)
35. Venkatesh, V., Morris, M.G., Davis, G.B., et al.: User acceptance of information technology: toward a unified view. MIS Q. **27**(3), 425–478 (2003)
36. Wright, R., Keith, L.: Wearable technology: if the tech fits, wear it. J. Electron. Resour. Med. Libr. **11**(4), 204–216 (2014)
37. Wu, J.-H., Wang, S.-C.: What drives mobile commerce? An empirical evaluation of the revised technology acceptance model. Inf. Manag. **42**(5), 719–729 (2005)

Green Information System Adoption and Sustainability: A Case Study of Select Indian Banks

G.P. Sahu and Monika Singh[(✉)]

Motilal Nehru National Institute of Technology Allahabad, Allahabad, India
{gsahu, rmsl502}@mnnit.ac.in

Abstract. This paper investigates the Critical Success Factors (CSFs) for successful adoption and implementation of Green Information System (Green IS) in organizations. Extensive literature review conducted to identify the CSFs and these CSFs are validated through case studies of two Indian banks- State Banks of India (SBI) and Housing Development Finance Corporation Limited (HDFC). Nineteen CSFs are identified, namely: Leaders Obligation, Environment Changes, Industry's Vision and Strategy, Resource Allocation, Expert Selection, Communication, Conflicts Resolution, Standard Adoption, Human Resource Induction and Training, Efficient Organization Structure, Cost-Benefit Analysis, Inspection/Audits, Financial Support, Technological Advancement, Customer Demand, System Integration, Rivalry Pressure, Awareness, and Government Policies. An interrelationship among these nineteen CSFs is established and a model is developed for effective Green IS implementation. Interpretive Structural Modeling (ISM) used to develop the model with the opinion of IT Experts and academicians. Moreover, this paper explores sustainability issues of Green initiatives. This study will enrich existing literature and assists researchers and policy makers in this area.

Keywords: Green information system · Green IS adoption · Sustainability process · Green IS · CSFs · Green banking · ISM

1 Introduction

"We don't inherit the environment from our ancestors; we borrow it from our children".

Stated by a renowned ecologist David Brower [11] indicating the necessity of Green initiatives adoption and its sustainability. While information system and information technology are the sources of industry/country growth, but on the other hand it is responsible for Greenhouse Gases (GHGs) emission contributing 1.6 % share of total emission and expected to be account for 2 % by 2020 [20]. It is required to use the IT/IS resources in a power competent and cost-effective manner [18, 70], thus Green IS/IT emerged as an essential strategic tool to reduce organizations carbon footprints [12, 14, 67] resulting in conservation of natural resources and the environment. The increasing demand of green product/services, public and consumers awareness towards for environmental issues [1, 24, 53] and restricted policies over manufacturing and

Y.K. Dwivedi et al. (Eds.): I3E 2016, LNCS 9844, pp. 292–304, 2016.
DOI: 10.1007/978-3-319-45234-0_27

providing eco-friendly products/services [50] encourages public and private organizations to manage their activities' impact on the environment and to achieve good reputation with avoiding additional expenditure [66].

Banking sector, being the less pollutant industry, is observing increasing rate of GHGs emission due to the massive use of electronic equipments and appliances [65]. These issues necessitate the adoption of Green initiatives. Green IS adoption affects the reputation, quality of assets and rate of return on long term basis [56]. The social responsibilities of banks encourages them to finance the green projects and adopt the innovative Green initiatives to control their business activities [4, 5].

Green IS refers to the developing and using Information Systems to assist and enable ecological sustainability programs tends to have an indirect and positive [35]. Green IS facilitates waste and energy reuse, and routing effectively [10, 15]. Green manufacturing strategy is essential on a long term implementation basis and a five-layer model is proposed by authors for implementation and planning [39]. The identified research gap is, limited literature available on factors influencing effective and efficient adoption of Green IS and barriers of implementation that because majority of available literature is on significance of the Green IS/IT. This paper fills this gap by identifying nineteen factors and few barriers through literature review and two Indian banks.

This research paper is an attempt to identify the factors influencing the implementation of Green IS in the banking sector through extensive review of existing literature and in-depth personal interview of policy makers and IT experts of SBI and HDFC banks at Allahabad branch. The case studies these banks explored barriers in Green IS adoption. Nineteen CSFs identified and validated by these case studies. ISM model is used to determine relationship among these CSFs and to develop a model. Later, sustainability issues of Green initiatives are discussed. The entire research methodology is present in the third section. Paper is ended up with discussion and conclusion.

2 Literature Review

In the current era, when ICT is responsible for growth and development of countries by providing IT/IS services products, on the other hand it is accountable for contribution of 1.6 % GHGs emission in the environment [20]. Worldwide firms and government move towards adopting Green practices due to exponentially increasing rate of GHGs emission and increasing demands of green products and services. [1, 12, 14, 24, 53, 67]. According to Dedrick [18] and Watson [70], it is required to use the IT/IS resources in power efficient and economical manner through implementing Green IS.

Firms adapting ISO 140001 certifications or other eco-friendly practices certificate rewards in many ways such as: reductions in incurred cost, waste production and in GHGs emission increment in savings; enhanced communication; reduction in penalties; well improved corporate reputation; and improved operational processes [13, 17, 28, 38, 43, 47, 59, 72, 73]. Henningsson and Hedman [31] found that Green IS is a bottom–up practice that attracts and make expert the individuals worried about environment, to investigate the problems and resolve it. Majority of the literature found on the antecedents of Green IS [37, 46] and its role in environment sustainability [9, 14, 29, 41, 45].

Sarkar and Young [57] suggested effective cost model and awareness programmes as influencing factors for Green IT adoption. Schmidt et al. [60] found corporate administration, ecological commitment and initiatives from IT workforce as predictors of Green IS adoption. Butler [12] found that institutional essentials persuade the acceptance and implementation of Green IS initiatives. González [19] identified external factors (organization position, relations, policies) and internal factors (organizational strategy, technology and financial capacity) influencing adoption of clean technologies.

The benefits of GIS, augmented public awareness of environmental issues and regulatory instructions forced the organizations to Go Green through implementing Green IS [15]. Consequently Green IT/IS policy, design, and practice initiatives in recent times emerged into a vigorous research area in the Information System area. However, the existing literature represents a major gap of nonexistence research [14], conceptual and empirical both, that can aid organizations to build up strategy and framework to adopt and implement Green IS and practices.

3 Research Design

Extensive literature review is conducted for identification of CSFs, while IT experts and academician's opinion (via personal interview) are used to validate these driving and restraining factors of Green IS implementation. ISM methodology is used to find out the relationship among the identified nineteen CSFs and thereafter, to develop a model to aid the researcher in this area and policy makers for smooth implementation of Green initiatives. The entire research design is presented in the Fig. 1.

The research is based on the case studies of two banks: SBI, largest public bank in India and HDFC, among the top most private banks of India to examine and analyze the factors driving and restraining the implementation of Green IS in banking sector.

The first phase involves the extensive literature review and interview of 5–6 IT experts and policy makers from these two banks using structure and open ended questions in order to gain deep information about process and significance of Green IS implementation. Second phase includes synthesizing the case study to identify the CSFs and barriers of Green IS adoption and to validate them. ISM model is a tool to structure the various directly-indirectly interrelated elements into a complete systematic structure [3, 56, 64]. According to Gupta and Sahu [27] this is the best technique to

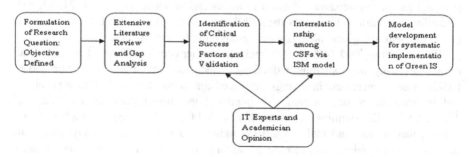

Fig. 1. Research process of the study

examine the interdependency among the CSFs. Therefore, ISM model is used and a model is developed to draw the interrelationship among these nineteen CSFs.

3.1 Case Study 1: State Bank of India

The first largest and oldest bank of India, SBI, is on the 46th position all over world ranking with brand value of $6.56 for FY 2014–15. According to Annual Report-2015 of SBI, this bank is practicing accountable banking to reduce its carbon footprints and to improve eco-sustainability through introducing Green initiatives and adopting the electronic mode of operations. SBI has been providing Green Channel Counters (GCC), financial support to construction of wind farms in India, Online banking, Solar ATMs, beginning of a pilot project to calculate the carbon footprint levels, funding to renewal energy projects. Currently SBI has more than 16,333 computerized branches and more than 22 millions netbanking users, since 2009–10 and faced various favored and disfavored factors in implementation of Green IS. By interview of IT experts and managers at SBI Allahabad main branch it is observed that various factors like government policies, financial support, customers and employees' awareness towards degradation of environment, technological innovation, customer demand are encouraging the branch to adopt Green initiatives. They are using old heritage building, in order to minimize the use of cooling systems, Kiosks, GCC for environment sustainability. However they are facing various problems like old aged customer's rigidness towards acceptance of new technologies, lack of trust in online services, threat of online theft etc. Sometimes villagers or old aged person come to the banks (not using online banking) only to visit/walk or for gossiping with other customer.

3.2 Case Study 2: Housing Development Finance Corporation Limited

HDFC, established in 1994 in India, is second largest private lender in asset volume and 45th global rank holder. With the brand value of $12.6 billion for FY (2014–15), HDFC is one of the dynamic branches in the field of environment sustainability, accountable for operations effects on environment, adopted various Green initiatives as an essential elements of its business practices to control GHG emission and reduce carbon footprint. HDFC is signatory to the Carbon Disclosure Project and was amongst 16 firms in India to achieve Carbon Disclosure Leadership Index score 17 in 2012. Interview of IT experts and policy makers at HDFC Allahabad branch it is explored that through multi-channel delivery and E-statement it has reduced the consumption of papers; using Energy-Efficient Lighting concepts HDFC have achieved 10 % reduction in electricity consumption. Also, it has adopted the 'Phase-out' policy to change inefficient lighting options, green infrastructure concept for water management and energy savings. The employees promote and conduct green awareness campaigns in order to change the behavior and attitude of stakeholders towards environment sustainability. According to them, Green IS implementation influencing factors are leader's commitment, government policy, customer's awareness and green services demand and cost-benefit analysis.

4 Green IS Critical Success Factors

Through extensive literature review and interview of policy makers, IT experts of SBI and HDFC, and academician nineteen CSFs for implementation of Green IS are identified and listed in Table 1. Maximum of the influencing factors identified in the study are general in character and could be used in any type of organizations despite of the nature, sector and size of the industry.

Table 1. Critical success factors for implementation of Green IS

SN	CSFs	Description	Study
1.	Leaders obligation	Top management support importance in adopting environmental sustainability strategy	[13, 16, 22, 28, 31, 36, 38, 47, 48]
2.	Environment changes	Dynamic process of changing of organization environment in adapting new technologies	[19, 47, 53, 69, 73]
3.	Industry's vision and strategy	Firm's vision and plans to encourage employees and to give them a sense of purpose	[2, 9, 14, 19, 30, 46, 70, 73]
4.	Resource allocation	Allocation of resources (like money, technologies, personnel etc.) and their continuous availability	[27, 31, 61, 62, 73]
5.	Expert selection	Appointment of individual/s to identify and resolve Green IS issues	[30, 49, 73]
6.	Communication	2-way communication between the organization & stakeholders	[13, 19, 47, 71, 73]
7.	Conflicts resolution	Evade personality clashes and keep the egos behind	[26, 45, 73]
8.	Standards adoption	Standard guidelines requirements e.g. ISO14001 standards	[7, 53, 60, 73]
9.	Human resource induction and training	Training of all stakeholders in order to trim down or eliminate their resistance and to develop awareness	[6, 17, 19, 30, 34, 42, 44, 48, 54, 61, 73]
10.	Efficient organization structure	Required IT equipments along with network infrastructure	[19, 32, 73]
11.	Cost-benefit analysis	Incurred cost-benefit calculation results from Green IS adoption	[18, 19, 27, 46, 48, 73]
12.	Inspection/Audits	Periodical audit/inspection for process review and expenses	[19, 32, 40, 68, 73]
13.	Financial support	Funds availability from organization and other financial agency	[19, 58, 73]
14.	Technological advancement	Innovative technologies to meet environment-customers demand	[17, 19, 46, 73]

(Continued)

Table 1. (*Continued*)

SN	CSFs	Description	Study
15.	Customer demand	Customer demands for eco-friendly products and services	[19, 25, 52, 73]
16.	System integration	Ability of integration of different organization functionalities	[18, 27, 46, 51]
17.	Rivalry pressure	Global rise of competition to provide green products/services	[21, 27, 33, 63]
18.	Awareness	Understanding of Green IS as a means of reducing carbon footprints	[18, 21, 23, 29, 60]
19.	Government policies	Government laws, regulations and enforcement of penalties	[27, 37, 46, 63]

It is observed from Table 1 that these nineteen factors are critical factors for organizations if they want effective and smooth implementation of Green IS/initiatives. Many authors as shown in the table found in their studies these factors critical for implementation and also, IT experts, policy makers and academicians have supported and validated these factors as critical factors for Green IS implementation in their organizations.

5   ISM Methodology and Model Development

According to Sage [55], ISM modeling technique is an interactive learning process, aid to determine interdependency and direction among the variables of a system. This is a superior interactive planning method that enables people of a team to build up a structure to define/establish relationships among factors in a set [8]. To build up the structure, a set of questions are answered by Experts of the relevant field.

This model is used by various authors to interpret the relations and direction among the known variables relevant to the problem and to develop a structured model for better understanding of interdependency [27, 33, 64]. Therefore, ISM model is used and all steps followed to develop the model. The process consisted several steps: (1) Identified Critical Success Factors/elements via literature review and experts/academician's opinion (Table 1); (2) Developed Structural Self-Interaction Matrix (SSIM) pointing to pair-wise connection between elements; (3) Developed a Reachability matrix from SSIM, and checked whether the matrix is transitive or not i.e. if factor 1 is related to factor 2 and factor 2 is related to factor 3 then, definitely factors 1 and 3 are directly-indirectly related to each other according to ISM assumption (Table 2); (4) Developed Antecend Set and Intersection Set from SSIM, followed by partitioning of Reachability matrix into different level (Table 2). Based on the results from step 4, a directed graph is drawn resulting into a model by removing transitive relationship (Fig. 2).

It is depicted from the Table 2 that all nineteen factors influencing implementation of Green IS into an organization are categorized under eight levels from I to VIII. Green IS implementation is on level I and Awareness is on Level VIII. The Table 2 shows the antecend of the factors and their Reachability to the other factors. A model is

Table 2. Reachability set and levels of factors

Factors	Reachability set	Antecend set	Intersection set	Level
1 Leaders obligation	1,3,4,5,6,8,9,10,11,14, 16,20	1,2,6,8,11,13,14,15,17,18,19	1,6,8,11,14	V
2 Environment changes	1,2,4,6,7,9,15,17	2,3,6,8,10,11,14,15,17,18,19,20	2,6,15,17	IV
3 Industry's vision and strategy	2,3,4,5,6,8,9,10, 12, 13,14,16,20	1,3,8,11,12,13,14,15,17,18,19	3,8,12,13,14	IV
4 Resource allocation	4,5,9,10,14,20	1,2,3,4,6,7,8,10,11,13,14,15,16,17,18,19	4,10,14	II
5 Expert selection	5,6,8,10,11,12,14,16,18,20	1,3,4,5,6,8,9,10,12,13,14,15,17,18,19	5,6,8,10,12,14,18	VI
6 Communication	1,2,4,5,6,7,9,10,11,14,16,20	1,2,3,5,6,8,9,10,12,15,16,17,18	1,2,5,6,9,10,16	IV
7 Conflicts resolution	4,7,9,10,12,17,20	2,6,7,14,16,17	7,17	II
8 Standards adoption	1,2,3,4,5,6,8,9,10,12,14,16,20	1,3,5,8,11,13,14,15,17,18,19	1,3,5,8,14	V
9 Human resource induction and training	5,6,9,10,13,20	1,2,3,4,6,7,8,9,10,11,12,13,14,15,16,17,18,19	6,9,10,13	II
10 Efficient organization structure	2,4,5,6,9,10,11,12,14,15,17,20	1,3,4,5,6,7,8,9,10,11,13,16,18,19	4,5,6,9,10,11	IV
11 Cost-Benefit analysis	1,2,3,4,8,9,10,11,13,14,16,20	1,5,6,10,11,12,13,15,17,18,19	1,10,11,13	VI
12 Inspection/Audits	3,5,6,9,11,12,13,20	5,7,8,10,12,13,17,18,19,20	5,12,13,20	IV
13 Financial support	1,3,4,5,8,9,10,11,12,13,14,16,20	3,9,11,12,13,18,19	3,9,11,12,13	VI
14 Technological advancement	1,2,3,4,5,7,8,9,14,16,20	1,3,4,5,6,8,10,11,13,14,15,16,17,18,19	3,4,5,8,10,14,16	V
15 Customer demand	1,2,3,4,5,6,8,9,11,14,15,16,17,20	2,10,15,18	2,15	VII
16 System integration	4,6,7,9,10,14,16,20	1,3,5,6,8,11,13,14,15,16,17,18,19,20	6,14,16,20	III
17 Rivalry pressure	1,2,3,4,5,6,7,8,9,11,12,14,16,17,20	2,7,10,15,17,18	2,7,17	VI
18 Awareness	1,2,3,4,5,6,8,9,10,11,12,13,14,15,16,17,18,19,20	5,18,19	5,18,19	VIII
19 Government Policies	1,2,3,4,5,8,9,10,11,12,13,14,16,18,19,20	18,19	18,19	VII
20 Green IS implementation	2,12,16,20	1,3,4,5,6,7,8,9,10,11,12,13,14,15,16,17,18,19,20	12,16,20	I

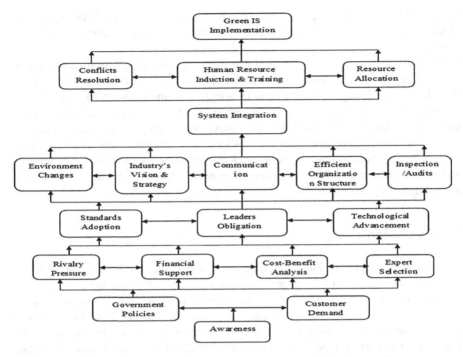

Fig. 2. Model for critical success factors for Green IS implementation

developed (refer Fig. 2) from Table 2 i.e. ISM model of CSFs for better understanding of interdependency on each other.

All factors were categorized under eight levels through Reachability matrix and a model developed from the Table 2 representing systematic directly-indirectly relationship among these CSFs. Figure 2 shows (Bottom –up approach) that factor 18, at level VIII, is the predictor of factor 19 and 15 (at level VII), where these two factors are interrelated and predictors of factors 5, 11, 13 and 17 (at level VI). Again these four factors are interrelated and predictors of 1, 8 and 14 (at level V). Similarly all these interdependent factors at level V are predictors of factors 2, 3, 6, 10 and 12 (at level IV). These interdependent factors at level IV are predictors of factor 16 (at level III). Further, factor 16 is the predictor of three interrelated factors 4, 7 and 9 (at level II).

At level I the factor 20 i.e. Green IS implementation is the objective factor of this study is predicted by factors 4, 7 and 9 and indirectly with all rest sixteen factors. Therefore, this model provides a clear directed vision of inter-dependent CSFs of Green IS implementation in the banking industry as well as other similar organizations.

6 Discussion

In the current fast growing industries where government policies, stakeholders awareness towards environment sustainability, and market competitions are the major factors encouraging firms to adopt Green IS, few factors are pushing back the firms to accept the new Green IT/IS. On other side, if some firms have adopted the Green IT/IS and indulge in providing green services they are unable to sustain due to poor performance or lack of reward.

From the case studies it is observed that many factors like lack of trust (mainly of senior citizens), proper training and awareness programmes for public etc. are responsible for no or slow growth of Green IS adoption in the firms. Also, major factor responsible for slow growth is huge population, which takes time to train/learn, additionally other factors are lack of buy-in of management/employees, insufficient financial sources, lack of experts, undefined goal, lack of communication, inefficient IT infrastructure [9, 38]. Authors find in their research that the companies offering green services and implemented green policies are not earning more profit in comparison to other firms not indulged in green practices.

7 Conclusion

This research paper has identified nineteen Critical Success Factors for effective implementation of Green IS in organizations, with special reference to banking sector, to reduce their carbon footprints. The environmental accountability of industries, laws created by government, customer's awareness etc. are forcing firms to implement Green initiatives as an integral part of their business activities. This study will be helpful to IT Experts/Mangers to gain insight about Green IS/IT and its antecedents and to take appropriate actions to link Green IS with firm's strategy. The research is conducted with special reference to banking sector, but the results can be implemented to any company indulge in adopting green initiatives or Corporate Social Responsibility (CSR). Study is also helpful in creating increased revenue as the running cost of Green information technology and information system is very low. The proposed model in this study aid banks in adopting Green IS smoothly and efficiently.

Case studies of SBI and HDFC banks used to validate these factors and explored the sustainability issues of Green IS in these banks. Relationship among identified nineteen factors had been established using ISM model. Research model is developed representing the interdependency of all the factors showing that Awareness, Government Policies and Customer Demand are the major drivers of Green Is implementation in the firms.

References

1. Akenji, L.: Consumer scapegoatism and limits to green consumerism. J. Cleaner Prod. **63**, 13–23 (2014)
2. Andrews, C.J.: Putting industrial ecology into place: evolving roles for planners. J. Am. Plann. Assoc. **65**(4), 364–375 (1999)
3. Attri, R., Dev, N., Sharma, V.: Interpretive structural modelling (ISM) approach: an overview. Res. J. Manag. Sci. **2**(2), 3–8 (2013)

4. Bahl, S.: Role of green banking in sustainable growth. Int. J. Market. Financ. Serv. Manag. Res. **1**(2), 27–35 (2012)
5. Bihari, S.C.: Green banking-towards socially responsible banking in India. Int. J. Bus. Insights Transformation **4**(1), 82 (2010)
6. Blacklow, S., Waddell, D.: Resistance: an impediment to integrating environmental principles. In: Proceedings of the 5th International and 8th National Research Conference on Quality and Innovation Management, 12–14 February, pp. 49–65. The University of Melbourne, Melbourne (2001)
7. Boiral, O., Sala, J.M.: Environmental management system: should industry adopt ISO 14001? Bus. Horiz. **41**(1), 57–64 (1998)
8. Bolaños, R., Fontela, E., Nenclares, A., Pastor, P.: Using interpretive structural modeling in strategic decision-making groups. Manag. Decis. **43**(6), 877–895 (2005)
9. Bose, R., Luo, X.: Integrative framework for assessing firms' potential to undertake Green IT initiatives via virtualization – a theoretical perspective. J. Strateg. Inf. Syst. **20**(1), 38–54 (2011)
10. Boudreau, M.C., Watson, R.T., Chen, A.: From Green IT to Green IS. Cut. Benchmark Rev. **8**(5), 5–11 (2008)
11. Brower, D.R., Chapple, S.: Let the Mountains Talk, Let the Rivers Run: A Call to Those Who Would Save the Earth. HarperCollins West, New York (1995)
12. Butler, T.: Compliance with institutional imperatives on environmental sustainability: building theory on the role of Green IS. J. Strateg. Inf. Syst. **20**(1), 6–26 (2011)
13. Chandrashekar, A., Dougless, T., Avery, G.C.: The environment is free: the quality analogy. J. Q. Manag. **4**(1), 123–124 (1999)
14. Chen, A.J., Boudreau, M.C., Watson, R.T.: Information systems and ecological sustainability. J. Syst. Inf. Technol. **10**(3), 186–201 (2008)
15. Chen, A.J., Watson, R.T., Boudreau, M.C., Karahanna, E.: Organizational adoption of Green IS & IT: an institutional perspective. In: Thirtieth International Conference on Information Systems, Phoenix: IS, p. 142 (2009)
16. Daellenbach, U.S., McCarthy, A.M., Schoenecker, T.S.: Commitment to innovation: the impact of top management team characteristics. R&D Manag. **29**(3), 199–208 (1999)
17. Daily, B.F., Huang, S.: Achieving sustainability through attention to human resource factors in environmental management. Int. J. Oper. Prod. Manag. **21**(12), 1539–1552 (2001)
18. Dedrick, J.: Green IS: concepts and issues for information systems research. Commun. Assoc. Inf. Syst. **27**(1), 11–18 (2010)
19. Del Río González, P.: Analysing the factors influencing clean technology adoption: a study of the Spanish pulp and paper industry. Bus. Strateg. Environ. **14**(1), 20–37 (2005)
20. Ericsson: Ericsson Mobility Report November 2015. http://www.ericsson.com/res/docs/2015/mobility-report/ericsson-mobility-report-nov-2015.pdf. 7 Mar 2016
21. Famiyeh, S., Kuttu, S., Anarfo, E.B.: Factors influencing the implementation of environmental management systems in Ghanaian firms. Environ. Manag. Sustain. Develop. **3**(2), 18 (2014)
22. Fielding, S.: ISO 14001 delivers effective environmental management and profits. Prof. Saf. **43**(7), 27–28 (1998)
23. Fiorentino, R., Garzella, S.: An integrated framework to support the process of green management adoption. Bus. Process Manag. J. **20**(1), 68–89 (2014)
24. Gabler, C.B., Butler, T.D., Adams, F.G.: The environmental belief-behaviour gap: exploring barriers to green consumerism. J. Customer Behav. **12**(2–3), 159–176 (2013)
25. Gholami, R., Sulaiman, A.B., Ramayah, T., Molla, A.: Senior managers' perception on green information systems (IS) adoption and environmental performance: results from a field survey. Inf. Manag. **50**(7), 431–438 (2013)

26. Green, D.D., McCann, J.: Benchmarking a leadership model for the green economy. Benchmarking: Int. J. **18**(3), 445–465 (2001)

27. Gupta, B., Sahu, G.P.: Towards a model for adoption of Green IS practices. Int. J. Manag. Res. **4**(2), 29–42 (2011)

28. Hanna, M.D.W., Newman, R., Johnson, P.: Linking operational and environmental improvement through employee involvement. Int. J. Oper. Prod. Manag. **20**(2), 148–165 (2000)

29. Hedman, J., Henningsson, S.: Developing ecological sustainability: a green IS response model. Inf. Syst. J. **26**, 259–287 (2016). doi:10.1111/isj.12095

30. Henningsson, S., Hedman, J.: Industry-wide supply chain information integration: the lack of management and disjoint economic responsibility. Int. J. Inf. Syst. Supply Chain Manag. **3**(1), 1–20 (2010)

31. Hersey, K.: A close look at ISO 14000: the quest to improve environmental safety. Prof. Saf. **43**(7), 26–29 (1998)

32. Hormozi, A.: ISO 14000: the next focus in standardization. SAM Adv. Manag. J. **62**(3), 32–41 (1997)

33. Iacobelli, L.B., Olson, R.A., Merhout, J.W.: Green/Sustainable IT/IS: concepts and cases Green/Sustainable IT/IS: concepts and cases. In: Proceedings of the Sixteenth Americas Conference on Information Systems, p. 104 (2010)

34. Imberman, W.: Your key to quality: employee commitment. Adv. Battery Technol. **35**(6), 22–27 (1999)

35. Jenkin, T.A., Webster, J., McShane, L.: An agenda for 'Green' information technology and systems research. Inf. Organ. **21**(1), 17–40 (2011)

36. Knights, D., McCabe, D.: Do quality initiatives need management? TQM Mag. **8**(3), 24–26 (1996)

37. Kuo, B., Dick, G.: The greening of organisational IT: what makes a difference? Australas. J. Inf. Syst. **16**(1), 81–92 (2010)

38. Lee-Mortimer, A.L.: Waste not, want not. Works Manag. **53**(5), 42–44 (2000)

39. Li, C., Liu, F., Wang, Q.: Planning and implementing the green manufacturing strategy: evidences from western China. J. Sci. Technol. Policy Chin. **1**(2), 148–162 (2010)

40. Maltby, J.: Environmental audit: theory and practices. Manag. Audit. J. **10**(8), 15–16 (1995)

41. Marcus, A.A., Fremeth, A.R.: Green management matters regardless. Acad. Manag. Perspect. **23**(3), 17–26 (2009)

42. Marguglio, B.W.: Environmental Management Systems. ASQC Quality Press, Milwaukee (1991)

43. Maxwell, J., Rothenberg, S., Briscoe, F., Marcus, A.: Green schemes: corporate environmental strategies and their implementation. Calif. Manag. Rev. **39**(3), 118–134 (1997)

44. McPherson, M., Nunes, M.B.: Organisational issues for e-learning. Int. J. Educ. Manag. **20**(7), 542–558 (2006)

45. Melville, N.P.: Information systems innovation for environmental sustainability. MIS Q. **34**(1), 1–21 (2010)

46. Molla, A., Cooper, V.A., Pittayachawan, S.: IT and eco-sustainability: developing and validating a green IT readiness model. In: Thirtieth International Conference on Information Systems, Phoenix: AIS, p. 141 (2009)

47. Nattrass, B., Altmore, M.: The Natural Step for Business: Wealth Ecology and the Evolutionary Corporation. New Society Publishers, Gabriola Island (2013)

48. Pawar, M.W., Rissetto, C.: A tool for improvement: environmental management systems. Publ. Manag. **83**(11), 10–17 (2001)

49. Petts, J., Herd, A., O'Heocha, M.: Environmental responsiveness, individual and organisational learning: SME experience. J. Environ. Plann. Manag. **4**(6), 711–730 (1998)

50. Porter, M.E., Van der Linde, C.: Toward a new conception of the environment-competitiveness relationship. J. Econ. Perspect. **9**(4), 97–118 (1995)
51. Ram, J., Corkindale, D., Wu, M.L.: Implementation critical success factors (CSFs) for ERP: do they contribute to implementation success and post-implementation performance? Int. J. Prod. Econ. **144**(1), 157–174 (2013)
52. Russo, M.V., Harrison, N.S.: Organizational design and environmental performance: clues from the electronics industry. Acad. Manag. J. **48**(4), 582–593 (2005)
53. Russo, M.V., Fouts, P.A.: A resource-based structure on corporate environmental performance and profitability. Acad. Manag. J. **40**(3), 534–559 (1997)
54. Ruth, S.: Green IT: more than a three percent solution. IEEE Internet Comput. **13**(4), 74–78 (2009)
55. Sage, A.P.: Interpretive structural modeling: methodology for large-scale population density. Small Bus. Econ. **6**, 291–297 (1977)
56. Sahoo, P., Nayak, B.P.: Green banking in India. Indian Economic Journal (2008)
57. Sarkar, P., Young, L.: Managerial attitudes towards Green IT: an explorative study of policy drivers. In: Proceedings of the 13th Pacific Asia Conference on Information Systems, Hyderabad, India, p. 95 (2009)
58. Sayeed, L., Gill, S.: Implementation of Green IT: Implications for a Dynamic Resource. In: Proceedings of the Fifteenth AMCIS, San Francisco, California, 6th–9th August 2009, (1998), pp. 1–8 (2009)
59. Schaarsmith, J.H.: ISO 14001 lowers environmental risks. Bus. Insur. **34**(28), 12 (2000)
60. Schmidt, N.H., Erek, K., Kolbe, L.M., Zarnekow, R.: Examining the contribution of Green IT to the objectives of IT departments: empirical evidence from German enterprises. Australas. J. Inf. Syst. **17**(1), 127–140 (2011)
61. Schmidt, N.H., Erek, K., Kolbe, L.M., Zarnekow, R.: Predictors of Green IT adoption: implications from an empirical investigation. In: Association for Information Systems: Proceedings of the 16th Americas Conference on Information Systems, Lima, Peru, p. 367 (2010)
62. Scrimshire, D.: What's involved in implementing ISO 14001? Modern Casting **86**(12), 32–34 (1996)
63. Simula, H., Lehtimäki, T.: Managing greenness in technology marketing. J. Syst. Inf. Technol. **11**(4), 331–346 (2009)
64. Singh, M.D., Kant, R.: Knowledge management barriers: an interpretive structural modeling approach. Int. J. Manag. Sci. Eng. Manag. **3**(2), 141–150 (2008)
65. Sudhalakshmi, K., Chinnadorai, K.M.: Green banking practices in Indian. Int. J. Manag. Commerc. Innov. **1**, 41–54 (2014)
66. Taib, M.Y.M., Udin, Z.M., Ghani, A.H.A.: The collaboration of Green design & technology towards business sustainability in Malaysian manufacturing industry. Proc.-Soc. Behav. Sci. **211**, 237–242 (2015)
67. Viaro, T., Vaccaro, G., Azevedo, D., Brito, A., Tondolo, V., Bittencourt, C.: 2P a conceptual framework to develop Green IT–going beyond the idea of environmental sustainability (2010)
68. Vinten, G.: The objectives of the environmental audit. Environ. Manag. Health **7**(3), 12–21 (1996)
69. Wagner, J.: Company-wide ISO 14001 certification. Pollut. Eng. **33**(9), 216 (2001)
70. Watson, R.T., Boudreau, M.-C., Chen, A.J.: Information systems and environmentally sustainable development: energy informatics and new directions for the IS community. MIS Q. **34**(1), 23–38 (2010)

71. Wilson, M.: Larry's features 'Green' market special. Chain Store Age **73**(6), 82 (1997)
72. Zingale, R., Himes, T.: Environmental management systems: making better business sense. Ind. Heat. **66**(8), 18–34 (1999)
73. Zutshi, A., Sohal, A.S.: Adoption and maintenance of environmental management systems: critical success factors. Manag. Environ. Qual.: An Int. J. **15**(4), 399–419 (2004)

Exploring XBRL-Based Reporting System: A Conceptual Framework for System Adoption and Implementation

Dhata Praditya[✉], Reni Sulastri, Nitesh Bharosa, and Marijn Janssen

Faculty of Technology, Policy and Management,
Delft University of Technology, Delft, Netherlands
{D.Praditya,n.bharosa,M.F.W.H.A.Janssen}@tudelft.nl,
ReniSulastri@student.tudelft.nl

Abstract. XBRL has been established as a financial reporting standard in the last 15 years. Many countries already adopting XBRL-based reporting system. In some countries it mandated by the government and for the other voluntary. IT adoption and implementation already existed as a separate process. To get more comprehensive analysis, this article aims to propose a unified conceptual model for IT adoption and implementation processes. A literature review on inter-organizational system (IOS) was conducted to reach that objective. This resulted in a conceptual framework represented by factors influencing adoption and implementation, levels of adoption and arrangement of the system. This framework will be used in further empirical study of XBRL reporting system or in broader, analysing the implementation of inter-organizational system.

Keywords: XBRL · IT/IS adoption · IT/IS implementation · Conceptual framework · Inter-organizational system · Information sharing

1 Introduction

Companies need to report various types of information, for example tax, statistical, inspection or annual statements regularly to several government agencies. This causes an increase on the amount of work on both sides. Processing a huge number of reports from businesses can be challenging, time consuming and error-prone for governments [1]. On another side, there is a high cost for enterprises for preparing several different reports and sometimes reproducing the same or partially already created data in various formats. Recently, organizations are able to share information with each other [2] due to the advancement of information and communication technology (ICT). The approach in exchanging data is shifting from bilateral information exchange to more advanced system, and this beneficial for private and public sector.

One of the examples of such system is XBRL-based reporting system. XBRL, an acronym of eXtensible Business Reporting Language, is an open standard to report financial and business information electronically [3] that enable the preparation, publication, exchange, and analysis of the financial and business statement [4]. Since introduced in the early 2000, XBRL has been already implemented in several countries such

Y.K. Dwivedi et al. (Eds.): I3E 2016, LNCS 9844, pp. 305–316, 2016.
DOI: 10.1007/978-3-319-45234-0_28

as the Netherlands [5], Australia [6], the United States [7], the United Kingdom [8], China [9], India [10], South Korea [11], Israel [12], Saudi Arabia [3] and Italy [13].

Perdana et al. [14] summarized potential effects of XBRL and divided the effects into three aspects: (1) accounting, (2) auditing, and (3) decision-making process. These affect three different parties: providers, intermediaries, and requesters. In accounting, potential impacts of XBRL include an integrated accounting and financial information supply chain [15], improved accounting data and financial information quality by facilitating information exchange [16], and achieving good corporate governance by providing more transparent financial processes [17]. In auditing, XBRL provides opportunity and capability to handle continuous auditing [18], which realized by traceability of the data on the system. With this capability, auditors can focus on the evaluation of financial information rather than on extracting and calculating financial data [19]. Last, with the improvement in information quality and capability of data tracing and aggregating, XBRL also can potentially improves the decision-making process of organizations.

Apart of the importance and benefits of XBRL, Perdana et al. [14] highlighted that only few XBRL literature discussing its implementation in public organizations, where public organization can be considered as the requesting party or information users. Since most implementations of XBRL reporting system mandated by the government, there should be some information available that can be extracted concerning how implementation of this system affects their business processes.

Moreover, literature in XBRL implementation focuses on technical development; mostly discussing the taxonomy [14], and only few focus on system arrangement: IT architecture, data management or system governance. In order to get more comprehensive view for the adoption and implementation of the system, this research will also include system arrangement in the proposed model. System governance, for instance, should be clearly established since the early implementation to avoid conflict between users, and become even more important to realise the next implementation phases.

The main objective of this research is to propose a model which can be used to analyse the adoption and implementation of XBRL. This research reviewed existing IT adoption models that used in investigating inter-organizational system (IOS) and resulted in the selection of TOE model to structure the determinants in system adoption and implementation. TOE model then assembled with XBRL adoption strategy model and system arrangement.

This paper is structured as follows. In the next section, a brief overview of literature in inter-organizational system (IOS) is given, specifically about the business and government relationship, and also the implementation concept. Then, methodology used in this research is described, whereas the proposed model is presented and discussed later. Finally, conclusions are drawn in the last section.

2   Literature Review

2.1   XBRL

Government has the responsibility to control the market, as a safeguard that maintain equality in a competitive market [1]. This can be achieved by ensuring that businesses comply with established laws and regulations [20]. For this purpose, businesses have to deal with a huge number of reports sent to several government agencies. In the traditional information exchange, human-to-human or human-to-system communications, human can be considered as weak link because many activities are vulnerable of errors, take a lot of time to process and costly [20]. On the other side, government also burdened with aggregating, comparing, and evaluating the information [20].

Inter-organizational system (IOS) can be defined as "an automated system distributed in two or more organizations which provide the collection of information resources, such as common databases, infrastructure and applications that extend beyond organizational borders and facilitate information sharing to support the business process of the organization" [21, p. 2]. System-to-system information sharing among organizations not only minimize the paper-based process, but also simplify the processes, and improves formulation and implementation of policy that lead to many other benefits [22].

XBRL-based reporting system is an example of IOS. XBRL, often referred as 'barcodes for reporting', is an open international standard for the electronic communication of financial and business information [23]. The first generation of XBRL was developed by Charles Hoffman in 1998, with the main objectives facilitate data sharing in financial report and to invent the new method that simplifies the way financial data prepared, validated, consumed and analysed [24]. Today, XBRL international, a global and not-for-profit organization, which consists of approximately 600 public and private organizations has been developed to consistently support the enhancement of reporting and analysis to meet global business practice [23].

An XBRL consists of four main elements: (1) XML standard, (2) XBRL taxonomy, (3) instance document, and (4) XBRL specification [25]. The XML standard and syntax allow the semantic meaning, expression and information modelling in XBRL [26]. A taxonomy contains the metadata that corresponding with a particular XBRL entity in the instance documents [27], and by using this metadata, taxonomy manages *the elements* and *elements' relationships* which support data validation [28]. XBRL instance document is basically the financial statements which are formatted with tag [29]. XBRL specification includes the rules and technology that defines how XBRL works by allowing multiple instance documents of different taxonomies to be processed by the same software tools [29].

2.2   IT/IS Adoption and Implementation

In this research, XBRL is viewed as IS innovation in the financial sector. Magalhaes [30] defined IS implementation as "a process of change aimed at the integration of technological artefacts into the social structure and processes of the organization" [30, p. 10].

Furthermore, Thompson [31] explained the process of innovation divided into three-stage process, initiation which consists of the need of change, gathering information and evaluation, led to adoption stage. Adoption stage explains the decision to use innovation and to allocate resources to the innovation. Implementation stage refers to the development and installation of innovation to ensure the benefits of innovation are realized. IS implementation used in this research mainly focus on adoption and implementation stages.

Table 1. Comparison of established IT adoption models

Models	Main focus	Limitations
TAM [39]	1. Behavioural theories with focus on beliefs, attitudes, and behaviour [40] 2. Provides a room for intervention of individual behaviour via external variables [41] 3. Reflects mutual relationship between adoption intention and attitudes, perceptions, and beliefs [42]	1. Pays more focus on initial adoption rather than continuous adoption [40] 2. Focus on prediction of behaviour on the exploitation stage, and lack of focus on possibility of failure on development and testing stage [43] 3. Deals mostly with the voluntary adoption [42]
TOE [44]	1. Provides theoretical perspective of contextual factors [44] 2. Presents variables that assess project complexity from theoretical aspects and practical aspects [45] 3. Supports the assessment to investigate the dynamic of project complexity [45]. 4. Includes environmental context in the analysis [46] 5. Provides a solid theoretical foundation, consistent empirical basis, and the potential of application for IS adoption [46]. 6. Free from industry and firm-size restrictions [47]	1. Some predictors are more suitable for large organizations instead of for small and medium enterprises [48] 2. Does not explaining the decision process and causality within the factors [49] 3. Offer not more than a taxonomy for categorizing variables and does not provide an integral conceptual model or a comprehensive theory [50]
IASAM [51]	1. Combines socio-economic aspects and socio-technical aspect of technology [43] 2. Addresses technology acceptance issue and sustainability issue [51] 3. Takes into account technical, social, financial, and sustainability assessment [51] 4. Assessing potential failure of a new technology since the development phase [43]	1. Relatively too complex [43] 2. Need relatively more time to analyse [51]

Myers [32] stated that IS implementation research developed into two dominant categories: factor and process. Factor research tried to identify variables related with implementation success and failure. In the area of XBRL implementation, there is plenty research focus on this aspect [3, 29, 33–35]. Process research tried to explain how and why the implementation running over time. Several research in XBRL implementation falling into this aspect [36–38].

XBRL reporting system is used by organizations as a tool for preparing and reporting their financial statement. Even though the real users of the system and the decision maker in the organization might be individuals or groups, from the system perspective the user is an organization. In this regards, from many IT adoption models available in literature, this research only focus with models that used in organizational level. There are three dominating models found in the literature: (1) Technology Acceptance Model (TAM), (2) Technology-Organization-Environment Model (TOE), and (3) Integrated Acceptance and Sustainability Assessment Model (IASAM). Table 1 summarizes the focus and limitations of each model.

3   Methodology

In order to achieve the objective, this research using multi-stages literature review. First, articles discussing IOS, for instance electronic data interchange (EDI), Public Safety Network (PSN), and especially XBRL reporting system from academic journals in information system area such as Management Information System Quarterly (MISQ), Government Information Quarterly (GIQ), or Information System Research (ISR), were collected. These articles were combined with papers from international conference proceedings in information system and electronic government area. This list includes the newest version of e-government references library.

Second, those articles were reviewed. Only relevant articles were selected as we wanted to identify which IT adoption model to be used in proposed model. As a result, prior research mainly using TAM [3, 52, 53] and TOE frameworks [33, 35, 54] in analysing the adoption and implementation of IOS.

Third, original papers which proposed those IT adoption models were studied. Most cited papers that using the models were also studied to gain information about the limitations and advantages of each model to be considered as a proper model in explaining XBRL reporting system (as shown in Table 1). Based on this, TOE were selected for the proposed model. ✦

Fourth, other important elements for the proposed model were identified. In this stage, one article proposed a model to explain in specific IOS adoption [55], one article propose adoption strategy of XBRL [56], and another article propose level of adoption of the XBRL reporting system [57] were studied. These three models then were combined to analyse how organizations adopt XBRL in their organization. Further, the importance of system arrangement was also recognized [58, 59] in implementing IOS.

Last, from aforementioned affluent sources, factors, adoption level, implementation stage and other information related to inter-organizational system were collected and used to propose a conceptual framework in investigating XBRL reporting system.

4   Model Construction

As a system that involving many organizations, implementing XBRL reporting system is a complex endeavour. Learning from existing implementations may be critical for the future implementation. In this regards, the objective of this research is to propose a conceptual model for analysing this system. As shown in the Fig. 1, the IT/IS implementation concept from [30] which describe adoption as a part of implementation process is used. Therefore, the successful of implementation reflected by the successful of system adoption in users. The blue line represents the adoption process in an organization that influenced by several factors structured using TOE. Some factors are also influencing system arrangement. Then, according to [58], architecture and governance of IT system are influenced by the willingness of organization to adopt the system. Some elements were identified during the research and explained in detail as follow:

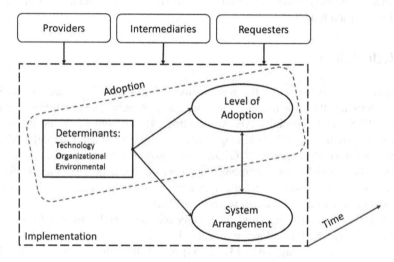

Fig. 1. Proposed conceptual model

(a) Determinants

There are many factors influencing implementation of XBRL provided from literature, even more if other IOS implementations are included. Perceived benefits and perceived risk, both mainly refer to return on investment, were usually used in explaining why an organization has to use an innovation [29, 60–62]. Other determinants were also used to explain the adoption of innovation such as complexity [29, 54, 60], compatibility [54, 60, 63, 64], organizational readiness [29, 33, 61, 64], system security [65, 66], management support [1, 54], power and trust [65, 67], firm structure, size and culture [68–70], external pressure [33], regulation [1, 71, 72], and incentive [1, 37].

In order to make factors found from literature more structured, TOE model is adopted in this research. The TOE framework at first described by [44] in explaining how the organization context plays as important role in adopting and implementing innovations. As an organization-level theory, this framework explains three elements of an organization that influence their adoption decision of technological innovations: *technological, organizational,* and *environmental context.* The technological context refers to existing technologies that are currently used by the firm and other technologies available in the market but has not been used by the organization [73]. The organizational context includes characteristics and resources of the organization [71]. The environmental context refers to external condition that might stimulate the firm in technology adoption [73]. The used of TOE as synthesizing model is also because it offers flexibility of factors in each context [73].

(b) Levels of Adoption

As XBRL can be implemented for inter-organizational purpose and internal purpose [33], levels of adoption variable need to be included in the model. Research from [57] provides four adoption levels of XBRL: (1) non-adopters, which is irrelevant for the proposed model; (2) low adopters, by outsourcing the XBRL conversion; (3) medium adopters, reflected by retaining their current financial system and converting their financial data to XBRL in-house; (4) high adopters, which have potential to gain the optimal benefits from the system. Findings from (57) show that organization who decide to use XBRL mainly choose to be low adopters or high adopters.

On another literature, Sledgianowski et al. [56] offers three XBRL adoption strategy for organization: (1) bolt-on, using XBRL conversion at the end of traditional reporting chain; (2) built-in, integrating XBRL as part of reporting process without interfering other domains reporting system that still need manual conversion; (3) embedded, standardizing the reporting process using XBRL. However, XBRL might not suitable for different domains reporting process, thus adoption using embedded strategy might not feasible in present day.

In the inter-organizational perspective, levels of adoption can also be demonstrated by actively or passively contributing in the system governance, participating in decision-making process, involving in problem solving and information sharing [62].

(c) IT/IS Arrangement

The terminology arrangement that used in this study is referring to prior study from [74] that provide explanation about how the interplay between IT architecture and IT governance ensures IT activities in supporting organizational objective by providing IT agility. The system arrangement refers to governance and architecture of IOS system that support information process. Level of adoption and system arrangement are used to address TOE limitations by providing better correlation and causality of each element in the proposed model.

(d) Time

As indicated in SBR (Standard Business Reporting) implementation in Netherlands, system arrangement could be changed during the implementation process, factors influencing or key actors and their roles in each implementation phase could also be different [36]. For this reason, time variable need to be added in the proposed model to show that all variables in the model may change throughout the implementation phase.

(e) Actors

Another variable that should also be added in the model is actors, including their roles in each implementation phase [8]. For example, at the early phase, system owner and developer plays an important role to developing the system. Then the system will be tested by the user, to find out if there is any bugs or errors in the system. This process then being followed-up by the developer to create an adjustment in order to solve issues found by users. By adding this variable, the governance of the system can also be explained, including the decision making process, monitoring and formal communication.

5 Conclusion

This article aims to propose a conceptual model to be used for investigating XBRL reporting system. The proposed model presented was acquired by assembling IT adoption models with XBRL adoption strategy model. Further, to get more comprehensive result, system arrangement in term of system architecture and system governance included in the model, this will fill a gap in XBRL research which lack of system perspective research.

The proposed model indicates that an interrelation between adoption and implementation is exist, which means if there is any change in the determinants, in may affect adoption, implementation or both. For example, changes on the regulation and legal framework of XBRL reporting system, from voluntary to mandatory, will have an impact on adoption process and system arrangement. With the changing, there is an additional incentive for organizations to adopt the system and this resulted in a significant raise of data transactions need to be handled by system.

XBRL is still considered in the initial stage of maturity. This proposed will be tested using survey and case study in the future research. The objective is to collect empirical data in identifying factors influencing of the implementation, identifying actors and their responsibility in the implementation process, explaining how and why implementation running over time, and evaluating gap between theoretical and practical of XBRL reporting system. This data can be used to develop a comparative study of the cross-nation boundary and develop future system that can solve XBRL reporting system issues and challenges identified.

References

1. Chen, Y.-C.: A comparative study of e-government XBRL implementations: the potential of improving information transparency and efficiency. Gov. Inf. Q. 29(4), 553–563 (2012)
2. Yang, T.-M., Pardo, T., Wu, Y.-J.: How is information shared across the boundaries of government agencies? An e-Government case study. Gov. Inf. Q. 31, 637–652 (2014)
3. Rawashdeh, A., Selamat, M.H.: Critical success factors relating to the adoption of XBRL in Saudi Arabia. J. Int. Technol. Inf. Manag. 22(2), 4 (2013)
4. Jones, A., Willis, M.: The challenge of XBRL: business reporting for the investor. Balance Sheet 11(3), 29–37 (2003)

5. Bharosa, N., et al.: Managing the transformation to standard business reporting: principles and lessons learned from the Netherlands. In: 12th Annual International Conference on Digital Government Research (dg.o 2011). ACM, College Park (2011)
6. Azam, M.S.: Intention to adopt standard business reporting in Australia: an application of the technology-organization-environment framework. RMIT University (2012)
7. Chen, Y.-C.: Improving transparency in the financial Sector: e-Government XBRL implementation in the United States. Publ. Perform. Manag. Rev. **37**(2), 241–262 (2013)
8. Dunne, T., et al.: Stakeholder engagement in internet financial reporting: the diffusion of XBRL in the UK. Br. Acc. Rev. **45**(3), 167–182 (2013)
9. Liu, C., et al.: The impact of XBRL adoption in PR China. Decis. Support Syst. **59**, 242–249 (2014)
10. Gauri, M.: XBRL: in India. Glob. J. Finan. Manag. **6**(6), 517–522 (2014)
11. Jeong, J.-S., Na, K.-S., You, Y.-Y.: A case study of financial statements reporting system based on XBRL taxonomy in accordance with Korean Public Institutions adoption of K-IFRS. Cluster Comput. **17**(3), 817–826 (2014)
12. Markelevich, A., Shaw, L., Weihs, H.: The Israeli XBRL adoption experience. Acc. Perspect. **14**(2), 117–133 (2015)
13. Avallone, F., Ramassa, P., Roncagliolo, E.: The pros and cons of XBRL adoption in Italy: a field study. In: Mancini, D., Dameri, R.P., Bonollo, E. (eds.) Strengthening Information and Control Systems. LNISO, vol. 14, pp. 157–170. Springer, Berlin (2016)
14. Perdana, A., Robb, A., Rohde, F.: An integrative review and synthesis of XBRL research in academic journals. J. Inf. Syst. **29**(1), 115–153 (2014)
15. O'Riain, S., Curry, E., Harth, A.: XBRL and open data for global financial ecosystems: a linked data approach. Int. J. Acc. Inf. Syst. **13**(2), 141–162 (2012)
16. Baldwin, A.A., Brown, C.E., Trinkle, B.S.: XBRL: an impacts framework and research challenge. J. Emerg. Technol. Acc. **3**(1), 97–116 (2006)
17. Kim, J.W., Lim, J.-H., No, W.G.: The effect of first wave mandatory XBRL reporting across the financial information environment. J. Inf. Syst. **26**(1), 127–153 (2012)
18. Rezaee, Z., Elam, R., Sharbatoghlie, A.: Continuous auditing: the audit of the future. Manag. Audit. J. **16**(3), 150–158 (2001)
19. Khadaroo, M.I.: Business reporting on the internet in Malaysia and Singapore: a comparative study. Corp. Commun.: Int. J. **10**(1), 58–68 (2005)
20. Bharosa, N., et al.: Tapping into existing information flows: the transformation to compliance by design in business-to-government information exchange. Gov. Inf. Q. **30**(Suppl. 1), S9–S18 (2013)
21. Robey, D., Im, G., Wareham, J.D.: Theoretical foundations of empirical research on interorganizational systems: assessing past contributions and guiding future directions. J. Assoc. Inf. Syst. **9**(9), 4 (2008)
22. Landsbergen Jr., D., Wolken Jr., G.: Realizing the promise: government information systems and the fourth generation of information technology. Publ. Adm. Rev. **61**(2), 206–220 (2001)
23. XBRL-International, XBRL Specification 2.1. (2013)
24. Kernan, K.: XBRL around the world. J. Acc. **206**(4), 62 (2008)
25. Müller-Wickop, N., Schultz, M., Nüttgens, M.: XBRL: impacts, issues and future research directions. In: Rabhi, F.A., Gomber, P. (eds.) FinanceCom 2012. LNBIP, vol. 135, pp. 112–130. Springer, Heidelberg (2013)
26. Rawashdeh, A.: Suggested model for XBRL adoption. Int. J. Res. Commer. Manag. **3**(5), 93–96 (2013)
27. Zhu, H., Wu, H.: Interoperability of XBRL financial statements in the US. Int. J. E-Bus. Res. (IJEBR) **7**(2), 19–33 (2011)

28. Chang, C., Jarvenpaa, S.: Pace of information systems standards development and implementation: the case of XBRL. Electron. Mark. **15**(4), 365–377 (2005)
29. Doolin, B., Troshani, I.: Organizational adoption of XBRL. Electron. Mark. **17**(3), 199–209 (2007)
30. Magalhaes, R.M.: The organizational implementation of information systems: towards a new theory. The London School of Economics and Political Science (LSE) (1999)
31. Thompson, V.A.: Bureaucracy and innovation. Adm. Sci. Q. **10**, 1–20 (1965)
32. Myers, M.D.: A disaster for everyone to see: an interpretive analysis of a failed IS project. Acc. Manag. Inf. Technol. **4**(4), 185–201 (1994)
33. Henderson, D., Sheetz, S.D., Trinkle, B.S.: The determinants of inter-organizational and internal in-house adoption of XBRL: a structural equation model. Int. J. Acc. Inf. Syst. **13**(2), 109–140 (2012)
34. Troshani, I., Rao, S.: Drivers and inhibitors to XBRL adoption: a qualitative approach to build a theory in under-researched areas. Int. J. E-Bus. Res. **3**(4), 98 (2007)
35. Rostami, M., Nayeri, M.D.: Investigation on XBRL adoption based on TOE model. Br. J. Econ. Manag. Trade **7**(4), 269–278 (2015)
36. Janssen, M., van der Voort, H., van Veenstra, A.: Failure of large transformation projects from the viewpoint of complex adaptive systems: management principles for dealing with project dynamics. Inf. Syst. Front. **17**, 1–15 (2014)
37. Enachi, M., Andone, I.I.: The progress of XBRL in Europe – projects, users and prospects. Proc. Econ. Finan. **20**, 185–192 (2015)
38. Mousa, R.: E-Government adoption in the UK: XBRL project. Int. J. Electron. Gov. Res. (IJEGR) **9**(2), 101–119 (2013)
39. Davis, Jr. F.D.: A technology acceptance model for empirically testing new end-user information systems: theory and results. Massachusetts Institute of Technology (1986)
40. Premkumar, G., Bhattacherjee, A.: Explaining information technology usage: a test of competing models. Omega **36**(1), 64–75 (2008)
41. Davis, F.D., Bagozzi, R.P., Warshaw, P.R.: User acceptance of computer technology: a comparison of two theoretical models. Manag. Sci. **35**(8), 982–1003 (1989)
42. Hossain, M.A., Quaddus, M.: The adoption and continued usage intention of RFID: an integrated framework. Inf. Technol. People **24**(3), 236–256 (2011)
43. Aizstrauta, D., Ginters, E., Eroles, M.-A.P.: Applying theory of diffusion of innovations to evaluate technology acceptance and sustainability. Proc. Comput. Sci. **43**, 69–77 (2015)
44. DePietro, R., Wiarda, E., Fleischer, M.: The context for change: organization, technology and environment. In: Tornatzky, L.G., Fleischer, M. (eds.) The Processes of Technological Innovation, pp. 151–175. Lexington Books, Lexington (1990)
45. Bosch-Rekveldt, M., et al.: Grasping project complexity in large engineering projects: the TOE (Technical, Organizational and Environmental) framework. Int. J. Proj. Manag. **29**(6), 728–739 (2011)
46. Oliveira, T., Martins, M.F.: Information technology adoption models at firm level: review of literature. In: European Conference on Information Management and Evaluation. Academic Conferences International Limited (2010)
47. Gangwar, H., Date, H., Raoot, A.: Review on IT adoption: insights from recent technologies. J. Enterp. Inf. Manag. **27**(4), 488–502 (2014)
48. Awa, H.O., et al.: Integrating TAM and TOE frameworks and expanding their characteristic constructs for e-Commerce adoption by SMEs. J. Sci. Technol. Policy Manag. **6**(1), 76–94 (2012)
49. Rui, G.: Information systems innovation adoption among organizations-A match-based framework and empirical studies (2007)

50. Dedrick, J., West, J.: Why firms adopt open source platforms: a grounded theory of innovation and standards adoption. In: Proceedings of Workshop on Standard Making: A Critical Research Frontier for Information Systems, Seattle, WA (2003)
51. Ginters, E., Barkane, Z., Vincent, H.: Systems dynamics use for technologies assessment. In: 22th European Modeling and Simulation Symposium (EMSS 2010). DIPTEM University of Genoa (2010)
52. Janvrin, D.J., Pinsker, R.E., Mascha, M.F.: XBRL-enabled, spreadsheet, or PDF? Factors influencing exclusive user choice of reporting technology. J. Inf. Syst. 27(2), 35–49 (2013)
53. Chouhan, V.: Analysis of XBRL implementation by technology adoption model (TAM) in Rajasthan. SANJAY DIXIT, p. 18 (2015)
54. Borgman, H.P., et al.: Cloudrise: exploring cloud computing adoption and governance with the TOE framework. In: 46th Hawaii International Conference on System Sciences (HICSS-46). IEEE Computer Society, Wailea (2013)
55. Rahim, M.M., Shanks, G.G., Johnston, R.B.: Understanding IOS adoption processes in a first-tier automotive supplier company: an application of the theory of IOS adoption motivation. In: ECIS (2006)
56. Sledgianowski, D., Fonfeder, R., Slavin, N.S.: Implementing XBRL reporting. CPA J. 80(8), 68 (2010)
57. Garner, D., et al.: The different levels of XBRL adoption. Manag. Acc. Q. 14(2), 1–10 (2013)
58. Saha, P.: Advancing the whole-of-government enterprise architecture adoption with strategic (systems) thinking. In: Enterprise Architecture as Platform for Connected Government. NUS Institute of Systems Science, Singapore (2010)
59. Klievink, B., Bharosa, N., Tan, Y.-H.: The collaborative realization of public values and business goals: governance and infrastructure of public–private information platforms. Gov. Inf. Q. 33(1), 67–79 (2016)
60. Cooper, R.B., Zmud, R.W.: Information technology implementation research: a technological diffusion approach. Manag. Sci. 36(2), 123–139 (1990)
61. Liu, C.: XBRL: a new global paradigm for business financial reporting. J. Glob. Inf. Manag. (JGIM) 21(3), 60–80 (2013)
62. Barrett, S., Konsynski, B.: Inter-organization information sharing systems. MIS Q. 6, 93–105 (1982)
63. Hung, W.-H., et al.: Critical factors of adopting enterprise application integration technology: an empirical study on larger hospitals. Commun. Assoc. Inf. Syst. 36(1), 31 (2015)
64. Singerling, T., et al.: Exploring factors that influence information sharing choices of organizations in networks. In: AMCIS 2015: Americas Conference on Information Systems, Puerto Rico, 13–15 August 2015 (2015)
65. Savoldelli, A., Codagnone, C., Misuraca, G.: Understanding the e-Government paradox: learning from literature and practice on barriers to adoption. Gov. Inf. Q. 31(Suppl. 1), S63–S71 (2014)
66. Sayogo, D.S., Gil-Garcia, J.R.: Understanding the determinants of success in inter-organizational information sharing initiatives: results from a national survey. In: Proceedings of 15th Annual International Conference on Digital Government Research. ACM (2014)
67. Hart, P., Saunders, C.: Power and trust: critical factors in the adoption and use of electronic data interchange. Organ. Sci. 8(1), 23–42 (1997)
68. Sambamurthy, V., Zmud, R.W.: Arrangements for information technology governance: a theory of multiple contingencies. MIS Q. 23, 261–290 (1999)
69. Shan, Y.G., Troshani, I., Richardson, G.: An empirical comparison of the effect of XBRL on audit fees in the US and Japan. J. Contemp. Acc. Econ. 11(2), 89–103 (2015)

70. Laudon, K.C., Laudon, J.P., Brabston, M.E.: Management Information Systems: Managing the Digital Firm, vol. 12. Pearson, Upper Saddle River (2012)
71. Kuan, K.K., Chau, P.Y.: A perception-based model for EDI adoption in small businesses using a technology–organization–environment framework. Inf. Manag. **38**(8), 507–521 (2001)
72. Zhang, J., Dawes, S.S., Sarkis, J.: Exploring stakeholders' expectations of the benefits and barriers of e-Government knowledge sharing. J. Enterp. Inf. Manag. **18**(5), 548–567 (2005)
73. Baker, J.: The technology–organization–environment framework. In: Dwivedi, Y.K., Wade, M.R., Schneberger, S.L. (eds.) Information Systems Theory, pp. 231–245. Springer, New York (2012)
74. Tiwana, A., Konsynski, B.: Complementarities between organizational IT architecture and governance structure. Inf. Syst. Res. **21**(2), 288–304 (2010)

Information Sharing on Social Media

Exploring Theoretical Concepts for Explaining Sharing in the Social Media Environment

Cherniece J. Plume[✉] and Emma L. Slade

School of Management, Swansea University, Swansea, UK
cherniieceplume@hotmail.co.uk, {840406,e.l.slade}@swansea.ac.uk

Abstract. The concept of sharing has been amplified with the development of various social media platforms that enable consumers to share knowledge with each other and subsequently influence their attitudes and purchase intentions. However, recent studies have tended to utilise social psychological theories to explore sharing on social media and have concentrated on the behaviour of those that share rather than the underlying individual motivations that lead them to share. This paper outlines some of the theories used within the current sharing literature and suggests that combining uses and gratifications theory and self-construal theory is better suited to examining the underlying motivations of sharing.

Keywords: Uses and gratifications · Sharing · Motivations · Social media · Self-construal

1 Introduction

People have an inherent predisposition to share information with other people [1]. The evolution of social media has given consumers a variety of new platforms to share their consumption choices and has extended the reach of what they share. These technologies are truly becoming a steadfast tool to target audiences in a fast and efficient way [2]. The documented importance of sharing on consumers' purchase decision [3] makes understanding motivations to share on social media theoretically and practically important. Research that has examined sharing in a marketing or social media context has failed to identify a common theory to explain the phenomena, with many drawing from multiple theoretical underpinnings for example Hennig-Thurau et al. [4] who draw upon equity theory and balance theory, and Chiu et al. [5] who draw upon social cognitive theory and social capital theory. Therefore, this paper reviews the few dominant theoretical paradigms, paying particular attention to the motivations underlying social media sharing behaviour, to find out where their strengths and weaknesses lie to identify the most appropriate theory to explore sharing on social media. The remainder of the paper is as follows. The following section discusses theoretical concepts used in relation to sharing. This is followed by a brief discussion, highlighting the strengths and weaknesses of the current literature, forming the basis of future research suggestions. The paper is then briefly concluded.

© IFIP International Federation for Information Processing 2016
Published by Springer International Publishing Switzerland 2016. All Rights Reserved
Y.K. Dwivedi et al. (Eds.): I3E 2016, LNCS 9844, pp. 319–324, 2016.
DOI: 10.1007/978-3-319-45234-0_29

2   Theoretical Concepts Used in Relation to Sharing

Theories commonly used to explore sharing on social media are those from the social psychology discipline such as social cognitive theory, the need to belong concept, and social exchange theory. Social cognitive theory, which states that individuals observe others' behaviour and the ensuing consequences as a guide to inform their future behaviour, has been used to underpin the motivations of information sharing in social media [6], knowledge sharing intention in virtual communities [7], and sharing of tourism experiences on social media [8]. The need to belong concept, which suggests the innate human need of a sense of belonging [9], has been used to look at sharing behaviour in virtual communities [10] and positive WOM behaviour [11]. Highlighting the cost versus benefit self-interest of people, social exchange theory emphasises the importance of value in the exchange process [12], which has been used to underpin some sharing on social media studies [2], specifically in the context of online community [13] and content [14] sharing behaviour. It is normally combined with social cognitive theory as a way to provide theoretical underpinning to selected motivations for sharing in many studies [6, 7].

Both social exchange theory and social cognitive theory recognise the expectation of outcomes or reward, yet in the social media environment individuals do not necessarily expect to receive anything in return, rather relying on the hope that they will get help at another point in time due to its communal nature [6]. The need to belong concept focuses on the group aspect of sharing, thus failing to recognise the increasing heterogeneous nature of social media activities [15]. Despite their utility, these perspectives do not recognise the intrinsic satisfaction that an individual can get from sharing, failing to acknowledge more than just the consequences of the act itself [16]. In order to understand the appeal of using social media for sharing it is important to identify their motivations for using social media for this purpose and thus understand the individual user rather than just the communicator, establishing how and why they use this medium for sharing [17].

2.1   Uses and Gratification Theory

Uses and gratifications theory, which acknowledges the gratifications an individual seeks and receives from using particular media [18], is a more effective way to understand the mechanisms of sharing on social media. Focusing on how individuals use different types of media to meet their needs and the behavioural outcomes of this, it is considered one of the most effective theories at identifying the antecedents and consequences of media use [19], and is extremely useful to apply to new types of media, such as social media, to provide a more in-depth analysis of the motivations to use these platforms [20]. Individuals that use particular media are argued to have particular goals from doing so, thus make an active choice rather than a subconscious decision. This theory has been widely utilised to understand why and how people use social media sites in general [21] as well as sharing behaviours, such as Karnik et al. [22] who identified contribution, discovery, social interaction and entertainment as Facebook media sharing uses and gratifications.

Motivations are believed to be the influencing force that guides behaviour. The continuing evolution of media means that the list of motivations that have been identified by uses and gratifications theorists continues to expand, thus there are various classifications and ways of categorising them [23]. One of the most popular classifications includes entertainment, information, identity and social interaction [24], all of which are broad categories and cover varying sub-motivations. However, increasing use of the theory is bringing many more motivations to light, for example Oh and Syn [6] identify 10 motivations, including self-efficacy and altruism.

2.2 Brand Attitude and Purchase Intention

Brand attitude is the evaluation that a consumer has of a brand based on the information and knowledge they have accumulated - such as that acquired through sharing - and is an important element to social exchanges [25]. In a social media environment, where consumers are surrounded by networks of other individuals, they inherently learn their behaviours, attitudes and purchasing approaches through the knowledge these networks share. If a consumer holds a positive attitude towards a brand, then they are more likely to purchase that brand [26].

Consumers are influenced in their purchase decisions through what they gather and perceive from the sharing of knowledge from their peers about products or services [3]. The information that they receive through their social media networks, leads them to evaluate the product or service and thus result in their subsequent willingness to purchase in future [27].

2.3 Self-Construal Theory

Originally expanded from Hofstede's individualist-collectivist scale, which depicted cultural level differences [28], self-construal theory outlines individual-level differences not explained by the original theory [29]. It has been widely used within the marketing discipline as a way of studying the individual differences within consumers, particularly within consumer behaviour [30], and consumer psychology [31]. Defining two aspects of the self-concept, the independent and interdependent self-construals have become synonymous with differing motivations such as uniqueness and status seeking motivations (independent) or group focused, relationship oriented motivations (interdependent) [32]. Thus it can be argued that these differing self-views will have an impact on the uses and gratifications an individual seeks and obtains from utilising social media for sharing purposes, overcoming the identified lack of social psychological reasoning previously identified.

3 Discussion

Many studies have utilised social psychological theories to explain sharing on social media, yet few have considered the different dimensions of the self and how this impacts motivations to share on social media. Despite the seemingly strong argument for the selection of uses and gratifications theory, it has been suggested that this perspective is highly individualistic in its approach, failing to acknowledge the social aspects of media consumption [19].

Although the theories that have previously been used have made headway in identifying some of the behaviours of individuals who share, they fail to recognise intrinsic motivations that are extremely relevant to understanding sharing behaviour from an individual perspective [17]. It is suggested that the theories that have been used have all identified elements that can be classified under the uses and gratifications theory to identify motivations for sharing. For example, elements of social exchange theory could be classified under the remuneration motivation identified by Oh and Syn [6]. More unique theories that have been used to understand sharing such as social network theory [32], social capital theory [33], and social learning theory [34] also have the capacity to be incorporated into motivations for sharing and thus provide a better understanding of sharing as a whole. Uses and gratifications theory could be one way of making sure underlying propositions from many theories are incorporated to explain sharing behaviour.

It appears that much of the literature regarding sharing on social media is focused on behavioural tendencies rather than the underlying individual aspects of those who share. These individual characteristics are a much needed area for future research in sharing behaviour [35]. Understanding why they share would establish a more grounded understanding for their behaviour and allow brands to incorporate these motivations when approaching influential individuals. Kim et al. [36] used the uses and gratifications theory to examine motivations of the self-construal on Facebook in terms of use and satisfaction, but only distinguished between social and non-social motivations. Providing evidence for the need to incorporate these individual level differences into motivations for social media use, they suggested that future research should focus on alternative social media platforms other than Facebook. Munar and Jacobsen [8] also posit that motivations on social media differ depending on the type of content. Therefore, it is perhaps necessary to identify the differing motivations individuals derive from sharing different types of content on social media. Self-construal theory is one of the social psychological theories that are yet to be explored in depth within the realm of sharing on social media. Much of the literature points to the need for a more detailed look at the motivations of consumers who curate content [37] rather than those who initially create content. The opinion seeking, opinion passing, and opinion giving dimensions of eWOM would also provide a relevant addition to understand the motivations of sharing, as individuals within social media can take on these multiple roles and thus may be distinctly motivated to pursue each one [38]. The next step in addressing this topic will be to provide a stronger theoretical evaluation and development of relevant hypotheses.

4 Conclusion

This paper has explored the theoretical concepts for explaining sharing on social media and pointed to the areas of future research that are needed to further understanding on the topic, suggesting uses and gratifications theory combined with self-construal theory to be an appropriate way to address this gap.

References

1. Fehr, E., Bernhard, H., Rockenbach, B.: Egalitarianism in young children. Nature **454**(7208), 1079–1083 (2008)
2. Osatuyi, B.: Information sharing on social media sites. Comput. Hum. Behav. **29**, 2622–2631 (2013)
3. Wang, X., Yu, C., Wei, Y.: Social media peer communication and impacts on purchase intentions: a consumer socialization framework. J. Interact. Mark. **26**, 198–208 (2012)
4. Hennig-Thurau, T., Gwinner, K.P., Walsh, G., Gremler, D.D.: Electronic word-of-mouth via consumer-opinion platforms: what motivates consumers to articulate themselves on the internet? J. Interact. Mark. **18**(1), 38–52 (2004)
5. Chiu, C.-M., Hsu, M.-H., Wang, E.T.G.: Understanding knowledge sharing in virtual communities: an integration of social capital and social cognitive theories. Decis. Support Syst. **42**, 1872–1888 (2006)
6. Oh, S., Syn, S.Y.: Motivations for sharing information and social support in social media: a comparative analysis of Facebook, Twitter, Delicious, YouTube, and Flickr. J. Assoc. Inf. Sci. Technol. **66**(10), 2045–2060 (2015)
7. Ye, S., Chen, H., Jin, X.: Exploring the moderating effects of commitment and perceived value of knowledge in explaining knowledge contribution in virtual communities. In: The Tenth Pacific Asia Conference on Information Systems, pp. 239–254 (2006)
8. Munar, A.M., Jacobsen, J.K.S.: Motivations for sharing tourism experiences through social media. Tour. Manag. **43**, 46–54 (2014)
9. Baumeister, R.F., Leary, M.R.: The need to belong: desire for interpersonal attachments as a fundamental human motivation. Psychol. Bull. **117**(3), 497–529 (1995)
10. Ma, W.W.K., Yuen, A.H.K.: Understanding online knowledge sharing: an interpersonal relationship perspective. Comput. Educ. **56**, 210–219 (2011)
11. Sicilia, M., Delgado-Ballester, E., Palazon, M.: The need to belong and self-disclosure in positive word-of-mouth behaviours: the moderating effect of self-brand connection. J. Consum. Behav. **15**, 60–71 (2016)
12. Boardman, A.E., Greenberg, D.H., Vining, A.R., Weimer, D.L.: Cost-benefit analysis: concepts and practice, 3rd edn. Prentice Hall, Upper Saddle River (2006)
13. Pai, P., Tsai, H.-T.: Reciprocity norms and information-sharing behaviour in online consumption communities: an empirical investigation of antecedents and moderators. Inf. Manag. **53**, 38–52 (2016)
14. Shi, Z., Rui, H., Whinston, A.B.: Content sharing in a social broadcasting environment: evidence from Twitter. MIS Q. **38**(1), 123–142 (2014)
15. Weijo, H., Hietanen, J., Mattila, P.: New insights into online consumption communities and netnography. J. Bus. Res. **67**, 2072–2078 (2014)
16. Ryan, R.M., Deci, E.L.: Intrinsic and extrinsic motivations: classic definitions and new directions. Contemp. Educ. Psychol. **25**, 54–67 (2000)
17. Aitken, R., Gray, B., Lawson, R.: Advertising effectiveness from a consumer perspective. Int. J. Adv. **27**(2), 279–297 (2008)
18. Rubin, A.M.: The uses-and-gratifications perspective of media effects. In: Bryant, J., Zillmann, D. (eds.) Media Effects: Advances in Theory and Research, pp. 525–548. Lawrence Erlbaum Associates, Mahwah (2002)
19. Katz, E., Blumler, J.G., Gurevitch, M.: Utilization of mass communication by the individual. In: Blumler, J.G., Katz, E. (eds.) The Uses of Mass Communications: Current Perspectives on Gratifications Research, vol. 3, pp. 19–32. Sage Publications, Beverly Hills (1974)

20. Ruggiero, T.E.: Uses and gratifications theory in the 21st century. Mass Commun. Soc. **3**(1), 3–36 (2000)
21. Boyd, D.: Why youth (heart) social network sites: the role of networked publics in teenage social life. In: Buckingham, D. (ed.) Youth, Identity, and Digital Media, pp. 119–142. MIT Press, Cambridge (2008)
22. Karnik, M., Oakley, I., Venkatanathan, J., Spiliotopoulos, T., Nisi, V.: Uses and gratifications of a Facebook media sharing group. In: Understanding People's Practices in Social Networks, 23–27 February, San Antonio, Texas, USA, CSCW, pp. 821–866. ACM (2013)
23. Barton, K.M.: Reality television programming and diverging gratifications: the influence of content on gratifications obtained. J. Broadcasting & Electron. Media **53**(3), 460–476 (2009)
24. McQuail, D.: Mass Communication Theory. Sage Publications, London (1983)
25. Morgan, R.M., Hunt, S.D.: The commitment-trust theory of relationship marketing. J. Mark. **58**(7), 20–38 (1994)
26. Keller, K.L., Lehmann, D.: How do brands create value? Mark. Manag. **5**(May/June), 27–31 (2003)
27. Dodds, B.W., Monroe, K.B., Grewal, D.: Effect of price, brand, and store information on buyers product evaluation. J. Mark. Res. **28**(3), 307–319 (1991)
28. Hofstede, G.: Culture's Consequences: International Differences in Work-Related Values. Sage Publications, Newbury Park (1980)
29. Markus, H.R., Kitayama, S.: Culture and the self: implications for cognition, emotion, and motivation. Psychol. Rev. **98**, 224–253 (1991)
30. Millan, E., Reynolds, J.: Self-contruals, symbolic and hedonic preferences, and actual purchase behavior. J. Retail. Consum. Serv. **21**, 550–560 (2014)
31. Zhang, Y., Shrum, L.J.: The influence of self-construal on impulsive consumption. J. Consum. Res. **35**, 838–850 (2009)
32. Brown, J., Broderick, A.J., Lee, N.: Word of mouth communication within online communities: conceptualising the online social network. J. Interact. Mark. **21**(2), 2–20 (2007)
33. Wasko, M.M., Faraj, S.: Why should I share? Examining social capital and knowledge contribution in electronic networks of practice. MIS Q. **29**(1), 35–57 (2005)
34. Burke, M., Marlow, C., Lento, T.: Feed me: motivating newcomer contribution in social network sites. Proceedings of the SIGCHI Conference on Human Factors in Computing Systems, pp. 945–954. ACM (2009)
35. Wang, S., Noe, R.A.: Knowledge sharing: a review and directions for future research. Hum. Resour. Manag. Rev. **20**, 115–131 (2010)
36. Kim, J.H., Kim, M.-S., Nam, Y.: An analysis of self-construals, motivations, Facebook use, and user satisfaction. Int. J. Hum.-Comput. Interact. **26**(11-12), 1077–1099 (2010)
37. Villi, M., Moisander, J., Joy, A.: Social curation in consumer communities: consumers as curators of online media content. Adv. Consum. Res. **40**, 490–495 (2012)
38. Chu, S.-C., Kim, Y.: The determinants of consumer engagement in electronic word-of-mouth (eWOM) in social networking sites. Int. J. Advert. **30**(1), 47–75 (2011)

The Value Creation of Social Media Information

Tajinder Kaur Bahia[1(✉)] and Antonis Constantinou Simintiras[2,3]

[1] Marketing in New Times (MINT) Research, Warwick, UK
tajinderkbahia@gmail.com
[2] Gulf University for Science and Technology, College of Business Administration,
Kuwait City, Kuwait
Simintiras.A@gust.edu.kw
[3] Swansea University, School of Management, Swansea, South Wales, UK
a.c.simintiras@swansea.ac.uk

Abstract. Social media information is a useful barometer of value characterising the digital age. To identify the core contributors of value creation, value is in the 'eye of the beholder', and 'sharing' social media information is indicative of communicating such perceived value. Sharing allows for belongingness, as people do not simply connect with communities, they contribute to communities, and shape them too. Content that is shared needs to be credible, especially as the power to persuade is being co-created by consumers. This is facilitated by sharing content deemed truthful and relevant; accordingly, information conveyed needs to be accurate and timely. Drawing from social network theory and Buckner's (1965) theory on rumour transmission, we argue that the value of social media information is significantly created from an interplay of: (i) 'sharing', (ii) 'persuasion' and (iii) 'timing'. This interplay is not exhaustive, however, as other contributors may exist, thus further research is advocated.

Keywords: Social media information · Value creation · Sharing · Persuasion · Timing · Belonging · Accuracy · Speed

1 Introduction

This paper appraises the finer intricacies of value creation in the ever popular and fast-paced domain of social media. Social media may be defined as an array of Internet-based applications that develops and builds up from the conceptual ideology and high-tech fundamentals of Web 2.0, allowing for the formation and interchange of user-generated content (UGC) [1, 2]. This conceptualisation suggests that Web content is not simply consumed by users in a passive sense. Instead, it is created, shared and consumed by people who are actively generating content [1]. Indeed, a number of different research efforts exist that focus on the significance of UGC across differing contexts. Although there exist a many number of varied platforms for social media to include social networking, text messaging, photo sharing, wikis, weblogs, and discussion forums, it is mostly shaped by the more prevalent Internet-based applications to include 'YouTube', 'Facebook', 'Second Life', 'Wikipedia', and 'Twitter' [1, 2].

© IFIP International Federation for Information Processing 2016
Published by Springer International Publishing Switzerland 2016. All Rights Reserved
Y.K. Dwivedi et al. (Eds.): I3E 2016, LNCS 9844, pp. 325–331, 2016.
DOI: 10.1007/978-3-319-45234-0_30

When appraising the motivations for sharing experiences via social media, sharing practices emerge as valuable constructions of sociability and emotional support [3]. Social media is also understood as the digital version of word-of-mouth communication [4], as each and every individual is able to connect with many hundreds, if not thousands of other like-minded individuals on matters relating to the services and products, as well as the organisations that offer them [5]. Each and every individual is indispensable to the creation of value, and with the advent of 'influence marketing', this kind of marketing centres on main personalities and characters, rather than on a target market [5]. Accordingly, there seems to have been significantly more burden placed on organisations to source out key Social Media Influencers (SMIs) [6, 7], as a firm's collaboration with its customers may potentially result in entire marketing programs being co-created [8, 9].

In terms of marketing, social media is a hybrid constituent of the promotion mix considering that in the traditional sense it allows businesses to communicate with their customer base, yet also in the not so traditional sense, it allows customers to communicate openly and directly with one another [5]. Drawing insights from consumer culture theory, collectives deliver value to members via progressive sharing activities of numerous styles, thus consumer-based collectives constitute the basis of considerable value creation [9]. Arguably, as the information value constituents' shift, so too does the focus of marketing messages shift. Notwithstanding, the sharing of information and consumer experiences by brand communities on social media are found to be key to marketers' efforts to form relations with customers [2, 10, 11], which can serve to fulfil a person's need for belongingness [2, 12], and identity [9].

2   The Core Contributors of Value Creation for Social Media

As the bearing of consumer-to-consumer communications has become significantly exaggerated in the ever-virtual marketplace [5], to guide our research efforts that elucidate upon the core contributors of value creation for social media, established theoretical paradigms for examining and explaining how people develop networks, voice opinions, and share information include social network theory [4, 13], social exchange theory [4, 7], and social penetration theory [4]. Also of significance, the theory of rumour transmission (theory of communication) indicates the speed and accuracy of a rumour passing are affected by the structure of the network and the mind-sets (namely, critical ability) of the individuals in the network [4, 14]. Accordingly, people's interest and involvement serve to shape the content, timing, and frequency of information transmission [14].

As social media exchanges are beyond management's direct control [9], they are compelled to respond with credibility that is well-timed [15]. Similarly, sharing (and liking) social media can augment the effects of 'popular cohesion' and 'message diffusion' [16]. In particular, they explore how persuasive messages to encompass the notion of 'argument quality', can induce people to share and like messages. On a par with their research, we advocate that 'accuracy' ultimately underpins persuasive social media content that people want to share and relate to, with 'timing', explicitly 'speed' of response (comparable to that of message diffusion) being essential for firms seeking to cultivate the value creation process of social media information. Content that is shared calls for credibility, and as the power to persuade now also resides with the consumer, this can be facilitated by sharing content that is deemed persuasive, truthful and relevant (that is, accurate and timely). With this in mind, we argue that the value of social media information is significantly created from an interplay of: (i) 'sharing', (ii) 'persuasion' and (iii) 'timing'. These constituents are discussed in greater detail below.

2.1   Sharing - Belongingness and Identity

The sharing of social media information, also referred to as 'consumer-generated media', allows for a sense of belongingness [2, 12], as people do not simply connect with communities, they contribute to, as well as shape them too [17]. Three core attributes are deemed important for marketers to consider when persuasion is employed to engage a sense of ownership that leads to the sharing of social media information [6]. These are: (i) relevance, (ii) reach, and (iii) resonance. Relevance pertains to the actual content influencers are sharing deemed relevant to a business [6] by creating and negotiating meaning [2]. Reach refers to the number of people one could hypothetically influence in accord with an influencer's follower base, thus bringing value to a business [6, 17]. Resonance is understood as feeling engaged and identifying with an audience from sharing content that is relevant [6]. Hitherto, creating reflections of an extended digital self is facilitated by the practice of sharing content [18, 19]. Responses by others and retweets add value to a person's collection of social media information [19].

What is more, by creating social presence the awareness of connectedness and the feel of being in touch with others can endure as an experience deemed to be extremely engaging [1, 20]. To tap this aspect of human communication, a 'Connectedness Questionnaire' has been developed that focuses upon the affective advantages of the awareness systems [20]. Hypothesised affective gains span the feeling of companionship, a resilient group pull, a feeling of remaining in touch, of staying informed with other people's lives, as well as a sense of sharing, belonging, and closeness [20]. In a nutshell, awareness systems are not perceived as substituting prevailing communication means, but more so as a way to enhance them, to fortify social bonds, and enable new varieties of interaction [20].

2.2   Persuasion – A Need for Accuracy

Leading SMIs espouse and voice opinions that other people listen to, and are persuaded by [7]. It is important to see what this means for business [6]. By engaging with SMIs an organisation is able to intensify levels of awareness underpinning its brand, as well as build brand advocates, augment online reputation, and escalate page rank. Thus, whether the objective of one's business is to augment awareness or to increase SEO (search engine optimisation) traffic, SMIs constitute a viable source of business support [6] and contribute to effective communication strategies [7].

In certain instances, word of mouth updates are deemed as extremely persuasive, and are even professed as more dependable and truthful than more mainstream broadcasting mediums [21]. In a recent survey more than 90 % of the communication practitioners surveyed were confident that blogs and social media now influence mainstream news [21]. Social media is considered by consumers as being a more trustworthy source of information regarding products and services than corporate-sponsored communications transmitted via the traditional elements of the promotion mix [5, 22]. Reputation becomes a key factor. For instance, when appraising the SMI, a person's reputation online is found to factor in the strength and credibility of social media influence. Thus, the more persuasive and influential an individual is, the better the reputation of the individual [6].

SMIs facilitate marketing agendas via the practice of creating relationships. Even if an influencer's audience is niche or mass, an influencer can go about reaching a target group of consumers via their blogs and social networks that a brand in and of itself may not be able to influence [6]. Truth and accuracy are the building blocks of such relationships. Experts, for example, are always advised to be truthful and endeavour for accuracy, as truth and accuracy are basic principles, which ought to be endorsed as far as is feasibly possible [23]. Still, that is not to say there are many experts [24]. Transparency and accountability are called for to function efficiently, with impunity, particularly in a setting where people are actively immersed in online conversations [25]. Consumers are also more refined, visibly dubious and extremely demanding. The speed with which such changes are directly impacting marketing communication is remarkable [17], and indisputably necessitates a redrafting of the rules for handling matters such as reputation and brand management [25]. With this in mind, and tying in with the discussion on 'timing' to follow, we advocate the influencer's speed of response plays a significant part in shaping reputation.

2.3   Timing – Speed is of the Essence

Unlike any other platform of communications, including TV and radio, social media reach has proved to be the speediest in terms of reach and influence [17]. YouTubers upload in excess of 100 h of video each and every minute on a daily basis. That is approximately equal to 500,000 full length movies uploaded per week. More video is broadcast on YouTube in a month, compared with the last 60 years on broadcasting networks such as ABC, NBC, and CBS combined [17]. Time, in terms of speed and reach, is certainly of the essence when engaging with the throes of social media. Arguably therefore when it comes to mastering the domain of social media, survival of the fittest today may be better framed as 'survival of the fastest' [26]. Investments in new communication and information technologies serve to transcend geographic boundaries [5], to greatly alter traditional conceptualisations and perceptions of space, time, and interaction, and especially due to how efficiently, if not speedily, such technologies are facilitated [27–30].

In light of today's changing conceptualisations of time and space as a result of advancing technology, the speed of transactions and the transference of information have elevated to heights of incomparable importance [1, 31–34]. Indeed, when appraising the significance of speed, over recent years global communication has advanced at an unprecedented speed [28–30, 34]. As each day passes the sway of social media magnifies as more and more people become a part of new online communities [1, 17]. As an illustration, Facebook is a social utility that offers synchronous relations, which take place in real time, as when people text back and forth with friends, as well as asynchronous relations, which do not necessitate replies are made instantaneously, as when sending an email to a friend and a reply is received the following day. Also on offer with Facebook are opportunities for content sharing of pictures, music/audio, video footage, games, apps, groups, spanning in excess of 1.2 billion active users [17].

Potentially therefore, it may be that the speed of response can be construed as a measure of relational strength imbibed with a particular sense of significance. Undeniably, the power of web-based networks has amplified the speediness, scope of influence and interactivity of social media information and communication [1, 25]. In the present age of the social web, disclosed informal boardroom discussions can appear on the Internet in a matter of seconds, and records leaked through mass mail can be published and commented upon in blogs within a few minutes [25]. Invariably, the speed of such undertakings can potentially impair the image of a company and generate opinions of corporate negligence and a lack of responsibility [25]. Hence, timely action imbibed with speed is called for.

3 Conclusions and Directions for Future Research

The present paper has argued that the value of social media information is created from an interplay of sharing, persuasion, and timing. As it is accepted that this interplay is not exhaustive (as other contributors may exist), further research efforts by academics and marketers are encouraged. Accuracy of social media information is argued to give way to persuasion. Future research may seek to explore this relationship in terms of brand involvement/engagement/loyalty, honing in on the marketing efforts of SMIs specifically. As loyalty and engagement are significant to the value creation of social media information, future research may seek to explore if this is actually more apparent by regular and timely acts of sharing credible content with significant others that render a collective sense of belonging (identity).

Future research may seek to explore the darker side of value creation of social media information. That is, in terms of the value creation of social media information, anyone, anywhere with access to technology can share such information to feel belongingness and carve out an identity, yet the darker side of this chain is that if the means to engage and persuade in the domain of social media was taken away from people, would all types of social networks (to include digital natives and SMIs) habitually feel lost, alone, and at a loss for what to do [17]?

References

1. Kaplan, A.M., Haenlein, M.: Users of the world, unite! The challenges and opportunities of social media. Bus. Horiz. **53**, 59–68 (2010)
2. Laroche, M., Habibi, M.R., Richard, M.O.: To be or not to be in social media: How brand loyalty is affected by social media? Int. J. Inform. Manag. **33**, 76–82 (2013)

3. Munar, A.M., Jacobsen, J.K.S.: Motivations for sharing tourism experiences through social media. Tour. Manag. **43**, 46–54 (2014)
4. Pan, B., Crotts, J.: Theoretical models of social media, marketing implications, and future research directions. In: Sigala, M., Christou, E., Gretzel, U. (eds.) Social Media in Travel, Tourism and Hospitality: Theory, Practice and Cases, pp. 73–86. Ashgate, Surrey (2012)
5. Mangold, W.G., Faulds, D.J.: Social media: the new hybrid element of the promotion mix. Bus. Horiz. **52**, 357–365 (2009)
6. Cisnero, K.: To Engage and Create A Lasting Relationship with Social Media Influencers. https://blog.hootsuite.com/how-to-find-social-media-influencers
7. Ngai, E.W., Tao, S.S., Moon, K.K.: Social media research: theories, constructs, and conceptual frameworks. Int. J. Inform. Manag. **35**, 33–44 (2015)
8. Lusch, R.F., Vargo, S.L.: Service-dominant logic as a foundation for building a general theory. In: Lusch, R.F., Vargo, S.L. (eds.) The Service-Dominant Logic of Marketing, pp. 406–420. M.E. Sharpe, Armonk (2006)
9. Schau, H.J., Muñiz Jr., A.M., Arnould, E.J.: How brand community practices create value. J. Marketing. **73**, 30–51 (2009)
10. De Vries, L., Gensler, S., Leeflang, P.S.: Popularity of brand posts on brand fan pages: an investigation of the effects of social media marketing. J. Interact. Mark. **26**, 83–91 (2012)
11. McAlexander, J.H., Schouten, W.J., Koening, F.H.: Building brand community. J. Mark. **66**, 38–54 (2002)
12. Gangadharbatla, H.: Facebook me: collective self-esteem, need to belong, and internet self-efficacy as predictors of the iGeneration's attitudes toward social networking sites. J. Interact. Advert. **8**, 5–15 (2008)
13. del Fresno García, M., Daly, A.J., Segado Sánchez-Cabezudo, S.: Identifying the new influences in the internet era: social media and social network analysis. Rev. Esp. Invest. Sociol. **153**, 23–40 (2016)
14. Buckner, H.T.: A theory of rumor transmission. Public Opin. Quart. **29**, 54–70 (1965)
15. Moreno, A., Navarro, C., Tench, R., Zerfass, A.: Does social media usage matter? An analysis of online practices and digital media perceptions of communication practitioners in Europe. Public Relat. Rev. **41**, 242–253 (2015)
16. Chang, Y.T., Yu, H., Lu, H.P.: Persuasive messages, popularity cohesion, and message diffusion in social media marketing. J. Bus. Res. **68**, 777–782 (2015)
17. Tuten, T.L., Solomon, M.R.: Social Media Marketing. Sage, London (2014)
18. Carroll, E., Romano, J.: Your digital afterlife: When Facebook, Flickr and Twitter are your estate, what's your legacy?. New Riders, Berkeley (2011)
19. Belk, R.W.: Extended self in a digital world. J. Consum. Res. **40**, 477–500 (2013)
20. IJsselsteijn, W., van Baren, J., van Lanen, F.: Staying in touch social presence and connectedness through synchronous and asynchronous communication media. In: Stephanidis, C., Jacko, J. (eds.) Human-Computer Interaction Theory and Practice (Part II) of the Proceedings of HCI International, vol. 2, pp. 924–928. Lawrence Erlbaum, Hillsdale (2003)
21. Veil, S.R., Buehner, T., Palenchar, M.J.: A work-in-process literature review: Incorporating social media in risk and crisis communication. J. Conting. Crisis Manag. **19**, 110–122 (2011)
22. Foux, G.: Consumer-generated media: Get your customers involved. Brand Strat. **8**, 38–39 (2006)
23. Murphy, D.G., Loeb, S., Basto, M.Y., Challacombe, B., Trinh, Q.D., Leveridge, M., Morgan, T., Dasgupta, P., Bultitude, M.: Engaging responsibly with social media: the BJUI guidelines. BJU Int. **114**, 9–11 (2014)

24. Solis, B., Breakenridge, D.K.: Putting the public back in public relations: how social media is reinventing the aging business of PR. FT Press, Upper Saddle River (2009)
25. Jones, B., Temperley, J., Lima, A.: Corporate reputation in the era of web 2.0: the case of primark. J. Mark. Manag. **25**, 927–939 (2009)
26. Greengard, S.: The need for speed. Workforce **79**, 20–21 (2000)
27. Harvey, D.: The Condition of Postmodernity. Blackwell, Oxford (1989)
28. Kaufman-Scarborough, C.: time use and the impact of technology: examining workspaces in the home. Time Soc. **15**, 57–80 (2006)
29. Turner, J.W., Grube, J.A., Tinsley, C.H., Lee, C., O'Pell, C.: Exploring the dominant media: how does media use reflect organizational norms and affect performance? J. Bus. Commun. **43**, 220–250 (2006)
30. Turner, J.W., Reinsch, N.L.: the business communicator as presence allocator: multicommunicating, equivocality, and status at work. J. Bus. Commun. **44**, 36–58 (2007)
31. D'Aveni, R.A., Gunther, R.: Hypercompetition: Managing the Dynamics of Strategic Maneuvering. The Free Press, New York (1994)
32. Fine, C.H.: Clockspeed: Winning Industry Control in the Age of Temporary Advantage. Perseus, New York (1998)
33. Rubin, D.: Velocity management rush. IIE Solut. **33**, 36–39 (2001)
34. Bianchi, C., Mathews, S.: Internet marketing and export market growth in Chile. J. Bus. Res. **69**, 426–434 (2015)

The Intersection of Source, Message, and Recipient Characteristics on Information-Exchange Activity via Twitter

Mohammad Alajmi[✉] and Huda Farhan

Public Authority for Applied Education and Training, Kuwait City, Kuwait
maa.alajmi@paaet.edu.kw, hudafarhan@gmail.com

Abstract. The purpose of the research is to explain how Twitter supports real-time information exchange in popular domains, and examine the influence of source, message, and recipient characteristics on information exchange. University students were surveyed using a structured questionnaire. A model was developed and statistically tested to examine the influence of characteristics on information exchange via Twitter. Different characteristics were demonstrated to be significant predictors of information exchange. For source characteristics, authoritative knowledge, social connections, and attractiveness have a positive influence, while for recipient characteristics, prior knowledge, community engagement, and demographics influence information exchange. For message characteristics, information usefulness and information quality are effective. Overall, influences vary based on the domain. The results help Twitter operators and users to understand the most important source, message, and recipient characteristics for information exchange. This study informs sources about the characteristics that make tweets more informative, and more likely to be exchanged by recipients. It assists Twitter operators to understand what characteristics are important in future system designs.

Keywords: Source characteristics · Message characteristics · Recipient characteristics · Microblogging · Information seeking · Information sharing · Information exchange

1   Introduction

The recent development of social networking sites (SNSs) has transformed the World Wide Web into a social and participatory place in which users create, broadcast, modify, and share information and knowledge [1]. [2] stated that "online communities, including discussion forums, blogs, social networking sites, and microblogs, appear to be the most active places where users' information sharing behavior takes place" (p. 604).

Twitter, a social networking and microblogging service, is now used widely for broadcasting and exchanging messages, including information in various domains [3]. Twitter is a valuable source of user-generated content, with users able to send and receive messages ("tweets") freely. Therefore, Twitter use potentially differs from other means of communication because of its timeliness and convenience within a context of reduced control and direct access to personal thoughts and opinions [4]. According to

© IFIP International Federation for Information Processing 2016
Published by Springer International Publishing Switzerland 2016. All Rights Reserved
Y.K. Dwivedi et al. (Eds.): I3E 2016, LNCS 9844, pp. 332–353, 2016.
DOI: 10.1007/978-3-319-45234-0_31

statistics from Statistic Brain Research Institute, in March 2015 Twitter had 645 million Twitter users, posting an average of 58 million tweets per day.

This raises the question of what type of information is exchanged via Twitter and what are the most efficient characteristics that influence this activity. One of Twitter's key advantages is that users can interact with others and exchange information and knowledge. According to [5], users engage in information exchange by seeking and sharing information with each other within a communication medium. Users may aim to exchange information to discover more about topics of interest, evaluate particular information, and benefit others by sharing information. Thus, users typically inspect information that they exchange and determine what is valuable and what is not.

In recent years, Twitter has emerged as a popular research topic [4, 6–9]. Studies have identified several motivations, gratifications, and drawbacks affecting Twitter usage, and have generally concluded that Twitter is an important platform for information seeking and sharing during real-time events. Research has examined the factors affecting information adoption, credibility, diffusion, and exchange via social media, focusing on a particular domain or event [2, 8, 10, 12–14].

Although research has shown the importance of Twitter in information exchange, little is known about the effect of source, message, and recipient characteristics on the success of information exchange when users share and seek information and in particular domains. Previous studies suffer from conflicting conclusions, restrictions in the factors considered, and limitations of subjects or events. This study examines how Twitter supports information exchange in various domains, and comparatively examines the influence of source, message, and recipient characteristics on the most popular information-exchange domains.

2 Literature Review

2.1 Information Exchange and Social Media

Studies of collaborative information use in electronic environments have indicated that users are amenable to information exchange in terms of sharing experiences and recommendations, and connect with others who have similar concerns via social networks [15, 16]. A number of studies discussed the use of social media as a communication and information-sharing and -seeking resource in the context of different events and subjects [10, 12, 17]. According to [18–20], people seek and share information for comfort, support, empowerment of the knowledge they have, or simply to learn. Some information can simply be stored and recalled, while in other cases, it can be passed to others to make decisions and/or affect attitudes and behaviors.

Theories such as uses and gratifications, diffusion of innovation, and technology acceptance model promote an understanding of the use and acceptance of SNSs and identify determinants that influence SNS usage. Among several factors, the motivation for information exchange has played a sufficient role in SNSs general usage [21], features [22, 23], and usage types [7, 10]. In the context of health, [10] investigated the factors that influence cancer patients and their companions in using blogs for health information. They found that blogging activity is most helpful for information sharing, and this is affected by perceived credibility and posting comments on others' blogs. [7] examined which motivational and constraint factors impact sport Twitter consumption with regard to athletics. Information motivations were found to guide sport organizations and practitioners in utilizing social media as an information source. Most, if not all, studies, explain that the need for information is an essential motivation to use SNSs.

Information exchange is a sufficient and necessary condition for knowledge creation and collaboration [24]. Because of the importance of information exchange in knowledge creation and construction, substantial research has investigated a wide variety of factors for information diffusion via SNSs [2, 17, 25]. [17] classified the motivations for information exchange into four types: environmental, personal, interpersonal, and socio-cultural. They identified motivational factors for participation in information exchange that are different from the motivations for hindering contribution. While previous studies focused on the use of SNSs for information exchange, these still suffer from a lack of theoretical framework in understanding information-exchange activity via SNSs.

2.2 Information Exchange and Twitter

Twitter has recently developed rapidly because of its sufficient characteristics in relation to information pervasiveness [3]. Because of its timeliness, convenience and large number of users, Twitter has been widely adopted by the public to publish/share information on different topics, such as marketing, sport, politics, health, and education. Unlike traditional media and other SNSs, Twitter provides real-time information and status updates in these domains. [6] investigated the effect of collective intelligence from Twitter information on predicting events in the stock market. [26] studied Twitter as a platform for online word-of-mouth branding, suggesting that Twitter could play an important role in marketing. Twitter information was also used in predicting trends in health [10], as well as airline products and services [8] and enterprise collaboration [27].

Understanding information-exchange activity and its determinants on Twitter can help in the design of information systems and in assisting users to gain influence. A growing body of research explores factors that contribute to the process of information diffusion via Twitter [13, 28–31]. [31] analyzed 1.6 million tweets to identify their attributes and relative influence for disseminating information. [13] focused on the features of Twitter, including the features of tweets and retweets, that affect information diffusion and exchange. Overall, the research on information exchange via Twitter is still restricted to some determinants, and conducting research on other factors is highly recommended.

2.3 Twitter Use in Arabic Cultures

In developing countries, particularly the Arab region, Twitter has grown strongly in terms of the number of Arabic users and the amount of content posted in Arabic, indicating that Twitter is being adopted by broad segments of society. A growing body of work has started to identify the effect of national culture on information/knowledge sharing, diffusion, and adoption [2, 17]. Many studies have focused on cultures in the

Far East, Europe, or North America. However, and despite the substantial increase in Twitter use in the Arab world to disseminate information and raise awareness of local and global events, to our knowledge, no research has explored in detail the domains of Twitter usage and the determinants that influence information exchange via Twitter in Middle Eastern cultures.

3 Research Model and Hypotheses Development

In order to build knowledge via social media, information exchange is a necessary condition that needs to be investigated [32]. Social media makes it very convenient for users to share and seek information. Users log on to different social media sites to gather information to support their knowledge, and to make decisions. Our work extends existing research in two ways. First, we investigate the type of information that users share and seek via Twitter. Second, we investigate several characteristics to identify which are most related to information-exchange activity on Twitter.

Several theories have been applied to interpret how people are influenced by receiving information, such as Yale's model (exposure, attention, comprehension, acceptance, retention, and action) [33, 34] dual-process theory of normative and informational influences, the elaboration likelihood model (ELM) [35], and the heuristics systematic model (HSM) [36]. These four theories concentrate on three major factors: source, message, and recipient. Yale's model posits that three factors—message, source, and audience—influence people's attention, comprehension, and acceptance of a message, which could later affect their opinions, perceptions, and actions. Dual-process theory of human information processing considers how different types of influences (normative and informational factors) affect processing information, establishing its validity assessments, and ultimately form decision outcomes. ELM and HSM are the most prevalent dual-process models in information-processing research. ELM posits that attitudes and behaviors are influenced by a message both centrally and peripherally. The former entails high-cognitive efforts to observe information, while the latter uses the environmental cues of the message to form judgments. HSM also posits that there are two types of information processing: heuristic and systematic. Heuristic processing uses cognitive heuristic or learned knowledge structure to assess a message, whereas systematic processing examines all relevant pieces of a message to form a decision.

Other categorizations have also been used. [17] classified the motivations for information exchange in social information spaces into environmental, personal, interpersonal, and socio-cultural. [37] examined trust in bloggers of marketer and non-marketer sources using three categorizations of characteristics, namely bloggers, blog, and blog-reading outcomes. [13] proposed a conceptual model based on HSM to investigate the determinants of information retweeting during emergency events, while [30] investigated a number of features that might affect information diffusion via retweeting based on content features and context features.

We propose a theoretical framework with three categories of characteristics—source, message, and recipient—to comparatively identify the factors determining information-exchange activity in different domains on Twitter. We have formulated a number of hypotheses focusing on these categorizations (Fig. 1).

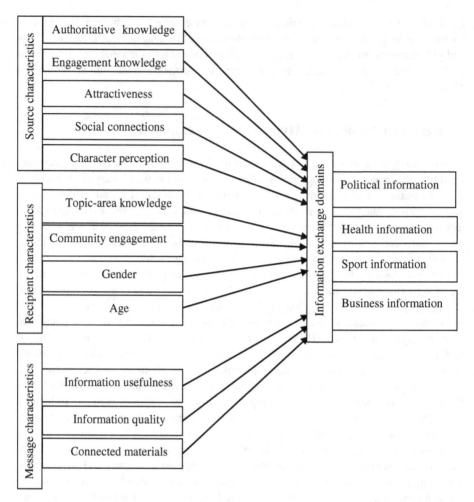

Fig. 1. Research model representing the hypotheses of the study

3.1   Source Characteristics

Source characteristics refer to the extent to which the tweet's writer is perceived by recipients to be capable of providing high-quality information. [13, 38] investigated the influence of source trustworthiness, expertise, and attractiveness on information retweeting in emergency events. [37] identified several blog authors' characteristics in the trust domain, including authoritative knowledge, engagement knowledge, character of the author, author's character claims, and author's social connections. Liu et al.'s and Doyle et al.'s characteristics, with some modifications, are detailed enough to represent the source characteristics in this study.

Sources are judged as credible based on perceived knowledge, competence, and expertise [39]. The knowledge of an information communicator depends on factors such as personal work, social experience, and personal background. Perceived knowledge can be assessed based on authoritative knowledge and engagement knowledge [37]. Authoritative knowledge is the extent to which the source is perceived to be capable of making accurate assertions in a particular topic area; it accrues over time, depending on factors such as personal work and personal background. [40] discussed the essential role of the positivist tradition, academicians, and portable knower-independent knowledge on authoritative knowledge. The accuracy of authoritative knowledge is supported by formal credentials, for example university degrees, and signs of accomplishment, such as awards.

Engagement knowledge refers to the extent to which tweets' sources are perceived to be capable of providing information, on a longitudinal basis, from personal efforts and social interaction. Unlike authoritative knowledge, which develops primarily through detached inquiry of the topic area, engagement knowledge develops through involvement "within" the topic area [40]. Engagement knowledge depends on topic-area passion, involvement, and wide-ranging experience. Participating in a topic-area Twitter community, for example, by posting strong comments on other tweets and retweets, requires Twitter users to read as much topic-area content as possible. Thus, engagement knowledge is mostly consistent with the tasks of experience in other studies. [13] explored the positive effect of source experience on information retweeting. [37] found that engagement knowledge has more influence than authoritative knowledge on trust formation in the blogosphere.

Source attractiveness—the extent to which writers are preferred by others in social media—can be measured through profile features, namely number of followers and followees, age of the account, number of favorited tweets, and frequency of tweets. [13, 38] identified the importance of source attractiveness on information retweeting.

Source characteristics are also assessed through social connections deriving from social capital. Social capital is the resources available through the structure, relational, and cognitive characteristics of interpersonal connections [41, 42]. Individuals with a large, diverse network of contacts allow users to exchange information with others, who willingly share information about their activities, actions, and experiences [43]. Although research has underlined the necessary role of social capital in receiving and accruing information [44, 45], indicators of its role in information exchange via social media do not exist. [37] investigated the effect of bloggers' social connections on trust intention and blog-reading outcomes, but neither trust intention nor blog-reading were predicted by bloggers' social connections.

The character of sources revolves around the totality of their personal integrity and benevolence toward readers. Perceived integrity is the extent to which a source is seen as honest, based on neutrality and commitment to moral and ethical conduct, whereas perceived benevolence is a source's caring and motivation toward members' needs and inquiries [46, 47]. Research in the context of the blogosphere has found that character has a significant influence on both trust intentions and blog-reading outcomes [37]. Thus, we hypothesize the following:

H1: Source characteristics (authoritative knowledge, engagement knowledge, attractiveness, social connection, and character claims) influence information exchange in topic areas ((a) politics, (b) health, (c) sport, (d) business).

3.2   Message Characteristics

[48] reviewed the literature on credibility of information and stated that "obviously, the message itself is critical for information credibility" (p. 140). Content, relevance, currency, accuracy, and usability have been identified as strongly influencing information credibility in electronic media.

Twitter messages cannot exceed 140 characters, so tweets typically consist of short phrases and comments. Despite this limit, governments, institutions, enterprises, and organizations have adopted Twitter to facilitate formal and informal communication, to share information and to discover topics of interest. In their study of airline users' tweets, [8] identified the main themes of information exchange, such as gathering information, sharing compliments, seeking and sharing information, providing community support, collaborating and helping with each other's problems, and reporting daily routines. Thus, Twitter users obviously perceive sources' tweets to be useful. This paper investigates the constructs of information usefulness and information quality. Information usefulness is the extent to which recipients find the information of messages useful for topic-area knowledge; information quality is the accuracy, comprehensiveness, and timeliness of information provided by messages.

Twitter users can mitigate the information volume deficiency using three mechanisms: URLs, mentioning, and multimedia. The short URL allows a link to be inserted into a message, through which users can access further information. Mentioning allows other users to be referenced in a tweet using the "@" symbol. To some extent, [13] realized the analogy between URLs and "mentioning" roles in providing a higher volume of information. Multimedia enables Twitter users to attach videos, images, and audios to tweets, creating richness, which relates to a message's depth, intensity, and vividness of information. Recent studies indicated that these mechanisms positively influence the action of information retweeting [14, 38] and partly influence retweeting in emergency events [13], but the efficiency of these attempts in the form of information exchange need to be explored within various domains. Thus, we hypothesized the following:

H2: Message characteristics (information usefulness, information quality, and connected materials) influence the information exchange in topic areas ((a) politics, (b) health, (c) sport, (d) business).

3.3   Recipient Characteristics

This refers to both stable factors, such as demographics, and variable personal characteristics. Understanding the information described in SNSs is a sufficient way to exchange information and build knowledge [37]. Twitter users introduce information from different domains, so information on Twitter comes from users with different knowledge. Using SNSs as an information-exchange strategy places the responsibility on recipients to share and find information that needs to be compared with the knowledge they hold, and measure the outcomes [49]. Thus, the importance of information exchange via Twitter might be determined by recipients' knowledge.

According to the motivational models, community engagement is an important determinant for adopting social media. [1] studied the importance of social relations on the expressive usage (social usage) and instrumental usage (information-sharing and -seeking usage) of social media. They identified the importance of community relations in expressive usage, but not in instrumental usage. In the community of practice, [17] underlined the importance of social-culture factors for increasing information exchange; their findings support the assumptions of the social influence model of technology use [50].

The influence of gender and age has been directly and indirectly explored in the context of SNSs [1, 22, 51–53], though not in relation to information exchange across different domains via Twitter. Some studies found that younger users are more likely to use SNSs frequently and have more SNS friends than older users [54, 55]. Regarding gender, the Arab Social Media Report found that about 64 % of male respondents used Twitter, while the percentage for female respondents was 34 % [56] (Salem et al., 2014). Men have been found to use SNSs for developing new contacts, whereas women use SNSs for maintain existing relationships [57]. Men use SNSs more for task-oriented and less for interpersonal reasons [58]. In measuring the effect of age and gender differences on the information value of SNSs, [49] found no notable effects on respondents' perceived usefulness of the acquired everyday information in meeting their daily needs. Based on this background, we infer that recipients' characteristics bolster information-exchange activity via Twitter. Thus, we assume the following:

H3: Recipient characteristics (topic-area knowledge, community engagement, gender, and age) influence information exchange in topic areas ((a) politics, (b) health, (c) sport, (d) business).

4   Research Methodology

4.1   Questionnaire Design

One of the most efficient means of data collection when the researcher knows what data is required to answer the research questions and measure the research variables is the questionnaire [59]. Participants were directed to answer questions on information-exchange activities in four domains (sport, health, politics, and business) using five-point Likert scales (5 = "always"; 1 = "never"). We selected these domains for three reasons. First, they are the most frequently identified domains in social media research [1, 8, 60]. Second, an Ipsos study in Kuwait identified these as the most popular domains for Twitter users [61]. Finally, these are the top domains for information seeking for graduate and undergraduate students [49, 62].

This study measures the influence of source, message, and recipient characteristics on the domains mentioned. Source characteristics comprise engagement knowledge, authoritative knowledge, attractiveness, social connections, and character claims; message characteristics comprise information quality, information usefulness, and connected materials; and recipient characteristics comprise topic-area knowledge, community engagement, age, and gender.

4.2 Sample and Data Collection

We collected data from Twitter users from Kuwait. A pilot study was used to validate the questionnaire after it was translated into Arabic and double-checked by specialists to ensure the accuracy of the translation. Based on feedback, a few minor changes were made to the wording. For convenience sampling, paper versions of the questionnaire were distributed to 900 undergraduates at a Kuwaiti university, within classes that all students are required to take. We described the purpose of the study and how the questionnaires should be completed via an oral presentation by the principle investigators. All students were informed that their answers would be anonymous and would be used for academic purposes. We collected 872 responses, and after discarding incomplete questionnaires, the number of effective responses was 820.

4.3 Data Analysis

We used a series of multiple regression analyses to test the hypothesized relationships among the theoretical model presented in Fig. 1. In order to screen potential multi-collinearity problems, an exploratory factor analysis (EFA) and the correlation matrix were computed for the variables.

Because several items were loaded at 0.3 and 0.4 in previous studies, and further items were suggested for some constructs, EFA was used to identify relationships among items using the maximum likelihood analysis extraction in SPSS. The factor loadings presented in Table 1 demonstrate that the items were well grouped with

Table 1. Results of constructs' descriptive statistics, reliability and validity

Variables	Alpha	Factor loadings	Mean	SD
Authoritative knowledge	0.69			
Has written a book about the topic		.791	3.54	0.98
Teaches courses on the topic		.501	3.71	0.86
Organizes events on the topic area		.524	3.81	0.89
Engagement knowledge	0.82			
Has extensive experience in the topic area		.630	4.26	0.76
Has resources that others do not have		.686	4.13	0.86
Is heavily involved in the area		.772	4.12	0.82
Is passionate about the topic		.714	4.09	0.84
Is interested in topic-area improvements		.568	3.93	0.77
Attractiveness	0.88			
Has a high number of followers		.842	3.67	1.12
Has a high number of followees		.832	3.52	1.08
Has a high frequency of tweets		.830	3.61	1.08
Has a high number of favorited tweets		.815	3.68	1.07

(Continued)

Table 1. (*Continued*)

Variables	Alpha	Factor loadings	Mean	SD
Social connections	0.73			
Attends major events on the topic area		.647	3.82	0.90
Has contact with other topic experts		.615	3.75	0.75
Character claims	0.72			
Says their information is trustworthy		.648	4.07	0.84
Says they are accurate, fair and unbiased		.759	3.77	0.98
Says they are trustworthy		.535	3.96	0.99
Information usefulness	0.70			
Improves outcomes of topic-area decisions		.636	4.26	0.67
Improves topic-area value that people receive		.723	4.16	0.67
Increases topic-area knowledge effectively		.524	4.20	0.75
Information quality	0.76			
Is well written		.500	4.10	0.81
Is accurate		.612	4.15	0.88
Is up-to-date and immediate		.831	4.28	0.80
Is easy to understand		.700	4.25	0.77
Connected materials	0.77			
Has URL links		.778	3.68	0.93
Has a number of mentions		.800	3.65	0.94
Has multimedia materials		.574	3.93	1.00
Topic-area knowledge	0.81			
I am satisfied with the topic-area tweets I read		.672	4.10	0.75
My previous information on the topic has been reinforced		.924	4.02	0.84
My appreciation of the topic has increased		.525	3.99	0.89
Community engagement	0.64			
I can relate to the others in the community		.750	3.99	0.86
I feel I am a part of the community		.551	3.81	1.10

Note: −, Negatively significant influence.

acceptable and high loadings. Since the results indicated that all factor loadings are $\geq$ .5, it can be said that the instruments are reliable and valid. The correlation matrix of all predictor variables was calculated to assess the possible correlation between factors. No high correlation between the variables was found. Table 2 shows the factor correlation of the variables.

Table 2. Correlation between constructs

	M	SD	1	2	3	4	5	6	7	8	9	10
Attractiveness	3.62	.94	1.00									
Engagement knowledge	4.10	.62	.401	1.00								
Information quality	4.19	.62	.359	.543	1.00							
Topic-area knowledge	4.03	.71	.278	.404	.542	1.00						
Connected materials	3.75	.79	.346	.100	.311	.193	1.00					
Authoritative knowledge	3.69	.72	.147	.420	.239	.288	.125	1.00				
Information usefulness	4.21	.55	.310	.478	.566	.418	.296	.315	1.00			
Character claims	3.93	.75	.494	.521	.414	.366	.369	.256	.425	1.00		
Community engagement	3.90	.85	.156	.309	.270	.480	.229	.305	.308	.207	1.00	
Social connections	3.78	.82	.255	.354	.118	.098	.204	.477	.194	.304	.206	1.00

5 Results

5.1 Sample Characteristics

The respondents' demographic information is shown in Table 3. Women accounted for 66.3 % and men 33.7 % of responses. One explanation is that the proportion of women in the population is larger than the proportion of men, and the sample reflects this. Most respondents (84.1 %) were aged 18–24 years.

Table 3. Demographic information of respondents ($N = 820$)

Demographics	Value	Frequency	Percentage
Gender	Male	276	33.7
	Female	544	66.3
Age	18–24 years	690	84.1
	25–34 years	110	13.4
	35 and over	20	2.4

5.2 Information-Exchange Domains

Information-exchange activity in the four domains identified was measured by identifying respondents' level of interest in information sharing and seeking through Twitter (Table 4). The results indicate that Twitter users exchange health information (M. 3.15) more than political (M. 2.53), sport (M. 2.33), and business (M. 2.09) information. However, users are generally more interested in seeking information (M. 2.70) than sharing information (M. 2.35) in the four domains.

Table 4. Activity rates for information sharing and information seeking through Twitter

Activity[a]	Mean	SD
I share political information via Twitter with others	2.15 (2.53)	1.19 (1.11)
I actively seek information about politics via Twitter	2.91	1.36
I share sport information via Twitter with others	2.25 (2.33)	1.41 (1.38)
I actively seek information about sport via Twitter	2.41	1.48
I share business and economic information via Twitter with others	2.01 (2.09)	1.15 (1.12)
I actively seek information about business via Twitter	2.18	1.22
I share health information via Twitter with others	3.00 (3.15)	1.26 (1.17)
I actively seek information about health via Twitter	3.30	1.23
Activity in all information-sharing domains	2.35	.81
Activity in all information-seeking domains	2.70	.80

Notes: Parentheses contain the means and SD of information-sharing and information-seeking activities for each domain.
[a]Five-point Likert-type scale, 1 = never, 5 = always

5.3   Hypotheses Testing and Results

Multiple regression analysis was used to examine the effect of a combination of two or more predictor variables on a criterion variable [63]. The results of the four multiple linear regressions are presented in Table 5. It is worth noting that the R2 for sport information exchange (38.3 %) was much higher than it was for politics (11 %), health (6.4 %), and business (4.3 %).

Politics. With regard to source characteristics (H1.a), authoritative knowledge (β = .153, p < 0.001) and social connections (β = .090, p < 0.05) were positively significant, while engagement knowledge (β = −.125, p < 0.01) had a negative influence. Sources who attend major political events and have social connections with other experts positively influenced political information exchange. Character claims and attractiveness (p > 0.05) were insignificant in this domain. Message characteristics were also assessed (H2.a), with none of the characteristics found to have a positive influence. However, connected materials (β = −.154, p < 0.001) negatively influenced political information exchange. With regard to recipient characteristics (H3.a), topic knowledge (β = .226, p < 0.001) was statistically very significant. The age hypothesis (β = .111, p < 0.01) was also confirmed: the youngest in our sample are less likely than the oldest to use Twitter for political information exchange. Gender was negatively significant (β = −.168, p < 0.001), with women less interested than men in political information exchange. Community engagement was insignificant.

Sport. In terms of the effect of source characteristics (H1.b), social connections (β = .127, p < 0.001) were positively significant, while authoritative knowledge (β = −.066, p < 0.05) and engagement knowledge (β = −.096, p < 0.05) were negatively significant. However, when sources have higher social connections, their tweets are considered significant by users. Two of the message characteristics were also supported (H2.b). Information usefulness (β = .034, p < 0.01) and connected materials (β = −.080, p < 0.05) were statistically significant. Connected materials negatively contributed to sport information exchange. Regarding recipient characteristics (H3.b), topic-area knowledge (β = .123, p < 0.01) and community engagement (β = .079, p < 0.05) positively affected sport information exchange. However, gender (β = −.630, p < 0.001) negatively contributed in the model, with women less likely than men to exchange sport information.

Business. The effect of source characteristics on business information exchange (H1.c) was influenced by the characteristics of attractiveness (β = .126, p < 0.01) and character claims (β = −.104, p < 0.05). However, character claims negatively contributed to business information exchange. Interestingly, none of the message characteristics (H2.c) were significant in business information exchange. Regarding recipient characteristics (H3.c), topic-area knowledge (β = .106, p < 0.05) was the only characteristic that was positively statistically significant. As in the political and sport domains, gender contributed negatively to business information exchange: women were less likely than men to use Twitter for business information exchange. Community engagement and age characteristics were insignificant.

Table 5. Results of the regression analysis on the hypotheses

	Politics information exchange		Sport information exchange		Business information exchange		Health information exchange	
	B(SE)	β(t-value)	B(SE)	β(t-value)	B(SE)	β(t-value)	B(SE)	β(t-value)
Constant	1.34(.355)	(3.78)***	3.99(.366)	(10.91)***	2.11(.371)	(5.69)***	1.13(.383)	(2.96)***
Source characteristics								
Authoritative knowledge	237(.062)	.153(3.824)***	-.126(.064)	-.066(-1.975)*	.055(.065)	.035(.847)	.174(.067)	.107(2.606)**
Engagement knowledge	-.222(.081)	.125(-2.753)**	-.212(.083)	-.096(-2.549)**	-.100(.084)	-.055(-1.179)	-.031(.087)	-.017(-.357)
Social connections	.122(.058)	.090(2.096)*	.212(.060)	.127(3.537)**	-.033(.061)	-.024(-.540)	-.074(.063)	-.052(-1.187)
Character claims	.032(.062)	.022(.510)	-.028(.064)	-.015(-.431)	-.153(.065)	-.104(-2.353)*	-.085(.067)	-.055(-1.265)
Attractiveness	.008(.046)	.007(.168)	-.034(.047)	-.023(-.719)	.151(.048)	.126(3.144)**	.193(.049)	.155(3.914)***
Message characteristics								
Information quality	.016(.083)	.008(.195)	.259(.086)	.105(3.026)*	.158(.087)	.078(1.821)	.354(.089)	.169(3.953)***
Information usefulness	.025(.075)	.014(.340)	.075(.077)	.034(.971)**	-.016(.078)	-.009(-.199)	.036(.081)	.019(.442)
Connected materials	-.216(.052)	-.154(-4.114)***	-.139(.054)	-.080(-2.560)*	-.059(.055)	-.042(-1.070)	-.043(.057)	-.029(-.757)
Recipient characteristics								
Topic-area knowledge	.353(.068)	.226(5.170)***	.238(.071)	.123(3.378)**	.168(.072)	.106(2.348)*	-.049(.074)	-.030(-.660)
Community engagement	.040(.051)	.030(.779)	.129(.053)	.079(2.442)**	-.078(.053)	-.059(-1.454)	.045(.055)	.033(.811)
Gender	-.395(.087)	-.168(-4.527)***	-1.840(.090)	-.630(-20.418)***	-.279(.091)	-.117(-3.053)***	-.089(.094)	-.036(-.945)
Age	.276(.085)	.111(3.252)**	-.160(.088)	-.052(-1.819)*	.067(.089)	.027(.755)	.096(.092)	.036(1.046)
F value	8.30***		41.70***		3.30***		4.57***	
R^2	.110		.383		.043		.064	
Adjusted R^2	.097		.374		.029		.050	

* $p < 0.05$. ** $p < 0.01$. *** $p < 0.001$. Gender: Dummy-coded with male = 0 and female = 1. Age: Dummy-coded with 18–24 years = 0, 25–34 years = 1, and 35 and over = 2.

Table 6. Summary of the results of hypotheses test

Hypotheses	Information exchange activity			
	Politics	Sport	Business	Health
Source characteristics				
Authoritative knowledge	√	−√		√
Engagement knowledge	−√	−√		
Social connections	√	√		
Character claims			−√	
Attractiveness			√	√
Message characteristics				
Information quality				√
Information usefulness		√		
Connected materials	−√	−√		
Recipient characteristics				
Topic-area knowledge	√	√	√	
Community engagement		√		
Gender	−√	−√	−√	
Age	√			

Note: − Negatively significant influence.

Health Source characteristics (H1.d) were significant through sources' authoritative knowledge (β = .107, p < 0.01) and attractiveness (β = .155, p < 0.001); the other source characteristics were insignificant. With regard message characteristics (H2.d), only information quality (β = .196, p < 0.001) was significant. No recipient characteristics (H3.d) were significant (Table 6).

6 Discussion and Conclusions

Health information was found to be the most prominent of the four domains for information exchange on Twitter. This indicates that Twitter is an important resource for finding more than for sharing health information. Twitter allows users to seek and share information on sensitive health topics, such as drug use, sexual health, or depression. Political information exchange is the next most popular domain, but the results show a remarkable gap between information seeking and information sharing. Twitter users prefer to seek rather than share political information. This might relate to recent legislation and judicial rulings that restrict the freedom to participate in political issues. Sport is the third most active domain for information exchange. Consistent with the other domains, users seek rather than share sport information. Thus, the top priority for users is to find sport news, results, or upcoming events rather than share such information. Business information is the domain with the lowest rate of information exchange, with a small difference in information-seeking and information-sharing activities. Because most of the respondents are young students, business information is not a priority for them. To our knowledge, there is no directly comparable research on the importance ratings of the information-exchange activity for this population. Therefore, comparisons are made with literature that has a slightly different focus. While not a study of SNSs, [62] surveyed over 8,000 American undergraduates and identified news or current events, product and purchasing information, and health and wellness information as the top three everyday information needs. [49] surveyed international students in the USA and found the top five information needs among SNSs to be finance, health, news of one's home country, housing, and entertainment. [61] showed the greater importance of Twitter for political issues than for health, sport, or business issues. It is remarkable that the top five domains are similar in nature, with a slight difference in ranking. Extending the domains is encouraged to test whether different samples would yield similar results to this study.

With regard to the factors that influence information-exchange activity, regression analysis showed that source characteristics partially correlated with information exchange for the four domains. The traditional knowledge sources, authoritative knowledge and engagement knowledge, do not efficiently drive all information-exchange topics. Political and health tweets posted by sources who have academic degrees and awards and conduct accomplishments are most likely to be sought and shared by Twitter users. However, these characteristics significantly detract from sport tweets in information exchange. Twitter users were dubious of the activities of engagement knowledge in information exchange, especially for political and sport tweets. Many Twitter accounts that tweet sensitive information use pseudonyms, but users may not trust and interact with information from such accounts. [13] identified the role of source expertise on information retweeting, which is consistent with our findings in political and health information exchange. Inconsistently, [37] found that trust formation is predicted by engagement knowledge of a blogger. It is also interesting that social network connections have more of a role in political and sport information exchange than in business and health information exchange. Therefore, a source with personal, professional, or institutional connections with political and sport experts and events provides information that is likely to be sought and shared by Twitter users. Character claims do not correlate with information-exchange activity, and actually detract from information exchange, especially in business tweets. This suggests that Twitter users consider sources' claims unnecessary in information exchange. It can be asserted that character claims do not influence information diffusion via SNSs, the blogosphere [37], and Twitter in particular. Source attractiveness affects business and health information exchange. Sources whose accounts have high numbers of followers, followees, tweets, and favorited tweets are of interest to Twitter users. Active sources in business and health on Twitter should have higher numbers of followers, followees, tweets, and favorited tweets. A source's credibility might be influenced by the number of followees, followers, tweets and favorited tweets in some subjects. These findings are in line with research on information retweeting on emergency events [13]. Generally, if sources are qualified with authoritative knowledge, are active in terms of social connections, and have accounts with high numbers of followers, followees, tweets, and favorited tweets, recipients seek out and share their tweets.

Message characteristics partially influence information-exchange activity. Information quality was important in health and sport information exchange, suggesting that Twitter users are highly motivated to seek and share health and sport information if tweets contain high-quality information. Because health information is necessary and sensitive for everyone [48], it must be accurate, up to date, and easily understood. Information quality acts as a trust signal for information acquirement and communications [64], but the findings suggest that it is not related to knowledge acquirement on all topics [37]. The nature of the sample generation is sensitive due to the rapidly changing actions and behaviors in general. Therefore, using social media as a credible main source of information might be vital for their future health and decisions. This requires special efforts by information specialists and health professionals to develop a mechanism to monitor information flow on one side and publish high-quality information through Twitter on the other side. Information usefulness impacts only sport information exchange. It may be normal for sport to be the most useful domain for gaining information for our sample. This suggests that the length limitation of tweets might be efficient for sport information, but weak for political, health, and business information. Some topics might need additional content length to attract Twitter users' interest and encourage them to seek and share. Although previous research found that information usefulness is highly correlated with information adoption and electronic word-of-mouth communication [65, 66], our findings suggest that information usefulness influence varies between domains. Contrary to expectations, none of the connected materials were found to be useful in information exchange, particularly for politics and sport. This suggests that users prefer tweets without URLs, mentions, or multimedia materials. This is in line with [13] findings, particularly for URLs and mentions, but completely contrasts with studies by [14, 38] regarding information retweeting. Future studies should consider particular situations within each domain and compare the characteristics of the current study on certain phenomena belong to different domains.

Information-exchange activity in politics, business, and sport appears to be driven primarily by recipient interaction to gain knowledge. Although Twitter users realize the limited usefulness of tweets in general, they are still determining the impacts of the tweets in supporting their current knowledge, except in health information exchange. Thus, the source must provide contents that facilitate goal attainment for recipients [37]. Community engagement was found to facilitate information-exchange activity only in the sport domain. It is interesting that sport information exchange connects Twitter users with their communities more than those who exchange political, business, and health information. Gender is a significant, but negative, characteristic of information exchange, except in health information exchange. Women are less likely than men to be interested in politics, business, and sport information exchange via Twitter. It seems that women do not interact with short contents as much as men do, so they may prefer other SNSs that do not limit message length. Also, the topics of the study might be more relevant to men than women. Research on the expressive and instrumental usages of Web 2.0 did not find gender differences [1].

Age is also important, though only in political information exchange. Older participants were more interested than younger ones in political information exchange, suggesting that older users engage more with in-depth topics.

6.1   Implications

This study uniquely investigated the influence of source, message, and recipient characteristics on information-exchange activity via Twitter. Unlike previous research, this study comparatively investigated the determinants of the most popular domains of information exchange. Previous studies examined the factors affecting information retweeting or information exchange on a particular subject or situation [13, 17], while this study aimed to explain the cognitive process underlying information-exchange activity and enhance the understanding of information seeking and sharing via Twitter. Thus, the findings extend the literature on information diffusion, and information exchange in particular, in various domains on Twitter.

This study facilitates an in-depth understanding of the key characteristics of information exchange based on source, message, and recipient characteristics. Information-exchange activity is influenced not only by the various characteristics, but also by the domains of information exchange. Not all subjects of information exchange might be influenced in the same way by the same characteristics. We also identify which tweets need to include URLs, mentions, or multimedia.

In this paper, sources' knowledge was distinguished between two human-capital ability resources: authoritative knowledge and engagement knowledge. As both contributed as predictors in this study and in [37] research, further research should consider the contribution of human-capital resources across populations, contexts, and social media applications.

These findings have practical implications for Twitter users. To increase information-exchange activity, sources should have particular characteristics, and these vary according to the specific domain. Although message characteristics had limited influence on information exchange, such characteristics still suggest some guidelines for posting tweets. Again, this varies according to the domain.

In terms of system design, Twitter needs to be an effective system not only for seeking and sharing information but also for categorizing tweet subjects. The length limit of tweets needs to be reviewed, especially for particular domains, to assist sources to provide more information. Some tweet contents should be excluded from the length limit, such as hyperlinks and character claims. Number of followers, followees, tweets, and favorited tweets are likely to attract users, and setting additional profile characteristics would increase information exchange and diffusion.

6.2   Limitations

The limitations of this study represent opportunities for future research. First, data were collected from a convenience sample of undergraduates. Although students are heavy users of social media, a convenience sample limits the validity of findings. Respondents might not represent the whole population because most SNS users are young people [67, 68]. Also, the favorite Twitter domains of the sample might restrict the influence of characteristics and the generalizability of the study to other groups. Future research should use samples across different generations and communities.

Second, this study focused on general information rather than a particular situation or event in each domain. Future research should comparatively investigate the influence of the current research's characteristics on information-exchange activity in particular situations, such as financial or political events.

Third, the findings found low variance within the models in terms of information-exchange activity. Further characteristics need to be investigated to increase the R2 value of our models. Finally, only gender and age were examined as antecedents in information-exchange activity. Other demographic factors should be examined as antecedents and moderators in future studies.

6.3   Conclusion

This research contributes to information-diffusion literature in general, and research on information exchange via Twitter in particular, by understanding the comparative influence of source, message, and recipient characteristics on exchanging information within four popular domains on Twitter. Source and recipient characteristics play a more important role than message characteristics in information-exchange activity. In source characteristics, authoritative knowledge, social connections, and attractiveness have a positive influence on information exchange, while in recipient characteristics, recipients' prior knowledge, community engagement, and demographics influence information exchange. In messages characteristics, information usefulness and information quality were demonstrated to be effective. However, overall the influences vary based on the domain of information exchange. This avenue of research will not only extend the scope of information diffusion and SNSs research; it will also facilitate the effective design and use of SNSs for different users and domains.

Acknowledgments. This work supported and funded by The Public Authority of Education and Training, Research project No. (BF-15-12), Research Title (The Intersection of Source, Message, and Recipient Characteristics on Information-Exchange Activity via Twitter).

References

1. Ribière, V., Haddad, M., Wiele, P.: The impact of national culture traits on the usage of web 2.0 technologies. J. Inf. Knowl. Manag. Syst. **40**(3/4), 334–361 (2010)
2. Shen, X., Zhang, K., Zhao, S.: Understanding information adoption in online review communities: the role of herd factors. In: 47th Hawaii International Conference on System Science, 6–9 January, Waikoloa, Hawaii, USA (2014)
3. Java, A., Song, X., Finin, T., Tseng, B.: Why we Twitter: understanding microblogging usage and communities. In: 9th WEBKDD and 1st SNA-KDD Workshop, 12–15 August, San Jose, CA, USA (2007)
4. Peterson, R.D.: To tweet or not to tweet: exploring the determinants of early adoption of Twitter by house members in the 111th congress. Soc. Sci. J. **49**(4), 430–438 (2012)
5. Wilson, T.: Models in information behavior research. J. Doc. **55**(3), 249–270 (1999)
6. Johan, Y., Mao, H., Zeng, X.: Twitter mood predicting the stock market. J. Comput. Sci. **3**(1), 1–8 (2011)

7. Witkemper, C., Lim, C., Waldburger, A.: Social media and sports marketing: examining the motivations and constraints of Twitter users. Sport Mark. Q. **21**, 170–183 (2012)
8. Sreenivasan, N., Lee, C., Goh, D.: Tweeting the friendly skies: investigating information exchange among Twitter users about airlines. Electron. Libr. Inf. Syst. **46**(1), 21–42 (2012)
9. Scanfeld, D., Scanfeld, V., Larson, E.: Dissemination of health information through social networks: Twitter and antibiotic. Am. J. Infect. Control **38**(3), 182–188 (2010)
10. Chung, D., Kim, S.: Blogging activity among cancer patients and their companions: uses, gratifications, and predictors of outcomes. J. Am. Soc. Inform. Sci. Technol. **59**(2), 297–306 (2008)
11. Cheung, M., Lou, C., Sia, C., Chen, H.: Credibility of electronic word-of-mouth: information and normative determinants of on-line consumer recommendation. Int. J. Electron. Commer. **13**(4), 9–38 (2009)
12. Liu, Z., Liu, L., Li, H.: Determinants of information retweeting in microblogging. Internet Res. **22**(4), 443–466 (2012)
13. Zarrella, D.: Science of retweets (2009). http://cdn2.hubspot.net/hub/53/file-13207809-pdf/docs/science-of-retweets-201003.pdf
14. Hersberger, J., Murray, A., Rioux, K.: Examining information exchange and virtual communities: an emergent framework. Online Inf. Rev. **31**(2), 135–147 (2007)
15. Virkus, S.: Use of Web 2.0 technologies in LIS education: experiences at Tallinn university, Estonia. Program: Electron. Libr. Inf. Syst. **42**(3), 262–274 (2008)
16. Matschke, C., Moskaliuk, J., Bokhorst, F., Schummer, T., Cress, U.: Motivational factors of information exchange in social information spaces. Comput. Hum. Behav. **36**, 549–558 (2014)
17. Belkin, N.: Information concepts for information science. J. Doc. **34**(1), 55–85 (1978)
18. Buckland, M.: Information as thing. J. Am. Soc. Inf. Sci. **42**(5), 351–360 (1991)
19. Dervin, B.: Useful theory for librarianship: communication not information. Drexel Libr. Q. **13**(3), 16–32 (1977)
20. Kim, S.: Factors affecting the use of social software: TAM perspectives. Electron. Libr. **30**(50), 690–706 (2012)
21. Smock, A., Ellison, N., Lampe, C., Wohn, D.: Facebook as a toolkit: a uses and gratifications approach to unbundling feature use. Comput. Hum. Behav. **27**(6), 2322–2329 (2011)
22. Holton, A., Baek, K., Coddington, M., Yaschur, C.: Seeking and sharing: motivations for linking on Twitter. Commun. Res. Rep. **31**(1), 33–40 (2014)
23. Earp, J., Ott, M., Pozzi, F.: Facilitating educators' knowledge sharing with dedicated information systems. Comput. Hum. Behav. **29**(2), 445–455 (2013)
24. Mir, I., Rehman, K.: Factors affecting consumer attitudes and intentions toward user-generated product content on YouTube. Manag. Mark. Chall. Knowl. Soc. **8**(4), 637–654 (2013)
25. Jansen, B., Zhang, M., Sobel, K., Chowdury, A.: Twitter power: tweets as electronic word of mouth. J. Am. Soc. Inf. Sci. Technol. **69**(9), 1–20 (2009)
26. Zhang, J., Qu, Y., Cody, J., Wu, Y.: A case study of microblogging in the enterprise: use, value, and related issues. In: Proceedings of the 28th International Conference of Human Factors in Computing Systems CHI 2010 (2011)
27. Romero, D., Meeder, B., Kleinberg, J.: Differences in the mechanics of information diffusion across topics: idioms, political hashtags, and complex contagion on Twitter. In: Proceedings of the 20th International Conference on the World Wide Web in New York, 28 March–1 April 2011, Hyderabad, India, pp. 695–704 (2011)

28. Remy, C., Pervin, N., Toriumi, F., Takeda, H.: Information diffusion on Twitter: everyone has its chance, but all chances are not equal. In: International Conference on Signal-Image Technology and Internet-Based Systems, 2–5 December, Kyoto, pp. 483–490 (2013)

29. Suh, B., Hong, L., Pirolli, P., Chi, E.: Want to be retweeted? Large scale analytics on factors impacting retweet in Twitter network. In: IEEE International Conference on Social Computing, pp. 177–184 (2010)

30. Bakshy, E., Hofman, J., Mason, W., Watts, D.: Everyone's an influencer: quantifying influence on Twitter. In: WSDM 2011, Proceedings of the Fourth ACM International Conference on Web Search and Data Mining in Hong Kong, 9–12 February, pp. 64–74. ACM, New York (2011)

31. Cress, U.: Mass collaboration – an emerging field for CSCL research. In: Rummel, N., Kapur, M., Nathan, N., Puntambekar, S. (Eds.) To see the World and a Grain of Sand: Learning Across Levels of Space and Scale: CSCL 2013 Proceedings, vol. 1, pp. 557–563. International Society of the Learning Sciences Madison, USA (2013)

32. Hovland, C., Janis, I., Kelley, H.: Communication Change and Persuasion: Psychological Studies of Opinion Change. Yale University Press, New Haven (1953)

33. Deutsch, M., Gerard, H.: A study of normative and informational social influence upon individual judgments. J. Abnorm. Soc. Psychol. **53**(3), 629–636 (1955)

34. Petty, R., Cacioppo, J.: Communication and Persuasion: Central and Peripheral Routes to Attitude Change. Springer, New York (1986)

35. Chaiken, S.: Heuristic versus systematic information processing and the use of source versus message cues in persuasion. J. Pers. Soc. Psychol. **39**(5), 752–766 (1980)

36. Doyle, J., Heslop, L., Ramirez, A., Cray, D.: Trust intentions in readers of blogs. Manag. Res. Rev. **35**(9), 837–856 (2012)

37. Bongwon, S., Lichan, H., Peter, P., Chi, E.: Want to be retweeted? Large scale analytics on factors impacting retweet in Twitter network. In: Proceedings of the 2010 IEEE International Conference on Privacy, Security, Risks and Trust, pp. 177–184 (2010)

38. Burgoon, J., Bonito, J., Bengtsson, B., Cederberg, C., Lundeberg, M., Allspach, L.: Interactivity in human-computer interaction: a study of credibility, understanding and influence. Comput. Hum. Behav. **16**(6), 553–574 (2000)

39. Chen, W., Hirschheim, R.: A paradigmatic and methodological examination of information systems research from 1991 to 2001. Inf. Syst. J. **14**(3), 197–235 (2004)

40. Nahapiet, J., Ghoshal, S.: Social capital, intellectual capital and the organization advantage. Acad. Manag. Rev. **23**(2), 242–266 (1998)

41. Tsai, W., Ghoshal, S.: Social capital and value creation: the role of intrafirm networks. Acad. Knowl. Manag. **41**(4), 464–476 (1998)

42. Steinfield, C., Ellison, N.B., Lampe, C.: Social capital, self-esteem, and use of online social network sites: a longitudinal analysis. J. Appl. Dev. Psychol. **29**, 434–445 (2008)

43. Lin, N.: Building a network theory of social capital. Connections **22**(1), 28–51 (1999)

44. Dike, S., Singh, K.: Applications of social capital in educational literature: a critical synthesis. Rev. Educ. Res. **72**(1), 31–69 (2002)

45. Mayer, R., Davis, J., Schoorman, F.: An integrative model of organizational trust. Acad. Manag. Rev. **20**(3), 709–734 (1995)

46. McKnight, D., Choudhury, V., Kacmar, C.: Developing and validating trust measures for e-commerce: an integrative typology. Inf. Syst. Res. **13**(3), 334–359 (2002)

47. Wathen, C.N., Burkell, J.: Believe it or not: factors influencing credibility on the web. J. Am. Soc. Inform. Sci. Technol. **53**(2), 134–144 (2002)

48. Sin, S.J., Kim, K.: International students' everyday life information seeking: the information value of social networking sites. Libr. Inf. Sci. Res. **34**(2), 107–116 (2013)

49. Fulk, J., Schmitz, J., Steinfield, C.W.: A social influence model of technology use. In: Fulk, J., Steinfield, C. (eds.) Organizations and Communication Technology, pp. 117–140. Sage, Newbury Park (1990)

50. Awad, N.F., Ragowsky, A.: Establishing trust in electronic commerce through online word of mouth: An examination across genders. J. Manag. Inf. Syst. 24(4), 101–121 (2008)

51. Katungi, E., Edmeades, S., Smale, M.: Gender, social capital, and information exchange in rural Uganda. J. Int. Dev. 20(1), 35–52 (2008)

52. Liu, C.: Gender differences in the determinants of sharing information via mobile phones. J. Int. Technol. Inf. Manag. 19(4), 61–75 (2010)

53. Pfeil, U., Arjan, R., Zaphiris, P.: Age differences in online social networking: a study of user profiles and the social capital divide among teenagers and older users in myspace. Comput. Hum. Behav. 25(3), 643–654 (2009)

54. Valenzuela, S., Park, N., Kee, K.: Is there social capital in a social network site? Facebook use and college students' life satisfaction, trust and participation. J. Comput.-Mediat. Commun. 14(4), 875–901 (2009)

55. Salem, F., Mourtada, R., Al-Shaer, S.: Citizen engagement and public services in the Arab world: the potential of social media. Arab Social Media Report, pp. 1–54 (2014)

56. Mazman, S.G., Usluel, Y.K.: Gender differences in using social networks. Turkish Online J. Educ. Technol. 10(2), 133–139 (2011)

57. Lin, K., Lu, H.: Why people use social networking sites: an empirical study integrating network externalities and motivation theory. Comput. Hum. Behav. 27(3), 1152–1161 (2011)

58. Easterby-Smith, M., Golden-Biddle, K., Locke, K.: Working with pluralism: determining quality in qualitative research. Organ. Res. Methods 11(3), 419–429 (2008)

59. Bosman, D., Boshoff, C., Rooyen, G.: The review credibility of electronic word-of-mouth communication on e-commerce platforms. Manag. Dyn. 22(3), 29–44 (2013)

60. Kabe, K.: Twenty five influenced tweets in the general political issue. Al Qabas, 22 January 2015

61. Head, A., Eisenberg, M.: How college students use the web to conduct everyday life research. First Monday 16(4) (2011)

62. Gall, M.D., Gall, J.P., Borg, W.R.: Educational Research: An Introduction. Pearson Education, Boston (2007)

63. Zhou, T., Li, H., Liu, Y.: The effect of flow experience on mobile SNS users' loyalty. Ind. Manag. Data Syst. 110(6), 930–946 (2010)

64. Sussman, S.W., Siegal, W.S.: Informational influence in organizations: an integrated approach to knowledge adoption. Inf. Syst. Res. 14(1), 47–65 (2003)

65. Cheung, C., Thadani, D.: The impact of electronic word-of-mouth communication: a literature analysis and integrative model. Decis. Support Syst. 54(1), 461–470 (2012)

66. Shin, D.: What do people do with digital multimedia broadcasting? Path analysis of structural equation modeling. J. Mob. Commun. 6(1), 258–275 (2008)

67. Kim, K.H., Yun, H.: Crying for me, crying for us: relational dialectics in a Korean social network site. J. Comput.-Mediat. Commun. 13(1), 298–319 (2007)

Persuasiveness of eWOM Communications: Literature Review and Suggestions for Future Research

Elvira Ismagilova[✉], Emma Slade, and Michael Williams

School of Management, Swansea University, Swansea, UK
{e.ismagilova.840405,e.l.slade,m.d.williams}@swansea.ac.uk

Abstract. Electronic word-of-mouth (eWOM) plays an important part in consumer purchase decision. The way consumers perceive the persuasiveness of eWOM message can affect their attitude, and purchase intention, and hence sales. Thus, the topic of persuasiveness of eWOM communications has received much attention from scholars. The objective of this paper is to provide a brief review of the existing literature related to the effectiveness of eWOM communications and offer an overview of the determinants of eWOM persuasiveness. This paper contributes to the existing eWOM literature by reviewing the existing studies on eWOM communications, identifying gaps in the current research and providing directions for future research.

Keywords: Electronic word-of-mouth · eWOM · Persuasiveness · Literature review · Research gaps

1 Introduction

Word-of-mouth (WOM) is one of the oldest and most important channels of information dispersion between people and is recognized as an important determinant of consumer purchase behavior. Nevertheless, traditional WOM communications are limited between network boundaries and become weaker over distance and time [1]. Development of the Internet and popularity of e-commerce have led to the growth of electronic WOM (eWOM). Even though eWOM may be less personal, mostly anonymous and happens between people with weak ties in comparison with traditional WOM, it is seen as a more powerful tool because it is credible, publicly available and has significant reach [2]. The influence of eWOM can affect attitude and purchase intention of consumers, and hence sales [3]. Therefore, eWOM communications have received much attention from scholars [1].

Even though many studies have been conducted on eWOM, a structured analysis of this research stream is still limited [3]. A review of previous literature is valuable because findings are spread across different disciplines and thus difficult to acquire a consolidated view on this topic [4]. A few attempts to assess the literature on eWOM communications have been done [3, 4]. However, these studies have not considered persuasiveness of eWOM in detail and how it is affected by social media. Hence, the objective of this paper is to provide a brief review of the exiting literature on

Y.K. Dwivedi et al. (Eds.): I3E 2016, LNCS 9844, pp. 354–359, 2016.
DOI: 10.1007/978-3-319-45234-0_32

persuasiveness of eWOM. This paper contributes to the existing literature, structuring and summarizing studies on eWOM communications, identifying existing gaps in the current research and providing directions for future studies.

The collection of appropriate research papers commenced through exploration of suitable articles found via Web of Science and SCOPUS. For this purpose the following search terms included "Electronic word-of-mouth", "Electronic word of mouth", "eWOM", "Internet word-of-mouth", "Internet word of mouth", "iWOM", "Online word-of-mouth", "Online word of mouth", "Helpful", "Useful", "Persuasive", and "Credible". Articles written in English, regardless of the research methods were collected. As a result of this search, 57 relevant scholarly articles were found that related, in various forms, to the persuasiveness of eWOM communications.

The remainder of the paper is as follows. First, the review of the literature about how consumers evaluate persuasiveness of eWOM communications is presented. After, the limitations of the existing studies are outlined with the proposed directions for future research. Finally, the paper is briefly concluded.

2 Persuasiveness of eWOM Communications

Consumers use eWOM as one of the most important sources of information to make purchase decisions [5]. Researchers suggest that consumers rely on eWOM communications if they perceive them persuasive [6]. Studies on the persuasiveness of eWOM mostly use the Elaboration Likelihood Model [7–12]. In order to be persuasive, message should be considered as helpful and credible. A number of studies prove the link between credibility and usefulness of eWOM and information adoption [6, 13, 14], which can influence consumers' attitudes and purchase intentions.

A number of studies investigate factors which influence persuasiveness of eWOM communications [7, 11, 13]. Studies propose that message, source of information and reviewer characteristics affect perceived eWOM helpfulness and credibility [5, 13]. Also, it is found that the effectiveness of eWOM communications can be moderated by platform type and type of product [9]. Determinants of eWOM persuasiveness are presented in Table 1 and briefly discussed below.

Message. Quality, argument strength, content, valence and other factors can influence the persuasiveness of eWOM message. For example, from conducting an on-line survey of 159 participants of a consumer discussion forum in China, Cheung et al. [13] found that argument strengths, recommendation consistency, and rating affect credibility of eWOM. Another study by Kim and Gupta [10] found that valence and emotions embedded in the online review affect usefulness of eWOM messages. Additionally, previous studies find that reviews with negative valences have more impact on persuasiveness of eWOM compared to those with positive valences [6, 15].

Source. Characteristics of information source can affect the credibility of eWOM communications and thus persuasiveness. Existing studies focus on expertise and trustworthiness of information source [6, 8, 14]. A study conducted by Teng et al. [6] using social media platform QQ, finds that source expertness and trustworthiness, as well as

Table 1. Determinants of eWOM persuasiveness

Construct	Details	References
eWOM message		
Rating	Rating inconsistency, overall star rating, average product rating in target category, aggregated rating	[7, 11, 13, 14]
Content	Length, per cent of negative words, image, valence, objectivity/subjectivity, emotions, detailed information, explained actions and reactions, review diagnocity, technical information, persuasive words, argument strength	[6, 8–10, 13, 16]
Quality	Relevance, timeliness, accuracy, comprehensiveness	[5, 11, 12, 17]
Volume	Total number of posted online reviews	[15, 18]
Recommendation consistency	The degree to which the eWOM message is consistent with other consumers' reviews about the same product or service	[11, 13, 17]
Source of eWOM		
Source Credibility	Expertise and trustworthiness	[6, 8, 14, 19]
Reviewer ranking and number of followers	Evaluation of the reviewer by other individuals	[7, 8]
Attractiveness	Similarity, familiarity and likability	[6, 19]
Profile picture	The reviewer has profile picture	[16]
Perceived social relationships	Tie strength and homophily	[6]
Receiver of eWOM		
Confirmation with receiver's prior beliefs	The degree of confirmation/disconfirmation between receiver's prior beliefs and the received information about the product/service	[13]
Trust propensity	Willingness to rely on other individuals	[17]
Cultural characteristics	Individualism-collectivism orientation	[11]
Level of involvement	The degree of psychological identification and emotional ties the receiver has with the product/service	[14, 15, 20]
Prior experience with seller	Previous experience with the provider of product/service	[18]
Prior knowledge	Previous knowledge about the reviewed product or service and the platform	[12, 20]

source attractiveness (familiarity and likeability), social tie, and homophile influence affect eWOM persuasiveness.

Receiver. The evaluation of eWOM can vary from person to person. As a result, the same message can be considered differently by consumers. Studies find that consumers' characteristics such as, trust propensity, previous experience with seller, prior knowledge, involvement, prior beliefs, and cultural characteristics can moderate the persuasiveness of eWOM communications [11, 15].

Development of Web 2.0 technologies and growth of social media introduced a new form of eWOM communication, social word-of-mouth [6, 21], which is "detailing evaluation by consumers about a product using social media" [21]. Using social media, consumers can communicate in online communities using different Web 2.0 technologies (recommendations, ratings, reviews, forums) [21]. Some studies investigate how social media affects eWOM persuasiveness [6, 21]. For example, a recent study conducted by Hajili [21], which used TripAdvisor as an example of a travel forum, finds that social media makes eWOM seem more credible and useful, which leads to information adoption. The results of this study show that characteristics of social media such as continuing contact, relationships with familiar peers, social media interactivity, and disclosure of individuals identity improves perceived credibility of eWOM communications.

3   Literature Gaps and Recommendations of Future Research

There are some issues, which have not yet been considered by existing studies on the persuasiveness of eWOM communications. This section highlights limitations, providing opportunities for future research.

Studies on eWOM communications have been conducted in China [1, 6, 11, 13, 17], Taiwan [5, 8, 19], South Korea [9, 12, 20], Germany [14] and USA [10, 15, 16, 18] which can limit generalizability the findings to other countries. Also, studies reported different results regarding persuasiveness of eWOM communications. For example, study [6] which is conducted in China finds that homophily of the source affects eWOM persuasiveness, while the other study [14] conducted in Germany shows the opposite results. It is important for future research to study effects of eWOM from the point of view of UK consumers to discover any differences due to cultural and social factors.

Most of the studies have considered just written eWOM [6, 7, 17, 20]. As a result, persuasiveness of visual eWOM is an under-researched area. Future research should consider the need of visual information for different industries and product categories. Also, researchers could consider how the perception of the message changes once it is presented in a visual form. Understanding consumers' visual orientation will help to conduct effective marketing communications.

There is a lack of studies on the impact of emotions on perceived persuasiveness of eWOM. Investigating the impact of emotions on eWOM can help mangers to improve attitude towards product and brand, and increase product sales. Also, previous studies have not considered moderators of this relationship (e.g. product type).

Studies mostly employ quantitative research approach, such as surveys [1, 6, 11, 13, 14, 17, 19, 20] and experiments [5, 9, 12, 15, 16] to investigate factors influencing persuasiveness eWOM communications. Future studies can use qualitative research approach such as interviews and focus groups in order to investigate new factors which can affect persuasiveness of eWOM communications.

Some studies investigate the role social media plays in eWOM persuasiveness, using platforms such SNS, forums and chatrooms [6, 8, 21]. However, factors which affect persuasiveness of eWOM may vary as a result of differences in technology base, communications methods, and conduct of members on different platforms. As a result, future research exploring and comparing how different types of social media platforms can influence persuasiveness of eWOM communications, will allow marketers to develop better strategies for particular online platforms.

4 Conclusion

To summarize, this literature analysis presented the state of current knowledge in the evaluation of eWOM communications by consumers. The researchers show that message, source and receiver characteristics affect eWOM persuasiveness. This paper assists future research by reviewing previous studies and proposing future research directions. The review presented has been limited by space constraints but provides a useful starting point for conceptualization of a research model, which can be enhanced further by a deeper review of current research.

Attending to some of the gaps identified, the researchers now plan to focus on the effect of embedded emotions in eWOM messages on usefulness of social media eWOM in the context of UK consumers.

References

1. Cheng, X., Zhou, M.: Empirical study on credibility of electronic word of mouth. In: Paper Presented at the 2010 International Conference on Management and Service Science, MASS 2010 (2010)
2. Hennig-Thurau, T., Gwinner, K.P., Walsh, G., Gremler, D.D.: Electronic word-of-mouth via consumer-opinion platforms: what motivates consumers to articulate themselves on the Internet? J. Interact. Mark. 18(1), 38–52 (2004)
3. Cheung, C.M., Thadani, D.R.: The effectiveness of electronic word-of-mouth communication: a literature analysis. In: Proceedings of the 23rd Bled eConference eTrust: Implications for the Individual, Enterprises and Society, pp. 329–345 (2010)
4. Trenz, M., Berger, B.: Analyzing online customer reviews-an interdisciplinary literature review and research agenda. In: ECIS, p. 83 (2013)
5. Tsao, W.C., Hsieh, M.T.: eWOM persuasiveness: do eWOM platforms and product type matter? Electron. Commer. Res. 15(4), 509–541 (2015)
6. Teng, S., Wei Khong, K., Wei Goh, W., Yee Loong Chong, A.: Examining the antecedents of persuasive eWOM messages in social media. Online Inf. Rev. 38(6), 746–768 (2014)
7. Baek, H., Ahn, J., Choi, Y.: Helpfulness of online consumer reviews: readers' objectives and review cues. Int. J. Electron. Commer. 17(2), 99–126 (2012)
8. Cheng, Y.-H., Ho, H.-Y.: Social influence's impact on reader perceptions of online reviews. J. Bus. Res. 68, 883–887 (2015)
9. Jeong, H.-J., Koo, D.-M.: Combined effects of valence and attributes of e-WOM on consumer judgment for message and product. The moderating effect of brand community type. Internet Res. 25(1), 2–29 (2015)
10. Kim, J., Gupta, P.: Emotional expressions in online user reviews: how they influence consumers' product evaluations. J. Bus. Res. 65, 985–992 (2012)
11. Luo, C., Wu, J., Shi, Y., Xu, Y.: The effects of individualism-collectivism cultural orientation on eWOM information. Int. J. Inf. Manag. 34, 446–456 (2014)

12. Park, D.-H., Kim, S.: The effects of consumer knowledge on message processing of electronic word-of-mouth via online consumer reviews. Electron. Commer. Res. Appl. **7**(4), 399–410 (2008)
13. Cheung, M.Y., Luo, C., Sia, C.L., Chen, H.: Credibility of electronic word-of-mouth: informational and normative determinants of on-line consumer recommendations. Int. J. Electron. Commer. **13**(4), 9–38 (2009)
14. Lis, B.: In eWOM we trust a framework of factors that determine the eWOM credibility. Bus. Inf. Syst. Eng. **5**(3), 129–140 (2013)
15. Park, D.-H., Lee, J.: eWOM overload and its effect on consumer behavioral intention depending on consumer involvement. Electron. Commer. Res. Appl. **7**(4), 386–398 (2008)
16. Xu, Q.: Should I trust him? The effects of reviewer pro-file characteristics on eWOM credibility. Comput. Hum. Behav. **33**, 136–144 (2014)
17. Guo, G., Chen, K., He, F.: An empirical study on the influence of perceived credibility of online consumer reviews. J. Chin. Mark. **3**(1), 13–20 (2009)
18. O'Reilly, K., Marx, S.: How young, technical consumers assess online WOM credibility. Qual. Mark. Res. **14**(4), 330–359 (2011)
19. Yu, Y.-W., Natalia, Y.: The effect of user generated video reviews on consumer purchase intention. In: 2013 Seventh International Conference on Innovative Mobile and Internet Services in Ubiquitous Computing (Imis 2013), pp. 796–800 (2013)
20. Doh, S.-J., Hwang, J.-S.: How consumers evaluate eWOM (Electronic Word-of-Mouth) messages. Cyberpsychol. Behav. **12**(2), 193–197 (2009)
21. Hajli, N.: Ethical environment in the online communities by information credibility: a social media perspective. J. Bus. Eth., 1–12 (2016). doi:10.1007/s10551-016-3036-7

Impact of Anonymity and Identity Deception on Social Media eWOM

Payal Shrivastava Kapoor[1(✉)] and Srinivas Gunta[2]

[1] FORE School of Management, New Delhi, India
payal@fsm.ac.in
[2] Indian Institute of Management, Indore, India

Abstract. Brand-related consumer to consumer communication, eWOM, is taking place in many forms across the social media space. Rules that governed credibility assessment of brand-related communication, WOM, in the Face to Face context may vary on social media, specifically because of anonymity that is afforded on different social media sites. The current study looks closely on the impact of anonymity in typical eWOM behaviour context on social media by drawing observations from a recent case in point and literature. The paper concludes with a list of relevant factors and propositions that must be tested empirically to draw greater understanding of the phenomenon.

Keywords: Anonymous communication · eWOM · Credibility · Computer-mediated communication

1 Introduction

Communication and interaction using social media has spread across cultures globally. Survey data suggests that more than 1.5 billion people, worldwide, are connected via social media communities. Users converse and interact via social media communities, discussion boards, weblogs, social networking sites etc. Increasingly they are turning to social media to socialize and broadcast their views. This has enabled users' of the world to seek and share brand-related experiences and opinions (eWOM) with the click of a few buttons which in turn has significantly altered consumer decision process [4, 15].

It is averred that social media is changing the fundamentals of communication in several ways. Intimacy of a face to face (FtF) communication has been replaced with a "broadcast-like ability to communicate with the masses" [1, p. 3]. Technology has enabled interpersonal communication to be visible on a more transparent public domain, simultaneously accessible to a very large set of audience. It abundantly supports consumer to consumer conversations, participation, interaction and collaboration which in turn influence behaviour. Therefore while interacting on social media users are hugely influenced by other outside their known circle [10]. Moreover, user interaction, quite like other computer mediated-communication (CMC), may be influenced by "disinhibition", enabling them to communicate and behave freely, feel "less restrained, and express themselves more openly" [15, p. 321]. At the same time, similar to other forms

Published by Springer International Publishing Switzerland 2016. All Rights Reserved
Y.K. Dwivedi et al. (Eds.): I3E 2016, LNCS 9844, pp. 360–370, 2016.
DOI: 10.1007/978-3-319-45234-0_33

of CMC, communication via social media may vary in the degree of anonymity. Anonymity, a social condition, permits user to conceal her identity which further complicates the process of communication on social media. Different social media interface permit different levels of anonymity, which may further reinforce the impact of deindividualisation and hyperpersonal [14].

This article explores the behavioural impact of anonymous eWOM communication by building on a recently observed case of a local establishment - Lemp Brewpub & Kitchen, Gurgaon, India. An anonymous weblog detailing a bad experience faced by a set of customers went viral which tarnished the reputation of the establishment beyond repair and resulted in its shutting down. This case, similar to many other recent cases, raises the question of how an anonymous communication (blog post in Lemp's case), reshared by many via various Social Networking Sites (SNSs), can cause serious harm to a brick and mortar establishment? A single bad experience shared in form of an anonymous blog, damaged Lemp's reputation permanently. This article enquires why despite of anonymity, deindividualisation and possible threat of identity deception, anonymous communication is influential, believable and gathers credibility. The paper explores how in the absence of traditional sources of credibility, users of social media explore alternate heuristics to assess credibility. It is further suggested that these subtle embedded alternate heuristics not only influence user disposition but also their behaviour, observed by the act of resharing of the anonymous blog post. Network-related features like homophily and perceived social conformity further provide explanation to the behaviour of resharing. The article concludes with several propositions derived from the experience of Lemp and support found in literature which may be further tested as future research.

The remainder of the article is organised like this: it starts with the details of the Lemp case followed with review of related literature and concludes with propositions.

2   The Case - Lemp Brewpub, Gurgaon, Haryana, India

2.1   Anonymous Blog

On Monday, 10th June 2013, an anonymous blog was posted by a group of eight friends who called themselves "Gurgaon victims" (from here on – group of friends). According to their blog on Sunday, 9th June 2013, based on a promotion they read on a www.zomato.com (a popular online restaurant database and review site, Zomato from here on, Exhibit 1), they decided to go to Lemp Brewpub & Kitchen, a local pub located in Gurgaon (satellite city to New Delhi, India), to enjoy a fun filled Hawaiian Brunch. Unfortunately Lemp could not deliver the Hawaiian Brunch and a series of occurrences led to altercation between the group of friends and staff. The anonymous blog post recounted how, as the events unfolded, the expected fun filled Hawaiian Brunch turned into a harrowing experience that ended for the group of friends at the local police station, with their parents having to settle the matters. Blog iterated the chronological occurrences of the incident along with photographs of the incident taking place (Exhibit 3). There were no photographs of the group of friends themselves. The tonality, flow of details and the facts mentioned in the blog post clearly portrayed the group of friends as victims and denounce the staff of Lemp as a bunch of goons.

2.2 After Effects

The anonymous blog went viral and the next day, users across social media sites like Facebook and Twitter woke up to the blog post trending as "How a lunch at Lemp Brewpub turned out to be the most horrid experience ever" (Exhibit 4). Users, many who had never dined at Lemp, were sharing and resharing the blog post in abundance. The Facebook page and Twitter handle of Lemp saw no response for a very long time.

Within a few hours, most of the users of social media, who had read the blog were completely consumed by it. They had declared Lemp to be the villain. They not only empathised with the group of friends but they extended support by action: posting supportive comments on the blog; sharing police information on where a formal complaint can be lodged; re-sharing the blog with more and more people; cracking "Lemp" jokes on Twitter and elsewhere (Exhibit 5), there by spreading negativity about it; posting bad reviews on Zomato despite having no first hand experience of the pub. As the anonymous blog went viral, it pulled the ratings of Lemp down drastically on Zomato. Within few hours, the number of reviews rose from 382 (before blog) to 900 plus (after blog) with majority of them being negative. The ratings dropped to a poor 1.3 based on 2975 votes (Exhibit 2). Users not only wholeheartedly believe the anonymous blog, they also indulged in supportive behaviour by resharing the post.

2.3 Epilogue

Even after months, Lemp failed to recover. On Zomato the ratings stood at a poor 1.3, based on 2101 reviewers. Post this incident whenever similar instances are shared on social media, users of social media are prone to say "don't do another Lemp!" Anonymous bloggers, who concealed their identity, not personally known to many, successfully influenced thousands of social media users and stained the reputation of an establishment in the most serious manner.

3 Theoretical Understanding

3.1 Computer-Mediated Communication and Anonymity

Web 2.0 and new media now provide many virtual avenues for users to engage and indulge in eWOM, both negative and positive [8]. The above case is an example of other similar cases that have gone viral on social media in the recent times. A single bad experience of a consumer is read, shared and reshared by thousands significantly damaging brand reputation with the spread of internet and the changing media consumption habits, several studies have found eWOM to be more credible, therefore influential, than traditional marketer generated communication [7].

eWOM via social media has intrigued researchers in the recent times for several reasons. From traditional FtF (face to face) WOM interactions, CMC eWOM diverges significantly. As already stated, users that connect via social media are diverse and the environment "opens up the WOM network from one's immediate contacts to the entire Internet world" [3, p. 9] therefore eWOM may take place between users who have no significant prior relationship. Furthermore, just like other CMCs, eWOM via social media may lack both non-verbal and social context cues, yet users adjust to the new environment and use alternative linguistic and other forms of heuristics for judgement [16, 17].

Critical enquiry of the current research is the influence of anonymity. Social media interactions take place in environment which may afford different degrees of anonymity to users. SNS like Facebook enables "social interactions through profile-based user accounts", identity creation is quite integral to the site hence user anonymity is lower [12, p. 439, 22]. Weblogs on the other hand provide "a more remote space with less interactivity that may reduce users' awareness of their audiences", hence anonymity varies [9, p. 285]: user identity information may be completely anonymous, pseudonymous, or identifiable. Completely anonymous blogs may still offer a few selective self-disclosures [16], as was seen in this case of anonymous blog against Lemp. The anonymous blog revealed no identity information about the bloggers. Level of anonymity of a social media site may further lead to identity deception. Since Identity is separated from physical Self "One can have as many electronic personas as one has time and energy to create" generating convenient possibilities for online deception [5, p. 2, 22, 9]

Therefore the critical question that needs to be asked is - Why did the users of social media, who read the anonymous blog, felt positively assured of the intentions and motives of a group of unknowns who reveal no personal information about themselves? In other words, why do anonymous eWOM communication on social media influence when source information is either not shared or could be incorrect?

3.2   Credibility of Anonymous Social Media EWOM

The traditional understanding of credibility, based on the extant literature on the subject, is that it may be derived as a result of interaction of source characteristics, message characteristics and receiver characteristics [20]. According to Metzger (2007, p. 2078) "credibility of a source or message is a receiver-based judgment which involves both objective judgments of information quality or accuracy as well as subjective perceptions of the source's trustworthiness, expertise, and attractiveness". Therefore it is the interaction of both source credibility, message credibility and receiver based triggers that influences judgements.

Weblogs, Facebook posts and Twitter tweets are the new age platforms that allow users to interact. On these platforms traditional understanding of credibility assessment can vary as the source can be anonymous and messages are technology-enabled and asynchronous. Credibility may not be derived solely from familiarity of source or believing others as they part of a physical social network, it will be assessed using all the other information available on the platform itself [2]. "Variety of stored-information of others", heuristics or cues, are embedded in these platforms which allow assessment of credibility [18, 19, p. 230]. If the heuristics are limited or peculiar, users adapt [21]. Therefore perceptions of credibility may not be based on the traditional sources of credibility, it may be based on all the (limited) informational heuristics available on the social media platform. Specifically, it is posited, readers of the anonymous blog of Lemp assessed credibility based on heuristics embedded within the anonymous blog post itself.

Credibility Heuristics – Source and Message Characteristics. Despite of the blog being anonymous, there were few identity related self-disclosures made in the blog. The bloggers described themselves as "young, 25-year old, working, well educated, aware, well-travelled, well spoken". This indirect self-disclosure helped in building the perception of source credibility. Other set of credibility came from the message itself and manner in which the anonymous blog was written. According to the Language Expectancy Theory, influence of the message can be attributed to its language characteristics. Users are influenced if language characteristics meet or violate the expected norms even if the message is anonymous [11]. Language of the blog was detailed, refined and informational. Furthermore numerous other heuristics, embedded in the anonymous blog, lend credibility: screenshot of Hawaiian Lunch promotion on Zomato; photograph of the display board; selective negative reviews; photographs of the staff of Lemp carrying a mean disposition; sly looking photograph of the owner with one of his staff member; detailed information of the sequence of events - all worked towards increasing the believability of the blog.

Despite the lack of real information regarding the identity of the bloggers, message characteristics and alternate heuristics together made the anonymous blog believable and credible. Therefore following propositions are iterated:

P1 – In the absence of identity information even limited self-disclosures in anonymous communication may lead to significant source credibility.

P2 – In the absence of identity information, message characteristics and content-related heuristics may lead to significant message credibility.

P3 – Believability of anonymous blog increases when the source credibility of the 'friend' who has shared the blog is significantly positive.

3.3 eWOM Behaviour - Why Share and Reshare an Anonymous Blog?

Receiver Characteristics – Social Conformity, Subjective Norms. Anonymous blog was abundantly shared by users and one of the primary reasons for the same was conformity to social behaviour. Social conformity refers to the "act of matching attitudes, beliefs, and behaviours to group norms" [6, p. 591]. Where there are numbers the others will join! Users shared as others before them had shared and they were expected to adhere to the subjective norm of resharing. "Subjective norm refers to how a user perceives ways people important to him or her would behave" [13, p. 334] and therefore how they must also match their behaviour to meet the social expectation. There is no evidence to reveal identity of the first few people who shared the blog on Facebook and Twitter. May be it was simply a few friends of the blogger, or maybe they were people unknown to them. But once the blog started going viral thousands of people re-shared. They believed it simply because a lot of people before them have already liked, shared, favorited or retweeted it. To that extend there may have been a "flow of source credibility" derived from the immediate network of "friends" who have shared the blog on their timeline, whose behavioural expectation had to be met. Therefore the following proposition is iterated:

P4 – In the absence of identity information subjective norms are positively associated with behaviour of resharing by the user.

Homophily. Homophily, or the perception of similarity [14], also had a role to play for the spread of the anonymous blog. Blogger by calling themselves "young and 25 year something" tried to connect with others like them. Users may have perceived similarity of lifestyle, age and background. Therefore homophily, perception of similarity, further influenced the reshare behaviour. Therefore the following proposition is iterated:

P5 – Perception of homophily with the blogger, based on limited self-disclosures, is significantly related to the behaviour of resharing by the user.

4 Conclusion and Future Research

This article discussed the behavioural impact of anonymous communication as observed in the case of Lemp. The article draws understanding from literature for a real case of a business establishment that loses its reputation permanently. The article in accordance with the traditional understanding of credibility, as a source, message and receiver characteristic based judgement, identified factors that would lead to believability of anonymous eWOM. The anonymous blog may have damaged Lemp's reputation significantly and permanently. The article highlights despite of absence of pre-existing familiarity, trust and anonymity, credibility can be established based on several subtle alternate heuristics embedded in the communication. It further explained how receiver network-related features like homophily, subjective norms and social conformity may be responsible for the anonymous blog going viral. With the help of the observations of this case and literature the article posites several research directions that can be explored.

New media has altered several aspects of interpersonal communication and influence. Consumer to consumer communication is taking place in abundance and marketers need to appropriately listen and engage. A single bad experience is capable of damaging an organisations reputation severely, as was seen in the case sited. Anonymity afforded by social media sites needs to be understood better so that marketers can have better control over their brands reputation. Therefore this paper is an attempt to have greater understanding of this phenomenon. Empirical verification of the propositions can lead to greater understanding of behavioural impacts of anonymous communication.

Exhibits

1 Zomato & Its User Review and Rating Mechanism

Zomato started its journey as an online restaurant guide under the name of Foodiebay.com in 2008. After aiding the taste buds of Delhi NCR food lovers it expanded to other cities such as Kolkata and Mumbai[1] and soon, other prominent cities across the country as well. In 2010, with funding from Info Edge, it rebranded itself to Zomato[2] and 2012 saw it launching its first international services.[3] With additional funding from Sequoia Capital it has forayed into many other international markets and is expected to eat into the market share of Yelp.[4] It has the following services; it is a restaurant database and guide which allows a user to search information, allows uers to review restuarants and recently it has started online food ordering service.

Restaurants, pubs and clubs detailed on Zomato can be rated by a reviewer on a scale of 1 to 5, where ratings denote the following:

Rating	1.0	1.5	2.0	2.5	3.0	3.5	4.0	4.5	5.0
Significance	Avoid	Very Bad	Blah!	Well..	Average	Good enough	Great	Loved it!	Insane!

A registered user may also leave a review of minimum 50 words. Registered users are categorised as: Foodie; Big Foodie; Super Foodie; Connoisseur. Based on a user's engagement with the site, he/she may get upgraded to the next levels.[5]

2 Lemp's Rating on Zomato

Source: https://www.zomato.com/ncr/restaurants?q=Lemp retrieved on June 13th2013

[1] http://www.dnaindia.com/lifestyle/report-for-the-love-of-food-1284846 retrieved on 28th Nov 2013.

[2] http://www.nextbigwhat.com/foodiebay-rebrands-to-Zomato-297/ retrieved on 28th Nov 2013.

[3] http://www.khaleejtimes.com/kt-article-display-1.asp?xfile=/data/todayevent/2012/August/todayevent_August29.xml&section=todayevent retrieved on 28th Nov 2013.

[4] http://techcrunch.com/2013/11/06/Zomato/ retrieved on 28th Nov 2013.

[5] http://www.Zomato.com/leaderboard retrieved on 28th Nov 2013.

3 Anonymous Blog Post (First Page)

The entire incident in detail   11/06/13 11:31 PM

Yesterday   The entire incident in detail

For a lot of reasons, we have thought a lot before writing this. It is a very detailed account and we suggest you read it with patience. There is a lot to learn for us customers and a lot to be learnt by the restaurant owners community also.

A few of us friends (young, 25-year old, working, well educated, aware, well traveled, well spoken) were searching for a place to go to for Sunday brunch and on Zomato.com we came across a "Hawaiian Sunday Brunch" at Lemp Brewpub, Gurgaon. We decided to try out the Hawaiian brunch. As you can see from the image below, the cost is Rs. 999 all inclusive of taxes, and the same was also confirmed to us by the manager, Mr. Robin.

To put it out there, it wasn't the first time we were going to Lemp.

[http://4.bp.blogspot.com/-IayOs4CF2t0/UbWhIwPXAI/AAAAAAAAAM/DjrwUq2QRXi/s1600/IMG-20130608-WA0001.jpg]
The Zomato screenshot of the "Hawaiian Sunday Brunch" at Lemp Brewpub

From the above image [http://www.zomato.com/ncr/lemp-brewpub-and-kitchen-sector-30-gurgaon/events#tabtop] you can read the promises:

Hawaiian food - NONE to be found.
Tiki bar serving exotic cocktails - there was no such bar.
Live music and dancing - There was no music playing at all. After we asked they switched on the speakers and regular music played in the background. For the dancing, there were never any plans for dancers. On a serious note we were told by the manager, Robin, that customers were the ones supposed to dance.

http://lempexperience.blogspot.in/2013/06/the-entire-incident-in-detail.html   Page 1 of 18

Source: http://lempexperience.blogpost.in/2013/06/the-entire-incident-in-detail.
html retrieved 12th June 2013

4 Immediate Social Media Reactions

Source (Left to Right): http://www.facebook.com retrieved 13th June 2013; https://twitter.com/search?q=lemp&src=typd retrieved 13th June 2013.

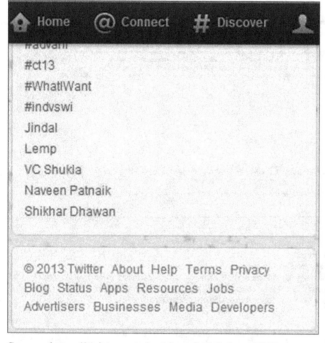

Source: https://twitter.com/ retrieved 11th June 2013

5 Don't Do a Lemp!

Source (Left to right): https://twitter.com/NitinBajaj/status/344449051997138944/ photo/1 retrieved on 7th September 2013; https://twitter.com/asraghunath/status/ 344817283119599617/photo/1 retrieved on 7th September 2013

References

1. Blackshaw, P., Nazzaro, M.: Consumer-generated media (CGM) 101: Word-of-mouth in the age of the web-fortified consumer, 2nd edn. A Nielsen BuzzMetrics White Paper, New York (2006)
2. Castillo, C., Mendoza, M., Poblete, B.: Information Credibility on Twitter. In: Proceeding of WWW 2011, March 28–April 1, 2011, Hyderabad, India, ACM (2011). ISBN 978-1-4503-0632-4/11/03
3. Cheung, M.Y., Luo, C., Sia, C.L., Chen, H.: Credibility of electronic word-of-mouth: informational and normative determinants of on-line consumer recommendations. Int. J. Electron. Commer. **13**(4), 9–38 (2009)
4. Chu, S.C., Kim, Y.: Determinants of consumer engagement in electronic word-of-mouth (eWOM) in social networking sites. Int. J. Advert. **30**(1), 47–75 (2011)
5. Donath, J.S.: Identity and deception in the virtual community. Commun. Cyberspace **1996**, 29–59 (1999)
6. Cialdini, R.B., Goldstein, N.J.: Social influence: compliance and conformity. Annu. Rev. Psychol. **55**, 591–621 (2004)
7. Hajli, M.N., Sims, J., Featherman, M., Love, P.E.: Credibility of information in online communities. J. Strateg. Mark. **23**(3), 238–253 (2015)

8. Hennig-Thurau, T., Gwinner, K.P., Walsh, G., Gremler, D.D.: Electronic word-of-mouth via consumer-opinion platforms: what motivates consumers to articulate themselves on the internet? J. Interact. Mark. **18**(1), 38–52 (2004)
9. Hollenbaugh, E.E., Everett, M.K.: The effects of anonymity on self-disclosure in blogs: an application of the online disinhibition effect. J. Comput.-Mediat. Commun. **18**(3), 283–302 (2013)
10. Jansen, B.J., Zhang, M., Sobel, K., Chowdury, A.: Twitter power: tweets as electronic word of mouth. J. Am. Soc. Inform. Sci. Technol. **60**(11), 2169–2188 (2009)
11. Jensen, M.L., Averbeck, J.M., Zhang, Z., Wright, K.B.: Credibility of anonymous online product reviews: a language expectancy perspective. J. Manag. Inf. Syst. **30**(1), 293–324 (2013)
12. Keenan, A., Shiri, A.: Sociability and social interaction on social networking websites. Libr. Rev. **58**(6), 438–450 (2009)
13. Lee, S.Y., Hansen, S.S., Lee, J.K.: What makes us click "like" on Facebook? Examining psychological, technological, and motivational factors on virtual endorsement. Comput. Commun. **73**, 332–341 (2016)
14. McCroskey, J.C., Richmond, V.P., Daly, J.A.: The development of a measure of perceived homophily in interpersonal communication. Hum. Commun. Res. **1**(4), 323–332 (1975)
15. Metzger, M.J.: Making sense of credibility on the web: models for evaluating online information and recommendations for future research. J. Am. Soc. Inform. Sci. Technol. **58**(13), 2078–2091 (2007)
16. Qian, H., Scott, C.R.: Anonymity and self-disclosure on weblogs. J. Comput.-Mediat. Commun. **12**(4), 1428–1451 (2007)
17. Suler, J.: The online disinhibition effect. Cyberpsychol. & Behav. **7**(3), 321–326 (2004)
18. Walther, J.B.: Computer-mediated communication impersonal, interpersonal, and hyperpersonal interaction. Commun. Res. **23**(1), 3–43 (1996)
19. Walther, J.B., Van Der Heide, B., Hamel, L.M., Shulman, H.C.: Self-generated versus other-generated statements and impressions in computer-mediated communication a test of warranting theory using facebook. Commun. Res. **36**(2), 229–253 (2009)
20. Wathen, C.N., Burkell, J.: Believe it or not: factors influencing credibility on the Web. J. Am. Soc. Inform. Sci. Technol. **53**(2), 134–144 (2002)
21. Westerman, D., Spence, P.R., Van Der Heide, B.: A social network as information: the effect of system generated reports of connectedness on credibility on Twitter. Comput. Hum. Behav. **28**(1), 199–206 (2012)
22. Zhao, S., Grasmuck, S., Martin, J.: Identity construction on Facebook: digital empowerment in anchored relationships. Comput. Hum. Behav. **24**(5), 1816–1836 (2008)

Consumer Intentions on Social Media: A fsQCA Analysis of Motivations

Patrick Mikalef[(⊠)], Ilias O. Pappas, and Michail Giannakos

Department of Computer and Information Science,
Norwegian University of Science and Technology,
Sem Saelandsvei 9, 7491 Trondheim, Norway
{patrick.mikalef,ilpappas,michailg}@idi.ntnu.no

Abstract. With social media gaining rapidly in popularity, a large number of companies have initiated attempts to capitalize on the large user base present on such platforms. Yet, it still remains unclear how affordances that social media facilitate can influence consumer intentions to purchase and engage in word-of-mouth. This paper builds on the distinction between utilitarian and hedonic features, and empirically examines how these aspects present on social media platforms affect consumer behavior. Using survey data from 165 social media users we perform fuzzy set Qualitative Comparative Analyses (fsQCA) to extract patterns of factors that impact both purchase, and word-of-mouth intentions. The outcomes of the analyses demonstrate that realizing high purchase and word-of-mouth intentions can be achieved through multiple ways which also depend on gender and spending history. Practical and theoretical implications are discussed, particularly concerning how these findings can guide the design of successful social media outlets for commerce.

1 Introduction

Social media have managed in very short period of time to radically change the way Internet users communicate and interact with each other. With the large user base present today on social media, business executives have been particularly attracted to the potential provided by these platforms to enact their competitive strategies [1]. The diversity of media supported by social media platforms, in combination with the vast user base and the rich profile and navigational information, have elevated the interest particularly for marketing and commerce purposes [2]. Indicative of this trend, the term social commerce has been coined to refer to the various types of commercial activities used on social media in order to enhance customer participation [3] and achieve greater economic value [4]. Within the scope of social commerce activities are marketing new products through interactive campaigns, enabling product browsing and purchasing in social commerce marketplaces, and facilitating interactions between consumers during the search and purchase of products [5].

Despite these very promising prospects for leveraging social media to gain a competitive advantage, a number of studies have revealed that in certain occasions companies have rushed into social media without formulating a clear plan [6]. Due to the relative novelty of deploying marketing and commerce strategies on social media,

© IFIP International Federation for Information Processing 2016
Published by Springer International Publishing Switzerland 2016. All Rights Reserved
Y.K. Dwivedi et al. (Eds.): I3E 2016, LNCS 9844, pp. 371–386, 2016.
DOI: 10.1007/978-3-319-45234-0_34

not much is known about how consumers respond to such campaigns and what features activate their behaviour. To date there are only a limited number of studies that empirically examine the concept of social commerce and how features available on social media impact consumer conduct [7]. It has been argued that in order to deploy successful marketing strategies and fully harness the potential of social media, it is necessary to understand how consumers utilize the affordances that such platforms offer. While there have been several studies that examine how the influence of specific motivations on social commerce websites impact consumer behaviour, they fail to examine the synergies that these affordances have and how the different combination of elements trigger specific actions.

Therefore, this research aims to address the question of how affordances present on social media influence consumer conduct. More specifically we seek to understand the mechanisms that promote intentions to purchase and word-of-mouth. To do so, we distinguish characteristics of social media in two major categories, utilitarian and hedonic ones. Analysing data from 165 social media users through the novel data analysis technique fuzzy set Qualitative Comparative Analysis (fsQCA), we aim to identify patterns of characteristics on social media that promote purchase and word-of-mouth proclivity. The statistical technique fsQCA builds on the ideas of complexity theory and is aimed at uncovering patterns of factors that stimulate purchasing and word-of-mouth intentions. In contrast with other statistical methods, it builds on the notion of *equifinality*, meaning that a specific outcome can be caused by more than one combination of factors. By doing so, we aim to highlight that there are different profiles of consumers and that their actions are triggered by different combinations of social commerce affordances.

In the next section we introduce the theoretical background on online commerce motivations as described under the utilitarian and hedonic motivation lens. In Sect. 3 we present the research propositions to be explored, while in Sect. 4 the data collection method and construct development process are discussed. Section 5 introduces the data preparation and analysis procedure along with results. In Sect. 6 these outcomes are discussed from a theoretical and practical point of view, concluding with Sect. 7 which suggests future directions for research based on the shortcomings of existing studies.

2 Background

Research on purchasing and word-of-mouth motivations is not new. The shopping process has been delineated and decomposed in a series of sequential activities, along with the underlying motivations which lead to a purchase decision. Consumers may be motivated to purchase a product due to the potential use it may have to them. On the other hand, it is becoming increasingly apparent that a vast majority of consumers engage in the buying process motivated by their need to socialize, to pass their time, or to discover new trends and fashions [8]. The main premise of these findings are that individuals do not only engage in the shopping process for the utility of the items to be purchased, but also for the satisfaction perceived in the process of doing so. As such, two broad categories of motivations have been defined in literature, i.e. utilitarian and hedonic motivations [9]. Utilitarian and hedonic motivation theory attempts to explain why people are inclined to perform a particular behaviour while purchasing. The idea of examining motivations from a utilitarian and hedonic point of view has gained eminence is recent years, with several research studies applying them for both purchasing and word-of-mouth intentions [10–12].

The reason for explicitly differentiating between utilitarian and hedonic based motivational factors is that they differ fundamentally. Utilitarian motivations are regarded as rational and goal oriented [13]. Applied to the online shopping context, utilitarian motivations perceive the benefit as stemming from efficiency, completeness, and usability of the process or medium [14]. Contrarily, hedonic motivations are triggered by the search of emotions such as happiness, enjoyment, and adventure experienced during the procedure [15]. In online shopping environments, hedonic motivated consumers are primarily interested in the enjoyment of the process rather than its utility [16]. Hence, hedonic consumers receive satisfaction from the experience itself and from the emotions perceived during it. The combined effect of utilitarian and hedonic motivations was put to test by Babin et al. [10] who argues that hedonic factors influence unplanned shopping whereas utilitarian ones do not. In addition, Jones et al. [11] point out that word-of-mouth is a result of heightened interest in a product, which in turn creates a psychological pressure which is relieved through sharing information. As such, aspects that enabled such hedonic reactions will likely be the cause of word-of-mouth. However, research has also shown that word-of-mouth is associated with cognitive processes, such as perceptions of value and equity evaluations [11].

Although a number of studies have provided insight over the factors that affect consumer behaviour, further exploration of how online shopping mediums stimulate consumer motivations are required. A prominent stream of research has shifted attention towards how motivations are influenced by the design of online mediums [17]. In this direction, the majority of studies have identified utilitarian factors as being the prime motivators of engaging consumers to purchase and word-of-mouth [18, 19]. Some commonly researched utilitarian factors include convenience, information availability, product selection, and customization [20, 21]. Despite the dominance of utilitarian design factors in influencing consumer behaviour, research on hedonic factors has also revealed some interesting outcomes. A study by Falk and Campbell [22] argued that when consumers are faced with a storefront or a commercial website of retailer, sensual stimulations and the ability to navigate freely are important. In line with Falk and Campbell's arguments, Eroglu et al. [23] stress that consumers do not navigate through online media solely to gather product-related information and make a rationale decision to purchase products they may need, but also do so to fulfil their needs of experience, emotion, and adventure. As such, similarly to traditional means of shopping, online consumer behaviour is influenced by aesthetics and the overall enjoyment of the experience [24].

The aforementioned studies signal a broadening in perspective with regard to hedonic and utilitarian motivations and aspects present on online media that may trigger them. With past studies arguing the impact that these motivations may have on consumer behaviour, and especially purchase and word-of-mouth intentions, it is important to examine their synergistic impact. In particular, in the novel context of social media understanding how affordances present on them affect behaviour is critical in designing marketing strategies.

3 Research Propositions

Following the studies described above, researchers in the area of e-commerce have begun to examine how utilitarian and hedonic aspects present on social media influence consumer behaviour [19, 25]. The potential of social media for product and brand marketing has been quickly realized by business executives, with early attempts yielding very promising results [26]. These outcomes have increased the interest of companies to deploy marketing strategies on social media in order to attract new customers and increase revenues. However, the interaction that consumers develop with the affordances present on social media as well as how these interactions impact the behaviour is a subject that remains relatively unexplored. Thus, there is a need to understand what aspects of social media motivate consumers to take action, and how these differ based on their profiles. We argue that there is diversity in the utilitarian and hedonic factors that influence consumer intentions to purchase and word-of-mouth. As such, it is critical to first distinguish between the primary utilitarian and hedonic aspects present on social media websites.

With a vast majority of studies focusing on utilitarian aspects of online shops, several important factors have been identified to date [27]. In the present study we follow the aspects put forth by Wolfinbarger and Gilly [28], who identify between convenience, information availability, and product selection. We also include personal recommendations as an important utilitarian aspect since through the profile developed on social media, consumers are presented with products that are tailored to their likings [16]. These factors are recurring in literature with numerous studies indicating their importance as part of the utilitarian motivation. The selection of the aforementioned factors has been based on their applicability to the social media context, and on past studies signalling the significance in other settings [12].

Concerning hedonic aspects, past studies have put forth a number of different factors such as trend discovery (keeping up with new trends and browsing new products), socializing (ability to socialize with friends and other shoppers), adventure (the stimulation felt during the browsing of products) and authority (the feeling of being able to control the medium in a way that suits the shoppers needs) [29–31]. As with utilitarian aspects, it is important to distinguish aspects of a hedonic perspective that are applicable on social media. Therefore, a number of hedonic factors that were related only to conventional stores were omitted.

Our research also identifies between profiles of consumers on social media. Gender differences in online shopping behaviour have been noted in several past studies [32, 33]. The differences noted have been traced back to how males and females differ in their perceptions of web technologies and the aspects they focus on or find important [34]. Further to gender differences, a significant factor for distinguishing between profiles of online consumers is their purchase history. Consumers that tend to buy frequently and are more likely to spend money online have been found to be influenced by different aspects during their shopping process [35]. The main premise of our research framework is that multiple types of consumers exist, and all have a different combination of factors (utilitarian and hedonic) that influence their shopping behaviour; be it to purchase or word-of mouth. In contrast with past studies, we assume that both purchase intentions and word of mouth intentions are triggered by a multitude of different combinations of affordances. This leads us to the following research propositions:

Proposition 1. *There is no single best configuration of consumers' demographics, utilitarian and hedonic motivation aspects that leads to high intention to purchase or word-of-mouth; instead, multiple, equally effective configurations of causal factors exist.*

Proposition 2. *Single causal motivational values may be present or absent within configurations for consumers' high intention to purchase or word-of-mouth, depending on how they combine with other causal conditions* (Fig. 1).

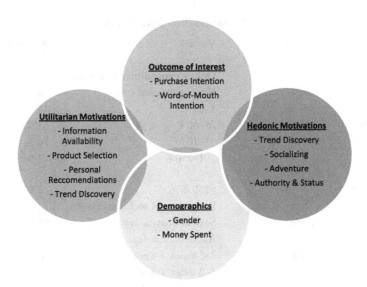

Fig. 1. Factors that affect consumers' intentions to purchase and word-of-mouth on social media

4 Methodology

4.1 Sampling

In order to explore the research propositions of this study a custom-built survey instrument was developed. The target population for administering the survey were individuals that had prior experience with using social media, and specifically for purposes including product browsing. The questionnaire was divided into three main parts. The first asked respondents to fill out information about their demographics and their habits concerning the use of social media. The second part was targeted in measuring the importance they attribute to utilitarian and hedonic aspects of social media. Finally, the third part was aimed at measuring the intentions of users to purchase and share product-related information found on social media. To ensure that there was no bias in the sample, multiple sources were used including a mailing list of over 600 respondents of an academic institution, approximately 20 forum boards of difference topics (fashion, computers, hobbies etc.). In total, the questionnaire contained 55 questions divided into the three aforementioned parts. The final number of fully complete responses were 165 which were then used for further analysis.

The descriptive statics of the final sample of respondents are depicted in Table 1 below. In terms of gender, the final sample presents an almost equal distribution between male and female respondents. The largest proportion of responses were from young users, however, this is in coherence with the demographics of social media users [36]. In addition, most respondents were from a relatively high educated background, with experience in online shopping, and a high frequency of using social media.

Table 1. Sample descriptive statistics

Variable	Percentage (N = 165)	Variable	Percentage (N = 165)
Gender		**Online expenditure (€/month)**	
Male	56 %	Never purchased online	6 %
Female	44 %	1–24 €	44 %
Education		25–50 €	25 %
Primary school	1 %	51–100 €	16 %
Junior high school	1 %	101–250 €	7 %
High school	14 %	>250 €	2 %
University	56 %	**Frequency of social media use**	
Post-graduate	28 %	Several times a day	55 %
Age group		About once a day	21 %
<24	50 %	3–5 times a week	8 %
25–34	37 %	1–2 times a week	4 %
35–44	7 %	Every few weeks	4 %
45–54	6 %	Less often	7 %
>55	0 %		

4.2 Measures

The constructs used in the study included adapted measures of past research studies as well as previously empirical tested ones. Operational definitions as well as key references for construct development are provided in Table 2. All items were measured on a 7-point likert scale in which respondents were asked to evaluate how much they agreed or disagreed with several sentences related to the constructs they were assigned to measure. The full questionnaire along with statistics on the item level are presented in Appendix A.

Table 2. Construct operational definitions

Construct	Operational definition	Key references
Convenience	The level of convenience perceived when browsing products or services on social media	[30, 37, 38]
Information availability	The amount of available information regarding products or services on social media	[28, 30]
Product selection	The diversity of products or services on social media	[28, 30]
Personal recommendation	The compatibility of customized advertisements presented to users on social media based on their profiles	[30, 37, 39]
Trend discovery	The effectiveness of social media in providing the latest information about new trends and fashions	[29, 30]
Socializing	The level of use of synchronous or asynchronous means of communication with fellow peers during product or service browsing on social media	[28, 30]
Adventure	The degree to which social media provide a novel and interesting browsing experience towards users, and the sense of excitement perceived during use	[40]
Authority and status	The sense of authority perceived over social media when browsing products	[41]
Purchase intention	The intention to purchase a product seen on a social media	[42, 43]
Word of mouth intention	The intention to share information with peers about products or services with peers on social media	[43, 44]

4.3 Reliability and Validity

Since latent variables were measured through a reflective mode, they were subjected to reliability, convergent and discriminant validity tests. To evaluate reliability, tests were performed at both the construct and item level. At the construct level all Cronbach Alpha (CA) values were above the lower threshold of 0.7. To determine item-level reliability, construct-to-item loadings were assessed, with all items having loadings greater than 0.7, thus indicating that they are reliable measures of the overall construct. Convergent validity was established by examining if Average Variance Extracted (AVE) scores were above the lower limit of 0.50. As indicated in Table 3, all AVE values exceed the threshold, indicating that convergent validity of constructs is established. Discriminant validity was tested through two ways. The first was by identifying if all constructs AVE square root was greater than its highest correlation with any other construct (Fornell-Larcker criterion), while the second was by examining if each indicators outer loadings on its assigned construct was greater than its cross-loadings with any other construct. Confirming reliability, convergent and discriminant validity indicates that the data are valid to use for further analysis.

Table 3. Inter-construct correlations and validity measures

	(1)	(2)	(3)	(4)	(5)	(6)	(7)	(8)	(9)	(10)
(1) CNV	**0.93**									
(2) IA	0.77	**0.90**								
(3) PS	0.83	0.83	**0.94**							
(4) PR	0.32	0.39	0.39	**0.87**						
(5) TD	0.77	0.86	0.82	0.47	**0.90**					
(6) SC	0.54	0.69	0.60	0.54	0.76	**0.85**				
(7) ADV	0.50	0.43	0.52	0.55	0.55	0.49	**0.89**			
(8) AUT	0.64	0.63	0.65	0.48	0.69	0.58	0.67	**0.92**		
(9) PI	0.62	0.60	0.64	0.49	0.66	0.57	0.68	0.71	**0.85**	
(10) WOMI	0.42	0.42	0.42	0.53	0.51	0.57	0.51	0.51	0.59	**0.84**
Mean	4.69	4.84	4.34	3.10	4.27	4.05	2.67	3.54	3.13	3.07
Standard deviation	2.00	1.80	1.84	1.91	1.81	1.96	1.74	1.81	1.97	2.01
Cronbach alpha	0.93	0.88	0.93	0.85	0.88	0.80	0.87	0.90	0.90	0.89
AVE	0.87	0.81	0.88	0.76	0.81	0.72	0.80	0.84	0.73	0.71

5 Analysis

5.1 Methodology and Calibration

To determine user profiles and the combinations of aspects on social media that enhance their intentions to purchase and word-of-mouth this study employs a fuzzy-set Qualitative Comparative Analysis (fsQCA). FsQCA adheres to the principles of configuration theory which in essence allows for the examination of interplays that develop between elements of a messy and non-linear nature [45]. The main difference of fsQCA with other statistical methods is that it supports equifinality, meaning that a particular outcome (e.g. high purchase intention) may be caused by different combination of elements. This is particularly relevant to the context of online shopping since consumers differ in the aspects that trigger their behaviour. As such, it is important to isolate what combination of affordances present on social media motivate specific consumer groups to purchase and share information. FsQCA follows such a paradigm since it is geared towards reducing elements for each patterns to the fundamentally necessary and sufficient conditions. In addition, fsQCA further supports the occurrence of causal asymmetry. Causal asymmetry means that, for an outcome to occur, the presence and absence of a causal condition depend on how this causal condition combines with one or more other causal conditions [46].

The first step in conducting an fsQCA analysis is calibrating dependent and independent variables into fuzzy or crisp sets. The fuzzy of fuzzy sets may range anywhere on the continuous scale from 0, which denotes an absence of set membership, to 1, which indicates full set membership. Crisp sets are more appropriate in categorical variables that have two, and only two options. The procedure followed of transforming continuous variables into fuzzy sets is grounded on the method proposed by Ragin [47]. According to the procedure, the degree of set membership is based on three anchor values. These represent a full set membership threshold value (fuzzy score = 0.95), a full non-membership value (fuzzy score = 0.05), and the crossover point (fuzzy score = 0.50) [48]. Since this study uses a 7-point likert scale to measure constructs, the guidelines put forth by Ordanini et al. [49] are followed to calibrate them into fuzzy sets. Therefore, full membership thresholds are set for values over 5.5, the cross over point is set at 4, and full non-membership values at 2.5. The gender of respondents is coded as 1 for males and 0 for females, while low spenders (marked with a value of 0) are those that spend up to 24€/month and high spenders (marked with a value of 1) those that spend over 25€/month based on median split.

5.2 Fuzzy Set Qualitative Comparative Analysis

By performing two separate fsQCA analyses truth tables of 2^k rows each are produced, where k represents the number of predictor elements, and each row indicates a possible combination (solution). Solutions that have a consistency level lower than 0.75 are disregarded [50]. Consistency is a measure of the degree to which a subset relation has been approximated. In addition, a minimum of two cases for each solution is set [50]. Having established these parameters, the fsQCA analyses are then performed using high purchase and word-of-mouth intention as the dependent variables. The outcomes of the fuzzy set analysis are presented in Table 4. The solutions are presented in the columns with the black circles denoting the presence of a condition, the crossed-out circles indicating an absence of it, while the blank spaces represent a "don't care" situation in which the causal condition may be either present or absent [50].

The outcomes of the analysis for high purchase intentions yield four different solutions. The first two concern male consumers while the latter two female ones. Specifically, solution 1 proposes that males that are flagged as high spenders are propelled to purchase on social media due to convenience, the product selection, and well as the ability to discover new trends on social media. Solution 2 differs in that it addresses low spending consumers whom are found to be influenced by the convenience of social media, personal recommendations presented to them, as well as the sense of adventure perceived while browsing products. Solutions 3 and 4 are oriented towards females with high spending habits. The former of these two solutions places emphasis on information availability, the product selection, and the ability to socialize on social media, while the later on personal recommendations and the capacity to discover new trends.

The analysis for high word-of-mouth intentions results in four different solutions, in which one is directed towards males and the other three towards females. Solutions 1 indicated that males are highly likely to engage in word-of-mouth when there is a lack of information, there is a large product selection, personal recommendations are present, and they are able to discover trends. Solutions 2 and 3 explain high word-of-mouth intentions for females that have a high spending profile. These type of consumers are influenced either by the convenience of social media combined with a broad product selection and an ability to socialize, or by a wide product selection, personal recommendation affordances, and the ability to discover new trends. Finally, solution 4 concerns females with low spending behaviour. This profile of user is

Table 4. Configurations for high purchase and word-of-mouth intentions

Configuration	Purchase Intentions				Word-of-Mouth Intentions			
	1	2	3	4	1	2	3	4
Demographics								
Gender	●	●	⊗	⊗	●	⊗	⊗	⊗
High Spending	●	⊗	●	●		●	●	⊗
Utilitarian Motivations								
Convenience	●	●				●		
Information Availability			●		⊗			
Product Selection	●		●		●	●	●	
Personal Recommendations		●		●	●		●	
Hedonic Motivation								
Trend Discovery	●			●			●	
Socializing			●			●		●
Adventure		●						●
Authority and Status					●			
Consistency	0.822	0.864	0.935	0.752	0.902	0.781	0.741	0.793
Raw Coverage	0.335	0.182	0.132	0.069	0.235	0.203	0.099	0.096
Unique Coverage	0.215	0.062	0.012	0.021	0.183	0.126	0.027	0.038
Overall Solution Consistency	0.785				0.805			
Overall Solution Coverage	0.432				0.416			

propelled to engage in word-of-mouth primarily based on hedonic motivations sparked by social media, such as socializing and feeling a sense of adventure.

6 Discussion

The present paper suggests that consumer intentions to purchase and engage in word-of-mouth on social are propelled by a combination of different factors present on such mediums. To examine what aspects facilitate consumer intentions to purchase and word-of-mouth, a conceptual model is proposed which distinguishes between utilitarian and hedonic aspects of social media platforms. While utilitarian and hedonic motivations have been extensively examined in research studies relating to shopping, at both physical and electronic shops, limited studies have examined their impact on social media platforms to date. Building on this gap, the present study has explored how these two types of motivations influence consumer intentions to purchase and word-of-mouth. Taking also into account personal characteristics such as gender and money spent, outcomes of the fsQCA analyses indicate that multiple solutions exist in influencing consumer intents. The results highlight the importance of focusing on specific combinations of aspects to enhance consumer engagement.

More specifically, our outcomes demonstrate that all the examined aspects of social media can trigger consumer intentions, but not all are effective in the same settings. The gender of consumers and spending habits do in fact regulate the affordances that are responsible for initiating purchase and word-of-mouth intentions. These outcomes demonstrate that not all consumers operate in the same way on social media, thus, requirements in terms of functionality and content may differ. This poses an interesting practical implication for companies that want to formulate commerce strategies over social media. Depending on the profile of consumers that are targeted, attention can be given to different aspects of the medium such as the diversity of products and the accompanying information, attributes that enhance adventure such as gamification techniques and rewards, socializing initiatives, or customization features based on consumer information [51]. Literature has recognized two primary types of social commerce initiatives; e-commerce website that utilize social media tools and concepts (e.g. Amazon), and those that are built on social media platforms that add e-commerce affordances (e.g. Facebook) [52]. As such, the combination of utilitarian and hedonic aspects can be accentuated in either of these two settings.

From a theoretical point of view this study confirms that it does not make sense to categorize consumers as solely utilitarian or hedonic, since during the purchasing process both types of motivations influence their intentions. In addition, considering utilitarian and hedonic aspects of social media platforms as a whole does not provide any guidance, but what is more beneficial is to distinguish factors pertinent to each category. The use of the fsQCA methodology also demonstrates that there is no aspect that is superior than the other in terms of initiating consumer behaviour, but rather, that each is valuable when coupled with others. In addition, our findings confirm the suggestion of past studies that gender differences exist in terms of shopping and motivations. We find that this is also applicable in the social commerce context for both purchasing and word-of-mouth intentions. The same applies for the money they tend to spend online, with the patterns of elements influencing low spenders being different than those of high spenders. Ultimately, these findings showcase that there is no universally optimal way of deploying social commerce strategies for companies. What is necessary is that a careful customer segmentation is performed and the main target groups are located correctly. Since social media provide a rich background of information of consumers, it is highly probable that in the future social commerce interfaces will be highly personalized, not only with respect to content, but also in terms of structure and functionality [53, 54].

7   Conclusions

While results of this study have shed some light on the utilitarian and hedonic aspects of social media that promote consumers' intentions to purchase and word-of-mouth, they must be considered under their limitations. First, the distinction of consumers based on gender and purchasing expenditure can be expanded to further refine their profiles. Elements such as product type, price, availability, computer literacy, trust, and age can also result in different aspects that are found as important. Second, the robustness of results could be increased by utilizing a larger sample size. Third, although the intention to word-of-mouth is examined as an outcome of motivations, the scope and audience to which it will be addressed is not controlled for. Based on the abovementioned limitations, future studies could direct efforts towards better understanding the actions taken by consumers and how the design and content of social media influences these decisions. Towards this direction, the use of fsQCA could provide a useful tool in thinking of non-linear and synergistic effects on desired outcomes [55].

Acknowledgments

 This project has received funding from the European Union's Horizon 2020 research and innovation programme under the Marie Sklodowska-Curie grant agreement No. 704110.

This work was carried out during the tenure of an ERCIM "Alain Bensoussan" Fellowship Programme.

Appendix A: Questionnaire Items

Construct	Items	Mean	S.D
For each of the following sentences please indicate how much you agree or disagree with them (1 – totally disagree, 7 – totally agree)			
Convenience			
[CNV_1]	Social Media websites are a convenient medium since I can browse products whenever I want to	4.37	2.052
[CNV_2]	It is convenient to browse products through Social Media since I can do so in the comfort of my own space	4.85	2.005
[CNV_3]	Through Social Media I can browse products/services in accordance with my schedule	4.85	1.940
Information availability			
[IA_1]	Social Media provide me with quick access to large volumes of information about products/services	4.90	1.792
[IA_2]	Comments by other users of Social Media websites help in giving feedback about a product/service advertised	4.89	1.796
[IA_3]	I can collect useful information about a product/service I want through Social Media websites	4.79	1.773
Product selection			
[PS_1]	Social Media help me find more products that I was unfamiliar with before	4.47	1.832
[PS_2]	I can find a wide selection of products in one website through Social Media	4.26	1.843

(Continued)

(Continued)

Construct	Items	Mean	S.D
[PS_3]	With Social Media I can browse through a large array of products	4.36	1.833
Personal recommendations			
[PR_1]	I find that through information from my profile on Social Media websites, I am presented with product advertisements that are more compatible to my likings	3.73	2.072
[PR_2]	Products presented to me on Social Media platforms are customized to my needs	3.37	1.841
[PR_3]	Product recommendations on Social Media websites make me feel as an important customer	2.23	1.640
Trend discovery			
[TD_1]	Social Media provide me with access to new trends	4.34	1.825
[TD_2]	Through social media I am able to keep up with new fashions	4.50	1.855
[TD_3]	I can see what new products are available on social media	4.26	1.780
Socializing			
[SC_1]	Social Media provide a great platform in order to exchange information with my friends regarding products	4.39	1.715
[SC_2]	Through Social Media I can effectively share my experience of a newly purchased product or service with others	4.64	1.830
[SC_3]	I can engage in friendships with other shoppers through Social Media websites	3.15	1.988
Adventure			
[ADV_1]	I find browsing products through Social Media to be stimulating	2.86	1.726
[ADV_2]	To me, browsing products via Social Media websites is an adventure	2.49	1.691
[ADV_3]	I get drawn in to a world of my own when browsing products on Social Media Platforms	2.60	1.774
Authority and status			
[AUT_1]	When browsing products on Social Media websites I feel I am in control	3.41	1.863
[AUT_2]	Through Social Media websites I feel that I have a good understanding on the product features which I am browsing	3.70	1.818
[AUT_3]	Social Media enable me to control my product browsing	3.60	1.777
Purchase intention			
[PI_1]	I purchase some of the products or services which I have browsed through Social Media	3.40	1.995
[PI_2]	After some time of thought I buy one or more products which I have browsed on Social Media sites	3.17	1.970

(Continued)

(Continued)

Construct	Items	Mean	S.D
[PI_3]	Some of my recent purchases were based on information which I found via Social Media sites	3.42	2.197
[PI_4]	I buy products I see advertised on Social Media through e-shops	2.85	1.893
[PI_5]	I buy products I see advertised on Social Media through shops nearby me	3.01	1.856
Word-of-mouth intentions			
[WOMI_1]	I sometimes share with my friends through Social Media, products, brands or services that I like	3.75	1.958
[WOMI_2]	I send invitations to my friends to join a group of a product/brand on a Social Media site	2.37	1.792
[WOMI_3]	When I see a product I like on a Social Media website I use a "Like" or "+1" function to show my appreciation	3.09	2.112
[WOMI_4]	I would say positive things through a Social Media website about products I like	3.72	2.001
[WOMI_5]	I send invitations to friends so that they can join groups of brands and products which I believe they would like	2.54	1.918

References

1. Mangold, W.G., Faulds, D.J.: Social media: the new hybrid element of the promotion mix. Bus. Horiz. **52**, 357–365 (2009)
2. Berthon, P.R., Pitt, L.F., Plangger, K., Shapiro, D.: Marketing meets web 2.0, social media, and creative consumers: Implications for international marketing strategy. Bus. Horiz. **55**, 261–271 (2012)
3. Kim, Y., Srivastava, J.: Impact of social influence in e-commerce decision making. In: Proceedings of the Ninth International Conference on Electronic Commerce, pp. 293–302 (2007)
4. Parise, S., Guinan, P.J.: Marketing using web 2.0. In: Hawaii International Conference on System Sciences, Proceedings of the 41st Annual, pp. 281–281. IEEE (2008)
5. Liang, T.P., Turban, E.: Introduction to the special issue social commerce: a research framework for social commerce. Int. J. Electron. Commer. **16**, 5–14 (2011)
6. Fournier, S., Avery, J.: The uninvited brand. Bus. Horiz. **54**, 193–207 (2011)
7. Wang, C., Zhang, P.: The evolution of social commerce: the people, management, technology, and information dimensions. Commun. Assoc. Inf. Syst. **31**, 1–23 (2012)
8. Childers, T.L., Carr, C.L., Peck, J., Carson, S.: Hedonic and utilitarian motivations for online retail shopping behavior. J. Retail. **77**, 511–535 (2002)
9. Tauber, E.M.: Why do people shop? J. Mark. **36**, 46–49 (1972)
10. Babin, B.J., Lee, Y.K., Kim, E.J., Griffin, M.: Modeling consumer satisfaction and word-of-mouth: restaurant patronage in Korea. J. Serv. Mark. **19**, 133–139 (2005)
11. Jones, M.A., Reynolds, K.E., Arnold, M.J.: Hedonic and utilitarian shopping value: investigating differential effects on retail outcomes. J. Bus. Res. **59**, 974–981 (2006)
12. Mikalef, P., Giannakos, M., Pateli, A.: Shopping and word-of-mouth intentions on social media. J. Theor. Appl. Electron. Commer. Res. **8**, 17–34 (2013)

13. Batra, R., Ahtola, O.T.: Measuring the hedonic and utilitarian sources of consumer attitudes. Mark. Lett. **2**, 159–170 (1991)

14. O'Brien, H.L.: The influence of hedonic and utilitarian motivations on user engagement: the case of online shopping experiences. Interact. Comput. **22**, 344–352 (2010)

15. Pappas, I.O., Kourouthanassis, P.E., Giannakos, M.N., Chrissikopoulos, V.: Explaining online shopping behavior with fsQCA: the role of cognitive and affective perceptions. J. Bus. Res. **69**, 794–803 (2016)

16. Mikalef, P., Giannakos, M., Pateli, A.: Exploring the business potential of social media: an utilitarian and hedonic motivation approach. In: Proceedings of the 25th Bled eConference eDependability: Reliable and Trustworthy eStructures, eProcesses, eOperations and eServices for the Future Proceedings, Bled, Slovenia, pp. 1–14 (2012)

17. Chitturi, R., Raghunathan, R., Mahajan, V.: Delight by design: the role of hedonic versus utilitarian benefits. J. Mark. **72**, 48–63 (2008)

18. Cheung, C.M., Lee, M.K.: What drives consumers to spread electronic word of mouth in online consumer-opinion platforms. Decis. Support Syst. **53**, 218–225 (2012)

19. Mikalef, P., Pateli, A., Giannakos, M.: Why are users of social media inclined to word-of-mouth? In: Douligeris, C., Polemi, N., Karantjias, A., Lamersdorf, W. (eds.) Collaborative, Trusted and Privacy-Aware e/m-Services. IFIP AICT, vol. 399, pp. 112–123. Springer, Heidelberg (2013)

20. Alba, J., Lynch, J., Weitz, B., Janiszewski, C., Lutz, R., Sawyer, A., Wood, S.: Interactive home shopping: consumer, retailer, and manufacturer incentives to participate in electronic marketplaces. J. Mark. **61**, 38–53 (1997)

21. Morganosky, M.A., Cude, B.J.: Consumer response to online grocery shopping. Int. J. Retail Distrib. Manag. **28**, 17–26 (2000)

22. Falk, P., Campbell, C.: The shopping experience. Sage, London (1997)

23. Eroglu, S.A., Machleit, K.A., Davis, L.M.: Atmospheric qualities of online retailing: a conceptual model and implications. J. Bus. Res. **54**, 177–184 (2001)

24. Mathwick, C., Malhotra, N., Rigdon, E.: Experiential value: conceptualization, measurement and application in the catalog and Internet shopping environment. J. Retail. **77**, 39–56 (2001)

25. Kim, H.W., Gupta, S., Koh, J.: Investigating the intention to purchase digital items in social networking communities: a customer value perspective. Inf. Manag. **48**, 228–234 (2011)

26. He, W., Zha, S., Li, L.: Social media competitive analysis and text mining: a case study in the pizza industry. Int. J. Inf. Manag. **33**, 464–472 (2013)

27. Keeney, R.L.: The value of Internet commerce to the customer. Manag. Sci. **45**, 533–542 (1999)

28. Wolfinbarger, M., Gilly, M.C.: Shopping online for freedom, control, and fun. Calif. Manag. Rev. **43**, 34–55 (2001)

29. Arnold, M.J., Reynolds, K.E.: Hedonic shopping motivations. J. Retail. **79**, 77–95 (2003)

30. To, P.L., Liao, C., Lin, T.H.: Shopping motivations on Internet: a study based on utilitarian and hedonic value. Technovation **27**, 774–787 (2007)

31. Chung, C., Austria, K.: Social media gratification and attitude toward social media marketing messages: a study of the effect of social media marketing messages on online shopping value. In: Proceedings of the Northeast Business and Economics Association (2010)

32. Brown, M., Pope, N., Voges, K.: Buying or browsing? An exploration of shopping orientations and online purchase intention. Eur. J. Mark. **37**, 1666–1684 (2003)

33. Van Slyke, C., Comunale, C.L., Belanger, F.: Gender differences in perceptions of web-based shopping. Commun. ACM **45**, 82–86 (2002)

34. Gefen, D., Straub, D.W.: Gender differences in the perception and use of e-mail: an extension to the technology acceptance model. MIS Q. **21**, 389–400 (1997)

35. Bellman, S., Lohse, G.L., Johnson, E.J.: Predictors of online buying behavior. Commun. ACM **42**, 32–38 (1999)
36. Correa, T., Hinsley, A.W., De Zuniga, H.G.: Who interacts on the web?: The intersection of users' personality and social media use. Comput. Hum. Behav. **26**, 247–253 (2010)
37. Burke, R.R.: Do you see what I see? The future of virtual shopping. J. Acad. Mark. Sci. **25**, 352–360 (1997)
38. Chiang, K.P., Dholakia, R.R.: Factors driving consumer intention to shop online: an empirical investigation. J. Consum. Psychol. **13**, 177–183 (2003)
39. Han, J., Han, D.: A framework for analyzing customer value of internet business. JITTA: J. Inf. Technol. Theory Appl. **3**, 25 (2001)
40. Westbrook, R.A., Black, W.C.: A motivation-based shopper typology. Retail.: Crit. Concepts. Environ. Retail. **2**, 82 (2002)
41. Parsons, A.G.: Non-functional motives for online shoppers: why we click. J. Consum. Mark. **19**, 380–392 (2002)
42. Van der Heijden, H.: User acceptance of hedonic information systems. MIS Q. **28**, 695–704 (2004)
43. Brown, J., Broderick, A.J., Lee, N.: Word of mouth communication within online communities: conceptualizing the online social network. J. Interact. Mark. **21**, 2–20 (2007)
44. Hennig-Thurau, T., Gwinner, K.P., Walsh, G., Gremler, D.D.: Electronic word-of-mouth via consumer-opinion platforms: what motivates consumers to articulate themselves on the Internet? J. Interact. Mark. **18**(1), 38–52 (2004)
45. Fiss, P.C.: A set-theoretic approach to organizational configurations. Acad. Manag. Rev. **32**, 1180–1198 (2007)
46. Leischnig, A., Kasper-Brauer, K.: Employee adaptive behavior in service enactments. J. Bus. Res. **68**, 273–280 (2015)
47. Ragin, C.C.: Redesigning Social Inquiry: Fuzzy Sets and Beyond. University of Chicago Press, Chicago (2008)
48. Woodside, A.G.: Moving beyond multiple regression analysis to algorithms: calling for adoption of a paradigm shift from symmetric to asymmetric thinking in data analysis and crafting theory. J. Bus. Res. **66**, 463–472 (2013)
49. Ordanini, A., Parasuraman, A., Rubera, G.: When the recipe is more important than the ingredients a Qualitative Comparative Analysis (QCA) of service innovation configurations. J. Serv. Res. **17**, 134–149 (2013)
50. Ragin, C.C.: Set relations in social research: evaluating their consistency and coverage. Polit. Anal. **14**, 291–310 (2006)
51. Zhang, H., Lu, Y., Gupta, S., Zhao, L.: What motivates customers to participate in social commerce? The impact of technological environments and virtual customer experiences. Inf. Manag. **51**, 1017–1030 (2014)
52. Huang, Z., Benyoucef, M.: From e-commerce to social commerce: a close look at design features. Electron. Commer. Res. Appl. **12**, 246–259 (2013)
53. Yadav, M.S., De Valck, K., Hennig-Thurau, T., Hoffman, D.L., Spann, M.: Social commerce: a contingency framework for assessing marketing potential. J. Interact. Mark. **27**, 311–323 (2013)
54. Pappas, I.O., Kourouthanassis, P.E., Giannakos, M.N., Chrissikopoulos, V.: Shiny happy people buying: the role of emotions on personalized e-shopping. Electron. Mark. **24**, 193–206 (2014)
55. Mikalef, P., Pateli, A., Batenburg, R.S., Wetering, R.V.D.: Purchasing alignment under multiple contingencies: a configuration theory approach. Ind. Manag. Data Syst. **115**, 625–645 (2015)

Impression, Trust, and Risk Management

The Role of Non-social Benefits Related to Convenience: Towards an Enhanced Model of User's Self-disclosure in Social Networks

Tristan Thordsen, Matthias Murawski, and Markus Bick[✉]

ESCP Europe Business School Berlin, Berlin, Germany
tristan.thordsen@edu.escpeurope.eu,
{mmurawski,mbick}@escpeurope.eu

Abstract. Despite the overwhelming and unabated popularity of social networks in the past years, the motivation behind an individual's registration to such platforms is still largely uncharted. Based on an in-depth review of leading Information Systems literature, this paper investigates which factors potentially influence individual's self-disclosure in social networks. The literature review reveals information privacy violation as the primary risk of online platform use. Regarding benefits, two categories are identified: *social benefits*, like reciprocity, relationship building and maintenance, or self-presentation as well as *non-social benefits* related to convenience, like personalization, entertainment, and safety and security. The later ones are mostly neglected in existing models. The main contribution of this paper consists of filling this gap by developing an enhanced research model of the user's self-disclosure in social networks.

Keywords: Convenience · Privacy concerns · Self-disclosure · Social and non-social benefits · Social networks · Structured literature review

1 Introduction

Social networks enjoy impressive popularity. Facebook, as an example, counts approximately 1.55 billion active users [1]. In 2015, 3.17 billion people in the world had access to the Internet. This means that close to 50 % of all Internet users are Facebook members [2]. Generally, a social network is an online community where registered users present themselves on personal profiles and can interact with other users [3]. Other global social networks are for example Twitter, with around 320 million users [4], or Snapchat with approximately 200 million users [5]. Following the postulation of [6] that social networks should not be treated as one of a kind, we focus on the previously mentioned *public* social networks, which have a *hedonistic* purpose. Due to its size and importance, this group of social networks is already targeted by researchers such as [3] but requires further analysis [6].

Through the registration and subsequent creation of individual profiles, users reveal sensitive personal information. Publically the disclosure of personal data in social networks is debated controversially as it bears significant risks [7, 8]. The disclosed

© IFIP International Federation for Information Processing 2016
Published by Springer International Publishing Switzerland 2016. All Rights Reserved
Y.K. Dwivedi et al. (Eds.): I3E 2016, LNCS 9844, pp. 389–400, 2016.
DOI: 10.1007/978-3-319-45234-0_35

personal information can be a valuable asset to several agents in today's digitalized society. Companies for example have great interest in personal data as they can use it to gain insights and thus generate a technology-based competitive advantage [9]. Public authorities seek to understand dynamics of the society with the help of the data collected. However, criminals might also profit from the disclosed data [10]. Presenting sensible information about oneself in social networks can have severe tangible and intangible consequences such as identity theft, fraud, and misuse [8]. Despite these threats, social network users are willing and forthcoming with regards to sharing personal information with other users that may be complete strangers [11]. Literature in the field of self-disclosure coherently suggests that social benefits are key motivators behind personal information disclosure. Scholars base their argumentations on Social Exchange Theory [12] and its successors like the Privacy Calculus Model [13], which state that self-disclosure is an essential part of relationship building, ultimately resulting in an individual's social benefits and increased well-being.

Self-disclosure in social networks comprises the interaction of humans and technology and requires an interdisciplinary research approach [14]. Thus, this topic has caught the focus of the Information Systems (IS) community. Besides the focus on social aspects, recent IS literature dealing with behavior in social networks provides some hints on non-social benefits an individual can reap from self-disclosing in the networks. These additional benefits seem to be convenience-related [3]. However, they are neither clearly elaborated nor comprehensively presented in current research so far. This paper solely concentrates on motives of the individual. In doing so, we focus on enabling individuals to self-reflect and thus to create a practical additional value for the user. Aiming on developing an enhanced model of self-disclosure in social networks containing both social benefits and non-social benefits related to convenience, we formulate the following two research questions (RQ):

- RQ1: *What are social benefits that affect individuals to disclose personal information in social networks?*
- RQ2: *What are non-social benefits related to convenience that affect individuals to disclose personal information in social networks?*

This paper contributes on a theoretical level by building the foundation for a revised research model stating the factors that affect users to disclose personal information in social networks. Based on that, hypotheses for future empirical research are formulated. The remainder of this paper is organized as follows. First, the literature review is presented. Results are discussed subsequently leading to the revised model and respective hypotheses. The paper ends with a conclusion.

2 Literature Review

Our method of choice is a structured literature review that analyzes and summarizes findings from available papers, while identifying research gaps and giving direction for future research [15]. The literature review objectively identifies different points of view for specific keywords or phrases and clusters a heterogeneous collection of literature available [16].

Recent studies discuss the cross-functional and cross-disciplinary nature of research activities concerning social networks and emphasize the central role for IS scholars, given the longstanding tradition of the IS field dealing with such questions [17]. Consequently, our focus lies on IS literature. Thus, publications from other related disciplines like law and psychology are excluded in this paper. Our objective is to work out to what extend the academic discipline of IS has engaged in exploring and analyzing the phenomenon of user's self-disclosure in social networks until today. Therefore, this work is based on a discussion of renowned IS literature published between 2008 and October 2015. This timeframe appears to be especially relevant as starting from 2008 a sharp increase of social network user numbers around the world is perceivable [1]. For identifying relevant IS literature, the VHB Jourqual 3 ranking of 2015 for "Wirtschaftsinformatik" (IS) published by the German Academic Association for Business Research is taken as basis [18]. Although a multitude of different journal rankings exists [19], the VHB Jourqual 3 is chosen because of both its topical character and scope regarding IS journals. For this literature review, only academic IS journals with a VHB Jourqual rating of "leading scientific journal in business administration and its subdomains, Category A" and "outstanding, worldwide leading scientific journal in business administration and its subdomains, Category A+" are taken into consideration for research [20]. Moreover, *Business & Information Systems Engineering*, a leading European journal is included to provide additional geographical and thematic diversity. Last, in order to gain a meta-perspective on the phenomenon of online self-disclosure, publications of the A + Business Administration journal *Science* are analyzed based on the given timeframe and parameters. In total, 13 academic journals have been identified for the literature review. This choice of literature fulfills a number of important criteria. The chosen journals all enjoy high acceptance and relevance in their fields and represent topical, as well as geographical diversity. As claimed by [21], major contributions in IS are most likely to be found in the leading journals. Finally, our journal selection covers the "Senior Scholars' Basket of Journals" ("SenS8" in list below) that comprises the eight "top IS journals" [22]. This set of journals is commonly used when analyzing the IS field [23]. The complete list of the 13 selected journals in alphabetical order is *Business & Information Systems Engineering* (Jourqual 3 rating: B), *European Journal of Information Systems* (A, SenS8), *Information Systems Journal* (A, SenS8), *Information Systems Research* (A+, SenS8), *INFORMS Journal on Computing* (A), *Journal of Information Technology* (A, SenS8), *Journal of Management Information Systems* (A, SenS8), *Journal of Strategic Information Systems* (A, SenS8), *Journal of the Association for Information Systems* (A, SenS8), *Management Information Systems Quarterly* (A+, SenS8), *Mathematical Programming* (A), *Science* (A+), and *SIAM Journal on Scientific Computing* (A).

Search strings used for identifying topic related literature are: Internet, data, Social Media, Social Network, privacy, disclosure. These keywords have been obtained by a first explorative search in three of the journals, namely *Information Systems Research*, *MIS Quarterly*, and *Journal of Management Information Systems*. Within these journals and the given timeframe, six relevant articles were identified. Based on common subject terms of these articles the above keywords for further literature search were generated. In order to lay a wide focus and to increase accuracy, these keywords are applied one after the other during the research process. The search resulted in 26 articles which are subject to further analysis. Given the diversity and nature of the publications at hand, directed content analysis is chosen as analyzing tool for the literature review. This qualitative research method provides knowledge and understanding of the subject under study by coding or categorizing information and identifying key topics and patterns [24]. This method can also be interpreted as a deductive category application since it clusters qualitative content according to key theoretical concepts while identifying relationships and networks in the literature pool [25].

As a result of the literature review, three main foci of the papers at hand have been identified: *self-disclosure*, *data analytics*, and *privacy*. Seven articles are aggregated under the topic *self-disclosure*. The topic of *data analytics* accounts for nine articles. The largest category *privacy* comprises the remaining ten papers. It is important to note that topic foci of the literature tend to vary in accordance with the respective year of publication. As concepts determine the organizing framework of a high-quality literature review, it is important to detect the most prominent concepts used in the literature at hand [21]. *Social Exchange Theory*, *Privacy Calculus* and *Privacy Concerns* appear most frequently in the articles. It has to be pointed out that the articles [3, 11, 26, 27] refer to all of the three respective concepts. They use *Social Exchange Theory* as basis for their research. The concepts of *Privacy Calculus* and *Privacy Concerns* are then employed as an extension of *Social Exchange Theory* in a social network context, meaning that a certain interrelatedness between the three theories can be observed. The majority of articles thus analyzes the factors behind self-disclosure from a social sciences point of view. However, while often being unstructured, certain non-social benefits are mentioned, as well.

Referring to our research questions, Fig. 1 illustrates the scope of factors that affect individuals to self-disclose in social networks presented in the literature at hand. It comprises the main findings of our literature review related to both social motives and non-social benefits that affect individuals to self-disclose in social networks.

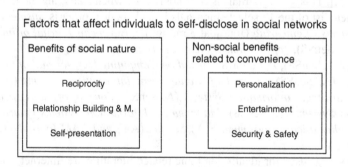

Fig. 1. Social and non-social benefits that affect individuals to self-disclose in social networks

3 Discussion

This chapter discusses our findings while giving answers to our research questions. Section 3.1 focuses on the social benefits that are considered to have an influence on user's self-disclosure in social networks. Non-social benefits related to convenience, which are often neglected in recently published models, are elaborated in Sect. 3.2 before mediating factors are shortly discussed (Sect. 3.3). Our revised model is presented in Sect. 3.4.

3.1 Social Benefits

The majority of the analyzed literature has identified reciprocity, relationship building and maintenance, and self-presentation to be the major benefits that individuals can reap from online self-disclosure (cf. Fig. 1). These dimensions are interrelated and overlapping. However, they are the answer to RQ1. Compared to the non-social benefits related to convenience, the social benefits are presented rather briefly, which is caused by the general agreement upon these aspects. However, their discussion is required due to the aim of developing a comprehensive model.

Reciprocity. Often also referred to as reciprocation, reciprocity can be seen as quid pro quo communication, a fair exchange of information between two individuals, synonymous with a "you tell me and I'll tell you" orientation [3]. Reciprocity is a signal between the communicating parties that they are willing to agree to a certain degree of vulnerability through the disclosure of personal information to advance their relationship [26]. This signal of mutual acknowledgement and appreciation of the relationship is perceived as a very positive message by the interacting parties. It fosters intimacy and social connection or bonding. Reciprocity lays the basis for any interpersonal relationship and is the primary benefit of self-disclosure [28]. The phenomenon of reciprocity can be seen as a driver for the intensification of relationships [3]. It leads to a greater willingness to provide further personal information, therefore increasing a person's vulnerability. However, individuals perceive an effect of increasing intimacy through the advancement of the relationship which is highly rewarding and "maximizes the benefit of the interactions" [26, p. 170].

Relationship Building and Maintenance. In social networks, it is possible to foster existing relationships and to gain new social contacts, which leads to the positive feeling of social connection and bonding [11]. A newly gained network of contacts and relations can then be easily maintained through the social network services [3]. One can interact conveniently and efficiently with a large number of friends. In [29] this argument is supported based on a Delphi study classifying user's overall active behavior on social networks. In this context, it is essential to point out that only a small fraction of about 10 % of users is seen as continuously active in social networks. Relationship building and relationship maintenance was defined part of the active behavior of over 85 % of all users in the Delphi study.

Self-presentation. Studies in the field of social networks confirm that benefits from self-presentation positively influence individuals to use social networks [3]. Driven by the desire for self-presentation, social network users disclose private information. Due to the asynchronous and selective forms of communication in social networks, users have the possibility to form an image of themselves that they wish to convey to others. Thus, self-presenting users only disclose information that seems desirable to them. This phenomenon is also called self-enhancement [27]. As described in [30], users engage in impression management when designing their social network profiles. By doing so, they seek to influence the impressions others hold about them. Such action helps the individual to feel comfort. Another kind of self-presentation in social networks can be the use of the service as online Curriculum Vitae [10].

3.2 Non-social Benefits Related to Convenience

Scholars of the literature pool directly and indirectly point out further positive factors that users can profit from when registering to a social network. The defined benefits all link to the "one click away" approach that refers to an increased ease of access to a certain goal [3]. In e-commerce, convenience is described as the perceived economization of time and effort for an individual in acquiring a certain benefit [31]. Assuming that individuals try to maximize their subjective utility while minimizing their costs, users will choose the more convenient, thus easier and/or faster way to achieve an equally desirable goal. Convenience has a significant impact on an individual's behavior and decision making [32]. In [3] the concept of convenience is applied to social networks. The authors show that social networks provide relatively high convenience when building social relationships. Our findings show that social networks offer a great variety of convenience for the user in other fields, as well. Convenience can be seen as a core category of factors that is connected with a number of central categories [33]. It is essential to point out that due to the broad definition of convenience, the central categories we have identified are overlapping to a certain degree and are thus not perfectly distinct. Formulating an answer on RQ2, we have identified convenience through personalization, convenience in entertainment, and convenience in security and safety as the central categories. It must be noted that convenience through personalization is the most prominent non-social category in the literature we analyzed.

Convenience Through Personalization. Providers of social networks collect and analyze all personal data that is disclosed by its members on the platforms [7]. Due to the rising popularity of social networks, users release an unprecedented, massive and increasing stream of data that requires processing. The overwhelming amount of data accumulated through a great number of new data-generating sources, including social networks, has led to a new phenomenon in the fields of business intelligence and analytics [9]. This phenomenon is widely known as big data or big data analytics. These terms stand for "data sets and analytical techniques in applications that are so large and complex that they require advanced and unique data storage, management, analysis and visualization technologies" [34, p. 1166]. The aim of data analytics is to identify and extract actionable insights from the available data [35]. Personalization is significantly enabled by big data. However, an increased ability of customization is only one of the many outcomes of big data analytics. Making use of such techniques, social network providers process the detailed disclosed personal data to reveal preferences, tastes and other specific information that can give insights on an individual's personality [36]. Based on the identified set of preferences, social network providers propose tailored content that fits the user's profile. Furthermore, the appearance of the individual's profile start page, as well as communication of the providers with the member is designed according to the user's personality. The adaption of a service or product to a person's preferences is called personalization [37]. Theory suggests that "users favor personalized communication and content that matches their taste" [38, p. 132]. In social networks, features and appearance can be personalized in real time through data automation [9]. In addition to the individualized content, data gathered by social network providers enables firms to target individual customers with tailored ads and products. In [39] personalized products are identified as an important economic benefit for the user, while in [38] a similar view emphasizing an increased customer satisfaction due to customization is presented. Customer relationship management becomes more efficient and effective through the personalized communication in social networks [40]. The user saves time and effort due to the customization of content and communication within social networks. The data gathered in social networks also enables tailored communication and product recommendations to the user outside of the online networks [38]. In addition, social network users have the opportunity to log into other websites using their social network credentials and can thus automatically create new accounts, provide address information and preferences. The content of those websites is then often customized for the user as well [37]. This uncomplicated data transfer and ease of access to other websites results in considerable economization of time and friction costs for the social network user, even outside the networks. According to [41], these benefits can animate consumers to disclose personal information. In [37] it is shown that personalization comes at the price of an increased privacy trade-off. This is due to the augmented analysis and trade of personal data utilized to customize content for users both in and outside social networks.

Convenience in Entertainment. Studies revealed social networks as "purely hedonic platforms" where enjoyment is a stronger predictor of use and participation than perceived usefulness [42, p. 1221]. In 2009, according to Facebook, "more than 70 % of all users engaged with platform applications every month" [3, p. 116]. All of these platform applications are accessible through a single social network site. Therefore, the user economizes considerable time and effort in accessing the desired applications and most notably in changing between them, if necessary. In addition, these applications are well integrated into the platforms and the interaction and trading of virtual goods with other users is facilitated. In [3, 27] the positive influence of enjoyment in social applications within social networks on users' self-disclosure is outlined. The authors focus solely on applications that enable the user to reveal their preferences regarding hobbies and tastes. Nevertheless, it is important to consider the availability of other enjoyment-related resources such as short videos, music, newspaper articles and further entertaining content that does not provide social benefits to the user, as well. 90 % of social network members are qualified as lurkers, thus passive users, according to [29, p. 215]. These users predominantly engage in the consumption of information and entertainment. This form of entertainment and the convenient access to a great number of diverse applications and content constitutes an important additional benefit to social network users.

Convenience in Security and Safety. To date, this potential benefit hasn't found much attention in the journals' publications. Nevertheless, in order to provide an adequate and comprehensive analysis of all selected articles, the identified additional benefit to a social network user is also presented here. Detailed private information can contribute to safety and security. Similar to personalization, security and safety are strengthened by big data analytics. An individual's disclosure of personal information in social networks may contribute to public safety and security, and ultimately even to the wellbeing of the user himself. In many countries, social network users often provide their personal information automatically to intelligence, public safety, and security agencies when disclosing them in the networks [34]. Without further efforts, social network users thus conduce to the fight against terrorism and crime that may ultimately affect them personally. According to [9, p. 7], "the precise capture of individual online behavior and surrounding events" has amongst others a considerable impact on public safety. Given the convenient way in achieving this benefit, an additional value to the social network user related to convenience can be perceived.

3.3 Mediators: Trust and Social Pressure

Besides the previously discussed constructs that represent the core findings of many articles, the literature pool also suggests that trust and social pressure are potential mediators affecting the dynamics of an individual's behavior and perception of privacy risk in social networks [7]. Trust in the context of this article can be defined as a person's belief that the other party of interaction possesses "characteristics that inhibit it from engaging in opportunistic behavior" [3, p. 116]. From a Social Exchange Theory perspective, a certain amount of trust is a prerequisite for individuals to experience reciprocation and to build relationships. It mitigates the subjective risk perceptions of disclosing personal information to the other party and thus enables social exchange in general [28]. Individuals, who perceive their relational counterpart as to be trustworthy, tend to disclose more personal of themselves to the other party. This holds true in online communities as well [7]. Likewise social pressure or peer pressure can impact individual self-disclosure in online communities [3]. In order to be part of a group and thus to reap the resulting social benefits may encourage individuals to contribute and disclose personal information in social networks [26].

3.4 Towards an Enhanced Model of User's Self-disclosure in Social Networks

Based on the structure of the conceptual models of [3, 28], and further insights gained through the literature review, the following conceptual model is developed (Fig. 2). It illustrates factors that potentially influence an individual to disclose personal information in social networks. Social benefits hypothetically constitute a major factor influencing users to self-disclose in the online communities. Simultaneously, additional non-social benefits related to convenience are expected to have a considerable impact on the user's motivation to self-disclose. It is noteworthy that in contrast to existing concepts, the presented model examines benefits of self-disclosure in social networks from both the social perspective and the non-social convenience-related perspective. As opposed to the models that provide the structural basis, privacy concerns is chosen as a construct instead of perceived privacy risk. In [3, 28] perceived privacy risk is utilized as a privacy proxy built on complementary constructs such as trust in social network providers and members. Privacy concerns is a more recent concept and finds high acceptance in the IS community. Moreover, it is an adequate tool for measuring an individual's worries and beliefs regarding privacy [11]. Thus, in this context, privacy concerns are a more suitable privacy proxy to apply in this research model. Trust and social pressure are mediators influencing the relationships between privacy concerns and self-disclosure and social benefits and self-disclosure, respectively.

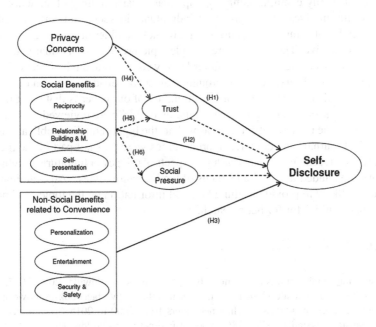

Fig. 2. Research model of user's self-disclosure in social networks, based on the literature review and structured according to [3, Fig. 1; 28, Fig. 1]

Based on our model, the following hypotheses can be derived:

- *H1: Privacy concerns have a negative impact on self-disclosure in social networks*
- *H2: Social benefits have a positive impact on self-disclosure in social networks*
- *H3: Non-social benefits related to convenience have a positive impact on self-disclo-sure in social networks*
- *H4: Trust acts as a mediator for the relationship between privacy concerns and self-disclosure*

- *H5: Trust acts as a mediator for the relationship between social benefits and self-disclosure*
- *H6: Social pressure acts as a mediator for the relationship between social benefits and self-disclosure*

4   Conclusion

Given the high relevance of research about user's self-disclosure in social networks, this paper contributes by highlighting non-social benefits that are related to convenience as an additional motivational factor for users. Combined with already established social benefits and the concept of privacy concerns, a revised research model was developed. This model enables us to derive six hypotheses, paving the way for future research opportunities. Until now, the theoretical model lacks empirical analysis. Similar empirical studies primarily examine sample groups that consist entirely of students. Future research on the motives and behavior of individuals in social networks based on a broader diversity of sample populations, e.g., to include older or working individuals, is a relevant objective. Thereby, a more complete picture of an individual's motives in social network use can be obtained. Studies largely concentrate on the Facebook online community in their observation. A thorough analysis of self-disclosure in other social networks would therefore be desirable. A limitation of our paper is that apart from the *Science* magazine, only leading journals in the field of IS were reviewed as we assume those to include the major contributions as well as the highest quality publications [21]. Lower-ranked journals and conference proceedings were thus not part of the literature pool. Moreover, research areas such as legal aspects of privacy or literature on behavioral science were excluded due to the IS focus of the literature review. An examination of these areas is likely to provide useful additional information on the topics and provide exciting opportunities for further research.

References

1. Statista: Facebook: number of monthly active users worldwide 2008–2015. http://www.statista.com/statistics/264810/number-of-monthly-active-facebook-users-worldwide/
2. Statista: Number of worldwide {Internet} users from 2000 to 2015 (in millions). http://www.statista.com/statistics/273018/number-of-internet-users-worldwide/
3. Krasnova, H., Spiekermann, S., Koroleva, K., Hildebrand, T.: Online social networks: why we disclose. J. Inf. Technol. **25**, 109–125 (2010)
4. Twitter Inc.: About Twitter. https://about.twitter.com/company
5. Statista: Global social networks by users 2015. http://www.statista.com/statistics/272014/global-social-networks-ranked-by-number-of-users/
6. Richter, D., Riemer, K., vom Brocke, J., Große Böckmann, S.: Internet social networking - distinguishing the phenomenon from its manifestations. In: Proceedings of 17th European Conference on Information Systems, Verona (2009)
7. Gerlach, J., Widjaja, T., Buxmann, P.: Handle with care: how online social network providers' privacy policies impact users' information sharing behavior. J. Strateg. Inf. Syst. **24**, 33–43 (2015)

8. Acquisti, A., Brandimarte, L., Loewenstein, G.: Privacy and human behavior in the age of information. Science **347**, 509–514 (2015)
9. Goes, P.B.: Big data and IS research. Science **38**, 3–8 (2014)
10. Tow, W.N.H., Venable, J.R., Dell, P.: Understanding information disclosure behaviour in Australian Facebook users. J. Inf. Technol. **25**, 1019–1028 (2010)
11. Jiang, Z.J., Heng, C.S., Choi, B.C.F.: Privacy concerns and privacy-protective behavior in synchronous online social interactions. Inf. Syst. Res. **24**, 579–595 (2013)
12. Thibaut, J., Kelley, H.: The Social Psychology of Groups. Wiley, New York (1959)
13. Ryschka, S.: Location-Based Services from a User' s Perspective Benefits and Risks (2015). http://opus.escpeurope.de/opus4/files/19/Dissertation_Stephanie_Ryschka_2015_online.pdf
14. Martensen, M., Börgmann, K., Bick, M.: The impact of social networking sites on the employer-employee relationship. In: Proceedings of 24th Bled eConference. eFuture: Creating Solutions for the Individual. Organisations and Society, Bled, 12–15 June 2011 (2011)
15. Rowe, F.: What a literature review is not - diversity, boundaries and recommendations. Eur. J. Inf. Syst. **3**, 240–250 (2014)
16. Boote, D.N., Beile, P.: Scholars before researchers: on the centrality of the dissertation literature review in research preparation. Educ. Res. **6**, 3–15 (2005)
17. Aral, S., Dellarocas, C., Godes, D.: Social media and business transformation: a framework for research. Inf. Syst. Res. **24**, 3–13 (2013)
18. VHB: Teilrating Wirtschaftsinformatik. http://vhbonline.org/service/jourqual/vhb-jourqual-3/teilrating-wi/
19. Harzing, A.-W.: Journal Quality List. http://www.harzing.com/resources/journal-quality-list
20. VHB: VHB Jourqual 3 Rating. http://vhbonline.org/en/service/jourqual/
21. Webster, J., Watson, R.T.: Analyzing the past to prepare for the future: writing a literature review. MIS Q. **26**, xiii–xxiii (2002)
22. AIS: Senior Scholars' Basket of Journals. https://aisnet.org/?SeniorScholarBasket
23. Sørensen, C., Landau, J.S.: Academic agility in digital innovation research. J. Strateg. Inf. Syst. **24**, 158–170 (2015)
24. Downe-Wamboldt, B.: Content analysis- method, applications, and issues. Health Care Women Int. **13**, 313–321 (1992)
25. Hsieh, H., Shannon, S.E.: Three approaches to qualitative content analysis. Qual. Health Res. **15**, 1277–1288 (2005)
26. Lowry, P.B., Cao, J., Everard, A.: Privacy concerns versus desire for interpersonal awareness in driving the use of self-disclosure technologies: the case of instant messaging in two cultures. J. Manag. Inf. Syst. **27**, 163–200 (2011)
27. Krasnova, H., Veltri, F.N., Günther, P.O.: Self-disclosure and privacy calculus on social networking sites: the role of culture. Bus. Inf. Syst. Eng. **4**, 127–135 (2012)
28. Posey, C., Lowry, P.B., Roberts, T.L., Ellis, T.S.: Proposing the online community self-disclosure model: the case of working professionals in France and the UK who use online communities. Eur. J. Inf. Syst. **19**, 181–195 (2010)
29. Chen, A., Lu, Y., Chau, P.Y.K., Gupta, S.: Classifying, measuring, and predicting users' overall active behavior on social networking sites. J. Manag. Inf. Syst. **31**, 213–253 (2014)
30. Richter, D., Riemer, P.D.K., vom Brocke, P.D.J.: Internet social networking research state of the art and implications for Enterprise 2.0. Bus. Inf. Syst. Eng. **53**, 1–89 (2011)
31. Izquierdo-Yusta, A., Schultz, R.J.: Understanding the effect of internet convenience on intention to purchase via the internet. J. Mark. Dev. Compet. **5**, 32 (2011)
32. Rao, H.K.: On risk, convenience, and internet shopping. Commun. ACM. **43**, 98–105 (2000)
33. Kacen, L., Rabinovich, M.: Qualitative coding methodology. Psychoanal. Psychol. **30**, 210–231 (2013)

34. Chen, H., Storey, V.C., Chiang, R.H.L.: Business intelligence and analytics: from big data to big impact. MIS Q. **36**, 1165–1188 (2012)
35. Dhar, P.V., Jarke, P.D.M., Laartz, D.J.: Big data. Bus. Inf. Syst. Eng. **6**, 257–259 (2014)
36. Zhao, X.I.A., Xue, L.: Competitive target advertising and consumer data sharing. J. Manag. Inf. Syst. **29**, 189–221 (2013)
37. Lee, D., Youngsok Bang, J.-H.A.: Managing consumer privacy concerns in personalization: a strategic analysis of privacy protection. MIS Q. **35**, 423–444 (2011)
38. Heimbach, I., Kostyra, D.S., Hinz, O.: Marketing automation. Bus. Inf. Syst. Eng. **57**, 129–133 (2015)
39. Pavlou, P.A.: State of the information privacy literature: where are we now and where should we go? MIS Q. **35**, 977–988 (2011)
40. Bruns, A., Neuberger, C., Stieglitz, S., Dang-Xuan, L.: Social media analytics: an interdisciplinary approach and its implications for information systems. Bus. Inf. Syst. Eng. **56**, 89–96 (2014)
41. Hui, K.-L., Tan, B.C.Y., Goh, C.-Y.: Online information disclosure: motivators and measurements. ACM Trans. Internet Technol. **6**, 415–441 (2006)
42. Rosen, P., Sherman, P.: Hedonic information systems: acceptance of social networking websites, Paper 162. In: Americas Conference on Information Systems, Acapulco, Mexico (2006)

Exploring How Individuals Manage Their Image When Interacting with Professional Contacts Online

Aparna Gonibeed[1](✉) and M.N. Ravishankar[2]

[1] Liverpool Hope University, Liverpool, UK
gonibea@hope.ac.uk
[2] Loughborough University, Loughborough, UK
m.n.ravishankar@lboro.ac.uk

Abstract. Social media is ubiquitous and most professionals feel compelled to use it for both personal and professional purposes. Although interacting with workplace colleagues and managers across online-offline and work-life offers several advantages, it also poses several image related challenges. This study aims to assess how individuals manage their image when interacting with professional contacts online. The article does this by studying individuals' experiences of interacting online and their responses to cope with emerging conflicts. For this purpose, 31 interviews were conducted among Indian IT professionals. The findings suggest that respondents exercised audience segregation and content segregation to convey a desired professional image. By focusing on the impact of interactions with professional contacts online, the study suggests that individuals enact a 'Restricted Self' online. In doing so, the article contributes to the literature on online impression management.

Keywords: Impression management · Social media · Cognitive demands

1 Introduction

Most employees now interact on social media. In these interactions, they must be cautious as image plays a vital role in gaining respect and liking from workplace colleagues. Hence, impression management is inevitable when interacting with professional contacts online. Within the wider literature on managing image online, it is seen that individuals tend to create a persona that closely relates to their offline selves. In other words, individuals try to maintain integrity between their online-offline selves and strive for accuracy with their offline and 'true' self [32]. However, given that individuals pursue diverse impression goals across work-life [8], they may experience some image related concerns. For instance, as employees increasingly socialize online, professional contacts may compare interactions across work-life and online-offline settings and express doubts on the validity of the information presented. Additionally, such comparisons may lead professional contacts to alter the image they have already constructed. Here, negative re-construction of an image by professional contacts may have adverse effects on respect and liking at the workplace. Consequently, the nature of interactions

Y.K. Dwivedi et al. (Eds.): I3E 2016, LNCS 9844, pp. 401–410, 2016.
DOI: 10.1007/978-3-319-45234-0_36

online is considerably changing as individuals use reflexivity and manage an image by using a variety of online boundary management strategies [17].

The dilemma outlined above influences the questions: How do individuals manage their image when they interact with professional contacts online? And given the risk of reputation loss, why do individuals interact with professional contacts online? To address this question, we conducted an in-depth qualitative study on Indian IT professionals and draw on extant scholarship on impression management to analyze the data.

The findings indicate that individuals exercise restraint in their interactions on social media. They do this by exercising two boundary management strategies: audience segregation and content segregation. Consequently, they enact a 'Restricted Self' or a restricted version of the self to protect their professional image. The article is organized as follows. First, we review the literatures on impression demands due to social media and appropriate coping strategies. Next, we describe research methods and discuss findings of the study. Finally, we examine the notion of 'Restricted Self' and discuss the implications of interacting with professional contacts online.

2   Background

People generate particular images of the self and thereby influence how others perceive and treat them. At the workplace, image plays a vital role and has important consequences for career progression and achievement of status and power [6, 10, 23]. Consequently, individuals spend considerable time at the workplace to convey a desired image that represents desirable qualities (e.g. intelligence, humor, initiative, trustworthiness) and elicit approval from key members [7, 8].

2.1   Challenges of Online Impression Management

In the modern workplace, individuals must rely on their interactions (for e.g. profile, status, photos) on social media to convey a desired professional image [9, 18]. Broadly speaking, impression strategies to convey an image via social media are characterized by the extent of accuracy of information that individuals share from their offline settings in their online interactions, also referred to as representativeness [30, 31]. By being representative in their interactions on social media, individuals wish to convey an image of the 'real', 'true' and 'authentic' self. However, when employees share 'real' and 'authentic' selves on social media and interact or socialize online, they face two impression related conflicts. One, online interactions may be viewed in the absence of any context thus opening up opportunities for misinterpretations by the audience [26, 28]. In such instances, it is important to note that while favourable stereotypes of professional competence and character can enhance one's image, unfavourable stereotypes detract from one's image. Additionally, individuals may find it challenging to correct unfavourable stereotypes arising from misinterpretations based on their self-presentations on social media [17]. Two, individuals tend to exercise 'region-behaviour'; different behaviours when with different kinds of audience [8]. As individuals pursue diverse image goals across work-life, they exhibit various aspects of their personality depending on the goal. However, such region-behaviour becomes meaningless as social media bridges work-life image and online-offline boundaries. Hence, employees risk loss of reputation, professional image and blurring of boundaries when employees view their colleagues exhibiting inappropriate behaviour on social media [17, 24]. Such instances have a direct and immediate negative impact on how individuals are perceived by colleagues at the workplace. Given these challenges to impression management online, the question of how do individuals manage their image online is a pertinent inquiry.

2.2 Coping Strategies

Existing literature suggests that employees cope with the above impression related challenges by choosing between strategies that apparently lay on a continuum. At one end of the continuum, scholars [14, 25] suggest that individuals exercise various online boundary management strategies and present a 'Restricted self' by exercising self-censorship and adjusting profile visibility. Some studies support this argument by suggesting individuals customize profiles to disclose different information to different individuals or create multiple profiles [13, 31, 32]. In this manner, scholars suggest that individuals seek control over their professional image by controlling the audience to their interactions and exercising caution in their status updates. Alternatively, on the other end of the continuum, few scholars [20, 33] argue that individuals are 'cyborgs' or 'hybrid selves' and integrate their online-offline self. In this notion of entanglement, individuals view their image as a set of characteristics that combine their physical and virtual identity into one image. In some ways, this hybrid self is similar to disembodied or dual selves, as the cyborgian self is fluid, malleable and occasionally, multiple. Although emerging literature pays attention to explanations that lay outside of the continuum [17, 24], we know little about how employees cope with impression demands online. This is important to understand because social media has a growing presence at the workplace. The remainder of this article describes the study that was conducted and the findings that emerged.

3 Research Method

In this study, we explored how a group of Indian IT professionals experience and respond to interacting with professional contacts on social media. To do this we adopted an interpretivist viewpoint which "does not predefine dependent and independent variables but focuses on the complexity of human sense-making as the situation emerges" [12]. From this viewpoint, the same physical institution, artefact or human action can have different meanings for different human subjects as well as the observing social scientist [15]. In this process, the researcher gets involved with the respondents in the process of negotiating meaning and research is inevitably influenced by the values of the researcher [2, 16].

3.1 Research Context

The Indian IT industry competes on a global level and provides employment opportunities in large numbers to graduates [5, 19]. In terms of IT-work, broadly three categories are identified: software solutions, products and services; the term 'IT professionals' refers to all those individuals employed by the IT-industry. The current IT professional workforce consists of software engineers and other non-engineering graduates who are educated, well paid, mobile and closely linked into the global services economy, whether working in India or abroad [29]. IT remains a viable career choice for many educated Indians today, for whom it offers competitive salaries compared to other sectors as well as an opportunity to live and work outside of India [29]. Within the wider literature, the IT workplace is associated with power imbalances and IT professionals are viewed within a post-colonial context aspiring a bourgeois lifestyle [1, 3, 4, 20].

3.2 Sample

This study is based on data collected from qualitative interviews with 31 Indian IT professionals who had a graduate degree or above. The sampling approach adopted in this study was non-probability using purposive and snowball sampling techniques. Non-probability sampling refers to sampling without random selection methods [11]. Purposive sampling is when a researcher targets a specific subset of people who meet the exact criteria of respondents or target group. In this case, the research targeted a sub-group: Indian IT professionals. Next, snowball sampling techniques were used; that is, respondents recommended their friends to the researcher and assisted the researcher in marketing the study on popular social networking sites like Facebook and Twitter. Further, ad-hoc quota system was followed to eliminate gender bias in the sample. Within this category, we sought to include in the study IT professionals from multi-national companies (MNC) and Indian IT companies (focused on software IT companies) so that the results can be generalized to the occupational group of respondents.

In addition to interviews, field notes were produced in the process. Table 1 summarizes the interviews with respondents across various forms of IT companies by grouping them into four basic categories: Manager (greater than ten years experience), Program Analyst (between 7 to 10 years experience), Associate-Projects (between 3 to 7 years experience) and Human Resource Manager (5 years experience).

Table 1. Interviews and role of respondents

Group	Role of respondents	No. of interviews
1	Managers	12
2	Program analyst	9
3	Associate – projects	8
4	Human resource managers	2

During interviews that lasted an hour on average, in response to questions like: "Would you say you are concerned about how a recruiter in the future may look at all your interactions on twitter before hiring you?" and "Have you experienced any conflicts at work by adding or not adding contacts from the office?" respondents spoke at length about their experiences of interacting on social media with colleagues, clients and other professional colleagues. They also reflected on potential consequences for their careers, respect and liking by workplace colleagues and such impact on their image at the workplace. Further, respondents spoke about anxieties, fears and cognitive demands when interacting online. Of noteworthy mention is that managerial interference was noted as a predominant issue among respondents which exacerbated their anxiety when interacting with professional contacts on Facebook.

3.3   Data Analysis

The interviews were transcribed; the length of the transcript accurately reflects the respondents' experience in identifying suitable coping strategies. Data analysis was an on-going and iterative process through the data collection period. Through such a process, we achieved theoretical saturation; that is, no additional themes emerged with additional data [2]. In the first step of data analysis, we used principles of grounded theory [27] to analyze the data. In this phase, we used sentence analysis to look for the major idea in each sentence, open coding to group the concepts into categories and axial coding [27], whereby we searched for the relationships between the sub-categories at a

Table 2.   Theme illustrations

First-order categories	Exemplary quotes
Theme I (second-order): Audience segregation	You don't want that if you put a status message, it should be shown to everyone. People perceive things in a different way, right. They see your pictures, and they may not always know the context right. A lot of the cultural associations would be lost. A lot of the cultural contexts would be lost. So the entire information is not being conveyed, all they can see is maybe a photograph (AN, 30)
	I'm very close to the team that I work with and it's easy for the lines to blur. But at the end of the day my boss is my boss and my colleague is still somebody that I have to go to work with and I maybe I'm just cautious. I haven't had a bad experience or anything, but I prefer to make sure the lines don't gel (AR, 25)
Theme II: Content segregation	The process of writing a blog is a search for your identity. I have a private blog that I keep. Even if someone finds out everything about it, I'm not afraid that it's there. It's just that I chose to not make it public. The process of blogging will reveal things to you that you did not know and it will help for yourself and others (SA, 39)
	One thing I realized is that Twitter for instance is a tool for others to understand about you as a personality. I'm very conscious about that. So I use Twitter as a way to express my opinion in a way that reflects my personality or reflect my knowledge about something or reflect my opinion, through which people understand who I am (RA, 36)

conceptual level and categorized them into higher-order themes (represented in Table 2). This process facilitated quick reference to similar concepts and their representative examples that could be collapsed into fewer categories and themes. Finally, we looked for relationships across the themes through an iteration process between emerging data and existing literature to determine possible explanations. Such an eclectic approach to the data helped to clarify the dynamics associated with impression management theory and how individuals respond to the conflicts that arose.

4 Findings

The data and analyses demonstrate that individuals take caution while building profiles and accepting friendship requests online due to concerns related to impression management. Broadly, respondents managed impressions online by audience segregation and content segregation. We discuss these findings in this section.

4.1 Audience Segregation

Consistent with previous findings, the respondents in this sample exercised various online boundary management strategies to segregate their online audience [14, 25, 32]. In analyzing the data, we focused on why respondents attached significance to audience segregation. At first sight, it appeared that respondents segregated among professional contacts in order to avoid socially awkward situations at the workplace, however, a deeper analysis suggests that respondents sought symbolic rewards in the form of liking and respect. Additionally, respondents also used these interactions to convey a desired image. For instance, SA explains that he uses his interactions on social media to convey an image of a multidimensional self:

> A bunch of folks think of me as the uber engineer, while others think I am a Marketer and one doesn't necessarily link me to the other. On Facebook page or LinkedIn network, they get to know who I am, so that's a way of getting a feel for the bigger person and a composite personality (SA, 39).

Another respondent explains that adding a professional contact to her network increases her likeability and makes it easy to approach the professional contact for any work-related favors in the future:

> You add people because it is an additional glimpse of you that they can see apart from what you already told them and as long as they are in your network it is an easier way to reach out to them if you need something (AI, Female, 32).

In addition to various online boundary management strategies, respondents were cautious of the audience at the workplace as well. In other words, respondents were keen to ensure that they were not 'caught' interacting online at the workplace as this had immediate negative implications on their professional image. For instance, NA explains how interacting at the workplace had implications on his professional image and performance rating:

I have lot of friends in the company so I used to chat and although I did my work, my manager never liked it. He would see communicator windows popping and me chatting at the workplace. He raised it many times and did not like me for that. There were (performance) rating issues and I had to bear it. It is an image which I had made up. (NA, Male, 30).

Overall, these experiences make them cautious when interacting online especially with professional contacts. In response, respondents appear to use a variety of online boundary management strategies which appear to alleviate impression demands.

4.2 Content Segregation

Misinterpretations by professional contacts signals failed impression management efforts and exacerbates impression demands. Almost all respondents feared consequences like loss of respect and liking by professional contacts. However, some (40 % of the sample) felt particularly threatened by it. This was because some respondents experienced some form of negative experiences that shaped their responses. For instance, online messages on public forums by managers like *"Don't you have some work to do?"* were specific incidents that triggered changes in how respondents interacted online. One respondent explains an incident that impacted him considerably was when he was told he may be fired as he openly commented on a company policy online:

I voiced my opinion against one of the policies that affected my training batchmate and myself. So we were called directly and asked, "You don't want to lose your job, do you?" I was only 6 months into the job and I really got scared at that time. So after that, I changed the way I wrote my mails you know and started talking to the right people and not talking to everybody in the world (GA, Male, 31).

In this sense, although the strategy altered slightly, the general response was still the same. Some respondents took particular steps like avoiding oversharing personal information online and reinforcing work-life boundaries. For example, many respondents said *"I might enjoy that privately but exercise caution online"* and *"It is about maintaining your image, you are giving them an opportunity to find out something about you"*; thus, expressing awareness of consciously using social media to build an image for professional contacts.

Although a handful of respondents claim that they exercise full disclosure by synchronizing their interactions across all social media sites, they did not share any personal information online. For instance, one respondent said, *"Although I share information openly across public networking sites, I do not discuss family or other things."* Similarly, another respondent said that his accounts are linked and he accepts all professional contacts on any social network, however, he does not share personal information publicly:

All my bosses are on my social network. My Twitter feed, LinkedIn and Facebook pages are connected. But, I also have a private blog where I write everything and I chose to not make it public. Even my wife cannot see the blog. (SA, Male, 39).

The respondents perceive that social media inevitably blurs work-life image and the further notion that interactions on the internet are permanent forced them to exercise caution.

In the process, respondents attach significance to their interactions online and invest considerable time and effort in impression management related activities. Respondents who exercised strategic disclosure responded to negative experiences by establishing various forms of self-censorship to alleviate impression demands.

5 Discussion

Motivated by recent research on online impression management [27, 24], this study set out to explore how individuals manage their image when interacting with professional contacts online. The empirical data presented above provides us with a deeper and alternative understanding of how individuals manage image online. It also vividly documents the rewards and conflicts that impact how individuals respond to impression related conflicts. This study supports literature that suggests that individuals are representative in their interactions online and extends a broader theoretical understanding of individuals' interactions online.

5.1 Restricted Self

In response to impression demands arising from impression management online, respondents chose to exercise control over their professional image by continually evaluating their boundary management strategies and exercising reflexivity. The data offers insights as to why respondents exercised control on professional image. One, respondents perceive the workplace audience to be in a powerful position. Since the workplace audience constitutes the 'key audience' in regard to professional image [6, 10, 21], respondents sought control over how they were perceived by restricting their interactions on social media. Additionally, power imbalances are popularly associated with the research setting of Indian IT professionals [4, 21, 22]. As evident in the data, the respondents are aware of such power imbalances and use social media to reinforce the same. Second, respondents pursue diverse impression goals in their work-life, consequently, as a boundary management strategy, respondents restrict their interactions online. This is evident in the data when respondents accept professional contacts to increase likability and respect yet use online boundary management strategies to control what their professional contacts can see online. Finally, when interacting with professional contacts online, respondents realize how visible they are in the offline setting. Previous research [17, 25] suggests that individuals seldom perceive the social consequences of their interactions on the internet. This is evident in the data when some respondents critically evaluate their interactions online to prevent any negative stereotypes that may arise in the future.

It is important to note that individuals enact a 'Restricted Self' because they fear consequences like loss of respect and liking by professional contacts. Further, the asynchronous and asymmetric movement across online-offline settings made them particularly aware of their diverse work-life image and helped them decide how to manage their professional image.

6   Conclusion

In any workplace, impression management serves many purposes and individuals experience cognitive demands while managing a professional image. In addition to the vivid differences in work-life impression goals, the respondents in this study experienced heightened impression demands when interacting with professional contacts online due to complex power asymmetries and fear of negative social consequences and stereotypes arising from interacting with professional contacts on social media. They coped with these demands by choosing between strategies to control the audience to their interactions (audience segregation) and controlling the content of their interactions (content segregation) online. Consequently, it appears that the respondents are in part representative or 'real' and practicing 'region-behavior' for the workplace audience by enacting a 'Restricted Self'. Of particular significance in this study is that despite the cognitive demands which inevitably lead to scrutinizing strategies that take up a significant portion of their time, the respondents find a way to interact online.

Overall, this study adds to the growing literatures on interacting with professional contacts online. It provides an alternative explanation on how employees resolve conflicts arising from interacting with professional contacts online. The findings have implications for similar occupational groups across geographies.

References

1. Brosius, C.: India's middle class: new forms of urban leisure, consumption and prosperity. Routledge, New Delhi (2010)
2. Corbin, J., Strauss, A.: Grounded theory research: procedures, canons, and evaluative criteria. Qual. Sociol. **13**(1), 3–21 (1990)
3. D'Mello, M., Eriksen, T.: Software, sports day and sheera: culture and identity processes within a global software organization in India. Inf. Organ. **20**(2), 81–110 (2010)
4. Fernandes, L.: Nationalizing 'the global': media images, cultural politics and the middle class in India. Media Cult. Soc. **22**(5), 611–628 (2000)
5. Friedman, T.: The World is Flat. Penguin Books, London (2005)
6. Gardner, W., Martinko, M.: Impression management in organizations. J. Manag. **14**(2), 321–339 (1988)
7. Giacalone, R., Rosenfeld, P.: Self-presentation and self-promotion in an organizational setting. J. Soc. Psychol. **126**(3), 321–326 (1986)
8. Goffman, E.: The Presentation of Self in Everyday Life. Anchor Books, New York (1959)
9. Hathi, S.: How social networking increases collaboration at IBM. Strateg. Commun. Manag. **14**(1), 32–35 (2009)
10. Ibarra, H.: Provisional selves: experimenting with image and identity in professional adaptation. Adm. Sci. Q. **44**(4), 764 (1999)
11. King, N.: Template analysis. In: Cassell, G., Symon, C.M. (eds.) Essential Guide to Qualitative Methods in Organizational Research. Sage Publications Ltd., London (2004)
12. Klein, H., Myers, M.: A set of principles for conducting and evaluating interpretive field studies in information systems. MIS Q. **23**(1), 67–93 (1999)
13. Lampinen, A., Tamminen, S., Oulasvirta, A.: All my people right here, right now: management of group co-presence on a social networking site. In: Proceedings of the ACM 2009 International Conference on Supporting Group Work, pp. 281–290. ACM, May 2009

14. Leary, M., Allen, A.: Self-presentational persona: simultaneous management of multiple impressions. J. Pers. Soc. Psychol. **101**(5), 1033–1049 (2011)
15. Lee, A.S.: Integrating positivist and interpretive approaches to organizational research. Organ. Sci. **2**(4), 342–365 (1991)
16. Lincoln, Y.S., Guba, E.G.: Naturalistic Inquiry. Sage Publications, Beverly Hills (1985)
17. Malaterre, A., Rothbard, M.P., Berg, J.M.: When worlds collide in cyberspace: how boundary work in online social networks impacts professional relationships. Acad. Manag. Rev. **38**(4), 645–669 (2013)
18. Majchrzak, A., Cherbakov, L., Ives, B.: Harnessing the power of the crowds with corporate social networking tools: how IBM does it. Manag. Inf. Syst. Q. Executive **8**(2), 151–156 (2009)
19. Nilekani, N.: Imagining India: The Idea of a Renewed Nation. Penguin Books, New York (2009)
20. Orlikowski, W.J.: Sociomaterial practices: exploring technology at work. Organ. Stud. **28**(9), 1435–1448 (2007)
21. Raghuram, S.: Identities on call: impact of impression management on Indian call center agents. Hum. Relat. **66**(11), 1471–1496 (2013)
22. Ravishankar, M.N., Pan, S.L., Myers, M.D.: Information technology offshoring in India: a postcolonial perspective. Eur. J. Inf. Syst. **22**(4), 1–16 (2012). May 2011
23. Roberts, L.M., Dutton, J.E., Spreitzer, G.M., Heaphy, E.D., Quinn, R.E.: Composing the reflected best-self portrait: building pathways for becoming extraordinary in work organizations. Acad. Manag. Rev. **30**(4), 712 (2005)
24. Sayah, S.: Managing work-life boundaries with information and communication technologies. New Technol. Work Employ. **28**(3), 179–196 (2013)
25. Schoneboom, A.: Workblogging in a Facebook age. Work Employ. Soc. **25**(1), 132–140 (2011)
26. Skeels, M., Grudin, J.: When social networks cross boundaries: a case study of workplace use of Facebook and LinkedIn. In: Proceedings of the ACM (2009)
27. Strauss, A., Corbin, J.: Basics of Qualitative Research, vol. 15. Sage, Newbury Park (1990)
28. Tufekci, Z.: Grooming, gossip, Facebook and Myspace. Inf. Commun. Soc. **11**(4), 544–564 (2008)
29. Upadhya, C.: Management of culture and managing through culture in the indian software outsourcing industry. In: Upadhya, C., Vasavi, A.R. (eds.) In an Outpost of the Global Economy: Work and Workers in India's Information Technology Industry, pp. 101–135. Routledge, New Delhi (2008)
30. Utz, S.: Show me your friends and I will tell you what type of person you are: how one's profile, number of friends, and type of friends influence impression formation on social network sites. J. Comput.-Mediated Commun. **15**(2), 314–335 (2010)
31. Vaast, E.: Playing with masks: fragmentation and continuity in the presentation of self in an occupational online forum. Inf. Technol. People **20**(4), 334–351 (2007)
32. Vasalou, A., Joinson, A., Banziger, T., Goldie, P., Pitt, J.: Avatars in social media: balancing accuracy, playfulness and embodied messages. Int. J. Hum. Comput. Stud. **66**(11), 801–811 (2008)
33. Veerapen, M.: Encountering oneself and other: a case study of identity formation in second life. In: Peachey, A., Childs, M. (eds.) Reinventing Ourselves: Contemporary Concepts of Identity in Virtual Worlds, pp. 81–100. Springer, London (2011)

Norm of Reciprocity – Antecedent of Trustworthiness in Social Media

Shweta Aggarwal[1(✉)], Sumita Rai[1], M.P. Jaiswal[1], and Henrik Sorensen[2]

[1] Management Development Institute, Gurgaon, India
aggarwal.shweta@gmail.com, {sumitar,mpjaiswal}@mdi.ac.in
[2] Aarhus University, Aarhus, Denmark
here@bcom.au.dk

Abstract. Social media is an important platform to seek advice from its members. It is important to consider members of social media as trustworthy before one may seek advice. Reciprocity is a defining feature of social media. Trust propensity of a trustor is considered an important antecedent of trustworthiness and is cited more than 10,000 times. However, it is not clear how norm of reciprocity affects trustworthiness. This study asserts that Norm of reciprocity may be a more important antecedent of trustworthiness than trust propensity Partial least squares-structured equation modelling was used to model constructs. This study extends the Mayer's model of trustworthiness. It has important implications for computer scientists and organization consultants working in area of trust in social media.

Keywords: Determinants · Norm of reciprocity · Social media · Trustworthiness · Trust propensity

1 Introduction

"If people can be seen as nodes, and the connections are their relationships, trust improves its 'bandwidth" [1, p. 12].

Social media is an important platform to seek advice from its members, it is important to consider members of social media as trustworthy before one may seek advice. Reciprocity is a defining feature of social media. Trust propensity of a trustor is considered an important antecedent of trustworthiness and is cited more than 10,000 times. However, it is not clear how norm of reciprocity affects trustworthiness. This study asserts that Norm of reciprocity may be a more important antecedent of trustworthiness than trust propensity Partial least squares-structured equation modeling was used to model constructs. This study extends Mayer's model of trustworthiness. It has important implications for computer scientists and organization consultants working in the area of trust in social media.

Y.K. Dwivedi et al. (Eds.): I3E 2016, LNCS 9844, pp. 411–418, 2016.
DOI: 10.1007/978-3-319-45234-0_37

1.1 Trustworthiness

Perceived trustworthiness of others is a precursor of trust [2, 3]. Therefore, it is important to find out factors which may affect trustworthiness. In this article, Trustor means a source of trust and trustee refers to the target of trust. The source of trust is an individual and target of trust is other members of social media. Context is trust in other members of social media to seek advice.

1.2 Context-Social Media

The sporadic use of social media has changed the way we seek information and professional advice. It is important to have a generalized trust in social media while seeking advice. Reciprocity is central to social media [4]. Therefore, it is essential to know how reciprocity affects trustworthiness in social media.

1.3 Norm of Reciprocity

The norm of reciprocity refers to the choice between being stingy or generous when returning help. The norm of reciprocity may be categorized as positive or negative [5]. This paper refers to the positive norm of reciprocity i.e. being generous while returning help.

The norm of reciprocity may be divided into direct reciprocity and indirect reciprocity. The first has to do with the exchange of information, goods, or services of the same value and the second has to do with paying forward [5]. This paper refers to the indirect reciprocity of the trustor. This norm is crucial because it goes beyond the inner circle of family and friends and extends to the outer circle. This outer circle includes people who are just our acquaintances, colleagues, and strangers [6]. Most of the members in a social network like LinkedIn, research gate are members of the outer circle. Members participate in a social network through indirect reciprocity.

2 Literature Review

For trust to be established there should be a source of trust and a target of trust. The source of trust is called trustor and target of trust are called trustee [7]. In this study, trustor is individual and trustee other members of social media.

2.1 Antecedent Related to Trustee- Trustworthiness

There are different antecedents of trust. These antecedents include trustee's reciprocity [8], social ties [9], and reputation [10]. Trustworthiness is one of the main antecedents of trust in the trustee. Perceived dimensions of trustworthiness of trustee include ability, benevolence, integrity [11, 12]. Trustworthiness means *"the trustor is confident that the trustee has attributes that are beneficial to the trustor"* [12, p. 4].

2.2   Antecedent Related to Trustor-Trust Propensity a Norm of Reciprocity

Researchers have studied different antecedents which affect trustworthiness. Characteristics of a trustor which affects another's trustworthiness includes propensity to trust [11, 12], personality [13–17], gender [18], and attitude [19]. Though generalized trust or trust propensity has been widely studied, there is a dearth of research focusing on the relationship between the norm of reciprocity and trustworthiness.

2.2.1   Norm of Reciprocity

The norm of reciprocity is the basis for exchange. Reciprocity is the main basis for social networks and cooperation [4]. In an ethnographic study of a music file sharing system, it was found that reciprocity was a vital factor for the viability of community [20]. Trust and reciprocity depend on culture, and they are essential for the generation of social networks [21]. Individuals achieve better results by building conditions where the norm of reciprocity and trust propensity can help to overcome strong temptations of short-term self-interest [22]. Although trustee's reciprocity is researched widely [13–17]. There are almost no studies on how a trustor's reciprocity affects perceived trustworthiness. Though there are economic investment studies on the relationship between the norm of reciprocity and trust, there is almost no psychometric-based research on the norm of reciprocity as an antecedent of trust. There are research studies on the effect of trust propensity on trustworthiness. However, there is a need to research on the norm of reciprocity effect trustworthiness in social media as reciprocity is a central mechanism for social media [4].

2.2.2   Trust Propensity

Trust propensity/generalized trust is a *"tendency to be willing to depend on general others across a broad spectrum of situations and persons"* [12, p. 3]. It is one of the most cited antecedents and is cited more than 10,000 times in different context [2].

3   Research Model

Mayer's model is the basis of this paper. Mayer's model is selected because it is a parsimonious model with a manageable number of factors. Parsimony provides a sound foundation for empirical research. Mayer's model has clear definitions for trust, has clarity in antecedents and has a distinction between source and target of trust [2]. According to Mayer's model, trust propensity is an important antecedent of trustworthiness and is rooted in Ericson's development theory.

3.1   Erikson's Development Theory

Trust develops during childhood as infant seeks or receives help from his or her caregiver. People develop trust propensity as they grow up. It is a generalized reaction to life's experiences with other people. Trust propensity does not mean that one believes others are trustworthy. It is a tendency to depend on others. It is an invisible colored glass that alters our interpretation of situations [23, 24].

3.2　Research Model

See Fig. 1.

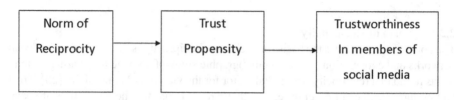

Fig. 1. Proposed research model

3.2.1　Norm of Reciprocity and Trust Propensity

Social exchange is the foundation of interaction among humans. Norms or rules have a central place in interactions. These rules guide the nature of relations and ties among actors, and these ties shape the exchange of resources and benefits [25]. Personal ties are based on trust, reciprocation, and reward. Therefore, the norm of reciprocity and trust propensity affects the exchange [25].

Colquitt emphasized that high trustors show a tendency to act in a cooperative way across most contexts and situations. Those with a high trust propensity, or high trustors, would be good at building exchange relationships because they have greater tendency to stick to the norm of reciprocity, which leads to long-term commitment and protection of the relationship. These, in turn, result in the development of social networks which would provide information to aid a trustor's decision making and thus result in action [24, 26, 27].

The greater the positive norm of reciprocity, the more positive is the local social exchange relationship will be. Therefore, the positive norm of reciprocity would lead to increased propensity to place trust in strangers [28].

Hypothesis H1: Norm of reciprocity would affect trust propensity.

3.2.2　Trust Propensity and Trustworthiness

Trust propensity of the trustor has been researched widely and is considered an important antecedent of trustworthiness [29]. Trust Propensity would lead to trustworthiness in the members of social media [1, 26, 30–33].

Hypothesis H2: Trust propensity would affect trustworthiness in members of social media.

4   Methodology

A systematic positivist approach to research using quantitative methodology involves formulating a hypothesis, collecting data, and ensuring the validity and reliability of the instrument selected for research. Trustworthiness is formative construct whereas trust propensity and norm of reciprocity are reflective construct. Data was analyzed using PLS-SEM due to the presence of the formative construct in the model. PLS-SEM is a causal modeling approach. It aims at maximizing the explained variance of the endogenous constructs [34].

4.1   Measures

A standardized version of questionnaires for trust propensity [3] and norm of reciprocity [5] was selected. A survey for constructing "trustworthiness" [3] was modified to measure trustworthiness in members of social media. There were 23 items in the questionnaire. All responses were asked on Likert scale. An expert panel reviewed items to assess the content validity of key constructs.

4.2   Data Collection

Survey was filled by professionals and students in India. The sample was restricted to a region as it is necessary to control for cultural factors as trust propensity and norm of reciprocity depend on culture. These respondents were avid users of LinkedIn and Facebook and frequently access these networks for seeking advice. Data was collected through offline and online channels. Subjects consisted of Males (37 %) and females (63 %). Out of 200 responses, 162 responses were valid.

5   Results

This section explains parameters for the construct validity of constructs and results of the structural model. For construct validity, measures for internal consistency, convergent, and divergent validity were noted. For Internal consistency of construct, Cronbach alpha should be above 0.7, and Composite reliability of constructs should be above 0.8. All the values were above the threshold value of 0.7 for Cronbach alpha and above 0.8 for composite reliability. Criteria for internal consistency and reliability were satisfied (Table 1).

Table 1. Construct validity-Cronbach alpha and composite reliability

	Composite reliability	Cronbach alpha	AVE
Trust propensity	0.779	0.694	0.44
Norm of reciprocity	0.75	0.701	0.49
Trustworthiness	0.861	0.822	0.4522

Bootstrapping was done with 5,000 subsamples. Trustworthiness is a second order reflective-formative construct. Latent scores of the second order construct were evaluated and imported into the model. T-stats were greater than 2.57, and VIF (Variation inflation factor) values were less than the threshold of 3.3. Table 2 shows the weights, VIF, and p-values of formative constructs.

Table 2. Construct validity of Formative construct Trustworthiness and its sub constructs

Trustworthiness dimensions	Beta	T-stats	VIF
Benevolence	0.337	5.83	1.6
Integrity	0.424	16	1.7
Competence	0.431	17	1.8

5.1 Structural Model Evaluation

In the structural model, all path coefficients were found to be statistically significant. R-square for endogenous constructs was moderate and were 0.28 (H1), and 0.198(H2). Both the hypothesis H1 and H2 were accepted (Table 3). The effect size for Norm of reciprocity (0.393) was greater than effect size of trust propensity (0.24).

Table 3. Structural model statistics

No	Beta	R2	P-value	f	Accept/reject
H1	0.527	0.28	.0001	0.393	Accept
H2	0.414	0.198	0.05	0.24	Accept

6 Discussion

Firstly, this is a first psychometric study to emphasize the role played by the norm of reciprocity in measuring trustworthiness in members of social media. The norm of reciprocity is an important construct especially in the social media context because it is the basis of the existence of the online social network [4]. Our analysis shows that positive norm of reciprocity may be more important than trust propensity as it has greater path coefficient (0.527), greater statistically significance (0.001) and greater effect size (0.393) than that of trust propensity (beta-0.414, p-0.05, effect size-0.24).

Secondly, it is important to validate Mayer's model [2] in the social media context. The importance of construct in trust research is determined by its context. This study proposed a new construct, "norm of reciprocity" as a determinant of trustworthiness.

7 Conclusion

This study validates Mayer's model. Mayer's model [2] was developed for interpersonal trust in an organizational context. Different antecedents have different importance in different context. As reciprocity is central to the existence of social media, the norm of reciprocity may be an important antecedent [4].

Non-probability sampling, single source bias, common method bias, and focus on variance evaluation rather than goodness of fit were limitations of this study.

7.1 Future Research

This research opens many areas for further studies. Firstly, future studies may focus on using qualitative methods such as ethnography, grounded theory, and case studies.

Secondly, collaborative economy is based on social media in general and social network in particular. Trust is an important organizing mechanism. Therefore, this research may be further progressed by taking it into the context of the design of collaborative organizations, social networks, and virtual communities.

Thirdly, this study was done in the context of social networks while seeking professional advice. Researchers may design studies in other countries to understand how culture and institutions affect the norm of reciprocity, trust propensity, and trustworthiness.

7.2 Implications

This study has implications in different areas. Firstly, this study has implication for computer scientists working in the area of social media. The norm of reciprocity is strongly correlated with trust propensity and could be used as a proxy to measure perceived trustworthiness and the trustor's trust propensity.

Secondly, employees' trust propensity affects the way they perceive things around themselves, t, and in turn their decision making and performance. Organization consultants can design programs to enhance the norm of reciprocity in virtual organizations like social networks, which would, in turn, enhance trust propensity.

References

1. Ten Kate, S.: Trustworthiness within social networking sites: a study on the intersection of HCI and sociology. Unpublished Business Studies Master, University of Amsterdam, Amsterdam (2009)
2. Mayer, R.C., Davis, J.H., Schoorman, F.D.: An integrative model of organizational trust. Acad. Manag. Rev. **20**(3), 709–734 (1995)
3. Mcknight, H.D., Chervany, N.L.: What trust means in e-commerce customer relationships: an interdisciplinary conceptual typology. Int. J. Electron. Commer. **6**(2), 35–59 (2002)
4. Lewis, S.C.: Reciprocity as a key concept for social media and society. Soc. Media Soc. **1**(1) (2015)
5. Eisenberger, R., Cotterell, N., Marvel, J.: Reciprocation ideology. J. Pers. Soc. Psychol. **53**(4), 743–750 (1987)
6. Falk, A., Fischbacher, U.: A theory of reciprocity. Games Econ. Behav. **54**(2), 293–315 (2006)
7. Fulmer, C.A., Gelfand, M.J.: At what level (and in whom) we trust: trust across multiple organizational levels. J. Manag. **38**(4), 1167–1230 (2012)
8. Ridings, C.M., Gefen, D., Arinze, O.: Determinants of Trust and Use in Virtual Communities. Drexel University, Philadelphia (2000)
9. Chai, S., Das, S., Rao, H.: Factors affecting bloggers' knowledge sharing: an investigation across gender. J. Manag. Inf. Syst. **28**(3), 309–342 (2011)

10. Koufaris, M., Hampton-Sosa, W.: The development of initial trust in an online company by new customers. Inf. Manag. **41**(3), 377–397 (2004)
11. Jarvenpaa, S.L., Shaw, T.R., Staples, D.S.: Toward contextualized theories of trust: the role of trust in global virtual teams. Inf. Syst. Res. **15**(3), 250–267 (2004)
12. McKnight, D.H., Choudhury, V., Kacmar, C.: Developing and validating trust measures for e-commerce: an integrative typology. Inf. Syst. Res. **13**(3), 334–359 (2002)
13. Furumo, K., de Pillis, E., Green, D.: Personality influences trust differently in virtual and face-to-face teams. Int. J. Hum. Resour. Dev. Manag. **9**(1) (2009)
14. Lumsden, J., MacKay, L.: How does personality affect trust in B2C e-commerce? (2006)
15. Mooradian, T., Renzl, B., Matzler, K.: Who trusts? Personality, trust and knowledge sharing. Manag. Learn. **37**(4), 523–540 (2006)
16. Rotter, J.B.: Generalized expectancies for interpersonal trust. Am. Psychol. **26**(5), 443–452 (1971)
17. Tan, F.B., Sutherland, P.: Online consumer trust: a multi-dimensional model. J. Electron. Commer. Organ. **2**(3), 40–58 (2004)
18. Awad, N., Ragowsky, A.: Establishing trust in electronic commerce through online word of mouth: an examination across genders. J. Manag. Inf. Syst. **24**(4), 101–121 (2008)
19. Fen Crystal Yap, S., Christina Kwai, C.L.: Leveraging the power of online social networks: a contingency approach. Mark. Intell. Plan. **32**(3), 345–374 (2014)
20. Beekhuyzen, J., von Hellens, L.: Reciprocity and sharing in an underground file sharing community. In: ACIS 2009 Proceedings, p. 44 (2009)
21. Häuberer, J.: Social Capital Theory: Towards a Methodological Foundation. VS Verlag für Sozialwissenschaften, Wiesbaden (2010)
22. Ostrom, E.: Governing the Commons: The Evolution of Institutions for Collective Action. Cambridge University Press, Cambridge (2006)
23. Erikson, E.H.: Identity: Youth and Crisis. W. W. Norton, New York (1994)
24. Rotter, J.B.: Interpersonal trust, trustworthiness, and gullibility. Am. Psychol. **35**(1), 1–7 (1980)
25. Blau, P.: Exchange and Power in Social Life. Wiley, New York (1964)
26. Colquitt, J.A., Scott, B.A., LePine, J.A.: Trust, trustworthiness, and trust propensity: a meta-analytic test of their unique relationships with risk taking and job performance. J. Appl. Psychol. **92**(4), 909–927 (2007)
27. Gouldner, A.W.: The norm of reciprocity: a preliminary statement. Am. Sociol. Rev. **25**, 161–178 (1960)
28. Opper, S., Holm, J., Nee, V.: Social Exchange and Generalized Trust in China. Department of Economics, Lund University (2014)
29. Schoorman, F.D., Mayer, R.C., Davis, J.H.: An integrative model of organizational trust: past, present, and future. Acad. Manag. Rev. **32**(2), 344–354 (2007)
30. Gefen, D.: Reflections on the dimensions of trust and trustworthiness among online consumers. SIGMIS Database **33**(3), 38–53 (2002)
31. Serva, M.A., Benamati, J.S., Fuller, M.A.: Trustworthiness in B2C e-commerce: an examination of alternative models. SIGMIS Database **36**(3), 89–108 (2005)
32. Ben-Ner, A., Halldorsson, F.: Trusting and trustworthiness: what are they, how to measure them, and what affects them. J. Econ. Psychol. **31**(1), 64–79 (2010)
33. Toma, C.L.: Perceptions of trustworthiness online: the role of visual and textual information. In: Proceedings of the 2010 ACM Conference on Computer Supported Cooperative Work, pp. 13–22 (2010)
34. Petter, S., Straub, D., Rai, A.: Specifying formative constructs in information systems research. MIS Q. **31**(4), 623–656 (2007)

Effect of Social Media on Trust in Virtual Project Teams of Construction Sector in Middle East

Sukhwant Kaur[1(✉)], Mohammed Arif[1], and Vishwesh Akre[2]

[1] School of Built Environment, University of Salford, Greater Manchester, UK
S.Sagar1@edu.salford.ac.uk, m.arif@salford.ac.uk
[2] Higher College of Technology, Dubai, UAE
vakre@hct.ac.ae

Abstract. Social media has greatly affected the way the virtual teams in construction sector of UAE collaborate and share information among each other. The social media is needed to support synchronicity, a shared pattern of coordinated behavior among individuals as they work together. Research shows that, although computer-supported collaborative work has increased, many distributed virtual teams are facing a number of issues in managing and controlling the teams which leads to distrust among the team members. Trust among virtual team members is considered to be one of the primary concerns that affect the performance of virtual teams in Construction Sector. This paper is a result of literature review of around 150 papers which dealt with positive and negative effect of social media interactions on trust among virtual team members. Through Literature review, it was found that conflict and cohesion within the team members greatly affects the role of communication on trust among virtual project team members.

Keywords: Collaborative tools · Middle East · Construction sector · Virtual teams · Trust · Performance · Social media

1 Introduction

The United Arab Emirates (UAE) has become the destination for many multinational companies attracted by the massive development programme, especially that in construction. The continuing market pressure for construction industry to achieve reduction in costs, improvement in quality, and reduced time to market, is becoming a threat. With the latest technologies, regulations, global alliances and changing customer needs, many organizations have adopted global virtual project teams for their business activities [15].

Social media's effect on virtual teams' ability to interact and communicate is visible throughout all areas of society. It's been found that there has been a shift in the way project teams communicate, rather than face to face interaction, they prefer mediated communication. Various studies have shown that interactions on social media tend to be weak ties—that is, project team members don't feel as personally connected to each other as at the other end of communication as they do when they are face to face [28].

© IFIP International Federation for Information Processing 2016
Published by Springer International Publishing Switzerland 2016. All Rights Reserved
Y.K. Dwivedi et al. (Eds.): I3E 2016, LNCS 9844, pp. 419–429, 2016.
DOI: 10.1007/978-3-319-45234-0_38

Due to the pressure from globalization, it is becoming necessary for construction organizations to adopt virtual project teams in order to deal with the challenges of the contemporary business environment [8]. Implementing virtual project teams success-fully within the construction context requires an in-depth understanding of the unique challenges that are not necessarily akin to the challenges encountered in face-to-face teams [18]. Against this backdrop, construction literature has been criticized for the scarcity of studies conducted about virtual project teams [9, 18].

It has been found that the failure of virtual project team is directly related to the difficulties of building trust and positive relationships across the three boundaries of geographical distance, time zones, and cultural differences [23]. Trust increases the motivation of the team members which help them to share information among them which is needed for greater performance of the virtual team. Virtual project teams face particular challenges involving trust, communication, deadlines, and team cohesiveness [18]. The building of trust becomes even more critical because the virtual teams work in different geographical locations and rely on social media for their day to day opera-tions. The communication between the virtual team members play very strong role in building trust in virtual team members. Therefore, this paper focuses on the role of communication in building trust in virtual teams of construction sector in Middle East after doing a comprehensive literature review.

Following this introduction, the remainder of this paper will be organized as follows: In Sect. 2, we present the need of virtual project teams in construction sector along with its definition, types of virtual teams and layers of trust in virtual teams. Section 3 discusses about the challenges faced by the virtual project teams. The issue of trust in virtual teams is discussed in Sect. 4. Section 5 deals with effect of communication on trust among virtual team members.

2   Need of Virtual Teams

The construction industry has been facing continuously increasing and sophisticated demands, which call for most efficient use of resources [35]. Project life cycles are shrinking virtually in all areas. In response to this, the construction industry has evolved, with the fragmentation of the production responsibilities into many sub-processes split amongst many participants, who belong to different organizations with different policies,

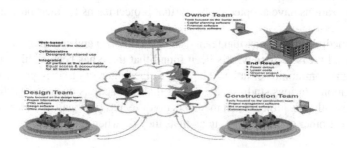

Fig. 1. Concept of virtual project teams in construction industry [Source: www.tes.com]

objectives and practices [4]. For this to happen, the construction industry has to rely on foreign skills and technologies leading to the evolution of virtual teams. Such teams are expected to comprise of capable individuals representing the relevant departments in the organization as shown in Fig. 1.

The following reasons are stated for the possible need of virtual project teams in any construction project [21]:

- The specific competence(s) needed is/are not available in the nearby area.
- Procurement of the projects design phase has resulted in the project involving participants that are geographically distributed.
- Material suppliers are non-local and their specific product influences the design of other disciplines.
- The client is non-local and is not represented locally by an agent.
- The project is a joint venture between different companies located in different geographical places.

For the construction industry, distributed teams could be defined as "groups of geographically, organizationally and/or time dispersed intelligent workers with different skills and in different positions of the hierarchy heavily relied on ICTs to accomplish engineering tasks which for all are held accountable" [18, p. 1103]. From the perspective of [25], virtual teams are groups of individuals collaborating in the execution of a specific project while geographically and often temporally distributed, possibly anywhere within (and beyond) their parent organization.

2.1 Types of Virtual Teams

Generally, the virtual project teams can be differentiated depending on the number of persons involved and the degree of interaction between them [15]. The different forms of virtual teams are clarified by classifying it with respect to two primary variables namely: the number of location (one or more) and the number of managers (one or more) [7, 27]. Therefore there are four categories of teams:

- Teleworkers: A single manager of a team at one location.
- Remote team: A single manager of a team distributed across multiple locations.
- Matrixes teleworkers: Multiple manager of a team at one location.
- Matrixes remote teams: Multiple managers across multiple locations.

Additionally, in their book 'Mastering Virtual Teams', the virtual teams have many different configurations and that they can be categorized into seven basic types of teams: project or product-development teams, which are the focus of this research, networked teams, parallel teams, work or production teams, service teams, management teams, and action teams [14, p. 4].

Our focus in this research is virtual project development teams. These teams are geographically distributed and may operate from different time zones. Project development teams are mainly focused on creating new products, information systems or organizational processes for users or customers. For our purposes, vendors and customers are not included in the definition of a virtual project team. If one were to include these two categories of team members in the definition of a virtual project team, almost 100 % of project teams would be distributed or virtual. Virtual project teams can be further characterized as having dispersed team members, knowledge, systems and workplaces, and as having a charter to make decisions [33, p. 4]. In other words, a virtual project team can cross time, distance, and organizational boundaries and make decisions to meet task goals. Team members may rotate on and off a project as their expertise is needed. This is often done in order to reduce project costs and efficiently utilize employee time and skills across the organization [14, p. 7].

2.2 Layers of Trust in Virtual Teams

The trust is a multi-dimensional concept that originates from different routes. Trust is developed at many levels [44] from societal to industrial, organizational, project and inter-personal. The development of inter-personal trust [31] between key team members [37], but contextual data and other studies showed that there were a variety of contexts that impacted the levels of trust in inter-personal context.

- The organizational trust context is driven by the norms and values of the organization. Trusting organizations are those that trust their own staff [49], supporting a no-blame culture [54]. Individuals within these types of organization have the authority to act and respond flexibly to partners in the project context, key issue for the development of trust [5].
- The inter-personal is a trust that occur between two individuals. Inter-personal trust between individual can be seen to start from two aspects of trust: global trust [10], which may be considered an individual's propensity to trust generated from wide variety of factors, and emotive trust [13], which is an individual's non-cognitive assessment of another individual on initial meeting.

In the light of the literature review on trust, it is proposed that trust be categorized into System-based, Cognition-based and Affect-based [55]. The formation and maintenance of trust in virtual teams are often temporary, depending more on the cognitive element than the affective element [29].

3   Challenges Faced by Virtual Project Teams

While there are great advantages that come with the adoption of the virtual teams, new challenges rise with them [40]. Evidence has demonstrated that overlooking the challenges facing distributed teams and failure in tackling such challenges would end up in disappointing results with distributed teams [34]. Virtual team may allow people to collaborate more productivity at a distance, but the trip to coffee corner or across the hallway to a trusted colleague is still the most reliable and effective way to review and revise a new idea [16]. Some of the problems that virtual project teams experience include the following: time delays in replies, lack of synergy among cross-cultural team members, communications breakdowns due to cultural variances, unresolved conflicts among culturally different members, different holidays [51]. The key findings reported by [50] were the challenge of leadership, managing virtual aspects of communication and developing trust. Further to this, it is understood by the literature that virtual teams face particular challenges involving trust, communication, deadlines, and team cohesiveness [18].

From the literature, the researcher has understood that there are social, technical and structural issues involved in the operation of the virtual teams which are discussed as follows:

- **Trust:** The issue of trust is very important particularly in the context of virtual teams because virtual team members are "geographically dispersed" and lack "shared social-context" and "face-to-face encounter" that are considered by many researchers as irreplaceable for building trust and repairing shattered trust [20]. Trust development in virtual teams presents significant challenges because it is difficult to assess teammates' trustworthiness without ever having met them [32]. Moreover, as the life of many virtual teams is relatively limited, trust must quickly develop [20].
- **Communication:** Because of the distributed nature of their work unit, virtual team members have to rely heavily on information and communication technologies [46]. The selection of the right technology is considered very important for most effective communication in virtual teams. As noted by [19], "if technology is the foundation of the virtual business relationship, communication is the cement" [19, p. 33].
- **Team Cohesiveness:** Cohesion is an important aspect of the virtual team. When compared to traditional team members, virtual team members generally report weaker relational links to teammates [32, 52]. These results are attributed to the significant reliance of virtual teams on electronic communication and the difficulties associated with such communication modes [48].
- **Diversity or Group Heterogeneity:** Virtual teams cut across organizational culture, national cultures, and functional areas. These all add to diversity or group heterogeneity, which may result in increased conflict among team members and less effective performance of the team [38]. One key reason for the use of functionally diverse teams may be because of external knowledge sharing. Team members who exchange information, technical knowledge, and feedback with those outside the team may be able to enhance the performance of the team [12]. Empirical research, however, has shown that diversity can be either a positive or a negative force on a team, both by helping and hindering team processes and performance [30, 53].
- **Leadership:** Managing the virtual team is a task in itself. Team leaders and supervisors must be aware of particular issues in order to avoid any potential problems [8]. In building the virtual corporations, the managers must be able to understand the diversity in international cultures so that understanding the trait is a success [36]. In addition, ineffective leadership [22] and cultural differences [22, 45] have been found to negatively impact communication effectiveness.

4   Issue of Trust in Virtual Teams

The Middle East is a multicultural region with people coming from various backgrounds and different countries to work on various kinds of projects, and hence, it's very important to understand the phenomenon of these groups who relate across multiple cultures.

Trust between project participants is clearly an important ingredient when working in a virtual project team. It is considered as one of the primary concerns that affect the performance of virtual teams. A great deal of literature has pointed to the importance of trust as a facilitator of positive relationships among project stakeholders. It is generally assumed that a critical factor in the successful completion of a project is trust in fellow team members to deliver their share of the work on time and with sufficient quality [20]. Trust has become a key research area within construction management, as well as in the wider business and management literature. In construction industry, the challenge of building trust, team identity and team cohesiveness has to be critically evaluated in order for the successful operations of virtual project team [8].

Trust has been defined as the "willingness of a party to be vulnerable to the actions of another party, based on the expectation that the other will perform a particular action important to the person in whom trust is placed, irrespective of the ability to monitor or control that other party" [29]. Trust is defined in terms of the faith and belief in another individual or group that the relevant party will fulfill expectations in the future [28]. Trust is the most difficult issue associated with virtual teams [17]. Trust can depend on situations and have its limitations. In some relationships, trust is only dependent on simple basic variables but as relationships mature and members get to know each other, individuals learn to trust or distrust the team members according to their characteristics [26]. Building trust is not an easy task. It is probably the most complicated issue in forming a successful and effective team [56]. With distance between team members, trust must be earned in order for the team to work. Trust and relationships between group members' increases creativity and critical thinking, as well as creating a more positive environment [41]. Trust encourages members to devote time to projects, keep their focus on joint objectives, help each other, and work harder [24].

Trust is especially important in cross-disciplinary work setups, as those during the design phase of a construction project. This due to that many sub-tasks are interdependent of each other and the team members are then forced to trust the other team members' competence to perform the interdependent tasks in such a way that the final product meets the expectations of the client [57]. Studies by [20] suggest that trust in geographically distributed virtual project teams are very fragile compared to the trust between members of co-located teams. Virtual team failure is directly related to the difficulties of building trust and positive relationships across the three boundaries of geographical distance, time zones, and cultural differences [23].

5   Effect of Communication on Trust Among Virtual Teams

The virtual environment presents considerable challenges to effective communication including time delays in sending feedback, lack of a common frame of reference for all members, differences in interpretation of written text, and assurance of participation from remote team members [11]. Thus, teams operating in the virtual environment face greater obstacles to orderly and efficient information exchange than their counterparts in the traditional context, a difficulty that is compounded when the virtual team is global in nature.

Team member communication was analyzed on the effectiveness of virtual teams and indicated that the most satisfied team members were in virtual teams with effective coordination and communication [39]. It is also indicated that teams performed more effectively when members developed effective communication norms, communication technology usage norms, and the like. The communication among virtual team members can be either Synchronous (Chat, Net meeting) or Asynchronous (email, electronic bulletin boards). As per studies by [6], there are mainly three barriers to communication in a project. These are (1) difference in language between business and systems, (2) difference in perception and (3) lack of a project communication plan. Controlling these aspects of communications is of utmost importance for project managers for successful completion of the project.

The development of trust is linked to increased communication among members [20]. The communication aspect of team members consists of communication tool and type used by the team members. It also deals with variation in time difference and holidays for the geographically dispersed teams and requirement of training by the team members of the virtual project teams. Managers can send employee for training to acquire skills and experiences that will make them good team players [2]. The training could allow employees to experience the satisfaction that teamwork can provide. The training could be in the form of workshop to help employees improve their problem solving, communication, negotiation, conflict management, and coaching skills.

The effective use of communication, especially during the early stages of the team's development, plays an equally important role in gaining and maintaining trust [3]. Communication is an ongoing challenge in virtual teams, difficulties are intensified when the team members are globally distributed [32]. Furthermore, mutual understanding within the team diminishes and overall understanding is hampered when a shared language is lacking among members, and communication becomes more strained when some members are co-located while others are geographically distributed [11]. Virtual teams that send more social communication achieve higher trust [20] and better social and emotional relationships [42]. Trusting team members where there is little to no relationship can be difficult [43]. Compared with face-to-face teams, distributed teams exhibit weaker relational links among team members [52]. Researchers attribute the weaker relationships to the significant reliance on communication tools and technologies and the difficulties of communicating with team members across time and space [39]. The high reliance on technology to communicate also contributes to lack of cohesion among team members [52]. However, greater cohesiveness may be achieved over time and as more social cues are exchanged among team members [8]. Research also indicates that as teams become more efficacious with the communication technologies, higher levels of trust tend to develop among members [20].

Dispersed members often assume that co-located team members are talking and sharing information that is not communicated to them and private exchanges has been identified as the cause of friction between team members [11, 45] which results in conflicts among virtual team members. The characteristics of communication technology, especially in a virtual team, may contribute to team conflict [1]. Thus, the very nature of the electronic exchanges within virtual teams may be a source of conflict; when the level of information richness is low because of a lean medium of communication.

The end result may be confusion, differing interpretations, and ultimately conflicting points of view. The "richer" means of communication such as face-to-face interaction are more effective in task and conflict resolution, as compared to 'leaner' means of communication as in virtual teams where merely exchange of written words or only vocal exchange of information is possible [47].

Therefore, this study through the above discussion and extensive literature review concludes the following points containing the effect of communication on trust:

- *Conflict among team members of virtual team decreases the positive effect of communication on trust in virtual project teams.*
- *Cohesion among team members of virtual team mediates the positive effect of communication on trust in virtual project teams.*

6 Conclusion

Strong business and social pressures are driving the adoption of virtual team working. Though virtual teams offer many benefits to organizations striving to handle a more demanding work environment, they also present many challenges and potential pitfalls. While awareness of these issues can result in improved coordination, distributed work introduces huge coordination overheads. Cross-functional cooperation and effective teamwork are some of the crucial ingredients for making these virtual teams work. Trust among virtual team members is considered to be one of the primary concerns that affect the performance of virtual teams.

One of the main contributors in developing trust among virtual teams is role played by social media. The kind of communication tool and its frequency greatly effects the trust among team members of virtual teams. This paper discusses the challenges faced by the virtual project teams focusing on the trust, which greatly affects the performance of the virtual team. Further, this paper yields the result of comprehensive literature review of technical papers, on the effect of communication on trust among team members of virtual teams of construction sector in the context of Middle East and proposes the two hypotheses showing the effect of cohesion and conflict on the role of communication on trust among virtual project teams.

7 Limitations and Future Scope

The limitation of this study is that we have identified the various factors effecting the trust in virtual teams through extensive literature review and pilot study needs to verify the actual factors. The conceptual model developed in this research is based on the variables extracted from the literature further improvement in the proposed model would include:

- Data collection through online survey and quantitative analysis of data through SPSS software.
- Development of Trust model by using Structural Equation Modeling (SEM) using AMOS Version22 software.

- Developing a hierarchy system by using Interpretive Structural Modeling (ISM) and Interpretive Ranking Process (IRP) to see the relative importance of the factors needed for building trust in virtual teams.   □

It is our belief that these findings will provide an important step in studying how trust in virtual team members can be enhanced which will lead to increase in the performance of virtual project teams.

Acknowledgements. I would like to express my sincere gratitude to my supervisor Dr. Mohammed Arif for the continuous support in my Doctoral research. I sincerely appreciate his patience, his motivational skills, and immense knowledge and experience that he has seamlessly shared with me. I would take this opportunity to acknowledge my local advisor, Dr. Vishwesh Akre, for his constant guidance at every phase of the study.

References

1. Kankanhalli, A., Tan, B., Wei, K.-K.: Technology, culture, and conflict in virtual teams: a case study. In: Proceedings of the 11th Australian Conference on Information Systems (2000)
2. Amah, E., Nwuche, C.A., Chukuigwe, N.: Result oriented target setting and leading high performance teams. Ind. Eng. Lett. 3(9), 47–60 (2013). www.iiste.org
3. Anderson, A.H., Mcewan, R., Baland, J., Carletta, J.: Virtual team meetings: an analysis of communication and context. Comput. Hum. Behav. 23, 2558–2580 (2007)
4. Aniekwu, A., Nwachukwu, J.C.: Understanding the Nigerian Construction Industry. Mindex Publishing Co. Ltd., Benin City (2002)
5. Black, C., Akintoye, A., et al.: An analysis of success factors and benefits of partnering in construction. Int. J. Project Manag. 18, 423–434 (2000)
6. Carvalho, M.M.: Communication issues in projects management. In: PICMET 2008, Portland International Conference on Management of Engineering and Technology, pp. 1280–1284. IEEE (2008). doi:10.1109/PICMET.2008.4599739
7. Cascio, W.F., Shurygailo, S.: E-leadership and virtual teams. Org. Dyn. 31, 362–376 (2003)
8. Chen, C., Messner, J.: A recommended practices system for a global virtual engineering team. Architectural Eng. Des. Manag. 6, 207–221 (2010)
9. Chinowsky, P.S., Rojas, E.M.: Virtual teams: guide to successful implementation. J. Manag. Eng. 19(3), 98–106 (2003)
10. Couch, L.L., Jones, W.H.: Measuring levels of trust. J. Res. Pers. 31, 319–336 (1997)
11. Cramton, C.D.: The mutual knowledge problem and its consequences for dispersed collaboration. Organ. Sci. 12, 356–371 (2001)
12. Cummings, J.N.: Work groups, structural diversity, and knowledge sharing in a global organization. Manag. Sci. 50, 352–364 (2004)
13. Doney, P.M., Cannon, J.P., et al.: Understanding the influence of national culture on the development of trust. Acad. Manag. Rev. 23(3), 601–620 (1998)
14. Duarte, D.L., Snyder, N.T.: Mastering Virtual Teams: Strategies, Tools, and Techniques That Succeed. Jossey Bass, San Francisco (2001)
15. Ebrahim, N.A., Ahmed, S., Taha, Z.: Virtual teams: a literature review. Aust. J. Basic Soc. Sci. 3(3), 2653–2669 (2009)
16. Gassmann, O., Vonzedtwitz, M.: Innovation Processes in Transnational Corporations. Elsevier Science Ltd., Amsterdam (2003)

17. Haywood, M.: Managing Virtual Teams: Practical Techniques for High-Technology Project Managers. Artech House, Boston (1998)
18. Hosseini, M.R., Chileshe, N.: Global Virtual Engineering Teams (GVETs): a fertile ground for research in Australian construction projects context. Int. J. Project Manag. **31**(8), 1101–1117 (2013)
19. Hulnick, G.: Doing business virtually. Commun. World **17**(3), 33–36 (2000)
20. Jarvenpaa, S.L., Knoll, K., Leidner, D.E.: Is anybody out there? Antecedents of trust in global virtual teams. J. Manag. Inf. Syst. **14**, 29–64 (1998)
21. Karlsson, E.: Building effective virtual project collaboration. A study of the benefits and challenges of geographically distributed virtual project work (2014)
22. Kayworth, T.R., Leidner, D.E.: Leadership effectiveness in global virtual teams. J. Manag. Inf. Syst. **18**, 7–40 (2001)
23. Kimble, C.: Building effective virtual teams: how to overcome the problems of trust and identity in virtual teams. Global Bus. Organ. Excellence **30**(2), 6–15 (2011). doi:10.1002/joe. 20364
24. Kramer, R.M.: Trust and distrust in organizations: emerging perspectives, enduring questions. Ann. Rev. Psychol. **50**, 569–598 (1999)
25. Leenders, R.T.A.J., Engelen, J.M.L.V., Kratzer, J.: Virtuality, communication, and new product team creativity: a social network perspective. J. Eng. Tech. Manag. **20**, 69–92 (2003)
26. Lewicki, R.J., McAllister, D.J., Bies, R.J.: Trust and distrust: new relationships and realities. Acad. Manag. Rev. **23**(3), 438–458 (1998)
27. Liz, L.K., Tim, S.: Global virtual teams for value creation and project success. Int. J. Project Manag. **25**, 51–62 (2007)
28. Maura, K.: Social media and interpersonal communication. Social Work Today **13**(3), 10 (2013)
29. Mayer, R.C., Davis, J.H., Schoorman, F.D.: An integrative model of organizational trust. Acad. Manag. Rev. **20**(3), 709–734 (1995)
30. Meyerson, D., Weick, K.E., Kramer, R.M.: Swift trust and temporary groups. In: Kramer, R.M., Tyler, T.R. (eds.) Trust in Organizations: Frontiers of Theory and Research, pp. 166–195. Sage Publications, Thousand Oaks (1996)
31. Milliken, F., Martins, L.: Searching for common threads: understanding the multiple effects of diversity in organizational groups. Acad. Manag. Rev. **21**, 402–433 (1996)
32. McDermott, P., Khalfan, M., Swan, W.: Trust in construction projects. J. Financ. Manag. Property Constr. **10**(1), 19–32 (2005)
33. Mcdonough, E.F., Kahn, K.B., Barczak, G.: An investigation of the use of global, virtual, and collocated new product development teams. J. Prod. Innovation Manag. **18**, 110–120 (2001)
34. McMahon, P.E.: Virtual Project Management: Software Solutions for Today and the Future. St. Lucie Press, Boca Raton (2001)
35. Mukherjee, D., Renn, R.W., Kedia, B.L., Mukherjee, D.: Development of interorganizational trust in virtual organizations: an integrative framework. Eur. Bus. Rev. **24**(3), 255–271 (2012)
36. Nathaniel, A., Anthony, C.I.: Barriers to the uptake of concurrent engineering in the Nigerian construction industry. Int. J. Eng. Bus. Manag. **4**, 1–8 (2012). doi:10.5772/51607
37. O'Hara-Devereaux, M., Johansen, B.: Global Work: Bridging Distance, Culture, and Time. Jossey-Bass, San Francisco (1994)
38. Oskamp, S.: Introduction: studying interpersonal processes. In: Oskamp, S., Spacapan, S. (eds.) Interpersonal Processes, pp. 7–24. Sage, Newbury Park (1987)
39. Paul, S., Seetharaman, P., Samarah, I., Mykytyn, P.P.: Impact of heterogeneity and collaborative conflict management style on the performance of synchronous global virtual teams. Inf. Manag. **41**, 303–321 (2004). doi:10.1016/S0378-7206(03)00076-4

40. Powell, A., Piccoli, G., Ives, B.: Virtual teams: a review of current literature and directions for future. Database Adv. Inf. Syst. **35**(1), 6–36 (2004)
41. Precup, L., O'sullivan, D., Cormican, K., Dooley, L.: Virtual team environment for collaborative research projects. Int. J. Innovation Learn. **3**, 77–94 (2006)
42. Reina, D., Reina, M.: Trust and Betrayal in the Workplace. Berre-Koehler Publishers Inc., San Francisco (1999)
43. Robey, D., Koo, H., Powers, C.: Situated learning in cross-functional virtual teams. Tech. Commun. **47**(1), 51–66 (2000)
44. Rolf Trautsch, B.: Managing Virtual Project Teams (2003). doi:10.1017/CBO9781107415324.004
45. Rousseau, D.M., Sitkin, S.B., et al.: Not so different after all: a cross disciplinary view of trust. Acad. Manag. Rev. **23**(3), 393–404 (1998)
46. Sarker, S., Lee, A.S.: Using a positivist case research methodology to test three competing practitioner theories-in-use of business process redesign. J. Assoc. Infor. Syst. **2**(7), 1–72 (2002)
47. Saunders, M., Lewis, P., Thornhill, A.: Research Methods for Business Students, 5th edn. FT/Prentice Hall, Harlow (2009)
48. Saxena, A., Burmann, J.: Factors affecting team performance in globally distributed setting. In: Proceedings of the 52nd ACM Conference on Computers and People Research – SIGSIM-CPR 2014, pp. 25–33 (2014). doi:10.1145/2599990.2599995
49. Sproull, L., Kiesler, S.: Reducing social context cues: electronic mail in organizational communication. Manag. Sci. **32**(11), 1492–1512 (1986)
50. Tschannen-Moran, M.: Collaboration and the need for trust. J. Educ. Adm. **39**(4), 308–331 (2001)
51. Vakola, M., Wilson, I.: The challenge of virtual organisation: critical success factors in dealing with constant change. Team Perform. Manag. **10**(5/6), 112–120 (2004). doi:10.1108/13527590410556836
52. Vinaja, R.: Major challenges in multi-cultural virtual teams. In: 33rd Annual Conference of the Decision Sciences Institute Southwest Region, Houston, TX, vol. 78541(956), pp. 341–346 (2003)
53. Warkentin, M., Sayeed, L., Hightower, R.: Virtual teams versus face-to-face teams: an exploratory study of a web-based conference system. Decis. Sci. **28**(4), 975–996 (1997)
54. Williams, B., Brown, T.: Exploratory factor analysis: a five-step guide for novices. Australas. J. Paramedicine **8**(3), 1–13 (2010)
55. Woodward, D., Widward, T.: The efficacy of action at a distance as a control mechanism in the construction industry when a trust relationship beaks down: an illustrative case study. Br. J. Manag. **12**, 355–384 (2001)
56. Wong, W., Cheung, S., Yiu, T., Pang, H.: A framework for trust in construction contracting. Int. J. Project Manag. **26**, 821–829 (2008). doi:10.1016/j.ijproman.2007.11.004
57. Zaheer, A., McEvily, B., Perrone, V.: Does trust matter? Exploring the effects of inter-organizational and interpersonal trust on performance. Organ. Sci. **9**(2), 141–159 (1998)

Trust Management in Social Internet of Things: A Survey

Wafa Abdelghani[1(✉)], Corinne Amel Zayani[1], Ikram Amous[1], and Florence Sèdes[2]

[1] MIRACL Laboratory, Sfax University, Sfax, Tunisia
abdelghani_wafa@hotmail.fr,
{corinne.zayani,ikram.amous}@isecs.rnu.tn
[2] IRIT, Paul Sabatier University, Toulouse, France
florence.sedes@irit.fr

Abstract. Social Internet of Things is a new paradigm where Internet of Things merges with Social Networks, allowing people and devices to interact, facilitating information sharing and enabling a variety of at-tractive applications. However, face to this new paradigm, users remain suspicious and careful. They fear disclosure of their data and violation of their privacy. Without trustworthy technologies to ensure user's safe communications and trustworthy interactions, the SIoT will not reach enough popularity to be considered as a well-established technology. Accordingly, trust management becomes a major challenge to ensure reliable data analysis, qualified services and enhanced security. It helps people exceed their fears and promotes their acceptance and consumption on IoT services. However, current research still lacks a comprehensive study on trust management in SIoT. In this paper, we expose basic concepts, properties and models proposed for the trust management in SIOT environments. Furthermore, we discuss unsolved issues and future research trends.

Keywords: Social Internet of Things · Social networks · Trust management · Trust attacks

1 Introduction

The Internet of Things is expected to be dominated by huge content-oriented traffic, intensive interactions between billions of persons often on the move and heterogeneous communications among hosts and smart objects. It provision a millions of services, with strict real-time requirements and striking flexibility in connecting everyone and everything [13]. Interconnected things such as sensors or mobile devices sense, monitor and collect all kinds of data about human social life. Those data can be further aggregated, fused, processed, analyzed and mined in order to extract useful information to enable intelligent and ubiquitous services.

Integrating social networking concepts into the Internet of Things has led to the Social Internet of Things (SIoT) paradigm which enables people and connected devices to interact, facilitating information sharing and enabling a variety of attractive applications.

© IFIP International Federation for Information Processing 2016
Published by Springer International Publishing Switzerland 2016. All Rights Reserved
Y.K. Dwivedi et al. (Eds.): I3E 2016, LNCS 9844, pp. 430–441, 2016.
DOI: 10.1007/978-3-319-45234-0_39

However, face to this new paradigm, users remain suspicious and careful. They fear disclosure of their data and violation of their privacy. Without trust-worthy technologies to ensure user's safe communications, and trustworthy inter-actions, the SIoT paradigm will not reach enough popularity to be considered as a well-established technology, and all its potential will be lost.

Accordingly, trust management becomes a major challenge in SIoT to ensure reliable data analysis, qualified services and enhanced user's security. It helps people face and exceed their fears and uncertainty and promotes user's acceptance and consumption on IoT services and applications.

In the literature, trust mechanisms have been widely studied in various fields. However, existing models cannot be entirely applied in SIoT environments be-cause they are not adapted to its specific constraints (mobility, constrained re-sources,..). Current research has not comprehensively investigated how to man-age trust in such environments. This paper is a survey about the trust management in SIoT environments, its basic concepts, its properties, its models and its unsolved issues.

The paper is organized as follows. In Sect. 2, we expose an overview about the SIoT paradigm, its definitions, its evolution and its network structure. In Sect. 3, we address the notion of trust in SIoT environments, its properties, trust related attacks and the main constraints of trust management in SIoT. In Sect. 4, we present a classification of SIoT trust models. In Sect. 5, we provide literature review of trust models in Social Internet of Things. We conclude the paper in Sect. 6.

2   Social Internet of Things Paradigm

The Social Internet of Things (SIoT) is a new paradigm where IoT merges with social networks, allowing people and connected devices as well as the devices themselves to interact within a social network framework to support a new social navigation [12].

The structure of the SIoT network can be shaped as required to facilitate the navigability, to perform the discovery of objects and services and to guarantee the scalability like in human social networks. A level of trustworthiness must be established for leveraging the degree of interaction among things and social networks models can be adapted to address SIoT [9].

2.1   From Smart Things to Social Things

IoT embodies a large number of smart objects that, through standard communication protocols and unique addressing schemes, provide information and services to final users. Making objects smart was only the first step of an evolutionary process that affected modern communication devices and has been triggered by the advent of IoT in the telecommunication scenarios. The second step consists of the evolution of objects with a certain degree of smartness to objects with an actual social consciousness. These objects can interact with the surrounding environment and feature a pseudo-social behavior with "neighbors" or within "circles" and "communities".

The third step consists of the birth of social objects that act in a social com-munity of objects and devices [2]. Those social objects are able to autonomously establish relationships with other objects, to join communities and to build their own social network which may be different from their owners ones. This has given a specific structure to SIoT networks that is different from the structure of common social networks and that brings up new types of relationships.

2.2 SIOT Network Structure

[1, 3] address basic aspects to fully achieve an effective social networks of intelligent objects. In analogy with "human" social networks, [3] propose various forms of socialization among objects. The parental object relationship is defined among similar objects, built at the same period by the same manufacturer. Moreover, objects can establish co-location object relationship and co-work object relationship, like humans do when they share personal (e.g., cohabitation) or public (e.g., work) experiences. A further type of relationship is defined for objects owned by the same user (mobile phones, game consoles, etc.) that is named ownership object relationship. The last relationship is established when objects come into contact, sporadically or continuously, for reasons purely related to relations among their owners (e.g., devices/sensors belonging to friends); it is named social object relationship.

These relationships are created and updated on the basis of objects features (such as: object type, computational power, mobility capabilities, brand) and activity (frequency in meeting the other objects, mainly). Notice that, the establishment and the management of such relationships should occur without human intervention. Human is responsible only to set the rules of objects social interactions and then enjoys services resulting from such interactions.

Another structure was proposed by [6], who propose an SIOT network based on three kinds of social relationships connecting objects owners: (i) friendship relationship, which represents intimacy, (ii) social contact relationship, which represents closeness and proximity and (iii) community of interest relationship, which refers to common knowledge or experiences.

We note that when designing a structure for SIoT network, authors are divided between those who base on peer to peer networks and only opt for inter-objects social relationships and others who base on social networks and only consider social relationships between objects owners. However SIoT is a combination of both and should consider both objects and humans stakeholders. Thus, different kinds of relationships may operate between them such as: human-human, object-object and human-object social relationships.

3 Trust in Social Internet of Things

The concept of trust has been studied in many disciplines ranging from psychology to computer science. It is hard to precisely define the term "trust" because of its multidimensional, multidisciplinary and multifaceted aspects. A trust relationship involves at least two entities: a trustor and a trustee, reliant on each other for mutual bene t and the context in which reside the trust relationship, such as the purpose of trust, the environment of trust (e.g., time, location, activity, devices being used, their operational mode, etc.), and the risk of trust. It specifies any information that can be used to characterize the background or the situation of involved entities [8]. Trust management is an important feature in networking systems like SIoT. We present here some properties of trust in general which depends on authors vision and hypothesis. Then we present specific challenges and constraints of trust management in SIoT environment.

3.1 Trust Properties

In literature, trust was computed in several ways depending on considered properties.

- **Trust can be direct:** This property says that trust is based on direct interactions, experiences or observations between the trustor and the trustee.
- **Trust can be indirect:** The trustor and the trustee here don't have any past experiences or interactions. The trust here is build on the opinion and the recommendation of other nodes. We talk about transitive trust.
- **Trust can be local:** It depends on the couple trustor/trustee considered and differs from one couple to another, which means that a node i can trust a node j whether another node k can distrust the same node j.
- **Trust can be global:** The global trust also called reputation means that every node has a unique trust value in the network which can be known by all other nodes.
- **Trust should be asymmetric:** Which means that two people tied by a relationship may have different levels of trustworthiness each other. The fact that A trusts B does not imply that B should trust A [13].
- **Trust should be subjective:** Trust is inherently a personal opinion which is based on various factors or evidence, and that some of those may carry more weight than others [10].
- **Trust can be objective:** In some case, such as when trust is computed based on QoS properties of a device.
- **Trust can be context-dependent:** Where the trust of a node i in a node j varies from one context to another.
- **Trust can be a composite property:** Trust is really a composition of many different attributes: reliability, dependability, honesty, truthfulness, security, competence, and timeliness, which may have to be considered de-pending on the environment in which trust has been specified [10].
- **Trust can depends on history:** This property implies that past experience may influence the present level of trust [16].
- **Trust should be dynamic:** Trust is non-monotonically changing with time. It may be periodically refreshed or revoked, and must be able to adapt to the changing conditions of the environment in which the trust decision was made [10].

3.2 Trust Related Attacks

A malicious node aims to break the basic functionality (e.g. service composition) of the IoT. In addition, it can perform the following trust-related attacks [5]:

1. **Self-promoting attacks (SPA):** it can promote its importance (by pro-viding good recommendations for itself) so as to be selected as the service provider, but then stop providing services or provide malfunction services.
2. **Bad-mouthing attacks (BMA):** it can ruin the reputation of well behaved nodes (by providing bad recommendations against good nodes) so as to decrease the chance of good nodes being selected as service providers.
3. **Ballot stuffing attacks (BSA):** it can boost the reputation of bad nodes (by providing good recommendations for them) so as to increase the chance of bad nodes being selected as service providers.
4. **Whitewashing attacks (WA):** a malicious node can disappear and rejoin the application to wash away its bad reputation.
5. **Discriminatory attacks (DA):** a malicious node can discriminatory at-tack non-friends or nodes without strong social ties (without many common friends) because of human nature or propensity towards friends in social IoT systems.
6. **Opportunistic service attacks (OSA):** a malicious node can provide good service to opportunistically gain high reputation especially when it feels its reputation is dropping because of providing bad service. With good reputation, it can effectively collude with other bad node to perform bad-mouthing and ballot stuffing attacks.

3.3 SIoT Trust Management Requirements/Constraints

SIoT networks are different from social networks because a large number of requirements and constraints such as characterizes them:

- Huge amount of entities and devices involved.
- Limited storage space capacity of entities and devices.
- Limited computation resources of entities and devices.
- High dynamism due to the large number of nodes joining and leaving the networks at any moment.
- Energy consumption, which is one of the biggest challenge of entities and device needing battery.
- Criticality and sensitiveness of used services and applications since they act on the real world.
- Power efficiency, making trust management algorithms and mechanisms faster and less energy consuming to support small things constraints.

Thus, trust management protocols must accommodate and ensure some important criteria such as scalability, adaptability, survivability, power efficiency and resiliency of the SIoT network.

4 SIoT Trust Models Classification

[11] propose to classify trust computation techniques on four design dimensions: trust composition, trust propagation, trust aggregation and trust update.

4.1 Trust Composition (TC)

In SIoT environment we distinguish two kind of trust based on the type of relationship: (i) the trust between a user and its device also known as quality of service (QoS) Trust and (ii) the trust between a user and other users also known as Social Trust. Trust composition refers to what factors to consider in trust computation especially QoS trust and social trust.

QoS Trust: QoS trust refers to the belief that an IoT device is able to provide quality service in response to a service request. QoS trust in general refers to performance and is measured by competence, cooperativeness, reliability, task completion capability, etc.

Social Trust: Social trust derives from social relationship between owners of IoT devices and is measured by intimacy, honesty, privacy, centrality, and connectivity, etc. Social trust is especially prevalent in social IoT systems where IoT devices must be evaluated not only based on QoS trust, but also based on the trust degree on their owners.

4.2 Trust Propagation (TP)

Trust propagation refers to how to propagate trust observations between entities. In general, there are two trust propagation schemes: (i) distributed and (ii) centralized.

Distributed: In the distributed trust propagation scheme, IoT devices prop-agate trust observations to other IoT devices they encounter or interact without the use of a centralized entity. The management of such propagation is arduous but it offers more scalability.

Centralized: The centralized trust propagation scheme requires the presence of a centralized entity (i.e. physical cloud) and uses structures like Distributed Hash Table (DHT).

4.3 Trust Aggregation (TA)

Trust aggregation consists of aggregating trust observations to get a unique convergent value. In the literature, the main aggregation techniques investigated are static weighted sum (SWS), dynamic weighted sum (DWS), Bayesian Model (BM) and Fuzzy Logic (FL).

4.4 Trust Update (TU)

Trust update concerns when trust is updated. In general, there are two schemes - event-driven scheme and time-driven scheme.

Event-Driven: In the event-driven scheme, all trust data in a node are updated after a transaction or an event is made.

Time-Driven: In the time-driven scheme, trust observations are collected periodically and trust is updated by applying a trust aggregation technique.

5 State of Art

5.1 Overview

Authors of [4] are the first to consider social relationships in trust management for IoT. They propose a new protocol based on three trust factors: (i) Honesty, (ii) Cooperativeness and (iii) Community interest. (i) Honesty refers to the belief of a node i that another node j is honest based on direct observations. Using a set of anomaly detection rules, node i count suspicious or dishonest experiences he had observed during a period Δ_t such as discrepancy in recommendation, interval, retransmission, repetition,... A dishonest node is a malicious node which aims to disturb the functionality and the performance of the IoT network giving improper recommendations to himself or to other nodes. (ii) Cooperativeness reflects the willingness of a node j to help other nodes in some task such as pro-viding a service to a service requester. An uncooperative node is not a malicious node. It does not aim to harm the basic functionality of IoT, but, it acts only for its own interest. [4] assume that friends are likely to be cooperative toward each other and compute cooperativeness value as the ration of the number of common friends over the total number of friends. (iii) Community interest represents the degree of common interest or same capabilities between two nodes and is computed as the ratio of the number of their common community/group interests over the total number of community/group interests.

Authors consider both direct and indirect trust. Direct trust is an aggregation of honesty, cooperativeness and community-interests values which are assigned by a node i to a node j based on direct observation and interaction between the two nodes. If the two nodes had never interacted in the past, the node i will consider the indirect trust which is based on the observations and the past experiences of other nodes with the concerned node. The honesty assessment and the indirect trust are used to increase the protocol resilience against some trust related attacks.

In summary, [4] propose a trust protocol which is both direct and transitive (indirect). The considered trust value is composite (depending on three factors), subjective and asymmetric (the trust of a node i in a node j differs from the trust of a node j in a node i). This value is dynamic because it varies over time and depend on history (past interactions) but not on the context. Trust values are aggregated with the static weighted sum and propagated in a distributed way.

Despite the fact that [4] are the first to consider social relationships in trust management for IoT, the proposed measure for computing cooperativeness (the percentage of common friends) is very simple and does not really reflect the willingness of a node i to cooperate and collaborate with others. The kind of social relationship exploited for measuring trust between object is the social relation-ship between their owners. However, in SIoT, an object is able to build its own social network which is different and independent of the social network of its owners. Furthermore the resiliency of the proposed protocol face to the trust related attacks has not been proven by evaluations. Finally, the proposed solution does not consider the specific constraints of the IoT environments such as storage management and energy consumption.

In [5], the authors aim at improving the trust management protocol pro-posed in [4]. They reuse the same trust measure, which is an aggregation of honesty, cooperativeness and community-interest. But they take into consideration other aspects such as the scalability, the adaptivity and the survivability of the protocol. As in the old protocol, the update of trust values is always events-driven and the trust values are computed only for a limited set of nodes to minimize computation and to maintain scalability. However, a new storage management strategy is proposed which permits to use limited storage space and to enhance scalability.

[6] propose an adaptive and scalable trust management protocol for SOA-based IoT systems. Distributed collaborating filtering technique is used to select trust feedback from owners of IoT nodes sharing similar social interests and three social relationships are considered for measuring social similarity and filtering trust feedback based on social similarity: (i) friendship, (ii) social contact, and (iii) community of interest. An adaptive filtering technique is employed for combining direct trust and indirect trust into the overall trust to minimize convergence time and trust bias of trust evaluation.

The proposed approach avoids Self-promoting, Bad-mouthing, Bal-lot stuffing and Opportunistic service attacks. It also take into consideration some SIoT constrains such as scalability and limited storage and computing capacity of IoT devices by computing trust only for the limited set of nodes of interest. However, authors don't consider social relationship between objects but only social relationship between their owners. The trust value is the same for all the objects and device owned by the same person. But the different characteristics of those different devices must influence the trust value. Moreover, QoS trust is not considered which is an important factor in Object-connected environments. Finally, considering a limited set of node is not a radical solution which can really ensure scalability. It is only a temporal solution.

[13] focused on the trustworthiness management in the social IoT by proposing subjective and objective approaches. The subjective approach has a slower transitory response, which is particularly obvious when dealing with nodes with dynamic behaviors. However, it is practically immune to typical behaviors of social networks, where a malicious person modifies his actions based on the relationships. On the contrary, the objective approach suffers from this kind of behavior, since a nodes trustworthiness is global for the entire network and this includes both the

opinion from the nodes with which it behaved maliciously and the opinion from the nodes with which it behaved benevolent. Direct service quality trust assessment and feedback propagation is used to avoid Self-promoting attacks. Credibility is used to avoid Bad-mouthing and Ballot stuffing attacks and quality trust assessment is used to remedy to Opportunistic service attacks. Distributed hash table are used for enhancing resiliency and scalability.

In [7] an access service recommendation scheme for efficient service composition and malicious attacks resistance in SIoT environments is proposed. To address issues in trustworthiness evaluation of SIoT services/devices including vulnerability, dynamic behavior, and resource restriction, they present a recommendation metric which integrated the timeliness properties of transactions and the social relationships between devices into the evaluation of access service in dynamic environment. An energy aware mechanism is also considered for workload balancing and network stability. The proposed approach permits to avoid Self-promoting and Bad-mouthing, Ballot stuffing. However, authors don't propose specific solutions for SIoT constraints such as scalability and limited storage and computational capacities. The presented works are classified and summarized in the Table 1.

Table 1. Classification of existing works based on SIoT network structure

	Human to Human social relationship	Object to Object social relationship
[5]		X
[6]		X
[13]	X	
[4]		X
[7]		X
[14]	X	
[15]		X

[14] proposed a trust service platform that offers trust evaluation of two any entities to SIoT services. Authors modulate the human trust information process and social relationship to create a trust model by incorporating three factors namely Reputation, Recommendation, and Knowledge. Recommendation represent surrounding suggestions (e.g. from friends, relatives, and colleagues) and reputation represent the global opinions on the trustee (e.g. ranking/ratings levels in public media). Knowledge is the information provided by trustee to evaluate its trustworthiness. Authors use ontology for representing user's knowledge which can be not suitable for limited resource objects. They don't explain how their protocol can face trust related attacks and don't propose solution to ensure the scalability of the SIoT network.

In [15], propose a trust model based on guarantor and reputation for SIoT environments. Every object has a reputation rating associated with it, which is stored in the object itself and which can only be updated by a reputation server. Agents are built into the objects to update the reputation. Objects are associated with their owners. If the owner buys a new object and associates it with oneself then that objects baseline reputation will be the same as other SIoT objects owned by the same person. The nodes use credits to get services. If a node provides the correct service then he is paid some credits as commission. If he acts maliciously then it has to give some credits to the other nodes as forfeit payment. The commission and forfeit rates act as guarantees for an objects behavior. This approach ensure scalability because information about objects are stroked in a distributed way. However, it consider only social relationship between human and attribute the same trust value for all objects owned by the same person. Limitation of storage and computing capacity of objects as well as energy consumption are not taken into account.

5.2 Discussion and Comparison

In the previous subsection, we review the majority of work in the area of trust management on SIoT environments. We also highlight their limits. In this section, we provide a classification of those related work based on specific criteria. In Table 1, We compare them based on the involved SIoT network structure. In Table 2, we classify them based on adopted trust properties. In Table 3, we compare their resiliency face to the different kinds of trust related attacks. In Table 4, we compare them based on their willingness to respond to the specific SIoT constraints. And finally, in Table 5, we classify them according to Trust-Model dimensions.

Table 2. Classification of existing works based trust properties

	Direct	Indirect	Local	Global	Subjective	Objective	Asymme tric	Composi te	Dynamic	Contextu al
[5]	X	X	X		X		X	X	X	
[6]	X	X	X	X	X		X	X	X	
[13]		X		X	X	X	X	X		X
[4]		X		X	X		X		X	
[7]		X	X	X			X			
[14]		X		X			X	X		
[15]	X	X		X	X		X	X		

Table 3. Classification of existing works based resiliency face to trust related attacks

	SPA	BMA	BSA	OSA	DA	WA
[5]	X	X	X			
[6]	X	X	X			
[13]	X	X	X			
[4]	X	X	X			
[7]	X	X	X			
[14]	X	X	X	X		X
[15]	X					

Table 4. Classification of existing works based on considered SIoT constraints

	Scalability	Adaptability	Power efficiency	Survivability	Resiliency
[5]	X	X			X
[6]	X	X			X
[13]	X	X			X
[4]	X				X
[7]					X
[14]					X
[15]				X	

Table 5. Classification of existing works based on trust model dimensions

	Trust composition		Trust propagation		Trust aggregation				Trust update	
	QoS T	Social T	D	C	BM	SWS	DWS	FL	E-d	T-d
[5]	X	X	X				X		X	
[6]	X	X	X				X		X	X
[13]	X	X	X		X				X	
[4]	X	X	X		X				X	
[7]	X	X	X				X		X	
[14]		X	X					X	X	
[15]		X						X	X	

This comparison allow us to state that there is many progress in the area of Trust Management in SIoT systems. However, the majority of related works simply apply the trust protocols used in traditional social networks. These protocols prove their efficiency face to trust related attacks. But, they don't take into account, the novel structure and the novel constraints related to SIoT. Scalability is partially ensured and power efficiency is practically ignored. The majority of related works consider either human to human social relationship or object to object social relationship. However both of them are implied in this environments. A trust management protocol which is specifically designed for SIoT systems is still required.

6   Conclusion

In this survey, we pointed out the importance of trust management in SIOT. We first expose an overview about the SIOT paradigm, its evolutions and its network structure. Second, we address the trust notion and its related concepts. We demonstrate its role in SIOT environments and present its main properties.

Third, we present the main trust related attacks cited in literature. Fourth, we expose a classification of SIOT trust models based on specific criteria. Then, we provide a literature review of trust models in Social Internet of Things. Finally, we discuss unsolved issues.

References

1. Atzori, L., Iera, A., Morabito, G.: Siot: giving a social structure to the internet of things. IEEE Commun. Lett. **15**(11), 1193–1195 (2011)
2. Atzori, L., Iera, A., Morabito, G.: From "smart objects" to "social objects": the next evolutionary step of the internet of things. IEEE Commun. Mag. **52**(1), 97–105 (2014)
3. Atzori, L., Iera, A., Morabito, G., Nitti, M.: The social internet of things (siot) when social networks meet the internet of things: concept, architecture and net-work characterization. Comput. Netw. **56**(16), 3594–3608 (2012)
4. Bao, F., Chen, I.R.: Dynamic trust management for internet of things applications. In: Proceedings of the 2012 International Workshop on Self-Aware Internet of Things, pp. 1–6. ACM (2012)
5. Bao, F., Chen, I.R., Guo, J.: Scalable, adaptive and survivable trust management for community of interest based internet of things systems. In: 2013 IEEE Eleventh International Symposium on Autonomous De-centralized Systems (ISADS), pp. 1–7. IEEE (2013)
6. Chen, R., Guo, J., Bao, F.: Trust management for soa-based iot and its application to service composition. IEEE Trans. Serv. Comput. **2**(1), 1 (2015)
7. Chen, Z., Ling, R., Huang, C.M., Zhu, X.: A scheme of access service recommendation for the social internet of things. Int. J. Commun. Syst. (2015)
8. Dey, A.K.: Understanding and using context. Pers. Ubiquit. Comput. **5**(1), 4–7 (2001)
9. Geetha, S.: Social internet of things. World Sci. News **41**, 76 (2016). Avinashilingam
10. Grandison, T., Sloman, M.: A survey of trust in internet applications. IEEE Commun. Surv. Tutorials **3**(4), 2–16 (2000)
11. Guo, J., Chen, R.: A classification of trust computation models for service-oriented internet of things systems. In: 2015 IEEE International Conference on Services Computing (SCC), pp. 324–331. IEEE (2015)
12. Kim, J.E.: Architecting social internet of things. Ph.D. thesis, University of Pittsburgh (2016)
13. Nitti, M., Girau, R., Atzori, L.: Trustworthiness management in the social internet of things. IEEE Trans. Knowl. Data Eng. **26**(5), 1253–1266 (2014)
14. Truong, N.B., Um, T.W., Lee, G.M.: A reputation and knowledge based trust service platform for trustworthy social internet of things. Innovations in Clouds, Internet and Networks (ICIN), Paris, France (2016)
15. Xiao, H., Sidhu, N., Christianson, B.: Guarantor and reputation based trust model for social internet of things. In: 2015 International Wireless Communications and Mobile Computing Conference (IWCMC), pp. 600–605. IEEE (2015)
16. Yan, Z., Holtmanns, S.: Trust modeling and management: from social trust to digital trust, pp. 290–323. IGI Global (2008)

Combating Misinformation Online: Identification of Variables and Proof-of-Concept Study

Milan Dordevic, Fadi Safieddine[✉], Wassim Masri, and Pardis Pourghomi

The American University of the Middle East, P.O.Box: 220, 15453 Dasman, Kuwait
{Milan.Dordevic,Fadi.Safiedinne,Wassim.Masri,
Pardis.Pourghomi}@aum.edu.kw

Abstract. The spread of misinformation online is specifically amplified by use of social media, yet the tools for allowing online users to authenticate text and images are available though not easily accessible. The authors challenge this view suggesting that corporations' responsible for the development of browsers and social media websites need to incorporate such tools to combat the spread of misinformation. As a step stone towards developing a formula for simulating spread of misinformation, the authors ran theoretical simulations which demonstrate the unchallenged spread of misinformation which users are left to authenticate on their own, as opposed to providing the users means to authenticate such material. The team simulates five scenarios that gradually get complicated as variables are identified and added to the model. The results demonstrate a simulation of the process as proof-of-concept as well as identification of the key variables that influence the spread and combat of misinformation online.

Keywords: Misinformation · Information · Simulation · Social media · Authentication

1 Introduction

The process by which information and misinformation travels online and specifically by social media users has been the subject of several publications [1–5]. The challenges in combating misinformation on social media could be greatly enhanced should researchers be able to simulate the different scenarios of information and misinformation cascades. Specifically here, researchers need to consider the factors involved in the travel of misinformation and the factors involved in combating the spread of misinformation. In this paper, the authors identify the factors that influence the travel of information and misinformation as both theoretically start from one single node and travel across a network of nodes and points. Variables are identified for which the authors develop a fuller picture of what influences the process, speed, and success pace of fighting misinformation online. In the process of identifying these variables, the team simulates five scenarios as new variables are identified with each simulation and added to the model.

© IFIP International Federation for Information Processing 2016
Published by Springer International Publishing Switzerland 2016. All Rights Reserved
Y.K. Dwivedi et al. (Eds.): I3E 2016, LNCS 9844, pp. 442–454, 2016.
DOI: 10.1007/978-3-319-45234-0_40

2 Literature Review

Oxford Internet Survey of 2013 results show online social networks as becoming one of the key sources of information and news especially among younger generations [6]. Thus, the spread of misinformation has increased as a result of the increase in the number of people using social networks [7]. Due to the lack of accountability of social media users spreading information and not having appropriate filtering techniques similar to reviewing and editing information in traditional publishing, social media have become a significant media for the spread of misinformation [4]. Thus, the spread of diverse forms of information, misinformation, and propaganda involves the distribution of false information through an information diffusion process involving users of social networks where the majority of users may not be attentive to the untruth story. In one study, researchers state that the acceptance of misleading information by the people greatly depends on their prior beliefs and opinions [8]. In another study [9], researchers state that the spread of misinformation in online social networks is context specific with topics such as health, politics, finances, theology, and technology trends are key sources of misinformation. People believe things which support their past thoughts without questioning them [10]. We have used the term misinformation to denote any type of false information spreading in social networks.

Considering the dark side of social networks, the environment facilitates the arrangement of groups and campaigns with the intention of undertaking unethical activities as well as mimicking widespread information diffusion behavior [4, 10]. Consequently, this facilitation of potential misconducts in online environments has encouraged some users to spread misinformation that results in greater support to cult-like views in a variety of topics [5]. What is more, those views are sometimes contagious and the individuals behind them make great efforts to spread them to others. The persistence of misinformation in the society is dangerous and requires analysis for its prevention and early detection [10–12]. The lack of accountability and verifiability however afford the users an excellent opportunity to spread specific ideas through the network while not discouraging freedom of expression and freedom of ideas [4].

In online social networks, the enormous distribution of data has resulted in persistent pockets of misinformation. Thus finding reliable information requires sifting-out the different types of misinformation in online social networks which has become a computationally puzzling task [10].

2.1 Related Work

In a research conducted by Lee et al. [1], the authors aimed at identifying and engaging "information propagators" which refers to people willing to help propagate information on social media. By modelling their characteristics and using that model to predict their willingness to propagate information in the future, the authors have been able to identify three characteristics of people willing to propagate information and misinformation online. These characteristics are: (1) personal traits of users such as personality and readiness to share or pass on that information; (2) the wait-time of a user based on the previous time lapses between passing on the information to predict the next time they share that information again; and (3) a recommender system based on the two previous components to select the right set of users with a high likelihood of Re-sharing of information. While the paper focuses on Twitter as an example, parallels could be drawn to other social media applications.

In a research conducted by Hoang and Lim [2], the authors aimed to identify and model factors that contribute to viral diffusion based on the interrelationships among items, users, and the user-user network. This time the team categorized these factors into two sets. The first set includes external factors such as advertising, while the second set includes internal factors such as: (a) Item virality which is the ability of an item to spread the adoptions by users through the follow links; (b) the virality of the users diffusing the item which is their ability to spread the adoptions to other users through the follow links; and (c) the susceptibility of the user adopting the item, which is the ability of a user to adopt items easily as other neighbouring users diffuse the items to others. The authors then proposed a Mutual Dependency Model that measures all three factors above simultaneously based on a set of principles that help to distinguish each property from others in viral diffusion.

In a research conducted by Jin et al. [3] the authors applied epidemiological modelling techniques to understand information diffusion on Twitter, in relation to the spread of both news and rumours. Epidemiological models are usually used to better understand how information diffuses by dividing users into several groups that reflect their statuses. The possible groups in which a user has been classified are: susceptible (S), exposed (E), infected (I), and recovered (R). Users could move from one group to another with a certain probability that could be estimated from data. Several models were introduced such as the SI model in which a susceptible (S) user can get infected (I) by one of his neighbours and will stay permanently in this state; SIS model where users can move back and forth between being (S) susceptible and (I) infected; the SIR model where users could move to a recover (R) state which is not really used to in news cascades models; and a model called SEIZ model (susceptible, exposed, infected, sceptic) proposed originally by Bettencourt et al. (2006) [13] which added a new state: exposed (E). Jin et al. (2013) suggested instead to represent the case where a user may take some time while in the exposed (E) state before believing a rumour (i.e. move to an infected (I) state).

For simulating spread of misinformation online, Budak et al. [4] presented a network algorithm that could be tested in case of two competing campaigns using two variations of the Independent Cascade Model (ICM) termed: (1) Multi-Campaign Independent Cascade Model (MCICM) and (2) Campaign-Oblivious Independent Cascade (COICM) to consider how information and misinformation spreads online. The paper, theoretically, relies on the design of the system itself and the input of 'influential' people to counter 'bad' campaign and limit misinformation. This could potentially be useful during time-sensitive political campaigns or breaking news events. Budak et al. acknowledge a limitation shared by other publications in this area when it comes to lab modelling of information diffusion acknowledging that lab models may not reflect the full extent of influences in real life. Thus, lab simulations will still need to be tested in the real world of social media [4] p. 667.

While previous work has provided important literature into the behaviour and challenges of spreading and combating misinformation online, there does not seem to be one uniform method to how the spread of information is modelled. Nor does there seem to be uniformed agreed method for modelling the spread of misinformation. In addition, despite repeated review of the literature, the team could not find any viable or applied proposal on how to combat the spread of misinformation online.

2.2   The 'Right-Click Authenticate' in Combating Misinformation Online

In a prior publication [5], the authors suggested an approach to combating misinformation on social media. The team proposed an automated approach, dubbed as 'Right-click Authenticate' option that could review, rank, and identify misinformation using tools already found online. However, these tools have not been combined together in a setup that helps online users in their pursuit of authentication of the information they view. Three categories of authentication have been identified: textual, imagery, and video misinformation, however the paper focused on the first two: Textual and imagery authentication. In that process, users who are unsure about the content could right-click and select authenticate as conceptualized in Fig. 1.

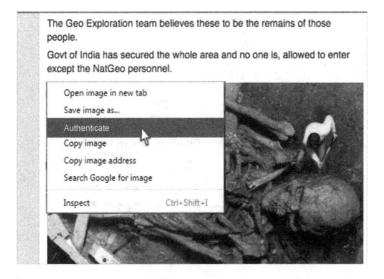

Fig. 1.   Conceptualizing a right-click 'Authenticate' option [5]

Using reverse image search [14], a search that requires the user to upload an image or copy the image's web address to search for matches to that actual image online, users are able to identify the sources and dates of the first appearances of that image online as well as the context in which the image is presented. Some of the highly refined reverse image searches are able to detect even modifications of the image including color tones changes, photo editing, cropping and writing made onto the original image. Second layer is to validate any meta-data linked with the questioned image including the camera used, date it was created, and what photo-editing tools have been used. Meta-data may also help detect if any image editing tools have been used [15, 16].

The third part is an editorial feedback written in the same format and style Wikipedia operates authentication of information [17] with regards to the authenticity of that image. Image editorial feedback is combine with explanations based on the origin, date, meta-data, where the image appears online, or article that dismisses or confirms that image. Finally, a crowdsourcing of feedback is represent the final indication on what the majority of users judging this information. These four sections are combined as: Image Match, Image Metadata, Editorial, and Feedback respectively. The solution is the bundling of these four sections into one single right-click option as conceptualized in Fig. 2. To ensure the successful results, the same algorithm used for online search engines to be used here. Thus, images that get frequently selected as a match to get higher ranking than those images that do not get selected as a match.

Fig. 2. Conceptualization of the 'Authenticate' outcome [5]

The right-click search authenticate option can also be used to authenticate a selection of news by title or text since the option to select and search text is already a well-established right-click search option on variety of browsers [5]. Another benefit for this right-click authenticate for images and text is that copyright infringements on intellectual rights are become more easily detected. In the paper, the authors acknowledge that new images and breaking news to require longer time to be authenticated. This proposal just based on theory and has not been simulated, implemented, or tested.

3 Research Questions and Methodology

The team acknowledges that the 'right-click authenticate' method for tackling the spread of misinformation needs to be demonstrated and proven as proof-of-concept. This paper attempts to further develop this theory to answer some key questions:

1. What variables are influencing the spread of information and misinformation on social media?
2. By means of simulation, can the process by which information and misinformation be modeled as proof-of-concept?

The team used graph theory computational simulation with observational research method [18]. In the process of identifying variables, the team used reflective analysis [19] to review progressively different scenarios in the spread of information and misinformation on social media. This approach is comparable to other approaches identified in the literature [1–4].

In lab conditions, the team observed the different two-dimensional simulations of information as it travelled from the source to a theoretical maximum reach. The two-dimensional simulation represents a slice of what a real-world multi-dimensional simulation of information would likely resemble. Successively analyzing and observing simulations of scenarios, the team subsequently evolved their model of simulation to identify and introduce new variables. With the introduction of new variables, a reflective analysis considered the logical impact of the new variable. Changes to the simulation and the justifications are then considered. While conducting the simulation, the team suggested values for such variables that are not based on any specific scenario or research, but solely for the purpose of facilitating a reflective analysis to re-evaluate the simulation and considering missing factors.

One of the main assumptions agreed at the start of the simulation is that the phenomena by which information and misinformation travels can be simulated despite unpredictability generally dominating human behavior online. This assumption is consistent with other academic publishers in this area of research. Without a preset of simulation scenario or the number of variables, the team developed five simulations and identified a total of ten variables. The demonstration, simulation, and identification of variables presented in this paper will be extended in further research aiming to design a formula by which success rate of combating misinformation online could be used for computational simulation.

4 Variables and Graph Modelling

Spread of misinformation in social networks can be modeled by using graph theory. The team considered a weighted directed graph $G = (V, E)$ consisting of V vertices and edges E. V can be viewed as the users of the social network. Among the vertices in V, the team distinguishes two types of vertices:

(1) Vertices which belong to set S, the set of sharing vertices, which represents users that send and receive information;

(2) Vertices which belong to set R, the set of reading vertices, which represents users who only receive information- accordingly $R \subseteq S$. A vertex r is a neighbor of a vertice s if and only if there is $e_{s,r} \in E$, an edge from r to s in G. Furthermore, all vertices from V can be divided into subsets (layers) depending on length l. Where $V = V_1 \cup V_2 \cup \ldots \cup V_l$ from Fig. 3.

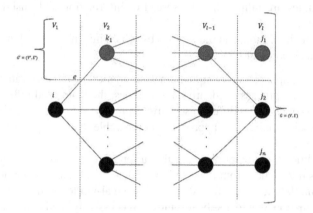

Fig. 3. Graph of misinformation modeling (Color figure online)

Assuming i and j are any vertices of the given graph, the vertices i and j_n are connected by certain chains of edges going through different layers. The main goal of the team's approach is to see the effect of cascade labeling in models that they created. Note that cascade labeling symbolizes pressing the Right-click 'Authenticate'.

As illustrated in Fig. 3, by selecting edge e, *where* $e \in E$, the entire sub graph G' from $k_1 \in V_2$ to $j_1 \in V_l$, where l stands for length, is colored in red. This step is known as cascade labeling. Subsequently, this cascade labeling results in coloring some of the vertices from G into red. Coloring in red symbolizes the node authentication of the information to be untrue and the exclusion of sharing misinformation. The authors assume that pressing the 'Right-click Authenticate' can happen more than once in a demonstrated model.

Given graph G by sequentially repeating the cascade labeling process i.e. pressing the 'Right-click Authenticate' button, the number of vertices colored in red increases while the number of vertices colored in black decreases.

Since selecting an edge e results in coloring some vertices of sub graph G' into red, repeating the same process on any other edge from E in a graph G will result in coloring some more vertices into red.

Eventually, after n repetitions of this process in graph G, all vertices from subset V_l can be colored in red. Therefore, by implying cascade labeling procedure, some of the destination vertices $j_1, j_2, \ldots, j_n$ will be preserved of receiving misinformation.

The model in Fig. 3 is assuming that only one vertex authenticates the information and passes that information on. The first vertex to authenticate and turn from black to

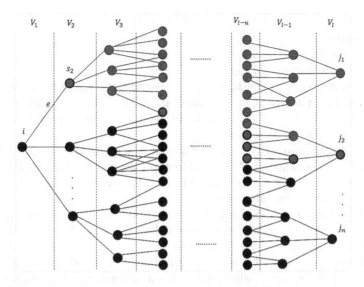

Fig. 4. Extended graph of misinformation modeling (Color figure online)

red is modeled as red with black line and labeled as vertex $s_2 \in S_2$, where $S_2 \subseteq V_2$. The extended version of that model is shown in Fig. 4.

In the next scenario, the team studied next three variables that need to be considered in combating misinformation online: rate of authentication, rate of sharing, and rate of cross-wire.

The rate of Authentication (A) is a variable that represents the rate of users willing to authenticate the information. This usually occurs when online users are not sure of an information or when they get conflicting information. Thus, these users might decide to authenticate such information to start a correction cascade or at least stop the cascade of misinformation from their part.

The rate of Authentication (A) could be anything between 0 and 100 %; although the team acknowledges it is unlikely to be either extreme. For the simulation in Fig. 5, the team predicts that the percentage of users who will authenticate to be around 30 %. Thus for the simulation purposes, the team have assumed the probability of authentication as $A = 0.3$.

The passing on Rate (P) is a variable that represents the ratio of users who read the information and then perform an action of actively disseminate it further. Thus, the ratio shows the probability that vertex which authenticate will pass that correct information to anyone else as well as the ratio of those vertex that pass on misinformation.

The synonyms used for passing on rate are average of forwarding, liking, and sharing rate. We assume that the rate of willingness to share is probably the same for those who believe the misinformation. To demonstrate this scenario, the team assumed the probability of sharing information by online users regardless they believe it or not to be $P = 0.5$. Although if the research determines differences in sharing between those who believe and those who do not believe the information, variations of this variable could be created as P_1 for those who believe the information to be true and P_o for those who do not believe it.

The Cross-Wire (Cw) is a variable that represents the probability that user who received different information from different sources will react to validate. In such a case, online users exposed to misinformation are sufficiently skeptical to question it and use the 'Right-click Authenticate' to validate it. In Fig. 5 vertex c_1 received different information from sources a and b and accept the information received from a while discard the misinformation received from b.

For the purpose of simulation, the team assumed $Cw = 0.3$. The simulation in Fig. 5 shows the usage of variables A, P and Cw. Moreover, the figure shows how the speed of misinformation spread is slowed down compared to the scenario in Fig. 4 and again for those who authenticate the information.

As demonstrated in Fig. 5, providing means of authentication can have important impact on the spread of misinformation online. Red nodes are shown to be playing a role in limiting the spread of misinformation.

For the next simulation, the team considers Same Level Communication (Sl) as a variable that represents the probability that users who authenticate information and leave feedback encourages other users from the same level also to authenticate. That includes passing on vertices on the same level thus turning several of these vertices from black to red. For example, in Fig. 6, vertices c_1 and c_2 have validated the misinformation. Provided c_1 or c_2 left a feedback, this turns the remaining vertices from black to red. The same happens to $c_3, c_4,$ and c_5.

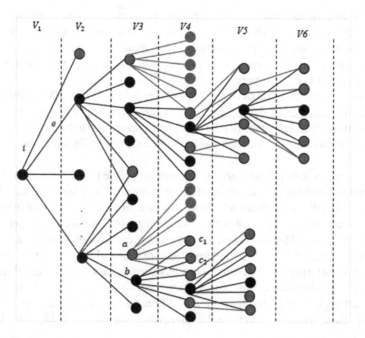

Fig. 5. The authenticate, passing on rate, and cross-wire rate simulation (Color figure online)

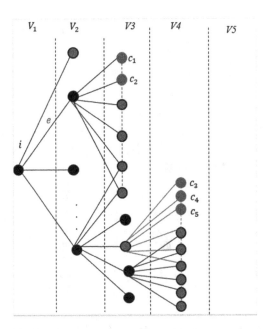

Fig. 6. Reverse validation (*Rv*). (Color figure online)

The team assumes that all other variables and assumptions are kept in place.

A vertex that is red or just turned red with probability 0.5 will alert other online users that the information is not true. In such scenario, the team assumes that other vertices will, in turn, discard the misinformation and turn into red. The reason behind this assumption is that the first online user to authenticate has a greater impact on subsequence online users. So the team assumed that probability of Same Level Communication is $Sl = 1$.

Considering the rate of authentication A, passing on information rate P, average cross-wire rate Cw, success rate of Same Level communication rate Sl, where $A = 0.3$, $P = 0.5$, $Cw = 0.3$, and $Sl = 1$ respectively, excluding misinformation does not extend beyond V_4. The simulation of this scenario specific lab scenario, demonstrated in Fig. 6, where at level V_4 all vertices are red.

For the final simulation, the authors have considered Reverse Validation (*Rv*) Variable. *Rv* represents a probability that the user who initially believed the misinformation, while being informed by other users through their feedback that the information is not true, either removes the post or rectify the post, thus turning red node themselves. However, to differentiate them from other red node, the team decided to label such node green. This is a backflow to a previous or source vertex. The output of applying the *Rv*, is shown in Fig. 7 as green vertices. The team considered this final variable at probability that the source vertex will take action to rectify the misinformation as $Rv = 0.5$.

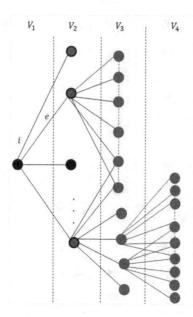

Fig. 7. Same level communication (*Sl*) (Color figure online)

5   Results and Limitations

The combinations of all these variables and the assumptions that the team made to understand how combating misinformation works has resulted in identifying some key variables where i is the first vertex and j_n is the last vertex of the given simulation. V_1 represents the first phase of spread of misinformation and l represents the maximum possible reach of information through the network. The authors conclude that combating misinformation online is also be influenced by the following variables: rate of authentication A, passing on information rate P, average cross-wire rate Cw, success rate of Same Level communication rate Sl, and Reverse Validation rate Rv. Thus the paper demonstrates by means of simulation how misinformation travels online. The paper also shows how 'right-click authenticate' process can reduce the spread of misinformation online. Thus suggesting a viable solution for combating misinformation online by identifying and demonstrating key variables and factors.

The proof-of-concept has been constrained with assumptions that are based mostly on observations of computer simulation and reflective analysis subjective to individual experiences of the team. However, the approach has been backed by similar observations done in other academic publications [1–3]. The team acknowledges that the proposed variables may not be exclusive, and that further research may reveal additional factors influencing the travel of information and the means of combating misinformation online. Furthermore, the identification of the variables is lab based and further proof should be drawn from examples from existent event observations once the formula is developed. This is a limitation acknowledged in the literature when it comes to lab modeling as opposed to real life simulation [4]. The 'right-click authenticate' process has two key limitations in application and implementation [5]. In application, the authors acknowledge that the 'authentication' option has little or no real impact at authenticating breaking news. For the process to work, time is needed for the information or image to be authenticated and a review written. For the implementation limitation, the building of the 'right-click authenticate' option requires authorization and collaboration from a reverse image search engine, which may not be forth coming.

6   Conclusion

The team set out to demonstrate a proof-of-concept and identified the variables involved in the travel of information and the 'Right-click Authenticate' idea suggested in a previous publication [5]. The team believes that some headway has been achieved but that still work to be done to develop the formula and conduct simulations to further validate the concept. Two parallel lines of further research are expected to follow. First, the team will be working towards developing the formula and run computational simulations of the formula using MATLAB and BioLayout Express for three dimensional simulation. Second and equally important, the team intend to develop a prototype browser based on an existing open source applications that allows demonstration of the concept and the running of actual simulations thus allowing lab and field simulations.

References

1. Lee, K., Mahmud, J., Chen, J., Zhou, M., Nichols, J.: Who will retweet this? automatically identifying and engaging strangers on twitter to spread information. In: The 19th international conference on Intelligent User Interfaces, pp. 247–256. ACM (2014)
2. Hoang, T.A., Lim, E.P.: Virality and susceptibility in information diffusions. In: ICWSM (2012)
3. Jin, F., Dougherty, E., Saraf, P., Cao, Y., Ramakrishnan, N.: Epidemiological modeling of news and rumors on twitter. In: Proceedings of the 7th Workshop on Social Network Mining and Analysis, p. 8. ACM (2013)
4. Budak, C., Agrawal, D., El Abbadi, A.: Limiting the spread of misinformation in social networks. In: Proceedings of the 20th International Conference on World Wide Web, pp. 665–674. ACM (2011)
5. Safieddine, F., Masri, W., Pourghomi, P.: Corporate responsibility in combating online misinformation. Int. J. Adv. Comput. Sci. Appl. (IJACSA) 7(2), 126–132 (2016)
6. Dutton, W.H., Blank, G., Gorseli, D.: Cultures of the internet: the internet in britain. Oxford Internet Survey 2013 Report, University of Oxford (2013)
7. World Economic Forum Report.: Top 10 trends of 2014: the rapid spread of misinformation online (2014)
8. Libicki, M.C.: Conquest in Cyberspace: National Security and Information Warfare. Cambridge University Press, New York (2007)
9. Karlova, N.A., Fisher, K.E.: Plz RT: a social diffusion model of misinformation and disinformation for understanding human information behaviour. Inf. Res 18(1), 1–17 (2013)
10. Kumar, K.K., Geethakumari, G.: Detecting misinformation in online social networks using cognitive psychology. Hum. Centric Comput. Inf. Sci. 4(1), 1–22 (2014)

11. Lewandowsky, S., Ecker, U.K., Seifert, C.M., Schwarz, N., Cook, J.: Misinformation and its correction continued influence and successful debiasing. Psychol. Sci. Public Interest **13**(3), 106–131 (2012)

12. De Neys, W., Cromheeke, S., Osman, M.: Biased but in doubt: conflict and decision condence. PLoSONE **6**, e15954 (2011)

13. Bettencourt, L.M., Cintrón-Arias, A., Kaiser, D.I., Castillo-Chávez, C.: The power of a good idea: Quantitative modeling of the spread of ideas from epidemiological models. Phys. A Stat. Mech. Appl. **364**, 513–536 (2006)

14. Martin, J.: How to do a reverse Google Image search on Android or iPhone. PC Advisor (online) (2016)

15. Buchholz, F.: On the role of file system metadata in digital forensics. Digit. Invest. **1**(4), 298–309 (2004)

16. Castiglione, A., Cattaneo, G., De Santis, A.: A forensic analysis of images on online social networks. In: IEEE Conference, pp. 679–684 (2011)

17. Wikipedia Contributors.: Wikipedia: Version 1.0 Editorial Team. Wikipedia, The Free Encyclopedia. https://en.wikipedia.org/wiki/Wikipedia:Version_1.0_Editorial_Team/ Assessment

18. Osmond, J., Darlington, Y.: Reflective analysis: techniques for facilitating reflection. Aust. Soc. Work **58**, 3–14 (2015)

19. Altmann, J.: Observational study of behavior: sampling methods. Behaviour **49**(3), 227–266 (1974)

Breaking Anonymity of Social Network Accounts by Using Coordinated and Extensible Classifiers Based on Machine Learning

Eina Hashimoto[1], Masatsugu Ichino[1], Tetsuji Kuboyama[2],
Isao Echizen[3], and Hiroshi Yoshiura[1(✉)]

[1] University of Electro-Communications, Tokyo, Japan
{e-hashimoto,yoshiura}@uec.ac.jp
[2] Gakushuin University, Tokyo, Japan
[3] National Institute of Informatics, Tokyo, Japan

Abstract. A method for de-anonymizing social network accounts is presented to clarify the privacy risks of such accounts as well as to deter their misuse such as by posting copyrighted, offensive, or bullying contents. In contrast to previous de-anonymization methods, which link accounts to other accounts, the presented method links accounts to resumes, which directly represent identities. The difficulty in using machine learning for de-anonymization, i.e. preparing positive examples of training data, is overcome by decomposing the learning problem into subproblems for which training data can be harvested from the Internet. Evaluation using 3 learning algorithms, 2 kinds of sentence features, 238 learned classifiers, 2 methods for fusing scores from the classifiers, and 30 volunteers' accounts and resumes demonstrated that the proposed method is effective. Because the training data are harvested from the Internet, the more information that is available on the Internet, the greater the effectiveness of the presented method.

Keywords: Social network · Privacy · de-anonymization · re-identification

1 Introduction

Online social networks enrich human communication. They are used not only for communication among friends and family members but also for job hunting, marketing, branding, and political communication such as among political activists. On the other hand, they can reveal personal information and cause privacy problems. They can also reveal confidential information and enable posting of copyrighted, offensive, or bullying contents.

To mitigate the privacy problems, social network services provide mechanisms that enable users to limit the disclosure of posted content (text, photos, etc.) to friends, followers, etc. However, because defining an appropriate disclosure range for each post is cumbersome [1], users tend to use the same range for all their posts, resulting in too much disclosure for sensitive content and/or unnecessarily limited disclosure for less sensitive content. Furthermore, disclosure by friends and followers, such as retweets, is a big loophole in disclosure control. Another approach to privacy protection is

Y.K. Dwivedi et al. (Eds.): I3E 2016, LNCS 9844, pp. 455–470, 2016.
DOI: 10.1007/978-3-319-45234-0_41

anonymizing social network accounts. Users omit, change, or obscure identifying and pseudo-identifying information, such as name, age, address, affiliation, face, in their posts and profiles so that only friends can recognize the poster. Such anonymization is widely used in Japanese social networks for example [2].

The anonymization approach can be compromised, however, by linking an anonymized account to an account in another social network. For example, Narayanan and Shmatikov showed that accounts in two social networks used by the same person can be identified by finding similar social graphs in the two networks [3]. Goga et al. also identified accounts used by the same person by comparing location information and time stamps attached to posts and writing styles [4]. Almishari et al. and Narayanan et al. also pursued the same objective by using machine learning to compare writing styles [5, 6]. Their methods, however, are indirect because they simply link accounts and/or blogs—knowing that account-1 and account-2 are used by the same person does not directly reveal the person's identity.

In contrast, we have developed a method that links a social network account to a resume, which directly represents a person. Given social network accounts and resumes, the method matches accounts to resumes. Because most organizations, e.g. companies, universities, and public institutions, have resumes or resume-like information for their members, and governments have similar information on residents, the proposed method has generality.

Our research thus clarifies a serious privacy risk; that is, persons of concern to organizations and governments can be identified and their freedom of speech can be suppressed. Besides clarifying a privacy risk, the proposed method can be used for protective purposes. It can be used to identify a person in an organization who misuses a social network (e.g. by revealing confidential information or posting copyrighted contents). It does this by linking the misused account to a candidate resume.

Although our method uses machine learning as did previous research, we encountered a difficulty in preparing training data that did not arise in the previous research. Almishari's method, for example, uses a naïve Bayes classifier to learn writing styles of texts posted from one account [5]. It then identifies texts posted from another account that has similar writing styles, and that account is considered to probably be used by the same person. The training data for Almishari's method are texts posted from the first account, which are not difficult to obtain. The training data for Narayanan's method, which identifies blogs posted by the same person, are not difficult to obtain either [6]. Preparing training data for these methods is not difficult because the linking falls into a particular pattern, i.e. learning features of texts and identifying other texts having similar features. However, preparing training data is not easy if the linking falls outside this pattern.

Our problem of linking an account to a resume does not fall into the pattern. Our method could learn writing styles of texts posted from the account but cannot identify a resume by using the learned writing styles. This is because a resume is not conventional text consisting of sentences but a list of keywords that represents characteristics of the person.

To overcome this difficulty, we use machine learning to implement a component classifier for each characteristic described in the resume, e.g. a component classifier for whether a social network account is used by a person whose hobby is dancing and one for whether the account is used by a person who is a computer engineer. We then compose a classifier for the resume itself by combining these component classifiers and use this classifier to determine whether an account is used by the resume owner. We can search the Internet for social network accounts that have specific characteristics (hobby of dancing) and use the text from them as training data for learning the component classifiers.

This work makes three contributions to social network privacy.

(1) In contrast to previous methods, our proposed method links social network accounts directly to identities by linking them to resumes, which are held by most organizations and governments. It revealed a privacy risk more serious than that revealed in previous research and can be widely used to deter misuse of social networks.

(2) We overcome a difficulty in preparing training data, which most previous research did not encounter, by decomposing the learning problem into subproblems for which we can harvest training data from the Internet.

(3) The greater the amount of information available from the Internet, the greater the amount of training data, which makes our proposed method more effective.

2 Related Work

Much work has been done on extracting personal information from social networks. Earlier work mainly focused on estimating users' sensitive information by using keyword and graph matching with heuristic algorithms. In 2007, Backstrom et al. de-anonymized anonymous social network accounts by searching the social network for subgraphs of known human relationships and identifying the subgraphs' nodes that represented users and friends [7]. In 2008, Lam et al. correctly estimated the first names of 72 % of the users of a social network and the full names of 30 % of the users by keyword-matching analysis of comments from friends [8]. In 2011, Mao et al. identified tweets containing sensitive information about travel and medical conditions with 76 % precision and tweets posted under drinking with 84 % precision by using learning algorithms of naïve Bayes and support vector machine (SVM) [9]. The training data were tweets that had been labelled by hand as either sensitive or non-sensitive. In 2012, Kótyuk and Buttyan estimated age, gender, and marital status, which were not disclosed in the user profiles, from disclosed parts of the profiles, friend information, and user group memberships by using learning algorithms of neural networks [10]. In 2014, Caliskan-Islam et al. used naïve Bayes and AdaBoost to classify users into three levels of revealing private information [13].

Recent related work has generally focused on linking a target account or post with another account or post. In 2009, Narayanan et al. reported a linking method based on subgraph matching that had been used to link the Twitter and Flicker accounts of the same users with an error rate of 12 % [3]. In 2010, Polakis et al. reported a method for linking the names of social network users to their e-mail addresses [11] and used it to match 43 % of the user profiles extracted from Facebook to the user e-mail addresses. In 2012, Goga et al. proposed a method for identifying users who used different social networks (Yelp, Twitter, Flickr, and Twitter) by analysing and combining the features of geo-location, timestamp, and writing styles from their posts [4]. In the same year, Narayanan used several machine learning algorithms including SVM and linear discriminant analysis to identify blogs posted by the same person [6]. In 2014, as mentioned above, Almishari et al. used a naïve Bayes classifier to identify Twitter accounts used by the same person [5].

3   Linking Social Network Account to Resume

3.1   Representative Application

Given social network accounts and resumes, our method identifies pairs of matching accounts and resumes, thus linking accounts to resumes, which represent identities. A representative application of our method is use by a company that finds that posts from an anonymous social network account include objectionable content such as content criticizing the company or exposing company wrongdoing. The company determines whether the account belongs to an employee by calculating the linkability between the account and each resume it holds and assuming the most linkable resume probably represents the target person, whom the company may punish.

Note that a company obtains a person's resume when the person joins the company and maintains it. Additional information about salary, promotions, changes in job, family members, addresses, etc. are collected over time. Here we refer to all this information simply as "resume".

3.2   Difficulty in Using Machine Learning

One of the biggest challenges in using machine learning is preparing the training data because the effectiveness of the learning critically depends on that data. As mentioned in Sect. 1, previous methods, which link accounts and/or blogs, learn writing styles of texts (posted from an account or included in a set of blogs) and identify texts posted from another account or included in another set of blogs that have similar writing styles [5, 6]. Training data for these methods are text at hand and are not difficult to prepare. In the method proposed by Kótyuk and Buttyan, learned correlations between disclosed attributes (age, gender, marital status, number of friends, language used, etc.) are used to infer undisclosed attributes [10]. The training data for this method are attributes disclosed in profiles and texts on social networks and are not difficult to obtain.

However preparing training data is not always that easy. Mao used known sensitive and non-sensitive tweets as positive and negative examples of training data. Because these training data are manually labelled "sensitive" or "non-sensitive" [9], preparing the training data is time consuming. Mao's method therefore does not work on a large scale and requires manual preparation of training data whenever it is used for new kinds of sensitive tweets (ones related to income, addresses, drug use, etc.). Caliskan-Islam et al. mitigated this problem by socially outsourcing the labelling task [13]. They did not solve the problem, however, because the time and effort needed were not reduced but simply shifted from the researchers to outsourced workers. Hart et al. used corpora for training data [14], but time and effort are needed to prepare such corpora.

Preparing training data is much more difficult for our problem in which an anonymized social network account is linked to a resume. Our method could learn writing styles of texts posted from the account but cannot identify a resume by using the learned writing styles because a resume is not a conventional text consisting of sentences. The use of outsourced workers is not an option because the training data could not be labelled by such workers. We overcome this difficulty as described in the next section.

3.3 Our Method Using Machine Learning

A resume consists of pairs of attributes and attribute values, for example, gender = female, current address = "Chofu city, Tokyo", hometown address = Osaka, affiliation = Company A, educational history = "Ph.D. from Tokyo Univ. in 2000, Master's degree from Kyoto Univ. in 1997, etc.", and hobbies = "dancing, painting". The attribute values represent the characteristics of the owner of the resume. We use machine learning to implement a component classifier for each attribute value. For example, we implement a classifier for determining whether a social network account is used by a woman[1], one for determining whether the account is used by a person from Osaka (based on Osaka dialect), and one for a person with dancing as a hobby.

We then compose a classifier for the resume itself by combining the component classifiers for all the attribute values on the resume. This classifier is used to determine whether an account is used by the owner of the resume, i.e. a person having all attribute values on the resume. The number of component classifiers used for the resume classifier depends on the number of attribute values on the resume. The score for the resume classifier is the aggregation of the scores of the component classifiers.

Given social network accounts and resumes, our method identifies matching accounts and resumes as follows (Fig. 1).

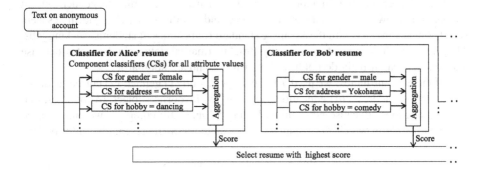

Fig. 1. Proposed model for de-anonymization

---

(1) Implement component classifiers for all attribute values on resumes.
(2) Compose a classifier for each resume.
(3) Obtain text posted on each social network account.
(4) Input the text from each account into the classifier for each resume. Then output the classifier score for each resume for each account. Each score represents how likely the account is used by the resume owner.
(5) For each account, the resume with the highest classifier score is selected. The selected resume is assumed to represent the account owner.

Effective component classifiers can be implemented for gender and address attributes as shown in [15, 16]. It may also be possible to implement component classifiers for other attributes as did Pennacchiotti et al. for political affiliation, ethnicity, and coffee brand preference [17]. Collecting positive examples of training data is automatized by using a tool such as TwiPro [12], which searches the Internet for social network accounts for which the user profile includes a given attribute value (e.g. hobby = dancing). This search works for most attribute values though the tool cannot collect a sufficient number of accounts for unusual attribute values such as "hobby = cooking eel". Collecting negative examples of training data is easier—the same tool is used to search for social network accounts for which the user profile does not include a given attribute value.

4   Data Description

4.1   Sample Data from Volunteers

Hereafter we abbreviate "social network account" as "account". We obtained Twitter accounts and resumes from 30 volunteers attending our university. Table 1 shows their demographics. The tweets and resumes were originally written in Japanese and are translated into English here.

The volunteer resumes included 12 attributes such as name, birthdate, gender, current address, hometown address, educational history, and qualifications. These attributes were selected in accordance with the Japanese standard for resumes of students' seeking jobs. They do not include job history or family structure (marital status, children, etc.) because students in Japan usually do not have job histories and are not married.

Of these 12 attributes, we used 7 in our experiment: (1) gender, (2) current address, (3) hometown address, (4) educational history, (5) favourite subject, (6) hobbies, and (7) qualifications. Because educational history is generally complex, we simply used the departments in which the volunteers were studying as representative information.

Table 1.   Volunteer demographics

(a) Gender		(b) Age				(c) School year			(d) Department		
Male	Female	20	21	22	23	2nd	3rd	4th	Informatics	Electronics	Machanical engineering
20	10	10	14	5	1	4	21	5	24	2	4

We also obtained access to the Twitter accounts of the 30 volunteers and to their tweets. The number of tweets obtained from each account ranged from 2167 to 3000 (2771 on average). All of the account profiles and tweets were anonymized by the volunteers themselves, who omitted, changed, or obscured identifying and pseudo-identifying information. In the evaluation described in Sect. 6, the number of tweets for the test data was 2771 (all tweets), 1000, 250, 60, or 15 per account. Among the previous methods mentioned in Sect. 2, the method of Almishari et al. [5] is most similar to ours because it uses tweets for linking but is different in that it matches writing styles while our method matches attribute values. Almishari et al. used 100, 50, 20, 10, or 5 tweets per account for their test data. We used more test data because attribute values (e.g. dancing as a hobby) do not often appear in tweets while writing style can be observed in a few tweets.

For these data, the sample problem in our experiment was to match the 30 Twitter accounts to the 30 resumes. Although this is a small problem, it was sufficiently difficult to evaluate our method. We therefore used it for an initial evaluation. The problem is difficult because the resumes were very similar, so the classifiers were provided with little information. For example, all the volunteers were undergraduate students at the same university and were in one of three departments (informatics, electronics, or mechanical engineering), which are in neighbouring buildings. Their current addresses are close to the university and close to each other. The Informatics and Electronics Departments share many subjects such as computer architecture, programming, and signal processing. The Electronics and Mechanical Engineering Departments also share many subjects, and the Informatics and Mechanical Engineering Departments share some basic subjects such as physics. The volunteers therefore had similar educational experiences. Their daily schedules were also similar. They were similar in age and school year as well, and none of them were married or had job histories.

The problem derived from the representative application described in Sect. 3.1, i.e. a company is to identify an employee of concern, is larger in scale but is probably easier to solve. The resumes of employees include much more information because employees are different in terms of job history, position, salary, and family structure while the resumes of the student volunteers did not include such information at all. Employees have different daily schedule depending on their job and more qualifications than students. Their ages have a wider range, and their addresses vary greatly if they work in different parts of the company that are in different geographic areas.

4.2   Training Data

We obtained training data by using TwiPro [12], as mentioned in Sect. 3.3. For positive examples of training data, we collected tweets from 30 random Twitter accounts, each having more than 1000 posted tweets, and used up to the latest 3000 tweets from each account. For the attribute values on a resume for which we could not collect data from the 30 accounts, we used data from as many accounts as possible as long as we could collect data from at least ten accounts. Otherwise, we did not implement a classifier for that attribute value. Negative examples of training data were similarly prepared.

5 Preliminary Experiment

We carried out a preliminary experiment to identify the attributes in the resumes most effective for the linking and the sentence features that should be extracted from tweets as well as to test the machine learning algorithms and methods for aggregating the component classifier scores. We evaluated all attributes on the resumes and evaluated bag-of-words (frequency of words appearing in tweets) and binary (appearance or non-appearance of words) models for feature extraction. Random Forest, linear SVM, and logistic regression were tested as the learning algorithm for component classifiers.

When texts from M accounts are input into N component classifiers, M vectors consisting of N scores are output, each of which represents an account. Machine learning could also be used to generate resume classifiers that classify these N-dimensional vectors in accordance with the resumes. However the implementation of such learning needs more research because training data are sparse in a high dimensional learning space[2]. We therefore used simple score fusion methods to generate resume classifiers for the experiments described here. That is, we used the score average and score product from the component classifiers to clarify the viability of our approach. The use of machine learning algorithms (e.g. SVM, Random Forest, and boosting) will be studied in future work.

Table 2. Attributes and values used for preliminary experiment

Volunteer	Gender	Current address	Hometown address	Department	Favourite subjects	Hobbies	Qualifications
1	F	City A, Kanagawa	City E, Saitama	Informatics	Programming	Comedian, Audrey, eye glasses	Driving license
2	F	City A, Kanagawa	County F, Nagano	Informatics	German	Playing piano, piano circle	Driving license
3	F	City B, Tokyo	City B, Tokyo	Electronics	Physical exercise, music, mathematics	Martial arts of Aikido, basketball, music, reading, baking sweets	Driving license
4	M	City C, Kanagawa	City C, Kanagawa	Mechanical engineering	Plastic & cutting processing	Robot mechatronics, engineering circle	Driving license
5	M	City D, Tokyo	City G, Hokkaido	Informatics	Art	Tennis, futsal, watching TV, football	Driving license, sales representative, financial planner
6	M	City D, Tokyo	City H, Aomori	Electronics	Electronic circuits, electromagnetics, web design, programming	Baseball, baseball circle, watching social network	–

---

[2] For example, there are 119 attribute values in the 30 sample resumes mentioned in Sect. 4.1, so we have only 30 samples in 119-dimensional space.

5.1   Sample Data

In the preliminary experiment, we used sample data for three of the female and three of the male volunteers. Table 2 shows the attributes and attribute values extracted from their resumes (city names have been anonymized for privacy). There were 7 attributes and 46 unique attribute values. We implemented only 40 component classifiers as we could not obtain a sufficient number of positive examples of training data for 6 of them (the underlined values). We used all tweets of the 6 volunteers for the test data.

5.2   Calibration

The scores for the component classifiers were calibrated using the following formula before fusion by averaging. We do not explain the rationale for using this formula because it is standard in data analysis and other researchers of de-anonymization (e.g. Narayanan [6]) have used it.

$$\alpha_{ij} = \frac{x_{ij} - \overline{x_j}}{\sigma_j} \tag{1}$$

where M and N are the number of accounts and number of component classifiers, respectively. They were set to 6 and 40 for the preliminary experiment. The x_{ij} is the original score of the j-th component classifier calculated for the i-th account, where $1<=i<=M$ and $1<=j<=N$. Note that the j-the component classifier was implemented with respect to the j-th attribute value. The α_{ij} is the calibrated value of x_{ij}, and $\overline{x_j}$ and σ_j are, respectively, the average and standard deviation of x_{ij} over $1<=i<=M$.

5.3   Results

Figure 2 shows the distribution of scores for the component classifiers with the bag-of-words model used for the sentence features and Random Forest used as the learning algorithm. The horizontal axis represents the component classifier for each attribute value. The vertical axis represents the value of the calibrated scores. The distribution of the M scores calculated using a classifier is represented by a box, lines above and below the box, and dots. The left most ones, for example, represent the score distribution of the classifier for "current address = City A in Kanagawa". The box represents the scores between the lower and upper quartiles of the distribution (i.e. 50 % of the scores). The two lines above and below the box represent the top and bottom 25 % of the scores, and the two dots represent the scores for the two accounts belonging to the two volunteers who actually live at this address. Thus, the higher the dots, the more correct the classifier.

Table 3 shows the rankings of the accounts that actually had the corresponding attributes (shown by dots in Fig. 2). The rankings were averaged over each sentence feature, algorithm, and attribute. For example, the average of the six classifier scores represented by dots for the current address attribute in Fig. 2 was 3.83, which is shown in the corresponding (upper-left) cell in Table 3. The smaller the value of the average

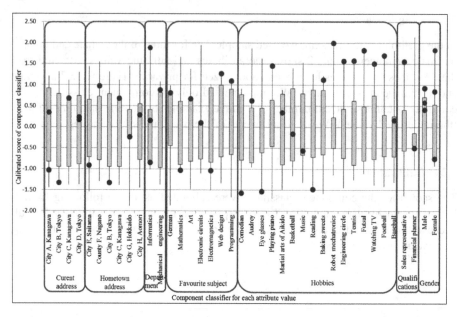

Fig. 2. Score distribution of component classifiers with bag-of-words and Random Forest

Table 3. Ranking of accounts that actually had corresponding attributes

Feature	Learning algorithm	Current address	Hometown address	Department	Favourite subjects	Hobbies	Qualifications	Gender	Average over all attributes	Average over 4 attributes
Bag-of-words	Random Forest	3.83	3.83	2.75	2.86	2.75	3.00	2.67	3.17	2.76
	Linear SVM	3.50	2.83	3.00	1.86	2.88	2.00	2.00	2.68	2.43
	Logistic regression	3.33	3.00	3.00	2.14	2.69	2.00	2.00	2.69	2.46
Binary	Random Forest	3.50	2.67	4.00	3.43	3.13	4.50	3.50	3.54	3.51
	Linear SVM	3.17	3.67	2.75	3.14	4.06	2.00	4.00	3.13	3.49
	Logistic regression	3.83	3.50	4.00	3.86	3.13	5.50	2.83	3.97	3.45

ranking, the more correct the score of the component classifier. Note that the expected value for ranking is 3.5 because there are six possible rankings (1 through 6). From Table 3, we can see that bag-of-word was a better model than binary and, when we focus on rankings in bag-of-word model, we can see that the attributes most effective for de-anonymization were department, favourite subject, hobbies, and gender.

We therefore considered 12 cases: one of the three learning algorithms (Random Forest, linear SVM, or logistic regression), all attributes or the four most effective attributes (department, favourite subject, hobbies, and gender), and fusion by average or by product with the bag-of-words model used for the sentence features. Table 4 shows the results for the first case (Random Forest, all attributes, and average). The classifier scores in Table 4 were calibrated again using the method described in Sect. 5.2. The highest score in each row is shown in bold italic and, positioning on the

Table 4. Resume classifier scores for case of random forest, all attributes, and average

		Resume no.					
		1	2	3	4	5	6
	1	-1.8772	-1.8091	-1.7393	-0.6563	-0.5510	*-0.2724*
	2	0.5327	*1.4159*	1.2572	0.4543	0.0738	-0.2863
Account	3	-0.7332	*0.0897*	-0.5668	-1.3735	-1.6809	-1.5570
no.	4	0.7635	0.4048	0.9986	*1.8512*	0.7651	1.7652
	5	0.9798	0.4715	0.2185	-0.0616	*1.5058*	-0.1729
	6	0.3344	-0.5728	-0.1682	-0.2141	-0.1128	*0.5234*

diagonal (shaded cells) indicates that the account was correctly linked to the resume of the account owner. Four accounts were correctly linked here.

Table 5 shows the number of times the correct resume (i.e. the resume of the account owner) was ranked top or second for each case. The best cases were (a) Random Forest - all attributes – average, (b) Random Forest – four effective attributes – product, (c) Logistic regression – all attributes – average, and (d) Logistic regression – four effective attributes –average, which we will evaluate in detail in the next section.

Table 5. Number of times correct resume was ranked first or second

Learning algorithm	Attributes	Fusion method	First	Second
Random Forest	all	product	2	1
		average	4	1
	Department, favourite subject, hobbies, gender	product	4	1
		average	3	1
Linear SVM	all	product	3	1
		average	3	1
	Department, favourite subject, hobbies, gender	product	3	1
		average	3	1
Logistic regression	all	product	4	0
		average	4	1
	Department, favourite subject, hobbies, gender	product	4	0
		average	4	1

6 Evaluation

6.1 Results

We evaluated the four cases ((a), (b). (c) and (d)) described in Sect. 5.3 for the accounts and resumes of the 30 volunteers described in Sect. 4.1. We implemented component classifiers for 119 attribute values on 30 resumes using Random Forest and logistic regression, and thus implemented 119 × 2 component classifiers.

Figure 3 shows the results for case (b) (Random Forest - four effective attributes – product). The horizontal axis represents each of the 30 accounts, and the vertical axis represents the resume classifier scores calculated for the corresponding accounts. The distribution of each score calculated by 30 classifiers is represented by a box, lines above and below the box, and dots. Symbols •, ▲, □, and × represent the score of the account owner's resume. The • indicates that the account owner's resume was the top resume, meaning that the resume (i.e. the person) was correctly identified. The ▲ and □ indicate that the account owner's resume was in the top 10 % (top 3) and 20 % (top 6), respectively, and the × indicates otherwise. For example, the resume of account 1's owner was in the top 20 %.

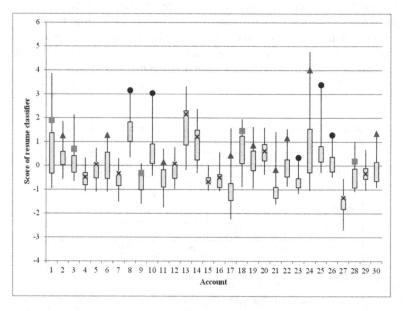

Fig. 3. Distribution of resume classifier scores with Random Forest, four attributes, and product

Table 6 shows the numbers of correct resumes being on top, in the top 10 %, and in the top 20 % for the four cases. The two best cases were case (b), in which 5 resumes were correctly identified, 14 resumes (including the 5 resumes) were in the top 10 %, and 19 were in the top 20 %, and case (c), in which 6 resumes were correctly identified, 12 resumes were in the top 10 %, and 16 were in the top 20 %.

Figures 4(b) and (c) show the performance of the proposed method with less data in the best cases. The horizontal axis represents the number of tweets per account for the test data. The vertical axis represents the number of correct resumes being on top, in the top 10 %, and in the top 20 %. Basically, the less data, the less precisely the method performs though there are some fluctuations. The number of correct resumes

Table 6. Number of correct resumes being on top, in top 10 %, and in top 20 %

Case	Learning algorithm	Attribute	Fusion method	Top	Top 10%	Top 20%
(a)	Random Forest	All	Average	3	10	15
(b)	Random Forest	Department, favourite subject, hobbies, gender	Product	5	14	19
(c)	Logistic regression	All	Average	6	12	16
(d)	Logistic regression	Department, favourite subject, hobbies, gender	Average	2	12	18

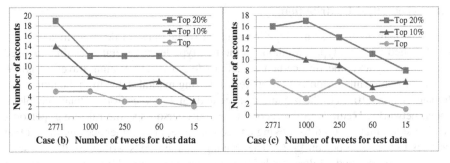

Case (b) Number of tweets for test data

Case (c) Number of tweets for test data

Fig. 4. Performance of proposed method with less data

approached the expected value with random choice (i.e. 1 for the top, 3 for the top 10 %, and 6 for the top 20 %) with 15 tweets.

6.2   Analysis

The results for accounts 10 and 25 were good for all cases. This was because the tweets posted from those accounts contained words related to attribute values in the corresponding resumes, especially those related to favourite subjects and hobbies. Resume 10 included, for example, "favourite subject = differential and integral calculus" while tweets from account 10 included phrases related to this subject such as "Let's practice on partial differential equations". The account owners' resumes were ranked 10, 12, and 3 for the accounts 13, 16, and 22 for case (b) but they were ranked 5, 5 and top for case (c). We may be able to improve these results by fusing scores in both cases, i.e. combining the scores for Random Forest and Logistic regression.

The results for accounts 7 and 14 were bad in all cases. Tweets from account 7 mostly contained words such as "Good morning" and "Sleepy", which were not related to the corresponding resume. Our de-anonymization method using resumes cannot work well for this kind of account. Resume 14 included "hobby = music", and tweets from account 14 mentioned music pieces and singers. However, because those music pieces and singers are not well known, the words in those tweets did not overlap words in the positive training data, i.e. the tweets of 30 music lovers. To handle this case, we need some abstraction, e.g. to learn using music and singer categories instead of words that directly appear in tweets.

While the number of attribute values described on the 30 resumes was 169, we implemented and used component classifiers for only 119 attribute values because we could not obtain sufficient numbers of positive training data for the other 50 attribute values from the Internet. This means that we could implement component classifiers for more attribute values and could improve the precision of the de-anonymization if a larger number and a wider variety of accounts were available on the Internet.

7   Summary of Our Contribution

7.1   Theoretical Contribution

Previous methods that use machine learning for social network de-anonymization can be classified into two types. Methods in the first type learn general rules that are used for identifying texts meeting certain conditions (e.g. tweets revealing travel plans) [9, 13] and for inferring attributes of users (e.g. inferring marital status from the number of female friends) [10, 17]. The training data are texts and profiles from ordinary people in social networks. Methods in the second type learn person-specific rules (e.g. person's writing style) that are used for linking an account or text to another account or text that belongs to the same person [5, 6]. The training data are texts written by that person.

Our proposed method does not belong to either type. Though its purpose is similar to that of the second type, i.e. linking two objects belonging to the same person, one of the objects (i.e. resume) is not a conventional text while the other is a conventional text (tweet). Writing styles learned from the conventional text cannot be used for resume identification. Our method therefore learns general rules (e.g. those for identifying texts written by females) as do methods of the first type. It then composes person-specific rules (e.g. those for identifying texts written by the owner of a resume) from the learned general rules. The training data for our method are texts written by ordinary people. Thus, we have enabled linking different kinds of objects that belong to the same person by composing person-specific rules though learning general rules.

7.2   Implications to Stakeholders

There are four main stakeholders for our proposed method, the attacker who uses the method to identify the poster of content, the victim who is identified, the potential victim who would be identified if content was posted, and the system developer who implements the method into a real system. Our theoretical contribution most helps the system developer. Because the training data are texts from ordinary people (e.g. texts disclosed in Twitter), the system developer can obtain them without permission from a specific person. He or she can thus harvest a huge amount of training data through social networks, and the more text available in networks, the more effective the method.

8 Conclusion

8.1 Summary

We have presented a method that uses machine learning to link social network accounts to resumes, which directly represent identities. In this method, a classifier is implemented for each resume that quantifies how likely the owner of a social network account is the owner of the resume. The difficulty in using machine learning for de-anonymization, i.e. preparing training data, is overcome by decomposing the classifier for a resume into component classifiers for characteristics (such as having dancing as a hobby and being a computer engineer) described on the resume so that training data for the component classifiers can be obtained from the Internet. Because the training data are harvested from the Internet, the more information available on the Internet, the more effective the method. It can be used widely because most organizations and governments have resume or resume-like information.

Our research clarifies a serious privacy risk: persons of concern to organizations and governments can be identified and their freedom of speech can be suppressed. The proposed method can also be used to identify a person who misuses a social network (e.g. revealing confidential information, posting copyrighted contents) by linking the misused account to a candidate resume.

8.2 Future Research Directions

(1) For the component classifiers, we will test other learning algorithms such as basic ones like naïve Bayes and more sophisticated ones like non-linear SVM and deep learning, and their combinations.

(2) For the resume classifiers, we will test learning algorithms instead of simple average and product methods. Resume classifiers need to cope with hundreds or more scores from component classifiers to precisely identify the corresponding resumes. Boosting, which adaptively optimizes the weights of scores by focusing on erroneously classified data at each stage, is therefore a promising algorithm for resume classifiers.

References

1. Gurses, S., Rizk, R., Gunther, O.: Privacy design in online social networks: learning from privacy breaches and community feedback. In: Proceedings of 29th International Conference on Information Systems, pp.1–10, Paris (2008)
2. Mixi: Infographics for finding out the newest data of mixi. http://pr.mixi.co.jp/entry/2011/06/01/infographics.html. (in Japanese)
3. Narayanan, A., Shmatikov, V.: De-anonymizing social networks. In: Proceedings of 30th IEEE Security & Privacy, pp.173–187, Oakland (2009)
4. Goga, O., Lei, H. et al.: On exploiting innocuous user activity for correlating accounts across social network sites. ICSI Technical reports - University of Berkeley (2012)

5. Almishari M, Kaafar, M., et al.: Stylometric linkability of Tweets. In: Proceedings of 13th Workshop on Privacy in the Electronic Society, pp.205–208, Scottsdale (2014)
6. Narayanan A., Paskov, H., et al.: On the feasibility of internet-scale author identification. In: Proceedings of 33rd IEEE Symposium on Security and Privacy, pp.300–314, San Francisco (2012)
7. Backstrom, R., Dwork, C., Kleinberg, J.: Wherefore art thou R3579X? anonymized social networks, hidden patterns, and structural steganography. In: Proceedings of 16th International World Wide Web Conference, pp. 181–190, Banff (2007)
8. Lam, I.-F., Chen, K.-T., Chen, L.-J.: Involuntary information leakage in social network services. In: Matsuura, K., Fujisaki, E. (eds.) IWSEC 2008. LNCS, vol. 5312, pp. 167–183. Springer, Heidelberg (2008)
9. Mao, H., Shuai, X., Kapadia, A.: Loose tweets: an analysis of privacy leaks on Twitter. In: Proceedings of 10th ACM Workshop on Privacy in the Electronic Society, Denver (2011)
10. Kótyuk, G., Buttyan, L.: A machine learning based approach for predicting undisclosed attributes in social networks. In: Proceedings of IEEE 4th International Workshop on Security and Social Networking, pp.361–366, Budapest (2012)
11. Polakis, I., Kontaxis, G., et al.: Using social networks to harvest email addresses. In: Proceedings of 9th ACM Workshop on Privacy in Electronic Society, pp.11–20, Chicago (2010)
12. TwiPro: Searching profiles of Twitter users. http://twpro.jp/. (In Japanese)
13. Caliskan-Islam, A., Walsh, J., Greenstadt, R.: Privacy detective: detecting private information and collective privacy behavior in a large social network. In: Proceedings of 13th Workshop on Privacy in the Electronic Society, pp. 35–46, Scottsdale (2014)
14. Hart, M., Manadhata, P., Johnson, R.: Text classification for data loss prevention. In: Fischer-Hübner, S., Hopper, N. (eds.) PETS 2011. LNCS, vol. 6794, pp. 18–37. Springer, Heidelberg (2011)
15. Burger, J., Henderson J., et al.: Discriminating gender on Twitter. In: Proceedings of Conference on Empirical Methods in Natural Language Processing, pp.1301–1309, Edinburgh (2011)
16. Cheng, Z., Caverlee, J., Lee, K.: You are where you Tweet: a content-based approach to geo-locating Twitter users. In: Proceedings of the 19th ACM International Conference on Information and Knowledge Management, pp.759–768, Toronto (2010)
17. Pennacchiotti, M., Popescu, A.-M.: A machine learning approach to Twitter user classification. In: Proceedings of 5th International AAAI Conference on Weblogs and Social Media, pp. 281–288, Barcelona (2011)

Controlling and Mitigating Targeted Socio-Economic Attacks

Prabhat Kumar[(✉)], Yashwanth Dasari, Shubhangee Nath, and Akash Sinha

Department of Computer Science and Engineering, National Institute of Technology Patna, Patna, India
{prabhat,dasari134763,shubhangee134784,akash.cse15}@nitp.ac.in

Abstract. The transformation of social media has paved a way to express one's views, ideas, and opinions in an effective and lucid manner which has resulted in its increased popularity. However, there are both pros and cons of this socio-technological revolution. This may lead to its misuse with planned and targeted attacks which often have the potential of massive economic effects. This paper articulates the negative aspects, especially, of how the social media is being misused for greedy needs. Spammers may defame the product to achieve their greedy goal of earning more profit by decreasing the competing effect of their opponents. This paper discusses, analyzes and proposes two novel techniques by which one can either decrease or completely abolish these types of socio-economic attacks.

Keywords: Social media · Economic · Target attack · False content prevention · False content tolerance

1 Introduction

Social media has been the ever expanding realm since a decade and has taken the technological advancements to its pinnacle. Social media helps the business in a variety of ways especially in promotion which is economically viable and effective than the traditional ways of promotion. Table 1 enlists the percentage of B2B marketers who use various social media sites to distribute their content. The increasing popularity of social networking sites such as Twitter, Facebook and LinkedIn has attracted a large number of bloggers, content writers and article creators [1]. Social media has removed all the communication and interaction barriers and bridged the gap amongst the earthlings.

Another positive aspect of social media is uniting a large number of people on a huge platform which is necessary to induce positivity in the society. On the other hand, it has many bad and ugly impacts [3]. As stated above our aim is to control or totally mitigate the false content (uploading fake videos which have no authentication, posting vulgar images) making the platform more trust worthy and reliable than the former. Some of the bad and ugly aspects are that some spammers are forging multiple identities (also called Sybil) in order to harm the users of the media [4]. This is due to the fact that no mechanism for authentication is provided when any video or picture that addresses the

Y.K. Dwivedi et al. (Eds.): I3E 2016, LNCS 9844, pp. 471–476, 2016.
DOI: 10.1007/978-3-319-45234-0_42

Table 1. Percentage of marketing people using social media [2]

Company name	Percentage(%) of marketing people using social media
Linkedin	91
Twitter	85
Facebook	81
Youtube	73
Google+	55
SlideShare	40
Pinterest	34
Instagram	22
Vimeo	22
Flickr	16
StumbleUpon	15
Foursquare	14
Tumblr	14
Vine	14

issue of public interest gets uploaded. One can easily post some false and vulgar content and raise some sensitive issues which may damage the goodwill of the product as it is just a matter of creating a fake identity and uploading a video or some morphed photograph. Cautious content filtration of objectionable or adulterated content is necessary because it is high time to control the evil abuse widely prevalent in the society. This paper provides various approaches to control this at various levels starting from the very root level. The work concentrates on all types of false content detection, false content tolerance and vulgarity issues. The aim is not to undermine the great contributions that the social media has made to social progress and technological advancement but rather to make it more trust worthy, reliable and transform it to a better facilitative tool which supports social cohesion and benign societal relations by abolishing such false content.

2   Related Work

Content-based filtering in online social networks has good results in the case of text or information. Content-based filtering can be applied concurrently at the same time when the text is getting uploaded [9, 10]. But this is not the case with videos or photographs. Daily millions of videos get uploaded and content filtration is not possible. Even the technique of content-based filtration is context based. Much of the literature work is not available in this context of socio-economic attacks. Some of the available instances are Maggi incident and many messages spreading that soft-drinks are contaminated with AIDS blood etc. Such incidences clearly elucidate some of the ugly aspects of social media.

Ying-Chiang-Cho addressed various negative aspects of social media such as (1) Cyber Bullying, (2) Role of social media in organization of negative social events such as the 2011 UK riots, (3) Social-media-assisted infidelity and promiscuity [3]. He has discussed various instances of the misuse of social media in different public domains. One of them is Cyber bullying which describes the situation of a child or a teenager when he/she is harassed, humiliated, embarrassed, threatened or tormented using the digital technology. Cyber bullying includes sending mean messages or threats, spreading rumors, posting hurtful or threatening posts, sexting (circulating sexually suggestive pictures or messages about a person) and so forth [5, 6]. He articulated the ugly side of social media by various examples. Some of them are as follows:

- A 13-year old school boy, Ryan Halligan took his life because of cyber bullying.
- A 15-year old girl, Phoebe Prince hanged herself because of the threatening messages and called names at school.

There are still many instances which have not come under the limelight in the society. His work has addressed the issues very well but has provided no means of abating or eradicating the serious threat from the society. His work also lacks the discussion of any socio economic attacks [3]. R. Gandhi et al. has addressed the economic issues related to security [8]. His work has paved ways for the future extension of such critical issues in the context of economy such as damaging the reputation of perishable goods. This work includes providing solution to this critical issue at various stages. The work includes abating it at the very rudimentary level, tolerating it at the middle and the peak stages. Posting of fake videos and photographs may damage the goodwill of the good to a major extent. We are paying special attention to this type offensive videos and photographs which publicize the objectionable and fake content which has no source of authentication in it-self.

3 Strategies

We propose two techniques namely 1. FALSE CONTENT TOLERANCE and 2. FALSE CONTENT PREVENTION. To illustrate these techniques let us consider the following scenario. Say, a plate contains five types of fruits namely apples, oranges, mangoes, bananas and grapes that constitute the daily supplements of an individual in the country, India. The usual cost of apples and grapes is higher than the others. So we can categorize these as costly fruits. The cost of mangoes and oranges is greater than that of bananas but cheaper than apples and grapes. So these can be categorized as medium cost fruits. The cost of bananas is far cheaper than the others. So this fruit can be categorized as a low cost fruit.

The country India exhibits a large proportion of population of average and low salaried people. This infers that an average salaried person generally resorts to buying or ordering either medium cost fruits or low cost fruits. So the demand for medium and low cost fruits is higher, again amongst these, the demand for low cost fruit dominates. Without loss of generality the restaurant managing personnel will have a greater quantity of bananas, a medium quantity of mangoes and oranges, and a lower quantity of apples and grapes. Suppose the managing staff of mango production unit wishes to raise the demand for mangoes in the market so as to increase the net profit of the production unit. To achieve this, the unit plans a scheme to decline the popularity of other fruits in the market. The competitors in this scenario are apples, grapes, oranges and bananas. As the cost of apples and grapes are higher, the competing effect of these fruits can be neglected. So the real competitors are oranges and bananas in which the competing effect of bananas is higher than that of oranges. Hence they would like to target the sales of bananas and oranges. The plot is as follows: The production unit will create a video which tarnishes the popularity of the target fruits, oranges and bananas. In the video, they may use all types of defaming contents which shows that eating these fruits will spoil the health of common mass and will show side effects in the upcoming future. Also the video may make some false claim that this video is approved by some of the well known, reputed doctors or health societies. Further as the present social media does not provide any authentication for posting of these types of videos, this video may go viral in the social media negotiating the genuineness of the target fruits, oranges and bananas achieving the goal of the production unit successfully. In due course of time, the video gets popularized in all the sections of the society. This may not have any drastic effect on consumption of that particular fruit if an individual is considered. But as a whole this may have a serious decline in consumption of the target fruits and therefore also reducing the profits. This may have a drastic impact on the sales of these target fruits. Everyone may start to pick a mango instead of taking an orange or a banana. Gradually the demand for mangoes will sharply increase and the market price of mango will soar. Thereby the target of mango production units is achieved easily just by posting a fake video which has no authentication at all. The same thing can be done by many adversaries for spoiling the goodwill of their opponents in one or the other way. This is a serious issue which needs urgent consideration.

To cater the need of addressing such issues we propose techniques to reduce or possibly diminish the effect of this false content. The FALSE CONTENT TOLERANCE approach aims at minimizing the fake post by associating the information of the user with the post he uploads. In this strategy, the social media allows all types of videos to get posted. Possibly the video may be seen by an individual and he/she starts sharing it. If a video is getting shared, it should be shared along with the source id's URL (who posted it for the first time) should also be shared. If this type of control mechanism is implemented these false content videos may reduce to an appreciable amount as the source identity can be known easily from the URL. So the spammers may have the fear of their identity getting easily traced. For example, instances of false content promotions or defamation of rival products administered through uploading and sharing of videos and other media are witnessed on the social networking sites like Facebook, Twitter etc. on a routine basis. Now if it is made mandatory to reveal one's source id and that the aforementioned detail is displayed publicly along with the given video or other media then the culprit might get apprehensive about being publicly shamed or subjected to persecution through law. He knows that now he can be traced till a certain point. So, it is safe to conclude that a general disinclination towards uploading of such false videos and other media may be evident post implementation of the aforementioned technique. This requires very few changes in the existing framework and the present architecture of the social media. As it requires very few changes, it only requires a minimum effort to do this work. But still the users can make Sybil accounts (fake id) and do this type of unethical things to fulfill their greedy need of tarnishing a product. Hence the problem still persists which can be resolved by using FALSE CONTENT PREVENTION technique.

The second technique is illustrated as below: When a video is posted the social media authorities ask for the user's telephone number as an authentication mechanism. The OTP mechanism can be used to verify the user's telephone number. If this type of authentication is done successfully then those videos are called certified videos. The user's telephone number will not be shared and will be kept safe and secure by the social media authorities. If the user refuses to reveal his identity the social media still allows to post the video but these videos are called uncertified videos. Such videos can still be shared but they lose their credibility. This ensures that the video having fake content may not get popularized. The additional changes in the settings of giving the option to show only certified videos help to reduce the effect in a very effective manner. This requires more effort than the tolerance technique but ensures that the fake content is not encouraged in any manner.

4 Analysis

The tolerance strategy though requires minimal changes in the existing architecture and the present framework is not at all a viable solution because it is just a matter of few minutes to create one fake id. These types of fake ids persist in all types of social networks. Albeit the prevention strategy requires much effort and time but it guarantees the addressing of the problem from the very root level. The effort involves changing the settings architecture, an overhead of time and effort during authentication and also verifying whether the video is certified or not during the time of sharing. This technique has an authentication mechanism by which the user can be tracked easily by the means of telephone number which is re-verified using OTP (One Time Password). So the user cannot simply escape by giving a false telephone number. As the certified videos can only be shared by using this technique, it has an indirect effect of gradually diminishing this sort of misuse in all contexts. If an annotation of 'recommended for most of the users' is provided along with the option of show only certified videos, then most of the users will go for it. Gradually it gets popularized and spreads from one user to another resembling the chain effect. Consequently, only the certified videos get posted and also only those videos are shared.

Just like prevention is better than cure, the prevention strategy stated above is better than the tolerance strategy.

5 Conclusion

Careful and selective content filtration is essential so as to stop socio economic back-stabbing which may have a serious business effect [7, 8]. Our proposed methods work well in all platforms. The technique of false content prevention is much viable and reliable than the false content tolerance though it requires more effort. Validation of fake videos (if reported by an organization or a company to social media authorities) and posting new videos along with certification to counter the false attacks (counter videos) addresses the problem in an effective way. Further this can also be applied to contents such as textual posts which are abusive and non-ethical. However, the proposed techniques suffer with certain limitations as in case of FALSE CONTENT TOLERANCE which can be defeated by using Sybil accounts. The prevention approach provides an improvement over the tolerance strategy but requires a certain overhead from implementation point of view. These techniques can be improved in the future by real time implementation and proper feedback integration. In addition, the rating of videos based on its authenticity may help to make the platform more trustworthy.

References

1. Spisak, K.: Social Media Statistics (2015). http://www.business2community.com/social-media/social-media-statistics-2015-01393793#IPjuq80WDr2XirGf.97
2. Pulizzi, J.: B2B Content Marketing: 2014 Benchmarks, Budgets, and Trends—North America (2014). http://contentmarketinginstitute.com/wp-content/uploads/2013/10/B2B_Research_2014_CMI.pdf
3. Cho, Y.C.: Violence and aberration in the age of social media: transforming the advanced communication technology into a better facilitative tool. IEEE Consum. Electron. Mag. 3(4), 69–74 (2014)
4. Koll, D., Li, J., Stein, J., Fu, X.: On the state of OSN-based Sybil defenses. In: Networking Conference 2014 IFIP, Trondheim, pp. 1–9 (2014)
5. Bullying Statistics. http://www.bullyingstatistics.org/content/cyber-bullying-statistics.html
6. Cyberbullying Case Studies. http://cyberbullying.ua.edu/index.php/casestudies/
7. Oehri, C., Teufel, S.: Social media security culture. In: Information Security for South Africa, ISSA 2012, Johannesburg, Gauteng, pp. 1–5 (2012)
8. Gandhi, R., Sharma, A., Mahoney, W., Sousan, W., Zhu, Q., Laplante, P.: Dimensions of cyber-attacks: cultural, social, economic, and political. IEEE Technol. Soc. Mag. 30(1), 28–38 (2011)
9. Thilagavathi, N., Taarika, R.: Content based filtering in online social network using inference algorithm. In: International Conference on Circuit, Power and Computing Technologies, ICCPCT 2014, Nagercoil, pp. 1416–1420 (2014)
10. Vanetti, M., Binaghi, E., Carminati, B., Carullo, M., Ferrari, E.: Content-based filtering in on-line social networks. In: Dimitrakakis, C. (ed.) PSDML 2010. LNCS, vol. 6549, pp. 127–140. Springer, Heidelberg (2010)

Data Acquisition, Management
and Analytics

Social Sensor Web: Towards a Conceptual Framework

Salman Qayyum Mian[1(✉)], Matti Mäntymäki[2],
Jukka Riekki[1], and Harri Oinas-Kukkonen[1]

[1] University of Oulu, Oulu, Finland
{salman.mian,jukka.riekki,harri.oinas-kukkonen}@oulu.fi
[2] University of Turku, Turku, Finland
matti.mantymaki@utu.fi

Abstract. Sensor technology has become increasingly pervasive, leading to its use in many areas, such as health care and wellness. Current technologies and services are based on one-way connectivity, such that sensors are primarily used to transmit information. Though data generation is essential to the pursuit of meaningful information, having the right information at the right time in the right context is what successfully integrates the social web into real-world situations. This paper extends the concept of the Internet of Things and develops a conceptual framework of the Social Sensor Web that employs sensors to elaborate context-aware information in order to determine an effective approach to social interaction. The paper also highlights the importance of dual connectivity of sensor devices through workshops based on the state of the art. We present five dimensions of the Social Sensor Web that can serve as a guide for designing future health and wellness technologies.

Keywords: Social web · Sensor · Monitoring · Context awareness · Dual connectivity · Health · Wellness

1 Introduction

The rapid development and increasing affordability of sensor technologies, together with the spread of Internet connectivity, have led to a massive number of connected sensors. In the health care context, connected sensors are used to transmit individuals' blood glucose levels and blood pressure information to health care professionals. Such functions can improve the quality and decrease the costs of health care [1].

Furthermore, in the domain of personal wellness, heart rate monitors and fitness tracking devices enable users to share information about their exercise routines and training progress with other people. Today, consumers who are interested in monitoring their health and wellbeing have access to several commercial applications, devices, and personal solutions for fitness, sports activities, and wellbeing [2].

Given this plethora of options, people utilize technological tools to monitor their health in various ways. For example, 'lifelogging' is an emerging concept referring to the continuous recording of physiological data and everyday life activities. Similarly, the 'quantified self' is a movement incorporating technology into the data acquisition

© IFIP International Federation for Information Processing 2016
Published by Springer International Publishing Switzerland 2016. All Rights Reserved
Y.K. Dwivedi et al. (Eds.): I3E 2016, LNCS 9844, pp. 479–492, 2016.
DOI: 10.1007/978-3-319-45234-0_43

of inputs (e.g. food consumed, quality of surrounding air), states (e.g. mood, arousal, blood oxygen levels), and performance (e.g. mental and physical) from users' daily lives. These trends of self-monitoring and self-sensing make use of wearable sensors (electrocardiogram, electroencephalogram, video, etc.) and wearable computing [3].

While the use of sensor technologies creates significant value for both individuals and society, this value could be increased through further advancements. For example, transmitting blood glucose levels or physiological data through sensors represents only one-way web connectivity. Sensor devices could play an expanded role if, first, their information they gather could be combined for realistic contextual perception and, second, if the sensor devices themselves could be empowered with basic interactive capabilities for consuming and producing meaningful information.

In this paper, we propose the concept of the Social Sensor Web. We define the Social Sensor Web as the interplay between sensors and the social web phenomenon, such that sensors elaborate on contextual space in order to determine an effective interaction approach. The essence of this concept sheds light on the dual connectivity between sensors and the web, such that sensors take on the form of social entities [4]. For example, information from the social web can be used to predict the spread of flu; this information could be refined and transmitted to users (e.g. to suggest changes in their workout programs). Thus, social sensor technologies could be used in the healthcare sector to design more efficient interventions or to persuade people to develop and sustain healthier lifestyles.

We present the results of two workshops, in which interdisciplinary groups of experts discussed and assessed the state of the art related to social sensor technologies and identified the most prospective applications of social sensors. Based on the findings of these workshops, we developed the conceptual framework of the social sensor web. Further, by setting a research agenda, the paper contributes to the research on social sensor technologies; its framework can serve as a guide for designing future applications based on the collaboration of sensors and the social web.

2   Context-Aware Sensors in the Social Web

Sensors that measure physical quantities, such as pressure or light, have grown increasingly pervasive. Smartphones and mobile devices typically feature sensor technologies (e.g. touch screens), which collect different types of data from changes to the environment or an object (e.g. temperature, vibrations, or movement) [5].

As sensor technologies have developed, people have changed their ways of using the Internet. Due to the large-scale adoption of social media and online social networking, the Internet has become a social space, to the extent that Oinas-Kukkonen and Oinas-Kukkonen [4] proposed the concept of the *social web*. This idea highlights the role of the web as a social space characterized by connectivity and interactions, both among people and between people and information [4]. Oinas-Kukkonen and Oinas-Kukkonen [4] describe the social web as follows:

*The term **social web** refers to a pattern of thinking in which end-users jointly create or generate much of the content for the web, whereas companies try to harness the end-users with tools with which they can participate and engage themselves in content production and sharing. [...] An essential feature of the social web phenomenon is that social web is not only a virtual world; what is remarkable about it is its interconnection with one's own life.*

Since the majority of people and an increasing share of physical objects have online digital presences, we propose the concept of a "Social Internet of Things" (SIoT). Whereas the Internet of Things focuses on devices that are connected to the Internet, SIoT shifts the emphasis to objects that interact on the web [6]. Sensors equipped with basic interactive capabilities (e.g. reception and processing capabilities) could interact with other sensors, people, and social web applications.

Aggarwal and Abdelzaher [7] discussed the drivers of integrating sensors with the social web, focusing primarily on social networks. One of the key incentives for users is real-time awareness of others' updates. Such integration could facilitate a better understanding of users' global behaviors. Sensors could also enable measurements of users' environments, thus facilitating context awareness.

Humans' role in this phenomenon is particularly important in terms of data generation and social relations. Although users who use contextual sensors might decrease their self-report data production, their activities will produce more data. Therefore, humans still play a critical role in terms of user-generated activities.

Recent sensor applications have sought to collect data that can be directly associated with individuals' real-time personal information. Some examples of such applications include GPS applications on mobile devices, accelerometers, and location sensors designed to track humans or vehicular traffic. These types of sensors can support a rich variety of applications in which sensor data can be used to model underlying relationships and interactions [1].

At an aggregate level, behavior measurements can be used to investigate and predict traffic conditions through collecting and processing massively distributed data (e.g. the collection of vehicular GPS trajectories to develop street maps) [8]. Currently, this use of sensor data involves very little, if any, social component. However, the same sensor-generated information can also be used on a real-time, daily basis to avoid traffic congestions. As an example of the viability of this vision, Google has acquired Waze, a company specializing in social mapping techniques. Google plans to use Waze's crowd-sourced data on users' locations to suggest alternate routes to outsmart traffic congestions [9].

Furthermore, an application called City Sense, a subscription that provides information on where the people in a city are through GPS-enabled phones, can be used to plan activities [10]. For instance, the service can inform a user walking in the city that his/her friends are sitting in a nearby cafeteria. Turning sensor devices into intelligent objects that communicate with users' social network sites can challenge the conventional information flow between a sensor object and the social web.

Networked sensor data have also been applied in social web applications to aid in the detection of earthquakes [11]. Integrating data from sensor networks into the web would further enhance the web integration of everyday devices and objects, resulting in a giant sensor network and wide-scale connection between the social web and the physical world [4]. In addition, the nomadic nature of the web, which can be accessed from anywhere through mobile devices, requires portable and environmental sensors.

According to O'Reilly and Battelle [12], the new direction of the web is on a real-time collision course with the physical world. Hence, using information generated by sensors requires real-time context awareness. This is where contextual information developed by sensors can complement information from other sensors by better utilizing their measurements. Schmidt [13] considers context awareness to be the key enabler for understanding situations in urban environments with ubiquitous devices. The goal of system context awareness is to arrive at a close representation of the user's perception of the surrounding world. Though the user's perceptions are multi-faceted and based on human senses, multiple sensors are required to develop contextual awareness close to human perception. This will help the system provide users feedback related to situation-based decision-making. Tamminen et al. [14] point out that the social acceptability of a context-aware system is dependent on how well the system fits into the routine processes of everyday life in a society. Therefore, the better a system is able to develop context awareness, the greater its chances succeeding in the race to technological adoption.

To address the issues discussed in this section, we now discuss the workshops held in this study and present the conceptual framework for the Social Sensor Web.

3   Towards the Social Sensor Web

3.1   Study Setting

We collected empirical data from two expert workshops on social sensor technolo-gies, comprising a total of 14 experts from various fields, such as information systems, mobile technologies, and physical education. The participants had diverse cultural backgrounds in terms of gender and countries: Most were PhDs who are actively engaged in research, and half also had industry experience. The workshops were organized and facilitated by the first author. The objective of the workshops was

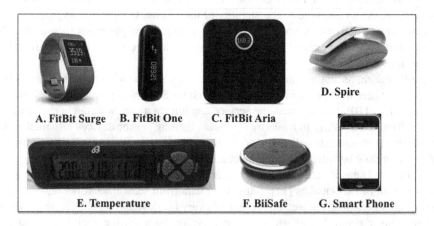

Fig. 1. State-of-the-art sensors and technologies.

to obtain participants' perceptions regarding social sensors and, ultimately, to develop a conceptual framework of the social sensor web.

The purpose of the first session was to familiarize the participants with one another, the research objectives, the focal concepts, and the state of the art of social sensor technologies. To this end, the participants were presented a number of different sensor devices (see Fig. 1), which they were then asked to scrutinize and discuss.

The first was *FitBit Surge* (device A), a fitness wrist device [15] with a built-in GPS; continuous heart rate monitoring capabilities; and tracking for daily activities, such as distance, steps taken, sleep pattern, and floors climbed. It synchronizes measurements wirelessly with a smartphone and presents the data in the FitBit app, as shown in the first two screenshots in Fig. 2. Additionally, the device displays calls and notifications from the smartphone, as shown in Fig. 3A later. The *FitBit One* (device B) is a limited version [15] of the Fitbit Surge; it lacks heart rate monitoring and is used with the FitBit Surge to provide measurement accuracy. The *FitBit Aria* (device C) is a non-wearable wireless device [15] that tracks weight and Body Mass Index (BMI) to determine body fat percentage. The device allows users to analyze weight data in relation to data on calories burned. Alternatively, the FitBit app can be used to manually log diet information, including food plans, water intake, etc., while also displaying all kind of measurements in graphical charts.

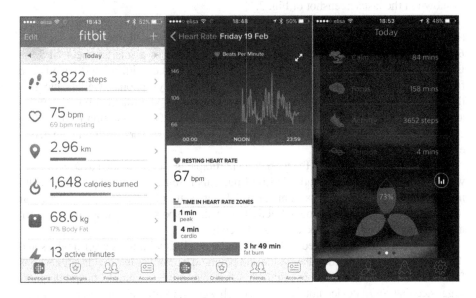

Fig. 2. Synchronization and presentation of physiological data.

Spire (device D) is waist-worn [16] device that monitors a user's breathing pattern in real time and assesses stress levels accordingly. It categorizes breathing patterns into three types: "low and uniform" corresponds to a user being calm, "high but uniform" corresponds to focus, and "high and erratic" corresponds to stress. Based on the collected data, the device sends notifications to the user's smartphone. For example, it may suggest

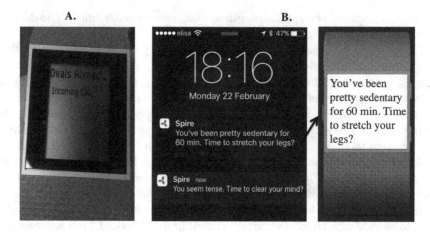

Fig. 3. *FitBit Surge* display and *Spire* notifications on the smartphone.

that a stressed user needs to relax or encourage a user who has been sitting idle to stretch his/her legs (see Fig. 3B). The device synchronizes with a smartphone app, which lets the user set goals and presents statistical analyses of their everyday breathing patterns, as shown in the last screenshot of Fig. 2.

Temperature (device E) is a non-wearable device that measures indoor and outdoor temperature using a small sensor probe that needs to be placed outside the window. *BiiSafe* (device F) is a smartphone accessory [17] that uses a smartphone's GPS via Bluetooth to enable users to share their locations to connect with or alert friends and family and help them find important lost items, such as keys, phones, wallets, etc. It is the only product on the market to combine location sharing, alert/distress functionalities and lost-item finding capabilities. A *smartphone* (device G), in addition to providing communication services and social web apps, has several sensors, including an accelerometer, a gyroscope, etc.

In addition to these items, the workshop participants were provided access to three weeks of data from the first author's Life Log. This Life Log included personal health measurements and assessments from the use of these state-of-the-art sensors; a calendar for the past three weeks of logged activities such as sport sessions, locations, work meetings and travel; and a mockup of social contacts.

The participants were asked to familiarize themselves with the sensor devices and their features and to consider their value and potential, as well as to provide suggestions for additional functionalities that could add value to users. For example, the participants suggested that *Spire* device notifications, which were currently displayed on the smartphone (Fig. 3B), could additionally be displayed on the device itself, as in the *Fitbit Surge* device (Fig. 3A).

In the second workshop, the same participants were divided into three groups. Whereas the purpose of the first workshop was to familiarize participants with state-of-the-art technologies, the second workshop encouraged participants to think "outside of the box" regarding sensor-based solutions not limited to the presented sensors. In consultation with the participants, the use scenarios were created to target three different domains: healthcare monitoring, fitness and wellness, and social interaction. The participants worked in teams for an hour, collaborating on how state-of-the-art sensors could provide effective solutions to the use scenarios. The scenarios ranged from monitoring the elderly at home, to child safety, to decreasing stress through personalized activities, to keeping in touch with family and friends.

The participants then presented their solutions and identified their core solution concepts. The teams' work was discussed, and remarks were noted, merged, and deliberated for the rest of the workshop. Ultimately, a consensus was reached; this consensus formed the dimensions of the framework.

3.2 The Framework

The following are quotes from the participants during their collaboration efforts in the second workshop:

> *One of the exciting aspects of sensors is their ability to work continuously and all the time, whether it's controlling traffic signals or monitoring my health.* - Participant 2

> *It is great that sensors can know more about me in order to help me, but it scares me to think that this information, unless controlled, might get out of the circle of people I trust.* - Participant 5

> *I think, no matter how much information sensors can generate, it still needs to be taken into account with artificial intelligence in parallel to precisely identify real-life context issues and provide solutions accordingly.* - Participant 11

Our conceptual framework of the Social Sensor Web is based on the participants' consensus and feedback, which can serve as guidance for designing future applications based on the combination of sensors and the social web. The framework contains four horizontal dimensions: keep alive monitoring, context awareness, interaction intelligence, and the personal social web (presented in Fig. 4).

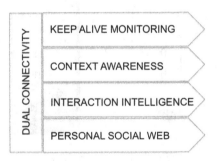

Fig. 4. The conceptual framework of social sensor web.

These four horizontal dimensions are connected via the fifth, vertical dimension: dual connectivity. The concept of monitoring serves as a basis for contextual awareness in systems, which is critical for determining suitable interaction approaches. Social interactions towards a target must take place within users' own social web. Within this exemplary system, dual connectivity allows the dimensions to coexist and work together in an effective way. Further sections elaborate on each dimension's importance and potential.

3.2.1   Dual Connectivity

The conventional information flow between a sensor and the social web has traditionally been one-way, meaning information extraction or placement: either sensor data are shared on the social web or a request is sent from the sensors and information is retrieved from the social web. Both cases require the user of the sensor device to initiate the information flow. Though this certainly serves a purpose, it involves minimal intelligence. A more sophisticated sensor could automatically invoke the social web to collect relevant information that could influence the user. Alternatively, the social web could serve as the initiator and provide useful information to the sensor [4].

The dual connection perspective presented in Fig. 5A can completely change the way we think about new solutions of information flow. For example, consider an individual's daily fitness workout, which is planned through a sensor that is a part of the social web. With one-way connectivity, workout data are shared on the social web. However, let us assume that a flu is spreading throughout the user's region and a local hospital shares information on the social web. If the social web were able to share this information with the sensor, this would allow the sensor to modify the user's workout to address the risk of flue. This is a clear case of a dual connection between sensors and the social web, in which each can invoke the other. For instance, in Fig. 5B, a notification is displayed to the user depicting information gathered from the social web by the sensor device, and the user can use the device's left button to let a nearby friend know of his/her proximity.

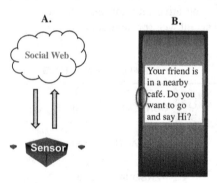

Fig. 5. Dual connectivity.

3.2.2   Keep Alive Monitoring

One of the key benefits of technology is its ability to keep working to serve its purpose 24/7. Increasing costs of healthcare are a major problem [18]. Remote health monitoring provides not only a way to address these rising costs but also opportunities to monitor petty health issues, which can turn into major health problems over time [19]. On a technical level, this has been possible due to the development of wireless devices and sensing equipment [20]. Many research groups are investigating novel and cheaper ways to support healthcare issues related to diverse groups, including the elderly and disabled, chronic disease patients, and sports enthusiasts [21].

To achieve continuous health and wellbeing management, monitoring and timely interventions are extremely important. For sensor-based systems to become instruments of continuity and control for end users, monitoring must remain alive for extended periods [22, 23]. This notion of *keep-alive monitoring*, which provides information on users' health and surrounding contexts at all times, can only fulfil its potential if the information can help in identifying threat-related information patterns. This is only possible if such information is reliable and continuously monitored.

Power consumption in these technologically advanced devices remains a concern. As a precaution, these boundary conditions should, by default, be considered within the overall monitoring scheme, where a sensor's power consumption is monitored. According to Satyanarayanan [24], the monitoring capabilities of futuristic sensing devices should make use of smart spaces and involve minimal user distraction; this will allow them to achieve both user satisfaction and their goals simultaneously. As Mark Weiser [25] stated: "The most profound technologies are those that disappear. They weave themselves into the fabric of everyday life until they are indistinguishable from it."

3.2.3   Context Awareness

The value of "context" in the field of human–computer interaction has been widely acknowledged, particularly as the use of sensors to obtain context information has been widely practiced in the domains of robotics and machine vision [26]. Recently, the concept of context has received growing attention due to developments in mobile computing, which have led to the emergence of pervasive computing [13]. Context refers to a description of facts that add meaning. This is best described by Dey [27] as, "any information that can be used to characterize the situation of an entity. An entity is a person, place, or object that is considered relevant to the interaction between a user and an application, including the user and applications themselves."

Knowledge of both the physical environment and the situational environment is important. Schmidt [13] presented a model for the concept of context, which is a context feature space that distinguishes context related to human factors from context related to the physical environment over time. The human factor categories rely on user information, biosensor readings, the user's social environment (e.g. social interaction), and the user's tasks (e.g. goals). The model's physical environment aspects also hold importance (e.g. tracking location and indoor/outdoor temperature).

One distinguishable feature of wearable computing is awareness of both a user and his/her environment. For instance, a heart rate measurement of 90 beats per minute (bpm) is considered to be average; however, for an individual whose average heart rate is 76 bpm, this is high and a possible cause for alarm. Here information revealing that the elevated heart rate is caused by jogging makes a difference.

Location is the most commonly used context information in present technology. However, detailed and reliable context awareness of various parameters would allow systems to make proper judgments concerning not only providing context-based services but also automatically executing these services for an enhanced user experience. Active context awareness, in which a service or application automatically adapts to discovered context through changes to its behavior, is required [28]. Santos et al. [29] summarized several system prototypes for context identification that support social networking services.

3.2.4   Interaction Intelligence

This dimension is the nucleus of the decision-making process based on contextual awareness. In its most simple form, interaction can comprise the act of notifying some social contact or user of the nature of a context. The type of interaction is dependent on the system domain and the type of contact.

In real-life scenarios, actions taken by a system can be proactive, preventive, or reactive, depending on the goals of the system or the problem domain. For example, in the case of healthcare, *proactive* measures or actions could include suggestions to eat healthy, while *preventive* actions could include specific suggestions such as to avoid obesity. Finally, *reactive* actions could correspond to emergency situations, such as a heart attack. For each of these actions, further decision-making on the part of the target recipient is needed. For instance, information related to personal fitness goals may be transmitted to the user or the trainer; the location of a kid in emergency care may be transmitted to parents or teachers; and, in the case of the elderly, information on heart issues may be transmitted to a caretaker or a hospital.

3.2.5   Personal Social Web

A user's personal social web comprises the user's network connections. The increased use of these connections through social web applications has increased people's comfort working with real-life social network connections at the technology level. Figure 6 presents a conceptual illustration of a personal social web as a network.

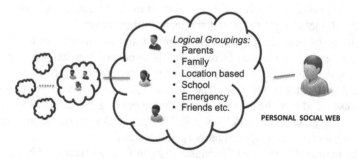

Fig. 6. Personal social web.

It is common for users to create logical groups of the connections in their own networks (e.g. family, friends, or work colleagues), typically based on static parameters. However, a personal network could also be divided into logical groups based on dynamic parameters, such as current location. Engagement with a dynamic social network based on, for example, location could benefit from the use of sensors that are part of the network in real time. In a dance group, meaningful information generated from sensors and the dynamic dance-group social web regarding the participants' wellness and the class environment can help teachers perform better. In school, a child's school sub-network has priority in case of an emergency. The logical groupings of an individual's personal social web can be utilized to achieve social interaction targets based on the contextual nature of the situation.

4   Discussion and Conclusion

The purpose of the study was to develop a conceptual framework for Social Sensor Web. Recent increases in lifestyle mobility increase the need for context-aware solutions based on sensor technologies. In practice, contextual awareness, when combined with the social web and sensor data, creates large volumes of data that need to be assessed. This information is collected through various sources; then, an accurate context is developed, and a meaningful result is given to the user in a presentable way. To achieve this, not only does the stream of information need to be intelligently processed, but, on a technological level, physical user interfaces (UIs) need to be dynamically advanced.

Figure 7 shows the inherent concept behind this part of discussion. The user is considered to be the center of the information hierarchy, and streams of information are expected from the user's Social Sensor Web. In the current state-of-the-art, as well as in the workshops, *sensors* (right in Fig. 7) are primarily connected to users' *smartphones* for wireless synchronization. However, for this user, the *FitBit Surge* is the main interaction device. The sensor's dynamic interface emphasizes the information that is most useful to the user based on a meaningful analysis of data from all streams. The streams of information from all channels are necessary to develop contextual awareness in the smartphone. This involves extensive real time data analysis on the smartphone, while simultaneously emphasizing the need for intelligent UIs in sensor devices like the *FitBit Surge*.

FitBit Surge

Smartphone

Sensors

Fig. 7. Dynamic interface.

Insufficient protection of users' private information is a major security risk related to the extensive use of sensor-generated information. Mancini et al. [30] proposed that the investigation of mobile privacy requires a diversified approach, in which cross-interpretations of data from complementary studies should be mandatory.

Mobile privacy issues are difficult to study and poorly understood because direct observation methods are typically intrusive to study settings. On the other hand, exploiting user information is critical to success in proactivity, self-tuning, and behavioral change. Greater dependence on pervasive computing systems makes users aware of their own movements, behavior patterns, and habits [24]. However, Patil et al. [31] found that the motivations for using location sharing data were connecting and coordinating within own circles to project an image of 'checking in' and receiving rewards.

From a critical perspective, sensors can be noisy, and machine-learning algorithms are not always accurate. The concept is too technology-centric, and the expectation of exposing users to extensive physiological monitoring is an issue. Morozov [32] gives a detailed and interesting perspective of the nonsense raised by the advent of the Internet, the rise of the social web, and the smart gadgets that are making humans "dumb." Further, David Berry, a critical theorist [33] has pointed out that conceptualizing the world of digital media can have implications on society norms.

Accurate context detection is a challenging problem, as mentioned by Paul Dourish in his book, *Where the Action Is* [34]. Many assumptions might fail to hold true in challenging real-world situations. However, the pace at which the technology is progressing, the proposed framework presents an opportunity to be better prepared for future technology utilization. In this regard, it is essential for future research to focus on the robustness of the framework dimensions, and the links among these dimensions should be thoroughly studied.

The insights from our workshops suggest that the determination of context through sensors is emerging. The framework may have been limited by the participants' cultural backgrounds, professions, and the provided sensors, which may have introduced bias variables. The concept of a dynamic interface to give simple and reliable information is another issue in terms of user experience. In particular, content provided to a user needs to be credible and filtered in a such a way that objectivity and information value needs are maintained and the user's needs are addressed. This, in turn, calls for understanding the ethical implications related to social sensor technologies. Interestingly, however, ethical aspects have not been extensively discussed in relation to persuasive systems [35].

Finally, our findings are subject to limitations which offer avenues for future research. First, our research approach was highly exploratory. Hence, additional research in the area is needed to increase the trustworthiness of the results and their interpretations. Second, in order to keep the scope of the study manageable, several important issues, such as security, privacy, trust, and user experience were excluded from our investigation. We thus suggest future research covering these areas.

References

1. Aggarwal, C., Abdelzaher, T.: Social sensing. In: Aggarwal, C.C. (ed.) Managing and Mining Sensor Data, pp. 237–297. Springer, New York (2013)
2. Sellen, A.J., Fogg, A., Aitken, M., Hodges, S., Rother, C., Wood, K.: Do life-logging technologies support memory for the past? An experimental study using sensecam. In: SIGCHI Conference on Human Factors in Computing System, pp. 81–90 (2007)

3. Neff, G., Nafus, D.: Self-Tracking. Essential Knowledge Series. The MIT Press, Cambridge (2016)
4. Oinas-Kukkonen, H., Oinas-Kukkonen, H.: Humanizing the Web, Change and Social Innovation. Palgrave Macmillan, Basingstoke (2013)
5. Sensors: Sensors, convert the measurement into a signal. www.what-is-a-sensor.com/
6. Antonio, I.: The social Internet of things: from objects that communicate to objects that socialize in the Internet. In: 50th FITCE, University Mediterranea, August 31–September 1 2011 (2011)
7. Aggarwal, C., Abdelzaher, T.: Integrating sensors and social networks. In: Aggarwal, C.C. (ed.) Social Network Data Analytics, pp. 379–412. Springer, New York (2011)
8. Ahmed, M., Karagiorgou, S., Pfoser, D., Wenk, C.: A comparison and evaluation of map construction algorithms using vehicle tracking data. GeoInformatica **19**(3), 601–632 (2015)
9. Google Blog, Google maps and Waze, outsmarting traffic together. www.google blog.blogspot.fi/2013/06/google-maps-and-waze-outsmarting.html
10. Sensor Networks. www.citysense.com
11. Kurata, N., Spencer, B.F., Ruiz-Sandoval, M.: Risk monitoring of buildings with wireless sensor networks. Struct. Control Health Monit. **12**, 315–327 (2005)
12. O'Reilly, T., Battelle, J.: Web Squared: Web 2.0 Five years on, Web 2.0 Summit (2009). www.web2summit.com
13. Schmidt, A.: Context-Aware Computing: Context-Awareness, Context-Aware User Interfaces, and Implicit Interaction. The Encyclopedia of HCI, 2nd edn. (2013)
14. Tamminen, et al.: Understanding mobile context. Pers. Ubiquit. Comput. **8**, 135–143 (2004)
15. FitBit Products: Surge, One, and Aria (2016). www.fitbit.com/uk/store
16. Spire Product: Discover your calm (2016). www.spire.io
17. BiiSafe Product: More than a key finder (2016). www.biisafe.com
18. Orszag, P.R., Ellis, P.: The challenge of rising healthcare costs – a view from the congressional budget office. N. Engl. J. Med. **357**, 1793–1795 (2007)
19. Lymberis, A., Dittmar, A.: Advanced wearable health systems and applications - research and development efforts in the European Union. IEEE Eng. Med. Biol. Mag. **26**(3), 29–33 (2007)
20. Leijdekkers, P., Gay, V., Lawrence, E.: Smart homecare system for health tele-monitoring. In: First International Conference on the Digital Society (2007)
21. Telegraph (2016). http://www.telegraph.co.uk/news/health/elder/12113536/NHS-remote-monitoring-will-allow-dementia-patients-to-stay-at-home.html
22. Biswas, J., Tolstikov, A., Jayachandran, M., Foo, V., Wai, A., Phua, C., Huang, W., Shue, L., Gopalakrishnan, K., Lee, J., Yap, P.: Health and wellness monitoring through wearable and ambient sensors: exemplars from home-based care of elderly with mild dementia. Ann. Telecommun. **65**(9–10), 505–521 (2014)
23. Loe, M.: Doing it my way: old women, technology and wellbeing. Sociol. Health Illn. **32**(2), 319–334 (2010). Blackwell Publishing Ltd
24. Satyanarayanan, M.: Pervasive computing: vision and challenges. IEEE Pers. Commun. **8**(4), 10–17 (2001)
25. Weiser, M.: The computer for the 21st century. SIGMOBILE Mob. Comput. Commun. Rev. **3**(3), 3–11 (1999)
26. Schmidt, A., Beigl, M., Gellersen, H.W.: There is more to context than location. Comput. Graph. **23**(6), 893–901 (1999)
27. Dey, A.K.: Understanding and using context. Pers. Ubiquit. Comput. **5**(1), 4–7 (2001)
28. Chen, G., Li, M., Kotz, D.: Data-centric middleware for context-aware pervasive computing. Pervasive Mobile Comput. **4**(2), 216–253 (2008)

29. Santos, A., Cardoso, J., Ferreira, D., Diniz, P., Chainho, P.: Providing context for mobile and social networking applications. Pervasive Mobile Comput. **6**, 324–341 (2010)
30. Mancini, C., Thomas, K., Rogers, Y., Price, B.A., Jedrzejczyk, L., Bandara, A.K., Joinson, A.N., Nuseibeh, B.: From spaces to places: emerging contexts in mobile privacy. In: 11th ICUC, 30 September – 3 October, pp. 1–10 (2009)
31. Patil, S., et al.: Reasons, rewards, regrets: privacy considerations in location sharing as an interactive practice. In: SOUPS, 11–13 July 2012 (2012)
32. Berry, D.M.: Critical Theory and the Digital. Bloomsbury Publishing, New York (2014)
33. Morozov, E.: To Save Everything, Click Here: Technology, Solutionism, and the Urge to Fix Problems That Don't Exist. Penguin, UK (2013)
34. Dourish, P.: Where the Action Is: The Foundations of Embodied Interaction. MIT, Cambridge (2004)
35. Torning, K., Oinas-Kukkonen, H.: Persuasive system design: state of the art and future directions. In: 4th International Conference on Persuasive Technology. ACM (2009)

Towards Process Patterns for Processing Data Having Various Qualities

Agung Wahyudi(✉) and Marijn Janssen

Faculty of Technology, Policy and Management,
Delft University of Technology, Jaffalaan 5, 2628 BX Delft, The Netherlands
A.Wahyudi1@tudelft.nl, M.F.W.H.A.Janssen@tudelft.nl

Abstract. Organizations become more data-intensive and companies try to reap the benefits from this. Although there is a large amount of data available, this data has often different qualities which hinders use. Creating value from big data requires dealing with the variations in quality. Depending on their quality, data need to be processed in various ways to prepare this data for use. Although the processes vary, dealing with certain levels of data quality is a recurring challenge for many organizations. By developing generic process patterns organizations can reuse each other solutions. In this paper, process patterns for dealing with various levels of data quality are derived based on a case study of a large telecom company that employs all kinds of data to create operational value. The process patterns can possibly be used by other organizations.

Keywords: Big data · Data quality · Data processing · Process patterns · Telecom

1 Introduction

Today's organizations collect more and more data due to datafication. Datafication refers to activities that digitalize all objects which are related to the organizations' processing chain [1, 2]. Data can originate from internal and external sources and might have different qualities. Data quality refers to data that are fit for use by data users or data consumers [3, 4]. The definition of data quality captures a broad perspectives by including by the quality conveyed by the data and the use of the data.

Many studies suggest that organizations can gain benefits from the data if they succeed in unlocking value from the data. This can result in greater efficiency and profits [5] as well as competitive advantages [6–8]. Therefore, organizations are seeking ways to realize the value from their big data [8].

Value creation requires the processing of data. Data can be processed in various ways (e.g. [9–11]). Although the idea of drawing value from the data seems to be straightforward, many organizations failed to do so. According to a recent study by Reid et al. [12], two third of businesses across Europe and North America failed to unlock value from big data. In this paper, we identify generic process patterns that can be used by any organization to deal with data which have various data qualities. The various data qualities of internal and external sources require organizations to deal with them in various manners. Which process should be followed depends on the data

© IFIP International Federation for Information Processing 2016
Published by Springer International Publishing Switzerland 2016. All Rights Reserved
Y.K. Dwivedi et al. (Eds.): I3E 2016, LNCS 9844, pp. 493–504, 2016.
DOI: 10.1007/978-3-319-45234-0_44

qualities. These variations have some similarities that create process patterns of how organizations deal with them. Which process should be followed depends on the data qualities. The data quality provides the initial set of conditions to select the process steps that are necessary to prepare the data for use. Such patterns can be viewed as a practice which can be reused or from which others can learn. We view a process pattern as a recurring sequence of steps that results in the accomplishment of a certain value. Given certain starting conditions, the patterns can be followed to create value form the data. Process patterns should be independent on the technology implementation. They should enable organizations to more easily create value from the data.

The objective of this research is to derive process patterns for creating value from data. For this purpose, a case study in the Telecom industry is investigated and typical process patterns are derived. The research approach is presented in Sect. 2. On the basis of state-of-the-art literature in Sect. 3 and a case study at a telecom in Indonesia presented in Sect. 4, the patterns will be presented in Sect. 5. Finally, conclusions will be drawn in Sect. 6.

2   Research Approach

The purpose of this study is to identify process patterns. First, the concept of big data quality, data processing, and process patterns were identified from a rigorous review of literature. Since this study aims at enhancing our understanding of how an organization overcame big data quality challenge to create value from the data, a qualitative case study-based approach was used to inductively arrive at process patterns [13]. Qualitative case study research is widely used in information systems research, and is well suited to understanding the interactions between information technology-related innovations and organizational contexts [14]. According to Yin [13], the case study includes a variety of data collection instruments to ensure construct validity.

The following criteria were used for the selection of the case: (1) the case is in an information-intensive organization context; (2) the case employs and combines many datasets to create operational value; and (3) case study information should be available and accessible. We conducted a case study within the context of PT Telekomunikasi Indonesia Tbk., the biggest telecom in Indonesia, which provided the researchers with unlimited access to subject matter experts and internal documentation for all the cases. This helped to perform triangulation to ensure the construct validity of the case study [13].

3   Literature Review

3.1   Data Quality (DQ)

Data quality (DQ) is a prominent challenge mentioned in the big data literature [8, 15–21]. As described by Redman [22], low DQ impacts on operational level, tactical level, and strategic level of organizations, e.g. cost increase (to 8–12 % of revenue), poorer decision making, and difficulties in setting strategies.

Wand and Wang [23] define DQ as "data that are fit for use by data users or data consumers" (p. 6). This definition draws the attention to the view that DQ is not only related to the data it conveys, but also to the use of the data. Wang and Strong [4] classify DQ into four types based on data of consumers' point of view, namely (1) intrinsic DQ that denotes that data have quality in their own right (e.g. accuracy); (2) contextual DQ that highlights the requirement that DQ must be considered within the context of the task at hand (e.g. value-added); (3) representational DQ describing that DQ is related to data representation (e.g. interpretability); and (4) accessibility DQ that emphasizes the importance of computer systems that provide access to data (e.g. accessibility). High DQ is explained by Wand and Wang [23]: "high quality data should be intrinsically good, contextually appropriate for the task, clearly represented, and accessible to the data consumer" (p. 22).

In order to unlock value from the data, organizations very often combine many datasets from various data sources whether internally or externally. Those datasets may have varieties of DQ which organizations should take into account when they process them. When DQ is low, often a process are started to deal with the low quality, before the data can be used. In this way, 'garbage in is garbage out' is avoided.

3.2 Data Processing

Due to the variability of DQ in datasets, there is no uniform way to process them. As such, which process should be followed depends on the DQ. Normally, data are processed sequentially in data lifecycles which encompass all facets of data generation to knowledge creation [10]. There are many models of data lifecycles in the literatures. Some prominent ones are Data Documentation Initiative (DDI) Combined Lifecycle Model [9], DataOne Data Lifecycle [10], and ANDS Data Sharing Verbs [11]. The DDI Combined Life Cycle Model has eight activities in a data lifecycle, namely (1) study concept; (2) data collection; (3) data processing; (4) data archiving; (5) data distribution; (6) data discovery; (7) data analysis; and (8) repurposing. Meanwhile, activities defined in the DataOne Data Lifecycle are (1) planning, (2) collecting, (3) assuring, (4) describing, (5) preserving, (6) discovering, (7) integrating, and (8) analyzing. The ANDS Data Sharing Verbs consist of: (1) create, (2) store, (3) describe, (4) identify, (5) register, (6) discover, (7) access, and (8) exploit.

Although these models use various terminologies, all models of the data lifecycles have common activities which reflect data provider's and data consumer's point of view. Our study focuses on data consumer's point of view because we focus on the process of unlocking value from many data which have varying DQ.

From data consumer's perspective, the first step of data processing is to discover relevant data from data providers. It could be conducted by using searchable interfaces to locate the data or by making agreements with data providers. This step may require user registration and signing in.

The next step is to access the data. Data can be accessed either through an automated system (i.e. using a Web link, perhaps passing through an authentication barrier and/or licensing agreement), or by an application to a data consumer.

Third, data need to be exploited. Data exploitation requires good technical metadata (fields, descriptions, metrics, etc.), which provide contextual information about the way the data were created. Cleansing, parsing, and other functions to prepare the data to be fit for analysis are also involved in this step. Moreover, it also includes the transformation of several different datasets into a common representation (format, coding scheme, and ontology), accounting for methodological and semantic differences while preserving a provenance trail. In addition, the dataset very frequently needs to be combined with other datasets so that more insights or knowledge could be obtained.

The final step is to analyze the data. We apply statistical and analytical models to the data in order to extract meaningful answers to the prior research questions.

3.3   Process Patterns

The aforementioned data lifecycle provides the bases for creating process patterns. Data processing may vary based on DQ of the data. For example, internal data which have a high DQ need not to be assessed as this is already known, but external data (e.g. Twitter data) should be assessed first and maybe cleansed prior to exploitation. The variation of data lifecycle for dealing with a dataset results in a process pattern.

The terminology process pattern is comprised of "process" and "pattern". According to Davenport [24], a process is "a specific ordering of work activities across time and place with a beginning and an end, and clearly identified inputs and outputs: a structure for action" (p. 21). Inline with this, Ambler [25] defines a process as "a series of action to produce one or more outputs from one or more inputs" (p. 2). He also defines a pattern as "a general solution to a common problem, one from which a specific solution may be derived" (p. 4). Patterns have been applied in various domains, e.g. architecture, economics, telecommunication, business, and software engineering [26]. Patterns in software engineering come in many flavors, including (but are not limited to) analysis patterns, design patterns, and process patterns. Hagen and Gruhn [27] define process patterns as "patterns that represent proven process which solves a frequently recurring problem in a pattern like way" (p. 1). Process patterns provide flexibility in their use since one can select and apply a suitable process pattern according to the situation under study.

In the literature, there is no consensus about what should be included in a process pattern. Buschmann et al. [26] mentions that a pattern must consist of contexts, problems, and solutions. A context of a pattern describes a design situation that gives rise to a design problem. The problem describes a concrete situation which may emerge in the contextual application. A pattern should mention internal and external forces, e.g. influences of customers, competitors, component vendors, time and money constraints and requirements. The solutions describe the process that consists of a set of activities that are supposed to solve the problem if they are executed. Process patterns of overcoming DQ challenges assist organizations in creating value from the data. They also serve as catalogs and repositories to the organizations for future use.

4 Case Study

The goal of the case study was to derive process patterns. For this reason, the case study involved multiple methods for collecting data. In the case study, the primary processes of PT Telekomunikasi Indonesia Tbk., a state-owned telecom company in Indonesia, were selected for analysis.. The primary processes of the CDMA marketing department were focused on, as the marketing department dealt with various sources of data having a variety of data qualities.

The traditional way of marketing based on intuition mostly resulted in ineffective targeting, segmenting, and positioning of products. As a result, the program often ended with unsatisfactory returns on marketing investments. The program did not have sufficient justification and it was hard to predict its success. Moreover, the marketing activities sometimes unexpectedly turned back to the rise of customer complaints, customer churn, and financial loss. The tight competition in the market and the increasing power of customers kept forcing them to respond competitor moves and customer voices with attractive programs. On the other hands, the programs should be designed very carefully not to impact their customers' satisfaction and long-term profitability, e.g. discounting cash-cow products for which customers were willing to pay or giving massive national-wide promotion which would result in network over-load and congestion in dense cities.

Many data generated by the telecom, e.g. transaction data, customer data, machine logs, network performance data, etc., and external data such as social media, crowd-sourced maps, could potentially be used to target customers better. By com-bining those data, they designed an attractive discount program. As mentioned by Verhoef et al. [28], organizations can obtain value from the data in a bidirectional way, i.e. value to customer and value to organization. From the program, customers of the telecom benefited by obtaining budget communication solution and perceived quality. Meanwhile, as the impact of customer experience, the telecom benefited by increasing

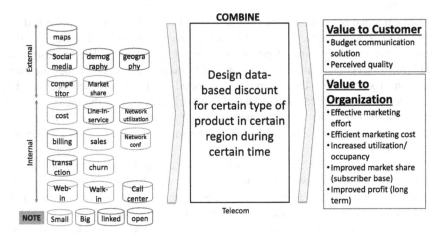

Fig. 1. Case Study: a telecom designed a data-based discount program

its market share, improved brand recognition, and high return on marketing cost. The way the telecom turned the data into value is illustrated in Fig. 1.

The company built the information system that had a number of functionalities to process the big data. Prior to running the program, an initial kick-off meeting that included data providers and related departments was held. The marketing and IT department proposed a model that described how to turn the data into decision. From the model, they listed all the required data and made agreements with the data providers on access, metadata, cut-off time, etc. The IT department built a data lake to pool data that had been retrieved with restricted/limited access and some data from machines with concurrency issue. They also employed a number of tools to cleanse the low quality data and parse the data that had unfit representation for the further process. Syncsort DMX-h Hadoop application was utilized to exploit the data. The application had extracting, transforming, aggregating, and loading functionalities. Many datasets were combined and transformed based on the task at hand. The processes involved a number of execution activities that include one or more datasets, e.g. joining, aggregating, then manipulating fields, rejoining, etc. Furthermore, the data were analyzed using trade-off analytics and visualized using Microsoft Excel. The program was then proposed to the board of executives for decision. Sometimes, iterations between the aforementioned processes occurred.

Initially, drawing value from the data seemed straightforward using the functions provided in the information system. However, it was found to be complex in terms of data quality variation. Since the telecom incorporated many datasets, the DQ of the datasets varied greatly. Internal big data and partners' data usually come with high intrinsic DQ because these data were self-managed (e.g. by periodic calibration of data-generating sensors, quality control, or using service-level agreements with partners). However, the datasets may have low accessibility DQ, contextual DQ and representational DQ. For example, call center recordings which were mostly unstructured caused difficulties for technical staffs to process (ease of operation); many data were just thrown to the data lake but never used (value-added); machine logs had varied representation depending on the machine's manufacturer (consistent representation).

Unlike internal big data, external big data such as social media very often had low intrinsic DQ. For example, Twitter data might have a data-biased issue (i.e. they represent only certain groups of people, e.g. young generation). The unbiased data could lead to inaccurate outcomes if employed to make a conclusion about the entire population. External big data were also reported to have low accessibility DQ (e.g. license/subscription fee which leads to no/limited access to the data), low representational DQ (e.g. no metadata which causes a problem in understanding and interpreting the data), and low contextual DQ (e.g. outdated statistical data which was not fit in the task).

As a result, there were many ways of data processing based on DQ of the data. Fortunately, some patterns were indicated in the case that showed specific solutions for particular problems of DQ. From these, process patterns could be derived. Recurring specific processes were found, namely data processing, for a particular DQ problem, from which a process pattern was derived. For example, accuracy problem was solved by cleansing the data before exploitation.

5 Discussion

The objective of this paper was to identify process patterns for dealing with different DQ. To do so, the organizations developed an information system having various functionalities. Data were processed in a data processing sequence, which followed the data lifecycle from a high level of abstraction. From the literature and the case study, we derived the following typical data lifecycle. We used similar steps as found in the literature (See Sect. 3.2), but we extended this by including a managing process that could occur in any step of data lifecycle. It consists of connecting, controlling, and integration functions so that the data processing sequences can be executed. Moreover, we listed all functionalities related to every step of nominal data lifecycle. The nominal data lifecycle together with the functionalities used to process the data is shown in Fig. 2.

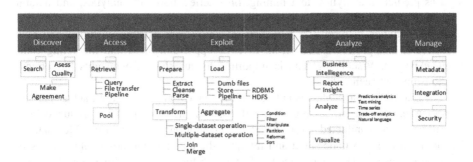

Fig. 2. Functions used in each step of a nominal data lifecycle

The first step in the nominal data lifecycle was the "discover data" step. In this step, some functions such as search, assess quality, and make agreement were employed. Search functions assisted them to quickly find relevant data from many datasets in the data lake. Assessing quality is important to determine whether actions to improve the quality are needed in the subsequent steps. In order to use the data properly, organizations make agreements with the data providers on: (1) what data should be included in the process?; (2) how to retrieve the data?; (3) when was the cut-off time or the retrieval time?; (4) how to read the data?; and (5) what if the data were not intrinsically good (e.g. corrupted)?

The "access data" step consists of retrieving and pooling the data. Retrieving the data is strongly related to accessibility. A number of activities were used, such as query, flat file transfer, or process pipeline. Sometimes organizations pool the data in the data lake for several reasons, such as limited/restricted access, concurrency issue, etc.

The third step, "exploit data" is one of the most challenging steps in terms of the application complexity. Because there is seldom a single application that has all the functionalities, various applications having separate functions are composed together to perform data exploitation. Interoperability and standardization are key success factors to get all applications working together. Some functions in this step are preparing, transforming, aggregating, and loading the data. In the "preparing step", some data might need to be extracted because they are retrieved as compressed flat files, cleansed because they contain low intrinsic quality (e.g. low accuracy), or parsed because their original representation is not fit for the further process. The organizations transform the data using single-dataset and multi-dataset operations. Functions such as conditioning, filtering, manipulating, partitioning, reformatting, sorting, joining, and merging are selected based on the task in hand. The combination and iteration of those functions are found very often. Aggregating the data is supposed to reduce the data based on certain fields. The outputs are loaded either to dumb flat files, stored in the relational databases, passed to HDFS, or put into the pipeline to the next process.

The next step was to "analyze" the data. Functions included in this step are business intelligence, analyzing, and visualizing the data. Business intelligence has been used extensively to generate reports. Analyzing the data is the most difficult task because it creates the value of the data. The data were analyzed using various analytical methods such as predictive analytics, text mining, time series, trade-off analytics, and natural language, depending on the task in hand. In the case study, the telecom exhibited trade-off analytics between the projected revenue (from existing customer and new subscribers) and projected cost (from revenue opportunity loss and marketing campaign expense). Visualizing data is important to quickly grasp insights (e.g. trend, relationship) between datasets.

The step of "manage" data is not part of the sequential process, but manages all the aforementioned data processing steps. It ensures the data pressing sequence run smoothly. It is conducted thru metadata, integration, and security. Metadata is important in order to understand and interpret the data so that they could be reused. Integration ensures the involvement of many actors and the utilization of many applications could run smoothly.

From the case study, we found that every dataset had a variation of data processes depending on its DQ. Figure 3 shows a data process pattern for the situation in which all datasets have high DQ.

However, if any dataset has a low DQ, the data processing takes different paths, different from the typical process. Combining the concept of DQ from Wang and Strong [4] and the case study, we derived four process patterns as described in Table 1. The process patterns consist of DQ context, problem, and the solution that reflect the modification of the typical data process.

Process pattern 1 represents the change of typical data processing to take low intrinsic DQ into account. The example of dataset from the case study is customer complaint from social media (e.g. Twitter). The data have low accuracy because some

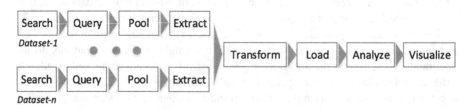

Fig. 3. Typical data process pattern when all datasets have high DQ

Table 1. Process patterns of DQ challenge: the context, problem, and solution (the red words indicates different patterns from the typical process)

DQ dimension	Dataset	Problems	Process Pattern
Intrinsic - Accuracy - Objectivity	Customer complaint from social media	Some data were from real customers, other data maybe from black campaigners	1 Search→ Assess accuracy → Query → Pool → Extract → Cleanse → Transform → Load → Analyze→ Visualize
Representational - Interpretability - Consistent representation	Network performance data	Varied terminologies and data representation across vendors' machines	2 Search → Make agreement → Metadata→ Integration → Query → Pool → Extract → Transform: Manipulate→ Load→ Analyze→ Visualize
Accessibility - Accessibility - Security	Transaction data	- Existing machines were not capable of handling many concurrent access (scalability) - Very restricted access - Privacy issue	3 Search→ Access securely → Query → Pool: Data lake → Extract → Transform: Manipulate → Load → Analyze → Visualize
Contextual - Value-added	Many datasets	Lack of knowledge of how to derive value	4 Search → Metadata → Query → Pool → Extract → Transform → Load → Analyze: Model → Visualize

conversations were not generated by real customers, but maybe driven by fake accounts and black campaigners. Moreover, not the entire customers are represented in the social media, e.g. the old generation. Therefore, prior to exploitation, the data should be assessed for their accuracy. Because we are unable to improve their accuracy, cleansing is the only way to remove data with low accuracy.

Process pattern 2 considers the low representational DQ. From the case study, the network performance data generated by machines from many vendors are hard to interpret because varied terminologies are used across vendors' machines. Therefore, metadata are very important to understand so that they can be reused. The data also have inconsistent representation, because each vendor has different formulations of performance indicators (e.g. drop call). Organizations should make agreements on performance indicators (e.g. standardization) that are applied across vendors' machines. In the exploitation step, the fields containing performance indicators need to be manipulated so that they represent consistently for the subsequent process. In a multi-software vendor environment, often different methods of access are used, e.g. direct query to databases, file transfer, query from the vendor's application, SNMP logs, etc. Therefore, integration ensures that the information system could handle multiple ways of access.

Low accessibility DQ is represented by *process pattern 3*. From the case, the transaction data were generated by the machines that were not designed to process many concurrent connections. Therefore, organizations create a data lake to store the data so that they access the source once but reuse the data many times from the data lake. Moreover, organizations may have strict regulations about access to the machines. Hence, accessing data from the data provider in a secure way is very important. Privacy issue could concern organizations. Therefore, in the exploitation process, they may manipulate the fields related to privacy to be anonymous.

Process pattern 4 addresses low contextual DQ. Most of datasets have unknown value prior to the use. Therefore, the model to use the data in the analysis step is important for the organizations to create value from the data. Metadata are also important so that the data could be put into a contextual use.

The process patterns describe the recurring problems of big data quality together with the solutions that consist of certain functions to solve the problem. The process patterns can be reused for any organization in order to create value from the data.

6 Conclusion

The objective of this paper is to derive process patterns for creating operational value from data in information-intensive organizations. Four patterns have been identified based on differences in data quality. A case study in a telecom was investigated. In the case, the telecom combined many data, including internal and external data, to design a big data marketing program in order to increase market share and profit.

The creation of value from the data depends heavily on the data quality. Various data need different data processing steps based on the quality they have. This led us to look for process patterns for every big data quality problems. Combining literature review and the case study, we proposed four process patterns that map big data quality problems in data processing, together with the following solutions. Process pattern 1 deals with low intrinsic data quality, e.g. inaccurate and biased. Functionalities such as accessing accuracy and cleansing are added to the typical data processing pattern. Low representational data quality is encountered by process pattern 2. Challenges like interpretability and consistent representation are solved by the functionalities such as metadata, making agreements, integration, and manipulation. Process pattern 3 considers low accessibility data quality. Secure access, building a data lake, and data manipulation are needed from dealing with restricted access, concurrency, and privacy. Process pattern 4 copes with low contextual data quality. To turn the data into value, models to use the data and metadata are two important elements in this pattern.

A limitation of this study is that the patterns were derived using a single case study in a particular field. It is recommended that more empirical research is conducted in other fields to test and refine the proposed process patterns as well as to evaluate the process patterns and the significance of their elements.

References

1. Mayer-Schönberger, V., Cukier, K.: Big Data: A Revolution That Will Transform How We Live, Work, and Think. Houghton Mifflin Harcourt, Boston (2013)
2. Bauer, F., Kaltenbock, M.: Linked Open Data: The Essentials (2011)
3. Lee, Y.W., et al.: AIMQ: a methodology for information quality assessment. Inf. Manag. **40**(2), 133–146 (2002)
4. Wang, R.Y., Strong, D.M.: Beyond accuracy: what data quality means to data consumers. J. Manag. Inf. Syst. **12**(4), 5–33 (1996)
5. Gantz, J., Reinsel, D.: Extracting value from chaos. IDC iview **1142**, 9–10 (2011)
6. Manyika, J., et al.: Big data: the next frontier for innovation, competition, and productivity (2011)
7. Zikopoulos, P.C., et al.: Understanding Big Data. McGraw-Hill, New York (2012)
8. LaValle, S., et al.: Big data, analytics and the path from insights to value. MIT Sloan Manag. Rev. **21** (2013)
9. Green, A., Kent, J.-P.: The metadata life cycle. In: MetaNet Work Package 1: Methodology and Tools, pp. 29–34 (2002)
10. Michener, W.K., Jones, M.B.: Ecoinformatics: supporting ecology as a data-intensive science. Trends Ecol. Evol. **27**(2), 85–93 (2012)
11. Burton, A., Treloar, A.: Designing for discovery and re-use: the 'ANDS data sharing verbs' approach to service decomposition. Int. J. Digit. Curation **4**(3), 44–56 (2009)
12. Reid, C., et al.: Seizing the information advantage: how organizations can unlock value and insight from the information they hold (2015)
13. Yin, R.K.: Case Study Research: Design and Methods. Sage publications, Thousand Oaks (2013)
14. Nag, R., Hambrick, D.C., Chen, M.J.: What is strategic management, really? inductive derivation of a consensus definition of the field. Strateg. Manag. J. **28**(9), 935–955 (2007)
15. Zuiderwijk, A., et al.: Socio-technical impediments of open data. Electron. J. e-Government **10**(2), 156–172 (2012)
16. Chen, C.L.P., Zhang, C.-Y.: Data-intensive applications, challenges, techniques and technologies: a survey on big data. Inf. Sci. **275**, 314–347 (2014)
17. Fan, J.Q., Han, F., Liu, H.: Challenges of big data analysis. Nat. Sci. Rev. **1**(2), 293–314 (2014)
18. Marx, V.: The big challenges of big data. Nature **498**(7453), 255–260 (2013)
19. Millard, I., et al.: Consuming multiple linked data sources: challenges and experiences (2010)
20. Zhou, Z.H., et al.: Big data opportunities and challenges: discussions from data analytics perspectives. IEEE Comput. Intell. Mag. **9**(4), 62–74 (2014)
21. Zicari, R.V.: Big data: challenges and opportunities. In: Big Data Computing, pp. 103–128 (2014)
22. Redman, T.C.: The impact of poor data quality on the typical enterprise. Commun. ACM **41**(2), 79–82 (1998)
23. Wand, Y., Wang, R.Y.: Anchoring data quality dimensions in ontological foundations. Commun. ACM **39**(11), 86–95 (1996)
24. Davenport, T.H.: Process Innovation: Reengineering Work Through Information Technology. Harvard Business Press, Boston (2013)
25. Ambler, S.W.: More Process Patterns: Delivering Large-Scale Systems Using Object Technology. Cambridge University Press, New York (1999)

26. Buschmann, F., et al.: A System of Patterns: Pattern-Oriented Software Architecture. Wiley, Chichester (2004)
27. Hagen, M., Gruhn, V.: Towards flexible software processes by using process patterns. In: IASTED Conference on Software Engineering and Applications (2004
28. Verhoef, P.C., Kooge, E., Walk, N.: Creating Value with Big Data Analytics: Making Smarter Marketing Decisions. Routledge, Abingdon (2015)

Business Intelligence from User Generated Content: Online Opinion Formation in Purchasing Decisions in High-Tech Markets

Karan Setiya[1], Jolien Ubacht[2(✉)], Scott Cunningham[2],
and Sertaç Oruç[3]

[1] Deloitte Consulting, Almere, The Netherlands
ksetiya@deloitte.nl
[2] Faculty of Technology, Policy and Management,
Delft University of Technology, Delft, The Netherlands
{j.ubacht,s.cunningham}@tudelft.nl
[3] Sybo Games, Copenhagen, Denmark
sertac@sertacoruc.com

Abstract. User Generated Content (UGC) requires new business intelligence methods to understand the influence of online opinion formation on customer purchasing decisions. We developed a conceptual model for deriving business intelligence from tweets, based on the Classical Model of Consensus Formation and the Theory of Planned Behaviour. We applied the model to the dynamic high-tech smartphone market by means of three case studies on the launch of new smartphones. By using Poisson regression, data- and sentiment-analysis on tweets we show how opinion leadership and real-life events effect the volume of online chatter and sentiments about the launch of new smartphones. Application of the model reveals businesses parameters that can be influenced to enhance competitiveness in dynamic high tech markets. Our conceptual model is suitable to be turned into a predictive model that takes the richness of tweets in online opinion formation into account.

Keywords: Business intelligence · User Generated Content · Twitter · Sentiment analysis · Opinion formation · Smartphones · High-tech markets

1 Introduction

Nowadays having an online presence is the norm for enterprises. At the same time, the amount of data produced on the Web is increasing rapidly. Consequently, the ability of handling this data is becoming increasingly important for enterprises in order to gain competitive advantage [6] and retain market position. In our study, we specifically focus on how this phenomenon of the increased importance of User Generated Content (UGC) fits into high-tech industries. High-tech industries are characterized by high sunk costs, high risks and being dynamic with rapidly changing customer requirements and product characteristics/features [3]. Obtaining and sustaining competitive advantage requires different methods in such fast-paced industries compared to other (low-tech) industries where the operating environment is less prone to rapid change.

Published by Springer International Publishing Switzerland 2016. All Rights Reserved
Y.K. Dwivedi et al. (Eds.): I3E 2016, LNCS 9844, pp. 505–521, 2016.
DOI: 10.1007/978-3-319-45234-0_45

This leads us to raise the question of whether the analysis of UGC can help generate better insights into a fast moving consumer market with short production cycles. In the smartphone industry, we recognize the aforementioned trends of increased data being generated from (mobile) devices; there is an increasing amount of mobile UGC and UGC is increasingly influencing public image and sales of products [16]. The smartphone industry itself is characterized by short product life cycles, rapid product and feature imitation, aggressive pricing strategies, highly price sensitive end-consumers and high barriers to entry [4]. In our study, we developed a conceptual model for deriving business intelligence from microblog posts. The objective of applying this model is to obtain new insights into the way that prevailing opinions are formed within UGC by analysing tweets. We applied the conceptual model on three real life cases of new smartphones. The main research question in this study is *"What kind of business intelligence on opinion formation of end users can be derived from tweets?"*.

Business intelligence applications of UGC is a relatively new field of academic study, a literature review yielded a limited number of studies where UGC is used to relate to real world phenomena such as predicting movie box office returns based on tweets [2] or presidential election polls [15]. In both studies the UGC analysis produced more accurate predictions than traditional methods. While many studies have recognized the potential of UGC analysis for business intelligence, only very few provide a methodology and apply this methodology to real cases, whereas the importance of understanding the potential of UGC in business-settings is increasing. Therefore, by means of developing a theoretical model on the role of opinion formation, we shed light on the types of business insights that can be derived from User Generated Content.

In Sect. 2 we present the conceptual model that we developed for measuring online opinion formation, based on the *Classical Model of Consensus Formation* and the *Theory of Planned Behaviour*. Next, in Sect. 3, we present the empirical data and the statistical analysis that we performed in order to further understand the process of opinion formation, which in turn can be influenced by companies to their own (competitive) advantage. The outcomes of the empirical twitter analysis are presented in Sect. 4, in which we present a descriptive statistical model to describe the data, our Poisson regression analysis which shows the effect of our main independent variables (influencers, real world events and spam bots) on the tweets volume and sentiment and we show several aspects of User Generated Content that can be input for company (marketing) strategies. A reflection on our conceptual model is presented in Sect. 5. Finally, in Sect. 6 we answer our research question, reflect on limitations of the conceptual model and the empirical data analysis and formulate future research topics.

2 Conceptual Model

In order to develop our conceptual model for measuring online opinion formation, we examined two of the most important established models in the domain of online opinion formation and the drivers of (purchasing) behaviour (and in turn, competitive position): the *Classical Model of Consensus Formation* [5] and the *Theory of Planned Behaviour* (TPB) [1].

2.1 Classical Model of Consensus Formation

We used the adaptation of the Classical Model of Consensus Formation by Jackson [10] as a basis to explore the online opinion formation in the cases analysed. The original model by De Groot [5] describes that in a group of agents, no agent will simply share or strictly disregard the opinion of any other agent. Each agent in the network will take others' opinions into account when forming their own opinion. Repeatedly averaging this process of influencing leads to the newly formed opinions of the agents to either be brought closer to each other or be taken further apart. This can either lead to convergence into agreement or to divergence into disagreement. Jackson introduced opinion leaders to this Classical Model of Consensus Formation [10]. In the exploration and critical assessment of the model by De Groot [5] he states: *"Opinion leaders will arise naturally in the model, as individuals who are listened to by others and who have non-negligible influence on the opinions of at least some other agents."* (p. 296). He further states that when a network is strongly connected, such that there is a direct path from any agent to any other agent, and aperiodic, then it is convergent. Literature often presumes that this is the case; there are no agents who are not influenced by another agent's opinion. Translated to our research context this entails that if every person in a social network is, to some extent, influenced by the opinion of every other person in the same network, then a prevailing opinion will arise (convergence). The original model was adapted in our study to fit our more open context where the agents are in fact not strongly connected but linked via open social media. We used this model to describe the formation of the prevailing opinion from the collected tweets. Note that in our open context, a prevailing opinion which is carried by a majority of people in a network is not guaranteed since not every person in our data set is necessarily connected to every other person via a direct path. Therefore, multiple prevailing opinions can arise. This is important to acknowledge because multiple prevailing opinions adds complexity to understanding the formation of the prevailing opinion(s) and possible efforts to influence these.

2.2 Theory of Planned Behaviour (Subjective Norms)

The Theory of Planned Behaviour (TPB) by Azjen [1] is originally a theory from the psychology field. This theory describes the relation between beliefs and action and was proposed to build upon the Theory of Reasoned Action [9]. The TPB describes that human behaviour, specifically the intent to act, can be predicted by three types of considerations. The first consideration is attitude towards a certain behaviour: the way a person feels about the behaviour, personally. The second consideration is subjective norms: whether or not the specific behaviour is encouraged by friends and family. The third predictor of intention is *perceived behavioural control*: the extent to which the person feels able to overcome barriers to the behaviour. According to the TPB, these three considerations form the most important predictors of intention, subsequently intention is the most important predictor of behaviour. In our study, we consider prevailing online opinion as a proxy for *subjective norms*, which is one of the predictors of human behaviour.

2.3   Conceptualization

In Fig. 1 we present our conceptual model based on elements from the Classical Model of Consensus Formation with our own additions. The model illustrates how business insights can be derived from online chatter that leads to opinion formation by electronic word of mouth (eWOM). We consider online chatter as a continuous process of opinion formation. In our context the opinions are formed about products, specifically smartphones. Next, from the online opinion formation process we identify a number of key parameters that are expected to be the main determinants of the prevailing online opinion (in De Groot's model this is the formed consensus). The key implications are that firstly this prevailing opinion, in a way, is already a business insight. When we are able to discover a certain opinion about a product emerge from online chatter, this is grounds for a company to formulate a strategy to respond to this online product sentiment in order to influence it for the better (or in order to damage competitors' online product opinions). Although not tested in our study, we also suggest that these parameters are valuable sources for predicting intention to buy according to the Theory of Planned Behaviour. In turn, this can potentially contribute to improve the competitive advantage of companies in the high-tech market, given that appropriate actions are taken to utilize these insights. Here, the prevailing online opinion would be a proxy for subjective norms. In other words, the online opinion about a product is highly valued when making a purchasing decision or even in creating the intention to buy. This intention to buy, in turn, is a predictor for actual buying behaviour [1]. If future studies provide evidence that there is indeed a relationship between the online opinion formation via eWOM and purchasing behaviour, businesses could make use of this in their strategy to improve their competitive position. In our study, we focused on the continuous process of online opinion formation. From this, we recognised a number of key parameters that shape the prevailing opinion that yield business insights in the role of opinion formation in high-tech markets.

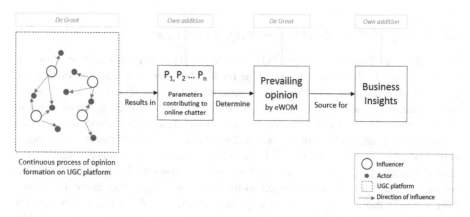

Fig. 1. Conceptual model for deriving competitive advantage from UGC analysis

3   Data Collection and Analysis Method

In this section we explain the methodology and technical architecture to make the operationalization and the practical application of our conceptual model explicit. First, we present our key design choices for the empirical data (analysis) such as the selection of tweets as a proxy for UGC and the rationale behind the selection of the specific cases. Next, we explain the high-level technical architecture which was used for data-collection and, in part, for data analysis. Finally, we explain how we interpreted the data by means of our conceptual model.

3.1   Data Collection

In order to test our conceptual model, we made a number of important design choices. First, we chose tweets as our UGC source. We consider tweets to be representative for a wider range of UGC (however not all UGC), similar to, amongst numerous other studies, [2, 11, 15]. Public tweets are relatively simple to collect through the Twitter APIs. Over 90 % of tweets are public, and can thus be captured programmatically, without the need to obtain special permissions to collect this (public) data. Also, it is important for businesses to be able to respond quickly to rapidly changing customer requirements in a dynamic market environment. Tweets lend themselves for such an objective as tweets can be collected almost in real-time, unlike most other forms of UGC. We collected tweets pertaining to the launch of three new smartphones in the market. We then used volume and sentiment of the tweets as metrics to find out the prevailing opinion about each product. According to Liu et al. [14], other studies of online word of mouth (eWOM), and research on traditional word of mouth (WOM), have identified volume (measured as the number of messages) and valence (classification of positive or negative) as two important measures of WOM activity.

The three smartphones selected for our case study are: Samsung Galaxy S5, Sony Xperia Z2 and HTC One (M8). Our case selection was based on both pragmatic considerations and an attempt to maximize the reliability versus construct validity trade-off. The three key considerations for our case selection were: (1) *the timing of the product launch*: we expected most online chatter about the products around the launch date, due to anticipation and buildup of online and offline hype (due to e.g. marketing efforts from manufacturers and brand loyalty from customers); (2) *similar product features*: each smartphone caters to a similar target market. With similar target markets, we can compare the opinion formation for the three cases and recognize specific capabilities that the companies show (such as employing a certain parameter to influence the prevailing opinion); (3) *Expected volume of online chatter*: for our statistical analyses, we needed to maximize the collected tweets in order to have a representative sample of the population of tweets. For collecting the tweets, we developed a web application which automatically queries the Twitter API with relevant key words for each case, processes the response by parsing the returned data and saving it in a database.

Figure 2 illustrates the high level technical architecture. Our web application queries Twitter's streaming API for tweets about our search terms such as "Samsung Galaxy S5". The response is dumped into our cache table of the database without

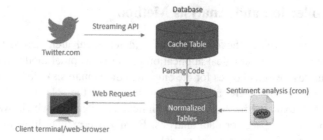

Fig. 2. High level technical architecture

parsing the data. Next, the raw data is parsed and saved to the respective tables in a MySQL database. This process of translating the raw data into our own data structure is known as *database normalization*. Our normalized data in the populated database is now ready for analysis. In our analysis, the key parameters that shape the prevailing opinion of each product are those factors that influence the volume and sentiment of our collected tweets. Before finding these parameters, we first needed to do a sentiment classification of our data set. To this end, we implemented a PHP class which classified our collected tweets into positive, neutral and negative sentiments based on natural language processing techniques. This sentiment classifier would run automatically each day to tag each tweet with its corresponding sentiment class. Once our populated, normalized database was classified, we used this dataset to analyse and interpret the data. Sentiment and volume of tweets are our dependent variables, and the key parameters that shape these variables become the independent variables.

3.2   Data Analysis

In total, we collected 1,448,799 tweets, which is a 369 days worth of tweets (with three simultaneous data streams for approx. 120 days). The analysis of the tweets was subdivided into two major parts. First, we built a descriptive statistical model, in order to help explain the data trajectory and its distribution. An important trade-off in building this model is: the more parameters we add, the more data-specific the model becomes, but this also sacrifices the level of generalizability of the model. With this trade-off in mind, based on the theoretical underpinning described in Sect. 2, and a first inductive exploration of the data, we considered the following parameters to be the most important contributors to the expected rate of tweets per day (volume):

$$\lambda = N + E(t) + C + O + B$$

Where:

- λ: Poisson expected rate of daily tweets
- N: Base rate of daily tweets. This is the number of "noise" tweets that is more or less constant throughout the data collection. This number of tweets was picked up for the given query, regardless of any other (external) factors

- **E(t)**: An event that triggers tweets as a function of time. For example a large-scale mobile conference, a feature announcement or the launch of the smartphone in question. From our data, it becomes apparent that the tweets triggered from such a real world event are a function of time because the tweet rate often shows anticipatory and spillover increase in tweet rate surrounding the event
- **C**: The manufacturing company-specific capabilities. Brand equity and the ability of a manufacturer to directly or indirectly effect the online and offline chatter about their product is the third building block of the expected daily rate of tweets. Note that measuring this brand equity and quantifying its contribution to λ is out of scope of our study. Brand equity is a composite variable, built up from among others: performance, value and social image [12]
- **O**: Presence of opinion leaders or key influencers. We use two metrics to identify the key influencers in our data set: the number of mentions per user account in our collected tweets, and the number of retweets for each tweet. This gives us the most popular user accounts and the most popular tweets and with these two metrics, we were able to indicate the most influential user accounts and show the most popular tweets in each case
- **B**: The presence of spam bots. Spam bots can dilute the opinion formation and the classification of sentiment. If a negatively classified tweet is repeated many times by a spam bot, this could unjustly skew the prevailing opinion toward negative opinions. Therefore, we attempted to identify such tweets by calculating the likelihood of every user to tweet more than the overall average number of tweets per day (Poisson likelihood distribution). If a user's tweeting frequency has a likelihood of less than 1 %, we consider this a spam bot (account)

The second major part of the statistical analysis consists of a number of Poisson regression analyses and modeling the interaction effects of the main independent variables to answer the main research question. The Poisson regressions model the volume of tweets based on the three parameters *tweets from influencers, occurrence of events* and *tweets from spam bots* (these are the independent variables). We also modeled the effect of these parameters on the sentiment of tweets and volume of tweets (the dependent variables). By manipulating the aforementioned parameters, we derived company-specific capabilities which were identified in terms of inducing online chatter.

4 Statistical Analyses and Interpretation

A summary of the main findings from our descriptive statistical analysis is presented in Table 1. The base rate of tweets (N) is clearly different in each case, from 154 tweets per day for the Sony Xperia Z2, to 1729 tweets per day for the HTC One (M8). Further, in all three cases, the kinds of opinion leaders were similar. Each case showed that the highest number of mentions and retweets came from three categories of opinion leaders: the smartphone manufacturer, a number of mobile network operators (such as T-Mobile, Verizon etc.) and a number of well-known technology bloggers/vloggers.

The HTC case yielded the most tweets per day, however the Samsung case yielded similar numbers in terms of volume of tweets per day and the fraction of (spam) bots.

Table 1. Overview of cases essential statistics

	Total # tweets	Λ	N	# Event days	O	B	% Positive	% Negative	% Neutral
Samsung Galaxy S5	679,704	5,189	268	48	4,634	357,400	32.72	8.29	58.99
HTC One (M8)	677,383	6,048	1,729	31	2,896	424,933	29.17	7.45	63.39
Sony Xperia Z2	91,712	728	154	42	830	41,397	34.48	4.08	61.43

In both cases, the fraction of spam was well over half (53.5 % and 65.4 % for Samsung and HTC, respectively). The Sony case yielded far less tweets, however also relatively less spam with 46.4 % coming from spam accounts. This indicates that products from smartphone manufacturers with higher market share and online presence will also induce more spam.

The case with the most positive online chatter is the Sony Xperia Z2, which is surprising since this is the least popular in terms of volume of tweets. Not only does the Sony case produce the highest percentage of positive tweets, it also has the least negative tweets. This indicates that Sony is able to create a more positive buzz online than larger players on the smartphone market such as HTC and Samsung.

The second part of our statistical analysis is the Poisson regression analysis, where we tested a number of hypotheses in order to model the effect of the identified parameters on the daily rate of tweets and sentiment.

In Table 2, we present the results of the Poisson regression for the overall tweet rate and tweet rates per sentiment class. The model predicts nearly 810 tweets per day *without* the effect of influencers, bots or events (when independent variables have no effect). The values of the independent variables (Poisson parameters) are a factor increase or decrease on the predicted rate of daily (positive, negative or neutral) tweets if that independent variable increases by 1 unit, *all else being unchanged*. From the table it becomes evident that the occurrence of a real-world event triggers the strongest effect on overall daily tweet volumes (factor 2.028) as well as for each of the sentiment classes. This is in line with expectations; real world events such as the Mobile World Conference or the announcement of a specific functionality of the new smartphone are, to a great extent, marketing and promotional methods for manufacturers, meant to create awareness and buzz around their products. These events are the strongest determinant of daily tweet rate.

Table 2. Poisson regression: daily tweet rate

	Prediction (# tweets)	Influencers	Event	Bots
Daily tweet rate	809.97 ***	0.993 ***	2.028 ***	1.0002 ***
Daily positive tweet rate	243.47 ***	0.994 ***	2.131 ***	1.0002 ***
Daily negative tweet rate	68.92 ***	0.995 ***	1.85 ***	1.0002 ***
Daily neutral tweet rate	512.35 ***	0.992 ***	1.999 ***	1.0002 ***

Signif. codes: 0: "***" 0.001: "**" 0.01: "*" 0.05: "." 0.1: " " not significant: "n.s." (as given by R)

In addition, influencers and spam bots also significantly affect the daily tweet rate. Here, it is noticeable that influencers have a dampening effect on the daily tweets volume from 'real users' (non-influencers and non-spam bots). This could indicate that an increase of tweets from influencers shift 'real users' into a more passive role of publishing tweets about the product.

Furthermore, in terms of sentiment, we see that the occurrence of events are a stronger determinant of an increase in positive tweets (increase by 213 %), than on negative tweets (increase of 85 %). Events also trigger a stronger increase in positive tweets than the overall increase of 103 %. The data analysis shows that events trigger a relatively strong positive sentiment as compared to negative and neutral sentiment online chatter (tweets).

Diving deeper into our statistical analysis, we modeled the autonomous effect of our independent variables on the daily tweet volume and sentiment per case. The results of this analysis can be found in Table 3.

Consistent with the base rate of tweets (N), the Poisson regression predicts the most tweets for the HTC case and the least tweets in the Sony case, when none of the independent variables (influencers, events, bots) are at play. Furthermore, spam bots and events are the strongest determinants of tweet volume and sentiment in the Sony case and influencers have the strongest effect in the Samsung case. Surprisingly, influencers have a slightly decreasing effect on the real users' tweets in the HTC case. This is not the case in the Samsung and Sony case. However, since most of these results are not more than 0.1 significant in the HTC and Sony cases, further analysis would be needed in order to determine the validity of this specific effect.

4.1 Company Specific Capabilities

By comparing the case-specific regression results, we identified company specific-capabilities which can help the smartphone companies recognize their strengths, weaknesses, opportunities and threats in the process of online opinion formation. If we assume that each company's objective is to increase the number of tweets from real users about their product, then according to the results of our analysis, Sony has been most effective in using real world events to trigger additional tweets from real users. At the same time, spam bots (which may also have been employed by Sony), have the strongest effect out of all three cases.

Samsung was most effective in using influencers to drive chatter from real users. Specifically, when looking at the most retweeted tweet in the Samsung data, we found that a tweet by football star Cristiano Ronaldo, promoting the Samsung Galaxy S5 as part of Samsung's marketing campaign, was most influential.

In terms of the effect on sentiment of real users, a few things stand out from our results. Firstly, the strongest increasing effect on positive tweets by influencers is found in the Samsung case, at the same time, they also have the strongest increasing effect on negative tweets. Comparing the effects of the parameters on sentiment of real users, we found that in the Sony case, the effect of real world events have the strongest increasing effect on positive tweets. Another notable result is that the effect of events on negative tweets is stronger than the effect on positive tweets in the Samsung case. Although the

Table 3. Poisson regression: total and sentiment tweet rate per case

		Prediction	Influencers	Event	Bots	Pseudo R^2
Samsung Galaxy S5	All	2,411.49 ***	1.002106 ***	1.774112 ***	1.00012 ***	0.644
	Positive	206.43 ***	1.00491 ***	1.776597 ***	1.000118 ***	
	Negative	87.97 ***	1.006669 ***	1.839144 ***	1.000096 ***	
	Neutral	714.0836 ***	1.002693.	1.693674 ***	1.00012 ***	
HTC One (M8)	All	3,238.935 ***	0.9964912 **	1.773402 ***	1.000117 ***	0.723
	Positive	324.4074***	0.9984911	1.951503***	1.000095***	
	Negative	96.93106***	0.996837	1.510892**	1.000115**	
	Neutral	655.239***	0.998553	2.443912***	1.000089.	
Sony Xperia Z2	All	358.2151 ***	1.000198	1.951005 ***	1.001031 ***	0.642
	Positive	63.68824***	1.019967	3.553738***	1.000089	
	Negative	9.18002***	1.007648	1.125418	1.001048.	
	Neutral	135.9369***	0.9905421	2.245549***	1.000704*	

absolute number of predicted negative tweets is arguably negligible, this is an important finding which Samsung could use to strategically engage with their (potential) customers in order to improve the prevailing opinion(s) about their product online and offline. Each company in our analysis has their own specific capabilities and with our data-driven analysis, we can shed light on these capabilities, allowing these companies to act upon them.

4.2 Interaction Effects

In the previous section, we modeled the isolated effect of the independent variables influencers, events and spam bots on the daily tweeting volume and sentiments. In order to understand the dynamics and interaction between the independent variables and the effect of those interactions, we also modeled the effects of a combination of independent variables on the dependent variable: the real user tweet rate. Since we are dealing with an open multi-actor and multi-variable environment where numerous factors can have an effect on both sentiment and volume of tweets, it is important to consider these interaction effects.

In Fig. 3 we can see that, for the pooled tweets of all cases, there is a positive trend line for the daily tweets volume of real users as a function of the tweets coming from influencers. This is different from what we found in our isolated effect of influencers in the Poisson regression in the previous section. This difference can be explained by the fact that in Fig. 3, the effect of the other parameters (bots and events) are not unchanged. Therefore, it seems that there is an interaction between the events, spam bots and influencers in their effect on the daily tweet volume from real users. Again, we use Poisson regression to model this interaction. An interaction between independent variables A and B implies that the effect of A depends on the value of B and that the effect of B depends on the value of A [7]. In Table 4 the results of the modeled interaction effects are presented. The interaction for events and influencers has the strongest effect on the predicted daily rates of tweets from real users. Also, the three-way interaction of events, influencers and bots results in a slight increase of predicted daily

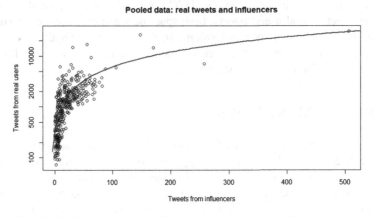

Fig. 3. Pooled tweets from influencers and daily tweets from real users

Table 4. Pooled data: interaction coefficients

Interaction	Coefficient
Events and influencers	0.9590 ***
Influencers and bots	0.9999 ***
Bots and events	0.9995 ***
Events and influencers and bots	1.00002 ***

tweets. This tells us that when influencers tweet and there is also an event, the tweets from real users (non-influencers and spam bots) decrease. This same effect is apparent for the modeled two-way interactions of events, influencers and spam bots.

However, when the interaction of all three parameters are modeled, the predicted number of tweets from real users increases slightly. This slightly unintuitive effect of events and influencers' interaction leading to a decrease in tweets from real users might be explained by the nature of the interactions between influencers and real users. Similar to traditional media (TV, radio etc.), when an event occurs, the media is the first to publicize this to a passive audience. Similarly, key influencers such as smartphone manufacturers, technology bloggers and mobile network operators are expected to tweet more on days of events in order to report on these events and real users are then adopting a more passive role as they are consuming the newly published information before expressing their own opinions.

4.3 Synthesis of Findings

When we consider both the isolated effects and interaction effects on volume and sentiment of tweets from real users, it seems that in our (pooled) data, interaction effects do occur (as seen in Fig. 3) as the coefficients of the effect in our individual parameters show a decrease in tweets volume when influencers increase their tweets volume. Whereas the interaction effect of all three parameters shows an increasing coefficient (1.00002) as can be seen in Table 4. Our analyses thus show that when there is an interaction of all three (core) parameters then the tweets from real users are predicted to increase. In short, in the HTC case, influencers have the strongest decreasing effect on real users' tweets. Both spam bots and events have the strongest increasing effect on real users tweet volume in the Sony case. Finally, the effect of events on real users' tweets volume are very similar in the Samsung and HTC case (coefficients of 1.774 and 1.773 respectively).

5 Conceptual Model Applied

In Fig. 4 we present the application of our conceptual model, as illustrated in Fig. 1, by starting with analyzing the process of opinion formation. To this end, we took a snapshot of this continuous process of opinion formation with our dataset of 369 days worth of tweets. We then recognize a number of opinion leaders (or influencers). Similar to previous studies such as Kim and Hovy [13], we classified the tweets in

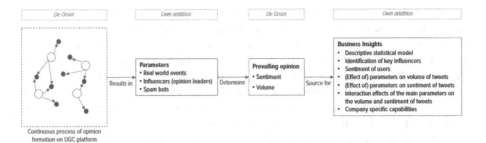

Fig. 4. Application of conceptual model

positive, negative or neutral tweets. With this classification we were able to model the effect of our identified opinion leaders and events on the sentiment as presented in the previous sections. By aggregating the tweets with these classifications, we could indicate the prevailing opinions surrounding the respective topics (smartphones). This prevailing opinion is seen as the subjective norms as described in the TPB [1]. We suggest that these subjective norms can be strategically shaped by incentivizing actors in the network and in this way steering the (sentiment of) online chatter about a product. By analyzing tweets, we recognized three key parameters that shape the prevailing opinion: the first two are real-world events and a small number of opinion leaders who determine the prevailing opinion amongst these agents. The third parameter is spam-bots. It is important to recognize that spam-bots can potentially influence this opinion as well since popular products and brands tend to elicit more spam-messages which misuse the brand recognition in order to attract people to their websites. The main 'real' influencers however, are the handful of opinion leaders and real-world events. In turn, the resulting prevailing online opinion, has a number of important implications in terms of a product's potential performance. Some of the most important business insights derived from our applied model are the identification of key influencers and events, and their effect on the tweets volume and sentiment surrounding a specific topic. With such insights, companies can actively steer the online (and consequently offline) conversation about their products by strategically engaging with (potential) customers, influencers and organizing events. Our conceptual model can be further developed into an 'always-on' solution where, based on the parameters, simulations can be run which provide predictions into the consequences of managerial decisions. For example, such a decision support system could simulate real world events and its repercussions on sentiment based on historical data to support management decisions with regard to e.g. marketing strategy or product release timing, etc.

6   Conclusion

In this section we present our overall conclusions while answering our main research question *"What kind of business intelligence on opinion formation of end users can be derived from tweets?"*. The purchasing behavior of customers is increasingly being influenced by the online chatter about products and services. Therefore, methods to steer this online opinion formation are becoming increasingly valuable for companies. Understanding the online opinion formation and strategically acting upon the insights gained from the analysis of user generated content underlie the ability to steer this prevailing opinion about specific topics. With the application of our conceptual model, we presented a number of methods to find such valuable insights in tweets.

Firstly, in order to understand the formation of prevailing opinions online, we can identify opinion leaders. These key influencers contribute to the subjective norms surrounding a product, online. *Top-down (proactive):* Proactively understanding the drivers of online opinion formation will enable companies to establish strategies to influence the prevailing opinions that are bound to arise. More concretely, one of the main drivers of prevailing (online) opinions are opinion leaders. By measuring the influence of opinion leaders upon the sentiment and volume of tweets from (potential) customers, companies can employ such opinion leaders in order to drive the online opinion. However, the objectivity of influencers such as technology vloggers is imperative to their credibility and, by extension, their core business. These influencers will less likely promote a product in exchange for compensation from the manufacturer as the risk of being exposed and losing credibility as an objective technology reviewer would be detrimental. *Bottom-up (reactive):* At the same time, with an online and social media presence, companies can get much closer to their customers than ever before. By actively measuring the online sentiment surrounding a product or service, companies can leverage online channels to engage with their customers on a personal level. The offline world and the online realm cannot be considered independently of each other. We have seen in our twitter analyses, that real world events strongly influence the online chatter and sentiment about smartphones. Finally, we are dealing with a multi-variable and open context where influencing factors upon tweets volume and online sentiment do not operate in isolation. Therefore, it is important to understand the interaction effects of the influencing factors. Here, the objective should be to find the right combination of influencing factors (events, opinion leaders and (spam) bots) and effectively formulating a strategy to employ these factors to influence the online opinions about a product or service. Our conceptual model, in combination with the concrete application of this model in our study, can serve as a basic framework for operationalizing such a strategy.

The main business insights that we were able to derive from our method of UGC analysis are:

- **Description of the buildup and trajectory of the data with a descriptive statistical model**: $\lambda = N + E(t) + C + O + B$. Each of these parameters can be influenced to shape online opinion formation.
- **Identification of key influencers (opinion leaders)**: Smartphone manufacturers, technology bloggers/vloggers, mobile network operators. Each of these influencers can be employed to influence the prevailing online opinion.
- **Sentiment of real users (over time)**: The trajectory of sentiment about the respective products can be analysed so that triggers for negativity and positivity can be identified and acted upon.
- **Main parameters that determine volume of tweets**: Events, influencers and (spam) bots. These main parameters will have a relatively strong impact on the prevailing opinion.

- **The effect of the main parameters on volume of tweets**: Events trigger the strongest uplift in tweets volume. Therefore, events are an important tool for manufacturers to consider when attempting to steer the online opinion formation.
- **The effect of the main parameters on sentiment of tweets**: Similar to the volume of tweets, events trigger the strongest uplift in positive tweets.
- **The interaction effects of the main parameters on the volume and sentiment of tweets**: When influencers tweet and there is also an event, the tweets from real users decrease.
- **Company specific capabilities**: Sony has been most effective in using real world events to trigger additional tweets from real users. Samsung was most effective in using influencers to drive chatter from real users. In the Sony case, the effect of real world events have the strongest increasing effect on positive tweets. Each company has specific capabilities which we can recognize with our data-driven analysis. This allows these companies to act upon them in order to shape the online opinion regarding their product.

Our main academic contributions lie firstly in our way of analyzing UGC for business insights based on a theoretical model. Second, by using a modern application of the Classical Model of Consensus Formation we found concrete–new- parameters i.e. real world events and spam bots (in addition to opinion leaders) that shape online opinion formation. We discovered the roles of the diverse sources of tweets and their influence on volume and sentiment of tweets. This differs from the offline world as there are more sources and types of agents forming the prevailing opinion. The application of this model in the online world enabled these nuances as we could work with large volumes of data, as opposed to an offline setting with much more limited and more indirect data. Third, we found categories of opinion leaders who each showed significant effect on the formation of online opinion, namely: manufacturers, mobile network operators and technology bloggers/vloggers.

6.1 Limitations

In order to increase the reliability such that the results of our study become generalizable for a wider range of products or industries, the application of our conceptual model should be done on more cases, while maximizing representativeness of the respective product-group or industry. Nonetheless, we have made a first step toward delivering more insight into this field of study, where academic research is sparse. Our technical implementation is modular and scalable such that it can be applied to other products and topics where online chatter is expected. Furthermore, we collected data from one source: Twitter. Although tweets have proven to be a relevant, effective and rich source of data for our purposes, gathering data from various social media sources to cover a wider demographic and build a richer data set could improve the application of our conceptual model.

A number of improvements could be made on the text analysis techniques. Natural language processing is a complex and strongly-evolving discipline. Basic techniques were combined in this study in order to classify the tweets into sentiments and finding spam tweets. Some ways to improve the classification accuracy are: (1) expanding the matching dictionary used to classify each tweet's sentiment, (2) expanding the classifications to more nuanced sentiment based on severity of language and (3) considering word order, grammar and punctuation. In general, similar to sentiment detection, spam detection is considered a text classification problem [8, 13]. By using e.g. a Naïve Bayes approach, similar to our sentiment classifier, spam classification in the application of our model can be improved in future research.

6.2 Future Research

In our research, we revealed insights which answer important questions in the domain of business intelligence from UGC as well as identify knowledge and theory gaps. First, we have laid the ground work for obtaining business insights from tweets and in future research, we suggest to measure the competitive advantage that can be derived from these insights. Moreover, explicit measurement of the relation between online opinion (as subjective norms) and buying behaviour (expressed as business performance metrics such as sales or profit) can be measured as part of this competitive advantage from UGC analysis. Second, our descriptive statistical model identifies the five main parameters that contribute to the expected tweets volume per day. This descriptive model can be combined with our Poisson regression analysis and be further developed into a predictive model. An implementation of our conceptual model can automatically draw from historical data and compute predictions based on influencing coefficients similar to our analysis (influence of events on positive tweets from users etc.). In closing, our study has laid ground work for understanding online opinion formation, UGC analysis and the implications on competitive advantage. Understanding the interactions between the online and offline world, in a business context and also in social and cultural contexts is paramount in today's rapid technological advancements, ubiquity of technology and online media in our lives.

References

1. Ajzen, I.: The theory of planned behavior. Organ. Behav. Hum. Decis. Process. **50**(2), 179–211 (1991)
2. Asur, S., Huberman, B.A.: Predicting the future with social media. In: Paper Presented at the 2010 IEEE/WIC/ACM International Conference on Web Intelligence and Intelligent Agent Technology (WI-IAT) (2010)
3. Baer, W.J., Balto, D.A.: Antitrust enfocement and high-technology markets. Mich. Telecomm. Tech. L. Rev. **5**, 73 (1998)
4. Cromar, S.: Smartphones in the US: Market analysis (2010). https://www.ideals.illinois.edu/bitstream/handle/2142/18484/Cromar,%20Scott%20-%20U.S.%20Smartphone%20Market%20Report.pdf. Accessed 18th April 2016
5. De Groot, M.H.: Reaching a consensus. J. Am. Stat. Assoc. **69**(345), 118–121 (1974)
6. El Sawy, O., Pereira, F.: Business Modelling in the Dynamic Digital Space. An Ecosystem Approach. Springer, Heidelberg (2013). doi:10.1007/978-3-642-31765-1_1
7. Evans, S.M., Janson, A.M., Nyengaard, J.R.: Quantitative Methods in Neuroscience: A Neuroanatomical Approach. Oxford University Press, Oxford (2004)

8. Fawcett, T.: In vivo spam filtering: a challenge problem for KDD. ACM SIGKDD Explor. Newsl. **5**(2), 140–148 (2003)
9. Fishbein, M.: A theory of reasoned action: some applications and implications. Nebr. Symp. Motiv. **27**(1979), 65–116 (1979)
10. Jackson, M.O.: Social and Economic Networks. Princeton University Press, New Jersey (2010)
11. Jansen, B.J., Zhang, M., Sobel, K., Chowdury, A.: Twitter power: tweets as electronic word of mouth. J. Am. Soc. Inf. Sci. Technol. **60**(11), 2169–2188 (2009)
12. Keller, K.L.: Conceptualizing, measuring, and managing customer-based brand equity. J. Mark. **57**(1), 1–22 (1993)
13. Kim, S.-M., Hovy, E.: Determining the sentiment of opinions. In: Proceedings of the 20th International Conference on Computational Linguistics (2004)
14. Liu, Y., Chen, Y., Lusch, R.F., Chen, H., Zimbra, D., Zeng, S.: User-generated content on social media: predicting market success with online word-of-mouth. IEEE Intell. Syst. **25**(1), 75–78 (2010)
15. O'Connor, B., Balasubramanyan, R., Routledge, B.R., Smith, N.A.: From tweets to polls: linking text sentiment to public opinion time series. ICWSM **11**, 122–129 (2010)
16. Tirunillai, S., Tellis, G.J.: Does chatter really matter? Dynamics of user-generated content and stock performance. Mark. Sci. **31**(2), 198–215 (2012)

Discourse Analysis of Blogs: Analyzing Language to Maximize the Value of Consumption-Oriented Blogs as Data Source

Carmela Bosangit[1(✉)], Scott McCabe[2], and Sally Hibbert[2]

[1] School of Management, Swansea University, Swansea, UK
c.a.bosangit@swansea.ac.uk
[2] Nottingham University Business School, University of Nottingham, Nottingham, UK
{scott.mccabe,sally.hibbert}@nottingham.ac.uk

Abstract. The value of blogs to consumer research has been established; however, its full potential is still to be realized as empirical analyses into their use have been dominated by quantitative studies. There is a fundamental research gap in the range of methods adopted by researchers which has limited blogs as a source of valuable insights. This paper asserts the importance of language and the rhetorical functions of blogs as social interaction contexts where meanings are created and channeled; thus, offering a route to develop better understandings of authors and their narratives. Using discourse analysis to examine blogs, the paper demonstrates how a focus on language can provide rich insights to understand consumption experiences. Discourses of travel that emerged from the analysis were presented and theoretical and practical implications were outlined.

Keywords: Blogs · Discourse analysis · Consumer narratives · Travel stories

1 Introduction

Extant literature on consumption-oriented blogs has provided evidence on how blogging has empowered consumers to self-publish their experiences and marketers and researchers have recognized the opportunities for these naturally occurring data as a data source (See work of Lu & Stepchenkova, 2015; a systematic review of user-generated content applications in tourism and hospitality research [1]). Consumption oriented blogs are valuable to marketers because they are accounts of products and experiences that relate to consumers' lives and which allow them to internalize the symbolic meanings embedded in their experiences [2]. Although there is an increase in empirical work demonstrating the potential of blogs in marketing these are dominantly quantitative in nature. This has also been observed in existing literature on travel blogs. According to Banyai and Havitz (2012), content of travel blogs has commonly been reduced to statistical data and mere categories [3]. There are only a few studies on travel blogs using qualitative research methods such as narrative analysis, qualitative content analysis and discourse analysis [4–8]. Most empirical work mining travel blog content has been quantitative content analysis focused on specific destinations and extracting common themes

© IFIP International Federation for Information Processing 2016
Published by Springer International Publishing Switzerland 2016. All Rights Reserved
Y.K. Dwivedi et al. (Eds.): I3E 2016, LNCS 9844, pp. 522–532, 2016.
DOI: 10.1007/978-3-319-45234-0_46

related to destination image, tourist evaluation of the destination and actual tourist behavior [7]. On the other hand, netnography has been used to analyze consumption-oriented blogs in different consumption contexts [2, 9]. One reason for the use of more quantitative techniques could be the huge amount of data that are available, and the fact that the data is in a digital format at source. Thus researchers may feel tempted into more technologically driven methods of data cleaning, manipulation and analysis. Yet we argue that much valuable interpretive analysis is omitted from such a myopic approach to these rich, naturally occurring datasets.

Using quantitative research methods limits the potential of blogs for understanding the writers/narrators and how they reconstruct their consumption experiences. There is a missed opportunity because blogs are personal and deeply subjective in nature and represent fruitful opportunities for qualitative researchers, offering investigators a publicly available conduit to backstage thoughts and feelings of others [10]. For example, using qualitative approaches in analyzing blogs can provide insight into the processes by which events and activities are transformed into personally meaningful experiences [11], which cannot be captured using quantitative research methods. Bosangit, McCabe and Hibbert (2009) call for researchers to explore other frameworks that are appropriate to maximizing the use of blogs in understanding rapid and continuously changing consumption experiences such as tourism [7]. Banyai and Havitz (2012), suggest that a realist evaluation approach could maximize the potential of travel blogs by using qualitative techniques alongside quantitative methods [3].

Blogs represent a vast, diverse and idiosyncratic range of content which presents challenges for qualitative researchers. There are some useful guides to using qualitative approaches to blog data collection and analysis [12–14]. However, researchers and marketers may need more guidance and persuasion to adopt qualitative approaches. There is scant empirical work using qualitative techniques for the analysis of blogs both in the general field of marketing and tourism marketing. This paper therefore contributes to this research gap by illustrating how discourse analysis can be used to understand consumption experiences. Focusing on the language used by bloggers, the discourse analysis aims to address the following research questions: a. what type of stories are told by bloggers? and b. what are embedded in these stories that provide insights to consumption experiences?

Theoretically, this paper contributes to works highlighting how stories which are also embedded in blogs are fundamental to the conceptualization of consumption experiences, particularly tourist experiences [15, 16, 22]. For practical implications, marketers can use blogs to understand the non-visible and rarely stated elements in experiences (i.e. hedonic and subjective dimensions of experience) [11, 17] and provide insights to the development and design of marketing communication strategies. As the main purpose of this paper is to demonstrate the potential of using qualitative approach in examining blogs as a data source, the next section focuses on the process of discourse analysis of travel blogs.

2 Discourse Analysis of Blogs

Discourse analysis (DA) is appropriate for studying blogs because it is concerned with the way texts are constructed, the functions they serve in different contexts and the contractions that run through them [18]. There are several different approaches to social constructionist discourse analysis such as discourse theory, Foucauldian perspectives, critical discourse analysis and discursive psychology (see Jorgensen and Philipps, 2002 for the differences among these approaches) [19]. This paper draws on discursive psychology (DP) as it allows examination of how blogs are constructed [20, 21] and how texts are socially organized to achieve local actions such as identity management [22]. DP favors the analysis of records of natural interaction or textual materials produced as part of life's activities rather than using experiments, surveys and interviews to generate research data, because of its emphasis on how both "reality" and "mind" are constructed by people conceptually, in language, in the course of their performance of practical tasks. Blogs are one form of this textual material.

In the tourism context, discourse analysis is a rarely used method. Jaworski and Pritchard (2005) note how discourse and communication scholars historically have little dialogue with scholars in tourism [23]. According to McCabe and Foster (2006: 195) [24], the work of Dann (1996) remains the cornerstone for researchers interested in socio-linguistic interpretation of discourses of tourism [25]. Compared to other popular methods for analyzing travel blogs such as content analysis and narrative analysis [8], DA can provide a deeper understanding of travel blogs beyond a mere listing of destination attributes. Willig (2008) described DA as a particular way of reading – reading for action orientation (what is the text doing?), rather than simply reading for meaning (what is this text saying) [24]. Potter and Wetherell (1987) confirmed that there is no mechanical procedure for producing findings from an archive of transcript [27, 28]. However, several discourse analysts have suggested guidelines for doing DA such as Potter and Wetherell's (1987) 10 stages in the analysis of discourse [27]; Billig's (1991) procedural guide for DA [29]; Wiggins and Potter's (2008) detailed and comprehensive guidance on the practicalities of DP research [30], and Antaki et al.'s (2003) evaluating DP research [31].

For this paper, Potter and Wetherell's (1987) 10 stages for a DP analysis was adopted [27] by the authors as it is appropriate for analyzing travel blogs as the data source of consumption experience. The stages include: (1) research questions; (2) sample selection (3) collection of records and documents; (4) interviews; (5) transcription; (6) coding; (7) analysis; (8) validation, (9) the report and (10) application. As travel blogs were used as the data source, and the study does not involve interview and transcription, stages 3, 4 and 5 were replaced by the authors with downloading of blogs for the analysis. These stages are grouped into three phases of the study: pre-discourse analysis, discourse analysis and post-discourse analysis. Figure 1 below illustrates these three stages in detail.

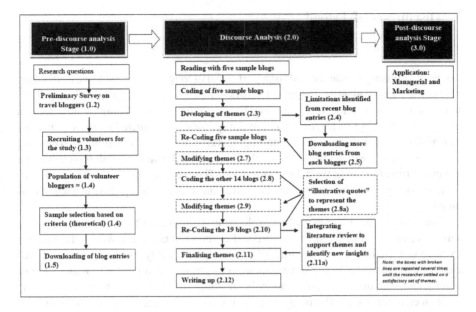

Fig. 1. Discourse analysis process (developed by the authors)

The pre-discourse analysis involved the following: setting of the research objectives; a survey among travel bloggers as there was a lack of relevant data on travel bloggers during the research period; and the identification of sample travel blogs to be used for the discourse analysis. The survey was conducted to gain an understanding of bloggers' profiles, motivation and practices which facilitated the identification of a sample of bloggers and blogs that would be appropriate for addressing the research questions. From the 1,214 respondents to the survey, volunteers for the discourse analysis were recruited. 19 travel bloggers met the following criteria set: bloggers have blogged about long-haul and multiple destination trips that are longer than three weeks; have written between 25 and 50 blogs; blogs should have more text than pictures and be written in English. With their consent, blogs were downloaded for the next stage.

The second stage which formed the discourse analysis was comprised of reading and a reiterative process of coding to identify the themes from the data set. During the initial stages of coding five blogs (steps 2.2 and 2.5), important extracts were put into a matrix against each blogger to clearly show variability and consistency among these bloggers. However, as coding reached steps 2.8 and 2.10. NVivo, qualitative software, was used to deal with the huge amount of data and categorize it into five established themes. After coding the data into these themes, another round of coding produced a better selection of illustrative quotes which best represent a theme. This stage ended with the writing up of the findings which fed into the third stage; the post discourse stage where management and marketing implications were identified.

3   Discourses of Travel

3.1   Stories of Risk and Challenge

Stories of voluntary or unexpected risks are typical of long-haul and multiple destination travelers' narrative identity and reflect self-development or self change [32, 33]. Risk-taking behaviors are expected of tourists because they perceive being on holiday as a "license for thrill" [34]. Hence, there are many stories constructed as risky situations such as skydiving, rafting, bungee jumping, trekking and mountain climbing. There are also "tourist risks" which refers to possible misfortunes that might befall travelers in the process of travelling or at their destination [35]. These are in stories of long, dangerous bus rides, being scammed, and being attacked by an animal or being close to a dangerous animal.

The construct of challenge is less explored in the tourism literature on its own as it is always associated with risk, adventure and frontier travel [36]; however, the analysis revealed that challenges are not limited to those particular types of experience. Challenges are personal and come in various forms – physical and mental – or any form of activity and situation that test someone's capability of dealing with them. Common forms of challenges retold by bloggers to their readers are experiences of physical challenges; conquering a specific fear (e.g. snorkeling, heights) and challenging practices and norms of a long-haul and multiple destination traveler. Below is an example of an account where the blogger highlighted the danger, the skills required and described the experience as an achievement.

> "Well, today we were risking life and limb on what has been dubbed ... 'the most dangerous road in the world' ...It was highly exhilarating and great fun and with the ability to go as fast or as slow as you wanted, it meant that you could squeeze as much or as little adrenaline out of you as you wished. One or two of our group came off their bikes gathering some flesh wounds to add to their travelling tales but most came off unscathed. Over the last few hours we had/ travelled about 60 km and descended by over 3000 m in altitude,...we had also cheated death on the World's most dangerous road, something to be proud (and relieved) about! What an excellent experience!" (Chrissie and Mark)

Bloggers also shared accounts of failure of achieving their set goals, and in these stories, self-presentation technique such as self-handicapping were used [37]; where the blogger produces obstacles to success with the purpose of preventing observers from making dispositional references about one's failure. Outcomes can either be positive or negative but what was important was to challenge one's limit as it is important for an evolving self [38]. These stories are integrated in the life story of the blogger and contribute to their identity work.

3.2   Accounts of Learning and Reflection

The analysis showed bloggers sharing what they learn about the destination (the place and the people) and how they personalized their experience by integrating their reflections on what they have seen within their previous experience or even existing knowledge prior to the visit. This confirms that learning experiences are more gratifying when they can take their own personal meaning [40]. How they construct these stories may also indicate an aspect of their identity as a "learner" or their interests. This extract from a blogger's account on Nazca lines is an example of how he personalized his experience.

> *"There are a whole host of theories as to why these lines in the desert were created approximately 2000 years ago...A German mathematician has spent her life dedicated to the cause and theorised that the lines are an astronomical calendar mapped out by complex mathematics, another theory is that they map the routes to water, which in the harsh desert is a valuable commodity. There are of course the usual extraterrestrial landing site theories but the most widely accepted is that they're connected to ritual walkways from a religious based cult. I have my own theory of course... I believe there is someone in the afterlife looking down and laughing at us. "Look at all those crazy Gringos's paying good money to ogle something some friends and I scratched in the dirt when we were bored". Whatever reasons the lines came to be, I was sure they'd be pretty spectacular" (Michael)*

Bloggers differ in their use of linguistic techniques, style of writing, use of emotional words and integrating their opinions with facts and stories about the places. They filter and expand on their stories as they want to share to their readers. Travel blogs indeed provide a good access to the learning and reflections of the travelers which are less explored in the tourist studies literature. Pearce (2005) posited that what tourists learn is seen to have limited commercial interest [41]. However, the analysis has shown how bloggers value this aspect of their experiences as these stories enhance their social status hoping to get recognition from their readers for "discovering" or experiencing the place before them which gives them some authority to talk about it because they have been there like any frontier travelers [36].

3.3   Accounts of Novelty and Difference

Novelty and strangeness are essential elements in the tourism experience [42]. These concepts are based on the perception of what the individual knows or is familiar with. There are stories of novelty in activities they engaged in enhanced by its location and participants. The stories that bloggers tell of their encounters with the locals are equivalent to what Jasinki (2001) call "rhetorics of othering" [43]. The extract below shows a blogger's reaction to what she has witnessed, a memorable experience to share with her readers.

> *"I was saddened to witness several cremations as well as babies' body being thrown directly in the river. Such intimate rituals of life and death take place in public which is a shock to me but merely the crossing between the physical and spiritual world in the Hindu culture" (Meltem)*

Other examples of these stories include accounts of playing pool with a lady boy in a Vietnamese bar and playing football with the Indians in the Andes in Cusco, Peru. Some bloggers pay closer attention to how the locals live which facilitates their appreciation of their home culture and enhances their identity as they use the differences to know the self. The construct of novelty is vague but personal and subjective; it can cover anything that a blogger writes about and points out to their readers as something that is strange, unique and bizarre or interesting and has produced emotions of surprise, shock, amazement. The analysis confirm that the element of novelty is still crucial in creating memorable experiences [44, 45].

3.4 Accounts of Self-expansion

Social interaction with fellow tourists is both an integral and functional aspect of back-packing [46]. But the analysis reveals that there is more to the social interaction of travelers, these interactions have helped them with their self-expansion. Self-expansion is achieved when an individual enters into a close relationship with another person, in which they include the other in their concept of self in the sense that they feel as if the other's perspectives, resources and identities are to some extent similar to their own [47:218]. Interaction with fellow tourists gave bloggers specific resources such as knowledge, status and a sense of belonging to a community by identifying themselves with these people. Knowledge or the sharing of information is the most common resource gained from other travelers which ranges from prices of accommodation, how to get to certain place, best accommodation and additional tips. These practices are common features of backpacking [33, 49]; and are considered ways of gaining road status [51] which enhances their identity as a backpacker or traveler.

Some bloggers talk about other travelers they meet on their travels and associate with themselves. For example, a blogger described her friends as "great minded trav-elers" and sharing the same passion (for traveling) which enhances her identity to her readers. Identifying themselves with people who they think are exceptional is also seen in this account:

> "He was here in Vietnam flying helicopters ...he got shot in the leg by a machine gun ...He has spent a huge amount of his time back in Vietnam and has helped local people achieve the most extra ordinary things that they may never have even dreamt of doing if they had not met him. Luckily for me he was here, this time he was busy learning the Viet language. Kent, Stu and I spent hours chatting, it was so good meeting someone like him and I soon realised with our conversations that us travel bloggers really experience and see within the more finer details of this big wide world, what with all our endless questions, unique experiences, trusty cameras and note books always at hand" (Claire)

In this extract the blogger was able to present an aspect of herself as a travel blogger and formalize her belonging to that group. In the tourism literature, this self-expansion model is not explored and these stories signal that this concept needs to be recognized as one of the benefits of travelling.

3.5 Stories of Escape

This is the least dominant theme; however, it represents an important part of tourist experience as it covers moments when bloggers take a break from travelling. According to Cohen and Taylor (1992) escape depends on a reality that individuals escape from [50]. Hence, these stories of escape are unique from the construct of escape established in the literature which is usually an escape from boredom or everyday routine. Bloggers' reality over the period they have been traveling have changed as their everyday life is now filled with work of traveling, making travel their "occupational career".

Escape comes in various forms. First, it can take the form of rest and relaxation or at least a less active day for some bloggers. Stories of escape are usually short, with some bloggers even saying there is not much to post in the blog because they "just chilled out for the day", email people, chat or even did the laundry. Second, the beach paradise as an escape is a dominant feature in their stories. Despite travelers being in different places with varied travel motivations, the beach is one of the places they consumed commonly. Third, sleep is one of the most mentioned words albeit in varying contexts such as letting their bodies recuperate from any strain they subjected them to, in preparation for a strenuous activity or simply because they want a lazy morning and to get up late. Below is a short extract from a blogger admitting the need to rest after travel.

> *"...the past 3 months of travelling was starting to catch up with me... so I would take time out relaxing in my room reading, watching tv and sleeping"(Meltem)*

Despite its importance to travelers, sleep in tourism literature has not been explored. In fact, only the work of Valtonen and Veijola (2011) recognized the theoretical and industry-related insights of the tourist experience of the embodied state and practice of sleeping [51]. They emphasized that sleep has always been seen as an indicator of development and success in tourism in terms of overnight stays; but sleep itself has been left untouched.

4   Conclusion

This study has demonstrated how discourse analysis of blogs as naturally occurring data can provide insights on consumption experiences that may prove elusive when applying more commonly used-researcher led approaches such as direct interviewing techniques [11]. The discourse analysis provided in-depth understanding of the subjective reality of bloggers and the meanings they have assigned to their travel experiences [8]. Focusing on the language used by bloggers, five dominant types of travel stories emerged through the discourse analysis of blogs written by 19 British travel bloggers. These themes reflect common types of stories which constitute a tourist experience that bloggers felt worth sharing with their readers. Embedded within these stories are memorable experiences of the bloggers, which also provide insights on their self-presentation strategies and techniques used as well as the value and meaning of these travel experiences to them.

This research contributes to the literature on conceptualizing tourist experiences as it confirms the role of blogs in empowering travelers to share their stories to their readers. In terms of marketing implications, this research has provided empirical evidence on how blogs can reveal core consumption experiences as remembered and reconstructed by the consumers. Blogs have provided their readers access to their feelings, thought processes and reflections. Further, the research confirms that travel experience remains to be used for identity construction [21, 29, 31]. Therefore, marketers in their formulation of a destination brand should pay particular attention in offering experiences that will give tourists opportunities to present or enhance their identities through the stories they tell.

References

1. Lu, W., Stepchenkova, S.: User-generated content as a research mode in tourism and hospitality applications: topics, methods, and software. J. Hosp. Mark. Manag. **24**(2), 119–154 (2015)

2. Zhao, X., Belk, R.W.: Live from shopping malls: blogs and Chinese consumer desire. Adv. Consum. Res. **34**, 131 (2007)
3. Banyai, M., Havitz, M.E.: Analyzing travel blogs using a realist evaluation approach. J. Hosp. Mark. Manag. **22**(2), 229–241 (2013)
4. Tussyadiah, I.P., Fesenmaier, D.R.: Marketing places through firstperson stories—an analysis of Pennsylvania roadtripper blog. J. Travel Tour. Mark. **25**(3–4), 299–311 (2008)
5. Berger, I.E., Greenspan, I.: High (on) technology: producing tourist identities through technologized adventure. J. Sport Tour. **13**(2), 89–114 (2008)
6. Bosangit, C.: Understanding consumption experiences: a discourse analysis of travel blogs. Doctoral dissertation, University of Nottingham (2012)
7. Bosangit, C., McCabe, S., Hibbert, S.: What is told in travel blogs? Exploring travel blogs for consumer narrative analysis. Inf. Commun. Technol. Tour. **2009**, 61–71 (2009)
8. Banyai, M., Glover, T.D.: Evaluating research methods on travel blogs. J. Travel Res. **51**(3), 267–277 (2012)
9. Kulmala, M., Mesiranta, N., Tuominen, P.: Organic and amplified eWOM in consumer fashion blogs. J. Fash. Mark. Manag. **17**(1), 20–37 (2013)
10. Chenail, R.J.: Ten steps for conceptualizing and conducting qualitative research studies in a pragmatically curious manner. Qual. Rep. **16**(6), 1713 (2011)
11. Bosangit, C., Hibbert, S., McCabe, S.: "If I was going to die I should at least be having fun": travel blogs, meaning and tourist experience. Ann. Tour. Res. **55**, 1–14 (2015)
12. Wakeford, N., Cohen, K.: Fieldnotes in public: using blogs for research. In: Fielding, N., Lee, R.M., Blank, G. (eds.) The Sage Handbook of Online Research Methods, pp. 307–326. Sage, London (2008)
13. Ward, R.: Blogs and wikis a personal journey. Bus. Inf. Rev. **23**(4), 235–240 (2006)
14. Hookway, N.: Entering the blogosphere': some strategies for using blogs in social research. Qual. Res. **8**(1), 91–113 (2008)
15. McGregor, I., Holmes, J.G.: How storytelling shapes memory and impressions of relationship events over time. J. Personal. Soc. Psychol. **76**(3), 403–419 (1999)
16. Moscardo, G.: The shaping of tourist experience: the importance of stories and themes. In: Morgan, M., Lugosi, P., Ritchie, J.R.B. (eds.) The Tourism and Leisure Experience: Consumer and Management Perspectives, pp. 3–26. Channel View Publications, Bristol (2010)
17. Carù, A., Cova, B.: Small versus big stories in framing consumption experiences. Qual. Mark. Res. Int. J. **11**(2), 166–176 (2008)
18. Parker, I.: 5.19 Discourse analysis. In: Flick, U., von Kardoff, E., Steinke, I. (eds.) A Companion to Qualitative Research, p. 308. Sage, London (2004)
19. Jørgensen, M.W., Phillips, L.J.: Discourse Analysis as Theory and Method. Sage, London (2002)
20. Potter, J.: Discourse Analysis and Constructionist Approaches: Theoretical Background. British Psychological Society, Leicester (1996)
21. Burr, V.: Social Constructionism. Routledge, London (2015)
22. Augustinos, M., Every, D.: Contemporary racist discourse: taboos against racism and racist accusations. In: Watson, B., Galloise, C.A. (eds.) Language, Discourse and Social Psychology, pp. 233–255. Palgrave MacMillan, Hampshire (2007)
23. Jaworski, A., Pritchard, A.: Discourse, Communication and Tourism. Channel View Publications, Bristol (2005)
24. McCabe, S., Foster, C.: The role and function of narrative in tourist interaction. J. Tour. Cult. Change **4**(3), 194–215 (2006)

25. Dann, G.: The Language of Tourism: A Sociolinguistic Perspective. CAB International, Oxon (1996)
26. Willig, C.: Introducing Qualitative Research in Psychology: Adventures in Theory and Method, 2nd edn. Open University Press, Berskshire (2008)
27. Potter, J., Wetherell, M.: Discourse and Social Psychology: Beyond Attitudes and Behaviour. Sage, London (1987)
28. Langdridge, D., Hagger-Johnson, G.: Introduction to Research Methods and Data Analysis in Psychology. Pearson Education Limited, Essex (2009)
29. Billig, M.: Ideology and Opinions. Sage Publications, London (1991)
30. Wiggins, S., Potter, J.: Discursive psychology. In: Willig, C., Stainton-Rogers, W. (eds.) The Sage Handbook of Qualitative Research in Psychology, pp. 73–90. Sage, London (2008)
31. Antaki, C., Billig, M., Edwards, D., Potter, J.: Discourse Analysis Means Doing Analysis: A Critique of Six Analytic Shortcomings (2003). https://dspace.lboro.ac.uk/dspace-jspui/handle/2134/633
32. Desforges, L.: Travelling the world: identity and travel biography. Ann. Tour. Res. **27**(4), 926–945 (2000)
33. Noy, C.: The trip really changed me: backpackers' narratives of self-change. Ann. Tour. Res. **31**(1), 78–102 (2004)
34. Wickens, E.: Licensed for thrill: risk taking and tourism. In: Clift, S., Gabowski, P. (eds.) Tourism and Health. Pinter, London (1997)
35. Tsaur, S., Tzeng, G., Wang, K.: Evaluating tourist risks from fuzzy perspectives. Ann. Tour. Res. **24**(4), 796–812 (1997)
36. Laing, J., Grouch, G.: Extraordinary journeys: an exploratory cross-cultural study of tourists on the frontier. J. Vacat. Mark. **11**(3), 209–223 (2005)
37. Berglas, S., Jones, E.E.: Drag choice as a self-handicapping strategy response to noncontingent success. J. Pers. Soc. Psychol. **36**, 405–417 (1978)
38. Cziksenthmihalyi, M.: The Evolving Self. HarperCollins, New York (1993)
39. Danziger, P.: Shopping: Why We Love It and How Retailers can Create the Ultimate Customer Experience. Kaplan Publishing, Chicago (2006)
40. Falk, J., Dierking, L.: Learning from Museums: Visitor Experiences and the Making of Meaning. AltaMira Press, Walnut Creek (2000)
41. Pearce, P.: Tourist Behaviour: Themes and Conceptual Schemes. Channel View Publications, Clevedon (2005)
42. Cohen, E.: Towards a sociology of international tourism. Soc. Res. **39**(1), 164–182 (1972)
43. Jasinski, J.: Sourcebook on Rhetoric: Key Concepts in Contemporary Rhetorical Studies. Sage, Thousand Oaks (2001)
44. Poulsson, S., Kale, S.: The experience economy and commercial experiences. Mark. Rev. **4**, 267–277 (2004)
45. Toffler, A.: Future Shock. Bantam Books, New York (1970)
46. Murphy, L.: Exploring social interactions of backpackers. Ann. Tour. Res. **28**(1), 50–67 (2001)
47. McLaughlin-Volpe, T.: Understanding stigma from the perspective of the selfexpansion model. In: Levin, S., van Laar, C. (eds.) Stigma and Group Inequality: Social Psycholgical Perspectives. Lawrence Erlbaum Associates Inc., New Jersey (2008)
48. Riley, P.: Road culture of international long-term budget traveler. Ann. Tour. Res. **15**(3), 313–328 (1988)
49. Sorensen, A.: Backpacker ethnography. Ann. Tour. Res. **30**(4), 847–867 (2003)

50. Cohen, S., Taylor, L.: Escape Attempts: The Theory and Practice of Resistance to Everyday Life. Routledge, London (1993)
51. Valtonen, A., Veijola, S.: Sleep in tourism. Ann. Tour. Res. **28**(1), 175–192 (2011)

Insights from Twitter Analytics: Modeling Social Media Personality Dimensions and Impact of Breakthrough Events

Akshat Lakhiwal[✉] and Arpan Kumar Kar

Department of Management Studies, IIT Delhi, IV Floor, Vishwakarma Bhavan,
Hauz Khas, New Delhi 110016, India
akshatlakhiwal@gmail.com, arpan_kar@yahoo.co.in

Abstract. Social media and big data have been in high focus due to their potentially huge impact on business, society and polity. This research contributes to the same domain and peruses the twitter community before and after an event which is a major breakthrough for an economy. Here, the event being monitored is the Union Budget-2016 in India. The research taps the occasion to understand the various groups which participate in the online discussion amongst 43,924 tweets from 22,896 users and the pre and post budget twitter metrics are analyzed, deducing the sensitivity of the groups to the day of proposal of the budget. The research framework incorporates twitter analytics and relies on visual and quantitative data, drawing inferences from the intelligence. How the personality dimensions change before and after the event, is also analyzed. This change in dimensions can directly account for the influencing nature of the social media group.

Keywords: Twitter analytics · Social media · Big data · Network analytics · Content analytics · Sentiment analytics · Brand personality · Dimensions

1 Introduction

The emergence of big data has created a new awakening in the business and research community. Such a large pool of data, being incremented every single second presents tremendous opportunity to analyze and reasonably pre-empt certain trends with a fair amount of certainty. Social Media [1, 17], out of all has been one of the main sources of generating data and has drawn interest of businesses for marketing purposes, which includes product development, service promotion, customer engagement as well as brand promotion. Research groups from diverse areas have been involved in observing and utilizing the opportunities presented by social media analytics to a great effect. Significant amount of work has been done in collecting and processing data through various portals to gain insights into several areas such as stock price prediction, Relief measures, Crisis Management, early event prediction, election prediction, public relations and public opinion [2, 3]. However, the analysis of the data presents its challenges due to its high variety, veracity, volume and velocity with which it is created and generated.

© IFIP International Federation for Information Processing 2016
Published by Springer International Publishing Switzerland 2016. All Rights Reserved
Y.K. Dwivedi et al. (Eds.): I3E 2016, LNCS 9844, pp. 533–544, 2016.
DOI: 10.1007/978-3-319-45234-0_47

Twitter [38–40], in particular, has been actively leveraged in facilitating social media analytics. Users active on twitter and interested in certain topics can easily communicate with one another using rapid and ad hoc establishment of shared 'hashtags' [33–35] which integrates the users even if they are not following each other. These hashtags along with the other metadata forms a basis for data extraction and analysis. Due to its open [3] architecture, twitter allows researchers to integrate smoothly to its API [4] and search for the desired content by using keywords such as the hashtags. A key aspect of twitter's persona is its real time nature [5, 40]. Research has shown that the reactionary nature of twitter is highly sensitive and the twitter posts can promptly reflect the occurrence of an event through generation of hashtags, formation of opinion based clusters and intermittent mentions to a certain group of twitter users. Tweets comprising of such content and sentiments [6] hold significant gravity as it can rapidly divide the social front into opinion groups like the political community, business groups, economists or individual users.

This social media segregation is the cornerstone of this research and puts forward the possibility of a relative sensitivity in several social media dimensions by analyzing 43,924 tweets from 22,896 users. The objectives of this paper are as follows: In the first step, we shall find observe how the social media community is split based on their opinion. Further, we shall assess the brand's social personality dimensions which can be associated with a twitter handle and consequently the sensitivity of the opinion group to the occurrence of the event.

2 Literature Review

The literature review has been organized into three subcategories beginning with the identification of the dimensions associated with a brand and its personality, studying social media and social media analytics.

2.1 Dimensions of Brand Personality

Considerable amount of work has been done in past in analyzing the consumer behavior, particularly to the association of human like attributes to a brand, referred to as brand personality [7, 15]. This personality of the brand allows the consumer to express him or his personality dimension through the use of the brand. The extensive study done in the past suggests that there are five characteristic personality attributes most commonly associated with a brand. These five personality dimensions [7, 16] viz. Sincerity, Excitement, Competence, Sophistication and Ruggedness can be understood by fifteen distinct dimensions (Fig. 1).

The possibility of dispersing a personality into several dimensions is crucial for our research as it allows deeper understanding [19] of the defining elements of the personality. With such an understanding, penetrating the consumer mind and adapting as per its need becomes a relatively simpler proposition. This framework has been extensively utilized by marketing researchers and business groups in the past to define the personality of a brand and align it with that of the target consumer group.

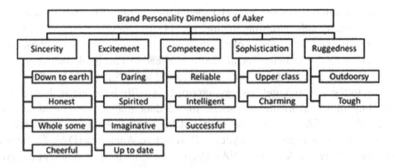

Fig. 1. The personality dimensions which constitute a brand's personality [7, 16].

This research aims at drawing coherence of the dimensions of brand personality with those of a social media entity and that of the defining facets with metrics [18] of web analytics.

2.2 Social Media and Its Classification

Social media in many capacities can be deemed as layer of functionality over Web 2.0 [8] sites. Web 2.0 facilitates greater and dynamic commotion of information through a greater collaboration among internet users, content providers and enterprises. Through this unique integration it truly allows the interfacing of different platforms of information, services and products through integration. Heavily reliant on user-generated and user-controlled content, it condones the use of any heavyweight infrastructure to access and use services, thereby empowering users and promoting larger collaboration. This strong support to information sharing and open expression has drawn significant attention on getting this data collected to uncover hidden patterns. Innovative business models are leveraging this strong social media layer to track and discover gaps in the real world. There can be numerous social media website categories [9, 36]: social networking sites, creativity sharing sites, intellectual property sites, user sponsored sites, company sponsored causes, company sponsored support sites, business networking sites, collaborative web, e-commerce sites, podcasts, news sites, educational sharing sites, open source communities, and social bookmarking websites. These platforms based on the functional blocks [9] facilitate management of identity, presence, relationships, reputation, groups, conversation and sharing, and thus project discrete utility to its users. Therefore, based on these blocks of functionality, present a different unique opportunity for greater exploration for researchers, since factors of brand personality would vary.

2.3 Social Media Analytics

Every social media entity has six broad functionalities [10] associated with it which serve as the building blocks for social media analytics. Figure 2 [9, 10] shows these user controlled functionalities. Based on these functionalities, the user's social media identity finds a unique spot in the social media topography. The progression of these over time eventually aids in settling the metrics [11] for analysis. In this context we will pay attention to one social media platform, Twitter [38–40]. We have chosen twitter because it is the fastest growing social platform, ahead of Facebook and Google+ [12] and unlike Facebook data, twitter data is considered to be 'open' [13]. It thus provides opportunity to the research and business groups by swiftly integrate with its API. This understanding of social media and social media data shall be leveraged to perform Twitter Analytics (TA) [12] on the twitter data. Twitter Analytics can broadly be categorized into three types of analytics – Descriptive Analytics (DA), Content Analytics (CA) and Network Analytics (NA). Each of these focuses on different dimensions of the data. Descriptive Analytics focuses on descriptive statistics [21, 22] such as number of tweets, distribution of different types of tweets and the number of hashtags. Such statistics are gateways to other metrics [12] like user activity and visibility [12]. Content analysis [23, 24] employs text mining and machine learning algorithms to perform word, hashtag and sentiment analysis [26]. Content analysis enables extraction of intelligence from Web2.0 [25], which must be preceded by meticulous text cleaning and processing. Network Analysis [27] leverages the network of @replies and re-tweets existing on twitter to perform topological [37] or community analysis. This network topology refers to a layout of nodes and edges based on the information of reply and re-tweet in Twitter. Network Analysis is useful in drawing significant number of community specific metrics [28] from the data.

3   Proposition

In the light of the above discussion, we can clearly identify the five personality dimensions which are associated with a brand and also observe that social media identities have a certain set of user controlled functionalities which define the extent of depth and breadth of the identity on the social media network. Taking twitter as the medium, every twitter identity has an alphanumeric nomenclature known as the twitter handle. The twitter handle is the unique name of the identity on the twitter network. Every time a user tweets, content is generated. This content comprises of a textual tweet which is upto 140 characters long, along with other data points such as the geo-location information, sending user's ID, time of posting, number of replies received, number of re-tweets and so on. These data points are known as metadata [11] and hold tremendous significance in establishing the social media functionality of the twitter identity. This research begins with identifying standard metrics prevalent over the twitter network which defines the functionality of a unique twitter handle. On identifying these metrics, an analogy can be drawn between them and the brand personality framework to obtain the personality dimensions of a unique twitter handle. Every dimension of the twitter personality can be aligned to a unique twitter metric which would serve as a facet to the dimensions, analogous to the brand personality framework. Consequently, the research proposes analytics as a tool to observe the sensitivity of these dimensions on the online forefront due to the occurrence of a major breakthrough event in the social arena. These metrics are the number of original tweets per total tweets, re-tweets received per total tweets tweeted, mentions received per total tweets tweeted, average favorite count received per tweet, visibility [12] of the twitter handle and the average sentiment [3] of the twitter handle.

Figure 2 shows one of the ways by which these social media metrics can be categorized by mapping them with the brand personality framework suggested above. Only the 5 most suitable of these metrics has been used in this study. By using this framework, we have mapped some of the social metrics with the five dimensions. This mapping was obtained as a result of a Delphi study [29–31] yielding a consensus amongst 12 social media experts in 3 iterations. By observing the percentage change (sensitivity) in the value of these metrics to the breakthrough event, the sensitivity of the dimensions of a twitter handle or a larger social media group can be obtained. In order to facilitate the clearer observation of any transition, the research looks at a large pool of twitter handles, and divides them into broader social media groups. This segregation is done on the basis of the nature of tweets tweeted by the twitter handle as well as the real life manifestos `which the account holder carries.

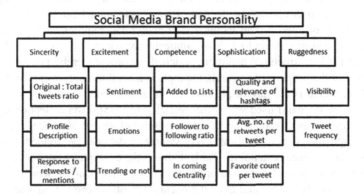

Fig. 2. Indicative social media metrics relevant to brand personality dimensions

For example, the twitter handle of a consultancy company offering an unbiased view forms the part of a different social media group as compared to the twitter handle of an individual affiliated with a particular political community. Similar analogy can be drawn for the twitter handles of a business group and an independent social media influencer or a Media Network such as a News Agency. Such twitter identities with similar real life affiliations can be clubbed together and hence an observation of the transition of the personality dimensions of a larger social group due to the occurrence of a major breakthrough event can be observed. Statistical tools are used to determine a change in the means of these dimensions due to the occurrence of the event at different confidence levels. This kind of clubbing was done to divide twitter users into broader groups.

Table 1. Example of a data sample along with metadata

Tweet	#Budget2016- 88% the survey respondents hope to see #tax reforms for minimisation of litigation. Our report: https://t.co/FYef8tew8z		
Metadata	**Value**	**Metadata**	**Value**
favorited	FALSE	replyToUID	NA
favoriteCount	0	statusSource	<a href="http://..
replyToSN	NA	screenName	GrantThorntonIN
created	2/28/2016 23:46	retweetCount	1
truncated	FALSE	isRetweet	FALSE
replyToSID	NA	retweeted	FALSE
id	7.04E+17	longitude	NA
		latitude	NA

4 Research Methodology

The process of calculating a change in the personality dimensions of social media groups begins with collecting twitter data (tweets and metadata) by identifying the topics or the area of interest. The acquisition of twitter data requires the use of API [12] which allows acquiring of up to 1 % of publically available data on twitter. The data thus obtained is less structured and more enriched in content thereby posing numerous challenges. For the purpose of research, the topic is a breakthrough event for the Indian social fabric, which is the day of proposal of the annual budget for the calendar year 2016-2017. The keyword used was '#Budget2016' [33–35]. Data collection was done for a period of 20 days, comprising of equal periods before and after occurrence of the event. Through analytical algorithms, every sample of data can be divided into a tweet and sixteen distinct metadata points. Table 1 shows the example of such a sample. The next step is to separate the data samples of those twitter handles which have been tweeting consistently before and after the occurrence of the event from the rest. This step becomes imperative because the transition of personality dimensions of a twitter handle can only be gauged if it continues to stay active on twitter after the occurrence of the event. Those twitter handles which are active for only one half (either pre or post occurrence) of the research are hence of little importance. These consistent twitter handles are then divided into well identifiable and distinct groups based on several factors like their real life manifestations, nature of tweets, relation with the event or their span of social influence. Once the data samples are consistent and divided, the six key metrics are calculated for every twitter handle for before and after the occurrence of the event. The visibility of the twitter handle can be calculated by adding the number of @replies received and the number of re-tweets received by it. The sentiment for a tweet can be calculated using several natural language algorithms [26] such as 'Sentistrength' [14]. Through these metrics, we can now transitively gather a fair idea of the personality dimensions of each of the social groups both before and after the event. By a comparison of these values, we can compare the sensitivity in the form of percentage change in every dimension of each social media group. This change in personality dimensions can also be tested using statistical tools like paired T-test on the means of the data corresponding to each social group identified. Let us assume that there are n social groups identified in the data set comprising of consistent twitter handles.

For each of these social groups there would be 5 personality dimensions. Each of these dimensions will have a mean value both before and after the event. Let us denote this mean by μ (before the event) and μ' (after the event). Thus, to check the difference in means occurring due to the event, paired T-test can be conducted as follows:

$$H_0 : \mu^{ij} = \mu'^{ij} \tag{1}$$

and

$$H_1 : \mu^{ij} \neq \mu'^{ij} \tag{2}$$

Here, H_0 refers to the null hypothesis, i.e., the means of the dimensions remain unchanged due to the occurrence of the event; while H_1 refers to the alternate hypothesis 'i' refers to the ith personality dimension ranging from 1 to 5 and 'j' refers to the jth social media group ranging from 1 to n. μ^{ij} = mean value of ith dimension corresponding to j^{th} social media group before the occurrence of the event. μ'^{ij} = mean value of ith dimension corresponding to j^{th} social media group after the event occurs.

5 Findings

A corpus of **43,924 twitter data** was extracted with the keyword '#Budget2016'. This comprised of tweets both before and after the occurrence of the event, separated by date. The data comprised of **22,896 distinct users**, out of which **1,534 users** were consistent in their activity and held relevance for the research. These tweets were further scanned and the tweets which were either not relevant to the research or were outliers were removed from the corpus. For example, tweets pertaining to the budget announcements in countries other than India were irrelevant to the research and were removed. Eventually, **10,231** tweets from the **1,534 unique users** were found to be relevant to the research and were used for the analysis. The final data set comprised of **6,050 (~59 %)** re-tweets. The unique users corresponding to the set of tweets were further classified into 11 distinct social groups as shown in Table 2. This categorization of the data set was developed as a result of the consensus obtained during the Delphi study [30–32] conducted amongst 12 social media experts in three rounds of iterations. The data samples which constituted each of these groups were used to calculate the personality dimensions for these groups before and after the event.

These dimensions were compared and the absolute percentage change in their values implied the sensitivity of these groups to the breakthrough event. Table 3 shows the transition in these personality dimensions for the social media groups.

It can be observed that the discrete social media groups which were identified have different sensitivities, showcased by the sensitivity of the social media metrics for different dimensions of the framework. This sensitivity enables us to break down and identify the susceptible regions in the social media fabric which are most impacted by any breakthrough event on the social media forefront. Statistical analysis using paired T test shows a significant change in means of dimensions corresponding to social groups as shown in Table 4.

Table 2. The consistent twitter handles were classified into 11 distinct social media groups

Social Media Group	Description
Business Group	Real life Business Groups and Profitable Organizations. Eg: 99acres, indiamart
Consultancy / Advisory	Consultancy firms across domains (Taxation, IT/ITeS, Financial services, etc). Eg: KPMG
Entrepreneural Community	Individuals or groups affiliated with the Entrepreneural Community. Eg: Startup India
Financial / Economic research	Individuals or group affiliated with the Financial research community. Eg: CRISIL India
Financial Markets	Individuals or group providing news and views of the financial markets. Eg: BSE India
Government Agency	Groups and Organizations endorsed by the Govt. of India. Eg: NITI Ayog
Social Influencers	Individuals, bloggers or groups, with high social influence. Eg: WeAllareIndians
Individual User	Twitter handle of an independent individual user.
Political Community	Individual or group, affiliated with a Political community or agenda. Eg: ModiforIndia
Industrial Community	Groups for Industrial Affiliations. Eg: CII India, Indiaretailbiz
Media Network	Individual or groups, affiliated with the Mass News Media. Eg: ETIndia, Forbes

Table 3. Changes in the Sensitivity of the Social Media Personality Dimensions after the event

	Excitement	Sincerity	Influence	Susceptibility	Reliability	Ruggedness
Business Group	36.78%	2.85%	7.65%	86.22%	5.72%	17.50%
Consultancy / Analysis	0.82%	6.11%	15.37%	25.77%	12.46%	69.30%
Entrepreneural Community	6.67%	1.82%	70.04%	22.73%	0.45%	23.45%
Financial / Economic research Community	19.44%	10.10%	25.68%	51.98%	0.00%	5.39%
Financial Markets	71.69%	5.32%	12.83%	59.75%	5.27%	14.80%
Government Agency	62.81%	10.46%	13.41%	50.87%	14.91%	82.72%
Independent Social Influencers	9.83%	12.50%	100.02%	15.64%	6.49%	114.60%
Individual User	5.21%	5.12%	69.59%	27.49%	3.66%	80.57%
Political Community	15.58%	0.71%	53.90%	9.20%	1.93%	72.40%
Industrial Community	8.67%	24.52%	12.26%	1.02%	3.96%	42.46%
Media Network	78.51%	2.94%	64.74%	38.28%	4.44%	56.05%

In the Table 4, S denotes a significant change, while NS denotes an insignificant change in means with 95 % confidence level. Major differences are perceived in excitement, sophistication and ruggedness of the brand personality through the Twitter profiles across user categories or groups. However, the context specificity (i.e. type of event being studied) of this outcome may not be ignored.

Table 4. Results of the paired T-test performed on the means corresponding to the dimensions.

	Excitement	Sincerety	Competence	Sophistication	Ruggedness
Business Groups	S (0.033)	NS	NS	NS	NS
Consultancy Groups	NS	NS	NS	NS	NS
Entrepreneural Community	NS	NS	NS	NS	NS
Financial / Economic research Community	NS	NS	NS	NS	NS
Financial Markets	S(0.044)	NS	NS	NS	NS
Government Agency	NS	NS	NS	S(0.044)	NS
Independent Social Influencer	NS	NS	NS	NS	NS
Individual Users	S(0.004)	NS	NS	S(0.000002)	S(3.25E-11)
Iindustrial Community	NS	NS	NS	NS	NS
Media Network	S(2.254E-07)	NS	S(0.0029)	NS	S(0.002)
Political Community	NS	NS	NS	S(0.005)	S(0.064)

Table 5. Most sensitive social groups based on overall change in personality dimensions

DIMENSION	MOST SENSITIVE AND SIGNIFICANT SOCIAL GROUPS IN THE DATA SET	TOTAL TWEETS
Sincerity	Industrial Community, Independent Social Influencers	495
Excitement	Business Groups#, Media Networks*, Financial Markets*, Individual users#	8763
Competence	Independent Social Influencers, Entrepreneurial Community, Media Network#	1643
Sophistication	Business Groups, Financial Markets, Government Agency#, Individual Users#, Political Community#	7940
Visibility	Independent Social Influencers, Government Agencies, Individual Users#, Media Network#, Political Community#	7579

A closer investigation highlights that majorly the individual users show a change of personality after breakthrough events, followed by media networks. Financial markets and business groups also highlight some statistically significant changes in personality in terms of their excitement.

6   Concluding Discussion

The research successfully manages to observe that the Social media universe can be judiciously divided into opinion groups. These groups comprise of entities which can exist in the form of twitter handles, Facebook groups or profiles. By identifying social media metrics which are coherent with the distinct facets of the brand personality framework, the five personality dimensions have been success fully associated with each of the opinion groups identified in the data.

In Table 5, asterisk (*) represents groups depicting both a high sensitivity and a significant change in mean. Hash (#) represents groups depicting a significant change in mean but with a low sensitivity. The framework brings out the most and least sensitive or rather susceptible social groups based on the percentage change in the values of the metrics mapped to these dimensions, due to the occurrence of the breakthrough event. The results of the analysis can be seen in Table 3. This framework of social media analytics is particularly useful in identifying the dimensions which are most susceptible intrinsically to these groups due to the occurrence of major events. Both the research and business community can gain significant insight into the Social media behavior of these groups by tracing the sensitivity of these frameworks. For people working in public policy, insights are provided on who are the most sensitive groups whose social discussion may polarize sentiments of an economy. How communities may interact may also be understood by NA.

In conclusion, this framework is a novel road-step in penetrating deeper into the social media fabric and dismantling the intricacies of social media analytics. The brand personality framework is one of the many methods which can be used to map the different social media metrics with the personality dimensions of a social media entity and remains one of the limitations of the research. However which parameters of brand personality get affected and among which user group may be a factor of the type of break-through events being explored. Generalizing the nature of personality change over different types of events may be considered in future research directions. Other parameters of brand personality dimensions based on social media can be explored in future research. Also variations in outcome may be observed if a different platform of social media (e.g. Facebook) is used for such a study. However, despite these limitations, the intuitive association between brand and social media personalities reveals an intriguing exploration which can be taken forward in future research.

References

1. Aral, S., Dellarocas, C., Godes, D.: Social media and business transformation: a framework for research. Inf. Syst. Res. **24**, 3–13 (2013)
2. Ranco, G., Aleksovski, D., Caldarelli, G., Grčar, M., Mozetič, I.: The effects of Twitter sentiment on stock price returns. PLoS ONE **10**(9), e0138441 (2015)
3. Bruns, A., Liang, Y.E.: Tools and methods for capturing Twitter data during natural disasters. First Monday **17**(4), 1–8 (2012)
4. Makice, K.: Twitter API: Up and Running: Learn How to Build Applications with the Twitter API. O'Reilly Media, Inc., Sebastopol (2009)
5. Sakaki, T., Okazaki, M., Matsuo, Y.: Earthquake shakes Twitter users: real-time event detection by social sensors. In: Proceedings of the 19th International Conference on World Wide Web. ACM (2010)
6. Kouloumpis, E., Wilson, T., Moore, T.D.: Twitter sentiment analysis: the good the bad and the OMG!. In: ICWSM 2011, pp. 538–541 (2011)
7. Aaker, J.L.: Dimensions of brand personality. J. Market. Res. **34**, 347–356 (1997)
8. O'reilly, T.: What is Web 2.0: design patterns and business models for the next generation of software. Commun. Strat. **1**, 17 (2007)
9. Kaplan, A.M., Haenlein, M.: Users of the world, unite! The challenges and opportunities of social media. Bus. Horiz. **53**(1), 59–68 (2010)
10. Kietzmann, J.H., et al.: Social media? Get serious! Understanding the functional building blocks of social media. Bus. Horiz. **54**(3), 241–251 (2011)
11. Bruns, A., Stieglitz, S.: Towards more systematic Twitter analysis: metrics for tweeting activities. Int. J. Soc. Res. Methodol. **16**(2), 91–108 (2013)
12. Chae, B.K.: Insights from hashtag# supplychain and Twitter analytics: considering Twitter and Twitter data for supply chain practice and research. Int. J. Prod. Econ. **165**, 247–259 (2015)
13. Gurstein, M.B.: Open data: empowering the empowered or effective data use for everyone? FirstMonday **16**(2) (2011)
14. Thelwall, M.: Heart and soul: sentiment strength detection in the social web with SentiStrength. In: Proceedings of the CyberEmotions, pp. 1–14 (2013)
15. Caprara, G.V., Barbaranelli, C., Guido, G.: Brand personality: how to make the metaphor fit? J. Econ. Psychol. **22**(3), 377–395 (2001)
16. Geuens, M., Weijters, B., De Wulf, K.: A new measure of brand personality. Int. J. Res. Market. **26**(2), 97–107 (2009)

17. Glynn, M.W., Faulds, D.J.: Social media: the new hybrid element of the promotion mix. Bus. Horiz. **52**(4), 357–365 (2009)
18. Clifton, B.: Advanced web metrics with Google Analytics. Wiley, New York (2012)
19. Ekinci, Y., Hosany, S.: Destination personality: an application of brand personality to tourism destinations. J. Travel Res. **45**(2), 127–139 (2006)
20. Kar, A.K.: A group decision support system for selecting an open source tool for social media integration. In: Sengupta, S., Das, K., Khan, G. (eds.) Emerging Trends in Computing and Communication. Lecture Notes in Electrical Engineering, vol. 298, pp. 407–413. Springer, India (2014)
21. Bruns, A., Highfield, T.: Political networks on Twitter: tweeting the Queensland state election. Inf. Commun. Soc. **16**(5), 667–691 (2013)
22. Xiang, Z., Gretzel, U.: Role of social media in online travel information search. Tourism Manag. **31**(2), 179–188 (2010)
23. Holsti, O.R.: Content Analysis for the Social Sciences and Humanities, pp. 602–611. Addison-Wesley, Reading (1969)
24. Riff, D., Lacy, S., Fico, F.: Analyzing Media Messages: Using Quantitative Content Analysis in Research. Routledge, New York (2014)
25. Chau, M., Jennifer, X.: Business intelligence in blogs: understanding consumer interactions and communities. MIS Q. **36**(4), 1189–1216 (2012)
26. Pang, B., Lee, L.: Opinion mining and sentiment analysis. Found. Trends Inf. Retr. **2**(1–2), 1–135 (2008)
27. Burt, R.S., Kilduff, M., Tasselli, S.: Social network analysis: foundations and frontiers on advantage. Ann. Rev. Psychol. **64**, 527–547 (2013)
28. Scott, P.J., Wasserman, S. (eds.): Models and Methods in Social Network Analysis, vol. 28. Cambridge University Press, Cambridge (2005)
29. Schmidt, R., Lyytinen, K., Keil, P.C.M.: Identifying software project risks: an international Delphi study. J. Manag. Inf. Syst. **17**(4), 5–36 (2001)
30. Osborne, J., et al.: What ideas-about-science should be taught in school science? A Delphi study of the expert community. J. Res. Sci. Teach. **40**(7), 692–720 (2003)
31. Gokhale, A.A.: Offshore outsourcing: a Delphi study. J. Inf. Technol. Case Appl. Res. **9**(2), 6–18 (2007)
32. Dyer, L., Blancero, D.: Workplace 2000: A Delphi-Study (1992)
33. Wang, X., et al.: Topic sentiment analysis in Twitter: a graph-based hashtag sentiment classification approach. In: Proceedings of the 20th ACM International Conference on Information and Knowledge Management. ACM (2011)
34. Small, T.A.: What the hashtag? A content analysis of Canadian politics on Twitter. Inf. Commun. Soc. **14**(6), 872–895 (2011)
35. Lau, J.H., Collier, N., Baldwin, T.: On-line trend analysis with topic models: \#Twitter trends detection topic model online. In: COLING (2012)
36. Hanna, R., Rohm, A., Crittenden, V.L.: We're all connected: the power of the social media ecosystem. Bus. Horiz. **54**(3), 265–273 (2011)
37. Jiang, B., Claramunt, C.: Topological analysis of urban street networks. Environ. Plann. B: Plann. Des. **31**(1), 151–162 (2004)
38. Kwak, H., et al.: What is Twitter, a social network or a news media? In: Proceedings of the 19th International Conference on World Wide Web. ACM (2010)
39. Java, Akshay, et al.: Why we Twitter: understanding microblogging usage and communities. In: Proceedings of the 9th WebKDD and 1st SNA-KDD 2007 Workshop on Web Mining and Social Network Analysis. ACM (2007)

40. Huberman, B.A., Romero, D.M., Wu, F.: Social networks that matter: Twitter under the microscope (2008)
41. Sakaki, T., Okazaki, M., Matsuo, Y.: Earthquake shakes Twitter users: real-time event detection by social sensors. In: Proceedings of the 19th International Conference on World Wide Web, pp. 851–860. ACM (2010)

Analysis of the Value of Public Geotagged Data from Twitter from the Perspective of Providing Situational Awareness

Aragats Amirkhanyan[✉] and Christoph Meinel

Hasso Plattner Institute (HPI), University of Potsdam, Potsdam, Germany
{Aragats.Amirkhanyan,Christoph.Meinel}@hpi.de
https://hpi.de

Abstract. In the era of social networks, we have a huge amount of social geotagged data that reflect the real world. These data can be used to provide or to enhance situational and public safety awareness. It can be reached by the way of analysis and visualization of geotagged data that can help to better understand the situation around and to detect local geo-spatial threats. One of the challenges in the way of reaching this goal is providing valuable statistics and advanced methods for filtering data. Therefore, in the scope of this paper, we collect sufficient amount of public social geotagged data from Twitter, build different valuable statistics and analyze them. Also, we try to find valuable parameters and propose the useful filters based on these parameters that can filter data from invaluable data and, by this way, support analysis of geotagged data from the perspective of providing situational awareness.

Keywords: Analysis · Statistics · Big data · Location-based social networks · Geotagged data · Georeferenced data · Situational awareness · Public safety awareness

1 Introduction

Nowadays, social networks are an essential part of modern life for millions of users around the word. Users use social networks to communicate with friends and share what happens with them, what they feel and so on. One of the biggest social networks is Twitter that, according to the recent statistics [3], has more than 300 million active monthly users, who post every day more than 600 million tweets (messages) [6]. Twitter is not only the social network, but it is the source of real-time news feeds and it is the place where breaking news appear firstly, before we read it in the newspapers, listen at the radio or watch on TV [12]. The amount of data produced by social networks increases dramatically every year. And, also, there is a trend, that users post geotagged messages that reflect the situation around them. For research, it is important, because it gives us

© IFIP International Federation for Information Processing 2016
Published by Springer International Publishing Switzerland 2016. All Rights Reserved
Y.K. Dwivedi et al. (Eds.): I3E 2016, LNCS 9844, pp. 545–556, 2016.
DOI: 10.1007/978-3-319-45234-0_48

more possibilities for visualization and analysis of social data, since we can be interested not only in the content of messages but also in the location, from where these messages were posted.

Analysis of public social geotagged data is a big topic and there are many papers and enterprise solutions, which cover different aspects and challenges of social data analysis. One of the most popular cases is to use geotagged data for analyzing and detecting natural disasters. For example, Sakaki et al. [17] used Twitter users as social sensors to detect earthquake shakes. They investigated the real-time interaction of events, such as earthquakes, in Twitter and proposed an algorithm to monitor tweets and to detect an earthquake target event. Another use case of using public social data is to analyze natural disasters was presented by De Longueville et al. [10]. In their paper, they showed how location-based social networks (LBSN) can be used as a reliable source of spatiotemporal information, by analyzing the temporal, spatial and social dynamics of Twitter activity during a major forest fire event in the South of France in July 2009. Later in 2013, the amount of public social geotagged data increased and researchers had a possibility to detect not only global but, also, local geo-spatial events [18].

In 2013, Kalev Leetaru et al. [13] presented their deep study of geography of Twitter. They analyzed data from Twitter posted around the world and built many statistics, such as total tweets per day, average tweets per hour, all exact location coordinates and the top 20 cities by percent of georeferenced tweets. Also, their study includes linguistic, textual and user profiles analysis of data. In 2014, Muhammad Adnan et al. [7] presented their results of analysis geotagged data from Twitter. In their work, their concentrated on social dynamics of Twitter usage based on data from London, Paris and New York City. They showed the areas of tweeting activity, they provided the results of ethnicity analysis of Twitter users, geography of tweets of different ethnic groups and gender analysis. Another analysis of geotagged data, Diansheng Guo et al. [11] presented in 2014. In their work, they were aimed to detect non-personal and spam users on geotagged Twitter network. Their approach contains extracting user characteristics, constructing training datasets, conducting supervised classification for detecting non-personal users and the evaluation of the approach. In 2015, Umashanthi Pavalanathan et al. [16] presented interesting results. They showed that young people and women more often write geotagged tweets; users, who geotag their tweets, tend to write more, making them easier to geolocate; and text-based geo location is significantly more accurate for men and for older people.

Based on papers of previous years including mentioned in this section, we see how geotagged data are valuable and what we can obtain from analysis of them. Therefore, in this paper, we provide our research results of analysis of geotagged data in the scope of our specific challenge, which is analysis of the value of geotagged data from the perspective of providing situational awareness. For that, we start with Sect. 2, in which we provide the description of our research project, in the scope of which we address the current challenge, and our motivation for that. The remainder of the paper is organized as follows: in Sect. 3, we describe how we collect data and what data we have for analysis. Afterwards, in Sect. 4, we provide statistics and our analytic results of collected data. Based on that, we try to propose methods for making data more valuable for analysis of situational awareness and public safety awareness. We conclude the paper and provide future directions of research in Sect. 5.

2   Project Scope and Motivation

In the scope of our main research project, we are aimed to analyze and visualize in real-time publicly available social geotagged data to provide situational and public safety awareness. This challenge requires a complex solution, therefore, during work on the project, we face with many additional challenges that come from the practice [8,9], such as real-time clustering and visualization of massive geotagged data, provision of advanced methods for searching and filtering, provision of real-time valuable statistics and so on. Nowadays, there are a lot of social analytics tools, such as TweetDeck, Twitonomy, Hootsuite, Tweepsmap, Geofeedia and so on. Many of them provide powerful functionality for analysis and visualization of data for different purposes and solve some challenges mentioned above. But mostly, they are aimed to support marketing and business, therefore, their solutions of filtering and providing real-time statistics are not always can be applied to our research project that has other focus.

We have our specific goal, which is provision of situational and public safety awareness. To achieve this goal, we want to work with social geotagged data that describe the situation around the place, from which they were posted. But it is not always the case, and we have to work with a huge amount of data that are useless for our analysis and they do not reflect valuable information and do not describe the situation around. Therefore, we face with the challenge that presented in this paper. This challenge is analysis of the value of public geotagged data from Twitter from the perspective of providing situational awareness. In the scope of this challenge, we want to understand what and which parameters can help us to recognize whether some concrete message does have any value in describing the situation around or not, based on which characteristics we can fully exclude invaluable data from our dataset and which statistics of data can help us to better understand the situation around. All together should support our research project. Therefore, we are aimed to collect social geotagged data, build statistics and analyze them. Results of these statistics can help us to exclude invaluable data and develop advanced filters to support analysis of data from the perspective of providing situational awareness.

3   Data

Data is an essential part of any research. For our research, we use public social geotagged data from Twitter. Twitter provides a quite powerful API to fetch required data [1,5]. One of them is commercial Twitter's Firehose, which guarantees access to 100 % of tweets, and other one is public Streaming API, which does not guarantee the percentage of receiving data in real-time. More comparisons between data from Twitter's Streaming API and Twitter's Firehose, you can find in the paper of Fred Morstatter et al. [15]. But we want to mention that, according to some studies [1], using Twitter's Streaming API users can expect to receive anywhere from 1 % of the tweets to over 40 % of tweets in near real-time. Also, you can increase the percentage of receiving tweets by applying more strict criteria. The criteria can be keywords, usernames, locations, named places, etc. In our case, we use location as a criteria and we collect data from London, because London is one of the world's most active Twitter cities [4]. To collect data, we use the Java-based application that connects to Twitter's Streaming API, specifies needed criteria and starts to receive tweets in real-time. For our experiments we decided to collect data from the area that covers London and its neighborhood. The coordinates of monitored area are {51.247948, -0.569042; 51.727184, 0.303813}, where the first pair is latitude and longitude coordinates of the south west and the second pair is latitude and longitude coordinates of the north east. We parse all received data, normalize them and save them into the database for further analysis. For research and further analysis, we collected 1 million tweets that cover about 12 days: from the 28th of January 11:37:30 AM until the 8th of February 12:41:48 PM.

4   Analysis

This section is the main part of the paper. In this section, we provide different valuable statistics and full description and analysis of them. Also, we try to find out how our results could be used to support analysis of situational and public safety awareness. It means that based on our statistic and statistics results, we try to propose (1) methods for reducing the amount of data by excluding (removing) invaluable data and (2) filters that can support analysis of geotagged data. Both proposals (excluding data and filters) are aimed to support analysis of situational awareness based on social geotagged data.

Table 1. Tweets' languages statistics

English	Undefined	Spanish	Arabic	Portuguese	French	Others
83.80 %	6.76 %	1.66 %	1.37 %	1.16 %	0.92 %	4.33 %

We start with the statistics in Table 1. In this table, you can see the most popular languages of tweets posted from London. Information about languages we take from the tweet object, which is provided by Twitter [5]. Firstly, we can see that the official language is in the first place. About 83.80 % of all tweets are posted in English. Then we can see that for 6.76 % of tweets, Twitter was not able to identify the language. In most cases, it means that tweets without the language do not contain sentences or even words. They are just a set of hashtags, user mentions, symbols and URLs. So, such tweets do not have semantic sense. In the

Table 2. Tweets' place types statistics

City	Admin	Country
79.08 %	18.50 %	2.42 %

next places, we have Spanish (1.66 %), Arabic (1.37 %), Portuguese (1.16 %), French (0.92 %) and so on. Now, we need to consider how we can use obtained information to support analysis of data. Firstly, we definitely can exclude all tweets with the undefined language, because they bring no sense and we can not use them to analyze situational awareness. By this way, we can reduce the amount of data by 6.76 %. Other thing that we can do, we can use the knowledge about used languages to filter dataset by languages or filter dataset from tweets in other foreign languages. It can support analysis of data, because we would fetch only relevant data.

Usually tweets contain the place information, because users are asked to attached a geographic place to the tweet before to publish it. Additional, Twitter asks users to attach exact coordinates. So, the final tweet could have the exact geo coordinates and attached place. Places could be *city*, administrative area (*admin*), *country* or some concrete place of interest (*poi*), for example, Big Ben in London. In our dataset, almost all tweets have attached places (only 5 tweets do not have a place), but only 11.53 % of data have exact coordinates. In Table 2, you can see which place types are usually attached to tweets. In the first place we have the *city* with about 79.08 %, then the *admin* (administrative area) with about 18.50 % and in the last place we have the *country* place type with about 2.42 %. In our research, we are interested only in the tweets that have the *city* place type or more narrow as a place of interest (*poi*). Place types, such as *country* and administrative area (*admin*), are too big areas and we can not use such data for analyzing situational awareness. It means that we can easily exclude such data from our dataset, but with one assumption. We exclude tweets with irrelevant place types only if these tweets do not have exact geo coordinates. Because if the tweet contains exact geo coordinates, we should not consider to which place the tweet is attached. So, if we exclude tweets with *country* and *admin* place types, we can reduce dataset by maximum 20.92 %.

Not all content published in Twitter is original. Some tweets come from other social networks or have links to the external web sites or services, such as Facebook, Instagram, Swarm (Foursquare) and son on. If the tweet contains several links, we consider only the last link, because usually the last link refers to the original source of information. According to Table 3, the main external source

Table 3. Statistics of external sources of tweets

twitter.com	instagram.com	bit.ly	swarmapp.com	goo.gl	trendinalia.com	youtube.com
8.46 %	6.54 %	1.51 %	0.98 %	0.47 %	0.44 %	0.44 %

of tweets is twitter.com (8.46 %). It means that users post tweets that contain links to other tweets. Then we have instagram.com (6.54 %), bit.ly (1.51 %), swarmapp.com (0.98 %) and so on. We can suppose that if user posts a tweet about what happens around him, he does not include links to external websites into the tweet, otherwise, user likely does not really describe the situation around him. But this statement does not work if the tweet has link to another social network, because, in this case, it could be that user posted about the situation around in Instagram but then he reposted the message to Twitter. Therefore, it is not always obviously, which data we can exclude from dataset. It requires more detailed analysis. But some of them we can definitely exclude. For example, we can exclude tweets that refer to Foursquare, Swarm or Yelp, to social networks that have nothing with describing the situation around. Usually, tweets, which refer to Swarm, have information, such as "Hi, I am in London" or something similar to it. So, if we exclude tweets at least only from Swarm, we can reduce dataset by about 0.98 %.

Table 4. Statistics of the most demanding geo coordinates

gcpe6rh4k4j9	gcpvjc9kxvpg	gcpuuqtyeztv	u120jz6zfbbe	gcpusn4djt0k	gcpvnqvtp20z
5.79 %	5.75 %	4.93 %	4.33 %	4.15 %	3.34 %

We have 1 million tweets but only 11.53 % of tweets have exact geo coordinates, others have geo coordinates based on an attached geographic place (the center of the place). It means that if tweets have the same attached places then they have the same coordinates. Based on our dataset, we calculated that from 1 million possible geo coordinates, we have only 37650 unique geo coordinates, which is about 3.76 % of all possible coordinates. This percentage is less than the percentage of tweets with exact coordinates. So, we can conclude that tweets with exact geo coordinates can have the same coordinates. Usual case for that is when tweets are reposted from other social networks. Additionally, we analyzed which geo coordinates are the most demanding. In Table 4, you can find the calculated statistics. The coordinates are presented in geohash[1] form to simplify the represent. They can be easily converted back to latitude and longitude by the geohash function. According to our statistics, about 5.79 % of tweets have coordinates *gcpe6rh4k4j9* (51.23513843, -0.59857568), which is in the area of the city Guildford. The next, about 5.75 % of tweets have coordinates *gcpvjc9kxvpg* (51.51294588, -0.09681718), which is the center of London. By this statistics, we can see which places are the most attractive by Twitter users. Above we mentioned that about 79.08 % of tweets contain attached places of the *city* type. But these places are different. If user posts a tweet in London and he attaches the place as London then his tweet would have coordinates of the center of London. But if he attaches some concrete district of the city then the tweet would have

---

[1] https://en.wikipedia.org/wiki/Geohash.

more concrete location. For example, such district of London can be Barnet, Hackney, Lambeth and so on. Actually, Twitter suggests the closest and the most appropriate place when user wants to attach the place to the tweet, and it helps more correctly determine the location for the tweet even if user did not attach the exact geo coordinates. Now, the question is what we can do with this statistics to support analysis of situational awareness. We can use this statistics to design a filter. This filter would use statistics from Table 4 and provide filtering data from tweets, which were posted from the most demanding geo coordinates. In some cases, it can facilitate visual analysis of situation.

In Sect. 3, we mentioned that we subscribe for data from London and its neighborhood defined by the following coordinates {51.247948, -0.569042; 51.727184, 0.303813}. But Twitter usually returns not only data from the specified area but also from areas that overlap that area. For example, we receive, also, tweets with coordinates of the entire country UK. Therefore, additionally, we calculated the percentage of tweets that have coordinates inside of the specified area. The result is 82.51 %, which is close to the percentage of tweets containing a *city* place type. If we exclude tweets outside the monitored area, we can reduce the amount of data by 17.49 %. But this percentage will be less, if we, firstly, exclude tweets with inappropriate place types *admin* and *country*.

In Introduction, we mentioned that some tweets contain location information, such as hashtags or words of locations, and they can be geolocated. Therefore, we want to find out how many tweets in our dataset contain additional location information. In some cases, it can help to identify the location more precisely than it is specified. For example, we could have the tweet "The house is on fire in Carnaby Street" and this tweet could have an attached place as the entire London, which has coordinates of the city center. But in this case, this message would be more valuable if it would have more concrete location. We can see this concrete location in the text message "in Carnaby Street". Therefore, we want to find out how many tweets in our dataset contain such additional location information. To find out it, we used Stanford Named Entity Recognizer (NER) [2]. And after applying this library for our dataset, we obtained that about 9.51 % of tweets contain additional location information in their text content. It means that potentially 9.51 % of tweets could be more accurate geolocated than it is specified.

The next thing, in which we are interested in, is how many unique users we have. We calculated that in our dataset we have 107105 unique users, and it means that we have about 9.37 posts per user. Not all users are equally active. Therefore, we want to find out which users produce more tweets than others. In Table 5, you can find partial statistic results. In the first place, we have user *tegrenade*, who produced about 1.40 % of all tweets from our dataset. It is about

Table 5. The most active Twitter users

tegrenade	hesjkr94	trendinaliagb	orgetorix	blankiiam015	don_jide	a_rockas	biggucci_idz
1.40 %	0.61 %	0.50 %	0.26 %	0.23 %	0.22 %	0.22 %	0.20 %

14004 tweets during 12 days, which means 1167 tweets per day. The Twitter accounts in the next palaces produced also huge amount of data, you can see it in Table 5. Some of these active users we can consider as a non-personal or spam users. It is an interesting challenge to identify it and Diansheng Guo et al. [11] presented their approach of detecting non-personal and spam users. But in the scope of our paper, we would like to use found statistics to design a filter. And this filter would be aimed to filter data from the most active users by using statistics from Table 5. In some case, it can facilitate analysis of data.

Now, we consider hashtags, user mentions, symbols, URLs and media objects in tweets, and how they are mentioned by users. We start with symbols. The symbol is the character started with $ dollar sign and it is often used in the financial area, for example, to put price information or to include the name of the company in the stock market. Examples of symbols are AMZN, GOOG, FB, GBPUSD, where AMZN - Amazon, GOOG - Google, FB - Facebook, and GBPUSD - British Pound to Dollar. So, we can suppose that tweets with symbols have nothing with describing the situation around, therefore, we can exclude them. But they constitute just about 0.01 %, so the benefit is small.

Table 6. The percentage of tweets that contain URLs in their text content

has URL	1 URL	2 URLs	3 URLs	4 or more URLs
25.70 %	23.96 %	1.71 %	0.03 %	0.003 %

Many tweets contain URLs. According to our statistics, about 25.70 % of tweets contain URL. Mostly, tweets contain only one URL (23.96 %), but some of them have more links. Details statistics you can find in Table 6. Such URLs could be links to other social networks or to some external websites with some news. We can suppose that if user posts the tweet about what he sees now, likely, he will not include a link to the external resources, but with the exception when user reposts the tweet from other social networks. Therefore, we can assume only one or maximum two links. Others tweets we can exclude from dataset.

Some tweets contain media objects: image or video. According to our statistics, 14.24 % of tweets contain media object, and 14.238 % of them contain only one media object and 0.002 % of them contain 2 media objects. Media-based tweets are produced by 35.81 % of users. So, it is common to include one media object to the tweet, but existence of media objects in tweets does not tell us about the relevance of the tweets from the perspective of describing the situation around. Therefore, we should not consider this parameter for filtering data.

Users often mention other users in their tweets to start or to keep discussion. For that, they use @ character and the account name of the user. From Table 7, we can see that about 51.68 % of tweets contain user mentions. We could suppose that the number of user mentions can affect how the tweet describes the situation around. More user mentions in the tweet then more likely that this tweet is just

Table 7. The percentage of tweets with user mentions in their text content

has mention	1 mention	2 mentions	3 mentions	4 or more mentions
51.68 %	36.35 %	9.58 %	3.12 %	2.63 %

Table 8. The percentage of tweets with hashtags in their text content

has hashtag	1 hashtag	2 hashtags	3 hashtags	4 or more hashtags
22.71 %	12.04 %	5.04 %	2.23 %	3.40 %

a part of the discussion, but not describing the situation around. Therefore, we are interested in a filter that can filter data by number of user mentions. For example, we could want to filter data from tweets that contain 3 or more user mentions. It can reduce dataset by 5.74 % for further analysis.

In Table 8, you can see the statistics of hashtags in tweets. According to our results, about 22.71 % of tweets contain hashtags. About 12.04 % of them contain only one hashtag, about 5.04 % of them contain two hashtags, about 2.23 % of them contain 3 hashtags and about 3.40 % of them contain 4 or more hashtags. We can suppose that when user wants quickly to post a tweet about the situation around, he would not consider about including a huge amount of hashtags into the tweet. But we can not fully rely on this statement. We should consider another additional parameter.

In Table 9, we provide the statistics of the most utilized hashtags during the time periods of collected data. 799 hashtags appear every day (12 days) in our dataset, 580 hashtags appear in 11 days (91.66 % of the entire date range), 548 appear in 10 days (83.33 %) and so on. Some hashtags, which appear every day, could be useless hahstags from our perspective, for example, the hashtag *#happybirthday*. Whereas among these hashtags, there are hashtags that represent geographic places, for example, *#london*. The hashtag *#london* appears every day, but we assume that this hashtag can be included into the tweet to describe the situation around. Therefore, we need to consider an additional parameter that can help us to understand the value of tweets with popular hashtags. Therefore, we built the statistics of the distribution of the most popular hashtags among users. You can find this statistics in Table 10. From that statistics, we can see that, for example, the hashtag *#london* is used by 5.07 % of users. This hashtag is used by significant amount of users and it appears every day, therefore, we can not exclude tweets with this hashtag. Whereas, the hashtag *#happybirthday*, which appears also every day, is used only by 76 users (0.071 %

Table 9. The count of hashtags and the count of days when these hashtags appear

12 (100 %)	11 (91.66 %)	10 (83.33 %)	9 (75.00 %)	8 (66.66 %)	7 (58.33 %)	6 (50.00 %)
799	580	548	606	720	988	1286

Table 10. Statistics of usage concrete hashtags by the percentage of users

london	love	cbb	superbowl	uk	sb50	art	fridayfeeling	valentinesday	tbt
5.07 %	0.71 %	0.70 %	0.60 %	0.53 %	0.52 %	0.50 %	0.49 %	0.44 %	0.43 %

of users). This fact could give us a guess that such hashtag does not bring any situational information into the tweet. Therefore, we can think about filtering them.

We have three parameters related to the hashtags: the number of hashtags in the tweet, the distribution of hashtags during the date period of dataset and the distribution of hashtags among users. We want to filter tweets that do not describe the situation around. For that, we need to use all three parameters. Therefore, our filter should assume that an invalid tweet should have more than n hashtags, at least m of these hashtags should appear every day during the monitored period d (in our case it is 12 days, but it can be customized), and less than p percents of users should use these m hashtags. We need to point out that we do not consider which values of parameters n, m, p, d to choose to obtain the best filtering results, but we have only showed the parameters that should be considered. Finding the concrete optimal values is a part of future work.

5 Conclusion and Future Work

We devoted this paper for analysis of the value of social geotagged data from the perspective of providing situational awareness. We were motivated to do it because we have to work with a huge amount of invaluable data and we wanted to reduce this amount of invaluable data, design filters and build statistics that can support analysis. During work on analysis of data, we built statistics by different parameters and different compound parameters, and we presented the most valuable found results from our perspective.

It is always important to point out that we do analysis of social geotagged data from the perspective of providing situational awareness and, all statistics which we built, we analyzed for our concert use case that makes our research different from many existing social analytics tools focused mostly on business and marketing. For example, in the statistics of the most popular languages in Table 1, we tried to find out how this statistics can help us to remove partially invaluable data. And we found out that the indicator of invaluable data, from the perspective of providing situational information, can be the undefined language. We went further and we tried to heuristically find out how number of different entities in the text content can affect the situational value of data. We had an assumption that if the tweet has many URLs, user mentions, hashtags and symbols then such tweet has less the situational value. Based on this assumption, we built statistics by mentioned parameters that showed us what the benefit we can obtain if we exclude much littered tweets. Another example of analysis of geotagged data from perspective of providing situational awareness is the statistics of original sources of tweets. We found out that some sources of tweets can be indicators of invaluable data, but it requires manual analysis and making the list of irrelevant sources, such as Swarm and Foursquare, which do not bring situational information in their content.

To evaluate the benefit from analysis of data and built statistics, we applied some recommendations for our research project. If we remove data with inappropriate place types (*country*, *admin*), data outside the specified monitored area, data from irrelevant services: Swarm and Foursquare, data with symbols and data with undefined languages, then we exclude 28.86 % of invaluable data. Meanwhile, we can expect the higher percentage of removed invaluable data, if we apply more advanced methods for filtering based on compound parameters from built statistics. Therefore, we would like to continue research and, for that, we determine some future work directions.

As a future work, we would like to build and visualize in real-time presented in the paper statistics. Also, we would like to use statistics from this paper to develop proposed filters. These filters can help to better analyze data and provide more accurate situational awareness. Such filters could be filters of the spam hashtags, inappropriate URLs, inappropriate geo location coordinates, tweets that contain too much user mentions and so on. Also, we need to find the optimal values of the parameters for filters from the perspective of providing the optimal filtering to have mostly data that describe the situation around. With results in this paper and future work mentioned in this section, we plan to go further to achieve the main goal of the research project - real-time situational and public safety awareness based on public social geotagged data.

References

1. Bright planet. http://www.brightplanet.com/2013/06. Accessed 08 Mar 2016
2. Stanford Named Entity Recognizer (NER). http://nlp.stanford.edu/software/CRF-NER.shtml. Accessed 08 Mar 2016
3. The number of monthly active Twitter users worldwide. http://www.statista.com/statistics/282087/number-of-monthly-active-twitter-users/. Accessed 08 Mar 2016
4. The world's most active Twitter cities. http://www.forbes.com/sites/victorlipman/2012/12/30/the-worlds-most-active-twitter-city-you-wont-guess-it/. Accessed 08 Mar 2016
5. Twitter api documentation. https://dev.twitter.com/overview/api. Accessed 08 Mar 2016
6. Twitter statistics. http://www.internetlivestats.com/one-second/#tweets-band. Accessed 08 Mar 2016
7. Adnan, M., Longley, P.A., Khan, S.M.: Social dynamics of twitter usage in London, Paris, and New York City. First Monday **19**(5) (2014). http://firstmonday.org/ojs/index.php/fm/article/view/4820
8. Amirkhanyan, A., Cheng, F., Meinel, C.: Real-time clustering of massive geodata for online maps to improve visual analysis. In: 2015 11th International Conference on Innovations in Information Technology (IIT), pp. 308–313, November 2015
9. Amirkhanyan, A., Meinel, C.: Visualization and analysis of public social geodata to provide situational awareness. In: 2016 Eighth International Conference on Advanced Computational Intelligence (ICACI), pp. 68–73, February 2016

10. De Longueville, B., Smith, R.S., Luraschi, G.: Omg, from here, i can see the flames!: a use case of mining location based social networks to acquire spatio-temporal data on forest fires. In: Proceedings of the 2009 International Workshop on Location Based Social Networks, LBSN 2009, NY, USA, pp. 73–80. ACM, New York (2009). http://doi.acm.org/10.1145/1629890.1629907

11. Guo, D., Chen, C.: Detecting non-personal and spam users on geo-tagged twitter network. T. GIS **18**(3), 370–384 (2014). http://dx.doi.org/10.1111/tgis.12101

12. Kwak, H., Lee, C., Park, H., Moon, S.: What is twitter, a social network or a news media?. In: Proceedings of the 19th International Conference on World Wide Web, WWW 2010, NY, USA, pp. 591–600. ACM, New York (2010). http://doi.acm.org/10.1145/1772690.1772751

13. Leetaru, K., Wang, S., Cao, G., Padmanabhan, A., Shook, E.: Mapping the global twitter heartbeat: the geography of twitter. First Monday **18**(5) (2013). http://firstmonday.org/ojs/index.php/fm/article/view/4366

14. Mao, H., Shuai, X., Kapadia, A.: Loose tweets: an analysis of privacy leaks on twitter. In: Proceedings of the 10th Annual ACM Workshop on Privacy in the Electronic Society, WPES 2011, NY, USA, pp. 1–12. ACM, New York (2011). http://doi.acm.org/10.1145/2046556.2046558

15. Morstatter, F., Pfeffer, J., Liu, H., Carley, K.M.: Is the sample good enough? comparing data from twitter's streaming API with twitter's firehose (2013). CoRR abs/1306.5204. http://arxiv.org/abs/1306.5204

16. Pavalanathan, U., Eisenstein, J.: Confounds and consequences in geotagged twitter data (2015). CoRR abs/1506.02275. http://arxiv.org/abs/1506.02275

17. Sakaki, T., Okazaki, M., Matsuo, Y.: Earthquake shakes twitter users: real-time event detection by social sensors. In: Proceedings of the 19th International Conference on World Wide Web, WWW 2010, NY, USA, pp. 851–860. ACM, New York (2010). http://doi.acm.org/10.1145/1772690.1772777

18. Walther, M., Kaisser, M.: Geo-spatial event detection in the twitter stream. In: Serdyukov, P., Braslavski, P., Kuznetsov, S.O., Kamps, J., Rüger, S., Agichtein, E., Segalovich, I., Yilmaz, E. (eds.) ECIR 2013. LNCS, vol. 7814, pp. 356–367. Springer, Heidelberg (2013)

Social Media Use During Emergency Response – Insights from Emergency Professionals

Mahshid Marbouti[✉] and Frank Maurer

University of Calgary, Calgary, AB, Canada
{mmarbout,fmaurer}@ucalgary.ca

Abstract. This paper analyzes issues in organizational needs for extracting information from social media during emergency response. By interviewing 16 Canadian emergency professionals, we gained insight into such things as: how they currently monitor social media; what types of information they are interested in, what challenges they encounter and what strategies they use to overcome those challenges. The most frequent requirements mentioned by participant were the need for prioritization and categorization of social media data to mitigate information overload. These professionals are also concerned about the reliability of information and counteracting the rumors.

Keywords: Social media · Emergency response · Requirement gathering · Information overload · Information reliability

1 Introduction

When an emergency happens, social media may provide information from the public that can contribute to situation awareness of emergency operation centers (EOCs) and impact their decision-making. For example, Twitter reported that during Hurricane Sandy in 2012, people sent more than 20 million tweets about the storm within 6 days. During the event, people actively broadcast different kinds of emergency-related information. The information can be descriptions of the event, impact on the community, requests for help, and expressions of fear [1, 2].

This study describes the current status of the use of social media by Canadian practitioners through semi-structured interviews. We gather requirements elicitation on support tools for those who are monitoring and analyzing social media information posted by public to enhance situational awareness. Our goal is to bring insight into the challenges that these practitioners are facing when trying to extract information from social media, and try to identify what kinds of information types are needed. We discuss strategies that organizations are currently using to tackle those challenges.

Y.K. Dwivedi et al. (Eds.): I3E 2016, LNCS 9844, pp. 557–566, 2016.
DOI: 10.1007/978-3-319-45234-0_49

2 Related Work

Many recent studies discuss the importance and rise in the usage of social media. A group of studies discuss social media usage by exploring datasets of social media posts across various emergency events [3–5]. Hughes et al. [6] analysis across four emergency events shows the importance of social media in extracting on the ground information and the adoption of people to social media during events. Takahashi et al. [7] explores how ordinary people and organizations use social media and what factors impact this use by analyzing tweets during Typhoon Haiyan in the Philippines Bruno. An analysis of tweets from hurricane sandy demonstrates that retweet activity increased during the event [8]. Some studies analyze rumors in twitter datasets to extract and analyze propagation patterns and the content of the rumor related tweets [9–11]. Imran et al. [12] surveys different studies for processing social media in mass emergencies.

Another group of studies explore social media usage and the issues around that by gathering requirements from practitioners. Tapia et al. [13] conducted semi-structured interviews to understand the usage of micro blogged data by emergency related organizations. They showed the landscape of the microblogged data usage among different organizations is varied. They found microblogged data useful when responders are in lack of information. However, there are concerns with quality and reliability of microblogged data. Another study [14] discuss the results of interviews with US emergency managers about their barriers and wish lists when using social media. They identify three main barriers for using social media: lack of resources, lack of policies and guidelines for social media use, and concern about the trustworthiness of the posts. A survey [15] of 241 U.S. emergency managers at the county level explores if organizations use social media and discuss how they can improve these usage. This study states that only about half of these organizations use social media in any way.

The use of social media is evolving rapidly and it's different from one event to another and from one organization to another [3, 16]. The use and requirements for social media can vary by geo-political region. As previous studies are mostly US centered, we intend to reveal the usage of social media within Canadian organizations and to understand if the challenges are the same and what specific strategies Canadian organizations have to tackle those challenges. To the best of our knowledge this paper is the first study that focus on requirement elicitation of Canadian practitioners. We target both emergency managers and social media analysts across Canada in the emergency field.

3 Methodology

We conducted semi-structured interviews with 16 participants across different organizations (see Table 1). The organizations can be divided to two main types: End users and Service providers. End users belong to public organizations (e.g. Emergency Operation Center, police department, etc.) or private sectors (e.g. Oil and Gas sector). We target participants who have the experience of managing and respond to at least one emergency event (e.g. Slave lake Fire, Alberta Flood 2013, Calgary Snow Storm 2014). The interviews performed starting March 2015 until December 2015. We asked participants about their use of social media, how they monitor and extract information from public posts, and what challenges they are facing when using social media. Each interview lasted between 60-90 min and was audio taped and transcribed. To analyze the notes we followed a process inspired by grounded theory [17]. Grounded theory involves iterative coding of concepts (open-coding) and finding patterns apparent in the text (axial coding) in order to form typologies. Our goal is to determine current usages of social media across different organizations. We used the saturate (http://www.saturateapp.com/notebooks) application to analyze the interview notes.

Table 1. Requirement elicitations user profiles

Participant	Title	Years of experience in emergency field	Type of organization
P1	Researcher at Center of child, family, and community research	4-5	Service Providers
P2	Police officer	19	End Users – Public org.
P3	Director, national security and strategic foresight	6	Service Provider
P4	Director of emergency communication	30	End Users – Public org.
P5	Fire chief	24	End Users – Public org.
P6	Senior safety coordinator	20	End Users- Private sector
P7	Emergency manager	16+	End Users – Public org.
P8	Emergency manager	12	End Users – Public org.
P9	Police officer	20	End Users – Public org.
P10	Executive director of operations	28	End Users – Public org.
P11	Police officer	unknown	End Users – Public org.
P12	Emergency center communications officer	unknown	End Users – Public org.
P13	Strategic communications specialist	unknown	End Users – Private sector
P14	Team lead communications	10	End Users –Public org.
P15	Digital communications officer	11	End Users –Public org.
P16	Vice President	unknown	Service Provider

4   Results

We will describe our findings in this section. In our results, we will not use any percentages or "statistics" since this would not be suitable for the size and nature of the sample studied. Instead, we will describe the main themes, based on counts of coding categories, and then give examples of descriptions of these themes in the words of the interviewees themselves.

4.1 Patterns of Use

Most of the participants agreed that social media has became a central element in emergency response planning. *"It's not a part you can ignore or a piece that can wait."* They were familiar with the potential and importance of using social media during an emergency event. *"Manage public relation if you do not manage it, it manages you."* Twitter, Facebook and Instagram were the mostly used social media services mentioned by participants. Depending on the resources and the size of the organization they were managing, the degree of their involvement with social media was different. Some mentioned that they monitor social media "very intensively" and others mentioned that they only communicate out and do not monitor social media, mainly because of "lack of resources" due to the sheer volume of information.

Public sector end-users mostly monitor social media for *"watching the conversation, communication and identify trends, reporting urgencies, ... [seeing] impact on community."* They care about people and their safety, properties and environment. It is important for these organizations to know the topics that people talk about and how they feel about those topics. *"We push information but we are also very interested and keen on what people are talking about."* However the usage differs between everyday monitoring and when an emergency happens. As many participants stated during an emergency the volume of messages increases but a participant pointed out another interesting difference: *"during a crisis event that conversation is very elevated and very focused ... in non-crisis in 5 min I see 20 different topics that people are talking... maybe there is a higher need for filtering during non-crisis event since the conversation is much wider... [while during the crisis] it comes about how to filter out the noise."* On the other hand emergency events have more challenges as they usually happen fast and it takes time for authorities to get a grip of the online story. For example, one participant stated about a shooting, *"Social communication was huge and it took authorities three hours to become part of that conversation. Speculations and accusations were occurring; investigators were required on follow up noise to track the efforts. It's a mess and we don't know what the formula is"*.

The police social media analysts described some additional usages in regards to social media. Their tasks include general enquiries tasks such as *"less formal questions, legal advice type questions"*, proactive community policing such as *"sharing infographics about the latest crime trends"*, reactive to crimes for example *"ask public to help find and identify suspects"*, and investigative support for example: *"the officers are reaching out to me asking for assistant on social media... They found a wallet they have a name but they can't find the contact detail of the owner... Can we find this person on Facebook?"* Another police officer stated that when there is a risk of further incidents, they monitor social media intensively to determine where and what is being said to help mitigate the risks.

We also interviewed few private sector end-users. They pointed out that their companies usually do minimal monitoring on a daily basis. One of them stated that during an emergency event they are looking for information about what people are saying about the emergency, what negative comments or inaccuracies are being reported about the company then craft a response to the posted information. She mentioned,

"[The company] hired a public relations company to monitor the social media feeds in the recent oil spill because traffic was so high. Otherwise [the company] do very minimal monitoring on a day-by-day basis, really only during an emergency."

4.2 Types of Information

We asked participants what kind of information social media provides that they are interested in. We extracted the following categories from their responses:

1. Detail: As a communication officer mentioned in an emergency event they try to extract the impact of event on people and environment. A social media post can contain information that shows this impact. People can provide details in messages, photos, and videos as a participant commented: *"People post about things they're in the middle of or post pictures, videos, comments"*. According to our participants Details can be regarding properties, their conditions, and damages during an event. Details can also be regarding affected people, their injuries, their evacuation, their needs of resources such as food, blankets, water, etc.
   Questions: A post can contain a question that the author seeks an answer for. As an emergency manager stated they *"Try to answer questions quickly – before someone non-authoritative can answer."* They may ask questions regarding different subjects such as evacuation orders, volunteering and donation, or rescue processes: *"For flood people asking us with evacuation areas. there were 3 communities that they want to evacuate and then 4,5 were going to be and then they started asking ... people started asking questions where should we go, where are the community help centers, ..."*

2. Misinformation: A post can contain a rumour or false information. According to recent analysis on emergency-related social media posts [9], a considerable portion of emergency-related microblogs can be incorrect. Rumours or false information can spread quickly, either purposefully or accidentally, and lead to wrong decisions and actions by the public. Hence, identifying microblogs that contain false information can help analysts to counteract them. A participant mentioned: *"Another critical piece, [we] need to be able to dispel rumors. In tornado, there were two rumors: I heard that there [were] two separate touchdown points."*

3. Urgencies: An emergency related posts can contain request for help. For example, somebody needs help or rescue immediately. These kinds of posts are highly prioritized for emergency people. They try to find these posts by scrolling through lists of incoming messages but are challenged by the high volume of incoming posts, e.g. *"We had posts like I can't find my mom, can somebody go and check the house OR my neighbour has been handicapped can someone go and check;"*

4. Sentiment: The public perception regarding an event was another category that the participants mentioned. While these posts often do not have any operational information, understanding the public sentiment can help the authorities prioritizing resources. One participant mentioned the importance of sentiment, which helped discover problems that are about how people feel and react to the situations the authorities were already familiar with.

4.3   Information Overload – the Need for Filtering and Categorization

One of the obvious problems that all participants mentioned was the volume of information coming from the public. According to the interviews, analysts receive thousands of messages every day and the situation is worse during an emergency. The Calgary flood infographic [18] shows there were 857,000 tweets for the most popular hashtags during the first two weeks of flooding. A considerable percentage of incoming messages are operationally irrelevant which makes it hard to extract urgency type posts: *"Got 10 s of thousands of messages of support from around the world. People would report people who might need to be checked on, but this could get overwhelming fast." "If somebody needs help we should make sure to catch that by scrolling through and its challenging and things get messed up."*

Another participant stated sometimes businesses try to promote themselves by attaching their advertisement to the trending hashtags in twitter. As an analyst stated one drawback of current tools is that they represent posts in a reverse-chronological order that makes it challenging for them to make sense of thousands of incoming posts with a short amount of time in an emergency situation. Another participant mentioned: *"It takes a significant amount of time and effort to sort through the incoming posts, we get thousands of incoming messages on a daily basis, we try from a corporation perspective to acknowledge or respond messages, right now we are performing about 3 %!"* On the other hand, the use of social media by the public has enormously increased during the last decade and community members now expect help when they send a social media message, *"There is an increase in the expectation from public that if they tweet asking for help they will generate help or a response, we are not there yet!"*

Some organizations have strategies to mitigate the information overload. For example, one participant mentioned that they were creating a role called "Audience Intelligence". The role monitors news and streams to determine what the trends are and understand what people are saying. This can help the rest of the social media monitoring team to catch stories online. The digital communication officer in the police department also mentioned that since they lack resources to monitor social media posts during the night shift, they put the geo-tagged ones on the map view so that everybody can see what is going on in social media.

4.4   Degree of Separation

The pressure that people within emergency operation centers face makes the analyst job difficult as the responders are often local people who see their friends and families in danger. The participants who had experienced the Alberta floods in 2013 or the huge fire at Slave Lake in 2011 mentioned that the magnitude around those events were unprecedented. Responders may not sleep for several days and bear lots of pressure. As one participants mentioned *"you may start crying in a corner after working several hours"*. As they stated, having a degree of separation and use the help of outsiders for monitoring social media can be useful, *"during the flood we had one person that worked remotely, I think that was one of the keys in the success, having that degree of separation... since that person was not influenced by the crazy energy that was present in the Calgary Emergency Operation Center".*

4.5   Collaboration and Communication

We frequently heard from participants that communication and collaboration among people is more important than technology. In emergencies, integration between different organizations happens through people. Some participant mentioned that emergency managers might satisfy their informational needs through their trustworthy sources of information. Hence, it is important to establish those links before an emergency happens. This could also be applied in the social media space by helping analysts identify active users within a community. It is important to be involved in social media before an emergency happens and establish the communication links. As a participant explained, *"One of the big messages that we've been getting again and again in emergency management is that relationships in terms of people and organizations sits above technology and capability, even if you do have technology unless you have personal relationships build and trusted ahead of time still you are going to struggle!"* Another participant mentioned that during the Alberta Flood 2013, twitter shut down the Calgary police twitter account as it was treated as spam due to exceeding the daily limit of tweets.

4.6   Reliability of Social Media

Although social media contains information that can contribute to situation awareness, one of the concerns is the reliability of the information. Almost all participants had concerns regarding the reliability of a source when talking about social media.

"Can you verify the information, who is the source of the info?"

Source Reliability.   One aspect of reliability was regarding how much the source of information is reliable. When asked about what characteristics they consider to assess the reliability of a source, the answers were: is the twitter account valid? Do they follow their organization? Is there a known/verified follower? What past posts does this user have? How recent was the account made? What is the number of followers/friends? How active is the user? How many times is the user being reposted? Is the user an eyewitness or inside the emergency region? How old is the user account? What is the profile picture of the user? As one participant mentioned, going through all these characteristics takes time.

Dispel Rumors.   Another concern that many of participants mentioned was the spread of rumors over social media. As mentioned by many participants, one of the tasks of a social media analyst is to counteract rumors. A rumor is information where the analyst knows that the information is wrong. According to our participants, rumors might spread intentionally by malicious people but they can also spread unintentionally by lack of understanding or technical information, accidental misinformation or simply people's frustrations. For example, a communication officer stated that during the Calgary flood, there was a rumor that the drinking water is not safe in the city. One person found a boil water advisory from the same day but different year on the city website and tweeted that the water was not safe. This incorrect information spread rapidly. The city responded by dispelling the rumor but needed to repeat this many times. Some participants mentioned this concern that sometimes by counteracting a rumor, the number of people that hear about it increases – which might undesirably spread the rumor. Authorities need to target a select audience when counteracting a rumor. One participant wished that they could filter social media recipients based on different factors like geographical location or demographics so that they could target communities of interest. *"During a crisis who is your audience?... We are less interested to counteract the rumour to a global audience. Need to know that and ensure the messaging and efforts are directed to those audience members and not spend energy dispelling rumours that are unrelated to the event and that audience."*

5 Current Tools

In this section we are going to discuss what are the practitioners expect from social media monitoring tools and what are the state of current tools to manage these expectations. Most of the participants expected two common features from a social media monitoring tool: simplicity and the ability to manage multiple social media sources. They were using commercial tools: geo-feedia[1], Radian 6[2], Hootsuite[3], and SproutSocial[4]. Hootsuite and Sprout Social are broadcasting tools. They let users schedule updates to communicate with public. Radian 6 lets users listen and engage within multiple social media sources. In the listening part, users can track specific keywords. Finally, Geo-feedia's main advantage is to provide location-based filtering of geo-tagged posts and keyword based filtering. One of the participants commented that in an emergency situation they usually prefer Hootsuite because of its simplicity. However none of these tools help users automatically prioritize the social media posts based on their importance or the level of information. The chronological order makes it challenging for analysts to make sense of thousands of incoming posts within a short period of time in an emergency situation. End users currently lack advanced filtering tools to help identify and categorize relevant information. The tools should let analyst identify and track key influential users within their community. Future tools should be able to view the sequence of posts not just based on time but also based on the amount of information the posts are carrying. We noticed that none of the tools that are currently being used by these big emergency related organizations has been developed specifically for emergencies but they have been built for a broader market. This reveals that there is a need to design and develop practical tools specifically for emergency response and management.

---

[1] https://geofeedia.com.
[2] https://login.radian6.com.
[3] https://hootsuite.com.
[4] http://sproutsocial.com.

Assessing the reliability of sources is another requirement that analysts need. Although participants knew some characteristics that can determine how much a source is reliable, they did not have enough time to check those characteristics in emergency chaos. Exploring how we can assign reliability scores to social media sources is a current research direction to address this issue. Researchers are exploring different features (e.g. user profile characteristics, content of a message) to be able to derive a reliability scores for social media users [19, 20].

6 Conclusion

This paper addresses the organizational requirements in response to emergency events. We conducted semi-structured interviews and gathered information about the usage and challenges of social media in emergencies. Based on our interviews we realized that social media information is considered both essential and high risk. It was essential as it helped people communicate easier, faster and opened a two-way communication road. It is considered high risk, as there were lots of speculations regarding what has happened. We discussed what strategies the practitioners are using to mitigate the current challenges and what can be the features of future tools to help them in identifying situational awareness information. Social media analysts require tools that help them automatically prioritize and categorize social media posts according to their informational needs. They also require tools to facilitate quickly assessing the reliability of sources. Finally they need to be able to target communities of interest to dispel the rumors.

References

1. Hughes, A., Palen, L.: Social media in emergency management: academic perspective: critical issues in disaster science and management: a dialogue between scientists and emergency managers. In: FEMA in Higher Education Program (2014)
2. Hiltz, S.R., Plotnick, L.: Dealing with information overload when using social media for emergency management: emerging solutions. In: Proceedings of the 10th International ISCRAM Conference, pp. 823–827 (2013)
3. Landwehr, P.M., Carley, K.M.: Social media in disaster relief. In: Chu, W.W. (ed.) Data Mining and Knowledge Discovery for Big Data, pp. 225–257. Springer, Heidelberg (2014)
4. Dashti, S., Palen, L., Heris, M.P., Anderson, K.M., Anderson, S., Anderson, S.: Supporting disaster reconnaissance with social media data: a design-oriented case study of the 2013 Colorado floods. In: Proceedings of the 11th International ISCRAM Conference (2014)
5. St Denis, L., Palen, L., Anderson, K.M.: Mastering social media: an analysis of Jefferson county's communications during the 2013 Colorado Floods. In: Proceedings of 11th International ISCRAM Conference (2014)
6. Hughes, A.L., Palen, L.: Twitter adoption and use in mass convergence and emergency events. Int. J. Emer. Manag. 6, 248–260 (2009)
7. Takahashi, B., Tandoc, E.C., Carmichael, C.: Communicating on Twitter during a disaster: an analysis of tweets during Typhoon Haiyan in the Philippines. Comput. Hum. Behav. 50, 392–398 (2015)

8. Marina, K., Leysia, P., Kenneth, M.A.: Think local, retweet global: retweeting by the geographically-vulnerable during Hurricane Sandy. In: Proceedings of the 18th ACM Conference on Computer Supported Cooperative Work & Social Computing, pp. 981–993. ACM (2015)

9. Starbird, K., Maddock, J., Orand, M., Achterman, P., Mason, R.M.: Rumors, false flags, and digital vigilantes: misinformation on Twitter after the 2013 Boston Marathon bombing. In: iConference 2014 Proceedings (2014)

10. Oh, O., Kwon, K.H., Rao, H.R.: An exploration of social media in extreme events: rumor theory and Twitter during the Haiti Earthquake 2010. In: ICIS 2010, p. 231 (2010)

11. Marcelo, M., Barbara, P., Carlos, C.: Twitter under crisis: can we trust what we RT? In: Proceedings of the First Workshop on Social Media Analytics, pp. 71–79. ACM (2010)

12. Imran, M., Castillo, C., Diaz, F., Vieweg, S.: Processing social media messages in mass emergency: a survey. ACM Comput. Surv. 47(4), 1–38 (2015)

13. Tapia, A.H., Moore, K.A., Johnson, N.J.: Beyond the trustworthy tweet:a deeper understanding of microblogged data use by disaster response and humanitarian relief organizations. In: Proceedings of the 10th International ISCRAM Conference, Baden-Baden, pp. 770–778 (2013)

14. Hiltz, S.R., Kushma, J., Plotnick, L.: Use of social media by US public sector emergency managers: barriers and wish lists. In: Proceedings of ISCRAM (2014)

15. Plotnick, L., Hiltz, S.R., Kushma, J.A., Tapia, A.: Red tape: attitudes and issues related to use of social media by US county-level emergency managers. In: Proceedings of ISCRAM (2015)

16. Houston, J.B., Hawthorne, J., Perreault, M.F., Park, E.H., Goldstein Hode, M., Halliwell, M.R., Turner McGowen, S.E., Davis, R., Vaid, S., McElderry, J.A., Griffith, S.A.: Social media and disasters: a functional framework for social media use in disaster planning, response, and research. Disasters 39(1), 1–22 (2015)

17. Glaser, B.G., Strauss, A.L.: The Discovery of Grounded Theory: Strategies for Qualitative Research. Transaction Publishers, Brunswick (2009)

18. Yablonski, C.: The impact of social media on the Calgary Flood. In: Inbound Interactive (2013)

19. Diakopoulos, N., Choudhury, M.D., Naaman, M.: Finding and assessing social media information sources in the context of journalism. In: Proceedings of the SIGCHI Conference on Human Factors in Computing Systems, Austin, Texas, USA (2012)

20. Xia, X., Yang, X., Wu, C., Li, S., Bao, L.: Information Credibility on Twitter in Emergency Situation. In: Chau, M., Wang, G., Yue, W.T., Chen, H. (eds.) PAISI 2012. LNCS, vol. 7299, pp. 45–59. Springer, Heidelberg (2012)

Predicting Stock Movements
using Social Network

Sunil Saumya, Jyoti Prakash Singh$^{(\boxtimes)}$, and Prabhat Kumar

National Institute of Technology Patna, Bihar, India
{sunils.cse15,jps,prabhat}@nitp.ac.in

Abstract. According to "Wisdom of Crowds" hypothesis, a large crowd can perform better than smaller groups or few individuals. Based on this hypothesis, we investigate the impact of online social media, a group of interacting individual, on financial market in Indian context. The interaction of different users of www.moneycontrol.com, a popular online Indian stock forum, is put to a social graph model and several key parameters are derived from that social graph along with the user's suggestion such as (*Buy, Sell or Hold*) related to a stock. The user's impact in that forum is then calculated using the social graph of the users. Stock price movement is then predicted using user's suggestions and their impact in that forum. As per our knowledge, this is the first paper which considers the impact of www.moneycontrol.com user's suggestions and social relation to predict the stock prices.

Keywords: Sentiment analysis · Wisdom of crowd · Page rank · Stock price movement

1 Introduction

Stock market investment decisions are mainly driven by the market information available to investor. In earlier days, the main source of new information was news articles containing information related to a company, such as the company fundamentals, future plans and so on. The stock price of a company was driven by these publications. The rise of internet and finance related websites and applications has changed the scenario as the new information about a company is readily available. Some of the websites are developed as a forum where number of interested users interact with each other and give their opinion on different stocks. A system which can utilize this data and peoples opinion to predict future changes in prices is highly required to support the decision making of investors and traders.

There are two popular hypothesis regarding stock price prediction (i) Efficient Market Hypothesis (EMH) [1] and (ii) Random Walk [2]. The EMH [1] states that it is impossible to "beat the market" because stock market efficiency causes existing share prices to always incorporate and reflect all relevant information. The random walk hypothesis states that stock market prices evolve

© IFIP International Federation for Information Processing 2016
Published by Springer International Publishing Switzerland 2016. All Rights Reserved
Y.K. Dwivedi et al. (Eds.): I3E 2016, LNCS 9844, pp. 567–572, 2016.
DOI: 10.1007/978-3-319-45234-0_50

according to a random walk and hence cannot be predicted which is consistent with the EMH.

Inspite of both the hypothesis stating stock price can not be predicted, some automated systems, which use the financial news to help in decision making of investors and traders have been proposed [3]. Another research [4] has shown that there is a strong relationship between stock price fluctuations and publications of relevant news. Schumaker and Chen [5] proposed a system to prove the effect of news items on the stock prices using stock's history data. The other notable works using historical data to predict the stock prices are by Patel et al. [6,7] using Auto Regressing model and Moving Average model, Zuo et al. [8] using Bayesian network and Auto Regressive Moving Average model. All these works used historical stock prices or company related news to predict future prices using some statistical techniques.

"Wisdom of Crowd" (WoC) [9] hypothesis states that a diverse and independent "crowd" can make more precise predictions than a few people. They can even beat professionals. Crowd is defined as "potentially large and unknown population" [10]. The WoC can also be viewed as collective intelligence [11]. With the rise of social networking sites, this phenomenon has got a boost as diverse people from different places in the world interact with each other on websites, blogs and message boards. It has attracted a lot of researchers to use this crowd's intelligence to predict the stock related information. Ruiz et al. [12] studies the impact of twitter activity on financial market. Latoeiro et al. [13] tried to predict the stock market activity using Google search queries. Although, there have been some studies involving financial industry using crowd's opinions for their investments but there is hardly any practical evidence. The user-generated contents were also used in [14–16] to identify the share returns. But very few work have been done which show a good prediction result on a huge consistent data for long duration of time [17].

All the previous studies were done on developed country markets. Whether those studies are really useful in a developing country like India seems an interesting research problem. Mukherjee [18] compared the Indian stock market with international markets and pointed out a lot of differences. That motivated us to investigate the impact of online social forum on Indian stock market involving Indian stock exchanges such as National Stock Exchange (NSE) and Bombay Stock Exchange (BSE). In this paper, we have considered an Indian financial forum www.moneycontrol.com as our data source and two representative stocks namely State Bank of India (SBIN) and Reliance Communication (RCOM) for our study.

2   Data Collection

The forum data was collected from mmb.moneycontrol.com for two stocks namely SBIN and RCOM. We used data scraping technique to collect the data. Data scraped from mmb.moneycontrol.com were then filtered and pre-processed to collect the following fields, (i) User_Name, (ii) User_Level, (iii) Num_Messages,

Table 1. The details of fields of a user message

Sl. no	Field	Description
1	User_Name	The screen name of the user participating in the forum
2	User_Level	Different levels of the user
3	Num_Messages	Total messages written by the user
4	Followers	The number of other users who follow this user
5	Following	The number of other users this user is following
6	Stocks_Tracked	The number of stocks tracked by a user
7	Time	The date and time on which the message was written
8	Message_Text	The message about a stock written by the user
9	Rating	The rating given by other users to a message
10	Replies	The number of replies given to a message

Reliance 💬 17 comments

Price when posted : BSE: Rs. 954.15 NSE: Rs. 954.10

New Member
18 Followers

no, i can not. btw, where can i find block deals data? exchanges report only the big ones at the eod. thanks,

about 2 hrs 52 min 31 sec ago

Reply | Rate | Click if offensive | Share | Repost

Fig. 1. A general format of message on mmb.moneycontrol.com

(iv) Followers, (v) Following, (vi) Stocks_Tracked, (vii) Time, (viii) Message_Text, (ix) Rating, and (x) Replies. The details of the fields are given in Table 1. A typical message on mmb.moneycontrol.com is given here in the Fig. 1 and the details of the user is given in Fig. 2.

Some of the messages were discarded as they did not convey any sentiment about the stocks. Those were just informative or enquiry messages as shown in Fig. 1. After discarding those messages, we worked with 490 reviews for SBIN and another 389 reviews for RCOM. The custom-developed program in Python was then used to extract the suggestions given by users in terms of *"Buy"*, *"Sell"*, or *"Hold"*.

3   Proposed Method

We extracted the suggestions *(Buy, Sell, or Hold)* of the users through their messages using Natural Language Toolkit (NLTK) [19] package in Python. The message text was tokenized and Part of Speech (POS) tagging was done. The verbs from those tagged words were taken and if they match *Buy, Sell, or Hold*, then they were associated with the tag. In some messages, users have not directly

New Member

1046 Messages   6 Tracked (Stocks)
18 Followers   17 Following

Mostly writes on :Reliance,TCS,Pincon Spirit,Maruti
Suzuki,United Brewerie,

FOLLOW   Post a message

Fig. 2. A general format of Member information on mmb.moneycontrol.com

written whether to *Buy, Sell or Hold* but they have given the next price (target) of the stock. We have extracted the current price of the stock using *nsetools* which is a Python library for extracting real time data from National Stock Exchange (India). If the current price of the stock is less than the target given by the user then the suggestion is taken as *Buy* else *Sell*. After extracting the suggestions of the users from their messages, we created a network of users and their suggestions. A sample network showing the interaction of different users and their suggestions such as *Buy, Sell, or Hold* is shown in Fig. 3.

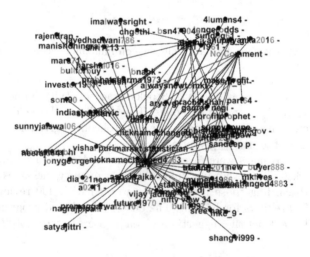

Fig. 3. The user interaction graph

The network was made using tool known as "Gephi" [20] which supports calculation of features such as degrees, page rank etc. Degree refers to how many links a user has with other users. PageRank [21] algorithm estimates the importance of a website by counting the number and quality of links to other websites. This concept is used here to find how important a user is by counting

Table 2. Weighted average Vs. real stock movement

Sl. no	Stock name	Weighted average	Real stock movement
1	SBIN	0.01283	Upward
2	SBIN	−0.3276	Downward
3	RCOM	−0.3713	Downward
4	RCOM	−0.00242	Downward

the number and quality of links with other users of the system. The importance of the users (weight) is a real number ranging between 0 and 1 with 0 being less important and 1 being most important. The user's suggestions *(Buy, Sell, Hold)* are encoded with *(+1, -1, 0)* respectively. The stock movement is then decided by finding the weighted average of encoded suggestions with respect to user's weight. The results are shown in Table 2.

As can be seen from the Table 2, +ve weighted average indicates an upward movement in stock price whereas -ve average indicates downwards movement.

4 Conclusion

We have tried to model the financial market on the concept of WoC using data from www.moneycontrol.com. The users are assigned weights based on their social interaction in the forum. The user's weight along with their suggestions is then used to predict the stock price movement. The results looks promising on the small datasets we have considered in this work. The finding indicates that the online financial forum can be used as a data source for stock market movement prediction. One of the major limitation of the current work is small data size. This work can be further extended to predict the exact % of swing in stock price as well as the future price of the stock including more parameters such as historical prices, recent news related to company etc.

References

1. Malkiel, B.G.: Efficient market hypothesis. In: Eatwell, J., Milgate, M., Newman, P. (eds.) The World of Economics, pp. 211–218. Springer, Heidelberg (1991)
2. Godfrey, M.D., Granger, C.W., Morgenstern, O.: The random-walk hypothesis of stock market behaviora. Kyklos **17**(1), 1–30 (1964)
3. Mitra, G., Mitra, L.: The Handbook of News Analytics in Finance, vol. 596. Wiley, Hoboken (2011)
4. Fung, G.P.C., Yu, J.X., Lu, H.: The predicting power of textual information on financial markets. IEEE Intell. Inf. Bull. **5**(1), 1–10 (2005)
5. Schumaker, R.P., Chen, H.: A quantitative stock prediction system based on financial news. Inf. Process. Manage. **45**(5), 571–583 (2009)
6. Patel, J., Shah, S., Thakkar, P., Kotecha, K.: Predicting stock and stock price index movement using trend deterministic data preparation and machine learning techniques. Expert Syst. Appl. **42**(1), 259–268 (2015)

7. Patel, J., Shah, S., Thakkar, P., Kotecha, K.: Predicting stock market index using fusion of machine learning techniques. Expert Syst. Appl. **42**(4), 2162–2172 (2015)
8. Zuo, Y., Kita, E.: Stock price forecast using Bayesian network. Expert Syst. Appl. **39**(8), 6729–6737 (2012)
9. Surowiecki, J., Silverman, M.P., et al.: The wisdom of crowds. Am. J. Phys. **75**(2), 190–192 (2007)
10. Poetz, M.K., Schreier, M.: The value of crowdsourcing: can users really compete with professionals in generating new product ideas? J. Prod. Innov. Manage. **29**(2), 245–256 (2012)
11. Kittur, A., Kraut, R.E.: Harnessing the wisdom of crowds in wikipedia: quality through coordination. In: Proceedings of the 2008 ACM Conference on Computer Supported Cooperative Work, pp. 37–46. ACM (2008)
12. Ruiz, E.J., Hristidis, V., Castillo, C., Gionis, A., Jaimes, A.: Correlating financial time series with micro-blogging activity. In: Proceedings of the Fifth ACM International Conference on Web Search and Data Mining, pp. 513–522. ACM (2012)
13. Latoeiro, P., Ramos, S.B., Veiga, H.: Predictability of stock market activity using google search queries. Working Papers ws130605, Universidad Carlos III de Madrid, March 2013
14. Antweiler, W., Frank, M.Z.: Is all that talk just noise? the information content of internet stock message boards. J. Financ. **59**(3), 1259–1294 (2004)
15. Bollen, J., Mao, H., Zeng, X.: Twitter mood predicts the stock market. J. Comput. Sci. **2**(1), 1–8 (2011)
16. Avery, C.N., Chevalier, J.A., Zeckhauser, R.J.: The "CAPS" prediction system and stock market returns. Rev. Finan. **20**(4), 1363–1381 (2016)
17. Nguyen, T.H., Shirai, K., Velcin, J.: Sentiment analysis on social media for stock movement prediction. Expert Syst. Appl. **42**(24), 9603–9611 (2015)
18. Mukherjee, D.: Comparative analysis of indian stock market with international markets. Great Lakes Herald **1**(1), 39–71 (2007)
19. Bird, S.: NLTK: the natural language toolkit. In: Proceedings of the COLING/ACL on Interactive presentation sessions, pp. 69–72. Association for Computational Linguistics (2006)
20. Bastian, M., Heymann, S., Jacomy, M.: Gephi: An open source software for exploring and manipulating networks. In: International AAAI Conference on Weblogs and Social Media (2009)
21. Page, L., Brin, S., Motwani, R., Winograd, T.: The pagerank citation ranking: bringing order to the web (1999)

Coordinating Data-Driven Decision-Making in Public Asset Management Organizations: A Quasi-Experiment for Assessing the Impact of Data Governance on Asset Management Decision Making

Paul Brous[(✉)], Marijn Janssen, and Paulien Herder

Delft University of Technology, Delft, The Netherlands
{P.A.Brous,M.F.W.H.A.Janssen,P.M.Herder}@tudelft.nl

Abstract. Public organizations are facing increasing challenges to the management of their infrastructure assets. New sources of data, such as social media and IoT, can provide new insights for organizations to help them deal with these challenges. Yet data must be of sufficient quality in order to be acted upon. The objective of this study is to develop and approach to evaluate how data governance improves decision-making in asset management organizations. This paper describes a quasi-experiment which identifies and quantifies relationships between data governance and improvements in asset management decision-making. The quasi-experiment focusses on data requirements for determining current and future asset conditions, which is critical for assessing remaining service life and risk of failure. The quasi-experiment utilizes a pre-test post-test control group design. We expect that the inclusion of data governance improves the quality of data which allows for improved decision-making in asset management organizations.

Keywords: Data · Data governance · Data quality · Data management · Experiment

1 Introduction

Public asset management organizations are facing increasing challenges to the management of their infrastructure assets, technological advances, political shifts, changing stakeholders, or economic fluctuations. Many public asset management (AM) organizations routinely store large volumes of data in an attempt to find ways to improve efficiency and effectiveness of their AM processes through data-driven decision-making [8, 15]. Increasing the complexity is the development of techniques which utilise other data sources such IoT and Social Media data to provide information which may provide more timely information than more traditional methods. We follow Mohseni's [24] definition of AM as being a discipline for optimizing and applying strategies related to work planning decisions in order to effectively and efficiently meet the desired objective [17, 22, 24]. AM is therefore essentially a matter of understanding risk, followed by

© IFIP International Federation for Information Processing 2016
Published by Springer International Publishing Switzerland 2016. All Rights Reserved
Y.K. Dwivedi et al. (Eds.): I3E 2016, LNCS 9844, pp. 573–583, 2016.
DOI: 10.1007/978-3-319-45234-0_51

developing and applying the correct business strategy, and the right organization, process and technology models to solve the problem [24].

This study is centered on the AM process of determining current and future asset conditions, which is critical for assessing the remaining service life of assets and to prevent the risk of failure of assets. This knowledge has a direct impact on decisions regarding the provision of logistic and maintenance support for assets and disposing of, or renewing assets. The objective of this study is to evaluate how data governance supports data-driven decision-making in asset management organizations. Data governance specifies the framework for decision rights and accountabilities to encourage desirable behavior in the use of data [19], ensures that data is aligned to the needs of the organization [13], monitors and enforces compliancy to policy [36], and ensures a common understanding of the data throughout the organization [26].

According to Brous et al. [6], data infrastructures can be seen as a shared, evolving, heterogeneous, set of resources (including human resources, or agents), which are capable of providing facts required to fulfil a social need. Data infrastructures often have a unique character and behave differently. This makes it difficult to implement data governance in different environments and achieve similar outcomes [16]. It is difficult to attribute the contribution of data governance to asset management decision-making to one or more specific factors [4]. This article starts with the introduction and identification of the problem in sections one and two. Subsequently, the design propositions of the quasi-experiment are derived in sections three and four, which encompass an overview of data-driven decision-making in asset management organizations and the potential functional elements of data governance in asset management organizations respectively. In section five we describe the design of the quasi-experiment and the gaming approach whose purpose is to identify the effect that the design propositions have on data quality. In section six we discuss the possible limitations of the quasi-experiment. The paper concludes with a summary of the theory and approach in section seven.

2   The Need for Data Governance

Data quality can be affected by a broad range of outside influences at indiscriminate moments in time [37]. It is because of this that it is exceptionally difficult for asset management organizations to effectively manage their data. Asset management organizations may thus not always be well equipped to handle data [23]. The reasons for this often do not lie in the technology, but rather originate in a wide variety of areas such as organization, or culture [12, 24]. Because data infrastructures are complex [6], there is an interrelationship between their social and technical dimensions.

New sources of data, originating from sources such as social media and IoT, can provide new insights to help organizations face these challenges. But data must be of sufficient quality in order to be acted upon [25, 39] and too much data can create "noise" which detracts van the quality of the information. A widely adopted definition of high quality data is data that is "fit-for-use" [35, 40]. Using the definition provided by Strong et al. [35], the characteristics of high-quality data have intrinsic, accessibility, contextual, and representational aspects. This also means that usefulness and usability are important aspects of quality [13, 35]. Having data infrastructures which produce data of a quality that is aligned to the needs of the organization is therefore essential for asset management organizations which rely on data-driven decision-making processes [2].

According to Panian [28], enforcing policies and processes around the management data is the foundation of an effective data governance practice. The enforcement of data management policies and processes requires coordination. Coordination is the management of dependencies between activities [20]. Coordination mechanisms, such as hierarchies and networks, denote the way interdependent activities and decisions are managed [21]. Coordination mechanisms need to be established to ensure accountability for data quality through a combination of incentives and penalties [2], as accountability can unlock further potential by addressing relevant issues related to data stewardship. Governing data appropriately is only possible if it is properly understood what the data to be managed means, and why it is important to the organization [34]. Attention to business areas and enterprise entities is the responsibility of data stewards [38] who have the entity-level knowledge necessary for development of data for which they are responsible [34].

3   Data-Driven Decision Making in AM

In more and more AM organizations, managerial decisions rely on data-based analytics [8]. Many AM organizations gather extremely detailed data from and propagate knowledge to their consumers, suppliers, alliance partners, and competitors. Also, there are many more opportunities for data collection outside of operational systems. According to Brynjolfsson et al. [8], mobile phones, vehicles, factory automation systems, and other devices are routinely instrumented to generate streams of data on their activities. AM organizations can use sensors to track the performance of their assets, and they can use the data these sensors provide to improve the management of their assets. Similarly, data collected from social media may make the user experience visible and may provide insights into the real-time condition of the assets. However, the use of data for decision-making in processes such as prognostics [18] is still relatively undeveloped, and there are still serious ethical [4] and technical [12] issues which need to be addressed.

More precise and accurate information should facilitate decision making [1, 33]. In this paper, we develop an experiment for measuring the effect of data governance on data-driven decision-making within the context of determining current and future asset conditions. In this research, the assumption is made that all asset management decision-making is data-driven and that better quality data results in better decision-making.

4   Functional Elements of Data Governance in Asset Management Data Infrastructures

According to Brous et al. [6], data infrastructures can be viewed as complex adaptive systems (CAS). In this research we model the elements of data infrastructures viewed from a CAS perspective. In this way, this research builds on previous work published by Brous et al. [6, 7]. According to Brous et al., data infrastructures can be conceptualized as consisting of data and technology, which are stable and simple building blocks and are the basic parts of the system. These building blocks are manipulated by agents who interact with one another, operating within a certain schema. Schema refers to the shared rules which are embodied by norms, values, beliefs, and assumptions [11]. Agents use rules to make decisions within frames of reference or schemata by which they interpret and evaluate information. In this regard, the schema of data infrastructure is defined and maintained by data governance processes which provide coordination for data management activities [6].

As discussed in the previous sections, data governance specifies the framework for decision rights and accountabilities to encourage desirable behavior in the use of data [19], ensures that data is aligned to the needs of the organization [13], monitors and enforces compliancy to policy [36], and ensures a common understanding of the data throughout the organization [26].

A common metric used to measure the effectiveness of data governance is data quality [26, 31, 39]. Data governance, data quality and data (quality) management are closely linked and are often handled by the same individuals in organizations [26, 29]. In this regards, data governance is important for decision making with regard to data quality management [19, 26, 27]. According to Strong et al., data quality is typically determined by the data's fitness for use, which is the capability of data to meet the requirements of the user in order to accomplish a certain goal in a given context. A user can only decide whether or not data is fit for use if the quality of the data is known and reported. This makes it important for organizations to define data quality metrics, which can be used to measure and report the quality of data based on well-defined data quality dimensions. Wang and Strong [37] identify four dimensions of data quality and one hundred and eighteen aspects of data quality. This research follows Otto [26] and Wang & Strong [37] and addresses only the commonly used quality aspects of completeness, consistency, accuracy, relevancy, and timeliness [26, 37]. In this research we follow the definitions of these data quality aspects provided by Pipino et al. [30] pp 212 (see Table 1 below).

Table 1. Definitions of data quality aspects (adapted from [30] p. 212)

Data quality aspect	Definition
Completeness	"The extent to which data is not missing and is of sufficient breadth and depth for the task at hand"
Consistency	"The extent to which data is presented in the same format"
Accuracy	"The extent to which data is correct and reliable"
Relevancy	"The extent to which data is applicable and helpful to the task at hand"
Timeliness	"The data to which data is sufficiently up-to-date for the task at hand"

Propositions for the design of a data governance prototype were created based on the elements of data governance discussed above. According to Denyer et al. [14], a design proposition is a general template for the creation of solutions for a particular class of field problems. The design propositions suggest on a high level which functional infrastructure elements may be used to improve data governance in asset management data infrastructures. We propose four key elements to improve data governance: 1. coordination mechanisms; 2. definition of data quality requirements; 3. monitoring of data quality; 4. shared data commons. Although there may be other ways to improve data governance, these infrastructure elements were found to be critical. Based on these key elements, the following design propositions were generated:

1. Coordination mechanisms positively influence data quality in asset management organizations
2. Defining data quality requirements positively influences data quality in asset management organizations
3. Monitoring data quality positively influences data quality in asset management organizations
4. Creating a shared data commons positively influences data quality in asset management organizations.

5 Evaluation Method: The Quasi-Experiment and the Use of Serious Games

In section five we discuss the structure of the quasi-experiment and the use of serious gaming to explore system behavior and to simulate data governance in an asset management setting.

5.1 Gaming Approach

According to Shadish et al. [32], an experiment is a study in which an intervention is deliberately introduced to observe its effects. Experiments have factorial designs where independent variables are systematically varied, and the dependent variable(s) are quantitative, objective measures of system performance [1]. A quasi-experiment [9] is an empirical study used to estimate the causal impact of an intervention on its target population [1]. According to Adelman [1], quasi-experiments share similarities with experimental design, but they lack the element of random assignment to treatment or control. Instead, the researcher controls the assignment of the treatment condition to the quasi-experiment using criterion other than random assignment such as an eligibility cutoff mark. In this study the choice was made for a quasi-experiment as opposed to a true experiment as full control over the scheduling of experimental stimuli that make a true experiment possible is lacking [9] and we wish to retain control over selecting and scheduling measures and how the treatment will be organized [32].

The quasi-experiment detailed in this paper uses gaming as a tool to simulate data governance in data-driven decision making in an asset management setting. According to Bekebrede [3], serious gaming can be a useful tool to simulate complex socio-technical infrastructure systems and supports policy makers and designers in understanding the complexity of the planning and design of these systems from the observer perspective [3]. With a support tool is meant a tool or instrument which can contribute to the planning, design, implementation and management of data infrastructures in different ways. Gaming can thus be used as a support tool for understanding the complexity of asset management data infrastructures and the impact of these on asset management decision-making. At the same time, gaming is an experience space in which participants can experience the complexity themselves and increase their understanding of the system, from the player perspective. We aim to evaluate data governance in a game setting in which participants use a prototype application to specify the coordination mechanisms for decision rights and accountabilities, to ensure that data is aligned to the needs of the organization, to monitor and enforce compliancy, and to ensure a common under-standing of the data. At the same time we aim to control the variables to test our prop-ositions and to ensure that the effects can be contributed to data governance. Figure 1 shows the variables involved in the quasi-experiments.

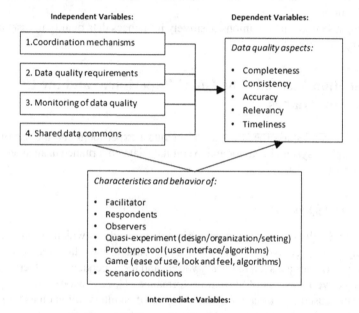

Fig. 1. Variables involved in the quasi-experiments

In this quasi-experiment, participants will be required to maintain assets in Mine-craft, a virtual world, using data provided to them by the "game-master". Virtual worlds, such as Minecraft, allow researchers to explore existing theory and develop new theory in a variety of fields, including information and social sciences [23]. Minecraft is a multiplayer sandbox-building game focused on creativity, building and survival in which players can acquire resources and must maintain their health and hunger at acceptable levels. The core gameplay revolves around construction [10]. In this quasi-experiment, players play as a team, but operate as individuals. The team consists of 5 players.

Within their virtual world, each team will be allocated "assets" which they will be required to manage and maintain based on the data provided to them. The state of the assets will degrade during the course of the game, and will need to be maintained. In a second application, players will be able to govern their data using the functional elements described in the design propositions. Depending on their allocated group, players will have access to varying degrees of functionality. This allows the researcher to manipulate the variables within the game setting in order to test the four design propositions. For example, at the start of the game, teams may be given the opportunity to define the required quality of the data provided to them, and, depending on the game settings, define who is responsible for maintaining the quality of each dataset. During the course of the game, the game master will degrade the quality of the data unless appropriate action is taken. The control group will not have any access to the second application, but will be granted access to the same data. The researchers will be able to monitor the fluctuating quality of all the datasets throughout the game.

5.2 Structure of the Quasi-Experiments

The quasi-experiments will be conducted as follows (see Fig. 2 below). Firstly, the quasi-experiment will be introduced to the participants and instructions will be given. Secondly, the pre-test, a participant survey, will be conducted to measure various background characteristics of the participants, as well as their experience with asset management, data governance, and with serious gaming. Thirdly, participants will be asked to complete scenario tasks within the game environment.

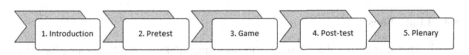

Fig. 2. Structure of the quasi-experiments

While the participants are playing the game, time measures and observations will be made to obtain additional information. Time measures will be made to examine how long it takes to conduct the scenario tasks and to investigate whether there are significant

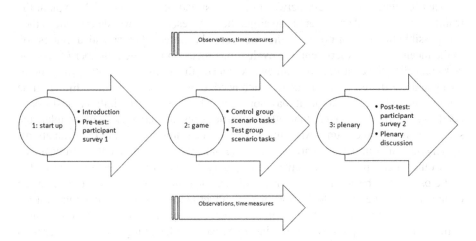

Fig. 3. Approach of the quasi-experiment

differences between the time used to conduct the scenarios by the treatment group and the time used by the control group. Fourthly, a post-test in the form of a second participant survey will be used to measure the extent to which data governance influences the completion of the scenario tasks within the game. Finally, in a plenary discussion the participants will be questioned as to the levels of difficulty of the tasks and if they have any suggestions to improve the game or the prototype tooling (Fig. 3).

5.3 Treatment Versus Control Condition

Five groups will be tasked with completing the scenario tasks within the game to test the effect of the introduction of coordination mechanisms for decision rights and accountabilities, the alignment of data to the needs of the user, options to monitor and enforce compliancy, and options to ensure a common understanding of the data. The fifth group is a control group to establish a base-line. Quasi-experiments will be conducted with at least five groups of 5 people to ensure that sufficient participants are involved and that the responses to the questionnaire can be analysed with statistical tests. Ideally, at least 10 experiments will be conducted to ensure statistical validity. The conditions for the treatment groups and the control group should remain as equal as possible.

5.4 Limitations

Quasi-experiments are subject to concerns regarding internal validity, because the treatment and control groups may not be comparable at baseline [5]. With quasi-experimental studies, it may not be possible to convincingly demonstrate a causal link between the treatment condition and observed outcomes. This is particularly true if there are confounding variables that cannot be controlled or accounted for, such as if the design of the experiment does not control for the effect of other plausible hypotheses that could have improved performance between the pretest and the posttest [1]. For example, external influences may occur between the pretest and posttest that could explain the results. If the selected group represent either the very best or very worst performers, then it is possible that pretest-posttest differences could be affected by statistical regression to the mean. In this experiment, the evaluations focus on a limited number of specific tasks related to the coordination framework, data quality definitions, data quality monitoring and the shared data commons which need to be conducted within a limited time frame. Due to time limitations it may not be possible to conduct additional tasks or to conduct scenario tasks longer than 50 min. Participants may not be able to complete the scenarios in this time frame. Also, three types of measures are used in the evaluations, namely time measures, observations and questionnaires. In addition to these three measures, other measures, such as other data quality aspects, of the performance of the participants may be used. By using additional measures, more information may be obtained regarding the contribution of data governance to decision-making in asset management organizations. Moreover, other factors may influence the outcomes, such as the user interface, quality of the tooling, experience with gaming, and experience with information management in general. The final results may therefore not only be attributed to the coordination framework, the definition of quality requirement, the monitoring of data quality or the shared data commons.

6 Summary

Public organizations are facing increasing challenges to the management of their infrastructure assets and many AM organizations are looking for ways to improve the efficiency and effectiveness of their AM processes through data-driven decision-making. New sources of data such as IoT and social media data may provide more timely information than more traditional techniques. In this paper, we develop a measure of data governance for data-driven decision-making within the context of determining current and future asset conditions. The assumption is made that asset management decision-making is data-driven and that better quality data results in better decision-making. It is important to realize that there are still ethical, organizational and technical barriers to the adoption of data driven decision making. In this paper we describe a quasi-experiment to assess how aspects of data governance - a coordination framework, data quality definitions, data quality monitoring and a shared data commons - affect the commonly used quality aspects of completeness, consistency, accuracy, relevancy, and timeliness. The quasi-experiment detailed in this paper uses gaming as a tool to simulate the implementation of data governance in data-driven decision making in an asset management setting. This experiment does have limitations as quasi-experiments are subject to concerns regarding internal validity, because the treatment and control groups may not be comparable at baseline and it may not be possible to convincingly demonstrate a causal link between the treatment condition and observed outcomes.

References

1. Adelman, L.: Experiments, quasi-experiments, and case studies: a review of empirical methods for evaluating decision support systems. IEEE Trans. Syst. Man Cybern. **21**(2), 293–301 (1991)
2. Al-Khouri, A.M.: Data ownership: who owns "my data". Int. J. Manag. Inf. Technol. **2**, 1–8 (2012)
3. Bekebrede, G.: Experiencing Complexity: A Gaming Approach for Understanding Infrastructure Systems. Delft University of Technology, Delft (2010)
4. Bhidé, A.: The big idea: the judgment deficit. Harv. Bus. Rev. (2010)
5. Blackwell, D.: Equivalent comparisons of experiments. Ann. Math. Stat. **24**(2), 265–272 (1953)
6. Brous, P., et al.: Data infrastructures for asset management viewed as complex adaptive systems. Procedia Comput. Sci. **36**, 124–130 (2014)
7. Brous, P., et al.: Towards modelling data infrastructures in the asset management domain. Procedia Comput. Sci. **61**, 274–280 (2015)
8. Brynjolfsson, E., et al.: Strength in Numbers: How Does Data-Driven Decisionmaking Affect Firm Performance?. Social Science Research Network, Rochester (2011)
9. Campbell, D.T., Stanley, J.: Experimental and Quasi-Experimental Designs for Research. Wadsworth Publishing, Boston (1963)

10. Canossa, A.: Give me a reason to dig: qualitative associations between player behavior in minecraft and life motives. In: Proceedings of the International Conference on the Foundations of Digital Games, pp. 282–283. ACM, New York, NY, USA (2012)
11. Choi, T.Y., et al.: Supply networks and complex adaptive systems: control versus emergence. J. Oper. Manag. 19(3), 351–366 (2001)
12. Coff, R.W.: human assets and management dilemmas: coping with hazards on the road to resource-based theory. Acad. Manage. Rev. 22(2), 374–402 (1997)
13. Dawes, S.S.: Stewardship and usefulness: policy principles for information-based transparency. Gov. Inf. Q. 27(4), 377–383 (2010)
14. Denyer, D., et al.: Developing design propositions through research synthesis. Organ. Stud. 29(3), 393–413 (2008)
15. Bertsimas, D., Thiele, A.: Robust and data-driven optimization: modern decision making under uncertainty. In: Models, Methods, and Applications for Innovative Decision Making, pp. 95–122. INFORMS (2006)
16. Grus, L., et al.: Spatial data infrastructures as complex adaptive systems. Int. J. Geogr. Inf. Sci. 24(3), 439–463 (2010)
17. Hastings, N.A.J.: Physical Asset Management. Springer, London (2010)
18. Heng, A., et al.: Rotating machinery prognostics: state of the art, challenges and opportunities. Mech. Syst. Signal Process. 23(3), 724–739 (2009)
19. Khatri, V., Brown, C.V.: Designing data governance. Commun. ACM 53(1), 148–152 (2010)
20. Malone, T.W., Crowston, K.: The interdisciplinary study of coordination. ACM Comput. Surv. 26(1), 87–119 (1994)
21. Malone, T.W., Crowston, K.: What is coordination theory and how can it help design cooperative work systems?. In: Presented at the ACM Conference on Computer-supported Cooperative Work, New York, USA (1990)
22. Mathew, A.D., et al.: Understanding data management in asset management: a survey. In: Presented at the World Congress for Engineering Asset Management, Beijing, China, 27 October 2008
23. Mehdi, K.-P.: Inventive Approaches for Technology Integration and Information Resources Management. IGI Global, Hershey (2014)
24. Mohseni, M.: What does asset management mean to you?. In: Presented at the Transmission and Distribution Conference and Exposition, Greenwood Village, USA, 7 September 2003
25. Otto, B.: On the evolution of data governance in firms: the case of Johnson & Johnson consumer products North America. In: Sadiq, S. (ed.) Handbook of Data Quality, pp. 93–118. Springer, Heidelberg (2013)
26. Otto, B.: Organizing data governance: findings from the telecommunications industry and consequences for large service providers. Commun. Assoc. Inf. Syst. 29(1), 45–66 (2011)
27. Otto, B., et al.: Towards a framework for corporate data quality management. In: ACIS 2007 Proceedings, p. 109 (2007)
28. Panian, Z.: Some practical experiences in data governance. World Acad. Sci. Eng. Technol. 38, 150–157 (2010)
29. Pierce, E., et al.: Industry report: the state of information and data governance. IADQ (2008)
30. Pipino, L.L., et al.: Data quality assessment. Commun. ACM 45(4), 211–218 (2002)
31. Redman, T.C.: Data Driven: Profiting from Your Most Important Business Asset. Harvard Business Press, Boston, USA (2008)
32. Shadish, W.R., et al.: Experimental and Quasi-Experimental Designs for Generalized Causal Inference. Wadsworth Publishing, Boston (2001)
33. Shannon, C.E.: A mathematical theory of communication. Sigmobile Mob. Comput. Commun. Rev. 5(1), 3–55 (2001)

34. Smith, A.: Data Governance And Enterprise Data Modeling – Don't Do One Without the Other! — Enterprise Information Management Institute. http://www.eiminstitute.org/library/eimi-archives/volume-1-issue-2-april-2007-edition/data-governance-and-enter-prise-data-modeling-dont-do-one-without-the-other
35. Strong, D.M., et al.: Data quality in context. Commun. ACM **40**(5), 103–110 (1997)
36. Thompson, N., et al.: Government data does not mean data governance: lessons learned from a public sector application audit. Gov. Inf. Q. **32**(3), 316–322 (2015)
37. Wang, R.Y., Strong, D.M.: Beyond accuracy: what data quality means to data consumers. J. Manag. Inf. Syst. **12**(4), 5–34 (1996)
38. Weber, K., et al.: One size does not fit all—a contingency approach to data governance. J. Data Inf. Qual. **1**(1), 4:1–4:27 (2009)
39. Wende, K.: A model for data governance – organising accountabilities for data quality management. In: Presented at the Australasian Conference on Information Systems, Toowoomba, Australia, 5 December 2007
40. Wende, K., Otto, B.: A contingency approach to data governance. In: Presented at the International Conference on Information Quality, Cambridge, USA, 11 October 2007

e-Government and Civic Engagement

Political Social Media in the Global South

Joyojeet Pal[(✉)] and Andre Gonawela

University of Michigan, Ann Arbor, USA
{joyojeet,andregon}@umich.edu

Abstract. We examine the evidence of growing social media use among political elites in low- and middle-income countries, including in places where the proportion of actual voters on social media is small. We propose three ways to view this phenomenon of– first, as signaling, second, as a means for politicians to access elite populations, and third as a way to circumvent mainstream media and exercise direct control over political communication.

Keywords: Twitter · Social media · Political communication · Global south

1 Introduction

In the last decade, engagement with major social media outlets such as Twitter and Facebook has become a central element of political communication, particularly around major elections. Social media have challenged media logics in several parts of the world, most recently in the United States, where politicians have been able to reach citizens directly and even channel their mainstream media engagements through social media. Although scholarly attention to political social media has drawn its empirical basis in developments in the Western world, the trend of social media use is now global. The World Bank lists 135 countries as low- and middle-income, and the Twiplomacy study found social media use among politicians in 119 of those countries, including in 25 of the 31 low-income countries [1]. At the same time, despite claims that social media drive election results [2] there is little evidence that social media influence election outcomes, and indeed evidence suggests that online popularity can be deeply misleading in predicting results [3]. Events around the Egyptian pro-democracy movement and election-related protests in Iran were early drivers on subjects of social media and citizen action in the Global South [4, 5]. Commentary on social media has since taken a cautionary tone, noting its purpose as a means for media capture by entrenched institutions and powers [6–8]. We propose a lens to approach the motivations of political actors for whom social media use is not a means of winning elections but is nonetheless an important media strategy.

2 Approach

We identified 73 nations listed as low- and middle-income where the head of government had a verified account on Twitter or Facebook. In each of these, we searched, where

Y.K. Dwivedi et al. (Eds.): I3E 2016, LNCS 9844, pp. 587–593, 2016.
DOI: 10.1007/978-3-319-45234-0_52

relevant, for at least one known electoral opposition figure. Overall, we gathered the details of 113 politicians – including their date of joining social media and scale of following. Our goal here is not to analyze the tweets in detail but rather to document the broad use of social media, so we primarily gathered basic data on rate of messaging, duration on social media, and online following. We also kept a database of the 3,200 recent tweets (till May 2016) of politicians with more than 1 million followers, and we conducted a discourse analysis of the tweet content to qualitatively observe the language in the messaging. Rather than provide a comprehensive account of social media use in low- and middle-income countries, our purpose here is to propose reasons for its presence and potential growth. Since Tweets are typically mirrored as Facebook updates, we focused primarily on public Twitter data, using Facebook only for illustrative purposes.

3   Findings

Fifty-three of the politicians had active accounts on both Facebook and Twitter, 27 had a following of 1 million or more on either Twitter or Facebook, and 14 had a following of more than 1 million on both Facebook and Twitter. Some leaders such as Enrique Peña Nieto of Mexico and Najib Razak of Malaysia were early adopters, getting on social media prior to the extremely successful Obama campaign of 2008. The majority of politicians in our sample have joined social media since 2009. Some of the most recent accounts include those of Jimmy Morales of Guatemala, José Serra of Brazil, Abdel Fatah al-Sisi of Egypt and Muhammadu Buhari of Nigeria, each of whom had more than 500,000 followers on Twitter within a year of joining.

In Table 1, the politicians in our sample with the highest number of either Facebook likes or Twitter followers, as a ratio of the number of internet users in their home country, are arranged in descending order, to allow a snapshot into popularity trends. Domestic internet use is not necessarily a reliable value to peg a political leader's popularity against (we also have no way of telling whether these likes or follows are authentic). From the sample of accounts with more than 1 million followers, we find that fame independent of politics can be useful for candidates – thus Imran Khan of Pakistan, Morales of Guatemala, and Michel Martelly of Haiti gain followers for their other activities (cricket, comedy, music). Reach on social media can reflect the potential media footprint that politicians control, as is visible among the nation–states with a relatively smaller internet penetration such as Afghanistan, Niger and Cambodia, where a leader can dominate the local social media following. Even among countries with large and diverse social media use, politicians can directly reach upward of 10 % of their countries' entire populations – Recep Erdoğan of Turkey, Luis Solís of Costa Rica, and Rafael Correa of Ecuador all command a social media following that crosses this threshold.

Table 1. Selected highly followed political figures as proportion of national internet penetration (min followers:150,000).

Country	Internet users ('000)	Political figure (* = head of govt.)	Facebook likes ('000)	Twitter followers ('000)
Jordan	3,200	Rania Al Abdullah	5,623	4,480
Myanmar	1,118	Aung San Suu Kyi*	1,715	0
Cambodia	1,362	Sam Rainsy	2,063	0
Afghanistan	1,955	Ashraf Ghani*	1,046	171
Rwanda	1,248	Paul Kagame*	515	1,340
Guatemala	3,620	Jimmy Morales	925	52.5
Costa Rica	2,407	Luis Solís*	600	179
Iraq	3,815	Haider Al-Abadi	914	65.2
Indonesia	42,727	Prabowo Subianto	9,080	2,380
Turkey	38,216	Recep Erdoğan*	8,048	7,720
Pakistan	25,136	Imran Khan	5,237	3,300
Haiti	1,176	Michel J. Martelly*	201	142
Ecuador	6,767	Rafael Correa*	1,141	2,540

Politicians' sphere of influence may extend beyond the regional boundaries of their nation–states, such as in the case of countries with large diaspora populations such as Cambodia, Vietnam and Guatemala. We see a spectrum of political systems – while in 28 countries, electoral issues are arguably crucial (both the elected leader and the most recent major opposition leader have presences), there are also leaders from single-party systems like Paul Kagame of Rwanda and Nguyễn Tấn Dũng of Vietnam who are online despite limited electoral opposition in their respective nations.

4   Why Social Media?

Based on our study of language of the tweets, we identify three recurrent themes in the politicians' social media messaging. The first is signaling – i.e. what the brand of social media suggests about the kind of politician standing behind it. The second is elite access – i.e. reaching out to elite populations in a country or in the world who respond to social media. The third is media logic – i.e. creating channels to circumvent the mainstream media to reach citizens directly.

4.1   Signaling

Social media exist as an outward brand presence. India's Narendra Modi is Asia's most followed politician, Rwanda's Kagame is Africa's. The two leaders use discussions around development as signaling for what their respective regimes stand for. Both leaders have complicated political histories – Modi was known for his involvement in religious riots in India, and Kagame has run Rwanda without credible opposition for more than two decades. On Twitter, both propose images of tech-savvy modernists, re-creating political images around a discourse more directly controlled by their teams than by mainstream media.

The two tweets in Fig. 1 exemplify this spirit. The messages are crafted as aphorisms that use aspirational language but are delivered as enlightened counsel. The speakers emerge as leaders who appreciate modernity. In Rwanda's case, the message underlines the need for a continuing Kagame regime. In India, Modi's message nods at an aspirational discourse around technology and development for a rising India.

Paul Kagame ✔
@PaulKagame   ✿   👤 Follow

People should not worry too much about technology instead adopt& adapt them for their enabling capacity n wider use.Dangers can be mitigated

Narendra Modi ✔
@narendramodi

Digital technology has a vital role in making democracy stronger & in overall human resource development. nm4.in/1gSEYPZ
9/24/15, 10:09 PM

Fig. 1. Twitter messages from Rwandan President Paul Kagame and Indian Prime Minister Narendra Modi

Although there is a broad literature on political communication and the role of the internet in political branding [9], little work looks at the Global South. The more complex question – that of how the association with the technology artifact is seen as playing a role in building positive online capital for a political leader – lies at the intersection of communications and development studies. There is also little work on political signaling in the Global South, and much of the existing work around traditional image management of former (or current) strongmen through signaling neoliberal reforms, tourism, etc., has been critiqued for its overt courting of Western approval [10]. Politicians' use of social media in these settings opens up the possibilities of examining the content of their social signaling, the nature of its spread, as well as theoretical work on what the technology artifact means to the political brand. Such work builds upon a wealth of research into aspiration in technology that has interrogated what technology artifacts themselves come to represent for modernity [11], and how these have impacted geopolitical discourses [12].

4.2   Elite Affiliation

Because social media access is restricted largely to the educated wealthy in the Global South, these media are more likely to reach an elite demographic both within countries and in the diaspora. The imagination of social media as a technology associated with the West and with the younger generations can extend to the political branding of the user and who the user appeals to. Pakistani politician Imran Khan, himself critiqued as a Cambridge-educated elite, has been credited with reaching the otherwise apolitical "burger population" (young Americanized Pakistanis) with the use of social media, compensating for weaker grass-roots organization compared to the major Pakistani parties. Social media here offer an alternative and arguably complementary means of outreach that might not have the same electoral draw as grass-roots presence but creates value by attracting the attention of mainstream media.

Besides wealthy expatriates, the elite access of social media also extends to young voters. In Pakistan, the ruling party is represented on social media not by the prime minister but by his young daughter, who posts messages as well as pictures of her father, Nawaz Sharif, at various events. Social media are used as a means of performing filial duty while also emphasizing the leader's anointed nod to the technology and aspirations of younger Pakistanis. Young voters have traditionally not been a useful political constituency in many countries because of apathy, but these cases suggest that political actors see the potential to change this culture. The tweet from former military coup leader and Nigeria's current President Buhari (Fig. 2) has three nested messages: first, by posting first-person messages on Twitter he signals a social media user challenging opponents' claim that he has never finished school; second, his message reaches out to the younger voters, not a natural constituency for him, being part of an older generation with ties to military dictatorship; finally, he shouts out to Nigerians abroad – signaling that he stands not for his tribal affiliations (a major factor in elections) but for a pan-regional identity.

Fig. 2. Twitter message from Pakistani cricketer and opposition politician Imran Khan and Nigerian President Muhammadu Buhari

4.3 Media Logic

Studies of social media in the Global South have generally been enthusiastic about its potential for democratizing, drawn in part by events surrounding the Arab Spring [13]. Less attention has been paid to the potential for institutional capture of social media – which we see early signs of here in the massive reach of some political leaders in their home countries. Social media create a means for politicians to avoid the media logics that would dictate that only those messages seen as interesting to the mainstream media would find voice in their channels [14]. With increasingly ubiquitous access to mobile devices, a tech-savvy politician can craft a media flow straight to the citizenry. Politicians need not ignore mainstream media, which in most countries have a far more significant reach to voting citizens. Rather these politicians integrate social media channels to complement their mainstream media strategies.

Social media allow the political movement represented by a leader to be organized into one space – the same channel that serves as a voice can also serve as a means to troll or silence oppositional voices. Not only do leaders like Modi, Erdoğan, Joko Widodo of Indonesia and Noynoy Aquino of the Philippines have more followers on social media than any single mainstream media channel in their respective home states – they have all started using social media as their primary means of outreach, which in turn acts as a feeder into mainstream media. This enables politicians to better control their message and also to decide what stories they wish to give momentum to, because that power now rests in their networks.

5   Conclusions

Focusing primarily on messaging such as tweets restricts our understanding of the online networks of political leaders but helps us to understand the ways politicians wish to be perceived. Countries that have big enough electorates and international presence increasingly need political leaders who look "global" – this adds an external-facing dimension to the social media that goes beyond wooing an electorate.

There is clear evidence that political social media will stay and likely grow in much of the Global South. However, the confluence of ideas from multiple bodies of work means more than ever that an inter-disciplinary frame is needed to make sense of these developments. Politicians' use of social media to project themselves as representing a modern vision for their respective states is tied to the symbolic value of technology as a means for aspiration in the Global South, particularly as technology has become elemental to our collective perception of what constitutes development. As the next modern selfie-shooting political star turns the corner, it is imperative that the community of e-society researchers consider how our theoretical tools can help to understand the ways that political communications and indeed power relations are changing permanently as Twitter and Facebook become household names even in the places where they don't translate all that well.

References

1. Lufkens, M.: Twiplomacy Study 2016. Burson-Marsteller, Editor, Geneva (2016)
2. Barclay, F.P., et al.: India 2014: facebook 'like' as a predictor of election outcomes. Asian J. Polit. Sci. 23(2), 134–160 (2015)
3. Leng, H.K.: Marketing politicians on facebook: an examination of the Singapore general election 2011. Stud. Bus. Econ. 7(1), 101–109 (2012)
4. Sabadello, M.: The role of new media for the democratization processes in the Arab world. The Arab revolutions. Reflections on the role of civil society, human rights and new media in the transformation processes, SAFRAN schlaininger arbeitspapiere für friedensforschung, abrüstung und nachhaltige entwicklung, p. 11 (2011)
5. Grossman, L.: Iran's protests: why twitter is the medium of the movement. Time (2009). http://content.time.com/time/world/article/0,8599,1905125,00.html

6. Morozov, E.: Iran: downside to the "Twitter Revolution". Dissent **56**(4), 10–14 (2009)
7. Mungiu-Pippidi, A., Munteanu, I.: Moldova's "Twitter Revolution". J. Democracy **20**(3), 136–142 (2009)
8. Burns, A., Eltham, B.: Twitter free Iran: an evaluation of twitter's role in public diplomacy and information operations in Iran's 2009 election crisis (2009)
9. Dahlgren, P.: The Internet, public spheres, and political communication: dispersion and deliberation. Polit. Commun. **22**(2), 147–162 (2005)
10. Fisher, J.: 'Image management' in East Africa: Uganda, Rwanda, Kenya and their donors. Images of Africa: Creation, negotiation and subversion (2015)
11. Pal, J.: Rajnikant's laptop: computers and development in popular Indian cinema. Inf. Technol. Int. Dev. **6**(2), 39 (2010)
12. Burrell, J.: Invisible Users: Youth in the Internet Cafés of Urban Ghana. MIT Press, Cambridge (2012)
13. Lotan, G., et al.: The Arab Spring| the revolutions were tweeted: information flows during the 2011 Tunisian and Egyptian revolutions. Int. J. Commun. **5**, 31 (2011)
14. Vergeer, M., Hermans, L., Sams, S.: Online social networks and micro-blogging in political campaigning: the exploration of a new campaign tool and a new campaign style. Party Polit. **19**(3), 477–501 (2013)

Opportunities and Challenges
of Using Web 2.0 Technologies in Government

Uthayasankar Sivarajah[✉], Vishanth Weerakkody, and Zahir Irani

Business School, College of Business, Arts and Social Sciences, Brunel
University London, Uxbridge, UK
{Sankar.Sivarajah,Vishanth.Weerakkody,Zahir.Irani}
@brunel.ac.uk

Abstract. Public administration has endured signification transformation over the last decade enabled largely through Information and Communication Technology. In recent times, second generation web technologies (Web 2.0) such as social media and networking sites are increasingly being used by governments for its digital activities ranging from public relations to knowledge management. However, as Web 2.0 technologies are more interactive than the traditional models of information provision or creation of digital services, these technologies have brought about a new set of opportunities and challenges to those government authorities. This study draws on the extant literature to examine the opportunities that Web 2.0 technologies offer to public authorities and the challenges they may need to overcome when integrating these technologies into their work practices.

Keywords: Web 2.0 · Social media · Opportunities · Challenges · Digital government

1 Introduction

Governments around the world have placed great emphasis on ensuring they exploit the power of rapidly evolving ICTs to transform both internal operations and the external delivery of its services [9, 11, 23]. The use of a broad class of technologies ranging from personal computers to mobile devices has enabled governments to offer convenient and enhanced accessibility to government services and information to citizens, businesses and governmental units [44]. The internet and the developments around Web in particular has been able to provide a new generation of instruments to facilitate social networking, information sharing and collaborative work [24, 31, 38]. It has opened new sets of possibilities for governments, ranging from the joint production of public services in cooperation with citizens, social organisations and businesses, from the wide distribution and re-use of government information to the introduction of new forms of democratic participation. Governments are aware of these new possibilities and have actively started exploring them. However, the use of ICT in government and public services is about far more than simply introducing new technologies and involves major changes in internal organisational structures as well as the need to convince potential users that digital government is in their interests [28]. Despite

© IFIP International Federation for Information Processing 2016
Published by Springer International Publishing Switzerland 2016. All Rights Reserved
Y.K. Dwivedi et al. (Eds.): I3E 2016, LNCS 9844, pp. 594–606, 2016.
DOI: 10.1007/978-3-319-45234-0_53

spending enormous amounts on web-based initiatives, government agencies often fail to meet users' needs online. Baumgarten and Chui [4] posit that this trend can be reversed by employing new governance models and embracing user participation through second generation web based technologies that extend beyond one-to-one digital communication. However, in order to do this, government agencies will need to assess the business case and the requisite organisational and governance changes that a shift to Web 2.0 entails prior to adopting these modern technologies [18]. In addition, the internet itself is constantly changing as social media sites such as Facebook, Twitter, Instagram, etc. gain and lose popularity. This means that public agencies who embrace the second generation web based communication methods are facing a moving target making the decision making process regarding which channels to use challenging [41].

This paper provides a conceptual review of the opportunities and challenges that the use of Web 2.0 technologies may have for government authorities. To do so, this paper draws on the extant literature and contributes to the emerging field of Web 2.0 use by government organisations through providing a descriptive account of both opportunities and challenges of using technologies in a governmental context.

2   The Role of Web 2.0 in Government Organisations

Web 2.0 tools such as social media and networking sites have empowered government organisations to create, distribute and gather information outside the customary hierarchical information flow. There has been an increasing urge by public sector organisations to deliver services online and pay greater attention to Web 2.0 technologies due to the ever-increasing trend in the use of online environments by citizens and the rise in adult and younger generations involved in social networking and virtual community activities [31, 39]. Nevertheless, this is not the only reason for the growing interest in Web 2.0 technologies by these organisations. Web 2.0 facilitates the public services institutions with a key platform for citizen engagement and collaboration with the community to improve transparency and accountability [1, 29]. This new form of technology-enabled participation is becoming more accustomed as governments are investing in these technologies to enable more effective communication with their stakeholders. In effect, Web 2.0 approaches allow local government to gather feedback from citizens on the priorities and effective organisation of public services.

Governments and officials at every level are leveraging Web 2.0 technologies for various purposes [2]. The use of Web 2.0 tools in the government organisations can be categorised to two main areas of application; (a) internal use and (b) external use [3, 37]. The internal uses of these technologies facilitate government agencies and its employees to network and share internal organization and work processes using Web 2.0 technologies. Some of the internal uses of Web 2.0 tools are as follows:

Internal Staff and Cross-Agency Collaboration: The use of Web 2.0 technologies such as internal wikis and other collaboration tool for data sharing among their colleagues and storing work materials using sites such as DropBox [15]. In addition, Web 2.0 tools is also being used for collaboration between institutional levels, agencies, departments in order to increase efficiency and time-saving.

Knowledge Management: Though traditional knowledge management systems are applied to structured knowledge, Web 2.0 applications (social software, folksonomies, and wiki) are particularly effective in enabling the sharing of informal and tacit knowledge internally, among employees [37].

Facilitating Policymaking: policy makers have launched Web 2.0 applications such as YouTube channels and other applications to communicate with its constituency and facilitate a platform to encourage citizens to participate in policymaking [15]. This kind of engagement enhances the government's effectiveness and improves the quality of its decisions [22].

On the other hand, the external uses of Web 2.0 tools by the governments have been to better facilitate better service provision, external governance and stakeholder relations [3]. Some government organisations are developing a presence on Web 2.0 applications recognising its interactive potential in order to strengthen the relationship with citizens and solicit their feedback [44]. The following is a list of the external uses of these technologies:

Local Reporting and Problem Solving: government agencies especially local councils facilitating the citizens who want to engage or report issues that affect their neighbourhood, community, region, or county by either adopting or partnering with Web 2.0 integrated websites such as FixMyStreet.com (e.g. road repair, graffiti removal, traffic concerns, etc.) Web 2.0 technologies such as Twitter, Facebook and other similar applications make this possible with unprecedented speed and efficiency [6].

Political Participation: the most drastic change in the government organisations occurring is the utilisation of social networking for the purpose of elections. Through the use of applications such as Facebook, YouTube, Blogs and various other tools; Web 2.0 has been actively used for political campaigns and debates especially during the times of elections for all emerging public officials [2]. In this respect, convincing potential users that note will be taken of electronic interaction in terms of policy formulation is important [20] or there is a risk of cynicism undermining any engagement.

Public Relations: the most prevalent Web 2.0 tools adopted by among government agencies have been communication and information sharing tools, such as Twitter and RSS feed which facilitate quick communication or short messaging for keeping the general public constantly informed with its activities [3].

The list of uses is not comprehensive by any means as Web 2.0 philosophy is far from mature, and its future development and adoption is difficult to envisage [37]. However, they do indicate the key uses of these technologies in government organisations. Nonetheless, it is important to recognise that the success in any online services depends on strategic use of ICT together with an organisation's ability to reorganise its back-office and internal processes effectively [16]. Therefore, the use of Web 2.0 technologies for public service delivery by the organisations requires not only technological innovation but also organisational, legal and social innovation in order to successfully embrace and reap the benefits from these technologies [18]. The aforementioned uses of Web 2.0 technologies in government organisations are illustrated in Fig. 1.

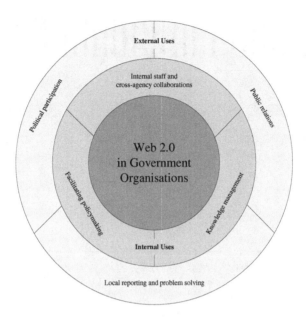

Fig. 1. External and internal uses of Web 2.0 in government organisations

3   The Significance of Web 2.0 Technologies for Government Organisations

Much government activity is now focused on Web 2.0, and social media has become a central component of digital government context in a very short period of time. In this respect, social media are applications that enable the sharing of information including wikis, blogs and social networks [9]. There are various innovative examples of using Web 2.0 technologies by government organisations. The Web 2.0 initiatives such as NASA's internal social networks and virtual worlds, and the U.S. intelligence community's "intellipedia" are just a few of the recent efforts launched within central government. Table 1 presents these examples in a systematic manner by first highlighting the government organisation and at which level (i.e. central, regional and local) these tools are being utilised within. Secondly, the type of Web 2.0 technologies adopted is mapped against these organisations and finally, an application scenario of a Web 2.0 technology used by the organisation is presented.

As illustrated by Table 1, the most popular Web 2.0 tools that has been adopted by the government organisations have been social networking sites (i.e. Facebook), Microblogging (i.e. Twitter), online video and photo sharing sites (i.e. YouTube and Flickr) and RSS feeds. Some local government authorities are also leveraging cloud computing services (e.g. Google Apps for business) in an effort to provide public

Table 1. Government organisations adopting Web 2.0 Technologies

Government organisation (Domain)	Web 2.0 Technologies												Example Web 2.0 application scenario	Reference (s)
	Blogs	Microblogging	Wikis	Social networking	Social bookmarking	Video sharing sites	Picture sharing sites	RSS	Deliberation platforms	Virtual worlds	Mashup	SaaS platforms		
Her majesty's armed forces (UK – central government)	✓	✓		✓		✓							British army utilises Facebook to provide latest news and other information (i.e. photos, videos etc.) to the public.	[26]
Westminster city council (UK – local government)	✓	✓				✓		✓			✓	✓	The council uses YouTube channel to raise awareness of services and shape policy developments.	[13]
Open town hall (US – regional government)	✓	✓		✓					✓				The Open Town Hall platform gathers public input to help government agencies make better decisions. It encourages widespread and inclusive citizen participation in deliberation.	[36]
Central intelligence agency (US – central government)			✓			✓	✓	✓					Uses wiki system for collaborative data sharing among the US Intelligence Community (e.g. Intellipedia)	[15]
Washington state department	✓	✓		✓		✓	✓	✓					Utilises Twitter to broadcast	[45]

(Continued)

Table 1. (*Continued*)

Government organisation (*Domain*)	Web 2.0 Technologies													Example Web 2.0 application scenario	Reference (s)
	Blogs	Microblogging	Wikis	Social networking	Social bookmarking	Video sharing sites	Picture sharing sites	RSS	Deliberation platforms	Virtual worlds	Mashup	SaaS platforms			
of transportation (*US - regional government*)														up-to-date urgent news feeds and other relevant information of the department to the public.	
Data.gov (*US - central government*)								✓			✓			Data.gov utilises mashup techniques to provides citizens access to congressional calendars and voting records, political district maps, etc.	[42]
Front national (French political party) (*France – central government*)		✓		✓		✓	✓	✓		✓				Front national Party set up virtual headquarters in SecondLife for promoting their presidential campaigns	[37]

services while using fewer resources, reducing carbon emissions, and thus producing financial savings for the organisations [25]. Although Table 1 presents a clear idea of the significant role of Web 2.0 in governments, it is too early to deduce the importance of these technologies by only reviewing the Web 2.0 experiences in the government organisations. Therefore, to fully understand the real value of these technologies for government organisations, it is necessary to evaluate and articulate the implications of Web 2.0 in the digital government context.

4 Discussion: Opportunities and Challenges of Web 2.0 in Government

In any consideration of adopting new technology, attention must be paid to the opportunities and challenges of such adoption [21, 43].The emergence of Web 2.0 and the rise of social networks have opened up both new perspectives and challenges for the public institutions [44]. Nevertheless, cutting edge digital communication comes filled with both potential opportunities and risks. As a result, the implications of these new digital frontiers and opportunities are also on the governmental agenda [30]. The following sections therefore presents a review of the potential opportunities and challenges that the government organisations might face when using Web 2.0 technologies.

4.1 Opportunities of Web 2.0 Technologies for Government Organisations

One way to evaluate Web 2.0 technologies is to consider them to be a 'disruptive technology' for government, creating 'disruptive innovation' in the digital government as well as augmenting digital government with better services and management [15]. Implications of these new technologies and opportunities from the perspective of administrations are now also on the governmental agenda [30] especially as there is the potential for Web 2.0 tools to create a change in public sector processes. The following is a list of some of the opportunities that Web 2.0 technologies have to offer for government organisations.

Revive Civic Engagement: Web 2.0 tools such as social networking sites and deliberation platforms can be powerful tools that the governments can deploy to help revive civic engagement and harness the wisdom of crowds. The government can especially enlist important niche audiences, leverage their insights for policymaking and improve the citizen-government relationship [27].

Enhance External Transparency: Web 2.0 applications can help improve external transparency for government organisations. The integration of online collaboration tools and interactive maps into government websites can enable governments to become more inclusive and responsive to individual citizens throughout the policy life cycle resulting in improved policy outcomes [33].

Rapid Dissemination of Information: The viral nature of Web 2.0 tools such as Microblogging and social networking sites can help disseminate information over the internet much faster compared to traditional methods (e.g. postal letters, pamphlets, static websites etc.) of information delivery [10]. This can draw a larger pool of audience and promote awareness of existing government services to the public.

Efficient Gathering of Collective Intelligence: Gathering intelligence from the citizens for crowdsourcing has revolutionarily changed with the use of some Web 2.0 technologies such as Wikis [35]. It has enabled the government organisations efficient and effective collection of geographically dispersed collective intelligence from the citizens with less effort in comparison to traditional crowd-sourcing methods such as public forums and workshops.

Lower IT Costs: As the model of Web 2.0 at times requires the use of intermediaries especially mashup applications, these intermediaries can enable governments to provide enhanced, customized services to their citizens at much lower costs than the government's centralized provision of service [12]. In addition, they provide a means for public service organizations to disseminate information about public services, to educate citizens about matters that affect their quality of life, to solicit people's feedback and to enrol them as co-producers in a timely and cost effective way.

Streamline Internal Operations: The collaboration tools such as wikis can streamline internal operations within government agencies especially among disparate teams and across agencies enabling individuals to engage in open discussions leading to a potential build-up of knowledgebase [1].

It seems that the advent of the emerging web technologies creates an unexpected dilemma for governments. On one hand, governments seek to use the new opportunities to deliver services but on the other hand governments have significant problems embracing these emerging web technologies due to many challenges and risks.

4.2 Challenges of Web 2.0 Technologies for Government Organisations

Despite the potential opportunities of Web 2.0 not all government agencies have explored the possibilities of these technologies [19, 32]. Most public services organisations find it difficult to overcome the perception that some Web 2.0 technologies such as social networking sites (e.g. Facebook) have limited business value and are more a distraction to employees than a means to deliver digital government services [40]. Moreover, government models for leveraging internet technologies is rather different from that of commercial enterprises [21], especially as government agencies are more cautious and slow in adopting new emerging technologies in comparison to commercial organisations. The following are a list of potential challenges that government organisations could face by adopting Web 2.0 technologies.

Development of New Service Model: As the Web 2.0 model requires the use of external platforms (e.g. Facebook, YouTube and Twitter), it can prove as a challenge to develop a new service model that integrates these Web 2.0 platforms with existing digital government systems in a manner that is secure and improves the quality of services to citizens [21].

Additional Staff: Once Web 2.0 tools such as blogs have been adopted by government organisations, it may require some level of moderation to ensure that comments and contributions do not turn out to be a platform where the public discussions are monopolised by a vocal minority or extremist activists groups. This level of moderation may be costly in terms of time and effort spent by the organisations where additional staff might be required to be moderators of content [21].

Loss of Control: Government organisations can face loss of control due to excessive transparency using Web 2.0 applications such as blogs. For instance, blogging by ministers and civil servants has led to release of sensitive information in an incorrect and sometimes illegal manner [38]. In addition, the technique of application mashups and content syndication on to existing government platforms can also be an issue leading to loss of ownership control and authenticity of the final products.

Restricted User Participation: The investment on Web 2.0 applications on the government front can potentially result in restriction to exclusive user participation. Web 2.0 applications are mostly used by well-educated young and adult generation in the developed part of the world which can lead to wider societal divides by giving more voice to those that already have it or use it [17]. In addition there is also the risk of older people not likely to participate in Web 2.0 because of the lack of Web 2.0 confidence or because of the lack of technical ability [8].

Social Isolation: Though Web 2.0 can stimulate social interactions and communication between different individuals, there is also the risk of people isolating themselves from the real world as they become too addicted the use of internet [17].

Risk of Information Overload and Reliability: There is a risk of information overload and poor quality of content shared by public users when using some Web 2.0 applications such as blogs and wikis, as concerns can be raised against their reliability, accuracy and authority of information [27].

Security and Privacy Threat: The open nature of Web 2.0 presents significant challenges to the traditional enterprise approach to controlling intellectual property over information shared and surety of these applications. The increase in functionality and interactivity has increased the ways in which an application can be attacked successfully by hackers and viruses and therefore proves to be a security concern for organisations. There are also risks when sharing information using social networking sites where it could lead to possible abuse of personal information, hacking and stalking [7].

Threat of Cyber Extremisms: These new, interactive, multimedia-rich forms of communication provide effective means for extremists to promote their ideas, share resources, and communicate among each other [14].

Critical Reviews: While the advent of Web 2.0 technologies has played an important role in the providing people with useful assessments of products and services, it has also meant that there is now a greater risk of these assessments damaging the image of people and organisations without a fair reason. This is because it is difficult to find out of assessment are fair or the result of the personal resentment [17].

In spite of the abovementioned challenges, some government agencies still want to harness the collaborative power of Web 2.0 and many scholars believe the opportunities that the Web 2.0 developments can offer cannot be ignored by the public sector as it can take the evolution of digital government agenda in new directions [34]. Instead of avoiding these new technologies, governments should develop an overall strategic plan for agencies at all levels to participate in social networks, and develop a coordinated effort to develop and implement these tools. In this context, being clear why Web 2.0 is being introduced is important. This clarity will help ensure that any development meets a stated goal and this will assist in ensuring an effective adoption across the organisation [5]. More importantly, whether governments are initiating small-scale pilot projects or contemplating a larger roll-out of Web 2.0 technologies, it is essential for them to be aware of the impact of these tools in order for successful implementation [12].

5   Conclusions

Based on a conceptual review, this paper has contributed to the existing knowledge of Web 2.0 use by governments by articulating a descriptive account of the opportunities and challenges of Web 2.0 technologies that need to be considered when adopting these tools by governments. Through this review, several salient opportunities were identified that would significantly enhance both internal and external business process in public administration. These ranged from reduced cost of operations and streamlined internal work practices to increased transparency and civic engagement. However, the review also exposed several challenges that need to be considered when implementing Web 2.0, such as, exclusion of certain user groups or communities, security and privacy risks and capacity to deal with large volumes of information. These factors suggest that government authorities already using and/or planning to use Web 2.0 technologies as part of their digital transformation journey need to have in place the necessary strategies to deal with the challenges posed by the technologies while embracing the opportunities they present. This study is of significant relevance to public sector and the IS research community, policy makers, local government authorities and practitioners as it provides them with a deeper better understanding of the factors that encourage and hinder adoption of Web 2.0 technologies in government. In doing so, this conceptual review of the opportunities and challenges offer a foundation for management when taking decisions regarding the adoption of Web 2.0 technologies in government organisations for internal work purposes and external engagement and service delivery to citizens. The next stage of this study will be to contextualise these opportunities and challenges by empirically examining the influence they have on the ICT enabled transformation efforts across both central and local government authorities.

References

1. Accenture: Web 2.0 and the Next Generation of Public Service, Accenture, United States (2009)
2. Adams, M.O., Smith, L.D.: Changing the face of public affairs: a look at how social networking is impacting the business of the public sector. Natl. Soc. Sci. J. **34**(1), 10–16 (2010)
3. Anttiroiko, A.: Innovation in democratic E-Governance: benefitting from web 2.0 applications in the public sector. Int. J. Electron. Gov. Res. **6**(2), 18–36 (2010)
4. Baumgarten, J., Chui, M.: E-government 2.0. McKinsey & Company, New York (2009)
5. Baxter, G.J., Connolly, T.M., Stansfield, M.H.: Organisational blogs: benefits and challenges of implementation. Learn. Organ. **17**(6), 515–528 (2010)
6. Bertot, J.C., Jaeger, P.T. Grimes, J.M.: Crowd-sourcing transparency: ICTs, social media, and government transparency initiatives. In: Proceedings of the 11th Annual International Digital Government Research Conference on Public Administration Online: Challenges and Opportunities Digital Government Society of North America, p. 51 (2010)
7. Al-Tameem, A.B., Chittikala, P., Pichappan, P.: A study of AJAX vulnerability in Web 2.0 applications. In: First International Conference on the Applications of Digital Information and Web Technologies, ICADIWT 2008, p. 63 (2008)
8. Blank, G., Reisdorf, B.C.: The participatory Web. Inf. Commun. Soc. **15**(4), 537–554 (2012)
9. Bonson, E., Royo, S., Ratkai, M.: Citizens' engagement on local governments' Facebook sites. an empirical analysis: the impact of different media and content types in Western Europe. Gov. Inf Q. **32**(1), 52–62 (2015)
10. Buchanan, E., Luck, E.: The electronic village: the digital challenges in communication strategies for sporting organization. Int. J. Bus. Environ. **2**(2), 258–279 (2008)
11. Cabinet Office: Government ICT Strategy. Cabinet Office, London (2011)
12. Chang, A., Kanna, P.K.: Leveraging Web 2.0 in Government. IBM Center for The Business of Government, Washington, D.C (2008)
13. Charlton, J.: Public sector use of social media takes off [Homepage of Guardian News & Media Limited], 06 July 2011. http://www.guardian.co.uk/public-leaders-network/2011/apr/06/public. Accessed 06 Apr
14. Chen, H., Thoms, S., Fu, T.: Cyber extremism in Web 2.0: an exploratory study of international Jihadist groups. In: IEEE International Conference on Intelligence and Security Informatics, ISI 2008, Taipei, Taiwan, p. 98 (2008)
15. Chun, S.A., Shulman, S., Sandoval, R., Hovy, E.: Government 2.0: making connections between citizens, data and government. Inf. Pol. **15**(1,2), 1–9 (2010)
16. Commission of the European Communities: eEurope 2005: An Information Society for All. Commission of the European Communities, Brussels (2002)
17. de Kool, D., van Wamelen, J.: Web 2.0: a new basis for E-Government? In: 3rd International Conference on Information and Communication Technologies: From Theory to Applications, ICTTA 2008, p. 1 (2008)
18. Dovey, T., Eggers, W.: Web 2.0: The Future of Collaborative Government. Deloitte Research, Washington, D.C (2009)
19. Eggers, W.D.: Government 2.0: Using Technology to Improve Education, Cut Red Tape, Reduce Gridlock, and Enhance Democracy. Rowman & Littlefield Publishers Inc., Lanham (2007)
20. Ferro, E., Loukis, E.N., Charalabidis, Y., Osella, M.: Policy making 2.0: from theory to practice. Gov. Inf. Q. **30**(4), 359–368 (2013)

21. Freeman, R.J., Loo, P.: Web 2.0 and e-Government at the municipal level. In: World Congress on Privacy, Security, Trust and the Management of e-Business, CONGRESS 2009, p. 70 (2009)
22. Gayo-Avello, D.: Social media, democracy, and democratization. IEEE Multimedia **2**, 10–16 (2015)
23. Gov.uk. Social media guidance for civil servants: October 2014 — GOV.UK (2014). https://www.gov.uk/government/publications/social-mediaguidance-for-civil-servants/social-media-guidance-for-civil-servants. Accessed 20 Apr 2015
24. Grimmelikhuijsen, S.G., Meijer, A.J.: Does Twitter increase perceived police legitimacy? Public Adm. Rev. **75**(4), 58–607 (2015)
25. Guardian: Hillingdon goes for Google Apps [Homepage of The Guardian], 03 August 2012. http://www.guardian.co.uk/government-computing-network/2011/dec/19/hillingdon-council-google-apps/print. Accessed 19 Nov 2011
26. HM Armed Forces: HM Armed Forces|Facebook [Homepage of HM Armed Forces] (2011). http://www.facebook.com/ukarmedforces. Accessed 6 Jul 2011
27. Huijboom, N., Broek, T., Frissen, V., Kool, L., Kotterink, B., Nielsen, M.M., Millard, J.: Public Services 2.0: Impact of Social Computing on Public Services. European Communities, Luxembourg (2009)
28. Irani, Z., Love, P.E.D.: Information systems evaluation: a crisis of understanding. In: Irani, Z., Love, P.E.D. (eds.) Evaluating Information Systems: Public and Private Sector. 1st edn, Butterworth-Heinemann, UK, p. 20 (2008)
29. Johnston, P., Craig, R., Frissen, V., Stewart-Weeks, M., McCalla, J.: Realizing the Potential of the Connected Republic: Web 2.0 Opportunities in the Public Sector. Cisco Internet Business Solutions Group, San Jose (2008)
30. Klischewski, R.: Drift or Shift? propositions for changing roles of administrations in E-Government. In: Wimmer, M.A., Chappelet, J.-L., Janssen, M., Scholl, H.J. (eds.) EGOV 2010. LNCS, vol. 6228, pp. 85–96. Springer, Heidelberg (2010)
31. Mainka, A., Hartmann, S., Stock, W.G., Peters, I.: Looking for friends and followers: a global investigation of governmental social media use. Trans. Gov. People Process Policy **9**(2), 237–254 (2015)
32. Meijer, A., Thaens, M.: Alignment 2.0: Strategic use of new internet technologies in government. Gov. Inf. Q. **27**(2), 113–121 (2010)
33. Meijer, A., Thaens, M.: Alignment 2.0: Strategic use of new internet technologies in government. Gov. Inf. Q. **27**(2), 113–121 (2010)
34. Mergel, I.A., Schweik, C.M., Fountain, J.E.: The transformational effect of Web 2.0 technologies on government. In: Social Science Research Network Working Paper Series (2009)
35. Nam, T.: Suggesting frameworks of citizen-sourcing via government 2.0. Gov. Inf. Q. **29**(1), 12–20 (2012)
36. Nelimarkka, M., Nonnecke, B., Krishnan, S., Aitamurto, T., Catterson, D., Crittenden, C., Garland, C., Gregory, C., Huang, C.C.A., Newsom, G., Patel, J.: Comparing three online civic engagement platforms using the "spectrum of public participation" framework. In: Proceedings of the Oxford Internet, Policy, and Politics Conference (IPP), pp. 25–26 (2014)
37. Osimo, D.: Web 2.0 in Government: Why and How? European Communities, Luxembourg (2008)
38. Osimo, D., Campbell, D., Kerr-Stevens, J., Bishop, C., Bryant, L.: Public Services 2.0: Web 2.0 From the Periphery to the Centre of Public Service Delivery. European Commission Information Society and Media, Brussels (2009)
39. Randall, C.: e-Society. The Office for National Statistics, South Wales (2010)

40. Sander, T.: Government 2.0: Building Communities with Web 2.0 and Social Networking. e. Republic Inc., California (2008)
41. Saulles, M.: Social media and local government in England: who is doing what? In: Proceeding of the 11th European Conference on e-Government, Ljubljana, Slovenia (2011)
42. Schweik, C.M., Mergel, I., Sandfort, J.R., Zhao, Z.J.: Toward open public administration scholarship. J. Public Adm. Res. Theor. **21**(suppl 1), i175–i198 (2011)
43. Sivarajah, U., Irani, Z., Jones, S.: Application of Web 2.0 technologies in E-Government: a united kingdom case study. In: 2014 47th Hawaii International Conference on System Sciences (HICSS), pp. 22–21 (2014)
44. Sivarajah, U., Irani, Z., Weerakkody, V.: Evaluating the use and impact of Web 2.0 technologies in local government. Gov. Inf. Q. **32**(4), 473–487 (2015)
45. Dadashzadeh, M.: Social media in government: from eGovernment to eGovernance. J. Bus. Econ. Res. (JBER) **8**(11), 81–86 (2010)

Political Factors for the Adoption of Different Governance Models in the Provision of Public Services Under Web 2.0 Technologies

Manuel Pedro Rodríguez Bolívar[✉]

University of Granada, P.O. Box: 18071 Campus Universitario de Cartuja s/n, Granada, Spain
manuelp@ugr.es

Abstract. This paper contributes to the current debate on Web 2.0 technologies and their implications for local governance through the analysis of the perceptions of policy makers of local governments about the governance model to be adopted in the management of Web 2.0 applications for the delivery of public services. Also this paper analyses political factors as attributes that could explain the governance patterns to be adopted by municipalities. To achieve this aim, an e-survey has been performed by policy makers in Spanish municipalities. Findings indicate that policy makers are mainly prone to implement Web 2.0 technologies under the "Bureaucratic Model" framework, keeping the leading role in this implementation. Nonetheless, right-wing ideologists and majority governments are prone to implement collaborative models of governance, whereas left-wing ideologists and minority governments are in favor to implement non-collaborative models of governance.

Keywords: Web 2.0 technologies · Governance models · Public services · Political factors

1 Introduction

The use of Web 2.0 technologies in the public sector could be relevant to undertake the transformation of the roles played by citizens, who will no longer be mere 'end-users', but will become partners and co-creators of information and services [16], with the aim at obtaining more citizen-oriented services, which has led to a blurred distinction between production and consumption. Nonetheless, the use of social media introduces a number of policy problems, such as the interpretation of the information shared in networks or the loss of significant control over the content and applications [12].

So, the implementation of Web 2.0 technologies in public administrations is forcing a reconsideration of the administrative structures of governments and the fostering of open, user-driven governance [3]. In fact, a lively debate in the political arena is the governance model to be used in managing Web 2.0 technologies, which has led to the service-focused uses to be the holy grail of social computing, possibly the most difficult to implement successfully but most impactful if successful [6].

© IFIP International Federation for Information Processing 2016
Published by Springer International Publishing Switzerland 2016. All Rights Reserved
Y.K. Dwivedi et al. (Eds.): I3E 2016, LNCS 9844, pp. 607–618, 2016.
DOI: 10.1007/978-3-319-45234-0_54

This paper is focused on the field of public sector management and the influence that political variables could have in the perceptions of policy makers to choose the governance model if public administrations embrace Web 2.0 technologies in public sector delivery. To achieve this aim, a questionnaire has been designed and sent to policy makers of local governments in Spain. The findings indicate that policy makers want to play the leading role in the implementation of Web 2.0 technologies using the Bureaucratic model of governance.

This paper is structured as follows. Section 2 discusses the governance models under the Web 2.0 era and the influence of political attributes. Section 3 describes the empirical research and, finally, the discussion and conclusions bring the paper to an end.

2   Web 2.0 Technologies. A New Way for Co-production of Public Services and Public Sector Governance

2.1   Web 2.0 Technologies in Delivering Public Services and Public Governance

The implementation of Web 2.0 technologies has emphasized the idea of co-production in public sector services [8]. Four citizen co-production initiatives in the age of social media can be identified, termed "Citizen Sourcing" (G2C), "Government as a Platform" (C2G) and "Do it Yourself Government" (C2C) and "Bureaucratic Model" (G2G), in accordance with the interaction between citizens and government and with how citizens are involved in the co-production of public services [18, 33].

Under the "Bureaucratic Model" of governance (G2G), the government designs the strategy for the use of Web 2.0 technologies, produces the content and manages the network. Governments only seek to provide an innovative channel for its online representation and for broadcasting of government information about public services via social media sites [38] in order to reach a wider spectrum of citizens, what has been called as "screen-level bureaucracy" [5].

In the model termed "Citizen Sourcing" (G2C), citizens help governments improve public sector delivery in a participative framework [26] and share their opinions with government through social media channels [18]. Citizen-sourcing is, therefore, conducive to civic learning and may change the government's perspective on the public to "makers and shapers" of policies and decisions [19].

Under the label "Government as platform" (C2G), the government urges citizens to actively collaborate in the design and creation of public services. Social media channels are used to increase interactivity with citizens or to work in collaboration with government stakeholders on innovative ideas to fulfil the mission of government [38].

Finally, under the "Do It Yourself Government" (C2C) environment, citizens govern themselves with little or no interference from the government. Citizens are inter-connected through social media applications [7] and form an important addition to the government-centric form of public service provision, by fostering both the exchange of experiential information and social-emotional support [22].

All previous governance models should not be viewed as mutually exclusive. By contrast, governments can experiment some of these governance models over time as if

Co-production initiatives/Role of Governments	Non-collaborative	Collaborative	
	Executor (commissioner)	Partner (co-producer)	Initiator (facilitator)
"Bureacratic Model" (G2G)	X		
"Citizen Sourcing" (G2C)		X	
"Government as a Platform" (C2G)		X	
"Do it Yourself Government" (C2C)			X

Fig. 1. Classifying citizen co-production initiatives and role of government in the age of social media (Source: 19, 36).

they were a continuum in a line of development of governance of Web 2.0 technologies for providing public sector services. It determines the role played by local governments as a continuum of top-down to bottom-up processes from "executor (commissioner)" to "initiator (facilitator)" [35] – Fig. 1.

2.2 Models for Governance Web 2.0 Technologies in Delivering Public Services and Political Attributes

Political structures could affect both the likelihood and nature by which e-government activity enhances citizen participation [1] and the decisions taking regarding public services [40]. According to [2, 40], politicians have preferences for some policies over others according to their ideological attitudes. Indeed, political Ideology refers to a set of political beliefs or a set of ideas that characterize a particular culture. Right-wing parties have been linked to more pro-private business values (privatization) and to adopt e-government for collaboration with third parties to achieve efficiency and a cost reduction [11, 39], whereas left-wing organizations are conventionally associated with public values (public production). Under this framework, left-wing ideologists see the "do-it-yourself-state" as an instrument for empowerment whereas right-wing ideologists do not see a need for empowerment since this would challenge the existing order [23]. Therefore, our first political hypothesis is derived:

H1: Governments that operate in a more conservative political environment (right-wing governments) are more likely to adopt collaborative governance models of Web 2.0 technologies in the delivery of public services for ideological reasons.

On the other hand, [34] argue that political competition plays a key role in the decision of politicians to devolve institutional power to citizens. Political competition is the rivalry for the capacity to influence or determine official governmental decision-making and action on questions of public policy. Majority governments are those with increased political leadership of the government team and robustness in the face of managing public services [11], whereas minority governments are in the opposite situation. By contrast, prior research demonstrates that a high degree of political competition can create a favourable environment for technological reforms [39] and e-governance [37]. Thus the following hypothesis is derived:

H2: Minority governments are less likely to adopt non-collaborative models of governance of Web 2.0 technologies for political reasons because of political checks and balances.

Another political incentive of the development of e-government is the political stability [11, 17]. Although political stability is not a well-defined concept, it means the durability and integrity of a current government regime. In accordance with prior research, technological infrastructure and political stability are crucial factors for ICT-led development because its payoff will become apparent only in the medium to long term [11]. In addition, [24] emphasized that the level of political stability has the potential to influence the level of engagement by local citizens in productive economic activity. Therefore, the following hypothesis is derived:

H3: Governments in a more stability environment of the ruling party are more likely to adopt e-participatory government and, therefore, collaborative models of governance of Web 2.0 technologies for providing public sector services.

Finally, another political incentive to adopt participatory governments is the political strength, which can be defined as the party fragmentation of the local council. According to [33], coalition governments may experience some kinds of weakening due to internal conflicts. These governments show some problems of coordination and are less effective in undertaking budgetary reforms, which can affect to the implementation of e-government technologies. Therefore, the following hypothesis is derived:

H4: Governments with a high political strength are more likely to adopt e-participatory government and, therefore, collaborative models of governance of Web 2.0 technologies for providing public sector services.

3 Policy Makers' Perceptions on Web 2.0 Implementations in Spanish Local Governments

3.1 Sample Selection

Large cities have been at the forefront in the adoption of e-government innovations [14, 25] and use mechanisms that permit direct citizen involvement [30] due to the tradition of citizen participation at the local level [28]. Thus, this paper focuses on large Spanish local governments due to the managerial devolution process implemented in Spain in the 1990s [10] and their rapid introduction of new technologies to provide e-services [29]. Sample Spanish municipalities are those with a population of over 50,000 inhabitants, together with those which, although smaller in terms of numbers are provincial capitals, regional capitals or in which the headquarters of regional institutions are located. In total, 148 Spanish municipalities meet these conditions, and account for over 50 % of the total population of Spain [36].

Data were obtained by sending a link to perform an e-survey, which was sent to the policy makers of sample local authorities via email. The contact details were obtained from the Spanish central government's website. 7 sample municipalities had not yet introduced social networks, and thus neither had experience of Web 2.0 nor dedicated human resources to this area. Therefore, the questionnaire was sent to 141 local governments and 46 complete replies were received from policy makers - response rate, 32.62 %. Nonetheless, there were 107 incomplete responses to the questionnaire and,

Table 1. Characterization of the sample and Web 2.0 applications embraced by the local governments that answered all the e-survey questions.

Descriptive Statistics						
Web 2.0 application	Frequency		Number of Web 2.0 applications used/municipality	Frequency	Main Statistics	
	Number of municipalities (N)*	% Total sample municipalities				
RSS	34	73.91	1	7	Mean	3
Facebook	30	65.22	2	10	Median	3
Twitter	27	58.70	3	11	Mode	3
YouTube	20	43.48	4	6	Maximum	8
Official Blogs	10	21.74	5	9	Minimum	1
Flickr	11	23.91	6	2	Standard deviation	1.64
Tuenti	6	13.04	7	0		
Friend Feed	5	10.87	8	1		
Linked in	5	10.87	TOTAL	46		
Delicious	1	2.17				
Slice	0	0.00				
Formspring	0	0.00				
TOTAL	149					

NOTE:
* This column indicates the number of local governments that use each one of the Web 2.0 applications. In this regard, one local government can use more than one Web 2.0 application at the same time, as noted in the following columns of this table. The column named "%Total sample municipalities" is calculated using the number of municipalities that use the Web 2.0 application and the total number of municipalities that responded the e-survey (46 municipalities).

in consequence, for some questionnaire items, the response rate exceeded the above-mentioned minimum – Table 3 in Annex.

The official web pages of sample municipalities of the respondents were re-visited to obtain information regarding the use of Web 2.0 technologies. These technologies are being used by governments for the delivery of public services but in different ways. The blogs are used to provide updated information and to debate about a topic. Facebook is used to promote social and personal relations, which makes this tool useful for projecting a communicative image of governments. YouTube is more addressed to broadcasting, which allows governments to give full access to videos. And, finally, Twitter has a more hybrid character. So, the objective of each one of these tools and the level of citizen engagement are mainly different according to the technology used.

Table 1 shows that the Web 2.0 applications most commonly used for providing public services by the local governments sampled are RSS channels (73.91 %), Facebook (65.22 %), Twitter (58.70 %) and YouTube (43.48 %). In addition, the 93.47 % of the municipalities use up to 5 Web 2.0 applications at the same time in order to be communicated with citizens and they usually use 3 different Web 2.0 applications at the same time to be in touch with citizens (median, media, mode and the low value of the standard deviation in Table 1). Despite previous comments, data indicate that whereas some local authorities use eight different Web 2.0 applications (for example, Vitoria-Gasteiz), others only use one of them (for example, Alcobendas or Manresa).

3.2   Methodology of Research

To address the research questions established, a questionnaire was designed and sent to all policy makers in the sample municipalities with the aim at capturing their perceptions on the issues that are analysed in this paper. Policy makers were addressed in this survey taking into account not only their significant role in the policy-making process within local government, but also their direct involvement in the possible implementation of Web 2.0 technologies in public sector delivery.

The questionnaire was made up of 16 questions covering the role that local governments must play in delivering public services with the implementation of Web 2.0 technologies – Table 3 in Annex. Two draft versions of the survey were pre-tested on a selected group of stakeholders, to refine the design of the questionnaire items. First, the research team drafted a preliminary version based on the conclusions of previous work in the field of Web 2.0 technologies [7, 18, 36]. Then, the initial text was presented to two specialists on Web 2.0 technologies and to ten policy makers, to ascertain their opinions on the understandability and clarity of the questionnaire and the possible inclusion of other questions relevant to the study aims. Comments and suggestions made were analysed and incorporated into the text of the questionnaire. The link to the second version of the questionnaire was provided to the policy makers of each sample local government. Also, they were offered the possibility of clarifying any remaining doubts before completing the questionnaire.

Based on prior studies on attitude analysis [8], respondents were asked to describe their degree of agreement with each statement on a five-point Likert scale (from strongly disagree, "1" to strongly agree, "5"). Although the Likert scale has some limitations [15], they do not invalidate conclusions about the numbers [27] and the results obtained have proven to be robust, reliable and valid [27].

After the questionnaire was completed, each item was analysed separately using the median and the mode of the responses, because the mean can have scale problems [4]. Also, the tests of the hypotheses were performed using the multi-regression analysis and cluster analysis. In this regards, we estimate the following OLS regression:

$$y_i = \alpha + \beta_1 \text{POL IDEOLOGY} + \beta_2 \text{POL COMPETITION} + \beta_3 \text{POL STABILITY} + \beta_4 \text{POL STRENGHT} + \varepsilon_i$$

where y_i is the dependent variable (total score for "Do it Yourself", "Citizen Sourcing", "Government as a Platform" and "Bureaucratic" models of governance"), α is the constant of the equation, each of the independent variables analysed in this paper is represented by their name (Political ideology, Political Competition, etc.), β_i is the parameter to be estimated and ε_i is the error term.

Besides, based on [31], cluster analyses were performed using the k-means algorithm with the aim at identifying homogenous groups of attributes. Variables' description and basic statistics of political incentives are displayed in Table 2 in Annex.

3.3   Analysis of Results

Although the policy makers who responded to the questionnaire believe local governments could play any of the roles identified in prior research (initiator, partner or executor), the results obtained reflect their preference to act as executor (or commissioner) (mean scores for items 1.13, 1.15 and 1.16 – Table 3). Nonetheless, the respondents also showed their preference for greater openness in the information exchanged (median score: 4.5; mode score: 5) as well as for sharing government knowledge, infrastructure and other assets for use by the public (median and mode scores: 4). Thus, Information and Nudging is also a model in which respondents could be interested, while the municipal authorities would retain a leading role in the design and execution of public services delivery. This could be a means of enhancing e-democracy and at the same time help improve the government's image.

By contrast, the least-favoured model of governance of Web 2.0 technologies in providing public services is that of the Do-it-yourself Government model (C2C) (the median and mode scores for items 1.1, 1.2, 1.3 and 1.4 – Table 3) and policy makers are opposed to the creation of associations to represent citizens in managing the provision of public services (median and mode scores: 1). The co-production model of governance, too, obtained scores lower than those for the Bureaucratic model and the Informing-and-Nudging model. Respondents believe that, although effective collaboration between citizens and local governments should be encouraged (median and mode scores: 4), this collaboration should be conducted mainly in terms of enhancing the quality of information (median score: 4; mode score: 5) rather than via the co-execution of public services (median score: 3; mode score: 4).

Regarding the hypothesis testing, Table 4 in Annex shows OLS coefficients and Table 4 in Annex depicts the clusters analysis for each one of the governance models. Based on the OLS models, results indicate that the political ideology is a determinant factor for the model chosen to manage Web 2.0 technologies in providing public services ("Do it Yourself" and "Bureaucratic Model" – Table 4). By contrast, no significant association has been found regarding political competition, political stability and political strength. In Table 4, clusters analysis seem to indicate that right-wing parties are prone to implement the "Do it Yourself" whilst the left-wing parties are prone to implement "Bureaucratic Model" of governance. Thus, H1 is supported and we can conclude that countries ruled by conservative parties are more likely to adopt collaborative governance models of Web 2.0 technologies in the delivery of public services, than countries ruled by progressive parties.

The political competition is not significant for choosing a model of governance of Web 2.0 technologies for the delivery of public services. Therefore, H2 is not supported by the data. Nonetheless, it seems that majority governments are more prone to collaborative models of governance whereas minority governments are in favour of the Bureaucratic Model of governance (Table 4). This result does not support prior research which indicates that governments with broad electoral majorities are not motivated to remain cued to citizens' feedback [11].

Finally, regarding political stability and political strength, results indicate that these variables do not impact on the governance model to manage Web 2.0 technologies in providing public services. Therefore, H3 and H4 are not supported. This result does not confirm prior research that indicates that the higher level of political stability and the higher political strength have the potential to influence the level of engagement of citizens, promoting participatory governments [24, 33]. Also, no differences exist in the cluster analysis performed regarding these variables (Table 4).

As for the cluster analysis, results in Table 4 in Annex indicate that political ideology and political competition could have influence on the perception of policy makers regarding the model of governance when Web 2.0 technologies are used for e-services delivery. Collaborative models are characterized for being supported by right-wing ideologists and majority governments (clusters 1, 3 and 5 in Table 4), whilst non-collaborative models are preferred by left-wing ideologists and minority governments (cluster 7 in Table 4). In fact, right-wing ideologists think that "Government as a platform", "Citizen Sourcing" and "Do it Yourself" models of governance are the best models of governance with a focus on the "Do it Yourself" model of governance – clusters 1, 3 and 5 in Table 4 in Annex. By contrast, left-wing ideologists seem to prefer the "Bureaucratic Model" of governance (cluster 7, Table 4).

4 Discussions and Conclusions

Although social networks are forcing governments to foster open and user-driven governance [3], findings indicate that the main goal pursued by governments is the representation of the agency function through all available online channels. In fact, sample policy makers show a preference for the "Bureaucratic Model" and the "Government as a Platform" models, and wish to retain a predominant role in the implementation of Web 2.0 technologies for the delivery of public services, monitor and manage the Web 2.0 technologies directly, and are less favourable to the inclusion of citizens in the generation of content and information. This model of Web involvement shows that social media services are by no means immune to government censorship or government-sponsored censorship [20].

Also, findings indicate that the "do it yourself" model is preferred by right-wing ideologists, which indicate their preference for privatizing public services and leaving them to the market [2]. By contrast, the left-wing ideologists think that government must design and provide the e-services. So, senior officials are responsible for the coordination of all municipal Web 2.0 activities, which is agree with the findings of prior research regarding open communication [13]. Nonetheless, employee training could be a highly significant factor for networking and network management [9].

On the other hand, although political competition is not found a statically significant variable in governance models. Results indicate that majority governments are prone to implement collaborative models of governance whereas the minority governments are not. This result does not support prior research which has demonstrated that political competition plays a key role to devolve institutional power to citizens [34].

Finally, political stability and political strength do not impact on the governance model to manage Web 2.0 technologies for e-services delivery. This finding is confirmed in both statistical methods used (OLS and cluster analysis) and it is not agree with prior research which indicates that political conditions must be stable for e-government success [17]. Therefore, future studies should examine the relationship between the political stability and the use of e-participation as a medium of citizen participation, especially regarding e-services.

In brief, although the political value of e-participation applications has been seen as instruments of bureaucratic reform [1], our findings confirms other recent research findings according to which social media have their own logic, but it is only manifest when it encounters fertile ground within a government bureaucracy [21]. Only right-wing ideologists and policy makers of majority governments have indicated the collaborative models of governance, as the "Citizen Sourcing" or the "Do it yourself" models, and the role of co-producer as mainly relevant. But, are these findings influenced by the public administration style of countries?; Will the introduction of Web 2.0 technologies widen the digital divide? Can we use different modelling techniques to analyse this topic? For example, data panel techniques could be used if we can collect multiple data over time and its application could help to know trends in the topic analysed in this paper. All these questions remain to be addressed in future research.

Acknowledgments. This research was carried out with financial support from the Regional Government of Andalusia (Spain), Department of Innovation, Science and Enterprise (Research project number P11-SEJ-7700).

Annex. Results of the Research

Table 2. Definition of variables and descriptive statistics.

Variable	Description	Calculation	Source	Hypothesis	Cases	Mean	Median	Mode	Standard deviation	Min	Max
Total "Do it Yourself"	Total score in favour of this model of governance	$\sum_{i=item\ 1.1}^{item\ 1.4} q_i$	Based on data collection		46	12.76	13.00	12.00	3.11	5.00	20.00
Total "Citizen Sourcing"	Total score in favour of this model of governance	$\sum_{i=item\ 1.5}^{item\ 1.8} q_i$	Based on data collection		46	13.87	15.00	15.00	3.59	6.00	20.00
Total "Government as a Platform"	Total score in favour of this model of governance	$\sum_{i=item\ 1.9}^{item\ 1.12} q_i$	Based on data collection		46	16.17	17.00	17.00	2.76	7.00	20.00
Total "Bureaucratic Model"	Total score in favour of this model of governance	$\sum_{i=item\ 1.13}^{item\ 1.16} q_i$	Based on data collection		46	14.34	15.00	16.00	2.82	5.00	20.00
Political Ideology	Political Ideology of the ruling party	0-Right wing 1-Left wing 2-Others	Spanish Ministry of Public Administrations database	H1	46	0.61	0.00	0.00	0.74	0.00	2.00
Political Competition	Majority vs. minority governments	1-Majority 0-Minority	Spanish Ministry of Public Administrations database	H2	46	0.65	1.00	1.00	0.48	0.00	1.00
Political Stability	Numerical variable that proxies for the popularity of the party in office	Difference in percentage of votes of the ruling party with respect to the second most-voted party	Spanish Ministry of Public Administrations database	H3	46	0.23	0.19	0.12	0.15	0.04	0.56
Political Strength	Numerical variable that reflects the local governments' level of political strength.	$\dfrac{\sum_{i=1}^{n} p_i^2}{(\sum_{i=1}^{n} p_i)^2}$	Based on data collection. Herfindahl index is used, from 0 (maximum fragmentation) to 1 (minimum fragmentation)	H4	46	0.42	0.42	0.38	0.07	0.29	0.56

Source: Own elaboration.
Key: (1) dependent variables; (2) independent variables.

Table 3. Results for items related to the governance model and the role of local governments in the use of Web 2.0 technologies.

Questionnaire	Frequency	Response Rate	Mean	Median	Mode	Standard Deviation	Min	Max
RQ1. Governance model and role of local governments in the use of Web 2.0 technologies								
a) Initiator (Facilitator) (C2C). "Do it Yourself" model								
1.1. For Web 2.0 technologies to be efficient as a means of interaction between local governments and citizenry, citizens should be represented by associations but they should not interact directly with the local government as individuals.	46	32.62%	1.73	1.00	1.00	1.56	1.00	5.00
1.2. The creation of public/private/user/academic communities for the delivery of public services should be encouraged and developed.	53	37.59%	3.58	4.00	4.00	0.97	1.00	5.00
1.3. The implementation of Web 2.0 in providing public services gives an essential role to users of these services.	54	38.30%	3.72	4.00	4.00	1.00	1.00	5.00
1.4. Social networks and blogs are suitable spaces in which discussion topics and issues of interest for citizens can be put forward.	48	34.04%	3.83	4.00	4.00	0.95	1.00	5.00
b) Partner (Co-producer) (G2C) Co-production. "Citizen sourcing" model								
1.5. Web 2.0 technologies foster effective collaboration between citizens and government.	54	38.30%	3.67	4.00	4.00	0.95	1.00	5.00
1.6. Citizens may participate in the generation of content and information.	53	37.59%	3.15	3.00	4.00	1.20	1.00	5.00
1.7. The local government opens up a problem or activity for resolution or co-execution by citizens in order to tap into the unique skills, talents, and knowledge of the population.	54	38.30%	3.13	3.00	4.00	1.20	1.00	5.00
1.8. User contributions enhance the quality of information, and Web 2.0 describes these contributions.	53	37.59%	3.96	4.00	5.00	1.14	1.00	5.00
c) Partner (Co-producer) (C2G) Informing and Nudging. "Government as a platform" model								
1.9. The local government uses Web 2.0 technologies to openly share government knowledge, infrastructure, and other assets for use by citizens.	55	39.01%	4.20	4.00	4.00	0.85	2.00	5.00
1.10. Public sector information is released for use by citizens.	50	35.46%	3.70	4.00	4.00	0.99	1.00	5.00
1.11. Greater openness of all kinds of information is obtained.	48	34.04%	4.31	4.50	5.00	0.88	1.00	5.00
1.12. The local government uses Web 2.0 technologies to disclose information pro-actively, to open up the inner workings and performance of government and thus empower citizens to hold their government to account.	48	34.04%	3.92	4.00	4.00	0.85	2.00	5.00
d) Executor (Commissioner) (G2G). "Bureaucratic Model"								
1.13. A plan is created to document security controls, and this plan is reviewed at regular intervals.	46	32.62%	4.26	5.00	5.00	0.95	1.00	5.00
1.14. For Web 2.0 management, external advisors are hired to monitor government policies and procedures with respect to external communications activities.	46	32.62%	1.96	1.00	1.00	1.73	1.00	5.00
1.15. Local governments should designate a senior official responsible for the coordination of their Web 2.0 activities.	48	34.04%	4.35	5.00	5.00	1.08	1.00	5.00
1.16. Local governments must always play the lead role in the implementation of Web 2.0 technologies regarding the delivery of public services.	48	34.04%	4.42	5.00	5.00	1.43	1.00	5.00

Source: Own elaboration.

Table 4. Regressions and cluster analysis.

Regressions	Dependent Variable				Variance Inflation Factors (VIF) (no multicollinearity)
	Total "Do It Yourself"	Total "Citizen Sourcing"	Total "Government as a Platform"	Total "Bureaucratic Model"	
Constant	29.925 (3.396)***	22.663 (2.077)**	24.782 (2.492)***	21.354 (2.685)**	
Political ideology	-1.977 (-2.485)**	-1.062 (-1.078)	-0.944 (-1.241)	-1.980 (-2.758)***	1.711
Political Competition	0.000 (0.000)	-1.061 (-0.620)	-0.861 (-0.652)	-0.687 (-0.551)	2.160
Political Stability	1.896 (0.380)	7.889 (1.278)	3.568 (0749)	0.799 (0.178)	2.657
Political Strength	-7.595 (-0.603)	-3.370 (-0.216)	-5.474 (-0.454)	-4.469 (-0.393)	3.392
N	46	46	46	46	
R^2	0.196	0.074	0.064	0.203	
Durbin-Watson Test (no autocorrelation)	1.680	1.837	1.893	2.151	

Cluster analysis	Governance Models							
	"Do It Yourself"		"Citizen Sourcing"		"Government as a Platform"		"Bureaucratic Model"	
	Cluster 1	Cluster 2	Cluster 3	Cluster 4	Cluster 5	Cluster 6	Cluster 7	Cluster 8
Total score	20.00	5.00	20.00	6.00	20.00	7.00	20.00	5.00
Political ideology	0.00	0.00	0.00	2.00	0.00	1.00	1.00	2.00
Political Competition	1.00	1.00	1.00	1.00	1.00	0.00	0.00	0.00
Political Stability	0.07	0.19	0.07	0.24	0.40	0.08	0.15	0.19
Political Strength	0.47	0.45	0.47	0.43	0.38	0.43	0.35	0.37
N	24.00	22.00	28.00	18.00	37.00	9.00	37.00	9.00

Source: Own elaboration.
a) *Key for regressions analysis:*
Notes: None of VIF exceeded 4.79, which suggests that no strong multicollinearity exists.
t-value in parentheses.
Significance: ***1%, ** 5%, *10%.
b) *Key for clusters analysis:*
  (1) Political Ideology: 2.00 (Others), 1.00 (Left wing) and 0.00 (Right wing).
  (2) Political Competition1: 1.00 (Majority Governments) and 0.00 (Minority Governments).

References

1. Ahn, M.J., Bretschneider, S.: Politics of e-government: e-government and the political control of bureaucracy. Pub. Adm. Rev. **71**(3), 414–424 (2011)
2. Bel, G., Fageda, X.: Why do local governments privatise public services? A survey of empirical studies. Local Gov. Stud. **33**(4), 517–534 (2007)
3. Bertot, J.C., Jaeger, P.T., Grimes, J.M.: Crowd-sourcing transparency: ICTs, social media, and government transparency initiatives. In: Proceedings of the 11th Annual International Conference on Digital Government Research, Puebla, Mexico (2010)
4. Bertram, D.: Likert scales. From the University of Calgary, Department of Computer Science Web Site (2007). http://poincare.matf.bg.ac.rs/~kristina/topic-dane-likert.pdf. Accessed 28 June 2014
5. Bovens, M., Zouridis, S.: From street-level to system-level bureaucracies: how information and communication technology is transforming administrative discretion and constitutional control. Pub. Adm. Rev. **62**(2), 174–184 (2002)
6. Chang, A.-M., Kannan, P.K.: Leveraging Web 2.0 in Government. E-Government/ Technology Series, IBM Center for the Business of Government, Washington, D.C. (2008)
7. Dunleavy, P., Margetts, H.Z.: The second wave of digital era governance. Paper presented at American Political Science Association Conference 2010 Annual Meeting Papers, Washington, DC, USA (2010)
8. Emerson, T.L.N., Conroy, S.J., Stanley, W.: Ethical attitudes of accountants: recent evidence from a practitioners' survey. J. Bus. Ethics **71**(1), 73–87 (2007)
9. Ferro, E., Loukis, E.N., Charalabidis, Y., Osella, M.: Policy making 2.0: from theory to practice. Gov. Inf. Q. **30**(4), 359–368 (2013)
10. Gallego, R., Barzelay, M.: Public management policymaking in Spain: the politics of legislative reform of administrative structure, 1991–1997. Governance **23**(2), 277–296 (2010)
11. García-Sánchez, I.-M., Rodríguez-Domínguez, L., Gallego-Álvarez, I.: The relationship between political factors and the development of e-participatory government. Inf. Soc. Int. J. **27**(4), 233–251 (2011)

12. Graells-Costa, J.: Administración colaborativa y en red. El profesional de la información **20** (3), 345–347 (2011)
13. Harrison, J., Wessels, B.: A new public service communication environment? Public service broadcasting values in the reconfiguring media. New Media Soc. **7**(6), 834–853 (2005)
14. Ho, A.T.K.: Reinventing local governments and the e-government initiative. Pub. Adm. Rev. **62**(4), 434–444 (2002)
15. Hodge, D.R., Gillespie, D.: Phrase completions: an alternative to likert scales. Soc. Work Res. **27**(1), 45–55 (2003)
16. Johnston, E., Hansen, D.: Design lessons for smart governance infrastructures. In: Ink, D., Balutis, A., Buss, T. (eds.) American Governance 3.0: Rebooting the Public Square? National Academy of Public Administration, USA (2011)
17. Krishnan, S., Teo, T.S.H.: Moderating effects of governance on information infrastructure and e-government development. J. Am. Soc. Inf. Sci. Technol. **63**(10), 1929–1946 (2012)
18. Linders, D.: From e-government to we-government: defining a typology for citizen co-production in the age of social media. Gov. Inf. Q. **29**(4), 446–454 (2012)
19. Lukensmeyer, C.J., Torres, L.H.: Citizensourcing: citizen participation in a networked nation. In: Yang, K., Bergrud, E. (eds.) Civic Engagement in a Network Society, pp. 207–233. Information Age Publishing, Charlotte (2008)
20. MacKinnon, R.: Flatter world and thicker walls? Blogs, censorship and civic discourse in China. Pub. Choice **134**, 31–46 (2008)
21. Meijer, A., Thaens, M.: Social media strategies: understanding the differences between North American police departments. Gov. Inf. Q. **30**(4), 343–350 (2013)
22. Meijer, A.: Networked co-production of public services in virtual communities: from a government-centric to a community approach to public service support. Pub. Adm. Rev. **71** (4), 598–607 (2011)
23. Meijer, A.: The do it yourself state. The future of participatory democracy. Inf. Policy **17**(3–4), 303–314 (2012)
24. Meso, P., Musa, P., Straub, D., Mbarika, V.: Information infrastructure, governance, and socio-economic development in developing countries. Eur. J. Inf. Syst. **18**(1), 52–65 (2009)
25. Moon, M.J.: The evolution of e-government among municipalities: rhetoric or reality? Pub. Adm. Rev. **62**(4), 424–433 (2002)
26. Nam, T.: Suggesting frameworks of citizen-sourcing via Government 2.0. Gov. Inf. Q. **29** (1), 12–20 (2012)
27. Norman, G.: Likert scales, levels of measurement and the "laws" of statistics. Adv. Health Sci. Educ. **15**(5), 625–632 (2010)
28. Oakerson, R.J.: Governing Local Public Economies: Creating the Civic Metropolis. ICS Press, Richmond (1999)
29. Orange Foundation: eEspaña. Informe anual 2014 sobre el desarrollo de la sociedad de la información en España. Fundación Orange, Madrid (2014)
30. Peters, B.G.: The Future of Governing. University Press of Kansas, Lawrence (2001)
31. Rapkin, B.D., Luke, D.A.: Cluster analysis in community research: epistemology and practice. Am. J. Commun. Psychol. **21**(2), 247–277 (1993)
32. Rodríguez Bolívar, M.P.: Governance models for the delivery of public services through the web 2.0 technologies a political view in large Spanish municipalities. Soc. Sci. Comput. Rev., 1–23 (2015, in proof)
33. Roubini, N., Sachs, J.D.: Political and economic determinants of budget deficits in the industrial democracies. Eur. Econ. Rev. **33**(5), 903–938 (1989)
34. Smith, D.A., Fridkin, D.: Delegating direct democracy: interparty legislative competition and the adoption of the initiative in the American states. Am. Polit. Sci. Rev. **102**(3), 333–350 (2008)

35. Span, K.C.L., Luijkx, K.G., Schols, J.M.G.A., Schalk, R.: The relationship between governance roles and performance in local public interorganizational networks: a conceptual analysis. Am. Rev. Pub. Adm. **42**(2), 186–201 (2012)
36. Spanish National Statistics Institute (SNSI): Internet document (2014). http://www.ine.es/inebmenu/mnu_padron.htm
37. Sriramesh, K., Rivera-Sánchez, M.: E-government in a corporatist, communitarian society: the case of Singapore. New Media Soc. **8**(5), 707–730 (2006)
38. The White House. The Open Government Initiative (2009). http://www.whitehouse.gov/open
39. Tolbert, C.J., Mossberger, K., McNeal, R.: Institutions, policy and e-government in the American states. Pub. Adm. Rev. **68**(3), 549–563 (2008)
40. Ya Ni, A., Bretschneider, S.: The decision to contract out: a study of contracting for e-government services in state governments. Pub. Adm. Rev. **67**(3), 531–544 (2007)

Mobile Governance in Indian Urban Local Bodies: An Exploratory Study

Somnath Mitra$^{(\boxtimes)}$, M.P. Gupta, and Jaijit Bhattacharya

Indian Institute of Technology Delhi, New Delhi, India
somnathmitra@gmail.com, mpgupta@dms.iitd.ac.in,
jaijit@gmail.com

Abstract. This paper attempts to collate and derive insights from various initiatives on mobile governance by Urban and local bodies in India. The first generation e-governance initiatives by urban local bodies resulted in computerization of the legacy systems/practices in government with limited ability to internalize the advances in information and communication technologies (ICT). The paradigm shift from e-governance tom-governance results in radical differences in the key processes of creating, maintenance and usage of knowledge, creation of secure mobile transaction and delivery system, establishment of the appropriate infrastructural support for multi-mode direct citizen interface and delivery mechanisms. The paper identifies the various mobile app use case scenarios for residents, urban local body managers, system integrators, telcos, data services provider, and other stakeholders. Based on these mobile apps, it is attempted to classify the cities in various categories.

Keywords: Mobile app · Smart cities · Urban · Waste · Water · Energy · Transport · Governance · Mobile governance · Transformation Index · User Index · Environment Index

1 Introduction

The basic and universal corner stone of good governance are quality of service, quick response mechanisms and above all accountable and transparent process mechanism. The first generation e-governance initiatives resulted in computerization of the legacy systems/practices in government with limited ability to internalize the advances in information and communication technologies (ICT). M-government aims to make the interaction between government and citizens (G2C), government and business enterprises (G2B), and inter-agency relationships (G2G) more friendly, convenient, transparent, and inexpensive in designing, managing and administering public realm in urban local body as per Diatha [1]. New Urbanism principles and transect analysis should be conducted, followed by formulation of regulation plan, built form standards, public space standards, architectural standards, landscape standards, environmental resource standards and administration for the study area and are presented in the web for responses from public and to seek alternative design from citizen or friends of the city living world over. Experts examined how different types of knowledge are incorporated in governance processes, a swell as the extent to which spatial dimensions are included

© IFIP International Federation for Information Processing 2016
Published by Springer International Publishing Switzerland 2016. All Rights Reserved
Y.K. Dwivedi et al. (Eds.): I3E 2016, LNCS 9844, pp. 619–627, 2016.
DOI: 10.1007/978-3-319-45234-0_55

in such knowledge-building processes (e.g. GIS-based; maps, visualizations). Baud [2] examined mainly digitized processes of knowledge management. These are hybrid KM systems, with several modes of interaction (mobile phones, internet, face2face) coordinated by municipal administrations. Today's cities not only have to be interconnected, transit oriented, walkable and cycle-able, they have to be the smart cities of the future. As per Datta residents can drive urbanization through the back of your mobile phone [3]. Pfeffer provides a comprehensive state-of-the-art review of geo-technologies for spatial knowledge co-creation (crowdsourcing) and management for urban governance focusing on (1) the kinds of geo-technologies that feature in the urban governance area; (2) the discourses with respect to geo-technologies in urban governance processes; (3) the kinds of knowledge produced, used, exchanged, and contested in relation to quality of life, economic development and the ecosystem; and (4) the transformative potential of geo-technologies in urban governance processes. Through this review it draws out the capacities and challenges of geo-technologies for inclusive and sustainable urban development [4]. Janowski examined a range of digital technologies have become available to potentially help address such pressures including: government as a platform, i.e. "a common core infrastructure of shared digital systems, technology and processes on which it's easy to build brilliant, user centric government services"; mobile platforms to provide mobile apps to mobile devices; local big data and data mining; wearable devices and mobile health apps; and ad-hoc networks, compute continuum and Internet of Things [5]. Even more remarkably, these citizens are not necessarily concentrated in large cities (as in the case of the cluster "Countryside citizens"). This population may represent an important "market" to target in order to develop a habit of e-Government usage, for instance through innovative platforms and systems(e.g., mobile apps). As per Lamberti (2014) a balanced multichannel PA service provision, where online and offline channels are opened is required to meet the diverse expectations and needs by the different profiles [6]. Mobile App for Urban Local Bodies should be for three actors – Citizen, Technical Person, and City Stakeholder. This paper provides a comprehensive state-of-the-art review of geo-technologies for spatial knowledge production and management for urban governance.

2 Mobile Governance Ecosystem

Mobile Governance ecosystem consists of following stakeholder – Residents, Telecom Service Providers, Urban Local Body management, System Integrators, Special Interest Groups (like environmental groups, animal rights groups, Differently abled groups, senior citizen groups, women empowerment groups, cyber security groups, data privacy groups, academia and the likes), Regulators (TRAI), and Mobile Vale Added Service Providers (like Google, Facebook, WhatsApp, Twitter, Mygov.in, City Open Data, and the likes). The Smart City Mobile Data Ecosystem consist of (Fig. 1) namely - Mobile Value Added Service Providers (Telcos, GIS service providers, advertisers, and the likes), Basic Free Mobile Service Providers (DBT, Waste Monitoring, Water Delivery, Public Safety, Public Toilets, Services for Senior Citizen and the likes), Premium Mobile Service Providers (Traffic congestion, Utility Bill Payment, Weather data, Air quality data, Job data, Entertainment data, and the likes), Data Service Provider s

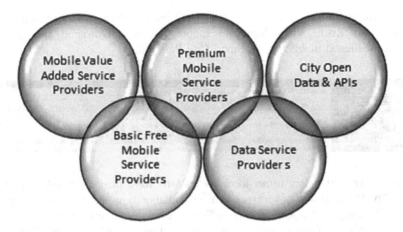

Fig. 1. Mobile app stakeholders in smart cities /urban local bodies

(Google, Facebook, Twitter, You Tube, Snapdeal, Amazon, Flipkart, Oyorooms, Zomato, DHL, FedEx, and other supply chain companies), City Open Data and APIs. Smart City Mobile Data Ecosystem is an intersection of mobile value added services, basic free mobile services, premium mobile services, data services, and city open data-APIs. The seamless flow of flow data/information will generate city knowledge for the city's residents, city's students, city tourists, city's senior citizens, city's pets and animals, city's economically weaker section, and other demographic segments.

3 Smart City Ranking and Number of Mobile Apps Proposed in Smart City Proposal

Service driven indices may be helpful in categorizing city into leader or laggard. Extending Linders (2015) [7] these are based analysis of Transformation Index, Customer (User) Index, and Environment Index of planned Mobile App of Top 20 Indian Urban Local Bodies (Table 1). These indices are leverage for Qualitative analysis and competitive analysis of top 20 urban local bodies in India. Transformation Index refers to relative impact of the mobile governance adoption by top 20 urban local bodies on transforming the governance, service delivery, and accountability of the urban local body, as assessed by the researcher. Customer (User) Index refers to relative impact of the mobile governance adoption by top 20 urban local bodies on resident engagement, resident collaboration, crowdsourcing, and community development within the urban local body precinct, as assessed by the researcher. Environment Index refers to relative impact of the mobile governance adoption by top 20 urban local bodies on air quality, energy saving, water quality, efficient water usage, waste collection-reuse-recycle-reduce, as assessed by the researcher. Urban local body of Bhubaneshwar, Pune, Jaipur scores highest in our research on urban governance using mobile app. Urban local body of Surat, Ahmedabad, Jabalpur, Sholapur score relative second highest. Urban local body of Dhavanagere, Delhi NDMC, Coimbatore, Belgaum / Belgavi, Udaipur,

Chennai, Bhopal lowest among the urban local bodies planning mobile app. Urban local bodies of Kochi, Vishakhapatnam, Indore, Kakinada, Guwahati, and Ludhiana have not mentioned mobile app in Smart City Proposal.

Parameter	Purpose
Smart City Rank	As declared by Government of India, Ministry of Urban Development
City Name (with score)	As declared by Government of India, Ministry of Urban Development
Number of Mobile App(s) in Smart City Proposal (SCP)	Smart City proposal as submitted by various urban local bodies to Government of India, Ministry of Urban Development
Transformation	The relative qualitative urban transformation impact the mobile app has on the urban local body vis-à-vis other urban local bodies.
Customer (Users)	The relative qualitative citizen engagement the mobile app has on the urban local body vis-à-vis other urban local bodies.
Environment	The relative qualitative environmental impact the mobile app has on the urban local body vis-à-vis other urban local bodies.

Summary. Top 20 Indian urban local bodies who have planned mobile app in the Smart City Proposal for governance, citizen collaboration and grievance redressal, energy efficiency, revenue collection efficiency, seamless service to tourists, and healthcare delivery. Transformation Index reflects transformation is urban local body governance, financing, and transparency. Customer (User) Index reflects ease of delivery urban local body services, complaints & redressal, and accountability of officials. Environment Index reflects cost saving due to efficient energy distribution, power distribution, water distribution, waste management, and the likes. This index also reflects air quality, water quality, and sustainable living.

Smart City Proposal of several urban local bodies carries plan to roll out mobile app for citizen engagement, service delivery efficiency, and innovative value added services. The competitive position of top 20 Indian urban local bodies in terms of Technology Adoption and Governance for Transformation Index, Customer (User) Index, and Environment Index, as assessed by the researcher (Figs. 2, 3 and 4). Based on discussion with experts (urban planning experts, policy experts, technology experts, and environment experts), this papers demonstrates high technology adoption in Bhubaneshwar, Pune, & Jaipur is translating higher degree of transformation. In the cities like Surat, Ahmedabad, Jabalpur, & Solar marginally low technology adoption (as compared to high technology adoption cities), demonstrates marginally low transformation. Cities likes Dhavanagere, Delhi NDMC, Belgaum, Udaipur, Chennai, & Bhopal low technology adoption, however mid-range transformation, because of matured municipal service delivery processes. Cities like Kochi, Vishakhapatnam, Indore, Kakinada, Guwahati, & Ludhiana are low on technology adoption, and so low on transformation. As per experts there is high technology adoption in Bhubaneshwar, Pune, & Jaipur and is translating higher degree of customer (user) index. In the cities like Surat, Ahmedabad, Jabalpur, & Sholapur substantially low technology adoption (as compared to high technology adoption cities), demonstrates marginally low customer (user) index, since in these cities customer (user) participation. Cities likes Dhavanagere, Delhi NDMC, Belgaum, Udaipur, Chennai, & Bhopal are low on technology adoption, and low on customer (user) index. Cities like Kochi, Vishakhapatnam, Indore, Kakinada, Guwahati, & Ludhiana are relatively high on technology adoption, however low on customer (user) index, because in-efficiencies in delivery of municipal services. As per experts there is high technology adoption in Bhubaneshwar, Jaipur, & Surat and is translating higher degree of environment index. In the cities like Pune, Ahmedabad, Chennai, Bhopal & Sholapur marginally low technology adoption (as compared to high technology adoption cities), demonstrates marginally low environment index, since in these cities environment data is effectively analyzed. Cities likes Jabalpur, Dhavanagere, Delhi NDMC, Belgaum, and Udaipur are low on technology adoption, and so low environment index, since environment data not properly collected. Cities like Kochi, Vishakhapatnam, Indore, Kakinada, Guwahati, & Ludhiana are very on technology adoption, and so low on environment index, because environment monitoring infrastructure is in-efficiencies and in-effective.

Table 1. Qualitative analysis of top 20 Indian urban local bodies

Smart City Rank	City Name (with score)	Number of Mobile App(s) in Smart City Proposal (SCP)	Transformation	Customer (Residents)	Environment	Remark
1.	Bhubaneswar (78.83%)	03	Mobile app planned to transform service for and Parking Mobile App. "Mo Sathi" women's safety, and Emergency response.	The app addresses safety concerns of only 50% of the residents.	The planned mobile app will help service delivery more energy efficient.	The apps promised in smart city proposal are towards women safety, better space utilization, and energy efficiency.
2.	Pune (77.42%)	03	Public transport ITMS transformation leveraging GPS, real-time tracking, health monitoring in buses, Smart bus stops. Grievance redressal and bill payment through website and mobile app. Pan-city Water Mobile App and Website to be completed by Dec 2016. Passenger Mobile App for passenger convenience. Advertisement on Mobile App for Passengers for location based services.	Potential to provide transport convenience to commuters and travelers.	The planned mobile app will help service delivery more energy efficient.	The apps promised in smart city proposal are towards citizen convenience, energy efficiency, and improvement of municipal service delivery.
3.	Jaipur (73.83%)	02	Transformative Smart Card Module-Register My Card, Check my balance, Recharge my card, and Help My reward points. Journey planning – Live Bus Time Module, Live Metro Times, Find nearest bus stop, Plan my journey and Help. Incident Reporting Module – Report Bus Breakdown, Report against driver, Report against conductor, Report bus delay, and Help. Transformation of Women empowerment using *MohallaNigraniSamiti* Module - Report Daily Collection by field staff, Report Missed, Collection or delay, Report improper ward cleaning Report Weekly Recyclable Collection. Incident Reporting Module – Report broken bin, Report overflowing bin, Report complaint against field	Seamless city wise smart card for multiple services has the potential to add convenience to residents and tourists.	Seamless city wise mobile app based smart card will help service delivery more energy efficient, water efficient, and waste efficient.	The apps promised in smart city proposal are towards for convenience to tourists, residents, energy-water efficiency and efficient service delivery.

(Continued)

Table 1. (*Continued*)

Smart City Rank	City Name (with score)	Number of Mobile App(s) in Smart City Proposal (SCP)	Transformation	Customer (Residents)	Environment	Remark
			staff, and Help.			
4.	Surat (68.16%)	02	Healthcare transformation "Aarogyam" Smart Health Mobile App and "Smile" Health Mobile Lab. Citizens are provided various options for easy complaint registration like through Whatsapp, single no. helpline, mobile app, website, etc. Centralized service delivery by developing SMAC Center (**SMArtCity** Center) for Mobile Apps, Mobile tickets, Social Media, M-Id (Mobile Id).	The app address one part of the Telemedicine value Chain. SMAC centralized plan to centralized resident and visitor management system.	Centralized service delivery center for mobile app service fulfillment request will help service delivery more energy efficient, water efficient, and waste efficient.	The apps promised in smart city proposal are towards mobile app based healthcare delivery (only ULB to promise that), and efficient municipal service delivery.
5.	Kochi (66.98%)	00	Not reported	Not reported	Not reported	Not reported
6.	Ahmedabad (66.84%)	02	Transformative public safety by Monitoring of CCTV feeds through mobile apps to improve safety and service standards for Citizen Safety and Integrated Transit Platform: Mobile App platform for planning and tracking commutes.	The app plans to enhance public safety and security using technology based intelligence and integration drones.	There is specific no focus of planned mobile app on improvement of environment related measurements.	The apps promised in smart city proposal are towards proactive public safety, and energy efficiency in public safety (fewer number of vehicles per residents).
7.	Jabalpur (63.03%)	01	Transformation planned by developing Unified Service Platform providing Government services of all departments and Online access to all the information and data.	An unified mobile app platform plan to get 360 degree of the services that are delivered to residents.	The planned mobile app improves water distribution efficiency, as residents do not have travel to register grievance and solution.	The apps promised in smart city proposal are towards ICT and mobile app based municipal service delivery.
8.	Vishakhapatnam (61.12%)	00	Not reported	Not reported	Not reported	Not reported
9.	Sholapur (60.83%)	00	The city aspires to have free wifi zones across the city.	Free Wifi service will enable easy access to mobile based municipal services.	There is specific no focus of planned mobile app on improvement of environment related measurements.	The apps promised in smart city proposal are towards mobile app based municipal service delivery.
10.	Dhavanagere (59.63%)	01	Plans to ensure the 24 x 7 energy supply with metering as well as pre-paid metering system to be controlled online and complaints suggestions exchanged through mobile apps.	The mobile app by municipality will ensure seamless delivery, billing, and grievance management of utility services.	The planned mobile app improves water distribution efficiency, as residents do not have travel to register grievance and solution.	The apps promised in smart city proposal are towards efficient delivery of municipal services and energy efficiency.
11.	Indore (59.89%)	00	Not reported	Not reported	Not reported	Not reported
12.	Delhi NDMC (59.63%)	01	Grievance redressal planned using 'PleaseFix' mobile app. Mobile app - POOCHO has been developed, which can help citizen to locate a vacant parking space and guide it through the traffic to reach it.	The mobile app by municipality will ensure seamless delivery, billing, and grievance management. The second mobile app is already available for residents and taxi drivers for usage, and improved collection from parking lots.	The planned mobile app improves energy efficiency of residents, as they do not have travel to register grievance and solution. Already rolled out mobile improves fuel efficiency of private cars and taxis.	The apps promised in smart city proposal are towards efficient delivery of municipal services and energy efficiency.
13.	Coimbatore (58.74%)	01	Plan to build Mobile Governance for Citizen Engagement transformation.	Mobile app plan to enhance collaborative citizen participation.	There is specific focus of planned mobile app on improvement of environment related measurements.	The apps promised in smart city proposal are towards citizen collaboration, and energy efficiency.
14.	Kakinada (58.19%)	00	Not reported	Not reported	Not reported	Not reported
15.	Belgaum / Belgavi	01	Plans to transform citizen engagement by various	Mobile app plan to enhance collaborative citizen participation.	There is specific no focus of planned mobile app on	The apps promised in smart city proposal

(*Continued*)

Table 1. (*Continued*)

Smart City Rank	City Name (with score)	Number of Mobile App(s) in Smart City Proposal (SCP)	Transformation	Customer (Residents)	Environment	Remark
	(57.99%)		mediums including mobile app and internet for every citizen upto ward level in smart city plan preparation, the same procedure will be adopted for all future projects.		improvement of environment related measurements.	are towards resident collaboration.
16.	Udaipur (57.91%)	01	Plan to transform tourist facilities by providing information regarding differently-abled friendly established, availability of wheel chair, audio guide, etc.	Mobile app plan to enhance ease of tourism to visitors, service providers, and municipalities.	There is no specific focus of planned mobile app on improvement of environment related measurements.	The apps promised in smart city proposal are towards for tourists, residents, energy-water efficiency and efficient service delivery.
17.	Guwahati (57.66%)	00	Not reported	Not reported	Not reported	Not reported
18.	Chennai (56.16%)	01	Plan to transform leveraging mobile apps based utility services, Public grievance redressal system using mobile app and SMS based systems.	The mobile app by municipality will ensure seamless delivery, billing, and grievance management.	There is specific focus of planned mobile app on improvement of environment related measurements.	The apps promised in smart city proposal are towards energy-water efficiency and efficient service delivery.
19.	Ludhiana (55.84%)	00	Not reported	Not reported	Not reported	Not reported
20.	Bhopal (55.47%)	02	Plan to transform heritage and tourist sites. Citizen participation transformation for maintaining cleanliness of these sites and capture tourist complaints. Mobile app based enabled transformed Government Services.	The mobile app plan to make the tourist friendly, contribute towards *Swaach Bharat*, and seamless delivery of services.	Mobile app indirectly help quality of air, quality of water, and efficient usage of vehicle.	The apps promised in smart city proposal are towards convenience to tourists, residents, energy-water efficiency and efficient service delivery.

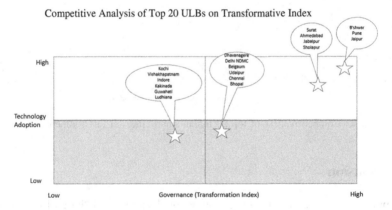

Competitive Analysis of Top 20 ULBs on Transformative Index

Fig. 2. Competitiveness of top 20 Indian smart cities on Transformation Index

Competitive Analysis of Top 20 ULBs on Customer (User) Index

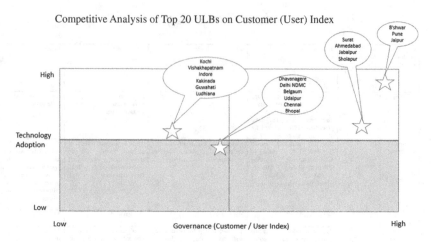

Fig. 3. Competitiveness of top 20 Indian smart cities on Customer (User) Index

Competitive Analysis of Top 20 ULBs on Environment Index

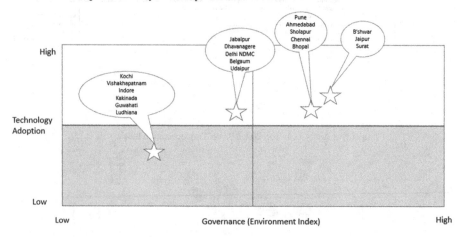

Fig. 4. Competitiveness of top 20 Indian smart cities on Environment Index

4   Conclusion

The rapid uptake of mobile technologies in remote locations and "base-of-the-pyramid" communities – together with the emergence of many innovative mobile applications and services, has increased the potential for ICTs to play a positive role in supporting and establishing good governance. In upcoming time, urban local bodies worldwide will be challenged by the need to look into developing m-government by adopting strategies that will enable them to harness the opportunities offered by mobile technologies and maximise their benefits (energy saving, water saving, power saving, and human capital saving) in order to provide better governance of the urban local body. Despite all its promise though, m-governance in urban local bodies still in its nascent stages and needs more research to improve the effectiveness of m-services development and to attain wide public acceptance and there are still limits in the capacity of m-governance in urban local bodies to reach out to "base-of-the-pyramid" segments of the population, and in order to not widen the digital gap, urban local bodies should avoid enforcing the use of mobile channels, and provide access to new technologies only to those who are willing to use them.

References

1. Sundar, D.K., Garg, S.: m-Governance: a framework for Indian Urban Local Bodies. In: The Proceedings of Euro mGov (2005)
2. Baud, I., Scott, D., Pfeffer, D., Sydenstricker-Neto, J., Denis, E.: Digital and spatial knowledge management in urban governance: emerging issues in India, Brazil, South Africa, and Peru. Habitat Int. **46**, 501–509 (2014)
3. Datta, A.: New urban utopias of postcolonial India: entrepreneurial urbanization in Dholera smart city. Gujarat. Dialogues Hum. Geogr. **5**(1), 3–22 (2015). Sage
4. Pfeffer, K., Martinez, J., O'Sullivan, J., Scott, D.: Geo-technologies for spatial knowledge: challenges for inclusive and sustainable urban development. In: Gupta, J., Pfeffer, K., Verrest, H., Ros-Tonen, M. (eds.) Geographies of Urban Governance, pp. 147–172. Springer International Publishing, Switzerland (2015). ISBN 978-3-319-21272-2
5. Janowski, T.: Digital government evolution: from transformation to contextualization. Gov. Inf. Q. **32**(3), 221–236 (2015)
6. Lamberti, L., Benedetti, M., Chen, S.: Benefits sought by citizens and channel attitudes for multichannel payment services: evidence from Italy. Gov. Inf. Q. **31**(4), 596–609 (2014)
7. Linders, D., Liao, C.Z., Wang, C.: Proactive e-Governance: flipping the service delivery model from pull to push in Taiwan. Gov. Inf. Q. pp. 01–09 (2015)

Smart Governance for Smart Cities: A Conceptual Framework from Social Media Practices

Harish Kumar[✉], Manoj Kumar Singh, and M.P. Gupta

Department of Management Studies, Indian Institute of Technology,
IIT Delhi, New Delhi 110016, India
harishkr08@gmail.com, manojksiet@gmail.com,
mpgupta@dms.iitd.ac.in

Abstract. The governance for smart cities must improve democratic processes, transparency in governance, citizen-centric development and political strategies for the cities. To achieve this, the government needs to gather information about citizens' perceptions, demands, development priorities, grievances, and feedbacks about policies that are being developed or implemented. To involve the citizens in governance, governments should facilitate multiple ways to citizens to communicate. Social media platform empowers the citizens to use technology oriented common platform to communicate among themselves as well as with government. This study proposes a conceptual framework for smart governance illustrating how the governance could be transformed towards smart governance through social media platform.

Keywords: Smart cities · Citizen-centric development · Smart city governance · Social media

1 Introduction

The governance includes all governing processes of political, social, economic, educational, development, city infrastructure and administrative work to enhance the prosperity and growth in the cities as well as country. The quality of governance [25] affects the development of cities. The smart cities are an ICT enabled city, which facilitates fast communication, real-time information to citizens, quality life, well connected transport, better civic services, health facilities, continuous energy and water supply, environment conservation and appropriate use of natural resources.

To maintain the self-aware nature of smart cities, citizens are expected to retrieve all information and participate actively in the government actions, development plans, and future policies etc. For the successful smart cities, citizens' suggestions, participation and feedbacks in government process are essential. Therefore, there is need for an efficient governance structure [8] and the two ways communication channels to make the city government smart.

© IFIP International Federation for Information Processing 2016
Published by Springer International Publishing Switzerland 2016. All Rights Reserved
Y.K. Dwivedi et al. (Eds.): I3E 2016, LNCS 9844, pp. 628–634, 2016.
DOI: 10.1007/978-3-319-45234-0_56

2 Literature Review

The smart administration, integration of various services, and multiple channels of communications [22] are required for the development of the smart cities. Social media has the unique ability to enable politicians and policymakers to mine user-generated data and content from their Facebook pages and twitter accounts to look for reactions to various policy proposals [23, 27]. The participation, collaboration and transparency in governance could be improved via open government policies [6, 19, 24]. The evaluation criteria of social media use in the Korean government [29] was developed among four dimensions i.e. openness of information, Promptness of information, mutuality of information, and control of information.

The social media could be used for citizen empowerment [16] and crisis situations [12]. Automation in governance [1] through e-governance has improved the efficiency and transparency in the government processes and services [9]. The government can use social media to discuss about implementation challenges, new services, monitoring the process, crowdsourcing over various issues to get the appropriate solutions.

3 Selection of Indicators for Smart Governance

Some indicators have been identified from the various research articles (Table 1) which are considered essentials for smart governance.

Table 1. Various indicators for smart governance

Citizen centric government [13]	Interactive monitoring process [2]
Quality of policy making [18]	Strategic urban planning [2]
Expanding the number and types of participants [18]	Transparency in government processes [2, 13, 18, 23]
Providing information to citizens [2, 18]	Public engagement [28]
Easy access to information for the citizens [13]	Planning and regional development [17]
Equality of participation [13, 18]	Citizens' feedback systems to government [2, 23]
Open governance [3, 14, 20]	Public perception [20]
Government innovations [7]	Increased degree of government openness [13, 23]
Response from target audience [18]	Collection of valuable opinions [5]
Decision making planning [28]	Public and social services [10]
Resource efficiency [8]	Understanding citizens' problems and context [23]
Responsible resource consumption [8]	Open government for direct and indirect effects [19]
Decision making process [18]	Citizen satisfaction [11]

(Continued)

Table 1. (*Continued*)

Political strategies [10]	E-participation [11]
E-Consultation [18]	E-empowering citizens [18]
Increased efficiency and effectiveness in government processes outcomes [2, 13]	Use of social media for crisis situations (traffic and weather etc.) [12]
Accountability [2, 8, 13, 23]	Creating a digital space from social space [23]
Increased collaborative ability [13, 18, 24]	Promote citizens trust [23]
Trust in government [21]	Crowdsourcing solutions and innovations [4]
Public Participation in decision making [10, 13]	Reduce difference in communications among govt. vs regions vs citizens [23]
City policy making [2]	Encouraging citizens participation [23]
Social Interaction [3]	Sharing of Information to create awareness [13, 15]
Organizational capacity [8]	Citizens' co-production [16]
Transparent governance [10, 23]	Public forum over social media [26]
Use of social media for critical situations (earthquakes and floods etc.) [12]	Direct communication channels between government and citizens [23]

4   Conceptual Framework and Discussions

Social media meliorate the government's vision, strategies, planning, leadership and resources utilization. The rapid increase in the internet usage and social media have forced government to show presence on social media for public engagement and mobilizing individuals. The study designs a conceptual framework with five dimensions to find the social media role to improve the city governance (Fig. 1).

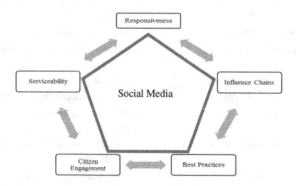

Fig. 1. A conceptual framework to achieve smart governance through the social media practices.

Table 2. Characteristics features of each dimension

Citizen engagement	Serviceability	Responsiveness	Influence chains	Best practices for smart governance
Public participation in decision making (E-participation)	Understanding citizens' problems and context	Response from targeted audience	Equality of participation	Citizen centric government
Improved decision making process and well informed citizens	Easy access to information for the citizens	Sharing of Information to create awareness	Expanding the number and types of participants	Providing information to citizens
Public forum for discussion over social media	Improved organizational capacity	Government accountability	Increased transparency in government processes	Transparent government
Citizens' co-production in development	Adoption of open data usage to innovate new services	Government innovations	Increased degree of government openness	Open governance
E-empowering citizens	Increased efficiency and effectiveness in government processes outcomes	Citizen satisfaction	Encouraging citizens participation	E-Consultation
Public engagement in policy making process	Responsible resource consumption	Taking public perception into consideration	Increased social interaction among government officials and citizens	City policy making
Citizens' feedback systems to government	Direct communication channels between government and citizens	Promote citizens' trust in government activities	Reduce difference in communications among govt. vs regions vs citizens	Interactive monitoring process
Collection of valuable opinions	Crowdsourcing solutions and service innovations	Resource efficiency	Quality of policy making	Planning and regional development
Creating a digital space from social space	Use of social media for crisis situations and critical situations	Increased collaborative ability	Strategic urban planning	Multichannel information delivery

The indicators for smart governance (Table 1) have been classified into framework dimensions (Fig. 1) based on social media involvement towards the smart governance. Table 2 shows the key role of social media in improving the city governance.

Citizen Engagement Through Social Media. Social media encourages the citizens to participate in government processes as a co-producer in the policies, decisions making and planning for the city development. The citizens can play an active role in giving feedbacks or suggestions to the government schemes and programs. The citizens may take part in government process at anytime from anywhere.

Improved Serviceability Through Social Media. The citizens may inform their problems and requirements directly to government officials through social media. Adoption of open data and crowdsourcing solutions through social media could lead to the new innovations and wisely resources consumption.

Social Media and Government Responsiveness. Information could be shared in fast pace over social media to create the awareness or to manage the disasters. Adoption of social media by government officials and responses over these sites would increase the government accountability and trust among the citizens.

Social Media and Influence Chains. Influence chains enhances the capacity of government to mobilize changes in the city as per citizens' requirements. E-participation over social media enlarges the scope of citizen participation and equality of participation among the citizens in decision making. Social media increases the transparency and openness in government via reducing the middleman in the government procedures.

Best Practices for Smart Governance. The facility for E-information, E-consultation and E-participation through social media fulfills the basic criteria of smart governance for a smart city. The interactive monitoring process for planning and policy implementations increases the transparency in the government.

Thus, the framework suggests that the social media improves government functionality, planning and reachability, and user participations for the cities development. Therefore, the social media plays a crucial role in the transformation of city governance into smart governance.

5   Conclusions, Limitations and Further Research

Social media is a two way medium for sharing the thoughts, feelings and opinions that could be used to deliver the smart solution for smart cities. It increases the potential of city government to grow into effective, responsible and well-resourced unit to improve the urban conditions. The smooth functioning of all systems, good strategies, integrated operations & maintenance, and controlled civic services to the citizens are the main keys of smart governance for the smart cities.

Government needs to set up the privacy and security solutions and also legitimacy check of the information spread over the social media. The effects of social media issues like privacy, authenticity of data, fake social accounts, hacking of the personal accounts, and misuse of social media to get political or religious benefits could also be considered while making the social media as an open governance platform.

References

1. Abdelsalam, H.M., Reddick, C.G., Gamal, S., Al-shaar, A.: Social media in Egyptian government websites: presence, usage, and effectiveness. Gov. Inf. Q. **30**(4), 406–416 (2013)
2. Baud, I., Scott, D., Pfeffer, K., Sydenstricker-Neto, J., Denis, E.: Reprint of: digital and spatial knowledge management in urban governance: emerging issues in India, Brazil, South Africa, and Peru. Habitat Int. **46**, 225–233 (2015)
3. Bertot, J.C., Jaeger, P.T., Hansen, D.: The impact of polices on government social media usage: issues, challenges, and recommendations. Gov. Inf. Q. **29**(1), 30–40 (2012)
4. Bertot, J.C., Jaeger, P.T., Grimes, J.M.: Crowd-sourcing transparency: ICTs, social media, and government transparency initiatives. In: Proceedings of the 11th Annual International Digital Government Research Conference on Public Administration Online: Challenges and Opportunities, pp. 51–58. Digital Government Society of North America (2010)
5. Bonsón, E., Torres, L., Royo, S., Flores, F.: Local e-government 2.0: social media and corporate transparency in municipalities. Gov. Inf. Q. **29**(2), 123–132 (2012)
6. Chun, S.A., Reyes, L.F.L.: Social media in government. Gov. Inf. Q. **29**(4), 441–445 (2012)
7. Criado, J.I., Sandoval-Almazan, R., Gil-Garcia, J.R.: Government innovation through social media. Gov. Inf. Q. **30**(4), 319–326 (2013)
8. de Oliveira, J.A.P., Doll, C.N., Balaban, O., Jiang, P., Dreyfus, M., Suwa, A., Moreno-Peñaranda, R., Dirgahayani, P.: Green economy and governance in cities: assessing good governance in key urban economic processes. J. Clean. Prod. **58**, 138–152 (2013)
9. Dixon, B.E.: Towards e-government 2.0: an assessment of where e-government 2.0 is and where it is headed. Public Adm. Manag. **15**(2), 418 (2010)
10. Giffinger, R., Fertner, C., Kramar, H., Kalasek, R., Pichler-Milanovic, N., Meijers, E.: Smart cities. Ranking of European medium-sized cities, Final report. Centre of Regional Science, Vienna UT (2007)
11. Jinmei, H.: Quality evaluation of e-government public service. In: 2011 International Conference Management and Service Science (MASS), pp. 1–4. IEEE, August 2011
12. Kavanaugh, A.L., Fox, E.A., Sheetz, S.D., Yang, S., Li, L.T., Shoemaker, D.J., Natsev, A., Xie, L.: Social media use by government: From the routine to the critical. Gov. Inf. Q. **29**(4), 480–491 (2012)
13. Kim, P.S., Halligan, J., Cho, N., Oh, C.H., Eikenberry, A.M.: Toward participatory and transparent governance: report on the Sixth Global Forum on Reinventing Government. Public Adm. Rev. **65**(6), 646–654 (2005)
14. Lee, G., Kwak, Y.H.: Open government implementation model: a stage model for achieving increased public engagement. In: Proceedings of the 12th Annual International Digital Government Research Conference: Digital Government Innovation in Challenging Times, pp. 254–261. ACM, June 2011
15. Li, H., Sakamoto, Y.: Social impacts in social media: an examination of perceived truthfulness and sharing of information. Comput. Hum. Behav. **41**, 278–287 (2014)

16. Linders, D.: From e-government to we-government: defining a typology for citizen coproduction in the age of social media. Gov. Inf. Q. **29**(4), 446–454 (2012)
17. Maas, L.T.: The effect of social capital on governance and sustainable livelihood of coastal city community Medan. Procedia Soc. Behav. Sci. **211**, 718–722 (2015)
18. Macintosh, A.: Characterizing e-participation in policy-making. In: Proceedings of the 37th Annual Hawaii International Conference System Sciences 2004, pp. 10. IEEE, January 2004
19. Meijer, A.J., Curtin, D., Hillebrandt, M.: Open government: connecting vision and voice. Int. Rev. Adm. Sci. **78**(1), 10–29 (2012)
20. Mueller, M.L.: Hyper-transparency and social control. Telecommun. Policy **39**(9), 804–810 (2015)
21. Nam, T.: Citizens' attitudes toward open government and government 2.0. Int. Rev. Adm. Sci. **78**(2), 346–368 (2012)
22. Odendaal, N.: Information and communication technology and local governance: under standing the difference between cities in developed and emerging economies. Comput. Environ. Urban Syst. **27**(6), 585–607 (2003)
23. Picazo-Vela, S., Gutierrez-Martinez, I., Luna-Reyes, L.F.: Understanding risks, benefits, and strategic alternatives of social media applications in the public sector. Gov. Inf. Q. **29**(4), 504–511 (2012)
24. Stamati, T., Papadopoulos, T., Anagnostopoulos, D.: Social media for openness and accountability in the public sector: cases in the Greek context. Gov. Inf. Q. **32**(1), 12–29 (2015)
25. Stead, D.: What does the quality of governance imply for urban prosperity? Habitat Int. **45**, 64–69 (2015)
26. Stewart, K.: Designing good urban governance indicators: the importance of citizen participation and its evaluation in Greater Vancouver. Cities **23**(3), 196–204 (2006)
27. Sobkowicz, P., Kaschesky, M., Bouchard, G.: Opinion mining in social media: modeling, simulating, and forecasting political opinions in the web. Gov. Inf. Q. **29**(4), 470–479 (2012)
28. White, J.T.: Pursuing design excellence: urban design governance on Toronto's waterfront. Prog. Plann. (2015)
29. Yi, M., Oh, S.G., Kim, S.: Comparison of social media use for the US and the Korean governments. Gov. Inf. Q. **30**(3), 310–317 (2013)

Expression in the Social Age: Towards an Integrated Model of Technology Acceptance, Personality, Civic Engagement and Social Capital

Vishnupriya Raghavan[1](✉), Marya Wani[2], and Dolphy Abraham[3]

[1] Manipal Global Education Services, Bangalore, India
vishnupriyaraghavan@gmail.com
[2] Institute of Product Leadership, Bangalore, India
malikmarya@gmail.com
[3] Alliance University, Bangalore, India
dolphy.abraham@alliance.edu.in

Abstract. We investigate the factors that affect the use of social media for civic engagement and social capital, and examine if online civic engagement also results in offline civic engagement. Using data from 282 university students, we find significant relationships between social media use, social capital, online and offline civic engagement. This study also tests the relationship between personality traits of individuals and how these traits relate to the use of social media for civic engagement and social capital. While agreeableness and conscientiousness are strongly associated with perceived usefulness of social media use, agreeableness was found to have a negative association with perceived usefulness of social media in the context of civic engagement.

Keywords: Social media · Civic engagement · Social capital · Technology acceptance · Big five model · Personality traits

1 Introduction

The use of social media presents new opportunities for citizens to express their opinions, discuss issues and initiatives of public interest, and display their commitment for a social cause [1]. Studies have shown that social media use helps mobilize social protests and movements influencing offline civic participation [1]. Social media use positively influences civic engagement through participatory behaviors, i.e., through free information exchange on news about civic matters, news and current events and interaction between users which may motivate more citizens to join a cause [2]. Prior research also suggests that online civic engagement promotes offline civic engagement [3] and it is seen as a precursor for engagement in physical communities, amongst young adults in particular [4]. Few studies on social media have noted that the discussion of community/societal issues in social media can encourage individuals to become engaged citizens [5] and this may also lead to social capital [6].

© IFIP International Federation for Information Processing 2016
Published by Springer International Publishing Switzerland 2016. All Rights Reserved
Y.K. Dwivedi et al. (Eds.): I3E 2016, LNCS 9844, pp. 635–645, 2016.
DOI: 10.1007/978-3-319-45234-0_57

The above arguments motivate our interest in investigating the use of social media in a culturally diverse and a young developing country like India. The use of social media during the 2014 General Elections [7] provides evidence to suggest that the use of social media has been gaining momentum in the country. Focusing on the role of social media for civic engagement, we address three important gaps in the extant literature.

First, although civic and political organizations use social media, empirical research on the effects of social media use on civic engagement is limited [6]. Second, online political groups may have an ability to foster offline political participation [8]. However, further investigation on the effects of online participation on political participation and civic engagement can help researchers understand the civic and political processes [8]. Third, there are few systemic studies that examine the factors that influence the use of social media [9] and effect of social media use on civic engagement [10].

It is important for policy makers and governments to understand how social media is used for civic engagement. Uncovering the underlying motivations to use social media would help academia and researchers to understand user behavior, and the *why* and *so-what* of social media use. Some studies have focused on the effect of personality on social media use and the resulting social capital and civic engagement [6]. However, studies report that the relation between personality and social media use (being a technology) may be mediated by technology acceptance factors [11, 12]. The mediating effect of technology acceptance variables will help researchers explain the effect of social media use on civic engagement more comprehensively. We use an integrated model that studies the effect of personality traits using the Big Five model, on social media use mediated by variables of the technology acceptance model (TAM), the effects of online civic engagement on offline civic engagement and the effect of social capital on online civic engagement.

2 Prior Research and Hypotheses

In this section we present the prior literature in the areas of social media use, civic engagement, personality and technology acceptance. We also present an integrated model that builds on linking personality, technology acceptance models, social media and civic engagement.

2.1 Social Media, Social Capital and Civic Engagement

Civic engagement commonly refers to "knowledge of, interest in and discussion of public affairs, as well as participation" (Haller et al. 2011 p. 5 – [13]). Civic engagement through social media includes knowledge, interest, discussion and participation, and information gathered about public affairs through social media [13]. Civic participation leads to empowering community members, developing critical awareness and performing citizenship [14].

Past work [15] has demonstrated the positive relationship between social media use and two forms of civic engagement; offline civic engagement and online civic engagement. Hence we hypothesize:

H1: Social media use is positively associated with online civic engagement

Online communities that promote civic engagement have been found to facilitate offline civic engagement [4, 16]. In order to study this phenomenon of online civic engagement through social media leading to offline civic engagement, we hypothesize:

H2: Online civic engagement through social media is positively associated with offline civic engagement

Social capital is defined as the "resources embedded in one's social networks, resources that can be accessed or mobilized through ties in the network" (Lin, 2008, p. 51 – [17]). Research suggests that social capital can be created from online relationships and interactions [18] and is referred to as 'virtual' or online social capital. We also measured social capital in the form of online social capital. Studies have found social media use to have a positive association with social capital [19] and also an antecedent for civic participation [4]. Based on the literature above, we hypothesize:

H3: Social media use has a positive association with social capital

H4: Social capital is positively associated with online civic participation

2.2   TAM and Social Media

A few studies have used a theory-driven approach to examine the psychological antecedents of civic engagement and of online civic engagement in particular [15]. Prior studies have found that perceived usefulness is positively associated with the intention to use social media [20]. Literature suggests that PEOU's influence on technology acceptance is moderated by PU [21]. Hence, we hypothesize the following:

H5: Perceived usefulness is positively associated with social media use

H6: Perceived ease of use is positively associated with perceived usefulness

2.3   Personality and TAM

Personality can be conceptualized as an individual's behavioral, emotional, and attitudinal response patterns [22]. For measuring personality we used the "Big Five" framework as it is one of the most widely used models in academic research [22, 23] which defines five personality traits of conscientiousness, extraversion, openness, emotional stability and agreeableness [24]. Prior research has empirically examined the effect of personality on behavioral intention (of using technology) mediated by TAM variables of perceived usefulness [11, 12, 25] and ease of use [11, 25]. These studies have mostly found support for the hypotheses studying the effect of personality traits on TAM variables.

People high in extraversion are likely to be high performers in tasks requiring social interaction like civic activities [26]. Such people are also likely to act based on their perceptions of what others think about them. In the context of civic engagement, high performers are likely to use the tools like social media to present themselves as competent in front of their peers.

H7: Extraversion is positively associated with perceived usefulness of social media for civic engagement

Agreeable people are generally viewed as kind, considerate, likable or cooperative [27]. In the context of civic engagement, these traits may be less apparent as individuals motivated to take part in an activity pertaining to solving a civic problem are more likely to be angry or disturbed about the status quo. Therefore, we posit that individuals who are less agreeable are more motivated to use social media for civic engagement activities.

H8: Agreeableness is negatively associated with perceived usefulness of social media for civic engagement

Conscientious people possess an intrinsic motivation for accomplishment. They are more likely to try to use the tools available to improve the performance of the task at hand [25]. They are more able to follow directions and make use technology effectively than people who are non-conscientious [28]. We therefore posit that conscientious people are more likely to see the benefits of using social media to support their civic activities.

H9: Conscientiousness is positively associated with perceived usefulness of social media for civic engagement

We use the construct of emotional stability to measure the emotional status of the individual based on prior studies [25]. Individuals taking part in civic engagement activity and who wish to interact and work with others need to be able to allow others to observe their work and to be able to handle criticism from others. Hence, emotional stability

H10: Emotional stability is positively associated with perceived usefulness of social media for civic engagement

People who rank highly on openness are more likely to learn new things and find new ways to carry out tasks [26]. The use of social media presents the opportunity for individuals to try a new platform to accomplish a social objective. Therefore, we posit that individuals who rank highly on openness will also be more likely to use social media for their civic activities.

H11: Openness is positively associated with perceived usefulness of social media for civic engagement

3 Method

The above review of literature reveals that although a number of studies have studied the impact of social media on civic engagement, and likewise of personality on social media use, the mediation effect of TAM factors has not been studied in a comprehensive and integrated model. In the following sections we explain our research design and analysis of data.

3.1 Sample and Procedure

To examine the relationship between social media use and civic engagement and to examine the factors that influence social media use, an online survey was conducted among undergraduate and graduate students including Executive MBA and PhD students of a university in Bangalore, India between January 2016 and March 2016. All the students received the survey's URL through an email invitation and three reminders were sent subsequently. A total of 2954 survey links were sent and 298 responses were received out of which 282 usable responses were used for data analysis making the response rate 9.6 %. Socio demographics included gender (female = 45 %), age (range: 18 to 84), and educational qualification (undergraduate = 60.9 %, graduate = 36.8 %).

3.2 Measures

All the subjective scales employed in this study are extracted from prior literature. The perceived ease of use and perceived usefulness were measured based on earlier studies [29], which was employed in the TAM literature [25, 30] in the context of personality traits and technology use. The personality traits were measured using part of the 10-item personality inventory [24] that has been shown to have adequate levels of reliability, validity and external correlates [24].

Social media use is operationalized using the attitudinal scale developed by earlier studies [31]. The respondents' online and offline civic engagement and social capital was gauged using the scale developed by earlier studies [6, 15].

3.3 Preliminary Measurement Validation

The pilot study helped establish content and face validity. Our examination of the psychometric properties of the scales showed Cronbach's alpha > 0.7 confirming acceptable reliabilities.

3.3.1 Reliability and Validity

Table 1 shows that acceptable ranges for composite reliability, and average variance extracted (AVE).

The two important validity measures, convergent validity and discriminant validity can also be inferred from Table 2. The AVE of all constructs are larger than 0.5 as

Table 1. Reliability and convergent validity

Variable	Cronbach's α	Composite reliability	AVE
Perceived ease of use	0.7384	0.8477	0.6502
Perceived usefulness	0.7552	0.8601	0.6726
Social media Use	0.8468	0.8909	0.6211
Social capital	0.9003	0.9226	0.6659
Online civic engagement	0.8980	0.922	0.6641
Offline civic engagement	0.8725	0.9066	0.6622

shown in Table 2 confirming convergent validity. Discriminant validity can be inferred as the indicators load higher on their measured construct than on other constructs; and the square root of the average variance extracted (AVE) is larger than its correlations with other constructs [32].

3.3.2 The Fornell-Larcker Criterion

Discriminant validity can also be assessed by the Fornell-Larcker criterion [33] which states that a construct has to share more variance with its corresponding indicators than with other constructs (Refer Table 2).

Table 2. Inter-construct correlations: The Fornell-Larker Criterion for Discriminant Validity

	AVE	PEOU	PU	SM_USE	SOC_CAP	CIV_ONL	CIV_OFF
Perceived ease of use	0.6502	**0.8063**					
Perceived usefulness	0.6726	0.4431	**0.8201**				
Social media use	0.6211	0.3695	0.6214	**0.7881**			
Social capital	0.6659	0.3669	0.6658	0.5915	**0.8160**		
Civic engagement online	0.6641	0.2254	0.2986	0.3700	0.4007	**0.8149**	
Civic engagement offline	0.6622	0.0646	0.2194	0.1565	0.2015	0.5942	**0.8138**

3.4 The Structural Model: Hypotheses Testing

Hypotheses are tested using the structural model. A 5 % significance level is used as a statistical decision criterion. The validated model with the structural path coefficients and their significance is illustrated in Fig. 1. The hypotheses that are supported are shown in Table 3.

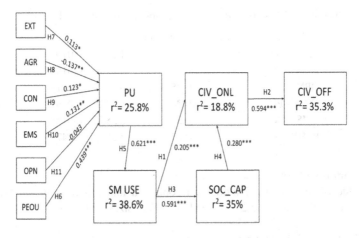

Fig. 1. The validated research model

Table 3. Test of PLS Path with Bootstrap

Path	Mean for path coefficient	Standard deviation for path coefficients	T statistic	Hypothesis
EXT→PU	0.1087	0.665	1.6946[c]	Supported
AGR→PU	−0.1401	0.0512	2.6826[b]	Supported
OPN→PU	−0.0445	0.0611	0.6954	Not Supported
CON→PU	0.1277	0.0677	1.8225[c]	Supported
EMS→PU	0.1281	0.0549	2.3836[b]	Supported
PEOU→PU	0.4459	0.0527	8.3313[a]	Supported
PU→SM_USE	0.6269	0.0362	17.1876[a]	Supported
SM_USE→CIV_ONL	0.2086	0.066	3.1012[b]	Supported
SM_USE→SOC_CAP	0.5948	0.0441	13.4065[a]	Supported
SOC_CAP→CIV_ONL	0.2796	0.0627	4.4581[b]	Supported
CIV_ONL→CIV_OFF	0.5996	0.0496	11.9774[a]	Supported

[a]denotes the significant path at 0.001; [b]denotes the significant path at 0.01 and [c]denotes the significant path at 0.05

3.5   Additional Validity Tests

3.5.1   Effect Size

The PLS structural model can be assessed by f^2 that is obtained by $(R^2\ incl - R^2\ excl)/(1- R^2\ incl)$ [34]. The f^2 values of 0.02, 0.15 and 0.35 denote small, medium and large effects respectively [35]. The effect sizes of various independent variables are presented in Table 4.

Table 4. Effect size - Relevant indicators for the structural model

Path	R^2 included	R^2 excluded	T value	f^2
EXT→PU	0.258	0.25	1.6946	0.0107
AGR→PU		0.244	3.573	0.0188
OPN→PU		0.257	0.6954	0.0013
CON→PU		0.246	1.8225	0.0161
EMS→PU		0.244	2.3836	0.0188
PEOU→PU		0.074	8.3313	0.2479

3.5.2 Goodness of Fit

A GoF value of the structural model was obtained and found to be 0.3478 which exceeds the cut-off value of 0.25 for medium effect sizes of r squared [36].

3.5.3 The Stone-Geisser Test

The Stone-Geisser test [36] also called as the Q^2 indicator is also used to assess the predictive relevance of the structural model. Using the blind folding procedure, the cross-validated redundancy of Perceived Usefulness (0.1559), Social Media Use (0.2312), Online Civic Participation (0.1176), Offline Civic Participation (0.2209) and Social Capital (0.2205) are found and are greater than 0 signifying the predictive relevance of the model.

4 Results and Discussion

We empirically tested the effect of social media use on online civic engagement (H1) and social capital (H3); social capital on online civic engagement (H4) and also the effect of online civic engagement on offline civic engagement (H2) and found support for all the hypotheses. We also studied the effect of personality traits identified by the Big Five model on social media use with extraversion, agreeableness, conscientiousness, and openness, having a significant effect on perceived usefulness of social media while emotional stability had no significant effect on perceived usefulness. It is important to note that we found agreeableness to have a negative significant effect on social media use for civic participation as was hypothesized. The results affirm our belief that in the context of civic engagement, agreeableness may not be a personality trait that the users of social media possess as individuals motivated to take part in an activity pertaining to solving a civic problem are more likely to have angst or be disturbed about the status quo. Perceived ease of use had a significant impact on perceived usefulness of social media. Perceived usefulness had a significant positive impact on social media use (H5).

It is interesting to note that social media is able to generate civic interest. This is an important finding for governments, civic action groups and other parties interested in using social media as an enabling tool for democracy. This may be because of the participatory nature of the medium as compared to other traditional media which may encourage users of social media to exhibit civic engagement. Another reason as to why social media fosters civic engagement could be the trust factor [6]. Social media use can create reciprocity and trust among its members which in turn fosters civic engagement and social capital [6].

Prior research shows that a significant part of discussions related to civic matters do happen online particularly amongst young adults. This means that, the more the respondents were involved in online civic engagement, the more they participate in offline civic engagement. The results corroborate with earlier findings [19, 37]. The fact that social media can be used as a platform for civic engagement is significant in the light of the fact that younger generations are more ardent users of social media and hence social media can be considered as potentially potent tool for civic activities in the future. The results help us understand how citizens use social media to spur civic action both online and offline [6, 23].

4.1   Conclusions

We believe that our study has advanced the scholarly debate on the transformative role played by social media. Our research has developed and empirically validated a new integrated theoretical framework that relates personality traits and technological factors on social media use and its outcome on civic engagement and social capital. We studied the role of social media in civic engagement using both, personality traits and technology perspectives, rather than just one of the approaches. The limitations of this study should be recognized. This study examined diverse age groups but the interpretation of the findings should be treated with caution as a majority of respondents belonged to the age group of 18 and 35. Our findings may be subjected to a self-selection bias, as younger adults having significant experience in using Internet technologies are more likely to respond to a web survey. Although this age group is best suited in the context of social media use, richer insights could be obtained with middle aged adults and senior citizens as well. While the model stresses the fact that personality traits do account for civic engagement, future research could include social traits such as life satisfaction, trust and personality factors such as loneliness. These types of traits can motivate people to express their emotions in social media. Future research can evaluate findings from information collected through qualitative and quantitative methods and also investigate moderator roles of socio-economic status, age group, education, income levels and network size. Despite these limitations, we believe our work strongly contributes to the growing field of social media research. The finding that online civic engagement positively influences offline civic engagement and also influences social capital is certainly promising for a country like India with weak infrastructure and civic apathy. Online civic engagement, if can spur offline actions that can become visible mass movements, engendering civic participation and engagement as the results demonstrate, can be a boon for developing economies in particular where citizens can work with the government to bring changes in the society.

References

1. Lee, F.L., Chan, J.M.: Digital media use and participation leadership in social protests: the case of Tiananmen commemoration in Hong Kong. Telematics Inform. **32**(4), 879–889 (2015)
2. Kim, Y., Chen, H.T.: Discussion network heterogeneity matters: examining a moderated mediation model of social media use and civic engagement. Int. J. Commun. **9**, 22 (2015)
3. Metzger, M.W., Erete, S.L., Barton, D.L., Desler, M.K., Lewis, D.A.: The new political voice of young Americans: online engagement and civic development among first-year college students. Educ. Citizsh. Soc. Justice (2014). doi:10.1177/1746197914558398
4. Raynes-Goldie, K., Walker, L.: Our space: online civic engagement tools for youth. In: Civic Life Online: Learning How Digital Media can Engage Youth, pp. 161–188 (2008)
5. Culver, S.H., Jacobson, T.: Media literacy and its use as a method to encourage civic engagement. Revista Comunicar **20**(39), 73–80 (2012)
6. Zúñiga, H.G.D., Jung, N., Valenzuela, S.: Social media use for news and individuals' social capital, civic engagement and political participation. J. Comput. Mediated Commun. **17**(3), 319–336 (2012)
7. Ahmed, S., Jaidka, K., Cho, J.: The 2014 Indian elections on Twitter: a comparison of campaign strategies of political parties. Telematics Inform. **33**(4), 1071–1087 (2016)
8. Conroy, M., Feezell, J.T., Guerrero, M.: Facebook and political engagement: a study of online political group membership and offline political engagement. Comput. Hum. Behav. **28**(5), 1535–1546 (2012)
9. Xu, Z., Zhang, Y., Wu, Y., Yang, Q.: Modeling user posting behavior on social media. In: Proceedings of the 35th International ACM SIGIR Conference on Research and Development in Information Retrieval, SIGIR 2012 (2012)
10. Bolton, R.N., Parasuraman, A., Hoefnagels, A., Migchels, N., Kabadayi, S., Gruber, T., et al.: Understanding Generation Y and their use of social media: a review and research agenda. J. Serv. Manag. **24**(3), 245–267 (2013)
11. Svendsen, G.B., Johnsen, J.A.K., Almas-Sorensen, L., Vitterso, J.: Personality and technology acceptance: the influence of personality factors on the core constructs of the technology acceptance model. Behav. Inf. Technol. **32**(4), 323–334 (2013)
12. Zhou, T., Lu, Y.: The effects of personality traits on user acceptance of mobile commerce. Int. J. Hum. Comput. Interact. **27**(6), 545–561 (2011)
13. Haller, M., Li, M.H., Mossberger, K.: Does E-government use contribute to citizen engagement with government and community? In: APSA 2011 Annual Meeting Paper, July 2011
14. Cicognani, E., Mazzoni, D., Albanesi, C., Zani, B.: Sense of community and empowerment among young people: understanding pathways from civic participation to social well-being. VOLUNTAS: Int. J. Voluntary Nonprofit Organ. 26(1), 24–44 (2014)
15. Jugert, P., Eckstein, K., Noack, P., Kuhn, A., Benbow, A.: Offline and online civic engagement among adolescents and young adults from three ethnic groups. J. Youth Adolesc. **42**(1), 123–135 (2012)
16. Bennett, W.L., Wells, C., Freelon, D.: Communicating civic engagement: contrasting models of citizenship in the youth web sphere. J. Commun. **61**(5), 835–856 (2011)
17. Lin, N.: A network theory of social capital. In: Castiglione, D., van Deth, J.W., Wolleb, G. (eds.) The Handbook of Social Capital, pp. 50–69. Oxford University Press, London (2008)
18. Yang, S., Lee, H., Kurnia, S.: Social capital in information and communications technology research: past, present, and future. Commun. Assoc. Inf. Syst. **25**(1), 23 (2009)

19. Park, N., Kee, K.F., Valenzuela, S.: Being immersed in social networking environment: Facebook groups, uses and gratifications, and social outcomes. Cyber Psychol. Behav. **12** (6), 729–733 (2009)
20. Lin, K.Y., Lu, H.P.: Why people use social networking sites: an empirical study integrating network externalities and motivation theory. Comput. Hum. Behav. **27**(3), 1152–1161 (2011)
21. Ma, Q., Liu, L.: The technology acceptance model: a meta-analysis of empirical findings. J. Organ. End User Comput. (JOEUC) **16**(1), 59–72 (2004)
22. Balmaceda, J.M., Schiaffino, S., Godoy, D.: How do personality traits affect communication among users in online social networks? Online Inf. Rev. **38**(1), 136–153 (2014)
23. Correa, T., Hinsley, A.W., Zúñiga, H.G.D.: Who interacts on the Web? The intersection of users' personality and social media use. Comput. Hum. Behav. **26**(2), 247–253 (2010)
24. Gosling, S.D., Rentfrow, P.J., Swann, W.B.: A very brief measure of the Big-Five personality domains. J. Res. Pers. **37**(6), 504–528 (2003)
25. Devaraj, S., Easley, R.F., Crant, J.M.: Research note —how does personality matter? Relating the five-factor model to technology acceptance and use. Inf. Syst. Res. **19**(1), 93–105 (2008)
26. Barrick, M.R., Mount, M.K.: The Big Five personality dimensions and job performance: a meta-analysis. Pers. Psychol. **44**(1), 1–26 (1991)
27. Russo, S., Amna, E.: The personality divide: do personality traits differentially predict online political engagement? Soc. Sci. Comput. Rev. (2015)
28. Rosen, P.A., Kluemper, D.H.: The impact of the Big Five personality traits on the acceptance of social networking website. In: AMCIS 2008 Proceedings, p. 274 (2008)
29. Davis, F.D.: Perceived usefulness, perceived ease of use, and user acceptance of information technology. MIS Q. **13**(3), 319 (1989)
30. Venkatesh, V., Morris, M.G., Davis, G.B., Davis, F.D.: User acceptance of information technology: toward a unified view. MIS Q. **27**, 425–478 (2003)
31. Ellison, N.B., Steinfield, C., Lampe, C.: The benefits of Facebook "Friends:" social capital and college students' use of online social network sites. J. Comput. Mediated Commun. **12** (4), 1143–1168 (2007)
32. Chin, W.W.: The partial least squares approach to structural equation modeling. Mod. Methods Bus. Res. **295**(2), 295–336 (1998)
33. Fornell, C., Larcker, D.F.: Structural equation models with unobservable variables and measurement error: algebra and statistics. J. Market. Res. **18**, 382–388 (1981)
34. Cohen, J.: Statistical Power Analysis for the Behavioural Sciences, 2nd edn. Lawrence Erlbaum Associates, Hillsdale (1988)
35. Ringle, C.M., Sarstedt, M., Straub, D.W.: Editor's comments: a critical look at the use of PLS-SEM in MIS quarterly. MIS Q. **36**(1), 3–14 (2012)
36. Tenenhaus, M., Vinzi, V.E., Chatelin, Y.-M., Lauro, C.: PLS path modeling. Comput. Stat. Data Anal. **48**(1), 159–205 (2005)
37. Vesnic-Alujevic, L.: Political participation and web 2.0 in Europe: a case study of Facebook. Public Relat. Rev. **38**(3), 466–470 (2012)

Predicting People's Intention Towards Sharing Political Contents in Social Media: The Moderating Effect of Collective Opinion

Mohammad Alamgir Hossain[1(✉)], Caroline Chan[1], and Yogesh Dwivedi[2]

[1] School of Business IT and Logistics, RMIT University, Melbourne, Australia
{mohammad.hossain, caroline.chan}@rmit.edu.au
[2] School of Management, Swansea University, Swansea, Wales, UK
y.k.dwivedi@swansea.ac.uk

Abstract. The purpose of this study is to establish and examine a model explaining sharing of political content in social media. From individuals' perspective, this study identifies two personal (i.e., altruism and social recognition) and two content related attributes (i.e., perceived truthfulness and value) that can directly affect sharing intention of political contents in social media. Moreover, the proposed direct effects are arguably contingent upon 'collective opinion'. The empirical results support all the hypotheses except the moderating effect of *collective opinion* between *perceived value* and *intention*. The implications of the findings and future research directions are also discussed.

Keywords: Political content · Social media · Altruism · Collective opinion · Perceived truthfulness

1 Introduction

The growing availability and affordability of high-speed Internet (especially using Smart phones) has increased the popularity and use of online social media and social networking sites (hereinafter, social media). Today, social media becomes an unprecedented way of providing information, comment, video, and image - content as a whole - to the community. One of the most attractive characteristics of social media is its support for user-generated content, transforming individuals from passive consumers of content to active producers [17, 26]. Social media has proved itself as strong enabler for political engagements demonstrated in recent political movements in the Middle East where political contents were consumed and shared very quickly, and by large numbers of people. However, the consequence of content sharing, especially political ones, are not always pleasant; in fact sometimes can result in ugly punishments. In social networking sites, some 'criminals' (read *activists*) may create a content that can be 'followed', 'liked' or shared by an innocent person who not necessarily supports the ideology of the content but still is vulnerable for trial. In December 2015, a man in Thailand has been arrested for 'liking' a doctored photo of the King and 'sharing' with 608 'friends' on Facebook; he could be jailed for 32 years [3].

Published by Springer International Publishing Switzerland 2016. All Rights Reserved
Y.K. Dwivedi et al. (Eds.): I3E 2016, LNCS 9844, pp. 646–657, 2016.
DOI: 10.1007/978-3-319-45234-0_58

In November 2015, another woman in Thailand was charged with 'sharing' of a similar type of photo; she had committed suicide [21]. In Saudi Arabia the penalty is as worse as execution for them who 'spread rumors' (not necessarily produce it) about the government on social media and 'cause confusion in societies' [1]. In spite of the susceptibility of such consequences, *"37 % of internet users have contributed to the creation of news, commented about it, or disseminated it via postings on social media sites like Facebook or Twitter"*, at least 17 % of the same respondents have shared these news [25, p. 4].

Despite the phenomenon and consequence of sharing political news in social media is growing, knowledge about the associated factors is not well documented in literature. Hence, it is imperative that researchers explore content sharing process - one best way is examining the determinants of content sharing in social media by individuals. Moreover, prior studies claim that, especially under uncertain conditions, factors might be influenced by collective opinion. Hence, the primary objective of this study is to identify the factors that influence people's intention to share political contents in social media; alongside, we try to understand how the roles of these antecedents are affected by collective opinion.

In order to answer the research questions, we developed a research model from literature. The model is validated by survey data using partial least square (PLS) modeling. We start this paper presenting the theoretical background and research framework, and then present data analysis techniques and discuss the results.

2 Theoretical Background

Looking at social media research in academia, reasonable efforts can be acknowledged that enriched the behavioral aspect of social media acceptance. However, relatively little is known about the mechanism of content sharing in social media. Yet, prior studies have identified some antecedents including perceived social attention/ recognition [9, 15], means of socialization [15, 17] or information and knowledge sharing [9], entrainment gratification (perceived enjoyment/hedonic benefit) [22], and users' prior experience [17]. In the context of political content sharing, we contend that some of the previously identified factors from generic content sharing in social media may still be relevant due to the inherent nature of participation. For example, seeking social status is relevant for political content sharing context too – a person might perceive that sharing political news in social media would support the belief that he is politically conscious, and sharing the news would enhance his social status than the people who do not. However, we recognize that some of the factors important for generic content sharing may not be applicable in our context. Factors such as *perceived enjoyment*, which is very important for generic content sharing might not be important for political content sharing [17]. Similarly, although prior studies documented that socializing is one of the strong drivers for using social media [22] and to participate in content sharing [17]; sharing political content, rather, may de-socialize a person with the people from opposite political mindset.

Our study incorporates both personal and content characteristics to provide an integrated model explaining people's intention for political content sharing in social media on the following rationales: (1) *altruistic motivation* provides an understanding explaining people's welfare tendency without consciously considering the benefits to own; (2) *perceived social recognition* is a fundamental dimension that explains why people share information with their reference groups; there are enormous political contents available over the Internet, but rational people would share the contents after (3) applying truthfulness judgment, and (4) evaluating the overall quality; and (5) people in a social media considers *collective opinion* as important to make a decision under uncertainty [27].

2.1 Altruistic Motivation

Altruism refers to one's sharing behavior that promotes welfare of others without conscious regard for one's own interest, and expectation of a return [7, 14]. Ma and Chan [20] proposed that altruism is performed voluntarily and is important for knowledge sharing particularly in social media environments where communities are formed based on common interests. They also suggest that, in online social environments, altruistic users are more likely to show their care for and offer help to others, intentionally. Other people contribute to communities because they enjoy helping others [10]. Similarly, other studies [e.g., 23] found altruism as a major incentive for sharing tourism information in online social media and claimed that, people show altruistic behavior from the mental obligation to repay the benefit they received earlier from the knowledge community. Also, Hsu and Lin [15] provided an account explaining the impact of altruism for sharing information in blogs. Proactive online activists come to know political contents from various sources and provide them to others as a one-stop source. They feel that they should share political content either to educate the community or to establish a statement. Therefore, we deduce the first hypothesis as:

> H1. Altruistic motivation will have a positive influence on people's intention for sharing information in online social media

2.2 Perceived Social Recognition

Theory of social exchange claims that, as opposed to altruism, individuals engage in social interaction and offer helps to other with the expectation to receive some forms of social rewards in exchange such as recognition, status, and respect [22]. Social recognition or reputation is a social variable that is evaluated and endorsed by other people in the society. In the current context, perceived social recognition (PSR) can be defined as the degree to which a person believes that active participation through sharing contents in social media platform would enhance his/her personal status among the other users [adapted from 15]. PSR is a highly acceptable variable in online knowledge sharing research illustrating that, people share information and knowledge because they want to be recognized (mostly informally) as an expert or aware individual than common individuals. Davenport and Prusak [7] emphasized that, PSR is an important factor in shaping behavior of the people in online information and knowledge sharing – people who share more knowledge receive higher social recognition. Thus, PSR significantly affect people's attitude towards participation in social blogging [15]. In fact, it is the strongest factor that enhances people's intention to share information within online investment communities [22]. Building on the above argument, we postulate that:

H2. Perceived social recognition (PSR) will have a positive influence on people's intention for sharing information in online social media

2.3 Perceived Truthfulness of Content

Literature is very limited on perceived truthfulness (PT), particularly in social media. Generally speaking, audience of any message tries to comprehend the truthfulness of it [24] before deciding its appropriateness [8]. Bauer and Greyser [2] found that PT of advertising, in general, is one of the dominant perceptual dimensions that explains people's reactions to it. Towards television advertising, Chan [5] claimed that PT is necessary to make people to like an ad and to attract their attention. The closest variable to perceived truthfulness is perceived credibility, which received reasonable attention in information sharing literature. For example, past studies suggest that when a credible source communicates a rumor, the believability and sharing of the rumor increase [18]. However, *"credibility is related to truthfulness in that more credible information should be perceived as more truthful"* [18, p. 279]. Social media contains millions of political contents and receive further hundreds every day; people are more likely to share the content, which they perceive as more truthful than be doubtable. Thus:

H3. Perceived truthfulness (PT) will have a positive influence on people's intention for sharing information in online social media

2.4 Perceived Value of Content

Perceived value (PV) or perceived usefulness has been consistently identified as a significant variable explaining user behavior; however, relatively is less studied in online social media research. PV can be defined as people's overall assessment about the quality and utility of an online content benefiting a given society. The utility theory stresses that – very often – customers do not buy a product or service for its own sake but they buy a 'bundle of attributes' which derive value [29]. For example, the value of an online content related to political issues is measured against few characteristics including informativeness, usefulness, derived value, helpfulness and so on [22]. Helkkula and Kelleher [11] claimed that the value perception process involves internal and external dialogue while it is created and co-created by customers to each other. Evaluating the value of a political content, people do not solely perceive the value to one but to include the society. In online social media, prior studies found that *perceived value* is a strong determinant of intention to share information [22]. Therefore, we propose that:

H4. Perceived value (PV) will have a positive influence on people's intention for sharing information in online social media

2.5   Collective Opinion

People do not find trouble accepting a good music or rejecting a bad one; popularity of the pieces in between vary depending on whether people know the number of download the music had [27]. Prior studies strongly claim that others' opinion influence ones' in online environments [18]. In social media environment, people liked a same news/story more when it had many existing supporters than had only a few [26]; interestingly, people even switched their preferences when the assumed numbers are flipped. In our context, people would share a message when they are certain about the truthfulness of it; but, for a statement that is debatable or uncertain, people tend to consider collective opinion (CO) and would likely share if it already received a good number of share or 'like'. Hence, a moderating effect of CO between perceived truthfulness and sharing intention of a message is plausible. Based on the prior work of Li and Sakamoto [18] who investigated the role of CO on perceived truthfulness and collective sharing likelihood of a statement in social media, our study investigates the moderating effect of CO on the antecedents to people's intention for sharing political content, which is:

H5. The relationship of altruism, social recognition, perceived truthfulness, and perceived value to intention for sharing content is moderated by collective opinion; that is, the relationships are weaker under conditions of low collective opinion and stronger under conditions of higher collective opinion.

3   Research Methods

3.1   Data Collection and Validation

We approached to seven online social networking groups in Facebook and Twitter that entertain political debates and contents. Among them, three agreed to host a link inviting people to our questionnaire. A total of 188 responses were usable for data analyses. Standard demographic measures were analyzed in order to characterize the sample. The sample is well distributed between male (54 %) and female (46 %). Among them, 45 % belong to 18-25 age group followed by 21 %, 12 %, 14 %, and 8 % within 26–33, 34–41, 42–49, and 50+, respectively. Majority of the respondents (73 %) have been using Internet for at least 4 years; and 47 % use social media for 2–3 h per day followed by 38 % for one hour or less. Majority of the respondents (57 %) follow the group as a source of entertainment, 21 % consider as a consolidated source of information (21 %), 15 % are highly concerned on politics, and 7 % are active in politics. We validated the collected data in two ways: first, testing non-response bias using Kolmogorov-Smirnov method; and then checking the common method variance (CMV) using marker variable (MV) technique [19]. Considering the exploratory nature of the research partial least squares (PLS), particularly *SmartPLS* (version 3.2.3, www.smartpls.de), has been employed for data analyses.

3.2   Measures

This study consists six constructs, measured using multiple-items used in prior studies. All of the indicators were considered as reflective and were based on a seven point Likert–type scale, evaluated and examined from users' perspective [11]. Specifically, *altruism* was measured by the instrument developed in [20, 28], *perceived social recognition* from [28], *perceived truthfulness* from [8], *perceived value* from [22, 29], and *collective opinion* from [26].

4   Results

4.1   Assessment of Measurement Properties

The measurement properties of the research model were assessed with convergent and discriminant validity of the measures. The first test of discriminant validity proves that a construct is more strongly related to its own measures than with any other construct in the model. Referring to Table 1, all constructs met the acceptable criterion for AVE (>=0.5), establishing reliability of the latent variables [6]. Moreover, the square root of AVE to construct correlations proves that each construct is more highly related to its own measures than with other constructs. Then, internal consistency for each block of indicators was examined applying two measures: Cronbach's α and composite reliability (CR) – Table 1 shows that all constructs met the 0.7 threshold value for both measures.

Chin [6] recommended that *"not only each measure be strongly related to the construct it attempts to reflect, but it should not have a stronger connection with another construct"* (p. 671). To address this, first, item loading of each item was calculated taking 0.6 as the minimum cut-off level [16]; following this rule, two items were discarded. Later, we compared the correlations of each item to all other constructs – Table 2 shows that no item loads higher value on other constructs than on the construct it represents, ensuring discriminant validity at item level. Then, convergent validity was examined. Although there is no set prescription, 'the narrower the range and higher the lowest loading' ensures convergent validity; our range of item loading (0.601-0.891) confirms no issue with convergent validity.

Table 1. Psychometric property of the constructs

CR	AVE	α	Constructs	AM	PSR	PT	PV	CO	INT
0.784	0.502	0.701	Altruistic motivation	**0.709**					
0.848	0.528	0.776	Perceived social recognition	0.501	**0.726**				
0.839	0.570	0.767	Perceived truthfulness	0.208	0.156	**0.755**			
0.808	0.521	0.706	Perceived value	0.509	0.581	0.241	**0.722**		
0.855	0.664	0.746	Collective opinion	0.279	0.439	0.202	0.397	**0.815**	
0.883	0.717	0.803	Intention to share	0.458	0.562	0.295	0.518	0.324	**0.847**

Table 2. Outer model loadings and cross-loadings

	Items		AM	PSR	PT	PV	CO	INT
Altruistic motivation (AM)	Feels good helping someone	AM1	**0.790**	0.365	0.239	0.428	0.248	0.391
	Sharing content gives pleasure	AM2	**0.736**	0.440	0.106	0.418	0.258	0.405
	I enjoy sharing	AM3	**0.614**	0.239	0.087	0.209	0.031	0.160
	I enjoy helping others	AM4	**0.609**	0.267	0.105	0.239	0.106	0.153
Perceived social recognition (PSR)	Sharing improves my image	PSR1	0.352	**0.658**	0.097	0.334	0.219	0.326
	Increases prestige when shared	PSR2	0.392	**0.745**	0.030	0.390	0.250	0.463
	Sharing improves recognition	PSR3	0.445	**0.684**	0.226	0.355	0.298	0.353
	I earn respect by sharing	PSR4	0.299	**0.754**	0.131	0.482	0.438	0.416
	Enhances personal status	PSR5	0.349	**0.783**	0.111	0.525	0.376	0.459
Perceived truthfulness (PT)	[#] Appear to be truthful	PT1	0.024	0.040	**0.601**	0.068	0.054	0.089
	[#] Are credible	PT2	0.219	0.186	**0.762**	0.286	0.224	0.265
	[#] Are believable	PT3	0.126	0.007	**0.757**	0.099	0.056	0.114
	[#] Are not exaggerated	PT4	0.171	0.167	**0.878**	0.175	0.171	0.291
Perceived value (PV)	[#] Are valuable	PV1	0.348	0.578	0.168	**0.811**	0.391	0.427
	[#] Offer high utility	PV2	0.417	0.476	0.092	**0.860**	0.345	0.487
	[#] Are helpful	PV3	0.444	0.324	0.208	**0.620**	0.183	0.265
	[#] Are informative	PV4	0.297	0.222	0.344	0.551^d	0.159	0.252
Collective opinion (CO)	[*] is important to me	CO1	0.223	0.301	0.184	0.334	**0.764**	0.241
	[*] shapes my judgment	CO2	0.243	0.384	0.153	0.332	**0.861**	0.298
	[*] receives higher attention	CO3	0.213	0.384	0.160	0.305	**0.817**	0.247
Intention to share (INT)	I try to share regularly	INT1	0.276	0.386	0.226	0.319	0.174	**0.757**
	My intention is sharing	INT2	0.450	0.483	0.213	0.466	0.287	**0.885**
	I intend to increase sharing	INT3	0.416	0.542	0.303	0.505	0.336	**0.891**
	I intend to recommend others	INT4	0.276	0.348	0.080	0.309	0.365	0.521^d

d - discarded; [#: political contents in online social media], [*: High numbers of like/share/follow]

4.2   Assessment of the Structural Model

For assessing the structural model, the direction of path coefficient, magnitude of t-statistics, and explanatory power of the independent variables (R^2) were checked. The results, summarized in Table 3, find that all four primary hypotheses are supported while our model 'moderately' explains 44.7 % of the variance of people's intention to share political content in social media [13, p. 303].

Table 3.   Structural properties of the constructs

Hypothesis	Path coefficient	Standard deviation	t statistics	p Values
H1: Altruistic motivation → Intention	0.157*	0.069	2.275	0.023
H2: Perceived social recognition → Intention	0.366***	0.067	5.469	0.000
H3: Perceived truthfulness of content → Intention	0.142**	0.047	3.053	0.002
H4: Perceived value of content → Intention	0.213**	0.076	2.806	0.005

Significance level *p < 0.05, **p < 0.01, ***p < 0.001

4.3   Assessing the Moderating Effect

In order to examine the moderating effect of *collective opinion*, we used PLS product-indicator approach. In this process, for *altruistic motivation* for example, we developed a dummy variable consisting 16 indicators (product term between the indicators of the exogenous variable and moderator) [see 12 for detail]. To claim a moderation effect, the path coefficient between interaction term and the endogenous variable has to be significant. In our case the moderating effect of *collective opinion* is established except for *perceived value*.

5   Discussion and Implication

Now a day, sharing political contents in online social media becomes a regular activity. It is not that people are becoming more politically concerned than before; rather they now have easy access to technologies (Web 2.0 and social networking applications) than in previous years. If the sacrifice is affordable, what one knows should be known by others. Moreover, they can now verify – to some extent – the credibility of the content. Hence, sharing political content online can be viewed as an agglomeration of the characteristics of the content itself and the sharer's perceptions.

5.1   Effect of Personal Characteristics

The results established that, overall, people intent to share political content in social media when they perceive that the content is truthful and possesses value to a given society. Interestingly, people share contents without expecting any external rewards or returns (altruism) but, at the same time, feel a strong need for personal recognition and prestige – consistent with prior studies [e.g., 4].

Supporting the first hypothesis, our results find that *altruistic motivation* (AM) is one of the influencing factors that drive people to share political content in social media ($\beta = 0.157$; $t = 2.275$; $p = 0.023$). Also, the moderating effect of *collective opinion* between AM and *Intention* is supported ($\beta = 0.561$; $t = 2.384$; $p = 0.017$). Despite some researchers' doubt, previous studies revealed that altruism 'does exist' and is a part of human nature and inner desire [24]. Helping others is a common tendency of most people [28]; such 'other-regarding sentiments' give them contentment by contributing to public goods but benefiting little to oneself. Specifically in online media, the sacrifice against fulfilling such desire is minimal; it requires relatively less effort, time, and costs than tradition media to share in. For political content in particular, a person feels mental obligation or social justice that other people in his group should know and be aware of. Generally, the contents related to corruption, incapability, conspiracy, and mockery of a government are most likely to be shared. Sharing such political content fulfill the need of forming collective outlook e.g., liking or detestation to a political entity. Such tendency is more prominent when the content receives substantial support from a collective group considering that it benefitted a numbers of people and thus would contribute to social justice, thus worthy of sharing.

As proposed in hypothesis H2, people perceive that their social recognition will be increased if they share political contents on social media; in fact, it came as the strongest antecedent ($\beta = 0.366$; $t = 5.469$; $p = 0.000$). Standing at the core of social capital literature, since the past to present, people feel a desire to be recognized. People who expect social recognition develop interpersonal relationships and are more likely to share political content with others in the communities, consistent with prior studies [e.g., 22]. Also, sharing a content would enhance prestige when the content's merit is already established by collective opinion, assuming that the content would be further shared a number of times and would contribute to one's prestige who share than who do not ($\beta = 0.679$; $t = 2.319$; $p = 0.021$). The outcome of this is that people do not usually share a political content, which failed to receive attention by prior readers (indicated by share/like with respect to elapsed time since the incident occurred).

5.2   Effect of Content Attributes

Every individual shares one of the two opposite opinions (e.g., for or against, true or false, believable or not believable) and share the opinion by interacting with its neighbors in a physical or virtual communication field. Assuming him/her as a rational social being, the tendency to let other people know about the content depends on the quality of the message such as credibility of it. Our third hypothesis exhibited a significant relationship between *perceived truthfulness* (PT) and *intention* to share

($\beta = 0.142$; $t = 3.053$; $p = 0.002$). People's intention to share political content should develop if the truthfulness is appropriately managed. As a means to enhance truthfulness, the content should contain some specific details including source and authenticity of the source, if verified and verification method, and so on [8]. Our data analysis established that *collective opinion* (CO) would have significant moderating influence on the relationship between PT and *intention* ($\beta = 0.364$; $t = 2.092$; $p = 0.037$). That means, the relation between PT and *intention* is more prominent under the influence of CO; i.e., when CO is low PT will have less effect on *intention* compared to when CO is high. Higher CO enhances people's confidence on the truthfulness of a political content trusting that less truthful contents are rejected by most people and are not disseminated.

Lastly, the fourth hypothesis posited that *perceived value* (PV) of the content would have a positive influence on people's intention towards sharing political content in social media. The study revealed a significant result ($\beta = 0.213$; $t = 2.806$; $p = 0.005$), and thus accepting the H4. It is evident that political content becomes viral when they attract readership and are shared by people, and thus in turn contributes to the popularity of the content generator. This finding implies that, content developers should pay close attention on enhancing value proposition. Also, PV is a relative term and is "uniquely and phenomenologically" determined by the user [30, p. 7] based on his/her expertise or knowledge about the subject matter; therefore the moderating role of collective opinion should have least effect – it is supported by our data analysis ($\beta = 0.279$; $t = 1.45$; $p = 0.148$). Therefore, targeting the audience of political contents based on people's socio-academic background is important for these to be shared.

5.3   Theoretical Contributions

The primary contribution of this study is investigating people's attitude in the context of political content sharing in social media. To the best of our knowledge, past research in online social media was silent if truthfulness judgment of a message affects its sharing – our study provided support in favor of it. As the second contribution, we contemplated in a single model that, people's attitude to share political contents not only is reflected by their inherent psychological factors (i.e., altruism motivation and social recognition) but the perceived merit of the message too (i.e., perceived truthfulness and value). Moreover, although previous studies claimed that one's decision is influenced by others' opinion but the nature of such impact was unclear in literature: do the opinions of others actually contribute to form one's perception of the story? Hence, the third theoretical contribution of the current study is to investigate the effect of *collective opinion* in content sharing. Now it is clear that *collective opinion* increases truthfulness of a political content but does not change the perception on its value, also a story liked/shared by many others is expected to contribute to the welfare of others, and improve people's reputation if further shared.

5.4 Limitations

Despite contributing new and valuable insights to social media literature, this study has some limitations. First, people's political orientation could be a strong predictor or moderator of political content sharing in social media – it is beyond the scope of this current study and would be worthwhile to study in future. Also, the use of political discussion groups only in the survey limits the perceptions of people who share political contents in common groups, and worthy to be included. Second, few prior studies claim that *perceived value* is a multi-dimensional construct which may include hedonic and social value in addition to utilitarian value [11], we considered it as a first-order construct. Future study could examine the contribution of the multi-dimensional constructs related to *perceived value* in a hierarchical model. Third, we used self-reported survey that might result self-selection bias. Although the CMB tests did not expose any concern on the data quality, still it was not possible to claim strongly that data are free from such bias. Future research could use actual data on political content sharing and thus would be more confident to claim the effect of the variables we discussed. Fourth, future research is urged to collect more data and replicate the study in other settings such as in cultures, nature of government (democracy or monarchy), etc. Finally, Chan [5] claims that older people trust less to media content; the investigation on the effect of control variables such as age, education, and previous experience using social media would enhance our further understanding.

References

1. Akbar, J.: Saudi Arabia warns Twitter and Facebook 'rumour-mongers' they risk death penalty in first ruling of its kind (2015). http://www.dailymail.co.uk/news/article-3261575/Saudi-Arabia-warns-Twitter-Facebook-rumour-mongers-risk-DEATH-PENALTY-ruling-kind.html
2. Bauer, R.A., Greyser, S.A.: Advertising in America: the consumer view (1968)
3. Bhutia, J.: Man faces 32-year jail term for Facebook 'like' of doctored photo of king (2015). http://www.ibtimes.co.uk/thailand-man-faces-32-year-jail-term-facebook-like-doctored-photo-king-1532851
4. Boe, G.P., Ponder, L.D.: Blood donors and non-donors: a review of the research. Am. J. Med. Technol. **47**(4), 248–253 (1981)
5. Chan, K.: Children's perceived truthfulness of television advertising and parental influence: a Hong Kong study. Adv. Consum. Res. **28**(1), 207–212 (2001)
6. Chin, W.W.: How to write up and report PLS analyses. In: Esposito Vinzi, V., Chin, W.W., Henseler, J., Wang, H. (eds.) Handbook of Partial Least Squares, pp. 655–690. Springer, Heidelberg (2010)
7. Davenport, T.H., Prusak, L.: Working Knowledge: How Organizations Manage What they Know. Harvard Business Press, Boston (1998)
8. Feldman, D.C., Bearden, W.O., Hardesty, D.M.: Varying the content of job advertisements: the effects of message specificity. J. Advertising **35**(1), 123–141 (2006)

9. Goh, D.H.-L., Ang, R.P., Chua, A.Y., Lee, C.S.: Why we share: a study of motivations for mobile media sharing. In: Liu, J., Wu, J., Yao, Y., Nishida, T. (eds.) AMT 2009. LNCS, vol. 5820, pp. 195–206. Springer, Heidelberg (2009)

10. He, W., Wei, K.-K.: What drives continued knowledge sharing? An investigation of knowledge-contribution and-seeking beliefs. Decis. Support Syst. 46(4), 826–838 (2009)

11. Helkkula, A., Kelleher, C.: Circularity of customer service experience and customer perceived value. J. Custom. Behav. 9(1), 37–53 (2010)

12. Henseler, J., Fassott, G.: Testing moderating effects in PLS path models: an illustration of available procedures. In: Esposito Vinzi, V., Chin, W.W., Henseler, J., Wang, H. (eds.) Handbook of Partial Least Squares, pp. 713–735. Springer, Heidelberg (2010)

13. Henseler, J., Ringle, C., Sinkovics, R.: The use of partial least squares path modeling in international marketing. Adv. Int. Market. (AIM) 20, 277–320 (2009)

14. Hoffman, M.L.: Psychological and biological perspectives on altruism. Int. J. Behav. Dev. 1(4), 323–339 (1978)

15. Hsu, C.-L., Lin, J.C.-C.: Acceptance of blog usage: the roles of technology acceptance, social influence and knowledge sharing motivation. Inf. Manag. 45(1), 65–74 (2008)

16. Igbaria, M., Guimaraes, T., Davis, G.B.: Testing the determinants of microcomputer usage via a structural equation model. J. Manag. Inf. Syst. 11(4), 87–114 (1995)

17. Lee, C.S., Ma, L.: News sharing in social media: the effect of gratifications and prior experience. Comput. Hum. Behav. 28, 331–339 (2012)

18. Li, H., Sakamoto, Y.: Social impacts in social media: an examination of perceived truthfulness and sharing of information. Comput. Hum. Behav. 41, 278–287 (2014)

19. Lindell, M.K., Whitney, D.J.: Accounting for common method variance in cross-sectional research designs. J. Appl. Psychol. 86(1), 114 (2001)

20. Ma, W.W., Chan, A.: Knowledge sharing and social media: Altruism, perceived online attachment motivation, and perceived online relationship commitment. Comput. Hum. Behav. 39, 51–58 (2014)

21. Matharu, H.: Man jailed for 30 years in Thailand for insulting the monarchy on Facebook (2015). http://www.independent.co.uk/news/world/asia/thai-man-jailed-for-30-years-for-face book-posts-insulting-monarchy-10445226.html. [cited 29 Feb 2016]

22. Park, J.H., et al.: An investigation of information sharing and seeking behaviors in online investment communities. Comput. Hum. Behav. 31, 1–12 (2014)

23. Parra-López, E., et al.: Intentions to use social media in organizing and taking vacation trips. Comput. Hum. Behav. 27(2), 640–654 (2011)

24. Piliavin, J.A., Charng, H.-W.: Altruism: a review of recent theory and research. Ann. Rev. Sociol. 16, 27–65 (1990)

25. Purcell, K., et al.: Understanding the participatory news consumer. Pew Internet Am. Life Project 1, 19–21 (2010)

26. Sakamoto, Y., Ma, J., Nickerson, J.V.: 2377 people like this article: the influence of others' decisions on yours. In: Proceedings of the 31st Annual Conference of the Cognitive Science Society (2009)

27. Salganik, M.J., Dodds, P.S., Watts, D.J.: Experimental study of inequality and unpredictability in an artificial cultural market. Science 311(5762), 854–856 (2006)

28. Shiau, W.-L., Chau, P.Y.K.: Does altruism matter on online group buying? Perspectives from egotistic and altruistic motivation. Inf. Technol. People 28(3), 677–698 (2015)

29. Snoj, B., Pisnik Korda, A., Mumel, D.: The relationships among perceived quality, perceived risk and perceived product value. J. Prod. Brand Manag. 13(3), 156–167 (2004)

30. Vargo, S.L., Lusch, R.F.: Why "service"? J. Acad. Market. Sci. 36(1), 25–38 (2008)

e-Society and Online Communities

Understanding Business Models in the Sharing Economy in China: A Case Study

Shang Gao[1(✉)] and Xuemei Zhang[2]

[1] School of Business, Örebro University, Örebro, Sweden
shang.gao@oru.se
[2] School of Business Administration,
Zhongnan University of Economics and Law, Wuhan, China
xuemo123@foxmail.com

Abstract. Along with a growing environmental consciousness and the advancement of information communication technology, car sharing and apartment sharing as the prominent examples of the sharing economy is becoming increasingly popular in China. This study aims to have a better understanding of business models in the sharing economy in China. Four research questions are presented. On the basis of a literature review on the business model and sharing economy, we proposed an analysis framework consisting of four major dimensions of business model concepts to study how the sharing economy works in China, including value network, value architecture, value proposition, and value finance. To address this, a case study with the Uber China is carried out. The key findings from the case study are presented in accordance with identified four dimensions of business model concepts.

Keywords: Business model · The sharing economy · Value network · Value proposition · Value architecture · Value finance · Uber

1 Introduction

The sharing economy refers to the phenomenon of turning unused or under-used assets owned by individuals into productive resources [25]. The emerging of the sharing economy has opened a new door for competitions across industries (e.g., Airbnb in the hotel industry, Uber in the taxi industry). Online services offered in the sharing economy enable people to share cars, accommodation, bicycles, and other items with others who are willing to pay to use them.

The key companies in the sharing economy are disrupting traditional industries across the globe. These companies bring significant economic and environmental benefits. For example, the car sharing service provided by Uber is a powerful way to reduce carbon emissions, to save money on transportation, and to reduce traffic [18].

In today's ever changing dynamic business environment, the business model plays an important role in the success of many companies [12]. The growth of sharing economies of production and sharing economies of consumption has attracted academic

Y.K. Dwivedi et al. (Eds.): I3E 2016, LNCS 9844, pp. 661–672, 2016.
DOI: 10.1007/978-3-319-45234-0_59

attention in recent times [17]. However, to our knowledge, there has not been much research on business models in the sharing economy in developing countries.

In this study, we focus on business models in the sharing economy in China, specifically focusing on the case of Uber China, a provider of car sharing services and a pioneer of the sharing economy. The objective of this study is to have a better understanding of business models in the sharing economy in China. To address this, we employ four key dimensions of business model concepts to formulate the question research questions to study business models in the sharing economy with the case Uber China. As a result, the following research questions (RQ) are proposed:

RQ1. What actors are involved in the sharing economy in China, and how are they related?

RQ2. What resources and activities are essential to the success of the business of an actor in the sharing economy in China?

RQ3. How do different actors make profits in the sharing economy in China?

RQ4. What are the key values offered by each actor in the sharing economy to its customers?

The remainder of the paper is organized as follows. Section 2 reviews the theory on business models. Section 3 introduces the research methods. Section 4 presents the analysis framework. A case study with Uber China is carried out in Sect. 5. This is followed by a discussion and conclusion in Sect. 6.

2   Literature Review

The literature about the sharing economy and business models is discussed in this section.

2.1   The Sharing Economy

Sharing economy has emerged as alternative suppliers of goods and services traditionally provided by long-established industries [27]. The sharing economy can be defined as a socio-economic ecosystem that commonly uses information technologies to connect different stakeholders-individuals, companies, governments, and others, in order to make value by sharing their excess capacities for products and services [13]. Moreover, Botsman and Rogers [5] indicated that sharing the economy underlies the business model in the operation of collaborative consumption, where people offer and share underutilized resources in creative, new ways.

Sharing economy activities fall into four broad categories: recirculation of goods, increased utilization of durable assets, exchange of services, and sharing of productive assets [22].

2.2   Literature on Business Models

The business model is a fundamental concept to manage strategic development of an organization. A business model tells what the business of an organization is all about.

A business model can be defined as the description of an organization or network of organizations involved in creating and capturing value based on technological innovation [6].

This concept can also inform the design of information systems and support sustainable development of an organization. Previous research have looked at the concept of business models in the context of specific domains (e.g., e-Business [3], e-Government [14], digital ecosystems [23], mobile ecosystems [12]).

However, there is a lack of literature on business models in the sharing economy, particularly in developing countries. Although the business model is very important to the success of many enterprises [10, 11], very few publication can be found to address the business model in sharing economy in the literature. Daunoriene et al. [9] provided an approach to address the sustainability of sharing economy business models. The following four perspectives have been identified in their study: economy, environment, society, and technology [9]. Zrevas et al. [27] studied the impact of Airbnb on the hotel industry in Texas. Their research findings provided some empirical evidences that the sharing economy is making inroads by successfully competing with, differentiating from, and acquiring market share from incumbent firms. In this research, we aim to complement current literature on business models in the sharing economy with a case study from China.

According to the literature review, while the term "business model" is extensively used, there is no widely agreed upon definition of what constitute this concept. Therefore, we had an overview on the existing definition on business model. Some of the different views of the concept of the business model are presented here.

As explained by Petrovic et al. [20], a business model is the logic of a "business system" for creating value that lies behind the actual processes. It gives a complete overview of an organization and the process of constructing a business model is part of any business strategy.

Afuah and Tucci [1] defined business models as a system of components (customer value, scope, pricing, revenue sources, connected activities, implementation, capabilities and sustainability) and relationships between these components.

Basically, the business model consists of three things: the type of goods/services provided, the business model archetype and a revenue model [21]. Further, Methlie and Pedersen [15] defined a business model as consisting of three dimensions: (1). Service strategy, this includes service value proposition, and market focus; (2). Governance form, this refers to the ways in which flows of information, resources and goods are controlled by the parties of the value-creating business network; (3). Revenue Model, this includes revenue valuation and sharing.

Amit and Zott [4] illustrates that the business model depicts the content, structure, and governance of transactions designed so as to create value through the exploitation of business opportunities. Furthermore, Morris et al. [16] defines that a business model is a concise representation of how an interrelated set of decision variables in the areas of venture strategy, architecture, and economics are addressed to create sustainable competitive advantage in defined markets. It has six fundamental components: value proposition, customer, internal processes/competencies, external positioning, economic model, and personal investor factors.

Based on the similarities among a wide range of business model conceptualizations, Osterwalder and Pigneur [19] proposed a reference model, called "Business Model Canvas" (BMC), including customer segments, value proposition, channels, revenue streams, key resources, key activities, key partners, customer relationships, and cost structure.

Al-Debei and Avison [2] employed a content analysis approach to review the existing business model literature and identified the following four major dimensions of the concepts of business models: value proposition, value network, value architecture and value finance.

3   Research Methods

The objective of this research is to investigate business models in the sharing economy in China. To address this, we firstly derived an analysis framework based on previous literature on business models. Then, we carried out a case study in terms of the derived analysis framework in China.

A case study [26] is useful in the early stages of research on an emerging research topic, when there is not much available literature. As indicated in the last section, there are only few studies addressing business models in the sharing economy. Therefore, we believe that case study is an established method designed for addressing the proposed research questions.

Data was collected mainly through four face-to-face interviews with staffs from Uber China and through some internal documents provided by the managers in Uber China in October 2015. The interviews were conducted based on the four research questions proposed in Sect. 1. We recorded the face-to-face interviews digitally. The interviews took on average 90 min. All the interviews were conducted in Mandarin. We retained and analyzed the data in the original language and only translated into English at the time of writing. A member of the research team who was proficient in both Mandarin and English preformed the translations to ensure consistency.

After data collection, the data was coded for further analysis. Strauss and Corbin [24] defined selective coding as the process of selecting the central or core category, systematically relating it to other categories, validating those relationships, and filling in categories that need further refinement and development. This coding approach fit well with the setting of this study. Therefore, we used selective coding technique [7] to code and organize the interview data. A coding schema was developed for business model in the sharing economy in terms of the analysis framework presented in above. The four dimensions in this framework are: value network, value architecture, value proposition, and value network. For example, if the emergent data was closely aligned with an identified dimension, we used selective coding to associate this piece of data to the dimension.

4   Analysis Framework

As presented in Sect. 2, following a comprehensive review of the literature on business models, Al-Debei and Avison [2] identified that the value proposition, value network, value architecture and value finance were the four key elements to be examined when designing, analyzing, and evaluating business models. In this research, we reused this analysis framework (see Fig. 1) to investigate business models in sharing economy in China. The four dimensions [2] in the framework were presented as following:

- Value network: describes inter-organizational relationship with a business model.
- Value proposition: refers to the way in which organizations create value for their customers and for each party engaged in service provision.
- Value architecture: represents how an organization's resources and core competencies are configured to create and provide value to customers.
- Value financial: relates to the way revenue are generated and costs are structured in the business model.

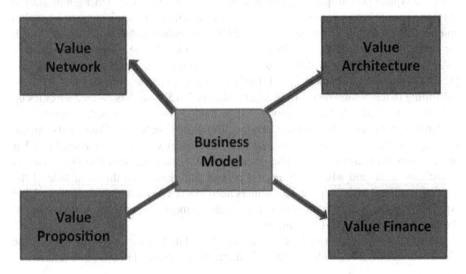

Fig. 1. Fours dimensions of business model concepts

The reason for basing the analysis of business models in sharing economy on the proposed four dimensions was that it is an established method for business analysis with clearly structured categories [2], which is highly associated with the objective of this study.

Some statements from the interviews contained key findings that could bring answers to the RQs. We also found that some other statements might not address the RQs directly. But these statements provided background information for the case analysis.

By analyzing the interview data based on the four dimensions of business model concept, we were able to extract elements to answer the RQs. The RQ1 can be addressed by studying value network dimension. The resources and activities in RQ2 are found as value architect dimension. Each actor' capability to make profits in RQ3 is associated with value financial dimension. The value offerings in RQ4 are linked with value proposition dimension.

We selected our cases based on two conditions. First, the organization should be a good representative organization in China. Second, the organization should have a strategic plan to engage in the sharing economy. Uber China is one of the most popular ride-hailing platforms engaged in the sharing economy in China. In addition, Uber China is also proactive in collaborating with other actors in the sharing economy. Thus, Uber China was chosen as our case in this research.

5   Case Study

5.1   Case Background

Uber is a typical peer-to-peer marketplace in the sharing economy. Uber got its start in 2009 as a private luxury car service in San Francisco. It then began raising venture capital and launched a mobile smartphone app in 2010 that enables potential customers to call for a ride, get a price quote, and then accept or reject it [8]. The company expanded to UberX in 2012, enabling customers to arrange for rides in smaller, less expensive cars [8]. Uber was officially launched in Mid-July 2014 and was expending very fast in China. According to the annual report from Uber China in 2015, Uber has entered 21 cities up to December of 2015 in China, among which Chengdu has the best performance.

Uber is able to provide real-time, and location based ridesharing. Consumers can use Uber app on their smart devices to submit a trip request which is then routed to Uber drivers who use their own cars. The Uber app on the smart devices allows consumers to indicate when and where they need a pickup, and drivers on the other side of the platform respond to the request. Consumers need to store payment information on Uber App. Neither the rider nor the driver deals with payments. Uber takes a percentage of the fare, and the rest goes to the driver.

The rest of this section analyzes the data collected in the case study according to the identified four dimensions in the analysis framework presented in the last Section.

5.2   Value Network

From the data collected from the four interviews, we have identified the following actors interacting with Uber China in the sharing economy:

1. Mobile device manufacturers: manufacturers that manufacture mobile devices to customers.
2. Platform operator (Uber).
3. Mobile network operators.
4. Consumers: individuals and organizations that use ridesharing services, and drivers.
5. Governmental regulatory agency: a governmental authority that issues the policy and regulations on ridesharing services.
6. Third party partners: partners that help Uber recruiting drivers, and provide navigation services for drivers.
7. Investors.
8. Competitors.

Uber provides its service to both customers and driver through mobile data networks. Therefore, the mobile network operators play an important role in the sharing economy. For example, Uber Wuhan (i.e., one of the local branches in China) has reached a strategic cooperation with Hubei Unicom, which one of the mobile network operators in China. For example, Hubei Unicom provided a customized SIM card with a good deal on data plan for Uber drivers in Wuhan. Consequently, Uber driver can save money when they are using mobile data with Uber app. And Uber highly recommends its drivers to purchase this SIM card. As a result, Hubei Unicom can get more subscribers from Uber drivers in Wuhan.

One of the interviewee indicated that Uber China had reached a strategic cooperation agreement with the governmental agency in Wuhan in October 2015. The world's largest operations center of Uber will be established in Wuhan in the near future. This center aims to provide a better service to both drivers and riders in China. Consequently, this operation center will provide hundreds of job opportunities for citizens in Wuhan. Thus, this creates a win-win situation for both Uber China and the local governmental agency.

Third party partners are also playing important roles in the sharing economy. For example, one of the interviewee indicated that local car leasing companies also help Uber recruit and manage drivers. Moreover, there are some navigation service providers (e.g., Google Map, Tomtom) to provide navigation services for both drivers and riders on Uber. Baidu is a well-known company for search in China. Baidu is also a key partner of Uber China. Baidu integrated the Uber API, which is available in Baidu Maps and the Mobile Baidu search app.

Uber's Chinese investors include HNA Group, CITIC Securities, China Pacific, China Life and Guangzhou Automobile Group, other investors including Vanke, Minsheng Bank and China Broadband Capital Partners. In addition, the Baidu Inc involved in China's A, B rounds of financing.

Lastly, a good competitor can also promote the development of sharing economy. Didi, which is a domestic ride-sharing company, is the biggest competitor for Uber in China. Both Uber China and Didi spent billions in their battle for market share. Both companies raised billions from investors in the past two years as they were trying their best to secure their positions in the fiercely competitive market by offering both drivers and passengers' subsidies that have proved as important incentives to attract Chinese consumers. As a result, consumers often switched between two platforms.

5.3 Value Proposition

Uber can provider better ride experience in contrast to the traditional taxi-hailing services in China. On one hand, Uber has its own requirements for being a qualified Uber vehicle. All Uber China vehicles have to be less than 5 years old in China. This means all the Uber China vehicles are quite new in Chinese market. On the other hand, Uber China has it's own specific requirements to become an Uber driver. Most interviewees indicated several times that good services ratings and good on-time rates are two of the important requirements to be Uber drivers in China.

Most interviewees also indicated that Uber was seen as a disruptive innovation to traditional taxi-hailing services. The objective of Uber China is to make sure that riders can get a car as easy as possible. Uber used some well-designed algorithms on dynmic pricing to helps supply meet high demand at specific areas.

Moreover, Uber China can help vacant vehicles to be better used to reach a high capital efficiency. Uber is able to generate value by matching unused cars and under-used cars with consumers willing to pay for the ride-sharing services.

5.4 Value Architecture

One of the interviewee indicated that human resources (e.g., experienced employees) are essential to the success of Uber China in the sharing economy. Uber China tended to employ local elites to manage their local business since these elites have a better understanding of the local market. When Uber China plan to start business in a new city, Uber China only operate the following two departments to mange the business under the general manager: the operational department and the marketing department. The local Uber team also has the authority to plan all kinds of localized operational and marketing activities according to consumers' demands.

Having a large user base is another key resources for Uber China. As a platform, the consumers of Uber include drivers and riders. Uber aimed to deploy least vehicles in a city to meet the consumers' demands most efficiently. One of the interviewees indicated that the market share of Uber China on the mobile transportation platform has been increased from 2 % at the beginning of 2015 to 35 % at the end of 2015.

Key activities capture the most important things an organization does to make its business model work. As for Uber China, the interviewees indicated that the key activities include recruiting qualified drivers, attracting riders, providing good customer services to both riders and drivers, having good relationships with third party partners.

Uber also made great efforts in localization with its operation in China. Uber China devoted itself in localizing the service. Most interviewees mentioned several times that one of the key strategies of Uber China was to increase their ability to localize effectively in China. For example, Uber China changes default map service into Baidu map in China. One of the interviewees referred to the following story as another example on localization. Chengdu is a city famous for being the home of the giant panda in China. To be in line with this local characteristic, Uber built many panda themed meeting points in Chengdu. As a result, these meeting points make it convenient for drivers to locate their passengers, and also for people new to the city to meet up for a ride.

Some of the interviewees also indicated some risks for Uber China. Some drivers may leave Uber's platform to other competitors in China. Moreover, the government's support is crucial for the success of Uber China in the mobile transportation marketplace in China as it decide if the private car's company with its ride-hailing services is legal or not. The governmental agency might issue detailed local policies that could negatively affect Uber's operation in China. Last but not least, unlike licensed taxi drivers, private citizens providing ride-hailing services do not always purchase commercial insurance for passengers.

5.5 Value Finance

One of the main sources of revenue is the platform commission. Uber China charges 20 % of each ride fare as platform commission. However, the tax issue is a grey area for Uber China. Many sharing economy companies are true intermediaries, providing a platform for consumers rather than providing services directly. However, there is no such role in the traditional economy. This also applies to Uber China. Thus, city regulators need to formulate relevant rules and tax policies for companies doing business in the sharing economy.

Table 1. The business model of Uber China in the sharing economy

	Uber China in the sharing economy
Value network	Mobile device manufacturers Platform operator (Uber) Mobile network providers Consumers: individuals and organizations that use the services, and drivers Governmental regulatory agency Third party partners: partners that help Uber recruiting drivers, and provide navigation services for drivers Investors Competitors
Value proposition	Better ride experience Used some well-designed algorithms on dynmic pricing to helps supply meet high demand at specific areas High capital efficiency
Value architecture	Human resources (e.g., experienced employees) A large user base Localization The key activities include recruiting qualified drivers, attracting riders, providing good customer services to both riders and drivers, having good relationships with third party partners Avoid some potential risks (e.g., formulating the regulation on insurance for passengers)
Value finance	Platform commission The governmental regulatory agency charges the tax on the service Mobile service operators charge users for data packages

On the other hand, some interviewees said that, actors involved in the sharing economy could benefit each other by exchanging resources. One of the interviewees took the following case in Uber China-Wuhan branch as an example. Uber China-Wuhan branch had reached a collaborative agreement with the largest local supermarket chain in Wuhan. Uber China-Wuhan branch purchased electronic shopping gift cards from the supermarket chain at a cost of 60 thousand RMB per week. These shopping gift cards were mainly used as incentives to attract both drivers and passengers on Uber China. In return, the local supermarket chain offered complimentary exhibition spaces to promote Uber China in its 38 physical stores.

Mobile network operators are another important actor in the Uber-based sharing economy. Customers' demands for mobile data and phone calls are increasing in the Uber-based sharing economy. This opens an opportunity for mobile network operators to increase their profits.

The key findings from this case study are summarized in Table 1 in the next page.

6 Conclusion and Future Research

This study has investigated business models in the sharing economy in China. Firstly, on the basis of a literature review on business models, we proposed an analysis framework consisting of four dimensions to study how the sharing economy works. We employed a case study methodology to understand business models in the sharing economy in China. The results revealed that the Uber-based sharing economy is a network composed of different actors, who can contribute to coevolution of each other in the network. The key to success is to build and sustain a sound network by incorporating helpful and complementary actors.

This research contributes to the literature on business models in the sharing economy by employing the analysis framework for analyzing key business model dimensions of the case on Uber China. It reveals how business models can support the development and evolution of the sharing economy in China. Some of findings from this case study in China are in consistent with previous research finding from Uber in other countries. For example, Cusumano [8] indicated that Uber is violating regulations for transportation services—insurance, training of drivers, and licenses in some countries.

Concerning the practical implications, this research provides some important insights for the development of the sharing economy in China. Uber China needs to further ensure users' safety, protect users' privacy, and self-regulate the health of itself in the sharing economy. At the same time, consumers should use ridesharing services with a clear understand of their rights and obligations. The sharing economy is a new concept and many local governmental agencies are not familiar with the business model in the sharing economy. The companied involved in the sharing economy can initiate some meeting to address some problems together with the local governmental agency. It would be better for the managers of sharing economy companies to explain their business to regulators rather than wait for regulators to approach relevant companies with a concern. As a result, the companies can possibly avoid some misperceptions about their business with the local governmental agency.

We are also aware of some limitations. First, the generalizability of our findings is limited by the fact that they are based on a single case study. This can be addressed by conducting more case studies in future both in China and in other countries. Second, our insights are subject to the data available from the conducted interviews, which may not completely reflect business models in the sharing economy in China. However, the coding scheme helped us analyze the data in a structured way.

The findings of this research also provide a good basis for further investigation. The analysis framework can be used for further research on business models in sharing economy. We also plan to carry out a comparative study to investigate the difference on business models between Uber China and Uber in some other countries in the future.

References

1. Afuah, A., Tucci, C.L.: Internet Business Models and Strategies: Text and Cases. McGraw-Hill Higher Education, New York (2000)
2. Al-Debei, M.M., Avison, D.: Developing a unified framework of the business model concept. Eur. J. Inf. Syst. **19**(3), 359–376 (2010)
3. Alt, R., Zimmermann, H.-D.: Preface: introduction to special section–business models. Electron. Markets **11**(1), 3–9 (2001)
4. Amit, R., Zott, C.: Value creation in e-business. Strateg. Manag. J. **22**(6–7), 493–520 (2001)
5. Botsman, R., Rogers, R.: What's Mine Is Yours: The Rise of Collaborative Consumption. Collins, London (2010)
6. Chesbrough, H., Rosenbloom, R.S.: The role of the business model in capturing value from innovation: evidence from Xerox Corporation's technology spin-off companies. Ind. Corp. Change **11**(3), 529–555 (2002)
7. Corbin, J., Strauss, A.: Basics of Qualitative Research: Techniques and Procedures for Developing Grounded Theory. Sage publications, Thousand Oaks (2014)
8. Cusumano, M.A.: How traditional firms must compete in the sharing economy. Commun. ACM **58**(1), 32–34 (2015)
9. Daunorienė, A., Drakšaitė, A., Snieška, V., et al.: Evaluating sustainability of sharing economy business models. Procedia-Social Behav. Sci. **213**, 836–841 (2015)
10. Gao, S.: High level modeling and evaluation of multi-channel services, Norwegian University of Science and Technology (2011)
11. Gao, S., Krogstie, J.: A combined framework for development of business process support systems. In: Persson, A., Stirna, J. (eds.) PoEM 2009. LNBIP, vol. 39, pp. 115–129. Springer, Heidelberg (2009)
12. Gao, S., Krogstie, J.: Understanding business models of mobile ecosystems in China: a case study. In: the proceedings of the 7th International Conference on Management of Computational and Collective IntElligence in Digital EcoSystems (MEDES'15). ACM (2015)
13. Hamari, J., Sjöklint, M., Ukkonen, A.: The sharing economy: why people participate in collaborative consumption. J. Assoc. Inf. Sci. Technol. (2015)
14. Janssen, M., Kuk, G., Wagenaar, R.W.: A survey of web-based business models for e-government in the Netherlands. Gov. Inf. Q. **25**(2), 202–220 (2008)
15. Methlie, L.B., Pedersen, P.E.: Business model choices for value creation of mobile services. Info **9**(5), 70–85 (2007)
16. Morris, M., Schindehutte, M., Allen, J.: The entrepreneur's business model: toward a unified perspective. J. Bus. Res. **58**(6), 726–735 (2005)
17. Nguyen, G.T.: Exploring collaborative consumption business models-case peer-to-peer digital platforms (2014)
18. Orsi, J.: The sharing economy just got real. Shareable. net (2013)
19. Osterwalder, A., Pigneur, Y.: Business Model Generation. Wiley, New Jersey (2010)
20. Petrovic, O., Kittl, C., Teksten, R.D.: Developing business models for eBusiness. In: International Conference on Electronic Commerce. Citeseer (2001)
21. Popp, K., Meyer, R.: Profit from Software Ecosystems: Business Models, Ecosystems and Partnerships in the Software Industry. BoD–Books on Demand, Norderstedt (2010)

22. Schor, J.: Debating the sharing economy. Great transition initiative (2014)
23. Sharma, R.S., Pereira, F., Ramasubbu, N., et al.: Assessing value creation and value capture in digital business ecosystems. Int. J. Inf. Technol. **16**(2), 1–8 (2010)
24. Strauss, A., Corbin, J.: Basics of Qualitative Research: Grounded Theory Procedures and Techniques. Sage Publications, Newbury Park (1990)
25. Wallsten, S.: The competitive effects of the sharing economy: how is Uber changing taxis? Technology Policy Institute (2015)
26. Yin, R.K.: Case Study Research: Design and Methods. Sage publications, Thousand Oaks (2013)
27. Zervas, G., Proserpio, D., Byers, J.: The rise of the sharing economy: estimating the impact of Airbnb on the hotel industry. Boston U. School of Management Research Paper (2013–2016) (2015)

Influences and Benefits of Role Models on Social Media

Lyndsey Jenkins[1](✉), Ruoyun Lin[2], and Debora Jeske[1]

[1] Edinburgh Napier University, Edinburgh, UK
{l.jenkins,d.jeske}@napier.ac.uk
[2] Leibniz-Institut für Wissensmedien, Tübingen, Germany
r.lin@iwm-tuebingen.de

Abstract. The current paper examined three research questions. First, what are the perceived benefits for social network users who have role models online? Second, to what extent does having role models online influence one's self-presentation on social media? And finally, are users who expect more in return (greater reciprocity) more likely to have role models on social media? Using two opportunity survey samples and exploratory analyses, study 1 ($N = 236$) demonstrated that having role models was associated with greater perceived support for one's career aspirations, and perceived access to information. The results of study 2 ($N = 192$) revealed that participants who had role models online reported that their online profile presented a more realistic self-presentation of values and priorities, as well as having higher reciprocity expectation.

Keywords: Role model · Social media · Information-seeking · Reciprocity expectations

1 Introduction

When we need information, support and guidance, we often seek help from those who are more qualified or experienced to assist us. These individuals may often include individuals that can be considered role models [1]. Role models are individuals that people look up to. In addition, role models may be individuals that you would hope to be like (now or in the future). This includes individuals who may be known to a person but who have not met yet [2]. Frequently, role models include people in authority or positions of respect. This often includes public officials and well known professionals (e.g., people serving in emergency services such as fire brigade, police and similar as well as educators, athletes, parents, celebrities or religious leaders [3, 4]). Role models are usually senior in experience and influence than other contacts [5, 6]. The specific status, gender, experiences and rank of contacts may likewise play a role as to whether or not these contacts are considered positive role models [3, 5].

Social media makes it easier for individuals to identify role models and get in touch with one another. Indeed, past evidence suggests that contacts on digital platforms play an important role in building social support and social capital [7] as these social media sites enable users to share information, create personal content and collaborate with

Y.K. Dwivedi et al. (Eds.): I3E 2016, LNCS 9844, pp. 673–684, 2016.
DOI: 10.1007/978-3-319-45234-0_60

other users on these sites [8]. Having a role model online may help us gain more informational benefits as they may post useful and relevant information about career paths and options publicly [2].

The 'virtual presence' of online role models may increase the effort that social network users make to connect with the role model and how they interact as well as present themselves 'in front' of others via their online profiles [2]. This may start by users paying careful attention to how they present themselves, as the role model may be aware of their interactions online [5]. At present, many of these findings about the benefits of role models on social media have not been substantiated. The purpose of the present work is to provide support for some of the hypothesized benefits whilst also paying attention to the role of reciprocity expectations.

In the following section, we outline three research questions and review the literature in an attempt to answer each. First, what are perceived benefits for social network users who have role models online? Second, to what extent does having role models online influence one's self-presentation? And third, to what extent do the expectations of social network users play a role? That is, are those who have higher reciprocity expectations more inclined to have role models because of their expectation that they would benefit from this association in the future?

1.1   Perceived Benefits for Social Network Users

Online contacts may form another source of support to those present in every-day life, as they can provide social support and mentoring opportunities (which have been explored as predictors of subjective career success, [9]). Past work [10] has demonstrated that people seek information by making connections through active seeking of sources, active scanning of the environment for information, and making connections through non-directed monitoring as well as connections by proxy (via other people's connections and searchers). Social networks offer information seekers several options in one place. This may play an important role in terms of young adults' readiness for career decision-making. This can be defined as the degree to which individuals feel capable to make career choices that take into account a personal circumstances and wider context variables, including social, economic and organizational variables [11]. Social networks may therefore be particularly beneficial to and shape career decision making due to their 24-hour availability and their potential to support information seeking.

Social network activities may similarly help mentees to obtain instrumental as well as emotional support [12, 13]. Previous research has emphasized the need to consider the role of multiple sources of information and advice in career decision making [14–16]. Especially among younger adults, being able to access more information and learn from positive role models may aid career decision-making when transitioning from school or university into the workplace. The contact and interaction during information seeking may increase the willingness and readiness of students to participate in various optional career-related opportunities. Contacting role models may also represent a career strategy of its own and complement parental support - as long as the role model's achievement appears to be obtainable by the less experienced individual [17]. We suggest that having role models online will increase social network users' access to information and career-related planning.

1.2   Self-presentation

Social Comparison Theory [18] suggests that people evaluate their own views and achievements in relation to other people's accomplishments to gain a good understanding of themselves. Through this comparison, usually with similar others or those they aspire to be like, individuals gain insight that allows them to personally define who they are in contrast to others. This process benefits from learning about others – a process facilitated by exposure to information about others. For example, after reading role model's career experience in their posts, the user might identify what it takes to achieve certain career stages successfully but also understand requirements to develop [4]. In turn, the information could help the individuals understand how to present themselves successfully online. The verifiability of information may furthermore increase their efforts to be present a realistic – or slightly flattering – profile online and reduce their tendency to share inaccurate information about themselves (e.g., idealized).

The contact and possible exchange with role models and external advisors via social networks may further help younger adults become more knowledgeable about themselves and their career options [19]. This may be particularly important when individuals want to learn about their own future career options from others. Yet, self-presentation plays an important role as well. Social networks not only allow users to learn from their role models via their posts, but may increase awareness of managing their interactions and profiles online. This is further reinforced by the fact that many network users are increasingly aware of the fact that even their personal profiles may be viewed by others outside of role model status, including employers and the general public [20]. As a result, social desirability may shape the degree to which social network users present a realistic versus a more social desirable image that may be more polished and slightly less representative of themselves. This links with idealistic versus realistic impression management online [21, 22].

1.3   Reciprocity Expectations

The Social Exchange Theory [23] suggests that social behavior is driven largely by the expectations of the individuals [24]. This means the interaction between individuals involves all partners negotiating and reflecting on the rewards and costs of their interpersonal relationship. The exchanges involved in relationships help build "feelings of personal obligation, gratitude and trust" (Blau, 1964, p. 94 – [25]). As a result, social network users have to balance several social expectations at the same time. This includes reciprocity expectations [26] as these may further shape online activity [27].

For example, social media users may expect that connections will be willing to reciprocate later. In other words, some users may intentionally connect with a role model with the hope that this connection will result in mutual benefits. Users who have greater reciprocity expectations may see role models as potentially useful connections than those who do not expect a return for favors. So users with higher reciprocity expectations might expect each other to endorse each other (LinkedIn, for example, allows users to submit small supportive statements about contacts that can be seen by other users). The 'followers' of a role model may be more willing to "like" and share the comments of their role models, reinforcing their popularity and status as a role model. In addition, network users may purposefully contact role models as they hope that mutual support and information exchange will lead to mutual long-term benefits. This raises the question of mutual expectations when social network users connect with one another (e.g., the expectation that favors will be returned) – the other side of benefits to having role models on one's network.

2   Study 1 – Benefits

2.1   Method

The focus of the first study was to examine, in the context of career-related information seeking, whether or not young adults experience potential benefits of having role models on social media when engaged in such information-seeking. The focus was to examine whether perceived career support and perceived access to information was improved amongst those social network users with role models on their social networks.

2.1.1   Participants and Procedure

Using an opportunity sample, we recruited 281 psychology students from three educational institutions in the American Midwest (n = 151, 53.7 %) and North East England (n = 130, 46.5 %) as part of a larger data collection effort. Data screening did not show any significant differences between the two datasets. For the purpose of the present research, we excluded all participants that did not use social media, who omitted questions on role model access, or completed only some of the questionnaire. This result in a final sample of 236 participants between the ages of 17 to 35 and on average about 20 years old (M = 20.53, SD = 2.61). Three out of four participants were women (77.1 %, n = 182). Male participants made up less than a quarter of the sample (22.9 %, n = 54).

Participants were invited via announcement in class or via email. Once participants had completed the consent form, they were asked to complete measures related to career-related decision making and information access, their social network connections (including role models) and demographics. This was followed by the debrief statement.

2.1.2   Measures

Study 1 included the following measures to capture career-related information seeking and engagement of young adults generally.

Occupational Engagement. This was measured using nine items from the Occupational Engagement Scale–Student, OES-S [28]. An example item is: "I volunteer in an area that I find interesting." Responses were made on a five point scale ranging from (1) unlike me to (5) like me (α = .81, M = 3.31, SD = 0.66).

Career Pursuit Support. Four items were used to measure support from family and friends in pursuing career goals [29]. This subscale measures perceived emotional and instrumental support from family and friends in pursuing career goals. An example item is "I receive the encouragement I need from others to meet my career goals." Responses were made on a five point Likert type scale ranging from (1) strongly disagree to (5) strongly agree ($\alpha = .85$, $M = 3.49$, $SD = 0.89$).

Likely Access to Information (Informational Support). In order to assess the extent to which individuals seek information from the online environment, the six-item Environment Exploration subscale was selected [30]. These were modified by including references to information sought from contacts on social media sites. The instructions presented to our participants stated that "How likely is it that you would ask your contacts/friends on your social media sites to get the following information?" These items did not imply that these contacts or friends had to be role models to capture general access to information from the social network. An example item is: "Information about potential career possibilities". Two items were added from the "External Search Instrumentality" subscale [30]. These items were (1) "Initiating conversations with friends and relatives about careers" and (2) "Initiating conversations with several other students about their career interviews." The response options ranged from (1) hardly ever to (5) almost always. A composite was created based on all eight items ($\alpha = .94$, $M = 2.48$, $SD = 0.80$).

Access to Role Models Online. In order to determine respondents' accessibility to role models online, they were asked "Have you used social media (e.g., social network sites such as Facebook, LinkedIn) to connect with potential role models?" Respondents answered either Yes = 1, or No = 2. Just a third of the participants ($n = 85$) reported that they had used social media to connect with a role model online, while two thirds had no such role models ($n = 151$).

Demographics. These included age and gender.

2.2   Results

Data screening showed unremarkable skew and kurtosis for all measures. Table 1 shows the correlations for the different measures.

In order to analyze differences in career-related and information behaviors amongst social network users with or without online role models, we used analysis of covariance. Each analysis involved age and gender as covariates as older and female network users may potentially also have more online connections but fewer role models [2]. No significant difference was observed in relation to occupational engagement ($F(1, 228) = 2.893$, $p = .090$, $\eta_p^2 = .013$). Having a role model online did not influence occupational engagement for these participants ($M = 3.41$, $SD = 0.68$, $n = 84$), compared to those who did not have such role models online ($M = 3.23$, $SD = 0.61$, $n = 148$). However, having role models online did influence the level of perceived support for career pursuit ($F(1, 228) = 6.553$, $p = .011$, $\eta_p^2 = .028$). Those with a role model reported higher perceived career support ($M = 3.69$, $SD = 0.72$, $n = 84$) compared to those who did not have such role models ($M = 3.42$, $SD = 0.84$, $n = 148$).

A significant influence was observed in relation to the perceived access to information ($F(1, 228) = 15.517$, $p < .001$, $\eta_p^2 = .064$). As anticipated, having a role model online significantly increased perceived access to information for those who had role models online ($M = 2.76$, $SD = 0.71$, $n = 84$) compared to those who did not

Table 1. Correlations between measures and age

	(1)	(2)	(3)	(4)
(1) Occupational engagement	1			
(2) Career support	.198[b]	1		
(3) Information access	.260[b]	.401[b]	1	
(4) Age	.153[a]	−.053	.047	1

Note. [a] $p < .05$, [b] $p < .01$

($M = 2.35$, $SD = 0.78$, $n = 148$). This difference also remained when taking into account occupational engagement as a covariate ($p < .05$), which suggests that individual engagement in career-related information seeking has a significant role in accessing information, although the benefits of having access to role models appear to be particularly prominent.

3   Study 2 – Self-presentation and Reciprocity Expectations

3.1   Method

The second study enabled us to explore whether having role models on social media influences online self-presentation, and the relationship with reciprocity expectation.

3.1.1   Participants and Procedure

Data collection involved two different samples ($N = 217$), including a UK student sample (n = 129) and a Facebook opportunity sample ($n = 63$). Preliminary data screening revealed no significant differences between the two samples. However, we only retained cases that provided full information about social media use, role models and the key constructs of interest. The final sample included 192 participants, including 43 males and 147 females (plus 2 missing values). Participants' age ranged from 16 to 69 ($M = 24.01$, $SD = 9.20$).

Participants were invited via a university research portal, email and short messages on social media. Once participants had completed the consent form, they were asked to complete measures related to reciprocity expectations, social media use (including role models), presentation on social media and demographics. This was followed by the debrief statement.

3.1.2   Measures

Realistic Self-presentation on Social Networks. We asked several questions. First, we asked about their own evaluation of how realistically the participants presented themselves online on their most used website. This question asked: "Overall, to what extent does your social networking profile that is visible to your network reflect your personality, priorities and values? Think about the site that you use the most (if you use more than one social media platform)" ($M = 6.52$, $SD = 1.88$). Second, we created slight variants of the same question by only changing the start of each question to ask about specific contacts. Therefore, we created a question for family: "To what extent your family members would agree that your social activities on this site reflect ...?" (*M* = 6.12, *SD* = 1.99). And third, "To what extent would your close friends agree that your social activities on this site reflect ...?" (*M* = 6.76, *SD* = 1.92). The final question asked: "To what extent your colleagues would perceive your social activities on this site reflect ...?" (*M* = 5.83, *SD* = 2.08). The response options for all questions were: (0) not at all to (10) to a great extent.

Reciprocity Expectations. This was measured using 10 items from the 27-item Reciprocity questionnaire by [25]. The scale was shortened to include only items that would be potentially transferable to the online context. An example item is: "If someone does a favor for me, I am ready to return it." Responses were made on a five point scale ranging from (1) very untrue to (7) very true (α = .63, *M* = 2.70, *SD* = 0.60).

Access to Role Models Online. All participants were asked "Do you have any contacts on your social networking sites that are role models for you?" More than half (*n* = 115) had contacts that were role models, with just over a third had no such role models (*n* = 77).

Demographics. This included gender and age.

3.2 Results

Data screening showed unremarkable skew and kurtosis for reciprocity and the presentation measures. Table 2 shows the correlations for the different measures.

In order to analyze differences in career-related and information behaviors amongst social network users with or without online role models, we used analysis of covariance. Each analysis involved age and gender as covariates. Efforts of realistic self-presentation (match between online profile and user's personality, priorities and values), as judged by the participants themselves, similarly differed amongst participants with and without role models ($F(1, 185) = 7.963$, $p = .005$, $\eta_p^2 = .041$).

Participants with role models actually reported higher scores – more realistic self-presentation online (*M* = 6.84, *SD* = 1.76, *n* = 113), than those without models (*M* = 6.05, *SD* = 1.97, *n* = 76). A similar result was obtained when we asked participants how true their family would rate their online presentation ($F(1, 185) = 7.800$, $p = .006$, $\eta_p^2 = .040$). Again, ratings were higher amongst participant with role models

Table 2. Correlations between measures and age

	(1)	(2)	(3)	(4)	(5)	(6)
(1) Reciprocity	1					
(2) Present. online: Self	.058	1				
(3) Present. online: Family	.016	.711[b]	1			
(4) Present. online: Friends	−.005	.774[b]	.753[b]	1		
(5) Present. online: Colleagues	−.029	.462 [b]	.622[b]	.578[b]	1	
(6) Age	−.251[b]	−.028	.020	−.028	.070	1

Note. [a] *p* < .05, [b] *p* < .01

($M = 6.44$, $SD = 1.95$, $n = 113$) than those without ($M = 5.64$, $SD = 1.95$, $n = 76$). However, no significant difference was noted when participants were asked about the perceptions of close friends ($F(1, 185) = 1.863$, $p = .174$, $\eta_p^2 = .010$) and colleagues ($F(1, 185) = .960$, $p = .329$, $\eta_p^2 = .005$).

With regard to reciprocity expectations, a significant difference was observed ($F(1, 182) = 10.277$, $p = .002$, $\eta_p^2 = .053$). Having a role model online was associated with greater expectations of reciprocity amongst these participants ($M = 4.61$, $SD = 0.58$, $n = 111$), compared to those who did not have such role models online ($M = 4.31$, $SD = 0.58$, $n = 75$).

4 Discussion

The presence of social media in everyday life, both at a personal and professional level, has provided new opportunities for individuals to connect to mentors and role models online. The current paper examined three research questions. First, what are the perceived benefits for social network users who have role models online? Second, to what extent does having role models online influence one's self-presentation on social media? And finally, are users who expect more in return (greater reciprocity) more likely to have role models on social media? In order to provide first answers to these exploratory questions, we used the results from two different studies, the participants of which were part of two opportunity samples.

The benefits associated with role models were explored in the first study. The results of group comparison showed that having role models was associated with greater perceived support for one's career aspirations and perceived access to information. These results suggest that having role models in one's networks may boost social network users' future-oriented engagement and improve information access. This is an important contribution to what has only been hypothesized previously. Further research may wish to consider the influence of online role models social network users engage with in person (as this might reinforce the influence of the role model). In our study, we cannot be sure which sources of influence had a greater impact beyond the two groups (parents or role models; see [16]) as role models may have included parental figures as well [31]. In addition, it would be interesting to replicate our research with professionals instead of students as age and experience may play an important role in terms of who is sought out as a role model. Future research may further wish to consider how participants seek out information: active seeking of sources, active scanning of the environment for information, and making connections through non-directed monitoring as well as connections by proxy [10].

A second area of interest in our work related concern was therefore how realistic social network users choose to present themselves online. This was examined in study 2 by considering the degree to which the online profile reflects the user's real personality, priorities and values. In our work, we focused on individual behavior rather than social norms as influences on strategic self-presentation (see work on social norms by [32]). In contrast to expectations, participants with role models reported more realistic self-presentation of values and priorities than those who did not have role models online. Results are in line with work by [33] who showed that true self-expression appeared to be positively associated with personal disclosure on Facebook walls. Moreover, those who expressed their 'true self' online tended to be more active social media users who posted content that was both personally revealing as well as emotional content that may increase the accuracy of self-presentation in front of all other contacts. The current findings further contribute to current knowledge about self-disclosure. This suggests that Goffman's [34] notion of 'performing the self' and impression management may not necessarily supported as the relationship between role models and their contacts may require a greater degree of honesty in order to maintain the trust and good will of this relationship. Similarly, impression management via social media may be impaired by the fact that it is difficult for social network users to interpret online cues when the interactions are entirely computer-mediated [35].

When the participants were asked to what extent their social networking profile visible to their network (e.g., newsfeeds, your posts, comments, shares and "likes") also reflects their personality, priorities and values, we saw a significant difference in terms of perceived fit, depending on who assessed this fit between the profile and the actual user's characteristics. A significant difference was observed when participants were asked their own perceptions of presentation fit (between profile and their actual personality, priorities and values) as well as how realistic their family would evaluate the fit of their online profile to the user's personality, priorities and values. The results suggest that individuals with role models believed that their online profile would match their personal characteristics – at least in their own eyes and close others such as their family members' perspective. This suggests that social network users want to portray their genuine self and be perceived as the 'real deal' in order to foster their relationship with role models. Researchers interested in this area may moreover review previous work on role transitions [36]. This work proposed that people strive to be authentic or true to themselves (in line with our work) in the process of exploring provisional selves.

However, our conclusions may need to be interpreted with caution. We did not collect a measure to assess social desirability efforts or impression management efforts. More polished profiles may influence the extent to which role models agreed to join on social media, especially when they know the real person and become aware of the discrepancy between their real self and their online persona. This suggests a form of backlash: Overly unrealistic self-presentation may actually reduce role model willingness to be connected – although this would have to be tested further. Some research suggests that role models may bring about change in those who admire them by helping them to reflect on values as well as identify those that are relevant and attainable [3]. This may actually reinforce more realistic self-presentation on online profiles over time – certainly an area for future research.

The results for the perceived perspectives from two other groups (friends' and colleagues') did not match those obtained for self-ratings and family. No significant differences were obtained when participants were asked to imagine their friends or colleagues rating their profile. These findings may be the result of two variables. First, familiarity – participants' genuine character may be less familiar to friends and colleagues than oneself and the family (who are more likely to know the real 'you'), in line with the idea of weak and strong social ties. In addition, people take different roles in different social environments. Unfortunately, we did not have enough information about the nature of the relationship between our participants and their role models (e.g., how often they interact online & offline, whether the role model's opinion has a determinant influence on one's future career, and so on). Future research may wish to examine this further as some networking may be driven by more utilitarian motives. For example, some contacts may be less interested in individual attributes of a social media connection, but rather look towards their usefulness due to their ties and connections within a social network. This might explain why friends and colleagues may not worry about the degree to which the profile of a user matches their characteristics (e.g., personality, priorities and values) – they may not judge their network contacts based on their realistic self-presentation but by what they can do for them by association [37].

Group comparisons in study 2 further revealed that those participants who had role models online did have higher reciprocity expectations. In other words, they expected that a good turn or doing a favor on their part would also be returned by others. That said, we acknowledge an important caveat: since the data are cross-sectional, we cannot exclude the possibility that people with higher reciprocity expectation (or occupational engagement in the first study) are more likely to add a role model on social media. In other words, reverse causality may play a role in our results as both studies make causal assumptions which need to be tested in follow-up experiments. We do not know if these reciprocity expectations are mutual as some role models may expect some (non-financial) return on investment. We do not know how actively and effectively the role models of our participants and our participants themselves communicated their expectations. Future research may wish to examine reciprocity expectations as a control variable rather than as an outcome variable.

4.1 Conclusions

The study explored the possibility that having a role model on social media may help individuals on social media to gain more career information (study 1). These results suggest that having role models in one's network may boost social network users' future-oriented engagement and improve information access. At the same time, the presence of role models may make social network users more cautious, resulting in more accurate self-presentation online (study 2). However, participants who had role models online also a higher reciprocity expectation (study 2), which suggests that they expect favors to be repaid in the future. This suggests that the benefits of having role models may align with expectations of future returns.

References

1. Kuperminc, G., Emshoff, J.G., Reiner, M.N., Secrest, L.A., Niolon, P.H., Foster, J.D.: Integration of mentoring with other programs and services. In: DuBois, D.L., Karcher, M. J. (eds.) Handbook of Youth Mentoring, pp. 314–339. Sage, Thousand Oaks (2005)
2. Gretzel, U., Bowser, G.: Real stories about real women: communicating role models for female tourism students. J. Teach. Travel Tourism **13**, 170–183 (2013). doi:10.1080/15313220.2013.786466

3. Brace-Govan, J.: More diversity than celebrity: a typology of role model interaction. J. Soc. Mark. **3**(2), 111–126 (2013). doi:10.1108/JSOCM-05-2012-0079

4. Buksa, I., Mitsis, A.: Generation Y's athlete role model perceptions on PWOM behavior. Young Consumers **12**(4), 337–347 (2011). doi:10.1108/17473611111185887

5. Boissin, J.-P., Branchet, B., Delanöe, S., Velo, V.: Gender's perspective of role model influence on entrepreneurial behavioral beliefs. Int. J. Bus. **16**(2), 182–206 (2011)

6. Collins, J., Cooke, D.O.: Creative role models, personality and performance. J. Manag. Dev. **32**(4), 336–350 (2013). doi:10.1108/02621711311326347

7. Vitak, J., Ellison, N.B., Steinfield, C.: The ties that bond: re-examining the relationship between Facebook use and bonding social capital. In: Proceedings of the 44th Hawaii International Conference on System Sciences, pp. 1–10 (2011). doi:10.1109/HICSS.2011. 435

8. Elefant, C.: The "Power" of social media: legal issues and best practices for utilities engaging social media. Energy Law J. **32**(1), 1–56 (2011)

9. Ng, T.W.H., Feldman, D.C.: Subjective career success: a meta-analytic review. J. Vocat. Behav. **85**, 169–179 (2014). doi:10.1016/j.jvb.2014.06.001

10. McKenzie, P.J.: A model of information practices in accounts of everyday-life information seeking. J. Documentation **59**(1), 19–40 (2003). doi:10.1108/00220410310457993

11. Sampson Jr., J.P., Peterson, G.W., Reardon, R.C., Lenz, J.G.: Using readiness assessment to improve career services: a cognitive information processing approach. Career Dev. Q. **49**, 146–174 (2000)

12. Higgins, M.C.: Changing careers: the effects of social context. J. Organ. Behav. **22**, 595–618 (2001). doi:10.1002/job.104

13. Higgins, M.C., Kram, K.E.: Reconceptualizing mentoring at work: a developmental network perspective. Acad. Manag. Rev. **26**, 264–288 (2001). doi:10.5465/AMR.2001.4378023

14. Creed, P.A., Hughes, T.: Career development strategies as moderators between career compromise and career outcomes in emerging adults. J. Career Dev. **40**, 146–163 (2013). doi:10.1177/0894845312437207

15. Metheny, J., Hawley McWhirter, E.: Contributions of social status and family support to college students' career decision self-efficacy and outcome expectations. J Career Assess. **21**, 378–394 (2013). doi:10.1177/1069072712475164

16. Slaten, C.D., Baskin, T.W.: Examining the impact of peer and family belongingness non career decision-making difficulties of young adults: a path analytic approach. J. Career Assess. **22**, 59–74 (2014). doi:10.1177/1069072713487857

17. Lockwood, P., Kunda, Z.: Increasing the salience of one's best selves can undermine inspiration by outstanding role models. J. Pers. Soc. Psychol. **76**(2), 214–228 (1999)

18. Festinger, L.: A theory of social comparison processes. Hum. Relat. **7**(2), 117–140 (1954). doi:10.1177/001872675400700202

19. Sampson, J.P., McClain, M.-C., Musch, E., Reardon, R.C.: Variables affecting readiness to benefit from career interventions. Career Dev. Q. **61**, 98–109 (2013). doi:10.1002/j.2161-0045.2013.00040.x

20. Joos, J.G.: Social media: new frontiers in hiring and recruiting. Employ. Relat. Today **35**(1), 51–59 (2008). doi:10.1002/ert.20188. Springer

21. Gosling, S.D., Augustine, A.A., Vazire, S., Holtzman, N., Gaddis, S.: Manifestations of personality in online social networks: self-reported Facebook-related behaviors and observable profile information. Cyberpsychology, Behav., Soc. Netw. **14**, 483–488 (2011). doi:10.1089/cyber.2010.0087

22. Sievers, K., Wodzicki, K., Aberle, I., Keckeisen, M., Cress, U.: Self-presentation in professional networks: more than just window dressing. Comput. Hum. Behav. **50**, 25–30 (2015). doi:10.1016/j.chb.2015.03.046

23. Homans, G.C.: Social behavior as exchange. Am. J. Soc. **63**(6), 597–606 (1958). http://www.jstor.org/stable/2772990
24. Reber, A.S.: Dictionary of Psychology, 2nd edn. Penguin Reference, New York (1995)
25. Perugini, M., Gallucci, M., Presaghi, F., Ercolani, A.P.: The personal norm of reciprocity. Eur. J. Pers. **17**, 251–283 (2003). doi:10.1002/per.474
26. Blau, P.M.: Exchange and Power in Social Life. Wiley, New York (1964)
27. Lampinen, A., Lehtinen, V., Cheshire, C., Suhonen, E.: Indebtedness and reciprocity in local online exchange. In: Proceedings of CSCW, 23–27 February, San Antonio, Texas, USA, pp. 1–11 (2013). doi:10.1145/2441776.2441850
28. Cox, D.W., Krieshok, T.S., Bjornsen, A.L., Zumbo, B.D.: Occupational engagement scale-student: development and initial validation. J. Career. Assess. **23**, 107–116 (2014). doi:10.1177/1069072714523090
29. Rottinghaus, P.J., Buelow, K.L., Matyja, A., Schneider, M.R.: The career futures inventory – revised: measuring dimensions of career adaptability. J. Career Assess. **20**, 123–139 (2012). doi:10.1177/1069072711420849
30. Stumpf, S.A., Colarelli, S.M., Hartman, K.: Development of the career exploration survey. J. Vocat. Behav. **22**, 191–226 (1983). doi:10.1016/0001-8791(83)90028-3
31. Direnzo, M.S., Weer, C.H., Linnehan, F.: Protégé career aspirations: the influence of formal e-mentor networks and family-based role models. J. Vocat. Behav. **83**, 41–50 (2013). doi:10.1016/j.jvb.2013.02.007
32. Uski, S., Lampinen, A.: Social norms and self-presentation on social network sites: profile work in action. New Media Soc. **18**(3), 447–464 (2016). doi:10.1177/1461444814543164
33. Seidman, G.: Expressing the "true self" on Facebook. Comp. Hum. Behav. **31**, 367–372 (2014). doi:10.1016/j.chb.2013.10.052
34. Goffman, E.: The Presentation of Self in Everyday Life. Doubleday and Anchor Books, New York (1959)
35. Lin, R., Jeske, D.: Impression management via content-dependent "liking" on social media. Int. J. Web Based Communities (in press)
36. Ibarra, H.: Provisional selves: experimenting with image and identity in professional adaptation. Adm. Sci. Q. **44**, 764–791 (1999). doi:10.2307/2667055
37. Kadushin, C.: Understanding Social Networks: Theories, Concepts, and Findings. Oxford University Press, New York (2012)

Using Facebook to Find Missing Persons: A Crowd-Sourcing Perspective

M.J. Hattingh$^{(\boxtimes)}$ and M.C. Matthee

Department of Informatics, University of Pretoria, Pretoria, South Africa
{Marie.Hattingh,Machdel.Matthee}@up.ac.za

Abstract. This paper explores the ways in which Facebook is used in the quest for finding missing persons in South Africa. Graphs are used to indicate differentiated roles of the Facebook communities: some communities act mainly as originators of the messages whereas others act more as distributors or end points of the messages. Crowd-sourcing is used as a conceptual tool to further our understanding of the way messages are shared among different Facebook communities. The four pillars of crowdsourcing as proposed by Hosseini et al., are used to analyse the network of communities as a crowd-source system. It is argued that Facebook can be effective as crowdsourcing system despite the fact that there is no guarantee that missing persons reported there will be found, since it most likely provides much needed emotional support to friends and relatives of the missing person.

Keywords: Crowdsourcing · Social media · Facebook · Missing people · Emotional support

1 Introduction

"A child goes missing in South Africa every five hours" [1]. This alarming fact is not just restricted to children and also not to just South Africa, but is a world-wide problem. Scoop [2] reported in 2013 that 4,432,880 people have disappeared in the past 20 years worldwide. The ubiquity of technology gives people/organisations additional tools to assist in the search for missing people. Centralized databases (registers) can be constructed and information can be shared with ease [3]. Previously, this type of information was usually controlled and distributed through formalized organisations such as the law enforcement services. However, with the rise in the uptake of social media, ordinary citizens can now contribute to the search of missing persons through Web 2.0 technologies. In South Africa, the social media platform adoption has changed significantly. The 2014 World Wide Worx and Fuseware report [4] has indicated that Facebook is the biggest social media platform in South Africa. The report indicated that there are 9.4 million active Facebook users in South Africa in 2014 compared to 6.8 million users in 2013. People use these social media platforms to create social networks. However, these social networks can now be used as a problem solving tool, where a problem is being "outsourced" to the "crowd", this is known as crowdsourcing [5]. Taking the problem solving abilities of networks of people in consideration this study is attempting to answer the following question: How do people use social media

Y.K. Dwivedi et al. (Eds.): I3E 2016, LNCS 9844, pp. 685–694, 2016.
DOI: 10.1007/978-3-319-45234-0_61

platforms, such as Facebook, to aid the search of missing persons? This problem is approached from a crowd-sourcing perspective. Crowds usually originates as an undefined network of people that contribute to a particular task [5]. We answer the research question by firstly mapping the interaction of Facebook groups/pages dedicated to finding missing persons in South Africa and secondly using crowdsourcing as analytical lens, to understand how Facebook communities interact in the quest for finding missing persons.

The paper will first provide in Sect. 2 some background on missing persons which is followed by a brief discussion on the use of social media as a crowdsourcing tool in Sect. 3. After this, in Sect. 4, data is presented on a snapshot taken from a particular network of Facebook groups. The snapshot is analysed in Sect. 5 using the four pillars of crowdsourcing. This is followed by the discussion and conclusion of the findings in Sects. 6 and 7 respectively.

2   Missing Persons and Social Media

According to the "Missing persons: A handbook for parliamentarians" [3], a missing person is defined as an "individuals of whom their families have no news and/or who, on the basis of reliable information, have been reported missing…" With the advent of technology, one would intuitively assume that the search for missing persons will be made easier. However, that is not always the case. Missing Children SA representative says that "Every year we see our success rate decrease. It's not necessarily because we're finding less people, it's just because more people are hearing about the service that "Missing Children SA" provides" [6].

Missing persons is a societal problem that extends beyond finding the missing person. Support to the families of the missing person is also important. According to Wayland [7] the police and non-police search agencies are the primary support mechanisms for the family members as the "the initial focus is on the physical location and return of the missing person and the emotional needs of the family are often set aside while these practical issues are dealt with". Social media can extend support to families of missing person by rendering emotional support. Johnson et al. [8] state that when people are embedded in a caring network, such as a Facebook community dedicated to the search of finding missing people, they are able to obtain social resources, such as instrumental and emotional support, to cope with daily stress or uncertainty. This is extended by Wang and Nayir [9] that stated informal and formal social networks, such as Facebook communities, offer access to resources, to social and emotional support and to practical help for coping with personal, economic and social problems.

3   Crowdsourcing

Hosseini et al. [10] identify four parts (or pillars) of crowdsourcing that describes the entire operation: (1) The crowd: describing the diversity of the people who take part in the crowdsourcing activity, whether they are known to the crowdsource or each other, whether they are enough to fulfil the task without being overloaded, how they were involved to take part and whether they are willing and able to take part, (2) The Crowdsourcer: the person or organisation that needs the help of the crowd to solve a problem The crowd-sourcer might rely on intrinsic or extrinsic motivation, extending the call to participate to the general public in an ethical way. (3) The Crowd-sourced task: This recognises the traditional way the task would have been completed if crowdsourcing did not occur as well as the complexity, solvability, ability to automate, the role of the crowd and the type of contribution made by the crowd. (4) The Crowdsourcing Platform: This refers to the interaction between the crowd and the platform such as social media, the interaction between the crowdsourcer and the platform, the functionalities provided by the platform.

There are a number of existing crowdsourcing tools that use social media to reach the crowd. One such an example is Ushahidi, an open source crises map platform, which was used for disaster relief during the earthquake in Haiti [11]. Rahwan et al. [12] explain how they used social media to crowdsource rapid information gathering in order to find five wanted persons during a manhunt challenge. Their biggest challenge was to mobilize participants to share messages. Gao [11:12] found that during disaster relief, social media as crowdsourcing mechanism provides "aggregate situational awareness, important and new communications pathways, and some opportunities for assistance on an individual level."

4 Method

On the 7th of March 2016, the lead researcher typed in "Missing people" in Facebook search engine. The first public South African Facebook group dedicated to locating missing people, was identified as "Missing People in Centurion" (MPC). The lead researcher then considered every post of the MPC Facebook group between 7 March 2016 and 1 October 2015, giving her approximately 6 months' posts to analyse. Table 1 below illustrates the data captured during the first search iteration.

Table 1. Data captured from first Facebook community

A	B	C																		
MPC	Missing people in Centurion	689 members																		
	Groups Posted																			
PL	Minors Missing - The pink ladies org for missing children	FC	MC	FA	MC	FA	MC	FA	FCD	FC	FA	FC	FA	FC	MC	MC	MA	MC	FC	MA
Hi5Kids	Hi5 Kids recovery	MC	FC	FC																
MCSA	Missing Children SA	MC	FA	FA	MC	FC	FA	FC	MC	FC	FC	MA	MA	MA	MA	MA	FA			
NP-BVEN	NewsPaper - Bedfordviewedenvalenews	MC																		
SAPS	South African Police Services	FCD																		
NP-RK	NewsPaper - Rekord	MA	MA	MA	MA															
NP-KM	NewsPaper -Kormorant	MC																		
NP-MM	NewsPaper - Maroelamedia	MC																		
PLC	People who live in centurion	FA	FA	FA																
BCPF	Vulnerable Citizens Support Initiative:Benoni CPF	MC	MC																	
Pvt	Private Posts	FA	MA	FA	MA	FA	FA	FA	FC	MA	MA	MC	MA							
KCF	Krugersdorp Community forum	MA																		
GPFW	GPF Wilgehof	MC																		
NP-MS	NewsPaper - Mobserver	MC																		
CCC	Centurion concerned citizens	FA	FA	MC																

For every Facebook community with its accompanying posts, she captured the following information in an MS Excel spreadsheet, (as illustrated by Table 1 above, which represents the data captured for the first Facebook community reviewed): (1) The group the post originated from (column B). An acronym was assigned to each group in column A. (2) Each post that was distributed by each of the groups (column C). Distinction was made between posts depending on whether it was an adult or child that was missing or found or deceased. The following codes were used: a missing child (MC), a missing adult (MA), child found (FC), found adult (FA). In a few instances the post reported that a child was found deceased (FCD) or an adult was found deceased (FAD). All duplicate posts from the same group were ignored. Finally, the lead researcher then repeated the above steps for the six dedicated "missing people" or community support Facebook groups that were listed in the first group (Table 1 column B), excluding newspapers and private pages, until saturation was reached (no new communities emerged).

5 Data Analysis

Table 2 below illustrates the data that was obtained from the Facebook review. Seven Facebook communities dedicated to finding missing people or community support communities were found, linked directly or indirectly to the first Facebook group. In total, 392 posts were reviewed within the given 6 month timeframe. These Facebook communities were connected to a total of 38 other communities (45 communities in total). Table 2 above summarises all the communities reviewed where the size of the community is indicated by both the number of members/likes of the community, and the types and number of posts distributed by each of these communities.

The connectivity between the different Facebook communities is illustrated by Figs. 1 and 2 which represents the connections (and thereby the reach) of the Facebook crowd. In Fig. 1 each Facebook community is represented by a node whereas each line represents a one-directional information flow between two Facebook communities. The arrow points to the community that shares the posts of the connected Facebook community. For example, the Pink Ladies is dedicated to finding missing persons and can therefore be seen as the originator of the posts. Indeed, Fig. 1 shows that the Pink Ladies (PL) has the most references (shared posts) by other communities, followed by the Missing Children SA (MCSA) group who is also dedicated to finding missing persons. The third most-shared posts originate from private people (PVT) reporting missing people. This is indicated by the sizes of the nodes.

Figure 2 illustrates a different kind of information flow. The lines of the graph and size of the nodes now refers to the number of posts shared by that specific community of other communities. It further shows in Fig. 2 that even though PL's posts were shared the most among different communities, PL did not share any posts associated with other communities (within the research period). Similarly, the posts of MCSA were widely shared, but MCSA did not share any other communities' posts on their page. Both these communities' nodes are therefore very small. However, the first Facebook group reviewed by the researchers, MPC, shares a lot of posts of other communities as indicated by the size of the node. The second and third biggest sharer

Table 2. Summary of Facebook Communities identified

Facebook Group/Page name	Members/likes	Connections	FA	FC	MA	MC	FCD	FAD
1. Missing people in Centurion (MPC)	689 members	15	18	11	17	19	2	0
2. Minors missing - the Pink Ladies org for missing children (PL)	28030 likes	0	5	7	95	31	0	0
3. Hi5 Kids Recovery (Hi5 K)	9193 likes	3	2	7	3	1	1	0
4. Missing Children SA (MCSA)	62621 likes	0	19	28	32	17	0	3
5. Vulnerable Citizens Support Initiative:Benoni CPF: Gauteng Community Alerts (BCPF)	7468 members	11	1	11	11	8	2*	3
6. People who live in Centurion (PLC)	31556 members	11	1	3	6	2	2*	0
7. Centurion Concerned Citizens (CCC)	24256 likes	5	13	7	3	0	1	0

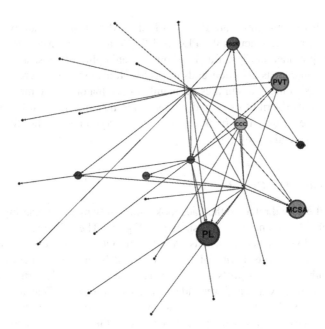

Fig. 1. Originators of posts

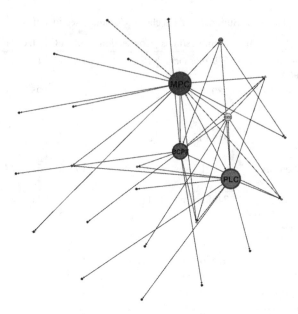

Fig. 2. Distributors of posts

of posts of other communities are PLC and BCPF. MPC is a community dedicated to finding missing people whereas the PLC and BCPF are community support groups.

The maps provided in Figs. 1 and 2 show the 'enlarging of the search party' across diverse geographic areas and thousands of people. It also shows differentiated roles of the communities: some communities act mainly as originators of the messages whereas others act more as distributors or end points of the messages. The following sections will analyse the above Facebook communities according to the four pillars of crowdsourcing as defined by [10].

5.1   Pillar One: The Crowd

In this paper the crowd refers to the Facebook community members sharing the posts of various Facebook communities (illustrated in Fig. 2). Their features are as follows: *Diversity:* The diversity needed in this crowd is from a geographical perspective. This was indeed reached since the initial group reviewed by the researchers is situated in Gauteng, South Africa, but posts as far as Kraaifontein in the Western Cape Province some 1000 km from Gauteng, were identified. *Unknownness:* Due to the nature of Facebook, the crowd will inevitably know about one another as anyone can have at least limited access to anyone's profile. However, the aim of this exercise is not anonymity but is in support of the crowdsourcer's task. In the majority of instances the missing person post/update was made by the specific Facebook community, as illustrated in Fig. 1 above, only 10 % of all the posts under consideration (26 of 393 posts) were private posts. *Largeness*: The largeness of the networked Facebook communities, is what makes the Facebook platform so successful in finding missing people.

Table 2 above illustrates, that between the communities under consideration, there is a crowd of 163 813 Facebook users that would be able to assist in the quest to find missing people. *Undefined-ness:* The vast amount of Facebook users is an illustration of the undefined-ness of the Facebook social network. All of the groups, bar the private posts, were public groups which allowed anyone access to their postings. *Suitability:* The Facebook communities referenced in this study all voluntarily participated in solving the "missing people" problem by posting the "missing people" information, or share the posted information. The number of communities referenced by particular communities is an illustration of their ability to collaborate with other communities and individuals. The Facebook communities' motivations are all intrinsic as no incentive, bar the possibility of locating the missing person is provided.

5.2   Pillar Two: The Crowdsourcer

In this paper the crowdsourcer refers to the Facebook communities and community members (in terms of private posts) who provide the posts of missing persons (illustrated in Fig. 1). A missing person post usually includes personal details with a photo as well as contact details of the authorities and a contact number of the missing persons community representative. The features of the crowdsourcer in this context are as follows: *Incentive provision:* There was no need for the crowdsourcers (the different communities listed in Table 2 or the private posts) to provide any incentives for "the crowd" to participate in posting or sharing missing people information. *Open Call:* As all the groups were public groups, it was open for any member of the public to participate in the posting or sharing of missing people. *Ethicality provision:* At any stage can a member of "the crowd" choose not to participate, or even "opt-out" of the Facebook group by unfollowing the page or removing themselves from the group. Furthermore, the crowdsourcer is ethically bound to provide feedback to "the crowd". From Table 2 it is seen that updates were made where available. *Privacy provision:* Due to the nature of Facebook it is near impossible for "the crowd" not to be aware of one another. However, it is possible for the crowd to private message the crowd-sourcer, which the crowdsource is not allowed to disclose to others.

5.3   Pillar Three: The Crowdsourced Task

In this paper the crowdsourced task refers to the activity of locating missing people. There features are as follows: *Traditional operation:* The missing people's communities work in conjunction with the authorities to locate the missing persons. In most cases, if the missing person's notice is released through a missing person's community (such as MCSA or PL) a police docket number is included (if available)). This allows for the traditional operations to continue parallel with the community's crowdsourcing initiative. *Modularity:* Although a number of posts can be posted daily regarding missing people, it is done one by one. Therefore, "the crowd" can choose the post which they would like to share. *Complexity:* Task of sharing a Facebook post is quite straightforward and the community was quick to assist if someone had trouble sharing a post. *Solvability:* Unfortunately, the act of sharing a post does not necessarily result in solving the missing person problem. However, a secondary activity of the ability to support the crowdsourcer emotionally (especially if it is a private post) can be seen as solving the emotional isolation problem. An example of this is a message posted on MPC (Missing Persons in Centurion): "Morning all, my brother has been missing for 2 weeks now. I ask that we all pray for his safe return where ever he might be, also if anyone knows or have seen him please contact me at this number" on which MPC replied: "Hi, why don't we all just re-share this and ask our contacts to share so the word spreads more and more". *Automation Characteristics:* The nature of Facebook allows for a measure of automation. Once a Facebook user "follows" a group he/she will automatically receive the post from the group (the crowdsourcer), however, the act of further sharing it is not automated. Furthermore, this is an inexpensive method of automation. *User-driven:* The particular problem that is attempted to be solved through "the crowd" is creating awareness and finding missing people. This is problem solving activity but also an example of an innovative way of using technology. *Contribution Type:* The Facebook communities allow for both an individual and collaborative contribution. Collectively the various communities are working together to find missing people. However, on an individual level, a community member renders support to the crowdsourcer (in the event of an individual/private post).

5.4   Pillar Four: The Crowdsourcing Platform

In this paper the crowdsourcing platform refers to Facebook. Its features are as follows: *Crowd-related Interactions:* Facebook as the chosen crowdsourcing platform in this instance provides clear mechanisms for enrolment and authentication (as far as user profiles are legitimate). In certain instances, especially when it's a private post, the community members were asked to share the missing person's details, however, in formal missing person's posts, the communities spontaneously shared posts without being "tasked" to do it. *Crowdsourcer-related Interactions:* The crowdsourcer in this study took two forms: dedicated missing people group administrators who generate and co-ordinate posts regarding missing people as illustrated in Fig. 1 above and secondly, individuals sharing private posts (usually about someone close to them) being missing. In both these instances, Facebook has clear rules in place regarding privileges of users and administrators. *Task-related Facilities:* The communities provided no restriction on the sharing of posts regarding missing people. Furthermore, the crowdsourcers (not in the case of private posts) usually work closely with the authorities in order to ensure the authentication of the "task". *Platform-related Facilities:* The online platform provided by Facebook is governed by the Facebook terms and conditions. Furthermore, the nature of Facebook allows the crowd to easily interact with the crowdsourcer.

6 Discussion

The discussion above illustrates the value of the concept "crowdsourcing" in reaching an understanding of the way in which Facebook is used to find missing persons. Certain members and Facebook communities in the network act as the "crowd" (Fig. 2) whereas others act as the crowdsourcers (Fig. 1) who have a specific task – finding missing people. The crowdsourcing platform is Facebook. Using crowdsourcing as analytical lens also shows the shortfall of using Facebook in the quest to find missing persons. Gao et al. [11] believe that social media as crowdsourcing tool lacks inherent coordination capabilities when used for disaster relief. Although the phenomenon of missing persons cannot be considered a disaster, there are similarities in the processes needed to react to the disaster and to find missing persons: there is a need to not only share but also coordinate information among different groups and organisations. We have found evidence of close cooperation be-tween the missing persons groups and the police in some of the posts. This means that Facebook is used not only as a way of mobilising crowds (sharing messages) in this context. We therefore believe that if authorities use social media in a more focused and coordinated way, or combine it with existing crowdsourcing tools, the "power of the crowd" can truly be realised in the search for missing persons. Despite the fact that "the crowd" might not literally result in the locating of a missing person (only two posts made reference to the locating of a missing person through the actions of the "the crowd"), the crowd seems to be effective in other ways. It renders emotional support to the crowdsourcer. Technological advances, such as the Internet, have created new opportunities for social interaction and support among community members [13]. The Internet supplements the traditional operations of locating a missing person – through the processes of authorities and at the same time extend emotional support to the crowdsourcers individually and collaboratively.

7 Conclusion

This research paper aims to understand how Facebook is used in the quest of locating missing persons. Crowdsourcing is used as analytical lens and explains the interaction between communities indicated in the graphs as those of the crowdsourcer (Fig. 1) and those of the crowd (Fig. 2). It further illustrates the "powerful propagation capability" [11] of Facebook as crowd-sourcing platform. It also points towards the necessity of a more coordinated effort in order to realise the benefit of Facebook as crowdsourcing platform. This might imply an expansion of the traditional search processes by authorities to officially include social media. In addition, it is argued that this network of communities act not only as a massive search party but also as a source of emotional support. This study can be seen as exploratory in the sense that it included data from a short time period. More research is needed to apply current research on crowd-sourcing to such systems to understand and improve its effectiveness.

References

1. A child goes missing every five hours in SA – MCSA, 4 June 2015. http://www.news24.com/SouthAfrica/News/A-child-goes-missing-every-five-hours-in-SA-MCSA-20150604
2. 4,432,880 Missing Persons Vanished In Past 20 Years Monday, 26 August 2013, 11:20 In Press Release: International Rewards Centre. http://www.scoop.co.nz/stories/WO1308/S00441/4432880-missing-persons-vanished-in-past-20-years.htm
3. Missing persons: A handbook for Parliamentarians, No. 17 (2009). http://www.ipu.org/PDF/publications/missing09-e.pdf
4. South African Social Media Landscape 2014 (2014). http://www.worldwideworx.com/wp-content/uploads/2013/10/Exec-Summary-Social-Media-2014.pdf
5. Howe, J.: The rise of crowdsourcing. Wired. Issue 14.06, June 2006. http://www.wired.com/wired/archive/14.06/crowds.html
6. NGO helps find more than 450 missing people, 22 December 2015. http://ewn.co.za/2015/12/22/NGO-helps-find-more-than-450-missing-persons
7. Wayland, S.: Supporting those who are left behind (2009). http://www.missingpersons.gov.au/~/media/mp/files/pdfs/supporting%20those%20who%20are%20left%20behind.pdf
8. Johnson, E.C., Kristof-Brown, A.L., Van Vianen, A.E., De Pater, I.E., Klein, M.R.: Expatriate social ties: personality antecedents and consequences for adjustment. Int. J. Sel. Assess. **11**(4), 277–288 (2003)
9. Wang, X., Nayir, D.: How and when is social networking important? Comparing European expatriate adjustment in China and Turkey. J. Int. Manage. **12**, 449–472 (2006)
10. Hosseini, M., Phalp, K., Taylor, J., Ali, R.: The four pillars of crowdsourcing: a reference model. In: 2014 IEEE Eighth International Conference on Research Challenges in Information Science (RCIS), Marrakech, pp. 1 – 12 (2014). doi:10.1109/RCIS.2014.6861072
11. Gao, H., Barbier, G., Goolsby, R.: Harnessing the crowdsourcing power of social media for disaster relief. IEEE Intell. Syst. **26**(3), 10–14 (2011)
12. Rahwan, I., Dsouza, S., Rutherford, A., Naroditskiy, V., McInerney, J., Venanzi, M., Jennings, N.R., Cebrian, M.: Global manhunt pushes the limits of social mobilization. Computer **46**(6), 68–75 (2013)
13. Sarason, I., Sarason, B.: Social support: mapping the construct. J. Soc. Pers. Relat. **26**(1), 113–120 (2009)

Social Media and Megachurches

Atish Sircar and Jennifer Rowley[✉]

Manchester Metropolitan University, Manchester, UK
atish.z.sircar@stu.mmu.ac.uk, j.rowley@mmu.ac.uk

Abstract. This paper contributes to the understanding of social media strategy by examining how, Hillsong, a megachurch, is using social media. Whilst there, is a growing body of research on megachurches, and on the use of social media by not-for-profit organisations, no prior studies have examined the use of social media in megachurches. The study uses a content analysis of Hillsong's social media platforms on Twitter, Facebook, YouTube and Instagram, to demonstrate the distributed model of social media presence adopted by Hillsong, and relates this to the various purposes for which Hillsong uses social media. Discussion and conclusions evaluate this approach to social media strategy.

Keywords: Megachurch · Internet · Social media · Engagement · Online communities

1 Introduction

Social media has emerged as an important medium for communication, and specifically, for organizations communicating with their customers [1]. A particular strength of social media is the opportunity it provides to engage in a two-way conversation [2]. Also, organisations have viewed social media as a means of protecting their corporate or brand reputation [3], increasing customer engagement [4] or increasing online sales [5]. But most research into social media tends to focus on its impact, on, for instance, customer engagement, satisfaction or relationships [6–8] and there is an absence of studies on social media strategy. Furthermore, although there is a growing body of research on the use of social media by not-for-profit organisations e.g. [9, 10], most of this research is concerned with commercial organisations. Given their focus on growth and community building, megachurches offer an interesting and different context in which to explore the use of social media. A megachurch is an evangelical Christian assembly with more than 2000 attendees, who meet in a large arena for teaching and worship. Such churches have succeeded in attracting young, professional and highly educated individuals who are typically 'digital natives', and therefore for whom use of the internet and engagement with others of like mind through social media is integral to their way of life. On the other hand, although there have been some prior studies on the megachurch phenomena [11] and some analysis of their use of the internet [12] there have been no previous studies on the way in which these churches are using social media.

Published by Springer International Publishing Switzerland 2016. All Rights Reserved
Y.K. Dwivedi et al. (Eds.): I3E 2016, LNCS 9844, pp. 695–700, 2016.
DOI: 10.1007/978-3-319-45234-0_62

The aim of this paper is to contribute to the understanding of how social media can be used to grow and support engagement in large scattered communities. It seeks to do this by conducting a case study analysis of the way in which Hillsong, a megachurch, uses social media in pursuit of its mission.

2   Literature Review

Megachurches have a significant role in rebuilding interest and engagement with the Christian religion. The phenomenon is worldwide, with several megachurches having venues in several cities, and some in several countries. Whilst megachurches are not a new phenomenon, an early example being the Methodist church which was founded in the 19th century [13], the current model of a megachurch dates from the latter part of the twentieth century when church leaders began to understand the potential of new media and technologies. Notwithstanding the importance of church buildings, many megachurches are classed as being a "digital ministry". Megachurches are branded, and since many of the churches are global, they need to manage a global brand, and hence must attend to their digital presence, reputation and identity.

A significant quantity of research has been carried out on megachurches. Some of this research analyses the factors that affect the development and success of mega-churches. For example, Martin et al. [14] studied 12 megachurches to understand their characteristics, while Karnes et al. [15] assessed the demographic and economic factors that explain the development of the megachurch movement. Other researchers have examined the way in which megachurches use the internet and websites. For example, Kim [16] studied Korean megachurches exploitation of the internet and their use of websites to support religious practice. Hackett [17] found that church leaders in three megachurches in Africa used websites to bolster their image, and to legitimise their authority. Sturgill's [18] research on UK-based megachurches is the only study to examine megachurch websites from the perspective of marketing and branding.

A few studies focus specifically on Hillsong. Connell [12] explained how the church had changed religious practices and civic, social institutions while creating social capital using modern technology. More recently, Klaver [19] conducted an ethnographic study in New York and Amsterdam to profile the transformation of sermon and preaching practices, when they are reproduced across time and place. Importantly, whilst there is considerable interest in the megachurch model, there has been limited previous research into the use of the Internet in megachurches and none on the way in which megachurches use social media.

The small, but growing body of research into the use of social media in not-for-profit organizations offers some useful insights and emerging theoretical frameworks. Some of these studies focus on the messages sent by the organisation [9] or on how they engage stakeholders [20]. Nah and Saxton [10] suggest that there are four factors that affect the adoption and use of social media by not-for-profit organisations: strategy, capacity, governance and environment, whilst Lovejoy and Saxton [9] develop a classification of the purposes for which microblogging is used that includes information, community, and action.

3   Research Methodology

3.1   Case Study – Hillsong Church

This research takes a single case study approach to the investigation of the use of social media by megachurches. According to Rowley [21], case studies are suitable for generating answers to 'how' questions; in this study the aim is to understand how megachurches use social media. Hillsong has been chosen as a case study, because it is a global church that has fully embraced a digital ministry and makes significant use of social media to communicate with members, build communities, and to promote the church and its merchandise and events. Starting in a rented hall in 1983 in Australia, Hillsong is now the most successful branded community church with three Australian campuses and twenty-four other locations around the globe in cities such as London, Kiev, Cape Town, Paris, Stockholm, Moscow and New York. The weekly attendance is around 34,083 worshipers.

3.2   Content Analysis of Hillsong's Social Media Presence

In order to explore how Hillsong uses social media, a content analysis of Hillsong UK's social media presences was conducted. The purpose of this analysis was two-fold: to profile the extent and nature of Hillsong's social media presence; and, to explore the purposes for which Hillsong and its community groups used the various social media channels. The content analysis focused on the four social media channels used by Hillsong, Twitter, Facebook, Instagram, and YouTube. Social media presences were identified through Hillsong's websites, supplemented by Google searches. In addition to these 'official' social media presences, there are also mentions of Hillsong, or, for example, its music, in various other social media presences; these were not included in this study.

   Analysis of each of the social media presences identified involved first establishing on which social media platforms the various leaders, churches and communities had a presence. Then for each presence the person posting on the site and the uses and were noted. Persons posting were classified as leaders (L) or members (M). The coding frame for the uses was developed inductively, based initially on inspection of two of the social media presences. This process identified five uses: sales (S), promotion (P), events (E), giving (G), and two-way communication (2C).

4   Findings

Hillsong UK has a number of social media presences, associated both with the church as a whole and individual community groups. In addition, the purposes for which the various different platforms are used differs between groups.

Facebook. Facebook is primarily used to support daily media-based worship. For example, the profile page is used to promote and communicate events, post multimedia files, music releases, music videos and campaign summaries. Hillsong uses Facebook to target particular communities or groups, in respect of, for instance, the sales of conference tickets. Also, the page allows community members to share the Hillsong Facebook page on their individual Facebook page. Community members can also post events and upload photos into albums, and share and advertise upcoming events. Also, music videos can be shared and liked, while pictures of recent events communicate a sense of a lively and interesting community. Five church leaders use Facebook to initiate two-way communication, promote events, charity fundraising, and sales. For example, the lead pastor of the church uses Facebook for promoting events and conferences and books. The emphasis is on one-way communication and promotion rather than on communication with members and community building. All church communities based in the five UK locations have a profile page that is used for promotion, communication, sales, and marketing. Visitors are able to like the page and share on their profile, comment, subscribe to new events, and buy tickets. Only three of the communities, family, wildlife, and sisterhood use Facebook for community building and for the promotion of events and publishing photos of past events. Some communities, such as the music community are closed groups.

Twitter. Twitter is used for communicating and advertising events and new products and services such as new music albums, outreach activities, fundraising and recent developments. Spiritual messages are posted to encourage users in their faith, to build social relationships and to stay connected to the church. On the other hand, compared to facebook, Twitter posting are mainly from Hillsong leaders, with very few postings from members of the community. All the five leaders of the church had a Twitter presence and used it variously for promotion, sales of events and regular communication with church members, globally. For example, the senior pastor, Brian Huston, uses Twitter for spreading Christian religious messages and promotion of his new published books, whilst his wife, Bobbie Huston, uses the page mainly to update the sisterhood community and for promoting events and the London pastor, Gary Clarke, uses Twitter for the promotion of new music albums and for spreading new biblical messages. As far as the church communities in the UK, Twitter is mainly used for posting events and for promotion of music albums. Only the London church, @HillsongLondon, uses Twitter to its full potential, including promotion, sales, fundraising, events and album sales. The remaining four church communities only use their profile page for promotion and communication from leaders. Amongst the UK communities, only the Kids community has a profile page, which is used mainly for promotion.

Instagram. Hillsong uses Instagram for updating its community members and others interested in Hillsong music and events. There are many comments from members on the photos that are posted on Instagram, and, in addition, these photos are shared on Hillsong member's individual social media platforms. However, all leaders, and the churches in the five locations use Instagram for promotion and sales. Posting is administered by community members who are allowed to post high definition photos; this helps the church to build its image. Amongst the communities, only Kids community has an Instagram profile page, which is used for promotion.

YouTube. Hillsong London's YouTube channel broadcasts music videos, past events and conferences and sermons from the lead pastors and musicians, as well as educational Bible courses such as the Alpha course. Anyone can view the videos, comment and share them on their profile pages. Text messages from interested people can also be seen. None of the other UK churches, nor any of the communities have a YouTube presence. Only the main lead pastor, Brian Huston, has a YouTube channel, which he uses to promote gospel music and sermons on a weekly basis.

5 Discussion, Conclusions and Further Research

This study shows that Hillsong has social media presences across Facebook, Twitter, Instagram and YouTube. Facebook is the most used social media platform, whilst YouTube is only used by the church leader, Brian Huston, and by the Central London church. Analysis of who posts on these social media presences, shows that both leaders and members post on most of the Facebook sites, and that there is evidence of two-way communication. On Instagram, there are also postings from leaders and members, but less two-way communication. However, on Twitter, the posting is mainly from church leaders, with no evidence of two-way communication. Some of the Hillsong communities, such as Family, also have Facebook presences, but many others do not. Kids does not have a Facebook presence, but does have a presence on Twitter and Instagram. Hillsong's uses of social media can be classified as sales, promotion, events, and giving. All of these uses are evident in the Facebook presences of the churches in the various locations, and, with the exception of events, are in evidence on the church leaders websites. Communities only use Facebook for events and promotion. The emphasis on sales and promotion is consistent with some earlier studies [5]. Contrary to expectations, Hillsong does not appear to be making full use of the capacity of social media to build member engagement and relationships [4, 7, 8]. There is some two-way communication in some social media presences, but, interestingly, as in [20] not in Twitter, nor in the Hillsong communities.

The overriding sense is that the social media presence of Hillsong is complex, being scattered across platforms, and having several groups on some platforms. It would appear that social media page 'owners' such as church leaders, both international, and local church, are using their Facebook pages and other social media presences to communicate their messages to Hillsong members, and that each is doing this in a way that is consistent with their personality and role. In other words, if Hillsong has a social media strategy it is distributed and emergent, rather than directed and specified.

This paper reports on an early stage of a larger project. The next stages will:

(1) Extend the content analysis of the Hillsong social media presences to other groups, and develop a more sophisticated classification for the types of use of social media.
(2) Contribute to understanding of the extent to which there are shared objectives and strategies regarding social media use, through interviews with key stakeholders in the church.

References

1. Wade, M.: Seeker-friendly: The Hillsong Megachurch as an enchanting total institution. J. Sociol. (2015). doi:10.1177/1440783315575171
2. Bacile, T., Ye, C., Swilley, E.: From firm-controlled to consumer-contributed: consumer co-production of personal media marketing communication. J. Interact. Mark. **28**, 117–133 (2014)
3. Lee, M., Youn, S.: Electronic Word of Mouth (eWOM): how eWOM platforms influence consumer product judgement. Int. J. Advertising **28**, 473–478 (2009)
4. Gummerus, J., Liljander, V., Weman, E., Pihlström, M.: Customer engagement in a facebook brand community. Manage. Res. Rev. **35**, 857–877 (2012)
5. Chen, Y., Fay, S., Wang, Q.: The role of marketing in social media: how online consumer reviews evolve. J. Interact. Mark. **25**, 85–94 (2011)
6. Kim, A.J., Ko, E.: Do social media marketing activities enhance customer equity? an empirical study of luxury fashion brands. J. Bus. Res. **65**, 1480–1486 (2012)
7. Okazaki, S., Díaz-Martín, A.M., Rozano, M., Menéndez-Benito, M.D.: Using twitter to engage with customers: a data mining approach. Internet Res. **25**, 416–434 (2015)
8. Trainor, K.J., Andzulis, J.M., Rapp, A., Agnihotri, R.: Social media technology usage and customer relationship performance: a capabilities-based examination of social CRM. J. Bus. Res. **67**, 1201–1208 (2014)
9. Lovejoy, K., Saxton, G.D.: Information, community, and action: how nonprofit organizations use social media. J. Comput.-Mediated Commun. **17**, 337–353 (2012)
10. Nah, S., Saxton, G.D.: Modeling the adoption and use of social media by non-profit organisations. New Media Soc. **15**, 294–313 (2013)
11. Thumma, S., Bird, W.: Changes in American Megachurches: Tracing Eight Years of Growth and Innovation in the Nation's Largest-attendance Congregations (2008). http://hdl.handle.net/1805/5657
12. Connell, J.: Hillsong: a megachurch in the Sydney suburbs. Aust. Geogr. **36**, 315–332 (2005)
13. Eagle, D.E.: Historicizing the megachurch. J. Soc. Hist. **48**, 589–604 (2015)
14. Martin, P.P., Bowles, T.A., Adkins, L., Leach, M.T.: Black megachurches in the internet age: exploring theological teachings and social outreach efforts. J. Afr. Am. Stud. **15**, 155–176 (2011)
15. Karnes, K., McIntosh, W., Morris, I.L., Pearson-Merkowitz, S.: Mighty fortresses: explaining the spatial distribution of American megachurches. J. Sci. Study Religion **46**, 261–268 (2007)
16. Kim, K.: Ethereal christianity: reading korean megachurch websites. Stud. World Christianity **13**, 208–224 (2007)
17. Hackett, R.I.J.: The new virtual (inter)face of African pentecostalism. Society **46**, 496–503 (2009)
18. Sturgill, A.: Scope and Purposes of church web sites. J. Media Relig. **3**, 165–176 (2004)
19. Klaver, M.: Media technology creating 'Sermonic Events' the Hillsong megachurch network. CrossCurrents **65**, 422–433 (2015)
20. Lovejoy, K., Waters, R.D., Saxton, G.D.: Engaging stakeholders through twitter: how nonprofit organisations are getting more out of 140 characters or less. Public Relat. Rev. **38**, 313–318 (2012)
21. Rowley, J.: Using case studies in research. Manage. Res. News **25**, 16–27 (2002)

'Unofficial' Presence of Higher Education Institutions in India on Social Media: Good or Bad?

Rakhi Tripathi[(✉)]

Centre for Digital Innovation, FORE School of Management, Delhi, India
rakhi@fsm.ac.in

Abstract. The objective of this paper is to analyze the unofficial presence of Universities in India on Social Media with a focus on Facebook and Twitter. Content analysis was used in terms of quantitative approach. A checklist was developed as the main research instrument based on other checklists and questionnaires. It was observed that all the selected institutions have online presence, however, some are very active online and some have static presence. One third of the institutions are on social media and surprisingly one-fourth has unofficial accounts on social media. Government institutions as compared to Private have larger unofficial presence on social media. Unofficial presence on Social Media can be a concern for higher education institutions in terms of security and branding.

Keywords: Website · Higher education · Social networking site · Interaction

1 Introduction

Online presence has never been as crucial for higher education as it is now. The projection of providing information is now been shifted to engaging students and other stakeholders online. The social media revolution has certainly entered education, carrying with it the notion that users add value through its participation [8]. The importance of social media in academics can be clearly observed in institutions in US and UK. By 2011 all the top institutions in US came on social media, Facebook and Twitter being prominent.

Digital presence is becoming an integral part of higher education in India too. Being a developing nation, India has approximately 700 higher education institutions (HEI). Though majority of the Universities have web presence in terms of website but limited universities are present on Social Media. Like in developed nations, Facebook and Twitter too are the leaders among the other social networking sites when it comes for higher education institutions in India. It has been observed that unofficial accounts on Social Networking Sites of many Universities have been created and University administration has no control over these accounts.

With an objective of analyzing the unofficial presence of Universities in India on social media this paper focuses on the research question of 'Why do the Universities have unofficial accounts on social media and what are the concerns related to it?'

© IFIP International Federation for Information Processing 2016
Published by Springer International Publishing Switzerland 2016. All Rights Reserved
Y.K. Dwivedi et al. (Eds.): I3E 2016, LNCS 9844, pp. 701–706, 2016.
DOI: 10.1007/978-3-319-45234-0_63

Reader may not get confused with this piece of research with role of social media for higher education. This paper is an attempt to understand concerns and issues Universities might have to face because of unofficial presence.

2 Related Work

Online presence of higher education institutions is on rise as it enhances learning, communication and engagement. Institutions are paying attention to their website and presence on social media. Every digital platform is different in terms of nature, features and projection [7]. Hence, it becomes important for higher education institutions to focus on all these platforms differently.

In past one decade there have been a number of studies on digital presence of higher education institutions from different directions. Majority of the papers from India and overseas are focusing on how academicians and students are employing social media and website [1, 6]. [5] have come to a conclusion that for Higher education institution's branding, social media plays a key role. The branding of HEI helps them in building their identity and image among their key stakeholders – students, parents, institution partners and society at large. The uprising competition for students and program recognition as well as demand for financial support tools prompt the higher education institutes to use strategic and planned PR and to allocate more efforts for communication in the internet [16]. In a longitudinal study for three years on "rules of engagement in the online world" it was found that colleges and universities in USA continue to embrace social media [2]. The higher education institutes attract and connect to their various stakeholders: students current and prospective, alumni, recruiters, Industry collaborators, International collaborators etc. through their brand communities on various social networking sites like Facebook, YouTube, Twitter, Blogging and Podcasting. It has also been identified through research that the communities which do not facilitate interaction and engagement tend to lose their audience. Study by [2] shows in a national sample of 456 of four-year accredited U.S. institutions that 100 % report using some form of social media, with Facebook (used by 98 %) and Twitter (used by 84 %) being the most prominent.

Social media is considered to be an essential part of Web 2.0 technologies. Use of social networking sites for education has been a popular topic. Some [12] studied the use of social networking sites by undergraduates, graduates, and faculty members at Yonsei Institution in Seoul, South Korea and [9] found that the youths at age group of 13–14 years based on gender, ethnicity and parental income, were using social networking sites more than at age group of 20–23 years. There have been studies on social media in higher education in different countries like in Oman [1], Dublin [14], USA [4].

3 Research Method

This study made use of content analysis methodology for the quantitative method. India has approximately 700 higher education institutions (including Government and private). 300 plus academic institutions for the present study were selected by combining the data from three reliable data sources: economics times (http://articles.economictimes), outlook (http://www.outlookindia.com) and India today (http://www.indiatoday). No ranks were given to the institutions. The following steps listed were carried out:

- Browsed through the 320 institutions websites to check the level of website and presence of social media.
- Social networking sites were independently searched to see the number of unofficial accounts of the institutions. By unofficial it is meant that these accounts/pages on social media of the institutions are not created and maintained by the intuition but by someone else and hence, institution has no control over its content.

Unofficial presence on social media of Universities in India was noted during the period of January 2016 through March 2016. The data was entered into an Excel spreadsheet, data was compiled and results reported.

4 Results

Total 320 websites of Universities in India were studied, out of which 300 were valid (approx 96 %). Websites which were either not opening or were redirected to other websites were considered invalid. Out of these 300 Universities 71 have unofficial accounts on social media.

After analyzing the unofficial accounts and pages further, it was found that most of accounts on social media are created by alumni or the present students of the institute. Digging deeper, data reveals that more than 90 % of unofficial accounts are of Government institutions (64 out of 71) and rest of Private institutions. Therefore it is eccentric to see that government institutions have more presence on social media unofficially as compared to officially.

The websites of these 71 universities were visited to check their online presence. Websites were analyzed to see at what stage they currently are at: *Information* stage where website provides basic information. The second stage *Interaction* provides a web site with some form of interaction with its stakeholders. *Transaction* stage provides monetary transactions available to its stakeholders. It was found that only two university websites are at Information level which includes one Government and one private university. Majority of the universities are at interaction level. More than 90 per cent of Government university websites are interactive. These institutions are interacting with its stakeholders in some way. These shows the universities are engaging its stakeholders through website but are still not present on social media. 3 out of 71 university websites are at the transaction level. These institutions, along with interaction, provide transactions, primarily student fee submission.

4.1 Visiting Unofficial Social Networking Sites of HEI

As already stated above 71 of 300 universities have unofficial accounts on social media. More than 95 % of these accounts/pages are either on Facebook or Twitter only. 69 Universities out of 71 have unofficial Facebook pages (Table 1) where 62 are Government and only 7 are private universities. These pages are formed after 2010. 50 % of them have more than 10, 000 likes which implies people are aware about the account and are following it. These accounts are also very active in updating status. Mostly the news is related to the institution only which might include alumni achievements. Moreover, these accounts engage its followers. Some statuses have 'comments' and 'likes' both. Two out of 69 Websites share same information with Facebook page (news updates only). Both these Websites are Government websites.

Table 1. Details of unofficial pages and accounts on facebook and twitter

Unofficial page/Account	Facebook	Twitter
Total number of Institutions	69	18
Government (Govt.)	62	17
Private (Pvt.)	7	1
More than 10, 000 likes	35 (Govt. = 32; Pvt. = 3)	–
More than 1000 followers	–	8 (All Govt. HEI)
Date of formation	after 2010	2009–2011
Regular updates	43 (Govt. = 38; Pvt. = 5)	7 (All Govt. HEI)
Not functional	26	11

As compared to Facebook, only 18 universities are present on Twitter unofficially. Same as in Facebook, majority of the unofficial presence on Twitter is of Government HEI. It must be also noted that 26 of these universities Facebook pages and 11 of twitter accounts are not functional (24 of Government and 2 private). Except one all the HIE that have unofficial twitter accounts also have unofficial Facebook pages. It has also been noticed here that the accounts with more followers/likes have regular updates and vice versa.

5 Discussion

This section confers some useful insights from the above results.

A large number of universities that are present on social media unofficially have interactive websites. These universities are engaging its stakeholders in some way. Unofficially too these universities are active on social media. Therefore, it would be better to have an official presence on social media and synchronize the content with its website. This will strengthen the online presence of the University.

It has also been noticed that there are Government universities that are at a higher level of website i.e. Transaction level and still are not on Social media. Digging deeper it was found that there are two primary reasons behind it. First, in Government Universities it is a long process to get approval [13]. Second, in these universities social media presence is not on their strategic goals.

There are Universities having more than one unofficial page. When searched for the University on social media several pages appear and it becomes difficult to find the authentic one. If the unofficial page on social media is made by alumni of the University then this shows high level of loyalty and eagerness to be connected online. This also shows that apart from administration of the University, others are also promoting the University. Any positive comment or news will improve the image of the University. According to [11] through social networking sites not only organizations can engage its stakeholders but also gain competitive advantage by marketing and creating awareness on social media.

On the contrary, unofficial presence on social media can be a matter of concern. As the university has no control over the content, any incorrect information can go against the image of the University [10]. The unauthorized administrator of the unofficial social media account can upload negative comments, news or images about the institution [15]. The result being aspirants and other stakeholders might be misguided.

6   Conclusion and Future Research

This is one of the first studies which explore the unofficial presence on social media of higher education institutions in India. The results from this exploratory study indicate one fourth of the surveyed top 300 higher education institutions in India have unofficial social media presence, Facebook being the leader. Previous studies have shown how Web 2.0 technologies are being used by institutions. This paper analyses and highlights pros and cons of being on social media unofficially.

As seen in this study majority of the universities are at interaction level and have unofficial social media presence. It is important for these universities to engage their stakeholders online not only through website but through social media.

For future research, a framework on digital strategy for higher education can be a useful research topic where all the departments of an institution are related and integrated and move towards online presence.

References

1. Al-Mukhaini, E.M., Al-Qayoudhi, W.S., Al-Badi, A.H.: Adoption of social networking in education: a study of the use of social networks by higher education students in Oman. J. Int. Educ. Res. 10(2), 143–153 (2014)
2. Barnes, N.G., Lescault, A.M.: Social media soars as Higher-Ed experiments and re-evaluates its use of new communications tools. http://sncr.org/sites/default/files/higherEd.pdf. Accessed 26 Jul 2015
3. Blankenship, M.: How social media can and should impact higher education. Educ. Digest 76(7), 39–42 (2011)
4. Boateng, F., Liu, Y.Q.: Web 2.0 applications' usage and trends in top US academic libraries. Libr. Hi Tech 32(1), 120–138 (2014)

5. Chauhan, K., Pillai, A.: Role of content strategy in social media brand communities: a case of higher education institutes in India. J. Prod. Brand Manage. **22**(1), 40–51 (2013)

6. Cheung, C.M., Chiu, P.-Y., Lee, M.K.: Online social networks: why do students use facebook? Comput. Hum. Behav. **27**(4), 1337–1343 (2011)

7. Kim, D., Kim, J.H., Nam, Y.: How does industry use social networking sites? an analysis of corporate dialogic uses of facebook, twitter, youtube, and linkedin by industry type. Qual. Quant. Int. J. Methodol. **48**(5), 2605–2614 (2014)

8. Mason, R., Rennie, F.: E-learning and Social Networking Handbook Resources for Higher Education. Routledge, New York (2013)

9. Mikami, A.Y., Szwedo, D.E., Allen, J.P., Evans, M.A., Hare, A.L.: Adolescent peer relationships and behavior problems predict young adults' communication on social networking websites. Dev. Psychol. **46**(1), 46 (2010)

10. Narayanaswamy, R., McGrath, L.: A holistic study of privacy in social networking sites. Acad. Inf. Manage. Sci. J. **17**(1), 71–85 (2014)

11. Nord, J., Paliszkiewicz, J., Koohang, A.: Using social technologies for competitive advantage: impact on organizations and higher education. J. Comput. Inf. Syst. **55**, 92–104 (2014)

12. Park, J.-H.: Differences among university students and faculties in social networking site perception and use: implications for academic library services. Electron. Libr. **28**(3), 417–431 (2010)

13. Sym, C.: Using Social Media in a Crisis: A Snapshot (2012). https://blog.case.org/2012/02/21. Accessed Mar 2016

14. Tapia, W.: An exploratory case study on the effectiveness of social network sites: the case of facebook and twitter in an educational organization (2012)

15. Xu, F., Michael, K., Chen, X.: Factors affecting privacy disclosure on social network sites: an integrated model. Electron. Commer. Res. **13**, 151–168 (2013)

16. Zailskaite, L., Kuvykaite, R.: Internet based communication with target audiences: case study of higher education institutes. Econ. Manage. **15**, 849–857 (2010)

Development of an Integrated Connectedness Model to Evaluate the Effectiveness of Teaching and Learning

Salah Al-Hamad[1], Laszlo E. Kollar[3], Taimoor Asim[2(✉)],
and Rakesh Mishra[2]

[1] Computer Engineering Department, College of Engineering, Ahlia University,
Manama, Kingdom of Bahrain
salhamad@ahlia.edu.bh
[2] School of Computing & Engineering, University of Huddersfield, Queensgate,
Huddersfield HD1 3DH, UK
{t.asim,r.mishra}@hud.ac.uk
[3] Savaria Institute of Technology, University of West Hungary,
Karolyi G. Ter 4, Szombathely 9700, Hungary
kollar.laszlo@nyme.hu

Abstract. Use of blended learning system in a structured manner results in achieving higher order skills in cognitive domain. However, there is a need to quantify skills improvements as the students go through lower level skills to higher level skills. To ascertain this progression, it is necessary to develop a mathematical model of learning which can indicate the effectiveness of teaching and learning methods on skills improvement. In this study, mathematical learning model has been developed, which predicts the students' knowledge, depending on the amount of instruction they receive. It is expected that this model will enable development of direct correlation between teaching and learning methods, and the skills level attained by the students. The model is applied for different categories of learning. Parameters in the model are determined after least-square fitting has been applied on observed student learning data.

1   Introduction

Teaching and learning processes that are being followed globally by education providers consist of conventional face-to-face approach. The globalisation, along with the interdependence of various economies, has resulted in creating an extra dimension to the higher order of skills requirements. Hence, there is a need to develop new teaching and learning methodologies that can comply with the ever increasing demands of the industry, regarding the skills of engineering students.

The present paper summarizes existing learning models, and proposes an integrated connectedness model (ICM) that is applicable to indicate and compare the effectiveness of different teaching and learning methods on skills improvement. The model is validated by using data available in the literature to quantify the usefulness of the teaching and learning process in cognitive learning [1]. The old version of levels of taxonomy was assumed in the study cited, and in the validation of the proposed model as well.

Published by Springer International Publishing Switzerland 2016. All Rights Reserved
Y.K. Dwivedi et al. (Eds.): I3E 2016, LNCS 9844, pp. 707–716, 2016.
DOI: 10.1007/978-3-319-45234-0_64

Then, cognitive learning evaluation, assuming the new version of levels of taxonomy, through the ICM have been carried out and presented in this paper.

2 Connectedness Model

Real learning usually involves some learning of both (i) students learn by memorization, and that learning is independent of prior knowledge, and (ii) students learn new knowledge by constructing an association between new and some prior knowledge. The first is known as Pure Memory Model while the latter is called Simple Connectedness Model. Pritchard et al. [2] developed a model which interpolates between, and even beyond, these two models. This model is called Connectedness Model, and the parameter that establishes the relationship between the pure models is called the connectedness parameter, denoted by γ. Connectedness Model can be effectively used for all skill levels of cognitive domain. This model determines students' knowledge K_T as a function of the amount of teaching or instruction i. Thus, K_T represents the fraction of the material that is known by the student, and another parameter, A_T represents what is unknown. K_T and A_T vary between 0 and 1. Initially $K_T = 0$, because students do not know anything about the subject to be learnt, or in other words, the subject knowledge is unknown, i.e. $A_T = 1$. Students are supposed to learn the subject completely by the end of the course, hence $K_T = 1$ and $A_T = 0$ at the end of the teaching period in the case of an ideal student. The governing differential equation takes the following form:

$$\frac{dA_T(i)}{di} = -A_T(i)(\delta_{con}\gamma(1 - A_T(i)) + \delta_{mem}(1 - \gamma)) \tag{1}$$

The model involves a differential equation for dA_T/di, i.e. for the rate of change of unknown knowledge. The equations are based on A_T, because given instructions are generally related to what students do not know. However, once the solution for A_T is found, K_T can easily be obtained. The parameter that expresses the probability that something taught sticks in the student's mind is the sticking coefficient δ, hence δ_{con} and δ_{mem} are the sticking coefficients from the pure memory and simple connectedness models. The solution for the known knowledge can be written as follows:

$$K_T(i) = \frac{(1 - K_{T0})(\delta_{mem}(1 - \gamma) + \delta_{con}\gamma)}{(1 - K_{T0})\delta_{con}\gamma + (\delta_{mem}(1 - \gamma) + K_{T0}\delta_{con}\gamma)\exp(\delta_{mem}(1 - \gamma)i + \delta_{con}\gamma i)} \tag{2}$$

where students' knowledge, during the teaching period, depends on their initial knowledge K_{T0}, which can be obtained by pre-instruction test scores, and can be used as input in the model. The model is equivalent to the pure memory model for $\gamma=0$, and it is equivalent to the simple connect model for $\gamma=1$. Pure memory model is particularly applicable to lowest skills in cognitive domain. The equation for the rate of change of unknown knowledge can be written as follows:

$$\frac{dA_T(i)}{di} = -\delta_{mem}A_T(i) \tag{3}$$

The solution for the known knowledge is obtained as follows:

$$K_T(i) = \frac{1}{1 + \frac{(1-K_{T0})exp(-\delta_{con}i)}{K_{T0}}} \tag{4}$$

3 Development of an Integrated Connectedness Model (ICM) for Different Learning Domains

The learning domains are distinguished in cognitive learning as knowledge, comprehension, application, analysis, synthesis, and evaluation. The proposed model relates the test results of any domain to the test results of the preceding domain. The model assumes identical importance to each of these domains, i.e. the total knowledge that may be gained in each domain takes 1/6 of the total knowledge in the subject that students learn. The initial knowledge for the knowledge test is assumed to be $K_{T0,kn}=0$, i.e. students do not know anything about the subject that they are about to learn. The knowledge gained in the knowledge domain is 1/6 of the total knowledge in the subject, and it is essential for gaining knowledge in the comprehension domain. Therefore, the initial knowledge for the comprehension test is $K_{T0,co}=1/6\ K_{T,kn}(i_{ins})$, where $K_{T,kn}(i_{ins})$ is the known knowledge in the knowledge domain at the end of the learning period. The initial knowledge can be determined similarly for all the other domains, ending with the initial knowledge for evaluation, which is $K_{T0,ev}=5/6\ K_{T,sy}(i_{ins})$ with $K_{T,sy}(i_{ins})$ being the known knowledge in the synthesis domain at the end of learning period.

The model also assumes that learning in knowledge domain is independent of prior knowledge, learning in the evaluation domain is based purely on association between prior and new knowledge, whereas learning in the other domains is a combination of both types. First, an appropriate model has to be chosen, and then the sticking coefficients δ_{mem} and δ_{con} as well as the connectedness parameter γ have to be determined. In practice, since the sticking coefficients always appear in the products δi in the models, the products $\delta_{mem}i$ and $\delta_{con}i$ are determined and used in further calculations. These parameters are determined by fitting the solution in the chosen model on test data. Consequently, the combined model is constructed as follows (see Fig. 1). Learning in the knowledge domain is modelled by the pure memory model, and the product $\delta_{mem}i$ is determined. Learning in the evaluation domain is modelled by the simple connect model, and the product $\delta_{con}i$ is determined. Then, the same sticking coefficients δ_{mem} and δ_{con} in the connectedness model are used to simulate learning in the remaining four domains, and the connectedness parameter β is determined for each of the four domains.

4 Teaching/Learning Groups

45 students were selected from the three mechanical engineering specialisations i.e. Automotive, Industrial Maintenance and Manufacturing Engineering. The students have then been divided into three separate groups. Each group consists of 15 students (5 students from each specialization), where the students have almost similar abilities. The details of these groups are as follows:

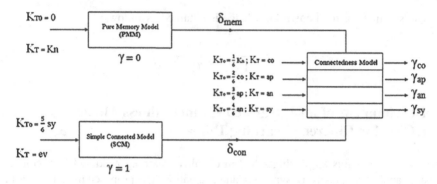

Fig. 1. Flowchart of combined model for cognitive learning

Group 1: Demonstration under the watchful eyes of the instructor (Teacher Centred, Interactive Dependent)

Teachers in this group serve as the centre of knowledge in both theory and practical sessions, and are primarily responsible for directing the learning process. During assessment phase (student's participation and demonstrations), teachers were focused almost exclusively on what had the students learned. Students were viewed as empty vessels, whereas the teacher imparts learning into these vessels within a given time period. Furthermore, learning was viewed as additive process [3].

Group 2: Students learn using computers and the teacher facilitates the process (Student Centred, Interactive Independent).

In this method, students were considered as knowledgeable and they can bring about engagement and personal responsibility in learning [4]. This supports the idea of knowledge construction by learners through their use of prior knowledge and experience, which assists them to shape meaning and acquire new knowledge. The mechanical engineering teachers, during their preparation, observed that in constructive learning students participated in class and they may have a wide range of previous learning experiences, which enable teachers to select teaching/learning methods at higher level of skills for optimal learning [5].

Group 3: Project Base Group, work with and without supervision (Interactive)

In this collaborative-interactive approach the lecturer provides computer tutorials including videos and animations, which show the students how to use tutorial instructions in order to warm-up to the lecture with the use of tutorial tasks and questions [6, 7]. The lecturer intends to use two ways of communication between the teacher and the students, combined with active learning to increases understanding. The method was established in cooperative environment where students work together. It allows learning to continue after the class session. Students teach each other. The most effective way to learn is to actually teach, because this requires the highest degree of mental processing (high level of thinking skills) and greatly increases the likelihood that long-term memories will be produced. The tutorial was provided with motivational animations to stimulate team work, and it has a greater likelihood of being incorporated into long-term memory.

5 Cognitive Skills Evaluation Techniques

The learner should achieve proficiency in lower levels of cognition, and then progress through higher levels. This analysis is similar to the one carried out by Zywno [8] for electrical engineering students. In mechanical engineering modules, various levels have been identified as per the developed model of cognitive level skills related to the knowledge (recall data), comprehension (understand information), application (applying knowledge to the new situation), analysis (separating information into part of better understanding), evaluating (justify a stand or decision by appraising, arguing, defending, judging, selecting, supporting, valuing and evaluating) and creating (create new product or point of view by assembling, constructing, creating, designing, developing and formulating idea).

Lecturer marked the students during maintenance and production of six tasks in Automotive, Industrial Maintenance and Manufacturing. The quality of students' results for each activity is determined by comparing their products with the checklist and awarding learning ability indicators for each student and task. The learning ability indicator shows how well the student has performed a certain task by comparing his/her application results with the checklist. Figure 2a shows the correlation between learning ability indicator (average marks obtained in the examination before entering this course) and the marks obtained for the three groups in the examination of the knowledge cognition level. Most groups show considerable improvement in knowledge but final marks for group 2 students are uniformly distributed between 80% and 95%. This indicates that student-centred approach has increased the level of achievement of learning outcomes for this heterogeneous group of students. The final marks for group 3 are spread between 65% and 85%. Hence, the interactive teaching and learning methods have produced a slight increase in the final marks but not too much like group 2.

Figure 2b presents the variation of students' marks in the examination of analysis cognition level. The final marks for group 2 are concentrated in the interval 75% to 95% so their level of achievement is the same as in previous cases (knowledge, comprehension, application). Furthermore, the students' final marks from group 1 are in the interval 55% to 80%. Hence, the teacher-centred approach does not increase the marks significantly at analysis cognition level. Figure 2c presents the variation of students' marks in the examination of evaluation cognition level. The students were evaluated for their abilities in analyzing and evaluating the machining operation and procedure and selecting, preparing tools and equipment and using measuring instruments facilities to calculate missing dimensions of engineering application. This also requires students to be capable of analyzing and verifying the manufacturing operations, assembling different parts to create prototype in final shape, designing a new shape and modifying one shape to another shape, arranging machine tools, materials and instruments for final manufacture and engineering maintenance preparation of parts and tools. The students' final marks from group 1 are clustered around the interval 55% to 65%. The teacher-centered approach does not enable the development of appropriate students' skills for evaluation cognitive level. Furthermore, students from group 1 obtained the lowest marks in comparison to those from group 2. Group 3 show less

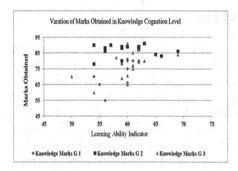
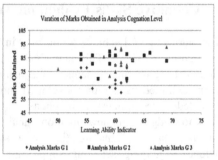

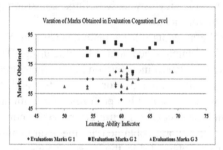

Fig. 2. (a) Comparison between teaching methods in Knowledge cognition level, (b) Comparison between teaching methods in Analysis cognition level, (c) Comparison between teaching methods in Evaluation cognition level

marks than the previous cases (knowledge, comprehension, application and analyses). This shows that the combination students-centred approached is far more useful in delivering learning outcomes at higher level of developed cognition skills.

6 Cognitive Learning Evaluation Through ICM

The combined model is applied here for the case of imparting cognitive learning skills through blended learning system. The procedure described in Sect. 3 is followed for different learning domains. The learning domains for this case are the following: knowledge, comprehension, application, analysis, evaluation and creating. The product $\delta_{mem}i$ for the knowledge domain as well as the product $\delta_{con}i$ for the creating domain were determined to be 1.33 and 0.57 for Group 1, 2.01 and 0.71 for Group 2 and 1.45 and 0.49 for Group 3 respectively. First, the product $\delta_{mem}i$ was determined from the pure memory model only, using the test results obtained for the knowledge domain and assuming no initial knowledge. Then, the product $\delta_{con}i$ was calculated from the simple connect model using the test results obtained for the creating domain and using test results obtained for the evaluation domain as input. The dependence of post-instruction knowledge on initial knowledge in the creating domain is shown in Fig. 3 together with the test data used for fitting.

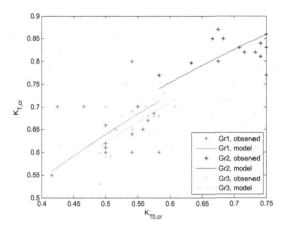

Fig. 3. Curve fitting on data for creating (simple connect model)

Once the sticking coefficients are known, the connectedness parameter was also determined for each learning domain, and results are summarised in Table 1. The connectedness parameter increases for the different domains from knowledge to creating, because the more advanced the students' learning in the subject, the more association they can construct between new and prior knowledge. The values that did not follow this trend are the connectedness parameters for the comprehension and analysis domains for Group 3. The value for the comprehension domain is negative, which means that the normalized gain slightly decreases with increasing pre-instruction test scores. This can happen when students with higher pre-instruction scores exert less effort, whereas students with lower pre-instruction scores make more effort to improve their results [2]. Furthermore, this group was not exposed to a very structured learning environment as instructor's input was least with this group. This might have caused skills development that cannot be explained from the model that has been used. The trends observed justify the choice of the model. If students learnt by memorization only or by constructing only association between new and some prior knowledge, then the values of the connectedness parameters would be close to 0 or 1, respectively.

The post-instruction knowledge as a function of initial knowledge is shown in Fig. 4. The normalized gains for the knowledge domain and for the creating domain are obtained from the pure memory model and the simple connected model, respectively,

Table 1. Connectedness parameters for all the learning domains in cognitive learning

	Group 1	Group 2	Group 3
Knowledge	0	0	0
Comprehension	–0.02	0.12	–0.37
Application	0.12	0.33	0.25
Analysis	0.64	0.48	0.18
Evaluation	0.94	0.66	1.03
Creating	1	1	1

and they are shown in Fig. 5. The normalized gains are calculated for the remaining four learning domains by using the connectedness model, and they are presented in Fig. 6. It can be seen that the knowledge as well as the normalized gain is always highest for Group 2. The knowledge and the normalised gain are lowest for Group 1 in the knowledge, comprehension and analysis domains, whereas these are lowest for Group 3 for the application, evaluation and creating domains. Thus, the teaching method applied for Group 3 is more effective at lower level skills, but the method applied for Group 1 is more effective at higher level skills. However, the most effective teaching method in all the cases is the one that has been applied with Group 2.

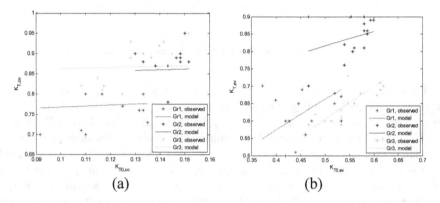

Fig. 4. Curve fitting on data (connectedness model) (a) comprehension (b) application (c) analysis (d) evaluation

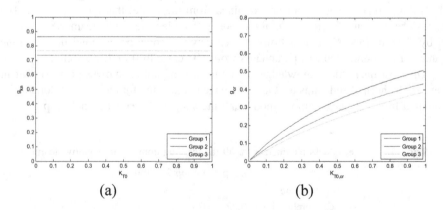

Fig. 5. Normalized gain for (a) knowledge domain (pure memory model) (b) creating domain (simple connect model)

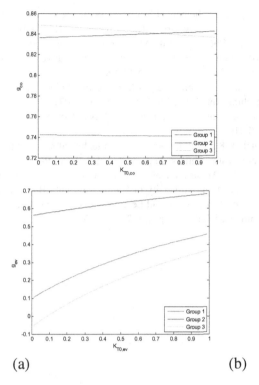

(a)   (b)

Fig. 6. Normalized gain for (a) comprehension (b) evaluation domains (connectedness model)

7 Conclusions

Mathematical models have been developed in the present study that quantifies the learning process at microscopic level within cognitive skills domains. In contrast to the macroscopic (conventional) evaluation methods used throughout the world, these models provides a much clearer picture of the teaching/learning taking place at different skills' levels enabling a better control over the quality of teaching and learning process. These models can be further modified in order to apply them to other fields of education.

The above study has clearly indicated that integrated connectedness model (ICM) represents skills development in cognitive skills domains fairly well. ICM can be used to monitor effectiveness of the teaching and learning strategies through well-developed assessment strategies. It can also dictate development of teaching and learning materials by providing important feedback on the effectiveness.

References

1. Abdulrasool, S., Mishra, R.: Using computer technology tools to improve the teaching-learning process in technical and vocational education: mechanical engineering subject area. Int. J. Comp. Tech. **15**(9), 155–168 (2008)

2. Pritchard, D.E., Lee, Y.J.: Mathematical learning models that depend on prior knowledge and instructional strategies. Phys. Rev. Spec. Top. Phys. Educ. Res. **4**, 010109 (2008)
3. Leung, M.Y., Lu, X., Chen, D., Lu, M.: Impacts of teaching approaches on learning approaches of construction engineering students: a comparative study between Hong Kong and Mainland China. J. Eng. Educ. **97**, 135 (2008)
4. Watters, D.J., Watters, J.J.: Approaches to learning by students in the biological sciences: implications for teaching. Int. J. Sc. Ed. **29**(1), 19–43 (2007)
5. Mehmet, S.: Blended learning model in mechanical manufacturing training. Afr. J. Bus. Man. **4**(12), 2520–2526 (2010)
6. Mumcu, F.K., Usluel, Y.K.: ICT in vocational and technical schools: teachers' instructional, managerial and personal use matters. Turk. Onl. J. Ed. Tech. **9**(1), 98–106 (2010)
7. Mayer, R.E.: Short Video About the Role of Video and Its Design for Effective Teching and Learning in Higher Education. University of California, Santa Barbara (2011)
8. Zywno, S.M.: Hypermedia Instruction and Learning Outcomes at Different Levels of Bloom's Taxonomy of Cognitive Global. J. Eng. Ed. **7**(1), 59–70 (2003)

Consumers' Attitudes Towards Social Media Banking

Dola Majekodunmi[1(✉)] and Lisa Harris[2]

[1] Web Science Doctoral Training Centre, University of Southampton,
Southampton, UK
oamlg14@soton.ac.uk
[2] Web Science Institute, University of Southampton, Southampton, UK
l.j.harris@soton.ac.uk

Abstract. "Social media banking" refers to the use of social media as a form of delivery channel for banking services. This research examines the attitudes and preferences for social media banking among users with emphasis on University of Southampton students. The purpose of the study was to examine the use of social media banking by students using the framework of Rogers Diffusion of Innovation theory and to gain an understanding of the factors which influence the adoption and usage of social media banking. A survey method was used to collect data from a sample of students at the University of Southampton. Data was analysed using an appropriate software which assessed factors that influence the attitude of students to social media banking. These factors were relative advantage, compatibility, complexity, trialability and observability. Descriptive, correlation and multiple regression analysis were used to analyse data. The findings show that three attributes of the diffusion of innovation namely relative advantage, compatibility and trialability were statistically significant in the attitude towards social media banking.

Keywords: Innovation · Diffusion · Social media banking · Attitudes · Innovation adoption · Innovation attributes

1 Introduction

The Web has transformed the nature of banking and the way bank customers access and use their accounts has changed over the years. There are several channels through which banking needs can be met now. Some of these channels are Web enabled which has brought about the concept of social media banking and digital banking. Some banks now use Web 2.0 as a channel for communication, interaction, customer engagement and marketing. Social media banking refers to the use of social media as a form of delivery channel for banking services. This could range from accounts opening, funds transfer, bill payments, as well as customer relationship management, and these activities can be done without visiting a physical branch. Some banks have also referred to this as social banking, Twitter banking and Facebook banking. Some objectives of social media banking include improving customer service, brand and reputation management and product marketing. There are a significant number of social

© IFIP International Federation for Information Processing 2016
Published by Springer International Publishing Switzerland 2016. All Rights Reserved
Y.K. Dwivedi et al. (Eds.): I3E 2016, LNCS 9844, pp. 717–727, 2016.
DOI: 10.1007/978-3-319-45234-0_65

media users (by December 2014, the UK had 57,266,690 internet users out of a total population of 64,767,115 representing 88.4 % of the population) of which 50.9 % were subscribed to Facebook [8]. However it was reported that even though social media banking adoption by banks is evidenced through their social media pages, sufficient attention has not been given to understanding the role of social media in banking [12] and its impact on attitudes of customers towards its adoption hence the need to investigate the factors that may affect the adoption of social media banking.

An innovation such as social media banking will usually bring about a change in the different levels of stakeholders be it the bank customer, the organisation offering the idea and the society at large. However as good as an innovation may be, if it is not adopted, it will be categorized as useless. The objective of this study was to investigate factors that influence attitudes towards social media banking. Diffusion of innovations is a theory developed by Everett M. Rogers in 1962 and this theory highlights the need to understand how innovation is accepted. Rogers's theory of diffusion is characterised by five innovation attributes namely relative advantage, compatibility, complexity, trialability and observability and these attributes are investigated in relation to social media banking in this paper.

2   Background

Some banks provide social media banking services and a few examples are discussed. Fidor bank in Germany has no physical branches and prides itself as the first bank to have an online only banking service. The bank only has an online presence and since its establishment in 2009 the bank has come up with innovative solutions such as the 'like for interest'. This means that the more likes the bank gets on Facebook the more the interest rate a bank customer gets on their savings rate and vice versa for their overdraft and loan rates.

Commonwealth Bank of Australia has a Facebook banking tool (CommBank Kaching app) that enables customers to make deposits and payments through Facebook app and also peer to peer payment using phone number and address. Barclays bank in the United Kingdom recently launched a payment system on Twitter called PingIt which allows bank customers to make payments via their Twitter accounts. Denizbank in Turkey prides itself as being the first bank to have a Facebook banking branch. It launched a Facebook application in 2012. Customers could transfer money through their Facebook accounts and could also monitor their current, savings and credit card accounts. Over 150000 people used the application within two weeks of its launch. In addition, customers can make credit applications through Facebook and Twitter and get special interest rates.

ICICI Bank India (Fig. 1) allows customer to get bank account information through Facebook. A debit card and password is required to perform this transaction though. Customers can also make payments to anyone on the Facebook list of friends. In addition, the bank launched payment services on Twitter at the beginning of 2015. With this new service, customers can make payments to anyone who has a Twitter account, they can also check their account balance and last three transactions on their account.

Fig. 1. ICICI bank India advert for banking on Twitter

Social media banking is relatively new and any idea that is perceived as new should be considered an innovation worthy enough to be studied. Few academic research is reported in the field of social media banking as it is relatively new and studies reported were limited to managerial perception of social media use [6], bank brand reputation and customer service through social media [5], social media strategies for banks [17] and adoption of social media marketing by banks [16]. There has been no research reported from the perspective of innovation adoption of social media banking services by the consumer hence the need for the present study.

Previous work has reported the use of the Diffusion of Innovation theory in the banking industry but this has only been for internet and mobile banking [2, 9, 10, 13, 15, 18]. Even though Internet and mobile banking are related and have made social media banking possible, there is still the need for more research as social media brings with it issues about privacy and trust, thus this present study was conducted to understand what customers attitudes are and what influences the adoption of this new technology.

3   Theoretical Framework and Hypotheses

In order to understand the factors that influence the adoption of a technology by consumers, it is essential to understand the theory that underpins how an innovation is adopted. There are existing models and theories that have been used to research the adoption of pre-existing technologies that existed before social media banking i.e. Internet banking and mobile banking. These theories include Theory of reasoned action, Theory of planned behaviour, Diffusion of Innovation theory and the Technology Acceptance Model and The Unified Theory of Acceptance and Use of Technology.

All of the above named theories have been used extensively with internet banking and mobile banking. For the purpose of this study, the diffusion of innovation theory will be reviewed as the focus of this study is investigating the attitudes and preferences of customers to adoption of social media banking with respect to the five attributes of diffusion of innovation theory. Everett Rogers in his book Diffusions of Innovation proposes that four main elements are responsible for the spread of new ideas namely communication channels, the innovation itself, time and a social system [14]. This approach in itself makes the research interdisciplinary as both the technicalities of the idea being proposed and the social system in which it would be used in would be considered, hence the reason for choosing this theory.

There has been research done investigating whether the attributes of diffusion of innovation theory have a relationship with the adoption of mobile and internet banking but none has been conducted on the use of social media by banks. The results of the previous studies on mobile and internet banking show that all of the attributes have a significant effect either positive or negative on attitudes towards adoption.

3.1 Diffusion of Innovation Theory

Definition of key terms that relate to the adoption of a new technology.

- Diffusion: The process by which a new product or idea is accepted by the users.
- Rate of diffusion: The speed with which an idea or product innovation spreads amongst users.
- Adoption: The process by which a user accepts a new idea or product.
- Innovation: "An innovation is an idea, practice or object that is perceived as new by individual or other unit of adoption" [14].

3.2 Attributes of Innovation

The perceived attributes of innovation explain the rate of adoption of an innovation. These five attributes are relative advantage, compatibility, complexity, trialability, and observability. It is imperative to take into consideration the words of [14] which says "The individuals perceptions of the attributes of an innovation, not the attributes as classified objectively by experts or change agents affect its rate of adoption" (p. 223).

3.2.1 Relative Advantage

This is the degree to which an innovation is considered better than an existing alternative. It is assumed that the greater the degree an individual perceives relative advantage, the greater the rate of adoption of the innovation. Earlier research suggested that relative advantage of an innovation has a positive relationship with the rate of adoption of that innovation [11]. When a user perceives the usefulness of a new technology over an existing one, they tend to adopt the new one [14]. Previous research on the perceived correlation between relative advantage and mobile and internet banking showed a positive trend [2, 15]. As social media banking is an offshoot of internet banking, it is hypothesized that relative advantage will have a significant effect on attitude and the intention to adopt social media banking by customers.

H1: Relative advantage will have a significant effect on attitude towards social media banking adoption.

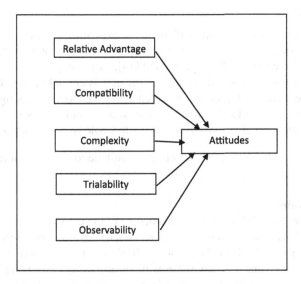

Fig. 2. The research model

3.2.2 Compatibility

This is the degree to which an innovation is consistent with existing values and past experience of adopters. It is assumed that innovations will be easily adopted if it fits an adopters existing values and experiences [14]. Previous research showed that compatibility is significantly relevant in the attitude of consumers towards the adoption of Internet banking [15]. Furthermore, it has been pointed out that perceived compatibility was statistically significant in the adoption of mobile banking [9]. Based on this review and on the premise that social media banking is an offshoot of both internet and mobile banking, it is hypothesized that perceived compatibility will have a significant effect on attitudes towards social media banking adoption.

H2: Compatibility will have a significant effect on attitude towards social media banking adoption.

3.2.3 Complexity

This is the degree to which an innovation is perceived to be difficult or easy to use. If an innovation is easy to understand then it would be adopted more than if it is complex to understand. [3] pointed out that perceived complexity influences the adoption of internet banking negatively. However [2] in their study on mobile banking adoption found that perceived complexity had no significant effect. Bank customers may not use social media banking services if it is frustrating or if it requires more effort than existing technologies (mobile and internet banking). Therefore it can be hypothesized that when a user perceives that an innovation is complex to use the less likely they are to adopt it.

H3: Complexity will have a significant effect on attitude towards social media banking adoption.

3.2.4   Trialability

This is the degree to which an innovation can be experimented with before actual use by the adopter. Rogers suggests that there is a faster rate of adoption of a technology if it can be tried before being fully implemented [14]. However [1] are of the opinion that this is not applicable to financial services as the user is not able to try the technology before implementation but previous research done on mobile banking and internet banking revealed that banks do provide demonstration tools on their websites which can be likened to being able to experiment the technology before actual use.

H4: Trialability will have a significant effect on attitude towards social media banking adoption.

3.2.5   Observability:

This is the degree to which the result the outcome of the use of an innovation is visible to others [14]. This original construct was redefined into two constructs visibility and result demonstrability by [11]. With mobile banking, it was assumed that access to banking services anytime and anywhere without any delay and seeing the results of transactions makes it an innovation that is perceived as being visible to others. The probability to adopt an innovation is higher when the benefits of using the innovation can be easily observed [4]. As the benefits of using social media banking can be easily observed by users, it can be hypothesized that perceived observability will have a significant effect on attitude towards its adoption.

H5: Observability will have a significant effect on attitude towards social media banking adoption.

4   Methodology

This research was exploratory in nature because there were no studies that provided an insight into consumers' attitudes and preferences for social media banking. For the purpose of this research, a quantitative approach was employed. This method was adopted as it is relatively quick to collect data and precise numerical data from quantitative research produce results which are independent of the researcher. A purposive sampling technique was used as this enabled specific group of people to be targeted in the study. The study was conducted in July 2015 and the target population was postgraduate students at the University of Southampton hence the small sample size of 107 as the undergraduates were on summer vacation and there were time constraints for data collection. The primary data for this study was collected using a structured questionnaire. The questionnaire had two sections- section one comprised of questions to obtain information on the demographics of the participants and section two contained questions that collected data related to the influence of the five attributes of innovation on the perception and attitude of participants to social media banking. A 5 point Likert scale (a psychometric scale) was used and they were coded accordingly. The questionnaire consisted of 34 questions measuring five variables. Cronbach alpha index was used to check if multiple items in the questionnaire were reliable as well as to determine the internal reliability of the items for each construct. The coefficients ranged between 0.774 to 0.900 which implied that all the items in the constructs were reliable as they are all greater than 0.7 [7].

Data collected from the survey questions was analysed using Statistical Package for the Social Sciences (SPSS) version 22. Frequencies, means, standard deviations, multiple linear regression and correlation analysis are reported. The first section of the questionnaire (questions 1–10, 12–14) was analysed using descriptive statistics and the second section (question 11) was analysed using regression and correlation analysis.

5 Research Findings

5.1 Descriptive Statistics

The total number of participants was 107 and demographics and descriptive statistics results showed that 52.3 % of the participants were female and 47.7 % were male suggesting that more females responded to the questionnaires. Majority of the participants were aged 18–25 and this is solely due to the fact that the survey sample is university students. Most participants (n = 48) preferred getting in touch with their bank in person compared to social media and other methods such as email. Only 8.4 % of participants preferred getting in touch with their bank through social media. The results showed that 37.9 % of participants used social media to view bank products and services, 25.3 % had used social media to make bank payments and 24.1 % to make complaints. Only a few customers (n = 3) had opened a bank account using social media. 25.3 % of participants had actually made a payment using social media channels. 4.6 % had not performed any of these activities. 10.4 % of the participants reported that they would rather not use social media banking services but a good number (89.6 %) were happy to perform one activity or the other using social media banking. 79.4 % of respondents indicated that data security was the most important factor that acted as a barrier towards their use of social media banking. The majority of respondents (64.5 %) were neither satisfied nor dissatisfied with social media banking which might have to do with the fact that majority of the respondents still preferred visiting a branch to perform their banking transactions. Only 31.8 % of respondents were satisfied with their use of social media banking.

5.2 Correlation Analysis

Pearson correlation coefficient investigates the relationship between variables and measures the strength of an association between two variables. In this model, the level of significance was set at 1 %, the strength of association between relative advantage and attitude was very large ($r = 0.885$, $p < 0.01$) while the strength of association between complexity and attitude towards social media banking is very low ($r = -.0317$). Relative advantage, compatibility, trialability and observability all had positive correlations with attitudes to social media banking.

Table 1. Association between the constructs

Construct	Attitude	Relative advantage	Compatibility	Complexity	Trialability	Observability
Attitude	1	0.885	0.869	-.0.317	0.861	0.715
Relative advantage	0.885	1	0.878	-0.342	0.846	0.762
Compatibility	0.869	0.878	1	-0.367	0.842	0.757
Complexity	-0.317	-0.342	-.0.367	1	-0.304	-0.217
Trialability	0.861	0.846	0.842	-0.304	1	0.679
Observability	0.715	0.762	0.757	-0.217	0.679	1

Note: Correlation is significant at the 0.01 level

5.3   Multiple Regression Analysis

Regression analysis was used to investigate the relationship between independent variables and a set dependent variables. In the present study, the independent variables were relative advantage, observability, trialability, compatibility and complexity whilst the dependent variable was the attitude to social media banking. The model was used to predict participants' attitude to social media banking. Table 2 below show the regression analysis results.

Table 2. Regression analysis results

Independent Variable	Unstandardized Coefficient β	Unstandardized coefficient Standard error	Standardized coefficient β	T	Significance Value
Constant	0.389	0.375		1.039	0.301
Compatibility	0.241	0.086	0.266	2.811	0.006
Complexity	0.013	0.069	0.008	0.188	0.851
Trialability	0.281	0.075	0.301	3.733	0.000
Relative Advantage	0.368	0.090	0.389	4.096	0.000
Observability	0.014	0.059	0.015	0.233	0.817

Dependent Variable: Attitude

The results (Table 3) showed that 84.2 % of the variance in the dependent variable (attitude) is accounted for by the five independent variables. This suggests that the model is fit for use to measure the significance of the attributes of innovation on the users' attitude to social media banking.

Table 3. Model summary

Model	R	R square	Adjusted R square	Standard error of the estimate	Change Statistics				
					R square change	F change	Df1	Df2	Sig F change
1	0.918[a]	0.842	0.834	0.432	0.842	107.771	5	101	0.000

[a]Predictors: (Constant), Observability, Complexity, Trialability, Compatibility, Relative Advantage

The regression analysis also showed how statistically significant the five attributes of the diffusion of innovation are on the model and identified whether the independent variables significantly predicted the dependent variable. There was a strong relationship between the dependent and the independent variable (R = 0.918). Observability and complexity recorded significance values of 0.817 and 0.851 respectively which were both greater than 0.05 which means these two attributes were not statistically significant. On the other hand, relative advantage, trialability and compatibility are statistically significant with values of 0.000, 0.000 and 0.006 respectively. The F statistic was very large (F = 107.771, p < 0.005) and because the p value is less than 0.05, the result is statistically significant. The equation that predicts the attitude to social media banking is represented by the model below.

$$Y = \beta_0 + \beta_1 X_1 + \beta_2 X_2 + \beta_3 X_3 + \beta_4 X_4 + \beta_5 X_5$$

Where Y represents attitude and β_0 is the constant which has a value of 0.389.

X1 = Relative advantage
X2 = Compatibility
X3 = Complexity
X4 = Trialability
X5 = Observability

Therefore the model is represented as

$$Y = 0.389 + 0.368(\text{Relative advantage}) + 0.281(\text{Trialability}) + 0.241(\text{Compatibility}).$$

6 Discussion

Findings of this study revealed that convenience and ease of use were the major incentives for the use of social media banking for participants. A third of the participants had made payments and viewed products and services using this channel. Few participants had opened a bank account using social media and perceived data security and privacy as barriers to adoption of social media banking indicating that security of transactions conducted on social media should be a priority to banks for attitudes towards the adoption of social media banking to improve. The study also found that participants were willing to receive financial advice and recommendations for products and services through social media banking as they found these to be more convenient to use even though they would still rather visit a physical branch to perform transactions. This highlights the need for awareness of social media banking services to be embarked upon by banks through other channels such as online and mobile banking so customers can be assured of getting the same form of service whether they visit a branch or virtually.

If customers perceive that social media banking is better than internet and mobile banking in terms of convenience and satisfaction, and perceive that it is consistent with existing values and can be experimented with before actual use, it would lead to an attitudinal change towards social media banking. Some participants reported that they preferred to have their social network accounts integrated with their bank accounts while others preferred to be able to apply for specific banking products through their social network accounts. Despite these positive perceptions, the majority of participants perceived data security and privacy as barriers to adopting this form of banking. Therefore issues of security should be of high importance to banks so they can reassure users of safety and increase their confidence in using social media banking. There is also the need for risk management policies to be put in place, for attitudes to change.

The regression results showed that relative advantage had a significant effect on the attitude of participants to use social media banking ($\beta = 0.389$). Pearson's correlation coefficient between relative advantage and attitude was a strong positive correlation and beta value for relative advantage was the highest among the independent variables which indicates that relative advantage had the highest contribution in explaining attitudes toward social media banking. Additionally significant positive correlations between attitudes to social media banking and relative advantage, compatibility, trialability and observability was observed, demonstrating the importance of these innovation attributes (Table 1).

The results showed that relative advantage, compatibility and trialability were statistically significantly associated with attitudes of participants towards social media banking. As of the time of writing this paper, there is a lack of literature on the influence of innovation attributes on attitudes to social media banking. Findings from this present study are however consistent with findings of [13, 18] who reported that relative advantage, compatibility and trialability significantly influenced attitudes towards mobile banking adoption and internet banking adoption respectively.

7 Conclusion

This study set out to investigate students' attitudes and preferences for social media banking using the theoretical framework of the diffusion of innovation with particular emphasis on the five innovation attributes namely relative advantage, compatibility, complexity, trialability and observability. Findings from the study has demonstrated that students are aware of social media banking channels, though majority are neither satisfied nor dissatisfied with the service. Majority of the participants reported hearing about social media banking through word of mouth, so there is the need for banks to embark on sensitization through adverts, these adverts should highlight the benefits of using social media banking which could include convenience, ease of use and reduced time of transaction among others.

This study has generated insight into which innovation attributes are predictive of attitudes towards social media banking. The present study utilised an online survey method limiting participants to only internet users. Future work should incorporate using other technology models such as the Unified Theory of Acceptance and Use of Technology model to get a more comprehensive outlook into social media banking acceptance and adoption. Although this research has been based on data sourced from users and non-users of social media banking services, there can't be a generalisation of the result findings as the sample is not large enough therefore a study of non-users intention to adopt this form of banking should also be carried out with a larger sample.

References

1. Aldás-Manzano, J., Lassala-Navarré, C., Ruiz-Mafé, C., Sanz-Blas, S.: The role of consumer innovativeness and perceived risk in online banking usage. Int. J. Bank Mark. **27**(1), 53–75 (2009)
2. Al-Jabri, I., Sohail, S.: Mobile banking adoption: application of diffusion of innovation theory. J. Electron. Commer. Res. **13**(4), 379–391 (2012)
3. Chaipoopirutana, S., Combs, H., Chatchawanwan, Y., Vij, V.: Diffusion of innovation in Asia: a study of internet banking in Thailand and India. Innovative Mark. **5**(4), 27–31 (2009)
4. Cruz, P., Barretto Filgueiras Neto, L., Muñoz-Gallego, P., Laukkanen, T.: Mobile banking rollout in emerging markets: evidence from Brazil. Int. J. Bank Mark. **28**(5), 342–371 (2010)
5. Dalziel, N., Hontoir, J.: A tale of two banks: customer services on Facebook. In: Proceedings of 2nd European Conference on Social Media (ECSM2015), 9–10 July (2015)
6. Dănăiață, D., Margea, C., Kirakosyan, K., Negovan, A.: Social media in banking. a managerial perception from Mexico. Timisoara. J. Econ. Bus. **7**(2), 147–174 (2014)
7. Field, A.: Discovering Statistics Using SPSS, 3rd edn. SAGE Publications, London (2009)
8. Internetworldstats.com, European Union Internet Usage and Population Stats (2015). http://www.internetworldstats.com/europa.htm#uk
9. Khraim, S., Shoubaki, Y., Khraim, A.: Factors affecting Jordanian consumers' adoption of mobile banking services. Int. J. Bus. Soc. Sci. **2**(20), 96–105 (2011)
10. Manoranjan, D., Pradhan, B., Snigdha, S.: Determinants of customers' adoption of mobile banking: an empirical study by integrating diffusion of innovation with attitude. J. Internet Bank. Commer. **19**(3), 1–21 (2014)
11. Moore, G., Benbasat, I.: Development of an instrument to measure the perceptions of adopting an information technology innovation. Inf. Syst. Res. **2**(3), 192–222 (1991)
12. Murray, L., Durkin, M., Worthington, S., Clark, V.: On the potential for Twitter to add value in retail bank relationships. J. Financ. Serv. Mark. **19**(4), 277–290 (2014)
13. Nor, K., Pearson, M., Ahmad, A.: Adoption of internet banking: theory of the diffusion of innovation. Int. J. Manag. Stud. **17**(1), 69–85 (2010)
14. Rogers, E.M.: Diffusion of Innovations, 5th edn. Simon & Schuster Adult Publishing Group, New York (2003)
15. Tan, M., Teo, T.: Factors influencing the adoption of internet banking. J. Assoc. Inf. Syst. **1**(5), 1–44 (2000)
16. Tarabasz, A.: The Use of Social Media in the Polish Retail Banking in the era of Marketing 3.0, University of Łódź, Poland (2013)
17. Taskiran, N., Bolat, N.: Globalization and social media strategies by financial institutions worldwide. In: Hacioglu, Ü., Dincer, H. (eds.) Managerial Issues in Finance and Banking, pp. 67–76. Springer, Switzerland (2013)
18. Yunus, M.: Diffusion of innovation, consumer attitudes and intentions to use mobile banking. Inf. Knowl. Manag. **4**(10), 12–18 (2015)

Author Index

Printed in the United States
By Bookmasters